FROMMER'S

SPAIN & MOROCCO PLUS THE CANARY ISLANDS ON $40 A DAY

by Darwin Porter

1987-88 Editio

Published by Prentice Hall Press
A Division of Simon & Schuster, Inc.
Gulf + Western Building
One Gulf + Western Plaza
New York, NY 10023

ISBN 0-671-62061-4

Manufactured in the United States of America

Although every effort was made to ensure the accuracy of price information appearing in this book, it should be kept in mind that prices can and do fluctuate in the course of time.

CONTENTS

MAPS

Acknowledgment

The author gratefully acknowledges the contribution of Margaret Foresman, longtime newspaper editor of Key West, Florida, for her editorial assistance.

INFLATION ALERT: I don't have to tell you that inflation has hit Spain and Morocco as it has everywhere else. In researching this book I have made every effort to obtain up-to-the-minute prices, but even the most conscientious researcher cannot keep up with the current pace of inflation. As we go to press, I believe I have obtained the most reliable data possible. Nonetheless, in the lifetime of this edition—particularly its second year (1988)—the wise traveler will add 15% to 20% to the prices quoted throughout these pages.

Introduction

SPAIN AND MOROCCO ON $40 A DAY

SPAIN IS EUROPE'S lady of mystery. Dressed in jet-black velvet, she softens her austerity with a red rose.

By the millions, suitors cross her courtyard. Some stay forever; others retreat at the sight of something brutal in her cold dark eyes; still others return again and again, as if by chance—on some off moment—they will seduce her.

She is the eternal enchantress, a cloak-and-dagger queen who only reluctantly embraces today.

For her glory she casts her eye on a more golden day when her star was in ascendancy. A day when her soldiers of fortune sailed throughout the world—Columbus to America, Balboa to the Pacific, Pizarro to launch the conquest of Peru, Cortés to begin his march through Mexico. On their heavily laden galleons, gold and silver were shipped back to her treasure chest.

She used this booty unwisely. Fortune turned against her. But in her deepest despair she never hid behind her fan, preferring to face the sight and sound of death. She remained—and is to this day—regal and proud, always the queen.

By all means, pay this lady of Spain a visit.

THE SPECTACLE OF SPAIN: Spain is a land of golden-brown plains, snow-capped mountains, valleys with terraces of grapevines, olive groves, unspoiled fishing villages, snug harbors, sandy beaches, ancient walled cities, great art treasures, romantic castles, Gothic cathedrals, cave dwellings, flower gardens, scrub grass, and palaces left over from the Golden Age.

Picture yourself as part of the life of this striking, dramatic country.

—You're in a flower-filled Moorish courtyard drinking cool sangría and listening to the splashing sounds of the same fountain that harem girls heard centuries ago.

—You're in the Plaza de Toros watching a savage, thick-necked black bull lift a horse and its rider off the ground and hurl them into the air.

—You're lying on the beach in Marbella watching as a bikini-clad French movie star emerges from the water.

—You're looking at a lantern that goes on at sundown, casting a faint glow against a background of the plains of La Mancha; and in the distance on the ridge of a hill, you think you see that lanky scarecrow, Don Quixote, on his weary Rozinante, trailed by his faithful, donkey-riding squire.

My aim is to aid you in a discovery of some of the beauty and mystery of a land that is often violent, always passionate, and forever intriguing.

EXOTIC MOROCCO: And after you've courted and wooed "the lady of Spain," you can make a very short crossing over the sea to visit a place that has long stood for romance and glamor, exotic Morocco. A short and inexpensive boat or hydrofoil trip (the latter taking only an hour) will deliver you into a completely different world.

Like Spain, Morocco is a kingdom, but there the similarity ends. From fertile plains rich with the aroma of citrus blossoms to the Atlas mountains capped with snow, the terrain is varied and the choice to the vacationer is immense. You can opt for the towns of the deep south that lie on the gateway to the Sahara, the "route of the casbahs," or else you may prefer one of the beach resorts strung along the Atlantic or Mediterranean. The country, even though small, has a staggering 2,000 miles of beaches. Perhaps one of the justly famed imperial cities, such as Fez, will tempt you into a "thousand and one nights."

In the world of Islam, the land is called al-Maghrib, or the "land of the West." Many visitors from dry, hot, and dusty Saudi Arabia come to Morocco for their vacations, as they want to visit an Arab country known for its fertile land. Of course, Morocco has its own deserts and lots and lots of sunshine, but it is still viewed as lush to the Arab world. It is that strip of land that connects the immense wastelands of the Sahara with Europe beyond the narrow Straits of Gibraltar.

The magic of Morocco has exerted its spell for a very long time. For Americans, perhaps no one did more to promote early tourism there than Hope, Crosby, and Lamour when they went on their *Road to Morocco,* which still is shown on late-night TV.

Rich in folklore and scenery, Morocco is considered a "safe" destination to the North American traveler, as its people are known for their hospitality and charm. They may harass you with overtures to buy their carpets, daggers, handcrafts, whatever, but they will rarely harm you. If you want to discover towns with exotic names such as Taroudannt, Tiznit, and Tafraoute, not to mention Zagora and Ouarzazate, then read on.

There are those who think that since Spain and Morocco are entirely different countries occupying different masses of land on separate continents, Europe and Africa, they should likewise be divided into separate books. Perhaps, but we've decided to combine them between one cover—a double feature, you might say, for the price of one admission.

THE QUESTION OF PRICE: Spain is a mecca for the traveler who craves beauty, a colorful and rich culture, comfort, and bountiful food.

In days gone by, the proud caballero was the world's greatest tourist, calling on the Incas or the American Indian. Now the tide has turned. The world is coming to Spain in armadas that would have dwarfed Philip's, making it the most popular tourist attraction in Europe. But the miles and miles of white-skinned northerners lining the beaches from the Costa Brava to the Costa de la Luz were bound to alter the price structure of Spain.

Unlike the always-plentiful bargains in the Spain of the past, today's values must be sought out; they won't come looking for you. Part of the purpose of this book is to help you find them quickly. Regrettably, the price structure of Spain has now caught up with continental Europe. However, in the less visited places, especially those not trampled by tourists, you'll find plenty of low-priced budget establishments.

On the other hand, Morocco hasn't caught up with the price structure of

Europe. If you avoid the deluxe places, you will find amazing bargains, particularly if you venture beyond such well-traveled oases as Marrakesh.

If you decide not to rent an expensive car, you'll find that rail travel is remarkably cheap. Likewise, meals in moderate restaurants often cost no more than $7 at dinner, and the portions are most generous.

Inexpensive rooms are found throughout the land in units that most often contain private bath. The going rate in more modest places ranges from $8.50 to $18 a night for a double, but you can pay much more, of course, depending on the rating of the hotel. In fact, many first-class hotels are so reasonable in price that we've included many of them throughout Morocco since they are such bargains. Many readers will want to pay slightly higher charges for the better amenities.

If you need to hire a guide in such confusing cities as Fez, you'll often be able to obtain an official one for only $10 a day.

THE $40-A-DAY BUDGET: The budget that I have allocated—$40 per day per person—covers the basic living costs of three meals a day and the price of a room. Naturally, the costs of sightseeing, transportation, shopping, laundry, and entertainment are *extra,* although I'll show you how to keep those expenses trimmed to a minimum.

Travel in Spain and Morocco offers several bonuses for $40 a day. For example, more often than not you will be given a private bath with your well-appointed bedroom. Similarly, for the price of the menu of the day (a fixed-price meal of the day), you'll always get three courses, plus the regional wine. Even the tip is included in the bill, but it's customary to leave something extra if the service has been good.

The $40-a-day budget roughly breaks down this way—$23 per person (based on double occupancy) for a room and a continental breakfast, $7 for lunch, and $10 for dinner.

Of course, for those who can afford more, I've included a lot of splurges, both hotels and restaurants that offer good value in the more medium-priced travel range.

The $25-a-Day Travel Club—How to Save Money on All Your Travels

In this book we'll be looking at how to get your money's worth in Spain and Morocco, but there is a "device" for saving money and determining value on *all* your trips. It's the popular, international $25-a-Day Travel Club, now in its 24th successful year of operation. The Club was formed at the urging of numerous readers of the $$$-a-Day and Dollarwise Guides, who felt that such an organization could provide continuing travel information and a sense of community to value-minded travelers in all parts of the world. And so it does!

In keeping with the budget concept, the annual membership fee is low and is immediately exceeded by the value of your benefits. Upon receipt of $18 (U.S. residents), or $20 U.S. by check drawn on a U.S. bank or via international postal money order in U.S. funds (Canadian, Mexican, and other foreign residents) to cover one year's membership, we will send all new members the following items.

(1) *Any two* of the following books

Please designate in your letter which two you wish to receive:

Europe on $25 a Day
Australia on $25 a Day

Eastern Europe on $25 a Day
England on $35 a Day
Greece including Istanbul and Turkey's Aegean Coast on $25 a Day
Hawaii on $45 a Day
India on $15 & $25 a Day
Ireland on $30 a Day
Israel on $30 & $35 a Day
Mexico on $20 a Day (plus Belize and Guatemala)
New York on $45 a Day
New Zealand on $35 a Day
Scandinavia on $50 a Day
Scotland and Wales on $35 a Day
South America on $25 a Day
Spain and Morocco (plus the Canary Is.) on $40 a Day
Turkey on $25 a Day (avail. May '87)
Washington, D.C., on $40 a Day

Dollarwise Guide to Austria and Hungary
Dollarwise Guide to Belgium, Holland, & Luxembourg (avail. June '87)
Dollarwise Guide to Bermuda and The Bahamas
Dollarwise Guide to Canada
Dollarwise Guide to the Caribbean
Dollarwise Guide to Egypt
Dollarwise Guide to England and Scotland
Dollarwise Guide to France
Dollarwise Guide to Germany
Dollarwise Guide to Italy
Dollarwise Guide to Japan and Hong Kong
Dollarwise Guide to Portugal, Madeira, and the Azores
Dollarwise Guide to the South Pacific (avail. Aug. '87)
Dollarwise Guide to Switzerland and Liechtenstein
Dollarwise Guide to Alaska (avail. Nov. '87)
Dollarwise Guide to California and Las Vegas
Dollarwise Guide to Florida
Dollarwise Guide to New England
Dollarwise Guide to New York State (avail. Aug. '87)
Dollarwise Guide to the Northwest
Dollarwise Guide to Skiing USA-East
Dollarwise Guide to Skiing USA-West
Dollarwise Guide to the Southeast and New Orleans
Dollarwise Guide to the Southwest
Dollarwise Guide to Texas

Dollarwise Guides discuss accommodations and facilities in all price ranges, with emphasis on the medium-priced.)

A Shopper's Guide to Best Buys in England, Scotland, and Wales
(Describes in detail hundreds of places to shop—department stores, factory outlets, street markets, and craft centers—for great quality British bargains.)

Bed & Breakfast—North America
(This guide contains a directory of over 150 organizations that offer bed & breakfast referrals and reservations throughout North America. The scenic attractions, businesses, and major schools and universities near the homes of each are also listed.)

Dollarwise Guide to Cruises
(This complete guide covers all the basics of cruising—ports of call, costs, fly-cruise package bargains, cabin selection booking, embarkation and debarkation and describes in detail over 60 or so ships cruising the waters of Alaska, the Caribbean, Mexico, Hawaii, Panama, Canada, and the United States.)

Dollarwise Guide to Skiing Europe
(Describes top ski resorts in Austria, France, Italy, and Switzerland. Illustrated with maps of each resort area plus full-color trail maps.)

How to Beat the High Cost of Travel
(This practical guide details how to save money on absolutely all travel items—accommodations, transportation, dining, sightseeing, shopping, taxes, and more. Includes special budget information for seniors, students, singles, and families.)

Marilyn Wood's Wonderful Weekends
(This very selective guide covers the best mini-vacation destinations within a 175-mile radius of New York City. It describes special country inns and other accommodations, restaurants, picnic spots, sights, and activities—all the information needed for a two- or three-day stay.)

Motorist's Phrase Book
(A practical phrase book in French, German, and Spanish designed specifically for the English-speaking motorist touring abroad.)

Swap and Go—Home Exchanging Made Easy
(Two veteran home exchangers explain in detail all the money-saving benefits of a home exchange, and then describe precisely how to do it. Also includes information on home rentals and many tips on low-cost travel.)

The Fast 'n' Easy Phrase Book
(French, German, Spanish, and Italian—all in one convenient, easy-to-use phrase guide.)

Travel Diary and Record Book
(A 96-page diary for personal travel notes plus a section for such vital data as passport and traveler's check numbers, itinerary, postcard list, special people and places to visit, and a reference section with temperature and conversion charts, and world maps with distance zones.)

Where to Stay USA
(By the Council on International Educational Exchange, this extraordinary guide is the first to list accommodations in all 50 states that cost anywhere from $3 to $30 per night.)

(2) A one-year subscription to *The Wonderful World of Budget Travel*

This quarterly eight-page tabloid newspaper keeps you up to date on fast-breaking developments in low-cost travel in all parts of the world bringing you the latest money-saving information—the kind of information you'd have to pay $25 a year to obtain elsewhere. This consumer-conscious publication also features columns of special interest to readers: **Hospitality Exchange** (members all over the world who are willing to provide hospitality to other members as they pass through their home cities); **Share-a-Trip** (offers and requests from members for travel companions who can share costs and help avoid the burdensome single supplement); and **Readers Ask . . . Readers Reply** (travel questions from members to which other members reply with authentic firsthand information).

(3) A copy of *Arthur Frommer's Guide to New York*

This is a pocket-size guide to hotels, restaurants, nightspots, and sightseeing attractions in all price ranges throughout the New York area.

(4) Your personal membership card

Membership entitles you to purchase through the Club all Arthur Frommer publications for a third to a half off their regular retail prices during the term of your membership.

So why not join this hardy band of international budgeteers and participate in its exchange of travel information and hospitality? Simply send your name and address, together with your annual membership fee of $18 (U.S. residents) or $20 U.S. (Canadian, Mexican, and other foreign residents), by check drawn on a U.S. bank or via international postal money order in U.S. funds to: $25-A Day Travel Club, Inc., Frommer Books, Gulf + Western Building, One Gulf + Western Plaza, New York, NY 10023. And please remember to specify which *two* of the books in section (1) above you wish to receive in your initial package of members' benefits. Or, if you prefer, use the last page of this book, simply checking off the two books you select and enclosing $18 or $20 in U.S. currency.

> Once you are a member, there is no obligation to buy additional books. No books will be mailed to you without your specific order.

THE FUTURE OF THIS BOOK: Spain and Morocco, let us remember, are volatile countries: today's undiscovered fishing village may be tomorrow's chicly fashionable beach resort. Therefore I'd like to encourage you to share your reactions to places already recommended—Has the service deteriorated? Have the prices gone up?—as well as any new finds you may have discovered. Have you stumbled upon an unheralded inexpensive restaurant? A small hotel that is colorful, clean, and comfortable? A village fiesta unique and impressive?

All of us have one common goal: to travel far and wide as comfortably and inexpensively as we can. Your assistance can be helpful in achieving that aim. Like its sister books, *Spain and Morocco on $40 a Day* has sections devoted to readers' suggestions. If yours is included in the next edition—and that goes for the chapter on the Canary Islands as well—you will have the pleasure of sharing a special treasure with others. For your suggestion to be used, it is imperative to include the complete street address and telephone number of the establishment you are suggesting.

Please send your comments, discoveries, or criticisms to Darwin Porter, Frommer/Pasmantier Publishers, Gulf + Western Building, 1 Gulf + Western Plaza, New York, NY 10023.

Part One

SPAIN, GIBRALTAR, AND THE CANARY ISLANDS

Chapter I

GETTING THERE

1. Plane Economics
2. Traveling Within Spain

IN RELATION TO the other Western European countries, Spain sometimes seems a bit remote, perched as it is on the seemingly isolated Iberian peninsula. But in terms of its distance from North America, Spain is one of the closest of all Western European countries. I'll first discuss the basic structure of air fares to Spain, then deal with methods of traveling within Spain and itinerary highlights once you arrive.

Spain is changing at a rapid rate. In just a short period of time it has moved from an essentially rural country, controlled by a reactionary despot with fascist leanings, to a highly industrialized democracy, and has done so at great cost and chaos to the old established order. A few of its Mediterranean coastal cities are almost ceasing to be Spanish, and are turning instead into international melting pots. Yet in its inland cities, this land of lore is responding to the world interest in its past by restoring its castles and palaces that have rested in decay for hundreds of years. Tourism is like a shot of adrenalin to a country that once appeared to the Western world to have become disillusioned with itself. Spain is hard to understand and almost impossible to generalize about. One reason for this is that Spain is made up of a group of nations: the Aragonese and the Castilians; the Catalans of the northeast and the Galicians of the northwest; and the Basques, the Andalusians, and others.

1. Plane Economics

If you wish to fly directly to Madrid from North America, as most visitors will, there are two major airlines which do so: **Iberia,** the Spanish international airline, and **Trans World Airlines** (TWA). As part of my continuing policy to travel on many carriers, I chose Iberia for my most recent flight to Madrid. I was pleased with the experience from the point of view of service, comfort, punctuality, and concern for safety.

Iberia, which claims with ample justification to be the airline that knows Spain best, offers more routes from North America to Spain than any other carrier. Among them are daily nonstop service from New York to Madrid, Málaga, and the Canary Islands; frequent direct service from New York to Barcelona; and a newly inaugurated nonstop service from Miami to Madrid. Just before press time, Iberia had negotiated new nonstop routes from Chicago and Los Angeles to Madrid, scheduled to begin some time in 1987.

Based on the number of passengers transported annually, Iberia is the third largest airline in Europe. It was established in 1927 as a domestic Spanish mail carrier between Barcelona and Madrid. Service to New York began in 1954, and, by 1961, Iberia's fleet was completely jet-powered. More than 13 million passengers flew on the airline in 1984–1985, using the airline's well-established routes to more than 66 cities in 52 different countries.

Except for some of the charter flights for which Iberia will supply details upon request, the least expensive regular fare to Spain is a **midweek APEX ticket,** which is available to passengers traveling in both directions on Monday through Thursday. Iberia requires a reservation and a prepayment at least 14 days in advance, a minimum stay of seven days, and a maximum stay of 60 days for passengers originating in Miami, 180 days for passengers originating in New York. Children receive a 33% discount, and a $75 penalty is imposed for cancellations or any changes in the itinerary.

APEX passengers who wish to travel in either direction on a Friday, Saturday, or Sunday pay a surcharge over the midweek APEX fare.

An **excursion ticket** costs more than either form of the APEX ticket, but requires the same 14-day advance payment and carries the same $75 penalty if the departure date is changed. An excursion ticket, however, has the advantage of no minimum stopover, a maximum stay of a full year, and the very attractive option of being able to change the return date without a penalty.

Yet another ticket, the **normal economy fare,** is the most expensive of all the coach class tickets, yet carries the advantage of having no advance purchase requirements, a validity of a full year, no minimum stopover, and a 50% discount for children.

Preference class is Iberia's equivalent of Business Class on other airlines, with rapid check-in and faster baggage service, an increased baggage allowance, free drinks, upgraded food service, and extra-comfortable seating.

Grand Class is the equivalent of First Class on other airlines. Both Grand and Preference Class offer special waiting lounges at major airports, away from the bustle of the terminal.

Fares vary with the season, costing the least in winter and the most in summer. For more information, consult your travel agent or one of Iberia's phone reservations clerks at their toll-free number (800/221-9741).

In addition to flights to Spain, Iberia offers more than 100 tours of different regions of the country, each loaded with extra values and options.

CHARTER FLIGHTS: Many travelers look to charter flights to provide less expensive air transportation. Such flights are characterized by lack of convenience and rigidity of scheduling. Charters to Spain can be arranged through **Nueva York Hispano,** 261 West 70th St., New York, NY 10023 (tel. 212/595-2400), which uses both Iberia, the national airline, and Spantax, a private Spanish charter firm.

You can also investigate the charter flights offered by **Spanish Heritage Association,** 116-53 Queens Blvd., Forest Hills, NY 11375 (tel. 212/520-1300). Sometimes their flights are a few dollars less than Nueva York Hispano.

2. Traveling Within Spain

With the exception of its government-owned airlines, **Iberia** and **Aviaco,** Spain's transportation facilities are, in general, a bit less developed and up-to-date than those of other Western European countries—but they make up for their relative dowdiness by the moderate cost of their fares.

THE TRAINS: The **Spanish State Railways (RENFE)** provide the most economic means of discovering the second-largest country in Europe. On peninsular routes, the main long-distance connections are normally served with night express trains with first- and second-class seats and with beds and bunks. There are also fast daytime trains of the TALGO, TER, Corail, or Electrotrain types, which have a high standard of comfort and high commercial speeds. There is a general fare for these trains, with supplements for bunks, beds, and certain superior-quality trains. Nevertheless, the Spanish railway is one of the most economical in Europe, a fact that makes this mode of transport the most advantageous in the majority of cases.

Direct trains connect Madrid with Paris and Lisbon; Barcelona with Paris and Geneva; and on the frontiers, at Valencia de Alcantara–Marvão (Portugal), Irun-Hendaye, and Port Bou–Cerbère (France), international connections are easily made. There is also an express from Algeciras to Hendaye with direct coaches.

EURAILPASS: Many in-the-know travelers to Europe have for years been taking advantage of one of its greatest travel bargains, the Eurailpass, which permits unlimited first-class travel in any country in Western Europe, except the British Isles (good in Ireland). Passes are purchased for periods as short as 15 days or as long as three months, and are strictly nontransferable.

Here's how it works. The pass is sold only outside of Europe and North Africa, and only to residents of countries outside those areas. Travelers may purchase the Eurailpass for 15 days for $260, 21 days for $330, one month for $410, two months for $560, and three months for $680. Children under 4 travel free providing they don't occupy a separate seat (if so, half fare), and children 5 to 12 pay only half fare.

Its advantages are tempting. No tickets, no supplements (simply show the pass to the ticket collector, then settle back to enjoy the European scenery). Seat reservations are required on some trains. With your Eurailpass, you can also purchase bus and steamship tickets at a reduction. In Spain, for example, you are allowed 15% on certain tours. A pamphlet issued by Eurailpass gives all details.

Those under the age of 26 can purchase a **Eurail Youthpass,** entitling them to unlimited second-class transportation for two months for only $370, or one month for $290. These passes are nontransferable, and if there is any evidence of alteration, the pass is nullified.

Travel agents in all towns and railway agents in such major cities as New York, Montréal, Los Angeles, or Chicago sell the tickets. The Eurailpass is available at the offices of CIT Travel Service, the French National Railroads, the German Federal Railroads, and the Swiss Federal Railways.

Eurail Saverpass is a money-saving ticket offered for three or more people traveling together. It is good for 15 consecutive days of unlimited first-class rail travel in the same countries and with the same privileges as Eurailpass. All it requires is that your group remain together throughout the trip. The price of the 15-day saver is $199 per person.

If you plan to travel a great deal on the European railroads, you will do well to secure the latest copy of the Thomas Cook Continental Timetable of European Railroads. This comprehensive but portable 500+-page timetable covers all of Europe's mainline rail services with detail and accuracy. It is available exclusively in North America from **Forsyth Travel Library,** P.O. Box 2975, Shawnee Mission, KS 66201 (tel. 913/384-3440), at a cost of $15.95, plus $2.50 priority postage.

THE BUSES: The bus lines are numerous, low priced, and often most comfortable. Reader Jim Marrion, Holyoke, Massachusetts, writes: "If you are going

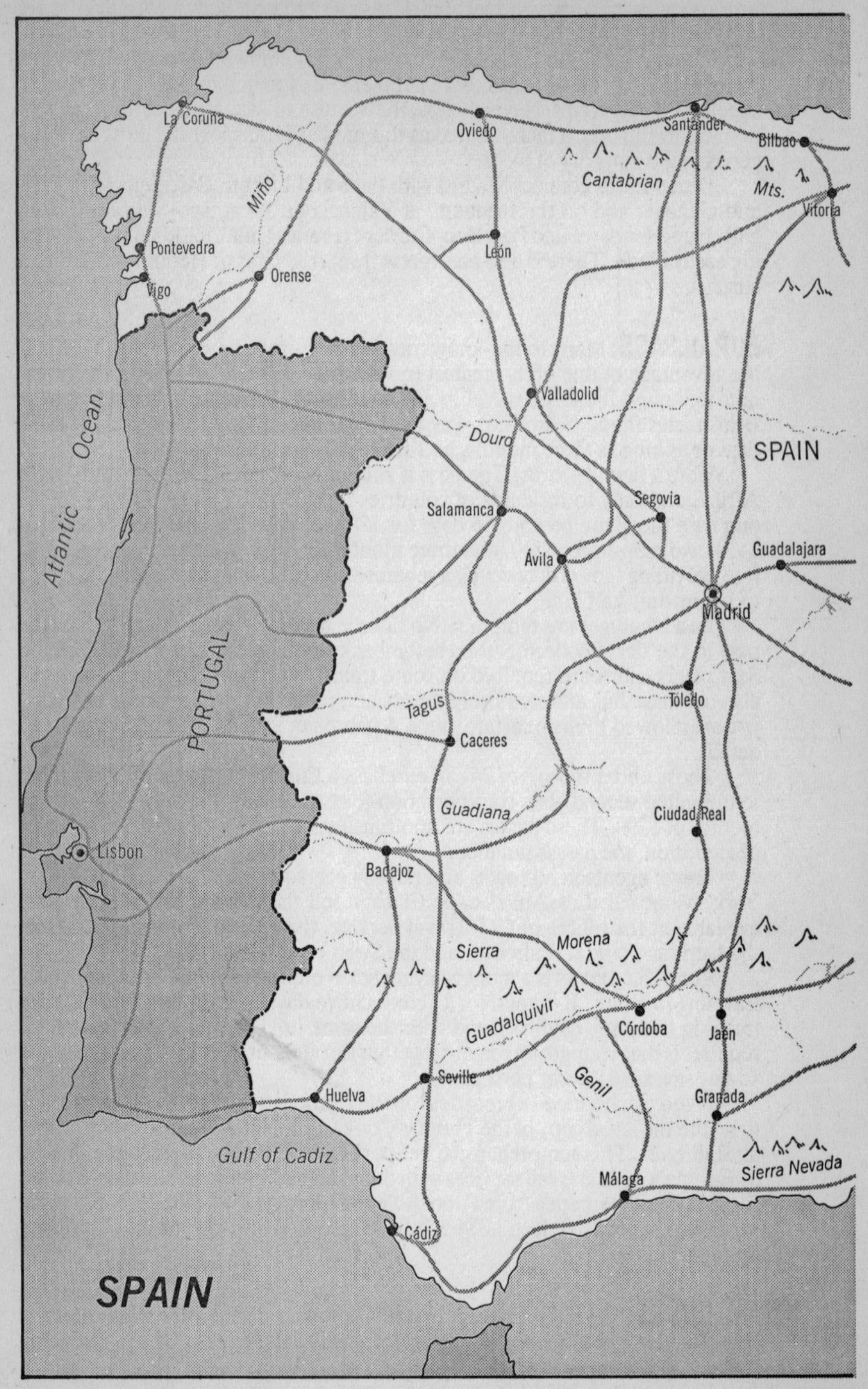
La Coruña
Oviedo
Santander
Bilbao
Cantabrian
Mts.
Vitoria
Miño
León
Pontevedra
Orense
Vigo
Atlantic
Ocean
Valladolid
Douro
SPAIN
Salamanca
Segovia
Ávila
Guadalajara
Madrid
PORTUGAL
Toledo
Tagus
Caceres
Guadiana
Ciudad Real
Lisbon
Badajoz
Sierra
Morena
Guadalquivir
Córdoba
Jaén
Genil
Seville
Huelva
Granada
Gulf of Cadiz
Sierra Nevada
Málaga
Cádiz
SPAIN

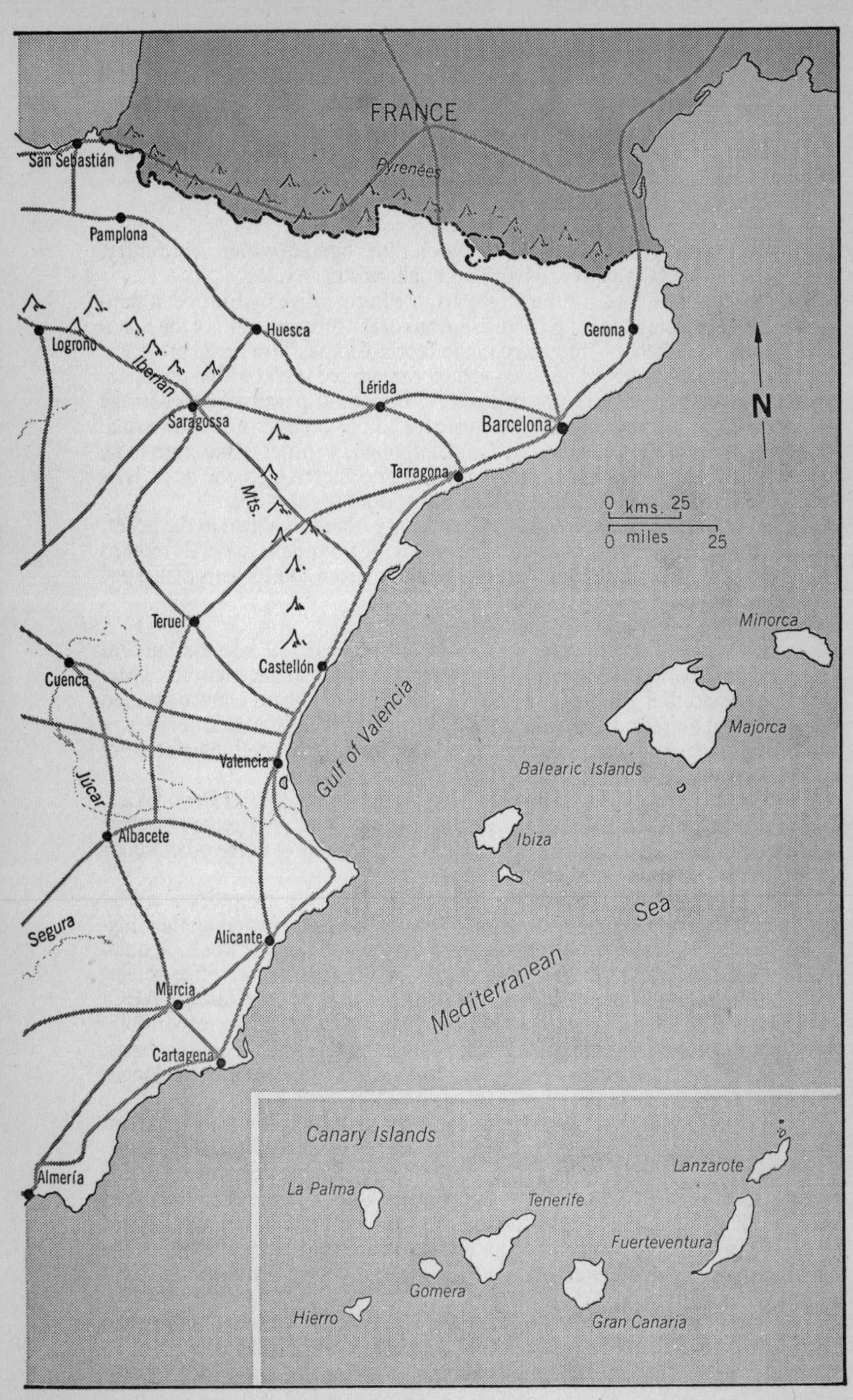
FRANCE
Pyrenées
San Sebastián
Pamplona
Huesca
Logroño
Iberian
Mts.
Saragossa
Lérida
Gerona
Barcelona
Tarragona
N
0 kms. 25
0 miles 25
Teruel
Castellón
Cuenca
Valencia
Júcar
Gulf of Valencia
Albacete
Segura
Alicante
Murcia
Cartagena
Almería
Minorca
Majorca
Balearic Islands
Ibiza
Sea
Mediterranean
Canary Islands
Lanzarote
La Palma
Tenerife
Fuerteventura
Gomera
Hierro
Gran Canaria

less than 100 miles, the bus is the only way to travel. You get to see more because the trains always leave you outside the center of the city."

You'll rarely encounter a for-real bus terminal in Spain. Sometimes the hub of transportation is a café, a bar, the street in front of a hotel, or simply a spot at an intersection.

Typical prices include the following: from Madrid to Toledo, a distance of 44 miles (70 km), 325 pesetas ($2.28) one way; from Madrid to Segovia, some 54 miles (87 km), 435 pesetas ($3.05).

AIR TRAVEL WITHIN SPAIN: Two major airlines operate within the country: the big daddy **Iberia,** and a hard-working smaller sister, **Aviaco.**

Domestic air flights, for the most part, are inexpensive by European standards. But if you plan to visit far-flung sections of the former center of the Spanish Empire, you might be interested in the Iberia Airlines **Visit Spain** program.

Iberia will issue an airline ticket valid for unlimited travel within the Spanish mainland and the Balearic Islands for $199 if round-trip transatlantic passage is purchased at the same time. Passengers need not predetermine the actual dates and times of the flights within Spain, although the order of the cities to be visited must be specified in advance and cannot be altered once the ticket is issued. The ticket is valid for up to 60 days after your arrival in Spain.

If an optional-passage journey to the Canary Islands is added to the ticket, the price rises to a nonetheless highly reasonable $249. Infants under 24 months of age pay only 10% of the adult fare, and children from 2 to 12 years of age pay half the adult fare.

CAR RENTALS: If you're planning to tour Spain, a car will ease the burdens considerably. Even if you're limited to extensive touring in the environs of Madrid, you'll find that a rented automobile will come in handy, allowing you to stop off at that *típico* roadside tavern for a sherry or to make that side detour to a medieval village. You'll be your own master, exploring at your leisure places not covered—or covered too hurriedly—on the organized tour.

On my most recent trip to Spain, I tried the services of **Budget Rent-A-Car,** whose offices are scattered strategically throughout Spain. My report on their facilities should give you an idea of the prices and procedures of the other major firms, which include ATESA, Hertz, and Avis.

The smallest—and least expensive—car in Budget's inventory is a Fiat Panda or its equivalent. Suitable for up to four passengers, including their luggage, the car is available at an unlimited-mileage rate of $138 per week. To qualify for this rate, clients must reserve through a Budget reservations office at least three business days in advance. An additional 33% I.V.A. (see Taxes in ABCs of Spain) is added to these figures, and all gasoline, of course, is the responsibility of the renter. For short rentals, it's possible to hire a car on a per-day basis, with a fee for each kilometer driven, but most visitors usually prefer the longer period.

An attractive medium-size car available through Budget would be a Ford Escort. With manual transmission, it costs $264 per week and offers the sometimes much-needed extra benefit of air conditioning. A more expensive choice is a five-passenger Volkswagen. It rents for about $495 a week, with unlimited mileage. If you are comfortable driving it, a car with manual transmission is much cheaper. (Some companies consider automatic transmission such a costly expense that they don't even offer it.) Likewise, if you're cutting costs, don't request air conditioning.

More information about the discounted rates available through Budget can be obtained by calling their toll-free U.S. number: 800/527-0700.

Other rental companies include the government-owned **ATESA,** whose offices are at 59 Gran Vía in Madrid (tel. 247/730-001). **Avis** is also well represented in Spain, with about 25 depots and kiosks, including ones at all the major airports (call Avis toll free within the U.S. at 800/331-2112). Finally, **Hertz** will accept your reservation before you leave North America. Their toll-free number is 800/654-3001.

Gasoline

Gas is easily obtainable throughout the country. Ask for regular, the normal fuel used in rented cars in Spain. The average Spanish vehicle—predominantly Seats or Fiats—gets close to 45 miles a gallon.

HITCHHIKING: This is no longer smiled upon as much as it used to be. It may be technically illegal. However, people still do it, tourists tending to pick up tourists. Finding space in cars driven by Spaniards, however, is not so easy (they're often at capacity with friends or relatives). I don't recommend that you stick out your thumb in the presence of the Civil Guard.

THE SIGHTS OF SPAIN: The sights of Spain are staggering. It takes at least two months to see all the major cities—and even that calls for some fast moving. Most of us don't have such an allotment of time, however, and will want to get the most out of Spain in a shorter number of city visits.

It is with this in mind that a personal selection of the "Top Ten Cities" has been made below. This list, of course, should not be taken to imply that Spain does not have country scenery of interest.

But the romance and magic of Spain are to be found in its cities, of which it possesses more legendary ones than any country other than Italy. These have altered their makeup dozens of times through waves of invasions by alien conquerors (such as the Moors).

Here, in no particular order, are my nominations for glamour and greatness: (1) Toledo; (2) Segovia; (3) Madrid; (4) El Escorial; (5) Salamanca; (6) Seville; (7) Granada; (8) Córdoba; (9) Barcelona; and (10) Santiago de Compostela.

PLANNING YOUR ITINERARY: From the standpoint of the visitor, Spain is roughly divided into these sections: **Madrid** and its environs; **Andalusia** (Seville, Córdoba, Granada, the Costa del Sol); **Barcelona,** a jumping-off point for Majorca and the Pyrenees; the **Atlantic Coast,** beginning in the east with San Sebastián and stretching west to La Coruña; and **Valencia** and the **Costa Blanca,** referred to as the **"Levante."**

Madrid is the major gateway. But it is not—or should not be—the prime target for pilgrims. The Prado aside, what makes the Spanish capital so intriguing is that it makes such a good excursion base for several of Spain's major attractions: Toledo, Segovia, El Escorial, Ávila, Salamanca, Burgos, Cuenca, and the royal palaces at Aranjuez and La Granja.

After winding up an affair with the cities of the heartland, you might head next for the biggest lure of all, Andalusia, with stopovers at Córdoba, Seville, Granada; and an afternoon spent getting intoxicated (free) in the bodegas at Jerez de la Frontera.

If time remains, you might tie in a trip to Andalusia with an excursion to nearby Tangier on the northwestern coast of Africa.

But you won't know Spain until you've visited **Catalonia,** the **Basque Country,** and **Galicia.** The capital of Catalonia is Barcelona. From there, you can continue with excursions in all directions; north to the Costa Brava, the Pyre-

MILEAGE BETWEEN MAJOR CITIES

Distance in Miles

	Almería	Ávila	Barcelona	Cádiz	Córdoba	Coruña	Granada	MADRID	Málaga	Oviedo	Pamplona	Salamanca	San Sebastián	Toledo	Valencia	Zaragoza
Alicante	182	333	319	427	326	639	219	262	299	541	417	393	475	255	103	309
Almería		411	502	300	206	727	103	349	136	629	601	473	640	348	285	470
Ávila	411		445	383	283	334	331	71	399	231	328	60	295	85	290	259
Badajoz	374	197	634	212	169	479	272	249	270	381	468	142	451	228	444	450
Barcelona	502	445		774	563	693	532	385	618	559	271	482	328	429	216	184
Cádiz	300	383	774		163	665	208	411	164	567	663	371	702	361	501	613
Córdoba	206	283	563	163		617	103	248	116	528	500	328	539	194	338	450
Coruña	727	338	693	665	617		647	378	715	281	458	298	473	419	596	516
Cuenca	317	175	348	439	276	481	297	104	381	383	332	233	394	116	136	207
Gerona	564	507	62	858	625	755	600	447	680	621	333	544	390	491	278	246
Granada	103	331	538	208	103	647		269	80	549	521	391	560	264	322	471
León	556	158	486	494	454	207	472	206	544	73	250	122	268	243	425	308
MADRID	349	71	385	411	248	378	269		337	280	252	131	291	44	218	202
Málaga	136	399	618	164	116	715	80	337		617	590	469	628	314	402	539
Oviedo	629	231	559	567	528	211	649	280	617		287	195	262	316	498	374
Pamplona	601	328	663	500	458		521	252	590	287		273	57	296	314	109
Pontevedra	735	338	700	649	606	75	655	386	715	242	466	278	484	423	605	516
Salamanca	473	60	482	371	328	328	391	131	469	195	273		291	145	350	299
San Sebastián	640	295	328	702	539	473	560	291	628	262	57	291		325	368	166
Segovia	403	42	403	465	308	347	323	54	391	225	229	102	266	98	272	219
Seville	262	306	649	78	86	587	159	334	136	489	586	294	624	284	432	535
Toledo	348	85	429	361	194	419	264	44	314	316	296	145	335		231	246
Valencia	285	290	216	501	338	596	322	218	402	498	311	350	368	281		202
Valladolid	469	75	411	443	358	282	389	120	457	156	202	71	219	273	338	228
Zaragoza	470	259	184	613	450	516	471	202	539	374	109	299	166	246	202	

nees, and to the little principality of Andorra; then to the monastery of Montserrat; west to Zaragoza; south to the old Roman city of Tarragona; east to the vacation resorts of Majorca, Ibiza, and Minorca.

For readers with the time, a trip along the Atlantic Coast of Spain may also rank as an exceptional travel experience. Beginning at the summer capital and Basque center of San Sebastián, you can journey along this "green coast" to Galicia, with its capital at La Coruña and its major stopover at Santiago de Compostela.

On the way back to Madrid, you can combine the cathedral city of León, the Castilian plain of Zamora, the university city of Salamanca, and the walled city of Ávila.

Of the coastal resorts, the **Costa del Sol** is the winner (with Marbella, Torremolinos, and Nerja recommended, in that order, for places in the sun); the **Costa Brava** is runner-up (Tossá de Mar is the brightest star on this sun strip); and the **Costa Blanca** comes in a poor third (with Benidorm and Alicante the chief centers). And one of the best spots is Sitges, south of Barcelona, on the so-called **Gold Coast (Costa de Oro).** The beach cities of San Sebastián and Santander are quite lovely on the Atlantic Coast—but the Spanish virtually acquire squatters' rights to all the hotel rooms there in July and August.

Valencia, surrounded by orange groves and rice paddies, has many sightseeing targets that can be shot down in a day—but it's not a place to linger in, as it's a big industrialized port city.

For specific distances between cities, refer to our mileage chart.

A **two-week itinerary** might run this way: Days 1 through 4 in Madrid (one to recover from the air flight or motor trip there, another to see the sights, including the Prado). While still based in Madrid, Day 3 could be spent on a trip to Toledo with a possible stopover in the morning at Aranjuez, and Day 4 could take in a morning visit to El Escorial and an afternoon at Segovia.

On Day 5 you could swing south to Córdoba, arriving in time to view its world-famed mosque, and for Day 6 you could head west to Seville, the capital of Andalusia. On Day 7 you could drive south to the sherry town of Jerez, perhaps pressing on to the Atlantic seaport of Cádiz for the night.

Day 8 could take you to Algeciras, east of Cádiz, with an afternoon visit to Gibraltar. From either port, you could spend Day 9 in Tangier if you have no further time in which to explore Morocco. Days 10 and 11 could be passed basking in the sun at one of the resorts along the Costa del Sol, and Days 12 and 13 could be spent in Granada, north of Málaga. On Day 14 you could drive back to Madrid, or else journey to Málaga and catch a flight there.

Chapter II

THE SCENE IN SPAIN

ENIGMATIC SPAIN is not Europe. Some have compared it to Africa, but it isn't Africa either. It is a unique country, a land that made an institution out of the bullfight, the flamenco dance, the fiesta, and the siesta. Spiritually it's pitch black or blood red; it recognizes few other colors in its spectrum.

1. Staying in Spain

Unlike the north of Europe, the hotels in Spain on our budget almost invariably will give you a private bath with either a tub or else a shower, perhaps a combination of both. As such, they constitute one of the great hotel bargains of the world. However, don't hit a city after dark and hope to grab up the best bargains: they are likely to be long gone, having been nailed down by the early birds.

Hotels in Spain, as I'll outline below, come in a wide variety of styles, shapes, forms, and prices. Within the same hotel there is often a different price structure. Therefore, if you want to cut corners drastically, ask for a room with a wash basin only and be prepared to share a corridor bath. In most establishments the public baths are adequate, particularly if you don't use them during peak hours between 7:30 and 9 a.m. and 6 to 8 p.m.

THE HOTEL OUTLOOK: Hotel clients will find a sign listing prices posted downstairs in the lobby. An individual card is also posted in the bedroom, since some rooms, of course, are more expensive than others. The hotel—not the government, as in days of yore—determines the price rate it will charge, but announces tariffs in advance. Minimum and maximum rates are set. Theoretically, the maximum rate should apply for the better rooms and the peak season—but this is rarely the case. The maximum rate is generally in effect all year. However, at some resorts in the slow season, the rates may be lowered by the management to attract added business. In all instances in this book, I have quoted the higher rate. If you should arrive at a hotel that has decided to charge you the minimum, then you can consider this as an added bonus.

The rate for full board is arrived at simply by adding the price of the meals to the price of the room. There is no obligation, however, to accept full board, except at *pensions* (boarding houses). In such establishments, it's recommended that you take half board, or "demi-pension" (that is, breakfast plus either lunch or dinner).

If there are three or more in your party, you may want to ask for an additional bed in your room. In a single room, an additional bed usually costs no more than 60% of the maximum price for the room (no more than 35% of the maximum price in a double room).

When you see the sign **Residencia,** it means you can't take any meal at the establishment other than breakfast.

The Spanish government rates hotels by stars. The most outstanding hotels in Spain are rated five stars, or deluxe, with leading first-class establishments earning four stars. However, for our limited budget, we'll stay mainly with three-star hotels, dipping often into the one- or two-star field for cheaper lodgings.

In addition to counting the stars on the blue sign at the door, note if there is a tiny *s* following the letter *H.* If there is, this symbol designates a *hostal.* A hostal is not to be confused with a hostel, which most often in the north of Europe caters only to students. A hostal in Spain is a modest hotel. The government grants it stars; however, a hostal with three stars is about the equivalent of a hotel with two stars. A hostal often doesn't have the services of a regular hotel, and lets you save money not only on the room rate but by carrying your own luggage or whatever.

Pensions are among the least expensive accommodations. A liberal sampling of the better pension establishments is included in this guide.

The cheapest places in Spain are designated by light-blue plaques outside the door, **CH** standing for *Casa Huespedes* and **F** for *Fonda.* These are invariably basic but respectable establishments, and some readers have found them "salubrious" as well. Readers John and Gail Pearce of Toronto say: "The magic word for finding cheap accommodations seems to be fonda rather than pension. A fonda proved a saving grace in Toledo."

Warning: As a general rule I always request a room in the rear if the hotel lies on a principal square or main artery. Spain, now that it's switched from the donkey to the automobile and motorcycle, has some of the noisiest city traffic I've encountered in Europe. Thundering buses rumbling through the major cities only add to the decibel count. Another alternative is to seek hotels on quieter side streets, and this guide has many of those.

Staying at Paradores and Albergues

The Spanish Department of Tourism has created some unique accommodations. Throughout the country, deserted castles, monasteries, and palaces have been taken over and turned into hotels. In some cases, first-class modern hotels have thus been created.

At great expense, modern baths, steam heat, and such have been added, yet the tradition that was and is Spain has been retained. These establishments have been furnished with antiques, excellent reproductions, and objects of art. Meals are also served in these government-run hotels. Usually, typical dishes of the region are featured. Whenever possible, try to avoid dining in a parador on Sunday at lunch. Many local residents frequent paradors at this time, and dining rooms are most often crowded. In-house guests are not necessarily given preference on the waiting list for tables.

The more ambitious of the establishments are called *paradores,* and are in historic as well as scenic areas. The *albergues,* on the other hand, are modern and are built substantially in the Spanish fashion. They are comparable to motels, as they are along the roadside, existing in hotel-scarce sections for the convenience of passing motorists who want overnight stopovers. A client is not allowed to stay in an albergue for more than 48 hours, and the management does not like to accept reservations. But reservations during the peak months at paradores are essential. In the case of the most popular parador, San Francisco, at Granada, it has been suggested that rooms should be reserved three to four months in advance.

In addition, the government also runs *refugios,* which are mostly in remote areas attracting hunters, fishermen, and mountain-climbers. One final establishment—a *hostería*—is a specialty restaurant, such as the one at Alcalá de Henares, near Madrid, which is decorated in the style of a particular province, and offers regional dishes at reasonable prices.

2. The Spanish

Ancestors of the Basques may have been the first settlers in Spain 10,000 to 30,000 years ago, followed, it is believed, by Iberians from North Africa. They, in turn, were followed by Celts who crossed the Pyrenees about 600 B.C., with resulting battles, which, as these things have a way of doing, finally left off after a long melding of the races into a Celtiberian people who inhabited central Spain. Others coming to the Iberian peninsula in prehistoric times were the Phoenicians, who took over coastal areas on the Atlantic beginning in the 11th century B.C. It is thought that these people were from the Mediterranean Sea's far eastern shores, as were those who established the city of Carthage. Perhaps half a millennium after the Phoenicians the Greeks came, lured by the gold, silver, and other metals found in the peninsula. The Greeks stayed and set up colonies before they were conquered by the Carthaginians from North Africa.

HISTORY: Around 206 B.C., the Romans, who were better record keepers than their predecessors, vanquished the Carthaginian lords of the Iberian peninsula, but they were resisted by the Iberians, by now quite a mixed lot. However, by the time of Julius Caesar, Spain (Hispania) was under Roman law and entered on a long period of peace and prosperity, eventually embracing Christianity. As in other Roman colonies and possessions, the steam ran out by the 4th century A.D., and the place was ripe for a Visigoth takeover. Christianity continued and gained even under Germanic invaders, but in A.D. 711, Muslims from Africa invaded and won, and the tone of the country changed drastically for the next few centuries.

The Moors, using as their capital Córdoba which had been the Romans' government center, called their new land "al-Andalus," or Andalusia. Mosques, palaces, gardens—much of beauty was introduced into the Arab-Spanish territory, and Muslim culture flourished in the areas under Islamic control. But the peninsula was not peaceful, with Christians clinging grimly to small sections of the country and wars large and small erupting constantly.

The Reconquest, the Christian efforts to rid the peninsula of the Moors, lasted more than 700 years, during which time the Muslims battled each other as well as the Christian forces. Caliphs strong and weak held all of the peninsula except for some northern fringe areas for several centuries, with the Islamic civilization bringing long prosperity to the fortified cities, and notable advances were made in agriculture, industry, literature, philosophy, and medicine. Jews were acceptable to the Moors and became a brilliant facet of the rich culture of Spain during this era.

Intermittent battles between Christians and Moors nibbled away at the Muslim holdings, with Catholic monarchies forming small kingdoms in the northern areas. By the middle of the 13th century, the kingdom of Granada was the only Muslim possession remaining in the Iberian peninsula. The portion that is now Portugal had broken its Moorish bonds by the 11th century, and in Spain rulers of some of the small kingdoms had successfully reclaimed former caliph-held areas. By the time of such kings as Alfonso I of Aragon (1104–1134), the final push was on to rid the land of Islamic control, a drive which reached completion in 1492. It was after the powerful kingdoms of Aragon and Castile had combined their forces under Ferdinand and Isabella that the last Moorish stronghold, Granada, was captured, marking the success of the Reconquest.

The policy of Ferdinand and Isabella was "one king, one law, one faith," although it really meant "one king and queen," since Isabella shared the throne with her royal mate. Foreign affairs were left to the administration of the king, but Isabella took over the rule of internal matters. In this province, she was closely involved with the establishment of the Holy Office, the dread Spanish Inquisition, aimed at firmly cementing Catholicism as the country's religion. Institution of this 300-year-long era saw man's inhumanity to man hold Spain in a stranglehold believed to be blessed of God. Christians, Jews, and Moors who had remained in Spain, which had been home to generations of their forebears, had for the most part peacefully co-existed until the Inquisition.

The year 1492 looms large in the history of Spain because of the completion of the Reconquest, of course, but this was also the year when Jews were given the choice of converting to Christianity or being expelled from the country, a choice which was given to the remaining Muslims of Granada in 1502. Most Jews left, but the great majority of Moors remained, converting to Catholicism and becoming known as the *Moriscos*. (They were nonetheless driven out of Spain in 1609–1611, under inexorable pressure from the Inquisition.)

These internal affairs may mean little to the average American, but the year 1492 was a banner year so far as the history of the New World is concerned —the year Christopher Columbus, that Italian from Genoa, sailed on a voyage funded by the Spanish monarchs to find China (Cathay) and discovered America. The era of this discovery was the immediate forerunner of the Golden Age of Spain.

In the first half of the 16th century, besides further voyages, discoveries, and claims to territories by Columbus, Balboa discovered the Pacific Ocean, Cortés seized Mexico for Spain, Pizarro took Peru, and Magellan (a Portuguese sailing in the Spanish service) and his Spanish successor circumnavigated the globe. The conquistadores took Catholicism to the New World and brought gold and other treasures back to their homeland. The Spanish empire was extended all the way to the Philippines, Spanish ships ruled the seas, and Spanish armies with their "unbeatable infantry" were feared all over Europe.

The intermarriage of royal families of Europe as a means of insuring continuation of dynasties didn't always work out as planned, and so it befell that a Habsburg grandson inherited the throne of Spain from Ferdinand and Isabella, thus embroiling the kingdom in a succession of wars. The Habsburg King of Spain also became head of the Holy Roman Empire in time to be deeply involved in religious wars, particularly with adherents of Martin Luther, and also in conflicts with France and the Turks in North Africa.

By the latter half of the 16th century, the Spanish sun had passed its zenith. Philip II, a fanatic Catholic, came to the throne at a time (1556) when his domain included Spain and its New World colonies; Naples, Milan, Genoa, Sicily, and other portions of Italy; Spanish Holland and Flanders (modern Belgium and the Netherlands); and portions of Austria and Germany. He also married Mary I (Bloody Mary), the British queen, in a bid to take over the British Isles and return them to Catholicism. However, neither this nor his later try to win

Queen Elizabeth I as his wife paid off, and his efforts to take England by force also failed. Spain's supremacy on the sea ended ignominiously in 1588 when the war fleet called the Invincible Armada was defeated by the British—with a little help from the forces of nature.

The might of Spain may have been weakened by the early 17th century, but culturally, it was still in a Golden Age, with such giants in the land as Cervantes, Lope de Vega, El Greco, and Velázquez (see "Art" below). But the country entered into an era of incompetent, ineffectual, and/or immoral rulers coupled with a tightening of the noose of the Inquisition. Many people emigrated to the New World, and without its supply of manpower, the army lost its old force, leading to the end of Spain's power in Europe through conflicts with France, England, and the Netherlands. Death ended the reign of the House of Habsburg at the dawn of the 18th century, and the Bourbon (Borbón) rule was begun, one which has extended, with a hiatus here and there, until today in the person of King Juan Carlos I. It was during the War of the Spanish Succession, to decide who would rule, that Great Britain laid claim to Gibraltar, in 1704, which it still holds. By the end of this war, Spain had lost Belgium, Luxembourg, Milan, Sardinia, and Naples.

During the 18th century, Spain's policies changed with the changing of sovereigns. Now one was for staying out of European battles and attending to internal matters. Next one or two would be for battle action, and changes were made of possession of New World territories back and forth between Britain, France, and Spain (Florida, Louisiana, and other properties). And then came Napoleon. He set up his brother Joseph Bonaparte as King of Spain in 1808, ushering in 90 years of turmoil. Britain and Spain joined forces to defeat Napoleon and return a Bourbon to the throne, but the conflicts had encouraged feelings of independence in the breasts of the Spanish colonists, leading to a time of revolt, which ended with the United States freeing from Spain's yoke the Philippines, Puerto Rico, and Cuba in 1898. Thus ended forever Spain's grip on the New World, although it held colonies in Morocco.

A spirit of liberalism developed and burgeoned in Spain after the defeat of Napoleon, and in the 19th and early 20th centuries, struggles ensued between absolute monarchy and the radical republicans. The 1812 Constitution of Cádiz, a move toward liberalism, was succeeded by the constitution of 1931, which declared Spain a democratic republic of workers and signaled the end of Roman Catholicism as the official religion of the country. After a vote overwhelmingly supported the idea of a republic, Alfonso XIII abdicated, but the Cortes, or parliament, couldn't come to grips with governmental problems, because neither the right nor the republican left had a majority.

This inability to compromise and set up a working government paved the way for the Spanish Civil War, which erupted in 1936, when army officers in Spanish Morocco revolted against the republic. Gen. Francisco Franco came from Morocco to Spain to lead the Nationalist (rightist) forces in the two and a half years of battle that ravaged the country. When the Republicans were beaten, Franco became chief of state, maintaining his hold on the powerful position until his death in 1975.

Spain was not involved in World War I or in World War II, although Franco's sympathies lay with Germany and Italy. They had aided him in his fight for power, and so Spain gave aid to the Axis as a non-belligerent. This fact influenced the diplomatic isolation into which the country was forced after the end of the war and its exclusion from the United Nations until 1955.

General Franco selected Juan Carlos de Borbón y Borbón to be King of Spain upon the demise of the généralissimo. After 1977 elections, the new Cortes initiated a new constitution, approved by the voters and the king, making official such reforms as removal of the status of the Roman Catholic Church as the church of Spain, as well as guaranteeing free enterprise and human and civil rights. It also granted limited autonomy to several regions. Among these were the Basque province and the Catalán province, both of which are still clamoring for complete autonomy.

GOVERNMENT: Spain is a constitutional monarchy, with the king as the head of state. Legislative power is vested in the Cortes, made up of two chambers—the Congress of Deputies and the Senate. All members of these two bodies are elected by popular ballot to four-year terms. The government, answerable to the Cortes, comprises the prime minister (president), vice president, and ministers. All these persons are appointed by the king. Spain has a "defender of the people," or ombudsman. All citizens of Spain can vote at the age of 18.

LANGUAGE: Spanish is the national language, with the Castilian dialect of the central and southern regions the most prevalent and the one used in schools and courts. Official in their own autonomous areas are Catalán, Galician, Basque, Bable, and Valencian tongues. Education is bilingual in those areas. The Spanish gypsies, believed to stem from long-ago migration from Asia, have their own language for communication among themselves.

ART: Spain's contributions to art are known throughout the world, from the 30,000 to 15,000 B.C. carvings and cave paintings in the northern Cantabrian Mountains to the works of the great masters—Velázquez, Goya, Picasso, and El Greco (not Spanish-born but a resident of the country for some four decades). The art of this country is a rich tapestry woven from threads of varied cultures—European, African, Mediterranean, and Atlantic—which have been drawn to and in this peninsula down through the centuries.

Unfortunately, the cave paintings of Altamira have been so damaged by bacteria brought in by visitors that they are no longer on public view. The work of later painters, however, can be seen all over the country in museums, cathedrals, churches, palaces, and monasteries, while sculptures, mosaics, and other works of art also abound. The influences of the ages can be traced in these works, with Phoenician, Greek, Celtic, Roman, Muslim, Romanesque, Gothic, Renaissance, classical, and modern all revealing that talent in art is an integral part of Spanish life.

To name the most outstanding artists and their works would demand more space than I have, but I strongly urge visitors to Spain to go to the Prado in Madrid and to at least some of the places elsewhere in Spain where art can be seen. Besides the four masters mentioned above, also high on the list of Spanish painters whose works should be viewed are Dali, Murillo, Zurbarán, Ribera, Gris, and Miró. The creativity, austerity, and passion evidenced in Spanish art is awesome.

ARCHITECTURE: Spain's architecture might well be nearly identical with that of other European countries had it not been for the long period of Muslim control of most of the Iberian peninsula. Because the Muslims (or Moors, as they were called by the Spaniards) believed in the enjoyment of life's pleasures today rather than in constructing for the ages, their architecture tended to be lavishly decorated on the surface but with flimsy substructure. Therefore, there are not many complete examples left of the monumental Saracenic structures of those centuries. However, enough exist, including great mosques, minarets, and palaces, to show how the influence of such building has come down to modern Spain. Various types of arches, colonnades, reflecting pools, fountains, columns, and filigree ornamentation are among the lasting characteristics.

The Alhambra at Granada and the Alcázar at Seville are the most outstanding examples of Moorish architecture extant in Spain. Both these structures (we'd probably call them complexes today) are the result of various caliphates and periods of Muslim architecture plus *Mudéjar* art. This latter is the name given work in the Spanish Muslim tradition after the Reconquest, either by Moors, converted Muslims, or their trainees. A Mudéjar style is still followed in Spain, especially in the villages, albeit a dim reminder of the grandeur of Muslim art of old.

Other architectural styles borrowed mainly from France and Italy are seen, but for truly original design, visitors should see the work of the controversial Catalonia-born António Gaudí, especially in Santander and Barcelona.

LITERATURE: The language of poets and the speech of the people have been the hallmarks of Spanish literature. Its great tradition of creative work influenced by the Roman heritage, the Moorish period, Jewish history, Catholic austerity, the remoteness of living on a peninsula cut off from its nearest neighbor by high mountains, and use through the centuries of a commonly understood tongue—all this is still reflected in the literary output of Spain. These influences have brought to the printed page a sense of God, salvation, death, tragedy, the world, and time, a combination that in translation may be remote from the interest of Americans in general. However, in much of Spain's medieval literature and even in today's, there is an earthy wit which is particularly enjoyable if you can read it in Spanish.

After the epic poetry of the late Moorish period and the popular poems by wandering minstrels came romantic ballads and Italian-influenced poetry. It wasn't until the 15th century that prose became widely recognized, with the publication of biography, novels, and moralizing treatises, these forms continuing on into the "Golden Age of Spanish Literature." This 16th-century age was marked mainly by religious and humanist writings, picaresque novels (the protagonist being a *picaro,* or rogue), pastoral novels, histories, books of chivalry, and plays. The Golden Age gave birth to a writer whose work has become known especially to most Americans through the medium of motion pictures if not through reading translations. Who has not heard of that "Man of La Mancha," *Don Quixote,* the creation of Cervantes?

Much modern Spanish literature dwells perhaps too much on social realism and philosophical problems to make for light reading, but there are some fine 20th-century poets, novelists, and playwrights whose work is best read in the language in which it is written but of which some good translations are available.

Four Spaniards have won the Nobel Prize for Literature since it was originated in 1901. Questions have been raised as to the wisdom of the awards committee in selecting José Echegaray, playwright, as co-winner in 1904, but more justification was seen in the naming of Jacinto Benavente, also a playwright, for the prize in 1922. The 1956 award went to Juan Ramón Jiménez, an Andalusian poet, and in 1977, the Nobel was presented to Vicente Alexandre, regarded as "the spiritual father of the younger generation of poets in Spain."

MUSIC AND DANCE: Perhaps the great Spanish musicians best known to North Americans are the pianist José Iturbi, classical guitarist Andrés Segovia, cellist Pablo Casals, and opera tenor Placido Domingo, although there are many others who may be favorites of yours.

The earliest music of Spain on written record springs from the early Christian era when the liturgy evolved into the Visigothic chant, which came to be called the Moorish chant. Before the Arab invasion, music was flourishing in Toledo, Zaragoza, and Seville, and it continued, with Christian Spain developing hymns and liturgical dramas in the monasteries, as well as other church music. These works became an element of court life in the little kingdoms that sprang up in opposition to the Moorish inroads, with secular tunes soon following.

The conquerors from Africa brought with them many instruments, some of which caught the fancy of the Spaniards and then of all Europe, with Zaragoza and Seville becoming centers for the making of musical instruments, crafts which outlasted the Moorish occupation. Among the instruments brought in were the square tambourine (*adufe* in Spanish), the standard tambourine (*pandarete*), a drum (*atabal*), a psaltery (*canón*), and metal castanets (*sonajas de azófar*). Three of the new instruments whose use spread through Europe were the lute, the rebec, and the naker (a small wood or metal kettledrum).

It wasn't until during the Renaissance, after the Moors were ousted, that instrumental music began to take its place as an important musical art form. This was especially true of music for a primitive guitar called the *vihuela,* typically Spanish but developed under Moorish auspices. (The six-course vihuela was replaced by the five-course guitar in the 17th century.) It was during this era that the pipe organ as a key element of sacred music gained stature.

Spanish opera, emerging in the 17th century, was strongly influenced by the work of the Italians, but the *zarzuela,* an 18th-century Spanish light musical similar to the Gilbert and Sullivan operettas (later a sort of variety show), was truly Spanish.

Traditional Spanish folk songs and dances have survived from early times, although these are giving way to TV and other modern mass entertainment, particularly in the urban areas.

Flamenco

From the lowliest taberna to the poshest nightclub, you are likely to hear heel clicking, foot stamping, castanet rattling, hand clapping, and the sound of sultry and tortured guitar music. This is flamenco. Its origins lie deep in the Orient, but the Spanish gypsy has given it an original and unique style.

It is a dance dramatizing inner tension. Performed by a great artist, flamenco can tear your heart out. But the growth and popularity of this art form have caused many a mediocre performer to enter the field, and these people are often more concerned with imitation and audience reaction than they are with any lost love. Occasionally you may have to sit through a parade of untalented performers, waiting for the true artist.

Chances are you are familiar with flamenco. But what most Americans consider flamenco is typical of Andalusia. Discovering variations on the theme may spark up many an evening for you.

The usual flamenco place in Spain is, in reality, a cabaret, where you pay a certain amount for the first drink—and this is tantamount to a cover charge.

Flamenco has no story line to follow. The leader, with insistent hand clapping, sets the pace, drawing each of the performers forward. He or she lurks behind and around the performers at all times, trying to infuse them with rhythm. If it is a good rhythm, it can be contagious. You may end up with the castanets yourself, stamping and crying out.

FIESTAS: Year in and year out, the Spaniard celebrates fiestas. Almost all of these events are religious in nature, but they offer entertainment to all, Catholic or not. Both religious and cultural motifs are combined to form this spectacle of Spanish life. Bullfights, parades of colorfully costumed locals, folk singing and dancing, concerts, games, and exhibits lift the fiesta out of merely regional interest.

During the fiesta, all semblance of a regularly scheduled life comes to a halt in the towns or cities. The gears shift rapidly, as the locals pour their energies and enthusiasms into these celebrations (the frenzied preparations leading up to them are almost as exciting as the actual events). When you see the hard life that many of the workers lead, you may better understand why the fiesta is such an important period in which to have an emotional overflow and release.

September, in particular, is one of the most crowded and varied months on the festival calendar, although August offers serious competition. **Semana Santa** (Holy Week) is celebrated all over Spain. **Corpus Christi** is another colorful observance time throughout the country. But the calendar is loaded year round.

Many of these fiestas have major variations—and are known by other names. For example, a *romerías,* which you may see along the road, is a pilgrimage to a particular historic site (everybody packs food, as the romerías sometimes last two days). In contrast, a *verbena* is held in a city (Madrid has one) or a town. At a verbena, the nightlife is festive, with a special emphasis placed on folk dancing. Finally, a *fería* (literally, fair) is a special event dear to the Spanish soul. The best-known one is the **Fería of Seville,** but there are countless others. Don't expect it to be devoted to cattle shows: singing and dancing are also the rule of the day.

How do you attend a fiesta? When and where are they held? Frankly, there are so many that it would take a thick volume to list and describe them. However, Tourist Bureaus throughout Spain distribute (free) a *Tourist Calendar,* which catalogues all of these folk traditions.

The most recent edition listed more than 3,000 such events.

3. Bullfights

THE SPECTACLE OF DEATH: A great number of Americans consider bullfighting a cruel and shocking sport. But Ernest Hemingway, in his encyclopedia of bullfighting, *Death in the Afternoon,* pointed out, "The bullfight is not a sport in the Anglo-Saxon sense of the word, that is, it is not an equal contest or an attempt at an equal contest between a bull and a man. Rather it is a tragedy; the death of the bull, which is played, more or less well, by the bull and the man involved and in which there is danger for the man but certain death for the bull." Hemingway, of course, became an aficionado. Perhaps you will too.

The symbolic inner drama of the bullfight is acted out almost like a ballet—it's certainly an art form. There are those who are convinced that it is not cruelty, but a highly skilled activity calling forth some of man's most important qualities: survival, courage, and style.

Regardless of how you view it—cruel sport, tragedy, art form—this spectacle in the afternoon is an authentically Spanish experience, and, as such, has much to reveal about the character of the land and its people.

In fairness, it should be pointed out that many readers have expressed horror upon viewing a bullfight. I take no official position on it, as it is largely a matter of personal taste. Go at your own risk.

Season and Tickets

The season of the *corridas,* as the bullfights are called, takes place from early spring until around mid-October, possibly earlier. Fights are held in locations ranging from the oldest ring in remote Ronda to the big-time Plaza de Toros in Madrid. Sunday is corrida day in most major Spanish cities, although Madrid and Barcelona may have fights on Thursday. Smaller towns that can't afford many bulls plan fights to coincide with their fairs or feast days.

How to purchase a ticket will be described in both the Madrid and Barcelona sections of this book, but these preliminary comments can be made. Tickets fall into three classifications: *sol* (sun), *sombra* (shade), or *sol y sombra* (a mixture of two—half in the sun, half in the shade, when the sun starts to set). Naturally, the sombra seats are the most expensive; the sombra-y-sol ticket falls into the medium-priced range.

A bullring is called a *plaza de toros.* Don't refer to a bullfighter as a toreador. The one who kills the bull is a *matador.* All the use of the word toreador may prove—other than resulting in a laugh from a Spaniard—is that you've seen *Carmen.*

The Fight Itself

The corrida begins with a parade, in which all participants take part. For many viewers, this may be the high point in the afternoon's festivities, as all the bullfighters are clad in their costumes called "suits of light."

The fight begins when the lance-carrying *picadores* on horseback go after the bull and jab him. This is the point in the game at which the first-time viewer often raises objections. The horses are sometimes gored, even though protected by mattresses. If not this, the horse and its rider may be tossed into the air.

Next come the *banderilleros,* whose job is to puncture the bull with pairs of gaily colored darts. This is a major step in preparation for the kill. When the matador places the darts, it is even more exciting, as chances are he'll be more stylized and skilled than the banderilleros.

After this fanfare, the action narrows down to the lone fighter and the bull. This is the highlight of the afternoon. Gone are the fancy capes. Instead, the matador uses what is known as a *muleta,* a small red cloth. He makes a challenge to the bull, perhaps one known as a *natural,* most often with the muleta held in his left hand. Hemingway called it "the fundamental pass of bullfighting, the simplest, capable of greatest purity of line and the most dangerous to make."

After a number of passes, the time comes for the kill, the "moment of truth." A truly skilled fighter may kill the bull in one thrust. However, a bullfighter's skill at killing is not judged by what happens to the bull after the sword thrust. Nevertheless, it's a common sight to see fighters who make repeated thrusts, arousing a spirit of revenge on the part of the audience. The angry spectators are likely to toss objects into the ring to vent their rage. After the bull drops dead, the highest official at the ring may award the matador an ear from the dead bull, or perhaps give him the tail. The bullfighter may be carried away as a hero, or, if he has displeased the crowd, be chased out of the ring by an angry mob.

Usually, six bulls are killed by three matadors in an afternoon.

4. Food and Drink

For the North American, the Spanish cuisine presents a number of tempting surprises—enough to rate an *Olé.* It also offers a number of gastronomic nightmares, enough to make the palate cry uncle and the stomach rumble something unprintable. Matadors, horsemen, flamenco dancers, the Spaniards are. Great chefs they often are not.

Still, in spite of this drawback, the tastebuds of today's pilgrim are in for better flavors than ever before. Those who traveled in Spain in the '30s, '40s, and '50s could tell a story to make gastronomes swear off food for life. But today the Spanish chef or just plain cook in the tourist-trodden Spain is faced with a dilemma. Tastebuds tell the Spaniard one thing; the sharp-tongued foreigner often disagrees. Being essentially hospitable, the Spaniard tries to adapt. If a foreigner likes hamburgers, then hamburgers it will be. But the Spanish chef reacts with wide-eyed hurt when the diner sends the plate back with a question: "Why did you saturate that burger in all that olive oil?"

The foreigner may one day succeed in changing the Spanish cuisine. Already all major hotels feature international cooking, which sometimes is another term to describe bland, uninspired fare.

By no means should you get the impression that all Spanish food is bad. Many dishes and regional specialties are excellent, as will be detailed in the coming chapters.

The food in Spain is often varied, the portions immense—and the price moderate by North American standards. Don't travel looking for a Kansas City steak. However, the roast suckling pig is so sweet and tender it can often be cut with a fork. The Spanish have superb cuts of veal that are unknown in North America. The Spanish *lomo (de cerdo)*—a loin of pork—is unmatched anywhere.

Here are some general rules to help guide you:

Breakfast: One starts the day off lightly in Spain with a continental breakfast—either hot coffee, hot chocolate, or tea, with assorted rolls, butter, and jam. A typical Spanish breakfast is *churros* (fried, finger-like "donuts") and a chocolate that is very sweet and thick. The coffee is usually strong and black, served with hot milk. Some Americans consider it too strong and bitter for their tastes, and therefore ask for Nescafé, which seems to have a virtual monopoly in Spain. You'll get a pot of hot water and an envelope of powdered coffee. Breakfasts are served in your room or in the hotel restaurant, although the best buys are available at the so-called *cafeterías*. The cafeterías are found on all major streets in all Spanish cities. Breakfast is obtainable at almost any time you want it.

Lunch: This is an important meal in Spain, comparable to the farm-style noonday "dinner" in America. There is rarely anything dainty about Spanish lunches—no watercress sandwiches or scoops of chicken salad on toast. Luncheons usually include three or four courses, beginning with a choice of a big bowl of soup or several dishes of hors d'oeuvres called *entremeses*. Often a fish or egg dish is served following this, and then a meat course with vegetables. Wine is always on the table. Dessert is usually a pastry, custard, or assorted fruit; this is followed by coffee. Lunch is late by American standards: 1 to 3:30 p.m. And now you know why the Spaniard has those little sandwiches at 11. If you want to be almost guaranteed a table in a popular restaurant, arrive exactly at 1 p.m. when the restaurant first opens. That way, you'll be well into your meal when the 2 p.m. rush occurs.

Tascas: After the early-evening promenade, many Spaniards head for their favorite *tascas*, or bars, where they drink wine and sample assorted *tapas*, such as bits of fish, eggs in mayonnaise, or olives.

Dinner: This is another extravaganza. A typical meal again starts with a big bowl of soup, followed by a second course, often a fish dish, and backed up by another main course, usually veal, beef, or pork, accompanied by vegetables. Again, desserts tend to run to fresh fruit, custard, or pastries. A large flask of wine always sits on the table, and you can generally drink as much as you want. Afterward, you might have demitasse and one of those fragrant Spanish brandies. The chic dining hour, even in one-donkey towns, is 10 or 10:30 p.m. Quite conceivably, you might get out by midnight. (In heavy tourist regions and hard-working Catalonia, you can usually get your dinner by 8 p.m.). In most middle-class establishments, people dine no later than 9:30 p.m. It's really a matter of taste.

Warnings: Know that the Spaniard loves to eat from the first hour in the morning until midnight.

North Americans who plunge wholeheartedly (or whole hog) into this experience all at once may be headed for trouble. The Spaniard's stomach is made out of genuine, rust-free cast iron. Yours may not be. Those who start sampling all the specialties the first day and drinking far beyond their usual intake of wine invariably will be suffering "Toledo tummy" before the sun rises on the third day. You might want to get Tanagel, sold in all pharmacies, to stop this malady.

Furthermore, two heavy Spanish meals a day are definitely not recommended at any time. Throughout Spain are sprouting up modern cafeterías (not self-service), featuring what is essentially American-inspired food. It might be better to patronize one of these establishments, as the light lunch is virtually unknown elsewhere in Spain. Perhaps a toasted ham sandwich, some fresh fruit or melon, and a drink for lunch, instead of a four-courser ranging from chicken paella to squid cooked in its own ink. Then you may be in the mood for a big Spanish dinner.

As a final caution, if you do consume a heaping lunch, don't behave like mad dogs and Englishmen and rush out into the noonday sun for a round of sightseeing, the Prado, the Royal Palace, Toledo at sunset. Do as the Spaniard does. Go home to sleep it off in a recuperative siesta.

Alternatively, you may strike a different balance, changing your regular eating habits. If you take your large meal in the middle of the day (chances are, you may be hungry by 1 p.m. since most breakfasts are skimpy), you might happily settle for a snack in the early evening in one of the tapas bars or else a selection from a pastry shop. By not eating a large meal at night, you may help prevent indigestion.

RESTAURANTS AND MENUS: Many restaurants provide a *menú turistico* or set menu where most everything is included for one price. Spain is currently undergoing a change in its eating habits, probably as a result of entertaining so many visitors. For many, this tourist menu is too large, too unwieldy, especially at lunch. Others, however, find it the best bargain.

The *menú del día,* or *cubierto,* emerges as a more viable selection. Offering a complete meal at a set price, the menu of the day is the finest dining bargain in Spain, although it rarely features the best food. Usually it includes a first course, such as fish soup or hors d'oeuvres, followed by a main dish, plus dessert, bread, and the wine of the house. You won't have a large selection, but enough to dine well, nevertheless. For this set meal, the cook decides what are the best buys of the day at the market. Lunches, especially in Madrid, are becoming briefer. The siesta may one day be a thing of the past.

Of course, in all restaurants you can order à la carte. Certainly many visitors have found this preferable to ordering the more standardized set meals.

Finally, with very few exceptions, the cost of any dish on a Spanish menu includes the service charge too, but it is customary to leave a 10% tip.

Most restaurants in Spain still adhere to the rigid Sunday closing. Have your hotel call ahead and check a particular establishment before heading there on a Sunday. On the other hand, hotel dining rooms are generally open seven days a week. There's always some food dispenser open, particularly in Madrid, Barcelona, and the Costa del Sol, but in smaller places staffs like a day of rest.

Cafeterías: These are springing up everywhere. But don't expect self-service. The latter are usually called *auto-servicio* in Spain. Unlike the American-style cafeteria, the cafetería in Spain is derived from café (coffee) and etymologically has nothing to do with self-service. Many of these cafeterías—rated one, two, or three cups—don't even serve hot meals. Others do. Many feature increasingly popular dishes known as combined plates—say, fried eggs, french fries, veal, a lettuce-and-tomato salad. Some of these combined plates may be mismatched, others quite adequate.

The cafeterías are responsible for the biggest change presently occurring in the Spaniard's eating habits. Although many serve hot Spanish meals, their menus generally offer lighter items, such as hot dogs and hamburgers.

The Question of Olive Oil and Garlic

Garlic is an integral part of the Spanish diet, and after the cooking revolution that occurred in North America in the '60s and '70s, visitors are no longer as shy of its wonderful flavor as they once were. However, know that the Spaniard probably loves garlic more than you do, and it appears often in the oddest dishes. Since there are still some people around who can't abide it, in any form, it's important to learn the expression *sin ajo* ("without ah-ho"). That tells a waiter who doesn't speak English that you don't want garlic in your dish.

Olive oil is so expensive today that it's considered a luxury. But if you don't want it in a certain dish, and prefer, say, your fish grilled in butter, the word is *mantequilla.* In some instances, you'll be charged extra for the butter. Some dishes, such as paella, require the oil in their basic preparation—and therefore it can't be avoided.

One reader, John R. Miller, Jr., in the U.S. State Department in Rabat, Morocco, writes: "I found that olive oil added a distinct and hearty flavor to my eggs, and now prefer them cooked that way instead of with butter."

Perhaps, if you're not addicted already, Spain will convert you to olive oil and garlic.

Some Notes on the Cuisine

Whenever possible, you may want to partake of regional specialties, as during your visit to the Basque country or Galicia. But many dishes, including Andalusian gazpacho and Valencian paella, have transcended their region and have become dishes of the world. Some items you may want to avoid; others should be included as part of your Spanish experience, even though they may seem odd or sound unappetizing.

To begin with, soups are quite good, and are usually served in big bowls, although some hotels are catching on to the dainty cup. The creamed soups, such as asparagus and potato, can be top-notch, and bland enough to be soothing to delicate stomachs. In fact, they are often made of powdered envelope soups such as Knorr and Liebig. The already-mentioned *gazpacho,* on the other hand, is heavy but tasty. It is chilled soup, served year round, but particularly popular during the hot months. The combination is pleasant: olive oil, garlic, ground cucumbers, and raw tomatoes with a sprinkling of croutons. Spain also offers a variety of fish soups—*sopa de pescado*—in all of its provinces, and many of these are superb.

In the paradores and top restaurants, the hors d'oeuvres can be tempting. Sometimes as many as 15 tiny dishes are served. In lesser-known places, these entremeses are something to be avoided, often consisting of last year's sardines and bits and pieces of sausage left over from the Moorish Conquest. In contrast, salads will probably be appreciated by most North Americans. They are usually fresh, with crisp lettuce and vine-ripened tomatoes.

Eggs—served in countless ways—loom large in the Spanish diet. An omelet is called a *tortilla.* But what is known as a Spanish omelet in America is not Spanish in Spain (they refer to it as Portuguese). A Spanish omelet—called a *tortilla española*—is one made with potatoes. A simple omelet is called a *tortilla francesa.*

In its fish dishes, Spain is a star. The residents prepare them in unique and tempting ways, varying from province to province. It is now possible to get safe fish even in inland cities, such as Zaragoza. Ice and speedy transportation have distributed the treats of the sea all over Spain. One of the most common types of fish offered is hake (*merluza*); it's sweet and white, quite good and very popular. *Langosta,* a variety of lobster, is seen everywhere—and it's a treat, but expensive.

The Portuguese, in particular, but some of the Spaniards too, go into rapture at the mention of barnacles. Gourmets eat them with gleaming eyes, and speak of the sea-water taste. Others find them a tasteless bore.

If you see *rape* suggested on a menu, don't be surprised. The Spanish Tourist Office defines it as a "sweet, wide-boned ocean fish, the texture of scallops."

Also recommended—at least once—are a few dozen half-inch baby eels. They rely heavily on olive oil and garlic for their flavor, but they're good to eat. Squid cooked in its own ink is suggested only to those who want to go native. A culinary delight, however, are charcoal-broiled sardines, a treat in the Basque provinces.

One of the most popular fish dishes in Spain is "trout Navarre." Most often this dish is a trout stuffed with bacon or ham. Many Spanish people prefer it this way. Some fish lovers consider that such a method of preparation destroys the flavor of the trout.

You can't go to Spain without trying *paella,* made in thousands of different ways (with whatever the chef happens to have in the kitchen). Flavored with saffron, paella is the most famous dish of Spain, obtainable almost anywhere. It is an aromatic and delightfully seasoned rice dish topped usually with shellfish, chicken, sausage, peppers, and other local spices. Served authentically, it comes in a metal pan called a *paellera* steaming hot from the kitchen. Incidentally, what is known in America as Spanish rice isn't Spanish at all. If you ask an English-speaking waiter for Spanish rice, he'll serve you paella.

As for chicken, it will sometimes qualify for the Olympics, in the sense that it is stringy and muscular. Spit-roasted chicken, however, often can be quite flavorful. Beef, on the other hand, would not satisfy a Texas rancher, but it's possible to get a thinly cut steak that's not too tough. Pork is at its best when it is suckling pig, spit roasted, and served crisp on the outside, tender inside. Lamb chops and veal crop up on almost all menus, particularly veal.

Except in summer, vegetables are weak on the Spanish menu. Green fresh vegetables seem hard to come by, and the diner often gets canned string beans, peas, or artichokes. Potatoes are also a staple. Avoid mashed potatoes.

The Spanish resemble the Chinese in that they do not put great emphasis on desserts. *Flan* is a home-cooked egg custard, and it appears on all menus—sometimes with a burnt-caramel sauce. Otherwise, it's a good bet to ask for a basket of fresh fruit, which you will wash at your table. Homemade pastries are usually moist and not too sweet. Ice cream is featured on nearly all menus as well. As a dining oddity, many restaurants serve fresh orange juice as a dessert. Lots of Madrileños love it!

DAYS OF WINE, SHERRY, AND SOLARES: Unlike the European, the North American is a water drinker—and getting the stuff in Spain used to be a problem, but that has long since ceased to be the case. The water is safe to drink in all the major cities and tourist resorts. But if you're traveling in really remote areas, you might play it safe and order bottled water. On all other occasions, bottled water is a waste of money, yet it's thought of as a most fashionable drink.

One of the most popular noncarbonated bottled drinks in Spain is *Solares,* which comes from a town in northern Spain known for its pure waters. Nearly all restaurants and hotels have it. If you'd like your water with a little kick, then ask for *agua mineral con gas.* You'll note that bottled water often costs more than the regional wine.

In the largest cities you get bottled milk, but it loses a great deal of its flavor in the process of pasteurization and tastes cooked. In all cases, avoid untreated milk and milk products. Sometimes it's safe—and sometimes it isn't—but why take the chance? About the best brand of fresh milk is called **Lauki.**

Beer (*cerveza*) is not native to Spain, but is now drunk everywhere as commonly as in the U.S. Domestic brands include San Miguel, Mahou, Aguila, and Cruz Blanka.

Sherry (*vino de Jerez*), made from grapes from the aristocratic vineyards at Jerez de la Frontera, south of Seville, has been called "the wine with a hundred souls." This is the drink to have before dinner (try the topaz-colored *finos,* a very pale sherry), or whenever you drop in to some old inn or bodega for refreshment. Many of them have rows of kegs with spigots. *Manzanilla,* incidentally, was extolled by no less an authority than Hemingway, who preferred it as an apéritif. Remembered from Edgar Allan Poe's *The Cask of Amontillado,* a golden-colored, medium-dry sherry of the same name is also extremely popular. The sweet cream sherries (Harvey's Bristol Cream, for example) are favorite after-dinner wines (called *oloroso*).

The French may be disdainful of Spanish wines, but they can be truly noble, especially two leading Spanish varieties, **Valdepeñas** and **La Rioja,** both from Castile. If you're fairly adventurous and not too demanding in your tastes, you can always ask for the *vino de la casa* (wine of the house) wherever you dine. The **Ampurdan** of Catalonia is heavy. From Andalusia comes the fruity **Montilla.** There are also some good local champagnes in Spain, such as **Freixenet.** One brand, **Benjamin,** also comes in individual-size bottles.

A word should also be said about Spanish cider (*sidra*), from the northern provinces. There are three basic types: (1) still cider, which is poured in a special way, and is usually obtained in Asturian taverns specializing in this; (2) plain bottled cider, similar to that served in England or France; and (3) champagne cider, tasting a bit like champagne.

Sangría is the all-time favorite refreshing drink in Spain. It is a red-wine punch that is festive looking, and mixed with oranges, lemons, seltzer, and sugar.

Imported whiskies are available at most Spanish bars, but at a high price. If you're a drinking person, it is better to switch to brandies and cognacs. The Spanish reign supreme with these two drinks. Try **Fundador,** made by the Pedro Domecq family in Jerez de la Frontera. If you're seeking a smooth cognac, ask for "103" white label.

You'll find many varieties of aromatic and potently sweet liqueurs—fine for after dinner if you have a sweet tooth.

Coca-Cola, and even Pepsi, have long since made inroads into Spain, but these drinks are more expensive than in America. In general, avoid the carbonated citrus drinks that are on sale almost anywhere. Most of them never saw an orange, much less a lemon. If you want a citrus drink, order old, reliable Schweppes. An excellent noncarbonated drink for the summer, now exported to France, is called **Tri-Naranjus** and comes in lemon and orange flavors. Your cheapest bet is getting a liter bottle of **gaseosa,** which comes in various flavors. In summer you should also try a drink I've had nowhere else outside Spain. It's called a **horchata,** a nutty, sweet milk-like beverage made of tubers called chufas.

5. The ABCs of Spain

I have gathered a collection of important miscellany—data that can be crucial to a visitor to Spain—to help make your trip more enjoyable. Typical queries, answered below, include: How much do I tip a porter? How do I make a telephone call? How do I find a doctor? etc. Practical facts pertaining only to Madrid will be found under that title in Section 1, Chapter III.

BANKS: You get a better exchange rate here if you're exchanging dollars into pesetas than you do at any of the exchange bureaus around the city. Banks are open from 9:30 a.m. (but it's best to go after 10 a.m.) to 2 p.m. Monday to Friday. Banks are also open on Saturday from 9:30 a.m. to 1 p.m.

CLIMATE: In summer, it's hot, hot, and hot again, with the cities of Castile (Madrid) and the cities of Andalusia (Seville and Córdoba) stewing up the most scalding brew. Madrid has dry heat; the temperature can hover around 84° Fahrenheit in July, 75° in September. Inland Seville has the dubious reputation of being about the hottest area in Spain in July and August, often baking under temperatures that average around 93°.

Barcelona is humid. The temperature in Majorca in high summer often reaches 91°. On the overcrowded Costa Brava, the essentially European clientele experiences around 81° in July and August. The Costa del Sol has an average of 77° heat in summer. The coolest spot in Spain is the Atlantic Coast from San Sebastián to La Coruña, with temperatures in the 70s in July and August.

In spite of attempts to change it, August remains the major vacation month in Europe. The traffic from France into Spain becomes a spectacular movement of humanity, and low-cost hotels are almost fully booked along the coastal areas. The top prices are in effect. To compound the problem, many restaurants and shops also decide it's time for a vacation, thereby limiting the visitor's selections for both dining and shopping.

Spring and fall are the ideal times to visit nearly all of Spain, with the possible exception of the Atlantic Coast, which experiences heavy rainfall in October and November.

In **winter,** the coast from Algeciras to Málaga is most popular, with temperatures reaching a warm 60° to 63°. It gets cold in Madrid, as low as 34°. Majorca is warmer, usually in the 50s, but often dipping into the 40s. Some of the mountain resorts have extreme cold.

Conclusion: May and October are the best months.

CLOTHING SIZES: For the most part, Spain uses the same sizes as the continent of Europe. The sizes of women's stockings and men's socks are international.

For Women

Junior Miss		Regular Dresses		Shoes	
U.S.	*Spain*	*U.S.*	*Spain*	*U.S.*	*Spain*
5	34	10	40	5	36
7	36	12	42	5½	36½
9	38	14	44	6½	37½
11	40	16	46	7½	38½
		18	48	8	39
		20	50	8½	39½
				9	40

For Men

Shirts		Slacks		Shoes	
U.S.	*Spain*	*U.S.*	*Spain*	*U.S.*	*Spain*
14	36	32	42	5	36
14½	37	34	44	6	37
15	38	36	46	7	38
15½	39	38	48	7½	39
15¾	40	40	50	8	40
16	41			9	41
16½	42			10	42
17	43			10½	43
				11	44
				12	45

Warning: This chart should be followed only as a very general outline, as in the same country there are big differences in sizes. If possible, try on all clothing or shoes before making a purchase. You'll be glad you did.

CRIME: See Chapter III, "Practical Facts," under Section 1 for advice on self-protection in Madrid, as issued by the American Embassy. More specific references to crime will be found under a Traveler's Advisory for cities such as Málaga and Seville. Terrorism is a major political problem for the country, but, chances are, the average visitor can go into every province of Spain and never encounter a Basque terrorist or know that one exists.

CURRENCY: Spain's unit of currency is the **peseta,** worth about $.007 in U.S. terms (as of this writing—*subject to change*). One U.S. dollar is worth about 143 pesetas. Spain also uses *centimos,* units of currency so low they're almost worthless. It takes 100 centimos to equal 1 peseta, which is worth about ½¢ in U.S. coinage.

Pesetas	U.S.$	Pesetas	U.S.$
2	.01	200	$1.40
3	.02	250	1.75
4	.03	300	2.10
5	.04	400	2.80
7	.05	500	3.50
8	.06	750	5.25
10	.07	1,000	7.00
15	.11	1,250	8.75
20	.14	1,500	10.50
25	.18	1,750	12.25
50	.35	2,000	14.00

Warning: There is now a 100-peseta coin. It is copper in color and about the same size as a 5-peseta coin. Therefore, it's quite easy to confuse the two.

CUSTOMS: Spain permits you to bring in most personal effects and the following items duty free: two still cameras with ten rolls of film each, one movie camera, tobacco for personal use, one liter bottle each of wine and liquor per person, a portable radio, a tape recorder and a typewriter, a bicycle, golf clubs, tennis racquets, fishing gear, two hunting weapons with 100 cartridges each, skis and other sports equipment.

Upon leaving Spain, citizens of the United States who have been outside the country for 48 hours or more are allowed to bring in $400 worth of merchandise duty free—that is, if they have claimed no similar exemption within the past 30 days. If you make purchases in Spain, it's important to keep your receipts.

ELECTRIC CURRENT: Most establishments now have either 125 or 200 volts. Carry your voltage adapter with you and always check at your hotel desk before plugging in any electrical equipment. It's best to travel with battery-operated equipment.

EMBASSIES: The American, Canadian, and British Embassies are located in Madrid. See "Practical Facts," Chapter III.

FILM: As one tourist official put it, film is "expensive as hell in Spain." Take in as much as Customs will allow. I suggest that you wait until you return home to process it.

HOLIDAYS: They include January 1 (New Year's Day); January 6 (The Epiphany); March 19 (Feast of St. Joseph); Good Friday; Easter Monday; May 1 (May Day); June 10 (Corpus Christi); June 29 (Feast of St. Peter and St. Paul); July 25 (Feast of St. James); August 15 (Feast of the Assumption); October 12 (Spain's National Day); November 1 (All Saints' Day); December 8 (Immaculate Conception), and December 25 (Christmas, of course). No matter how large or small, every city or town in Spain also celebrates its local saint's day. In Madrid it's on May 15 (Saint Isidro). You will almost never know what the local holidays are in your next destination in Spain. Therefore, don't use up all your pesetas, because you may arrive in town to find banks and stores shut tightly. In some cases, intercity bus services are suspended on holidays.

LAUNDRY: In most of the top hotels recommended in this guide, you need only fill out your laundry and dry-cleaning list and present it to your maid or valet. Same-day service usually costs from 25% to 50% more.

LIQUOR: Almost anyone of any age can order a drink in Spain. I've seen gypsy shoeshine boys who looked no more than 8 years old go into a tasca and purchase a glass of wine with their newly acquired tip. Bars, taverns, cafeterías, whatever, generally open at 8 a.m., and many serve alcohol until around 1 or 2 a.m. Spain doesn't have many stores devoted entirely to selling liquor and wine. Rather, you can purchase alcoholic beverages in almost any market, along with cheese and other foodstuffs.

METRIC MEASURES: Here's your chance to learn metric measures before they're common in America.

Weights

U.S.	*Spain*
1 ounce	= 28.3 grams
1 pound	= 454 grams
2.20 pounds	= 1 kilo (1,000 grams)
1 pint	= 0.47 liter
1 quart	= 0.94 liter
1 gallon	= 3.78 liters

Measures

U.S.	*Spain*
1 inch	= 2.54 centimeters
1 foot	= 0.3 meters
1 yard	= 0.91 meters
1.09 yards	= 1 meter
1 mile	= 1.61 kilometers
0.62 mile	= 1 kilometer
1 acre	= 0.40 hectare
2.47 acres	= 1 hectare

NEWSPAPERS: Most newsstands along the Gran Vía in Madrid or kiosks at the major hotels carry the latest edition of the *International Herald Tribune.* Spain also has an American weekly, a magazine known as the *Guidepost.* It is packed with information about late-breaking events in the Spanish capital: tips on movies shown in English, musical recitals, whatever. You may also want to become a regular reader of the *Iberian Daily Sun,* an English-language newspaper containing stories and listings of interest to both visitors from North America and Britain as well as expatriates. If you're traveling south, look out for *Lookout* magazine, a quality production in English, with stories focused primarily on Spain's Sun Coast, although the staff also runs articles of general interest to the traveler to Spain.

PASSPORTS: A valid one is all an American, British, or Canadian citizen needs to enter Spain. You don't need an international driver's license if renting a car. Your local one from back home should suffice if it is up-to-date.

PETS: Better leave them at home. Otherwise, before departure you have to bring documents to the Spanish consulate nearest you, revealing licenses and shots. In normal circumstances pets aren't welcome at public places; certain hotels will accept them, however. But these arrangements should be made in advance.

PHARMACIES: If you're trying to locate a drugstore at an odd hour, note the list posted outside the door to any drugstore that's not open. On the list are the names and addresses of pharmacies that are in service. The Spanish government requires drugstores to operate on a rotating system of hours—thereby assuring you that some will be open at all times, even Sunday midnight.

RADIO AND TV: You're out of luck if you want to watch your favorite TV shows in English. Every television network broadcasts in Spanish. However, on the radio you can pick up the voice of the American Armed Forces, listening to music, hourly newscasts, and sports reporting. You'll also get a weather report if you're planning to go touring that day.

RESTROOMS: The Spanish designations for restrooms are *aseos* and *servicios. Caballeros* are for men and *damas* for women. If you find no public facilities, you can go into a bar or tasca, but you should order something. Restaurants and hotels have toilet facilities, of course.

SMOKING: Temmie and Aubrey Baratz of Briarcliff Manor, New York, write: "Your readers should be forewarned that in Spain virtually everyone smokes. On buses. In the Metro. Everywhere. 'No Fumar' signs are ignored. With all that smoking, combined with inhaling diesel fumes, one wonders about the incidence of lung disease in Spain."

STORE HOURS: Major stores no longer take a siesta, and are open from 9:30 a.m. to 8 p.m. Monday to Saturday. However, smaller stores, such as the "mama and papa" operations, still follow the old custom and do business from 9:30 a.m. to 1:30 p.m. and 4:30 to 8 p.m. Of course, there is absolutely no set formula, and hours can vary from store to store.

TAXES: When Spain joined the Common Market (EEC) on January 1, 1986 (which it did simultaneously with Portugal), it committed itself to gradually eliminating most tariff barriers between itself and the rest of Europe. In consequence, internal sales taxes (known in Spain as I.V.A.) were immediately adjusted upward to between 6% and 33%, depending on the commodity being sold. Most of the basic necessities of a Spaniard's life, including food and most wines, are taxed at 6%. The majority of goods and services are taxed at the "ordinary" rate of 12%. Luxury goods such as jewelry, furs, motor yachts, rental cars, and private airplanes, carry a 33% tax. Luxury hotels are usually subject to the 12% tax, although the increase is almost always quoted as part of the rates. Unfortunately for drinkers and smokers, all imported liquors and all tobaccos (whether Spanish or foreign) are taxed at the 33% rate, making the prices of vices just a little bit higher. Most drinkers solve the problem by switching from scotch to Spanish wines, Spanish beers, or Spanish brandies with soda.

TELEPHONES: If you don't speak Spanish, you'll find it easier to telephone from your hotel. Know, however, that this is often a very expensive way of doing it, as hotels impose a surcharge on every operator-assisted call. If you're more adventurous, you'll find street phone booths known as *cabinas,* with dialing instructions in English. Local calls can be made by inserting two coins of 5 pesetas (4¢) each if you don't talk more than three minutes.

Normally, all Frommer travel guides list the telephone number of each establishment recommended. However, in Spain, particularly in a budget guide, that is not always possible. The major reason is that many of the smaller establishments, especially tascas, bars, discos, and restaurants, don't have phones. Surprisingly, one of the most popular French restaurants in Barcelona doesn't have a phone (how they manage to do business is their problem). One restaurant owner told me that the phone number of his place was listed in his wife's maiden name!

Unless you speak Spanish, in all its many variations, it is usually not necessary to call a restaurant listed in this guide for a reservation. Tables are generally plentiful, and restaurants are numerous in Spain, especially in the tourist zones. For first-class and deluxe dining, you should definitely call for a reservation, but most of those establishments do not fall in the price range of this guide.

Further, many discos and bars open only for the summer secure a phone for the season, and abandon that number when the autumn winds start to blow. Next spring, they apply for another number. In those cases, I don't give a phone number that would become hopelessly outdated during the lifetime of this edition. Pity the poor homeowner who gets reassigned the number for the Pango-Pango disco in Torremolinos.

TIME: Spain is six hours ahead of Eastern Standard Time in the United States.

TIPPING: It is not a problem if you follow certain guidelines, knowing that general rules are to be abandoned in the face of exceptional circumstances, such as someone performing a "life-saving feat." Tipping is simplified in Spain, since the government requires hotels and restaurants to include their service charges —usually 15% of the bill—in their tariffs or in the price of their food items. However, that doesn't mean you should skip out of a place without dispensing some extra pesetas. What follows are some guideline suggestions.

Hotels: A porter is tipped 50 pesetas (35¢) per piece of luggage he handles, but never less than 100 pesetas (70¢) even if you have only one small suitcase. If the maid has performed some extra task for you, you might give her 50 pesetas (35¢). Tip doormen helping with luggage at least 100 pesetas (70¢). If the doorman calls you a cab, give him 25 pesetas (18¢). In front-ranking hotels, the concierge will often submit a separate bill, reflecting your charges for newspapers, etc. If he's been helpful in performing extra services, such as wrapping packages or getting you tickets for the bullfight, you should tip him in addition to the bill he submits. Here I have no rule of thumb, as the tip will depend on the actual number of requests you have made of him.

Taxis: Add about 12% to the fare as shown on the meter. However, if the driver personally unloads or loads your luggage, increase that to approximately 20%.

Porters: At airports such as Barajas in Madrid and major terminals, the porter who handles your luggage will present you with a fixed-charge bill.

Restaurants: In both restaurants and nightclubs, 15% is added to the bill. To that, you should add another 3% to 5%, depending on the quality of the service. Waiters in deluxe restaurants and nightclubs are accustomed to the 5% —which means you'll end up tipping 20%. If that seems excessive, you must remember that the initial service charge reflected in the fixed price is distributed among all the help, including the dishwasher, so all of it does not go to your waiter.

Services: Barbers are tipped 100 pesetas (70¢); hairdressers for women, 200 pesetas ($1.40); manicurists, 50 pesetas (35¢). If you have a guide on a tour bus, it is not mandatory to tip, although 200 pesetas ($1.40) would be most appreciated. It is customary to tip an attendant in a gas station at least 25 pesetas (18¢). More generous Spaniards tip 50 pesetas (35¢). Likewise, an usher who shows you to your seat in a theater or at the bullfight expects from 25 to 50 pesetas.

TOURIST OFFICES: The headquarters of the main tourist office in Madrid is 50 María de Molina (tel. 411-40-19). The staff there dispenses folders and travel information not only about Madrid and its environs, but for the entire country. English is spoken.

Chapter III

MADRID

1. Orientation
2. Hotels in Madrid
3. The Restaurants of Madrid
4. The Top Sights
5. The Bullfight in Madrid
6. Shopping in Madrid
7. Madrid After Dark

AS SPANISH CITIES GO, Madrid is a young upstart. It was not significant until as late as 1561. It is the virtual nerve center of Spanish life, yet at times it seems so strangely removed from the country that the visitor would be left with only the dimmest impression of Spain if he or she saw only its capital city.

Once Barcelona was the major arrival and embarkment point for tourists to Spain, but that is no longer the case. The Castilians of Madrid have edged out the Catal‡ns of Barcelona, and Madrid has become the capital of the country—both in name and fact.

It is not my purpose to dispute the charm of either of these two venerated ladies. It's a question of preference and taste. However, if your time is pressed and you are forced to choose between them, then Madrid becomes the favored one, not only because of its own rich attractions, such as the Prado and the Royal Palace, but because of its satellites. Few European capitals are encircled with as many rich historical sites as Madrid.

Perhaps it was logical that Madrid became the capital: it is almost in the geographic center of the Iberian peninsula, which encompasses Portugal. As such, it is the loftiest capital city in Europe, sitting high on a plateau, some 2,133 feet above sea level. It is modern, increasingly industrial, noisy, animated, and ringed by new "cities" or apartment houses. Parts of it, particularly Old Madrid, are architecturally appealing. Other sections are graced with wide boulevards and landscaped parks—and there are splashing fountains, water shortage or not.

It is big and crowded, with hordes of visitors intermixing with the Spaniards during the summer months. In a country where birth-control propaganda is received with little enthusiasm, Madrid's population figure has topped the three million mark.

During the peak promenade hours—6 to 7:30 p.m.—on the Gran Vía, it would appear that every Spaniard in Castile goes out walking. For the most part, they are well dressed, animated, and apparently filled with so much to say that everybody seems to talk at once. The metallic sounds of conversation in the cafeterías, the tascas, or at the sidewalk tables are so overpowering that you may think a wholesale revolution is being organized. But nothing so dramatic. A wife's expenditures at the Galerías Precíados or the outrageously rising cost of langosta may send the Madrileño into a flight of fury. Such an outpouring of energy is often difficult for the more phlegmatic northern Europeans to understand. But how did it all begin?

A MINI-HISTORY: Madrid as a city was late in developing, but mention of an outpost at the site goes back to the 10th century. Once in the 14th century, and again in the 15th, parliament convened here, and Madrid also achieved some prominence as a royal hunting ground. However, it wasn't until 1561 that Philip II made it the capital.

From then on, the life of the town underwent rapid and dramatic alterations. During the War of the Spanish Succession, Madrid changed hands many times, but its greatest sympathy lay with the Bourbons in opposition to the House of Habsburg. Again, in opposition to Napoleon, a bloody uprising broke out in Madrid on May 2, 1808, that led to the Spanish War of Independence.

Following the war, Madrid, as the capital, entered upon a century of decline and defeat, presiding over the liquidation of an empire.

Madrid was the stronghold of the Republicans during the Spanish Civil War of 1936–1939, and it suffered the nightly raids of the German bombers. Large sections were destroyed, and others were bombarded when the Nationalists invaded in 1939. Franco made it his capital.

After the belt-tightening days of World War II, Madrid began to take on the appearance of a bustling metropolis, as the autonomy of the suburbs faded away. Nearly all traces of the destruction left by the Civil War vanished in the booming reconstruction days that followed.

1. Orientation

In modern Spain, all roads and rails—and all telephone lines—lead to Madrid, the center of a vast network of transportation and communication hookups. With such ever-increasing importance, the capital has overspilled whatever boundaries it may once have had—and is branching out in all directions. But the layout of this vast city need not perplex you, as there are many industrial and residential sections of Madrid that you probably will not concern yourself with as a visitor.

Every arrival must learn of the existence of the **Gran Vía,** which cuts a winding pathway across a large segment of the city beginning at the **Plaza de España,** containing one of the tallest skyscrapers in Europe, the **Edificio España.** Gran Vía was the original name of this street, although in recent years it was called Avenida de José Antonio. It has now reverted to the original designation. On this principal avenue in Madrid—Sinclair Lewis would have called it *Main Street*—you'll find the largest concentration of shops, hotels, restaurants, movie houses, whatever, of any other place in the city The **Calle Serrano** with its many shops and restaurants is a runner-up.

South of the avenue lies a large square known as the **Puerta del Sol,** which used to have the significance of, say, Piccadilly Circus in London. All road distances from Spain are measured from this gate. James Michener called it "Beloved of Madrileños for centuries as the focus of their life in a way that the popular squares of old European capitals could not equal." However, the significance of the Puerta del Sol has declined as the mainstream of life shifted elsewhere. At this gateway begins the **Calle de Alcalá,** a street that runs for 2½ miles.

Unlike the Puerta del Sol, the **Plaza Mayor** represents the heart of Old Madrid, enough so that I recommend that you treat it as an attraction. Whether it was an execution of a heretic or the scene of a bullfight, this huge square—ordered built by Philip III—was the center of life in Old Madrid. Its notoriety was achieved during the reign of Carlos II (1661–1700), called "The Bewitched One," the last of the line of the Spanish Habsburgs. Under the reign of this supposedly insane king, an *auto-da-fé*—literally, act of faith—was staged here in which nearly 20 persons lost their lives at the stake. Today the plaza is not addicted to violence and it doesn't necessarily look Spanish, but has a mixture of French and Georgian architecture. With its formality and tidiness, it makes for an interesting stroll—or a promenade. Through the arches pass pedestrians branching out onto the narrow streets of the old town, where one can find some of the capital's most intriguing restaurants and tascas. On the ground level of the plaza are colonnaded shops, many selling fun headgear such as that of a turn-of-the-century Spanish sailor or an officer in the kaiser's army.

Of all the sections of the capital, the area south of the Plaza Mayor—known as *barrios bajos*—merits the most exploration. The cobblestone streets are narrow and winding, the architecture often of the 16th and 17th centuries. Directly south of the plaza (reached by steps) is the **Arco de Cuchilleros,** a street of típico restaurants, such as the Casa Botín, flamenco clubs, and taverns—the poor people of Madrid, markets with fresh vegetables, *cuevas* (see the nightlife section), low dives with red lights and beaded curtains—it's the closest Madrid comes to evoking the rhythmic gypsy music and whirling dancers that *Carmen*-watching has led us to expect.

The Gran Vía ends its run when it merges with the Calle de Alcalá and becomes the **Plaza de la Cibeles,** with its fountain to Cybele, the mother of the Gods, and what has become known as the cathedral of post offices. From Cibeles, the wide **Paseo de Recoletos** begins a short run until it marches into the **Plaza de Colón.** From this latter square rolls the serpentine **Paseo de la Castellana,** the boulevard that one day may take all the attention away from the Gran Vía, flanked as it is by sophisticated shops, apartment buildings, such luxury hotels as the Castellana, Villa Magna, and the Luz Palacio, and foreign embassies. Once it was peppered with town houses in which rich Madrileños lived in the 18th and 19th centuries—but many of these, regrettably, are being torn down to make way for New Madrid. The boulevard bypasses the public ministries on its journey to the frontiers of Madrid.

Back at Cibeles again: heading south is the **Paseo del Prado,** housing Spain's major sightseeing attraction, the Prado, as well as the Botanical Garden. This paseo leads into the **Atocha Railway Station.** To the west of the garden lies the **Parque del Retiro,** the finest in Madrid, with restaurants, nightclubs, a rose garden, statuary, and two lakes. Once it was reserved for royalty.

TRANSPORTATION: No one ever claimed that knowing or getting around Madrid was easy. Surprisingly, many of the Madrileño taxi drivers are often unfamiliar with their own city, once they branch off the main boulevards. Everything in the Spanish capital is spread out, and this may cause you difficulty until you get the feel of it. The easiest, most sensible means of getting around among the widely scattered sights, restaurants, and hotels is by taxicab, but you may want to try some of the public transportation offered.

Airport

Barajas is the international airport of Madrid, and it's divided into two separate terminals—one for international flights, another for domestic. A shuttle bus runs between the two. For Barajas Airport information, telephone 205-40-90.

Air-conditioned yellow buses take you from right outside the arrival terminal at Barajas to the underground bus depot under the Plaza de Colón. You can also get off at several points along the way, provided you don't have your suitcases stored in the hold. The cost of the service is 150 pesetas ($1.05), and buses leave about every 20 minutes, either to or from the airport.

If you go by taxi into town, the approximate cost is 1,500 pesetas ($10.50), and the driver is entitled to assess a surcharge (either direction), not only for the trip but for baggage handling. If you should step into an unmetered limousine, it is important to negotiate the price in advance.

Taxi

In Madrid the rates are still reasonable enough that the taxi becomes a recommended way of getting about. The legendary antiquated cabs of the capital have been replaced by speedier and more efficient models. The increase in taxi rates has been high in Madrid, but they were originally below rock bottom.

When you flag down a taxi, the meter should register 85 pesetas (60¢)—but that fare will surely have gone up by the time of your visit. An average ride costs about 400 pesetas ($2.80). There are extras as well. Trips to the railway station or to the bullring carry a supplement, plus an additional fee tacked on to the fare on Sunday and holidays. It's customary to tip at least 10% of the fare or more.

Warning: So many of the taxi drivers of Madrid seem like such honorable fellows that it's hard to throw stones without hitting some of the good guys. But petty bandits often can be more annoying than professional Mafia types. Make sure that the meter is turned down when you get into a taxi. Otherwise, some crooked drivers will "assess" the cost of the ride, and their assessment, you can be assured, is involved with higher mathematics. This is a flourishing racket. Keep your guard up and the meter down.

Also, there are many unmetered taxis in Madrid that hire out for the day or for the afternoon. These are perfectly legitimate vehicles, but some of the drivers of these hired cars—particularly if business is slow—will operate like gypsy cabs. Since they are unmetered, they can charge you a high rate for just a short distance. They are easy to avoid. There are two types of taxis: black with horizontal red bands and white with diagonal red bands. Their rates are usually the same.

If you take a taxi outside the city limits, the driver is entitled to charge you twice the rate shown on the meter.

Subway (Metro)

The system, first installed in 1919, is quite easy to learn, and you can travel in the underground, if not comfortably, at least without any congestion or crushing, as in former years.

Line 7 is completely different from the rest, and as modern as some of Europe's newest underground systems. The future lines under construction will be the same type as no. 7. The central converging point of the subway is at the **Puerta del Sol.** The Metro fare begins at 40 pesetas (28¢). The Metro begins its runs at 6 a.m., shutting down at 1:30 a.m. It's best to try to avoid traveling on the subways during the rush hours, of course.

Bus

Madrid has two principal bus terminals—**Auto Rest,** 6 Glorieta Conde de Casals (tel. 251-66-44), and the large **Estación Sur de Autobuses,** 17 Canarias (tel. 468-42-00). Buses to the environs of Madrid, such as Toledo and Segovia, leave from numerous other stations; it's best to telephone 401-99-00 for the latest information about departures.

A network of buses also traverses the city, fanning out to the suburbs. The route of each bus is clearly marked at each stop on a schematic diagram. Buses are fast and efficient, traveling along special lanes made for them all over the city. The fare begins at 60 pesetas (42¢). Incidentally, an airport bus service is in operation.

Railway Stations

Madrid has three major railway stations, two of which are the Atocha and the Chamartín. At the **Atocha,** Glorieta de Carlos V, you can book passage for Lisbon, Toledo, Andalusia, the Levante (Valencia), and Aragón. The nearest Metro stop is Atocha. For trains to Barcelona and the French frontier, go to **Chamartín** in the northern suburbs at Agustín de Foxa. Metro: Chamartín. The third is **La Estación del Norte** (Príncipe Pío), which is the main gateway for trains to northwest Spain. Metro: Norte. For railway information, telephone 733-30-00.

Warning: In Madrid don't wait to buy your rail ticket or make a reservation at the train station. By this time there may be no tickets left—or at least no desirable tickets remaining. For most tickets, go to the principal **RENFE** office at 44 Alcalá (tel. 247-74-00).

PRACTICAL FACTS: Whatever your needs or travel problems, you'll find that Madrid has the answer to them. The single question is: How do you find what you're seeking quickly and conveniently? In an emergency, of course, your hotel is the best bet. But some of the smaller hotels aren't staffed with personnel entirely fluent in English; and sometimes—even if they are—the person at the desk can be amazingly apathetic about something of vital interest to you. The answers to some of your queries are found in "The ABCs of Spain," Chapter II. Some that pertain particularly to the capital are listed below.

Important warning: Increased thefts in Madrid have resulted in a warning by the American Embassy to American visitors, urging that you leave your passport and valuables in a hotel safe or other secure place while you visit sights of the city. Purse-snatching is prevalent, with the criminals working in pairs, grabbing purses from pedestrians, cyclists, and even from cars. If a car is standing still, a thief may open the car door or break a window in order to snatch a purse or package, even from under the seat. A popular scam against Americans in Madrid involves one miscreant smearing the back of a jacket or other clothing of the victim, perhaps with mustard or chocolate. An accomplice pretends to help the victim clean off the mess, meanwhile picking all pockets of valuables. The Embassy statement advises: Don't carry a purse; keep your valuables in front pockets; carry only enough cash for the day's needs; be aware of who is around you; and keep a separate record of your passport number, traveler's check numbers, and credit card numbers.

Every car can be a target, parked or just stopped at a light. Don't leave anything in sight in your car. Place valuables in the trunk when you park, and always assume that someone is watching you to see whether you're putting something away for safekeeping. Keep the car locked while you're driving and even for a one-minute stop.

American Express: For your mail or banking needs, the American Express office (tel. 429-57-75), at the corner of the Marqués de Cubas and the Plaza de las Cortés (across the street from the Palace Hotel), draws the visiting Yankee. The office is open weekdays from 9 a.m. to 5:30 p.m. and on Saturday until noon.

Babysitters: Nearly all major hotels in Madrid can arrange for babysitters. Usually, the concierge keeps a list of reliable nursemaids or young girls, and will get in touch with one of them for you, provided you give adequate notice. Rates vary considerably, but tend to be reasonable. More and more babysitters in Madrid speak English, but don't count on it. Chances are yours won't. You can request it, of course.

Bookstores: There are many all over the city, selling both English- and Spanish-language editions, along with touring maps. **Aguilar** has three outlets: at 24 Serrano (tel. 435-36-42), 18 Goya (tel. 275-06-40), and 154 Paseo Castellana (tel. 250-36-39). Or you could try **Editorial Hernando,** 8 José Garrido (tel. 471-77-62).

Currency Exchange: The currency exchange at Chamartín railway station is open 24 hours and gives the best rates of exchange in the capital. In exchanging money at a commercial bank, inquire not only about the percentage but the minimum commission charged.

Consulates and Embassies: The **American Embassy** is at 75 Calle de Serrano (tel. 276-36-00), and the **Canadian Embassy** at 35 Nuñez de Balboa (tel. 431-43-00). The **British Embassy** is at 16 Fernando el Santo (tel. 419-02-00).

Dentist: For an English-speaking dentist, get in touch with the **American Embassy,** 75 Calle de Serrano (tel. 276-34-00), which has a list of recommended ones. If you have a dental emergency, you may have to call several before you can get an immediate appointment—hence, the need of a comprehensive list.

Emergencies: If you need the police, call 091. In case of fire, dial 232-32-32, and if you need an ambulance, as in the case of an accident, telephone 256-02-00.

Hairdresser: Lis is a salon offering manicures and hairdressing for women, specializing in styling and dying. It's in the Torre de Madrid (tel. 241-54-39) and is open from 9:30 a.m. to 7:30 p.m.

Post Office: If you don't want to receive your mail at your hotel or American Express office, you can direct it to *Lista de Correos* at the central post office in Madrid. To pick up such mail, go to the window marked *Lista,* where you'll be asked to show your passport. The central office in Madrid is housed in what is known as "the cathedral of the post offices" at Plaza de la Cibeles (tel. 221-81-95). As for rates, they are rising faster than guidebooks can be printed. Remember that an airmail letter weighing only five grams, the legal limit before you pay an overweight charge, is a very slim letter indeed.

Religious Services: Most churches in Madrid are **Catholic,** and they're found all over the city. Catholic masses in English, however, are given at 165 Alfonso XIII. For more information, call 233-20-32 in the morning. If you prefer a non-Catholic ceremony, the British Embassy **Church of St. George** is at 43 Nuñez de Balboa (call 274-51-55 for worship hours). The interdenominational **Protestant Community Church** is at 34 Padre Damian (tel. 723-04-41), offering weekly services in the Colegio de los Sagrados Corazones, while the **Immanuel Baptist Church** offers English-speaking services at 4 Hernandez de Tejada (tel. 407-43-47). A **Christian Science church** is at 63 Alonso Cano (tel. 259-21-35), and a **Jewish synagogue** lies on Calle de Balmes (tel. 445-98-35). It opened in the late 1960s, the first one to do so since the expulsion of the Jews from Spain in 1492. Friday-night services begin at 7:30 p.m., while Saturday-morning services are at 9:30 a.m.

Restrooms: Some are available, including those in Retiro park in Madrid and on the Plaza del Oriente across from the Royal Palace. Otherwise, you can always go into a bar or tasca, but you should order something—perhaps a small glass of beer or even a bag of peanuts. The Spanish designations for rest rooms are *aseos* and *servicios. Caballeros* are for men, and *damas,* naturally, are for women. The major department stores, such as Galerías Precíados and El Corte Inglés, have good, clean rest rooms.

Telegrams: Cables may be sent at the central post office building in Madrid at the Plaza de la Cibeles (tel. 221-81-95). However, the dialing number for international telegrams is 241-33-00. In Spain it's cheaper to telephone within the country than it is to send a telegram.

Telephone: To make telephone calls in Madrid, follow the same instructions given in "The ABCs of Spain," Chapter II. However, it may be best for long-distance calls, especially transatlantic ones, to go to the main telephone exchange, Central de Teléfonos, 28 Gran Vía (tel. 004). You may not be lucky enough to find an English-speaking operator, but you can fill out a simple form which will facilitate the placement of a call.

Telex: You can send Telex messages from the central post office building in Madrid, Plaza de la Cibeles (tel. 221-81-95), and from all major hotels.

Temperatures: Average monthly temperatures in Madrid are as follows:

	High	*Low*		*High*	*Low*
January	46	34	July	91	65
February	48	34	August	90	66
March	52	39	September	76	65
April	65	45	October	65	52
May	75	52	November	55	48
June	78	58	December	50	41

Time: In Madrid, dial 093 to learn the time.

Tourist Offices: In Madrid, perhaps the most convenient one is at the 40-story Torre de Madrid (tel. 241-23-25), opening onto the Plaza de España. It's on the ground floor and is open during the lunch hours. If available, ask for a street map of the next town on your itinerary, especially if you're driving. The staff at the tourist office can give you a list of hotels and hostales, but cannot recommend any particular hotel over another. As listed in "The ABCs of Spain," Chapter II, the country's main tourist office is also in Madrid at 50 Maria de Molina (tel. 411-40-19). There are also English-speaking officers at the Chamartín railway station during the day and early evening.

2. Hotels in Madrid

Virtually everyone from retired bullfighters to Civil War field commanders has rented a floor and opened up a hotel or pension in Madrid. On our $40-a-day budget, it's possible to stay at many of the city's three-star hotels, and have a private bath too.

And if you think I'm planning to hustle you off to the boondocks for this cheap living, you're wrong. For the most part, I'll stick to the pick of accommodations on the Gran Vía. Some of the hotels lie a block or two off the avenue—and this may be even better, as that location offers some protection against the noise of traffic. This section will be followed by hotels in and around the Prado Museum and the most central Atocha Railroad Station, as well as those that lie off the fashionable Paseo de la Castellana in the north of Madrid.

My lead-off listings represent the cream of Madrid's value-packed hotels. However, those on the strictest of budgets—even those desiring to live cheaper than our budget—should read from the bottom of the list, booking into a one- or two-star hotel, or perhaps a clean, livable, albeit plain, pension (boarding house).

THREE- AND FOUR-STAR HOTELS: The principal feature of the following recommendations—in addition to the gracious and inexpensive living offered—is the sheer convenience of living on or near "Main Street," near the shops, movie houses, restaurants, bars, and cafeterías.

Off Plaza de las Cortés

Hotel El Prado, 11 Calle del Prado (tel. 445-71-00), doesn't compete with its more famous namesake, the museum, although its lobby is decorated with full-size copies of many of the art treasures that are the Spanish national heritage. While you sip a drink in the lobby, you can gaze upon the serene calm of a series of paintings whose size almost engulfs the otherwise simple room. The hotel has an unpretentious cafeteria on the premises, an underground parking garage (a rarity in this neighborhood), and some 50 clean bedrooms. Each has air conditioning, a mini-bar, and a private bathroom. Singles cost 5,800 pesetas ($40.60), doubles going for 8,300 pesetas ($58.10). The hotel, with its angular modern façade, is near the Teatro Español and the American Express office.

On or Near the Gran Vía

Lope de Vega, 59 Gran Vía (tel. 247-70-00), used to be a well-kept secret, attracting the Spanish gentry in town for the theater, fiestas, or shopping. Now it's gone international. But don't be misled by the entrance. Sandwiched between two shops, a tiny elevator will lift you to this well-run hotel. Once you enter the reception lounge and drawing room, you'll be in a world of graciousness and dignity. Attractive antiques are placed in the wood-paneled lounges and private rooms. A double with private bath rents for a maximum of 4,200 pesetas ($29.40). Top price for a single with bath is 2,600 pesetas ($18.20). Named after the great dramatist, the hotel is owned and managed by Mrs. Christina Belderrain Garin, who has trained her staff well, making for the atmosphere of a private club rather than a hotel. There's an underground 700-car garage across the street. The hotel has an American bar with television.

If you're a light sleeper, be duly warned that the front rooms opening onto the Gran Vía are noisy, of course.

Príncipe Pío (Holy Prince), 16 Onésimo Redondo (tel. 247-08-00). There are advantages as well as drawbacks to this selection. The whizzing traffic heard from the front rooms doesn't appeal to those seeking serenity. However, the location—within a short walk of the Royal Palace, the Plaza de España, and the Gran Vía—makes it bull's-eye center for many. In the words of one woman reader from Lowell, Massachusetts, "there's proper comfort and sanitation," a reference to the 167 modern bedrooms, all with private bath (many singles and doubles with shower, but no tub bath). The furnishings in both the public rooms and bedrooms are very much in the idiom of 1960s modern. Doubles cost 5,500 pesetas ($38.50); singles, 4,200 pesetas ($29.40). A lunch or dinner goes for 1,500 pesetas ($10.50). Because of its excellent facilities and standards, the government gives the Príncipe a high rating.

Mayorazgo, 3 Flor Baja (tel. 247-26-00), offers a warm Spanish experience. It's almost my preferred choice in the Gran Vía area, a mere fandango step away from the main boulevard. The hotel and its restaurant are owned by a Mexican family. Together, they have cast their know-how, skill, and outgoing charm into the running of this hotel—a case of the New World returning to the Old, for a switch. The bedrooms are pleasant, and more than half are spacious enough to offer sitting areas. Most of them have high-posted headboards and fringed bedspreads, set on islands of Oriental rugs. Reproductions of Iberian chests and armchairs have been placed throughout. All of the rooms have private bath. The rate in a single is 5,800 pesetas ($40.60), increasing to 8,000 pesetas ($56) in a twin-bedded room. You can have a meal here for 2,200 pesetas ($15.40).

Residencia Lar, 16 Valverde (tel. 221-65-92), is an 80-room hotel just off the Gran Vía. One gets personal attention here. A private bath goes with every room, and the most you'll be asked to pay for a double is 4,200 pesetas ($29.40). Singles, less preferred, rent for a maximum of 3,400 pesetas ($23.80). The rooms are clean, although a little creaky in the corners. There is a small sunken lobby, but no dining room. A continental breakfast is brought to your room for an extra 265 pesetas ($1.86).

Hotel Residencia Carlos V, 5 Maestro Vitoria (tel. 231-41-00), has long been a favorite of mine. I stayed there when I did the original research for this guide (then called $5 a Day) back in the 1960s. At that time you could get a double room with private bath for about $4 a day. However, regrettably, prices have gone up: today you are likely to pay from 4,200 pesetas ($29.40) in a single with private bath and about 5,500 pesetas ($38.50) in a double, also with private bath.

The seven-story art nouveau building, originally constructed in 1904, has been much altered over the years, with air conditioning added. Rooms have been considerably upgraded and improved. What hasn't changed is the unbeatable location: around the corner from the Galerías Precíados and just a short walk from the Gran Vía and the Puerta del Sol. Bathrooms have been modernized, and the lobby retains its air of elegance. Breakfast is served at the hotel, but one reader noted the locals walking a short block away to a café. There she noticed they had a morning "pick-me-up" of a small glass of anise or a combined brandy with anise. "A 'copa' of either put hair on my husband's chest, he claims, plus the vigor to walk for hours," she wrote.

Hotel Nuria, 52 Fuencarral (tel. 231-92-08), just three blocks from the Gran Vía, has some bedrooms with especially interesting views of the capital. Renovated in the late '60s, the 58-room hotel offers double rooms with private bath or shower for 3,800 pesetas ($26.60), breakfast included. The most expensive singles, with breakfast, rent for 2,200 pesetas ($15.40). The food is highly praised by those who have sampled it. The price of a complete luncheon or dinner is 1,200 pesetas ($8.40). The señora who double-checks the polishing and dusting maids makes the toughest marine drill sergeant look like a sissy, and guests thus get the benefit of immaculate rooms.

At Chamartín Railway Station

Hotel Chamartín, at the Chamartín Railway Station (tel. 733-90-11), is a 378-room hotel rising nine stories, part of the major transportation and shopping complex in this modern train station. The owner of the hotel is RENFE, the government's railroad system, and it's operated by Entursa Hotels, which is an organization best known for deluxe "museum" hotels. The Chamartín is the first of the company's budget properties. The director, who oversees a large staff, is José C. Moya. The hotel lies a 15-minute ride from the airport and a 5-minute jaunt from the city's major business and sightseeing areas.

All guest rooms are air-conditioned, featuring TV, radio, a refrigerator/bar, a private safe, and specially insulated windows for maximum quiet and privacy. Also available are 18 one-bedroom suites, some with balconies. Rates in the regular rooms are 5,800 pesetas ($40.60) in a single, from 8,200 pesetas ($57.40) in a double.

A coffee bar serves a continental breakfast daily, and room service is also available. A choice of drinks is featured at the bar off the main lobby. Guests can dine at a variety of restaurants and snackbars in the Chamartín complex.

Among the extensive facilities and services available to hotel guests are 13 shops, four movie theaters, a roller skating rink, a disco, and ample parking. Especially oriented to the business traveler, the Chamartín offers a currency exchange, travel agency, bank, car rental, and complete communication services. A screen in the lobby posting the arrival and departure of all trains affords special convenience to the traveler.

Off the Paseo de la Castellana

Far removed from the narrow streets of Old Madrid, the "New City" is booming northward. Beginning at the Plaza de la Cibeles, the Paseo de Recoletos runs into the Paseo de la Castellana, this wide boulevard wending northward. Once town houses stood in this principally residential sector of the city. Nowadays, luxury hotels such as the Villa Magna and the Luz Palacio line the avenue. To the west of the paseo is another wide boulevard, the Calle de Velázquez, which contains some good hotel bargains.

Hotel Tryp Velázquez, 62 Calle de Velázquez (tel. 275-28-00). The façade, facing an affluent residential street near the center of town, is pure art deco, although the interior is so filled with well-upholstered furniture and richly grained paneling that it defies a purely 1930s classification (it was actually built in 1947). Several public rooms lead off a central oval area lined with marble and 19th-century bronzes. One of them includes a warmly masculine bar area capped with a reproduction of a 17th-century hunting scene, as well as a cove-ceilinged feeder hallway adorned with astrological symbols in cerulean blue and gold. Farther on, there's an affluent-looking salon with parquet floors, statues, and russet-colored upholstery.

As in many hotels from this era, each of the bedrooms is different, some being large enough for entertaining, and all containing air conditioning. There's parking available on the premises. A double used as a single costs 7,200 pesetas ($50.40), while for double occupancy the rent is around 9,200 pesetas ($64.40), which is expensive for our budget but very low in price when you consider that this is a four-star hotel. This is really one of the most attractive medium-size hotels in Madrid, with great comfort and convenience.

Hostal Residencia Don Diego, 45 Calle de Velázquez (tel. 435-07-60), lies in a combination residential/commercial neighborhood that is relatively convenient to many of the monuments of the city. The hostal is on the fifth floor of an elevator building, whose vestibule contains an elegant winding staircase accented with iron griffin heads supporting its balustrade. The hotel is warmly inviting, filled with leather couches and a kind of comfortable, no-nonsense style of angular but attractive furniture. A bar stands at the far end of the main sitting room, and there's usually a collection of well-dressed business people waiting for a receptionist to take a few minutes to show up from whatever he or she is doing at the time. Singles begin at 4,100 pesetas ($28.70), with doubles going for 5,820 pesetas ($40.74).

Near the Plaza de España

Casón del Tormes, 7 Río (tel. 241-97-46), is an unusually attractive three-star hotel around the corner from the Royal Palace and the Plaza de España. It's a red brick, four-story structure with stone-trimmed modern windows looking over a quiet one-way street. The long lobby area fills most of the ground floor of the building, and is graced with glass display cases containing elaborate displays of silver and copper serving dishes, lots of richly grained vertical paneling, and a Spanish refectory table. Breakfast tables are set up on the marble floors, and a bar opens into a separate room. All of the accommodations are air-conditioned.

Attractive doubles with bath cost 5,400 pesetas ($37.80), while singles with bath rent for 4,000 pesetas ($28), plus tax, with a continental breakfast included in all tariffs. Public parking is available in the nearby Plaza de España.

Tirol, 4 Marqués de Urquijo (tel. 248-19-00), a short walk from the Plaza de España and the swank Meliá Madrid, is a good choice. A three-star hotel, it offers singles for 3,600 pesetas ($25.30) to 3,900 pesetas ($27.30) and doubles for 5,000 pesetas ($35), plus tax. Furnishings are simple and functional, somewhat characterless and old-fashioned, but adequate, and the 100 air-conditioned rooms have baths. In the cafeteria downstairs, you can order a snack or light meal. There's also a garage in the building.

Near the North Station

San Antonio de la Florida, 13 Paseo de la Florida (tel. 247-14-00). A lot depends on the room you get. I prefer those opening onto the Manzanares River and the former royal hunting grounds (now a public park), the Casa de Campo. The front rooms face a wide, traffic-heavy avenue, across from the North Station, and are less desirable, of course. But whichever room you get, it will be fairly modern, as the hotel was built in 1964, complete with 96 freshly created bedrooms, all with private bath.

For those who don't mind being slightly out of the center, or for those who are motorists (there is a garage), the San Antonio might be the ideal headquarters. The rates are reasonable: 4,000 pesetas ($28) in a double, 2,500 pesetas ($17.50) in a single. Breakfast is extra. The bedroom furnishings are functional, not exceptional, the balconies adding an extra bit of glamor. The public rooms have a quiet style, in a warm, contemporary sense, and the dining room is inviting. There's a cocktail lounge for predinner drinks, plus a grill room for light meals.

Near Glorieta Quevedo

Conde Duque, 5 Plaza Conde Valle de Suchil (tel. 447-70-00), is a good-size (138 rooms) hotel which was modernized way back in the '50s. It opens onto a tree-filled little plaza where children play. Be warned that this hotel is a long way north (about 12 blocks) of the Plaza de España, off the Calle de San Bernardo, which starts its run at the Gran Vía—too long to walk but a subway stop, the San Bernardo, is nearby, taking you into the heart of the city in a few minutes.

You pay 5,400 pesetas ($37.80) in a double room. All of these rooms contain a well-maintained private bath. Only a few singles are available, costing 3,500 pesetas ($24.50). A continental breakfast is extra. The furnishings include modified reproductions of 19th-century English pieces and modern built-in headboards. There are bedside lights and telephones. The three-star hotel is near a branch of the Galerías Precíados department store, in a residential sector filled with apartment houses.

Near the Puerta del Sol

Hotel Residencia Cortezo, 3 Doctor Cortezo (tel. 239-38-00), is off the Calle de Atocha, which leads to the railroad station, and it is only a few minutes' walk from the Plaza Mayor and the Puerta del Sol. A double room with bath rents for 5,000 pesetas ($35). Singles with bath are 3,300 pesetas ($23.10). A continental breakfast is extra. The accommodation is not only comfortable but attractive. The beds are springy, the colors well chosen, the furniture pleasantly modern, and often there is a sitting area with a desk and armchair. The baths are slickly contemporary, and the public rooms match the bedrooms in freshness.

The staff also furnishes guests with a lot of extras, such as an excellent map of the capital.

Hotel Victoria, 7 Plaza del Angel (tel. 231-45-00), is about as important to the legends of Madrid as Manolete himself. The famous bullfighter used to stay here, giving lavish parties in one of the reception rooms and attracting mobs in the square below when he went out on his balcony for morning coffee. Other clients have traditionally included historians, writers, and lesser bullfighters, all of whom enjoy the dozens of tapas bars in the neighborhood and the old-world charm of the ornate stone and metal façade.

The hotel was built in 1925 and named after the grandmother of the present King of Spain, Juan Carlos. Although the hotel is in a congested area in the center of Madrid, it opens onto its own little plaza, rich in tradition as a meeting place of intellectuals during the 17th century. Today the area is usually filled with flower vendors and older people catching rays of midafternoon sun. The rooms are quite comfortable, although not lavishly furnished, and a staid but polite atmosphere prevails. The hotel often rents out its banqueting room to middle-class Spanish families for wedding receptions. Doubles here rent for 6,500 pesetas ($45.50), with singles going for 4,500 pesetas ($31.50).

Hotel Ingles, 10-12 Echegaray (tel. 429-65-51). This hotel is more modern and perhaps a bit less personal than when Virginia Woolf made it her address in Madrid. Behind its red-brick façade, you'll find almost 60 unpretentiously contemporary bedrooms, each with its own bath and phone. The comfortable armchairs of the TV lounge, raised a few steps above the reception area, are likely to be filled to overflowing with avid soccer fans. Singles cost 2,800 pesetas ($19.60), doubles, 4,600 pesetas ($32.20). Motorists appreciate the adjacent garage. You'll find the hotel on a popular and very central street lined with local tascas.

On the Outskirts

Novotel Madrid, 1 Calle Albacete, corner of Avenida Badajoz (tel. 405-46-00), was intended to service the hotel needs of a cluster of multinational corporations whose headquarters lie 2½ miles east of the center of Madrid. But its rooms are so comfortable and its prices so reasonable that sightseers have begun using it as well. Its sparkling interior opened for the first time in 1986, making it one of the newest hotels in town, with an enthusiastic staff. It's a bit removed from the center of town, but late-arriving motorists find its position beside the M30 an attractive alternative to more centrally located hotels set within a maze of difficult-to-navigate inner-city streets.

Each of the comfortably furnished bedrooms offers a color TV with in-house movies, a well-designed bathroom, a mini-bar, radio, phone, and access to an English-speaking reception desk. The 240 bedrooms cost 8,100 pesetas ($56.70) for a single, 10,000 pesetas ($70) in a double, making it a splurge choice. Children under 16 stay free in their parents' room. There's a surprisingly attractive indoor/outdoor restaurant ringed with lattices, a cozy bar, and a swimming pool with a nearby cluster of trees and flowers. Motorists should exit from the M30 at the Barrio de la Concepción / Parque de las Avenidas just before they reach the city limits of central Madrid.

ONE- AND TWO-STAR HOTELS: For usually cheaper rates I'll have to desert the three- and four-star hotels in favor of the one-star and two-star establishments, the latter roughly comparable to a second- or third-class hotel. These accommodations are usually older, their furnishings frayed, but all of these recommendations are clean and moderately comfortable.

Near the Atocha Station

Hotel Mercátor, 123 Atocha (tel. 429-05-00), only about a three-minute stroll from the Prado, draws a clientele seeking a good, modern hotel—orderly, well run, and clean, with enough comforts and conveniences to please the weary traveler. Some of the rooms are more inviting than others, especially those with desks and armchairs. Color is often utilized effectively. The best twin-bedded rooms with private bath rent for 5,900 pesetas ($41.30). Singles peak at 3,900 pesetas ($27.30). The lower floors, as one reader put it, "are cold in design as a Nordic winter—but I had a good bedfellow." The Mercátor is a residencia—that is, it offers breakfast only. However, it has a bar and cafetería serving light meals such as *platos combinador,* or combined plates. There is an adjacent parking lot, and the hotel is within walking distance of the Iberia air terminal and American Express.

Near the Plaza Manuel Becerra

Ramón de la Cruz, 94 Don Ramón de la Cruz (tel. 401-72-00), is a 103-room, 103-bath modern hotel, on a relatively quiet street. It's just off the Plaza Manuel Becerra, which is reached from Retiro Park via the broad and attractive Calle de Alcalá. The subway, M. Becerra, stops near the hotel. The rooms are large enough to spread out your paraphernalia (unless you're returning from an African safari). They're styled with English reproductions, mainly mahogany pieces, such as chests and armchairs. The rate in a double is 4,000 pesetas ($28). Most singles with bath rent for 3,500 pesetas ($24.50). Two elevators service the eight floors, and there's a small breakfast room, plus an air-conditioned public lounge (no restaurant). The staff is friendly and cooperative.

Near the Puerta del Sol

Hotel Residencia Santander, 1 Echegaray (tel. 429-95-51), is a snug little hotel, just off the Puerta del Sol. You can get a fair to passable double room with private bath for 3,800 pesetas ($26.60). A single rents for 2,800 pesetas ($19.60). The Santander is on a teeming street, but you may appreciate the atmosphere if you like people and local color. The Santander is a refurbished old house, with 38 rooms.

Francisco I, 15 Arenal (tel. 248-02-04), offers 57 modern, clean rooms. Doubles with a shower-bath (sit-down tub) range from 4,500 pesetas ($31.50). Singles—only four in this category—with similar baths go for 3,200 pesetas ($22.40). There's a pleasant, if aseptic, lounge, a bar, Muzak, and on the sixth floor you'll find a comfortable, rustic-style restaurant where a set meal costs 1,400 pesetas ($9.80).

THE BEST PENSIONS: Now I turn to a decent bargain, the pensions, or hostales, of Madrid. In my opinion, they offer the cream of the crop in the Spanish capital. By and large, with notable exceptions, these accommodations are superior to the hotels rated one or two stars by the government.

Most of them occupy one large floor in an office or apartment building. All of them have fetching mid-city locations. Some serve breakfast only (and thus become an obvious lure for those who want to eat out); others dish up three meals a day.

Near American Express

Hostal Residencia Roso, 3 Plaza de las Cortés (tel. 429-83-29), is directly across the street from American Express, in an elevator building on the sixth floor. On a recent visit, a student from Arizona who was living here told me that it was the best pension he'd found in Spain—and he had been in all the provinces. But the owner enlarged upon this a bit, maintaining that it was the cleanest and best-kept pension in Europe. Unquestionably, it is good, immaculate, and tidy. Friends who know Madrid recommend it as a "very special and inexpensive little place to stay." Doubles with shower go for 2,800 pesetas ($19.60). No breakfast is served, and I extend my every good wish to the elevator.

Pension Aguadulce, 3 Plaza de las Cortés (tel. 429-83-65), is a family-run pension on the sixth floor of a grandly monumental building across from American Express and the posh Palace Hotel. The nine rooms are sheltered behind a hodgepodge of doors, some of which are covered with maroon leather. There's a view of the Plaza de las Cortés from the windows of the communal TV room. An elevator will take you up to the lobby, where you'll be quoted prices for bathless rooms at 1,500 pesetas ($10.50) in a single and 1,900 pesetas ($13.30) in a double. Units with bath are available only in doubles, which cost from 3,000 pesetas ($21), depending on the accommodation.

Hostal Principado, 7 Zorrilla (tel. 429-81-87), is rated two stars and it's a real find. In a well-kept town house near the American Express, it is run by the gracious Sra. Manuela Nuñez. She keeps everything immaculately clean, and has made many improvements since taking over the establishment. New tile, attractive bedspreads and curtains give everything a fresh look. A double with shower and water basin costs 3,200 pesetas ($22.40), rising to 3,800 pesetas ($26.60) in a double with complete bath. A bathless single rents for 2,300 pesetas ($16.10). No meals are served. At the entrance downstairs, you'll see where the residents of old arrived in their carriages.

Hostal Cervantes, 34 Cervantes (tel. 429-27-45), one of Madrid's most pleasant family-run hotels, has been widely appreciated by readers over the years of this guidebook. The Alfonso family maintain their floor of this stone and brick building in immaculate condition, scrubbing the terrazzo floors until they gleam. Each accommodation is simple, containing a bed with clean sheets and a few pieces of spartan furniture and a private bath. Singles cost 2,800 pesetas ($19.60), doubles, 3,500 pesetas ($24.50). No breakfast is served, but one of the Alfonsos will direct you to one of the cafés on the street below. To get here, take a tiny birdcage-style elevator to the second floor. The establishment is convenient to the Prado, Retiro Park, and the oldest sections of Madrid.

At Santa Bárbara

Santa Bárbara, 4 Plaza de Santa Bárbara (tel. 445-93-08), occupies the third floor of a building on a tree-lined street. The owner, Antonio Siragusa, is not allowed to put up a sign, so it is not quickly identified. He also pays for no advertisements, explaining he wants to keep prices as low as possible. The large apartment-turned-small-hotel has been renovated, and the bedrooms are, for the most part, of generous size, many furnished with antique beds. All the rooms have their own phone and bath with shower, as well as a balcony. There is a bright and airy breakfast/TV room. You'll be charged 3,600 pesetas ($25.30) in a double, 3,000 pesetas ($21) in a single. A continental breakfast is extra, served in a room that is a study in golden-oak furnishings. You can ride in the tiny iron-cage elevator.

Along the Gran Vía

The Gran Vía abounds in pensions, many of which are quite good. Others along the street are dubious as to service and facilities. The following represent what I consider the best buys in this classification. (Many of the boarding houses are not directly on the Gran Vía, but on streets jutting off from it.)

Hostal-Residencia Venecia, 6 Gran Vía (tel. 222-46-51), seems to have been created primarily for honeymooners, although nowadays non-newlyweds and single people are welcomed too. The Venecia still has its matrimonial beds in some of the rooms. It is a hotel high up in one of the older buildings on the Gran Vía, and is reached by one of those old-fashioned elevators. A bevy of scrubbing and polishing maids keeps the hotel as clean as a nunnery. The staff and guests combine to create a congenial atmosphere. The accommodation rates are from 1,500 pesetas ($10.50) to 2,000 pesetas ($14) in a double with some form of private bath. A bathless double, however, costs only 1,400 pesetas ($9.80). Depending on the plumbing, singles range from 1,400 pesetas ($9.80). A continental breakfast is additional.

Hotel Residencia Andorra, 33 Gran Vía (tel. 232-31-16), is one of the better pensions along this famed strip. Named after the principality in the Pyrenees, the Andorra is run by a young married couple, Mr. and Mrs. Angel Bertero Trossero, who speak English. They are most gracious as hosts, and surprisingly for such an inexpensive establishment, each of their accommodations has a phone and private bath and toilet included. A double room rents for 3,500 pesetas ($24.50), a single going for 2,400 pesetas ($16.80). The location is excellent, around the corner from the two major department stores of Madrid, El Corte Inglés and Galerías Precíados at the Plaza del Callao (also near the Callao Metro stop). The rooms, in spite of the central location, are quiet and peaceful, allowing you a good night's sleep. The residencia also has a bar, and can provide laundry service as well.

Margarita, 50 Gran Vía (tel. 247-35-49), is a pleasant haven run by English-speaking José A. Cacho and Margarita Pino. They are among the most hospitable pension owners I have encountered in Spain. Their house is warm and immaculate, lying on the fifth floor of an older building above the also-recommended Hostal Lauria. They have handsomely decorated their hostal and furnished it pleasantly with tasteful Spanish pieces. It is also one of the cleanest hostals along the Gran Vía, and you get plenty of water 24 hours a day, along with much comfort. Only eight comfortable rooms are rented, some of which contain a private bath and toilet. Coffee *con leche* along with fresh bread and butter are offered in their pleasant kitchen, where guests are welcome to use their refrigerator for storage of fruits and cheese. This two-star hostal charges from 2,600 pesetas ($18.20) in a double room with shower or private bath, 2,000 pesetas ($14) in a single with shower.

The **Hotel Alcázar Regis,** 61 Gran Vía (tel. 247-93-17), is part of the colorful past of Madrid. Conveniently perched on a corner—right in the midst of Madrid's best shops—it is an old-fashioned building, complete with a circular Greek-style temple as its crown. In a captivating atmosphere, you'll find long and beautiful rooms, wood paneling, leaded-glass windows, parquet floors, crystal chandeliers, and graciously proportioned bedrooms. There has been no chopping up of the rooms to install private baths. A single room with a water basin rents for 1,000 pesetas ($7), a similar double for 1,800 pesetas ($12.60).

Hostal Gaos, 14 Mesonero Romanos (tel. 231-63-05), offers guests the chance to enjoy a comfortable standard of living at moderate rates. A double bedroom with private bath costs 4,500 pesetas ($31.50), 3,400 pesetas ($23.80) if bathless. This residencia is on the second, third, and fourth floors of a building just off the Gran Vía; it lies directly north of the Puerta del Sol. Across the street is the popular flamenco club Torre Bermejas. There is a terrace solarium.

Hostal Lorenzo, 26 Calle Infantas (tel. 221-30-57), is an attractively informal hotel well recommended by several readers. It is housed on the third floor of an elegantly curving brick corner building with white shutters and iron railings, about two blocks from the Gran Vía and three from the Calle de Alcalá. Parquet floors lead to the comfortably old-fashioned bedrooms, which are well maintained by the couple operating the hostal. You're likely to have a serpentine dressing table or rows of flowerpots on your terrace, depending on the accommodation that's available when you show up. Each of the rooms has a private bath, and doubles cost from 3,000 pesetas ($21) to 3,400 pesetas ($23.80).

At the Puerta del Sol

Hostal Embajada, 5 Calle Santa Engracía (tel. 447-33-00), is a clean, pleasant three-star hotel about one block from the Plaza Alonso Martínez, a rather distinguished residential area. Still standing across the street is a great 19th-century palace. The Embajada has 84 rooms, and doubles with bath cost 5,200 pesetas ($36.40). Singles go for 4,000 pesetas ($28). You'll find the bedrooms tastefully decorated and the bathrooms modern. There's a modest lounge which has no bar.

Lisboa, 17 Ventura de la Vega (tel. 429-98-94), is perched right on Madrid's most famous restaurant street. My only warning is that during the evening the milling crowd of tasca hoppers tends to be noisy. The hotel is a neat and trim, modernized little town house, with compact rooms, each with private bath. Singles go for 1,600 pesetas ($11.20), doubles with shower or private bath for 3,200 pesetas ($22.40). In the cooler months there is central heating. The staff speaks five languages, sometimes amusingly so: "Our guests must not werry for transportations." True, everything seems near: American Express, the airline offices, the Puerta del Sol. The Lisboa has no restaurant, but it lies on a street of budget dining rooms and tascas.

Hostal Residencia Americano, 11 Puerta del Sol (tel. 222-28-22), is suitable for those who want to be in the bull's-eye center of Madrid, the Puerta del Sol, its so-called Times Square. Its owner-manager, A. V. Franceschi, has refurbished all the 42 bedrooms, which come with private bath. The hostal is surrounded by four streets, and 80% of the rooms are outside chambers with balconies facing the street. It's on the third floor of a five-story building, and Mr. Franceschi promises hot and cold running water 24 hours a day. The single rate is 2,200 pesetas ($15.40), increasing to 3,500 pesetas ($24.50) in a double. A continental breakfast costs extra.

Near the Plaza Mayor

Hostal La Macarena, 8 Cava de San Miguel (tel. 265-92-21). An establishment known for its reasonable prices and praised by readers for the warmth of its reception, this unpretentious but very clean hostal is run by the Antonio Juan family. Its 19th century façade is ornamented with belle époque patterns of acanthus leaves which offer an ornate contrast to the chiseled simplicity of the ancient buildings facing it. A dingy hallway and battered elevator will take you upstairs, where the family will greet you. The 18 accommodations cost 1,200 pesetas ($8.40) for a bathless single, 2,000 pesetas ($14) and 2,300 pesetas ($16.10) for a double, depending on the plumbing. The location is one of the establishment's strongest points: immediately behind the Plaza Mayor on a street with one of the most important clusters of tascas in Madrid. Metro: Sol.

Hostal La Perla Asturiana, 3 Plaza de Santa Cruz (tel. 266-46-00), is ideal for those who want to stay in the heart of old Madrid. It's a block off the Plaza Mayor and within two blocks of the Puerta del Sol. This small, family-run establishment has a courteous, helpful, and efficient staff member at the desk 24 hours a day, which is good both for security reasons and for the convenience of the guests. You can socialize with other visitors in the small, comfortable lobby adjacent to the reception desk. The bedrooms are clean, and some have a private bath. A twin-bedded unit with full bath costs 3,500 pesetas ($24.50); with shower, 3,200 pesetas ($22.40). Singles with bath rent for 2,300 pesetas

($16.10), while bathless singles go for 1,800 pesetas ($12.60). Clean towels are supplied daily and if you stay for a while, your sheets will be changed every four or five days. Breakfast, served in a small dining room, is included in the rates. No other meals are available, but there are inexpensive restaurants nearby, as well as the tapas bars on and off the Plaza Mayor. Reader Linda D. Metzler, assistant professor of Spanish at Kenyon College in Ohio, says she's stayed at the hostal during five summer visits to Madrid and has found it to be pleasant, reasonably priced, and accessible.

Near the Cortés

Hostal Residencia Olga, 13 Calle Zorrilla (tel. 429-78-87). Jeffrey and Marsha Silverstein, living in Badajoz, Spain, highly recommended this place to me—and theirs is a good choice. The location is behind the Cortes (Spain's House of Deputies), and Jeffrey finds it as clean as "my grandmother's kitchen —and that's pretty clean." It's family run, a single room with shower renting for 2,000 pesetas ($14), a double with shower for 3,000 pesetas ($21). Because the location is behind the Congreso, it is a secure area, relatively free of crime as there is 24-hour-a-day guard service. The host is known to me only as "García," and he and his wife are friendly and helpful. They do much to ease your adjustment into the capital.

A "CASA" OF BUDGET HOTELS: On the main drag, Gran Vía, close to many of Madrid's shops and restaurants, is an old-fashioned, 19th-century building filled almost exclusively with small hotels and pensions. The address is **44 Gran Vía.** The building has more hotel beds than the old woman who lived in the shoe had children. And some of the chambers are so small you may be as cramped as that prolific woman's niños.

Still, for the pilgrim who hops off the train in tourist-packed Madrid—armed only with luggage and minus a reservation—the house of hotels is a good bet for doorbell ringing. In some cases, there are two hotels on the same floor. An elevator makes the search easier.

Hostal-Residencia Continental, 44 Gran Vía (tel. 221-46-40), sprawls high, wide, and handsome over the entire third floor. The rooms are comfortable and tidy, the furnishings having undergone "a grand reform." Showers, baths, even paintings to enliven the decor, have been added. A twin-bedded room with bath costs 3,500 pesetas ($24.50). The price of a single with bath is 2,300 pesetas ($16.10), while a bathless single goes for 1,800 pesetas ($12.60). All tariffs include a continental breakfast. The lobby is dignified, and the desk clerk speaks English. Plaudits to a management that has tried to create a pleasant house in which to lodge.

Hostal-Residencia Miami, 44 Gran Vía (tel. 221-14-64), enjoys the vista from the eighth floor. Bearing no resemblance to its namesake, the 1920-ish Miami is a good bet for peseta watchers, as it charges only 2,100 pesetas ($14.70) for any one of its five doubles with water basins. Two of the special doubles, complete with private baths, rent for 3,600 pesetas ($18.20). Although somewhat cluttered, the residencia is clean and has a helpful staff.

Hostal-Residencia Tánger, 44 Gran Vía (tel. 221-75-85), on the top-floor roost, emerges with the quietest and sunniest disposition. The lobby is small but tasteful, and there is pleasantly old-fashioned furniture in the bedrooms. The passion of Mercedes Bilbao Ducable for knickknacks softens the rough edges and imbues the Tánger with a homey touch. Doubles with a shower (but no toilet) tally up at 1,900 pesetas ($13.30). Doubles with bath are 2,400 pesetas ($16.80). Only a continental breakfast is served.

STUDENT ACCOMMODATIONS: If you're a matriculated, degree-seeking student, your International Student Identity Card (ISIC) will be an open sesame for you in Madrid and the rest of Spain. The ISIC, which costs $10 (U.S.), entitles you to discounts and student reductions at some theaters and most museums; and it enables you to obtain discounts on air and bus transportation, as well as on tours; and provides sickness/accident insurance coverage. For information about the International Student Identity Card, request a copy of the latest *Student Travel Catalog* from the **Council on International Educational Exchange,** 205 East 42nd St., New York, NY 10017 (tel. 212/661-1414). The identification card issued you will give you access to most of the student lodgings of Madrid, such as those maintained *in summer only* by the University of Madrid.

3. The Restaurants of Madrid

The capital of Spain wraps a fringed shawl around a maze of restaurants. Most of my recommendations are in the heart of town, although dozens of restaurants have sprouted up overnight in every suburb. Time was when a traveler to Spain had to eat Spanish food almost exclusively. That is no longer true. Madrid has gone international, offering a wide spectrum of restaurants that range around the globe in cooking styles. They even do American food.

TOP-OF-THE-BUDGET DINING: My very favorite—and most expensive—recommendations will come first.

Casa Botín, 17 Calle de Cuchilleros (tel. 266-42-17), was founded in 1725, and is probably the most famous restaurant in Spain. Ernest Hemingway fanned the fires of its reputation when, in the final pages of *The Sun Also Rises,* Jake invited Brett to Botín to dine on roast suckling pig from Segovia and to drink rioja alta wine. "It is one of the best restaurants in the world," the author wrote. If that wasn't enough publicity, in *Death in the Afternoon,* he invited his mythical Lady there, the suckling pig, again distracting the characters from thinking "of casualties my friends have suffered."

Actually, the restaurant has everything on its side, especially its location near an edge of the Plaza Mayor, as well as its structure—an old building with beautifully preserved rooms that are furnished with imagination. Don't miss the early 18th-century oven; all visitors eventually inspect it. Out of that oven comes the justly praised roast suckling pig, that dish of Old Castile. Or if you prefer, the second-ranking dish is cordero asado (roast baby lamb). Don Antonio, one of the owners, assists with the language problem; he's greeted thousands of North Americans—so don't hesitate to call on him.

The service is tops, and a menú of the house goes for 3,000 pesetas ($21). This menú is offered only in autumn and winter, and includes garlic soup with egg, roast suckling pig, melon, or a small pitcher of wine or a glass of beer (mineral water if you prefer). Otherwise, the regular à la carte menu will cost 4,000 pesetas ($28) and up for a complete meal with wine. If you don't want the lamb or suckling pig, try instead the stewed partridge or the seasoned pork chops with potatoes. There is also a limited but well-chosen selection of fish dishes, including fried Cantabrian hake, baby squid in its own ink, and baby eels.

Classified as a two-fork restaurant, Botín has superb chefs, and you won't get any unpleasant surprises here. Lunch is served from 1 to 4 p.m., dinner from 8 p.m. to midnight. There is a small Andalusian bodega downstairs, where you can also order a complete meal (however, you can't drop in and tie up a table by ordering just a glass of wine). Nice atmosphere, as Papa would say.

El Mesón de San Javier, 3 Calle del Conde (tel. 248-09-25), has a long history going back to the 16th century, during which period it was owned by a secre-

erage traditionally associated with Spain. The management pumped much loot into making it modern and inviting. Hanging globe lights and spinning ceiling fans create an attractive ambience, as does the black-and-white marble checkerboard floor. You go here for beer, of course: la cerveza negra (black beer) costing 75 pesetas (53¢), or cerveza dorada (golden beer) at 65 pesetas (46¢). The local brew is best accompanied by homemade potato chips, a plate of them for 125 pesetas (88¢). Fresh shrimp, lobster, crabmeat, and barnacles are also served. The interior is quite large, dominated by a long counter and filled with huge tables. You can go directly to one of the wooden tables for waiter service, or stand at the counter. The nearest Metro stop is Alonso Martínez, and the hours are 11 a.m. till 11 p.m.

El Anciano Rey de los Vinos, 19 Bailén (tel. 248-50-51), may look like many other stand-up wine bars in Madrid, but the difference is in its connection with the sister of Isabela Segundo who used to slip away from the nearby Royal Palace for a tipple of wine whenever she could find an appropriate disguise as a commoner. Today the lower sections of its high-ceilinged walls are covered with hand-painted blue and green tiles, the designs of which face a curved wooden bar that is jammed during many parts of the day with crowds of talking, gesticulating, and flirting Madrileños out for a glass (or a carafe) of one of the four house wines. These range from dry to sweet and cost from 300 pesetas ($2.10) to 325 pesetas ($2.28) per pitcher, from 50 pesetas (35¢) to 60 pesetas (42¢) per glass. Beer is also served, as well as simple tapas priced between 75 pesetas (53¢) and 300 pesetas ($2.10) each. The establishment is closed every Wednesday.

Antonio Sánchez, 13 Mesón de Parades (tel. 239-78-26), was named in 1850 after the founder's son who was killed in a bullfighting ring. Memories of the bullfighter abound here, chief of which is the stuffed head of the animal that gored young Sánchez. Also featured on the darkly paneled walls are three valued works by the Spanish artist Zuloaga, who had his last public exhibition in this restaurant shortly before he died. A limited array of tapas, including garlic soup, is served with the Valdepeñas wine that a barman will draw from a barrel, although many guests ignore the edibles in favor of smoking endless cigarettes and arguing the merits of this or that bullfighter. A restaurant in the back serves Spanish food with a vaguely French influence. Tapas generally cost from 75 pesetas (53¢) to 300 pesetas ($2.10). The establishment lies in a warren of narrow streets near the Plaza Tirso de Molina.

SHERRY AND CONSOMMÉ: **Lhardy,** 8 Carrera de San Jerónimo (tel. 221-33-85), is a Madrid tradition, having opened its doors in 1839. This is a place with a great reputation as a gathering place of Madrid's literati. Upstairs is an expensive restaurant, but downstairs is a deli shop where you can buy some of the delicacies you tasted at the bar. It's traditional to come here to order a glass of sherry or else a cup of consommé from a large silver samovar, each costing 110 pesetas (77¢). The decor has been called "Isabella Segundo," and it definitely gives off the aura of another era. It is closed from the last week of July until mid-September.

CIDER DRINKING: **Casa Mingo,** 2 Paseo de la Florida (tel. 247-10-98), is a rarity in Madrid, left over from another era. It's a tavern-style cider bar, where you can order refreshing Asturian cider, hard or sweet, accompanied by crusty bread and goat cheese. The drink is served authentically. The waiter holds the glass as low as he can in his left hand and the bottle of cider as high as he can in his right. He then pours. Don't bother about the drops that may fall on the floor. You're participating in an age-old ritual. The price of a snack such as chicken and cider is 1,000 pesetas ($7). The perfect accompanying tidbit is a piece of

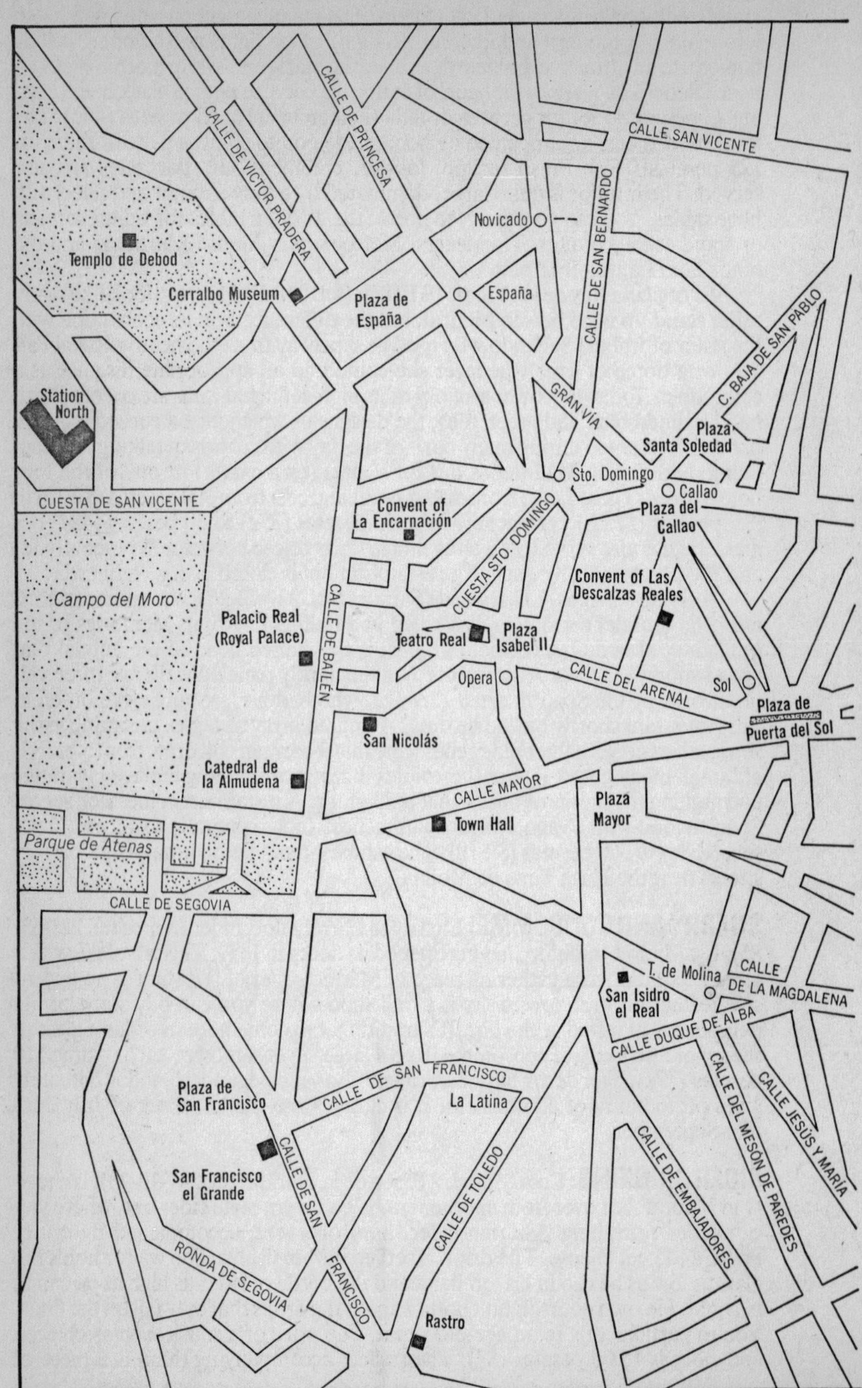
CALLE DE PRINCESA
CALLE DE VICTOR PRADERA
CALLE SAN VICENTE
Novicado
CALLE DE SAN BERNARDO
Templo de Debod
Cerralbo Museum
Plaza de España
España
C. BAJA DE SAN PABLO
GRAN VÍA
Station North
Plaza Santa Soledad
Sto. Domingo
Callao
CUESTA DE SAN VICENTE
Convent of La Encarnación
Plaza del Callao
CUESTA STO. DOMINGO
Campo del Moro
Convent of Las Descalzas Reales
Palacio Real (Royal Palace)
CALLE DE BAILÉN
Teatro Real
Plaza Isabel II
Opera
CALLE DEL ARENAL
Sol
Plaza de Puerta del Sol
San Nicolás
Catedral de la Almudena
CALLE MAYOR
Plaza Mayor
Town Hall
Parque de Atenas
CALLE DE SEGOVIA
T. de Molina
CALLE DE LA MAGDALENA
San Isidro el Real
CALLE DUQUE DE ALBA
CALLE DE SAN FRANCISCO
Plaza de San Francisco
La Latina
CALLE DEL MESÓN DE PAREDES
CALLE JESÚS Y MARÍA
CALLE DE EMBAJADORES
CALLE DE SAN FRANCISCO
San Francisco el Grande
CALLE DE TOLEDO
RONDA DE SEGOVIA
Rastro

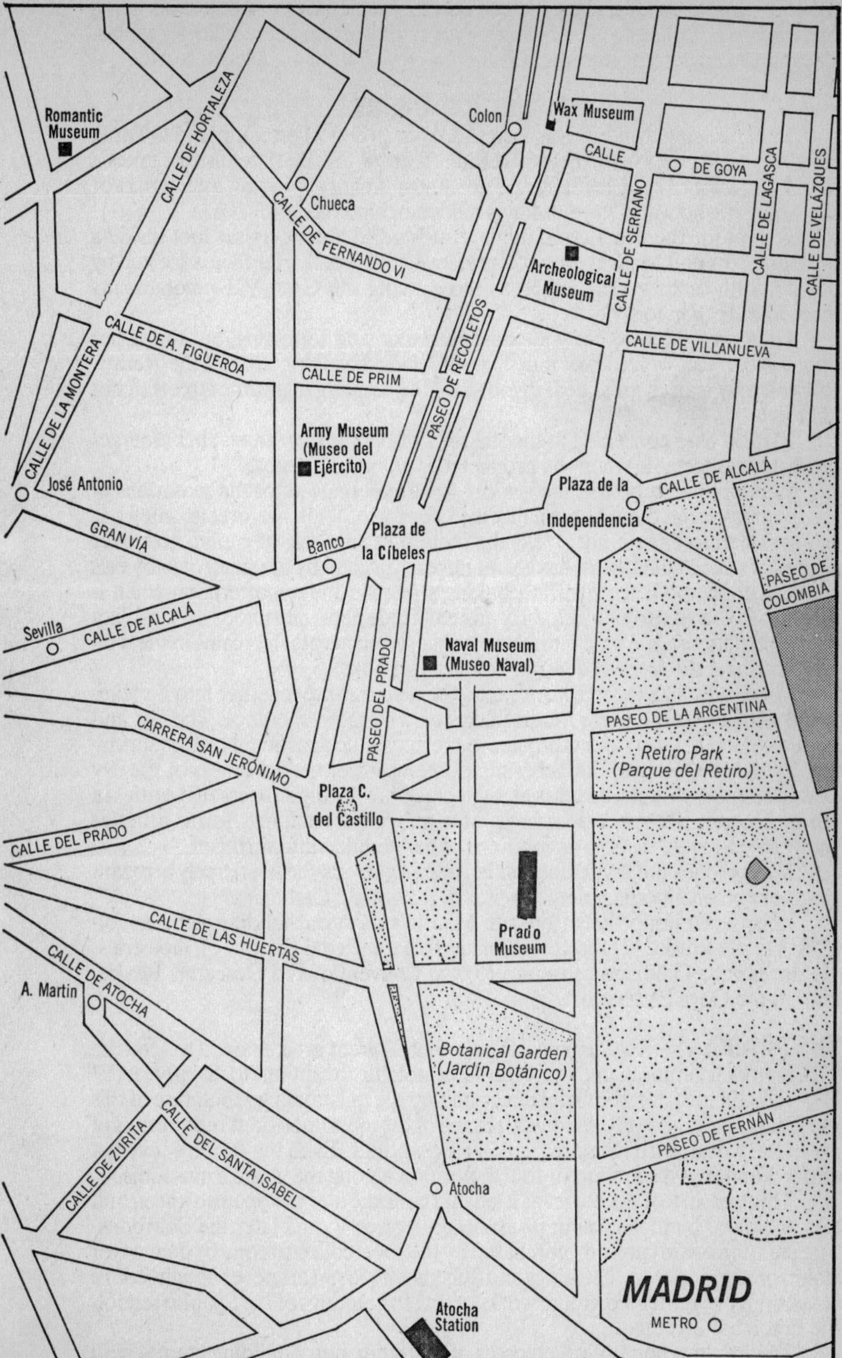

Romantic Museum
CALLE DE HORTALEZA
Colon
Wax Museum
CALLE DE GOYA
CALLE DE LAGASCA
CALLE DE VELÁZQUES
Chueca
CALLE DE FERNANDO VI
CALLE DE SERRANO
Archeological Museum
PASEO DE RECOLETOS
CALLE DE A. FIGUEROA
CALLE DE PRIM
CALLE DE VILLANUEVA
CALLE DE LA MONTERA
Army Museum (Museo del Ejército)
José Antonio
Plaza de la Independencia
CALLE DE ALCALÁ
GRAN VÍA
Banco
Plaza de la Cíbeles
PASEO DE COLOMBIA
Sevilla
CALLE DE ALCALÁ
Naval Museum (Museo Naval)
PASEO DEL PRADO
PASEO DE LA ARGENTINA
CARRERA SAN JERÓNIMO
Retiro Park (Parque del Retiro)
Plaza C. del Castillo
CALLE DEL PRADO
CALLE DE LAS HUERTAS
Prado Museum
CALLE DE ATOCHA
A. Martin
Botanical Garden (Jardín Botánico)
CALLE DEL SANTA ISABEL
CALLE DE ZURITA
PASEO DE FERNÁN
Atocha
Atocha Station

MADRID

METRO ○

cabrales (goat cheese) and bread. The decor is rustic, with wooden casks lining one wall. In fair weather, you can enjoy your drink at one of the sidewalk tables. The old tavern is across the street from the Goya Pantheon. Metro: Norte.

4. The Top Sights

In sightseeing, Madrid is as lean as a Spanish dog when compared to Paris, London, or Rome. Nevertheless, getting to know this Iberian mistress takes a long time, a lot of shoe leather, and an almost fanatical probing on the part of the stranger who wants to see what is hidden behind the fan.

Except for the Prado, you might visit Madrid and never set foot inside a museum. Not that Madrid proper is that lovely. She isn't. Her face is marred by dowdy, 19th-century relics, such as those lining the Gran Vía—monuments more to bulk than to style.

Of course, Madrid has wide paseos, parks, and fountains, but this is her public face. You won't learn much about Madrid walking around the Retiro. But you may learn a great deal if you stroll the teeming nighttime streets of her old town.

Madrid lives concealed in the shadows of her narrow streets, but emerges prudishly respectable when she promenades along her paseos.

Pretentious, stubborn, she is a city to be experienced for the sensations of the moment, even though sensuality isn't her forte. Walk her streets, smell her smells, listen to her sounds. Hear the indiscreet breaking of confidences over glasses of wine in the tascas; have your nostrils assailed by the smell of baby eels cooking in olive oil; feel the hot, baking streets in the midafternoon when it seems that you're strolling aimlessly around a pale ghost city under the Castilian sun; or experience the cold biting winds that sweep across the plains in the winter, punishing the faces of denizen and stranger alike.

Gradually, like a patchwork quilt, the pieces come together into a meaningful whole. After a while Madrid takes on a certain coherence. The dirt and squalor of her old town counterbalance the antiseptic apartment houses springing up on her skirttails; the bubbling fountains offset the harshness of the dry dust in summer; the shrill voices at night crack the deadly stillness that settles in the afternoon; the sheer dreariness of some of her buildings forms a better showcase to reveal the rich decorations of her architectural surprises.

Madrid does not invite unqualified admiration, as she is a fiercely arrogant city, her personality shaped by her proud, passionate Castilians.

In order of importance, I'd rate Madrid's most outstanding sights as follows: (1) the Prado, (2) the Royal Palace, (3) the Royal Factory of Tapestries, (4) the Lázaro Galdiano Museum, (5) the Convent of Las Descalzas Reales, and (6) the Goya Pantheon.

THE PRADO: There is a legend in Spain that all great art is shipped to Madrid. This is an exaggeration, and there are some notable exceptions to disprove it (El Escorial, Toledo), but the claim does point up the outstanding reputation of this museum. The Prado (tel. 468-09-50) is one of the most important repositories of art in the world, with its more than 7,000 paintings. Even the Prado's severest critics admit that it's in third or fourth position among the world's museums.

This treasury of art began as a private collection of the Spanish kings, and was enhanced by the Habsburgs, especially Carlos V, and later the Bourbons. The paintings were carefully purchased by the royal collectors one by one, never stolen or expropriated. The kings and queens who loved art never bought entire collections but rather individual works of art. In paintings of the Spanish school, the Prado has no equal.

The Prado is housed in a colossus of an 18th-century building littered with arcades and colonnades. The museum is not a storehouse of national art; it is a world museum, with works by many famed European painters. Still, on your first visit, you'll want to concentrate most heavily on the Spanish masters (Velázquez, Goya, El Greco, and to a lesser degree, Murillo). The average traveler can "do" the Prado in two visits of perhaps two or three hours' duration. Better yet, two weeks.

The Prado is open daily except Monday from 9 a.m. to 7 p.m., to 2 p.m. on Sunday and holidays (except Good Friday, Christmas, and New Year's, when it's closed). The entrance fee is 400 pesetas ($2.80). The Prado has galleries dedicated to the Spanish masters of the 19th century and the impressionists, among others. They are in the Casón del Buen Retiro, two blocks behind the Prado, on Calle Alfonso XII, opposite the Retiro park.

Currently, the painting stirring up the most excitement is Picasso's *Guernica.* Long banned in Spain, the painting rested for years in the Museum of Modern Art in New York before it was returned to its homeland. Picasso's work reflected his sadness at Generalissimo Franco's bombing of Guernica, a little Basque town. Picasso requested that *Guernica* not be returned to Spain until the death of Franco and the "reestablishment of public liberties." Behind a glass barrier, the painting covers almost a whole wall—some 12 feet high and about 25 feet long. Visitors are kept at a distance of some 25 feet from the world masterpiece.

The casón is open on Tuesday, Thursday, Friday, and Saturday from 9 a.m. to 7 p.m. It is closed on Monday.

For visitors who must see the Prado quickly (by far the majority), I have compiled a list below of a representative collection of outstanding paintings from the various schools.

With many notable exceptions (Goya's sketches), most of the major works of the Prado are exhibited on the first floor. You may want to head there first before your viewing power begins to fade.

You'll see art by Italian masters—such artists as Raphael, Botticelli, Mantegna, and Andrea del Sarto, along with Correggio. None of the works at the Prado represents the best of the output of these great artists, although an *Annunciation* is typical of the style of Fra Angelico (1400–1455).

The Italian cavalcade of art continues with the Venetian artists. Perhaps the most celebrated work here is Titian's voluptuous Venus being watched by a musician who can't keep his eyes on his work (two different versions are in separate rooms).

Don't miss the work of El Greco (1524–1614), the Crete-born artist who lived much of his life in Toledo. Philip II, a great patron of the arts, didn't take to El Greco's strangely distorted and elongated figures through which the artist expressed his spirituality. Although he was born in Greece and studied in Italy, many art historians have expressed the opinion that he was the most Spanish of all artists (Goya aficionados may differ). You can see a parade of "The Greek's" saints, Madonnas, Holy Families—even a ghostly *John the Baptist.* But El Greco's masterpiece hangs in a little church in Toledo (next chapter).

In the five-star showcase of the Prado is the work of the incomparable Velázquez (1599–1660), a "warts-and-all"-type painter who got away with many an unflattering portrait of his patron, Philip IV—the king even learned to like his likeness. The world, of course, considers Velázquez one of the all-time great painters. Spaniards, however, consider him *the* greatest. The Prado has the most splendid array of his works—notably the already-mentioned portraits of Philip IV, the highly praised *Drunkards,* and his series of four dwarfs. One of his best portraits is the little girl in the hoop dress, Margarita of Austria, daughter of his patron.

The most famous painting in all of the Prado is Velázquez's masterpiece. Entitled *Las Meninas,* it is considered by art critics to be a triumph in the use of light effects. Like so many of Velázquez's works, the painting contains a fascinating dwarf woman. The faces of the queen and king (presumably we are looking at the scene through their eyes) are reflected in the mirror in the painting itself. The artist in the foreground? Velázquez, of course. On center stage is Princess Margarita.

Rubens's peacock-blue *Garden of Love,* and his rendition of the *Three Graces* can be seen, and, going back to Spain, you'll see the art of Ribera (1591–1652), a Valencia-born artist who during his long sojourn in Italy refined and polished his tortured world on canvas. His best work is the *Martyrdom of St. Philip* in which we feel the somber tragedy of Spain.

Murillo's work, including *Bartholomé,* is also on display. This Seville-born artist (1617–1682)—often referred to as the "painter of Madonnas"—is not my favorite. A number of critics consider him extremely dated, at least for modern tastes. The sentimental cardmakers of yesteryear relied heavily on his works at Christmas. The most notable of his three Immaculate Conceptions displayed here is *La Immaculada de Soult,* returned to Spain by the French government during World War II.

The Prado contains one of the world's outstanding collections of Hieronymus Bosch, the Flemish genius who was born sometime in the mid-15th century and died in 1516. Through his paintings parade all the citizens of Hell—imps, hobgoblins, ghouls, ogres and ogresses, pigwidgeons, wraiths, and all sorts of creeping, crawling fiends—some only with a ghoulish head and a pair of mischievous legs trotting off to do no good. At his table of the *Seven Deadly Sins* you can stuff your eyes on gluttony. Also you'll see one of the Bosch's most famous works, his triptych, *The Hay Wagon.* Each selfish, greedy soul—even the pope—is trying to grab his share and more from the "hay wagon" of life as it rolls to Hell. Don't miss Pieter Brueghel's *Triumph of Death.* Brueghel, another Flemish painter, continues Bosch's ghoulish work.

One of "El Bosco's" finest triptychs (surely his best known work) is here, *The Garden of Earthly Delights,* which reveals his three stages of interpretation: (1) creation, (2) the struggle, and (3) hell.

The ground floor of the Prado is also rich in paintings and sculpture. But the first-timer, already exhausted, may want to confine his search to some sketches and paintings by Goya. Francisco de Goya (1746–1828) was considered a strange and eccentric genius, ranking along with Velázquez and El Greco in the trio of great Spanish artists. Hanging here also are the cruel portraits that Goya did of his patron, Charles IV, and his family. The queen looks like a chicken, the king a shadowy version of an overstuffed George Washington. Even a stallion and a chic riding costume couldn't disguise the fact that Maria Louisa Teresa looked like a scrubwoman. Goya painted at both the literal and figurative expense of royalty. Incidentally, the Goya paintings *Maja Vestida,* lying seductively clad in a white gown, and *Maja Desnuda* (the *Naked Maja,* believed to have been posed by the Duchess of Alba—and, later, on the screen by Ava Gardner), are on the ground floor.

Also displayed is the beginning of a series of sketches by Goya. Some of them, depicting the cancer of 18th-century Spain, caused the dragon fire of the Inquisition to breathe down Goya's neck. One of the artist's most reproduced works, *The Third of May (1808),* is recognizable by the outstretched arms of the man facing the firing squad. The scene is from the Napoleonic invasion of Spain. In addition, you'll see another important work, the battle scene from the *Second of May,* revealing a bloody event in 1808 as the Madrileños tried desperately to fight off the invaders. One of the strangest, gloomiest exhibits in the Prado reveals Goya in a black mood. And when Goya was in a black mood, he could make a painter such as Ribera look like a stand-up comic. The so-called "black paintings"—all expressionistic—were made at his country casa when Goya was deaf, perhaps even mad. To borrow the title from *Whistler's Mother,* the Goya paintings were arrangements in grays and blacks. After viewing these, you will have seen the best of his work, as well as the best of the Prado.

Buses going to the museum are numbered 10, 14, 27, 34, 37 and 45. Metro stations are Banco and Atocha.

THE ROYAL PALACE (PALACIO REAL): Owing a heavy debt to French architects, this huge royal palace on Calle Bailén (tel. 248-74-04) was begun in 1737, on the site of the Madrid Alcázar, which burned to the ground in the Christmas of 1734. Of its approximately 2,800 rooms—which that "Enlightened Despot" Charles III called home—some are open to the public, while others are still used for state business.

You are conducted through the royal showcase on a guided tour. Just say "Inglés" to the doorman who takes your ticket, so you'll hook up to an English-speaking tour. The inclusive tour encompasses the Tapestry Gallery, the Reception Room, the State Apartments, the Armory, the Royal Pharmacy, and the Library.

The reception rooms and state apartments should get priority here if you're rushed. They embrace a rococo room with a diamond clock, a porcelain salon, a Royal Chapel that is used whenever a new cardinal is sent to Spain, a Banquet Room where receptions for head of state are held, and a Throne Room with a chair on which Franco never sat.

The rooms are literally stuffed with objects of art and antiques—forming salon after salon of monumental grandeur, with no apologies for the opulence of a bygone era (damask, mosaics, stucco, Tiepoloesque ceilings, gilt and bronze, chandeliers, paintings, tapestries, and the inevitable chinoiserie).

The miles and miles of tapestries, both Flemish and Spanish, in the Tapestry Gallery comprise an impressive collection numbering in the hundreds. Many date back to the 15th century.

The palace was last used as a royal residence in 1931, before King Alfonso XIII and his wife Victoria Eugénie fled Spain. King Juan Carlos and Queen Sofia are more modest in their requirements. They have turned the Royal Palace over to history, choosing not to live there but in a much smaller palace, the Zarzuela, named after the Spanish operetta or musical comedy. Their palace is suburban.

After this, a short walk across the courtyard will bring you to the armory, where you'll see the finest collection in Spain, perhaps the world. Many of the items—powder flasks, shields, lances, helmets, saddles—are from the collection of Charles V (Charles I of Spain).

From here, the comprehensive tour takes you into the Royal Library, with volume after leather-bound volume, and the less interesting pharmacy containing bottles in which—conceivably—concoctions might have been mixed to help cranky Maria Josefa's migraines.

To visit all these sights, you pay 400 pesetas ($2.80). Hours in summer are from 9:30 a.m. to 12:45 p.m. and 4 to 5:45 p.m. (on Sunday from 9:30 a.m. to 1:30 p.m.). In winter, hours are from 9:30 a.m. to 12:45 p.m. and 3:30 to 5:15 p.m. (on Sunday from 9:30 a.m. to 1:30 p.m.).

Also known as the Palacio de Oriente, the Royal Palace is on the same-name Plaza de Oriente, a short ride from the center of town.

You may also want to visit the Carriage Museum (Carrozas), also at the Royal Palace, to see some of the grand old relics that Spanish aristocrats have been riding around in for the past two centuries. To visit it separately costs 85 pesetas (60¢).

Metro stops for the palace and its adjuncts are Opera and Plaza de España.

THE ROYAL FACTORY OF TAPESTRIES (REAL FÁBRICA DE TAPICES): At this factory, the age-old process of making exquisite (and very expensive) tapestries is still carried out with consummate skill. Goya is the superstar around here: nearly every tapestry seems to be based on one of his cartoons.

The artist, of course, was the most famous person who ever worked for the factory—employed between 1775 and 1792. During those years he designed more than four dozen "cartoons" that were used as models for tapestries. Many of these same patterns—such as *El Cacharrero* (The Pottery Salesman)—are still in production today. (To see Goya's original cartoons, you must go to the Prado.) Many of the other designs were based on cartoons by Francisco Bayeu, Goya's brother-in-law.

In 1835 the factory—known as Santa Bárbara when it was founded by Philip IV—was shut down. Now the industry's happily revived. Many of the workers hardly look at the pattern, they know it so well. Other more cautious artisans prefer to use a mirror.

As a superstitious lot, the artists may not want to show too much pride in their work. They remember Arachne, the Lydian maiden of Greek mythology who boasted of her weaving skill with such arrogance (even challenging Athene to a contest) that she was turned into a spider.

Admission is 50 pesetas (35¢). The factory, at 2 Fuenterrabia (tel. 251-34-00), is open from 9:30 a.m. to 12:30 p.m. Closed on Saturday and Sunday, the house also shuts down August 1 through September 1. Metro stop: Menéndez Pelayo.

GOYA MUSEUM AND PANTHEON (PANTHEON DE GOYA): Here, at the tomb of Goya, you can see one of his masterpieces, an elaborately beautiful fresco depicting the miracles of St. Anthony on the dome and cupola of the little hermitage of San Antonio de la Florida, which is on the Paseo de San Antonio de la Florida.

The tomb and fresco are in one of the twin chapels (visit the one on the right) that were built in the latter part of the 18th century. Discreetly placed mirrors will help you see the ceiling better. One of the figures in the paintings—a woman draped in fabric—is the best known segment of the fresco, used to symbolize Spain in travel posters throughout America and Europe. The hermitage is in a remote part of town at Glorieta de San António de la Florida (tel. 247-79-21), beyond the North Station. Take bus 46 or else the Metro to Norte. From July through September, the museum is open from 10 a.m. to 1 p.m. and 4 to 7 p.m. Hours from October through June are 11 a.m. to 1:30 p.m. and 3 to 6 p.m. On Sunday, it is open from 11 a.m. to 1:30 p.m. Closed Wednesday. Admission is 100 pesetas (70¢).

BULLFIGHTING MUSEUM (MUSEO TAURINO): At the Plaza de Toros de las Ventas, this museum (tel. 255-18-57)—the best of its kind in Spain—may serve as a fitting introduction to bullfighting before you actually see an event in the ring. Here you'll find such items as the death costume of Manolete, the traje de luce (suit of light) that he wore when he was gored to death at the age of 30 in Madrid's Plaza de Toros. The year: 1947. As one aficionado said at the time: "Manolete's fortunes were in the millions. He didn't know when to quit."

Other memorabilia evoke the heyday of Juan Belmonte, the Andalusian who in 1914 revolutionized bullfighting by performing so close to the horns that he became world-renowned for his bravery. His friend and rival, Joselito (José Gómez), is also represented, that matador who was gored 54 times. A bull finally ended the career of Joselito in 1920, although Belmonte retired and became (you guessed it) a bull breeder. Other exhibits include a Goya painting of a bullfighter (a guide will elaborately show you where to stand so that you may better appreciate the painting). Photographs and relics of the ring trace the history of bullfighting in Spain from its ancient origin to the present day.

The museum can be visited daily except Sunday, from 9 a.m. to 2 p.m. and 4 to 7 p.m. for an admission fee of 70 pesetas (49¢). Metro: Ventas.

MUSEUM OF LÁZARO GALDIANO: Imagine 37 rooms in a well-preserved 19th century mansion of the aristocracy bulging with artworks—including many by the most famous old masters of Europe.

Most visitors take the elevator to the top floor, then begin their descent, lingering long over many of the mementos. At the beginning of the collection, the hand-woven vestments (some dating from the 15th century), the display of swords (surely more than El Cid's army had), the daggers, the seals of kings (even one from Napoleon), hardly suggest what is in store. Case after case of Spanish fans are only mildly interesting (one belonged to Isabella II, who, the court considered, was in dire need of something to hide behind).

However, two works by the incomparable Bosch evoke his own peculiar brand of horror, his canvases peopled with creepy fiends devouring human flesh. Unexpectedly, Rembrandt's *Self-Portrait* adorns a wall nearby. The Spanish masters, naturally, are the best represented—a whole galaxy of them: Velázquez, El Greco, Zurbarán, Ribera, Murillo, and Valdés Leal.

Rare in Spanish museums is the section here devoted to works by English portrait and landscape artists: Sir Joshua Reynolds, Gainsborough, Gilbert Stuart (the American painter, noted for his three likenesses of George Washington), and Constable (one of his many interpretations of *Dedham Vale* in East Anglia). Italian artists exhibited include Tiepolo and Guardi, the latter with one of his never-ending, but always fascinating, scenes of Venice. Salon 30—for many, the most interesting—is devoted to Goya, and includes some of the paintings of his "black period" and a portrait of the cuckold, the weak Charles IV, and his unattractive but amorous Queen Maria Louisa.

Other exhibitions include enamel works (unsurpassed in Spain), 16th-century crystal from Limoges, French and Italian carvings from the 14th and 15th centuries (one of the most remarkable collections in the country), Byzantine jewelry, a Maltese cross from the 15th century, Italian bronzes from the Roman days to the Renaissance, and medieval suits of armor. In Salon 6 hangs a small portrait of a woman encased in a green velvet frame. Although the museum attributes this painting to Leonardo da Vinci, many art historians dispute this claim. The painting is more generally attributed to Ambrogio de Predis of Milan, with whom da Vinci lived his first years in that Lombard city. Calling it a da Vinci was denounced by one critic as "unwarranted and disturbing sensationalism."

At 122 Serrano, the museum (tel. 261-60-84) may be visited from 10 a.m. to 2 p.m. daily. Admission is 100 pesetas (70¢). It is closed in August and on Monday. Bus 9, 16, 19, 51, or 89.

CONVENT OF LAS DESCALZAS REALES: Following in the footsteps of Charles V's daughter, Juana of Austria, "gentle ladies" of the aristocracy—disappointed in love or "wanting to be the bride of Christ"—stole away to this mid-16th-century convent to take the veil. Of course, all of them brought a dowry, making the so-called "Royal Barefoots" one of the richest convents in the land.

However, by the mid-20th century the ladies of nobility were no longer in ascendancy, and recent arrivals had no problem at all taking the vow of poverty. True, the convent still contained a collection of art treasures valuable enough to have financed a revolution. But portraits by El Greco or Velázquez don't buy rice for the paella unless sold—and the sisters were forbidden to auction off anything. In sad fact, they were starving—the exposure of which brought on a nationwide scandal.

The state intervened, and the pope granted special dispensation to open the monastery as a museum. The good sisters, about 30 in all, are eating once again, happy to report; and much of the public is enthralled to get a look behind the walls of what was once a mysterious edifice on one of the most beautiful squares in Old Madrid.

An English-speaking guide will show you through. In the Reliquary are housed the dowries brought by the noble ladies, such as the last wife of Philip II. One of the relics is said to contain bits of wood from the cross on which Christ was crucified; another is alleged to hold some of the bones of St. Sebastian. The most valuable painting is Titian's *Caesar's Money,* valued in the millions (of pesetas). The Flemish Hall shelters the finest works, including one of the processional by Hans Van Baker. Other paintings are by Brueghel the Elder and Bernardino Luini, the Lombard artist. Sardonically, portraits of the sisters of Emperor Charles V reveal them to have the same faces as their ugly brother.

Many of the tapestries were based on Rubens's cartoons, displaying his chubby matrons. Gold and silver threads were woven into some of the vestments, dating mainly from the 16th and 17th centuries. In the cloisters, a guide will conduct you to the Chapel of Our Lady of Guadalupe, known for its Virgin sculpted in lead.

The convent (tel. 222-06-87) is open Tuesday to Friday from 10:30 a.m. to 1 p.m. and 4 to 5:30 p.m.; on Saturday and Sunday from 10:30 a.m. to 1 p.m., charging 100 pesetas (70¢) for admission. It stands on the Plaza de las Descalzas Reales, reached by heading down the Postigo de San Martín (so narrow the walls close in) from the Gran Vía. Metro stop: Plaza del Sol.

SOME MORE ATTRACTIONS: Those with more time for Madrid might want to check out the following sights:

Church of San Francisco El Grande

Ironically, Madrid, capital of cathedral-rich Spain, does not in itself possess a proper cathedral. But it does have an important church, with a dome larger than that of St. Paul's in London. At the Plaza de San Francisco El Grande (1 San Buenaventura), this 18th-century church is filled with a number of ecclesiastical works of art, notably a Goya painting of St. Bernardinus of Siena. A guide will show you through the building, taking you through the museum and pointing out the most interesting features in the chapels. On late fall or winter afternoons, you sometimes have to insist that the lights be turned on, or you'll see little. Admission is 50 pesetas (35¢). Metro: La Latina. You can also take a bus, line 3, from the Plaza de España, which goes right to the church.

The Rastro

If you're in the market for a gigantic wire figure of Don Quixote or a two-seater German motorcycle from World War II, then by all means visit the Rastro, the flea market of Madrid, which runs up and down several hilly streets south of the Plaza de Cascorro. You don't have to be in the market for anything. The Rastro is something to experience. The life of Madrid spills out here. There are legendary stories told about the discovery of fortunes in art treasures, but don't expect to uncover any such finds; instead, you'll often come up with interesting little things that can make ideal gifts, such as antique keys to castles. You can start a new vogue in America by placing them on your coffee tables; of course, you'll have to make up a spectacular story concerning their origins. But if you're interested in buying, there are many items that might tempt you, although frankly, most of the little thrown-together stalls are filled with plain unadulterated junk. One Spaniard claimed that someone stripped his motorcycle of parts on a Saturday night. On Sunday, he went to the flea market and, after an exhaustive search, found the stolen parts on sale. By 2 in the afternoon, most of the stallkeepers start shutting down. Often this is the best time to make quick purchases, as their desire to sell reaches a fever pitch then. *Bargain.* The nearest Metro station is La Latina, less than two blocks away.

The Retiro

Here in the heart of Madrid is a vast, shaded, once-royal park, which may be necessary to visit when the summer heat in Madrid becomes unbearable. A reminder of some of the large forests that once stood proudly in Castile, the park is filled with numerous fountains (one dedicated to an artichoke), statues (one honors Lucifer, strangely heretical in Catholic Spain), and a large lake where soldiers meet their girls during the hotter months.

In summer, the rose gardens are worth the visit, and you'll find a number of places where you can have inexpensive snacks and drinks.

From 8 a.m. to 8 p.m., you can rent a rowboat in the Retiro. If you're not so inclined, then a ride on one of the motorboats may make you completely forget that mean August sun. What to do afterward? Take a promenade.

The House of Lope de Vega

What Shakespeare is to the English-speaking world, Lope de Vega is to the Spanish. One of the most prolific writers who ever lived, this Madrid-born author dramatized Habsburg Spain as no one ever had before, earning a lasting position in Spanish letters. A reconstruction of his medieval house stands on a narrow street, ironically named Cervantes (knock on the ancient door at no. 11), his competitor for the title of the greatest writer of the Golden Age of Spain and a bitter enemy. It is within walking distance of the Prado. The dank, dark house is furnished with relics of the period, although one can't be sure that any of the furnishings or possessions actually belonged to this 16th-century genius. After a guide shows you through the house, you can visit the gardens out back. It is open from 11 a.m. to 2 p.m. on Tuesday and Thursday, and the price of admission is 100 pesetas (70¢). From mid-July and mid-September, the house (tel. 429-92-16) is closed to the public.

MUSEUM MISCELLANY: For those of you who have extra sightseeing time in Madrid, there are a number of museums that might be visited:

Archeological Museum (Museo Nacional Arqueológico)

For some reason, Iberian archeological museums tend to be dull—surprisingly, since so many civilizations (prehistoric, Roman, Visigothic, Muslim) have conquered the peninsula. An exception, however, to that generalization is this stately mansion in Madrid, a storehouse of artifacts from prehistoric times to the heyday of the baroque. One of the prime exhibits here is the Iberian statue *La Dama de Elche,* a piece of primitive carving—probably from the 4th century B.C.—that was discovered on the southeastern coast of Spain, as well as the splendidly polychromed *Dama de Baza* discovered in Granada Province, also from the same date.

A cache of treasures from the discovery of some of the finest Punic relics in Europe on the Balearic island of Ibiza, many of them found in a Carthaginian and Roman necropolis, are on display. Excavations from Paestum, Italy, are shown: some of the statuary of Imperial Rome, including a statue of Tiberius enthroned as well as one of the controversial Livia, wife of Augustus. The collection of Spanish Renaissance lusterware, as well as Talavera pottery and Retiro porcelain, is shown to good advantage, along with some rare 16th- and 17th-century Andalusian glassware.

The "classic" artifacts are impressive, and the contributions from medieval days up through the 16th century are highly laudable. Many of the exhibits were ecclesiastical treasures removed from churches and monasteries. A much-photographed choir stall from Palencia—hand-painted and crude, but remarkable nevertheless—dates from the 14th century.

At 13 Calle de Serrano (tel. 403-65-59), on the major shopping artery, the museum may be visited every day from 9:30 a.m. to 1:30 p.m. for 150 pesetas ($1.05). Worthy of a look are the reproductions of the Altamira cave paintings discovered near Santander in northern Spain in 1868. Joseph Déchelette called them "the Sistine Chapel of Quaternary art." The man-made *cuevas* in Madrid simulate the lateral chamber at Altamira—but with far more neck-craning room. The paintings—in blacks, reds, and violets—are chiefly of bison, horses, and wild boars. The simulated caves may be visited between 9:30 a.m. and 1:30 p.m. Metro: Colón.

Museum of Sorolla

Sorolla is an acquired taste. He was born Joaquín in Valencia in 1863, and died in Madrid in 1923. In his day he was celebrated, as autographed portraits from King Alfonso XIII and U.S. President Taft reveal. From 1912, he and his family occupied this elegant Madrileño town house off the Paseo de la Castellana. Two years after his death, his widow turned it over to the government—and it is now maintained as a memorial to the painter, inaugurated in 1932.

Except for the faded furniture and portraits, much of the house remains as Sorolla left it, right down to his stained paint brushes and pipes. In the museum wing, however, a representative collection of the artist's paintings is displayed. All of the works owned by the museum can't be exhibited, however, because of the lack of space.

Although Sorolla painted portraits of Spanish aristocrats, he was essentially interested in "the people," often in their native costumes, such as those once worn in Ávila and Salamanca. He was especially fond of painting beach scenes on what is now the Costa Blanca. His favorite subjects are depicted either "before" or "after" their bath, and he was interested in the subtle variations of the Spanish sunlight. One critic wrote that Sorolla "may fail to please certain individuals, contaminated by an unhealthy leaning towards things decadent, pessimistic and tragic."

Seek out not only the artist's self-portrait, but the paintings of Madame Sorolla and their handsome son.

Entered through an Andalusian-style patio, the museum is at 37 General Martínez Campos (tel. 410-15-84). It is open daily except Monday, from 10 a.m. to 2 p.m. and charges 200 pesetas ($1.40). The house and garden alone are worth the trip. At noon, a short video program depicts the painter's life and his work. Metro: Iglesia. Bus 5 or 16.

Fine Arts Museum

Right on Madrid's busy boulevard, an easy stroll from the Puerta del Sol, the **Museo de la Real Academia de Bellas Artes de San Fernando,** 13 Calle de Alcalá, is popular primarily because of its Goya salon. Works by that artist include a self-portrait, much reproduced, and a study of Manuel de Godoy, the confidant of the House of Bourbon and lover of Queen María Luisa at the time of the Napoleonic invasion of Spain. The two prized canvases by Goya here are his *The Crazy House* and a *Scene from the Inquisition,* brilliantly portraying his own brand of horror. Displayed also are works by other famous Spanish artists: Murillo, Ribera, Sorolla, and Zurbarán (his robed monks). In particular, search out Rubens's *Susanna and the Elders,* the latter lecherous indeed. The museum is open from 11 a.m. to 1 p.m. on Thursday and from 5:30 to 7:30 p.m. on Friday. Admission is 100 pesetas (70¢). Closed in August.

The Romantic Museum (Museo Romántico)

Of special interest and limited appeal, this museum attracts those seeking the romanticism of the 19th century. Decorative arts festoon the mansion in which the museum is housed: crystal chandeliers, faded portraits, oils from Goya to Sorolla, opulent furnishings, porcelain, jewelry, ceramics, even *la grande toilette.* Many of the exhibitions date from the days of Isabella II, the high-living, fun-loving queen who was forced into exile and eventual abdication of the throne (she lived in Paris until her death in 1904).

At 13 San Mateo, the Museo Romántico is open daily from 10 a.m. to 6 p.m., to 2 p.m. on Sunday. It charges 200 pesetas ($1.40) for admission. It is closed on Monday and from August 1 to September 15. For information, phone 448-10-71. Metro: Alonso Martínez.

Museum of Bottles (Museo de Bebidas)

In Madrid, Señor Chicote became a legend. His bar at 12 Gran Vía (tel. 232-15-12) is a mecca for foreigners and Spaniards alike, and was especially popular with Hemingway. In the cellar of the bar, the good señor collected beer, liquor, and wine bottles from all over the world. Many of the bottles were presented by celebrities, including Doña Fabiola de Mora y Aragón, who married the Belgian king, Baudouin; Cantinflas of Mexico; Onassis; Emperor Haile Selassie; as well as Tyrone Power and Ava Gardner, stars of *The Sun Also Rises.*

In all, there are more than 10,500 bottles, including one in the shape of a lightbulb, the gift of Phillips. Bottles come in odd shapes and sizes: one like a Rolls-Royce tank, another in the form of Charlie Chaplin. Many contain vintage whiskies, such as an 1820 Johnnie Walker.

All the bottles are now housed in an admission-free museum at 41 Paseo de Recoletos (tel. 410-30-13); Metro: Colón. Hours are 10 a.m. to 1 p.m. and 4 to 6 p.m.

The Wax Museum

The **Museo Colón,** Plaza de Colón (tel. 419-26-49), in the Centro Colón, charges 400 pesetas ($2.80) for adults and 200 pesetas ($1.40) for children. The museum is like London's Madame Tussaud's or Paris's Musée Grevin; there are scenes depicting events in Spanish history, such as Columbus calling on Ferdinand and Isabella. Contemporary international figures aren't neglected either. Thus, we see Jacqueline Onassis having champagne at a supper club and Garbo all alone. The heroes and villains of World War II—everybody from Eisenhower to Hitler—are enlivened by the presence of the "Blue Angel," Marlene Dietrich, singing "Lili Marlene." Out-of-work filmmakers created the 400 figures in

38 tableaux, succeeding best with backdrops, falling shortest in the depiction of contemporary celebrities. Two new galleries contain historical figures of Romans and Arabs from the ancient days of the Iberian peninsula, and a new show in multivision gives a 30-minute recap of Spanish history from the time of the Phoenicians to today. Admission to the small theater to see this show is 100 pesetas (70¢). The museum is open from 10:30 a.m. to 2 p.m. and 4 to 9 p.m. Metro: Colón.

Templo de Debod

This Egyptian temple once stood in the Valley of the Nile, 19 miles from Aswan. When the new dam built there was going to overrun its site with water, the Egyptian government agreed to have it dismantled and presented to the Spanish people. It was taken down stone by stone in 1969 and 1970, then shipped to Valencia. From that Mediterranean port, it was sent by rail to Madrid, where it was reconstructed and opened to the public in 1971. Photos upstairs in the temple depict its long history. It stands right off the Plaza de España, and can be visited daily from 10 a.m. to 1 p.m. and 5 to 8 p.m. (on Sunday, to 3 p.m.). Admission is free.

Army Museum (Museo del Ejército)

Behind the Prado, at 1 Méndez Nuñez (tel. 231-46-24), this museum has some outstanding exhibits from military history, including the original sword of El Cid. Isabella carried this same sword when she took Granada from the Moors. In addition, you can see the tent used by Charles V in Tunisia, along with relics of Pizarro and Cortés. The collection of armor is also exceptional. The museum is housed in the Buen Retiro Palace, which dates from 1631. Americans may be interested in seeking out a piece of the cross that Columbus carried with him when he discovered the New World. Charging 50 pesetas (35¢) for admission, the museum is open from 10 a.m. to 2 p.m.; closed Monday. Metro: Banco de España.

Museo Naval (Naval Museum)

The history of nautical science and the Spanish navy comes alive at 5 Paseo del Prado (tel. 221-04-19). For me, the most fascinating exhibit is the map the mate of the *Santa Maria* made to show the Spanish monarchs the new discoveries of land. There are also souvenirs of the Battle of Trafalgar, along with Juan de la Cosa's world chart. The museum, charging only 5 pesetas (4¢) admission, is open daily except Monday, from 10:30 a.m. to 1:30 p.m. Metro: Banco de España.

Museo Nacional de Artes Decorativas

In 62 rooms spread over several floors, this museum at 12 Montalbán, near the Plaza de las Cibeles (tel. 221-34-40), displays a rich collection of furniture, ceramics, and decorative pieces from all regions of Spain. It is especially rich in the 16th and 17th centuries, but the collection is eclectic, including many surprises—say, bronzes from the Ming dynasty in China. You're greeted by a Venetian 18th-century sedan chair in the vestibule. This bit of whimsy is only a preview of what awaits you: Gothic carvings, tapestries, alabaster figurines, vestments, festival crosses, elaborate dollhouses, Andalusian antique glass, elegant baroque four-poster beds, a chapel covered with leather tapestries, even kitchens from the 17th century. Just keep climbing one flight of steps after another; the surprises continue until you reach the top floor of what must have been one of the grandest mansions in Madrid. Hours are daily except Monday, from 10 a.m. to 2 p.m., and admission is 200 pesetas ($1.40).

THE CASA DE CAMPO: Most people aren't in Madrid too long before they hear about that once-royal park, the Retiro. But many tourists never make it to the former royal hunting grounds, the Casa de Campo, miles and miles of parkland lying south of the Royal Palace, across the Manzanares. You can see the gate through which the kings rode out of the palace grounds—either on horses or in carriages—and headed for the park. You, of course, will have to take less elegant transportation: the Metro to El Lago or El Batán.

The park has a variety of trees and a lake, which is usually filled with rowers. You can have drinks and light refreshments around the lake, or you can go swimming in an excellent, municipally operated pool.

The Madrileños like to keep the place to themselves; on a hot night or a Sunday morning, the park throngs with people trying to escape the heat. If you have an automobile you can go for a drive, as the grounds are extensive. The park is open until around 11 p.m. It's cool, pleasant, refreshing—a cheap way to spend an evening. In addition, the park has a zoo.

At the edge of the park is the Parque de Atracciones, previewed separately in the nightlife section. Take Autobus 33 from Plaza de Isabel, the Teleférico bus, or, on Saturday and holidays, buses from Ventas, Estrecho, and Puente de Vallecas.

Madrid's **Zoo** at Casa de Campo is modern and well organized, allowing you to see, through its division by continents, the wildlife of Africa, Asia, and Europe, with about 2,500 animals on display. Perhaps the most popular exhibit is the giant panda. Two of these animals were presented to Spain upon the occasion of a visit by King Juan Carlos to Beijing in 1978. Successful artificial insemination of the female, Shao-Shao, resulted in the birth of twins in 1982, one of which still survives and draws viewers constantly. Most animals are in a simulated natural habitat, with moats separating them from the public. There's an area where small animals may be petted by children. The zoo is open from 10 a.m. to sunset. Admission is 400 pesetas ($2.80). To reach the zoo, take the Metro from Batan Station, exiting on the right side for the park. Turn left for a walk up to the Plaza de España, which takes you directly to the zoo.

ORGANIZED TOURS: A large number of agencies in Madrid offer organized tours and excursions—among them is **Viajes Marsans,** with offices at 15 San Nicolas (tel. 242-55-00), owned by Gonzalo Pascual and Gerardo Diaz. The most popular full-day excursion is to the imperial city of Toledo, the complete jaunt costing 4,100 pesetas ($28.70). Other heavily booked full-day treks encompass El Escorial and the Valley of the Fallen for 4,100 pesetas ($28.70), or Ávila, Segovia, and the summer palace of the Bourbons at La Granja for 5,500 pesetas ($38.50). Full-day tours include lunch at a restaurant along the way. Half-day tours of Madrid, either artistic or panoramic, cost 2,600 pesetas ($18.20) for a morning trek, 1,700 pesetas ($11.90) for the afternoon.

An equally reliable company is the **Viajes Meliá,** 4 Evaristo San Miguel (tel. 242-2200). They offer tours to the same destinations as Marsans.

A WALKING TOUR: New Madrid is strictly for motorists, as it sprawls for miles in all directions. But in the center of Madrid, cars get in the way. Old Madrid is strictly for walking, the only way to savor its unique charm.

The tour begins on the **Gran Vía,** a street whose position as *the* boulevard of Madrid is being fast overtaken by the Paseo de la Castellana. Still the busiest street in Madrid, the shop-flanked Gran Vía was opened at the end of World War I. Until fairly recently, it was called Avenida de José António. Long before deluxe hotels started to sprout up on the Castellana, the hotels of the Gran Vía were the most expensive and elegant in the Spanish capital. The street ends at the Plaza de España, a vast square overshadowed by one of the tallest skyscrapers in Europe. From the square, you can walk up the Calle de la Princesa, turning to your left down the Ventura Rodríquez.

At 17 Ventura Rodríguez is the **Cerralbo Museum** (tel. 247-36-46), a town house dripping with the gilt and red-velvet romanticism of the 19th century—a place once inhabited by staunch nobility who posed stiff-backed and straitlaced for their family portraits. The family of the Marquis of Cerralbo lived in this splendid Madrileño mansion until the 1920s, filling its every nook and cranny with decorative bric-a-brac or art treasures. No one stinted on the crystal chandeliers or the fashionable, opulently colored glass imported from the factories of Venice where it was made to order. The Cerralbo clan were art collectors as well, purchasing well-known works from celebrated artists, including Zurbafan (an *Immaculate Conception*), Ribera (*Jacob with the Lamb*), and El Greco (*St. Francis*). As in every noble household, this one is richly endowed with tapestries, antique furniture, ecclesiastical sculpture from the Middle Ages, armor, marble busts, gilt mirrors, terracotta clocks, baby-fat cherubs, cabinets of porcelain (really exquisite), and chinoiserie. The Cerralbos apparently also had an interest in armaments, as exemplified by the pistols, helmets, and rifles. Especially intriguing is the library and study of the late marquis, just as he left it. Charging 200 pesetas ($1.40) for admission, it is open daily except Sunday afternoon and Monday, from 10 a.m. to 2 p.m. and 4 to 7 p.m.; closed during the month of August. Metro stop: Plaza de España or Ventura Rodríguez.

Returning to the Plaza de España, strike out down the Calle de Bailen until you reach the semicircular **Plaza de Oriente,** created in 1840. From that vantage point, you can explore the **Palacio Real,** or Royal Palace, described above.

After your tour, if you take a tiny side street to the northeast, the Calle Pavia, you'll arrive at the **Plaza de la Encarnación,** one of the most charming squares in Madrid. Sitting on the plaza is the **Convent de la Encarnación,** open daily except Monday, from 10:30 a.m. to 1 p.m. and 4 to 6 p.m., charging 100 pesetas (70¢) admission. On Sunday, it's open from 10 a.m. to 1:30 p.m. Finished in 1616, in the reign of Philip III and his Queen Margaret (sister of the emperor, Ferdinand II), this convent and its adjoining church stand right down from La Bola restaurant. The original architect was Juan Gómez de Mora, although work in another century was carried out by Ventura Rodríguez. A Spanish-speaking guide will show you around, pointing out the most important ecclesiastical paintings and a *John the Baptist* by Ribera. Other works include a gory Christ with serpentine hair by Gregorio Fernández. In the Reliquary rest a relic of St. Margaret and a skull said to be that of St. Alexander. The cloisters are filled with richly decorated chapels, one in the Pompeiian style.

From the square, walk down the Calle de Arrieta to the Plaza de Isabel II. There you can connect with the Calle del Arenal, leading to the **Puerta del Sol,** the "gateway to the sun," the historic heart of Madrid.

5. The Bullfight in Madrid

The Madrileños have a tremendous interest in action-packed events, an interest that reaches its peak in the bullring.

Chances are you'll see your first bullfight in Madrid, and you couldn't be more fortunate, because the capital draws the finest matadors in Spain. If a matador hasn't proved his worth in the major ring in Madrid, he just hasn't been recognized as a top-flight artist. The big season begins during the Feast of San Isidore, the patron saint of Madrid, on the 15th of May. This is the occasion for a series of fights, during which time the audience is filled with talent scouts. The men who distinguish themselves in the ring are signed up for Majorca, Málaga, or wherever.

If possible, try to buy your tickets where you see the official sign; otherwise you pay 20% more. Sometimes, however, the official center is out of tickets, and then you'll have to throw yourself upon the mercy of the scalpers if you're eager to see a particular fight.

For tickets to the biggest bullfight in Madrid, at the 26,000-seat **Plaza de Toros** at 237 Calle de Alcalá, go to the office at 3 Victoria (tel. 232-67-99). To reach it, head east from the Puerta del Sol, then walk two blocks down the Carrera de San Jerónimo, then turn south onto Victoria. You can save approximately one-fourth of the price of the ticket if you ask for *sombre y sol,* which means that during part of the fight you'll be in the sun.

Front-row seats are known as *barreras. Delanteras*—third-row seats—are available in both the *alta* (high) and *baja* (low) sections. The cheapest seats sold are *filas,* where you will have the worst view and be in the sun during the entire performance. Better count on spending at least 1,200 pesetas ($8.40) for a just passable seat all the way up to 6,000 pesetas ($42) or more for the more desirable seats in the shade. Bullfights are held on Sunday at 7 p.m. (also on holidays) from Easter to October, although in late September and October they often begin at 5 p.m. and are over at 7:15. Fights by neophyte matadors are sometimes staged at 11 on Saturday evening as well. These fights are less expensive.

On the day of the fight, take the Metro to Ventas, although you may be killed in the stampede if you arrive late in the afternoon shortly before the fight begins. Of course, you can take a taxi, although you'll never get one back unless you have the driver wait. A suggestion is that you take the Metro out early; that way you'll avoid the last-minute rush. After the fight, you can wait until the first two or three trains have gone before venturing underground.

READER'S SUGGESTION FOR PURCHASING TICKETS: "To avoid paying the 20% broker's fee tacked on when you buy a ticket at the downtown office, I suggest the tourist go down to the bullring, a few hours before the fight, and purchase a ticket at the window, *not* at the brown huts in front of the bullring, which also add a 20% surcharge. The seats are the same no matter where you obtain your tickets. Arriving within an hour of the bullfight will force one to stand in a terribly long line, and the better seats may no longer be available. For this reason, it is important to arrive at least two hours before the fight. To while away any time you have before the event, you can spend a delightful couple of hours at El Retiro park, which is full of people on Sunday afternoon. If you don't feel up to the half hour or so walk, the subway will take you there in a minute" (Kevin Corrigan, Miami University, European Center, Luxembourg).

6. Shopping in Madrid

Rivaled but not surpassed by Barcelona, Madrid offers the best buys for the bargain hunter of any city in Spain. Thousands of tourists pass through the Spanish capital yearly; and, frankly, many shops are designed chiefly for what the proprietors think the well-heeled foreigner will like.

On the other hand, Madrid is chiefly an industrial and commercial capital, in which the majority of the stores and shops exist primarily for the patronage of Spaniards. As the average income of a Spanish family is far below that of an American, Canadian, English, or Scandinavian, managers or shopkeepers must keep prices in line with what they think the local traffic will bear. Consequently, the city offers some of the most moderately priced high-quality merchandise of any European capital.

HANDCRAFT EXHIBITIONS: **Artespaña (Empresa Nacional de Artesanía),** 32 Gran Vía, 14 Hermosilla, 3 Plaza de las Cortés, and 33 D. Ramón de la Cruz, are the government-sponsored exhibition and sales centers for Spanish handcrafts, some of the best establishments at which to purchase handmade furniture and decorative items from all the regions of Spain. The buyers know their country well, bringing to their showrooms excellently made items. You'll find furniture reproductions, Toledo damascene work, wrought-iron work, ceramics, glassware, carved wood, jewelry, and hundreds of other accessories.

Much of the jewelry is made of sterling silver. Córdoban filigree boxes are a good buy. Other displays include tin lanterns (with inserts of ruby-red, amber, or midnight-blue glass), pewter ashtrays, handmade regional dolls, eccelesiastical woodcarvings, fringed pillow covers and bedspreads, handmade Catalán chairs, and Córdoban leather goods.

The showrooms are supervised by English-speaking attendants, who can arrange for packing and shipping. The hours are from 9:30 a.m. to 1:30 p.m. and 4:30 to 8 p.m. For information, telephone 411-13-62 or 261-64-00.

Kreisler, 19 Serrano (tel. 276-53-38), is owned and operated by a seemingly tireless American midwesterner from Akron, Ohio, Edward Kreisler, an entrepreneur of Spanish decorative handcrafts. Through his grapevine, he keeps in touch with artisans in obscure villages and towns, presenting their wares in his galleries in the Serrano shopping district. Within are most of the Spanish items that the North American visitor wants, including olive-wood articles, "El Greco chairs," mantillas, Toledo damascene work, woodcarvings, Spanish fans, purses in grained leather, and a line of Spanish soaps and dolls. Kreisler is also an official agency for Majorcan pearls and Lladró porcelain. Prices are competitive because Kreisler doesn't add on any percentage for commissions to guides. Purchases can be packed and shipped anywhere in the world.

At the **Galería Kreisler,** in a separate section, some of the fine painters and sculptors in the country have found an important showcase for their talents. Here you'll find both the old master and the avant-garde artist represented. The gallery features Spain's most reputable artists whose works are often in the permanent collection of the National Museum of Contemporary Art.

Galería Kreisler Dos, 8 Hermosilla (tel. 431-42-64), another Kreisler enterprise, presents contemporary paintings, sculpture, and prints. As at the other Kreislers, it is open from 10 a.m. to 2 p.m. and 5 to 9 p.m. It's about 75 yards around the corner from 19 Serrano.

MADRID'S LEADING DEPARTMENT STORES: **Galerías Precíados,** 28 Precíados (tel. 231-35-05), right off the Gran Vía, has greatly expanded and improved in recent years. It's really two stores connected by an underground passageway. It's more Macy's than Lord & Taylor, with quite presentable ready-made clothing for men, women, and children. There's a top-floor snackbar and restaurant. Some good buys I noted recently include guitars, men's suede jackets, Spanish capes for men, and women's full-length suede coats (the colors are exciting, including royal blue, kelly green, olive, and violet).

Men's suits: In the second-floor tailoring department, you can have a suit made to order. You're fitted with one of the basic "try-on" suits. The goodly selection of fabrics—plaids, solids, herringbones—are made into whatever style you prefer.

On the lower level is a department jam-packed with regional handcrafts, including ship models made in Catalonia, historical sword reproductions, regional dolls, tooled leather from Córdoba, damascene work from Toledo, Lladró porcelain figurines from Valencia, blown glass from Majorca, white ceramic pieces from Manises, handcrafts from Galacia, and ceramics from Gerona and Valencia.

The other big department store chain is **El Corte Inglés** (tel. 232-81-00), with outlets all around the country, including Málaga. At present, branches in Madrid are on Calle Precíados, near the Puerta del Sol in the center of the city;

on the Calle Goya, where it crosses the Calle de Alcalá; on the Calle Raimundo Fernández Villaverde, right off the Avenida del Castellana; and on Princesa Street. Rather than running about from boutique to tourist shop to boutique, many visitors will find it easier and often cheaper to make all their purchases in a department store. For example, at El Corte Inglés you can buy all types of souvenirs, such as swords from Toledo, typical flamenco dolls, the well-known Spanish shawls, and Lladró sculptures. The store has a multitude of special services available for tourists: interpreters, currency exchange, and parcel delivery to their hotels or overseas, and it arranges for all the necessary formalities for the **I.V.A.** refund, which can be up to 33% of the marked price, according to law.

CUSTOM TAILORING: Valdivia, 86 Gran Vía (tel. 247-96-40), is in the Edificio España (the Plaza Hotel building) at the Plaza de España. Mariano Valdivia inherited his skill and business from his father, and has won the respect and patronage of many a Spanish businessman or diplomat by turning out well-tailored suits for men. His staff can produce a suit in four or five working days, if you're available for fittings. Their shop offers an excellent choice of fabrics in all weather weights. Everything is made by hand, even the button holes. They can give you a conservative banker's look or outfit you in more trendy styled clothing. Senor Valdivia has expanded his shop to include women's clothing, blouses, and overcoats, many haute couture garments shipped in from Paris. The prices are quite reasonable for this ready-to-wear.

HEADGEAR: Casa Yustas, 30 Plaza Mayor (tel. 266-50-84), is an extraordinary hat emporium, especially popular in this day of strange headgear. If your sessions with the analyst have revealed a hang-up for unusual hats, you can satisfy your inclinations here. Picture yourself a Congo explorer, a Spanish sailor, an officer in the kaiser's army, a Rough Rider, a priest, even Napoleon. A straw sombrero is a conversation piece. Black berets are also sold here. One reader, a Spanish devotée, asserts that the beret, or *boína,* is used extensively in Spain. "France has stolen many ideas from Spain, including the beret," the reader, a former travel agent, claims.

ELEGANT LEATHER GOODS: Loewe, 8 Gran Vía (tel. 251-68-00), since 1846 has been the most elegant store for leather goods in Spain. Its gold-medal-winning designers have always kept abreast of changing tastes and styles. For the latest in luggage, handbags, jackets for both men and women (in leather or suede), along with stylish accessories, go here or to one of their branches, such as that at 26 Serrano or in the Hotel Palace. If you miss the Madrid store, you'll find outlets in such major tourist towns as Barcelona, Palma de Majorca, San Sebastián, Seville, and Valencia, as well as the Hotel Alhambra Palace in Granada.

A HOUSE OF CERAMICS: Antiqua Casa Talavera, 2 Isabel la Católica (tel. 247-34-17), is known as "the first house of Spanish ceramics." Its wares include a sampling of regional ceramic styles from every major area of Spain, including Talavera, Toledo, Manises, Granada, and Seville, among other sources. Sangría pitchers, dinnerware, tea sets, plates, vases—everything is handmade. Inside one of the showrooms, there is an interesting selection of tiles, ranging from reproductions of scenes from *El Quijote,* bullfights, dances, and folklore, to scenes from famous paintings at the Prado. At its present location for more than 60 years, the shop is only a short walk from the Plaza de Santo Domingo and the subway station there.

MAJORCAN TEXTILES: At **Casa Bonet,** 76 Calle Nuñez de Balboa (tel. 275-09-12), Ms Pilar Abrisqueta welcomes you. The store's specialty is the hand-worked textiles of Majorca, where women are famous for the quality of their needlework. A few examples are displayed on the walls, but a true concept of the establishment's inventory comes only when tablecloths, sheets, and pillow-cases are unrolled on Spanish tables covered with velvet. You'll find a full range of cottons, linens, and polyesters here, embellished with either hand embroidery or fancy machine stitching. English is spoken, and prices are usually competitive.

READER'S SHOPPING TIP: "For people who would like Nao or Lladró porcelain at a reduced price, on the lower level of the **Galerías Precíados** in the regional handcrafts section, find the corner that has damaged pieces. These have been repaired very skillfully. Take the one you like to the salesperson, who will take it to her supervisor, who will give you a discount price. You don't have to buy it if you don't agree with the price" (Lauretta B. Freeman, Montclair, N.J.).

7. Madrid After Dark

Madrid abounds with dance halls, tascas, cafés, theaters, movie houses, music halls, and nightclubs—but you have to proceed carefully through this maze, as many of these nightly offerings are strictly for the residents, or for Spanish-speaking people.

For the bizarre, you have to go to Hamburg or Paris, but if a good time is what you're looking for, Madrid won't let you down. The average visitor will want to find the flamenco places, as this is the highlight of Spanish nightlife, but there are other offerings that intrigue, too.

In most clubs a one-drink minimum is the rule, and you can nurse your drink through the entire evening's entertainment. It's a perfectly acceptable custom.

Because dinner is served late in Spain, nightlife doesn't really get under way until after 11 p.m., and it generally lasts till around 3 a.m. If you arrive at 9:30 p.m. at a club, you'll probably find that you have the place all to yourself.

Because Madrileños are said to be fond of prowling around at night, they are known throughout Spain as *gatos* (cats).

FLAMENCO SHOWS: The strum of a guitar, the sound of hands clapping rhythmically . . . and you know that flamenco is about to start. Soon colorfully dressed women, occasionally men, flounce onto the stage to swirl in time with the music. The staccato beat of castanets and the tapping of heels make the rafters ring. Flamenco . . . the incomparable Spanish art form.

Most of the major clubs in Madrid are patronized almost exclusively by foreigners. Hence, some of the very top ones are beyond the means of most budgeteers. However, two other leading and less expensive flamenco nightspots are Torres Bermejas and Arco de Cuchilleros. Neither one of them is cheap—but then you need only purchase one drink, as there is no minimum or cover charge.

Café de Chinitas, 7 Torija (tel. 248-51-35), is one of the swankiest and most expensive flamenco spots in town. In the old part of Madrid, between the Opera and the Gran Vía, it features the dancer La Chunga, as well as the guitarist Serranito. They join with 37 others to make up the *cuadro.* The show starts at 11 p.m., running until 3:30 a.m. The minimum, which entitles you to drink at a table, is 2,500 pesetas ($17.50). You can also go for dinner at about 9:30 p.m., and then stay on for the flamenco. Meals cost from 4,500 pesetas ($28). The café is open daily except Sunday all year. You sit in an elongated room at tables with fair visibility. The stage is at the far end of the room. The decor is amorphously elegant, sometimes in questionable taste, and doesn't quite live up to the promise of the street exterior. You enter through a staircase lined with old bullfighting posters and pictures, which takes you to two glass doors with bronze hands on them for handles.

Corral de la Morería, 7 Morería (tel. 265-84-46). In the old town, the Morería—meaning a quarter where Moors reside—sizzles more in its flamenco than in its skillets. The focus of attention is Lucero Tena, acclaimed as one of the leading flamenco stars in the world. Strolling performers, colorfully costumed, get the proceedings under way around 11 p.m., but they are there only to warm up the audience. A flamenco showcase follows, with at least ten dancers, all of whom have Gloria Vanderbilt waistlines. The star always appears late. The management has devised ways of putting tables in the most unlikely places. Reserve near the front and go early if you really want a ringside table. Your minimum drink consumption is from 2,000 pesetas ($14). À la carte dinners cost 4,500 pesetas ($31.50) to 5,000 pesetas ($35).

Torres Bermejas, 11 Mesonero Romanos (tel. 232-33-22), right off the Gran Vía, is an underground cellar decorated in the style of a harem from old Granada. Some of the best flamenco dancers in Spain appear here, usually a trio of gypsy stars. For 5,000 pesetas ($35), you can order a set meal, including wine. After 11:30 p.m., until 3 a.m., you can attend by ordering just a drink at 2,000 pesetas ($14).

If you're still on the flamenco trail, then you might try **Arco de Cuchilleros,** 7 Cuchilleros (tel. 266-58-37), near the Botiín Restaurant. Lots of single men and women come here. A flamenco show with a girlie twist is often presented. All in all, it's fun to be here if you don't take the proceedings too seriously. The one-drink minimum will cost you 2,000 pesetas ($14).

CULTURAL: For an authentic Spanish experience, you can attend a *zarzuela,* a Spanish musical variety show with turn-of-the-century music enlivened by bright costumes. Often these vaudevillian presentations sandwich flamenco numbers and musical revues between their regular acts.

One of the best places to view this musical theater is the **Monumental Theater,** 60 Calle de Atocha (tel. 227-12-14). Even non-Spanish-speaking visitors seem to enjoy performances here. Dance performances, ballets, and musicals are presented, with shows daily except Monday, at 7 and 10:30 p.m. Tickets cost from 500 pesetas ($3.50) to 1,200 pesetas ($8.40).

Along with opera and ballet, zarzuelas are also presented at the **Teatro de la Zarzuela,** 4 Jovellanos (tel. 429-12-86).

Ballet, Spanish style, is presented at the **Centro Cultural de la Villa,** Plaza de Colón (tel. 275-60-80).

DISCOS: The Spanish disco takes its inspiration from other Western capitals—in fact, many have English names. In Madrid, most of these clubs open around 6 p.m. for what is called a matinee. They usually go till 9 p.m., when they shut down to allow their young patrons to go out for dinner. Then around 11 p.m. they reopen, but they don't generally start to rock till around midnight.

Bocaccio, 16 Marqués de la Ensenada, off the Plaza Colón (tel. 419-10-08), is one of the poshest discos in the Spanish capital, done in glittering art nouveau, with tufted red velvet banquettes. In this elegant setting, you'll pay 1,200 pesetas ($8.40) for your first drink of a name-brand whisky. It's open daily from 7 p.m. to 3:30 a.m.

Joy Eslava, 11 Arenal (tel. 266-54-40), may be one of the most electronics-conscious nightspots in Madrid. It's filled with an array of up-to-date lights and sound equipment, with imitation lasers that fill the corners of this converted movie theater. If you don't feel like dancing, a collection of comfortable chaise longues are scattered throughout the establishment to help you forget how much you might be drinking. Libations range from 600 pesetas ($4.20) to 1,400 pesetas ($9.80), depending on the day of the week and the time you enter. It's slightly more expensive on weekends, although that's when it might be the most fun. The place is closed Monday.

Pacha, 11 Barceló (tel. 446-01-37), is the closest thing you'll find in Madrid to the old version of New York's Studio 54. Outfitted with special effects on the dance floor, this disco, like the Joy Eslava, is in a converted movie theater. Every Friday, Saturday, and Sunday, it's open at hours that any self-respecting Spanish nightcrawler would find horrifying—from 7 to 10 p.m., when drinks cost around 800 pesetas ($5.60) each. In addition to this session, the disco reopens for a late-night crowd from midnight until 4 a.m. except Monday and Tuesday. For the late-night hours, drinks cost from 1,500 pesetas ($10.50).

Mau Mau, 3 José Lázaro Galdino (tel. 250-27-57), in the Eurobuilding complex, is one of the leading nightspots of Madrid in the fickle world of discomania. Anyone with hopes of being included in the *tout Madrid* category will eventually show up or apply for membership in what is almost considered a private club, especially on those evenings when it's reserved for private parties. Open every evening except Sunday and from mid-July to mid-September, it serves drinks for around 1,500 pesetas ($10.50) each.

BELLE ÉPOQUE CABARET: Las Noches de Cuple, 51 Calle La Palma (tel. 232-71-15). If you don't mind going to bed as the rays of an Iberian sunrise filter through the narrow streets of the surrounding neighborhood, you might enjoy this updated version of the once-celebrated Madrileño cabaret. Its entrance is on a narrow but crowded street barely wide enough for the pedestrians and cars which compete for space. Inside, a long room with a vaulted ceiling and a tiny stage are the forum for the still-charming former beauty, Señora Olga Ramos. Ms Ramos conducts an evening of Iberian song with and sometimes without a mantilla. The charm of her all-Spanish act is increased by the discreet humor of an octogenarian accompanist with an ostrich-feather tiara and a fuchsia-colored boa. Your first drink will cost 2,000 pesetas ($14), plus a 400-peseta ($2.80) supplement for brand name liquors. Each additional drink costs from 700 pesetas ($4.90). The show, in theory, begins at 2 a.m., but occasionally the stars relent and go on earlier.

JAZZ: Whisky Jazz, 7 Diego de León (tel. 261-11-65), has the beat—in fact, it's Madrid's leading jazz center. It lies off the Calle de Serrano near the American Embassy. There is no number on the oak door (you may feel like you're attending a speakeasy of old, so tight is the security at the door). Inside the two-level brick structure is a main floor with a bar at the rear, plus an open staircase leading to a mezzanine of tables.

The memorabilia on the walls in the glass case reveal a reverence for jazz. Encased are letters and faded photographs of the "greats" from New Orleans, Kansas City, Chicago. Jazz groups appear with frequency; otherwise, the management plays recordings of their works. In the early part of the evening you pay 500 pesetas ($3.50), that tab increasing to 1,000 pesetas ($7) in the early morning when the live groups usually appear. On weekends and holidays the charge is 1,500 pesetas ($10.50).

Café Central, 10 Plaza del Angel (tel. 468-08-44), presents a deep-red façade to a satellite square of the Plaza Santa Ana at the side of the famed Hotel Victoria. The interior is vaguely art deco, with an unusual series of stained-glass windows representing what might be an urbanized Madrid. Many of the customers read newspapers and talk quietly at the marble tables during the day. At night, when jazz is played—at which time there's a supplement of 150 pesetas ($1.05) to 200 pesetas ($1.40)—the ambience is far more animated. Beer goes for 175 pesetas ($1.23). The establishment is open from 1 p.m. till 2 a.m. daily.

CAVE CRAWLING: To capture a peculiar Madrid joie de vivre of the 18th century, you can tune in the circuit of *mesones* and *cuevas,* many found in the old town, known as *barrios bajos.* From the Plaza Mayor, walk down the Arco de Cuchilleros until you find a gypsy-like cave that fits your fancy. Young people especially love to meet in the taverns and caves of Old Madrid for communal drinking and songfests. The sangría flows freely, the atmosphere is charged, the room usually packed, the guitars strummed into the night air. Sometimes strolling bands of singing students (known as *tuna*) go from bar to bar, colorfully attired, with ribbons fluttering from their outfits.

Mesón de la Guitarra, 13 Cava San Miguel (tel. 48-95-31), is my favorite cueva in the area. Of course, it's surrounded by many others on the same street, but it should be included in any evening of mesón hopping. It's about as warmly earthy as anything you'll find in Madrid, with ancient terracotta floors, antique brick walls, vaulted ceilings, hundreds of sangría pitchers clustered above the bar, murals of gluttons, old rifles, faded bullfighter posters, and "brown gravy" paintings. All of these form the setting for the crowds of working people, tourists, and loving couples, many of them here to meet their friends and listen to the sounds of three songs going all at the same time.

As Jerold Freier of Cambridge, Massachusetts, writes, "Yankee Stadium at game time sounds quiet by comparison. This is loud, exciting entertainment almost any night of the week. Like most things in Madrid, it doesn't get rolling until around 10:30 at night, although you can stop in for a drink and tapas much earlier if you want to. The mesón consists of three levels. The higher up and the farther you go, the louder it gets. Don't be afraid to start singing an American song if it has a fast rhythm. You'll find that about 60 people have joined in, even if they don't know the words."

There is no admission charge to enter this establishment, where beer costs from 125 pesetas (88¢) and a glass of Valdepeñas wine is 40 pesetas (28¢). Tapas, depending on how exotic they are, range from 350 pesetas ($2.45).

Mesón Asturias, 11 Cava San Miguel (no phone), is one of the several tapas bars on a street just behind the most beautiful square in Madrid, the Plaza Mayor. The interior is filled with vaulted ceilings and exposed brick. You'll find a rustic series of sit-down cells stretching off toward a second bar in the rear, but most customers seem to prefer standing up near the front entrance. There's often accordion music at night. Beer costs 125 pesetas (88¢), while a vodka and tonic goes for 250 pesetas ($1.75). A portion of grilled stuffed mushrooms is 225 pesetas ($1.58). This is the kind of place where you can either duck in, have a quick shot of wine, and leave, or stay for an extended period. In winter, the favorite spot is in front of the open fireplace in the front room, when a pitcher of sangría, 500 pesetas ($3.50), is the thing to order.

At **Mesón del Champiñon,** 17 Cava San Miguel (tel. 248-67-90), the barmen keep a brimming bucket of sangría behind the long stand-up bar as a thirst quencher for the many people who crowd in. It costs from 300 pesetas ($2.10). The name of the establishment translates as "mushroom," and that is exactly what you'll see delineated in various sizes along sections of the vaulted ceilings. A more appetizing way to experience a *champiñon* is to order a *ración* of grilled, stuffed, and salted mushrooms, served with toothpicks and accompanied by beer, for 225 pesetas ($1.58). Strange as it seems, the pair of tiny, slightly dank rooms in the back is where Spanish families jam in for the organ music produced by a stalwart musician performing in one corner. Unless you want to be exiled to the very back, don't expect to sit down here. Practically everybody prefers to stand.

Sesamo (Sesame), 7 Calle del Priíncipe (tel. 232-91-91), is in a class all by itself. This cueva, dating from the early 1950s, has drawn a clientele of young painters and writers to its ambience, described as "cosmopolita y bohemia." Hemingway was one of those early visitors (a plaque commemorates him).

When you first see it, you think you're walking into a tiny snackbar—and you are. But proceed down the flight of steps to the cellar. The walls are covered with contemporary paintings, and there are quotations from such writers as Byron or from such scholars as Unamuno. At squatty stools and tables, an international assortment of young people listens to piano music, perhaps folk singing, guitar playing—nothing formal. Conversation is also important. It's customary to order a pitcher of sangría for four at 650 pesetas ($4.55).

"DISNEYLANDIA": That's what the press of Madrid screamed when the **Parque de Atracciones,** Madrid's festive fun park, opened in 1969. There is a típico restaurant, a disco, an outdoor dance hall, a Greek theater presenting free concerts and flamenco, boats on canals, and many pleasure rides. Open all year, the park invites revelry.

To reach the park (on the edge of the **Casa de Campo,** the former royal hunting grounds) you can take a cable car from the intersection of the Paseo del Pintor Rosales and the Calle Marqués de Urgillo. Along the grassy parkway, there is a large overhead sign in yellow and orange (Teleférico) which you pass under, down along a path to the cable station, at the rear of the cafetería built on the hillside ledge. The ride takes about 11 minutes. The cable car operates from 11 a.m. to 2 p.m. and 4 to 9 p.m. in good weather only. For a group of three or four, a taxi would be more convenient and less expensive. The park is open from 6:30 a.m. to 1 a.m. on weekdays, from 6 a.m. to 2 a.m. on Saturday (rides shut down between 3 and 4 p.m.), and from noon to 1 a.m. on Sunday (again rides stop between 3 and 4 p.m.). The general admission is 50 pesetas (35¢) for adults, half price for children ages 3 to 10. The park is closed on Monday. You must buy tickets for the rides, and most adventures cost two or three tickets. Most rides cost 75 pesetas (53¢).

Some of the better rides, such as the Russian Mountain (in reality, a modified roller coaster), cost four tickets. Speedboats operate on the narrow canals, cutting through the grounds, past straw-thatched houses, twisted trees, and under bridges. There's an auto racetrack, with miniature cars and banks of rubber tires to ease the bumps. It's all here: "shoot the chute," a pond with boats for juvenile yachting types; a merry-go-round with stylized animals; a flight through "space," antique cars, a carousel, a maze of glass. You can ride throughout the grounds on an elongated puppy dog (a group of cars), or go writhing on an octopus (El Pulpo). At the center of everything is an illuminated tower, offering a bird's-eye view of the city, a miniature elevator taking you to the summit.

A final attraction is the Greek-style **Teatro,** which is free. This open-air theater has cast cement seats facing the bowl. Colored water displays shoot from the fountains, picked up by a reflection pool. From flamenco to ballet, from classic to comic, the bill of fare is wide. Weather permitting, one-hour shows are performed at 7:30 and 10:30 p.m. from May till the end of September.

A restaurant lies within the grounds. Although not super-expensive, its prices are high enough to make it a splurge.

THE PICK OF THE BARS: **Nuevo Oliver,** 3 Calle del Conde Xiqueña, off the Paseo de la Castellana (tel. 221-01-47). Would you like a private club for your headquarters in Madrid? Oliver is a hangout for show-biz people, with a good sprinkling of foreign personalities dropping by as well. The bar is like a drawing room or the library-study of someone's town house. There are two club rooms, each with its own personality. The street floor seems like a tasteful, although faded, stage setting, with sofas and comfortable armchairs arranged for home-like conversational gatherings—the tone set by the scenic mural on the ceiling, which is left over from the old grocery shop that used to occupy this site. On either side of the fireplace stand recessed shelves, with an eclectic collection of hi-fi records (you can pick the ones you want played), books on the theater, movies, and paintings. Drinks (and tapas) are brought unobtrusively to your table, and average 600 pesetas ($4.20) apiece. Reached by a graceful curving stairway, the downstairs room is softer, more secluded. The bar is open from noon till 2:30 a.m.

Café Madrid, 7 Calle Belén (tel. 419-99-19). Amid a black-and-white decor which pleasantly mingles art nouveau with high tech, you can enjoy one of the most sophisticated drink lists in town. This is what the Spanish call a *cocteleria,* where your pleasure might include gin fizzes, whisky sours, white and yellow ladies, brandy flips, or a dog's nose, perhaps a cousin to the Manhattan, a Bronx cocktail. There's even a wide selection of special coffees, including Irish and Jamaican. Drinks begin at 250 pesetas ($1.75). The establishment is open every day from 6 p.m. to 3 a.m.

Chicote, 12 Gran Vía (tel. 232-67-37). Whatever happened to Chicote, another favorite—some say, *the* favorite—bar of "Don Ernesto"? Created by the now-legendary Señor Chicote, it once attracted thousands of English-speaking readers, fans of Hemingway. The writer used it as a setting for his only play, *The Fifth Column.* Hemingway would sit here night after night entertaining his friends with such remarks as "Spain is a country for living and not for dying." The bar, a bit seedier today, still attracts writers, musicians, and artists. Drinks cost from 250 pesetas ($1.75).

Mr. Pickwick's, 48 Paseo Pintor Rosales (tel. 248-51-85), draws homesick English expatriates. No other establishment in Madrid recaptures the "pubby" atmosphere better. On the walls hang framed prints of characters from Dickens, brass hunting horns, pewter and ceramic beer mugs, even horse brasses. Loners can drink at the bar, or you can sit at one of the small tables, sinking into the soft sofas and armchairs. Most alcoholic drinks cost 350 pesetas ($2.45), including your tapas, usually salted nuts and Andalusian olives. The pub is about a ten-minute walk from the Plaza de España, and is open from 6 p.m. until 1:30 a.m.

Sportsman British Pub, 65 Alcalá (tel. 276-69-08). There are literally thousands of pubs in Madrid, as a quick review of the "bar" section of the phone book will show you. Many of them are recently established and pander to the modern taste of Madrileños. One of the most attractive is near the central post office in a beautifully paneled English-style club, ringed with banquettes and dotted with velvet. At the section near the entrance is a long bar area with comfortably padded elbow rests. The walls are covered with photographs of celebrities, especially Rita Hayworth and Ava Gardner. The restaurant Paddock is in back, with a bulletin board which seems to indicate that this is a gathering place of British expatriates in Madrid. Beer costs 250 pesetas ($1.75).

Casa Parra, 16 Echegaray (tel. 429-58-86). Its surprisingly stylish interior sets it a cut above many of the neighboring establishments that fill this popular, very Spanish neighborhood in Old Madrid. A monochromatic black-and-white interior—part Victorian, part high-tech—includes checkerboard tiles, marble tables on cast-iron bases, and rows of unusual graphics by Madrileño artists. The place is at its most dynamic between 11 p.m. and 3 a.m. when assorted painters, artists, and jazz musicians congregate here amid evocative music. Beer costs from 150 pesetas ($1.05) and is served every day from 7 p.m.

A FAMOUS OLD COFFEEHOUSE: **Gran Café de Gijón,** 21 Paseo de Recoletos (tel. 231-91-21). All old European capitals have a coffeehouse that traditionally has attracted the literati. In Madrid, the counterpart of Les Deux Magots in Paris or the Antico Caffè in Rome is Gijón, which opened in 1890 in the heyday of Madrid's *bella época.* Artists and writers (some look like Spanish versions of Tennessee Williams) patronize this venerated old café on one of Madrid's major boulevards. Many of them spend hours over one cup of coffee. The coffeehouse has open street windows looking out onto the wide paseo as well as a large terrace for sun-worshippers and birdwatchers. Along one side of the café is a stand-up bar, and on the lower level is a restaurant. In summer you can sit in the garden, enjoying, say, a blanco y negro (that's black coffee with ice cream), a popular drink. Mixed drinks cost from 400 pesetas ($2.80) and meals from 2,000 pesetas ($14).

Chapter IV

RING AROUND MADRID

1. Toledo
2. Aranjuez
3. El Escorial and the Valley of the Fallen
4. Segovia and La Granja
5. Alcalá de Henares and El Pardo
6. Chinchon
7. Ávila

MADRID IS ENCIRCLED by some of the major sightseeing treasures of Spain. As pointed out in the introduction to the capital, the most important reason for basing in Madrid is not only to view its own offerings, but the surrounding ones as well. In this chapter we'll take a tour of the environs of Madrid, on every major artery, shooting out in all directions from the capital. The distances are short enough—9 miles for the quickest one, 68 for the longest—so that you can leave Madrid in the morning, journey to a town and see its major sights, yet be back in your hotel by nightfall.

However, if you should want to stay over in any town along the way, I've included the best of the budget hotels in every place. The restaurants and the sights, however, will be the primary concerns of the average visitor.

The next two tours are included for those who have a couple of extra days to spend outside Madrid. Those who are so blessed can visit the beautiful little town from which Franco used to rule Spain, **El Pardo,** and they can go to the ancient university city that produced Cervantes, **Alcalá de Henares.** In addition, the walled city of **Ávila** looms heavily on many agendas.

All of these sites can be reached either by train or bus on a do-it-yourself basis.

1. Toledo

If El Greco were to return to Toledo today, I suspect he would not be shocked or even surprised at the appearance of the city that was the inspiration for so many of his paintings in the 16th century. The skyline of Toledo—officially declared a National Monument city—has remained that unchanged in spite of modern encroachments on its periphery. The residents dress differently, and El Greco might be puzzled at the strange hordes of camera-carrying tourists who pack into the city, but he could stroll through the familiar streets that are, in many instances, only alleyways, hardly big enough for a man and his donkey—much less an automobile.

Toledo still occupies its royal position, sitting like a queen on a high-hilled throne, overlooking the sparsely vegetated plains of New Castile. Surrounded on three sides by a loop of the River Tagus, it was an obvious choice as the capital of Spain, as it is a natural fortress near the geographic heart of Iberia. Even though Toledo is no longer the political center of the country, it remains the religious center, being the seat of the Primate of Spain.

Back in the 1500s Toledo resembled an old and faithful wife who had been deserted by an errant husband (Philip II) in favor of a simple young thing (Madrid). Toledo lost its status as the capital of Spain—and was never to regain it, although an attempt was made. But time has paid its alimony checks to this venerated city, which might safely be called a country town today, following its massive loss of population. If Toledo had remained the capital, the chances are that much of it would have been torn down and altered to keep pace with the expanding needs of modern Spain.

If you land in Madrid and your absurdly tight schedule allows you only one day for an excursion outside the capital, then that trip should be to Toledo. You still will not know Spain, but you will have seen a blending of the elements—Arab, Jewish, Christian, even Roman and Visigothic—that made Toledo great centuries before Columbus sailed to America.

GETTING THERE: Of all the means of transportation, the least expensive is:

By Bus: The bus route is shorter and more direct than the train, which goes through Aranjuez and leaves you too far from the heart of the city. The **Continental Auto** line (tel. 227-29-61) leaves from Estación Sur de Autobuses, 17 Calle Canarias (take the Metro to Palos de Moguer) in Madrid in both summer and winter (take the "directo" bus), and the trip takes about an hour and 15 minutes. Check bus schedules in advance. You purchase tickets upstairs, and the bus leaves from Madrid at the lower level. To be sure of a seat, it is necessary to purchase your ticket in Madrid the evening before your desired trip. You can take the Metro to the Palos de Moguer stop and enter the bus station directly from the platform.

By Car: As your own driver, you will go through the Puerto del Toledo in Madrid on the road south. A little more than halfway, 21 miles from Toledo, you'll come to the unspoiled medieval village of **Illescas,** where a stopover is recommended at the **Hospital and Sanctuary of Our Lady of Caridad.** The nuns who live here will show you their proud possessions, five paintings by El Greco. Admission is 35 pesetas (25¢). The view is worth far more. Hours are from 9 a.m. to 2 p.m. and 4 to 7 p.m. daily except Sunday.

Then it's on to Toledo. If you take your car inside the city gates, you must accustom yourself to blowing your horn gently—or driving slowly around the corners. Incidentally, remember to have some peseta pieces handy if you take your car around to some of the major sites, as there are many little old men there opening car doors. At the end of the day, the cost will be small.

About 3½ miles from the city the skyline of Toledo will come into view. It is spectacular. But the greatest surprise—and a moment of richer enchantment—will come later in the day when you cross over the 14th-century San Martín bridge spanning the Tagus for a view of the city from the other side. The setting is evocative of the moody, melancholy, storm-threatened *View of Toledo* hanging in the Metropolitan Museum in New York. It is said that El Greco painted that view from a hillside site on which the Spanish government has opened a parador, the **Conde de Orgaz,** named after the subject of El Greco's masterpiece (which, incidentally, is in Toledo, not New York). If you arrive at the right

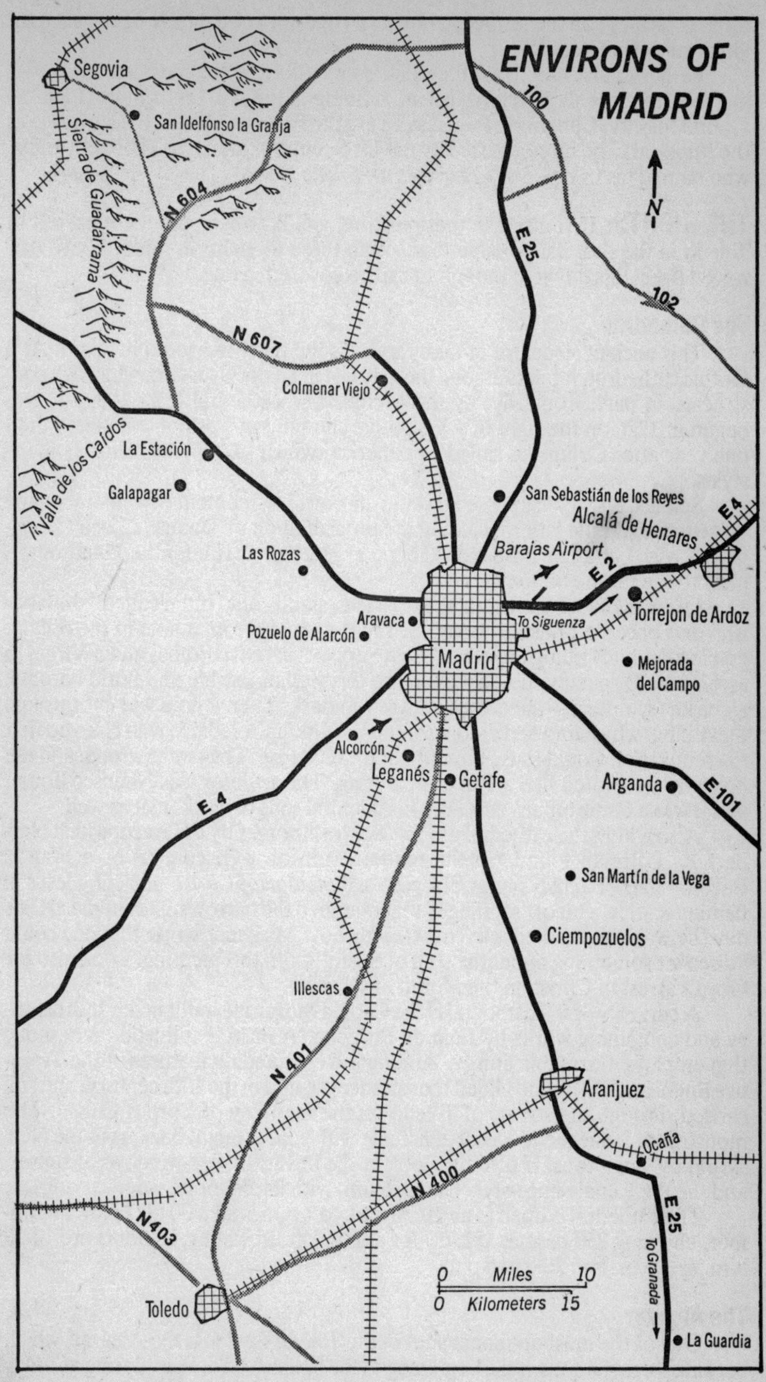
ENVIRONS OF MADRID
N
Segovia
San Idelfonso la Granja
Sierra de Guadarrama
N 604
100
E 25
102
N 607
Colmenar Viejo
Valle de los Caídos
La Estación
Galapagar
San Sebastián de los Reyes
E4
Alcalá de Henares
Barajas Airport
Las Rozas
E 2
Torrejon de Ardoz
Aravaca
To Siguenza
Pozuelo de Alarcón
Madrid
Mejorada del Campo
Alcorcón
Leganés
Getafe
Arganda
E 101
E 4
San Martín de la Vega
Ciempozuelos
Illescas
N 401
Aranjuez
Ocaña
N 400
E 25
N 403
To Granada
0 Miles 10
0 Kilometers 15
Toledo
La Guardia

time, you can sit on the terrace, enjoying an apéritif in what have been called the violet sunsets of Toledo.

Perhaps more important than all the sights outlined below is a road, known as the **Carretera de Circunvalación,** running along the Tagus in part and all around the city. Clinging to the hillsides are the rustic dwellings, the *cigarrales* of the Imperial City, immortalized by the 17th-century dramatist Tirso de Molina, who named his trilogy *Los Cigarrales de Toledo.*

THE SIGHTS: If you're like most visitors, you'll want to get the most out of Toledo in the shortest possible time. With these thoughts in mind, I have narrowed the sights down to those that can be covered in one day:

The Cathedral

This ancient structure of many styles is the most treasured in Spain. As a Gothic cathedral, it ranks among the greatest in all of Europe, having been constructed in part, ironically, by the Moors. The cathedral (tel. 22-22-41) was begun in 1226 on the sight of a Visigothic church, but was not completed until one year after Columbus sailed to America, which partially explains its many styles.

Spanish history has passed through its portals—moments to remember and those to forget, the latter including the proclamation of "Juana la Loca" (Joanna the Mad) and her husband, "Felipe el Hermoso" (Philip the Handsome), heirs to the throne of Spain.

Of its many treasures, its **transparente** stands out (often called "outlandish" and once "outrageous pomp"). Light pours in from a hole in the ceiling, gracing the high-riding angels, a "Last Supper" in polychrome, and a Virgin in ascension. Originally, no one could see this wall of marble and florid baroque alabaster sculpture—the cathedral was too dark. Then a hole was cut through the ceiling, which aroused a storm of protest among Toledans, who charged that the renovation would cause the cathedral to collapse. They were wrong, and the hole was decorated like a Rubens painting. The sculptor was Narcisco Tome, and it was a family affair, as he put his talented sons to work on it as well.

Also within the cathedral are the *Twelve Apostles* by El Greco, which Herbert R. Lottman found "in the modern vein of a Giacometti or a Francis Bacon." In the Sacristy hangs El Greco's *Spoliation of Christ,* depicting Jesus in flaming scarlet, a bit of "sacrilege" that offended the narrow minds of the artist's day (he was even hauled into court). James A. Michener wrote that one could "discover something about the soul of Spain" from this painting. Look also for Goya's arrest of Christ on the Mount of Olives.

A curiosity of the cathedral is the **Capilla Mozárabe,** built in the 16th century and containing works by Juan de Borgona. A mass is still held there today that employs mozarabic liturgy. Among the outstanding features of the **Treasure Room** is a 500-pound gilded monstrance created in the 15th century, and still carried through the streets of Toledo on the feast day of Corpus Christi. The monstrance is alleged to have been made with gold brought back from the New World by Columbus. If possible, look at the beautiful rose windows at sunset, and see the Renaissance-style **Choir Room,** with its elaborate woodcarvings.

The cathedral is open from 10:30 a.m. to 1 p.m. and 3:30 till 7 p.m. in summer, charging 250 pesetas ($1.75) for admission. In winter, its hours are 10:30 a.m. to 1 p.m. and 3:30 to 6 p.m.

The Alcázar

One of the most dominant sites of the Toledo skyline is the Alcázar, which became world famous at the beginning of the Spanish Civil War, during a 70-day siege in 1936. What person familiar with those events will ever forget the telephone call placed to the Nationalist general inside the Alcázar? The rebels had the son of the general and were going to kill him if the Nationalists didn't surrender the fortress. The general refused to surrender. The siege lasted from July 21 to September 28.

The Alcázar was practically destroyed, but this fortress had been devastated many times before that. Today it has been rebuilt, and has been turned into an Army Museum, housing such exhibits as a plastic model of what the fortress looked like following the Civil War, electronic equipment used during the siege, and photographs taken during the height of the battle.

In front of the museum is a monument honoring the heroes of the Alcázar. Admission is 100 pesetas (70¢), and the visiting hours are from 9:30 a.m. to 7 p.m. from March through August, to 6:30 p.m. in September and October, and to 6 p.m. in winter. The location is on the Plaza de Zocodover. A walking tour is laid out, giving a dramatic and realistic picture of the siege. Allow about an hour for a visit.

Museum of Santa Cruz

Formerly a 16th-century hospital, this magnificent Greco-Roman palace practically competes with the art it protects. It is a storehouse of the art treasures of Toledo. Built in the form of a Greek cross, the plateresque hospice was founded by Cardinal Mendoza, that dramatic nobleman—sometimes called "the third king of Spain"—who helped Ferdinand and Isabella gain the throne.

His handsomely constructed hospital, complete with paneled ceilings, is now a museum of fine arts and archeology. However, for all the cultures—Moorish, Visigothic—that have swept over Toledo, the city is weak in the latter. A rather unprepossessing display of Visigothic artifacts remains.

Look for El Greco's justly praised *The Assumption of the Virgin.* Goya and Ribera are also represented, along with a display of gold and opulent antique furnishings, as well as Flemish tapestries.

A short walk from the Plaza de Zocodover, the museum, on Calle de Cervantes, is open daily from 10 a.m. till 7 p.m. Admission is 200 pesetas ($1.40). You can visit the nearby **Museo de los Concilios y de la Cultura Visigoda** for another 100 pesetas (70¢).

The House of El Greco

In the old Jewish quarter of Toledo (known as the *antiguo barrio judio*) stands **Casa del Greco** on tiny Calle Samuel Leví. This building honors the artist, Domenico Theotocopouli, called El Greco because of his birth in Crete, who settled into Toledo in 1577 and lived there for most of his life until 1614. He lived with what could either have been his wife or mistress, Doña Jerónima, a noted beauty. Her face is said to have inspired El Greco's madonnas.

In 1585 he is known to have moved into one of the rundown palace apartments belonging to the Marquis of Villena. Pedro the Cruel's chancellor of the exchequer, Samuel ha-Leví, is said to have built a home on the same site in the 14th century. It was riddled with subterranean passages to hide his riches. In time the house was occupied by Don Enrique de Villena, who became notorious as a sorcerer. In the underground cellars he was said to have practiced black magic and alchemy.

The main part of the palace was rented to El Greco. From the windows he could look out onto his favorite views of the Tagus. He was to live at other Toledan addresses, although he returned to the Villena palace in 1604, remaining there until his death.

In the early part of the 20th century, the so-called Villena apartments were badly deteriorated and were torn down. However, the Marqués de la Vega-Inclán saved the only remaining part of El Greco's dwelling place. This was a small Moorish house, once believed to have been occupied by ha-Leví. In time it, along with a neighboring house, became the El Greco museum. Today it's furnished with authentic period pieces.

Without a guide, you can visit the studio of El Greco, complete with a painting by the artist. The garden and especially the kitchen merit your attention, as does a sitting room in the Moorish style. Jorge Manuel, the son of El Greco, also fancied himself an artist, as you'll see. The museum contains one of El Greco's *The Apostles,* as well as paintings of St. Francis, St. Bernardino, a view of Toledo, and three portraits, plus many pictures of various Spanish artists of the 17th century. For a 200-peseta ($1.40) admission fee, the house may be viewed from 10 a.m. to 2 p.m. and 3:30 till 6:45 p.m. Off-season hours are 10 a.m. to 1:45 p.m. and 3:30 to 5:45 p.m. The house is closed Sunday afternoon and Monday.

The Tránsito Synagogue

Down the street from El Greco's museum on the Paseo del Tránsito is this once important worshipping place for the large Jewish population that used to inhabit the city, living peacefully with both Christians and Arabs. This 14th-century building is noted for its superb stucco and Hebrew inscriptions. There are some psalms along the top of the walls and on the east wall a poetic description of this temple. The building of the synagogue was ordered by the chancellor of the exchequer to King Pedro the Cruel, Don Samuel ha-Leví. The name of the king appears clearly in a frame in the Hebrew inscription.

The synagogue is the most important part of the **Sephardi Museum** (Museo Sefardí), which was inaugurated in 1971 and contains in other rooms the tombstones with Hebrew epigraphy of the Jews of Spain before 1492, as well as other art pieces. The museum and synagogue can be visited from 10 a.m. to 1:45 p.m. and 4 to 5:45 p.m. in summer, until 6 p.m. in winter. It's closed Monday. Admission is 100 pesetas ($1.40). For information, phone 22-36-65.

San Juan de los Reyes

This church, at 21 Calle de los Reyes Católicos (tel. 27-38-02), was founded by King Ferdinand and Queen Isabella to commemorate their triumph over the Portuguese at Toro in 1476. Its construction was started in 1477, according to the plans of architect Juan Guas. It was finished, together with the splendid cloisters, in 1504, dedicated to St. John the Evangelist and used from the very beginning by the Franciscan friars. It is a perfect example of the Gothic-Spanish-Flemish style.

San Juan de los Reyes has been restored after being damaged in the invasion of Napoleon and abandoned in 1835. Actually, the national monument has been entrusted again to the Franciscans since 1954. The price of admission is 50 pesetas (35¢). You can visit the church from 10 a.m. to 2 p.m. and 3:30 to 7 p.m. in summer (it closes an hour earlier in winter).

The Church of Santo Tomé—Exposición Anexa

In a city that has as many historical sites as Toledo, this modest little 14th-century chapel on Calle de Santo Tomé (tel. 21-02-09) would have been overlooked if it did not possess El Greco's masterpiece, *The Burial of the Count of Orgaz.* In this painting, the spirituality of El Greco is revealed as never before; his elongated figures are at their most beautiful. The soul of the dead count is seen as an innocent baby ascending to heaven. The body of the count is surrounded by his friends (perhaps including El Greco), the men clad in black with starched white collars, totally unaware of the robed angels and *putti* appearing over their heads. El Greco did the work in 1586. The count reportedly died in 1323. You buy your ticket at the church for 70 pesetas (49¢), then sit in one of the hard-backed chairs placed in front of the painting. The longer you look at it, the more you realize its wealth of subtle details. The church, with its mudéjar tower, is open from 10 a.m. to 1:45 p.m. and 3:30 to 6:45 p.m. in summer (closes an hour earlier in winter). It's closed on Christmas and New Year's Day.

The Synagogue of Santa María la Blanca

In the closing part of the 12th century the Jews of Toledo erected an important synagogue in an art style known as almohade, which employs graceful horseshoe arches and ornamental horizontal moldings. However, by the early 15th century it had been converted into a Christian church. Much of its original look remains, nevertheless, and consists of five naves and elaborate mudéjar decorations—almost mosque-like in effect. Cloistered nuns have replaced its former Jewish occupants, and they're quite poor, judging by the signs outside advertising their embroidery. The synagogue is open in summer from 10 a.m. to 2 p.m. and 3:30 to 7 p.m.; from 10 a.m. to 1 p.m. and 3:30 to 6 p.m. in winter. Admission is 50 pesetas (35¢).

Hospital de Tavera

At the outskirts of the city, this private museum is near the Puerta Bisagra, off the Paseo de Madrid. A 16th-century Greco-Roman palace, it is a privately owned museum. Cardinal Tavera, who had the "ear of the royal family," originally built the place, ordering a façade called plateresque in Spain. Almost as if to perpetuate the aristocratic living style of the 16th century, the "hospital" has a spectacular art collection.

In the Banqueting Hall hangs a portrait of Charles V by Titian, and the collection of books in the Library has been called priceless. The museum owns five paintings by El Greco, including his *Holy Family,* the *Baptism of Christ,* and portraits of St. Francis, St. Peter, and Cardinal Tavera, the founding father of the hospital.

Ribera's freakish painting, *The Bearded Woman,* attracts many doctors who study it in detail. The hirsute female is nursing a baby, and the agonized look on the face of her husband reveals a lot.

The museum is open from 10 a.m. to 1:30 p.m. and 3:30 to 6 p.m. summer and winter. The entrance fee is 150 pesetas ($1.05). In the nearby church is the mausoleum of Cardinal Tavera, designed by Alonso de Berruguete.

WHERE TO EAT: Somewhere in the middle of your tour you'll want to take time out for lunch. This wonderful old city has several recommended restaurants, but the prices seem high—particularly for a lunch.

Maravilla (Wonder), 5-7 Barrio Rey (tel. 22-33-00), is a restaurant in a seasoned hotel that sits on a small satellite square of the historic Plaza de Zocodover, whose sidewalk cafés are featured heavily in Spanish novels and plays. The so-called Barrio Rey, the "quarter of the king," is friendlier and more intimate. It's like a living room somehow, filled with cheap restaurants and cafés that seemingly change their names so often it's virtually impossible to keep track of them.

Entered from the tiny cobblestone plaza, the hotel hides behind its bays and grillwork. The food in its dining room is passable—in fact, considering the price asked and the quality of the cuisine, it's about the best all-around dining bargain. You can get a four-course dinner (generous portions), including a carafe of the local wine, bread, and service for 900 pesetas ($6.30) to 1,200 pesetas ($8.40) on set menus.

Aurelio, 8 Plaza del Ayuntamiento (tel. 22-77-16), is a regional-style restaurant, lying within the shadow of the cathedral. It's one of the best restaurants in Toledo, offering very good value. Service is polite and efficient, and you couldn't be more centrally located with your dining choice. The menu is good and very familiar. You might begin with a sopa castellana, then follow with grilled hake, lubina a la sal (white fish cooked in salt), fresh salmon, roast lamb, and, if you're feeling elegant, Toledo partridge or roast suckling pig. A set menu is offered for 1,500 pesetas ($10.50) or else you can spend from 2,000 pesetas ($14) ordering à la carte. The restaurant is closed Tuesday.

La Parrilla, 8 Horno de los Bizochos (tel. 21-22-45), near the Alfonso VI Hotel, is a brick-built structure on a cobbled street. Rated two forks, it offers a set menu for only 850 pesetas ($5.95). If you order à la carte, you can expect to spend from 1,800 pesetas ($12.60) or more. It is a classic Spanish restaurant. That means you get no surprises on the menu but what you are served is reliable. The bill of fare is likely to include roast suckling pig, spider crabs, Castilian baked trout, stewed quail, baked kidneys, and La Mancha rabbit.

El Emperador Restaurant, 1 Carretera del Valle (tel. 22-46-91), is a modern restaurant on the outskirts of Toledo, reached via an arched bridge and by car or taxi. Its terraces overlook that memorable vista, the river below and the towers of Toledo. Inside, it is modified tavern style, with a spacious, attractive dining room with leather and wooden chairs, heavy beams, and wrought-iron chandeliers, and attentive service. Best news is that there is a set meal for 900 pesetas ($6.30), which might include a choice of three kinds of soup (beef, vegetable, or noodle) followed by a small steak with french-fried potatoes, then fresh fruit and wine. El Emperador is favored by the chauffeur guides from Madrid who almost always order from the à la carte menu the mountainous plate of roast lamb. It comes with potatoes, and one hardly needs any other food. If you order à la carte, expect to pay from 1,800 pesetas ($12.60).

Sinai, 7 Calle de los Reyes Católicos (tel. 22-56-23), is considered one of the best Jewish restaurants in Spain. Many of the specialties are kosher-style, and some derive from the Sephardic traditions of North Africa. Menu items include shaslik kebab, Tangiers-style beefsteak, Moroccan couscous, and paella. The house rioja wine is kosher. The establishment maintains family-style hours of 11 a.m. till 8 p.m. every day except Monday and during a changing series of annual vacations, which usually includes February. Full meals begin at around 2,200 pesetas ($15.40).

Parador Conde de Orgaz, Cerro del Emperador (tel. 22-18-50), combines some of the best Castilian regional cuisine with what surely must rank as one of the most spectacular views from any restaurant in Europe. Sheltered in one of the Spanish government's finest paradors, the restaurant is on the crest of a hill —said to be the spot that El Greco selected for his *View of Toledo.* From the heart of the city, you can either drive your car or take a taxi (the scenery along the way is well worth the extra pesetas).

On the upper level is a bar for an apéritif. Later you can select either a luncheon or dinner, both 2,200 pesetas ($15.40). Of course, you can order à la carte, but the fixed-price meal is cheaper, and can include, for example, some tasty Spanish hors d'oeuvres, followed by hake (a sweet white fish), then perhaps either veal or beef grilled on an open fire, plus dessert (some moist and light cakes here). If you're dining light (highly recommended on a hot August day), try a local specialty, tortilla española con magra.

Hostal del Cardenal, 24 Paseo Recaredo (tel. 22-49-00), is the best restaurant in Toledo, and the most expensive, but you may want to treat yourself to a splurge and enjoy its superb viands. It's owned by the same people who run the Casa Botín in Madrid, so beloved by Hemingway. In fact, the menu is very similar. For example, you might begin with "a quarter of an hour soup" (an excellent fish soup), using the same recipe as used in Madrid. Uniquely Toledan is partridge in casserole. Other dishes include white asparagus (an excellent beginning to your meal), as well as curried prawns, baked hake, filet mignon, smoked salmon, and many other main courses. Set menus are offered for 1,600 pesetas ($11.20), with à la carte dinners costing from 2,800 pesetas ($19.60). If you arrive early, you can enjoy a sherry in the charming little bar or else in the courtyard, entertained by the sound of chirping birds. The stone structure is built in the old style, and service is until 11:30 p.m.

Venta de Aires, 25 Circo Romano (tel. 22-05-45), is outside the city gates. Since 1891, when it was only a little roadside inn (*venta* means roadside inn), hungry Spaniards have made their way here to sample the pièce de résistance of Toledo, perdiz (partridge). "The French," confides a waiter, "know what a great dish this is. The Americans think it's spoiled or bad tasting. They're happy with roast chicken. But there are those exceptions. It always makes me happy when a Norteamericano likes our perdiz." This sought-after game dish, on the à la carte menu, is best with the red wine of Méntrida. However, if you want to keep your tab low, you'd better stick to the set meal, costing 2,200 pesetas ($15.40). For dessert you must try the marzipan, virtually an institution in Toledo and said to have been created by the Arabs who lived here. As a curiosity, see former President Nixon's entry in the guest book after he ate here in 1963.

STAYING OVERNIGHT: If you are among the fortunate few who can spend the night in Toledo, you will have a choice of widely varying accommodations. You can either stay in the city or across the river.

Hostal del Cardenal, 24 Paseo de Recaredo (tel. 22-49-00). The entrance to this very unusual hotel is set into the stone fortifications of the ancient city walls, a few steps from the Bisagra gate. After leaving the noise and dust of the parking lot outside, you'll enter an oasis of flagstone walkways, Moorish fountains, and burgeoning gardens of roses and cascading vines. The best restaurant in Toledo lies to your left, but to reach the hotel you must climb a series of verdant terraces to the top of the crenellated walls of the ancient fortress. There, grandly symmetrical and very imposing, rises the former residence of the 18th-century cardinal of Toledo, Señor Lorenzana. Containing 27 bedrooms, the establishment has intricately tiled walls, long and narrow salons, and a scattering of Iberian antiques. An inner courtyard uses the fortress walls as one of its sides. Each accommodation has a modern tile bath and dignified Spanish furniture. Singles cost 3,700 pesetas ($25.90), doubles, 6,200 pesetas ($43.40), plus tax.

Hotel Residencia Alfonso VI, 2 General Moscardó (tel. 22-26-00). It was built in the early 1970s, but its stately proportions and allegiance to the designs of old Spain make it seem much older. It sits near what might be the greatest concentration of souvenir shops in Toledo in the heart of the old city. Inside, you'll discover a high-ceilinged, marble-trimmed decor in a bland international style, with a scattering of Iberian artifacts and dozens of leather armchairs. Each of the 80 bedrooms, some of which lie within a newer wing, contain air conditioning, color TV, private bath, a phone, and copies of Spanish provincial furniture. Singles cost between 3,200 pesetas ($22.40) and 4,000 pesetas ($28); doubles, 5,000 pesetas ($35), plus tax. Fixed-price meals in the stone-floored angular dining room go for 1,500 pesetas ($10.50).

The **Hotel Carlos V,** 2 Plaza Horno de Magdalena (tel. 22-21-00), is an old favorite with visitors to Toledo. If you're driving, it's best to park at the garage on the Plaza de Zocodover, then walk to the hotel. Overlooking the cathedral, the hotel has a personality just as somber. But its rooms are well appointed and the service fine. When you see the handsome exterior of the Carlos V, you may be scared off, thinking it higher priced than it is. The tariff ranges in price from 4,000 pesetas ($28) in a single to 5,500 pesetas ($38.50) in a double. A lunch or dinner, ordered separately, costs 1,500 pesetas ($10.50).

Hotel Los Cigarrales, 12 Carretera Circunvalación (tel. 22-00-53). Many visitors find that its secluded position about a mile south of the city center offers a respite from the congestion of Toledo. It was built in the 1960s in a traditional red-brick style ringed with vegetation. It would be easy to mistake it for a private villa, except for the friendly reception genuinely offered by members of the Pedro Moron family. Most of the interior, including the upper hallway, is covered with blue-and-green tiles. A high-ceilinged dining room, always cool thanks to its thick walls and downstairs location, offers full meals for 2,200 pesetas ($15.40). You can see the towers of medieval Toledo from the flowering terrace of the pleasantly comfortable bar. Each of the very clean accommodations has a private bath and heavy Spanish furniture, air conditioning, a phone, and lots of sunlight. Singles cost 2,300 pesetas ($16.10); doubles, 4,000 pesetas ($28).

Residencia Imperio (Empire), 7 Cadenas, off the Calle de la Plata, just two minutes from the heartbeat Plaza de Zocodover (tel. 22-76-50), is the best bet for those who must keep costs rock-bottom. Run by Don José Gómez Prieto, it opened in 1967 and immediately attracted the attention of peseta-wise visitors. Most of the bedrooms overlook a little church with a wall overgrown with wisteria. You pay 3,200 pesetas ($22.40) for a double with private bath. Singles with shower go for 2,300 pesetas ($16.10). A continental breakfast costs extra. The rooms are not too large, but are fresh and comfortable.

Hotel Maravilla, 7 Barrio Rey (tel. 22-33-00), is a tiny bit of Spain that modern tourism is passing by. If your taste runs to small, very Spanish hotels with local color, then this will probably please you. First of all, it's 30 feet off the main square of Toledo, with its coffeehouses and sidewalk tables. The little old hotel, which was semi-modernized in 1971, opens directly onto a miniature cobblestone plaza. The building has many bay windows, the bedrooms are modest but adequate, and the furnishings are so-so. The cost for a double with bath is 4,400 pesetas ($30.80); singles with the same plumbing cost 3,000 pesetas ($21). You can order lunch for 1,300 pesetas ($9.10). You can hang out your laundry on the roof, and, on occasion, use an iron in the laundry room downstairs.

Across the Tagus

For readers who have a car or who don't mind one or two taxi rides a day, there are excellent accommodations in this area.

La Almazara, 47 Carretera de Piedrabuena (road number C781; tel. 22-38-66), takes its name from an old olive-oil mill that used to stand at this location. Providing one of the most offbeat accommodations in and around Toledo, it is hidden away up in the hills, discreetly approached via a private road. If you follow the road to the Parador or Ciudad Real, C781 turns off with road signs to Cuerva, about 1¼ miles out of the city. You arrive at an old-fashioned country villa, with its own courtyards and vineyards—a rare opportunity to soak up the atmosphere of old Spain, far removed from the pace of city life (exceptional view of Toledo).

La Almazara offers 21 rooms. A double with private bath costs 5,000 pesetas ($35); a single with private bath, 3,000 pesetas ($21). Only a continental breakfast is served. You may be assigned either a spacious chamber in the main house or a bedroom in the annex. The hotel is open from mid-March to October.

The Big Splurge

Parador Conde de Orgaz, Cerro del Emperador (tel. 22-18-50), is proof that when the Spanish government decides to recapture the spirit of the past—but with all the modern comforts of this century—it has no peer. Named after the subject of El Greco's masterpiece, this parador was recommended earlier for its restaurant. However, it also offers the most luxuriously appointed bedrooms in all of Toledo. On the ridge of a rugged hill, it was built on the spot where, as mentioned, El Greco is said to have painted his *View of Toledo* (although the artist arbitrarily turned a few buildings around to suit his sense of composition).

The Parador sits like a glorious large country inn, its spacious entry hall containing a long refectory table. A stairway and balcony lead to dark oak-paneled doors opening onto the bedrooms. The accommodations are spacious and beautifully furnished, each with reproductions of regional antique pieces. You pay 10,500 pesetas ($73.50) for a double room with private bath, 8,800 pesetas ($61.60) for a single with bath. Reserve well in advance.

The main living room-lounge has fine furniture, a wall of glass, old chests, brown leather chairs, thick-topped tables—all opening onto a sun terrace overlooking the Imperial City. On chilly nights, guests seek out the cozy recessed fireplace area.

YOUR PRE-DINNER ROUNDS: **Bar Ludeña,** 13 Plaza de la Horno Madeleña / 10 Corral de Don Diego (tel. 22-20-23), is a particularly charming bar serving delectable combinations of tapas to a loyal neighborhood clientele. The matter-of-fact owners sometimes open a small window and pass glasses of wine to clients who stand up outside, enjoying the view of the square. The bar is little more than a narrow corridor, serving racións of tapas for 300 pesetas ($2.10) that are so generous they become like little meals, especially when served with a plate of bread. The roasted red peppers are especially tasty, served with olive oil. There are also huge dishes of pickled cucumbers, onions, and olives, and a specialty is the stuffed crabs in their shells. What might be the smallest dining room in Toledo lies behind a curtain at the far end of the bar, serving inexpensive fare prepared in a tiny kitchen by the owner's female relatives.

WHEN NIGHT FALLS: Most people staying over have only one night to spend in Toledo, and they shouldn't lament the fact that the city's nightlife isn't terribly flamboyant. Toledo has something far more thrilling than flamenco: the walk through the old city on a trail that Cervantes might have taken. A strange air, bordering on the mystical, blankets the city at night, when it takes on an almost Oriental look. When the hordes of visitors have gone, when the sidewalk hawkers have closed down for the day, a mood descends that is both soothing yet curiously disturbing. The old city seems haunted, as if it had witnessed too much violence or had hidden too many secrets behind its walls. When the glare of the sun fades, the buildings become like silent ghosts leering down at you. The narrow streets at first appear foreboding, but they're safe—even though you might occasionally pass a figure in a long cape and a Napoleonic hat (a policeman). To spend the night in Toledo and to walk its ancient streets is to journey back into the Middle Ages. Well, almost.

2. Aranjuez

This Castilian town, about 29 miles south of Madrid, was the spring and fall home of the Bourbon kings, who found it too hot for the summer months (they headed then for La Granja near Segovia). With its manicured shrubbery, its stately elms, fountains and statues, Aranjuez still remains a regal garden oasis in what is otherwise an unimpressive agricultural flatland producing a great abundance of the strawberries and asparagus for Castilians.

An arm of the Tagus River cuts through the town on its way to Toledo. The Royal Palace goes back to the days of Philip II (1561) and is often compared with Versailles.

GETTING THERE: Aranjuez is easy to reach from Madrid. The road is good, and the trip takes less than an hour. If you don't have a car and you're on the do-it-yourself tour, then you can take a bus run by **Automnibus Interurbaños, S.A.,** 18 Paseo de las Delicias (tel. 230-46-07). Buses depart from the Estación Sur de Autobuses de Madrid, 17 Calle Canarias.

Tip: On the way to Aranjuez, look for what is known as **Cerro de los Angeles** (Angels' Hill), the geographic center of the Iberian peninsula. A huge white statue of Christ dominates the mountain.

THE SIGHTS: On your arrival in Aranjuez, it's best to purchase a ticket for 250 pesetas ($1.75), allowing you to visit the sleepy town's trio of attractions, including the Royal Palace, the Garden of the Island adjoining it, and the Casita del Labrador in the Jardín del Príncipe.

The Royal Palace

"Deception [is] . . . its dominant note," wrote an expatriate American. "In almost each of its widely varying rooms there is at least one thing that isn't what it first appears," William Lyon accurately put it. To prove his case, he cites mosaics that are made to fool the eye into thinking they are oils, or a flat ceiling in trompe l'oeil that achieves a startling three-dimensional effect.

As you enter the cobblestone courtyard, you can tell—just by the massive bulk of the palace—that you're going to see something spectacular. Ferdinand and Isabella came this way, as did Philip II (the former traveling about so much it was hardly possible for them to have a favorite oasis, the latter preferring the life he had created for himself at El Escorial). The Bourbons were the main force behind the flowering of Aranjuez. Philip V and Charles III were also fond of life as it was easily lived here.

The structure you see today dates principally from 1778 (the previous buildings were swept by fire). Throughout its salons parade the opulence of a bygone era, room after room a royal extravaganza. If it strikes you as a bit garish, remember that royalty in those days didn't have to apologize for ostentation.

Many styles, furnishings, and decorations are blended here: Spanish, Italian, Moorish, French. Of course, no royal palace would be complete without an Oriental salon, reflecting the popularity of chinoiserie that once swept over Europe. Of special interest also is the Porcelain Salon. The painting collection, relatively unimportant, does contain works by José Ribera and Lucas Jordan.

A guide conducts you through the huge complex and will expect a tip. The hours are 10 a.m. to 1 p.m. and 3:30 to 7 p.m. in summer (till 6 p.m. in winter).

Afterward, you're turned out on your own for an enchanting promenade through:

The Garden of the Island

It appears somehow forgotten, its mood melancholic. In back of the Royal Garden, it lies quietly, its special magic hard to convey. There once lived a Spanish impressionist, Santiago Rusiñol, who captured on canvas its evasive quality. One Spanish writer said it was "as if softly lulled by a sweet 18th-century sonata, beautifully portrayed by the composer Joaquín Rodrigo in his world-famous *Concierto de Aranjuez.*" "Non Plus Ultra" fountain is dazzling, although one observer found the black jasper fountain of Bacchus "orgiastic." Under linden trees, the fountain of Apollo is romantic, and others honor the king of the sea as well as Cybele, goddess of agriculture.

On your approach to the island, you may want to stroll through the **Parterre,** in front of the palace—much better kept than the Garden of the Island, but somehow not as romantic.

The Casita del Labrador

"The little house of the worker" is a classic example of understatement. Actually, it was modeled after the Petit Trianon at Versailles. If you visit the Royal Palace in the morning, you can spend the afternoon here. Those with a car can motor to it through the tranquil **Jardín del Príncipe,** with its black poplars, for a fee of 100 pesetas (70¢).

The little palace was built in 1803 by Charles IV, who later abdicated in Aranjuez. The queen came here with her youthful lover, Godoy (whom she had elevated to the position of prime minister), and the feeble-minded Charles didn't seem to mind a bit. Surrounded by beautiful gardens, the "bedless" palace is lavishly furnished in the grand style of the 18th and 19th centuries. The marble floors represent some of the finest workmanship of that day. The brocaded walls emphasize the luxurious living—and the royal john is a sight to behold (in those days, royalty preferred an audience). The clock here is one of the treasures of the house.

WHERE TO EAT: Between palace-hopping, you'll want to take time out for lunch. Be forewarned that most of Aranjuez's tourist-financed restaurants—especially those along the river—charge high prices.

But in the heart of town is a good low-cost dining recommendation, the **Casa Pablo,** 20 Almibar (tel. 891-14-51). Tables are set outside under a shade canopy, and as you dine here in garden chairs, you can enjoy the streets of trees and plants, the bed of roses, the red and pink geraniums. Usually, lottery sellers squat nearby, peddling their tickets. In cooler weather, you walk through the tasca to a cozy and clean dining room in the rear, or the one upstairs.

The two-fork tavern offers a complete meal for 1,500 pesetas ($10.50), including a carafe of wine, bread, and service. If it's a hot day and you don't want a heavy dinner, try a shrimp omelet, or half a roast chicken. Once, in asparagus season, I simply ordered a plate of those fresh morsels accompanied by white wine. If you want a superb dish, try a fish called mero (a Mediterranean pollack of delicate flavor), grilled over an open fire. If you dine à la carte, expect to pay from 2,500 pesetas ($17.50).

For some, the traditional choice remains **La Rana Verde** (The Green Frog), 1 Reina (tel. 891-32-38). The setting is next to a small bridge spanning the Tagus. The restaurant looks like somebody's summer house—the beamed ceiling stretching high and soft ferns drooping from hanging baskets. The preferred spots for dining are in the nooks overlooking the river (which eventually makes its lazy way to Portugal).

The least expensive way to eat here is to order a three-course set meal at 1,050 pesetas ($7.35). Strawberries are served with sugar or orange juice or ice cream. Asparagus, as in all the restaurants of Aranjuez, is a special feature. Especially recommended in season are the game dishes, particularly partridge, quail, and pigeon. Under the fish dishes, the fried hake is good as is the fried sole. Ordering à la carte will bring the tab up to 2,500 pesetas ($17.50).

WHERE TO STAY: **Hostal Castilla,** 28 Carretera Andalucía (tel. 891-26-27), is a 14-room establishment, each unit well furnished and containing a private bath and toilet. The rate is 2,400 pesetas ($16.80) in a double room, dropping to 1,900 pesetas ($13.30) in a single. The Castilla consists of a ground floor and part of the first floor of a well-preserved, early-18th-century house. Most of the accommodations look onto a courtyard with a fountain and flowers. The hall and entrance are a feature of the building (in days of yore, coaches entered here). The owner, Joaquin Suárez Parra, is a native of Aranjuez and his family are well-known local landowners. He has lived in England for several years and speaks English fluently. The hostal lies on one of the main streets of Aranjuez, quite near the Royal Palace and the gardens. There are many excellent restaurants nearby, and the hostal has an arrangement with a bar very close by for an inexpensive lunch. It makes a good center for visiting Aranjuez. Instead of the other way around, many visitors stay here and explore either Madrid or Toledo on a day trip.

An alternate choice is **Hostal Infantas,** 4 Avenida Infantas (tel. 891-13-41), which is a basic, two-star hostal, but it is well maintained and has reasonably up-to-date furnishings and modern plumbing. Open all year, it charges from 1,600 pesetas ($11.20) for a double without bath, 2,500 pesetas ($17.50) for a double with bath. In a peaceful zone, the hotel lies about a six-minute walk to the already previewed Royal Palace. Parking is available in front of the building. No meals are served, but you can enjoy a continental breakfast at the cafeteria nearby.

3. El Escorial and the Valley of the Fallen

Ranking next to Toledo as the most important excursion from Madrid is the austere monastery of El Escorial. Philip II ordered the construction of this granite-and-slate rectangular monster, and the building was begun in 1563, two years after the king moved the capital to Madrid. This combination palace–royal mausoleum is 30 miles from Madrid, on the slopes of the Guadarrama Mountains. A trip there is usually combined with an excursion to the Valley of the Fallen (nine miles away).

For years the haunt of aristocratic Spaniards, El Escorial has long been a summer resort. When the atmosphere of Madrid becomes unbearable, the air of El Escorial is like a tonic. Hotels and restaurants flourish in summer, as hundreds flock here to escape the heat of the capital.

GETTING THERE: If you're on the do-it-yourself tour, you can take either a train or bus. The **Autocares Herranz** has buses leaving from the station at 10 Calle Isaac Peral (tel. 243-36-45). Departures are at 8, 9, 10, and 11 a.m. and 1, 2, 3, 5:30, 7, 8, and 9 p.m. A one-way ticket costs 222 pesetas ($1.55). From El Escorial, the same line goes to the Valley of the Fallen, a round-trip fare costing 220 pesetas ($1.54). On holidays, the hours are likely to be different, so check in advance.

Trains leave Madrid from Atocha Station, and during the summer extra coaches are added to handle the overflow. Starting at 8:30 a.m., trains leave nearly every hour. For exact schedules and travel costs, consult the **RENFE** offices or the Spanish Tourism Office opposite the Palace Hotel in Madrid.

A VISIT TO THE MONASTERY: The **Royal Monastery of San Lorenzo del Escorial** is a huge granite fortress that houses a wealth of paintings and tapestries, and serves as a final resting place for Spanish kings. It is made foreboding, both inside and out, by its sheer size and institutional look, an aspect broken only by its steeples and towers. Built of rock from the nearby mountains, El Escorial took 21 years to complete, a remarkably fast time considering the bulk of the building and construction methods in those days.

El Escorial can proudly boast the following: 1,200 doors, 2,593 windows (if a guide tells you 2,673 windows, don't debate the point; his Spanish pride may force you into counting them), 86 staircases, 89 fountains, 16 courtyards or patios, and 300 cells. In addition, it contains more than 1,600 paintings and murals, including works by El Greco, Velázquez, Bosch, Titian, and Tintoretto, to name only a few, as well as tapestries by Goya.

The minimum time that you should allow—even for the most cursory visit—is two hours, although three would be more suitable, and even at that you'd be pushing it. The visiting hours are 10 a.m. to 1:30 p.m. and 3:30 to 6 p.m. daily except Monday. The comprehensive admission ticket is 350 pesetas ($2.45), but there are four different admissions and sights from which to choose.

Because the palace-monastery is so vast, you simply can't see it all—don't even try. But here are some of the highlights:

The **New Museo** is the picture gallery, containing the monastery's art collection. Philip II, who collected many of the paintings exhibited here, definitely did not like the mysticism of El Greco, and turned instead to his pet, Titian, for inspiration. Nevertheless you'll find El Greco's *The Martyrdom of St. Maurice* rescued from the mothballs where Philip stored it. In addition, you'll see such superb works as El Greco's *St. Peter,* Titian's *Last Supper,* and Velázquez's *The Tunic of Joseph.*

The **Royal Library** contains a priceless collection of books, estimated at 60,000 volumes—one of the most significant library storehouses in the world. Here you'll see displays ranging from the handwriting of St. Teresa to medieval instructions on how to play chess. Discover, in particular, the Muslim codices and a Gothic "Cantigas" from the reign of Alfonso X ("The Wise") in the 13th century.

You can also visit the **Philip II Apartments,** which he called the "cell for my humble self" that he ordered built in this "palace for God." By that time Philip had become a religious fanatic, and he requested that his bedroom be erected overlooking the altar. The apartments are strictly monastic, and you'll find Bosch's copy of his own work, *The Seven Capital Sins.* Its dome based on Michelangelo's drawings for St. Peter's, the **Basilica** has four organs, and measures approximately 300 feet from floor to ceiling. The choir contains a crucifix by Benvenuto Cellini. The **Throne Room** is, by comparison, simple. On the walls are many ancient maps.

The **Apartments of the Bourbon Kings** break from Philip's bleakness, and are more lavishly decorated in keeping with the latter-day tenants' taste for luxury. The tapestries displayed look like paintings until they are examined closely. Under the altar of the church you'll find the octagonal **Royal Pantheon,** where most of the kings of Spain from Charles I to Alfonso XII, including Philip II, lie buried. Here too are the tombs of the queens, the mothers of kings. This is one of the most regal mausoleums in the world (nearby, on a lower floor, is the "Wedding Cake" tomb for children). Just watch what you say in the **Whispering Hall,** and you may enjoy your visit to El Escorial.

Just as Philip II ordered it, El Escorial is dedicated to St. Lawrence, martyred by burning, and it commemorates the triumph of the soldiers of the Habsburg monarch at San Quintin in 1557. Juan Bautista de Toledo, the original architect, was replaced after his death by Juan de Herrera, the greatest architect of Renaissance Spain, who completed it in the shape of a gridiron. The total legacy of these men was summed up by a critic of European architecture as ". . . overwhelming, moving no doubt, but frightening."

If time (and interest) remains, you might visit the **Casita del Príncipe**

(Prince's Cottage), a small but elaborately decorated 18th-century palace that was a hunting lodge. The so-called cottage was built for Charles III by Juan de Villanueva. Near the gateway is a cafetería. *Warning:* It's almost impossible to visit the monastery and prince's cottage in the morning—at least before the casita closes for its staff to have lunch at 12:30 p.m. Most visitors stay in El Escorial for lunch, visiting the cottage when it reopens in the afternoon.

WHERE TO EAT: If you're not on an organized tour, you'll have to fend for yourself at lunch. And in El Escorial that can be a real problem. Some of the local eateries are overrun by the busloads of tourists who arrive as frequently as the rains in Galicia.

The diner seeking an economical noonday repast should bypass the highly advertised restaurants with their fat-cat menus and head instead for Plaza de la Constitucíon, right in the center of town. The restaurants here specialize in Castilian cooking, using the local produce and wines.

Castilla, 3 Plaza de la Constitucíon (tel. 890-52-19), stands right in the center of town; in summer tables are placed outdoors—in the shade, of course. The dishes featured here are typically Spanish, including a reliable paella. Another good-tasting dish is the veal scaloppine. Everything tastes better when you order a large pitcher of sangría. Expect to spend from 1,800 pesetas ($12.60) if you order à la carte. Closed Monday.

Mesón La Cueva (The Cave), 4 San Antón, (tel. 890-15-16), recaptures the world of old Castile. Built around an enclosed courtyard, it is a típico mesón. Everywhere you look it's nostalgia time—stained-glass windows, antique chests, scenic murals, a 19th-century bullfighting collage, time-soiled engravings, paneled doors, iron balconies.

The cooking is on target, the portions are generous. Some of the best-known regional specialties in Spain are served, including Valencian paella and fabada asturiana (the pork-sausage-and-bean dish). But a simple fresh trout broiled in butter may be the best of all. The most expensive items on the menu are roast suckling pig and roast lamb (tender inside, crisp on the outside, in the manner of Segovia). The tab here will range from 1,800 pesetas ($12.60) to 3,000 pesetas ($21). Opening off the courtyard, and entered through a separate doorway, is La Cueva's tasca, brimming over with Castilians in pursuit of their favorite pre-dinner drinks (many ending up not having dinner at all).

Charolés, 24 Floridablanca (tel. 890-59-75). Its sunny terrace, air-conditioned interior, and impeccable service are important reasons to seek this place out. But the real reason for its popularity is the array of fresh meats and fish the owner, Manuel Mínguez, imports every day from Madrid. The daily specials change with the availability of ingredients, but some outstanding dishes are likely to include a pastel of fresh vegetables with crayfish, pepper steak, temptingly herb-flavored chops of baby lamb, shellfish soup, and many other savory fish dishes. Kiwi tart is an appropriate dessert for a full meal likely to cost from 2,000 pesetas ($14). The restaurant is open daily from 1 to 4 p.m. and from 9 to midnight.

STAYING OVERNIGHT: If you'd like to break up your stay in Madrid, you might spend a night or two at El Escorial—or more if you have the time. The temperature in the summer is quite cool, primarily because of the bracing mountain air. What to do during the day need not be a problem. El Escorial makes an ideal base for visiting the cities and towns of Segovia and Ávila, the royal palace at La Granja, the Valley of the Fallen—or even the more distant university city of Salamanca. The hotels here are pleasant enough, and the rates are moderate.

Miranda & Suizo, 20 Floridablanca (tel. 890-47-11), is one of the leading two-star hotels, offering a double room with private bath for 3,600 pesetas ($25.30), singles—12 in this category—for 2,600 pesetas ($18.20), also including bath. A continental breakfast is extra. On a tree-lined street in the heart of town, this hotel is within easy walking distance of the monastery. An excellent middle-class establishment, the Miranda & Suizo is a simple, 47-room, Victorian-style building with balconies. Some of the quite good bedrooms open onto terraces. The rooms are amply furnished with comfortable pieces; the beds are often made of brass and sometimes you'll find fresh flowers on the table. In summer, tables and chairs are placed outside for dining.

The best low-budget accommodation in town is the **Hostal Cristina,** 6 Juan de Toledo (tel. 890-19-61). It offers only 16 rooms, but they are clean and comfortable, costing 2,800 pesetas ($19.60) nightly. Rooms contain a private bath. The staff is helpful and friendly, and because the food is good and plentiful, many Spanish visitors prefer to book in here on the full-board plan, paying 3,500 pesetas ($24.50) per person for everything. There's also a pleasant little garden.

Another possibility, less preferred, is the **Jardín,** 2 Leandro Rubio (tel. 896-10-07), a two-star hostal run by Don Fernándo Delgado Garcia, who offers 22 reasonably furnished and well-kept bedrooms. Doubles are modestly priced at 2,800 pesetas ($19.60) with private bath, only 2,100 pesetas ($14.70) with hot and cold running water. In summer you can order a good meal in the garden for 900 pesetas ($6.30).

A super bargain, if your needs are minimal, is **Hostal Malagón,** 2 San Francisco (tel. 890-15-76). There, Julián Cuena Esteban will welcome you into a very Spanish environment. He rents out only 10 rooms, each plain and basic but adequate for an overnight stay. Double rooms come with wash basins, costing from 1,600 pesetas ($11.20) a night. Singles go for 1,000 pesetas ($7). In the peak tourist months, you'll be requested to take one main meal at the hostal, a most filling repast for only 850 pesetas ($5.95).

The Big Splurge

Hotel Victoria Palace, 4 Juan de Toledo (tel. 890-15-11), is the finest hotel in town, lying in the heart of everything with a view of Philip's gargantuan compound. A traditional hotel of style and comfort, it has been modernized without losing its special character. Each of its 87 well-furnished and immaculately maintained bedrooms contains a private bath (in some cases, a private terrace as well). The rate is 8,500 pesetas ($59.50) for a double and 5,200 pesetas ($36.40) in a single. The price of the room, reasonable enough and a bargain for a four-star hotel, also includes the admission to El Escorial. The hotel is surrounded by beautiful gardens, and there is an outdoor swimming pool, a welcome relief in summer. The Victoria Palace's dining room serves some of the best food in town, a meal averaging around 2,200 pesetas ($15.40).

Whether you're planning to stay over—or are visiting El Escorial for the day—at some point most visitors head for:

THE VALLEY OF THE FALLEN: This architectural marvel—two decades in the making—might be called Franco's Escorial. It is dedicated to those who died in the Spanish Civil War. Its severest critics might suggest that this monument represents all the worst of neo-Fascist design; its kindest sympathizers say they have found renewed inspiration by coming here. Others not involved in the Spanish civil struggle might see it as a gigantic reminder of the folly of war.

A gargantuan cross, nearly 500 feet high, dominates the **Rock of Nava,** a peak of the Guadarrama Mountains. The funicular to the foot of the cross costs 100 pesetas (70¢) and is well worth it. However, it does not operate from 2 to 4 p.m. Directly under the cross is a basilica in mosaic, completed in 1959. Here is where the body of José Antonio, the founder of the Falangist party, is buried. When this nationalist hero was buried at El Escorial, a storm of protest arose—particularly from influential monarchists—who pointed up the fact that José Antonio was not royalty. Obviously infuriated, Franco decided to erect another monument. Originally it was slated to honor the dead on the Nationalist side only, but the intervention of several parties led to a decision to include all the caídos, so that in time the mausoleum claimed Franco as well.

On your way to the basilica you'll walk through six chapels. It's like going through a huge tunnel to the center of a mountain. By all means, wear your walking shoes.

If you go by car, you'll have to pay 300 pesetas ($2.10) to drive up the mountain to the monument. However, there is no charge for entering it. It's open from 10 a.m. to 7 p.m.

Valle de los Caídos, a three-fork restaurant (tel. 896-02-01), occupies a dramatic location halfway up the mountainside. After passing through the entrance gates, it's on your left and reachable only by car. It's a mammoth, modern structure, with wide suspended terraces and ceiling-to-floor windows. The menú del día is 1,000 pesetas ($7), which could include cannelloni Rossini as an opener, then pork chops with potatoes, a dessert and, of course, wine.

On the other side of the mountain is a monastery that has sometimes been dubbed "the Hilton of monasteries" because of its seeming luxury. It is inhabited by Benedictine monks.

4. Segovia and La Granja

Nowhere does the faded glory of Old Castile shine more brightly than in Segovia. Wherever you look, you'll see remains of a greater day, whether it be the most spectacular Alcázar on the Iberian peninsula or the well-preserved, still-functioning Roman aqueduct. The parade of armies of occupation—Romans, Visigoths, Moors—has disappeared, and Segovia is peaceful. It has little of the commercialism of Toledo, and the modern visitor can probe into the past at leisure.

Segovia lies on the slope of the Guadarrama Mountains. Two rivers, the Eresma and the Calmores, converge in the city.

Warning: If you're visiting in the early spring, wear warm clothes. It's cold at those altitudes.

GETTING THERE: If you go by automobile, the ride between Madrid and Segovia to the northwest will be approximately 54 miles by one road, 63 by another. At Villalba, the road forks and you have a choice of routes. Consider taking the southern one to reach it, returning via the northern route, but budgeting enough time for a stopover at La Granja.

If you're without an automobile, then you can catch a morning train at the Atocha Station in Madrid. You will be delivered to the train station in Segovia, where you can board a bus to the Plaza Mayor, the heart of the city.

It is also possible to go by bus. The **Empresa La Sepulvedana,** 16 Palos de la Frontera (tel. 230-48-00), runs a daily bus service, including Sunday and holidays. Hours are likely to vary, but on weekdays you should aim for the early departure, around 7:45 a.m., which will give you more time for exploring. Tickets go for around 455 pesetas ($3.19).

THE SIGHTS: This ancient city, whose history goes back to the dim Iberian past, lies in the center of the most castle-rich part of Castile. A major moment in its history came when Isabella was proclaimed Queen of Castile here in 1474. Walls still encircle the old part of town, but they are not as impressive as the ones you'll see at Ávila.

The narrow, winding streets of this hill city must be covered on foot if you're to have the experience that is uniquely Segovian. Basically, Segovia is a city rich in historical buildings—Romanesque churches, old mansions, 15th-century palaces.

Of the multitude of attractions in Segovia, I have selected six that I feel best represent the city.

Alcázar

If you've ever dreamed of castles in the air, then all the fairytale romance of childhood will return when you view this structure. Many have waxed poetic about it, comparing it to a giant boat sailing through the clouds. See it first from down below, at the junction of the Clamores and Eresma Rivers. It is on the west side of Segovia, and you may not spot it when you first enter the city. But that's part of the surprise.

The castle dates back many hundreds of years—perhaps to the 12th century. But a large segment of it—notably its Moorish ceilings—was destroyed by fire in 1862. Over the years, under an ambitious plan, the Alcázar has been restored.

Inside, you'll discover a facsimile of Isabella's dank bedroom. It was at the Alcázar that she first met Ferdinand, preferring him to the more "fatherly" king of Portugal. But she wasn't foolish enough to surrender her "equal rights" after marriage. In the Throne Room, with its replica chairs, you'll note that both seats are equally proportioned. Royal romance continued to flower at the Alcázar. Phillip II married his fourth wife, Anne of Austria, here.

After you inspect the polish on some medieval armor inside, you may want to walk the battlements of this once-impregnable castle, whose former occupants poured boiling oil over the ramparts onto their uninvited guests below. Or you can climb the tower, originally built by Isabella's father as a prison, for a view supreme of Segovia. (In particular, note the so-called pregnant-woman mountain.) Readers Temmie and Aubrey Baratz write: "We climbed it! It's not for the faint of heart or faint of leg. It's a long way up, but one doesn't know how long until the top is reached. The stairway is circular, often hazardous, with no railings, and dark in many places. But at the top the view is spectacular." The fortress is open from 10 a.m. to 7:30 p.m. (closes at 6 p.m. in winter). Admission is 100 pesetas (70¢).

The Roman Aqueduct

This aqueduct, an architectural marvel, is still used to carry water, even though it was constructed by the Romans almost 2,000 years ago. It is not only the most colossal reminder of Roman glory in Spain, but one of the best preserved Roman architectural achievements in the world. It consists of 118 arches, and in one two-tiered section—its highest point—it soars to some 95 feet. Another fact: you'll find no mortar in these granite blocks, brought from the Guadarrama Mountains. The Spanish call it **El Puente,** and it spans the Plaza del Azoguejo, the old market square, stretching out to a distance of nearly 800 yards. When the Moors took Segovia in 1072, they destroyed 36 arches. However, Ferdinand and Isabella ordered that they be rebuilt in 1484.

There are no visiting hours, of course; you can see it anytime night or day. It's an integral landmark of Segovia.

"The Lady of the Cathedrals"

This 16th-century structure lays claim to being the last Gothic cathedral built in Spain. Fronting the historic Plaza Mayor, it stands on the spot where Isabella I was proclaimed Queen of Castile. It's affectionately called *la dama de las catedrales*. Inside, it contains numerous treasures, such as the Blessed Sacrament Chapel (created by the flamboyant Churriguera), stained-glass windows, elaborately carved choir stalls, 16th- and 17th-century paintings, including a reredos portraying the deposition of Christ from the cross by Juan de Juni. Older than the cathedral are the cloisters, belonging to a former church destroyed in the "War of the Communeros." The museum of the cathedral contains jewelry, paintings, and a rare collection of antique manuscripts, along with the inevitable vestments. If you want to visit the cloisters, the museum, and the chapel room, the charge is 85 pesetas (60¢). In summer, the cathedral is open from 9 a.m. to 7 p.m. (from 9 a.m. to 1 p.m. and 3 to 6 p.m. in winter).

Church of Vera Cruz

Of all the Romanesque churches of Segovia, the one called Vera Cruz, on the Carretera de Zamarramala, is the most fascinating. Built in either the 11th or 12th century by the Knights Templar, it has an isolated view of Segovia, overlooking the Alcázar. Its major feature is its 12 sides. (The unusual design of this polygonal church is believed to have been taken from the Church of the Holy Sepulchre in Jerusalem.) Although the city was walled and protective, the knights boldly built this edifice outside. This is a gem of a Romanesque building. Inside there's a fascinating inner temple, rising two floors. It was here that the Knights Templar conducted a night-long vigil as part of their initiation rites. It is open from 10 a.m. to 1 p.m. and 3 to 6 p.m. Admission is 50 pesetas (35¢).

The Monastery of El Parral

The "monastery of the grape" enjoys a lonely position across the Eresma River—sitting as if abandoned (in fact, it has been recently restored). You arrive at the gateway like a pilgrim calling for his dole. Behind its plateresque façade, it is a church of many styles, including Gothic and Renaissance. It was established for the Hironymites by Henry IV, a Castilian king (1425–1474) known as "The Impotent." The chief art treasure of the monastery is a large retable, the work of Juan Rodríguez in 1528. The same artist also did the sarcophagi of the Segovian aristocratic family, the Villena clan. A robed monk shows you through. To reach the monastery, head out the Calle del Marqués de Villena anytime from 9 a.m. to 1 p.m. and 3:30 to 6:30 p.m. (from 9 a.m. to noon and 3 to 6 p.m. on Sunday and holidays). By all means, make a contribution to the cause.

The Church of San Martín

On the trail from the cathedral to the Roman aqueduct is the Church of San Martín, which was at one time among the most outstanding in Old Castile. A Romanesque structure from the 12th century, it is characterized by its outside porticoes. Except for the rare altar, the interior is less interesting. The square on which the church stands, the Plaza de la Sirenas, was modeled after the Piazza di Spagna in Rome. A fountain commemorates the legend of Juan Bravo, the hero of the War of the Communeros against Charles V. Nearby is the 15th-century **Mansion of Arias Davila,** one of the old houses of the Segovian aristocracy.

A MEAL IN OLD CASTILE: The natives of Segovia take a special pride in preparing roast suckling pig (cochinillo asado). Although this dish is popular throughout both Castiles, Segovia has acquired a particular reputation for it.

Perhaps you'd like to try it here; at any rate, you'll probably want to sample some of the Old Castilian cooking.

For years the **Mesón de Cándido,** 5 Plaza del Azoguejo (tel. 42-81-02), has maintained a monopoly on the tourist trade. An old Spanish inn, it is quite beautiful, and its popularity can be judged by the flocks of hungry diners who fill every one of the half-dozen dining rooms. In the shadow of the aqueduct, it offers an à la carte menu that includes cordero asado (roast baby lamb) or cochinillo asado. For a complete repast, including the local specialties cited, expect to spend from 2,500 pesetas ($17.50) to 3,500 pesetas ($24.50). The proprietor of "The House of Cándido" is known as *mesonero mayor de Castilla* (the major innkeeper of Castile). He's been decorated with more medals and has won more honors than paella has grains of rice, and has entertained everyone from King Hussein to Hemingway. His restaurant is open from 12:30 p.m. to midnight.

Less expensive is **Casa Duque,** 12 Calle Cervantes (tel. 43-05-37), founded in 1895. Below in the tavern decorated in the típico style, you may order a sherry or other pre-dinner drink before sitting down to your huge noonday repast. Duque, the *maestro asador,* as he calls himself, supervises the roasting of the pigs. The waitresses, wearing the traditional costume of the mayoress of Zamarramala, will serve you a menú del día for 1,600 pesetas ($11.20). If you want to enjoy Segovian gastronomic specialties, ask for sopa castellana, made with ham, sausage, bread, egg, garlic, and much more. For the main dish, roast suckling pig is the house specialty, or you may prefer roast lamb. To finish off, try a cake known as ponche alcázar. An à la carte choice will cost you anywhere from 2,200 pesetas ($15.40) to 3,000 pesetas ($21).

Restaurant José Maria, 11 Cronista Lecea (tel. 43-44-84), is a centrally located bar and restaurant that prides itself on the quality of its regional cuisine. The stucco and brickwork of its rustic interior lie behind an old-fashioned façade of stone, carriage lamps, and wooden doors. Before dinner, locals crowd in here to enjoy a selection of tapas at the bar. Later they retreat to the dining room for one of the flavorful meals. Menu items include many Castilian specialties and some nouvelle cuisine entries. Perhaps you'll get cream of crabmeat soup, roasted peppers, salmon with scrambled eggs, house-style hake, filet of sole, or a grilled veal steak. For dessert, try the ice-cream tart with whisky sauce. Full meals cost from 2,000 pesetas ($14). José Maria Ruiz has garnered several cooking awards during his career. Another good budget choice is **El Bernardino,** 2 Calle Cervantes (tel. 43-32-25), where the owner offers a menú del día for 1,000 pesetas ($7) that includes a huge paella (or hors d'oeuvres if you prefer), roast veal with potatoes, flan or ice cream, plus bread and wine. Expect to spend 1,800 pesetas ($12.60) if you order à la carte. El Bernardino is built like an old tavern, with lanterns hanging from the beamed ceilings, and a delightful view over the red tile rooftops of the city. The place is impeccable, the service excellent.

STAYING OVERNIGHT: Segovia is much cooler than Madrid, and for that reason it is ringed by a number of summer resorts, popular mostly with the Spanish. However, the hotels within the city are relatively modest, both in decor and price.

Gran Hotel Las Sirenas (The Sirens), 30 Juan Bravo (tel. 43-40-11), stands on the most charming old plaza of Segovia, opposite the Church of San Martín. Although modest, it's one of the leading hotels of Segovia, attracting those with traditional taste. Each well-kept accommodation—39 in all—has its own bath, telephone, and such contemporary fittings as bedside reading lamps. Its matrimonial doubles go for 5,200 pesetas ($36.40); singles, 3,200 pesetas ($22.40). A continental breakfast, costing extra, will be brought to your room. However, a more preferred spot is the drawing room's balcony, with its pots of red geraniums and a view of orange trees.

Hotel Acueducto, 10 Padre Claret (tel. 42-48-00), was built in the shadow of the Roman aqueduct in 1963. Behind its bandbox-modern façade are 73 bedrooms, most with streamlined furnishings and bed headboards with reading lamps and telephone. For the most expensive double rooms, you pay 6,000 pesetas ($42); singles average 4,500 pesetas ($31.50). A continental breakfast is extra. The dining room serves three complete meals a day, including a five-course luncheon or dinner costing from 1,500 pesetas ($10.50).

If you're seeking rock-bottom prices, try the **Hostal Florida,** 2 Calle Santa (tel. 425-881), where the owner, Juan Mingueia Gascón, will rent you a clean, basic room (only 11 in all) for 1,500 pesetas ($10.50) for two persons. Each accommodation contains a wash basin. You pay extra for a hot shower or a continental breakfast. The hosts are most accommodating, a good choice.

AFTER DARK: **Disco Oky,** 1-3 Carmen (tel. 43-21-28), is a trendy disco next to the Roman aqueduct, attracting the night lifers of Segovia. Different parties are held every week, and the programs are often broadcast over the most important radio chain in Spain. Drinks are moderate here, averaging around 400 pesetas ($2.80).

COCA CASTLE: If you're based in Segovia, you can make an excursion in the morning to Coca Castle, about 30 miles away. It is closed from mid-July to mid-August, but is usually open from 11 a.m. to 1 p.m. and from 3 to 5 p.m. (check, however, at the Tourist Office, 10 Plaza Mayor, tel. 430-328, in Segovia the day before heading there). It is closed on Sunday.

This fortress, which is both foreboding and impressive, is a flamboyant example of the Mudéjar military style of architecture and, as such, is considered the most impressive example in the country. It was constructed in the latter part of the 1400s by Moors who had been sent up from Andalusia. It is an architectural pile of turrets and towers, battlemented perimeters, and a huge keep. In the keep you can see some Romanesque wood carving. To get there from Segovia, take the C605 in the direction of Arevalo. Once you pass Santa Maria la Real de Nieva, turn off to Coca at the road sign.

LA GRANJA: Homesick for France, the Bourbon kings created a miniature slice of Versailles in Castile, with the snow-capped Guadarrama mountains in the background. The founder of the Bourbon dynasty in Spain, Philip V, grandson of Louis XIV, was born at Versailles on December 19, 1683. For his own gardens and summer palace in Spain, he chose a modest name, La Granja, meaning grange or farmhouse (a small farm originally stood on the site). In time La Granja became Philip's mausoleum (he is buried here, along with the body of his second queen, Isabel de Franesio, in the Collegiate Church).

La Granja is richly stocked with paintings and antique furnishings, mostly Empire. It is mainly noted for its tapestries, many of which were based on Flemish designs (others on cartoons by Goya), made at the Royal Factory of Tapestries in Madrid.

However, in the gardens—studded with elms and chestnuts—remain the abiding attractions of La Granja, luring tourists from the hot streets of Madrid every year. If you come either on a Thursday, Saturday, or Sunday afternoon (May through October), you'll see the fountains spewing forth. Gods, goddesses, and nymphs—captured in stone—cavort beneath the waters.

The palace is open from 10 a.m. to 1:30 p.m. and 3 to 5 p.m., charging an admission of 300 pesetas ($2.10). The entrance to the gardens is free, except when the fountains are turned on; then you pay 60 pesetas (42¢) at 5:30 p.m. only for the privilege of strolling through.

Buses run throughout the day between Segovia and La Granja, a distance of seven miles. La Sepulvedana, 21 Ezequiel González, operates regular service (check at the Tourist Office in Segovia for schedules). From Madrid, La Sepulcedana (3 Emilio Carrerre) runs a bus, in summer, to La Granja by way of the Puerto de Navacerrada. It leaves Madrid at 9 a.m. and returns at 8 p.m.

LEAVING THE AREA: After visiting La Granja, you can head back to Madrid via **Puerto de Navacerrada** (15 miles away), perched at an altitude of more than 6,000 feet. This mountain pass, somewhat reminiscent of Austria, has for years been the most popular skiing resort for Madrileños, and is jammed on winter weekends.

5. Alcalá de Henares and El Pardo

It is a strange combination, but in less than a day you can visit El Pardo, the site of Franco's former palace, and Alcalá de Henares, a sadly neglected town that gave the world Cervantes and Catherine of Aragon, the unfortunate first wife of Henry VIII. Perhaps you'll want to visit Alcalá de Henares first—maybe have lunch there—then go to El Pardo later in the afternoon.

ALCALÁ DE HENARES: Time has been unkind to this ancient town, which once flourished with colleges and monasteries, even palaces. A university was founded here in the 15th century, and Alcalá became a cultural and intellectual center. But in the 1800s everything was shut down, and a blanket of gloom and provincialism settled over the town. Decay destroyed most of the old buildings, and the bloody Civil War didn't help either.

However, in the last handful of years Alcalá has begun to attract visitors who come out from Madrid for the day, mainly to see the birthplace of the creator of *Don Quixote,* Cervantes, who was born here in 1547. Who knows? The town may soon experience a much-overdue renaissance.

The main stopover, then, is the rebuilt **Casa de Cervantes,** on Calle Mayor, an interesting 16th-century Castilian house constructed around a beautiful little courtyard, with a wooden gallery supported by pillars with capitals in Renaissance style, plus an old well. The house, maintained by the Community of Madrid, is open from 10 a.m. to 2 p.m. and 4 to 7 p.m. (from 10 a.m. to 2 p.m. on Sunday). Closed Monday. Admission is 100 pesetas (70¢).

After visiting this shrine, you should see the university, which adjoins one of the most interesting regional restaurants in Spain. Lope de Vega, and many other famous Spaniards, studied at the university; you can see some of their names engraved in plaques in the examination room. The university has a façade of plateresque, a style of ornamentation popular in the 16th century.

Hostería del Estudiante, 3 Calle de los Colegios (tel. 888-03-30), is a remarkable example of a 15th-century Castilian inn, an attraction in its own right (in fact, many visitors drive up from Madrid just to eat here). If you arrive early, you can lounge in front of a 15-foot open fireplace during the cooler months. At other times you may welcome this inn as a cool respite from the burning sun of Castile. Oil lamps hang from the ceiling; pigskins are filled with the locally made wine, and rope-covered chairs and high-backed carved settees capture the spirit of the past.

The restaurant is run by the Tourist Bureau, and offers a huge three-course lunch or dinner for 2,000 pesetas ($14), including everything. The restaurant features regional specialties such as the cocido madrileño, the hearty stew of Madrid, or trout in the style of Navarre. To finish, try the cheese of La Mancha.

The food, although quite good, reflects a heavy Castilian hand. The restaurant is closed Christmas through January.

After lunch, you might want to walk through the cloisters (floodlit at night for after-dinner strolls).

EL PARDO: After your visit to Alcalá de Henares, you should have time left for an afternoon jaunt to El Pardo (not to be confused with the Prado Museum), which lies about eight miles north of Madrid on another road. (El Pardo is easily reached by frequent bus service from Madrid.) A lot of Spaniards died in and around here during the Civil War. Much of the town was destroyed during the famous advance toward University City. But there's no trace of destruction today—the country is sleepy and peaceful. During Franco's reign, El Pardo—and not the capital—was the seat of government.

Palacio de El Pardo

The palace (tel. 736-03-29), the residence of Franco until his death, was opened to the viewing public in August 1976. Almost overnight it became one of the most popular sights around Madrid, with more than 2,000 people daily going through 30 of its 100 rooms from 10 a.m. to 1 p.m. and 3:30 to 6:30 p.m. in summer; 10 a.m. to 1 p.m. and 3 to 6 p.m. in winter. Sunday hours are from 10 a.m. to 1 p.m., and the palace is closed on Tuesday. If you want to visit only the main palace, the admission is 200 pesetas ($1.40). However, for 300 pesetas ($2.10) you can also visit the Palacio de la Quinta and the Casita del Príncipe.

The palace's exterior is like a large French-style château, which does little to reveal the surprising grandeur inside. It has been a royal residence since medieval times. Over the years it has been furnished lavishly, mostly with Empire pieces, and it boasts an outstanding collection of Flemish and Spanish tapestries.

Franco took over in 1940. Perhaps as an imperial conceit, he had many small salons to screen visitors before they were admitted to the reception hall. The former dictator's ornate gilt throne reveals royal pretensions. Of particular interest are mementos left by the Franco family, including an extensive wardrobe; see especially ten wax dummies modeling Franco's most important state uniforms. The tour takes about 45 minutes.

Highlights include a Tapestry Room, its 18th-century collection lit by a glittering bronze-and-crystal chandelier. Visiting ministers were received here. In the Salon de Consejos, with its 19th-century coved ceiling, ministers would gather for conferences or Franco would preside at large family dinners. Tapestries were based on cartoons by Goya, Bayeu, Aguirre, and González Ruíz. The next room is the office where Franco received ambassadors. While seated at his elaborately decorated and bronze-trimmed desk, he received more than 70,000 people. His most prized possession here was a 15th-century sideboard that once belonged to Queen Isabella.

A passageway takes you to a once-private room with English furnishings, used as a library. Next is the Goya Tapestry Salon, once a general reception area, mainly for friends of the general's wife. In the family dining room to follow, only lunch was served. The walls are covered with silk embroidery, the fabric matched on the chairs. The room is decorated with 17th-century Flemish paintings.

Other salons include a room used for after-dinner coffee, with many personal family photographs; an oddly shaped music room with classic English furniture; a private, simple Gothic chapel, which was the former bedroom of Alfonso XII who died there in 1884. Generalísimo and Mrs. Franco prayed there daily. What follows is a four-room suite once used by Franco's daughter.

Her bedroom is painted entirely in raspberry pink. Franco's former bedroom, with its green silk walls, has twin beds. But during the dictator's long illness a hospital bed was substituted. Next comes the official salon for Mrs. Franco, with its Louis XIII–style furnishings and Oriental chandelier. Franco's private theater is in white, red, and gold—classic and well-designed, a family gathering point for Sunday night motion pictures. Finally, the rooms Franco reserved for his most important overnight guests are perhaps the most tastefully decorated in the palace, done in the Marie Antoinette style. Outside the palace chapel is the place where Franco's body lay in state.

In back of Franco's former palace is the **Casita del Príncipe** (Prince's Cottage), a small hunting-lodge kind of palace that was built during the reign of Charles III in the 18th century. It was actually ordered by his son, the prince, or probably more accurately by his strong-willed wife, who was noted for needing a hideaway or two (the one at Aranjuez was simply too far away for quick "sneak-aways" in the night). Designed by architect López Corona, the cottage is lavishly furnished, including such adornments as embroidered silk walls. Eight paintings by Lucas Jordan are displayed, embracing six mythological scenes, an *Adoration of the Kings,* and *The Triumph of the Virgin.* Many of the furnishings are in styles of Louis XV and Louis XVI, as well as Empire. The small palace keeps the same hours as the main palace.

The crown took over the **Palacio de la Quinta** in 1745. Up to then, it had been the property of the Duke of Arcos. You can visit its gardens and fountains and explore its elegant interior, where the Museo de Papeles Pintados is installed.

El Pardo means a very dark green, and the surrounding countryside lives up to its title. If possible, go to the top of the hill and soak up the views in all directions. There are many places in the town where you can sit outside and have a cool drink.

WHERE TO DINE: **La Marquesita,** 4 Avenida de la Guardia (tel. 736-03-77), is one of a group of competing restaurants on the main boulevard, with an interior dining room and tables set across the street under a canopy for al fresco meals. It's a summer delight to dine under shady trees, a winter pleasure to have a meal in front of the inside fireplace. The front room is turned over to a tasca, where diners traditionally order a Tío Pepe before their meal. All the elements are there to suggest a Castilian inn—the crude regional chairs at the tables, the hams hanging from the beamed ceilings, even a see-through kitchen.

If you want a large dinner, consider the set meal for 1,500 pesetas ($10.50), including wine, bread, and service. On the à la carte menu, the fish dishes are fresh, especially the trout in the style of Navarre and the grilled sole with potatoes. The most expensive items in the chef's repertoire are the roast suckling pig and tournedos. The paella de mariscos (shellfish) for two is a savory treat, as is the fish soup, a light meal. An average dinner, selected from the à la carte menu, will cost from 2,500 pesetas ($17.50).

6. Chinchon

You might want to drive from Alcalá to Toledo, bypassing Madrid and taking the N111 along a pleasant country road. About halfway there, you'll see signs advertising the Cuevas de Chinchon, a reference to this ancient town famous for its manufacture of Anis de Chinchon, an aniseed drink. Of course, many visitors come here, a distance of 32 miles southeast from Madrid, to visit the cuevas or caves, but Chinchon deserves a visit because of its many historical attractions.

The Plaza Mayor is the center of town (the cuevas lie up a hill), and on this square you can purchase bottles of the liqueur inexpensively. The Romans, the Visigoths, and the Arabs have all passed through Chinchon. One of its most famous citizens, the Duchess of Chinchon, was immortalized by Goya.

In Chinchon, which is officially classified as a city, you can wander at will through its steep and narrow streets, noting many houses with large bays and spacious carriageways. Chinchon Castle, seat of the Condes of Chinchon, is not open to the public, but can be viewed from outside. It dates from the 15th century. The most interesting church is called Nuestra Senora de la Asunción, dating from the 16th and 17th centuries and containing a painting attributed to Goya.

The Spanish government has made this city even more desirable as a sightseeing goal by opening the **Parador Nacional** (tel. 894-08-36), which was installed in a restored convent from the 17th century. The building, over its long history, also served as a jail house and a hall of justice. It was handsomely converted, lying in the heart of town and containing 38 bedrooms. These rent for 7,500 pesetas ($52.50) for a single, 9,000 pesetas ($63) for a double. A hallway walled with glass opens onto a lovely Castilian courtyard. Many amenities and facilities were installed, including a swimming pool and two bars. The gardener works hard to maintain the beautiful grounds. Guests just dropping in for lunch or dinner in a choice of two dining halls can enjoy a filling repast for 2,200 pesetas ($15.40).

A second major attraction is the **Mesón Cuevas del Vino,** 13 Benito Hortelano (tel. 894-02-06), which is known for its wine cellars. You can come here not only to sample the wine, following in the footsteps of such personages as Carmen Sevilla, but also to order lunch or dinner at a cost ranging from 1,800 pesetas ($12.60) and up.

7. Ávila

The ancient walled city of Ávila, 68 miles west of Madrid, is completely encircled by its preserved 11th-century walls, which are among the most important medieval relics in all of Europe. The city has been declared a National Monument, and there is little wonder why. The walls aren't the only attraction, however: Ávila was the birthplace of St. Teresa of Jesus, and has a number of age-worn Romanesque churches, Gothic palaces, and a fortified cathedral.

Perhaps you've seen the walls already—for that was no Hollywood-created city in the old Frank Sinatra film *The Pride and the Passion.* When the citizens of Ávila ceased to be afraid, they started to move outside the city and erected houses backed up against the wall—but that was long ago, and all of those shanties have been ripped down. It is possible to drive the entire length of the walls, roughly about 1½ miles.

In all, the walls have about 88 semicircular towers and more than 2,300 battlements. The walls, which took nine years to build, were completed right before the dawn of the 12th century.

Warning: I sounded a caution to visitors going to Segovia in the early spring, and I'll sound the same warning here. Wear warm clothes as it's cold at these altitudes.

GETTING THERE: Ávila is about a two-hour train ride from Madrid. The 8 a.m. train from Atocha Station, arriving in Ávila at 10:22 a.m., is recommended. There are later morning trains and afternoon departures as well.

The buses from Madrid to Ávila leave from 11 Paseo Florida (Metro: Norte), in front of the Norte railway station. For information, telephone 248-48-91.

THE SIGHTS: Ávila lays claim to being the highest city in Spain (3,708 feet above sea level). It has changed hands many times—Romans, Visigoths, Moors—but in all the history of this walled city, no one has become more linked to its spirit and legend than St. Teresa, who was born here in 1515. This Carmelite nun, instrumental in the defeat of the Reformation, was a mystic, given to trances in which she conjured up the vision of the devil and of angels sticking burning hot lances into her heart. She also wrote about them. She was severely attacked and criticized in her lifetime (once she was imprisoned in Toledo), and she founded a number of convents, as she opposed the so-called looseness of the Carmelite order. Many legends sprang up after her death, including the belief that a hand severed from her body could perform miracles. Souvenir collectors later made keepsakes of her remains. In 1622 she was canonized. It is said that she developed an intense antagonism toward Ávila because of the harsh treatment she received there. However, one of the city's most interesting sights is the . . .

Convent of St. Teresa

This 17th-century convent and neoclassical baroque church (tel. 21-10-30) grew up on the site of the birthplace of this most important saint. It contains a number of relics associated with her life, including a finger that belonged to her right hand. One of the most bizarre displays in the church is the glass-enclosed body of a monk. You figure out if it is a real body or a clever reproduction. Look for some fine sculpture by Gregorio Hernández. You can also see a little garden spot where tradition says the saint-to-be, Teresa, played with her brother, Rodrigo, when they were children. The church is open from 9:30 a.m. to 1 p.m. and 3:30 to 8 p.m. There is no charge.

The Cathedral

This is both a cathedral and a fortress. Built into the old ramparts of Ávila, it is cold and austere, bridging the gap between the Romanesque and the Gothic—and as such, enjoys a certain distinction in Spanish architecture. One local writer likened it to a granite mountain. However, the interior is among the most unusual in Spain, built of a mottled red-and-white stone.

As in most European cathedrals, Ávila's has lost the purity of its original design, giving way to new chapels and wings (one completely in the Renaissance mode). The apse was built right into the walls, forming a large tower with machicolations. A Dutch artist, Cornelius, designed the seats of the choir stalls in the Renaissance style, and the principal chapel holds a reredos showing the life of Christ by Pedro Berruguete, Juan de Borgoña, and Santa Cruz. In back of the chapel is the tomb of Bishop Alonso de Madrigal (called "El Tostado" or "the parched one," owing to its brownish complexion)—the work a masterpiece of Vasco de Zarza.

The **Museum of the Cathedral** contains a ceiling laminated with gold, a 15th-century triptych, a copy of an El Greco painting, as well as "grande" vestments and 15th-century song books. The *Great Custodia* is by Juan de Arfe (1572). Admission to the museum is 50 pesetas (35¢).

The cathedral is open from 10 a.m. to 1:30 p.m. and 3 to 7 p.m. in summer, including holidays (till 5 p.m. in winter).

The Basilica of St. Vincent

Outside the city walls, this Romanesque-Gothic church, in faded sandstone, is the most interesting in Ávila. It consists of a nave and a trio of apses of monumental size. Like its mother church, the cathedral, it bridges the gap between Romanesque and Gothic, encompassing styles from the 12th to the 14th centuries. On the southern portal, a cornice depicts the eternal struggle between good and evil. The western portal dates from the 13th century and contains excellent Romanesque carvings.

The interior houses the tomb of St. Vincent, martyred on this site in the 4th century. The medieval carvings on the tomb, depicting his torture and subsequent martyrdom, are fascinating. Charging 25 pesetas (18¢) for admission, the church is open from 10 a.m. to 1 p.m. and 4 to 6 p.m. On Sunday, the hours are 10:30 a.m. to noon.

Church and Monastery of St. Tomás

Also outside the city walls, this Gothic monastery was built in the 15th century. Once it was the headquarters of the feared Inquisition in Ávila. For three centuries it had the dubious distinction of housing the tomb of Torquemada, the first General Inquisitor, whose zeal and role in organizing the Inquisition made him a conspicuous figure in Spanish history. According to some authors, after the friars were expelled from the monastery in 1836, a mob of Torquemada-haters ransacked the tomb and burnt the remains somewhere outside the city walls, casting the ashes on the fields. However, no documentary proof has been produced to support this opinion. It is historically true that the Inquisitor's tomb was in the southern part of the present sacristy, but nothing is known with certainty about the final destiny of his remains.

Prince John, the only son of Ferdinand and Isabella, was also buried here, in a sumptuous sepulchre in the transept of the church. During the French invasion the tomb was profaned, and now there is only a magnificent empty crypt. Don't miss a visit to the **Royal Cloisters,** in some respects the most interesting architectural feature of the place. In the 16th century a university was established in the King's Cloister that lasted until the 19th century.

Santo Tomás may be visited from 9 a.m. to 1 p.m. and 4 to 7 p.m. The cost for both the monastery and the cloisters is 75 pesetas (53¢). You can also visit the **Museum of Far Eastern Art** in the upper part of the third cloister. It exhibits works of art and fine handcrafts from Vietnam, China, and Japan. For more information, telephone 22-04-00.

Carmelitas Descalzas de San José

The Monastery of Discalced (Barefoot) Carmelite Nuns, 4 Las Madres (tel. 22-21-27), also known as the Convento de las Madres (Convent of the Mothers), is the first one founded by St. Teresa. She started the Reform of Carmel in this place in 1562, founding the order with four nuns. Two churches are here, the primitive one where the first Carmelite nuns took the habit and a second built by Francisco de Mora, architect of King Philip III, after the saint's death. This is a beautiful structure where St. Teresa and some of her relatives and friends are buried. In a museum, you can see many relics of the saint, the most important being the clavicle that was connected to her left arm. The churches and museum are open from 10 a.m. to 1 p.m. and 4 to 7 p.m. daily. There is no charge to visit the churches, but admission to the museum is 10 pesetas (7¢), free on Monday.

At this point in our journey, that bell you hear ringing is for dinner.

WHERE TO EAT: **El Rastro,** 1 Plaza del Rastro (tel. 21-12-19), is an old Castilian inn built right into the 11th-century town wall. From time unknown it has been an inn, putting up travelers for the night and feeding them well on the local produce. At the "Slaughterhouse," the dishes are typically Castilian, with more attention paid to the proper preparation of local produce than to tricky culinary maneuvers. You can enjoy a fair meal for 1,600 pesetas ($11.20). However, you'll pay more if you order the casa's specialties, such as cordero asado. The one supreme dish in Ávila is tender white veal. The dessert specialties originally came from recipes developed by nuns in the convent. Try, for example, the yemas de Santa Teresa (St. Teresa's candied egg yolk).

Mesón El Sol, 25 Avenida 18 de Julio (tel. 22-12-66). Your conversation may be distracted by the odors wafting out of the kitchen of what is one of the best of the low-budget inns of Ávila. It's mainly known for its food, which, although moderately priced, is served with dignity and style. Full meals, which could include seafood soup, fried hake, veal with garlic, and house-style flan, usually cost from 1,000 pesetas ($7). The establishment also rents out 15 simply furnished rooms at the Hotel Santa Teresa, ranging in price from 2,200 pesetas ($15.40) in a single to 3,000 pesetas ($21) in a double.

STAYING OVERNIGHT: Ávila is a summer resort. From its lofty plateau as Spain's highest city, it is cool in the hot months, and in Castile this is an attraction.

The hotels are few in number, comfortable without being spectacular—that is, all except the new parador, which is reason enough to make the trip to Ávila, even if, like Jericho, its walls came tumbling down. There is, as well, the four-star Palacio Valderrábanos. *Warning:* The Spanish book nearly all the hotel space in July and August, and it is hard to get an accommodation then without a reservation.

Parador Nacionale Raimundo de Borgoña, 16 Marqués de Canales de Chozas (tel. 21-13-40), is another triumph among the Spanish paradors. Within the ancient walls, skilled craftspeople have constructed an old-style inn, using salvaged stones, tiles, pillars, and timbers. The hotel is graced with a dignified entranceway for automobiles, and most of its public lounges open onto a central courtyard with an inner row of old columns. The furnishings are tastefully appropriate: tall stone fireplaces, highly polished tile floors, old chests, leather armchairs, paintings, and discreet sculpture. The price of the luxurious double bedrooms with private baths is 8,000 pesetas ($56) a night. Singles pay 6,600 pesetas ($46.20). The dining room, with its leaded-glass windows opening onto a terraced garden, serves good-tasting Castilian dishes. A large three-course dinner is wheeled out for 2,000 pesetas ($14).

If the parador is booked, try your luck at the **Hotel Reina Isabel,** 17 Avenida de José Antonio (tel. 22-02-00), once the most preferred choice in town—until the opening of the government parador. Near the railway station, outside the city walls, it charges 3,500 pesetas ($24.50) for a double with private bath. The most expensive singles with private bath cost 1,800 pesetas ($12.60). A continental breakfast is additional. The Reina Isabel, in spite of its regal name, is a good, substantial middle-class hotel—suitable for a night's stay.

Hotel Jardín, 38 San Segundo (tel. 21-10-74), has, as its name indicates, a small garden (in front). In this town of narrow streets and stone buildings, it is refreshing to see a little greenery. The Jardín is in a small park-like area near one of the old city gates. For 2,300 pesetas ($16.10), a couple can stay here in a clean double room with private bath. The other doubles, with less plumbing, are even more inexpensive at 1,800 pesetas ($12.60). Singles peak at 1,500 pesetas ($10.50) without bath. The accommodations are utilitarian, not the least bit fancy. A continental breakfast is extra. Meals are served in a skylit dining room: 800 pesetas ($5.60) for either lunch or dinner.

El Rastro, 1 Plaza del Rastro (tel. 21-12-19), is the best choice for the bargain hunter. The Rastro is my dining recommendation too, but few tourists know that they can spend the night at this old Castilian inn built right into the city wall. A double room with a private bath comes to only 2,000 pesetas ($14) a night. But if you're satisfied with a most basic, but clean, double room with a water basin—and the use of the bathroom in the corridor—then the rate for two is only 1,800 pesetas ($12.60) a night. For as little as 1,300 pesetas ($9.10), you can have a single room with water basin only. A continental breakfast costs extra.

Chapter V

CITIES OF THE HEARTLAND

1. Salamanca
2. Zamora
3. León
4. Valladolid
5. Burgos
6. Cuenca

FROM THE ARID PLAINS of Old Castile and the kingdom of León (and from Aragón) emerged the austere people who were to unify, and ultimately dominate, all of Spain. Modern Spain was conceived when Isabella of Castile married Ferdinand of Aragón on October 19, 1469. Five years later she was proclaimed Queen of Castile and of León. The chasing of the Moors from Granada, the conquest of all of Spain, the sailing of Columbus to America—all this would in time transpire because of these Catholic monarchs.

This proud and highly moral queen and her unscrupulous husband inherited a land largely treeless, with golden-brown plains. From this they fashioned an empire whose influence was to extend not only over all Spain, but throughout Europe and to the New World. The power once held by Old Castile shifted long ago to Madrid, but there have remained many reminders of a fabulous past.

The ancient kingdom of León once embraced the first three cities we are slated to visit: **Salamanca, Zamora,** and the provincial capital of **León.** Eventually this kingdom was annexed to the growing might of Castile. The district has been called the most castle-rich part of Spain. Walls of defense also grew up around the cities, particularly those near the Portuguese border, Salamanca and Zamora, although the walls at Ávila are the only well-preserved ones left.

In Old Castile we'll visit the inland provincial capital of **Vallodolid.** It was here that a broken-hearted Columbus died on May 19, 1506. On a happier day, Isabella married Ferdinand in this city. From there we journey to **Burgos,** once the capital of Old Castile. In **Vivar,** a small town near here, arose El Cid, Spain's greatest national hero. The Campeador was later to conquer the Moorish kingdom of Valencia.

Finally, we'll go to **Cuenca** in New Castile. Cuenca, of course, will not be visited because of any historical significance, but because it is an isolated, geographic freak (as you will soon discover).

1. Salamanca

This ancient university city is one of the most beautiful of Europe. It has passed its period of glory, but wears its fall from grace and prestige handsomely. Its fame began in the early 1200s when Alfonso IX founded a university here.

Today it is a well-preserved city, with many colleges that once attracted scholars from all over Europe plus turreted palaces, faded convents, and Romanesque churches. Great men have crossed the ancient Roman bridge that spans the Tormes, one of the routes leading into the city. Columbus came this way seeking—but not finding—support for his dreams. In this century, the Basque Unamuno, Spain's greatest scholar, spoke out against the actions of both the Nationalists and Republicans in 1936, but his voice was drowned by the clash of the Civil War. Broken and defeated, he died that year in Salamanca.

Now, in a more enlightened Spain, a large statue of Unamuno stands in one of the squares in the old part of town.

THE SIGHTS: After much visiting and eliminating, I have compiled the following list of "The Top Eight." All of them could be visited on one very busy day. I'll begin with . . .

The University

This, the oldest university in Spain, was the chief source of Salamanca's former glory. At one time it was considered the greatest university in Europe. In front of the plateresque façade of the building, a statue honors a Hebrew scholar, Fray Luís de León, who is connected with the university's best known legend. Once arrested on suspicion of being a heretic, Fray Luís was away for five years before he was finally cleared. When he returned, he began his first lecture (so the story goes): "As I was saying yesterday. . . ."

Inside this old building you can visit, first, the 16th-century classroom, cluttered with crude wooden benches. Light is practically nowhere to be seen. The remains of Fray Luís are kept in the chapel, which is worth a visit. The library is upstairs, but it cannot be visited. The university can be visited from 9:30 a.m. to 1:30 p.m. and 4 to 7 p.m. In winter, the afternoon hours are 4 to 6 p.m. In summer it is open on Sunday from 10 a.m. to 1 p.m. Admission is 75 pesetas (53¢).

The New Cathedral (Cathedral Nueva)

One would hesitate to call this a new cathedral at all—its origins, in fact, go back to 1513. It took so long to build a cathedral in those days (this one was completed in 1733) that the edifice represents many styles, but, roughly, it could be classified as late Gothic, although baroque and plateresque features are most evident. Churriguera with his rococo style also dabbled in this melting pot of architecture. The building has a grandly beautiful façade: gold on beige sandstone. It has elegant chapels, the best decorated dome in Spain, and bas-relief columns that look like a palm-tree cluster. Unfortunately, its stained glass is severely damaged. It doesn't cost anything to visit the cathedral, and you may do so from 10 a.m. till 1 p.m. and 3:30 till 6:30 p.m. (in winter, however, it closes at 5 p.m.).

The Old Cathedral (Cathedral Vieja)

Adjoining the new cathedral is this older version, which was begun in the 12th century, predating the university. Its simplicity is in dramatic contrast to the ornamentation of its younger but bigger sister. It is a Spanish version of Romanesque. Be sure to see the huge stone that once fell on a workman's head, but didn't kill him, causing the townspeople to claim it as a miracle. After inspecting the interior of the cathedral, venture forth into the enclosed cloisters with their Gothic-style tombs of long-forgotten bishops. The chapels here are of special architectural interest. The old cathedral, which keeps the same hours as the new one, charges 75 pesetas (53¢) for admission.

Casa de las Conchas

The restored 15th-century House of Shells was built by a doctor. The focal point of interest is its façade of simulated scallop shells, which creates a dramatic effect. The house is owned by Count Santa Coloma of Madrid and Seville. He rents his casa to the city of Salamanca for the symbolic sum of one peseta a year. In the patio, you can see the sculptured lions' heads.

Museo Provincial de Bellas Artes

The **Casa de los Doctores de la Reina,** 2 Patio de Escuelas, was built in the late 15th century by Fernándo Alvarez Abarca, physician to Queen Isabella. Along with the Casa de las Conchas, it is one of the most representative examples in existence of the Spanish plateresque style. The Fine Arts Museum is housed here, with a selection of paintings and sculptures ranging from the 15th to the 20th centuries. Hours from July 1 to September 30 are 9 a.m. to 2 p.m. On Sunday it opens at 10 a.m. During the off-season it is open from 10 a.m. to 2 p.m. and 4 to 6 p.m.

Convent of San Esteban

Few will have the time to visit all the old churches of Salamanca, but if you tour this one, you will have had the best. This edifice competes with the cathedral in magnificence—notably in its golden-brown plateresque façade. The late-Gothic church was built in the 16th century. Inside, José de Churriguera created a six-columned and garlanded high altar that is one of the greatest art treasures of Salamanca. The Gothic cloisters are open from 9:30 a.m. to 1 p.m. and 4 to 7:30 p.m., charging 50 pesetas (35¢) for admission.

Las Dueñas Convento

Diagonally across from San Esteban is one of the most visited sights of Salamanca, the convent of Las Dueñas, Plaza Concilio de Trento (tel. 21-54-42). Only the cloisters, dating from the 16th century, are open to the public, and these can be visited from 10 a.m. to 1 p.m. and 4 to 7 p.m. for an admission of 50 pesetas (35¢). You have a climb to the upper gallery for a close inspection of the carved capitals, which are covered, as one reader put it, "with demons and dragons, saints and sinners, and animals of every description." Some of the so-called saints and sinners are from the pages of *The Divine Comedy.* There is also a portrait of Dante.

The Plaza Mayor

This square is widely acclaimed as the most beautiful public plaza in all of Spain. It has enjoyed this reputation for a very long time, and I have no desire to dispute or detract from it. The plaza represents the 18th-century Spanish baroque style. No trip to the university city is complete unless at some point in your adventure you come here to walk through the arcaded shops and feast your eyes on the honey-colored buildings. After this inspection, you can understand why the Plaza Mayor (Town Square) is such an integral part of Spanish life.

STAYING OVERNIGHT: **Parador Nacional de Salamanca,** 2 Teso de la Feria (tel. 22-87-00), occupies a dramatically modern building set at the crest of a low hill just across the river from the center of the old city. Its modern façade looks a bit like a cluster of space-age town houses built like a self-contained vacation village near an ancient stone bridge crossing the Río Tormes. Inside, subtly contrasting shades of polished stone accent the dozens of contemporary paintings and leather armchairs of the public areas. Each of the well-furnished and comfortable bedrooms, 108 in all, contains a mirador-style balcony, a mini-bar, a private bathroom, air conditioning, and two or three framed lithographs. Singles cost 6,600 pesetas ($46.20); doubles, 8,000 pesetas ($56). Meals in the dining room go for 2,000 pesetas ($14). On the premises are a flowering garden, a parking garage, and an outdoor swimming pool.

The **Hotel Alfonso X,** 64 Toro (tel. 21-44-01), is attached in Siamese fashion to its more expensive sister, the Monterrey. Centrally positioned, about a four-minute walk from the Plaza Mayor, the Alfonso X offers a total of 66 rooms, each with private bath. For a double, the price is 6,500 pesetas ($45.50) nightly; it's 5,500 pesetas ($38.50) in a single. An added bonus—you can enjoy the facilities of the better equipped Monterrey, especially its outside terrace and open-air swimming pool, ideal for summer splashes. There's no restaurant, and breakfast costs extra.

Hotel Clavero, 21 Consuelo (tel. 21-81-08), is a good little modernized hotel near the 15th-century Torre del Clavero, a landmark tower of Salamanca. The hotel's location is top-notch, within walking distance of most of the city's major monuments. It's usually quiet and peaceful around here, and the hotel lies just off a small tree-decked plaza. A recent modernization job was carried out with reasonable skill, and the bedrooms are tidy, with suitable furnishings, plus a sprinkling of antique reproductions. For a double with private bath, you pay 3,500 pesetas ($24.50). Singles without bath cost 2,000 pesetas ($14). Dinner costs 1,000 pesetas ($7).

Las Torres is a small (29 rooms) hotel two flights up at 26 Plaza Mayor (tel. 21-21-00), which combines good comfort, low prices, and an unbeatable position. If you're lucky enough to get one of the rooms overlooking the Plaza Mayor, you're in for a treat indeed. A double with bath goes for 2,800 pesetas ($12.60). A continental breakfast is extra. Downstairs is a large cafeteria bustling with activity in the evening. A lunch or dinner costs 850 pesetas ($5.95).

The upcoming recommendations hardly qualify as hostales, much less hotels, but they are recommendable to those seeking to keep costs bone-trimmed in Salamanca without sacrificing either cleanliness or comfort.

Mindanao, 2 Paseo de San Vicente (tel. 23-37-45), rents out 29 simply furnished bedrooms with a minimum of plumbing. But the welcome is nice, and I recently encountered some lovely Spanish families visiting their offspring at the university. A single costs only 1,000 pesetas ($7), and a double rents for 2,200 pesetas ($15.40). You can also take your meals here. The portions are plentiful, a dinner costing from 750 pesetas ($5.25).

Also suitable is **Los Infantes,** 125 Paseo de la Estación (tel. 25-28-44), which is a breakfast-only place and much smaller than the Mindanao. It rents out 14 rather basic but clean accommodations at prices going from 1,800 pesetas ($12.60) in a single to 3,000 pesetas ($21) in a double, which makes it one of the better bargains of Salamanca.

Hostal Laguna, 13 Consuelo (tel. 21-87-06). Its location within the old city, about two blocks south of the Plaza Mayor and across from the Clavero Tower, is one of this simple hotel's finest virtues. Its three-story façade, dotted with iron balustrades, shelters an unpretentious handful of double rooms which, depending on their plumbing, range from 1,800 pesetas ($12.60) to 2,300 pesetas ($16.10).

WHERE TO EAT: **Candil Nuevo,** 1 Plaza de la Reina (tel. 21-90-27), puts the emphasis on quality Castilian cuisine—and the portions aren't skimpy either. Its commendable and recommendable dinner, 1,200 pesetas ($8.40), is served complete with bread and wine, plus service. The fresh-tasting fish dishes always come as a surprise in inland Salamanca. Candil is like a bodega, in the típico tavern sense, complete with stuffed bull's head. The roast suckling pig with parsley in its mouth spreads the word that the food is good. Most à la carte bills range from 3,000 pesetas ($21).

In addition, let's sample the wares at **El Mesón,** 10 Plaza Poeta Iglesias (tel. 21-72-22), opposite the Gran Hotel near the Plaza Mayor. One of the finest restaurants in the city, El Mesón serves good Spanish cooking in an inviting atmosphere. The set meal for 1,200 pesetas ($8.40) might include a choice of clam soup or gazpacho, followed by chicken cooked in its own juice or a breaded veal cutlet, and finally, fruit or flan, plus bread, wine, and service. The average à la carte bill is 1,400 pesetas ($9.80) to 2,800 pesetas ($19.60). Happy news: The Mesón is air-conditioned. It is closed in November.

Río de la Plata, 1 Plaza del Peso (tel. 21-90-05), is efficiently directed by the brother-sister team of Rafael (in the dining room) and Paulina (the chef). Together, they've made their centrally located restaurant one of the most desirable places in town. Using the freshest ingredients, the kitchens prepare versions of a traditional cocida castellana, house-style sole, roasted baby goat, many varieties of fish, and pungent rows of sausages. The napery is crisply ironed, and service is usually impeccable. Full meals begin at 1,800 pesetas ($12.60). The establishment is open for lunch and dinner daily except Monday and in July.

A whole slew of inexpensive restaurants can be found in the old part of town. Thus, opposite the Casa de las Conchas is **Las Conchas,** 2 Rue Antigua (tel. 21-53-94), with a cubierto for 650 pesetas ($4.55). Your first course is likely to be a sopa de mariscos (shellfish soup), followed by hake prepared in various ways.

If it's a hot day in Salamanca and you want what everybody else in the Plaza Mayor is drinking, order *leche helado*. It's an icy milkshake tasting of vanilla and almond—very refreshing and not too filling.

AFTER DARK: **La Coquette** (tel. 20-00-43) is the most recent investment of city entrepreneur José Montes, who did everything he could to create an impressive decor for this popular disco. All of it can be enjoyed for the price of a drink, around 300 pesetas ($2.10).

María (tel. 23-58-04), under the same management as La Coquette, draws a fashionable crowd of people who come to see and be seen amid the tasteful surroundings. Drinks begin at 300 pesetas ($2.10).

Rojo y Negro (tel. 21-88-94) is completely covered, bullfighter's style, in shades of red and black. The establishment, in addition to containing a disco, also has a piano bar and a café, all of which makes it one of the city's most complete entertainment facilities. It shuts down at 4:30 a.m., and your final tab for the evening is always more than you expect. Drinks cost from 300 pesetas ($2.10).

A SIDE TRIP TO CIUDAD RODRIGO: On the way to Portugal, Ciudad Rodrigo makes an ideal stopover, and it's a good day trip from Salamanca if you're based there. The ancient walled town is 54 miles from Salamanca.

Flanking its narrow streets are town houses from the 16th and 17th centuries, built by followers of the "Conquistadors." The cathedral dates from the 12th century, with some fine woodwork in the chancel by Rodrigo Aleman. The Plaza Mayor is a showpiece of 17th century architecture.

Installed in a 15th-century fortress is one of the handsomest paradors in

Spain, the **Parador Nacional Enrique II,** 1 Plaza del Castillo (tel. 46-01-50). The entrance is Gothic and bears the royal coat of arms and a plaque in Gothic letters. It offers 28 beautifully furnished rooms, doubles with private bath costing from 8,500 pesetas ($59.50). Singles are rented for the nightly rate of 7,000 pesetas ($49). A complete lunch or dinner costs from 2,000 pesetas ($14). The food is well prepared, and the service is friendly and polite. Facilities include a garden, central heating, air conditioning in the lounges and dining room, a garden, a foreign exchange, and a phone in every bedroom.

Hotel Conde Rodrigo, 9 Plaza de San Salvador (tel. 46-14-08). Its location inside the monumental heart of the city is one of this two-star hotel's strongest advantages. Behind thick and very old walls of chiseled stone are about three dozen simple but comfortable bedrooms whose quality has been praised by several readers. Each accommodation includes a private bathroom and mini-bar, plus a bouquet of thoughtful extras. Singles cost 4,000 pesetas ($28); doubles, 5,200 pesetas ($36.40). Full meals in the hotel's popular restaurant go for 1,500 pesetas ($10.50).

From Salamanca, we now head to Zamora, about 40 miles to the north. There is daily bus service from Salamanca's bus station at 27 Avenida Héroes de Brunete. Inquire at the Tourist Bureau for the exact time of departure. Some Zamora-bound trains also leave from Salamanca.

2. Zamora

Little known by tourists, Zamora (pronounced "tha-mora") is a most representative city of Old Castile. A blend of the old and the new, it has traces of its ancient city wall, yet is quite modern and commercial in parts. Capital of Zamora province, the frontier medieval city rises up starkly on the Castile flatlands, a reminder of life swept by, of conquering monarchs and forgotten kingdoms.

This is another city in which you're advised to walk and explore on your own. Stroll along the arcaded main square, walk across the arched Roman bridge built in the 1300s, pass by the decaying Romanesque churches. The river Duero flows peacefully by, and toward sunset it reflects the glow from the honey-colored stone buildings.

The one building that should be viewed from the interior is the 12th-century **cathedral.** Here, in this edifice topped by a gold-and-white Oriental-looking dome, you'll find rich hangings, interesting chapels, two 15th-century Mudéjar pulpits, and intricately carved choir stalls depicting religious figures on their backs. Later architectural styles, including Gothic, have been added to the original Romanesque features, but this indiscriminate mixing and blending of periods is typical of Spanish cathedrals—as you've probably noticed by now.

WHERE TO STAY AND EAT: Since Zamora is not on the main tourist route, its hotel and restaurant situation is sadly behind the times. But that has begun to change, especially since the opening of the following recommendation:

The **Parador Nacional Condes de Alba y Aliste,** 1 Plaza de Cánovas (tel. 51-44-97), is a government-owned and -run four-star parador. The tourist traffic didn't merit a large place in remote Zamora, so the planners wisely kept the rooms down to 19—each, of course, with private bath.

This magnificent parador, one of the most impressive in Spain, is right in the heart of the old part of Zamora, two blocks away from the Plaza Mayor. It is housed in a sumptuous old palace formerly belonging to the counts of Alba y Aliste, who built it in the late Middle Ages on the site of the Alcazaba. The palace was ordered by Enrique de Mendoza, first count and the uncle of King Ferdinand II of Aragon and Castile. The mansion was rebuilt in the 16th century. The parador reminds one of the New York Cloisters, with its splendid armor, antique furniture, tapestries, and old clocks. There is a large inner patio with a well in it, which is closed off by glass partitions in the winter. The lounges and public rooms have all been splendidly furnished with period pieces, carpets, comfortable chairs, plants, wood paneling, fireplaces, old mirrors, and chests, and no cluttering. The dining room is also furnished in what might be termed sumptuous rusticity, and provides a view of the swimming pool and surrounding countryside. There's also a cozy wood-paneled bar (open 12:30 to 11 p.m.). Doubles cost from 8,500 pesetas ($59.50); singles go for 7,000 pesetas ($49). A continental breakfast is extra. You can order a dinner for 2,000 pesetas ($14).

Cuatro Naciones (Four Nations), 7 Avenida de José Antonio (tel. 51-22-75), is one of the leading hotels in town, granted two stars by the government. Relatively small (40 rooms), it offers a double with complete private bath for 4,000 pesetas ($28). The best single rooms with private showers go for 2,900 pesetas ($20.30). The furnishings aren't inviting enough for more than an overnight stay, but they are adequate and comfortable, and many of the rooms are spacious. The food is also quite presentable, a complete luncheon or dinner costing 950 pesetas ($6.65).

If you're looking for a bargain, and you don't mind a few inconveniences, **the Chiqui,** 2 Benavente (tel. 51-14-80), is a very simple second-floor pension. It rents out only ten basic rooms, costing from 1,800 pesetas ($12.60) in a single, the tariff rising to 2,200 pesetas ($15.40) in a double. Only breakfast is served.

You might also try another hostal in the same building, the **Toary,** 2 Benavente (tel. 51-37-02), a 12-room, third-floor hostal. Here the simply furnished doubles rent for 2,400 pesetas ($16.80), a fine bargain. There is no restaurant, and for breakfast you'll have to go to a local café. But one thing is certain: you'll not be overcharged.

If you don't want to eat at either a main hotel or the parador, you'll find a number of regional restaurants, patronized mostly by the locals, serving fair and reasonably priced food.

Restaurant Paris, 14 Avenida de Portugal (tel. 51-43-25), is an elegantly decorated and air-conditioned restaurant where the affluent and sophisticated clientele seems to appreciate the drinks made by the polite barman almost as much as they do the well-prepared specialties. The establishment is known for its fish dishes, which often are made with a regionally inspired twist. Specialties include vichyssoise, Zamora-style clams, and shrimp and crayfish dishes. Meals range from 1,800 pesetas ($12.60) to 2,500 pesetas ($17.50).

Restaurant Serafin, 2 Plaza Maestro Haedo (tel. 51-43-16), offers an air-conditioned haven with an attractive bar for a relaxing stopover away from the sun. The menu specialties in this regionally inspired modern locale usually change with the seasons, but might, during your visit, include seafood soup Serafin, paella, fried hake, Iberian ham, and a savory form of cocido (stew). Full meals range from 1,500 pesetas ($10.50) to 2,800 pesetas ($19.60).

AFTER DARK: In all of Zamora, the street with the densest ratio of bars per square foot is the **Calle Los Herreros** or the "Calle de Vinos," which contains about 16 of them. Each is willing to accommodate a stranger for a quick drink of wine or beer and a selection of tapas. Each bar-going resident of Zamora has his or her particular favorite, and perhaps you'll discover yours. The most popular bars are the **Emilio, Los Angeles,** and the **Cooperativa.**

3. León

Once this was the leading city of Christian Spain. The old cathedral town was also the capital of the kingdom of the same name, a centuries-old empire that began to decline when it was united with Castile. León today is a sort of dividing point between the last remnants of Old Castile and the northwestern routes of Galicia. The principal interest in León focuses on the stained-glass windows of the cathedral, one of the most spectacular sights in Spain.

THE SIGHTS: Like most Spanish cities, León is divided into an old and a new quarter. The modern, commercialized León holds little interest (Papa H hated it), but the old quarter is well worth the visit.

The Cathedral

This 13th-century, early Gothic cathedral at the Plaza de Regla is called **Santa María de Regla.** Its cloisters, towers, flying buttresses—the usual architectural elements that one looks for in a cathedral—are virtually ignored, as one stands in awe of the yards of preserved stained-glass windows. To see a sunset through a rose window here is like watching the cathedral go up in incredibly beautiful flames. There are some 125 windows (plus 57 oculi) in all, taking up about 13,000 square feet. They weigh so much that they have threatened the walls of the cathedral. The oldest of the stained glass dates from the 13th century. Look for an illustration of the entombment depicted on a 15th-century altarpiece in the *capilla mayor,* and a Renaissance *trascoro* by Juan de Badajoz.

If possible, schedule time for a visit to the cloisters; 100 pesetas (70¢) for admission, and open from 9 a.m. to 1:30 p.m. and 4 to 7 p.m. (it opens at 11 a.m. in winter, closing at 5 p.m.), closed on Sunday afternoon. The nave dates in part from the 13th and 14th centuries, and the vaulting came much later, which explains why it is in a Renaissance style. You can see some faded frescoes, along with both Romanesque and Gothic tombs. After you visit here, you may want to see the second major sight in town . . .

The Royal Pantheon of St. Isidor

Here the flower of Spanish Romanesque blooms fully. The church was dedicated to San Isidoro de Sevilla in 1063, and contains as many as 23 tombs of Leonese kings. The pantheon marked the beginning of Romanesque art in León and Castile. It was mainly built in the 11th century, later embellished by the craftsmen and artists employed by Ferdinand I. The columns are magnificent, the capitals splendidly decorated. Covering the vaults are murals from the 12th century. See especially the ornate architecture of the southern portal and the central nave, as well as two portals at either end of the lateral naves.

Ferdinand I ordered that a new Romanesque church be erected on the foundations of a church built by Alphonsus V. Its consecration was to tie in with the arrival of the body of its patron saint from Seville. Unique in Spain, the **Treasury** holds such rare finds as a 10th-century Scandinavian ivory, an 11th-century chalice decorated with chalcedony, as well as an important collection of Oriental cloths from the 10th to the 12th centuries.

The **Library** alone contains many ancient manuscripts and rare books, including a Book of Job from 951 and a Visigothic Bible from the same period, as well as an 1162 Bible, plus dozens of miniatures.

The attractions may be visited in summer from 9 a.m. to 2 p.m. and 3:30 to 7:30 p.m. (in winter from 10 a.m. to 1:30 p.m. and 4 to 6:30 p.m.), for a 150-peseta ($1.05) admission fee. Closed on Sunday afternoon and Monday. For information, telephone 22-96-08.

For the third major sightseeing attraction of León, refer to the **Hotel de San Marcos,** below.

An Excursion to the Valporquero Cave

The most highly rated excursion in the environs of León, a distance of 26 miles north, is to the Cueva de Valporquero, which is possible to visit from mid-May until the end of October. Admission is 200 pesetas ($1.40), and the exploration takes at least an hour. Look for a signpost marking the trail near the Hotel San Marcos. The ride there takes about an hour or more, and the highway passes through a narrow gorge. The last part of the trip, a distance of several miles, is on a twisting, steep mountain road, so exercise caution.

Once there, you'll discover that the cave is still in formation. Nature has been working on it for centuries by underground streams. It's wise to wear hiking clothing. Once inside, be prepared for temperatures of 45° F. Only the hearty should explore inside the cave. Even though you are guided through, there are many steep inclines, a lot of slippery steps, and damp clay paths. Look for a stalactite "star" hanging from the ceiling. At the end of the adventure, you are taken along a narrow passage, about 5,000 feet in length, which has been tunneled out by underground waters.

STAYING OVERNIGHT: The **Hotel de San Marcos,** 7 Plaza de San Marcos (tel. 23-73-00), is a 16th-century former monastery, a top tourist attraction of León, lying on the east bank of the Bernesga River behind its celebrated plateresque façade. The Spanish government, at great expense, remodeled it, installing such luxury trappings as private baths, extravagant and authentic antiques, and quality reproductions. The old "hostal" used to put up pilgrims bound for Santiago de Compostela. It still does today—but not for the same amount of money the 17th-century pilgrims paid. A sumptuous double room with private bath goes for 12,000 pesetas ($84). Singles cost 7,500 pesetas ($52.50). The price of a complete dinner here runs to 2,200 pesetas ($15.40).

Even if you're not a guest of this five-star hotel, you can still visit it, as it contains both a church, its façade decorated with scallop shells, and an archeological museum. The museum is open from 10 a.m. to 2 p.m. and from 4 to 6 p.m. (in summer, until 8 p.m.). It is closed Sunday afternoon, otherwise charging 100 pesetas (70¢) for admission. The most stunning exhibit in the museum is the Crucifix of Carrizo, a Romanesque ivory from the 11th century.

Hotel Quindós, 24 Avenida José Antonio (tel. 23-62-00), is a rather functional hotel whose angularity has been tastefully relieved with examples of modern paintings, which enhance the establishment considerably. It lies about three streets south of the Plaza de San Marcos, in a commercial district in the center of town. The accommodations in the 96 bedrooms are sometimes better than those in more expensive hotels nearby. Singles rent for 3,600 pesetas ($25.30), while doubles cost from 4,500 pesetas ($31.50) per day.

The cheapest accommodation in León that you can stay at comfortably is the no-frills **Guzmán El Bueno,** 6 López Castrillón (tel. 23-64-12), a second-floor boarding house. The owner offers 29 simply furnished bedrooms, costing from 1,200 pesetas ($8.40) in a single and 1,900 pesetas ($13.30) in a double. The location is most central.

WHERE TO EAT: **Bodega Regia,** 8 Plaza San Martín (tel. 25-41-00). A loud-talking drinking crowd usually fills up the front room of this attractive restaurant in a building dating from the 12th century. In the oldest section of León, the establishment is decorated with Castilian artifacts, all of which have been carefully arranged by the owners, Marcos Vidal and his wife. A separate section is more sedate and is devoted to the consumption of such regional specialties as León garlic soup along with beef and veal dishes. Full meals range from 1,400 pesetas ($9.80) to 2,400 pesetas ($16.80) and are served daily except Sunday evening, the first two weeks of September, and the last two weeks of February.

Patricio, 24 Condesa de Sagasta (tel. 24-16-51), lies outside the monumental center of León, within a cluster of modern buildings. That doesn't prevent many local residents from trekking into its sparkling and air-conditioned interior. Patricio Turienzo, the owner, supervises the preparation of the fresh cuisine based on local recipes, with updated and sometimes fanciful twists. You might enjoy his gratin of shrimp, his fish concoctions, and his array of flavorful beef, pork, and chicken dishes. Full meals cost from 1,500 pesetas ($10.50) and are served at lunch and dinner every day except Sunday evening and Monday.

Casa Pozo, 15 Plaza San Marcelo (tel. 22-30-39). Gabriel del Pozo operates his namesake with all the flair that his central location deserves. What you'll find is an unpretentious restaurant which seems to have become a favorite with neighborhood residents who appreciate its clean napery, its unassuming style, and its flavorful cuisine. Menu specialties are made from fresh ingredients, including a flavorful combination of fresh peas with salty ham, shrimp with asparagus, roast pork or lamb laden with herbs and spices, and a delicate version of smothered sole known as estofado. Full meals cost from 1,500 pesetas ($10.50) and are served daily except Sunday, during the first two weeks of July, and for two weeks around the Christmas holidays.

AFTER DARK: The **Barrio Humedo,** Plaza San Martín, is one of the liveliest places in the city. It contains many regional restaurants, some serving only tapas and wine. A good example is **El Racimo de Oro,** 11 Plaza San Martín, where all the standard specialties are served amid a jostling crowd of jovial citizens.

Another choice would be the **Café Graja Victoria,** 25 Generalíssimo Franco (tel. 25-64-24), which serves tapas, traditional Spanish food, and drinks in a family-run ambience that is one of the most solidly established in town.

While the world is still rosy from the reflection of the stained glass in León, our tour of Old Castile moves to another provincial capital, that of . . .

4. Valladolid

From the 13th century until its eventual decay in the early 17th century, Valladolid was the on-again, off-again center of royalty (it saw the wedding of Isabella and Ferdinand, as was mentioned, and the birth of Philip II). Men who would one day be called saints came from Valladolid. Dreamers and philosophers searched to find reality, or escape it, here.

And, finally, came explorers, notably one named Columbus, who died here on May 19, 1506, broken in spirit and body. He was dead two years after the demise of his former patron, Isabella, and one year following the refusal of Ferdinand to reinstate him as a governor of the Indies. The death of Columbus somehow seems symbolic of Valladolid . . . of something lost, the golden opportunity in the New World that went astray, as Spain pursued short-sighted goals instead of long-term policies.

Valladolid lies in the heart of Old Castile, some 125 miles from Madrid. It is harshly cold in winter, harshly hot in summer.

Valladolid, a city that has seen greater days, is now living—perhaps grudgingly—with the realities of the present. Cervantes, Columbus, Philip II, the Catholic kings, are gone forever. After centuries of decline, the city is finding, not renewed glory, but greater economic health in such products as flour and ironware, and a huge Renault factory.

Many of Valladolid's treasures are buried in pollution, noise, and unimaginative structures of an industrialized city that seems to be swallowing up its historical past. Old parts of the city have given way to mindless, utilitarian structures, but there are also a number of quite obviously ancient structures scattered about here and there.

STAYING OVERNIGHT: **Hotel Melia Parque,** 17 García Morato (tel. 47-01-00), lies beside the peripheral road encircling the city. It was completed in 1982 and contains more than 300 efficiently compact bedrooms which are usually filled with business travelers unwilling to negotiate the labyrinth of Valladolid's central streets. Each of the air-conditioned bedrooms contains its own bath and many modern conveniences. Singles cost 4,000 pesetas ($28); doubles, 6,500 pesetas ($45.50).

Felipe IV, 16 Gamazo (tel. 30-70-00). When it was built, it was considered one of the grandest hotels in the city. Each of its almost 130 bedrooms was modernized in 1981, guaranteeing its position as one of the solidly acceptable hotel choices in Valladolid. Each accommodation contains a private bath, a mini-bar, and air conditioning. A garage provides parking for motorists. Singles cost 5,500 pesetas ($38.50); doubles, 7,500 pesetas ($52.50).

Enara, 5 Plaza de España (tel. 30-02-11), is arguably the best budget accommodation in Valladolid. Its heartbeat location is backed up by contemporary, pleasantly but simply furnished rooms. Each is well maintained. Singles are accepted for 2,200 pesetas ($15.40) nightly, and doubles are charged 3,800 pesetas ($26.60). Each unit has a private shower. There is no restaurant, but you'll be located near many low-budget dining rooms and cafés. However, a continental breakfast is offered.

WHERE TO DINE: **La Fragua,** 10 Paseo de Zorilla (tel. 33-71-02). The capable staff of this establishment serves what's probably the best food in town. Amid a rustic decor of hanging garlic, exposed masonry, and beams, you can enjoy beautifully prepared versions of Castilian cuisine fresh from the ovens. From the grill, you might begin with some spicy sausage as an appetizer, which will prepare you for the gastronomic pleasures to follow. This includes an array of beef, chicken, and lamb dishes, all heady with the right seasonings and served in copious portions. Fish from the Atlantic is imported fresh every day, with a wide selection available, prepared in many different ways. The huge collection of wines offers many lesser known vintages from the region, one of which the steward will select for you if you request it. Dessert could include a cheese tart or a melt-in-your-mouth version of chocolate truffles. The owner, Señor Garrote, proudly displays his culinary diplomas as if to justify the price of meals which cost from 2,500 pesetas ($17.50) and are worth it. The restaurant is open every day except Sunday evening.

Mesón Cervantes, 6 Calle del Rastro (tel. 30-85-53), is the kind of place where the owner (in this case Alejandro) works in the dining room, capably complemented in the kitchen by his wife (Julia) and occasionally his charming mother. Neighborhood residents make this place a favorite, partly because of its lack of pretensions and because of its flavorful and copious cuisine. Two particular favorites here are sole with pine nuts and seasonal river crabs. Many other fish dishes, including hake and monkfish, await your pleasure. Roast suckling pig and roast lamb are also popular. Meals in the air-conditioned interior cost from 1,800 pesetas ($12.60), and are served daily at lunch and dinner except on Monday and in November.

Mesón Panero, 1 Marina Escobar (tel. 30-70-19). The chef of this imaginative restaurant is reputed to be able to turn even the most austere of the traditional Castilian recipes into flavorful and, at times, sensual experiences. Set near the water, the establishment lures diners with fresh fish which, among others, includes a succulent brochette of sole and hake with fresh asparagus. At the beginning of every week, a featured favorite is the famous cocida castellana, a stew. Roast lamb and suckling pig are among other menu items, and an array of well-chosen wines can accompany your selections. Full meals cost from 2,000 pesetas ($14) and are served daily except Sunday night in winter.

THE SIGHTS: The College of San Gregorio, near the Plaza de San Pablo, houses the **National Museum of Sculpture** (Museo Nacional de Escultura). Gracing its galleries is illustrious, gilded, polychrome sculpture, an art form that reached its pinnacle in Valladolid. First, the figures were carved from wood, then painted with consummate skill and grace, achieving life-like dimensions.

Examples of this original and imaginative work that blended together the artistry of the painter and the sculptor are on display in the first three rooms of the museum. The most significant works here are those by Alonso Berruguete (1480–1561), son of Pedro, one of the great painters of Spain.

From 1527 to 1532 the younger Berruguete labored over a retable for the altar of the convent of San Benito. This work, housed at the museum, is considered a masterpiece. In particular, see his *Crucifix with the Virgin and St. John* in Room II and his *Sacrifice of Isaac* in Room III. Works by other artists such as Juan de Juni and Gregorio Fernández are also displayed.

After visiting the galleries, you may want to explore the two-story cloisters. The ground floor represents controlled simplicity, but the upper level is in the florid style, with jutting gargoyles and fleurs-de-lis. Then you may want to see the chapel where the confessor to Isabella I (Fray Alonso de Burgos) was buried. While here, you can't miss the gruesome sculpture of that favorite subject of Spain, *Death*.

The museum may be visited from 10 a.m. to 1:30 p.m. and 4 to 7 p.m. for 200 pesetas ($1.40). On Sunday it is open only from 10 a.m. to 2 p.m.

Adjoining the college is the **Church of San Pablo** (St. Paul), which was once a 17th-century Dominican monastery. Its façade—built in Isabelline-Gothic—is similar to that of the college above, but is more remarkable. Flanked by two towers, the main door supports level after level of lacy stone sculpture. The church may be visited from 7:30 a.m. to 1 p.m. and 5 to 9:30 p.m. (free).

There are a number of other churches and sights of interest in addition to San Gregorio and San Pablo. You can, as for example, visit the **cathedral** on the Plaza de la Universidad and the **Museo Diocesano** (Diocesan Museum), in the heart of the old quarter. The Calle Cascajares leads to it. Regrettably, this great cathedral seems to be in disrepair and is gradually falling to pieces. The reredos over the main altar is the work of Juan de Juni, and the Diocesan Museum contains numerous relics of artistic value (in particular the remains of collegiate churches built during the Romanesque and Gothic periods). For 75 pesetas (53¢), you can visit from 9:30 a.m. to 1 p.m. and 4 to 6 p.m.

The **Museo Oriental** (Oriental Museum), 7 Paseo de Filipinos (tel. 30-69-00), lies in the Royal College of the Augustinian Fathers, near the Campo Grande park. It consists of 13 rooms: nine for the Chinese section and four for the Filipino area. Here you'll find one of the best collections of Chinese art in Spain, with many bronzes dating from the 7th century B.C. up to the 18th century A.D.; wooden carvings; some 100 fine porcelain pieces from the 2nd century B.C. to the 19th century; paintings on paper and silk from the 12th century up to the 19th; and more than 1,300 Chinese coins dating from 770 B.C. to 1912; plus furniture, jade, and ivory.

In the Filipino section, the ethnological and primitive art is represented by shields, arms, and *anitos*. Religious art of the 18th century can be admired in an extraordinary collection of ivories, embroideries, painting, and silversmiths' work. Popular art of the 19th century can be seen in bronzes, musical instruments, and statuary. Valued keepsakes of the past of the Philippines are the flags and arms of *los últimos de Filipinas*. The museum is open daily from 4 to 7 p.m. and on holidays from 10 a.m. to 2 p.m. Admission is 150 pesetas ($1.05).

You can also make a quick tour through the house once occupied by Miguel de Cervantes, the immortal author of *Don Quixote,* who did much of his writing in Valladolid. The **Casa de Cervantes,** 14 Calle del Rastro, was occupied by Cervantes and his family (first-floor rooms) in 1605. It is now a museum, open from 10 a.m. to 6 p.m. in summer, charging 75 pesetas (53¢) for admission. It is closed on Monday.

AFTER DARK: **Recoletos,** 11 Plaza de Recoletos (tel. 22-94-15), is a musically oriented pub with a lively crowd of drinkers, who enjoy the 200-peseta ($1.40) drinks amid an antique decor. There's a DJ playing recently released music, but there's no dancing.

Bogui, 11 Recoletos (tel. 22-38-13), is an attractively trendy Spanish disco which has capitalized on the local rage for Humphrey Bogart. Drinks average around 360 pesetas ($2.53).

El Mascardón, 7-9 San José (tel. 27-56-54), is a popular bar where the entertainment may be either jazz or folk music, depending on who shows up. It goes through a series of transformations during the course of its business evening, which lasts from 7 p.m. to 3 a.m. Drinks start at 200 pesetas ($1.40).

5. Burgos

This Gothic city grandly lives up to its well-earned reputation as the "cradle of Castile," having sallied forth into life in the 9th century. Just as the Tuscans are credited with speaking the most perfect Italian, so the denizens of Burgos with their distinctive lisp ("El Theed" for El Cid) are supposed to speak the most eloquent Castilian.

When the Andalusians first heard that lisp, they thought the men of Burgos were rather an affected lot . . . until the heroism and valor of these lisping Castilians quickly dispelled that notion. And when I speak of heroism, El Cid Campeador marches into focus. The chivalrous knight is forever linked in legend and blurred reality to the city of Burgos. Spain's greatest national hero was born near here, and his remains are in the city's principal sightseeing attraction, its grand cathedral. El Cid was immortalized as the hero of the epic *El Cantar de Mío Cid.*

Like all the great cities of Old Castile that experienced early glory, Burgos declined seriously in the 16th century, to be revived later. In 1936, during the Civil War, right-wing Burgos was the headquarters of Franco's Nationalist army.

The city lies in the Arlanzón River valley, about 150 miles north of the once rebellious Madrid, and at almost equal distance from the French border. From Madrid, Burgos is easily reached by rail on the fast **TER** train.

Burgos is apt to be a cauldron in July and August. Following usually brilliant autumn days (the best time to visit), Burgos is likely to experience a long hard winter, with freezing cold winds rushing across the flat Castilian plains. Spring tends to be as clear as crystal, with the oak and beech forests in the provinces renewing their life under a luminous sky.

STAYING OVERNIGHT: The **Hotel España,** 32 Paseo del Espoleón (tel. 20-63-40), is the best budget choice in Burgos. It lies at the end of the city's major paseo, lined with sidewalk tables and full of promenading Castilians early in the evening. The bedrooms are adequate, lacking style and imagination, but completely comfortable. The prices are reasonable. The best double rooms with private bath cost 4,500 pesetas ($31.50). The choicest singles, with complete bath, go for 2,800 pesetas ($19.60). I extend a bravo to the cooperative and friendly management (when the España is filled to the rafters, desk personnel have been known to ring up other hostelries to find rooms for stranded tourists). A continental breakfast costs extra, and a lunch or dinner is 1,400 pesetas ($9.80).

The **Hotel Norte y Londres,** 10 Plaza Alonso Martínez (tel. 26-12-68), on a pleasant square deep in the heart of Burgos, possesses traces of its faded grandeur in its stained glass, leaded windows, and crystal chandeliers. Guests are assigned to good-size bedrooms, with basic furnishings. The super-size bathrooms come equipped with yesteryear's finest plumbing. Two persons in a room with private bath pay 3,800 pesetas ($26.60); singles in rooms with shower bath are charged 2,000 pesetas ($14).

The Big Splurge

Landa Palace, Carretera de Madrid N1 (tel. 20-63-43). Its prices launch it in the splurge category, but many readers have written in about this place, claiming that it deserves inclusion and praise. Its five-star rating qualifies it as one of the grand establishments of the region, as a quick once-over of its baronial entrance hall will reveal. Throughout its 14th-century confines you'll find carefully chiseled stone carved into Gothic arches, coffered or vaulted ceilings, richly detailed antiques, and sumptuous upholstery.

Elegant meals, costing from 4,000 pesetas ($28) apiece, are served beneath the medieval vaulting of the sun-flooded dining room, while after-dinner coffee is enjoyed on one of the flowering terraces. Even the hotel's swimming pool is ringed with palms and ficus, sheltered with an ogival roof, and flanked at one end with wrought-iron replicas of Gothic-style cathedral windows. An indoor garden provides a setting for contemplation. The clusters of antiques include tapestries and a collection of clocks. Singles cost from 9,000 pesetas ($63); doubles, 11,000 pesetas ($77). There's a parking garage for motorists, and the location is less than a mile outside Burgos on the road to Madrid.

WHERE TO EAT: The restaurants in the heart of Burgos—that is, surrounding the cathedral—usually feature prices that soar as high as a Gothic spire. Exceptions to that statement include . . .

Casa Ojeda, 5 Vitoria (tel. 20-64-40), is a top-notch restaurant which combines excellent Burgalese fare, cozy inn-like decor, friendly service, and medium prices. Downstairs there's a large, odd-shaped bar made of polished wood. Moorish-type tiles and low ceilings set a pleasant ambience for meals or munching. There are intimate nooks, old lanterns and fixtures, trellis work, and carpeting wherever you tread. Upstairs is the restaurant, which is divided into two sections: one overlooking the street and the other the Casa del Cordón where the Catholic monarchs received Columbus after his second trip to America, on April 23, 1497.

A menú del día costs 2,000 pesetas ($14), and might feature a Castilian soup, pork filets, dessert (ice cream, flan, fruit), bread, and wine. À la carte dishes are roast lamb (a specialty here), Basque-style hake, sole Harlequin, and chicken in garlic. However, if you order from this menu, the charge is likely to be 2,500 pesetas ($17.50) and up. Casa Ojeda is closed Sunday night in summer and Monday the rest of the year.

Mesón del Cid, 8 Plaza de Santa Maria (tel. 20-87-15). You'll find the solid 15th-century walls of this pleasant restaurant immediately opposite the façade of the cathedral. It was once the private home of the most powerful lords of the region, but today its allure stems from the flavorful specialties concocted by Jóse

López Algaza (known to his clients as Pepín), his wife, María Luisa, and their children. Menu selections are always fresh, and usually couched in the most flavorful regional traditions. You might be tempted by roast baby lamb laden with aromatic herbs, one of the selections of shellfish soups, roasted and stuffed peppers, pork, veal, and chicken dishes, perhaps one of the array of fresh fish brought in daily. The establishment charges from 1,800 pesetas ($12.60) for a full meal served daily for both lunch and dinner except on Sunday night.

Rincón de España, 11 Nuno Rasura (tel. 20-59-55), draws many discerning visitors. You can eat indoors in a rustic-type dining room, or outdoors under a large awning closed off by glass when the weather threatens. A special menu here costs 1,800 pesetas ($12.60) and includes an omelet, roast veal, flan, wine, and bread. The Spanish Corner also offers platos combinados. A more extensive special à la carte meal costs 2,500 pesetas ($17.50) and up and might include a spinach omelet, roast veal, ice cream, bread, and wine. The food here is fair, the portions large, the vegetables fresh, and the service friendly.

THE SIGHTS: From limestone quarries in 1221 came the first stones for the **Cathedral of Santa María,** Plaza de Santa María, in Burgos, an ecclesiastical structure destined to become one of the most celebrated cathedrals in all of Europe. Built in the flamboyant Gothic style, the cathedral was in the works for three centuries.

The exterior competes with the interior in sheer artistry and design. The three main doorways are flanked by two 15th-century ornamented, 275-foot-high bell towers by John of Cologne. Inside, the cathedral is cross-shaped, with enough chapels and appurtenances to create an architectural maze. The overall bastardized appearance stuns. Somehow, the effect of all the diversification of styles tends to heighten the drama and the impact on the first-timer.

Of all the chapels, the most outstanding is the 16th-century **Chapel of Condestable,** behind the main altar. This is one of the best examples of the Isabelline-Gothic style of architecture, relying heavily on such rich decorations as heraldic emblems with elaborate coats-of-arms, a sculptured filigree doorway, figures of apostles and saints, balconies, and an eight-sided "star" stained-glass window. The chapel contains the tomb of its founding Condestable and his wife.

Equally elegant are the two-story, 14th-century cloisters (note the splendid entrance) filled with some excellent examples of Spanish Gothic sculpture. The tapestries displayed, including one well-known Gobelin, are rich in art and detail. In one of the chapels is an old chest linked to the legend of El Cid. According to the story, it was filled with gravel, but used as security by the warrior to trick moneylenders into thinking that it contained great wealth.

In the **Chapel of El Santísimo Cristo** is a figure of Christ that, according to legend, was the work of Nicodemus. The model? Christ himself! (Spanish cathedrals are big on claims.) But this one is particularly interesting in a macabre way, in that it seems to be made of cowhide with what appears to be human hair.

Under the octagonal dome—often compared to a lantern—are buried the remains of El Cid and his wife, Doña Ximena. Finally, you may want to see the double **Escalera Dorada** (Stairway of Gold) in the north transept. This elaborate stairway was built in the 16th century, the work of Diego de Siloé.

From March to November, the cathedral is open from 9 a.m. to 1 p.m. and 3 to 7 p.m. (winter hours are 10 a.m. to 1 p.m. and 3 to 5 p.m.). For 100 pesetas (70¢) you can buy a ticket that entitles you to visit the chapels, the cloisters, and the treasury. This purchase is recommended, as many of the most important art treasures are behind bars. Stroll by at night, incidentally, as the cathedral is illuminated then.

At least one more sight in Burgos deserves a visit. It is the **Royal Monastery of Las Huelgas.** For a monastery whose name means restful retreat, this cloister outside Burgos has seen a lot of action. Built in the 12th century in a grand and richly ornamented style, it was once "a summer place" for Castilian royalty, as well as a retreat for nuns of royal blood. But today its old grandeur is just a shadow of itself, and it houses a small band of nuns of any blood type—that is, if they're Cistercian.

Inside, the Gothic church is built in the shape of a Latin cross. Despite some unfortunate mixing of Gothic and baroque, it contains much of interest—notably some 14th- and 17th-century French tapestries and a pulpit that revolves on a swivel. The tomb of the founder, Alfonso VIII, and his queen, the daughter of Henry II of England, lies in the Choir Room. A novelty is a photograph of the skeleton of the king's son, 13-year-old Henry I, revealing that he suffered an operation performed on his head.

Through the 13th-century doors we pass into the first cloisters, an appendage of the monastery. The cloisters were built in the 13th century in a blend of the Gothic and Mudéjar styles. The ceiling is severely damaged, but remains of Persian peacock designs are visible. In 1937 Franco and the Falangists met in the simple but beautiful **Chapter Room,** with its unusual 12th-century standard of the Moors (war booty). The second cloisters were built in the 12th century and were originally part of the palace.

Finally, the **Museo de Ricas Telas** is devoted to costumes—mostly 13th century—that were removed from the tombs. These remarkably preserved textiles give us a rare look at medieval dress.

The nunnery is reached by going out the Valladolid road for more than a mile (the turnoff is clearly marked). From the Plaza de José Antonio in Burgos, a bus bound for Las Huelgas leaves every 20 minutes. The convent is open daily except Monday from 11 a.m. to 2 p.m. and 4 to 6 p.m. Admission is 100 pesetas (70¢).

A SIDE TRIP TO SANTO DOMINGO DE LA CALZADA: Some 42 miles west of Burgos lies an interesting pilgrimage center, the small city of Santo Domingo de la Calzada. It can either be visited on a day trip or else as an overnight stopover (see below for details of its parador). The city is named after Saint Dominic, who is buried there. The town grew as a stopover for pilgrims traveling across Spain to worship at the shrine at Santiago de Compostela.

The crowning achievement of the town is its **Cathedral,** which is, for the most part, Gothic—with some exceptions, including Romanesque chapels. From the 13th century, the cathedral is a national monument, rich in architectural detail, including a Renaissance choir. A free-standing tower is in the baroque style, so it's really a bastardization of architectural elements. The namesake saint is buried in the crypt.

The cathedral still honors a centuries-old legend, as recounted in *Iberia,* the non-fiction book by James Michener. A cockerel is alleged to have stood up and crowed after it had been roasted. Supposedly, it was protesting the innocence of a pilgrim who had been accused of theft and sentenced to hang. To this day, a live cock and hen are kept in the cathedral in a big cage high up on a wall. Surprisingly you can often hear the rooster crowing at mass. The cathedral is open from 9 a.m. to 2 p.m. and from 4 to 8:30 p.m.

Food and Lodging

Parador Nacional de Santo Domingo de la Calzada, 3 Plaza del Santo (tel. 34-03-00). As they did during the Middle Ages, the thick stone walls of this former inn and hospital still shelter foreign travelers working their way through the north of Spain. The severely elegant arches of the interior are reputed to have been commissioned by the beneficent patron saint of the region, whose bridges and medical skills encouraged the tired pilgrims on their way to Santiago de Compostela. In the center of town, the handsome parador offers 27 comfortably furnished accommodations, each with a private bath and phone. Doubles cost 8,000 pesetas ($56), singles (only a pair), 6,600 pesetas ($46.20). Fixed-price meals emphasizing regional specialties go for 2,000 pesetas ($14).

For our next and final stopover, we leave Old Castile and head for what is known as "New Castile."

6. Cuenca

At last, the word is out—Cuenca is one of the most interesting towns in Spain. The citizens of this long-forgotten town—some 100 miles east of Madrid—could have spread the word years ago, but somehow they didn't, even though they could use a few tourist dollars around here. People sigh "Isn't it quaint?" after seeing Cuenca.

This medieval town—once dominated by the Arabs—has what the Spanish call *casas colgadas,* or what we would call cliff-hanging houses. With their multiple terraces, they are a sight to behold. The rivers Júcar and Huécar meet at the bottom of the deep ravine, and if you ever go inside one of these cliff dwellings, you'll really expect to take a sudden plunge to your death in one of the gorges that split Cuenca.

Cuenca-bound trains leave from Atocha Station in Madrid. Trains originating in Valencia also stop off at Cuenca to pick up passengers en route to the Spanish capital.

THE SIGHTS: The chief sight of Cuenca is Cuenca itself. It is cut off and isolated from the rest of Spain. One of the reasons for the belated interest is that it requires a northern detour from the heavily traveled Valencia–Madrid road. The gorges give it a quality of unreality, and about eight old bridges span the two rivers, connecting the ancient parts with the growing new. One of the bridges is suspended over a 200-foot drop.

What you do in Cuenca is walk and explore. The streets are narrow and steep, often cobbled, and even the most athletic tire quickly. But you shouldn't miss it, even if you have to stop and rest periodically. At night you're in for a special treat when the casas colgadas are illuminated.

When you enter the town, you know what is in store for you. The outskirts have an industrialized tinge, but press on. The best is yet to come. Stop off at the **Oficina de Información** at 34 Colón (tel. 22-22-31) and pick up a map of the town. You'll need one.

You should try to drive practically to the top of the castle-dominated hill, although the road gets rough as you near the end. The view is worth it, however. You'll notice that the gorges make the town appear freakish, somewhat reminiscent of little Ronda in Andalusia.

In summer, the mountain breezes are cool here; in winter you freeze. Fall and spring, too, can be nippy.

The one architectural site that merits a special visit is the Gothic **cathedral,** Plaza Pio XII, begun in the 12th century. It bears a resemblance to England's Norman style. Part of it collapsed in this century, but it has been restored. The cathedral, a National Monument filled with religious art treasures, can be visited from 10 a.m. to 1 p.m. and 5 to 6 p.m.

Spain's Most Modern Art Gallery

In this relatively obscure and remote town rests the **Museum of Spanish Abstract Art,** on Calle los Canónigos. The finest of its kind in Spain, it has been called "a rare gem" by critics. Behind the iron knocker on the oak door is a world whose art is as modern as tomorrow.

The museum is housed in one of the cliff-hanging dwellings; the salons are well arranged, particularly to allow the natural Spanish light in to illuminate the paintings whenever possible. Many visitors (and they're coming from all over the world now) erroneously attribute this museum to the government. Actually, it's financially independent, an idea born in the mind of painter Fernando Zóbel, who donated it in 1980 to the Juan March Foundation.

The most outstanding abstract Spanish painters are represented, including Rafael Canogar (especially his *Toledo*), Luís Feito, Zóbel himself, Tapies, Eduardo Chillida, Gustavo Torner, Gerardo Rueda, Millares, Sempere, Cuixart, Antonio Saura (see his grotesque *Geraldine Chaplin* and his study of Brigitte Bardot, a vision of horror, making the French actress look like an escapee from Picasso's *Guernica*). In one room, by contrast, there's a 15th-century mural discovered during the restoration of the building representing *The Banquet.*

Closed Monday, the museum is open weekdays from 11 a.m. to 2 p.m. and 4 to 6 p.m., on Saturday to 8 p.m., and on Sunday from 11 a.m. to 2 p.m. Admission is 150 pesetas ($1.05).

Toledo was originally considered as the site of the museum; admittedly, the "Imperial City" would have brought far more visitors. But Cuenca was chosen —lucky for Cuenca, and even more so for you if you can make the pilgrimage.

A Side Trip to an Enchanted City

If you're staying over in Cuenca—or otherwise have the time—you can visit what the citizens of Cuenca call their **Ciudad Encantada,** about 25 miles northeast of the capital. Here, a windy, rainy, violent Mother Nature fancied herself a sculptor. Backed up by her "artist's helpers" (underground waters), she created a city out of these large rocks and boulders, shaping them into bizarre designs. You don't have to accept the names that others have given to these images, comparing them to the likeness of such things as a seal, an elephant, a Roman bridge. Let your own imagination go to work.

WHERE TO STAY: **Xúcar,** 17 Cervantes (tel. 22-45-11), is the best economy bet for Cuenca—a modern little (28 rooms) hotel, built in the late '60s. Everything is immaculate, and the staff keeps the atmosphere informal. All the rooms contain a private tile bath, and rent for 3,500 pesetas ($24.50) in a double, 2,400 pesetas ($16.80) in a single. On the second floor is a lounge with TV, and the hotel boasts an elevator as well as a country-style dining room, with a tasca in front. Wood beams, fresh linen on the tables, and best of all, the friendly personal service make it inviting.

Posada de San José, 4 Julián Romera (tel. 21-18-00). The 17th-century cells that used to shelter the sisters of this former convent now house overnight guests who consider its views of the old city to be the best in town. It sits atop the cliff which juts above the town, near the cathedral and the forbidding depths of a gorge whose chasm yawns nearby. Antonio and Jennifer Cortinas are the imaginative owners who, in 1983, renovated this place into one of the most alluring hotels of the region. The bar, many guests find, is perhaps the most charming of the well-decorated public rooms. The two dozen bedrooms rent for 2,500 pesetas ($17.50) in a single, 3,600 pesetas ($25.30) in a double.

Avenida, 39 Avenida José Antonio (tel. 21-43-43), is a two-star hostal residencia, which means that it serves only breakfast. The host, Gregorio Mora Mora, runs a neat and tidy place, offering 33 comfortable bedrooms. A room with private bath costs 2,800 pesetas ($19.60) for two persons. Units which could be used either as singles or doubles but containing only a wash basin cost 2,000 pesetas ($14). The staff is friendly and helpful.

WHERE TO DINE: The **Mesón Casas Colgadas,** 3 Calle los Canónigos (tel. 21-18-22), offers one of the most spectacular dining rooms in Spain. The restaurant stands on (rather, clings to) one of the most precarious projected points in Cuenca. It's built five stories high, with sturdy supporting walls and beams. Pine balconies and windows overlook the ravine below and the hills beyond. In fact, it's the most photographed "suspended house" in town. Worth every centimo, the least expensive set meal begins at 1,600 pesetas ($11.20), although you could easily spend 2,500 pesetas ($17.50). The menu includes the most typical regional dishes and a wide variety of international cuisine. Before-dinner drinks are served in the tavern room on the street-floor level, which stays open till midnight. Even if you're not dining here, you may want to drop in for a drink and take in that view. (The abstract art museum is next door, incidentally, so why not combine the two?)

Togar, 3 Avenida República Argentina (tel. 22-01-62), is one of the least expensive restaurants in Cuenca that can be safely recommended. It offers homemade cookery in a simpático atmosphere. You can enjoy such classic dishes as fish soup, trout with ham, and loin of pork. Expect to spend from 1,600 pesetas ($11.20) for a good, filling meal, and never show up on a Tuesday.

Chapter VI

EXTREMADURA

THE LAND BEYOND THE RIVER DOURO it was called. In the west of Spain, along the Portuguese border, Extremadura gave the world the conquistadores. Famous sons included Cortés, Pizarro, Balboa, and many others less well known but also important, like Orellana and Hernando de Soto.

Many were driven from their homeland by economic necessity, finding it hard to make a living in this dry, sun-parched province. Many sent back money to their native land to finance the building of mansions and public structures that stand today as a monument to long-ago conquests and adventures in the Americas.

Because of the intense heat of summer, spring and fall are the best times to visit. The region lies between Andalusia and Castile, and shares many of the same characteristics. Much of the countryside is pastoral. Extremadura forms the provinces of Badajoz and Cáceres. It is not to be confused with the Portuguese province of Estremadura.

1. Guadalupe

Guadalupe lies in the province of Cáceres, 1,500 feet above sea level, 117 miles west of Toledo. The road you take to reach it (C401) is poor, but the wild scenery of the Extremadura Mountains is spectacular.

Reader Cork Millner writes, "The rough cobblestone streets that twist, a few yards wide, up and down the hills are stacked with tattered cottages that could have welcomed a serf centuries ago. The people are cheerful and contented, living on terms of friendship with the hens, pigs, and cows that inhabit the cottages with them. The only incongruity is the ubiquitous television antennas that crop up atop the cottages."

THE SIGHTS: The **Monastery of Guadalupe** is a treasure. In 1325 a shepherd searching for a stray lamb reportedly spotted a statue of the Virgin in the soil. In time, it was to become venerated throughout many parts of the world, honored in Spain by such personages as Isabella, Columbus, and Cervantes. Known as the Dark Virgin of Guadalupe, it is said to have been carved by St. Luke. You can see the Virgin enthroned above the altar.

A shrine was built to commemorate the statue. Riches of tribute poured in from all over the world, making Guadalupe one of the wealthiest foundations in Christendom. (The monastery of Hieronymites, founded by Alfonso XI in 1340, is now run by Franciscan friars.)

An expert on the subject, Walter P. Corrigan, North Miami Beach, Florida, writes: "The statue itself of Our Lady of Guadalupe with its magnificent treasure is very possibly one of the most remarkably beautiful pieces of religious art work in all of Christendom."

High above the altar in a small alcove, the Virgin is turned around to face her "subjects." The more devout among the audience can touch or kiss the jeweled garment.

In the magnificently decorated sacristy are eight 17th-century masterpieces by Zurbarán. Despite the uninspired subject matter forced on the artist—bald-headed friars connected with the monastery—he achieved richly imaginative canvases.

The Gothic cloister, dating from the 14th century, is in flamboyant style, with two galleries, a patio, and coffered ceilings. But the pièce de résistance, the Mudéjar cloister, is the most stunning of all. In its center is a Gothic Mudéjar shrine in brick and tiles from 1405. The Moorish fountain is from the 14th century.

In the form of a Latin cross, the church is noted for the wrought-iron railings in its naves. Be sure to see the museums devoted to ecclesiastical vestments and the choir books produced by 16th-century miniaturists. For 100 pesetas (70¢), you can visit the museum and the sacristy of the monastery.

Guided tours, lasting less than an hour, are conducted through the monastery from 9:30 a.m. to 1:30 p.m. and from 3:30 to 7 p.m. Winter hours are curtailed: 9:30 a.m. to 1 p.m. and 3:30 to 6 p.m.

WHERE TO STAY: In Guadalupe, the major hotel is the **Parador Nacional Zurbarán,** 10 Marqués de la Romana (tel. 36-70-75), which has 20 rooms installed in a 16th-century building with a beautiful garden. A double with bath costs 8,000 pesetas ($56); a single with bath rents for 6,600 pesetas ($46.20). Lunch or dinner goes for 2,000 pesetas ($14). The parador has a swimming pool and a bar. The hotel is in the center of town in a scenic spot.

The alternative to the parador is **Hospederia Real Monasterio,** Plaza Juan Carlos (tel. 36-70-00), once a way station for weary pilgrims visiting the shrine. Back then, lodging was granted in return for a small donation. Times have changed, but the prices remain low at this two-star hotel which, I think, deserves a higher rating. Some of the rooms contain high-vaulted ceilings. Doubles with bath cost 4,000 pesetas ($28). Triples with private bath go for 5,500 pesetas ($38.50). A continental breakfast costs extra. There is a bar, and visitors are generally pleased with the meals. A complete luncheon or dinner goes for 1,500 pesetas ($10.50). It is closed from January 10 to February 10.

2. Trujillo

Dating from the 13th century, Trujillo is celebrated for its noble sons, a string of colonizers and conquerors. Among the illustrious figures born at Trujillo were Francisco Pizarro, conqueror of Peru, and Francisco Orellana, the first man to explore the country of the Amazons.

Lying 56 miles east of Mérida, Trujillo was built on a granite ledge higher up the hillside from today's modern town and centers around the Plaza Mayor, one of the artistic landmarks of Spain.

A Moorish castle and a great variety of 16th- and 17th-century palaces, manorial houses, towers, churches, and arcades form a real symphony of stone around the plaza. They overlook the bronze equestrian statue of Pizarro, in the center, the work of the American sculptors Charles Runse and Mary Harriman. It is the twin of the one that stands in Lima, Peru, the second homeland of the great *extremeño.*

Steep, narrow streets and shadowy little corners evoke bygone times when native sons set out from here on their fantastic adventures. There is a saying that 20 American countries were "born in Trujillo."

Seek out the Santiago church with its Romanesque belfry and tower. Another beautiful church, Santa María, rebuilt in the 15th century, is the pantheon of some of Trujillo's greatest sons. The church contains a remarkable retable in the Gothic style.

Commanding a view over this proud town is its *castillo,* or castle.

FOOD AND LODGING: **Parador Nacional de Trujillo,** Plaza de Santa Clara (tel. 32-13-58), has been newly installed in the former 17th-century convent of Santa Clara in the heart of town. Parts of the original interior of the convent have been incorporated into the building. It contains 42 handsomely furnished and air-conditioned rooms, plus one elegant suite and two dining rooms, along with patios, comfortable lounges, a garden, a bar, and a garage. Although it has been classified as a "four-star" establishment by the government, its year-round rates are a reasonable 7,000 pesetas ($49) in a single, 8,500 pesetas ($59.50) for double occupancy. A three-course dinner of Spanish specialties costs 2,000 pesetas ($14).

3. Cáceres

The capital of the province, Cáceres is a national monument. Encircled by old city walls, it has many seignorial palaces and towers, a number of which were financed by gold sent from the Americas by the conquistadores. Allow about two hours to explore the monumental heartland of Cáceres.

THE SIGHTS: Heavily restored, about 30 old towers of the city's medieval walls remain. Originally the towers were much taller, a source of pride and independence to their builders. But when Queen Isabella took over, she ordered them "cut down to size."

The largest tower is at the Plaza del General Mola. Standing beside it is the **Estrella Arch,** or star arch.

The highest point in the old city is **San Mateo** (St. Matthew's), which dates from the 14th century. The church has a plateresque portal and a nave that is rather severe. However, some plateresque tombs add a more decorative touch.

Spared from the "lopping" ordered by the Catholic monarch, the **Casa de las Cigüeñas** (Storks' House) is next to San Mateo. Now the seat of the military government, it dates from the second half of the 15th century. Its slender tower is all that remains to reveal what the battlements looked like.

On the site of the old Alcázar, the **Casa de las Veletas** (Weather Vane House) has a baroque façade and a provincial archeological museum that is open from 10 a.m. to 2 p.m. and 5 to 8 p.m. (4 to 7 p.m. in winter). It is closed Sunday afternoon, otherwise charging 75 pesetas (53¢) for admission. It preserves the ancient Moorish cistern with five naves and horseshoe arches, and a patio and paneling from the 17th century. In the museum is a collection of Celtic and Visigothic remains, along with Roman and Gothic artifacts, as well as a numismatic collection.

Eventually you make your way to the **Plaza Santa María,** the heart of Old

Cáceres. On one side is a Gothic church from the 16th century, with three vaulted naves. Hidden behind heraldic shields are the remains of some of the proudest of the conquistadores of the province.

The **Church of Santiago** was begun in the 12th century and restored in the 16th century. It shelters the reredos of Alonso de Berruguete, carved in 1557, and a 15th-century figure of Christ.

La Casa de los Toledo-Moctezuma is a house built by Juan Cano de Saavedra. It was financed by a dowry from his wife, the daughter of Montezuma.

WHERE TO STAY: **Hotel Extremadura,** Avenida Virgen de Guadaloupe (tel. 22-16-00), was built in the mid-1950s in a style typical of the era and renovated sometime in the 1970s. Today it's surrounded by other recently constructed buildings in the commercial part of town, just beyond the gates of the old city. The friendly owners will rent you one of the 68 rooms for 3,500 pesetas ($24.50) in a single and 5,600 pesetas ($39.20) for a double. There's a swimming pool set into the garden, and you can use a parking garage that is on the premises.

Hotel Alcántara, 14 Avenida Virgen de Guadaloupe (tel. 22-89-00), contains 67 tastefully decorated bedrooms, most of which were renovated about a decade ago. It's in the commercial center of the city, in an area convenient to the old town. You'll appreciate the air conditioning and the mini-bar in each of the well-furnished units. These rent for 3,500 pesetas ($24.50) in a single, from 5,500 pesetas ($38.50) in a double. There is no restaurant, but a cafetería is on the premises.

WHERE TO DINE: **El Figón de Eustaquio,** 12-14 Plaza San Juan (tel. 24-81-94), offers a local form of Extremaduran cuisine that is taken seriously by the four brothers who own and run it. The Blanco family is the guiding force here. You will probably notice the family members doing practically every task, including preparing the amazingly large number of dishes, which might include all the typical Spanish specialties as well as honey soup, solomillo (filet of beef) de choto, tencas a la extremeña, and many other delicacies. Full meals range from 1,600 pesetas ($11.20) up. The air-conditioned interior is open every day.

4. Mérida

Once called Rome in miniature, Mérida was known as Augusta Emerita when it was founded in 25 B.C. Thirty miles east of the border town of Badajoz and 273 miles from Madrid, Mérida was the capital of Lusitania—and considered one of the most splendid cities of Iberia. It once ranked as the ninth town in importance in the Roman Empire.

THE SIGHTS: As a Roman city, Mérida was three times its present size. In western Spain in the province of Badajoz, its monuments, temples, and public works (such as aqueducts) have earned it a reputation for the finest Roman ruins on the Iberian peninsula. Michener wrote that a visit here "is like a trip to ancient Rome." An exaggeration, but Mérida is worthy, nevertheless.

The **Roman bridge** over the Guadiana was the longest in Roman Spain, consisting of 81 arches. It was constructed of granite under either Trajan or Augustus, then restored by the Visigoths in 686. Philip II ordered further restoration in 1610, and work was also done in the 19th century. It's about half a mile long.

At the head of the bridge, and guarding the entrance to town, is the **Alcázar,** commonly known as the Conventual or the Alcazaba. Built by the Moors, it is a square structure that was granted to the Order of Santiago in the 12th century.

The **Roman theater** is the greatest treasure of antiquity, and has been called "one of the best preserved Roman ruins in the world today." It was built by Agrippa in 18 B.C. to house an audience of 5,000 persons. Decorated even today with Corinthian columns and statues, it was one of the most celebrated buildings in Roman Spain. Today it's also the setting for classic dramatic presentations. Next to the theater is the amphitheater, dating from A.D. 8 and once seating about 15,000 spectators who thrilled at the sight of slaves being fed to the lions.

Both the theater and the amphitheater may be visited for 150 pesetas ($1.05) from 8 a.m. to 7 p.m. (winter hours are 10 a.m. to 2 p.m. and 4 to 6 p.m.).

Other sights of interest include the old hippodrome or **Circus Maximus,** which could seat about 30,000 people who were drawn to watch chariot races or boats engaged in naval battles (its basin could be flooded); the 50-foot-high **Trajan's Arch** (often called Arco de Santiago); the aqueducts; and some remnants of the **Roman wall** that once encircled the city.

Museo Nacional de Arte Romano (tel. 31-16-90) occupies a modern building immediately adjacent to the ancient Roman theater. It contains a collection of Roman statues, sarcophagi, columns, ceramics, ancient glassware, and coins. Entrance costs 200 pesetas ($1.40). The museum is open between 10 a.m. and 2 p.m. and from 4 to 6 p.m. every day except Monday. On Sunday and holidays, the museum is closed in the afternoon.

The latest monument to be excavated is the **Temple of Diana** (actually it was dedicated to Caesar Augustus). Squeezed between houses on a narrow residential street, it was converted in the 17th century into the private residence of a nobleman. He used four of the original Corinthian columns in his architectural plans.

READERS' SIGHTSEEING TIP: "After the theater, by far the most impressive other Roman remain is at the **Mithraeum,** a glorious second-century mosaic kept under cover in a locked shed. There are various other mosaics open to view (and to the elements), but make sure the curator unlocks the door to show you this exceptional one" (Mr. and Mrs. John Pearce, Toronto, Ontario, Canada).

WHERE TO STAY: The **Parador Vía de la Plata,** 3 Plaza Constitución (tel. 31-38-00), is in the heart of town, installed in the former Convento de los Frailes de Jesús. Opened in 1966, it offers air-conditioned rooms on different levels. Old stone stairs lead to the bedrooms, and in the cloister a salon has been installed. A double with bath costs 8,500 pesetas ($59.50), and a single with bath rents for 7,000 pesetas ($49). In addition you must pay for a continental breakfast. Should you want meals, the charge is 2,000 pesetas ($14) per person. In the center is a garden studded with shrubbery and flowers. The parador also contains a garage and bar.

The **Hotel Emperatriz,** 19 Plaza de España (tel. 31-31-11), is older, but a good value for a three-star hotel. Its doubles rent for 5,000 pesetas ($35), its singles for 3,200 pesetas ($22.40). All accommodations contain private bath. You can have a complete meal for 1,500 pesetas ($10.50). On the premises is a nightclub as well as a bar. Try to get a room facing the plaza where the intense activity of the locals can be watched until after midnight. On the rooftops around the square are many stork nests, and these birds seem to take a similar interest in all the activity.

WHERE TO DINE: **Restaurant Nicolas,** 13 Félix Valverde Lillo (tel. 31-96-10). It required the diligent efforts of three brothers, the Morenos, to transform what had been a very old, rundown house into one of the most charming restaurants of town. If the lower dining room isn't to your liking, you'll find more seating upstairs, as well as a pleasant garden for outdoor dining. Menu specialties are made with care from fresh ingredients. You might enjoy an array of fresh shellfish, roast baby goat, carefully seasoned roast of lamb, and flavorful concoctions of sole, hake, and monkfish. Full meals, costing between 1,200 pesetas ($8.40) and 3,000 pesetas ($21), are served daily except Sunday night.

5. Badajoz

The capital of the largest province in Spain, Badajoz is a frontier border town, lying on the left bank of the Guadiana near the once-turbulent Portuguese border. An old Roman bridge crosses the river, and a Moorish fortress recalls its past. If I gave stars for sightseeing interest, Badajoz would have none in its galaxy (Cáceres is far more interesting), but it does have some local color, especially in its huge ramparts and in its narrow streets built during the Middle Ages.

If you're driving to Badajoz from the northern approach, its fortified site can best be appreciated. It's a good idea to park outside and walk into the core of town. Along the way, you'll pass the Cathedral of Badajoz, which was constructed in the 13th century in the Gothic style. But it's seen many decorators since then.

WHERE TO STAY: The **Hotel Lisboa,** 13 Avenida de Elvas (tel. 23-82-00), is one of the major hotels of the city, containing 176 rooms, each with modern and comfortable appointments. It's at the edge of town and is rated three stars by the government. Singles cost from 3,800 pesetas ($26.60), doubles from 4,500 pesetas ($31.50).

Hotel Río, Avenida de Elvas (tel. 23-76-00). A grove of eucalyptus trees lies between the modern walls of this comfortable hotel and the river. There's an outdoor pool, as well as a parking garage, a disco pub and restaurant, and an encircling garden for the use of occupants of the 90 pleasantly furnished bedrooms. Each of the accommodations contains a private bath and mini-bar. Singles rent from 2,900 pesetas ($20.30); doubles, 4,000 pesetas ($28). You'll find this place near a bridge in Badajoz on the highway stretching between Lisbon and Madrid.

WHERE TO DINE: **Mesón el Tronco,** 17 Muñoz Torrero (tel. 22-20-76). You might not suspect that there's an attractively decorated restaurant in the back room after a quick glance at the popular bar near the front door, but the excellent tapas will give a hint of the regional delicacies that are available inside. The owner offers traditional Extremaduran dishes, as well as a changing repertoire of daily specials. Menu items include gazpacho, cocido of the region, lamb cutlets, and caldereta Extremadura style. Full meals begin at around 1,500 pesetas ($10.50), an affordable price for food you'll enjoy in air-conditioned comfort. The restaurant is open for lunch and dinner daily except Sunday.

Los Gabrieles, 21 Vicente Barrantes (tel. 22-42-75), is the personal domain of Gabriel Peláez, whose father established the restaurant 30 years ago. The extensive menu includes a range of carefully planned sauces, as well as both traditional and more unconventional dishes. These include soups, a regional stew, and a range of other local specialties. Full meals usually begin at around 1,800 pesetas ($12.60), although they can go much higher if you order one of the more adventurous featured dishes. Los Gabrieles is open for lunch and dinner daily except Sunday.

READERS' SIGHTSEEING TIPS: "For side trips in the Extremadura, we recommend visits to two towns. **Jerez de los Caballeros** is an interesting journey from either Badajoz (46½ miles south on N432) or Mérida (61½ miles southwest on N360). It is a small town of white houses extending from a cathedral on a hilltop down into a small valley below. Vasco Núñez de Balboa was born here, the first European to look westward on the Pacific Ocean. A statue in a small square at the bottom of the town commemorates him. Legend has it that he was born nearby in a small whitewashed house at 10 Calle Capitán Cortés.

"**Medellin,** some 25 miles east of Mérida, is a little town where Hernán Cortés, conqueror of Mexico, was born. The road approaches through irrigated farmland from which you get a first glimpse of the old whitewashed town on the opposite side of the Guadiana River. An old ruined castle on the adjacent hill dominated the town. The river is crossed on a Roman stone bridge. The cobblestone plaza of the town is surrounded by old stone buildings. In the center is a monument to Cortés, with the impressive ruined castle in the background. There is truly the atmosphere of ancient Spain here" (Dr. and Mrs. C. H. Chaffey, Dapto, N.S.W., Australia).

6. Zafra

One of the most interesting sightseeing targets in Extremadura, Zafra is filled with old streets and squares in the Moorish style. It lies 38 miles from Mérida. Its fair of San Miguel, on October 4, is famous throughout Spain. The castle of the dukes of Fería is the most important in the province. It is characterized by its sumptuous 16th-century Herrerian patio and its Sala Dorada with a richly paneled ceiling. The Ministry of Information and Tourism has opened a government-run parador in the restored castle.

It's the **Parador Hernán Cortés,** 7 Place Corazón de María (tel. 55-02-00), named after a former guest of the castle, one of the conquerors of Mexico. Cortés stayed with the dukes of Fería for a time before his departure to the recently discovered New World. The castle was originally built in 1437, on a square plan with four round towers. The interior of the parador is decorated in a beautiful, but restrained, style. It contains the chapel of the Alcázar, with an octagonal Gothic dome.

In addition to being decorated in splendid taste, the parador offers much comfort in its double rooms which rent for 7,500 pesetas ($52.50) and its singles which go for 6,200 pesetas ($43.40). All accommodations contain a private bath. A continental breakfast is extra. The magnificently decorated dining room offers regional meals for 2,000 pesetas ($14). In addition, there is a bar, a large lounge, a patio, a garden, and a swimming pool—first-class comforts in a setting of antiquity.

Puerta Honda, 36 Avenida López Azme (tel. 55-08-00). One of the best views of the citadel and the old city is available from the windows of the modern bedrooms of this Andalusian-style hotel. Each of the 50 rooms was recently renovated into a comfortably appointed and pleasant refuge, where a sauna, gymnasium, and outdoor pool are only some of the amenities. There's even a disco on the premises, as well as a garden and a flowered patio for midafternoon drinks. Single rooms range in price from 3,600 pesetas ($25.30), while doubles cost 7,200 pesetas ($50.40). The hotel also has one of the best restaurants in town, the Posada del Duque, offering meals from 1,500 pesetas ($10.50).

Chapter VII

ANDALUSIA

1. Jaén, Baeza, and Úbeda
2. Córdoba
3. Seville
4. Jerez de la Frontera
5. Cádiz
6. Costa de la Luz
7. Ronda
8. Granada

ANDALUSIA IS A PAGAN LAND. This vast, wild, rugged tract of southern Spain—quite interestingly—lives up to all the clichés you've ever heard about it. It's as if—for once—those travel posters didn't lie. Silvery olive trees vibrate in the wind; the scent of orange blossoms hangs in the air; mantilla-wearing señoritas, with carnations in their hair, run through the narrow streets on fiesta days; gypsies rattle their castanets in caves thousands of years old; and young men serenade their girls under balconies on hot Spanish nights.

This once-great stronghold of Muslim Spain is also rich in history and tradition. Of all the sections of Spain, it has the most celebrated sightseeing treasures: the world-famous Mezquita (mosque) at **Córdoba,** the Alhambra Palace at **Granada,** the great Gothic cathedral at **Seville.** It also has towns of which you may never have heard—places like **Úbeda,** castle-dominated **Jaén,** gorge-split **Ronda, Jerez de la Frontera** (the home of sherry), and the gleaming white port city of **Cádiz.** Give Andalusia at least a week, and know then you will have skimmed only the surface of its many offerings.

This dry, mountainous region also embraces the **Costa del Sol** (Málaga, Marbella, and Torremolinos), but this popular strip of Spain is dealt with separately in the following chapter. Go to the Costa del Sol for beach resorts, nightlife, and relaxation; visit Andalusia for its architectural wonders, its beauty, and a life that has come to symbolize—quite erroneously—Spain itself.

Crime alert: Anyone driving south into Andalusia and the Costa del Sol should be warned about thieves. Once one of the safest and most crime-free districts of Europe, southern Spain is now beset with incidents. A major problem is breaking into cars. Many motorists park their cars with all their luggage in it only to return from a sightseeing attraction to find they've been robbed.

Daylight robberies are very commonplace, especially in such cities as Seville, Córdoba, and Granada. It is not unusual for a car to be broken into while tourists are enjoying lunch in a restaurant. Some establishments have solved the problem by having guards (a service for which you should tip, of course). Under no circumstances should you ever leave passports and travelers checks unguarded in a car.

1. Jaén, Baeza, and Úbeda

The province of Jaén, with its three principal centers—the capital city of Jaén, Baeza, and Úbeda—lies in one of the most recently discovered tourist sections of Spain. But this country, at long last, is beginning to be accorded its proper interest. For too many years, visitors whizzed through Jaén on their way south to Granada, or bypassed it altogether on the southwest route to Córdoba and Seville. But the government is beefing up the sad lot of the hotels in the province with its excellent paradors, which now provide some of the best living accommodations in Spain. If you have an extra day, it is recommended that you spend it touring the capital city of Jaén and its two stepdaughters, Baeza and Úbeda.

To reach Jaén, take a train from the Atocha Station in Madrid, which will deliver you to the Linares and Baeza Station. From this point, you can then make frequent bus or electric train connections to either Úbeda or Jaén.

For our first stopover in the province, we'll pay our respects to the capital.

JAÉN: This city lies in the center of the major olive-growing district in Spain. It is sandwiched between Córdoba and Granada (each lying about 60 miles away, in opposite directions). Some 210 miles south of Madrid, the history-rich town of Jaén has been traditionally considered a gateway to Castile or a gateway to Andalusia, depending on which way one was headed. It has a bustling modern section of little interest to visitors, but its Moorish-influenced older part is reason enough for going there. A castle high on the hill dominates the capital, and it has been turned into a first-class parador. On a clear day, you can see the snow-covered peaks of the Sierra Nevada.

A historical note: The Christian forces gathered in their stronghold here before marching on Granada to oust the Moors in 1492.

The Sights

Jaén's most important National Monument is its honey-brown **cathedral,** Plaza de la Catedral, a blend of both baroque and Gothic architectural features, with a Romanesque façade—in all, an unfortunate wedding of styles that occurs too frequently in Spanish cathedrals. The interior is dominated by a huge dome. The formality and grandeur of the cathedral attest to Jaén's importance in days gone by. Note the richly carved choir stalls. The building is open from 7:30 to 11 a.m. and 5:30 to 9 p.m.; no admission charge. The cathedral museum contains an important collection of historic objects in two underground chambers, including some paintings by Ribera. It is open from 10:30 a.m. to 12:30 p.m. and 4:30 to 6 p.m., charging 40 pesetas (28¢) admission.

In addition to its cathedral, Jaén has a number of historic churches, but **La Magdalena** is the most interesting. A Gothic church, it was once an Arab mosque, and can be visited from 8 a.m. to 2 p.m. and 5 to 8 p.m. (free).

The city also has numerous mansions left over from the heyday of Spanish aristocracy that contrast dramatically with the Arabesque white and purple-washed tile-roofed dwellings. Its narrow, cobblestone streets hug the mountainside.

Where to Stay

Parador Castillo de Santa Catalina (tel. 26-44-11), a castle on the hill overlooking Jaén, is one of the government's showplace paradors. Just to stay here is a good enough reason for coming to Jaén. In the 10th century the castle was a Muslim fortress, surrounded by high protective walls and approached by a steep, winding road. When Christians did approach, the Moors were fond of throwing them overboard. The castle is still reached by the same road, but the hospitality has improved remarkably. Visitors enter through a three-story-high baronial hallway. The polite staff show guests to their balconied bedrooms (doubles only), all of which have been tastefully furnished, and with an eye to both comfort and style. The spick-and-span tile private baths (and the heating in winter) make living in this castle bearable after all. And the price for all this is about 9,500 pesetas ($66.50) for two persons, plus a supplement for a continental breakfast.

Dining at the castle is dramatic, both in atmosphere and cuisine. The high-vaulted dining chamber looks like a small cathedral, with its wrought-iron chandeliers, stone arches, a raised hearth, and a collection of copper kettles and ceramics. On either side of this lofty room are arched windows, opening onto a terrace on one side or a view of Jaén on the other. A big luncheon or dinner here, costing 2,000 pesetas ($14), includes the regional wine of Jaén province. The food is adequately prepared, and you can choose from typical Jaén dishes. The hors d'oeuvres consist of 20 tiny plates, including, of course, the olives for which Jaén is famous.

Hotel Rey Fernando, 7 Plaza Coca de la Piñera (tel. 25-18-40), is a fairly modernized establishment, a two-star hotel in Jaén. It's close to the monuments and transportation center, and makes for a comfortable overnight stay. Plain but livable doubles, with bathrooms, go for 4,200 pesetas ($29.40); singles cost 3,200 pesetas ($22.40).

Xauen, 3 Plaza Deán Mazas (tel. 23-40-91). Only breakfast is served at this simple, family-run establishment where motorists might have to park far away from the entrance. In spite of that, the handcrafted detailing of the building, its promising location in the center of the city, and its 35 air-conditioned bedrooms make it a popular choice. Singles cost from 3,800 pesetas ($26.60), doubles 5,200 pesetas ($36.40).

Where to Eat

Jockey Club, 20 Paseo de la Estación (tel. 25-10-18), is the leading restaurant in town, yet you can dine here at moderate cost. Owner Juan Pedro Millan works hard to maintain a comfortable ambience and a well-prepared cuisine, which includes rape (a white fish) "Jockey style," Milanese-style rice, salmon with green sauce, and a full range of meats and fish, including "smothered tongue." Full meals, served every day, range from 1,800 pesetas ($12.60) to 3,000 pesetas ($21).

Nelson, 33 Paseo de la Estación (tel. 22-92-01). Within a pedestrian walkway near the railway station, this successful restaurant relies on fresh produce and the gruff charm of its owners, the Ordónez brothers, for its acclaim. An impressive array of tapas greets clients at the bar where diners pause for drinks before heading in to dinner. In the air-conditioned dining room, you can enjoy full meals priced from 1,500 pesetas ($10.50). Your dinner might include any of the usual meat and fish dishes, or perhaps a savory filet steak prepared "house style," with plenty of herbs. Meals are served at both lunch and dinner daily except Sunday.

After lunch or an overnight stopover at Jaén, our tour continues to Baeza, 28 miles north.

BAEZA: This historic town of Gothic and plateresque buildings and cobblestone streets is one of the least spoiled in Spain, a fit rival for its bigger sister, Úbeda. In many respects, Baeza is like a fantasy of a small Andalusian town come true. At twilight lanterns hang on walls of plastered stone, flickering against the darkening sky and lighting the narrow streets.

The main square, Plaza de los Leones, a two-story open colonnade, is a good point to begin your exploration. But you may soon gravitate to the section bordering the **cathedral,** the most interesting area. Built in the 16th-century, the cathedral is a blend of Gothic and Renaissance architectural styles.

Even more enticing a sight is the **Palace of San Felipe,** with its intricately sculptured Gothic façade. Now a seminary, it contains a modern chapel opening off its 16th-century courtyard. A baroque stairway leads to another mosaic chapel. But in Baeza one doesn't want to spend too much time inspecting the interior of buildings, regardless of how fascinating. The town as a whole provides the architectural interest and drama.

Food and Lodging

Juanito, Paseo Arca del Agua (tel. 74-00-40). As you drive in from Úbeda, Juanito is on the outskirts of Baeza, serving regional specialties borrowed from both native Andalusia and nearby La Mancha. In season, game is served. Many of the vegetable dishes are cooked with ham. Juan Antonio Salcedo, the owner, is a devotee of the "lost art" of Jaén cookery. His wife, Luisa, assists with the revival of the ancient recipes that have made this place so well known. Each day Luisa prepares a different "suggestion of the day," except Sunday night when the restaurant is closed. It is usually savory and well prepared. You may choose habas beans, filet of beef with tomatoes and peppers, partridge salad, roast partridge, or loin in adobe. Meals cost from 1,800 pesetas ($12.60). The air-conditioned restaurant is also closed November 1 to November 15. If you'd like to spend the night here, around 20 rooms are available, unpretentious yet comfortable, ranging in price from 2,300 pesetas ($16.10) in a single to 3,000 pesetas ($21) in a double.

After a walking tour, it's only six miles by bus northeast to . . .

ÚBEDA: This former stronghold of the Arabs is a Spanish National Monument, a town filled with golden-brown Renaissance palaces, tile-roofed dwellings bathed in whitewash, and narrow cobblestone streets. Like its neighbor, Baeza, it offers the visitor a chance to see a relatively untouched, aristocratic town, often called the Florence of Andalusia. You can cut off the Madrid–Córdoba road and head east for Linares, then on to Úbeda, a detour of 26 miles. The government has installed a parador here in a ducal palace—so you might make it a luncheon stopover if you're pressed for time. You might also want to allow time to stroll through the town's many shops, which sell, among other items, leather craft goods, and *esparto* grass carpets.

The palaces and churches of the city are almost endless. You might begin your tour at the center of the monumental zone, the heartbeat **Plaza Vázquez de Molina,** which is flanked with several mansions, including the Casa de las Cadenas, which has been converted into the town hall. For centuries, a web of decay and dust has fallen over them, but now many are being restored. At present you can view the churches, but you'll have to settle for staring at the outside of the mansions. The charm of this town is to be discovered by wandering through its streets, and this charm isn't necessarily reflected in one particular sight. You'll probably get lost—but that's all right too.

The Sights

Iglesia El Salvador ranks along with San Pablo (see below) as the church in Úbeda having the most interest for visitors. This is considered one of the grandest examples of the Spanish Renaissance style, having been designed in 1536. Diego de Siloe was the designer, and work was carried out by Andrés de Vandelvira and Alonso Ruiz, because the original architect had died. The richly embellished portal is mere window dressing for the wealth of decoration inside the church. The pearl of the church is a sacristy designed by Vandelvira. The church has a single nave whose vaulting is colored in golds and blues. Seek out the many sculptures and altarpieces, and you can hardly miss the rose windows.

San Pablo (St. Paul's) has almost equal interest. Built in the Gothic style, it is known for its south door, constructed in the early part of the 16th century, and its chapels.

The **Hospital of Santiago,** on the edge of town, was completed in 1575, and it's still in use. It was built by Andrés de Vandelvira, often called "the Christopher Wren of Úbeda." Over the years, it has earned a reputation as the "Escorial of Andalusia," and although the title is misleading, it does point up the grandeur that this building once possessed. Happily, you can simply walk into its courtyard: no one charges admission.

Santa María de los Reales Alcázares is another intriguing Úbeda church, opposite the town hall. The cloisters, with their fan vaulting, are Gothic, and the interior with its tiled and painted ceiling is a blend of Gothic and Mudéjar. It stands on the ground that once held an Arab mosque. Inside the church you'll find a gruesome statue of a mutilated Christ—a real horror movie.

Living and Dining in a Ducal Palace

The **Parador Nacional del Condestabe Dávalos,** 1 Plaza de Vázquez de Molina (tel. 75-03-45), provides guests with a chance to live in a 16th-century palace, in a style superior to that of the duke who originally inhabited it back in the golden days of this ancient town. The palace shares an old paved plaza, deep in the heart of Úbeda, with La Iglesia del Salvador, a church with a dazzling façade. A formal entrance to this Renaissance structure leads into an enclosed patio, encircled by two levels of Moorish arches. Pots of palms and plants rest on the tile floors. An inner staircase leads to the balcony, off which lie the upper-level rooms. The bedrooms are nearly two stories high, and have beamed ceilings and tall windows. Antiques have been combined with reproductions: the beds are comfortable; and the private baths are roomy. The charge for all of this is 9,500 pesetas ($66.50) in a double room with private bath, 8,000 pesetas ($56) in a single with a private bath.

Before lunch or dinner, you might go into the low-beamed wine cellar, old and tavern-like, with stone arches, crude stools and tables, three giant kegs of wine, and a wall covered with a collection of ceramic vases and dishes. Dinner is served on the ground floor in a room representing restrained taste. Costumed waitresses bring good Spanish dishes to your table, and the bill for a luncheon or dinner is 2,000 pesetas ($14). This includes the wine and service. Why not have your after-dinner coffee in either of the living rooms, perhaps near the fireplace?

An Alternate Hotel Choice

Frankly, if you can stay at the parador, there doesn't seem to be any earthly reason for living elsewhere—unless you arrive without a reservation only to find the hotel fully booked. In that case, head for the **Hotel Consuelo,** 12 Avenida Ramón y Cajal (tel. 75-08-40). Not luxurious, but absolutely comfortable and utilitarian, this is a fairly modern, three-story building. The Consuelo's greatest asset, however, is its low rate structure: 2,800 pesetas ($19.60) for a double room with complete bath. The most expensive singles, those with private bath, rent for 2,300 pesetas ($16.10). A continental breakfast is extra. The Consuelo is on the other side of Úbeda from the parador, across from the Institute Enseñanza Media.

Now we move on. If you spend the night in the province of Jaén, you'll need to go 65 to 75 miles (depending on where you stayed) the next day to reach one of my most highly recommended "Top Ten Cities."

2. Córdoba

Ten centuries ago, Córdoba was one of the greatest cities in the world: it then had a population close to 900,000. The capital of Muslim Spain, it was not only Europe's largest city, but a cultural and intellectual center as well. Córdoba, the seat of the Western Caliphate, flourished with public baths, mosques, a great library, and palaces. But a lot of greedy, sacking hordes have since passed through Córdoba, tearing down its ancient buildings, carting off its art treasures, and pillaging its riches. Perhaps the proof of Córdoba's greatness lies in the fact that—despite these assaults—it still has enough traces of its former glory to make it a rival of Seville and Granada, and a contender for the title of the most fascinating city in Andalusia.

Today this provincial capital is known chiefly for its mosque, but it abounds with other artistic and architectural riches, especially its domestic dwellings. The old Arab and Jewish quarters are filled with streets narrower than most sidewalks. Like Seville, Córdoba is famed for its flower-filled patios, and it's perfectly acceptable to walk along the streets, gazing into the courtyards. This is rarely considered an invasion of privacy; rather, the citizens of Córdoba take pride in showing off their patios, part of the tradition of the city. For the most part, these homes are whitewashed, and plants hang from balconies.

If you are bypassing the province of Jaén and heading directly from Madrid to Córdoba, the distance is about 260 miles, a good day's drive from the capital. Córdoba lies on that much-traveled route between Madrid and Seville. Consequently, reaching it by rail from many centers in Spain is easy. It is serviced by both a **TER,** a fast express, and a slow train. The train trip from Madrid to Córdoba goes through some of Spain's most beautiful countryside. The **TALGO** is a fast, comfortable, and inexpensive ride.

Before I highlight the treasures of Córdoba, let's find a hotel.

WHERE TO STAY: The hotel situation here is varied. There are several that are modern and relatively impersonal, others more atmospheric and charming, and a few in both categories that are inexpensive.

Hotel Residencia Marisa, 6 Cardenal Herrero (tel. 47-31-42), is a real find, with a formal entrance and wrought-iron bars on its three floors of windows. Right opposite the mosque, it is a simple, friendly, and clean 28-room hotel where you can get a double with bath or shower for 4,500 pesetas ($31.50), a single for 2,800 pesetas ($19.60). No meals are served except a continental breakfast, not included in the tariffs. The rooms are comfortable and well furnished, and there's a pleasant white-walled lounge with dark wood doors. The service is polite and efficient. The major drawback is that the bells of the Mezquita church are likely to go off every 15 minutes and some readers have found it difficult to sleep.

Hotel Residencia El Califa, 14 Calle Lope de Hocles (tel. 29-94-00), presents a routine façade of slick walls and modern windows to a commercial street corner near the center of town. Attracting what seems to be a mainly Spanish clientele, the hotel has russet-colored marble floors, velour wall coverings, a spacious lounge, and an active TV set broadcasting soccer matches. Each of the 46 bedrooms contains air conditioning and private bath. Singles cost 4,900 pesetas ($34.30) and 6,500 pesetas ($45.50); doubles, 8,000 pesetas ($59.50). There is a restaurant, plus a bar and parking garage on the premises.

Hotel Selu, 7 Eduardo Dato (tel. 47-65-00). You'll find this modern hotel on a very narrow street in a dusty commercial part of town near the Paseo de la Victoria. Inside, some laudable efforts were made to add visual interest to the efficiently contemporary lobby. Spotlights illuminate the life-sized stone nude of a woman in the lobby-level café. Near the reception desk, masses of plants, dozens of velvet-covered armchairs, and a huge photograph of the Moorish columns of the Mezquita soften the angular lines. The hotel contains 118 simple bedrooms, each with private bath, phone, and air conditioning. Singles cost 2,500 pesetas ($17.50), doubles, 3,800 pesetas ($26.60). Motorists appreciate the in-house parking garage.

Hostal El Triunfo, 87 Cardenal Gonzalez (tel. 47-63-75). Set within an Andalusian building to the side of the Mezquita, this unpretentious 45-room hotel is owned and maintained by Señor Juan de la Rubia and his family. Each of the small but clean rooms has its own bath and phone, renting for 2,000 pesetas ($14) in a single, 3,500 pesetas ($24.50) in a double, with breakfast included. There's a family-style restaurant and bar adjacent to the reception area, frequented by neighborhood residents.

Hotel Riviera, 5 Plaza Aladreros (tel. 47-60-18). The genial and engaging owner of this modern hotel is José Palacios, who is likely to be staffing the reception desk on the day of your arrival. His establishment is set behind a five-story modern façade on a triangular plaza in a commercial section of town. The hotel offers 30 very clean "no-frills" accommodations, each with private bath, air conditioning, and phone. Only breakfast is served. Singles rent for 2,000 pesetas ($14), doubles, 3,600 pesetas ($25.30), taxes not included.

Hotel El Brillante, 91 Avenida del Brillante (tel. 47-58-00), is a third-class hotel five minutes from the heart of the city, at the foot of a hill that leads to the government's first-class parador. A typically Andalusian building, with white plaster and green trim, El Brillante has the characteristics of an old inn, with a patio (canopied in summer) filled with vines and potted plants. You'll be led up a staircase to a balcony, which winds around to the simple bedrooms. A double with bath rents for 2,800 pesetas ($19.60). Singles range in price from 2,000 pesetas ($14). The hotel is reached by bypassing the railway station and heading north up the Avenida de América. Cross the railway bridge and continue for half a mile. El Brillante is at the clearly marked turnoff to the parador.

Hotel Granada, 21 Avenida de América (tel. 47-70-00), is not the most elaborate or choicest hotel in Córdoba, but it shouldn't be written off. It's only a one-star hotel, across the street from a railway station—but what a railway station. Set back from the avenue, the station is colorful, with trees and a little flower garden. The Granada is also well built, fairly modern, and huddles beside this tree-lined avenue, luring guests with its combination bar-lounge at the entrance. The bedrooms are simply but adequately furnished. For a good-size double with private bath, the charge is 2,800 pesetas ($19.60). The best singles (with shower, no toilet) tally up to 2,500 pesetas ($17.50). Lunch or dinner costs 1,100 pesetas ($7.70) extra, including, for example, cream of mushroom soup, fried fish, filet of veal with vegetables, plus a choice of desserts.

Andalucía, 3 José Zorrilla (tel. 47-60-00), has made many friends since opening its doors in the late '60s. Off the Gran Capitán, it lies near the cathedral, making a presentable first impression with its admittedly modest trappings. "It always seems to be full," was one typical comment. "The word must be out." The word is that you can get a clean and comfortable double room for just 3,200 pesetas ($22.40), a single with shower bath for 1,900 pesetas ($13.30). The Andalucía serves breakfast, costing extra. Lunch or dinner goes for 950 pesetas ($6.65).

The Big Splurge

Parador Nacional de la Arruzafa, Avenida de la Arruzafa (tel. 27-59-00), is serenely placed on the rise of the Sierra de Córdoba, at the outskirts of the city. For its reasonable rates, it offers the conveniences and facilities of a luxurious resort hotel. It's one of the finest paradors in all of Spain, commanding not only the best view in Córdoba but featuring a swimming pool as well. The bedrooms—83 in all—are spacious and furnished in finely styled dark wood pieces. Some of the rooms have balconies for taking breakfast or relaxing over a drink. Doubles—all with complete private bath—cost from 10,000 pesetas ($70). A double rented to one person goes for 8,500 pesetas ($59.50).

Hotel Adarve, 15-17 Magistral González Francés (tel. 48-14-11). When it was built hundreds of years ago as a private villa, its triple rows of stone-trimmed windows and ornate iron balustrades aroused local envy. In 1986 it was tastefully renovated into one of the most attractive hotels in town. It sits opposite an unused, very ornate rear entrance to the Mezquita. The marble and granite sheathing of its airy lobby opens into an interior courtyard filled with seasonal flowers, a pair of splashing fountains, and a symmetrical stone arcade. There's no restaurant, but a coffeeshop and bar serves drinks and light snacks. Each of the 103 bedrooms contains a black-and-white marble floor, a modern bath, color TV, a phone, radio, and air conditioning. Singles cost 6,600 pesetas ($46.20) to 8,000 pesetas ($56); doubles, 10,000 pesetas ($70). The architects managed to fit in a parking garage nearby.

Los Gallos, 7 Avenida de Medina Azahara (tel. 23-55-00), is a modern hotel set in the midst of this ancient city. But it comes off winningly, perhaps because of its taste level and streamlined design. Half a block from a wide, tree-shaded boulevard, it stands eight floors high, crowned by an informal roof garden. The lifesavers in summer are the outdoor swimming pool and the air-conditioned bedrooms. For a double room with private bath, the charge is 11,000 pesetas ($77). Singles cost 8,500 pesetas ($59.50). The rooms have many built-in comforts and contain balconies. Finally, the hotel offers many additional facilities, such as a restaurant, a drinking lounge, and a spacious public lobby.

WHERE TO DINE: By all means, shake free of your hotel for at least one meal a day while you're in Córdoba. The restaurants are more like an evening adventure than they are places to pick up a quick bite. Often they combine food with flamenco—so make an evening of it.

El Caballo Rojo, entrances at 28 Cardenal Herrero, Plaza de la Hoguera, and 4 Judería (tel. 47-53-75), is the most elegant and expensive restaurant in Córdoba, a splurge choice. It is an atmospheric establishment within walking distance of the Mezquita in the old part of town. Its entrance is across from the Mezquita, but it requires a walk down a long open-air passageway flanked with potted geraniums and vines. You'll first see a popular bar belonging to the restaurant, and you may want to stop in there for your pre-dinner drink. Afterward, you can take the iron-railed stairs to the sun-flooded upper dining room with its immaculate napery and bare wood floors.

At "The Red Horse," a set meal begins at 1,500 pesetas ($10.50), and a typical one might include gazpacho, a main dish of chicken, then ice cream and sangría. The ice cream, incidentally, is likely to be homemade pistachio. To break the monotony of the usual gazpacho, you can order a variation here: almond-flavored broth with apple pieces floating in it. In addition to Andalusian dishes, the chef also knows how to prepare both Sephardic and Mozarabic specialties. The real aficionado comes here for rabo de toro, a stew that can be made with the tail of an ox or a bull. Unlike most rape served in Spain, the angler fish here is prepared in the Mozárabe style—that is, with pignolias, currants, carrots, and cream. It's easy to spend 3,500 pesetas ($24.50) for a dinner here if you order some of the more unusual (to the North American palate) delicacies.

La Almudaina, 1 Plaza de los Santos Martíres (tel. 47-43-42). The owners of this historic restaurant deserve almost as much credit for renovating a decrepit older building as they do for the excellent cuisine produced today by its bustling kitchens. In what used to be the Jewish quarter, which fronts the river, this establishment is considered by many residents to be one of the most attractive restaurants in Andalusia. Specialties include salmon crêpes, a wide array of fish and meats, and a not-too-sweet form of chocolate crêpe for dessert. Full meals range from 1,800 pesetas ($12.60) to 2,800 pesetas ($19.60), and are served daily except Sunday night.

Restaurant Oscar, 6 Plaza de los Chirinos (tel. 47-75-17), is hard to find even for seasoned residents of Córdoba. The location is in a quiet neighborhood about a block off the city's main commercial boulevard, Calle Cruz Conde. This is *the* seafood restaurant of town. You'll be tempted to stop for a drink in the comfortably appointed bar near the entrance before heading into the dining room in back. The food at the bar is most tempting, with rations of tapas priced from 350 pesetas ($2.45). Many guests fill up there. However, full meals are served in a tasteful decor of salmon-colored walls and timbered ceilings. Costing from 1,800 pesetas ($12.60), a meal might include different concoctions of shrimp, sea bass baked in salt, deep-fried squid, grilled hake, seafood soup, and such meat dishes as veal scalloppine with Roquefort. The huge selection of appetizers includes a savory seafood salad, smoked salmon, and fish soup. Meals are served at lunch and dinner daily except Sunday.

Ciro's, 19 Paseo de la Victoria (tel. 29-04-64). Since its co-owners established this restaurant in the late '60s, it's been transformed through various stages from a simple cafetería to the accommodating and comfortably air-conditioned restaurant you see today. Antonio and Edelmiro, the proprietors, mingle an almost impeccable service with a mixture of regional and nouvelle cuisine in the Andalusian style. Examples are a salmon and anchovy pudding, stuffed sweet peppers, hake in shrimp sauce, veal in red wine, and an array of dessert sorbets. Full meals range from 2,000 pesetas ($14) to 3,500 pesetas ($24.50).

El Churrasco, 16 Romero (tel. 29-08-19), is an unusually pleasant restaurant housed in an ancient stone-fronted building of the Jewish Quarter. Owned and operated by Rafael Carrillo, it serves elegant meals for 2,000 pesetas ($14) on two well-appointed floors of taste and charm. You'll pass a standup bar and an open grill before reaching the ground-floor dining room. Its view of the sky is covered, but you'll have the impression of being in a Moorish courtyard, thanks to the ring-around arches, the splashing fountain, and the drainage channels set into the brick floor between the plants and tables. Upstairs a more formal dining room is almost completely ringed with the owner's sometimes riveting collection of paintings, many of which were painted by his Córdoban friends. You can enjoy such specialties as grilled filet of beef with whisky sauce, succulent roast lamb, veal, and pork, grilled salmon, hake, swordfish, or rape (a whitefish) in a pine-nut sauce—all accompanied with immaculate napery and impeccable service. The establishment serves lunch and dinner daily except Thursday and in August.

THE SIGHTS: The principal reason for visiting Córdoba is its Mezquita, now a cathedral. But the old Alcázar, an ancient synagogue, museums, and galleries will round out your day. There's a lot to absorb, and visitors with more time may want to spend at least two days here. I'll begin with the star attraction.

The Mezquita

The origins of this mosque go back to the 8th century. It was the crowning architectural achievement of the Muslims in the West, rivaled only by the mosque at Mecca. It is a fantastic labyrinth of red-and-white, peppermint-striped pillars. Wandering inside is like taking a journey through an enchanted forest of jasper and marble.

To the shock and astonishment of most visitors, a cathedral sits awkwardly in the middle of this mosque, disfiguring the purity of the lines. The cathedral, mostly 16th century plus a lot of other styles, is impressive enough, what with its intricately carved ceiling and baroque choir stalls. But who can forgive it—or its builders—for desecrating one of the most magnificent architectural treasures in Europe? Additional ill-conceived annexes later turned the Mezquita into one of the freak architectural sights of the world. The one most interesting feature of the mosque is the *mihrab,* a domed chapel-shrine of Byzantine mosaics that once housed the Koran.

The Mezquita is open from 10:30 a.m. to 1:30 p.m. and 4 to 7 p.m. Admission is 150 pesetas ($1.05).

After your exploration of the interior, you may want to stroll through the Courtyard of the Orange Trees, which has a beautiful fountain. My heartiest readers will climb a 16th-century tower that was built here on the base of a Moorish minaret. The tower is high, and offers a panoramic view of Córdoba and its environs.

The Alcázar of the Christian Kings

Started in 1328 by Alfonso XI ("The Just"), the Alcázar de los Reyes Cristianos is one of the best examples of military architecture of its day. This fortress on the river was once lived in by Ferdinand and Isabella, who governed Castile from here, and made preparations for the reconquest of Granada, the last Moorish stronghold in Spain. Columbus journeyed this way round about then to fill Isabella's ears with his plans for discovery.

The building is a quadrangle, characterized by powerful walls and a trio of towers—the Tower of the Lions, the Tower of Allegiance, and the Tower of the River. The walls of the Tower of the Lions (Leones) contain ogival ceilings that are intricately decorated, and considered the most notable example of Gothic architecture in Andalusia.

The Alcázar is visited in particular for its beautiful gardens, which are illuminated at night, and for its Moorish baths. Of the many patios of the Alcázar, the Patio Morisco is perhaps the loveliest, its pavement decorated with the arms of León and Castile. Also while here, be sure to seek out a distinguished Roman sarcophagus, representative of the funereal art of the 2nd and 3rd centuries A.D. The collection of Roman mosaics is also outstanding—especially in a unique piece dedicated to Polifemo and Galatea.

The Alcázar is open year round from 9:30 a.m. to 1:30 p.m. In the afternoon from May 1 to September 30, it is open from 5 to 8 p.m. From October 1 to April 30, its afternoon hours are from 4 to 7 p.m. The admission is 100 pesetas (70¢). The gardens are illuminated from May 1 to September 30 from 10 p.m. till midnight.

The Synagogue (Sinagoga)

Córdoba possesses the most famous synagogue in Spain, one of three pre-Inquisition ones remaining (the other two are in Toledo). The Mudéjar edifice was built in 1350 on Calle Judío in the Barrio Judío (Jewish Quarter). The synagogue is noted particularly for its stucco work. The east wall contains a large orifice where the Tabernacle once was placed (inside were kept the scrolls of the Pentateuch). At the time Columbus was discovering America, the Jews were being expelled from Spain. The synagogue was then turned into a hospital, a role it played until 1588 when it became a Catholic chapel. The building may be visited during the day from 9:30 a.m. to 1:30 p.m. and 3:30 to 6:30 p.m. No admission is charged, but the attendant will expect a tip.

The Fine Arts Museum (Museo Bellas Artes)

Housed in an old hospital founded by the Catholic monarchs, this picture gallery is at the Plaza del Potro ("Pony Square"). The collection includes a group of medieval Andalusian paintings, examples of Spanish baroque art, and works by many of Spain's most important 19th- and 20th-century painters, including Goya. The museum was being renovated at press time, with its reopening schedule not yet known. Check at the tourist office.

Museo de Julio Romero de Torres

Reached across the patio from the Fine Arts gallery, this museum at Plaza del Potro honors a Córdoba-born artist who died in 1930. It has a certain novelty interest, for the artist particularly liked to paint nude women, such as the one seen in the celebrated *Naranjas y Limones* (oranges and lemons). When you glimpse this nude, figure out which are the lemons. Other notable works include *The Little Girl Who Sells Fuel, El Pecado* (Sin), and *A Dedication to the Art of the Bullfight.* A corner of the studio that the artist once occupied in Madrid has been reproduced in one of the rooms, displaying paintings left unfinished at his death. It is open from 10 a.m. to 2 p.m. in summer, from 10 a.m. to 1:30 p.m. and 4 to 6 p.m. in winter, charging no admission.

La Plaza del Potro, on which the museum stands, is one of the most characteristic of Córdoba. It is noted for its fountain, built in 1557, standing at one end of the square. The young stallion of the fountain has his forelegs raised, holding the shield of Córdoba.

Museo Municipal de Arte Taurino

Mementos of great bullfights are in a 16th-century building in the Jewish quarter, the same part of town that produced Maimonides. It was inaugurated in 1983 as an establishment connected to, but separate from, the Museo Municipal de Arte Cordobesas. Its ample galleries with splendid rooms contain memorabilia of the great Córdoba bullfighters, including stuffed bulls' heads, "suits of light," and pictures, trophies, and posters. That's Manolete over there in repose. You'll also see the blood-smeared uniform of El Cordobés. Both of these famed bullfighters came from Córdoba. The museum, at the Plazuela de Maimonides, may be visited from 9:30 a.m. to 1:30 p.m. and 5 to 8 p.m. in summer, from 9:30 a.m. to 1:30 p.m. on Sunday. Closed Monday. Admission is 100 pesetas (70¢).

Other Sights

Córdoba also contains a **Roman bridge** (Puente Romano) believed to date from the time of Emperor Augustus. It's hardly Roman anymore, as none of the

16 arches that support the bridge is original. In addition, the sculptor Bernabé Gómez del Río erected a statue to Saint Raphael in the middle of the bridge in 1651.

On the other side of the Roman bridge is the **Tower of the Calahorra.** Henry II of Trastámara ordered this tower built in 1369 to protect him from his brother, Peter I. The tower betrays Mudéjar architectural influences, as reflected in the arched ceilings of the chambers. In all, there are 14 good-size rooms, and the city of Córdoba uses them to house a museum of the town's history. For example, in one chamber are the three charters granted Córdoba by Ferdinand III. Another chamber honors Gonzalo Fernández de Córdoba, the Gran Capitán. Finally, one large room is called the Hall of the Americas. The tower keeps the same hours as the Alcázar, but admission here is 75 pesetas (53¢).

The **Provincial Archeological Museum** (Museo Arqueológico Provincial), Plaza Jerónimo Páez (tel. 47-40-11), is one of the three most important archeological museums in Spain (it's rated just behind those of Madrid and Barcelona). It's housed in a palace dating from 1505 that once belonged to Páez de Castillejo. Arranged chronologically, the collection depicts the goods left behind by the various peoples and conquerors who have swept through the province of Córdoba—everything from paleolithic times (400,000 years ago), neolithic (5th millennium before Christ), and Iberian hand weapons and ceramics to Roman sculptures, bronzes, ceramic, inscriptions, and mosaics. Especially interesting are some Visigothic artifacts. The most outstanding collection, however, is devoted to Arabian art and records the entire Muslim occupation. In between exhibits, take a few minutes to relax in one of the patios, with its fountains and ponds. Hours are 10 a.m. to 2 p.m. year round, 5 to 8 p.m. in summer, and 4 to 7 p.m. in winter. It's closed Sunday afternoon and Monday. Admission is 150 pesetas ($1.05).

One of the newest museums to open in Córdoba is the **Palacio de Viana** on the Plaza de Don Gome, which is open to the public from 9 a.m. to 2 p.m. in summer, charging 150 pesetas ($10.5) for admission. From the first of October until the end of May, hours are 10 a.m. to 1 p.m. and 4 to 6 p.m.; closed Wednesday. Córdoba was once known for its palatial palaces, but few of them are open to the public. Visitors are shown into a carriage house, where the elegant vehicles of another era are displayed. In a city famed for its leather, these carriages have much leather decoration. In the elegant rooms, look for the leather wall hangings, some of which date from the period of the reconquest by the Christians. There's also a collection of leather paintings. You can wander at leisure through the garden and patios.

SHOPPING: In Moorish times Córdoba was known for a peculiar kind of leather. This leather took its name from the city, whence is derived the word "cordwainer." This Córdoboan leather, so highly valued in 15th-century Europe, was studded with gold and silver ornaments, then painted with embossed designs (*guadamacil*). These large panels from Córdoba were used in many places in lieu of tapestries. Today the industry has fallen into great decline, the market filled with cheap imitations.

However, one shop in Córdoba continues the old traditions. **Meryan,** at 2 Calleja de las Flores (tel. 47-59-02), one of the most colorful streets in the city, is run by Angel Lopez-Obrero, aided by his two skilled sons, Alejandro and Carlos. They operate near the mosque in a building some 2½ centuries old. Their workshops are at the same address, and you can see artisans plying the age-old craft.

Usually items are custom ordered, but at a commercial retail outlet a selection of ready-to-go items is also sold, including cigarette boxes, jewel cases, attaché cases, book and folio covers, and ottoman covers, along with a large selection of other leather goods.

THE BODEGAS AND BARS OF CÓRDOBA: **Bodega Campos,** 32 Lineros (tel. 47-41-42), is the most festive-looking old tavern and wine cellar in Córdoba. It is accustomed to foreigners, who constantly seek it out near the Plaza del Potro (the entrance is by the little church of San Francisco). You can ramble through the long-beamed room, explore the rows of high-stacked barrels of aging wine, then perhaps have a glass of sherry in the courtyard, with its balcony and trailing flowers and vines. Don't miss the old iron gateway or the well with its rope and bucket. The bodega receives visitors from 10 a.m. to 2 p.m. and 4 to 8 p.m. Count yourself lucky if you hear some spontaneous flamenco while you're there.

Casa Pepe, 1 Romero (tel. 29-02-82), founded in 1930, is one of the most traditionally decorated bars of Córdoba, and one of the most securely established. Here you can have savory tapas and the kind of drinks that everyone in town has tasted at one time or another. It is located at the junction of two pedestrian streets within a two-story white stucco building whose balconies are festooned with flowers.

Bar Mezquita, 24 Cardenal Herrero (tel. 47-30-94), one of the oldest bars in Córdoba, has served glasses of beer and wine to clients within its cozy walls for many years. María and her husband, Rafael, are the genteel owners who maintain a tasty collection of tapas, served to standup clients in the postage-stamp bar in front or in the duet of old-fashioned rooms in back. The decor, with its Andalusian tiles and battered wooden tables, is nostalgically evocative of another era, and the bar has a loyal clientele. A glass of wine costs 35 pesetas (25¢), a draft beer 50 pesetas (35¢). The location is opposite the Mezquita, facing the monument's crumbling walls.

La Canoa, 18 Ronda los Tejares (tel. 47-17-61). Its rustic, almost monastic interior contrasts sharply with the covered pedestrian walkway on which it lies. However, its wine-barrel tables and Carthusian cellar decor appeals to its many clients. A wine press, terracotta floors, and an absence of chairs make a glass of wine or beer here more of a rapid pick-me-up than something to linger over for hours. You can order a ration of Serrano ham or a hefty platter of cheese if you're hungry. A beer costs 65 pesetas (46¢). The establishment is open daily except Sunday and for two weeks in August.

Casa Rubio, 5 Puerta de Almodóvar (tel. 29-00-64). You'll have to push back a thick curtain to enter this dimly lit enclave of pre-Franco Spain. Once inside, you'll find a gruff but accommodating welcome at the rectangular bar or in one of a pair of rooms partially covered with Andalusian tiles. My preferred place is within a plant-festooned inner courtyard, where iron tables and a handful of chairs wobble only slightly on the uneven flooring. Tapas include rations of Serrano ham or grilled squid, each 400 pesetas ($2.80). Beer costs 50 pesetas (35¢).

DISCOS: **Contactos,** 8 Eduardo Dato (tel. 29-24-66), in the center of town, is one of the city's most recent additions to the disco scene. A drink here averages 400 pesetas ($2.80) to 600 pesetas ($4.20). The disco is set behind a modern blue-green tile façade on a narrow pedestrian street. The entrance looks like a small art movie theater.

Saint-Cyr, 4 Eduardo Lucena (tel. 47-66-40), is the city's best choice for a disco with recently released and danceable music, and lots of the kind of people you might want to look at twice. Drinks cost 600 pesetas ($4.20).

3. Seville

Once in a great while, a city emerges with a personality so unique it becomes famed throughout the world for its beauty and romance. Seville, the capital of Andalusia, is such a place. It is the most charming of Spanish cities, because its mysteries cannot be unveiled in a night, or even in a month of nights.

Don Juan and Carmen—aided no small bit by Mozart and Bizet—have given Seville a romantic reputation. Perhaps because of the acclaim of *Don Giovanni, Carmen,* and *The Barber of Seville,* a cabal of debunkers has risen to challenge this reputation of the city. But if a visitor can see only two Spanish cities in a lifetime, they should be Seville first and Toledo second.

All the words used to conjure up an image of Andalusia—orange trees, mantillas, lovesick toreadors, flower-filled patios, castanet-rattling gypsies—seem to reach their fruition in Seville. But it is no mere fluff of a city decked out for tourists; it is rather a substantial river port, containing some of the most important artistic works and architectural monuments in Spain.

Seville had undergone radical change at the hands of history, but unlike most Spanish cities, it has fared rather well under most of its conquerors, be they Romans, Arabs, or Christians. Pedro the Cruel and Ferdinand and Isabella are only some of the many monarchs who have held court here. When Spain entered its Golden Age in the 16th century, Seville was the city that funneled gold from the New World into Spain. Columbus docked here after his journey to America.

Seville, romantic city that it is, was planned in my opinion more for the horses and buggy than for the modern motorist of today. Driving within its precincts is a nightmare. Nearly all the streets run one way toward the Río Guadalquivir. Locating a hard-to-find restaurant or hotel on a hidden little square might require more than patience, and even a little bit of luck.

A traveler's advisory: I sounded an alert against crime in the introduction to this chapter, and I doubly sound that alarm in Seville. With massive unemployment, the city has been hit by a crime wave in recent years, often daring daylight robberies, most often staged by gangs of rampaging youths. María Luisa Park is especially dangerous, as is the highway leading to Jerez de la Frontera and Cádiz. Take the same precautions in Seville that you would when strolling along New York's Times Square at midnight. Dangling cameras and purses are especially vulnerable. Cars are routinely broken into. Don't leave them unguarded with your luggage inside.

The police force recently has been beefed up, hoping to cut down on street crime. But those days of yore when you could wander at any hour of the day or night through the Santa Cruz district, or elsewhere, have gone the way of Franco's police state.

It takes at least two days to see most of the major sights of Seville, which means you'll need a roof over your head—

WHERE TO STAY: Seville's hotels, unlike its restaurants, are usually moderate in price—and several of them have Andalusian charm and style, antiquated but adequate.

Hotel América, 2 Jesús del Gran Poder (tel. 22-09-51), in the heart of town, is a 100-bedroom hotel that has many superior features. All units contain private bath, as well as phone and radio. The hotel is mercifully air-conditioned, and in high season it charges 5,800 pesetas ($40.60) in a double, from 3,800 pesetas ($26.60) in a single. Rooms are small, usually with tile floors, and everything is spick-and-span. Other superior features include wall-to-wall carpeting, and if you're there in winter, an individual heat control that works. One reader

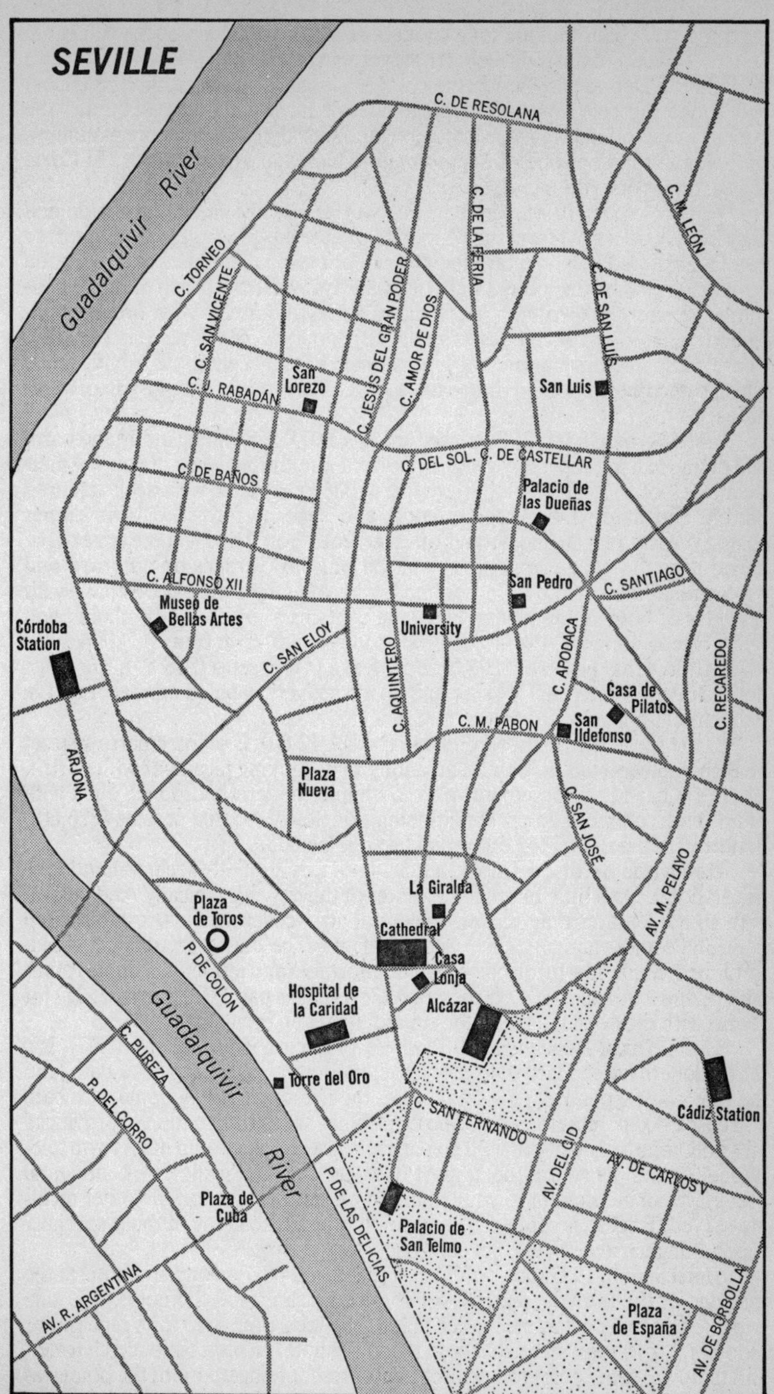
SEVILLE
Guadalquivir River
C. DE RESOLANA
C. M. LEÓN
C. DE LA FERIA
C. DE SAN LUIS
C. TORNEO
C. SAN VICENTE
C. JESÚS DEL GRAN PODER
C. AMOR DE DIOS
San Lorezo
C. J. RABADÁN
San Luis
C. DEL SOL. C. DE CASTELLAR
C. DE BAÑOS
Palacio de las Dueñas
C. ALFONSO XII
San Pedro
C. SANTIAGO
Museo de Bellas Artes
Córdoba Station
University
C. SAN ELOY
C. APODACA
C. AQUINTERO
Casa de Pilatos
C. RECAREDO
C. M. PABON
San Ildefonso
ARJONA
Plaza Nueva
C. SAN JOSÉ
AV. M. PELAYO
La Giralda
Plaza de Toros
Cathedral
Casa Lonja
P. DE COLÓN
Hospital de la Caridad
Alcázar
C. PUREZA
Guadalquivir
Torre del Oro
P. DEL CORRO
C. SAN FERNANDO
Cádiz Station
AV. DEL CID
AV. DE CARLOS V
River
Plaza de Cuba
P. DE LAS DELICIAS
Palacio de San Telmo
AV. R. ARGENTINA
Plaza de España
AV. DE BORBOLLA

liked the "real beds that are long enough—not the usual hammocks you get in Spain." Relaxing from sightseeing trips, you can rest in the TV lounge or order a drink in the Duque bar. Beside the hotel is a large car park, rising three floors and sheltering 600 cars. Although it doesn't have a major restaurant, the América does offer a tea room, cafetería, and snackbar, and if you're planning a shopping expedition, one of Spain's major chain department stores, El Corte Inglés, opens onto the same square.

Hotel Alcázar, 10 Menéndez y Pelayo (tel. 41-20-11). Set on a wide and busy boulevard across from the Murillo Gardens, this pleasantly contemporary hotel is sheltered behind a façade of brown brick. You'll register at a reception desk made cool by the lobby's slabs of striated gray marble. Each of the 93 bedrooms contains its own bath, phone, and air conditioning. With breakfast included, singles cost 4,200 pesetas ($29.40), doubles, 5,800 pesetas ($40.60). There's a Spanish restaurant and very pleasant bar adjacent to the lobby, above which a decorator installed three lattice structures reminiscent of a trio of miradores.

Hotel Fernando III, 21 San José (tel. 21-73-07). Its echoing lobby and baronial dining hall remind many visitors of what a wealthy hacienda in South America might look like. The building is modern, but constructed with richly textured marble and hardwood detailing, cooly and sparsely furnished with leather chairs, verdant plants, and wrought-iron accents. You'll find it at the edge of the barrio near the northern periphery of the Murillo Gardens on a narrow and quiet street. Many of the 156 accommodations offer a private balcony filled with cascades of burgeoning plants, and each contains a private bath, phone, and radio. Depending on the accommodation, singles cost from 3,700 pesetas ($25.90) to 4,200 pesetas ($29.40); doubles, 5,000 pesetas ($38.50), breakfast not included. There's a TV salon and an attractively paneled bar decorated in richly modern lines.

Hotel Reyes Católicos, 57 Gravina (tel. 21-12-00), is set on a narrow street near the railway station, behind an anonymous looking façade of white brick. There's a bar in the basement, plus 27 simple modern bedrooms, each with radio, bath, phone, and air conditioning. Singles cost 3,800 pesetas ($26.60), doubles 7,500 pesetas ($52.50), breakfast not included.

Residencia Sevilla, 5 Daoiz (tel. 38-41-61), is a quietly secluded and low-priced hotel. On a little plaza in the center of the city, it's typically Andalusian, with all the features that implies—a central glass-covered courtyard, a shaded patio, balconies, hanging vines, lots of plants. The entire first floor has old-fashioned, home-like furnishings. The comfortable and attractive double rooms with private bath peak at 4,000 pesetas ($28); singles pay 3,000 pesetas ($21) for rooms with showers. No meals are served, not even breakfast.

Hostal Ducal Residencia, 19 Plaza de la Encarnación (tel. 21-51-07), is a fairly modern hotel. Each of its airy, spacious double bedrooms has a bath, and the rate is 4,000 pesetas, ($28). Likewise, the five single rooms come with bath and cost 2,800 pesetas ($19.60). The furnishings are a combination of provincial and utilitarian, efficient but with no particular style. Each room has its own telephone, as well as central heating (it does get cold in Seville). A continental breakfast can be brought to your room for an extra charge, but no other meals are served. English is spoken. The location is handy to many of those specialty shops along narrow streets. Several buses stop nearby.

Hotel Simón, 19 García de Vinuesa (tel. 22-66-60), is a one-star hotel at the rear end of the Giralda, suitable for some who can stand the noise. The side street seems to be what one reader called "the local drag strip for Vespa motor scooters." If you can stand that, you'll find the hotel an old-fashioned charmer, and there are some quiet rooms. Before its present reincarnation, the hotel was a fine Sevillian private mansion, typical of those built in the city in the 18th and 19th centuries. Transformed to meet the standards of a hotel with up-to-date requirements, it is on a side street. The best singles rent for 2,400 pesetas ($16.80), the price going up to 3,500 pesetas ($24.50) in a double with private bath. The cheapest way for a couple to stay here is to take a double without bath for 2,400 pesetas ($16.80). The food is good, and the service is excellent. The chandelier-lit dining room is in the old Moorish style.

Residencia Murillo, 9 Lope de Rueda (tel. 21-60-95), is tucked away deep in the heart of Santa Cruz, the old quarter. In fact, it's almost next to the gardens of the Alcázar on a street so narrow you can practically peer into the bedroom in the house across the way—the houses in the "barrio" are that close together. The Murillo is named after the artist who used to live in this district. Inside, the lounges harbor some fine architectural characteristics and antique reproductions. Behind a grilled screen is a retreat for drinks. A double room with private bath rents for 6,500 pesetas ($45.50); singles pay 4,000 pesetas ($28) for rooms with bath. Many of the rooms I recently inspected were cheerless and gloomy, so ask to have a look before checking in. Like all the hotels of Seville, the Murillo is in a noisy area.

You can reach this residencia from the Menéndez y Pelayo, a wide avenue that lies west of María Luisa Park, where there's a sign that will take you through the Murillo Gardens on the left. Motorists should try to park in the Plaza de Santa Cruz. You can then walk two blocks to the hotel, which will send a bellhop back to the car to pick up your suitcases. If there are two in your party, station a guard at the car, and if you're going out at night, call for an inexpensive taxi to deliver you right to your door instead of strolling through the streets of the old quarter. It's less romantic that way, but a heck of a lot safer.

Hostal Goya, 31 Mateos Gago (tel. 21-11-70). Its location within a narrow-fronted town house in the oldest part of the barrio is one of its strongest virtues. You'll recognize it because of its gold and white façade, ornate iron railings, and picture-postcard demeanor. Each of the 20 cozy and simple bedrooms contains a private sink and shower, but guests of some of the less expensive accommodations must use shared toilets in the hallways. Singles cost 2,100 pesetas ($14.70), doubles 2,800 pesetas ($19.60) to 3,100 pesetas ($21.70), depending on the plumbing. Guests congregate in the marble-floored ground-level salon, where a skylight floods the couches and comfortable chairs with sunlight.

The Big Splurge

Hotel Doña María, 19 Don Remondo (tel. 22-49-90). Its location only a few steps from the entrance to the cathedral permits visitors to its rooftop terrace one of the most dramatic views in town. This four-star hotel represents a well-worth-it splurge, partly because of its tastefully chosen Iberian antiques which fill its stone-sheathed lobby and upper hallways. Its ornate neoclassical entryway is offset with a pure white façade and ornate iron balconies which hint at the building's origin in the 1840s as a private villa.

Amid the flowering plants of the uppermost floor, you'll find a postage-stamp swimming pool ringed with garden-style lattices and antique wrought-iron railings. Each of the 61 bedrooms contains a private bath, phone, and a hookup for optional TV. A few possess four-poster beds, others a handful of antique reproductions. Depending on the season, the accommodation, and the plumbing, singles cost from 4,000 pesetas ($28) to 8,000 pesetas ($56); doubles, 8,000 pesetas ($56) to 14,000 pesetas ($98), breakfast not included.

WHERE TO DINE: Nearly all of the major restaurants known and frequented by tourists in Seville have increased their prices considerably in the past few years. In response to the trend, budget-seeking Europeans have turned to other restaurants, seeking out less-frequented establishments where the Sevillians have been blissfully eating for years. Let's get off the main trail and follow their lead.

Warning: Avoid eating in the ridiculously cheap but not very hygienic restaurants near the train station. One reader wrote, "I ended up spending far more money on medical expenses after eating there than I had saved at the restaurant."

La Albahaca, 12 Plaza de Santa Cruz (tel. 22-07-14), on a prominent square in the old city, with an open-air terrace, offers a friendly welcome and a limited but savory menu that has become a favorite of the elite community of Seville. Specialties include seafood soup, grilled lamb chops, shellfish bisque, partridge braised in sherry, salmon in papillote, and for dessert, a chocolate pudding. The restaurant is in an old señorial house whose detailing you'll probably admire between courses. Full meals, served every day except Sunday, range upward from 2,000 pesetas ($14).

José Luís, 13 Avenida República Argentina (tel. 27-70-93), is a popular restaurant in a residential section of town. The Andalusian cuisine uses top-quality beef from Argentina and has a variety of individualized house recipes which include items such as filet Cleopatra, beef with rice, and oven-roasted lamb. Full meals range from 2,500 pesetas ($17.50). The restaurant is closed Sunday night.

Bodegón El Riojana, 12 Virgen de la Montanas (tel. 45-06-82), is owned by the same investors who direct two other restaurants in town. This usually assures good-quality meat and shellfish in the restaurant section, and the bar area is crowded with lovers of seafood tapas. There is much camaraderie. The adjacent two-fork restaurant section serves an international cuisine which includes pimientos (peppers) Riojanoa, Andalusian beefsteak, artichokes and mussels in green sauce, and several dessert soufflés. Full meals range from 2,200 pesetas ($15.40).

Enrique Becerra, 2 Gamazo (tel. 21-30-49). On my latest rounds, this restaurant provided me with one of my best meals. Near the cathedral, it has an intimate setting where the tapas bar is almost as popular as the well-known Andalusian restaurant. You are given a hearty welcome, and you are left with the feeling that your business is really appreciated. While perusing the menu, you can sip dry Tío Pepe and eat herb-cured olives given extra flavor by lemon peel. The gazpacho here is among the best in the city, and the sangría is served ice cold and not sickeningly sweet as is too often the case. Specialties include hake "real," sea bream Bilboan-style, and a wide range of meat and fish dishes. A meal costs from 2,200 pesetas ($15.40). The place is closed Sunday.

La Isla, 23 Arfe (tel. 21-26-31), extremely noisy, is unquestionably popular, although it's gone a bit high hat on us, adding such refinements as air conditioning. Once little more than a workingperson's dining spot, the Isla now appeals to tourists also. A meal costs from 2,000 pesetas ($14), and for that price, you get reasonably good cooking—including such typical dishes as sole covered with a tasty sauce, grilled liver, chicken croquettes. At an appealing bar at the front, guests can order a before-dinner sherry. The restaurant huddles close to a food market, giving you a view into the daily lives of Sevillians. It is closed in August.

El Bodegón Torre del Oro, 15 Santander (tel. 21-66-28), merits a resounding olé. The specialties of this three-fork house include Andalusian gazpacho (only in spring and summer), paella de arroz Bodegón (made with chicken, vegetables, and varied shellfish), and the most popular dish of all, pollo al ajillo (chicken cooked with garlic). You'll undoubtedly like the rustic atmosphere here—Spain itself, reflected in the hanging hams, the old oil paintings, crude tables and simple chairs. The evening begins in the bar section, where all sorts of wines are available, along with the traditional tapas of prawns, lobsters, etc. The Torre del Oro also offers a set menu for 1,800 pesetas ($12.60) that includes gazpacho, then veal or paella, and flan at the end. You can also eat at the bar, which is cheaper.

Restaurante Los Alcázares, 10 Miguel de Mañara (tel. 21-31-03), sits behind a colorfully tiled façade between the Alcázar and the Archives of the Indies. José Flores Fenández, the hard-working proprietor, prepares specialties such as a salad Andaluz (tomato, green pepper, and onion in about equal proportions), manchega garlic soup, sea bass or hake in fennel sauce, roast lamb cutlets, partridge in castellana sauce, or rabbit in cocotte sauce. The menu is in both English and Spanish and advertises meals that cost around 1,800 pesetas ($12.60) to 2,600 pesetas ($18.20). You'll enjoy a regional decor redolent of the Andalusian countryside. The establishment is closed on Sunday.

Mesón Don Raimundo, 26 Argote de Molina (tel. 22-33-55), is an attractively furnished restaurant whose entrance lies at the end of a flower-lined alleyway in the center of town. The interior of the building, which originated as a convent in the 17th century, contains lots of brick, terracotta, and gracefully carved columns which support the beamed or arched high ceilings. Your meal, illuminated with antique brass chandeliers and placed on immaculate multicolored napery, might include a fish stew of the day or one of the six kinds of soup (one with clams and pine nuts), then fresh grilled king shrimp, a casserole of partridge in sherry sauce, or wild rabbit casserole of the day. In winter, someone constantly feeds a glowing central fireplace, whose warmth makes the antique copper and wrought-iron art objects glow warmly. In summer, the place is comfortably air-conditioned. Full meals usually begin at 2,000 pesetas ($14).

Restaurant Rio Grande, 70 Betis (tel. 27-50-23), is named after the Guadalquivir River, which its panoramic windows overlook. It sits against the banks of the fabled river near the Plaza de Cuba, across the water from the oldest section of Seville. Some diners go here just for a view of the monuments of the city. But they quickly fall under the spell of the well-prepared Andalusian cuisine which has made the place famous. Full meals, priced from 2,200 pesetas ($15.40), might include cream of white asparagus soup, several kinds of salads, or a tempting appetizer of smoked salmon, smoked sole, and smoked anchovy (served with six different garnishes by the polite waiters). Main courses include a chef's special veal stew, swordfish with a ham-and-artichoke garnish, and hake filet in an almond-flavored eel sauce. It is open for lunch and dinner daily.

Hosteria del Laurel, 5 Plaza de los Venerables (tel. 22-02-95). Set inside one of the most charming buildings which ring this tiny, difficult-to-find square amid the labyrinth of the Barrio of Santa Cruz, this hideaway restaurant has two floors of dining rooms and iron-barred windows stuffed with burgeoning plants. Inside, amid Andalusian tiles and beamed ceilings, you can enjoy examples of typical regional cookery. Full meals are priced from 1,500 pesetas ($10.50) to 2,800 pesetas ($19.60). Many diners stop for a drink and tapas at the ground-floor bar before going into one of the dining rooms. It's more formal on the second floor.

El Mesón, 26 Calle del Dos de Mayo (tel. 21-30-75), was singled out for praise by James Michener in his now classic book, *Iberia*. In fact, the dessert favored by the novelist, membrillo and manchego cheese, is now called "The Michener Combination" on the menu. That menu is likely to feature fighting bull steak, as the Plaza de Toros is nearby. Many bullfighters frequent the establishment, and their presence, past and present, is commemorated in photographs and pictures decorating the walls. Look for the American bullfighter, John Fulton, as well as Kenneth Vanderford who was known as "the poor man's Hemingway." The restaurant owns several drawings of bulls and Spanish cowboys by Fulton. You might begin with a soothing dish of gazpacho, then go on to hake in the Navarre style if you don't want to face bull steak on your platter. Meals cost from 1,200 pesetas ($8.40) to 1,800 pesetas ($12.60). The restaurant is closed on Tuesday.

Restaurant El Tenorio, 11 Mateos Gago (tel. 21-40-30), sits behind a row of orange trees and a white-fronted façade between the cathedral and the barrio, a few steps from both. Its interior, dimly illuminated with a single window whose iron bars are festooned with ivy, is dotted with copper pots and pans, heavy timbers, and Spanish artifacts. Menu items prepared in the aromatic kitchen in back include roast lamb, an array of fresh fish, and succulent pork and beef dishes. Full meals cost from 2,000 pesetas ($14) each.

THE TOP SIGHTS: Seville has an astonishing number of palaces, churches, cathedrals, towers, and historic hospitals. Since it would take a great deal of time to visit all of them, I have narrowed the sights down to a handful of representative ones, which include all of the most famous and frequented places.

The Cathedral

This huge Gothic building, at the Plaza V. de los Reyes, ranks with St. Paul's in London and St. Peter's in Rome in size. Work began on it in the late 1400s, and it took centuries to complete. Built on the site of an ancient mosque, the cathedral claims that it contains the remains of Columbus, his tomb mounted on four sculptured men. (A digression: Many historians believe the remains of Columbus were taken to what is now the Dominican Republic sometime in the mid-16th century. However, in correspondence with me, the secretary of the Metropolitan Chapter maintains that the remains were moved to the Cathedral of Havana, Cuba, and finally, at the beginning of this century, in 1902, were shipped to the Seville cathedral. The Metropolitan Chapter keeps documents to this effect.)

The cathedral abounds in artistic works, many of them architectural, such as the stained-glass windows (some dating from the 15th century); the *rejas* (the iron screens closing off the chapels); the 15th-century choir stalls of gilt and velvet and elaborately carved; and, finally, the Gothic reredos above the main altar, a beautiful carving begun in the 15th century. During Corpus Christi and the Immaculate Conception observances, the altar boys do their dance of the castanets in front of the High Altar.

In the treasury you'll find minor works by Goya, Murillo, and Zurbarán; and here, in glass cases, a touch of the macabre shows up in the display of skulls.

After your tour of the dark interior, you can emerge into the sunlight again by entering the Patio of Orange Trees, with its fresh citrus scents and chirping birds. The cathedral soars into the sky, creating a sense of infinity. At night it is illuminated, and the effect of the Gothic fantasy is complete.

The cathedral may be visited from 10:30 a.m. to 1:30 p.m. and 4:30 to 6:30 p.m. (winter afternoon hours are 3:30 to 5:30 p.m.). Admission is 125 pesetas (88¢). Shorts and T-shirts are definitely not allowed. Also, depending on local circumstances, hours are likely to vary from those listed.

La Giralda Tower

This Moorish tower, at Plaza del Triunfo, next to the cathedral, is the city's most famous monument. Erected as a minaret in the 12th century, it has seen later additions, such as 16th-century bells. Just as the Big Ben tower symbolizes

London, La Giralda conjures up Seville. It is that important a landmark. To climb it is to take one of the walks of a lifetime. There are no steps—you ascend a ramp that seems endless. Should you make it to the top, the view of Seville is dazzling. The city is literally spread out at your feet. The old rule forbidding persons to go up alone has been done away with; authorities now assume you won't jump. Admission is 25 pesetas (18¢). It is open in summer from 10:30 a.m. to 1:30 p.m. and 4:30 to 6:50 p.m. (in winter from 10 a.m. to 1 p.m. and 4 to 5:30 p.m.). On holidays, it is open early in the morning.

The Alcázar

This is a magnificent Mudéjar palace, at Plaza del Triunfo, built in the 14th century by Pedro the Cruel. From the Dolls' Court to the Maidens' Court through the domed Ambassadors' Room, it contains some of the finest work of Sevillian craftsmen. Isabella and Ferdinand, who used to live here, also influenced its architectural evolution, as did Carlos V. On the top floor, the Oratory of the Catholic monarchs has a fine altar in polychrome tiles made by Pisano in 1504.

The Mudéjar style as exemplified by the façade was developed by Muslims working in Christian Spain following the final ousting of the Moors from Granada. Thus inspiration of the style is both Gothic and Muslim. This lavish palace in Seville is considered by some to be worthy of comparison with the Alhambra at Granada.

The well-kept gardens, filled with beautiful flowers, shrubbery, and fruit trees, are alone worth the visit. Hours are 9 a.m. to 1 p.m. and 3 to 5 p.m. On Saturday and Sunday it is open only in the morning. Admission is 125 pesetas (88¢).

Hospital de la Santa Carídad

This 17th-century hospital, 3 Temprado (tel. 22-32-32), is intricately linked to the legend of Miguel Manara. Such French writers as Dumas and Prosper Mérimée have portrayed him as a scandalous Don Juan. It has been suggested that he built this institution to atone for his sins. However, this has proved false. Manara had a "brave and chivalrous youth," but the death of his young and beautiful wife in 1661 caused such grief that he retired from society and entered the "Charity Brotherhood." There he spent the rest of his life, burying corpses of the sick and diseased as well as condemned and executed criminals. Today the members of this brotherhood of Saint Charity, as did their founder, look after the poor, the old, and invalids who have no one else to help them. Nuns show you through the courtyard, which is festive in colors of orange and sienna, and of different architectural styles. The baroque chapel contains works by Murillo and Valdés Leal, a 17th-century Spanish painter. As you're leaving the chapel, look over the exit door. Here you'll find one of the most macabre pictures I've ever seen—that of an archbishop being devoured by maggots. Somehow Leal's worms compensate for Murillo's pink cherubs. The hospital is open from 10 a.m. to 1 p.m. and 3:15 to 7 p.m. all year. Admission is 100 pesetas (70¢).

OTHER SIGHTS: The 12-sided **Tower of Gold** (Torre del Oro) overlooks the Guadalquivir River on the Paseo de Colón. Its lower base was built in the 13th century. Originally it was covered with gold tiles—hence its name—but someone long ago made off with them. Recently restored, the tower has been turned into a maritime museum. It is open from 10 a.m. to 1 p.m. daily except Monday. The price of admission is 25 pesetas (18¢).

To go to Seville and miss seeing an Andalusian palace would be a sad state of affairs. The Duchess of Alba no longer allows tourists to traipse through her inner sanctum, but it's quite easy to visit the **Casa de Pilatos,** the 16th-century palace of the dukes of Medinaceli, 1 Plaza de Pilatos (tel. 22-52-98).

Recapturing the splendor of the past, it combines the styles of Gothic, Mudéjar, and plateresque in its courtyards, fountains, and salons. According to tradition, this house was supposed to be a reproduction of Pilate's House in Jerusalem. Don't miss the two old carriages, or the rooms filled with Greek and Roman statues. The painting collection includes works by Carreño, Pantoja de la Cruz, Sebastiano del Piombo, Lucas Jordan, Batalloli, Pacheco, and Goya. The mansion may be visited from 10 a.m. to 1 p.m. and 3 to 8 p.m. in summer, from 10 a.m. to 1 p.m. and 3 to 6 p.m. in winter. The fee is 125 pesetas (88¢).

Continuing our exploration, in the lovely old convent off the Calle de Alfonso XII you'll find one of the most important art collections in Spain, housed in the **Museo de Bellas Artes** (Fine Arts Museum), 9 Plaza de Museo. A whole gallery here is devoted to two paintings by El Greco of his son, but Seville-born Murillo and his devoutly religious paintings are the highlights. Works by Zurbarán are also exhibited. The 17th-century artist Valdés Leal with his dramatic, macabre paintings is represented as well, with an entire wing devoted to his works. He did not believe in subtlety; in his painting of John the Baptist's head on a platter, he included his knife—in case you didn't get the point. I find the top floor less interesting, with its so-called modern paintings.

The art gallery is open from 10 a.m. to 2 p.m. and 5 to 7 p.m. (from 10 a.m. to 2 p.m. on Saturday and Sunday). It's closed on Monday. Admission is 150 pesetas ($1.05).

No sightseeing trip to Seville would be complete without a . . .

Stroll Through Santa Cruz

What was once a ghetto of Spanish Jewry is now the heart of Old Seville. The streets of Santa Cruz are no bigger than alleyways, and have such names as "Vida" or "Muerte" (Life, Death). Flower-filled balconies with draping bougainvillea jut out over this labyrinth, shading you from the noonday sun or lunar rays. Here you can look through numerous wrought-iron gates into the patios filled with fountains and plants. In the evening it is a common sight to see Sevillians sitting outside drinking icy sangría under the glow of lanterns. This old district, where Murillo used to live, can be entered through several streets, but the main one is northeast of the Alcázar. Its whitewashed houses are within easy walking distance of most of my hotel recommendations. Exercise caution strolling through this area, particularly at night, as it has been the setting for many robberies.

Now we head up the Avenida de Isabel la Católica for the . . .

Park of María Luisa

This vast tract of parkland—often considered dangerous to stroll through—in the eastern part of the city was once the private grounds of a palace. In 1929 Seville was to host the Spanish-American Exhibition, and many pavilions from the countries in the western hemisphere were erected here. The world-wide Depression brought havoc to the exhibition, but the pavilions still stand.

The principal one, at the Plaza de España, is a crescent-shaped building, accompanied by an arch-shaped lagoon with five arched and tile bridges leading to it. It's a fantastic palace and I commend the Sevillians for preserving it.

The **Archeological Museum** (Museo Arqueológico Provincial) is in the park at the Plaza de América, and it contains many artifacts from prehistoric times (Carambolo Treasure) and the days of the Romans, Visigoths, and Moors. It may be visited from 10 a.m. to 2 p.m., except Monday, for an admission fee of 150 pesetas ($1.05).

That Famous Tobacco Factory

At this point in your visit, you may wonder what happened to Carmen's tobacco factory (known more formally as the **Real Fábrica de Tabacos).** If you continue up the Calle San Fernando, you'll discover that the factory has gone to college . . . and so can we.

When Carmen waltzed out of the tobacco factory in the first act of Bizet's opera, this 18th-century building became world famous. But if you go there today, you'll find that serious students have replaced the "free-loving, cigarette-smoking Andalusian beauties."

By all means, explore the building at your leisure (although you may find it closed during part of the summer). It is near the landmark luxury hotel, the Alfonso XII. So far, no one charges admission.

The April Fair and Holy Week

Many tourists consider attending the April Fair in Seville reason enough for coming to Europe. Seville's April Fair is the most famous one in the country. It was inaugurated as "recently" as 1847, unlike some of the age-old fairs in Spain. The Andalusians—perhaps more so than most people—seem to know how to prepare a proper greeting for spring.

Holy Week comes first, from Palm Sunday until Easter. Through the streets of Seville are paraded the wooden figures called *pasos.* But by far the most interesting processions are those of the hooded and robed penitents, who look like—but certainly are not—members of the KKK.

The fería usually begins in mid-April lasting less than a week. The Andalusian women wear their traditional costumes; floats and carriages are festooned with flowers; horseback-riding men and their señoritas gallop through the traffic-free streets.

The April Fair is a showcase of Spanish folklore and customs, from bullfights (the best) to flamenco. Festively decorated tent-like pavilions—called *casetas*—are set up by the Sevillians, and they go camping until the fair is over. Lucky is the visitor who gets invited by one of the locals to his temporary home. Wine and food are constantly being served. At night, the fair is illuminated by miles of colored lights . . . a magnificent carnival atmosphere.

Despite all this gaiety and glamour, don't go to Seville at that time unless you have reservations (make them months in advance). Virtually every tourist on two continents, it would seem, including the Spaniards, floods into the city, occupying every accommodation from the most luxurious suite to the dankest room in the lowliest boarding house. To arrive for the fair without a reservation would be foolish indeed, unless you plan to book accommodations in a neighboring city and commute.

At any time of the year, however, you can enjoy:

FLAMENCO: When the moon is high in Seville—and the scent of orange blossoms is in the air—it's time to walk through the alleyways of Santa Cruz in search of the sound of castanets. Or, better yet, take a taxi and escape the muggers.

Los Gallos (The Roosters), 11 Plaza de Santa Cruz (tel. 21-69-81), is in a converted town house, transformed to provide a showcase for flamenco artists. In air-conditioned comfort, you can hear flamenco from 10 p.m. till dawn. Many clients sit transfixed throughout the night. You pay a total of 1,700 pesetas ($11.90), including the cover charge and your first drink. Marie J. Low of Anaheim, California, wrote: "There is absolutely no pressure to buy another drink. I consider it money very well spent." All of the seats have a clear view, even those on the tiny mezzanine. Reservations should be made before 6 p.m.

El Patio Sevillano, 11 Paseo de Cristóbal Colón (tel. 21-41-20), is a showcase of Spanish folksong and dance. The presentation includes flamenco and songs from Andalusia in many varieties, as well as classical Spanish music from such composers as Falla, Albéniz, Granados, and Chueca. The establishment is near the center of Seville on the bank of the river between two of the city's historic bridges. Two shows are presented nightly, one from 9:30 until 11 p.m. and another from 11:30 p.m. until around 1 a.m. When the demand is great enough, an additional show is offered beginning at around 7:30 p.m. The entrance fee and cover charge is 1,700 pesetas ($11.90), which includes the first drink. Each additional drink costs 300 pesetas ($2.10). Dancers, of course, wear the exotic costumes you'd expect, and work hard to produce a worthwhile program.

El Tablao de Curro Velez, 7 Rodó (tel. 21-64-92), is a non-touristy locale for the enjoyment of drinks and flamenco. Many types of dance are featured, usually beginning at around 9:30 p.m. and continuing till dawn. Each drink costs around 1,600 pesetas ($11.20), which justifies the salaries of the dancers. The establishment is closed during January and February.

La Trocha, 23-25 Ronda de Capuchinos (tel. 35-50-28), is known for its mixed revues. These include famous Spanish songs, inevitable flamenco, and regional dances. Sometimes women are invited up to join the male dancers (but men can never join the female performers). The audience is made up of both tourists and locals who frequent the place. The show has a lot of humor. Admission is 1,500 pesetas ($10.50), and drinks begin at 600 pesetas ($4.20). Take a taxi to reach the place.

TAPAS AND DRINKS: **El Rinconcillo,** 40 Gerona (tel. 22-31-83). Partly because of its age, and partly because of the refusal by its owners to change an iota of the decor, this is one of the most famous bars in Seville. It was founded in 1670, but seems to have stopped the clock sometime back in the 1930s. It sits on a street corner behind an ornate façade of multicolored tiles. Inside, amid dim lighting, heavy ceiling beams, iron-based and marble-topped tables, along with an un-chic clientele, you can enjoy a beer for 50 pesetas (35¢) and full meals for 2,000 pesetas ($14). The bartender will mark your tab in chalk on a well-worn wood countertop. Don't ignore the art nouveau tile murals of scantily clad maidens selling anise-flavored apéritifs: The establishment is open seven days a week.

La Alicantina, 2 Plaza del Salvador (tel. 22-61-22). Its interior is antiseptic modern, but its location on a very old square near verdant orange trees and a red-brick and sandstone church helps. It is not the visual allure of this bar that attracts clients, but its seafood tapas, said to be the best in town. That fact usually fills its sidewalk tables and bar to overflowing. Owner Manuel Postigo serves big rations of tapas for 650 pesetas ($4.55) and foreign liquor for 400 pesetas ($2.80) and up. However, you can order a beer for 65 pesetas (46¢). Tapas include clams marinara, fried squid, grilled shrimp, fried codfish, and clams in béchamel sauce. It is open seven days a week.

Milord, 3 Plaza de Cuba (tel. 27-96-49), tries to remain a cut above the other bars in town by stressing its image as a cocktail bar rather than a pub. It's stylish, chic, and located behind a screen of oleander at the edges of a plaza centered around jets of water across the river from the barrio. There are comfortable wicker chairs on the sidewalk in front and a glossy interior designed like a fantasy from an English hunting scene, with marble floors, horsey prints, and lots of green leather. Red-vested waiters serve beer for 70 pesetas (49¢), plus a wide array of international drinks.

Modesto, 5 Cano y Cueto (tel. 41-68-11), serves some of the best tapas in town made with "sea creatures." The location is at the northern end of Murillo

Park, opening onto a quiet square with flowerboxes and ornate iron railing. The bar has air conditioning, and you can often point to your choice of tapas such as a plate of black clams costing from 300 pesetas ($2.10). Upstairs there is a good-value restaurant, offering a meal for 2,000 pesetas ($14), including such dishes as fried squid, baby sole, grilled sea bass, and shrimp in garlic sauce. Closed Wednesday.

SEVILLE DISCOS: **El Coto,** 118 Luís Montoto (tel. 57-94-00), is in the basement level of the Hotel Los Lebreros. The place is popular and often crowded, especially after 11 p.m. when drinks average around 600 pesetas ($4.20).

Tukan, 66 Avenida República Argentina (tel. 45-25-45), is probably the most modern disco in Seville, filled with up-to-date light and sound. The youngish crowd pays around 550 pesetas ($3.85) per drink and dances energetically till dawn.

JAZZ IN SEVILLE: Thanks to its annual jazz festival, the tradition of improvised music is alive and well in Andalusia. Three clubs within Seville, each with their sometimes passionate aficionados, include **Bebop,** Calle Sol; **Contrapunto,** Plaza Jerónimo de Córdoba, and **Tatamba,** in the Edificio Resitur, 2 Calle Salado. The cover charge is usually included in the cost of the first drink, which averages around 900 pesetas ($6.30), with a beer costing 150 pesetas ($1.05) thereafter. Any big name jazz artist scheduled to appear in any of these clubs is usually advertised several days in advance throughout the city.

PRACTICAL FACTS: For **tourist information,** go to the tourist office at 9 Avenida de la Constitución (tel. 21-51-87). The office is open daily except Sunday from 9 a.m. to 7 p.m. From Holy Week to the end of September, it is also open on Sunday, from 9 a.m. to 1:30 p.m.

The **American Express** office in Seville is operated by Viajes Alhambra, 3 Teniente Coronel Segui (tel. 22-44-35).

For **medical emergencies,** go to the Hospital Universitario y Provincial, Avenida Doctor Fedriani (tel. 37-70-36).

The **post office** is at 30 Avenida de la Constitución (tel. 22-88-80). Hours are Monday to Friday from 9 a.m. to 8 p.m. and on Saturday from 9 a.m. to 1 p.m. The office is closed on Sunday.

While in Seville, you may want to attend a **bullfight.** The ring is called the Real Maestranza, and it's on the Paseo de Cristóbal Colón (tel. 22-64-37).

The phone to call for information about **rail travel** in Spain is 23-19-18. The **telephone office** is at 153 Calle Fería (for telephone service information, call 003). To send **wires** by phone, dial 22-20-00. If you want a **radio taxi,** call 25-08-59.

For information about flights, you can call the **San Pablo Airport,** Calle Almirante Lobo at 51-06-77.

The **Central Bus Station,** 1 Prado de San Sebastián (tel. 23-22-10), is the place to go for bus information in Spain.

Most **banks** in Seville are open from 9 a.m. to 2 p.m. Monday to Saturday. Always, but *always,* conceal your money before walking out of a bank in Seville. Never go out on the pavement counting money. Otherwise it won't be yours for long.

Shops, in general, are open from 9:30 a.m. to 1:30 p.m. and 4:30 to 8 p.m. Monday to Saturday. Most **department stores,** however, are open from 10 a.m. to 8 p.m. Monday to Saturday. Most of your routine shopping needs can be handled at **El Certe Inglés,** Plaza del Duque (tel. 65-40-11).

And, most important for Seville, the **police station** is on Plaza de la Gavidia (tel. 22-88-40).

If you've lost your passport (or had it stolen), go to the **U.S. Consulate, 7** Paseo de las Delicias (tel. 23-18-85).

A SIDE TRIP TO CARMONA: Easily visited on a day trip from Seville, Carmona is an ancient city, with a history dating back to Neolithic times. The town, 21 miles east of Seville, grew in power and prestige under the Moors. It established links with Castille in 1252.

Surrounded by fortified walls, Carmona has three Moorish fortresses, one of which has been turned into a luxurious parador (see below). The other two include the Alcázar de la Puerta de Córdoba and the Alcázar de la Puerta de Sevilla. The most outstanding attraction is the Seville Gate, with its double Moorish arch, standing opposite St. Peter's Church. There is also the Córdoba Gate which is reached by going along the Calle Santa María de Gracia (it was constructed into the ancient Roman walls in the 17th century).

The whole town is a virtual national monument, filled with once noble residences, narrow streets, whitewashed houses, and Renaissance mansions. Eventually you reach the Plaza San Fernando, the most important square, filled with elegant houses, some of which date from the 17th century. The most important church is dedicated to Santa María, standing on the Calle Martin López. You enter first into what was a Moorish ablutionary patio before exploring the interior with its white-painted vaulting, dating from the 15th century.

A Roman necropolis and amphitheater contain the remains of some 1,000 families who lived in and around Carmona some 2,000 years ago. There is also an archeological museum on the site which is visited on guided tours, lasting 45 minutes, between 9 a.m. and 2 p.m. and 4 to 6 p.m. daily except Monday. Admission is 150 pesetas ($1.05). One of the two important tombs, the Elephant Vault, consists of three dining rooms and a kitchen. The other, the Servilia Tomb, was as big as a nobleman's villa.

Parador Nacional Alcazar del Rey Don Pedro (tel. 14-10-10). Driving through Carmona's narrow streets, first into and then out of the ancient fortifications, is part of the charm of this parador. By following strategically located signs, you'll see it clinging by diagonal stilts to the rock face of a forbidding cliff. After parking in the shadows of a medieval courtyard, you'll enter the interior of one of the most attractive paradors in Spain. It's built around an Andalusian courtyard whose monumental fountain is ringed with Moorish columns, potted geraniums, and intricate tiles. A hallway crafted from brick, stone, and wooden beams—wide enough to accommodate a truck—leads to a lattice-shaded breakfast room where views of a patchwork quilt of fertile farmland stretches for miles.

The parador, which opened in 1976, contains 59 comfortably furnished bedrooms, each with private bath, phone, and rustically detailed accessories. For the most part, French doors open onto a panoramic view. Singles cost 6,500 pesetas ($45.50), doubles between 8,500 pesetas ($59.50) and 9,500 pesetas ($66.50), depending on the accommodation. Special features of the parador include a sloping flower garden, a tile-roofed gazebo, and a beautiful swimming pool set with herringbone patterns of blue and white tiles. A snack bar, 16 tile-roofed cabañas, and rosebushes encircle its waters. Fixed-price meals, costing from 2,300 pesetas ($16.10), are served under the stone vaulting of the restaurant.

AN EXCURSION TO ITALICA: Lovers of Roman history will flock to Italica, the ruins of an ancient city lying about six miles to the northwest of Seville, on the major artery to Lisbon, in the vicinity of the small town of Santiponce. Ideally, you might drive here. But if you don't have a car, you can take a bus leaving from Calle Marqués de Parada near the Córdoba railway station in Seville. The bus is likely to be marked Calle de Santiponce. Buses depart about every hour, and the trip takes about half an hour.

After the battle of Ilipa, Publius Cornelius Scipio Africanus founded Italica in 206 B.C. Two of the most famous of Roman emperors, Trajan and Hadrian, were both born at Italica. Master-building Hadrian was to have a major influence on his hometown.

In his reign, the amphitheater, the ruins of which can be seen today, was among the largest in the Roman Empire. Lead pipes that carried water from the Guadalquivir River can still be seen. A small museum displays some of the Roman statuary, although the finest pieces have been shipped to Seville. Many mosaics, depicting beasts, gods, and birds, can be seen, and others are constantly being discovered.

The ruins, including an Italica theater, can be explored from 9 a.m. until 7 p.m. (until 5:30 p.m. off-season) for an admission of 100 pesetas (70¢).

Where to Dine in the Area

Mesón Alija, 88 Réal, Castilleja de la Cuesta (tel. 16-08-58), lies three miles from Seville. In spite of the difficulty of finding this out-of-the-way restaurant, many visitors feel that the culinary rewards are worth the effort. Owner Don Baldomero prepares excellent seafood and meat specialties, each concocted with fresh ingredients, many of which are displayed in refrigerated cases near the entrance. You might enjoy several preparations of shrimp or crayfish, game dishes, succulent beef, lamb, or pork, or else such grilled tempters as a brochette of grouper and saffron-flavored shellfish-studded paella. Depending on what you order, full meals cost from 1,800 pesetas ($12.60) to 3,000 pesetas ($21), and can be consumed in cold weather beside the restaurant's blazing fireplace and in summer on a flower-ringed outdoor terrace. The restaurant stands opposite the Convent of Irish Nuns (yes, that's right) on the main street of town behind an unassuming entrance.

4. Jerez de la Frontera

After leaving Seville, those who have an extra day can take a change-of-pace adventure and visit the bodegas at Jerez (Sherry) de la Frontera as well as the Atlantic port city of Cádiz. I'll begin with Jerez, about 60 miles south of Seville.

This is that charming little Andalusian town that has made a bridge to England with the thousands and thousands of casks of golden sherry it has shipped there over the centuries. Steeped in the past, with origins going back nearly 3,000 years, Jerez today is primarily a modern, progressive town with wide boulevards, although it does have an interesting old quarter. Yet the reason that busloads of visitors pour in every year is to get those free drinks at one of the bodegas where wine is aged and bottled.

The town is pronounced either "Herez" or "Her-eth," depending on whether you're Andalusian or Castilian. The French, the Moors, etc., have called it various names—Hérès, Scheris—and somehow, as they are wont, the English corrupted this to Sherry (the "valour" of sherry was extolled by no less an authority than Shakespeare).

Jerez is easily reached by bus or rail from Seville. We'll begin our exploration with . . .

TOURING THE BODEGAS: Jerez is surrounded by the aristocratic vineyards of

Spain, and the ideal time to visit is during the grape harvest in September. However, visitors are assured of the finest in hospitality all year, because Jerez is widely known for its warm welcome.

There must be more than a hundred bodegas in and around Jerez, where you can not only see how sherries are made, bottled, and aged, but where you can get free samples as well. Among the most famous brands are Sandemar, Pedro Domecq, and Gonzalez Byass, the maker of Tío Pepe.

On a typical visit to a bodega, you are shown through several high-ceilinged buildings which house all of the makings of the sherries and brandies. One building will have facilities for the pressing and sorting of grapes; another will be a bottling plant; a third will be filled with thousands of large oak casks (probably imported from America).

Sometimes you are taken to a bodega or wine tavern and shown some bottles of the oldest wine in Jerez. Often such personages as Juan Carlos I, King of Spain, have come through here and autographed their favorite barrels.

After a typical tour, guests may go to an attractive bar where variously colored and different-tasting sherries—amber, dark gold, cream, something red, sweet, and velvety—can be sampled. *Warning:* These sherries are more potent than one might at first suspect. If offered, try the very dry La Ina or the brandy, Fundador, one of the most popular in the world.

If you're here at harvest time in the fall, by all means pay a visit to the vineyards, one of the most fascinating sights in Spain.

Most bodegas are open only from 9 a.m. to 1 p.m. and are closed in the afternoon. Regrettably, many of the bodegas are closed in August (some shut down in July). However, many reopen by the third week of August, while several others are closed until the first of September, when the wine festival gets going.

Since many people go to Jerez just to visit a bodega, they can be seriously disappointed. To avoid being thwarted, you can make a side trip to the village of **Lebrija,** lying about halfway between Jerez and Seville, 8½ miles west of the main highway.

Lebrija is a local winemaking center where some very fine sherries are made. At one small bodega, that of Juan García, you are courteously escorted around by the owner. However, there are several other bodegas in Lebrija, and the local citizens will gladly point them out to you if asked.

At Lebrija you can get a glimpse of rural Spain.

WHERE TO STAY: The town has no nightlife to speak of, and a minimum of hotels—but this works out reasonably well, since most bodega-hopping visitors come just for the day, then press on to Cádiz by nightfall, or head back to Seville. However, for readers staying over, here are my recommendations.

Nuevo Hostal, 23 Caballeros (tel. 33-16-00), is a little peseta-saver, frequented mostly by Spaniards. Rates are 3,500 pesetas ($24.50) for the best double rooms with shower, 3,000 pesetas ($21) for a double with less plumbing. Singles rent for 2,500 pesetas ($17.50). A large lunch or dinner is another 1,000 pesatas ($7). The entrance has superb 12-foot-high doors, with grillwork like a town house. Inside, the small lobby is three floors high and covered with glass in the Andalusian style. The bedrooms are large for the most part, pleasingly old-fashioned.

One of the best streets for those shopping around for budget hotels is the Calle Higueras, off Calle Fermin Aranda. Here you'll find such hostals as **Las Palomas,** 17 Higueras (tel. 34-37-73), where a bathless single room ranges in price from 1,800 pesetas ($12.60), and doubles are priced anywhere from 2,200 pesetas ($15.40).

Another good possibility, **Joma,** 22 Higueras (tel. 34-98-69), offers bathless singles at 1,800 pesetas ($12.60) and doubles with private bath for 3,000 pesetas ($21).

Best, but plastic new, is the **Hotel Mica,** 7 Higueras (tel. 34-07-00). Eight of its 38 rooms are singles. All have air conditioning, bath, and telephone. There's a pleasant bar downstairs for those espresso coffees, and a very modern breakfast lounge. Mica rates three stars. The best doubles rent for 4,800 pesetas ($33.60), a single going for 2,800 pesetas ($19.60).

Hotel Residencia Capele, 58 Corredera (tel. 34-64-00), is considered by some to be the second-best hotel in town, ranking just after the more highly rated Jerez. It is a contemporary structure, offering 30 well-furnished and maintained bedrooms. A double with bath costs 7,000 pesetas ($49), a similar single going for 5,000 pesetas ($35). The location is good, lying about a block or so from the heart of Jerez. There is no garage and no restaurant. A continental breakfast is served.

Hostal Ávila, 3 Ávila (tel. 33-48-08), might be your introduction to "hostal" living, as it's one of the better bargains of this sherry-producing town. One reader rated its comfort to that of a three-star hotel. Don't judge this hotel by its façade: inside, its 30 rooms are clean, comfortable and well maintained. The cost is 2,500 pesetas ($17.50) in a single, rising to 3,500 pesetas ($24.50) in a double. Most rooms have private bath or shower.

WHERE TO DINE: **Restaurante Tendido 6,** 10 Circo (tel. 34-48-35), is a combined restaurant and tapas bar whose loyal clients come from many walks of life within the city. Owner Juan Flor creates a dignified regional cuisine which includes grilled rumpsteak, fish soup, and a wide array of typical Spanish dishes. Full meals cost upward of around 2,000 pesetas ($14).

Gaitán, 3 Gaitán (tel. 34-58-59). The arrival of chef Antonio Arihuela to a location near the Puerto Santa María was favorably received by diners throughout the city. His establishment serves well-prepared meals costing from 1,800 pesetas ($12.60) at lunch and dinner daily except Sunday night, Monday, and in August. You might enjoy filet of hake smothered in an anchovy sauce, monkfish a l'americana, and one of the tempting array of lamb and beef dishes. The interior is air-conditioned and decorated in a regional style.

ARCOS DE LA FRONTERA: Only about 20 miles east of Jerez de la Frontera, this old Arab town was built in the form of an amphitheater. Sitting on a rock and surrounded by the Guadalete on three sides, it contains many houses which have been hollowed out of this formation. From the old city, it opens onto a high-in-the-clouds view that some visitors have found without rival on the Iberian Peninsula.

The city is filled with whitewashed walls and narrow winding streets that disappear into steps. It holds a lot of historical interest, and has a beautiful lake complete with paddle boats and a Mississippi riverboat. One can take the bus from Seville, Cádiz, or Jerez de la Frontera, as there is no train service to this little bit of paradise.

The best place to stay is the **Parador Casa del Corregidor,** Plaza de España (tel. 70-05-00), the government-run parador. From the balconies of the parador, one has views of the Valley of Guadalete, filled with farms, plains, and the river below. In good weather you can take your meals on one of these balconies (try the pork with garlic). Either lunch or dinner costs 2,000 pesetas ($14). Reader William C. Sano, Swampscott, Massachusetts, writes: "I spent one whole day reading my paperback novel on the balcony of our room, drinking in the view and watching the sun create unusual images in shadows as it moved across the sky. Then I went out exploring the Old Town at night." The parador offers 24 accommodations, some doubles with ballroom-size bath. Doubles rent for 9,500 pesetas ($66.50); singles for 8,000 pesetas ($56).

After our stopover in sherry country, we head south to the port city of—

5. Cádiz

This modern, bustling Atlantic port is a kind of Spanish Marseilles. It's a melting pot of Americans, Africans, and Europeans who dock or pass through here. The old quarter teems with native life, little dives, and seaport alleyways through which sailors from many lands wander in their search for adventure. But despite the thriving life, it is devoid of major interest, and has far more successful competitor cities in Andalusia.

At the end of a peninsula, Cádiz separates the Bay of Cádiz from the Atlantic. From numerous sea walls around the town, you have views of the ocean, to which the denizens of Cádiz have always looked. In fact, Columbus set out from here on his second voyage to the New World, on September 25, 1493. "Convert the infidels, settle the land," Isabella ordered him. She probably commanded that he speed up the gold shipments as well. Seventeen vessels were manned by anywhere from 1,000 to 1,500 men, including priests, doctors, even Chris's brother.

This ancient port city of Cádiz enjoyed varying states of prosperity, particularly after the discovery of the New World. Its origins go back into antiquity: Did Hercules really found the city? Or was it the trading Phoenicians? Arabs, Visigoths, Romans, and Carthaginians have passed through Cádiz, all leaving their imprints.

The most convenient point for a walking tour is Plaza de San Juan de Dios, which could easily provide the background for a movie about a North African port city. Anchor later at one of the sidewalk cafés, and watch the people pass by. Or perhaps stroll up San Antonio Abad for a glimpse of the seamy side of life. One reader from Bethesda, Maryland, found "the whorehouses all quite tidy and freshly painted, with pots of geraniums at the end of the San Antonio Abad." A right turn brought her to the street where gays congregate. But before we do too much exploring, let's settle into Cádiz.

WHERE TO STAY: Cádiz has a number of budget accommodations, some of which are quite poor. However, on our budget, we can afford some of the finest lodgings in the city.

Regio 1, 11 Ana de Viya (tel. 27-93-31), is a modern hotel which opened in the late 1970s on the main avenue of town. The more than three dozen bedrooms are filled with contemporary furniture and many conveniences. Singles rent for 3,000 pesetas ($21), doubles 5,000 pesetas ($35).

Regio 2, 79 Avenida Andalucía (tel. 23-30-05), contains the same number of rooms and the same proximity to the beach as its sister hotel (see above). This was constructed about five years after Regio 1 and contains all the conveniences of its slightly older sibling. Singles cost 3,500 pesetas ($24.50), while doubles run from 5,500 pesetas ($38.50).

Hotel Francia y Paris, 1 Plaza de San Francisco (tel. 21-23-18), is about a five-minute walk from the waterfront, on one of Cádiz's attractive tree-filled plazas in the heart of the old town. It's a modern structure of fair design; most of the bedroom windows are fitted with awnings to keep out the strong sun (Cádiz is called the "City of Light"). Fairly comfortable and medium-size double rooms with private bath rent for 5,000 pesetas ($35). Singles pay 3,000 pesetas ($35) and up. The hotel is run in a somewhat *comme ci, comme ça* manner. Many of the staff members speak English; and there is a cozy, wood-paneled bar and lounge.

Imares, 9 Plaza de San Francisco (tel. 21-22-57), is most Andalusian, an older hotel with a large entrance patio, a marble staircase, balcony, and all. The rooms in general are large and well kept; there are 37 in all, with a wide variation of plumbing. The most expensive doubles, with complete bath, are 3,000 pesetas ($21), 2,300 pesetas ($16.10) in a double with a shower bath. Singles go for 1,800 pesetas ($12.60). The hotel is run by a "simpático" staff who give good service. The only drawback is that since all the rooms face a cavernous inside patio, any noise reverberates through the whole building. Light sleepers, take note. The street sign for the hotel now only reads "Residencia" in white on red vertical letters.

WHERE TO EAT: Head to the heart of the city, the **Plaza de San Juan de Dios,** for good economy dinners. But here you must pick and choose carefully, as a number of eating establishments in Cádiz are more used to serving a rough-and-ready fleet than Mr. and Mrs. Smith of Lawrence, Kansas.

Restaurante El 9 is for real starvation budgeteers. It's at 4 Calle San Fernando (tel. 27-71-98), off the Plaza San Juan de Dios, and here you can get a meal for 800 pesetas ($5.60). I recently had a dish of rice with seafood, an egg (or a thin steak), a roll, a glass of wine, and some fruit for that sum.

Next door is another budget restaurant, the **Económica,** 2 Calle San Fernando (tel. 28-69-52), where a plate of lentils, paella, macaroni, or fish goes for 150 pesetas ($1.05). Two eggs and potatoes go for only 140 pesetas (98¢). Both the El 9 and the Económica have white tile walls and neon lights, but in some strange way exude a kind of budget charm all their own.

For upper-bracket dining in Cádiz, try one of the following recommendations:

Mesón del Duque, 12 Paseo Marítimo (tel. 28-10-87). Here, within the rough-hewn walls of a corner of the Edificio Madrid, near the waterfront, many guests come for what might be the most varied menu in Cádiz. Owner Arsenio Cueto makes personal visits to the food suppliers of town practically every day to provide the raw ingredients for his frequently changing house specialties. These include crayfish or dorado cooked in salt, crayfish with rice, and many other fish and meat dishes. A full meal in the air-conditioned interior usually begins at 1,500 pesetas ($10.52), going up. The restaurant is closed on Monday.

El Anteojo, 22 Alameda Apodaca (tel. 21-36-39). The ground-floor bar area is so pleasantly decorated and the seafood tapas are so savory that you might never get around to climbing a flight of stairs up to the dining room. There, however, a view of the sea is only one of the pleasant surprises waiting for you. Owner Pepe Iglesias, who has maintained this place for more than 40 years, still serves specialties based on Andalusian tradition, including seafood soup, tournedos, squid in its own ink, and a wide array of seafood. Dessert might be a chocolate soufflé, which would round out a full meal priced at 2,500 pesetas ($17.50) and up. The restaurant is open every day.

THE SIGHTS: The principal artistic treasures are found in the **Fine Arts** and **Archeological Museums** (Museo de Bellas Artes and Museo Arqueológico Provincial), both in the same building at Plaza de Mina. The Fine Arts Museum houses one of Spain's most important Zurbarán collections, including a series he did of a monk, as well as paintings by Rubens and Murillo (his picture of Christ is one of his most important works). The Museum of Archeology is known for its Roman, Phoenician, and Carthaginian collections. Both museums are open from 10 a.m. to 2 p.m. (closed on Saturday and Sunday), charging 75 pesetas (53¢) for admission.

The **cathedral** is a magnificent baroque building in the Plaza Pio XII, built in the 18th century by the architect Vicente Acero. The interior, composed of the finest materials, is in the neoclassic style forming an impressive group dominated by its outstanding apse-aisle. In its splendid crypt with a level vault lies the tomb of the Cádiz-born composer Manuel de Falla. The treasure museum contains a priceless collection of Spanish silver, embroidery, and fine paintings belonging to the Spanish, Flemish, and Italian schools. The cathedral can be visited, together with the treasure museum, from 10 a.m. to 1 p.m. and 4 to 6 p.m.

Branching out from the cathedral, incidentally, are cobblestone streets that will lead you to some of the most interesting alleyways in the old barrio.

READERS' SIGHTSEEING TIP: "Do mention the delightful park along the waterfront in the old quarter. It's straight out of *Alice in Wonderland,* with tropical plantings and fir trees sculptured into incredible corkscrew shapes. There's a little stand with tables where you can get beer, sherry, and simple tapas" (Lolli and Brian Sherry, Northfield, Ill.).

CÁDIZ AFTER DARK: **El Parisien,** 1 San Francisco (tel. 22-18-30). If you step in during daylight hours, this turn-of-the-century bar will usually be flooded with sunlight. At night, the flood is crowds of softly chattering locals who enjoy the well-prepared tapas and the drinks, priced at around 150 pesetas ($1.05) each. It's open every day except Sunday.

La Boîte, Edificio Isecotel, Paseo Marítimo (tel. 23-54-01), is one of the recently redecorated discos whose numbers flourish, although not often for long, throughout the south of Spain. A drink costs around 500 pesetas ($3.50). It is open from 9 p.m. till 3 a.m.

Pub Las Pergolas, Edificio Europlaya, Paseo Marítimo (tel. 25-11-10). You could meet just about anyone in this redecorated pub with a view overlooking the sea.

Cervecería del Puerto, 4 Zorrilla (tel. 27-18-37), is one of the most popular beer halls in town. It's usually loaded with an energetic crowd of drinkers who down large numbers of the well-prepared tapas in addition to their mugs of what is said to be the best brew in town. It's open daily except Wednesday.

El Maestrito, 8 Calle la Paz, is a local tapas bar open only in the evening, whose clients often come in for a glass of wine or beer, a few tasty snacks, and some animated conversation before going on to another establishment in the same part of town for the same purpose.

El Manteca, 66 Calle Mariana Pineda (tel. 21-36-03), has a bullfight ambience, typical in Cadiz. Homemade tapas are served. The place, open seven days a week, is managed by José Ruiz Manteca.

A SIDE TRIP TO MEDINA SIDONIA: This survivor of the Middle Ages is one of the most unspoiled of the hillside villages of Spain. It's about 29 miles east of Cádiz, 22 miles southeast of Jerez de la Frontera.

Medina Sidonia is one of those villages that time forgot. It has cobblestone streets, white tile-roofed buildings that cascade down the hillside, a Gothic church, a Moorish gate, and steep alleyways on which little old women in black and men on donkeys descend. The Arab influence is everywhere.

The surrounding countryside is wild and seldom visited. Pockets of fog sometimes settle over the land, and sunrise is often reminiscent of greeting the morning on the Yorkshire moors.

From Medina Sidonia, it's a 2½-hour drive to the port city of Algeciras, or you can take the Jerez road back to Seville.

6. Costa de la Luz

West of Cádiz, moving toward Huelva and the Portuguese frontier, lies the rapidly developing Costa de la Luz (Coast of Light), which is hoping to pick up some of the overflow from the Costa del Sol. The "Luz" coast stretches from the mouth of the Guadiana River, forming the boundary with Portugal, to Tarifa Point on the Straits of Gibraltar. Characterizing the coast are long stretches of sand, pine trees, fishermen's cottages, and lazy whitewashed villages.

The so-called Huelva district forms the northwestern half of the Costa de la Luz. The southern half stretches from Tarifa to Sanlúcar de Barrmeda. In traveling between these two portions of the Costa de la Luz, it is necessary to go inland to Seville. There are no roads going across the Coto Doñana and the marshland near the mouth of the Guadalquivir.

The national park authorities have organized Land Rover tours of the Coto Doñana. The tours last about three hours and begin every day except Monday, at 8:30 a.m. and in summer also at 5 p.m. The cost is about 1,500 pesetas ($10.50) per person. The tour includes the huge sand dunes, which are slowly moving inland. You're taken to the mouth of the Guadalquivir and shown the wildlife preserve, and the edge of marshland. Deer and wild pigs are usually seen, and in spring and fall you can also see large numbers of migrating birds that stop along the Costa de la Luz. It's a good idea to make a reservation by calling 955/430-432 some days in advance. However, it is possible to be taken along without a reservation if someone who reserves a seat does not show up.

At **Huelva** is a large statue on the west bank of the river commemorating the departure of Christopher Columbus on his voyage of discovery of the New World.

About 4½ miles up the Río Tinto, on the east bank on the waterfront of the little, sleepy town of **Palos de la Frontera,** is the actual spot from which Columbus departed. Here a monument marks the place.

His ships were anchored off this bank where the final victualing was carried out. About 3¾ miles south is the **Monasterio de la Rabida.** In the little white chapel in the convent grounds, Columbus prayed all night for the success of his voyage on the eve of his departure. The chapel may be visited. Even without the connections with Columbus, the monastery would be worth a visit, as it has a large number of paintings and frescoes from various periods on Columbian themes. A guide will show you around the Mudéjar chapel and a large portion of the old monastery. The monastery, 2½ miles southeast of Huelva, is open from 10 a.m. to 1 p.m. and 4 to 7 p.m. Models of the ships that Columbus sailed to the New World are on display.

From both places, the large white statue of Columbus at Huelva can be seen across the water downstream.

FOOD AND LODGING: Accommodations are severely limited in summer, and it's imperative to arrive with a reservation. You can stay at Mazagón (see below) at a government-run parador to the east of Huelva, or else perhaps consider anchoring at the western points—say, **Isla Cristina** (which is not an island) or at **Ayamonte,** which is even farther west, moving toward the Portuguese frontier.

Isla Cristina is almost an island, as it is surrounded by estuaries associated with the mouth of the Guadiana River. Both Isla Cristina and Ayamonte have collections of high-rise buildings near their beaches which, for the most part, are vacation apartments for Spaniards in July and August. Judging by their license plates, most of these visitors come from Huelva, Seville, and Madrid, so the Costa de la Luz is more Spanish in flavor than the overrun and more international Costa del Sol. In most places, no language other than Spanish is to be found on the menus, and that is a good indication of the clientele.

Many readers have found it hard to choose between Isla Cristina and Ayamonte. Both have excellent beaches—clean, wide, long sandy ones with dunes. The waves, for the most part, are small considering that this is the Atlantic Coast. Portions of the beaches are even calmer because of sand bars some 55 to 110 yards from the shore, which become virtual islands at low tide.

Ayamonte is the older resort, and it's the more interesting and colorful town, although the fishing harbor at Isla Cristina is uniquely beautiful. In Isla Cristina, the town is within walking distance from the beach, whereas in Ayamonte the town is separated by some miles from its beaches, Isla Canela and Moral.

Originally a rock castle, Ayamonte was erected on the slopes of the hill on which the castle stood. A natural desire to reach the sea explains why the buildings stand along the river on the plain.

For accommodations in either place, see below.

One of the best accommodations in the area is the **Parador Nacional Cristóbal Colón,** Carretera Mazagón-Moguer (tel. 37-60-00), at Mazagón (Palos de la Frontera), 12 miles from Huelva, a cheerful Andalusian town, with several churches dating from the 16th century. Open all year, this parador charges 9,500 pesetas ($66.50) in a double room, 8,000 pesetas ($56) in a single, all with private bath. One reader, Dr. A. C. Tarjan, Lake Alfred, Florida, writes: "The best place we've ever stayed at in Spain. Accommodations are quite good, with air conditioning, and there's a good view of the Mediterranean. Although a swimming pool is available, there is access to 40 miles of desolate beach. In the rooms are small refrigerators stocked with drinks (you pay as you go). The food prices are moderate—2,000 pesetas ($14) for a set menu. What is offered is simple."

At Ayamonte, the leading accommodation is the **Parador Nacional Costa de la Luz,** El Castillito (tel. 32-07-00). Overlooking the town, the parador was built so that it would command a sweeping view of the river and the surrounding towns and villages along its banks. Most people who are out touring for the day like to return for the memorable sunsets seen here. The parador is about 100 feet above sea level, and it stands on the same site as the old castle of Ayamonte.

Facilities include a swimming pool (a welcome relief in summer), a garden, central heating, air conditioning in the lounges, a dining room, and a bar. The parador, unlike most of its sisters, is built in a severe modern style with Nordic-inspired furnishings. The most expensive doubles rent for 9,000 pesetas ($63), with single occupancy costing 7,600 pesetas ($53.20). The dining room serves good regional meals costing from 2,000 pesetas ($14). Try, if featured, la raya en pimentón (ray with red pepper). El calamar relleno (stuffed squid) is another specialty.

In Isla Cristina, you can stay at the **Hotel Pato Azul,** 43 Gran Vía (tel. 33-13-50). It is quite comfortable, and the staff is pleasant. The hotel even has a swimming pool. The rooms are basic, however. They are also inexpensive: 3,500 pesetas ($24.50) for a single, 4,200 pesetas ($29.40) for a double. Guests are received from May to September. Isla Cristina has many bars and outdoor cafés where tapas or desserts may be eaten. But since most vacationers eat at their hotels or in their apartments, there are only a few restaurants.

Restaurante Acosta, 13 Plaza del Caudillo (tel. 33-14-20), is one of the best restaurants in town for the consumption of well-prepared fish dishes. Owned by a well-known local entrepreneur, José Acosta, who gave his family name to the popular restaurant, the establishment serves such specialties as seafood soup, oven-baked tuna, Andalusian meat stew, and several well-prepared veal dishes. Open every day except Monday and from October until June, the restaurant charges from 1,500 pesetas ($10.50) for a full meal.

7. Ronda

This little town, which sits proudly as a principality high (2,300 feet above sea level) in the Serranía de Ronda Mountains, is one of the oldest and most aristocratic towns in Spain. But that's not the chief reason it's visited. Ronda is split by a deep (500-foot) gorge, which in turn is spanned by a Roman stone bridge. On both sides of this "hole in the earth" are cliff-hanging houses, which look as if—with the slightest push—they'd plunge into the chasm.

Ronda is an incredible sight. The road to Ronda, once difficult to drive, is now a wide highway with guard rails. The town and the surrounding mountains were the legendary hideouts of bandits and smugglers, but today the Guardia Civil has put an end to that occupation. Smugglers today, it seems, either retire or become horse trainers.

You'll discover a town divided by the gorge into an older part, the Moorish and aristocratic quarter, and the newer part, on the southern side of the gorge, the section built principally after the Reconquest. The older quarter is by far the more fascinating; it contains narrow, rough streets, and buildings that show a marked Moorish influence (watch for the minaret). After the lazy sunny resort living of the Costa del Sol, a side excursion for the day to Ronda, with its unique beauty and refreshing mountain air, is like a tonic.

Ronda is great for the explorer. A native boy or two may attach himself to you as a guide: actually, if you give one a few pesetas, it might be worth it, since weaving your way in and out of the narrow streets may be a problem. There are the remains of the **Moorish baths;** the interesting **Palacio de Marqués de Salvatierra;** and the **Palacio de Mondragón,** overlooking the cliff, where the Moorish king lived before Isabella and Ferdinand moved in. However, at the latter, only the gardens can be visited, and they are not well maintained.

The oldest bullfight ring in Spain is in Ronda, built in the 1700s. Even if you don't want to watch a bullfight, the **Bullfighters' Museum,** reached through the ring, has an interesting collection of original, elaborately decorated clothing of famous bullfighters, lots of pictures, and trophies of some outstanding corridas on display.

Ronda is a three-hour ride from Algeciras.

STAYING OVERNIGHT: The **Hotel Reina Victoria,** 25 Jerez (tel. 87-12-40), with its spacious lounges and airy bedrooms, is similar to an English country home. In fact, it was built by an Englishman in 1906. It's at the edge of town, with terraces that hang right over the precipice, a 490-foot drop. Each bedroom has all the modern amenities; the rooms are big and comfortable, some with complete living room, including sofas, chairs, and tables. Outside many of the bedrooms is a private terrace with garden furniture. The beds are sumptuous, and the bathrooms have all the latest improvements. The simpler double rooms with bath rent for 7,600 pesetas ($53.20), the "semi-suites" for 8,500 pesetas ($59.50). The best singles, with private tub bath, cost 5,100 pesetas ($35.70), the least expensive singles going for 4,600 pesetas ($32.20). Dining here is recommendable, as the food is well cooked, a set meal costing 2,000 pesetas ($14).

Hemingway was a frequent visitor to this hotel, suggesting that it was ideal for a honeymoon "or if you ever bolt with anyone." But the hotel is mainly known for its memories of the poet Rainer Maria Rilke who, ailing in 1912, wrote *The Spanish Trilogy* here. He occupied a room on the third floor, which has now been preserved as a museum honoring him with first editions, manuscripts, photographs, and even a framed copy of his hotel bill. In a corner of the hotel garden is a life-size bronze statue of the poet.

Hostal Residencia Royal, 42 Virgen de la Paz (tel. 87-11-41), is the best choice for those who want to spend the night in an ancient section of Ronda. It is near the old bull arena, on a tiny cliff-edge plaza. From here you can easily reach most points of interest in the town. Every room of this comfortably conservative, Sevillian-style hotel has its own balcony, and you can enjoy the sunsets. Double rooms with bath cost 3,500 pesetas ($24.50). A single with bath (only two in this category) is 2,500 pesetas ($17.50). Rooms are reasonably well furnished.

Hotel Residencia Polo, 8 Mariano Soubirón (tel. 87-24-47), lies right in the heart of Ronda, close to a big shopping arcade for pedestrians. The Polo is run with professionalism, and its accommodations are pleasantly—not elegantly—decorated and are well kept. Bedrooms are spacious; even the closets and private bathrooms are large enough for your needs. You get good value here: 5,200 pesetas ($36.40) nightly in a double. Singles cost 3,500 pesetas ($24.50).

If you're on a real tight budget, try the **Hostal Biarritz,** 7 Cristo (tel. 87-29-10), which may have a chic name, but is one of the better bargains in town. In the lobby is an aquarium, but that is the only adornment. Everything is simple and plain, but well kept and maintained. Purificación Olveira Burgo rents out 21 rooms, charging from 1,800 pesetas ($12.60) to 2,200 pesetas ($15.40) in a double, depending on the plumbing. Meals, costing from 650 pesetas ($4.55), are also served.

WHERE TO DINE: **Don Miguel Restaurant,** 4 Villanuova (tel. 87-10-90), stands at the end of the bridge, with vistas of the upper gorge. A three-fork restaurant, it has tables set outside on two levels, enough to seat some 300 persons. The various menus range in price from 1,800 pesetas ($12.60) to 3,000 pesetas ($21). The food is fairly good, the rest rooms clean, and the chairs in the typical Andalusian style. The waiters are polite and speak enough English to get by. There is also a pleasant bar if you want to drop in just for a drink. Even if the food at Don Miguel weren't good (which it is), I'd still go here just to enjoy drinks and tapas (hors d'oeuvres) "inside the bridge," the old renovated prison. During the summer it's a bustling place. The restaurant closes from January 15 until February 20 and on Sunday in summer, Wednesday in winter.

Don Miguel also owns the **Mesón del Puente,** Plaza del Ayuntamiento, which is a bar built into the ancient bridge spanning the gorge. It makes an interesting stopover for refreshments. The Saturday night flamenco sessions attract mainly the locals.

Mesón Santiago, 3 Marina (tel. 87-15-59), is the domain of Santiago Ruíz Gil, who operates one of the best budget restaurants in Ronda, serving lunch only. A three-course menú del día, with bread and wine, is only 850 pesetas ($5.95), and it's not bad considering the price. If you order from what he calls his *especialidades de la casa,* count on spending around 2,000 pesetas ($14). At this family-run place, you can order caldo de cocido, almost a meal in itself. This is a savory stew with large pieces of meat cooked with such vegetables as garbanzos and white beans. You might also like the tongue cooked in wine and served with potato salad. All the servings are generous. Naturally, the à la carte menu is more expensive, but it is likely to include such dishes as partridge (in season), lamb, mountain trout, and regional meats. Fresh asparagus and succulent strawberries are also available at certain times of the year. Mr. and Mrs. Homero Argudín, of Guelph, Ontario, Canada, write: "We ate on a patio covered with a grapevine. It reminded us of the book, *El Sombrero de Tres Picos.* Local people of refined taste patronize this place. We saw a general and his party, also several bankers at nearby tables."

Pedro Romero, 18 Virgen de la Paz (tel. 87-10-61), attracts the bullfight aficionado. In fact, it stands opposite the bullring and gets extremely busy on fight days when it's almost impossible to get a table. The location is also just down the way from the already recommended Hostal Residencia Royal. One reader writes that "I had positively the best filet of sole in my life there on the recommendation of a Dutch film crew who had been there for several weeks." While seated under a stuffed bull's head, surrounded by photographs of young matadors, you might begin your meal with the classic garlic soup. Dinners begin at 1,800 pesetas ($12.60), going up. The namesake of the restaurant, of course, is famous in bullfighting circles. It was Francisco Romero who codified the rules of the game, introducing the muleta and cape as well. He was born at Ronda, and so was his grandson, the celebrated bullfighter, Pedro Romero. Romero was the namesake also of the young matador in *The Sun Also Rises* by Hemingway.

EXPLORING IN THE ENVIRONS: The **Cueva de la Pileta,** lying 15½ miles west of Ronda, plus about 1¼ miles' hard climb, near Benoaján, in the province of Málaga, has been compared to the Caves of Altamira, near Santander in the north of Spain. In an area of wild beauty known as the Serranía de Ronda, the caves were discovered in 1905 by José Bullón Lobato, grandfather of the present owners. More than a mile in length and filled with oddly and beautifully shaped stalagmites and stalactites, the caves contained five fossilized human and two animal skeletons.

In the mysterious darkness, cave paintings have been discovered, dating back to prehistoric times and depicting animals in yellow, red, black, and ochre. Many of the drawings contain symbols whose meaning is obscure. One of the highlights of the tour is a trip to the "chamber of the fish," a wall painting of a great black seal-like fish about three feet in length. The fish chamber is the innermost heart of the cave, ending in a precipice that drops vertically nearly 250 feet.

The easiest way to reach the cave is to drive there from Ronda. However, those without private transport can take the train to Benoaján. But, be warned, the cave lies at least an hour's walk from where the train deposits you. In the valley, just below the cave, lives a guide who will conduct you around the chambers, carrying artificial light to illuminate the paintings. You'll spend at least an hour here, and the cost is a well-spent 175 pesetas ($1.23). Hours are from 9 a.m. to 2 p.m. and 4 to 7 p.m.

Our next adventure is Granada, one of the top four tourist cities of Spain.

8. Granada

This former stronghold of Moorish Spain, at the foothills of the snow-capped Sierra Nevada mountain range, is part of the folklore of the world. Washington Irving (*Tales of the Alhambra*) used the image of this city of the pomegranate (*granada*) to conjure up a spirit of romance.

Perhaps because of all this excessive sentimentality, Granada, like Seville, has its debunkers. Admittedly, if Granada were to be judged by its 19th-century Lower City, it would be a dull, grayish Spanish town. Dozens of ill-conceived buildings were erected after the senseless destruction of the large Moorish part of the city. But the spirit of Granada is reflected more in its purple-red Alhambra, the 13th-century Moorish palace that is one of the most celebrated edifices in the world. Sitting high on a hill overlooking Granada, it is the city's crowning achievement.

Granada has played host to many "visitors," such as the Romans and the Visigoths; but it was the Muslim invaders who left the biggest imprint on the city. In 1492, after Isabella and Ferdinand took over this last remaining stronghold of the Arabs, the city entered a sad decline. But in the last century the Granadines began to prosper again. Granada today is one of the most important commercial cities of Spain.

Washington Irving may have helped publicize the glories of Granada to the English-speaking world, but in Spain the city is linked in legend to another writer: García Lorca. Born in 1898, this Spanish poet and dramatist, whose masterpiece was *The House of Bernarda Alba,* was shot in 1936 by Nationalist soldiers in the first months of the Spanish Civil War. During the rule of the dictator Franco, the works of García Lorca were banned in Spain, but, happily, that situation has changed now, and he is once again honored in the city in which he grew up.

Enjoying a mild climate, Granada is some 2,200 feet above sea level. It sprawls over two main hills, the Alhambra and the Albaicin, and it is crossed by two rivers, the Genil and Darro.

There are any number of ways to reach Granada. One of the most frequented routes is between Madrid and Granada, or Granada and Seville, or from the Costa del Sol. If you are visiting Granada from Madrid, it is suggested that you stop off at Jaén. But if this is impossible, then you can board a train at the Atocha Station in Madrid that will take you directly to Granada. In addition, regular scheduled Iberia Airlines flights go from Madrid to Granada's airport. In summer, in particular, many visit Granada from Málaga or Torremolinos. There is both train and bus service from Málaga. See the local RENFE or tourist offices about those constantly changing times of departure and return.

A warning note: A popular scam in Granada, usually practiced by gypsies, is to approach you, thrust a flower in your jacket, then pour out a rapid incantation (purportedly fortune-telling). You'll pay dearly for the experience, but only if you allow it.

WHERE TO STAY: The hotel and pension outlook is bright in Granada, and the choice of different styles of living is wide.

The **Parador Nacional San Francisco,** near the Alhambra (tel. 22-14-93), is one of the finest places at which to stay in Spain. The reasons are many, each crowding the others to be mentioned first. It is definitely romantic-style living, and the best double rooms rent for 11,500 pesetas ($80.50). Singles go for 9,600 pesetas ($67.20). It is imperative that you reserve weeks in advance, as this is one of the most sought-after places in the country.

The parador is part of the greater compound of the Alhambra, and that is recommendation enough. Its history goes back to the 15th century, when it was built as a convent following the reconquest of Granada by the Catholic kings. Queen Isabella was temporarily buried here, until her tomb in the Royal Chapel could be completed. The larger, Moorish-inspired patio at the parador is the older one, planted with time-aged vines and trees. The long gallery, opening onto the patio, must have been a chapel or a meeting hall; it is now a comfortable living room furnished with a mixture of antiques and upholstered pieces. The angular dining hall has remained the same, except that local women have replaced the nuns as waitresses.

The accommodations differ widely, the choice rooms being grabbed up first, of course. Many are large antique-filled bedrooms, but there are smaller and more simply furnished ones in the newer wing. From every window, you get a picture-postcard view. As for the food, most of the excellent dishes served are native to the province. You have assurance about the cleanliness of the food preparation, and you can come here to dine even if you aren't staying at the

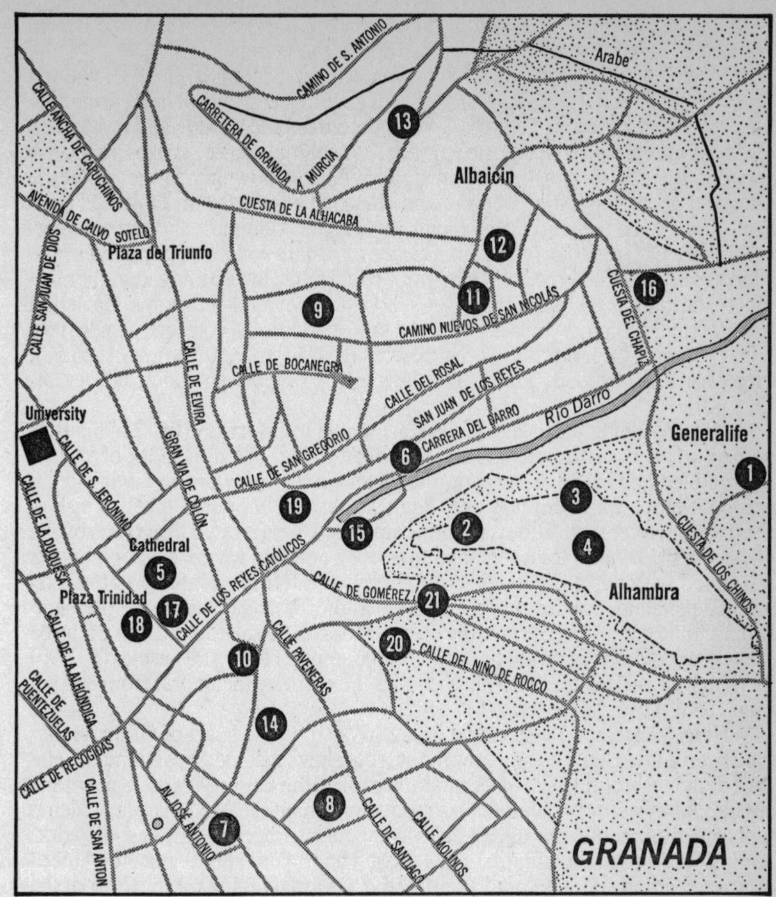

KEY TO NUMBERED SIGHTS:

1 Mirador
2 Alcazaba
3 Palacio Arabe
4 Palacio de Carlos V
5 Royal Chapel
6 Arab Baths
7 Castillo de Bibataubín
8 Santa Escolástica
9 Santa Isabel
10 Santa Teresa
11 San Nicolás
12 San Salvador
13 San Gregorio
14 San Matías
15 Santa Ana
16 Casa del Chapiz
17 Alcaicería
18 Archbishops Palace
19 Law Court
20 Torres Bermejas
21 Puerta de las Granadas

parador. A complete luncheon or dinner costs 2,100 pesetas ($14.70). Before your meal, join the guests by having a drink in the lounge.

Hotel Alhambra Palace, 2-4 Peña Partida (tel. 22-14-68). In 1922, about a dozen years after it was built, García Lorca gave a poetry recital here, accompanied by guitarist Andrés Segovia. Today, both from the outside and inside, this legendary hotel which is, like the parador, our splurge choice, evokes a Moorish fortress. It is complete with a crenellated roofline, a crowning dome, geometric tilework, and a suggestion of a minaret. It sits in a secluded and forested position, midway up the slope stretching between the Alhambra and the commercial center of Granada. Inside, in a decor of ornate ceilings, chastened brass, Moorish arches, and green and blue tiles, you'll find a high-ceilinged, rather formal restaurant, a grillroom, two bars, and 140 renovated bedrooms. Each unit has air conditioning, a private bath, and lots of additional comfort. Singles cost 5,000 pesetas ($35); doubles, 7,500 pesetas ($52.50) to 9,500 pesetas ($66.50), breakfast not included. Fixed-price lunches or dinners go for 2,200 pesetas ($15.40).

Hotel Washington Irving, Calle Carmen de los Martires (tel. 22-75-50), is named, of course, after the famous American writer. Set at the edge of a winding road leading to the Alhambra, this hotel was the only one in town when it was built more than a century ago. King Alfonso XII honored it with a visit at the turn of the century. Today, its more simplified form is rated three stars by the government. It occupies a dignified five-story building whose iron railings are festooned with vines. Its modernized lobby is tastefully sheathed with darkly grained paneling, but the public rooms are at their baronial best in the pleasantly masculine bar and in the lavishly ornate Moorish dining room. Each of the 63 bedrooms contains a private bath and phone, renting for 4,700 pesetas ($32.90) in a single, 7,000 pesetas ($49) in a double. Fixed-price meals cost from 800 pesetas ($5.60) to 1,850 pesetas ($12.95).

Hotel Victoria, 3 Puerta Real (tel. 25-77-00), in the heart of Granada, has long been a favorite. The gingerbread surrounding its domed tower and the elegant detailing around each of its windows evoke 19th-century Paris. You enter a circular lobby entirely sheathed in salmon- and cream-colored marble, which is replaced throughout the upper hallways with intricately geometric tilework. Amid a forest of Ionic columns on the second floor, you'll find a graceful American bar, a grand staircase, and an attractively formal dining room. Each of the 69 bedrooms contains its own TV, radio, private bath, phone, and air conditioning. Many have reproductions of antiques and walls upholstered in shades of terracotta. Singles cost 3,700 pesetas ($25.90); doubles, 6,200 pesetas ($43.40), breakfast not included.

Hotel Residencia Cóndor, 6 Avenida de la Constitución (tel. 28-37-11), is of a contemporary balconied design that contributes to its status as one of the best hotels in Granada. It's in the center of town, about a five-minute walk from the Alhambra and the cathedral. Many of the pleasant bedrooms have a terrace, and all have a private tile bath and an attractive combination of light-grained contemporary furniture with bentwood supports. Accommodations cost 4,000 pesetas ($28) in a single, 6,000 pesetas ($42) in a double. Only breakfast is served.

Hotel Guadelupe, Avenida de los Alijares (tel. 22-34-23), is set along the steep road that rises beside the entrance to the gardens of the Generalife and the Alhambra, near a cluster of other hotels and souvenir shops. It was built in 1969, but its thick stucco walls, rounded arches, and jutting beams of overhanging eaves make it seem older. A handful of its 59 rooms look out over the Alhambra, each containing a private bath, radio, and phone. Singles cost 3,200 pesetas ($22.40), doubles 6,000 pesetas ($42), breakfast and taxes not included. There's a fifth floor à la carte restaurant, plus a pleasant bar in the lobby.

Hotel Arrayanes, Avenida de los Alijares (tel. 22-34-23). Its location amid a cluster of other hotels and souvenir shops along the sloping road stretching beside the entrance to the Alhambra is one of its particular advantages. It was built in the early 1980s in a stark modern, pleasant format of marble floor coverings and pristine furnishings. Each of its 16 bedrooms has its own bath, phone, and radio. Rated three stars by the government, it contains few amenities other than its bedrooms, which rent for 3,200 pesetas ($22.40) in a single and 6,000 pesetas ($42) in a double, breakfast and taxes not included. However, residents are welcomed to patronize the bar and restaurant of its just-recommended sister hotel, the Guadelupe nearby.

Hotel Kenia, 65 Molinos (tel. 22-75-07), in many ways is an Andalusian dream come true. It sits behind a high wall in a residential neighborhood, amid a maze of sloping streets near the Alhambra. You'll pass through an ornate iron gate to enter the baroque gardens of what was originally built as a private villa in the 19th century. An ornate tower rises grandly above an architectural ensemble of yesteryear, presided over by Francisco Rodriguez Manzano and his polite, Spanish-speaking staff. The 19 bedrooms each contain a private bath, dignified and conservative furniture, and plenty of sunlight and quiet. Singles cost 2,500 pesetas ($17.50); doubles, 4,700 pesetas ($32.90). There's a formal parlor with a marble fireplace and Spanish versions of Eastlake period chairs, a dining room, and a graveled terrace where dining tables are placed between June and August.

Gran Hotel Brasilia, 7 Recogidas (tel. 25-84-50), is smack in the center of Granada, providing, among many comforts, full air conditioning. The rooms are well furnished, the hotel is efficient, the staff polite (English is spoken). In short, it's one of the best hotels in the city. All of the rooms, both single and double, have private tub-shower bath. Couples pay 5,500 pesetas ($38.50); singles, 4,000 pesetas ($28). You'll find other important facilities, such as an American bar, a roof terrace, and a grill for light snacks. The location is fine for shopping, too—only three blocks from the Puerta Real.

Macia, 4 Plaza Nueva (tel. 22-75-33), is an attractive modern hotel, right at the bottom of the hill going up to the Alhambra. Its 44 rooms rate two stars, so you're getting a real bargain in what I think should be a three-star hotel. All rooms have heating, private bath, and phone, and are clean and functional. Doubles cost 4,000 pesetas ($28), and singles run 3,000 pesetas ($21).

Sudán, 60 Acera Darro (tel. 25-84-00), is a two-star hotel, only a five-minute walk from the Puerta Real in modern Granada. A clean, comfortable, substantial hotel, it is one of the best places in the city: doubles cost from 4,000 pesetas ($28) daily. Singles with private bath rent for 2,500 pesetas ($17.50). Be sure to ask for one of the front rooms with bay windows, as they are the superior accommodations. The entire staff is most cooperative, and the food is quite good, with a lunch or dinner averaging 1,000 pesetas ($7).

Residencia Anacapri, 7 Joaquin Costa (tel. 22-55-63), is a quietly situated hotel, right off the Reyes Católicos in the heart of the modern city. The rooms are comfortable, nicely furnished; the hotel is well run, and has a look of old-world elegance to it. Doubles with private bath cost from 4,000 pesetas ($28). Singles with private bath start at 3,000 pesetas ($21), but are few in number. A continental breakfast will be delivered to your room, but no other meals are served. However, this need not be a problem, as the Anacapri is near many of Granada's budget restaurants. Because it is on a secluded street, the hotel offers rooms protected from the traffic noises of bustling Granada, the plague of most of the city's major hotels. You'll also be right in the center of the shopping section.

Hotel Inglaterra, 6 Cettie Meriem (tel. 22-15-59), is right near the cathedral, the peal of bells awakening you to another day in Granada. A corner hotel, it is built in an Andalusian style, with a glass-covered lobby. Recent modernization has brightened it up considerably, but while it still languishes in its 1920s heyday, it offers the fine service of bygone days. Not so old are the bathrooms, assigned to each bedroom. A double with bath goes for 4,000 pesetas ($28). Only three singles are offered, those with private baths costing 3,000 pesetas ($21). Triple rooms with bath rent for 5,600 pesetas ($39.20).

Hostal Carlos V, 4 Plaza de los Campos Elíseos (tel. 22-15-87), is an unpretentious, comfortable hotel on the upper floor of a building. Several of its rooms have balconies boasting some spectacular views of the city, and a double room with bath goes for 4,200 pesetas ($29.40), 3,500 pesetas ($24.50) without bath but with a terrace. Normally you're expected to have some meals in the hotel. These cost 1,000 pesetas ($7) for either lunch or dinner, plus a charge for a continental breakfast. The owner says he has special accommodations for four people, and all rooms have a telephone.

Hotel Manuel de Falla, 4 Antequeruela Baja (tel. 22-75-45), is a secret gem, known to discerning travelers. Within walking distance of the Alhambra, it is perched on a hill overlooking the city and has a small courtyard and air shaft. The view is perfect, and living here is like being a part of the life of a tiny village, far removed from the modern part of Granada. But don't expect a pad like Hugh Hefner's. It's bedrooms are basic, with decent furnishings and fairly reliable plumbing. For a double with private bath the rate is 4,500 pesetas ($31.50). Singles with shower bath are 3,000 pesetas ($21). You can order a meal here for an additional charge of 1,200 pesetas ($8.40).

Hostal América, 53 Real de la Alhambra (tel. 22-74-71), within the ancient Alhambra walls, is one of the leading boarding houses of Granada. You walk through a covered entryway right into the shady patio of what once was probably the villa of a wealthy family. It is both lively and intimate, with large trees, many potted plants and ferns. The plants run up the white plastered walls, leap over the doorways and windows, and twine themselves around the ornate grillwork. Garden chairs and tables are set out for the excellent, homecooked Spanish meals. This little oasis is a personal, homey retreat. The living room is graced with a collection of decorative objects from the region. The bedrooms occasionally have Andalusian reproductions, personal and pleasing, but without distinction. The cost of the best double room with private bath is 4,500 pesetas ($31.50), a single with bath going for 3,000 pesetas ($21). A complete lunch or dinner is an extra 1,400 pesetas ($9.80). It is open March 1 to October 31.

Pension California, 37 Cuesta Gomérez (tel. 22-40-56), is too often passed up as one whizzes up the hill toward the Alhambra. But don't miss it (on your left) if you're in need of an inexpensive and typically Spanish accommodation. It is run in an informal, family-like manner, totally unlike a hotel. The bedrooms are simply furnished, but well kept. A number of double accommodations with showers rent for only 2,400 pesetas ($16.80). Single rooms, with water basins only, cost just 1,800 pesetas ($12.60). A set lunch or dinner goes for 1,400 pesetas ($9.80), and a continental breakfast is extra.

WHERE TO DINE: From the heights of the Alhambra to the narrow, dark streets in the heart of the city, feasting on the rich and plentiful Andalusian cuisine is an important part of the day's activity in Granada. The lead-off restaurant recommendation is the government-run parador. **San Francisco,**

Alhambra (tel. 22-14-93), with its dinners for 2,100 pesetas ($14.70). In summer, meals are served on a terrace overlooking the Generalife.

Restaurante Cunini, 14 Pescaderia (tel. 26-37-01). Since a second entrance to this well-known fish house near the cathedral is at 14 Capuchina, it's easy to find. The array of seafood specialties extends even to the tapas served at the long, stand-up bar. Many guests move on to the ground-floor restaurant after a drink or two, where the cuisine served is from all over Spain, even the Basque country. Meals often begin with one of the soups offered, which include sopa Cunini and sopa sevillana (with ham, shrimp, and whitefish). Also popular is a deep fry of small fish called a fritura Cunini. Other specialties are stuffed sardines, a zarzuela, smoked salmon, and grilled shrimp. Meals, which are available every day for lunch and dinner except Sunday night, range from 1,200 pesetas ($8.40) to 2,200 pesetas ($15.40).

Los Leones, 10 Acera Darro (tel. 25-50-07). Since its establishment in the early 1920s, this restaurant has seen many of the changes modern times have brought to Granada. Today, owner Luís Salvador Ojeda, with his son Juan, is the proud owner of one of the best restaurants in town. The specialties are served impeccably and include hake with tartar sauce, Andalusian fish fry, a well-seasoned bull's tail, a frequently changing dish of the day, and fabada beans flavored with eggs and ham. Full meals, served daily except Monday night and Tuesday, range from 1,500 pesetas ($10.50) to 2,500 pesetas ($17.50).

Polinario, 3 Real de la Alhambra (tel. 22-29-91), is a simple two-fork restaurant within the ancient walls of the Alhambra, across the way from the Palace of Charles V. The Spanish cooking is reasonably good, and a complete buffet will set you back 1,200 pesetas ($8.40), including service and wine. This altitudinous restaurant earns its chief credits for its Andalusian dishes, such as chilled gazpacho, always a favorite with the summer crowd who flit in and out of here with copies of Washington Irving's book. Its rooms have been decorated with nondescript restraint, but this provides a soothing background for such dishes as lamb chops, ragoût, and hake fried Roman style. The inevitable but always-welcome flan is served for dessert. In summer, like the caliphs of old, diners eat in the garden. The restaurant closes at 5 p.m.

Restaurant Sevilla, 14 Oficios (tel. 22-12-23), opposite the Royal Chapel, is the Lorelei of Granada, luring a mixed crowd that spans the generation gap. The Sevilla, in the center of the city, is definitely típico with an upbeat elegance —like an owner's conception of what the foreign tourist wants an Andalusian decor to be. The menú del día goes for 1,800 pesetas ($12.60), and is available at either luncheon or dinner. My most recent repast included gazpacho, Andalusian veal, and a selection of desserts, such as caramel custard or fresh fruit, bread and the wine of Valdepeñas. To break the gazpacho monotony, you might try sopa virulé, which is made with pine kernels and chicken breast. For a main course, you should try the cordero (lamb) a la pastoril, which is cooked with herbs and paprika. The dessert spectacular is bananas flambé. If you order à la carte, expect to spend from 2,200 pesetas ($15.40). You can dine inside, where it is pleasantly decorated, or have a meal on the terrace. Sevilla also has a bar.

Los Manueles, 4 Zaragoza (tel. 22-34-15), is an old Granada standby on a narrow side street. It's not a street really—more like an alleyway, and the restaurant occupies the whole passageway. The location is right off the most central Puerto Real. It is unpretentious, with colorful tile walls and floors, and fans alternate with lanterns hanging from the ceiling. Above the counter hang dozens of tempting Serano hams. The king and queen of Spain have dined here. There are two small dining rooms, or you can sit on the no-traffic street outside in the summer. The tourist menu is 1,200 pesetas ($8.40). À la carte specialties include the pescada Manueles, which is hake with all kinds of peas, shrimp, and a sauce.

Finish with strawberries and cream or quince jelly. Ordering à la carte will cost from 2,000 pesetas ($14). The beef dishes are more expensive.

Chikito, 9 Plaza del Campillo (tel. 22-33-64), is set across the street from the famous tree-shaded square where García Lorca met with other members of "the little corner," or El Rinconcillo as they called themselves. These were 12 or so young men who were considered the beautiful and brightest in the 1920s when they brought a brief but dazzling cultural renaissance to their hometown. The café where they met has now changed its name, but it's the same building. Right in the center of Granada, the present-day Chikito is both a bar and a restaurant. In fair weather, guests enjoy drinks and snacks on tables placed on the square. In winter they retreat inside to the tapas bars for food and drink. There is also a complete restaurant facility, offering such dishes as sopa sevillana, shrimp cocktail, Basque hake, baked tuna, ox tail, osso buco, zarzuela (a seafood stew), grilled swordfish, and fried anchovies. Set menus are featured at 950 pesetas ($6.65), and it will cost about 1,500 pesetas ($10.50) or more to order à la carte. Closed Wednesday.

Torres Bermejas, 6 Plaza Nueva (tel. 22-31-16), opens onto one of the most charming squares of Granada. You enter a stylish bar area and can have an apéritif there before heading back to the warmly contemporary dining room. Main dishes include such delectable specialties as grilled swordfish, roast lamb, tournedos Rossini, veal chops, and shrimps pil-pil. A set menu is presented at only 1,000 pesetas ($7); dining à la carte is likely to cost from 2,200 pesetas ($15.40).

Mesón Andaluz, 17 Calle Elvira (tel. 22-73-57), is one of the best of the restaurants that lie near the Hotel Inglaterra in a maze of little streets. It is also in the vicinity of the cathedral. The pick of the places on this street of budget restaurants, it is decorated in a typical Andalusian style. You get efficient and polite service along with good food inexpensively priced. Set menus are offered for only 750 pesetas ($5.25), and you can dine à la carte for 1,500 pesetas ($10.50) and up. A menu is printed in English. From it you can make selections such as hake stew, rabbit prepared hunter's style, brains in the Roman style, fried chicken with garlic, and, to finish off, a whisky ice-cream tart.

Finally, I have found that one of the best lunches in Spain is served in any city that has a **Galerías Precíados** department store. Granada is no exception. The store is at Carrera del Genil (tel. 22-35-83). For shoppers in a rush, it offers a menu express for $5.50 (U.S.), which I consider one of the best bargains in the city. The meal begins with soup, and follows with, say, breast of chicken and french fries. For that low price, you also get bread and wine (or else beer or mineral water). Even better is the buffet, a selection of some 80 dishes and 25 desserts, costing from $7, including your beverage. I'd order a bottle of rioja red wine. Perhaps you will, too. Hours are from 10 a.m. to 8 p.m.

THE SIGHTS: The sights of Granada don't end with the Alhambra, they begin with it.

The Alhambra

When you first see the Alhambra, don't be surprised by its somewhat somber exterior. Remember that the Arabs applied the same principle to architecture that they did to their women: they kept the outside parts veiled. You have to walk across the threshold to discover the true treasures.

The Moorish palace is entered through the incongruous 14th-century **Gateway to Justice.** Tickets are sold in the office next to the uncompleted palace of the Habsburg king, Charles V. A comprehensive ticket, including both the Alhambra and the Generalife, costs 350 pesetas ($2.45). The Alhambra may be visited in summer from 9:30 a.m. to 5:30 p.m. In winter it opens at 10 a.m. and closes at 6 p.m. The average visitor does not need the services of an expensive guide, but should be content to stroll along in a quietly contemplative mood through the richly ornamented open-air rooms, with their lace-like walls and courtyards with fountains. Most of the Arabic inscriptions seem to translate: "Only Allah is conqueror."

The most photographed part of the palace is the **Court of Lions,** containing a highly stylized fountain of lions. This was the heart of the palace, the most private section, where the sultan wanted to be alone to enjoy his harem. Opening onto the court are such rooms as the **Hall of the Two Sisters,** where the favorite of the moment was kept, or the **Gossip Room,** that factory of intrigue. In the dancing room in the **Hall of Kings,** an early version of the striptease was performed nightly to amuse the sultan's party. In all, it's like a theater, around which the eunuchs of old guarded the gems of the harem. Apparently, these eunuchs weren't too diligent one night. One sultan, according to legend, beheaded 36 Moorish princes because one of them was suspected of having been intimate with his favorite.

You can see the room where Washington Irving lived (in the chambers of Charles V) when he was compiling his *Tales of the Alhambra*—the best known of which is the legend of the three beautiful princesses, Zayda, Zorayada, and Zorahayda, who fell in love with three captured Spanish soldiers outside their "La Torre de las Infantas." Irving did more than any other writer to publicize the Alhambra to the English-speaking world.

Although Irving credits the French with saving the Alhambra for posterity, these invaders blew up seven of the towers in 1812, but a Spanish soldier cut the fuse before more damage could be done. When the Duke of Wellington arrived a few years later, he chased out the chickens, the gypsies, and the transient beggars who were using the Alhambra as a kind of tenement dwelling, and set up housekeeping here himself.

Incidentally, don't miss the Roman-inspired **Royal Baths,** and the 13th-century **Alcazaba,** which is in ruins.

Charles V may have been horrified when he saw the cathedral placed in the middle of the great mosque at Córdoba, but he had his hand involved in some architectural incongruity as well. He built a Renaissance palace at the Alhambra. Although quite beautiful, it seems to have as much reason to be here as Anne Hathaway's cottage would at Times Square. Today it houses a **Museum of Fine Arts,** which you can visit for 75 pesetas (53¢), open from 10 a.m. to 2 p.m. daily except Sunday. It also shelters a National Museum devoted to Hispanic-Muslim art, which keeps the same hours, charging an additional 75 pesetas (53¢) admission. Ask at the Tourist Office, Casa de los Tiros, 19 Calle de Pavaneras (tel. 22-10-22) if the Alhambra will be illuminated during the time of your visit to Granada. Scheduling is erratic, so you must inquire locally about the *iluminado*.

From the Alhambra, you can proceed up the hill (road clearly marked) to . . .

The Generalife

The sultans spent their summers here at this palace, safely and serenely locked away with their dancing girls. Built in the 13th century to overlook the Alhambra, the Generalife depends on its gardens and courtyards for its glory. Don't expect an Alhambra in miniature: the Generalife was always meant to be a retreat, even from the splendors of the Alhambra. This palace was the setting of the story of the prince locked away from love in Irving's *Tales of the Alham-*

bra. It is open from 9 a.m. until 7 p.m. It opens at 10 a.m. in winter, closing at 6 p.m. The comprehensive ticket of 350 pesetas ($2.45), which most visitors purchase at the Alhambra, entitles you to admission to the Generalife.

The Cathedral and Royal Chapel

This richly ornate Spanish Renaissance cathedral, with its spectacular altar, is one of the great cathedrals of Spain. It is acclaimed primarily for its beautiful façade and interior gold and white decor. Work on it began in the 16th century, roughly some 30 years after Isabella and Ferdinand reclaimed the city. It is in the lower city, off the principal avenue, Gran Vía de Colón.

In back of the cathedral (entered separately) is the flamboyantly Gothic **Royal Chapel,** where Isabella and Ferdinand are buried. It was their wish to be buried in recaptured Granada, and not Castile or Aragón. The coffins are remarkably tiny by today's standards, which is a reminder of how short folks used to be. The tombs are properly accented by a wrought-iron grill, a masterpiece. Occupying much larger tombs are the remains of their daughter, Joan the Mad, and her husband, Philip the Handsome. Both the chapel and cathedral can be visited from 11 a.m. to 1 p.m. and 4 to 7 p.m.; the charge is 100 pesetas (70¢) for each monument.

The Albaicín

This old Arab quarter doesn't belong to the Granada of the 19th-century buildings and wide boulevards. It, and the surrounding gypsy caves of Sacro-Monte, are holdovers from the past. The Albaicín once flourished as the residential section of the Moors, even after the reconquest of the city, but it declined when the Christians finally declared the Muslims intolerable and drove them from the city. A narrow labyrinth of crooked streets, the Albaicín was spared the fate that many parts of Granada suffered when they were torn down in the name of progress. Happily, it has been preserved, as have its old cisterns, fountains, plazas, whitewashed houses, an occasional villa, and the decaying remnants of the old city gate. One catches a glimpse of a private patio filled with fountains and plants, a traditional way of life handsomely continuing. Be sure to follow the sign to the old Arab baths (free).

La Cartuja

This 16th-century monastery, right off the Albaicín, is sometimes called "the Christian answer to the Alhambra," owing to its ornate stucco and marble. Its most notable paintings are by Bocanegra, its outstanding sculpture by Mora. The church of this Carthusian monastery was decorated with baroque stucco in the 17th century. Its most outstanding feature is its sacristy, dating from the 18th century, an excellent example of the latter-day baroque style. Napoleon's armies killed Saint Bruno here, and La Cartuja is said to be the only monument of its kind in the world. Sometimes one of the Carthusian monks will take you on a guided tour. On the outskirts of Granada, but reached by bus #8 from the center, the monastery is open daily from 10 a.m. to 1 p.m. and from 3 to 7 p.m., charging an admission of 50 pesetas (35¢).

Huerta de San Vicente

At Virgen Blanca, poet Federico García Lorca spent many a happy summer with his family. It was their vacation home. As an 11-year-old, this dreamy-eyed schoolboy had moved to Granada in 1909, and he was endlessly fascinated with its life, including the Alhambra and the gypsies about whom he was later to write compassionately in his *Gypsy Ballads.* From a balcony of the house, you can look out at the Alhambra. The house, decorated with green trim and grillwork, is filled with family memorabilia, including furniture and portraits. Guests are allowed to inspect the poet's bedroom upstairs and see his oak desk stained with ink. Look for the white stool which he would carry to the terrace to watch the sunsets over Granada. For 35 pesetas (25¢), you can tour the house from 10 a.m. to 1 p.m. and from 4 to 7 p.m.

Casa Museo Manuel de Falla

The famous Spanish composer, known for his strongly individualized works, was not a native of Granada, but came to live there in 1919. He hoped to find a retreat, and he also sought inspiration from the city. He found a *carmen* (that's not a girl friend, but a small white house in local dialect) just below the Alhambra. In time he was to become friends with García Lorca, and they staged in 1922 the "Deep Song Festival" on the grounds of the Alhambra. Today, visitors can walk through the gardens of the man who wrote such works as "Nights in the Gardens of Spain," and see his collection of handcrafts and ceramics, along with other personal memorabilia. Lying on Calle Antequerela Alta, it is open daily except Monday from 10 a.m. to 2 p.m. and from 4 to 6 p.m., charging an admission of 35 pesetas (25¢).

Shopping in a Moorish Market

The **Alcaicería,** which huddles close to the cathedral in the lower city, is a rebuilt Moorish-style village of shops in the heart of Granada. Its narrow streets are filled with shops selling the típico arts and crafts of Granada province. For the souvenir hunter, the Alcaicería offers one of the most splendid assortments in Spain—everything from tiles to castanets to wire figures of Don Quixote chasing windmills. Lots of Spanish jewelry is to be found here, comparing favorably to the finest of Toledo work. For the window shopper, in particular, it makes for a pleasant stroll. In former days the Alcaicería was the silk market of the Moors.

The Gypsy Caves of Sacro-Monte

These inhabited gypsy caves have been the subject of much controversy. Admittedly, they are a tourist trap, one of the most obviously commercial and shadowy rackets in all of Spain. Still, the caves are a potent enough attraction, if you follow some rules.

Once thousands of gypsies lived in the caves of the "Holy Mountain," so named because of several Christians martyred here. However, many of the caves were heavily damaged in the flood-like rains of 1962, forcing hundreds of the occupants to seek shelter elsewhere. Nearly all of the gypsies remaining are in one way or another involved with tourism. As one newspaper writer put it, "Some gypsies do not even remain in the caves overnight. When the last bus has departed, they leave, too, for a modern apartment elsewhere in the city."

When evening settles over Granada, visitors in heavy loads descend on these caves near the Albaicín, the old Arab section. In every cave, you'll hear the rattle of castanets and the sound of guitars. Everybody in the gypsy family is doing an act.

Popularly known as the *zambra,* this can be intriguing entertainment *only* if you have an appreciation of the grotesque. Whenever a gypsy boy or girl comes along with a genuine talent, he or she is often grabbed up and hustled off to the more expensive clubs. Those left at home often amuse with their pathetic attempts to assume the image of glamour.

One of the main reasons for going, of course, is to see the caves. If you're expecting primitive living, you may be in for a surprise. Many are quite comfortable, with such conveniences as telephones and electricity, and often they are decorated with copper and ceramic items—and the gypsies need no encouragement to sell them to you.

If you want to see the caves, you can walk up the hill by yourself. By smoke signals or whatever, your approach will already be advertised before you get there. Attempts will be made to lure you inside one of the caves—and to get whatever money from you these cave-dwellers can.

You can also book one of the organized tours, arranged by the travel agencies in Granada. Even at the end of one of these organized tours—all expenses are theoretically paid in advance—there is likely to be another attempt (on the part of the gypsies, not the travel agencies) to extract more money from you. As soon as the *zambra* ends, hustle yourself out of the cave as quickly as possible. Even so, some señorita may chase you down the hill, jabbing her finger in your ribs and screaming, "Money, amigo, money." Readers have been critical of these tours. A typical comment, from a Syracuse University student: "The entire evening was unprofessional and un-typically Spanish and overpriced for the entertainment we received."

During the *zambra,* refuse to accept a pair of castanets, even if offered under the friendly guise of having you join in the fun. If you accept them, the chances are that you'll later be asked to pay for them. Buying anything in these caves is not recommended. Leave all your jewelry at your hotel (in itself risky), but don't take more money to the caves than you're prepared to let light-fingered Luís have.

A different point of view is reflected in the following letter:

"Several of the gypsies had superb figures, and they danced with fire in their feet. They were friendly to the tourists, offering them free drinks and castanets. The audience, which consisted mostly of Americans, sat rigidly and frigidly in their seats, contemptuously rejecting all attempts by the gypsies to establish friendly communications. Understandably, the gypsies were offended and hurt by the tourists' uncalled-for attitude of fear, hostility, and scorn. Though they felt rejected, the gypsies performed brilliantly—and all the while the audience looked guarded as if they were sitting in a robber's lair. It was painful to see. My wife and I feel very strongly that many of the gypsy performers, both in the Sacro-Monte caves and the nightclubs, are talented artists, the heirs of a colorful tradition, and worthy of our respect. As for the tourists, they will be well advised to show better manners. Otherwise, the gypsies have every right to regard them as barbarians" (Dr. Alfred Dorn, Long Island City, N.Y.).

GRANADA AFTER DARK: The best all-around flamenco show in Granada is staged at **Jardines Neptuno,** Calle Arabial (tel. 25-11-12). Maybe it's not the same show dancing girls performed for sultans centuries ago, but these acts are still "torrid," even though toned down considerably for today's audiences. In addition to flamenco, performers attired in their regional garb do folk dances and give guitar concerts. The show is in a garden setting and breezily expensive, as much as 1,800 pesetas ($12.60) for your first drink. But you can nurse it all evening, and that means three solid hours of entertainment. Don't arrive before 11 p.m.

If you want to hear "authentic" gypsy music, shun the caves and the tourist-oriented clubs, and head for the **Curro Club,** Calle Lavadero de las Tablas (no phone). Go late and be prepared to be entertained regally. In the upstairs bar are large pictures of García Lorca who was a hero to the gypsies. Drinks and admission cost from 1,200 pesetas ($8.40) per person.

Jardines Aben Humeya, 12 Carril de las Tomasas (tel. 22-46-76) in the Albaicín. A visit to its rose gardens and terraces is the best possible excuse for making an excursion into the winding alleyways of the ancient Arab section of

Granada. It was named after a legendary Moorish ruler who would probably have considered its greenery a welcome oasis. You'll recognize it by its string of colored lights stretching across the low stucco buildings of its entrance.

After passing a guard, you'll descend past a rose-flanked series of ivy-covered lattices into everybody's fantasy of a perfect Andalusian garden. There, by a thatch-covered bar, you can order beer for 275 pesetas ($1.93) and a full array of international drinks. There's an open-air dance floor, circular banquettes upholstered in soft cushions and dappled with shadows from the soaring trees, and a sound system broadcasting music. Be sure to climb to the top of the encircling fortifications for a stunning view of the Alhambra. The establishment is open from 8 p.m. to 3 a.m. daily between May and September.

READER'S TIP ON MOUNTAIN AND OCEAN SCENERY: "The traveler in his or her own car is able to drive up the highest mountain road in Europe, south of Granada, to a thousand feet below the highest peak in Spain, in the Sierra Nevada mountains, 11,500 feet high. Another magnificent road runs from Granada south to Lotril. The mountains rival those of Austria and Switzerland in their majesty, great cliffs, and deep gorges. The road from Lotril, which is on the sea, is another fine adventure, as it winds along the coast with many hairpin turns. Each curve presents a new view of the hills and the sea" (Calvin Keene, Lewisburg, Pa.).

Chapter VIII

THE COSTA DEL SOL

1. Algeciras
2. Tarifa
3. Estepona
4. Puerto Banús
5. San Pedro de Alcantara
6. Marbella
7. Fuengirola and Los Boliches
8. Mijas
9. Torremolinos
10. Málaga
11. Nerja
12. Almería

NOWHERE IS THE Spanish tourist boom more booming than on the sun strip named the Costa del Sol. This razzle-dazzle stretch of Mediterranean shoreline begins at the western frontier harbor city of Algeciras (gateway to Tangier), and stretches all the way east to the up-and-coming port city of **Almería.**

Sandwiched between these two points is a generally steep and rugged coastline, with poor-to-fair beaches, set against the Sierra Nevada. Along this stretch of land, you'll find sandy coves, whitewashed houses, olive trees, zillions of new apartment houses, fishing boats, golf courses, gimcrack souvenir stands, fast-food outlets, and a widely varied flora—both human and vegetable. In all, the Sun Coast's mild climate in winter and its virtually guaranteed sunshine in summer have made it a year-round attraction.

What were once sleepy fishing villages, with naked niños and little stoop-shouldered women in mourning black, have been knocked out of their slumber by the sound of rock music and the honking of a million horns.

Hotels, once scarce, are plentiful. Even the remotest, the most provincial of the villages, have erected hotels. Once the men fished for squid. Now their nets are turning up two-legged land creatures. With many exceptions, style and grace (two elements well known to the Andalusians) have gone the way of Garciá Lorca (he was executed) in this part of the world.

Many of the sun spots along the coast are strictly for low-income Europeans who book in here on a package deal for two weeks. For the average fun-loving gringo, I suggest **Marbella** and **Torremolinos.**

From June until deep in the heart of October, the coast is mobbed. If you should arrive during the peak months, make sure you've nailed down a reservation. If you go at other times, chances are the innkeeper will roll out the red carpet, kiss your hand, polish your shoes, and carry you to your pick of a chamber.

Visitors should be aware that on the Costa del Sol many restaurants close down about October 15 for a much-needed vacation. Also, October 12 is a national holiday, and travelers contemplating a visit at that time should be well established in a hotel long before the masses descend. It is also important to note that many supermarkets and other facilities are closed on Sunday. In addition, gasoline stations, for the most part, carry cube ice, which is sold inexpensively in small sacks.

The Costa del Sol is traversed by two bus lines, the best means of transportation for those planning to go resort hopping. The major run is from Málaga to Algeciras via Torremolinos and Marbella. If you're flying to the Costa del Sol from Madrid (Iberia has daily connections), you'll land at the Málaga airport, which is within easy reach of Torremolinos by taxi or private car. We'll begin our trip up this coast at:

1. Algeciras

This port town is the jumping-off point for Africa (it takes about three hours to reach either Tangier or Spanish Morocco). Algeciras reflects a heavy North African influence. It is a modern, efficient, and clean-looking port city. If you're planning a trip to Tangier from Algeciras, there is a baggage storage depot at the ferry terminal that is inexpensive.

Algeciras used to be a base for day trips to Gibraltar (see Chapter XV). In 1982 Britain and Spain lifted the 14-year Spanish blockade of Gibraltar. The border between Gibraltar and Spain (La Línea de la Concepción) is now open. However, remember that agreements are subject to change, and you really should check at the Turismo office on Avenida de la Marina (tel. 65-67-61) in Algeciras if you're contemplating a trip to "The Rock." There you'll be advised of the latest border-crossing situation.

Even if you don't have time to make the trip to Gibraltar, the habit of Gibraltar watching has always been popular in Algeciras. There it sits, in plain view, six miles out in the Bay of Algeciras. Gathering at the Algeciras docks, tourists aim either their binoculars or cameras at the formidable rock.

WHERE TO STAY: Algeciras is okay for the night, but is not recommended for long stopovers. If you must stay, try the following . . .

Hotel Término, 6 Avenida Villanueva (tel. 65-02-11), a short walk from the docking area. Some of its only fair bedrooms have views of the docks. For a double room with private bath, the charge ranges from 2,400 pesetas ($16.80) to 2,800 pesetas ($19.60); the best single rooms (with bath) cost 2,000 pesetas ($14). There's a terrace for drinks on the second landing. A continental breakfast is available. Término is a clean, comfortable, and cheap hotel.

Those wanting to get away from the port area should consider the three-star, 68-room **Hotel Alarde,** 4 Alfonso XI (tel. 66-04-08). A hotel which opened in 1971 in a quiet commercial area, it has double rooms with bath and balcony for 5,500 pesetas ($38.50), singles go for 3,000 pesetas ($21). There's a snack-bar, but no restaurant. In the center of Algeciras, the residencia is near the Park of María Cristina. Its furnishings are in the pure Andalusian style, with antique

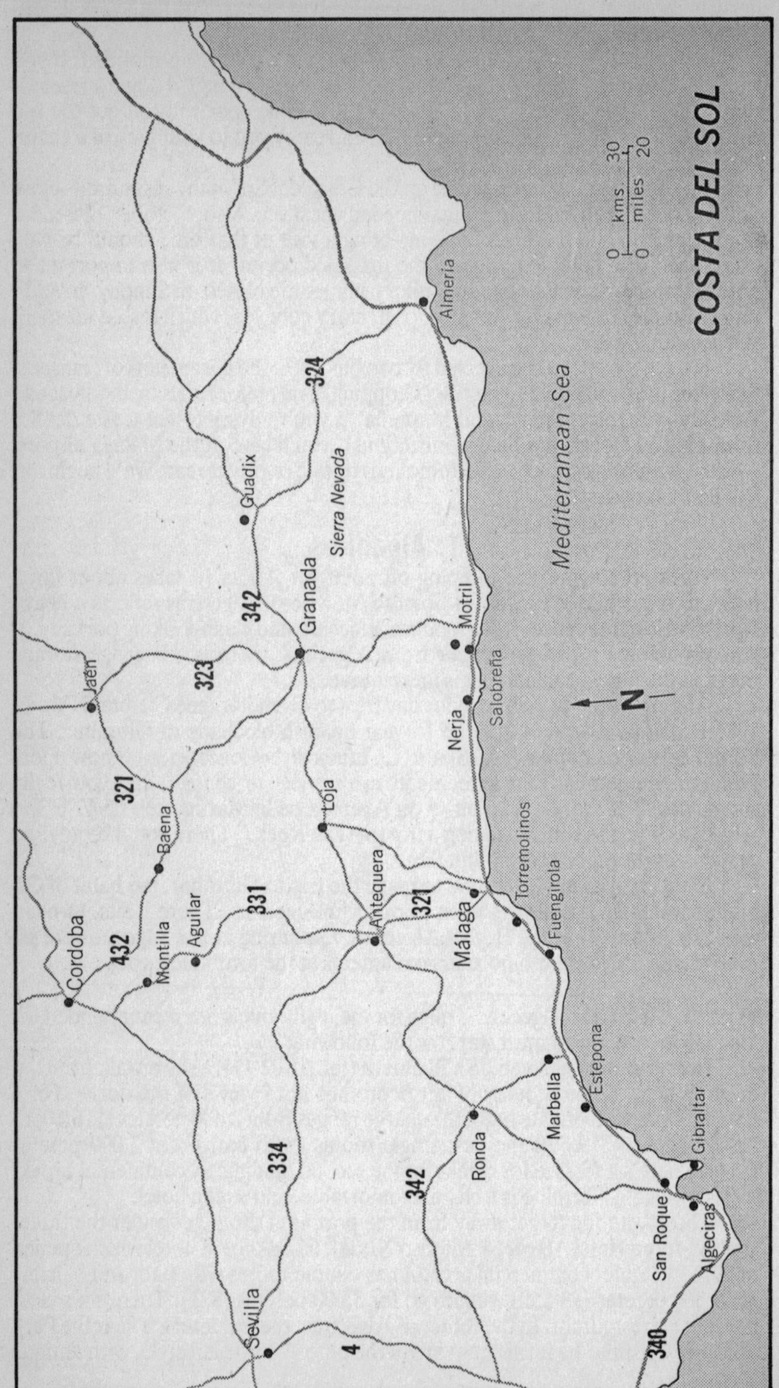
COSTA DEL SOL
Mediterranean Sea
Sierra Nevada
N
0 kms 30
0 miles 20
Almeria
Guadix
Granada
Motril
Salobreña
Nerja
Jaén
Loja
Baena
Torremolinos
Fuengirola
Málaga
Antequera
Cordoba
Montilla
Aguilar
Estepona
Marbella
Ronda
Gibraltar
San Roque
Algeciras
Sevilla
324
342
323
321
331
432
334
4
340

railings. The main floor is completely air-conditioned. On my most recent stay, I was left with a very favorable impression of the staff and the homey atmosphere created by management.

Hotel Octavio, 1 San Bernardo (tel. 65-26-50). Its reproductions of English antiques contrast sharply with the angular lines of its modern exterior. An American bar serves international drinks, and also on the premises is a pleasantly decorated restaurant, the Iris. Its 80 bedrooms each contain a private bath and air conditioning, with singles costing 4,500 pesetas ($31.50); doubles, 7,200 pesetas ($50.40). The hotel lies in a position convenient to the center of town.

Hotel Al-Mar, 2 Avenida de la Marina (tel. 65-46-61), is one of the newest hotels in town, filled with a blue and white decor of Andalusian and Moorish detailing. Giant in structure, it contains almost 200 bedrooms, most of which have a private bath, a panorama, and plenty of sunlight. The cost is 3,000 pesetas ($21) in a single, 5,500 pesetas ($38.50) in a double. On the premises are three restaurants, a handful of bars, and lots of verdant hideaways.

WHERE TO EAT: **Restaurant Marea Baja,** 2 Trafalgar (tel. 66-36-54), in the center of town, is effectively directed by Alejandro Fernández Gavilán and his wife, Natividad Mateo, who introduce newly created recipes frequently. You'll be greeted at the door with a friendly smile and the sight of a long tapas bar, which might serve to whet your appetite before you select something from the wide array of specialties. These include seafood crêpes, rape (a white fish), hake, and omelets. Meals range from 2,200 pesetas ($15.40) and are served daily except Sunday.

Across the canal is the **Casa Alfonso,** 4 Juan de la Cierva (tel. 67-12-39). For 800 pesetas ($5.60), you can get paella or bean soup, fried fish, a beefsteak with potatoes, bread, wine, and fruit. It's simple and unpretentious, an excellent bargain.

READER'S SIGHTSEEING TIPS: "**Getares** is a small village almost 2 miles south of Algeciras on the coast, with a lovely uncrowded beach with great views of the Rock. We seemed to be about the only foreigners on the beach.

"**Casares,** 8½ miles off the coast highway just south of Estepona, is a beautiful detour for those working their way north or south along the Costa del Sol. It is a small, unspoiled village in a spectacular setting against the Sierra Barmeja. Casares could be considered a prototype of the Andalusian village, glistening white, all hills, and topped by the ruins of an old fortress. The ride in from the coast offers outstanding views of the town" (James Wiley).

2. Tarifa

If you're in Algeciras, instead of rushing east along the Costa del Sol, I'd suggest a visit west to Tarifa, an old Moorish town that is the southernmost point in Europe. After leaving Algeciras, the roads climb steeply. In the distance you can view Gibraltar, the straits, and the "green hills" of Africa. In fact, you can actually see houses in Ceuta and Tangier on the Moroccan coastline. This road, between Tarifa and Algeciras, is one of the most splendid coastal routes in Spain, maybe in all of Europe.

Tarifa has retained much of its Moorish character, more so than any other town in Andalusia. Narrow, cobblestone streets lead to charming patios filled with flowers. The town was named for Tarik, one of the leaders of the Moorish forces.

At Tarifa is a five-mile-long beach. At one point this beautiful white sandy beach is a quarter of a mile wide. Tarifa is still a Spanish military zone, and that has hindered development—along with a wind that seems never to stop blowing.

Eight miles beyond Tarifa you can explore the ruins of the ancient Roman town of **Baelo Claudia,** lying off Route N340 along the Algeciras–Cádiz highway. The site is open daily except Monday, from 10 a.m. to 2 p.m. and from 3 to 6 p.m. (on Sunday from 10 a.m. to 1 p.m.). Admission is 100 pesetas (70¢). The town was founded in the 1st century but it was relatively forgotten for nearly 1,500 years. Once under the Romans it had been a flourishing fishing factory. Its population at one time was believed to have been 30,000 citizens. The archeological site was discovered only at the end of World War I. At present, excavations are far from complete. Some historians think Claudius may have founded the town. The old Roman theater dominates the ruins.

Mesón de Sancho, 340 Carretera General Cádiz-Málaga, Km. 94 (tel. 68-49-00), is a rambling, informal, hacienda-style inn, where you'll find a restful atmosphere, plus a swimming pool set out in the midst of olive trees and terraces. It's about ten miles southwest of Algeciras on the Cádiz road. A double with bath rents for 4,200 pesetas ($29.40). There are no singles as such; however, one person occupying a double room pays only 3,200 pesetas ($22.40). An intercommunicating two-room apartment with bath carries the highest price tag: 6,000 pesetas ($42) for four persons. Whenever I stay here, I request a bungalow, reached along a shady path, going for 3,500 pesetas ($24.50) nightly for two persons.

The room furnishings are modest-contemporary, with headboards, telephones, tile baths, and steam heating in the cooler months. Here you can relax in the afternoon, enjoying the potted geraniums, the flowering oleander, the graceful eucalyptus trees. In the country-style dining room, its walls of windows overlooking the garden, a complete luncheon or dinner is served for 1,500 pesetas ($10.50).

3. Estepona

A town of Roman origin, Estepona is a budding beach resort, 53 miles from Málaga. It is more unpretentious and less developed than Marbella or Torremolinos, and many prefer it for that reason, especially Europeans. Estepona contains an interesting 15th-century parish church and the ruins of an old aqueduct are nearby at Salduba.

Its recreational port is an attraction, as is its nude beach, Costa Natura, the first legal nude beach along the Costa del Sol. Its other beaches are La Rada, two miles long, and El Cristo, which stretches only 600 yards. One major reason for recommending Estepona is that it contains some of the major bargain stopovers along the Costa del Sol.

After the hot sun goes down, both locals and visitors can be seen strolling along the Paseo Marítimo, a broad avenue with well-maintained gardens on one side, the beach on the other. Estepona has had a long and sometimes turbulent history. The Moors called it Al Esstebuna.

The Estaponeros are happy to receive visitors and quick to announce that they have some 325 days of sunshine a year.

In the summer months, the cheapest way to eat in Estepona is to patronize one of the *merenderos,* which are little dining areas set up by local fishermen and their families right on the beach. Naturally, they feature seafood, including sole and sardine kebabs grilled over an open fire. Desserts are simple—perhaps ice cream—but you can usually order a fresh salad and there are, of course, fried potatoes.

After your siesta, you can head for the tapas bars. Most of them—called *freidurias* or fried fish bars—are at the corner of Calle de Los Reyes and La

Terraza. Tables spill onto the sidewalks in summer, and gambas (shrimp) à la plancha is the favorite (but not the cheapest) tapas to order.

ACCOMMODATIONS: In the town, your best bet, if you want to spend the money, is **Caracas,** 50 San Lorenzo (tel. 80-08-00), which lies just off the coastal highway. It is a gleaming white, five-story modern building with balconies and salmon-pink accents. Lying about 150 feet from the beach in the heart of Estepona, it offers 40 double bedrooms in the modern idiom. The rooms have no style, but are of generous size. A single rents for 3,500 pesetas ($24.50); a double, 5,200 pesetas ($36.40). The atmosphere is clean and jazzy bright. A complete luncheon or dinner goes for 1,500 pesetas ($10.50). Closed January 8 to February 8.

Buenavista, 180 Avenida de España (tel. 80-01-37), is a friendly, comfortable little residencia right on the coastal road. It's recommended for an overnight stopover or a modest holiday. Rooms are clean, but likely to be noisy in summer from the heavy traffic. Singles rent for 2,000 pesetas ($14); doubles, from 4,000 pesetas ($28). A continental breakfast is extra, and either lunch or dinner goes for 1,000 pesetas ($7).

El Pilar, 22 Plaza José Antonio (tel. 80-00-18), is a modest, two-story, tile-roofed hostal, opening onto the prettiest square in the village. There are tables set out for refreshments in the midst of orange trees and bougainvillea. The dining room is very provincial, and you can eat somewhat family style. A complete lunch or dinner costs 750 pesetas ($5.25). A single room is 1,500 pesetas ($10.50) without bath; a double, 1,800 pesetas ($12.60) if bathless to 1,900 pesetas ($13.30) with shower bath. The rooms are quite basic but clean, opening onto a covered central area.

La Malagueña, 1 Calle Castillo (tel. 80-00-11), is a very modest low-budget hostal. Many of its rooms open onto a three-story-high, glassed-in courtyard or else onto the street, overlooking the Plaza las Flores, with its border of orange-bearing trees. The courtyard of La Malagueña is rather simple with a fountain in the Andalusian style. The rooms are stripped-down basic, with water basins only and old beds. Linoleum covers the floors. The rates are 2,500 pesetas ($17.50) to 3,000 pesetas ($21) in a double, 1,500 pesetas ($10.50) in a single. A meal, taken separately, costs 750 pesetas ($5.25).

SPLURGE DINING: **El Molino,** Urbanización El Saladillo, Carretera Cádiz 172 (tel. 78-23-37), is set back from the coastal highway. It is named after a towering white windmill, surrounded by thick shrubbery and pine trees. Its two dining rooms are tavern style, with rustic furnishings and ceiling beams. In fair weather you can dine on the vine-covered terrace at the rear. Meals are offered every evening between 8 and 11:30 p.m. However, the restaurant is closed in February, the last two weeks in November, and on Tuesday. The cuisine is mainly French. I'd suggest, to get you started, shrimp cocktail, pâté of the casa, the snails, or perhaps turtle soup. For a main dish, you might prefer rack of lamb, veal chop, or the fish filets, which are always good. At the end of your meal, you may be tempted by the lemon sorbet or the fresh raspberries or wild strawberries in cream. Expect to spend from 2,800 pesetas ($19.60) for a complete meal.

4. Puerto Banús

This marine village, 5 miles east of Marbella, is a favorite resort of celebrities from all over the world. Almost overnight a village was created in the traditional Mediterranean style. There is no sameness here. Each building appears different in design, yet everything blends into a harmonious whole. Yachts can be moored at your doorstep. Along the harbor front is an array of sophisticated bars and restaurants, all of which are expensive.

Try, if you can, to wander through the quiet back streets as well, past elegant archways and grilled patios. The rich and the elegant rent apartments in this village for the season.

However, there are no inns that I know of, just restaurants. Go here for lunch or dinner and for sightseeing. It's a dream-like village, a Disneyworld creation of what a Costa del Sol fishing village should look like.

RESTAURANTS AND BARS: **La Poularde,** 14 Ribera (tel. 78-15-97). You have to climb a flight of outside stairs from the street below and negotiate a series of winding passages before you reach the expansive terrace set near the entrance of this restaurant specializing in a northern European cuisine, notably French. The owners are Joe, an American who used to run the well-known Joe's Bar in Marbella, and Daniele, an Italian mime actor. They have remodeled and created this restaurant-café-theater, offering top-class international entertainment. If you don't want to dine, you can occupy a seat in the comfortable bar or lounge area, enjoying the show (three nightly from 10:30 p.m.). There's even a late night snack menu, notably pastas for those who'd prefer one after midnight. But for dinner, costing from 3,600 pesetas ($25.30) and up, specialties include grilled sirloin with garlic, shrimp in cream sauce, fresh sautéed mushrooms bordelaise style, and duckling in a green pepper sauce, or perhaps roast quail with juniper berries.

La Crêperie, 4 Ribera (no phone), has something very northern European about its decor: it's filled, Paris-style, with turn-of-the-century accessories. Even the floor is composed of black and white marble checkerboards, upon which are set the glistening stone tables with cast-iron bases, bentwood chairs, and art nouveau posters showing elegant ladies on bicycles. The menu offers more than 30 different kinds of crêpes, ranging from full-meal pancakes stuffed with ham and grated cheese to delicate dessert crêpes loaded with chocolate and liqueurs. Light meals cost from 1,000 pesetas ($7).

Pizzería Don Carlos, Calle Ribera, is reached by climbing an exterior staircase. This informal pizzería is often frequented by members of the Atlantic Marine Club. Pizzas run the gamut of the world's varieties, costing from 500 pesetas ($3.50) up. A pizza specialty is the Four Seasons, with tomato, cheese, ham, artichokes, mushrooms, anchovies, and garlic. Two good plates are the lasagne al forno and tagliatelle homemade any way you like it. They also do macaroni and cheese, gnocchi romana, roast beef, fresh salads, and desserts. The most popular beverage seems to be one of the pitchers of sangría made to order at the bar.

Hollywood Bar, right on the port, offers the kind of place where you'll want to sit for an examination of the yachts bobbing a few feet away and of the pedestrians who may be admiring the boats as much as you are. The establishment contains a green and white decor of arched awnings and terracotta tiles focused around a series of collages of the best shots of the Hollywood stars of yesteryear. Monroe and Chaplin mark the entrance to the rest rooms, and the inner room has enough mirrors to entrance the starlets of any gender for a significant length of time. A "Hollywood burger" with everything on it costs around 500 pesetas ($3.50), a salad from 350 pesetas ($2.45).

Pizzería/Restaurant Horno Asador (tel. 78-01-48) is worth going to just for the view. The food is acceptable, but the other qualities are more appealing. The awning in front of the place directly on the water is just above a series of outdoor tables that command a view of the yachts floating in the harbor. The interior is centered around a glowing, stone-walled pizza oven whose fires are kept going all day, partially illuminating a plesantly proportioned inner room decorated in shades of yellow. The simple menu is limited to a standard collection of international food. Pizzas cost from 550 pesetas ($3.85). You can also order a seafood salad and a number of pastas, preceded, if you wish, by onion soup. Meats are often grilled. Count on spending from 1,800 pesetas ($12.60) up.

Sinatra Bar, 9 Muelle Ribera, is gravity center for people-watching. Here residents of the nearby apartments meet for early-morning coffee or drinks late in the evening. The preferred spot, if the weather is right, is on one of the chairs set out on the sidewalk. Only a few feet away, rows of luxury yachts await your inspection. Tables are usually shared, and piped music lets you hear Sinatra's voice. Hard drinks range from 600 pesetas ($4.20). It's also possible to order everything from an English breakfast at 700 pesetas ($4.90) to a hamburger plate, with an egg and salad for the same price. Snacks such as the "Mamaburger" are served throughout the day. Go here in the summer months only.

You might drop in at one of the piano bars in the heart of Puerto Banús. The most popular is **Duques,** Local 54, Muelle Ribera (tel. 78-35-38), with its long banquettes. It's owned by Duke Meets, an American with a skill for booking good acts. One night I heard an excellent jazz player, and you should count yourself lucky if you get to hear Duke perform. He specializes in country and western—that is, when he's not greeting guests. Drinks cost 450 pesetas ($3.15).

5. San Pedro de Alcantara

Between Marbella and Estepona, this attractive village, 43 miles west of Málaga, contains interesting Roman remains officially classified as a National Monument. In recent years it has been extensively developed as a resort suburb of Marbella, containing some colorful hotels, previewed below.

Pueblo Andaluz, Carretera de Cádiz, Km 172 (tel. 81-16-42), is built in the style of an Andalusian village, with patios and gardens planted with flowering shrubbery and trees. This self-contained resort world lies about a five-mile drive west from Marbella in the direction of Algeciras. However, the beach is only a five-minute walk from your bedroom door. It makes a good bet for families, as there's a special playground reserved for children, as well as a paddling pool. Bedrooms are decorated in the Spanish traditional style, costing 4,200 pesetas ($29.40) in a double, that tariff dropping to only 3,800 pesetas ($26.60) in a single. In the regional-style dining room, built like a hacienda, only breakfast is offered. The hotel is open from April 1 to October 31.

Cortijo Blanco, Carretera de Cádiz, Km 172 (tel. 78-09-00), a few miles west of Marbella toward Gibraltar, offers 162 bedrooms overlooking miniature patios overgrown with bougainvillea, canna, and roses. Built in the Andalusian hacienda style, it has modern accommodations, each with private bath. Tariffs vary according to the season, the highest rates in effect from mid-July to mid-September. Singles range from 5,000 pesetas ($35) to 5,600 pesetas ($39.20); doubles, 7,000 pesetas ($49) to 7,600 pesetas ($53.20), plus 2,500 pesetas ($17.50) per person extra for half board. Luncheon is served under a long covered garden pergola, dinner in the more formal dining hall, where the walls are lined with oils and tables surrounded by high-backed gilt and red Valencian chairs. During the day, the social center revolves around a large open-air swimming pool.

6. Marbella

Although it enjoys a broad base of tourism, Marbella is still, in part, the most exclusive resort along the Costa del Sol, ranking number two to Torremolinos in popularity. Once English expatriates and French countesses inhabited its shaded villas, and many still do. However, in recent years much Arab money has been pumped into Marbella. Marbella still has its bastions of posh, as reflected by the Marbella Club, but today it is completely overrun with tour groups and milling throngs, its heyday of avant-garde fashion a fading memory.

Marbella, a beach town in transition, is the first major resort the motorist approaches after heading east on the road from Algeciras (it's about 50 miles from Gibraltar). If it's approached from the east, it is about 37 miles from Málaga, 28 miles from Torremolinos. The big attraction is the beaches in and around Marbella—**El Fuerte** and **La Fontanilla** the two chief ones. But there are others, perhaps more secluded, if you have transportation and care to branch out. Yet keep in mind that the myth of a little hidden spot on the Sun Coast is just that: a myth.

Despite its overabundance of tourists, Marbella is a pleasant Andalusian town at the foot of the Sierra Blanca. It's bustling and modern, but there are traces of the old, such as its palace-like town hall, its medieval ruins, and old Moorish walls. Like most Spanish towns, its greatest charm is to be found in its old quarter, with its narrow cobblestone streets and Arabesque houses. However, many of the old houses have been hastily converted into shops that sell merchandise at inflated prices. Still, it makes for a good late-afternoon or before-dinner stroll.

WHERE TO STAY: Marbella, which is noted for charging about 15% higher prices than other places along the strip, quite surprisingly features a number of excellent budget and moderately priced hotels.

Hotel El Fuerte, Castillo de San Luis (tel. 77-15-00), is the most recommendable hotel in the center of Marbella. With a balconied and angular façade, it's right on the waterfront, its palm-fringed swimming pool with sapphire waters set across the street from a sheltered lagoon and wide-open beach. A handful of terraces, some shaded by flowering arbors, provide sun-dappled hideaways for quiet drinks. A restaurant with a panoramic water view and a bar are part of the facilities. The 146 comfortable, contemporary bedrooms, all with phone, private bath, and cool terrazzo floors, most with a balcony, rent for 7,000 pesetas ($49) in a single, 10,500 pesetas ($73.50) in a double.

Hotel Guadalpín, Carretera 340 Cádiz–Málaga, Km 186 (tel. 77-11-00), is right on the rugged coast, only 300 yards from the beach (a mile from the center of Marbella). You can live here at this three-star hotel for 6,500 pesetas ($45.50) in a double room with private bath. For a single with a full bath, the rate is 4,500 pesetas ($31.50), but only ten rooms are available in this category. Guests spend many hours relaxing around two swimming pools; or they walk along a private pathway lined with fir trees to the Mediterranean. The dining room has large windows overlooking the patio and pool, and the main lounge has been designed in ranch style with round marble tables and occasional leather armchairs arranged for conversational groups. The bar area of the spacious lounge is brick and natural wood, making it warm and attractive. Each room has not only two terraces, but a living room and bedroom combined; most of the rooms are furnished in "new ranch" style. They have all of the conveniences, such as telephones and central heating during the cooler months.

El Rodeo, 2 Victor de la Serna (tel. 77-51-00), is a modern hotel, just off the main coastal road of Marbella, yet it is quiet and cut off from traffic noises. It's a seven-story structure, with a swimming pool and sunbathing area at its crown. Two elevators whisk you to the second-floor lounges which are spacious, sunny, and furnished as in a country house. Stark white bamboo is used effectively in some areas, and the breakfast room is cheerful, with ladderback chairs and decorative fabric at the windows. There's also a bar with tropical bamboo chairs and tables. The bedrooms are well styled, with several shuttered closets and lounge chairs, white desks, and bentwood chairs. Each has a private bath. The highest tariffs are charged from April 1 to October 31, although the hotel is open all year. A single room with bath and terrace costs 3,800 pesetas ($26.60), rising to 5,000 pesetas ($35) in a double, also with bath and terrace. A continental breakfast is the only meal served. El Rodeo stands about a five-minute walk from the beach, another five-minute stroll to the old section with its boutiques and restaurants.

Las Chapas, Carretera de Cadiz, Km 198 (tel. 83-13-75), takes Spanish bullfight tradition seriously: most of its public rooms encircle a small bullring where mock "no-kill" fights are staged on weekends (sometimes with guests trying their skill) and matadors train with young bulls. Outside of that, it's a "regular" hotel, with air-conditioned bedrooms with private balconies and picture windows overlooking pine trees, mini-golf courses, tennis courts, and the Mediterranean across the main highway. The tone of the lounges and bedrooms is informal, with an accent on the traditional. A single room rents for 4,500 pesetas ($31.50), the cost increasing to 7,000 pesetas ($49) in a double. You can also stay here on full-board terms at a price of about 6,500 pesetas ($45.50) per person. The food is good. My most recent repast included an appetizer called simply "white garlic from Málaga." It proceeded to smoked salmon from the Bidasoa River and finally fresh pineapple with Morella cherries. Two swimming pools, a children's playground, a private beach area, and that bullring make this an interesting holiday center.

Residencia Lima, 2 Avenida Antonio Belón (tel. 77-05-00), a short skip to the sea, is a little bit more secluded, tucked away in a residential section of Marbella. Quite a modern structure, it stacks up its bedrooms for at least eight stories, then encircles them with private balconies. The Lima's furnishings, both in the bedrooms and the lounges, lean heavily on Spanish provincial. Open year round, the Lima charges a peak of 5,500 pesetas ($38.50) for a double with bath, 4,000 pesetas ($28) for a double with shower bath (there are four in this category). Singles with shower baths rent for 3,500 pesetas ($24.50).

Residencia Finlandia, Finlandia (tel. 77-07-00), is oddly placed in the "Huerta Grande," a residential section suitable for peace and quiet. Yet it's only a five-minute walk to the center of town, and a two-minute jaunt to the Mediterranean. This small hotel is a decent place in which to hole up for a while. It's clean, modern, and run by a friendly management. The rates are friendly too—3,800 pesetas ($26.60) for a double with bath, and 3,000 pesetas ($21) for single occupancy. The rooms are airy, spacious, and equipped with modern furnishings. You'll find your bed turned down at night, and you can have your continental breakfast on the terrace in the morning. Breakfast, the only meal served, costs extra.

Residencia San Cristóbal, 18 Ramón y Cajal (tel. 77-12-50), in the heart of Marbella, is a fine hotel—modern to the teeth, but not antiseptically so. Its five floors have long, wide terrace balconies, with window boxes filled with vines and flowers. The bedrooms contain many refinements, such as walnut headboards with telephones and overhead individual reading lamps. Room dividers separate the comfortable beds from the small living-room area. An added plus is the private terrace beyond—just right for a continental breakfast in the Marbella sunshine. Double accommodations with clean baths rent for 5,000 pesetas ($35) in high season. Only a continental breakfast is served.

El Castillo, 2 Plaza San Bérnabé (tel. 77-17-39), is perhaps the smallest hotel in town, perched in the old narrow-streeted town, at the foot of the castle, opening onto a minuscule triangular square used by an adjoining convent and school as a playground in the afternoon. There's a small covered courtyard, and the second-floor bedrooms have only inner windows. The spartan rooms are scrubbed clean, and contain white tile baths. Rates are 3,000 pesetas ($21) in a double, 2,000 pesetas ($14) in a single. No morning meal is served, and not one word of English is spoken. It's for the adventurous only.

Hostal Residencia Gogar, 5 Joaquím Chillida (tel. 77-00-11), is a tiny place right in the heart of Marbella. It's a gem if you can get in. It's ultra-clean and utterly simple, but you're right in the heart of the action, near Orange Tree Square. Only Spanish is spoken, but you can easily manage here. The señora who runs it is friendly and polite, proudly showing off her immaculate rooms, for which she charges just 2,400 pesetas ($16.80) in a bathless double, 1,600 pesetas ($11.20) in a single. Pots of geraniums are placed out on the balconies, and a jungle of bougainvillea climbs up the whitewashed walls.

Nagüeles, Carretera de Cádiz, Km 184, 2¼ miles from Marbella, heading west (tel. 77-16-88), stands near the luxurious Marbella Club on the fringes of Marbella, right on the main coastal road. Its entrance and restaurant are on the busy highway, but the two-story, whitewashed brick hotel has bedrooms set back from the traffic and protected by orange and willow trees. Red bougainvillea vines crawl through the railings of the balconies. There are 17 nicely, but simply, furnished bedrooms, which are clean and contain private bath. The rate is 2,400 pesetas ($16.80) in a single, 3,200 pesetas ($22.40) in a double. The hotel is open only from April to October.

Residencia Munich, 5 Virgen del Pilar (tel. 77-24-61), is an unassuming rather basic little three-story hotel, just a short walk from the water. It's owned by a German woman, Anneliese Gasteiger, who offers some rooms with a private bath, some with a balcony. A continental breakfast is the only meal she serves. The residencia is set back from the street, shielded by banana and palm trees. The little lounge and breakfast room are cluttered with knickknacks, a mixture of old and new furniture. There is definitely a home-like atmosphere. Doubles with shower or private bath peak at 2,800 pesetas ($19.60) and singles, also with private plumbing, go for 2,300 pesetas ($16.10).

Hostal-Residencia Enríqueta, 18 Joaquin Chinchilla (tel. 77-00-58). No breakfast is served at this unpretentious, family-run hotel a few steps from the Plaza los Naranjos, but if you're not driving, the location couldn't be better for tours of the old city. Concealed in a maze of winding, traffic-free walkways, it opens onto a simple and clean reception area filled with leather-upholstered chairs and eventually onto a garden-courtyard which ventilates some of the 23 rooms. If you arrive in the morning, you're likely to see a series of industrious maids polishing the paneling leading to the entrance of your room, which will rent for 1,500 pesetas ($10.50) in a bathless single, 2,200 pesetas ($15.40) in a bathless double, and 2,800 pesetas ($19.60) in a double with bath. The establishment is closed for about a month every midwinter, although the rest of the time it's open every day.

WHERE TO EAT: Restaurant prices are soaring in Marbella. In many instances, your hotel remains a good bet, but since so many of Marbella's hostelries are residencias, you'll need to seek out independent budget dining spots. I'll lead off with . . .

Restaurant La Cancela, 6 Misericordia (tel. 77-00-73), on one of the narrow streets of the old town, includes a collection of outdoor tables set up near the ivy-covered façade and a long bar area where you can enjoy your favorite drink. The interior might slightly need a coat of paint, but there's nonetheless an open fireplace and beamed ceilings which contribute to the rustic Andalusian atmosphere of this former private house. Your friendly English-speaking bartender may come from Germany or Holland, although the food items will be seasonally adjusted specialties from the region. These include roast lamb, stuffed pork, and a variety of inexpensive local fish dishes. The place offers menus for 1,800 pesetas ($12.60). The establishment is closed Sunday.

Metropol, 21 Avenida Ricardo Soriano (tel. 77-77-41), stands right on the main street. Its Dutch/Spanish patron, Leonardo Terol, will welcome you. He has taught his Spanish chef the skills he learned when he ran another restaurant in his native Netherlands. I've been dropping in here regularly for 20 years, and have found the cookery consistently good—in fact, much improved in recent years. The atmosphere in this warmly decorated restaurant is friendly and cozy, the ambience enhanced by soft-playing music in the background. Mr. Terol's cooking repertoire is international. Try, for example, his large shrimps l'Orly served with tartar sauce, and his superb chicken. I'd also suggest the filet of halibut, cooked au gratin in a well-flavored sauce. The paella is also good. Expect to pay about 1,800 pesetas ($12.60) for a meal at both lunch and dinner.

Crepería Marbella, 11 Plaza de los Naranjos (tel. 77-51-49), is the first of its kind in Marbella, set in the old town, overlooking Orange Tree Square from its second-floor precincts. Against the backdrop of an old-world atmosphere, it offers a variety of well-stuffed crêpes—both for your main course and dessert—prepared in the French manner. You might begin with French onion soup, or a mixed green salad. Main-course crêpes are likely to include everything from spinach soufflé to seafood (invariably featured). If you don't want a crêpe, or would rather save the experience for dessert, then you can ask for chicken Maryland. The dessert crêpes are spectacular (I've sampled apple, banana, and chocolate mint). Count on spending from 1,500 pesetas ($10.50). The crepería is reached by climbing a flight of stairs. It's entered through an arcaded patio with balconies which is an art gallery and shop. What you find is a small provincial room with a beamed ceiling, an overscale open fireplace, and Valencian chairs. Closed Sunday.

Casa Eladío, 6 Virgen Dolores (tel. 77-00-83), is on a narrow street that runs parallel to one side of the Plaza de los Naranjos, in the oldest part of Marbella. The feeling is Andalusian and elegant, with a garden setting, surrounded with immaculate blue, white, and yellow tiles, trickling fountains, heavily timbered ceilings, thick walls, and a series of brick arches around an open-air courtyard flanked with a colorful collection of local pottery set into wall niches. The place is undeniably attractive, yet it charges less than other restaurants nearby. Rich aromas filter forward from the kitchens, which prepare such dishes as swordfish with tarragon, jewfish with pineapple, house pâté, spaghetti carbonara, and kidneys with sherry. The menu is in English. Nearly everyone has pudding for dessert. If you dine here, expect a bill from 850 pesetas ($5.95) up. It's closed Wednesday.

The **Pizzería Sanremo,** Paseo Marítimo (tel. 77-43-33), right on the beach, draws devotees of the Italian kitchen who like to sample the viands of the owner, Stefano Vella. The menu is presented in English, and most diners prefer one of the pizzas, costing from 500 pesetas ($3.50), or perhaps one of the various spaghetti concoctions, averaging about 550 pesetas ($3.85) per plate. The raw carrot salad is an unusual item on menus in Spain, and the veal dishes are well prepared. For a complete meal, expect to pay about 1,800 pesetas ($12.60) and up. If you're in the resort on a Thursday, you can come here to order couscous, the North African specialty. The Sanremo is closed on Wednesday.

The Big Splurge

La Tricyclette, 14 Buitrago (tel. 77-78-00), is one of the most popular dining spots in Marbella. It is a converted home, courtyard and all, on a narrow street in the old part of town. It's easy to find if you ask, as it has become a local landmark. The customers come from all over Europe and North America. Sofas provide a living-room ambience in the bar, and twisting stairs lead up to an intimate dining room and an open terrace dining patio which is delightful except in the chilly months. The food is good, with a continental menu selection. A good beginning would be crêpes with a soft cream-cheese filling or grilled giant prawns. The fare consists of such delectable dishes as beef en daube, roast duck in beer, filet steak with a green pepper sauce, and chicken breast Leone (cooked in bread crumbs and topped with cheese and asparagus). An average meal here costs from 3,000 pesetas ($21). The wine list is extensive and reasonable. Reservations can be made between 8 p.m. to 1 a.m.; closed Sunday.

Gran Marisquería Santiago, 5 Paseo Marítimo (tel. 77-00-78). As soon as you enter this seaside restaurant, the bubbling lobster tanks will give you an idea of the kinds of dishes available. The orange and green decor, the stand-up tapas bar near the entrance, and the summertime patio join together with super-fresh fish dishes to make this one of the most popular eating places in town. On my most recent visit, I arrived so early for lunch that the mussels for my mussels marinara were just being delivered. The fish soup is well prepared, well spiced, and savory. The sole in champagne comes in a large serving, and the turbot can be grilled or sautéed. On a hot day, the seafood salad, garnished with lobster, shrimp, and crabmeat and served with a sharp sauce, is especially recommended. For dessert, I suggest a serving of Manchego cheese. A complete meal will cost from 2,800 pesetas ($19.60).

La Gitana, 2 Buitrago (tel. 77-66-74), has zoomed to the foreground in popularity in the old pueblo of Marbella. On a narrow street, the Gitana's restaurant section is open daily except Tuesday, only from 8 p.m. to midnight. You wine and dine under the stars on a rooftop in the old town. Specializing in barbecues, it also offers an array of other dishes, including fresh fish. From the barbecue, however, you can try the chef's honey-glazed chicken, spare ribs, sirloin steak, even lamb. Usually the catch of the day has turned up hake, sole, or swordfish, perhaps all three. The sauces served with the meat and fish here have zing. For dessert, you might top off everything with apple-and-raisin pie with fresh cream. The dining room is in the elegant tavern style. Expect to spend from 2,000 pesetas ($14) for a big, hearty meal. If you're watching your pesetas, you can patronize the bar, enjoying such excellent "snacks" as steak-and-kidney pie or chili con carne, a lunch costing from 750 pesetas ($5.25). Drinks are lowered at "happy hour," from 6 to 7 p.m. daily except Sunday and Tuesday.

Restaurante El Puchero, 3 Calle Panadería (tel. 77-29-78). Wrought-iron bars cover the windows of this house set at a corner of the Plaza de los Naranjos. When you enter, you might get a strong hint of the Spanish flavor of South America, especially from the simple wooden furniture, the rough stucco walls, the open fireplace, and the tiny enclosed courtyard sheltered from the sun by a white canopy. Roberto Noe Abraham, the owner, moved to Marbella from Buenos Aires to open this Argentinian restaurant in 1984. Specialties are the kind of Argentinian grilled meats made famous on the pampas, including churrasco (priced by the gram), a skewer of different kinds of meat, and a mixed grill for two. A full meal here costs around 2,200 pesetas ($15.40).

El Cóndor, 8 Calle Príncipe (tel. 77-73-43), is in the Old Town of Marbella above the famous Plaza de los Naranjos (Orange Square). It is a delightful old Spanish house converted into a comfortable and attractive bar, which also serves food at reasonable prices. Steaks are a specialty. The old house has Moorish stone archways and an intimate candlelit garden patio, where barbecues are served nightly in summer. In winter, a popular feature is the big log fire in the open fireplace. The owners, Brian and Maureen Hart from Nottingham, England, run their bar much like a house party, with an informal and homey atmosphere. El Cóndor is open from 8 nightly and from 1 p.m. on Sunday when they serve traditional English roasts and steaks. A meal costs from 1,200 pesetas ($8.40).

A MARBELLA TASCA CRAWL: No doubt about it—the best way to keep food costs low in super-expensive Marbella is to do what many Spanish families or expatriates do, and that is take your meals in the early evening in the tapas bars of the resort. You get plenty of atmosphere, low costs, good food, and might have fun while you're doing it. You can order a first course in one bar with a glass of wine or beer, a second course in another, and on and on as your stamina and appetite dictate. There is no need to call—in fact, many of the places don't have phones. Just show up. You can eat well in most of these places for 500 pesetas ($3.50).

El Mediterranito, Calle Tetuán, is tiny but good. Here you can on occasion order soused sardines or else stuffed eggs. The herb-flavored pork loin is also good. The owner, Miguel, will welcome you, perhaps suggesting a bottle of *montilla.*

Trebol, Calle Ancha, is not far from the Plaza Santo Cristo. A family-run concern, it is most inviting, and there's always plenty of food. My favorite dish is pinchitos, which are grilled bits and pieces of pork in a hot spicy sauce. Try also the mushrooms doused in olive oil and grilled, then served with a garlic-flavored dressing. One specialty is flamenquines, fish cakes wrapped in ham, coated with bread crumbs, and deep fried. Valdepeñas wine is served out of a barrel. It is closed Sunday. Never go before 7 p.m.

San Cristóbal, Calle San Cristóbal, is another family-run concern. The proprietor is Antonio. His wife does the cooking, and one of the family members serves. It is also open at lunchtime. Local residents, for reasons known only to themselves, refer to this place as the "California." The place enjoys a wide local reputation for the quality of its shellfish or "catch of the day," certainly not for its simple decor. Here you can get some of the finest of Mediterranean seafood, such as amberjack, spiky whelks, and spider crab, all at a low cost. If you can't make up your mind as to which fish to order, try a mixed fish fry and get a little bit of everything. The place is sometimes closed on Sunday.

Bar Figueredo, Calle Haza del Mesón, stands near the city market. There's no sign on the door, so you'll just have to follow the crowds when you get there. The place opens early in the morning, remaining so until 9 p.m. At night some of the best tapas in town are served here, including spareribs drenched in tomato sauce, a salad made with octopus, and pickled anchovies. This is very much of a workman's place, so don't expect any fancy airs. If you're there at lunch, you can order a plato del dia, which on occasion features paella. A catch of the day—often red bream—is also featured. The owner is Paco.

MARBELLA AFTER DARK: Marbella disco spots come and go with frequency, and those that survive are often "in" one year, "out" the next.

Ana Maria, 4-5 Plaza del Santo Cristo (tel. 77-56-46), offers an elongated tapas bar often crowded with garrulous locals and a frequently changing collection of singers, dancers, and musicians who execute everything from flamenco to popular songs. Drinks cost more than those in a place without entertainment —about 1,000 pesetas ($7) each.

Joy, Carretera de Cádiz, Km 186 (tel. 77-08-85), on the main highway leading to Puerto Banús, is marked by a vivid logo of a man in a sombrero accompanied by an attractive señorita. It's one of the most popular discos on the coast, with a disc jockey who seems to play the right music at the right moments. Drinks cost around 1,000 pesetas ($7).

Pepe Moreno, Carretera de Cádiz, Km 186 (tel. 77-02-79), not far from the disco Joy (see above), frequently shares its clientele with its neighbors, even though it seems more aggressive in its emphasis on Spanish decor, music, and ambience. A drink averages around 900 pesetas ($6.30).

IN THE SIERRA BLANCA: If the summer heat has got you, you may want to retreat north into the Sierra Blanca to **El Refugio,** 12½ miles north of Marbella on C337, outside Ojen (tel. 77-18-48). Reached by a winding road, this restaurant serves only dinner, except for Sunday lunch. Most motorists come early to enjoy the mountain scenery, then later the French cuisine. Dinner begins at 2,200 pesetas ($15.40). Meals are served in a rustic-style dining room, and there is an open terrace for drinks offering views of the Sierras. El Refugio is not unlike a fine Spanish villa, with a tile roof and iron grillwork at its windows. The lounge features an open fireplace and comfortable armchairs, along with a few antiques and Oriental scatter rugs. Closed Monday.

7. Fuengirola and Los Boliches

The twin fishing towns of Fuengirola and Los Boliches lie halfway between the more famous resorts of Marbella and Torremolinos, about 20 miles from Málaga. The promenade along the water stretches some 2½ miles. With their chalk-white houses and friendly residents, Fuengirola and Los Boliches don't have the facilities and drama of Torremolinos, nor the chicness of Marbella. But Fuengirola is cheaper, and that has attracted a horde of economy-minded European tourists.

On a promontory overlooking the sea, the ruins of San Isidro Castle can be seen. Los Boliches is just half a mile from Fuengirola and is less developed. The Santa Amalja, Carvajal, and Las Gaviotas beaches are broad and clean, and have fine sands.

Everybody—but everybody—goes to the big flea market at Fuengirola on Tuesday. To reach it from Torremolinos, take the Metro at La Nogalera station (under the RENFE sign). Trains depart about every 30 minutes. Just follow the crowds.

WHERE TO STAY: **Florida,** Paseo Marítimo (tel. 47-61-00), is a garden spot opening right onto the sea. In front of the hotel is a detached semitropical garden, providing areas for sunbathing and refreshments served under a wide, vine-covered pergola. The hotel offers 116 double or twin-bedded rooms with bath and shower. Most of them have a balcony overlooking the sea or mountains. The floors are tile, and the furnishings, particularly in the lounge, make much use of plastic. The cost of staying here for two persons is 5,000 pesetas ($35). Singles are 3,200 pesetas ($22.40). The full-board rate is 5,500 pesetas ($38.50) per person.

Hostal Sedeño, 1 Don Jacinto (tel. 47-47-88), occupies a tucked-away position three minutes from the beach, in the heart of town. Running between two streets, its entrance lobby is modest, but it leads to a larger adjoining lounge furnished with antiques and reproductions. You pass a small open courtyard, with stairs leading to the second- and third-floor bedrooms with balconies. These accommodations overlook a small garden with fig and palm trees, plus a glassed-in dining room with terrace. It's not unlike any early modern Florida motel. Doubles with full bath go for 3,500 pesetas ($24.50). Singles range in price from 2,500 pesetas ($17.50).

WHERE TO DINE: **Don Bigote** (Mr. Mustache), 39 Francisco Cano at Los Boliches (tel. 47-50-94), was a deserted century-old sardine factory and a row of fishermen's cottages before its transformation into one of the most popular restaurants in the area. In summer, a splashing fountain in the garden patio makes the right background for the well-prepared international menu. In cooler weather you have a choice of dining in one of the attractively decorated dining rooms, each furnished in a regional style. You might enjoy a pre-dinner drink under the rafters in the lounge bar. The chefs turn out a most recommendable Spanish and continental cuisine. Meals begin at 2,800 pesetas ($19.60), and the staff serves both lunch and dinner.

Shakespeare, Calle San Sebastián Elcano (tel. 47-36-30). If you're looking for a much-frequented Anglo-Saxon hangout serving the kinds of food you miss while traveling in Iberia, you'll enjoy this honest-to-goodness restaurant where the prices are as unpretentious as the ambience. The menu doesn't even try to make its listings sound fancier than they are. You'll have your choice of uncomplicated platters of the day such as five or six kinds of roasts (lamb, beef, duckling, turkey, and pork), river trout, or sole-on-the-bone with parsley sauce. You can begin your meal with several kinds of soup or pâté, and order à la carte if the spirit moves you (chicken curry, steak pie, or even steak Diane), followed by a "veddy British" trifle. A full meal, with wine, coffee, and extras, costs around 1,800 pesetas ($12.60).

Bar Club de Bote, Paseo Marítimo, Torreblanca (tel. 47-06-36), is one of the best and least expensive fish restaurants along a coast teeming with similar but inferior restaurants. The decor includes such unglamorous yet appropriate seaside accessories as paper tablecloths and simple cutlery. The tables are generous in size, and you're able to sit for an extended period in the comfortable chairs without squirming. Two brothers run both this place and the slightly more expensive (and excellent) **Restaurant La Barca** (tel. 47-50-84), next door, both of which are a stone's throw from the beach. Several readers have been so impressed with the budget prices of De Bote, however, that they've ordered fish delicacies that would be staggeringly expensive back home, only to discover that the portions are so generously served that they couldn't begin to finish them. The menu is predominantly fish in both restaurants, although a limited selection of chicken, pork, sausage, and beef is offered as well. Fish dishes include relatively oil-free combinations of rape (a white fish), hake, shrimp, crayfish, salmon, and a good paella served with wine in full meals that cost upward from 1,800 pesetas ($12.60) per person at the De Bote, slightly more at La Barca. The wine list at De Bote will be recited verbally by your waiter. In winter, the establishment closes every Wednesday, staying open every day in summer. It also shuts down for the month of November.

La Chuleta Flamenca, Calle Miguel de Cervantes, Perla 2 (tel. 47-38-70), in Fuengirola, is a typical mesón with tables out front under a canopy in an arcade half a block from the waterfront. At this two-fork restaurant, service tends to be friendly and courteous, but perhaps a little too forgetful during the rush of the tourist season in summer. The chef does a good job with steak, preparing it both Basque style and Provençale. For an appetizer, his pâté is a favorite, or you can select among an assortment of shrimp or snails. The chicken curry is also recommendable. For dessert, the homemade ice cream Grand Marnier is tempting, as is the Dame Blanche (ice cream with a hot chocolate sauce). For the à la carte specialties, you can expect to spend from 2,000 pesetas ($14). Open only for dinner in summer.

Belgica Antiqua, 67 Avenida Condes San Isidro (tel. 47-15-96), stands across the street from the city park, about a block from the Paseo Marítimo and the tourist office. This attractive restaurant offers exceptional value, with fixed-price meals for around 950 pesetas ($6.65). The menu advertises that the meals will follow Belgian and Dutch recipes, which is the case for most of the food items except for the obligatory hake which, with sole and a salmon or shrimp salad, makes up most of the fish choices. Other specialties include pepper steak, steak with mushrooms, a choice of à la carte vegetables, soups, and a traditional Belgian dessert called a Dame Blanche (a hot-chocolate sundae). À la carte meals cost from 1,200 pesetas ($8.40).

THE TIVOLI-WORLD OF THE COSTA DEL SOL: In what was once an olive grove on the highway near Fuengirola, the Tivoli-World of the Spanish Riviera was inspired by its famous namesake in Copenhagen. Much has been done to avoid a Coney Island atmosphere, although it is a pleasure garden, with more than 34 rides and attractions such as regional folk dances staged in an Andalusian square, a Chinese pagoda, a miniature Wild West frontier town with cancan shows, and a 4,000-seat theater where national and international stars perform on many special days. Among the 17 different fountains, there is one with coordinated light- and water-dancing cascades. You can eat anything from a light snack to a gourmet dinner in one of the many restaurants and snackbars, or have a drink in a variety of settings. All the shows and practically all the rides are included in the entrance price, which is about 995 pesetas ($6.97) for both adults and children.

8. Mijas

Just five miles up from the Costa del Sol perches a village known as White Mijas because of its marble-white Andalusian-style houses. Mijas is at the foot of a sierra near the turnoff at the emerging resort of Fuengirola. From its lofty precincts at 1,476 feet above sea level, a panoramic view of the Mediterranean unfolds.

Celts, Phoenicians, and Moors, as well as today's intrepid tourists, have traversed its cobblestone streets. The easiest way to get around town is to rent a burro taxi. All of Mijas is an attraction, and it's overrun with souvenir shops, but if you're seeking out a single destination, head for a park at the top of Cuesta de la Villa. There you'll see the ruins of a Moorish fortress dating from 833. If you're in Mijas for a fiesta, you'll be attending events in the only square bullring in the country.

WHERE TO STAY: **Hotel Mijas,** Urbanización Tamisa, Carretera Benalmádena (tel. 48-58-00), is one of the most charming hotels on the Costa del Sol. Built hacienda style, it sits on the slope of a mountain, with a flower patio that's partially enclosed. On white wicker furniture, you can rest on the terrace and enjoy the view. The drinking tavern is in the Andalusian style, with large kegs of wine. The more athletically inclined enjoy the swimming pool and tennis court. Later in the evening the guests retreat to the handsome lounge, furnished with inlaid chests and antiques, including an especially interesting collection of fans. The bedrooms maintain this stylish living, complete with private baths. Depending on the season, singles go for 8,000 pesetas ($56) to 9,000 pesetas ($63); doubles, 12,000 pesetas ($84) to 14,000 pesetas ($98). For such a small hotel, there is a wide range of facilities, including a sauna, gymnasium, boutique, hairdresser, barber, and a barbecue. Entertainment is provided (in season) in the evening, and during the day guests can play at the 18-hole Mijas golf course.

Those on the most limited of budgets, however, will prefer to seek lodgings at **Del Mirlo Blanco,** 13 Plaza Queipo de Llano (tel. 48-57-00), a little five-room establishment right off the main square. The hostal's kitchen is known for serving a particularly good Basque cuisine—and the Basques are some of the finest cooks in Spain. Visitors can drop in for a set meal at a cost of 1,400 pesetas ($9.80). Those seeking rooms will find a single with bath, costing 1,600 pesetas ($11.20); a double with bath, 2,200 pesetas ($15.40). The inn has a whitewashed exterior with black wrought-iron balconies and red shutters. Inside it is provincial style, with high-backed dining chairs. At the entrance stands a rack of home-baked desserts. A cozy living room has crescent-shaped couches and a fireplace. A rear dining room is bodega style, with an open fireplace. The aroma of good food permeates the atmosphere. During mealtimes the dueña of the house sits behind the tiny cash register, serenely smiling, wearing her hair up high on her head. English is spoken.

WHERE TO DINE: **El Padrastro,** Paseo del Compás (tel. 48-50-00), is the best place to dine within the town itself. It's a rival of the somewhat better-known Valparaíso on the Carretera de Fuengirola. Part of the fun of dining here is reaching the place. You go to the cliff side of town and walk up if you're athletic or else take the elevator to the highest point. There you will find El Padrastro, offering an international cuisine on its terraces with their panoramic views of the Mediterranean coast. If the weather is bad, you are seated inside. You can dine here inexpensively or more elaborately. If you select the latter, make it Chateaubriand with a bottle of the best Spanish champagne. If you stick to regional dishes, you'll come out cheaper. Expect to spend from 2,200 pesetas ($15.40) to 3,300 pesetas ($23.10), and know that in part you're paying for the view of not only the sea, but Fuengirola and the mountains as well. There is also a swimming pool.

The **Casa Jaime,** 3 General Mola (tel. 48-51-92), in the center of Mijas, serves one of the least expensive meals in the village. For just 950 pesetas ($6.65) you can order from the menú del día. On my latest rounds, this set meal began with a bowl of soup, followed by a baked white fish and salad, plus plenty of bread, a quarter of a liter of wine, and a basket of fresh fruit for dessert. The few outside tables go quickly in summer. Inside, the local men gather to watch bullfights on TV. The street is filled with souvenir shops, so you can combine a meal at Casa Jaime with a shopping excursion. If you're flush, try the pepper steak.

Continuing east, we come to the biggest resort on the Costa del Sol.

9. Torremolinos

This jet-age Mediterranean beach resort has become world famous in the past two decades—so famous and so discovered, in fact, that the arbiters of that which is chic have abandoned it and turned elsewhere for more fashionable oases. In summer, it is a gathering spa for international visitors.

It is a melting pot of Europeans and Americans who come from places ranging from North Dakota to the Boul' Mich, from Soho to Berlin. Many Americans have found Torremolinos the perfect place to relax after a whirlwind tour of Europe. The living's easy, the people fun, and you don't have to worry about visiting a lot of historical monuments.

Thus the sleepy fishing village that formerly was Torremolinos has been engulfed in a cluster of resort hotels. One visitor called the general style of the place "Andalusian Miamic." Prices have been on the upsurge in boom-town Torremolinos. Nevertheless, the town remains one of the vacation bargains of Europe, if you hunt and pick carefully through the ever-increasing maze of hotels. Comparable accommodations in Cannes would cost four times as much—maybe more.

Overlooking a bay, Torremolinos lies at the foot of the Sierra Mijas. It is nine miles west of Málaga, and it has a five-mile beach, its chief selling point. Once a summer resort, it has now arrived as an all-year-round vacation spot. For example, airplanes are flown in loaded down with low-income Danes, waving their meal tickets and stubs from en-masse hotel bookings. At the prices they pay in winter off-season, they save by *leaving* Copenhagen.

The sun does disappear occasionally, however, in Torremolinos, and the wind can blow hard and cold in winter. It is not unusual to see a woman decked out in a fur coat standing shivering on the windy central plaza, while others are lying in some secluded spot on the beach in the scantiest bikinis.

The old inhabitants who remember Torremolinos in the "hard" days cast a disdainful eye on these vacationing hordes. The attitude of the natives was best summed up by a black-shrouded Spanish dueña, who crossed herself at the sight of three German women in briefer-than-brief bikinis strolling down the street on a shopping expedition.

WHERE TO STAY: The competition is tough in Torremolinos. Consequently, a hotel generally has to be new—or look it—to compete successfully. The three-star hotels, for the most part, are superb, some of the finest resort accommodations in Spain today. The only catch is that when tourists are jumping as high as marlin, many of these establishments may insist on full or at least half board (breakfast, plus one other meal).

Miami, 10 Calle Aladino (tel. 38-52-55), is near the Carihuela section. It's the domain of Señora Vignale Gomez, who has furnished each accommodation differently, with dignity, style, comfort, and traditional trappings. Every room contains its own balcony and private bath. For all this, the high-season rate in a single is 2,500 pesetas ($17.50), rising to 4,000 pesetas ($28) in a double. A continental breakfast, costing extra, is the only meal served. The house, reminiscent of those built in Hollywood, California, is isolated by high walls and a private garden. There's even a small swimming pool. In the rear patio bougainvillea climbs over arches, and the tile terrace is used for sunbathing and refreshments. The living room is country rustic, with a walk-in fireplace, plus lots of brass and copper.

Alta Vista, 173 Apartado Correas (tel. 38-76-00), on the old marketplace, is right in the heart of Torremolinos, surrounded by little lanes of boutiques and patios with coffeeshops. It's a few minutes' walk from the beach, but the rooms have small balconies projected into the Costa del Sol sun. The entire roof is a tiled solarium with umbrella tables, lounge chairs, and a bar. For a double with private bath, the charge is 4,500 pesetas ($31.50), 3,200 pesetas ($22.40) in a single with bath. There are 106 rooms, offering ornate wrought-iron beds draped in decorative fabrics, reed-seated chairs, telephone, and bedside reading lamps. In the lounge (Andalusian wood and leather furnishings), guests gather for reading, conversation, or letter writing. The bar is inviting with its beamed ceiling and tiles. Lunches or dinners are served in a stylish dining room, with meals costing from 1,200 pesetas ($8.40).

Hotel Amaragua, Los Nidos (tel. 38-47-00), is right on the beach in the middle of the residential area of Torremolinos-Montemar, with a total of 198 rooms (12 of which are suites), all with complete bath, terrace, and sea view. The hotel has lounges, television, a bar, three large swimming pools (one heated), gardens, water sports, a children's playground, a sauna, parking facilities, and a tennis court. In a double with private bath, the rate is 5,200 pesetas ($36.40), 3,600 pesetas ($25.30) in a single with shower bath.

Los Nidos (tel. 38-04-00) is also in the residential area of Torremolinos-

Montemar, next to the beach. It's in the style of a small Andalusian village, with 70 rooms and bungalows, all with bath, central heating, private entrance, and terrace. Forty have a lounge and a safe. Double rooms with private bath rent for 5,200 pesetas ($36.40) nightly, singles for 3,800 pesetas ($26.60).

Hotel Edén, Las Mercedes (tel. 38-46-00), below the new town, is built on many levels on a cliff (the entrance is on the eighth floor). Two elevators take you down to the bedrooms—a "descent into the catacombs," as one reader put it. The 94 bedrooms have private terraces, which overlook the rooftops, a cultivated field, a stable renting riding horses, all climaxed by a vista of the Mediterranean. In a double with a complete private bath facing the beach, you pay 5,500 pesetas ($38.50), with taxes and service included. In a single, the rate is 4,300 pesetas ($30.10). The rooms are often decorated in resorty colors, but they're utilitarian and comfortable, although plumbing and maintenance may be shaky at times. On the lower level is a swimming pool and an adjoining terrace. An open veranda restaurant overlooks the sea.

One final temptation: Occasionally there is flamenco in the bar. Perhaps a gypsy guitarist will walk around the room singing, before a stamping, gaily costumed dancer goes into her act.

Sidi Lago Rojo, 1 Miami (tel. 38-76-66), stands in the heart of the still-preserved fishing village of La Carihuela, only 150 feet from the beach with its waterside fish restaurants and bars. The hotel, the finest place to stay in the fishing village, has its own surrounding gardens and swimming pool, along with terraces for sunbathing and a refreshment bar. The modern hotel offers studio-style rooms, tastefully appointed with contemporary Spanish furnishings, excellent tile baths, and terraces with views. Other facilities include radios, phones, air conditioning, and refrigerators. For a single with shower or bath, the charge is 4,000 pesetas ($28) in a single, 6,000 pesetas ($42) in a double. Set meals are offered for 1,500 pesetas ($10.50) at either lunch or dinner. The bar is a popular gathering point, with a sophisticated decor. In the late evening there is disco dancing.

Hotel Plata, 1 Pasaje Pizarro (tel. 38-00-70), is central, right on the coastal road to Málaga. It is surrounded on three sides by private terraces with folding chairs and tables set out for breakfast or drinks. The oddly shaped rooms are large; there's enough space to add extra beds if required. The modern doubles with bath rent for 3,500 pesetas ($24.50), singles for 2,800 pesetas ($19.60). Each bed has its own table and reading lamp. The air-conditioned dining room, which serves reasonably good meals, captures the Andalusian spirit with its beamed ceiling, crude yet comfortable chairs, and lots of bric-à-brac.

Hotel Blasón, 1 Avenida de los Manantiales (tel. 38-67-67), is right for those who want a simple hotel directly in the swim of things. Guests can sit on their little balconies watching the international parade of visitors pass beneath them. Regrettably, they get the noise until late at night, and the trucks and traffic as well. The hotel opens directly onto the Plaza de Costa del Sol. On its street level there are outdoor tables and chairs for drinks and snacks. The bedrooms in part are furnished with reproductions of Spanish provincial pieces, and all doubles contain a private bath. In all, 48 rooms are rented, with doubles costing from 3,400 pesetas ($23.80), and singles priced at 2,500 pesetas ($17.50).

Hotel Los Arcos, 192 Carlotta Alexandre (tel. 38-08-22), was once a grand old villa at the edge of what used to be a fishing village. It is somehow reminiscent of the Old Spanish houses built for movie stars in Beverly Hills in the '20s. Oddsy-endsy type furnishings are placed throughout, and the reasonably pleasant bedrooms attract a homing-pigeon clientele flying here in no small part because of the price: 3,200 pesetas ($22.40) for a double room with private bath;

single rooms with private baths are 2,200 pesetas ($15.40). A complete luncheon or dinner is an extra 1,000 pesetas ($7). All units have a garden view, telephone, and balcony.

Hotel Bristol, 112 Avenida Montemar (tel. 38-28-00), is built in the modern motel style, each room with a private balcony overlooking the free-form swimming pool. Perched on the western side of Torremolinos, it may escape the bedlam of the center of town, but it doesn't avoid the trucks and cement mixers roaring past its door. It is set off the main coast road, on an embankment covered with bushes and flowers. It is frequented by Nordic tour groups who want to return to Scandinavia sunburned and well fed. The Bristol's lobby is rather uninspired, but neat and streamlined. The spacious bedrooms are reasonably priced—2,400 pesetas ($16.80) for doubles with private bath, 2,000 pesetas ($14) for doubles with private shower bath.

Hostal Los Riscos, 40 Loma de los Riscos (tel. 38-14-20), is a redone private villa on the side of a hill, in a residential area of Torremolinos—not too far from the beach or the center of town. It has been well adapted to its present function of providing home-like accommodations at a low rate. True, it's a modern place —set back from the street by a low stone wall and an iron gate. It has a front portico, and the rooms open onto a small garden at the side. Guests like to gather here for a restful chat under the banana trees and bright umbrellas. The staff enjoys providing simple but nourishing home-cooked meals. You pay 2,400 pesetas ($16.80) for a double with private bath. The hostal has a restaurant, serving à la carte meals from 750 pesetas ($5.25) up.

Hostal Los Jazmines, Avenida del Lido (tel. 38-50-33), right on one of the best beaches in Torremolinos, at the foot of the shady Avenida del Lido, is a paradise for sunseekers who try not to get burned by sun or expense. It charges 2,800 pesetas ($19.60) to 3,600 pesetas ($25.30) in a double room with private bath. A complete meal costs 1,000 pesetas ($7). The hostal faces a plaza, and consists of a compound of modern buildings erected around terraces, lawns, and an odd-shaped swimming pool. Meals are served on the open-air terrace, or inside the appealing dining room, furnished with Spanish reproductions. The bedrooms are more impersonal, but they have their own little balconies, coordinated colors, and compact baths. It's a good hike up the hill to the center of town from here.

Samba, Urbanización La Colina (tel. 38-58-66), is a modern hillside hotel in a development just below the coast road to Málaga, about five minutes from the airport. Buses stop right outside the project, and the Torremolinos mini-rail has a stop in La Colina. Most of its no-frills bedrooms have projecting balconies and picture windows fronting the coastline. All rooms have a full private bath. Singles rent for 1,200 pesetas ($8.40), and doubles are modestly priced at 2,200 pesetas ($15.40). The lounge and dining room open off a lower floor onto a swimming pool play area. Within La Colina estate is a shopping complex with a supermarket, shops, boutiques, a drugstore, cafeterías, and restaurants, plus a disco for evening entertainment. Horseback riding and tennis courts are also available inside the estate, about a half-minute walk from Samba.

Hotel El Pozo, Calle Casablanca (tel. 38-06-02), winds itself around a cluster of pizzerias and boutiques in the commercial center. Its lobby-level bar has an open fireplace, heavy Spanish furniture, cool white tiles, and a view of a small courtyard. The 28 very clean rooms are behind carved doors in an environment of cool antiseptic stucco and masonry. Each contains a private bath, but there is no air conditioning. You'll have to leave your windows open for ventilation, and, for light sleepers, this could be a problem, as El Pozo lies in one of the liveliest sections of Torremolinos. From your window or terrace, you'll have a view of the promenades below. Singles cost 1,600 pesetas ($11.20) to 2,100 pesetas ($14.70), doubles 2,500 pesetas ($17.50) to 3,100 pesetas ($21.70).

WHERE TO EAT: The cuisine in Torremolinos, although somewhat slapdash, is varied, with lots of borrowing from America as well as continental Europe. The hotels often serve elaborate four-course meals, but at some point you may want to break free to sample the local offerings. At least the surroundings will be colorful, and the restaurants are clustered near each other, so you can do some window shopping in advance, waiting for that far-off fashionable dining hour of 10 p.m. Many establishments are expensive, but if you follow my clues, you'll find some good food bargains.

Restaurant Florida, 15 Calle Casablanca, La Nogalera (tel. 38-50-95), is a Danish and international restaurant on the lower level of a modern shopping complex, owned and run by a Dane, Jorn Lauvrits Hansen. The decor is South Seas, and the spread laid out inside is gargantuan, one of the best food values in Torremolinos. From 1 to 4 p.m. you can enjoy smörgåsbord, a vast array of dishes for just 750 pesetas ($5.25). Between 7 and 11 p.m. another deluxe buffet is offered at 1,300 pesetas ($9.10). Many diners go early and linger late, getting up for occasional forays to that groaning table. You get fine herrings, tasty salads, cold meats, and hot dishes, plus a lot of plates of food. A spread of cheeses and fruits is offered along with desserts. It's quite a bounty.

Restaurant Chef Manolo Fernández de Veigarrey, Eurosol Building, Carretera de Cádiz (tel. 38-95-25). The conscientious chef who lent his name to this relative newcomer works hard to keep his menus original and his prices reasonable. Within an impeccably clean dining room enhanced with light-brown tiles, roughly textured stone, and crisp white napery, he prepares a limited but frequently changing list of daily specials concocted from the freshest ingredients along the Costa del Sol. You might enjoy an asparagus mousse or a shrimp-and-leek tart as an appetizer, to be followed with medallions of angler fish in an orange sauce, tenderloin of beef in a Roquefort sauce, roast pheasant (seasonal), or a veal chop with green pepper sauce. The steward will suggest something from the short but well-chosen wine list to cap off full meals costing from 2,500 pesetas ($17.50). Reservations are suggested.

Annabelle's, Pasaje de Pizarro (tel. 38-09-07). You'll be greeted near the entrance to this engagingly garrulous place by the sight of an elongated bar where someone from about every nationality in Torremolinos is likely to be present. The posters of Marilyn Monroe, country western music, and the lighthearted ambience are the creative statement of an Englishman, Richard Copeland, a native of Yorkshire. A pint of Alsatian beer costs 240 pesetas ($1.68), and a bottle of Spanish beer goes for 100 pesetas (70¢). A corner grill and a handful of simple tables serves barbecues, chicken, Spanish-style ribs, entrecôte steaks, and chili con carne. A small mixed grill, usually ample for most appetites, costs 550 pesetas ($3.85), a full mixed grill 750 pesetas ($5.25). The place is usually open for English breakfasts, then closes between 11 a.m. and 4 p.m.

La Bovéda, 22 Cuesta del Tajo (tel. 38-11-85), is reached by walking down a steep flight of steps connecting Calle San Miguel to the beachfront at the Paseo Marítimo. Partners John Atkinson and Henri Cazade are in charge, and their hidden terrace has witnessed the preparation of some of the most sophisticated international food in town. The structure was originally built in the 16th century as a watermill, and today its cave-like interior contains all the accoutrements for fine dining. You might enjoy an apéritif in the concealed garden before heading in to your pre-reserved table. Menu items change with the availability of ingredients, showing a marked California influence, with overtones of France, Italy, and Spain thrown in. Inexpensive fixed-priced lunches cost from 900 pesetas ($6.30), with the more formal candlelight dinners going for 1,500 pesetas ($10.50) up to 3,000 pesetas ($21). A flamenco show is sometimes presented at 10:30 p.m., but it's best to inquire about that when you make a reservation.

El Gato Viudo, 8 Calle Nogalera (tel. 38-51-29), is a two-fork restaurant with sidewalk tables, right in the teeming heart of the action. The restaurant is decorated in the tavern style, with Kelly-green Spanish chairs and tartan cloths. The chef specializes in Spanish cookery, offering a set menu for just 650 pesetas ($4.55). The à la carte menu, in English, is small but interesting, including the familiar repertoire of national dishes—shellfish soup, paella, and roast chicken. Fresh fruit is your best bet to finish your meal. On the à la carte arrangement, the average meal ranges in price from 1,500 pesetas ($10.50). The atmosphere is informal, and the international clientele shows up in all ranges of attire. Closed in December.

Casa René, 19 Calle del Cauce (tel. 38-67-10), is a local restaurant whose sign in front advertises that "Swedish is spoken," yet still manages to maintain lots of authentic Spanish flavor. It's on a narrow and crowded traffic-free street which is so cramped that sometimes from outside you can make out the details of enlarged photographs of old Iberian cities hanging on the dark paneling. Sidewalk tables are available, but many guests prefer to eat indoors. House specialties include tournedos René, roast leg of lamb, steak maison, sole filet with asparagus in wine sauce, and grilled swordfish. A set meal is offered for around 850 pesetas ($5.95), and à la carte dinners begin at 1,800 pesetas ($12.60).

Restaurante Hong Kong, Calle del Cauce (tel. 38-41-29), is decorated Chinese-style with colors of gold, red, and white. It's the only restaurant on this crowded pedestrian walkway to have a piece of breathing space surrounding its outside tables, due to its partial seclusion on a tiny recessed area off the street. There's a long bar area lit with Chinese lanterns if you just want a drink. If you prefer dinner, the establishment offers a fixed-price menu at 850 pesetas ($5.95), and an array of à la carte Indonesian specialties including rijsttafel (a buffet of rice with many different garnishes). Among the Chinese dishes offered are hot spiced pork with vegetables, chop suey, and egg rolls. If you order à la carte, count on spending from 1,500 pesetas ($10.50).

Viking, 9 Casablanca (tel. 38-10-41), is one of the most popular budget restaurants of Torremolinos, drawing an international crowd to its colorful precincts at the end of the Calle San Miguel (where you can stop earlier at one of the tapas bars). Tove Jensen is the English-speaking host. The Viking has a 950-peseta ($6.65) menú del día that is far superior to those at many other establishments that will tempt you on the way to it. Specialties include such fare as pork chop with red cabbage, chicken American style, snails in garlic, and cucumber salad. Everything, of course, tastes better with Tubörg beer. Regular à la carte meals cost from 1,800 pesetas ($12.60).

Restaurante Canton, 23 Plaza de la Gamba Alegre (tel. 38-21-17), began as a hole-in-the-wall in the Edificio Begoña, but its popularity forced a move. For 950 pesetas ($6.65) you can order a complete dinner, including, for example, an eggroll, beef with onions, steamed white rice, and fresh fruit. Two specialties are the sweet-and-sour pork and the diced chicken with almonds. You might also try the sweet-and-sour fish. Richard K. Chang of Hamden, Connecticut, wrote: "Being Chinese, we are always quite critical of Chinese restaurants recommended by non-Chinese. However, the cuisine we enjoyed in the restaurant certainly came as a surprise (pleasantly so)." The Canton is open from 1 till 4 p.m. and from 7:30 p.m. till midnight, except Tuesday.

Salud Vegetarian Restaurant and Bar, Pueblo Blanco, Calle Casablanca (no phone). Maud and Christina welcome you to this little hole-in-the-wall, tucked away in a beautiful, but obscure, corner of Torremolinos. They are from Sweden and run this inviting little charmer. For your drink, you're offered a choice of fresh juices such as orange, apple, and carrot. Each day a hot soup is featured, as well as a salad. One hot dish of the day is also on the menu—on my most recent visit, a cauliflower-and-mushroom casserole. You sit on natural-wood shield-back chairs (very tiny). Maud and Christina don't like to call the place a health-food restaurant. They say, "It's not health food—it's the way people used to eat." With a homemade dessert, count on spending from 1,000 pesetas ($7). The restaurant is closed on Sunday.

The major gathering place in Torremolinos for the patrons of restaurants, boutiques, cafés, whatever, is called **La Nogalera.** Lying between the coast road and the beach (reached by walking down Calle del Cauce), this is a compound of modern, whitewashed buildings, with Andalusian flavor.

Open to pedestrian traffic only, it features a maze of colorful passageways, courtyards, patios for dining, fountains, trees, flowers—and lots and lots of people. If you're seeking anything from sandwiches to Belgian waffles to scrambled eggs to pizzas, you're likely to find it here.

Seafood at La Carihuela

If you want to get away from the brash high-rises and Coney Island-type honky-tonk, head to nearby Carihuela Village, where some of the best bargain restaurants are found. Tops with locals and visitors alike is **Casa Prudencio,** 41 Carmen (tel. 38-14-52), on the beach. À la carte dishes include gazpacho, lentils or soup, shrimp omelet, swordfish, and shish kebab. Try the special paella and strawberries with whipped cream (in the spring). The atmosphere is cordial, and you may make friends at the long tables where everyone sits together. There are also tables for four for the more fastidious. The boardwalk tables are almost always taken. If you want to splurge, order a lubina a la sal—a huge, boneless fish packed under a layer of salt, which is then prepared at your table and makes a singular gastronomical treat. Complete meals begin at 2,500 pesetas ($17.50).

El Cangrejo, 25 Calle Bulto (tel. 38-04-79), is a country-style tavern, with a beamed ceiling, open fireplace, and ships' models. Right in the colorful heart of La Carihuela, it has a picture-window view of the sea. One entrance is on the street (Calle Bulto) that runs parallel to the beach. Ignore the piles of shrimp heads and anchovy tails that often find their way to the floor. This is the perfect place for a big seafood dinner, and often Spanish families fill up all the tables, gorging themselves on such seafood as grilled shrimp, sea bass on a skewer, shellfish zarzuela, or chanquetes (a kind of local whitebait). For an appetizer, I'd suggest the shellfish soup. A half bottle of sangría is a good touch. The immense variety of seafood dishes is staggering, and you will probably be, too, when you leave "The Crab." A full repast will cost from 750 pesetas ($5.25) to 1,800 pesetas ($12.60).

TORREMOLINOS AFTER DARK: The nightlife of Torremolinos can be a romp. The scene of the action changes so rapidly in this town that it's hard to keep up with it. The fickle clique that decides what's hot seems to come up with a new disco two or three times a season.

The Bars

Bar Central, Plaza Andalucía (tel. 38-27-60), offers coffee, brandy, beer, cocktails, limited sandwiches, and pastries, served on a large, French-style covered terrace if you prefer. This place was made famous by Michener's *The Drifters.* Open from 9 a.m. to 1:30 p.m., it's a good spot to meet congenial people. Beer costs 100 pesetas (70¢).

Bar El Toro, 32 Calle San Miguel (tel. 38-65-04), is for aficionados (the bullfight theme is everywhere). Kegs of beer, bar stools, and the terrace on the main shopping street make it perfect for drinking a before-dinner sherry, or an after-dinner beer. A hamburger goes for 150 pesetas ($1.05). As a special attraction, the staff prepares a bullfight poster with your name between those of two famous matadors, for 350 pesetas ($2.45).

La Bodega, 38 Calle San Miguel (tel. 38-73-37). Its decor includes a smattering of everyday tiles, simple tables and chairs, and a long stand-up bar. Perhaps it relies more on its colorful clientele and the quality of its tapas to draw customers who seem to seek this place out above the dozens of other tascas within this very popular tourist zone. You'll be fortunate to find space at one of the small tables, since many clients consider the bar food plentiful enough for a satisfying lunch or dinner. Once you begin to order one of the platters of fried squid, pungent tuna, grilled shrimp, or tiny brochettes of sole, you might not be able to stop. Generous rations of tapas begin at 400 pesetas ($2.80), while a beer costs 50 pesetas (35¢).

Flamenco

El Jaleo at the Plaza de la Gamba Alegre (tel. 38-12-84) offers one of the best "tablao flamenco" showcases on the Costa del Sol, featuring singers, guitarists, and dancers. The price of a first drink (and this includes your cover) is 1,500 pesetas ($10.50). It is open from 10:15 p.m. till 1 a.m.

Discos

New Piper's Club, Plaza Costa del Sol (tel. 38-29-94), is a fun palace resembling a subterranean world, with ramps and tunnels connecting the various grottoes. Music, mostly for young tastes, is piped in on seven dance floors under strobe lighting reflecting fountains and pools. There is a swimming pool. The place is usually intimate and packed. In all, it's evocative of the disco heyday of the late '60s. Open nightly, the club charges 1,500 pesetas ($10.50).

Gatsby, 68 Avenida Montemar (tel. 38-53-72), stands on a major traffic-choked boulevard, and, wisely, has its own private parking. Taking its theme from Fitzgerald's 1920s, Gatsby has a loud, distortion-free sound system. The illumination employs strobes and spots, as you dance to up-to-the-instant disc selections. For your first drink, you pay 750 pesetas ($5.25). The attractive clientele seeks out the romantic tables or the tropical garden adjoining the building.

A Wax Museum (Museo de Cera)

One slightly offbeat way to spend time before dinner in Torremolinos is to go to the London Wax Museum, called the Museo de Cera de Londres, Avenida Palma de Mallorca (tel. 38-25-02), which is open daily from 10 a.m. to 10 p.m. In summer the museum is open from 10 a.m. to 2 p.m. and 4 p.m. to midnight. In 45 settings, it features almost a hundred lifelike wax figures—including bullfighters, famous painters, movie stars, plus the inevitable chamber of horrors. Adults are charged 360 pesetas ($2.53) for admission; children, 200 pesetas ($1.40).

Carihuela After Dark

For those who want to avoid the frenzied scene uptown, the little fishing village and beach district of La Carihuela is a nighttime target, much of the district evoking scenes in James Michener's *The Drifters*.

Rosie O'Grady's Pub, 37 Calle Bulto (no phone). On the nights when the Gaelic music resounds through the streets, it's hard to resist being pulled into the crowded confines of this charming pub. It's the personal statement of a dark-eyed, brunette Liverpudlian, Berica Neale, who is sometimes assisted by her husband, John. But for the most part she hires the singers, orders the inventory, and maintains order herself. It's the kind of place where happily romantic couples of all ages gather and are likely to be singing lustily before the end of their second drink. Music begins (usually) seven nights a week before 9 p.m. and includes everything from country western to English pop. Beer costs 100 pesetas (70¢), and there's no cover charge.

At **La Casita,** 44 Calle Bulto, drinks cost only 300 pesetas ($2.10). This is really a flamenco bar occupying what used to be a little fisherman's cottage. Shouts of *"Viva Andalucía!"* echo through the night. You're so close to the flamenco dancers at this bar that you'll feel part of the show yourself.

Intermezzo Piano Club, 4 Plaza del Remo (tel. 38-32-67), is by far the most sophisticated bar in Carihuela. The sea is visible from the front door, and the interior opens generously into a large almost-square room whose focus seems centered around a shiny black piano. Its curves are repeated in the undulating upholstered bar area which is skillfully lit with a series of spotlights. The decor might be called a combination of Victorian with modern, with dusty rose and black being the main colors and English hunting scenes hanging on the walls. There's a small dance floor if anyone wants to follow the live music, which begins every night of the week between 10 p.m. and 3 a.m. Drinks range upward from 200 pesetas ($1.40).

With Torremolinos behind us, we now head east to Málaga. It's a distance of only 9 physical miles, but at least 100 miles in spirit.

10. Málaga

This Mediterranean port city is first a bustling commercial and residential center, then a resort. Unlike Torremolinos, it could go on existing even if the sun-seekers disappeared suddenly, although tourism has undeniably beefed up the local economy considerably. Torremolinos is the unofficial queen of the Costa del Sol. Málaga, on the other hand, is official royalty.

The chief drawing card in Málaga is its mild off-season climate (summer can be a bit sticky); otherwise, it is devoid of a great deal of interest (its beaches are poor—the best one, **Baos del Carmen).**

Ranking next to Seville as the largest Andalusian city, Málaga has experienced a steady growth in population.

The city abounds with orange trees, flower markets, fishing boats, shops on narrow streets in the medieval section, hotels, parks, restaurants, and sidewalk cafés—and all this makes for a pleasant interlude.

The most festive time to visit Málaga is around the first week in August when the capital of the province celebrates the conquest of the city by the Catholic monarchs in 1487. This is an occasion for parades, bullfights, and a big *feria* (fair). A major, tree-shaded boulevard of the city, the **Paseo del Parque,** then becomes the scene of much building activity, as the avenida is transformed into a fairground featuring restaurants and amusements aimed at all purses.

Málaga's most famous son is Pablo Picasso, who was born here in 1881 at Plaza de la Merced, the center of the city. This co-founder of Cubism, who would one day paint his mural *Guernica* to express his horror of war, left little of his spirit in the city of his birth, and even less of his work.

A TRAVELER'S ADVISORY: Málaga is the unfortunate winner of a recent survey that declared it to have the highest crime rate in Spain. By far the most common complaint is purse-snatching, with an estimated 75% of the crimes committed by juveniles. The related problems of reported stolen passports to the U.S. consular office in Fuengirola has become a common story in a town where the pickings are rich for a floating population serviced by an understaffed police force.

As a warning to travelers, I stress that all precautions should be taken, including buttoning wallets and valuables into pockets (a moneybelt might be an even better idea). Drive with your doors locked and your windows rolled up (many incidents occur while motorists are waiting at traffic signals with their windows down).

In an era of changing social structures, when you are likely to be perceived as a "have" traveling in an area of "have-nots," it is wise to take special care of your valuables. Don't flaunt your possessions, especially jewelry. With the right precautions taken, you can still have a pleasant, care-free holiday, and the crime wave sweeping across Málaga need not darken the spirit of your traveling time spent there.

WHERE TO STAY: Málaga has a dearth of good hotels, but for the most part it charges prices compatible with our budget.

Parador Nacional de Gibralfaro, Monte Gibralfaro (tel. 22-19-02), has everything one could possibly desire in a Spanish accommodation: luxury, economy, seclusion, history, romance, and beauty. It sits high on a plateau, near the site of an old fortified castle, overlooking the city and the Mediterranean, with views of the bullring, mountains, and beaches. Originally a famous restaurant, the parador has been converted into one of the finest hotels in Spain. Built mostly of old stone, it is elegant—but the cost of a double accommodation with private bath is 8,500 pesetas ($59.50) a day. Singles pay 7,000 pesetas ($49). The bedroom suites have their own entranceway, a private bath, a combination bed-living room, tall and wide glass doors opening onto private sun terraces, complete with garden furniture. The decor of cowhide, handsome draperies, and the like, is tasteful; the furnishings are modern yet accented by reproductions of Spanish antiques; and all the necessities and several added amenities, such as armchairs, sofas, coffee tables, and a desk, enhance the comfort of guests. There are two dining rooms.

The parador is reached via a winding road through streets of old and new villas. If you have a car, drive north along the coastal road, Paseo de Reding. This becomes Avenida Casa de Pries, which in turn becomes the Paseo de Sancha. Turn left on Camino Nuevo, toward the hill.

Parador Nacional del Golf, Apartado 324 (tel. 38-12-55), is another tasteful resort hotel created by the Spanish government. Flanked by an 18-hole golf course on one side and the Mediterranean on another, it is arranged hacienda style, with several low, tile buildings. You're greeted by chirping birds and grounds planted with flowers. All bedrooms have a private balcony, with a view of the golfing greens, the circular swimming pool, or the water. The furnishings are attractive. There are no single rooms, but you can rent doubles and twin-bedded rooms costing from 7,500 pesetas ($52.50) to 9,500 pesetas ($66.50), plus tax, depending on the season. Use of the pool costs 600 pesetas ($4.20) to 800 pesetas ($5.60). Long tile corridors lead to the public rooms which, like the bedrooms, are air-conditioned. There are graciously furnished lounges and a bar and restaurant. The parador is less than 2 miles from the airport, 6½ miles from Málaga, and 2½ miles from Torremolinos.

Astoria, 3 Avenida Comandante Benítez (tel. 22-45-00), can be useful as a styleless hotel when you need an inexpensive place to sleep, and no glamour. It's a ten-minute walk from the center of town, opening onto the river, overlooking a wide street and gasoline station. There is no lounge, just a check-in counter. Rooms are simply furnished and clean, a single with shower (no toilet) costing from 2,700 pesetas ($18.90). Doubles, either with private shower or complete bath, range in price from 3,500 pesetas ($24.50). If you have a car, you'll generally find street parking.

Hostal Residencia Carlos V, 6 Cister (tel. 21-51-20), might serve as an emergency stopover if nothing else is available within the old city. It has a good central location near the cathedral, and an interesting façade is decorated with wrought-iron balconies and *miradores* in the style of La Coruña. The lobby, however, is fairly dark, but this is an old, safe haven. An elevator will take you to your room, which will cost from 1,800 pesetas ($12.60) in a single, from 3,200 pesetas ($22.40) in a double.

Casala, 3 Alameda de Colón (tel. 21-15-84), is suggested as an emergency shelter when a good bed and a clean room are all that you require. The hostal is near the river, within walking distance of the city center. The entrance is from a palm-tree-lined avenue. You enter a dark little lounge with an elevator which takes you to the simple, modest bedrooms. Singles with bath (hall toilet) cost 2,400 pesetas ($16.80). Doubles, also with bath (but no private toilets), go for 3,400 pesetas ($23.80). A continental breakfast, costing extra, is the only meal served.

El Cenachero, 1 Barroso (tel. 22-40-88), on the third floor, is a modest little (only 14 bedrooms) modern hotel. Each room is different and nicely carpeted—and all contain a shower. A double room with bath or shower costs 3,000 pesetas ($21). Singles with bath cost 1,900 pesetas ($13.30). Everything is kept clean. No meals are served. The little hostal, opened in 1969, is five blocks from Alameda.

Hostal Residencia Derby, 1 San Juan de Dios (tel. 21-13-01), is a recommendable boarding house on the fourth floor (take the elevator up). Right in the heart of Málaga on a main square, it overlooks fountains and the harbor. Some of the units have excellent views of the Mediterranean and the port of Málaga. On one recent visit guests crowded around to watch a Russian cruise ship come into port. The hostal is quite clean, and all rooms have hot and cold running water. The charge is 3,000 pesetas ($21) in a double, 1,900 pesetas ($13.30) in a single. The Derby is a real find in these inflationary times, and it's handy to transportation.

WHERE TO EAT: Málaga has a number of restaurants in its city center that are within our price range.

Restaurante Antonio Martín, 4 Paseo Marítimo (tel. 22-10-18), is set up in a tastefully designed brick building whose modern walls separate the seashore from a busy intersection on the coastal road in the commercial center of town. Unless you peer through one of the iron-grilled windows, you'll hardly be aware of the hysterical traffic outside, especially if you dine on the breezy outdoor terrace within full view of the Mediterranean. If you want to eat indoors, there are several areas for dining, one of which has half-timbered walls and immaculate napery. Menu items include stewed oxtail, grilled sirloin, kidneys in sherry sauce, leg of baby lamb, grilled salmon, mixed fried fish, grilled red mullet, fresh fried anchovies, shrimp cocktail, and shellfish soup. For a good meal, expect to pay from 1,800 pesetas ($12.60) to 2,500 pesetas ($17.50).

Restaurante La Alegría, 10 Marín García (tel. 22-41-43). This establishment opened more than a century ago and has been considered ever since as the grande dame of Málaga eateries. Regrettably, it felt it had to modernize and ripped out dozens of handcrafted accents just before the current wave of nostalgia swept across the world. Today the 1940s-style decor includes a dignified collection of full-grained cedar wall panels and solidly built chairs whose green-leather upholstery looks like the kind of thing you'd find in the dining room, or the games room, of an ocean liner.

It's the lead restaurant within the old city and definitely the best—and most expensive—one on a pedestrian street lined with cheaper *mesones típicos*. It's a four-fork eating place, and the prices are reasonable considering its rating. A uniformed and polite waiter will take your order for such specialties as veal from Ávila, grilled steak, kidneys in sherry sauce, fish soup, gazpacho, broad beans with ham, and an array of fish such as hake, sole, shrimp, and many kinds of shellfish. A full meal here will cost from 3,200 pesetas ($22.40).

The **Parador Gibralfaro,** Monte Gibralfaro (tel. 22-19-02), has long been the most exciting restaurant in Málaga. It enjoys a top-notch reputation for its fish dishes. From its hilltop retreat overlooking the city and the Mediterranean, it offers its guests a choice of two dining rooms. One is inside with walls of windows opening into the wide, covered terrace; the other is in the open air, with pleasant garden chairs and tables. The complete tourist menu, including wine and service, costs 2,000 pesetas ($14). At night, as the lights of Málaga go on, you can sip your Andalusian wine and look out over the world.

Another government-owned restaurant is the **Parador Nacional del Golf,** Apartado 324 (tel. 38-12-55). Its indoor/outdoor dining room opens onto a circular swimming pool, lawns, golf course, and private beach. The interior dining room, furnished with reproductions of antiques, has a refined country-club atmosphere. Pre-lunch drinks at the sleek modern bar tempt golfers and others, who then proceed to the covered terrace for their meal. A set menu costs from 1,800 pesetas ($12.60), and an à la carte menu is available. You can make it an afternoon, using the pool for 600 pesetas ($4.20) on weekdays, 800 pesetas ($5.60) on Sunday and holidays. You're given a 50% discount on the pool charge if you order a meal.

El Corte Inglés, 50 Avenida de Andalucía (tel. 30-00-00), offers two of the best value-for-pesetas dining selections in Málaga. Both are open only for lunch. The more formal of the two, the Steak House, is on the top floor of the huge department store. The establishment offers immaculate red-checked napery, comfortable seating, and rows of fish and meats in glass display cases. A formally dressed staff serves such specialties as green peppers stuffed with shellfish, filet of pork in a pepper cream sauce, and an array of temptingly seasoned brochettes. There is a complete wine list. Full meals cost from 2,200 pesetas ($15.40).

Immediately adjacent to the Steak House is a vastly popular buffet. You pay a set price of 1,350 pesetas ($9.45) (half price for children under six). That entitles you to access to more than 70 dishes. Wine is extra.

Restaurante Tormes, 2 Calle de San José (tel. 22-20-63). About the only decor in this alleyway restaurant a few steps from the Fine Arts Museum is a series of photographs of architectural curiosities throughout Spain. The ambience and the food are simple, but the cuisine is well prepared and generously served. The welcome is friendly and accommodating from the owner, Antonio Ramírez Macias, and his family. The restaurant has immaculate napery and offers a fixed-price meal for around 850 pesetas ($5.95), including the works. As an appetizer, gazpacho is a savory choice, or you might prefer the mixed hors d'oeuvres or even spaghetti. The *segundo plato* usually consists of fish, such as mero (Mediterranean pollack), followed by a poultry course such as roast chicken, and then dessert. The establishment is open every day.

El Cenachero, 5 Strachan (tel. 22-30-13), is the Málaga home of paella, served here with tender chunks of chicken, shellfish, peppers, and olives, all delicately flavored with saffron. It's on a quiet street leading up to the side of the cathedral. The atmosphere is full of local color, which would include a friendly welcome from the workers behind the marble-topped bar (which sits on a white-painted, hand-worked base). Its black surface is loaded with tapas that look savory and include the kind of shellfish delicacy that, if you're not careful, will totally spoil your appetite for dinner. If you're still in the mood, you can climb up to the mezzanine level where heavy ceiling beams and thick wooden tables are the setting for the consumption of the Spanish food. A simple meal which includes paella costs around 800 pesetas ($5.60) to 1,500 pesetas ($10.50). This two-fork restaurant is about as regional as you can get. It's open every day.

La Manchega "Mesón Típico," 4 Calle de Marín García (tel. 22-21-80), is one of several unpretentious bars and restaurants on this popular pedestrian-only street in a commercial part of downtown Málaga. When you enter, you pass sidewalk tables for drinking or dining. Inside, you'll see a ground-floor bar area with tile walls, a crowd of uniformed barmen, many of whom hint at having been sailors during earlier careers, and a decorator's attempt to create a type of indoor Andalusian courtyard. A *Salon Comedor* offers additional space for dining on an upper floor. Having been in business since 1924, the establishment offers years of experience at cooking such specialties as shrimp omelets, Málaga-style soup, beans with Andalusian ham, snails, eels, and a full array of shellfish, including grilled shrimp, clams, and mussels. There's also a good fish soup offered. Full meals range from 1,200 pesetas ($8.40).

Mesón Danes (Faarup), 1 Calle Barroso (tel. 22-74-42), provides Danish and Spanish snacks at medium prices. There's a menu for 950 pesetas ($6.65) that might include Danish or Spanish soup, fish, meat, and bread. The restaurant also has a special Faarup plate with assorted food. The Danish House stays open until midnight except on Sunday. It closes for vacation the entire month of August.

Drinks and Tapas

El Boquerón de Plata, 6 Alarcon Lujan, has long been one of the most famous bars of Málaga. You go there for good Spanish wine and tapas. If you're a local, the latest gossip will be the order of the day. Most guests have a beer and a helping of the prawns. The fish depends on the catch of the day—it's invariably fresh. A plate of the day ranges from 550 pesetas ($3.85). *Warning:* There are two other places in the region touting the same name.

La Tasca, 12 Calle de Marín García. If you're looking for a quiet and mellow tasca where no one ever raises his or her voice, this is not for you. Its crowded quarters contain elegantly carved bar panels gracefully fashioned into something that could have been built in the 18th century but probably is a good and more recent copy. This is really a hole in the wall, but it has style, conviviality, and a surprisingly large staff crowded behind the bar to serve the sometimes strident demands of practically everyone in Málaga, many of whom bring their children with them. You can have a choice of beer from the tap, wine, and an array of tapas. Try the croquettes (croquetas) and pungent shish kebabs (pinchon) laced with garlic and cumin. If you see an empty seat, try to commandeer it politely. Otherwise you'll stand in what might be awestruck observation of the social scene around you. The total bill for four beers, two croquettes, and two shish kebabs is around 550 pesetas ($3.85).

Bar Loqüeno, 11 Calle de Marín García, offers basically the same tapas as its neighbor, La Tasca. The entrance is behind a wrought-iron and glass door which leads into a stucco-lined room decorated in a "local tavern style" with a vengeance. There are enough hams, bouquets of garlic, beer kegs, fishnets, and sausages to feed an entire village for a week. There's hardly enough room to stand, and you'll invariably be jostled by a busy waiter shouting "calamari" to the cooks in the back kitchens. You can dine at a table outside for around 1,200 pesetas ($8.40). If you only want a drink, a beer costs from 110 pesetas (77¢).

THE SIGHTS: Unlike the rest of the Costa del Sol, Málaga has several historical sites of interest:

The Alcazaba

The remains of this ancient palace of the Moorish rulers of Málaga are within easy walking distance of the heart of the city (with plenty of signs to point the way up the hill). The government has improved the local landscape around it, and orange trees and purple bougainvillea make it look even more beautiful. The view overlooking the city and the bay from the palace is among the best on the Costa del Sol. This fortress was probably erected in the 9th or 10th century, although there have been later additions and reconstructions. Isabella and Ferdinand stayed here when they reconquered the city. Inside it is installed an **Archeological Museum.** The Alcazaba may be visited from 10 a.m. to 1 p.m. and 5 to 8 p.m. On Sunday it is open from 10 a.m. to 2 p.m. Admission is 50 pesetas (35¢).

The Cathedral (Catedral)

In the center of the city, this 16th-century Renaissance cathedral of Málaga suffered damage during the Civil War, but it remains impressive—big and vast, reflecting changing styles of interior architecture. Its most notable attribute is its richly ornamented choir stalls. The cathedral has been declared a National Monument. One statue of a lounging cardinal is definitely religioso camp. The cathedral, built on the site of a great mosque, may be visited from 10 a.m. to 1 p.m. and 4 to 6 p.m. all year. To see the choir by Ortiz, Mena, and Michael costs 50 pesetas (35¢).

Gibralfaro Castle

On a hill overlooking Málaga and the blue Mediterranean bay are the ruins of this ancient Moorish castle-fortress, the origins of which are unknown. It is near the government-run parador. (A visit to the castle might be tied in with a luncheon stopover. You can enter the old Arabic gate that leads to the inside of this fortress any time of the day free.) *Warning:* Do not walk to Gibralfaro Castle from the town. Several readers have reported muggings along the way, and the area surrounding the castle is considered very dangerous.

Fine Arts Museum (Museo de Bellas Artes)

This former Moorish palace is at 6 San Agustín, and it houses a modest collection of paintings, including a gallery devoted to native-born son Pablo Picasso. In addition, it also has works by Murillo, Ribera, and Morales, along with Andalusian antiques, mosaics, and sculptures. Visiting hours are 10 a.m. to 1:30 p.m. and 5 to 8 p.m. in summer (4 to 7 p.m. in winter). The entrance fee is 75 pesetas (53¢).

11. Nerja

Nerja dramatically perches on its handsome nest known as "The Balcony of Europe." Nearby is one of Spain's greatest attractions, the Cave of Nerja, a paleolithic panorama (see below). Nerja is some 32 miles east of Málaga.

The resort is known to hordes of European and North American vacationers who like its good beaches and small coves, its seclusion (off the main coastal route), and its atmosphere of narrow streets and courtyards, with whitewashed, flat-roofed houses.

WHERE TO STAY: Nerja may still be fairly small, but like David, it is a formidable contender for such Goliaths as Torremolinos. Its accommodations are excellent—top hotels, a government-run parador, and a scattering of moderately priced hostelries.

Hotel Balcón de Europa (tel. 52-08-00) occupies the best position in town, lying at the edge of the Balcón de Europa. Guests usually have private balconies of their own whose view stretches out over the water and the rocks. A private beach is set at the end of a narrow grassy area in back where parasol-shielded tables offer a place for a peaceful vista. The simple bedrooms are decorated in modern furniture set onto terracotta floors. There's a private garage a few steps away. Single rooms rent for 3,000 pesetas ($21) to 4,500 pesetas ($31.50), while doubles cost anywhere from 4,800 pesetas ($33.60) to 6,000 pesetas ($42), depending on the season of the year.

Hostal Fontainebleau, Calle Alejandro Bueno (tel. 52-09-39), is a personal favorite. The comfortable accommodations have been operated by English partners, Marlene and Peter Bainbridge, since 1982, and they have been joined at the front of the house by a sister-and-brother team, Kerry and Neil Anderson. The atmosphere is family-like. Each of the 22 pleasantly furnished rooms has a bath with shower, wall-to-wall carpeting, local and Gibraltar radio, and tea- and coffee-making facilities. Singles cost from 2,600 pesetas ($18.20), doubles from 3,400 pesetas ($23.80), and some family rooms suitable for three persons are available for 4,500 pesetas ($31.50). All rooms open onto an attractive fountain patio. You can order a continental breakfast served on the patio, weather permitting, or have a cooked breakfast in the restaurant. The hostal has a clients' telephone booth for metered calls worldwide; laundry, drying, and ironing facilities; and a foreign currency exchange desk open seven days a week. From December to April, video films in English are shown daily in the cozy lounge.

You can have drinks on the rooftop sun lounging terrace from May to October and in the Fountain Bar, resembling a British pub, any time. From the pub, you enter the Beefeater Steak Bar which features English home-style cooking. A three-course table d'hôte daily menu costs 1,200 pesetas ($8.40), including bread and wine. The hostal is about a ten-minute walk from the main beach, Playa Burriana, and a five-minute walk to the center of town. It's open all year except from early November to mid-December.

Cala-Bela, 8 Puerta del Mar (tel. 52-07-00), is a miniature hotel, much improved recently, just a one-minute walk from the Balcony of Europe. Like its more expensive next-door neighbor, the Portofino, it too has bedrooms opening onto the sea. The lounge is charming. For a double with bath, the charge is 3,000 pesetas ($21), dropping to 2,500 pesetas ($17.50) in a single. The rooms may be small, but they're clean—and what a view! Seated in a bone-white Valencian chair, you are served in a seafront dining room at a cost of 950 pesetas ($6.65). The food is good, so even if you're not staying at the hotel, you may want to patronize its restaurant, enjoying such dishes as filet of pork in a sherry sauce, the chef's paella, grilled crayfish, and trout with cream.

Villa Flamenca, in the Urbanización Nueva Nerja (tel. 52-18-69), offering a total of 88 rooms, was opened in 1969. The villa is a completely modern building near the beach, convenient for those quick dips. Guests are received all year, and the charge for doubles with bath is 3,200 pesetas ($22.40). No singles are available. A lunch or dinner is another 1,000 pesetas ($7).

Hostal Mena, 15 Alemania (tel. 52-05-41), is a modest little residencia which serves no meals for the residents of its 10 simple bedrooms. If your requirements are simple, there's a lot of charm about this place, including the central hallway whose back walls are lined with hundreds of blue and white Andalusian tiles. The white stucco façade with its green shutters is marred only by a vivid sign (orange plastic) announcing the name of the establishment. The family running the hostal is much in evidence and will sometimes occupy the small salon fitted snugly between the tile walls of the ground floor. Single rooms without bath cost 1,600 pesetas ($11.20), while bathless doubles go for 2,400 pesetas ($16.80). Doubles with bath cost 2,800 pesetas ($19.60).

Montesol, 230 General Franco (tel. 52-00-14). Four of the bedrooms of this humble guest house contain a private bath; the other three are fitted only with water basin. Owned by Manuel Guerrero Castillo, the house is quite modern and well kept (there is a vigorous ritual of scrubbing and polishing every day). Doubles without bath rent for 2,400 pesetas ($16.80); with bath, for 3,200 pesetas ($22.40).

Hostal Miguel, 31 Almirante Ferrándiz (tel. 52-15-23), is a pleasant yet unpretentious inn that contains only seven simply furnished rooms. They're housed in a 19th-century building whose iron-rimmed balconies serve as a base for more recent *miradores* which served to expand the façade. The hostal is on a quiet back street about a three-minute walk from the Balcón, across the street from the well-known Pepe Rico restaurant. No meals are served at the hostal other than breakfast, not included in the tariffs. The rooms rent for around 3,000 pesetas ($21) for a double.

The **Parador Nacional de Nerja,** Playa de Burriana (tel. 52-00-50), is worth saving up for. It's like an elegant California motel, blending modern concepts with traditional Spanish elements. Built low on the edge of a cliff, the parador is surrounded by lawns, spacious and sprawling, plus an outdoor swimming pool (or, if you prefer, an elevator will take you to the sandy beach below). The air-conditioned interior utilizes suitable furnishings, placed against a backdrop of beamed ceilings, tile floors, and homespun draperies. In high season (March through October), the rate is 10,500 pesetas ($73.50) in a double room with private bath. Singles pay 9,000 pesetas ($63). The double bedchambers are (1) worthy of a honeymoon, (2) worthy of a second honeymoon, or (3) reason enough to get married in the first place.

If you can't stay here, maybe you'll want to have a dinner—three big courses—after viewing the nearby caves. The price is 2,200 pesetas ($15.40) and a typical repast might include a shrimp cocktail, veal cooked in its own juice, accompanied by vegetables, and topped off by a piece of homemade cake. Before or after a meal you can go for a swim, nonresidents paying 600 pesetas ($4.20) for the privilege.

Pepe Rico Apartamentos, 28 Almirante Ferrándiz (tel. 52-02-47), gets an enthusiastic recommendation, both as a restaurant (see below) and as a secluded place to stay in a friendly atmosphere. It's the joint creation of Robert W. Holder and his wife, Kathy. German-born Holder worked in hotels and restaurants in Scotland, England, Greece, Switzerland, and France before finding his place in the sun in Nerja. He's also an amateur photographer, and with technical advice from his photographer father, produced a popular book, *Nerja—Balcón de Europa.*

Their attractive, comfortable, recently remodeled apartments are priced on a daily basis, but no reservations are accepted for less than a week. Each has a bedroom with twin beds and a living room, with daily maid service. The lowest rates are charged from January through March. Rates peak in July, August, and September. Apartments cost 1,200 pesetas ($8.40) per day in winter, rising to 3,000 pesetas ($21) per day in summer. The apartments are for two persons. It is closed in November.

WHERE TO DINE: **Pepe Rico Restaurant,** 28 Almirante Ferrándiz (tel. 52-02-47), was established in 1966 and is today one of the finest places for food in Nerja. It's run by Robert and Kathy Holder, who also rent apartments (see above). It is a gleaming white, Spanish-style building right on the street, with grill windows and little balconies. The rooms open onto a long rear balcony, overlooking a flower-filled courtyard. Dining is in a tavern-style room, half wood paneled, with handmade wooden chairs, rough plaster walls, and ivy vines. These vines creep in from the patio, where you can also order meals al fresco. Only dinner is served, and it's offered daily from 7:30 until 10 p.m. However, the restaurant shuts down on Thursday and is closed from the end of October until the middle of December.

Holder himself does the cooking with the help of one chef. The menu is international, and offers a separate specialty of the day, which might be a Spanish, German, Swiss, or French dish. These range from the Holders' own cold almond-and-garlic soup to Andalusian gazpacho, available only in the summertime. The list of hor d'oeuvres is impressive—Pepe Rico salad, smoked swordfish, an elegant selection, or else the pâté maison. Filet of pork, served Nerja style, and Hungarian kebab are popular main dishes. Also favored is the trout with crisp almonds. Considering the quality of the food, these prices are extremely reasonable—that is, from 2,500 pesetas ($17.50) for a meal. You could spend more, of course, if you order more expensively priced main dishes, such as roast pheasant with brandy cream sauce. Closed Thursday.

Portofino, 4 Puerta del Mar (tel. 52-01-50). For many visitors, this restaurant may offer just the ambience they're looking for, particularly if they crave well-prepared food, a sweeping view of the sea, and a tasteful but whimsical decor stressing strong sunlight and different shades of pink and white. Since the death of her Italian husband, the French-born owner, Theresa Torriglia, has maintained a personal stamp on virtually everything inside. The open hearth greets you near the front entrance, and white slipcovers cover the comfortable chairs pulled around it. Meals are eaten either behind the shelter of large sheets of glass or on the open terrace at the edge of the bay. Menu specialties include grilled veal, lamb, dorado, filet of beef béarnaise, a soup of the day, pâté of the chef, crayfish cocktail, and temptingly rich dessert profiteroles. A menú del día costs 1,600 pesetas ($11.20), while à la carte meals usually cost upward of 2,500 pesetas ($17.50). The Portofino is open only from March until November, during which time Theresa rents out about a dozen rooms which are usually booked long in advance for high-season occupancy. They cost 3,800 pesetas ($26.60) in a double and 3,000 pesetas ($21) in a single.

Restaurant Rey Alfonso, Paseo Balcón de Europa (tel. 52-01-95). Few of the visitors to the Balcón de Europa realize that they're standing directly above one of the better restaurants in town. The entrance to this panoramic dining room is at the bottom of a flight of stairs skirting some of the most dramatic rock formations along the coast. It is one of the most popular restaurants in Nerja, one whose menu doesn't hold many surprises but whose view, ambience, and clientele make it worthwhile. The establishment welcomes customers into the bar area if they don't want a full meal. If they do, menu specialties include paella valenciana, Cuban-style rice, five different preparations of sole (including everything from grilled to meunière), several versions of tournedos and entrecôte, beef Stroganoff, fondue bourguignonne, crayfish in whisky sauce, and, for dessert, crêpes Suzette. Meals here begin at around 2,000 pesetas ($14). The establishment is open for lunch and dinner daily except Wednesday.

Casa Luque, 2 Plaza de los Martíres (tel. 52-10-04), looks more like a dignified private villa than a restaurant, especially since its impressive canopied and balconied façade opens onto a sycamore-lined village square a few steps from the Balcón de Europa. The interior has an Andalusian courtyard that may make you want to linger over your meal, which might include pâté maison with raspberry sauce, shoulder of ham, osso buco, pork filet, hot pepper chicken Casanova, a full array of grilled meats, and a limited selection of fish, including grilled Mediterranean grouper. Full meals begin at 2,700 pesetas ($18.90) and will be supervised by the watchful eye of the owner. The restaurant is closed on Thursday, and for a few weeks sometime during the year on dates rarely specified long in advance.

Casa Paco y Eva, 50 Alemania (tel. 52-15-24), is a tavern restaurant where the first thing you may notice are groupings of fresh flowers set onto each of the wooden tables. It's on the ground floor of an apartment building, about a five-minute walk from the Balcón, in a relatively unfashionable part of town. However, once you're seated on one of the wood and leather chairs, tasting the array of house specialties, you'll forget about the location. Many of the featured menu items are seafood and include a fish soup, crayfish prepared in several different ways, and a house salad with more than its share of your daily vitamins. Full meals cost around 3,100 pesetas ($21.70), served daily in summer and daily except Thursday in winter.

THE CAVE OF NERJA: The most popular outing from Málaga, or Nerja itself, is to the **Cueva de Nerja,** which scientists believe was inhabited perhaps from 100,000 to 40,000 B.C. This prehistoric freakishly shaped stalactite and stalagmite cave lay hidden from the world as late as 1959, when it was exposed by a handful of men on a routine exploring mission from the nearby hamlet of Maro.

When fully opened, it revealed a wealth of treasures left from the days of the cave-dwellers, including some paleolithic paintings believed to be as old as 15,000 years. The paintings depict animals such as horses and deer, but as of this writing are not open to public view. The archeological museum in the cave contains a number of prehistoric artifacts. By all means, walk through its stupendous galleries, considered to resemble a drippy Gothic cathedral. In the **Hall of the Cataclysm,** the ceiling soars to a height of about 200 feet. From May 1 to September 1, hours are 9:30 a.m. to 9 p.m. Otherwise, the caves are open from 10 a.m. to 1:30 p.m. and 4 to 7 p.m. Admission is 175 pesetas ($1.23).

Nerja-bound buses leave from the Plaza Queipo de Llano in Málaga at 10 a.m. and again at noon, returning at 3 and 4:45 p.m. *Be warned:* The bus trip takes two hours each way, as the bus stops again and again between Málaga and Nerja.

12. Almería

This town was once known as the Spanish Hollywood. Its light is so pure and bright that it attracted a large colony of film people in past years who made epics in and around the town. When the celluloid folk aren't round, and you don't see as much of them these days, Almería can be dull. At first it appears to belong to a stretch of North African landscape. Actually it lies at the far eastern stretch of the Costa del Sol, a frontier outpost for many motorists traveling to and from Granada and Torremolinos.

This hot, provincial capital is dominated by the **Alcazaba,** its Moorish castle, and the **Castle of San Cristóbal.** Undoubtedly the most Oriental-looking city in southern Spain, it still reflects its Andalusian heritage as well in its narrow streets and white houses ending in terraces. To the Arabs it was known as the "Mirror of the Sea." Flowers grow abundantly, and orange groves and palm trees give the city a certain grace. Otherwise, most visitors find it hot and dirty.

The province of Almería is traversed by a series of high mountains, separated by narrow valleys, giving it a rugged relief. The coast is high and rocky.

Mini-Hollywood, Highway N340, lies in the small town of Tabernas between Almería and Murcia. Once upon a time, Hollywood's westerns were filmed in the Mohave Desert close to the California cities that provided the stunt men. Later, the producers of the "spaghetti westerns" of the '60s crossed the Atlantic toward the dusty plains of Spain. In time the filming of such epics as *Conan the Barbarian, Lawrence of Arabia,* and portions of *Reds* was also done here. Today, since movie audiences no longer seem to appreciate westerns as much as they once did, the set constructed by Sergio Leone some 22 years ago has been transformed into a tourist attraction where desperadoes are thrown through barroom doors every day at regularly scheduled brawls. There's a performance of violent and dastardly deeds twice a day. The rest of the time, it's possible to rent a horse and costume and ride through the main street of the re-created town past the sets where holdups and bank robberies used to be filmed with slightly more expensive equipment than your nephew's Kodak.

Today, nothing will prevent you from snapping away at Junior perched on top of Hi-ho Silver or renting a costume and getting a cowboy's-eye view yourself. Independent visitors pay around 175 pesetas ($1.23) for admission, although tours from Almería on Saturday at 3 p.m. are available from any Almería tourist agency at a price of 1,295 pesetas ($9.07) per person.

WHERE TO STAY: A suitable hotel is the **Costasol,** 58 Paseo de Almería (tel. 23-40-11), which is modern and functional, offering reasonable comfort. It doesn't have a restaurant, serving breakfast only, at an extra charge. The first-class hotel is in the center of town, and makes a decent overnight stop. It charges 4,000 pesetas ($28) in a single, 5,500 pesetas ($38.50) in a double. Most units contain a private bath or shower.

Residencia Nixar, 14 Antonio Vico (tel. 23-72-55), supplies a warm welcome and adequate, clean rooms, some with bath. Doubles rent for 1,800 pesetas ($12.60) to 2,800 pesetas ($19.60), depending on the plumbing, singles going for 1,400 pesetas ($9.80). Only breakfast is served.

WHERE TO DINE: **Rincón de Juan Pedro,** 6 Plaza del Carmen (tel. 23-53-79), is the best place to dine in Almería, and it can be expensive too, depending on what you order. Regional cookery is featured, and the atmosphere is immaculate, inviting, and pleasant enough. Located in a coastal province, the restaurant relies heavily on a varied fish repertoire, its typical dishes served with olive oil and plenty of spices. The cuisine is not only rich, but the ingredients are well prepared. In season, you might be able to order partridge, prepared in many different ways. Set meals begin at 1,800 pesetas ($12.60), although if you order à la carte your tab could easily reach 2,800 pesetas ($19.60).

Imperial Restaurant, 5 Puerta de Purchena (tel. 23-17-40), on the main square of the town, goes through a triangle at the intersection, giving it entrances on two streets. Run by Cristóbal Castillo, the air-conditioned restaurant has a menú del casa for 1,000 pesetas ($7), or if you order à la carte, expect to spend from 1,800 pesetas ($12.60). The Imperial specializes in fish and shellfish, with such appetizers as shellfish soup and fried fish. You might select as a main dish a large plateful of squid, flounder, and some other fried fish, unless you prefer the beef with red peppers or roast pork or veal. For dessert, I recommend the soufflé Imperial.

Chapter IX

VALENCIA AND THE COSTA BLANCA

1. Valencia
2. Benidorm
3. Alicante
4. Elche
5. Murcia

VALENCIA AND PARTICULARLY the Costa Blanca are Johnny-come-latelies in Spain's beach resort sweepstakes. As such, they are picking up a lot of the overflow from the more popular and extremely overcrowded Costa del Sol and Costa Brava, their chief competitors.

The Costa Blanca begins rather unappealingly at Valencia, but improves considerably as it winds its way south toward Alicante. It is dotted with little fishing villages and resorts known chiefly to vacationing Europeans or Spaniards.

Every coastal visitor to Spain seems to make it to **Valencia:** it's on the road to so many other points. But **Benidorm,** on the other hand, is more fitting for a longer stay. The success of Benidorm is fairly recent. It's the old story of Torremolinos again—a fishing village turned into an international resort.

Alicante is the official capital of the Costa Blanca. This provincial city enjoys a reputation as a winter resort because of its mild Mediterranean climate. **Murcia** is inland, but on the main road to the Costa del Sol; consequently, hordes of motorists pass through it. It makes for a pleasant stopover, as it's one of the most interesting cities in the Levante, a loose term, meaning east, often used to describe this part of Spain.

1. Valencia

The charms of Valencia—or lack of them—have been much debated. There are those who claim the city, where El Cid chased out the Moors, is one of the most beautiful on the Mediterranean. Others write it off as drab, provincial, and industrial. The truth lies somewhere in between.

Set in the midst of orange trees, and rice paddies, Valencia sidles up to Barcelona and Madrid for the title of Spain's third city. Admittedly, its reputation as a romantic city seems to be justified more by its past than its present looks. At one time, for instance, it was a walled city, and was believed to have been founded by the Romans.

Hidden between the modern office buildings and monotonous apartment-

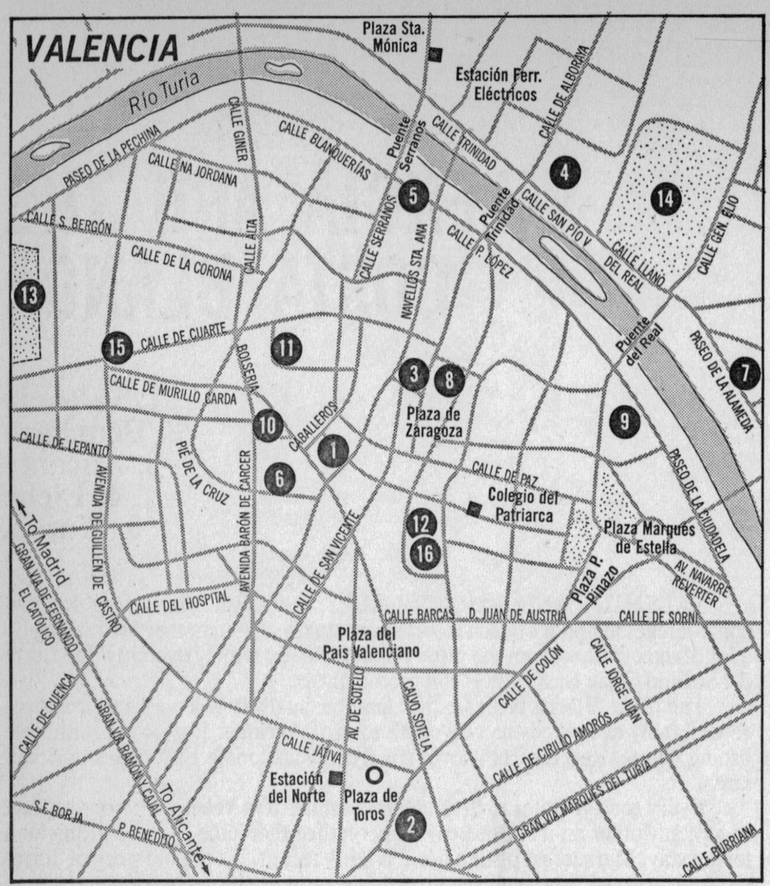

KEY TO NUMBERED SIGHTS:

1 La Lonja
2 Bullfighting Museum
3 Cathedral
4 Fine Arts Museum
5 Torres de Serranos
6 Mercado Central
7 Palacio de la Generalidad
8 Palacio Arzobispal
9 Convento de Santo Domingo
10 Santos Juanes
11 San Nicolás
12 Palacio del Marqués Dos Aguas
13 Botanical Garden
14 Royal Gardens
15 Torres de Cuarte
16 Ceramics Museum

house architecture are considerable remains of its illustrious past. However, nature, in the way of floods, and man, in the way of war, have been cruel to Valencia. The Valencianos have torn down a lot of buildings that today would be considered architectural treasures. But they are a determined and industrious people; you may recall that Valencia, the capital of the Loyalists, was the last to succumb to Franco's troops.

In the evening the city assumes a festive air, as throngs fill the streets for their nightly promenade. The scene is the liveliest at the central **Plaza del País Valenciano,** where you can walk through a heavily scented flower market.

With its life and vitality, Valencia makes for a suitable stopover, either on the way north from the Costa del Sol or south from Barcelona. However, its beach area, two miles away, is somewhat shabby—definitely third rate.

WHERE TO STAY: You have your choice of living inside the city or by the sea. I'll begin with my top recommendations.

Hotel Oltra, 4 Plaza País Valencia (tel. 352-06-12). Many of its almost 100 bedrooms overlook the colorful square below, which many residents consider the geographic center of town. Each of the air-conditioned bedrooms has its own bath and a freshly renovated look. Singles cost 3,800 pesetas ($26.60), doubles 5,800 pesetas ($40.60). There's no restaurant on the premises, but a cafetería serves drinks and light meals.

Llar, 46 Colón (tel. 352-84-60), fills a gap in the accommodation picture in Valencia. Built in 1967, the Llar was awarded three stars by the government, yet it charges reasonable rates. You pay 4,500 pesetas ($31.50) in a double room with private bath, 3,500 pesetas ($24.50) in a single, also with private bath. The Spanish modern lounge is decorated with tasteful and comfortable armchairs; a wrought-iron divider separates it from the bar. *Note:* Rooms in the back tend to be very stuffy (there's no air conditioning), and those facing the street noisy. So you'll have to choose which bothers you least.

Hotel Inglés, 6 Marqués de Dos Aguas (tel. 351-64-26), is for traditionalists. Placed in the heart of old Valencia, it stands right opposite a churrigueresque palace. The turn-of-the-century hotel has aged well by dint of care and respect. Most of its bedrooms have clear views of the tree-lined street below, and offer many old-fashioned comforts. The charge is 6,000 pesetas ($42) in a double room with private bath. No singles are available. The lounge and dining room have been nicely kept; the old furnishings have been retained—chandeliers, gilt mirrors, provincial armchairs, and murals. Spaniards who want the best of restrained service have been stopping here for years.

Sorolla, 5 Convento Santa Clara (tel. 352-33-92), is named after the famous Spanish painter. Built in 1968, it is a seven-floor modern hotel in the center of the city, near the Plaza del País Valenciano and the Plaza de Toros. Most of its 50 bedrooms have a narrow balcony and compactly placed and utilitarian furnishings. Comfort, not style, is the keynote, and everything is kept scrupulously clean. A double with private bath rents for 5,200 pesetas ($36.40); singles, also with baths, cost a peak 3,200 pesetas ($22.40). No breakfast is served.

Hotel Metropol, 23 Játiva (tel. 351-26-12), a three-star choice, is in front of the railway station, directly opposite the bullring, and only two blocks from the Plaza del País Valenciano. At first glance one would never suspect the hotel is so modern and well organized inside; its exterior suggests the architecture of a century ago, when builders incorporated balconies with tall French doors opening onto them. Many of the bedrooms are unusually large, even for Spain, and they are well furnished. Wall-to-wall draperies separate the sleeping area from the living room and its upholstered pieces. All the double rooms contain a private bath and cost 5,500 pesetas ($38.50) nightly. Singles with bath pay a top 4,500 pesetas ($31.50). All along the front of the Metropol are tables and chairs set out for drinks and meals.

Hotel Bristol, 3 Abadía San Martín (tel. 352-11-76), is clean, comfortable, and on a quietly secluded narrow street in the older part of the city, near the Church of San Martín. It is only a three-minute walk to the central shopping district. All of the doubles have either a private tub bath or shower, and rent for 5,000 pesetas ($35). Eight singles with bath or shower are available at 3,200 pesetas ($22.40).

Hostal Residencia Bisbal, 9 Pie de la Cruz (tel. 331-70-84), is conveniently located in the old city near the market and other points of interest. It is run by the owners, a husband and wife team who speak English and see to it that their place is kept sparkling clean. Doubles with shower cost 2,000 pesetas ($14), doubles with bath 2,700 pesetas ($18.90), plus tax. No meals are served, but this is no hardship as the hostal is near numerous bars and restaurants.

Sleeping by the Sea

The **Playa de Levante,** the Valencian beach, is about two miles from the city. It might be equally at home on the New Jersey coast. On the **Avenida de Neptuno** is a string of hotels, restaurants, and bathhouses, their backs facing the sands and the sea. The restaurants along here are expensive, the hotels inexpensive (many rooms cost what you'd pay for locker space at some resorts on either the French or Italian Riviera).

Hostal Chicote, 34 Avenida de Neptuno (tel. 371-61-51), is a fine place to stay when the temperature in the city starts keeping your plate of Valencian paella hot all evening. Decidedly unchic, as are all the "boarding houses" here, the 19-room Chicote offers rooms that are bare but clean, fairly comfortable, and a bargain. Most of the doubles contain a private shower bath and cost 3,200 pesetas ($22.40) nightly. Singles with shower bath rent for 2,200 pesetas ($15.40).

A Big Splurge for Drivers

The **Parador Nacional "Luís Vives,"** Carretera de Alicante, Km 6 (tel. 323-68-50), at El Saler, about 12 miles south of Valencia, is a government-owned and -operated parador, created by some of Spain's best architects and decorators. Many of the Spanish paradors try to evoke the romance and pageantry of medieva; Spain; but this one prefers to be modern, in a restrained and classic way. A double with private bath and terrace rents for 10,500 pesetas ($73.50).

The bedrooms are mammoth (ask for the ones at the back), with soft beds and large baths and "his and her" toilets. The furnishings throughout incorporate natural wood, leather, and homespun fabrics.

The air-conditioned parador is right on the coast, in the midst of sand dunes and a golf course. The oceanside terrace, wide and handsome, has a pathway leading through the dunes to the ever-pounding surf—one's own private beach. In all, it's just like a country club. Inside, the lounges are intimate and comfortable. The dining room on the ground floor has a good view; the kitchen manages to turn out distinguished food, with a big dinner costing 2,200 pesetas ($15.40).

WHERE TO DINE: Valencia has a lot of big sprawling restaurants, many emphasizing those combination plates that are popular in Europe. Often the hotels offer good enough dining; but the sidewalk-café restaurants usually have greater life and poorer food, generally speaking. The one dish to have in Valencia is paella—it's at home here. Follow the wafting aromas to:

Casa Cesáreo, 15 Guillén de Castro (tel. 351-42-14), is a discovery, an old-world tavern where you can eat very well. This long-established restaurant, within walking distance of the bullring and railway station, is on three floors. On the street level are counters and tables. If you order at the counter, prices are considerably cheaper—you're given a choice on the menu of *mostrador* (counter) or *mesa* (table). The menú del día—three plates, including bread and wine—costs 1,050 pesetas ($7.35) at the counter. Chef's specialties (ordered at the table) include Valencian paella, grilled red mullet, mariscada Cesáreo, and half a chicken cooked with garlic. For a complete meal on the à la carte menu, the charge is likely to range from 1,800 pesetas ($12.60). The Casa Cesáreo features a cuisine as typically Spanish as flamenco. Its walls are tile, its furnishings provincial, its guests colorful—in all, a memorable experience.

Restaurant Chapo, 3 Joaquín Costa (tel. 334-50-12). There's only a handful of tables within its air-conditioned interior, and, because of its size, you seem to get more personal service along with a tempting cuisine. Sometimes music is presented in the evening. Ingredients for the day's specials are exhibited in refrigerated cases, forming part of the decor. Menus depend on the shopping of the day. You might enjoy suckling pig (crisp roasted) or baby lamb with herbs, perhaps one of the fresh salad platters and a selection from the day's catch. Full meals cost from 1,500 pesetas ($10.50) and are served daily except Saturday at noon and Sunday in the evening.

El Cachirulo, 3 Cronista Almela y Vives (tel. 361-13-15). Connoisseurs of Aragonese decor and cuisine will quickly recognize that this restaurant is a specialist in both. You'll dine amid a restrained rusticity which some visitors describe as neo-Gothic, but which others describe as country style. There's an open fireplace, plus lots of scattered ceramics, and an attention to cuisine which most diners find satisfying. Your meal might include salmon, several preparations of roast pork and lamb, a wide array of Mediterranean fish dishes, rich desserts, and a full selection of regional wines. Full meals cost from 2,000 pesetas ($15.40) and are served daily except on Sunday night.

Barrachina, 2 Plaza del Pás Valenciano (tel. 351-87-50), is Valencia's super-deli. Only this is also a restaurant. The Barrachina must have one of the best selections of goodies in all of Spain; it's certainly got room for them, as it spreads maze-like over a whole block. Outside are café chairs and tables; inside are such specialties as sweets and candies, croissants, apple tarts, milkshakes (*batidos*) in all flavors, and about 25 combination plates. The place has a bit of a Coney Island atmosphere to it, right down to the odor of frying sweets. Of course there's sangría and horchata (which Valencia is famous for), hot dogs and sandwiches, cakes, and glazed fruit. Napoleons (called *mil-hojas* in Spain) are good as are the éclairs with whipped-cream filling (called *palonata*). There are several counters to sit at, and upstairs in a belle époque terrace are more chairs and tables.

There's also a separate restaurant which is open till 2 a.m. Here for 1,800 pesetas ($12.60), you get a salad, gazpacho, or other soup; macaroni gratin; hake or a quarter chicken; bread; wine or beer; and one of the excellent desserts. The least expensive paella is served with chicken, and you'll pay more for the version with shellfish. At the Barrachina counter, there's a daily combination plate special, which includes an omelet, veal steak with tomatoes and lettuce, plus bread, dessert, and wine.

Lionel, 9 Pizarro (tel. 351-65-66), is named after its owner, Lionel Tarzaón. This pleasant restaurant is filled with antique lamps and accessories. The competent cuisine offers good value at around 2,500 pesetas ($17.50) per meal. It could include such specialties as veal Orloff, beef filet, and duckling. The interior is air-conditioned, and your meal may depend on what's available as a daily special. Lionel is closed Sunday night.

La Strada, 22 Isabel la Católica (tel. 351-34-85). By this establishment's name you'd assume that most of the specialties would be Italian, but that's only partially true. Since the restaurant was taken over by Lionel, the cuisine has shifted to Valencian dishes based on the rice and meats available in the region. A fixed-price meal is offered every day for a reasonable 1,800 pesetas ($12.60), while à la carte meals cost around 3,000 pesetas ($21). You might enjoy the filet of beef Mexican style or one of the fish plates. La Strada, which is air-conditioned, closes for Saturday lunch and Sunday dinner.

Horchaterías

When in Valencia, you should stop at least once in one of the city's famous horchaterías, a kind of oldtime café where Valencianos drink that milky, nut-flavored beverage called horchata. The two best known horchaterías are the turn-of-the-century **El Siglo,** 11 Calle Santa Catalina (tel. 331-84-66), serving regular horchata from 85 pesetas (60¢), or the **Horchatería Santa Catalina,** 6 Calle Santa Catalina (tel. 332-22-28), which, a large plaque on a table assures us, was visited by royalty in 1903. Both places are open till about 9:30 p.m.

THE SIGHTS: From churrigueresque palaces to colorful city markets to exquisitely styled Gothic buildings, Valencia offers a number of important historical attractions, all of which can be covered in a day. I'll begin with:

The Cathedral (La Seo)

In the heart of the city, at the Plaza de la Virgen, this 13th-century cathedral, La Seo, represents a number of diversified styles. But the Gothic wins out. Its huge arches have been restored, and in back is a handsome domed basilica. Fortunate are those who visit it during one of the incense-burning ceremonies, a ritual little changed since the Middle Ages.

Of all the claims made by Spanish or Italian cathedrals, few exceed this one in Valencia. The cathedral for the past 500 years has had in its possession what it claims is the Holy Grail, that chalice used by Christ at the Last Supper. The subject of countless legends, the Holy Grail traditionally was used by Joseph of Arimathea to collect drops of Christ's blood as they fell from his body on the cross. It looms large in Sir Thomas Malory's *Mort d' Arthur,* Tennyson's *Idylls of the King,* and Wagner's *Parsifal.* In relatively recent times it got the Hollywood treatment in *The Silver Chalice.*

After seeing the cathedral, you can scale an uncompleted Gothic tower—known as **Miguelete**—for a panoramic view of the city and the fertile **Huerta** beyond. This octagonal tower is approximately 155 feet high. It is open from 10:30 a.m. to 1 p.m. and 5 to 8 p.m. weekdays. Admission is 75 pesetas (53¢). You may visit the **museum** of the cathedral (two works by Goya) from 10 a.m. to 1 p.m. and 4 to 7 p.m. The cathedral is free, but it costs 50 pesetas (35¢) for the museum.

Generalidad

Built in the 15th and 16th centuries, this palace at Plaza de la Virgen with its two square towers is one of the most fascinating in Spain. It has been handsomely furnished and restored, and is known for its carved wooden gallery. A Mediterranean Gothic building, this place is the headquarters of the Provincial Court, and may be visited with permission from the Secretaría de la Diputación (tel. 331-37-90). It is on the Calle de Caballeros in the old aristocratic quarter of Valencia.

La Lonja

At the Plaza del Mercado is the most splendid example of secular Gothic in Spain, completed in the 15th century. A beautiful, tasteful building, La Lonja has twisted spiral columns inside and stained-glass windows. Once it was a silk market. It may be visited (free) from 10 a.m. to 2 p.m. and 4 to 6 p.m. It is closed weekends and holidays.

The City Market (Mercado Central)

Across the street from La Lonja is one of the most fascinating city markets you're likely to encounter anywhere. When you see its more than 1,200 stalls (a rough estimate), you may never want to shop in a supermarket again. It has everything: dried herbs, homemade soup, black blood sausage, plucked poulets. To see the women of Valencia shop is sight enough. The market is in a giant railway station–like building, of stained glass, no less.

Ceramics Museum (Museo Nacional de Cerámico)

At the Palace del Marqués de Dos Aguas (tel. 351-63-92), you can see what looks like a surrealist decorator's masterpiece: a palace of rococo and churrigueresque. A bizarre building, its rooms compete with their exhibits. Next door to the Hotel Inglés, the palace has a vast collection of ceramics: lizards on plates, frogs on the backs of lambs. In addition, it has a Gallery of Humorists, with caricatures of everybody from Einstein on down. In keeping with its theme of unrelated items, it has a carriage museum and armor room downstairs. It may be visited from 10 a.m. to 2 p.m. and 4 to 6 p.m. daily except on Monday when it's closed, and on holidays when hours are from 10 a.m. to 2 p.m. The price of admission is 200 pesetas ($1.40).

Fine Arts Museum (Museo de Bellas Artes)

A treasure house of paintings and sculpture stands on the north bank of the Turia River, reached on the Calle de San Pío V. The collection is rich in Flemish artists, as well as the home-grown variety from Valencia—the latter school reflected especially in the 14th- and 15th-century Valencia "primitives." On the ground floor the archeological collection is displayed, including early Iberian, Roman, and early Christian finds. The most celebrated painting is a self-portrait by Velázquez, and you'll also see a whole room filled with works by Goya. Other paintings are by Morales, El Greco, Ribera, Murillo, Pinturicchio, Sorolla, and "El Bosco" (Bosch). Furthermore, the museum was given some important sculpture by Mariano Benlliure. Of special interest is a salon devoted to the works of contemporary Valencian painters. The visiting hours are from 10 a.m. to 2 p.m. and 4 to 6 p.m. Tuesday to Saturday; from 10 a.m. to 2 p.m. on Sunday and holidays; closed Monday. Admission is 200 pesetas ($1.40).

OUT-OF-TOWN EXCURSIONS: A great deal of the charm of Valencia is to be found in its environs, particularly in the fertile **Huerta** and the **Albufera** (a freshwater lake south of the city). The Huerta is Valencia's giant orchard of orange trees, alongside its rice paddies. The rice is grown here for Valencian paella. A trip makes for a pleasant afternoon or morning outing. It can be tied in with a visit to Albufera's **El Saler** beach (far superior to the Levante).

Behind the main street is a tiny docking area, where it's possible to board boats for a cruise of the lake. Negotiate with the owner about price.

VALENCIAN NIGHTLIFE: **Barcas 7,** 7 Barcas (tel. 352-12-33) seems isolated among the many banks and office buildings that surround it in the heart of town. The array of drinks can be augmented with small servings of paella at the stand-up bar. Tapas cost from 75 pesetas (53¢) up. At night there is often live music for the entertainment of guests. Despite the restaurant in back, where beef filet and veal dishes are house specialties, the establishment is more popular as a bar than as a restaurant.

Evening, 3 Joaquin Costa (tel. 334-50-12), is a bar where the nighttime ambience is heightened with South American music. Irish coffee might be a late-night drink you'll enjoy. Drinks begin at 350 pesetas ($2.45).

Mister Chus, 3 Conde Salvatierra (tel. 352-68-61). Despite its Chinese name, the orange and black decor of this popular disco couldn't be more Spanish. Clusters of sofas and chairs are placed between the carpeted walls. The music is upbeat, recent, and danceable, and the crowd often tends to be attractively mature. Drinks average 800 pesetas ($5.60). The rituals go on every night of the week except Monday.

Belle Époque, 8-10 Cuba (tel. 341-64-66), offers a place to drink, dance, chatter with friends, and appreciate the occasional drag show the management puts on. Because of the entertainment, drinks here cost around 1,800 pesetas ($12.60). It is open daily except Monday.

2. Benidorm

A gemütlich atmosphere prevails here as the yearly invasion from the north begins in late spring. Until it was discovered by the Germans, Benidorm was the tiniest of fishing villages. But in the summer, for every dozen natives, 12 dozen foreigners pour in. Long ago, the French and English also heard of its charm, its moderately priced hotels, and nightlife. It now awaits the Americans, who, so far, have just stuck a toe in the door.

The hotel builders of Benidorm must rock around the clock; you retire in the evening, and by the time you wake up, a new hotel has opened. Well, almost. Benidorm, because of its European influence, cracks through Spanish provincialism (or ignores it), and is the most sophisticated town this side of Torremolinos. It's recommended for stopovers or for longer stays—but reserve in advance for any stay between mid-June and September.

The town is reached by train from Alicante, also by bus from either Valencia or Alicante.

WHERE TO STAY: Benidorm, as mentioned, is increasingly being endowed with more and more hastily erected hotels—although no amount of building, it seems, can keep up with the popularity in the peak of the season. Pilgrims without reservations are practically laughed at when they innocently inquire for a room.

Since most of the hotel managers operate in a seller's market from June through September, they can slap the full-board requirement on their guests, despite protests by said guests that they simply don't want two stretch-your-girdle Spanish four-courses a day. The way to beat the board requirement is to book into one of my residencia recommendations. But residencias are rare in Benidorm. Every hotel proprietor either hires a chef, or fancies himself one . . . or is forced into giving the job to his mother-in-law.

I've avoided the hotels springing up along the coastal road, after having spent sleepless nights in them, watching and listening to the rumbling trucks going back and forth between Barcelona and the road south.

Hotel Cimbel, Avenida Europa (tel. 85-21-00). It sits on the sands of one of the most popular beaches in town, giving it tremendous appeal for sunworshippers who step virtually from the lobby onto the sands. Behind its balconied façade are around 150 comfortably furnished bedrooms, each with a full bath, air conditioning, and many extra touches. Considered a glamorous address by the resort's habitués, it charges 5,000 pesetas ($35) in a single, 9,000 pesetas ($63) in a double. There's a swimming pool, plus a parking garage and a disco on the premises, forming a complete resort complex.

Hotel La Peña, Avenida Gerona (tel. 85-06-94), is a modern hotel with 95 comfortable accommodations. Its bedrooms are streamlined, utilizing contemporary furnishings that, in part, were inspired by Spanish antiques. All of the rooms have air conditioning, plus telephone, large built-in wardrobes, and a functional and attractive bath. The price is 3,200 pesetas ($22.40) to 5,200 pesetas ($36.40) for a double room, 2,600 pesetas ($18.20) in a single. The lounge is restrained (in a nice sense), spacious and cool; the terrace opens onto a long private swimming pool, in case you prefer fresh water. In all, there are six floors of sea-view rooms with balconies.

Hotel Les Dunes, Avenida de Madrid (tel. 85-24-00), is like a big beach club. Built in 1958 on the Playa de Levante, this 110-room (all with private tub or shower), completely modern hotel is suitable for those who like plenty of activity, such as swimming . . . or whatever. In overall quality, the fairly spacious but simple bedrooms are above reproach. Many have a Juliet balcony opening onto Benidorm's greatest Romeo, the almost guaranteed sunshine. A guest pays 6,000 pesetas ($42) for a double room. Les Dunes is graced with a front-terrace swimming pool, near which is the dining area. Two bars take care of liquid sustenance. The hotel remains open all year (off-season reductions granted from November through February), and is heavily booked in summer by vacationers from Bristol, Bath, and Birmingham.

Hotel Brisa, Playa de Levante (tel. 85-54-00). From its beachfront perch, it is spotless, soulless, and simple, heavily outfitted with plumbing (private bath or shower in every room). This is a reasonable accommodation for both young and old moderns. The double rooms go for 3,200 pesetas ($22.40) to 3,800 pesetas ($26.60) a night, singles for 2,800 pesetas ($19.60). The rooms are bright, airy, and contain the necessary gadgets. There is elevator service, and a dining room where you can order one main meal a day for 1,500 pesetas ($10.50) per person extra. Its proudest feature is its swimming pool. The Brisa is open year round.

Residencia Don José, 2 Carretera del Alt (tel. 85-50-50), is rare as the dodo, in that it was built as a residencia to serve only breakfast—a definite plus as this pleasant little hotel is in the hub of a district containing Benidorm's best budget restaurants (and some intriguing, but touristy, shops). Lying a short walk from the sea, the Don José is a white brick multibalconied building. Its neat and clean bedrooms, up-to-date and attractively furnished, rent for 3,500 pesetas ($24.50) daily for doubles with private bath, 2,800 pesetas ($19.60) for singles. The hotel closes down from October till March.

Hotel Canfali, 1 Plaza de San Jaime (tel. 85-08-18), is a seaside villa, one of the best of the smaller hotels. Its position is a scene-stealer—at the end of the esplanade, perched on a low cliff, with a staircase winding down to the beach. The Canfali's functional, inviting doubles with private bath (either shower or tub) go for 4,200 pesetas ($29.40) to 4,800 pesetas ($33.60), the more expensive offering balconies with sea view. The hotel, open from April through October, is spacious and comfortable, but undistinguished in decor. Terraces overlook the sea, a perfect spot for morning coffee.

Hotel Levante, 4 Avenida de Martínez Alejos (tel. 85-88-12), a one-star hotel, won't romance you with glamour or special comforts—but its prices might. One of the older hotels of Benidorm—built back in the days (1958) when the resort was a target for German neocolonial activities—the Levante prices its doubles at only 2,500 pesetas ($17.50). Some of the rooms have a shower (no toilet); others have a water basin only. A few singles contain private bath, renting for 2,000 pesetas ($14). The hotel's utter simplicity is not helped by a formidable use of chrome and plastic, although the rooms open interestingly onto a courtyard. The hotel is open all year.

The Pick of the Pensions

Residencia Bristol, 1 Avenida de Martínez Alejos (tel. 85-40-28), is a winning little (30 rooms) one-star pension in the heart of Benidorm. Open from April to October, it is sheltered in a modernized elevator building that contains fairly comfortable bedrooms renting for 2,500 pesetas ($17.50) a night to couples (with private bath). However, most of the other adequately furnished bedrooms contain a shower (but no toilet), and these are offered at a reduced rate. Singles, for example, are only 1,800 pesetas ($12.60). The best rooms, parceled out on a first-come, first-served basis, are the front locations with the view.

Hostal del Mar, 4 Pintor Lozano (tel. 85-08-21), is only half a block away from the Playa de Levante. This homey, friendly hotel and restaurant has 23 rooms providing the bare essentials for overnighting. A double with bath rents for only 2,000 pesetas ($14), a single for 1,600 pesetas ($11.20). The hostal has a pleasant, old-world dining room. The tourist menu, costing 650 pesetas ($4.55), includes a special salad or consommé with egg, paella, pork chop, or chicken meunière.

On the Outskirts at Calpe

Paradero de Ifach, 50 Explanada del Puerto (tel. Calpe 83-03-00), is thrust out on the coast, 13 miles north of Benidorm, set back about two miles from the principal Valencia–Alicante highway. It huddles close to the giant Rock of Ifach (Alicante's Gibraltar). Built in the white flat-roofed North African style, the "paradero" offers sun-terrace living at moderate rates. Its living room is like a country home—traditional furnishings and groups of chairs arranged near the large sea-view window. Most of the 29 bedrooms are handsomely designed, making living here a pleasure. You pay 4,500 pesetas ($31.50) for a double room with bath, 4,000 pesetas ($28) in a room with a shower bath. The bedrooms can be quite special—some contain antiques. Perhaps you'll get a bed with a painted cut-out headboard and swan's neck footposts.

For dining, you can choose between a room with a beamed ceiling, an open fireplace, and red-and-white tablecloths, or the sun-room greenhouse, with its red tile floors, rows of arched windows overlooking the sea, a jungle of potted plants, hanging vines and ferns, and cages of singing birds. For dinner you pay 1,000 pesetas ($7) per person.

WHERE TO DINE: **La Caserola,** 7 Bruselas, Rincón de Loix (tel. 85-17-19), provides such northern specialties as fondue bourguignonne with a choice of five sauces, plus Spanish fish and rice dishes, but mainly it offers a French cuisine. The restaurant is on a quiet street at the edge of town. Filled with country-style accessories, it opens onto a warm-weather terrace. The medallions of veal gratinée are a good choice unless you prefer one of the fish plates. Full meals range from 1,800 pesetas ($12.60) up.

Restaurant Casa L'Esclau, Panaderos y San Miguel (tel. 85-64-15), is the kind of dining room which, if it doesn't remind you of Old Spain, will at least offer well-prepared regional dishes in a family-style atmosphere. There are no more than a dozen tables in the small place in the center of the old town. Owner

Juan Agullo receives deliveries of fresh fish daily, many of which go into his well-prepared specials. A popular dish is arroz a banda (paella without fish), and a caldero (a spicy form of fish stew) goes well with the house salads and the steamy rice dishes. Full meals cost 1,800 pesetas ($12.60) and up and are served every day.

BENIDORM NIGHTLIFE: As in Torremolinos, the nightlife in Benidorm has all the permanency of a sand castle. But here's the lay of the land as of this writing:

Benidorm Palace, Carreterra de Circunvalación (tel. 85-16-60), is considered one of the best discos of the region, partly because of its recently released music and its large dance floor, one end of which is reserved for the shows that the management occasionally brings in. There's an exterior garden for midnight trysts, expansive bars, and enough seating to allow customers to rest between dances. Drinks cost from 1,800 pesetas ($12.60).

El Calpi, 5 Plaza de la Constitución (tel. 85-30-97), is a popular tapas bar set in the middle of the old city. Many of the customers are from the neighborhood, here to enjoy a respite from the day's occupation as they sit at the outdoor tables in front. The on-tap beer can be a perfect accompaniment for the salty delicacies, most of which contain seafood. Examples are tuna with peppers, shrimp, crayfish, anchovies, oysters, and mussels. The place is closed Sunday throughout the year, plus Monday in summer. It's also closed in February.

International Club de Benidorm, 7 Avenida Alcoy (Edifício Iberia) (tel. 85-31-21). The nautical decor of this pub and snack restaurant (cafetería) is appropriate to its setting at the edge of the water. Despite that, it's only a few minutes' walk from the center of town and likely to be filled with well-heeled and relaxed clients enjoying Irish coffee and an array of cocktails. Drinks begin at 150 pesetas ($1.05).

3. Alicante

Often compared to Nice in France, Alicante for some visitors is the best all-around city in Spain. It is popular not only in summer but in winter, as it is one of the warmest spots on the Mediterranean Coast. Its position is 50 miles from Murcia to the north, and about 25 miles from Benidorm. There is direct rail service from Murcia, Valencia, and Granada, as well as extensive bus connections. If you're traveling up and down the Costa Blanca, it's better to stick to the buses, as they run more frequently.

With its wide, palm-lined avenues, it is a city that takes the promenade seriously in the early evening. The magnificent **Explanada de España** extends around part of the yacht harbor and also includes the great promenade under the palms with mosaic sidewalks. I suggest that you get out and walk it (or else jog), even if you're used to driving down to the corner in your hometown.

San Juan is the largest beach in Alicante, lying a short distance from the capital. A good promenade runs parallel to the sea, and it's lined with villas, hotels, and restaurants. The bay of Alicante has two capes, and on the bay is **Postiguet Beach.** The bay stretches all the way to the **Cape of Santa Pola,** a town with two good beaches, a 14th-century castle, and several seafood restaurants.

Like an amphitheater, Alicante rises from the seashore up a hill until it reaches the **Castle of Santa Bárbara** (tel. 20-51-00), which towers over the bay and the provincial capital. The Greeks called it "Akra Leuka" (White Peak), and its original defenses were believed to have been erected by the Carthaginians in 400 B.C. In time it was also used by the Romans and Arabs.

The size and grandeur of this fortress is evident in its moats, drawbridges, bastions with their embrasures and merlons, tunneled entrances, guardrooms, bakery, cisterns, underground storerooms, hospitals, batteries, powder stores, barracks, ruins of the former governor's quarters, the Matanza Tower and the Keep, high breastworks, deep dungeons, and barrel-vaulted entrance leading to the underground passage connecting the castle to the beach.

From here, there is a very impressive view over land and sea from the top of the castle. Access is either by asphalt road or by an elevator which one boards on the Explanada de España. In winter the castle is open from 9 a.m. to 7 p.m., in summer from 9 a.m. to 9 p.m. Admission is 75 pesetas (53¢) by elevator, 45 pesetas (32¢) by road.

Just north of the entrance to Santa Bárbara is the station of a 58-mile **narrow-gauge train** which takes people up along the sometimes wild, always beautiful rocky, sandy beach-lined coast to Denia.

The train passes through such places as Villajoyosa, Benidorm, Altea, and 26 other stations, almost all of which would be worth a visit. Just north along the coast, the first stations are at what appear to be endless sand beaches. Then you come to rocky inlets and ports which alternate with beaches. Various vacation houses and villages dot the landscape.

Now a tourist center, **Denia** is lively and bustling, stretching from the slopes of a hill to the seashore. It was inhabited by the Greeks, and its name, Denia, comes from an ancient temple that was dedicated to the goddess Diana. In the town hall, a building that dates from the beginning of the 16th century, there are remains of the temple. You'll also find the remnants of an old Iberian settlement and a great Moorish castle. Denia has fine beaches, and its fishing port is one of the best in the region.

Back in Alicante, you can explore on your own. I'd recommend checking out the **Barrio de Santa Cruz,** on the slopes of the Castle of Santa Bárbara. The section lies behind the cathedral and forms part of the **Villa Vieja** (as the old quarter of Alicante is called). It is a colorful sector with wrought-iron grilles on the windows, particularly the "bulging variety." Streets wind about, and one can view the entire harbor while dodging sheets hanging from the windows, or admire blocks of flowers.

In Alicante you'll also find several big and small plazas, some of which are paved with marble. The **Castillo de San Fernándo** has a panoramic view and can be visited during the day. It's not as awesome as Santa Bárbara, but impressive enough.

The city is characterized by its already-mentioned wide boulevards, all of which are clean and lined with shops and bookstores of every description. Alicante boasts seemingly unlimited shopping facilities, including its leading department store, Galerías Precíados, where you may find what you're seeking without being trampled to death by the mobs as in Madrid.

The traffic is easy-going—uncrowded and unhurried, so that one can wander about the city with a good chance of not getting killed. Along the way you'll encounter beautifully planted parks and apparently endless lines of palms and gardens. There are many pedestrian malls, some of them paved with marble or tile.

When it's time to eat you'll find shellfish and fish taking up a large part of the menu. Many restaurants that are close to the sea offer a wide variety of fish, as well as lobster and Dublin Bay prawns. The characteristic dish of Alicante is rice, which is served in many different ways. The most usual sauce is *aioli,* a kind of mayonnaise made from oil and garlic. Alicante rice is served with chicken, lean pork, and greens; there is an enormous variety of rice dishes with "fruits of the sea." But the greatest variety in the food line on the Costa Blanca is in desserts; Spanish nougat (*turrón de Alicante*) is the most popular of all.

WHERE TO STAY: Cristal, 11 López Torregrosa (tel. 20-96-00), is a seven-floor hotel with an all-glass façade, one of the best designed hotels to be erected in Alicante. Your bedroom (all have private bath) may have chalk-white walls, moss-green draperies, and matching counterpanes, beds set against the built-in headboards, telephone, reading lamps, service bell, and stereo music. Doubles rent for 4,100 pesetas ($28.70), singles for 2,400 pesetas ($16.80). In cooler months, there is central heating. The reception lounge is spacious, the comfortable furnishings arranged on islands of hand-loomed circular rugs. For drinks, there is a red and gold bar with low Chinese-style chairs and stools. The Cristal doesn't have a restaurant, but there's a snackbar on the premises. Built in the heart of Alicante, the hotel is, nevertheless, only a five-minute walk to the inner harbor and the esplanade.

Hotel Residencia Covadonga, 17 Plaza de los Luceros (tel. 20-28-44), offers 86 comfortable and spacious rooms and good service. It is in a good position with regard to the city's sights, the railway, buses, and the airport. Double rooms with bath rent for 4,200 pesetas ($29.40), and singles go for 3,000 pesetas ($21). The public rooms are roomy and inviting.

Residencia Navas, 26 Calle de las Navas (tel. 20-40-11), is a winner in the bargain sweepstakes in Alicante. Built in 1965, this 40-room hotel gets only a one-star rating from the government, but that is primarily because it serves only breakfast (a blessing really) and has only water basins in its fair-size single rooms —which rent, incidentally, for 1,000 pesetas ($7). Its clean, comfortable, and fairly handsome doubles with bath carry a price tag of 3,800 pesetas ($26.60). If you're determined to get blood out of every centavo, ask for one of the 24 doubles with water basin only—2,400 pesetas ($16.80) for two. Most rooms have their own balcony.

Portugal, 26 Portugal (tel. 22-32-44), opened in 1969, is modest and has 18 rooms spreading across its second floor. The accommodations are furnished in tasteful modern, and are kept immaculate. The most expensive doubles—those with private bath—go for 2,200 pesetas ($15.40). The few singles (with water basin only) rent for 1,200 pesetas ($8.40), whereas a double room with wash basin costs just 1,800 pesetas ($12.60). Only breakfast is provided, at extra cost. The Portugal is a corner hotel, one block from the bus station, about four blocks from the railway station, and a three-minute walk from the harbor.

Hotel Residencia San Remo, 30 Navas (tel. 20-95-00), is another low-budget selection. Most of its 20 bedrooms offer private bath. A white-plastered, seven-floor corner building, the residencia (breakfast only) offers clean, unpretentious, reasonably comfortable doubles with private bath for 2,800 pesetas ($19.60). Singles with wash basin cost 1,400 pesetas ($9.80); with private bath, 1,600 pesetas ($11.20). Some of the rooms have their own balcony.

WHERE TO DINE: Restaurant La Dársena, Muelle de Costa (Explanada de España) (tel. 20-75-89). Its glass-walled decor, recently renovated into a modern style, often reflects garrulous customers, but that's part of the fun. It's especially colorful at night, when everyone in town with something to celebrate seems to want to come in. If you decide on a meal here, order a drink and try to relax amid the hubbub. Paella is perhaps the best choice on the menu, and other rice dishes are commendable as well. A good one is prepared with duckling and green sauce. Full meals are served daily at lunch and dinner, except Sunday night and Monday. A complete meal will cost upward from 2,500 pesetas ($17.50).

Quo Vadis, 3 Plaza Santísma Faz (tel. 21-66-60), is considered one of the best restaurants in town. You'll pass through a sidewalk café and popular bar before reaching an air-conditioned dining room. There, amid a dignified country-style decor, you'll be able to watch the preparation of whatever you order, usually with touches of culinary theater. There's also an intimate terrace containing only about a dozen tables, each of which is covered with immaculate napery and candlelight. Menu specialties include a wide array of fresh seafood, including brochettes of sole, baked hake, shellfish, and such meat dishes as roast lamb with herbs, tournedos flambé with madeira, and a dessert specialty made with cream and ice cream (crêpes Brasil). Full meals cost from 2,200 pesetas ($15.40).

Pachá, 6 Haroldo Parres (tel. 21-19-38), is a pleasantly decorated restaurant whose dozen or so tables sit amid a country decor, which is appropriate to the establishment's location at the edge of the Plaza Estrella in the old city. Antonio Vilella, the owner and chef, produces house specialties, which are usually some form of rice dish laden with one or another kind of meat or the array of fish and shellfish that come steaming from the kitchen. You might enjoy the Catalán spinach or the eggplant in cream sauce as an accompaniment to your meat or fish, one of which is the entrecôte pizzaiola. Full meals begin at 1,800 pesetas ($12.60), although if you order the exotic forms of shellfish, the tab will go much higher. The restaurant is closed Wednesday.

Restaurant Jumillano, 64 César Elguezábal (tel. 21-29-64). The origins of this restaurant date from before World War II when it was a humble wine bar where a glass of local red cost half a peseta. Later, the place was upgraded to include the serving of food. Since the mid-'70s it's been directed and renovated by Juan José and Miguel Pérez Mejías. Many of the menu items are dedicated to locally inspired dishes whose original recipes probably developed long ago in the kitchens of the old city, which is just a few steps away. While sipping a draft beer, you can admire the bullfighter memorabilia attached to the walls and choose one of the well-prepared tapas at the stand-up bar. If you decide to eat, the specialties are a "festival of canapés," a full array of fresh shellfish and seafood, a savory filet of beef with garlic, and well-seasoned roasts. A full meal costs considerably more than it would have in the era of the half-peseta glass of wine, but it's worth the price at 1,800 pesetas ($12.60). The restaurant is closed Sunday.

ALICANTE AFTER DARK: **Frankfurt,** 16 San Fernando, is the only place where you can get food late at night. Serving typical German sausages, hot and cold sandwiches, and all kinds of beer, it's open daily from 7 p.m. to 3 a.m.

Taberna del Gourmet, 3 Romero, next-door to the Frankfurt, is a typical Spanish tavern, where you can enjoy the best Jabugo ham and tapas. Open from 10 a.m. to midnight seven days a week.

Nou Manolin, 3 Villegas (tel. 20-03-68). Many residents of Alicante appreciate the intricate tapas, costing from 95 pesetas (67¢), at this beer hall so much that they never get around to dining in the adjoining restaurant, which is under separate management. Owner Vicente Castelló hosts a wide array of local personalities, who usually seem to prefer the foamy beer on tap.

Sherezade, 17 General Lacy. You'll have to search hard to find a place at the elongated bar of this pleasantly decorated pub whose clientele, mostly youthful, seems to enjoy watching the antics and hearing the conversation of the driving force of the establishment, Josefo. There's likely to be music playing, and you may find an available seat below a potted palm on one of the establishment's divans. Drinks cost from 175 pesetas ($1.23).

Bugatti, 37 San Fernando (tel. 21-06-46). Anyone with any pretensions to being stylish has appeared once or twice at this trendy disco, which is one of the most modern on the Costa Blanca. The music is up-to-date and recent, and the entrepreneur who set it up has become a regular fixture in the night scene of the region. The establishment is open every day from 7 till 10 p.m., at which time it closes an hour for a quick clean-up, reopening at 11 p.m. and closing at 4 a.m. Drinks average 600 pesetas ($4.20).

4. Elche

Between Alicante (13 miles away) and Murcia is the little town of Elche, famous for both its age-old Mystery Play and the groves of date palms that grow in profusion. The play is reputedly the oldest dramatic liturgy performed in Europe. But unless you're visiting during August 15 and 16 when it's presented, the date palms will be the major attraction.

The palm forest is unrivaled anywhere in Europe. Many Spanish towns couldn't celebrate Palm Sunday properly if it weren't for this forest. But the local people don't sit around worshipping palms all day; shoe- and sandal-making are the other occupations around here. *La Dama de Elche,* the primitive sculptured bust in the Madrid Archeological Museum, was dug up in this area.

When you see the whitewashed houses in the setting of an immense date forest, you may feel you've been transplanted to an African, even an Oriental, oasis. Take time out to visit the gardens, which have been declared a national treasure.

The best place to stay is at the parador, **Huerto del Cura,** 14 Federico García Sanchez (tel. 45-80-40), which stands in the so-called priest's orchard. From your bedroom window, you'll have lovely views of the palm trees. The parador consists of a number of cabins in the date palm grove. Each accommodation has a private bath, along with phone, radio, TV, mini-bar, and heating or air conditioning. In low season a single rents for 6,100 pesetas ($42.70), going up to 6,500 pesetas ($45.50) in high season. A double in low season costs 8,100 pesetas ($56.70), climbing to 8,600 pesetas ($60.20) in high season. Although these tabs are high, it's a lovely, unique experience. Everything is beautifully furnished and immaculately kept, and the level of service is high. Built under the palms, a swimming pool separates the cabins from the main structure of the hotel. In the main building there is an attractive bar as well as an upstairs dining room, the four-fork Els Capellans, where the food is well prepared. Both regional and national dishes are featured, along with an array of international specialties. There is also a good wine list. You look out over the pool and date grove while dining. Dinner costs 2,200 pesetas ($15.40).

Peseta-watchers would be better advised to stay at the simple little **Residencia Cartagena,** 12 Gabriel Miró (tel. 46-15-50), which lies across the river in the more commercial part of town. The hotel is pleasant and comfortable enough, and is open all year. Singles are rented for 2,300 pesetas ($16.10), doubles rising to 3,800 pesetas ($26.60).

For dining, the locals prefer the **Parque Municipal,** Paseo Alfonso XIII (tel. 45-34-15), which is a large open-air restaurant and café, right in the middle of a public park. It's a good place to go for meals or drinks, and you'll get to study the people and the palms. Service is relaxed, the food of standard quality. Expect to spend from 1,400 pesetas ($9.80) to 2,800 pesetas ($19.60) for a complete meal here.

After a visit to the forest, we continue on to:

5. Murcia

This ancient Moorish city of sienna-colored buildings is an inland provincial capital on the main road between Valencia and Granada. Most motorists making this trip pass through it, and it's well worth a stopover. It lies about 52 miles from Alicante on the Costa Blanca.

The city abounds in grand houses built in the 1700s, but has many modern aspects as well, which have sprouted up at the expense of the old. Its principal artistic treasure is its 14th-century cathedral, a bastardized mixture of Gothic, baroque, and Renaissance. The Holy Week celebration here is known all over Spain, and this would be the ideal time to visit Murcia.

WHERE TO STAY: **Residencia Rincón de Pepe,** 34 Plaza de Apóstoles (tel. 21-22-39), is a surprise: a modern hotel hidden on a narrow street in the heart of the old quarter. Its entranceway is accented with marble, glass, and plants; there is a good-size lounge with many conversational areas, as well as a bar. The bedrooms are as up-to-date as the lobby, and they have many built-in conveniences. A double costs from 7,000 pesetas ($49) nightly, a single going for 5,500 pesetas ($38.50). Units are most comfortable, with air conditioning and complete baths. A continental breakfast (an extra charge) is the only meal served. Yet the residencia owns my first dining recommendation (see below).

Hotel Hispano 2, 3 Lucas (tel. 21-61-52). Their older hotel, the Hispano 1, was so successful that Joaquin and Ignacio Abellán decided to inaugurate this newer version in the late 1970s. The 36 comfortably furnished bedrooms, each of which contains TV, air conditioning, and a mini-bar, rent for 5,200 pesetas ($36.40) to 5,800 pesetas ($40.60) for a single, 6,400 pesetas ($44.80) to 7,200 pesetas ($50.40) for a double. Many of the clients might be conventioneers, attending conferences.

Hotel Condé de Floridablanca, 7 Corbalán (tel. 21-46-24), is ideally situated for explorations of the oldest part of the city. It's in the center of the Barrio del Carmen, in a building attractively decorated in local style with a baroque form of regional design. The neighborhood is fairly quiet at night unless a Vespa should happen to roar by, although that might be a problem anywhere in town. The five dozen air-conditioned rooms rent for 4,000 pesetas ($28) in a single, with doubles going for 5,500 pesetas ($38.50).

Hotel Majesti, 5 Plaza San Pedro (tel. 21-47-41). If you're looking for an unpretentious yet centrally located hotel, the Majesti, which adjoins the open-air market, may be the place for you. The approximately 70 rooms are air-conditioned and pleasant, costing from 1,800 pesetas ($12.60) in a single, and from 2,800 pesetas ($19.60) in a double.

WHERE TO DINE: **Rincón de Pepe,** 34 Apóstoles (tel. 21-22-49). Many residents of Murcia won't let foreign visitors leave town without taking them to this culinary landmark set up in the mid-1920s. Owned and operated by the nephew of the original founder, the establishment is under the direction of Raimundo González Frutos and his wife, Encarna, who do everything they can to produce the best food in town in menus that reflect the changing seasons. Specialties change frequently, but during your visit you might enjoy river salmon with lemon, artichokes with pine nuts, fish soup with rice, a skewer of marinated meats, and a dessert of, for example, pears cooked in wine. Full meals might cost upward of 2,600 pesetas ($18.20) and are served daily except Sunday between June and August. The rest of the year, Sunday lunch is served but the restaurant is closed Sunday night.

Casa Emilio, 17 Plaza de Camachos (tel. 21-13-25). The decor of this pleasant restaurant inspires references to a tastefully furnished private Spanish home. The owner, Emilio Martín, prepares a legendary paella, as well as grilled pepper steak, flavorful filets of veal, several kinds of soup, an array of fish and shellfish, and a succulent version of roast lamb. Full meals cost from 1,500 pesetas ($10.50) and are served daily except Wednesday and during the first two weeks of July.

MURCIA AFTER DARK: **Don Pepe,** 15 González Adalid (tel. 21-97-21), is decorated English style, with lots of paneling and a piano that is played softly as guests converse in quiet tones. It's open daily except in August. Drinks begin at 175 pesetas ($1.23).

La Tapa, Plaza Flores (tel. 21-13-17). In addition to being an unusual end point of a walk through the old city (the place is on one of the oldest squares of town), La Tapa offers richly flavorful beer on tap and a savory collection of tapas, costing from 80 pesetas (56¢). All kinds of people come here, including several reminders of old Spain.

Sirvent, 24 Gran Vía (tel. 21-21-23). There's an attractive outdoor terrace here for the increased enjoyment of your ice-cream sundae or whatever snack or drink you fancy. Many of the clients will simply be sipping coffee or drinks.

Rosa Rosae, Puerta Nueva, Centro Fama (tel. 26-60-13), is a youth-oriented disco open late on Thursday and Friday night, with slightly earlier closing on Saturday and Sunday. A drink averages around 900 pesetas ($6.30).

La Carroza, Pueblo Nuevo (tel. 24-35-31). The recorded music of this disco is likely to be complemented with live musical acts, which are performed to the enthusiastic approval of the audience. The hours are from 5:30 till 10:30 p.m. on Thursday, Friday, and Sunday, and from 5:30 p.m. to 3:40 a.m. on Saturday. Drinks begin at 600 pesetas ($4.20).

Bugatti, Plaza de Sta. Gertrudis (tel. 21-67-10), is the newest disco in town at press time. It's open daily from 7 to 10 p.m. and 11 p.m. to 4 a.m. Drinks average 600 pesetas ($4.20).

Chapter X

SETTLING INTO BARCELONA

1. Finding a Room
2. The Catalán Cuisine
3. The Top Sights
4. The City After Dark
5. Practical Facts

BARCELONA IS the most European of Spanish cities. The largest of Mediterranean ports, a formidable rival of Madrid, it lies between two hills, Tibidabo and Montjuïch. Staunchly independent and granted a sweeping autonomy, Barcelona is the reluctant bride of Spain. It has a separate language, Catalán, once outlawed, but now spoken as an assertion of independent pride.

This port is big, bustling, commercial, residential, cultural, artistic, new, and old, and often quite dangerous because of rampant crime. Sometimes these elements are at cross purposes. Barcelona has attained its present power and importance by the sheer work and determination of its proud people.

It is also a capital of contrasts. The narrow streets of the Gothic quarter are little changed since the Middle Ages, yet the wide boulevards and splashing fountains of the more commercial 19th-century town could be found in any number of Western European cities.

On the labyrinthine narrow streets branching off from the south of the Ramblas (near the Puerta de la Paz) walk Jean Genet's "whores, thieves, pimps, and beggars" ripped from the pages of *The Thief's Journal.* Today Genet would have had to add muggers. Also through the maze wander the sailors and foreigners in search of adventure, and they'll find more than they bargained for if they don't proceed carefully into the night.

Further evidence of Barcelona's contrasts is to be found in the burgeoning number of apartment houses that look as if they've been transplanted from the Bronx. These cold, impersonal structures exist in a city that was uniquely stamped with the work of Gaudí, the architect who "outrococoed rococo" with his architectural wonders.

Barcelona is a city of colorful restaurants and moderately priced hotels, reviewed in this chapter. Its winters are mild (palm trees flutter in the cool wind); its springs and autumns are ideal; its hot summers are almost bearable. And it has a beach.

The **Plaza de Cataluña** (in Catalán, Plaça de Catalunya) is the city's heart; the crime-riddled **Ramblas** with their evening promenades are its arteries. The

Ramblas begin at the **Puerta de la Paz,** with its 200-foot-high-monument to Columbus, and stretch all the way to the Plaza de Cataluña. Along the way you'll find chairs for sitting and viewing the parade, book shops and newsstands, and stalls selling birds and flowers. You'll also find half the muggers of the Mediterranean world in action here. Purse snatching and daylight robberies are commonplace. If you must see this world-famed tourist site, proceed with great caution. The southern part of the Ramblas, near the waterfront, is the most dangerous section.

The major wide boulevards are the **Avenida Diagonál,** the **Paseo de Colón,** the **Calle del Marqués del Duero,** and the elegant shopping street—the **Paseo de Gracia** (in Catalán, Passeig de Gràcia).

By all means, visit this capital of Catalonia. Its attractions are many. It's also an important center from which you can branch out on a number of excursions: to the Costa Brava, the principality of Andorra, the old Roman city of Tarragona, and the Monastery of Montserrat. The port is, finally, a jumping-off point—either by plane or boat—to the Balearic Islands. But if you're planning to do that in summer, make sure you have a reservation, both on a plane or boat and at a hotel once you get there, signed in blood.

LANGUAGE AND MAPS: Barcelona has two languages, Castilian Spanish and Catalán Spanish, the latter becoming more and more prominent with the rise of nationalism and the semi-autonomy of the government. Official notices are printed in both languages. For example, the Spanish word *calle,* meaning street, becomes *carrer* in the Catalonian language. Another word, such as *y* (meaning "and" in Spanish) is *i* in Catalán.

Maps and street addresses can be totally confusing. Franco and his generals aren't honored on Barcelona streets anymore. For example, the Avenida del Generalísimo Franco is now the Diagonal. The Avenida de José Antonio Primo de Rivera is now the Gran Vía (delles Corts Catalanes). Sometimes the street name has the new Catalán name; sometimes the old Spanish. Sometimes those in charge of street signs forgot, and there's a mixture of the two.

Often what's on your map (unless it's the last-minute, hot-off-the-press variety) isn't on the signpost, and finding an obscure address can be maddening.

GETTING AROUND BARCELONA: The city offers several adequate means of transportation: taxis, buses, subways.

Taxis: When you get into a taxi in Barcelona, a rate of 85 pesetas (60¢) is in force at the time of this writing, but will surely change during the lifetime of this edition. For each kilometer you travel in the city, you'll have to pay extra. As taxi rates go, these are low, and you'll find this means of transportation most efficient. You will have to pay extra if the taxi takes you to the bullring and extra if you go to the airport. You'll also have to pay extra for big pieces of luggage. *Warning:* Make sure that the flag is turned down when you enter the taxi. For a radio taxi, call 386-50-00.

Subway: The "Metro" is a low fare of 40 pesetas (28¢) on most rides, going up another 5 pesetas (4¢) on Sunday and holidays. The Gran Metro cuts across Barcelona from north to south, and the Transversal heads east to west. The best connecting station for subways in all directions is the Plaza de Cataluña.

Motorbuses: Barcelona has a system of motorbuses—45 pesetas (32¢) for most fares—and the routes are quite comprehensive. Buses on Sunday and holidays cost 50 pesetas (35¢).

Railroad: The terminal where most visitors arrive is the Estación de Francia (Estació de França in Catalán), next to the Ciudadela Park, on Avinguda

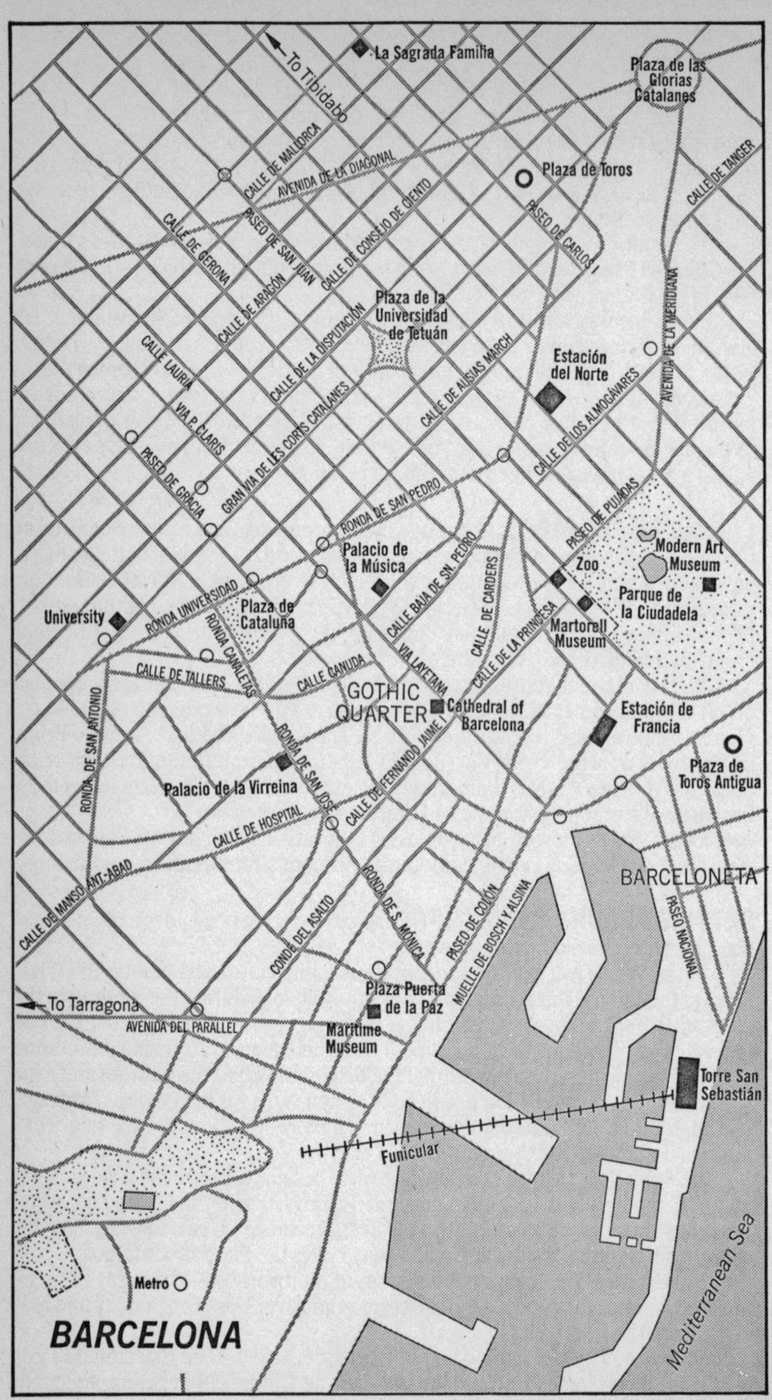
To Tibidabo
La Sagrada Familia
Plaza de las Glorias Catalanes
CALLE DE MALLORCA
AVENIDA DE LA DIAGONAL
Plaza de Toros
CALLE DE TANGER
CALLE DE GERONA
PASEO DE SAN JUAN
CALLE DE CONSEJO DE CIENTO
PASEO DE CARLOS I
CALLE DE ARAGÓN
Plaza de la Universidad de Tetuán
AVENIDA DE LA MERIDIANA
CALLE LAURIA
CALLE DE LA DISPUTACIÓN
CALLE DE AUSIAS MARCH
Estación del Norte
CALLE DE LOS ALMOGÁVARES
VIA P. CLARIS
GRAN VIA DE LES CORTS CATALANES
PASEO DE GRACIA
RONDA DE SAN PEDRO
PASEO DE PUJADAS
Palacio de la Música
Modern Art Museum
Zoo
Parque de la Ciudadela
RONDA UNIVERSIDAD
Plaza de Cataluña
CALLE DE CARDERS
CALLE BAJA DE SN. PEDRO
University
RONDA CANALETAS
CALLE DE LA PRINCESA
Martorell Museum
CALLE DE TALLERS
CALLE CANUDA
VIA LAYETANA
GOTHIC QUARTER
Cathedral of Barcelona
Estación de Francia
RONDA DE SAN ANTONIO
RONDA DE SAN JOSÉ
Plaza de Toros Antigua
Palacio de la Virreina
CALLE DE FERNANDO JAIME I
CALLE DE HOSPITAL
CALLE DE MANSO ANT-ABAD
BARCELONETA
RONDA DE S. MÓNICA
PASEO DE COLÓN
MUELLE DE BOSCH Y ALSINA
PASEO NACIONAL
CONDE DEL ASALTO
Plaza Puerta de la Paz
To Tarragona
AVENIDA DEL PARALLEL
Maritime Museum
Torre San Sebastián
Funicular
Metro
Mediterranean Sea
BARCELONA

Marqués Argentera (Metro: Término). Trains pull in here from Madrid, Zaragoza, Valencia, and Tarragona. There is another station, the Estació Sants-Central on the Avinguda Roma. Take the Metro to Sants-Estació. The number to call for railway information in Barcelona is 310-72-00.

From the Airport: To go into Barcelona from the international airport, you can board a RENFE train for a cost of 70 pesetas (49¢) for a one-way passage. Trains depart about every 20 minutes. You're deposited at the Sants-Estació, where the Metro will take you to wherever you're going. Many readers prefer the train to the airport bus.

1. Finding a Room

Hotels in Barcelona are plentiful, and are some of the most reasonable in Spain. However, the picture is not totally rosy. For some reason, Barcelona lags behind many Spanish cities in top-notch modern offerings in our price range (with a handful of exceptions). The top-rated hotels possible on our budget are a bit tarnished, but comfortable and adequate. Without question, they offer good value for the money they charge. However, because safety and security are important factors in selecting a hotel in Barcelona, you may want to spend more for better accommodations. If that is the case, make your selections from:

SOME TOP CHOICES: **Hotel Condes de Barcelona,** 75 Paseo de Gracia (tel. 215-06-16). One of the newest and most glamorous hotels of Barcelona is sheltered behind a unique neo-medieval façade at an angle of the architecturally splendid Paseo de Gracia. It was designed in 1895 as a private villa by Catalonian architect Vilaseca as part of Gaudí's modernist movement. Sadly, its heraldic shields, lion-shaped iron balustrades, and the palm-shaped patterns of its neo-Romanesque columns suffered a regrettable decline during the years the building had sheltered a bank. In 1986, following the arrival of its first client, German-born Baron von Thyssen, the building began a new lease on life as a very sophisticated hotel. Just enough hints of high-tech furnishings were added to make the lobby exciting, but everything else is as close to the original opulence as Vilaseca originally intended. Each of the public rooms is sheathed in glistening layers of polished travertine, dotted with streamlined furniture, and accented with plants. The curved, lobby-level bar and its adjacent stylish restaurant were designed with just a hint of art deco in mind.

The comfortable bedrooms contain marble baths, reproductions of Spanish paintings, soundproof windows, air conditioning, and a color scheme of salmon, green, or peach. Rated four stars, the hotel charges a bit less than many competitors with a similar rating. Singles cost 8,000 pesetas ($56), doubles 12,000 pesetas ($84), plus breakfast and taxes.

Hotel Wilson, 568 Diagonal (tel. 209-25-11). Set amid the belle époque grandeur of a neighborhood rich in architectural curiosities, this comfortable hotel is a member of the nationwide HUSA chain. The smallish lobby isn't indicative of the rest of this comfortable hotel, which opens on the second floor into a large and sunny coffeeshop/bar and TV lounge. Each of the 55 modernized bedrooms contains a TV, radio, phone, air conditioning, and soundproof windows. Singles cost 4,200 pesetas ($29.40) to 4,400 pesetas ($30.80), doubles, 6,500 pesetas ($45.50) to 6,600 pesetas ($46.20), plus breakfast and tax.

Hotel Hesperia, 20 Los Vergos (tel. 204-55-51). Its imaginative exterior rises amid the verdant gardens of one of Barcelona's most pleasant residential neighborhoods on the well-heeled northern edge of the city. Many habitués consider a stay in this area, about a 12-minute taxi ride from the center, to be worth the traveling time. You'll descend a flight of exterior steps, past a Japanese rock garden, to reach the stone-floored reception area with its adjacent bar. Each of the comfortable bedrooms has a modernized version of a many-angled corner window, whose quadruplicate panes of glass flood the monochromatic interior with sunlight. Singles rent for 5,900 pesetas ($41.30); doubles, 10,500 pesetas ($73.50), with a full buffet breakfast included. The impeccably uniformed staff is one of the establishment's strongest virtues. An underground parking garage is part of the package.

Hotel Tres Torres, 32 Calatrava (tel. 247-73-00), is set on the northern edge of the city in the Sarria district in a neighborhood of flowering gardens and expensive apartments. Built in 1966, its unpretentious five-story façade is sheathed in roughly textured stone slabs. Inside, above a pleasantly tasteful, conservative series of public rooms, are 56 clean bedrooms, each with its own bath, color TV, and phone. Singles cost 4,800 pesetas ($33.60); doubles, 7,500 pesetas ($52.50), with breakfast included. Taxes are extra.

Hotel Regencia Colón, 13-17 Sagristans (tel. 318-98-58). Set in a dignified, very stately stone-walled building behind the more prestigious Hotel Colón (with which it should not be confused), this comfortable hotel in the Gothic quarter offers 55 modernized accommodations at more reasonable rates than its better-known sister. You'll register in a formal, somewhat ecclesiastical lobby before heading upstairs to your room. Each contains a private bath, phone, and piped-in music. About half of the units have TV. Only breakfast is served, which is included in the daily rates of 3,300 pesetas ($23.10) and 3,700 pesetas ($25.90) in a single and 4,600 pesetas ($32.60) and 6,000 pesetas ($42) in a double; triples cost 8,300 pesetas ($58.10), plus tax. The establishment's location, within the shadow of the cathedral, is one of its chief virtues.

Hotel Astoria, 203 Calle Paris (tel. 209-83-11). Built in 1953, its severe façade was influenced enough by art deco to make visitors think it's 30 years older. The confusion carries through to the beautifully original public rooms, whose high ceilings, geometric designs, and brass-studded detailing could be Moorish or Andalusian. Within its price category, it is one of my favorite hotels in Barcelona. A sinuous staircase leads to the cedar doors of the 114 bedrooms, each of which contains a private bathroom, air conditioning, TV, radio, video movies, and soundproofing. About half of the rooms have been renovated into a slick international style of louvered closets and glistening white paint. The more old-fashioned chambers have warm textures of exposed cedar and Eisenhower-era accessories. Singles cost from 3,900 pesetas ($27.30); doubles, 5,900 pesetas ($41.30) to 7,000 pesetas ($49).

Hotel Zenit, 8 Santaló (tel. 209-89-11), is one of the rare buildings within this rich architectural zone whose exterior walls aren't embellished with chiseled ornamentations. This is an unpretentious and efficiently managed member of Spain's nationwide HUSA hotel chain. It shares the bottom two floors with the headquarters of the Catalonian Automobile Club, but above that are four balconied stories containing 61 clean and simple bedrooms, each decorated in a bland international style. Each has air conditioning and a private bathroom. Singles cost 4,700 pesetas ($32.90); doubles, 7,500 pesetas ($52.50), with breakfast included.

Hotel San Agustín, 3 Plaza San Agustín (tel. 318-16-58). Set on one of a duet of adjacent squares in the heart of the old city, near the covered produce markets, this five-story, tastefully renovated hotel overlooks the brick walls of an unfinished Romanesque church. Each of its 74 bedrooms contains a private bath, a phone, and adaptations of traditional Iberian furniture. Depending on the season, singles cost 2,700 pesetas ($18.90), doubles from 4,100 pesetas ($28.70) to 4,400 pesetas ($30.80).

LESS EXPENSIVE ROOMS: **Granvía,** 642 Gran Vía de les Corts Catalanes (tel. 318-19-00), provides old-style living in a great old city. On one of the most fashionable boulevards in the city, the hotel preserves accoutrements evoking another era. For example, the drawing room glitters with gilt furniture, mirrors, inlaid pieces, tables, and high-backed chairs. The long dining room is done in Wedgwood blue and white, with a row of crystal chandeliers, and French provincial chairs. Typical of the faded grandeur of the hotel, the elevator is also antiquated. Cacophonous sounds rising from the street below might disturb the light sleeper. In the two-story-high reception lounge is a grand balustraded stairway (worthy of *Sunset Boulevard*), leading to the arched balcony. In the Andalusian style, the courtyard is set with tables for al fresco drinks in the midst of palm trees and fountains. Behind the arches is a garden room serving continental breakfasts. The bedrooms are traditional, often featuring interesting reproductions of antiques—you might find an elaborate carving or painting in yours. Its not luxury, but good comfort. Rooms rent for 4,000 pesetas ($28) in a single to 5,800 pesetas ($40.60) in a double nightly. All of the bedrooms contain a private bath, and there is central heating as well.

Hotel Suizo, 12 Plaza del Angel (tel. 315-41-11). Only a few blocks from the cathedral, this symmetrical 19th-century building sits somewhat isolated from the taller structures that cluster across the streets surrounding it on three sides. The pleasantly modernized lobby has a floor covered with white marble slabs and a richly grained reception desk staffed with polite employees. Most of the ground floor is filled with an elaborate reproduction of a belle époque bar, where drinks and snacks are served either on white marble tables or at the curved bar. The bentwood chairs continue on an upper balcony for additional seating. The bedrooms, each with a private bath, air conditioning, music, color TV, and a phone, are pleasantly furnished with patterned wallpaper in antique-inspired designs and Spanish furniture. With breakfast included, singles rent for 5,000 pesetas ($35), while doubles cost 7,000 pesetas ($49).

Hotel Internacional, 78-80 Ramblas (tel. 302-25-66), is behind an exquisitely detailed peach and gray baroque façade. Many readers have wisely tended to avoid the Ramblas recently because it's considered unsafe—the list of people who have been mugged in daylight is almost endless. But if your heart is set on staying on one of the city's most legendary thoroughfares, the Internacional at least has the advantage of being at the upper, and slightly safer, end of it. The façade is noteworthy, but the interior has been drastically renovated into an early 1960s version of modernity. This includes a bar, a breakfast room, and high-ceilinged bedrooms with private baths, phones, and angular furniture. Members of a tour group might be filling up many of the rooms during your Barcelona stay, but if there are any accommodations available, a single will cost 3,500 pesetas ($24.50) and doubles go for 4,800 pesetas ($33.60), with breakfast included in these tariffs.

Montecarlo, 124 Rambla de los Estudios (tel. 317-58-00). The main lounge here features an elaborate carved ceiling, stylized carved doors, a crystal chandelier, and a baronial fireplace. The furniture has been renewed in the hall and in the rooms. Doubles with private bath cost 5,500 pesetas ($38.50); singles, also with bath, go for 3,400 pesetas ($23.80). There is a large covered garage in the same building, plus a coffeeshop on the premises.

Hostal Levante, 2 Bajada de San Miguel (tel. 317-95-65), is one of the nicest and most reasonable places to stay in Barcelona. It's housed in an imposing building, more than two centuries old, and it lies just a short distance from Plaza San Jaime, directly in the center of the Gothic Quarter. For 750 pesetas ($5.25), you're given a single room, or else you'll pay 1,400 pesetas ($9.80) in a double.

Units are clean and comfortable. There is central heating, and use of the hot showers in the corridors is included in the tariff. The hostal is removed from the noise of the streets. This 38-room establishment is run by a hard-working, helpful couple, Mr. and Mrs. Manuel Ibáñez, who speak English.

Hotel Residencia Habaña, 647 Gran Vía de les Corts Catalanes (tel. 301-07-50), has a gentility to it, an old-fashioned touch. It is a well-run hotel on an important street that is likely to be noisy and therefore can't be recommended to light sleepers. There is a modern reception room downstairs, and an elevator will take you up to the pleasantly appointed rooms. The Habaña, incidentally, has rooms in several price ranges. Doubles with bath go for 5,500 pesetas ($38.50). The most expensive singles, those with bath, rent for 3,900 pesetas ($27.30). A continental breakfast, costing extra, is the only meal served.

Hotel Inglés, 17 Calle Boquerí (tel. 317-37-70), is a small hotel in the old quarter, along a narrow street off the Ramblas. Because of its isolated position, this modest place is off the heavily trodden tourist trail, but a few minutes' walk will take you to the heart of the city. The management is helpful, and has set a moderate rate schedule: 3,200 pesetas ($22.40) for a double room with private bath. Singles with shower rent for 2,000 pesetas ($14). The rooms are fair, each with its own telephone. The level of cleanliness is adequate, and the Inglés can make for a pleasant stopover if your expectations aren't too high.

Hotel Continental, 138 Rambla de Canaletas (tel. 301-25-70), is a pleasant hotel that is scattered over two of the upper floors of a commercial building on the upper section of the Ramblas, the safer part. The reception area is flowery, slightly faded, accented with 19th-century bronze statues, and very clean. The friendly and attractive receptionist is guaranteed to melt the ice off any of your arrival's initial discomfort. The hotel is owned by Mrs. Malagarriga, a charming English-speaking blond whose family established the hotel in a nearby building in 1894. About 15 years ago she moved to the quarters you'll see today, where there's a pleasant, simple format. Each of the 34 rooms has a private bath, and ten have a semicircular balcony looking down on the Ramblas. Many of Mrs. Malagarriga's clients are teachers, professors from Oxford, TV crewmen from the BBC, and art lovers. A buffet breakfast, whose price is included in the room rent, is served daily from 8 a.m. to noon. Singles cost 3,400 pesetas ($23.80), while doubles go for 4,200 pesetas ($29.40).

Residencia Montserrat, 114 Passeig de Gràcia (tel. 217-27-00), is a surprisingly inexpensive hotel in what is one of the most desirable neighborhoods of Barcelona, at the top of the former paseo. This fourth-floor hotel is an aggressively simple, slightly drab collection of about 39 rooms, each relatively clean and located in a sector that is central and usually safe. The façade is grandly ornate and handsome, and the entrance leading up to the wrought-iron elevator cage is as high-ceilinged as a grand palace. The very small glass-and-wood elevator gives the impression of being in a jewel box as you ascend past a maid who might be singing a beautifully mournful chant from inside the echo chamber of the stairwell she's busily polishing. The hotel lobby is plain, but the straightforward receptionist will sign you into a serviceable bedroom (some with a terrace) which is only slightly rundown but quiet. All units have some form of bath. Singles cost 1,400 pesetas ($9.80), while doubles run 2,400 pesetas ($16.80).

Hotel Cortés, 25 Santa Ana (tel. 317-91-12). Each of the 50 bedrooms of this pleasant member of a Barcelona-based hotel chain contains a private bath. There's a small salon on the ground floor, with another slightly larger one one floor above. The hotel was entirely renovated in 1970, with an attractive, functional decor. Half the bedrooms look out over a quiet courtyard and about half overlook the street. Guests can take breakfast at a table in the bar that is connected to the hotel, and in the evening this is the place to enjoy a *cerveza* instead of a *café con leche*. Single rooms rent for 2,800 pesetas ($19.60), with doubles going for 4,300 pesetas ($30.10).

Hostal Roma, 11 Plaza Real (tel. 302-03-66), is on one of the most attractive squares in Barcelona, the center of much nightlife and a plaza filled with students or else rather dubious types of all nations. A third-class hotel, the hostal is basic and simply furnished, but clean. Depending on the plumbing, singles range from 900 pesetas ($6.30) to 1,400 pesetas ($9.80), with doubles going for 1,600 pesetas ($11.20) to 2,300 pesetas ($16.10). The more expensive units contain a private shower. In all, there are 60 bedrooms, half of which open onto the square and have sun, but are noisier. Pasquale Tarrason, the owner, is a young and charming host.

THE PICK OF THE PENSIONS: **Hostal Turín,** 9 Pintor Fortuny (tel. 302-48-12), given two stars by the government, is just off the Ramblas de los Estudios. The Turín is easily identifiable by its terracotta grillwork front. It's housed in a balconied, elevator building. Neat and simple, it is a good choice because of its streamlined bedrooms—small but comfortable. Most doubles are bathless but contain a water basin, and cost 2,600 pesetas ($18.20) a night. In one of the 18 doubles with private bath, the rate is 3,500 pesetas ($24.50). Bathless singles go for 1,900 pesetas ($13.30).

Hotel Universidad, 10 Ronda de la Universidad (tel. 317-13-41), is a postwar boarding house that has fewer amenities than some of the more preferred pensions previously recommended, but it's quite a bargain. Right in the heart of the city, the Universidad rates at least a bachelor's degree for running an efficient, well-kept, spotless, and friendly accommodation. The moderately attractive, but basic, double rooms with bath rent for 2,800 pesetas ($19.60) nightly, dropping to 2,100 pesetas ($14.70) if bathless. Singles, on the other hand, are equipped only with a wash basin, and cost 1,900 pesetas ($13.30). Dinner costs 1000 pesetas ($7).

Hostal Neutral, 42 Rambla de Cataluña (tel. 318-73-70), is just that—a neutral but very recommendable place, known for its cleanliness and efficiency. Like the Universidad, this is a postwar pension, but this time I'm referring to World War I. Still, its quite good doubles rent for only 2,800 pesetas ($19.60), and these have a private bath. But you may be assigned to a double with only a water basin for 2,100 pesetas ($14.70). The single rooms rent for 1,400 pesetas ($9.80) nightly. A continental breakfast is included. English is spoken.

Hostal Residencia Nilo, 17 José Anselmo Clavé (tel. 317-90-44), although modest, attracts a steady clientele of travelers from English-speaking countries. In the center of the city by the port, railway station, and Ramblas, the hostal is clean, and there is always hot water, fresh linen, and good friendly service. For 950 pesetas ($6.65) a bathless single is offered, increasing to 1,800 pesetas ($12.60) in a double. The hostal remains open all night.

Residencia Australia, 11 Ronda Universidad (tel. 317-41-77), is on the fourth floor of an old, centrally located building. The accommodations have all been redecorated and are clean and modern. The place is small (two singles and two doubles), but the welcome you receive from the Lorenzo family is big and warm. The single rooms cost 1,200 pesetas ($8.40), a double with bath going for 2,300 pesetas ($16.10) and a bathless double for 2,000 pesetas ($14). The Lorenzos, a Spanish family, all speak good English, having lived in Australia for 18 years. Mrs. Lorenzo is a friendly, helpful woman and an excellent cook, so I suggest you take breakfast here.

Hostal Residencia Pintor, 25 Gignás (tel. 315-47-08), is on the second floor of a building in the *casco antiguo* near the central post office and the Estacíon de Francia railway station. The hosts extend a warm welcome to guests and make them feel comfortable. They charge 1,300 pesetas ($9.10) for a large, double-bedded room with hot and cold running water. There are two spacious baths with tubs, showers, and basins.

2. The Catalán Cuisine

From the top of Montjuïch to the lowliest dive, Barcelona offers a wide variety of places at which to eat. If the Cataláns aren't always gourmets, they make up for it in the huge, filling portions they serve. The hotels and boarding houses offer good Catalán cooking, but large numbers of the visitors to Barcelona like to get out on the lively streets at night and search for a restaurant. Keep in mind that the city enjoys a large cult of midnight diners; if possible, have a late, late lunch. At least once you may want to order the Catalán sausage, *butifarra,* which is both white or dark (called blanca or negra). Another local specialty is a sweet round pastry called *ensaimadas.*

Finally, for your late-night snack, you might wander over to the Plaza Real, which many visitors consider a miniature version of the more famous Plaza Mayor in Madrid. Sometimes spontaneous live entertainment is presented to the guests seated at the outdoor cafés, enjoying shellfish such as grilled shrimp and beer until the wee hours.

THE BEST BARGAINS: The **Casa José,** 10 Plaza San José Oriol (tel. 302-40-20), wins, forks down, as the best all-around spot for rock-bottom economy dining in Barcelona. Placed on a medieval plaza, the restaurant draws an intriguing clientele—the local habitués, the mainstay, bending elbows with the transient foreigners, who often have to wait in line. An occasional frugal Catalán artist, with a Van Dyck beard, may be seen carefully ordering a well-prepared cubierto for 300 pesetas ($2.10), featuring, say, spaghetti, lamb stew, plus bread and dessert. For a big 350 pesetas ($2.45) you get roast chicken, french fries, salad, bread, and dessert. Paella is available for 350 pesetas ($2.45), although you must wait about half an hour for it to be prepared. More expensive meals are also available. This corner bistro overlooks the back of the old Church of Santa María del Piño. From the Rambla San José, it's only a three-minute walk up the Cardenal Casañas and Calle Boquería. Closed Saturday.

Nou Celler, 16 Princesa (tel. 319-90-24), is a pleasant corner of Catalán atmosphere near the Picasso museum. The establishment may be perfect if what you're looking for is a bodega-type meal, or even a drink or cup of coffee, in an ambience with country artifacts, hundreds of them, hanging from the beamed ceiling and high plaster walls. The back entrance is at 3 Barra de Ferro. If you come in that way, you'll be at the quieter end of the place, where, perhaps in honor of the nearby museum, someone has placed dozens of original artworks into a kind of collage of sketches. In the satellite dining room at the bottom of a few steps in back, a full meal costs around 1,500 pesetas ($10.50) à la carte. A set menu costs 650 pesetas ($4.55). You can choose zarzuela, paella, fish soup, Catalán soup, hake, and other classic Spanish dishes with few surprises—but also with few disappointments.

Ca la Maria, 76 bis Tallers (tel. 318-89-93). In Catalán, the name of the place translates as Casa (House of) María. Its façade is graced with blue and green tiles that mark the entrance to an interior filled with simple, half-paneled walls and tables covered with blue and white napery. It's on a quiet square opposite a church that looks almost Byzantine. The dining room is small enough to let you overhear many conversations around you. Service is competent and friendly. Menu items include roast goat, veal scaloppine, rape (a whitefish) in a pimiento cream sauce, sole with orange, and codfish in a garlic cream sauce. There are also daily specials that change frequently. Meals cost from around 1,800 pesetas ($12.60) and are served at lunch and dinner every day except Sunday night and Monday.

Bar/Restaurant Vegetariano, 41 Calle de Canuda (tel. 302-10-52), near the Gothic Quarter, a few blocks off the Ramblas, is affiliated with the Vegetarian Society of Barcelona, and as such, serves meatless meals to a host of regular clients. The decor is clean, simple, and modern, with a warmly tiled format. An illuminated glass case near the entrance contains desserts and salads. The cooks make fresh pastries, cakes, and good soups such as vichyssoise, and a large menu contains almost every popular fresh vegetable in Spain. Fixed-price meals are offered for around 400 pesetas ($2.80) and a dietetic menu for 750 pesetas ($5.25). Specialties include vegetable paella, vegetable cannelloni, and many omelets.

C'an Tripas, 16 Calle Sagues (tel. 200-85-40), is a good find, and is well known in Barcelona as a top budget restaurant. It has no frills, but still there's a certain charm about the place. The tables are laid out with oilcloth, and there are small chairs, arc lights, bottles standing on racks along the walls, sawdust on the floor, a television set, an open refrigerator, and a freezer in the small dining room. The walls are decorated with posters and coats hanging on hooks. You may select from a wide range of dishes, including, for example, fish soup, beef with brussels sprouts, brook trout, and Spanish melon. Meals cost from 1,200 pesetas ($8.40). The eatery lies on a street of sex-oriented nightclubs.

Restaurant Aquarium, 15 Calle del Cardenal Casañas (tel. 302-30-84), off las Ramblas de las Flores, is small and inviting, with one of the biggest and best cubiertos offered by a Barcelona bistro. For 1,100 pesetas ($7.70), a typical repast features fish soup, típico of the region; rice Cuban style; veal filet and tomatoes, hearty and filling; followed by a dessert (nothing special in this department), plus bread, wine, and service. Closed Sunday night

Restaurante Roma, Plaza Real (tel. 302-03-66), is another budget eatery, featuring a tourist menu for 850 pesetas ($5.95) that might include a soup or salad, cannelloni, omelet or eggs, then hake, breaded veal cutlet or chicken, plus bread and a dessert. If you're willing to pay a little more, you can get some surprisingly good fare, including a zarzuela (a mixed fish stew), tournedos, paella, rabbit, and grilled shrimp. The place is clean and otherwise pleasant. The Plaza Real is one of the most famous squares of Barcelona.

Pimpollo, 11 Calle Pintor Fortuny (tel. 318-22-97), near the Rambla de los Estudios, features golden-brown, spit-roasted chickens at prices to cluck about. In this narrow, modern "henhouse," diners roost on stools. For 500 pesetas ($3.50), diners can order a complete meal, drink included. Open from 1 to 5 p.m., the Pimpollo is a good way to keep food costs down in Barcelona without compromising your taste buds.

Burger King, 135 Rambla de Canaletas (tel. 320-54-29). You may like zarzuela, and a well-prepared paella may inspire a letter to someone back home, but from time to time what you really want is a hamburger. If that's the case, head for the most elegant Burger King in town, near the Plaça de Catalunya in what used to be the well-known Restaurant Canaletas. The change in Spanish food habits has helped hamburger chains to flourish in unlikely surroundings. This particular branch is lined with bronze bas-reliefs, marble walls, ornate iron columns, and a wrap-around upper balcony with finely crafted balustrades. This may be an overstated setting for having a Whopper with cheese at 275 pesetas

($1.93), or onion rings in olive oil at 130 pesetas (91¢). Still, it's convenient, inexpensive, and open every day from 10 a.m. to 1 a.m.

AT BARCELONETA: **Restaurant Peru,** 9 Passeig Nacional (tel. 310-37-09), dishes up savory viands, mostly sea creatures, near the harbor, a favorite haunt of both the Cataláns and foreign invaders during the summer months. Specialties are paella studded with shellfish and a distinctly Catalán bouillabaisse. For 2,500 pesetas ($17.50) you can dine very well indeed. You might begin with cannelloni, enjoying this pasta dish with some regional wine. The portions are large. You get hearty, vigorous Spanish fare daily except Monday.

Ramonet (Bar Xarello), 17 Maquinista (tel. 319-30-64). No one in this working-class restaurant near the seaport will coddle you if you expect old-world service, but if you want an unusual experience in serviceably masculine surroundings, this may be the place for you. The setting is inside an Andalusian-style villa on a narrow street where many of the shopowners, dock workers, and fishermen know one another. Many of the clients never move beyond the front room, where large wooden barrels serve as stand-up tables for seafood tapas or glasses of beer or regional wine.

Many Barcelonans come here for a quick meal, often at lunch but sometimes early in the morning after a long night's work. No one will sit down, since the well-prepared fish is served on the tops of stout barrelheads that cover much of the floor space. If you prefer, there are two inner dining rooms lined with wooden tables where a waiter will probably rattle off the names of the fish available that day (gambas, merluza, and rape are almost always present). If you want to pick your meal yourself, there's a beautifully arranged display of ocean denizens, whose names you may never have heard of, chilling on a bed of kale leaves near the door. Some menu items include a portion of pungent anchovies, grilled mushrooms à la plancha, braised artichokes, and a tortilla with spinach and beans. Mussels "from the beach" are also sold, along with fresh shrimp. The other fish are surprisingly inexpensive and usually prepared any way you like at bargain rates that are cheaper than those at more formal restaurants. A meal costs from 1,500 pesetas ($10.50) up.

OTHER TOP CHOICES: **Los Caracoles,** 14 Escudillers (tel. 302-31-85), flourishes in the labyrinth of the narrow, cobblestone streets of old Barcelona. That street, incidentally, is tawdry and potentially dangerous at night, so many clients like to go during the day. Most visitors to this Catalán capital write a memo to themselves: "See Gaudi's cathedral and dine at Caracoles." It's that popular. One of the port's most colorful restaurants, Los Caracoles is acclaimed for its spit-roasted chickens and for its namesake, snails. The spit is outside on the alleyway-like street, tempting the milling crowd of sailors, strollers, and Mr. and Mrs. Smith of Topeka with its wafting aromas. A long angular bar, filled with all the típico claptrap, is in front. This leads to a restaurant in back, with an upper level. You can look in at the busy preparations going on in the kitchen, dried spices, smoked ham shanks, and garlic bouquets hanging from the ceiling. In summer, tables are placed outside in the "cat alley." To dine here is a complete experience . . . but you'll be so close to the passersby they can inspect your chompers.

The food at the restaurant is excellent, with all sorts of Catalán specialties, but the caracoles and the chicken walk off with top honors. A typical repast will cost from 2,000 pesetas ($14), although your final tab could run much more.

Casa Leopoldo, 26 Calle de San Rafael (tel. 241-30-14). An excursion through the seedy streets of the Barrio Chino is part of the experience of coming to this celebrated restaurant. It's noted as a colorful and excellent purveyor of Barcelona's freshest seafood to a loyal clientele, many of whom visit from more glamorous sections of the city. It sits behind a double storefront covered with hospital-gray ceramic tiles on a street flapping with laundry and peopled by stray cats. This place has been serving wine since 1931 and dispensing food since 1939. In addition to a popular stand-up tapas bar, there are two dining rooms, one slightly more formal than the other. Full meals cost from 2,000 pesetas ($14) and include a large variety of seafood, featuring eel with shrimp, barnacles, cuttlefish, seafood soup with shellfish, and deep-fried inch-long eels. Other regional specialties include a Catalán version of tripe. The establishment is open daily except Monday and in August.

El 7 Portes, 14 Paseo Isabel II (tel. 319-30-46), is a lunchtime favorite of business people and an evening rendezvous for in-the-know clients who have, over the years, made it their preferred restaurant in Catalonia. Amid a decor of frequently polished hardwood paneling and rectangular mirrors, you can enjoy regional dishes such as fresh herring with onions and potatoes, a different rice dish for each day of the week (with shellfish, for example, or with rabbit), a wide array of fresh fish, succulent oysters, and an herb-laden stew of black beans and pork or white beans with sausage. The restaurant, it is said, has remained within the same family for 13 generations, and it is open daily from 1 p.m. to 1 a.m., charging from 1,800 pesetas ($12.60) for a full meal.

Duran Duran, 39-41 Alfonso XII (tel. 201-35-13), is one of the avant-garde and trendy new bars and restaurants developing in the Plaza Molina area. The decor, both in the spacious bar and in the dining room, is minimal, but there is nonetheless a feeling of warmth and well-being. This may be because of dramatic lighting, the Vivaldi that may be playing softly, the variegated pink-and-black marble tabletops, or all three. Amid bizarrely dressed but friendly waitresses, you can begin your meal with such appetizers as fresh foie gras of duckling or braised endive with romesco. This might be followed with a main course of brochette of filet of pork, rape (a whitefish) with a crab cream sauce, or four kinds of entrecôte. Many of the dishes are inspired by the nouvelle cuisine kitchen. Full meals cost from 2,400 pesetas ($16.80).

El Túnel, 33-35 Ample (tel. 315-27-59), is one of the best established and most prestigious restaurants in town for impeccable presentation of Catalán specialties. Owner Juan Palou is one of the city's most experienced restaurateurs, known for many years for the food coming from his kitchen. Featured dishes are cannelloni with truffles, kidney beans with shrimp, roast goat, a delectable fish soup, a stew of various kinds of fish, and filet of beef with peppers. All the items are served with a flourish and come with your choice of wine from the extensive cellar. The steward will be happy to select a reasonably priced beverage for you. Meals cost from 2,200 pesetas ($15.40) up. The establishment is closed Sunday night, all day Monday, and from July 15 to August 15.

Restaurant Pescallunes, 23 Carrer Magdalenes (tel. 318-54-83), is run by a group of friendly and charming Cataláns, while looking, feeling, and offering food items much like those of a French bistro. The smallish restaurant's entrance is a short walk from the cathedral, marked with an elaborate street lantern and an unpretentious sign. Inside, the ten tables have a view into the partially exposed kitchen and bask in the warmth of the fire in the Louis XIII–style fireplace. Open every day except Sunday, the restaurant serves specialties such as rape (a whitefish) with clams and tomatoes, a smooth vichyssoise, Chateaubriand with béarnaise sauce, sole cooked in cider, steak tartare, and dessert crêpes with Cointreau. If you've been dying for a fresh green salad, order the crispy endive with Roquefort. There's a different special feature each day. Full meals range from 2,000 pesetas ($14).

Llivia, 2 Copons (tel. 318-10-78), is a street-corner restaurant near the cathedral. It has a ground-floor bar lined with jars of spices, a white tile floor, and an upstairs dining room where you go for your meal after a drink below. Since seating in the restaurant is so limited (only eight tables set under a low-beamed ceiling), reservations are suggested. You can enjoy such dishes as vichyssoise, fish soup, goat cutlets, entrecôte, barbecued partridge, and Basque-style hake. You can order a menú del día at 1,000 pesetas ($7), or you can spend as much as 3,600 pesetas ($25.30) for à la carte fish specialties, which would include wine, coffee, and all the extras. Service is polite and concerned. The place is closed Sunday night and Monday.

El Caballito Blanco, 196 Calle Mallorca (tel. 253-10-33), is an old Barcelona standby, long popular with local gastronomes. The "Little White Horse," in the Paseo de Gracia area, is famous for its seafood, and features a huge selection. You can order rape (a whitefish) or mussels marinara, plus a wide selection of other fish platters. Their shrimp with garlic is excellent. If you don't want fish, try their grilled pork cutlets. Several different pâtés are offered, along with many varied salads. Count on spending from 2,000 pesetas ($14). On the left is a bar, with tables set in an elongated room lit by fluorescent bulbs. In lieu of decor, you'll find good food at medium prices. They are closed in August. The kitchen is also closed on Sunday night and all day Monday.

El Bodegón, 197 Calle Mallorca (tel. 253-10-17), is across the street and features similar fare at similar prices, but it's a bit cozier, with indirect lighting and a bistro atmosphere. Best here are the tapas and the seafood. Sometimes a guitar player comes around to entertain while you're dining. There are two dining rooms, with plastic chairs, paper tablecloths, paintings on the walls, and a low ceiling. The à la carte choice is particularly appealing, as it usually includes such selections as besugo (sea bream), kidneys in sherry, partridges (in season) served with fresh mushrooms that are on the market only in the autumn, and a civette of boar, again a seasonal dish. Meals cost from 1,800 pesetas ($12.60).

Restaurante d'España, in the hotel of the same name at 11 Calle Sant Pau (tel. 318-17-58), just off the Ramblas, has a large medieval-type dining room with huge chandeliers, bentwood chairs, and tile walls, a sort of art nouveau Gothic. It serves a tourist menu for 850 pesetas ($5.95) that'll include hors d'oeuvres or salad, paella or hake, followed by a grilled veal steak. The meal ends with ice cream, fruit, or flan. The location is in the teeming Barrio Chino.

A "DRUGSTORE": **El Drugstore,** 71 Paseo de Gracia (tel. 215-70-74), is a "plain Jane" sibling of similar establishments in Paris and Madrid. It features the usual "Drugstore" trappings: a snack-cafeteria, boutiques, toys, records, books, magazines, tobacco shop, a tea room, and shoeshine stand. At the snack delicatessen, combination dishes are available. The tourist dish of the day includes butifarra, a fried egg, mashed potatoes, tomato, bread, wine, and ice cream or coffee. There's a small dining area downstairs, plus a balcony. A self-service menu at 850 pesetas ($5.95) is one of the best food values in town. This Drugstore also has a pleasant sidewalk café, with white garden-type tables and chairs, pleasant for summer sitting. It's open till 5 a.m.

DEPARTMENT STORE DINING: The cafeterías at both **El Corte Inglés,** 14 Plaça de Catalunya (tel. 302-12-12) and 617 Avenida Diagonal (tel. 322-40-11), and **Galerías Preciados,** 19 Avenida Puerta del Angel (tel. 317-00-00), offer good value. Both have platos combinados as well as buffet selections. The maître d'hotel at El Corte Inglés gives out numbers for tables, and you'll pay

1,500 pesetas ($10.50) for a meal. At Galerías Precíados, getting a table may be more of an adventure as you have to make your own way if you choose the combination plate, for a charge of 1,400 pesetas ($9.80). The stores have separate sections for those who have a buffet lunch, which may include roast chicken, paella, seafood, cold salads, and desserts.

THE AMERICAN CORNER: **Henry J. Bean's Bar and Grill,** 14-16 La Granada del Penedes (tel. 218-29-98). As you walk down an unpromising street in a commercial sector, you'll suddenly come to speakeasy doors which swing open into a little corner of tongue-in-cheek America. Amid wooden tables festooned with checkerboard cloths and a giant salad bar, you'll discover a decor of advertisements from America's past, everything from George Wallace campaign posters to Marilyn Monroe promoting shampoo. Food is cheap, plentiful, and savory, with man-sized drinks of all descriptions. You can have one of the best smokehouse burgers in town, along with chili con carne, stuffed mushrooms, melt-in-your-mouth nachos, and an array of barbecued beef and chicken. No meal is complete without a slice of pecan or mud pie for dessert. You can eat for as little as 1,000 pesetas ($7). Half-price drinks are de rigueur during happy hour between 5 to 8 p.m.

The Chicago Pizza Factory, 300 Provenza (tel. 215-94-15). Its flamboyant red awning stretches across the street from one of Gaudí's most outrageous apartment buildings. Speakeasy scarlet-colored doors swing open to reveal a cavernous room where the posters, lampposts, and red-vested waiters all seem to glorify old Chicago itself. This is the Barcelona extension of a restaurant which proved enormously successful in London. It is filled with Windy City memorabilia. Like the decor, the food is whimsically informal. You can eat here for around 1,000 pesetas ($7), selecting such specialties as pizzas for between one and four persons, fried chicken, chili con carne, wine by the glass, fresh salads, stuffed mushrooms, and pecan pie. Don't overlook the possibilities of this place as a watering hole if you're in the neighborhood. At a pine-paneled bar near the entrance, a huge array of drinks are served beneath a sign proclaiming "My kinda town."

A MILK BAR: **Granja "La Palleresa,"** 11 Calle Petrixol (tel. 302-20-36). There are all kinds of bars sprouting up in Barcelona, but this particular one—a milk bar—offers a great number of creamy specialties instead of alcohol. It's a confection-lover's dream come true, tempting you with a crème de Cataluña (a special Catalán version of flan which makes French crème caramel look bland) and other specialties such as Spanish, French, and Swiss hot chocolate (made with water, milk, and Chantilly, respectively), mató de Montserrat (fresh cheese with sugar or honey), or the summertime favorite, horchata, which looks like a milkshake but is actually made with almonds. The bar is about a half block east of the Ramblas between Las Ramblas and the Plaza José Oriol. All but the most elaborate drinks cost around 130 pesetas (91¢), while desserts go for 150 pesetas ($1.05) and up.

SOME GOOD FINDS: **Casa Culleretes,** 5 Carrer Quintana (tel. 317-30-22), off the Ramblas, has a rightful claim as Barcelona's oldest restaurant. Founded in 1786, it still retains many of its original architectural features: all three dining rooms are decorated in a Catalán style, with tile dado and wrought-iron chandeliers. When you taste the food here, you'll know that someone has been at the stove long enough to perfect his or her craft. Specialties include sole Roman style, zarzuela a la marinara, cannelloni, and paella. Complete meals start at 1,500 pesetas ($10.50). From October to January, special game dishes are featured, including partridges (perdices). Celebrities, flamenco artists, bullfighters, have frequented this casa for its authentic dishes of northeastern Spain. They have left signed photographs on the walls to testify to their good times and meals here. The restaurant is closed Sunday night and Monday and July 1 to 20. Metro: Liceo-Ramblas.

Another real find is the **Restaurante Blanch,** off the Paseo de Gracia, 269 Diputación (tel. 302-40-24). Go through a bar area and enter a cozy, low-vaulted dining room where a good lunch is served for 1,000 pesetas ($7). It includes a big bowl of soup (brought in a tureen) or a mixed salad; paella, ravioli, sardines, or hors d'oeuvres; wienerschnitzel, a quarter chicken, or a steak. You end with dessert, and a half bottle of wine or beer is included. Portions are so large you can hardly finish them. The chef also prepares an array of international specialties. It's possible to order from the à la carte menu at a cost beginning at 1,800 pesetas ($12.60), which represents exceptionally good value. It's closed Sunday.

SPLURGE DINING: **El Dorado Petit,** 51 Calle Dolors Monserdà (tel. 204-51-53), is a chic dining rendezvous, with an elegantly informal garden. It's set within the vine-covered walls of what used to be a private villa with transitional elements of both art nouveau and art deco. A cluster of iron tables sits beneath a verdant linden tree within an enclosed courtyard in front, but the preferred enclave is within the glistening champagne-colored walls of the high-ceilinged interior. There you'll enjoy some of the most imaginative nouvelle cuisine in Spain, under the direction of Lluís Cruañas.

The dishes that have become the rage of Barcelona include carpaccio in the style of Harry's Bar, a brochette of crayfish, a delightful preparation which the menu calls a lasagne of fresh asparagus and salmon, and a delectable version of peppers stuffed with pâté of rascasse (a Mediterranean seafish), along with succulent pork, lamb, and fish dishes, many of them original. Full dinners cost from 4,000 pesetas ($28) and are served daily except Sunday and for two weeks in August.

Agut d'Avignon, Carrer de la Trinitat (tel. 302-60-34). One of my favorite restaurants in Barcelona is set near the Plaza Real on a tiny alleyway so small that you'll be able to find it only by knowing the cross street which it intersects (in this case, no. 8 Calle de Aviño or Avinyó). After passing through the curved enclosure of a tiny 19th-century vestibule, you'll enter a multi-level dining room whose beamed ceiling shelters two separate balconies and a main dining room. A batallion of impeccably uniformed and very polite waiters works hard to create an old-fashioned feeling of organized comfort.

Full meals cost from 3,500 pesetas ($24.50) and include some of the changing array of regional specialties which the owner, Mercèdes Giralt, exhibits flair and imagination in creating. You might need help in translating food items on the Catalán menu, which is likely to include chilled cream of crabmeat soup, shrimp in cognac sauce, clams marinara, stuffed squid, stew of rapefish, tournedos in a green pepper sauce, entrecôte with Roquefort, and a delectable version of sole with orange sauce, perhaps sweet and sour filet of pork. Reservations are suggested.

La Odisea, 7 Copons (tel. 302-36-92), sits near the cathedral in a 19th-century warehouse whose interior was redesigned along lines which were harmonious with the well-honed esthetic of its owner and chef. A meal here will whet your artistic sensibilities as well as your appetite. The moment you enter the elegantly simple bar, you're ringed with one of the most unusual collections of paintings in Barcelona. The art work is by friends of the owner, Antonio Ferrer, whose striking portrait (in full chef's regalia) hangs near the bar.

Later, in a dining room capped with heavy beams, with porcelain designed by local artist Guerrero Medina, you can order an elaborate set menu for 3,400 pesetas ($23.80). Menu specialties include sole Odisea, oysters gratinée, squid stuffed with crayfish, entrecôte with an anchovy-flavored cream sauce, veal kidneys in sherry sauce, and crêpes flambéed with Grand Marnier. If you order wine, be sure to ask for a look at the label, as the dream sequence pastels were designed by the Spanish artist, Francisco Artigau. The kind and very sophisticated maître d', Joaquin Cienfuegos, accepts reservations daily except Sunday, for both lunch and dinner.

A VISIT TO SOME TASCAS: The **Parrilla Grill Room,** 8 Calle Escudillers (tel. 302-40-10), off the Ramblas Capuchinos, is perfect for a before-dinner glass of wine. On this teeming street, it captures the spirit of old Barcelona, and the Gaudí-inspired art nouveau decor is a harmonious backdrop. Served until midnight, meals cost 1,200 pesetas ($8.40) to 1,500 pesetas ($10.50), but tapas cost less. A half bottle of wine goes for 165 pesetas ($1.16).

Taverna Kit Kat, 10 Calle Escudillers (tel. 318-87-29), near the above recommendation, is another way to pacify your stomach while waiting for the late dinner hour. The tasca is usually crowded at sundown with drinkers and munchers. It displays its wares under glass, and you can actually get real Mexican tortillas here. At a table lining the window, you can watch your fellow tasca hoppers eating and drinking as if both were going out of style. Cubiertos begin at 650 pesetas ($4.55), and a platter of Catalán sausage with beans costs 350 pesetas ($2.45). At night, you'll trip over the hookers and hustlers getting to the place, as the tavern lies on the most colorful (but not the safest) street in Barcelona. If you're easily intimidated, go to some of the newer, safer bars recommended in this chapter.

Bar Texido, 7 Plaza Real, is one of the most central and most popular tascas in Barcelona, especially on a Saturday night when the square becomes a fascinating "living room" for the city. Perhaps you'll order beer, maybe sangría. Either tastes good with the list of savory tapas, which include chorizo (the spicy Spanish sausage), Serrano ham, patates (potatoes) braves, grilled shrimp (gambas a la plancha), and calamari (squid). Snacks begin at 125 pesetas (88¢), and the entertainment is thrown in for free.

Bar Hispano, 21 Passeig Nacional (tel. 319-02-79). Its simple formica tables and unpretentious decor qualify it more as a tapas bar than as a full-fledged restaurant. Still, the array of food is so complete that many neighborhood families arrive in groups of five or six, camping out for a full meal of the delectably seasoned tapas. You'll find at least 30 kinds of tapas here, including tuna chunks, croquettes of minced fish, different preparations of squid, Russian salad, and anchovies. Two large mugs of beer and two rations of tapas cost about 800 pesetas ($5.60). You'll find this place beside the harborfront road in a colorful industrial and residential area known as Playa de la Barceloneta.

3. The Top Sights

From the top of Montjuich to the top of Tibidabo, there is much to see and do in Barcelona. The eccentric Tarragona-born architect, Gaudí, has left numerous art nouveau edifices to render us speechless; the Gothic quarter is fascinating, as are the seedy Ramblas; some art museums (medieval to Picasso), an entire village (an architectural melting pot of Spanish styles), and a surrealist park are only a few of the sights awaiting you. Give yourself at least three days, if you can spare them, to get acquainted with the city.

Incidentally, at some point during the day, you may want to pay a visit to the **Paseo de Colón** at the Barcelona harbor, dominated by a statue of Christopher Columbus. While here, you can see a good reproduction (go aboard if you wish) of the *Santa María* for 125 pesetas (88¢). It is open from 9 a.m. to 9 p.m. April to September, to 6 p.m. October to March.

You can also take a pleasant half-hour boat trip through the harbor. Boats depart about every 20 minutes or so from in front of the Columbus Monument at the Puerta de la Paz.

THE TEMPLE OF THE SACRED FAMILY (LA SAGRADA FAMILIA): This uncompleted work by the irrepressible Gaudí, who died in 1926, is a symbol of the defiant spirit of Barcelona. If you have time to see only one Catalán landmark, make it this cathedral. It is at Calle Mallorca and Provenza y Marina-Cerdeña. Begun in 1882, this incredible cathedral is one of the bizarre wonders of Spain. Its appearance is so odd that it's difficult to describe and must be seen to be appreciated, but this may give you a clue: art nouveau run rampant, ornamental figures, eight principal wall-ventilated tapering towers with celestially orbed peaks fringed with balls, and lots and lots of melting gingerbread draped in a majestic batter-like ooze over a forest of stalagmites and jutting brown icicles.

To enter the precincts costs 200 pesetas ($1.40), and for another 75 pesetas (53¢), you can see a 12-minute video of both the religious and secular works of Gaudí. An elevator in one of the towers will take you to the top (about 200 feet) for 50 pesetas (35¢). Hours are 9 a.m. to 9 p.m. April to September, to 7 p.m. October to March. Metro: Sagrada Familia.

THE CATHEDRAL: At the Plaça de la Seu, the **Cathedral of Barcelona** is a celebrated example of Catalán Gothic. Except for the west façade (built in the 19th century), the basilica was in the works from the end of the 13th century until the mid-15th century. Inside, the three naves, formerly dimly lighted, have now been cleaned and artistically illuminated, revealing their splendid Gothic details. This impressive cathedral is the grand old lady of the Barri Gòtic of Barcelona. With its large bell towers, its blending of medieval and Renaissance styles, its beautiful cloister, high altar, side chapels, sculptured choir, and Gothic-style arches, it is one of the most important cathedrals in Spain. In the cloister—artistically illuminated on Saturday and fiesta days—is a museum filled with medieval art. Open from 11 a.m. to 1 p.m., it may be inspected free. Hours are 7 a.m. to 1:30 p.m. and 4 to 7 p.m.

After viewing the cathedral, you may want to explore the excavations underneath, which were the site of a basilica dating from the 4th century and a Visigothic palace. You gain entry via the Excavation Museum, opposite the Plaza del Rey. At the square, incidentally, you can enjoy open-air concerts in the evening. Tickets, costing about 800 pesetas ($5.60), generally go on sale at 11 a.m. on the day of the concert.

At noon on Sunday, the best time to visit, you can see a sardana spontaneously danced in front of the cathedral. This is the most typical folk dance of Catalonia. Metro: Jaume I.

THE GOTHIC QUARTER (BARRI GÒTIC): This is the old aristocratic quarter of Barcelona that recalls to mind the days of the legendary counts. Spend at least two or three hours walking through its narrow streets and squares, preserved from the Middle Ages. A nighttime stroll takes on an added drama, but one should exercise extreme caution in traveling around after dark. The buildings, for the most part, are austere and sober. The cathedral is the crowning achievement, but the colonnaded, 18th-century **Bishop's Palace,** 5 Calle del Obispo Irurita (tel. 301-10-84), is also worth a visit. In addition, you'll find Roman ruins and the remains of the 3rd-century walls. The Gothic Quarter lies east of the Ramblas (the Calle del Carmen leads up to it).

THE PICASSO MUSEUM (MUSEO PICASSO): Three old converted palaces at 15-17 Calle de Montcada (tel. 319-63-10) have been turned into a museum, housing works by Pablo Picasso, the Málaga-born artist. Once belonging to one of the nobles of Barcelona, the splendid museum sits on a street left over from the Middle Ages.

In the winter of 1970 the artist donated some 2,500 of his works to the museum of Barcelona. Although other museums—certainly those in France—were hoping to receive the bequest, he favored Barcelona. Perhaps he remembered much of his youth spent there, during what biographers call his "formative years." The multimillion-dollar collection consists of engravings, paintings, and drawings. Richard Eder, in a press comment, called the collection "the extraordinary trail of Picasso's early assertions, disguises, concealments, reappearances, and transformations."

Some of the exhibit dates back to when Picasso was nine years old. Painted in 1896, one portrait depicts his stern aunt. Another, completed at the turn of the century and called *Science and Charity,* was painted by Picasso when he was 16 years old (his father was the model for the doctor).

Many of the works, especially the early paintings, show Picasso's debt to such artists as Van Gogh, El Greco, and Rembrandt. The so-called academic paintings reveal nude, bearded men. The famous series, the *Menines* (1957), are said to "impersonate" those of Velázquez. From his blue period, the *La Vie* drawings are perhaps the most interesting. Many sketches of scenes in Barcelona are in his notebooks.

The museum is open daily from 9 a.m. to 2 p.m. and 4 to 8:30 p.m. It is closed Sunday afternoon and Monday morning. The charge is 175 pesetas ($1.23). Metro: Jaume I.

GÜELL PARK (PARQUE GÜELL): At the slope of Tibidabo, overlooking the city from the north, is the park (free entrance) where Gaudí's imagination went to work again, this time for a wealthy count by the name of Güell. Gaudí created a surrealist's Disneyland with a mosaic pagoda, popular with children of all ages. The central architectural attraction looks like some ancient tomb of a lost civilization, what with its deliberately crooked columns and all. One sculptured piece resembles a prehistoric monster spitting water. Have a seat on the curvy mosaic bench, and contemplate what a schizoid dream must be like. Gaudí must have wanted to make his comment on the hanging gardens of Babylon. You can also visit Gaudí's House and museum next to the Carretera del Carmelo (tel. 204-52-50). It is open Sundays and holidays from 10 a.m. to 2 p.m. and 4 to 7 p.m., charging no admission. Metro: Lèsseps.

POBLE ESPANYOL: This Spanish Village in Montjuïch Park was built in 1929 for a world's fair. Even though that "bust" year wasn't a good one for a fair, somebody had the good sense to preserve this village, pieced together with the various types of architecture represented in the provinces of Spain, from the Levante to Galicia. At the entranceway, for example, is a facsimile of the gateway to the walled city of Ávila. On the Plaza Mayor, in the center of the village, you can sit outside and have drinks. Also, you can buy any number of handcraft and souvenir items from all of the provinces, and in some of the shops you can see craftspeople at work, printing fabric, blowing glass. The village can be visited from 9 a.m. to 7 p.m. Admission is 100 pesetas (70¢).

TIBIDABO MOUNTAIN: After seeing Gaudí's park, you can continue up the mountain to the top of Tibidabo, with its spectacular view of Barcelona. The ideal time to visit this hill, north of the port, is at sunset, when the city lights are being turned on. Quite a sight—and it should be. For as legend has it, Satan took Christ up here and tempted him with the world. Come here for the views of nature; the man-made attractions run a poor second. Tibidabo has been turned into a Coney Island of the sky; ferris wheels swing over Barcelona, some 1,600 feet above sea level. Being Spanish, the Cataláns also had to crowd a church into this carnival-like setting; it's called Sacred Heart. There are also restaurants and mountaintop hotels. From the Plaça de Catalunya, take a bus to the Avinguda del Tibidabo, where you can board a special bus that will transport you to the funicular. You can hop aboard and scale the mountain. A round-trip ticket is 80 pesetas (56¢). Metro: Tibidabo.

MONTJUÏCH PARK: At the south of the city, Montjuïch is an all-year delight. With its splashing fountains, gardens, outdoor restaurants, and museums, it makes for quite an outing. There are many walks you can take and places where you can peer out over the skyline of Barcelona. The park also contains the Poble Espanyol and the Joan Miró Foundation, dealt with separately as attractions. To reach Montjuïch, take the funicular leaving from the Paralelo underground station (line 3). On weekend nights, particularly Saturday, there is an illuminated fountain display—with dazzling color—near Plaza de España, lasting from around 9:30 to 11 p.m. In summer, the display is also staged on Thursday night. Metro: Pueblo Seco.

MUSEUM OF ART OF CATALONIA: At some point during your visit to Montjuïch Park, you may want to visit the Museo de Arte de Catalunya (tel. 223-18-24) at the National Palace, which has been turned into a treasure house of medieval art. Here is displayed a collection of Catalán Gothic retables, woodcarvings, medieval murals—endless Spanish and European baroque works, most of them religious in nature. The museum also houses an impressive collection of Romanesque murals.

A 12th-century painted front altarpiece depicts a saint being tortured and other Bosch-like scenes of horror, including victims boiled in a pot. You can see fragments of 12th-century decorative murals from the Church of Santa María de Tahull (Lérida). But the pinnacle of the 12th-century works is reached in the *Pantocrátor* (God the Majesty), a concave fresco removed from San Clemente de Tahull. Although it owes a heavy debt to the Byzantine influence, the fresco is a creative breakthrough in that it represents the attempt of a Spanish artist to make his personal statement.

You can also find woodcarvings and paintings from the Church of Esterri de Cardós, representing work from the 11th and 12th centuries. In another room are Gothic works of the 14th century—notably no. 26, a retable dedicated to St. Vicente. In yet another salon is a 15th-century Virgin of alabaster. Also displayed here are two especially outstanding retables—one by the Serra brothers from the Monastery of Gaulter in the province of Lérida; another by Jaume Serra, this latter one dedicated to the Virgin. A 14th-century retable is dedicated to Santa Catalina, interesting in that it depicts death, demons, and decapitation.

Also displayed is a notable collection of Gothic paintings, such as a Virgin nursing her child and an especially good *Resurrection.* There is another exceptional retable, this one a 14th-century work dedicated to San Juan Bautista, Santa Eulalia, and San Sebastian. See, in particular, a 15th-century triptych to Saint Estebán, and a well-known painting by Jaume Cireca, showing *Angels and Demons* in the mouth of hell, dating from 1433.

An important work, this one entitled *The Virgin of the Consellers,* is by Lluis Dalmau. Seek out works by Jaume Hugnet, a 15th-century Tarragona-born artist, known for his realistic faces (see his *Virgin and Child with the Angels*), plus a work by an artist a bit better known than those previously mentioned—El Greco's *Sts. Peter and Paul.*

The museum is open from 9 a.m. to 2 p.m. and charges 175 pesetas ($1.23) admission. Closed Monday. Metro: España.

FEDERICO MARÉS MUSEUM (MUSEO FEDERICO MARÉS): At 10 Carrer dels Comtes de Barcelona (tel. 310-58-00) is one of the biggest repositories in the region of medieval sculpture, most of it ecclesiastical. The entrance is just behind the cathedral, in back of a discreet metal sign placed near a blue and white tile background. The setting is actually an ancient Barcelona palace whose interior courtyards, chiseled stone, and soaring ceilings are impressive in their own right and certainly are the ideal setting for the hundreds of polychromed sculptures showing everything from a suffering Christ to a radiant Mary, in dozens of poses. The art dates from pre-Roman times to the 19th century, with sculpture coming from as far away as England. One wing of the collection is devoted to the display of the dusty ruins of an ancient Roman casa.

Marés is a collector and sculptor in his own right who bequeathed his treasures to the awesomely valuable museum. Open from 9 a.m. to 2 p.m. and 4 to 7 p.m., the museum is closed Sunday afternoon and all day Monday. Admission is 85 pesetas (60¢); free Sunday morning. Metro: Jaume I.

THE MARITIME MUSEUM (MUSEO MARÍTIMO): At the Porta de la Pau, at the edge of the harbor near the southern end of the Ramblas, this maritime museum (tel. 301-64-25) attracts visitors who have a love of the sea. Under stone-vaulted ceilings, it is rich in the lore of the sea, complete with figureheads and all the trappings that man has used to cross vast oceans. Its most outstanding exhibition is a reconstruction of La Galera Real of D. Juan de Austria, a lavish royal galley. As of this writing, no one is permitted to go aboard, however. One of the special exhibits is a map by Amerigo Vespucci, an explorer who lent his name to a continent. The nautical displays are housed in a 14th-century royal boatyard, called *Reales Atarazanas.* The museum is open from 10 a.m. to 2 p.m. and 4 to 7 p.m. It is closed on Monday and holidays. Admission is 100 pesetas (70¢). Metro: Atarazanas.

JOAN MIRÓ FOUNDATION (FUNDACIÓ JOAN MIRÓ): Born in 1893, Joan Miró went on to become one of Spain's greatest painters. He is known for his whimsical abstract forms and his brilliant colors. Some paintings by this Catalán surrealist, plus graphics and sculpture, have been collected at the foundation devoted to the artist, at Montjuïch Park. A large woven wall tapestry is about 14 feet high. This museum, open Tuesday to Saturday from 11 a.m. to 8 p.m., attracts art lovers from all over the world. On Sunday its hours are 11 a.m. to 2:30 p.m. Admission is 250 pesetas ($1.75). Josep Lluís Sert designed an attractive gray-painted modern building in which the collection is housed. In addition to the permanent body of work devoted to Miró, temporary exhibitions on contemporary art are frequently shown. The museum is reached by taking bus 61 on María Cristina at the Plaza de España and by bus 201 from the Parallel subway station. For information about the museum, telephone 329-19-08.

THE ZOO (PARC ZOÒLOGIC): Spain's top zoo (tel. 309-25-00) is in Ciutadella Park, near the Estación de Francia. It is a modern zoo, with barless enclosures, indoor and outdoor dolphin shows, and animals from Africa seldom seen. One of the most unusual attractions is the famous albino gorilla, Snowflake (Copito de Nieve), the only one of its kind in captivity in the world. The main entrances to Ciutadella Park are via the Passeig Pujadas and Passeig Picasso. Entrance to see all exhibits of the zoo is 300 pesetas ($2.10). Hours are daily from 9:30 a.m. to 7:30 p.m. Metro: Arc de Triomf (line 1) or Ciutadella (line 4).

READERS' SIGHTSEEING TIP: "For only subway fees in Barcelona one may enjoy the treat of viewing certain Gaudí buildings other than La Sagrada Familia. An especially enjoyable one is the **Casa Batllo,** 43 Passeig de Gràcia, at the corner of Gràcia and Aragó, a subway stop. We recommend taking the elevator up to the top floor (one can see out during the ride) and then walking down the steps. After that, going along Gràcia for a few blocks one can hardly fail to notice another Gaudí creation, **La Pedrera,** 92 Passeig de Gràcia. It is most enjoyable to view the sculpted stone outside, its inner courtyard, and, at a distance, the unique rooftop decorations" (Robert and Janice Titiev, Detroit, Mich.).

SHOPPING NOTES: If you're a window shopper, you may want to stroll along the Passeig de Gràcia (Paseo de Gracia) from the Diagonal to the Plaça de Catalunya (Plaza de Cataluña). Along the way, you'll see some of the most elegant—and most expensive—shops in Barcelona, along with an assortment of splendid turn-of-the-century buildings and cafés, many with outdoor tables.

You might also begin your shopping expedition at the **San José Mercado,** just off the Ramblas, near the Carrer del Carmen. Here you'll see a wide display of straw bags and regional products, along with a handsome display of the food you are likely to be eating later in a local restaurant: fruits, vegetables (beautifully displayed), breads, and cheese, along with meats and tanks filled with live fish. Go here for the fixings of a picnic.

Galerías Precíados, 19 Avinguda Puerta del Angel (tel. 317-00-00), and its neighbor a short distance away, **El Corte Inglés,** 14 Plaça de Catalunya (tel. 302-12-12), and 617 Avenida Diagonal (tel. 322-40-11), are the two biggest department stores in Barcelona. Each is loaded with merchandise, some of it the usual department-store fare you could find anywhere. Some sections, however, represent surprisingly good values at far lower prices than at the boutiques only a few blocks away. Galerías Precíados has reasonably priced Spanish leather in an extensive selection of wallets, purses, and passport cases.

Centro Anticuarious, 55 Passeig de Gràcia. If you're even vaguely interested in antiques, you shouldn't leave Barcelona without a stop at this shopping complex leading off one of the most aristocratic avenues in town. There are enough antiques of many different styles to furnish a palace, all of them assembled into a mutlilevel collection of boutiques whose treasures are visible through glass doors and windows. For an insight into who comes to town to unload bundles of pesetas, marks, dollars, or yen, you might have a coffee at the café/bar on the upper level, where the latest in disco music plays softly to encourage prospective customers to make that really grand splurge that they will probably keep forever. All of the shops keep slightly different hours, but usually the center opens around 10 to 11 a.m. daily except Monday.

If you're interested in purchasing espadrilles (in Spanish, *alpargatas*), head for **La Manual Alpargaters,** 7 Calle d'Avinyó (tel. 301-01-72). There you will find a huge selection of straw products such as hats, bags, and shoes. To reach it, turn off the Ramblas at Calle de Fernando, go for two blocks, and make a right. One woman reader wrote of the "individual attention, friendly service, and good prices," and I concur with her point of view.

Casa Arpi, 40 Rambla de los Capuchinos (tel. 301-74-04), although you wouldn't know to judge by its unprepossessing entrance, is one of the most famous camera shops in Europe. A multilingual staff will guide you to the best buys in both new and used cameras, including products manufactured by such names as Minolta, Nikon, Hasselblad, and Pentax. The "backup" equipment sold here is extensive, ranging from macro lenses to flash units. They even sell equipment to take care of the problems confronted by near- or far-sighted photographers. All the familiar names in film, Kodak or Fuji, are sold here, along with brands that you may never have heard of, particularly those imports from Eastern Europe. The firm also does quality processing, and the finished work should be ready within 24 to 48 hours after you drop it off.

Syra, 43 Passeig (Paseo) de Gràcia (tel. 216-01-76), is set into one of the most fascinating art nouveau buildings of Barcelona, one where virtually every angle has been exaggerated into super-voluptuous curves. Inside, you'll find items for sale such as Lladró porcelain, silverware, artwork, etchings, and a limited selection of furniture. Many of the items are small, perhaps reflecting the taste of the elderly women who sell them. The shop is closed Monday afternoon. The entrance is a few steps from the Passeig de Gràcia subway station.

Loewe, 35 Passeig de Gràcia (tel. 216-04-00), is the biggest branch in Barcelona of the most famous leather goods store in Spain. Everything is top-notch here, from the elegantly spacious showroom to the merchandise to the gracious sales people. This company exports its goods to branches throughout Asia, Europe, and North America.

Kastoria 2, 6-8 Avenida Catédral (tel. 310-04-11), is a large store near the cathedral. Here you'll find many kinds of leather goods, including purses, suitcases, and clothes, such as leather coats and jackets.

Artespaña, 75 Rambla de Cataluña (tel. 217-78-93), is a member of the nationwide government-owned chain that sells Spanish-made artifacts from throughout the country. This particular branch seems to specialize more in high-fashion household accessories and gift items than in the country-style, handmade products you might expect. They will ship your purchase home if you wish.

4. The City After Dark

Barcelona comes alive at night. Especially popular with the evening crowds is the funicular ride to Tibidabo or the waterworks of Montjuïch. The center of the club life is the cabaret-packed district at the south of the Ramblas, where you are likely to get mugged.

The Ramblas teem with excitement and danger. In the early evening a wide segment of the populace converges on this boulevard of cafés and bars. Later in the evening you may want to walk east down the **Calle Escudillers** (off the Plaza del Teatro, at the Ramblas Capuchinos). In the maze of narrow streets branching off from here are to be found out-of-the-way cabarets, some very good and some very bad restaurants, bars, tourist traps, and assorted nightlife catering to all tastes. It's not safe to go walking here. Women alone will feel intimidated, and men alone will be aggressively solicited by prostitutes, many of whom will brazenly grope them.

If you visit one of the dives in the old quarter, don't carry too much cash, because dimly lit, crowded cabarets are a haven for pickpockets. Many of the questionable establishments and gypsy joints are unabashed rip-off joints for sailors and their pickups. Take extreme care in selecting your slumming adventure for the evening, keep a healthy tongue-in-cheek attitude—and you're likely to have a good time.

My lead-off entertainment choice is a unique experiment.

AN EVENING WITH THE RED-HOT MAMAS OF YESTERYEAR: The incomparable **Bodega Bohemia** 2 Lancaster (tel. 302-50-61), off the Ramblas, is a Barcelona institution. In medieval-esque surroundings, the fading swan-like chansonniers and dying refugees from the cloak-and-dagger plays of Lope de Vega entertain you with their wit, irony, and satire—and what roughly might be called singing.

The bodega is a cabaret extraordinaire. Everybody from Marcello Mastroianni to Tennessee Williams to American collegiates to playgirls has frequented this place, which answers the question: *Whatever Happened to Baby Jane?* The Spanish Baby Janes are still belting one out for the boys in the back room.

As you may have gathered, the Bodega Bohemia is a talent showcase for theatrical personalities whose bones aren't so bouncy, but whose spirits are undimmed by rheumatism. It's not a freak show. Not at all, but more in the tragicomedy vein of the old Shakespearian actor in the long-running off-Broadway show *The Fantasticks.*

The woman who sits next to you may look like Count Dracula's great-grandmother, but when she gets up to perform, chances are she'll sound more like Florence Foster Jenkins. She's likely to sing "Granada," much to the delight of the rocking audience. Then the pinup queen of the boys who fought our boys in the Spanish-American War is likely to be followed by another love goddess of the octogenarians—this one a dead ringer for a drag version of Bela Lugosi. She'll probably play the accordion and do a few bumps and grinds that would have caused her to be arrested if she were only 30 years younger.

Curiously, most audiences fill up with young people, who cheer, boo, catcall, and scream with laughter—and the oldtimers on the stage love it. The show stretches on forever.

The cost? Only 500 pesetas ($3.50) for your first drink (no cover). In all, it's an incredible entertainment bargain if your tastes dip slightly into the bizarre. The street outside is none too safe, so it's better to have a taxi take you right to the door.

Also typical of Old Barcelona are shows at that octogenarian institution, the **Molino,** 99 Vila Vilá (tel. 241-63-83). The Molino is a regular theater, featuring variety shows and girlie acts, most of them pretty bad, but fun to watch nonetheless. Especially delectable are the give-and-take between audiences (often sailors and locals) and performers. You sit in regular theater chairs, and place your drink (a Coca-Cola, for example) on a ledge in back of the seat in front of yours. The 5:30 p.m. show costs 500 pesetas ($3.50) although the 10:45 one is raised to 1,200 pesetas ($8.40).

For more typical Spanish night-owl fare, sample:

FLAMENCO: **Los Tarantos,** 17 Plaza Real (tel. 317-80-98), offers some of the best flamenco in town. Its *tablao* is presented daily from 10 p.m. to 3 a.m. The price of admission is 2,000 pesetas ($14), which includes the cost of your first drink. Subsequent libations cost from 600 pesetas ($4.20) each.

CULTURAL: **Gran Theatre del Liceu,** 61 Rambla de Caputxins (tel. 301-67-27), was inaugurated in 1847, making it one of the grandest opera theaters in the world. It presents a classical repertoire of ballet, concerts, and opera. Front row and boxes are extremely expensive, and tickets are virtually impossible to obtain. However, one reader wrote in a budget tip. "Stop at the opera box office early in the evening and get a 400-peseta ($2.80) ticket for the fifth balcony (you'll enjoy the view of the ornate ceiling). When the curtain rises, you'll probably be able to move to a vacant and better seat as no one is admitted after the performance begins."

DISCOS AND CABARETS: **Dos Torres,** 300 Via Augusta (tel. 203-98-99), is one of the most sophisticated and fashionable late night bars in Barcelona. It lies in the affluent northern edge of the city, amid gardens which surround the private villas and expensive apartments of the Sarria district. In every season except winter, its triangular forecourt is filled to overflowing with well-dressed, articulate, and available young men and women. Inside the confines of what used to be the salons of an art nouveau villa, you'll find a minimalist decor with art deco accents, unusual lithographs, and a long and dramatically illuminated bar. The establishment is open daily except Sunday, from 1 p.m. to 3 a.m. Beer is 100 pesetas (70¢), while the 42 elaborate drinks (plus the daily creations of the bartender) begin at 300 pesetas ($2.10).

Studio 54, 54 Paralelo (tel. 309-54-54). Since the best days of Studio 54 in New York have faded, the energy seems to have crossed into a less disco-jaded culture across the Atlantic. Barcelona's version of the place where everybody used to want to be can sometimes get almost as wild as the establishment's namesake did in its heyday. If you look like you can afford the price of a drink, you'll probably be admitted into an enormous room where the crowd seems to be partially mesmerized by the several different light and slide shows and where the dance floor at the time of your visit might be filled with the more offbeat members of Barcelona's night scene. There's a cover charge, which varies according to your gender, the day of the week, and the time of night, from 500 pesetas ($3.50) to 1,100 pesetas ($7.70). Once you're inside, drinks will cost you around 400 pesetas ($2.80) each. The place is open Friday night, Saturday in the late afternoon and at night, and Sunday night. Like every nightclub in Spain, it's most crowded after around 11:30 p.m.

Barcelona de Noche, 5 Tapias, in the Barrio Chino (tel. 241-11-67), offers the kind of acts which, indeed, are best suited to very late-night viewing. The cabaret/mime/dance routine includes mostly men dressed as women, with the sole exception being one genetic female who seems tougher than many of her colleagues. Spaniards go for the exotics of it all, and maybe you will too. This place has been around for a long time and is well known in the city. Drinks, served every day except Tuesday, average around 2,000 pesetas ($14).

Belle Epoque, 246 Mutaner (tel. 209-73-85). The physical setting, with crystal chandeliers and plush accessories, strikes an opulent note for the productions, which often involve girls, glamor, and glitter. The amplification system is highly sophisticated, and the dance numbers are often accompanied by some of the most advanced lighting tricks in Barcelona. Drinks average around 2,000 pesetas ($14). The place is open daily except Sunday.

Arnau, 60 Paralelo (tel. 242-24-08). Just about any kind of musical act might be appearing during your visit here, but the enthusiastic crowd usually applauds warmly after the cabaret and music hall acts that show up. A drink costs around 850 pesetas ($5.95). Arnau is closed Wednesday.

Don Chufo, 618 Avenida Diagonal (tel. 321-30-11), is one of the best-known cabaret and disco institutions in town. It's in the Edifício Beethoven, which most taxi drivers will be able to find. It divides its functions between being an early-hours youth-oriented disco and a late-night cabaret with singers and comedians sometimes known throughout the Spanish-speaking world. Service is polite and people usually have a good time here. Drinks during disco hours are about 600 pesetas ($4.20), rising to around 2,000 pesetas ($14) at showtime.

2001, 406 Consejo de Ciento (tel. 245-00-84), is a two-level disco where many of the youthful clients move freely around the large space "checking things out" and meeting their friends, plus a terrace restaurant. Live music and shows are presented. The unusually potent drinks, many of them original recipes, average about 500 pesetas ($3.50).

BARS AND PUBS: Pub 240, 240 Aribau (tel. 209-09-67), near the Tuset area, is a place for the young. The elegant Pub, which has absolutely no resemblance to the English concept of a pub, features nightly guitar playing and rock, as well as South American folk music. There are three sections, one consisting of a bar, another a small amphitheater, yet another a lounge for talking and listening. It's all elegant and chic and is jammed every night. The action lasts till about 3 a.m. The average drinks go for 750 pesetas ($5.25) and up. However, the price of the first drink and the show ranges from 1,000 pesetas ($7) to 1,500 pesetas ($10.50).

Ideal Cocktail Bar, 89 Aribau (tel. 253-10-28), is a pleasant drinking spot, with paneling, stained-glass windows, comfortable leather-covered chairs whose model probably originated in the 19th century, white-jacketed waiters, and original artworks. Since Las Ramblas have become so unsafe, this area with its many bars has become the preferred nightlife center for many residents of Barcelona. Surprisingly, this is one of the few bars in town that not only understands the use of vodka but encourages it in such drinks as vodka and tonic, screwdrivers, vodka martinis, Tchaikovskis (vodka with Calvados), vodka with Drambuie, and vodka in a concoction called a Beso Cosaca (vodka with Grand Marnier and lemon juice). Beer costs from 225 pesetas ($1.58); mixed drinks, 300 pesetas ($2.10) to 450 pesetas ($3.15).

La Cova del Drac, 30 Tuset (tel. 217-56-42), is a pleasant neighborhood bar, which, between October and June, offers jazz every day from 11 p.m. till 2 a.m., except on Sunday night and Monday when it is closed. The concerts are held in a lower room where the admission price is 500 pesetas ($3.50) to 1,000 pesetas ($7). If you want just coffee, a beer, or a drink, there's no problem. Someone will serve you in a setting of medium-green walls, art nouveau iron-base marble tables, original artworks, and tropical rattan chairs. Sidewalk tables are available too.

Dirty Dick's, 2 Calle Marco Aurelio (tel. 200-89-52), is an English-style pub set behind an inwardly curving bay window in a residential part of town. The interior is darkly paneled and lined with stained pine, exposed brick, and tartan-covered banquettes set into cubicles for quiet conversations. If you sit at the bar, you'll be faced with a tempting array of tiny sandwiches that taste as good as they look. The pub is set at the corner of the Vía Augusta, a main thoroughfare leading through the district. Mixed drinks cost from 350 pesetas ($2.45).

Gold Lions Cocktelería Bar, 163 Aribau (tel. 239-50-53), is a recent example of the kind of very glamorous *whiskería* that is sweeping through Barcelona.

It has an angular bar stretching from the window in front in a long line past a chic, tasteful, richly trendy decor of plush upholstery, glossy black accents, and warmly inviting earth tones. An artistic display of the house drinks is set up "New Year's Eve" style, behind a screen of yucca plants. There's a second bar in the back where, if you want to play backgammon, someone will bring a playing board. Music is recently released disco tapes, and the entire atmosphere seems fun, relaxed, low key, and warmly permissive. It's open every day, as are many of the other unusual bars along this street. Beer costs around 180 pesetas ($1.26), while mixed drinks (which include things like a Coco Rico, a Favorita, five kinds of very potent coffees, an Alaska, and a Dumbo) begin at 350 pesetas ($2.45).

El Born, 26 Passeig del Born (tel. 319-53-33), is my favorite bar in this section of town. Its façade overlooks a green area that might almost be a village square in the country, especially since there isn't much traffic and the storefronts basically haven't changed much since before the neighborhood came into vogue. You enter a room that, when it was built, served as a local store for dried and salted codfish. The merchandise used to be washed and rinsed free of salt in the marble basins that today have been cleverly converted into part of the bar area. There are a few tables nearby, but my preferred spot is in the inner room where in winter a tiny stove sends out warmth and light and funnels its smoke up a black metal pipe stretching high above the rattan furniture and the modern paintings. There's a single ceiling fan, a rack of ceramic jugs and books, and music that could be anything from Louis Armstrong to Steely Dan. Surrounded by softly talking couples, you can order drinks for 300 pesetas ($2.10) and beer for 175 pesetas ($1.23) per glass.

Later, if you want dinner, you can ascend a flight of winding metal stairs to the upstairs buffet. There you'll find, carefully laid out, a simple but tasty collection of fish, meat, and vegetable dishes where a full dinner without wine costs around 1,500 pesetas ($10.50) per person. The somewhat cramped room contains a beamed ceiling, art nouveau posters, and a wine list for each of the tables where you'll dine.

El Copetin, 19 Passeig del Born, possesses a warmly wood-toned ambience in a long, narrow room which barely allows newcomers the space to squeeze past the bar stools to the seating area in the back. Recorded jazz music plays softly while one or another of the guests might get up to read what's posted on the bulletin board near the front door. Depending on the time of day, the bartender might be male or female. This is a pleasant stopping place, particularly if you want to cover a lot of bars in this corner of the oldest part of the city.

CHAMPAGNE BARS: Some observers say that Spain has done more to jet-propel itself into modern times within the last dozen years than virtually any other country in Europe. Although this applies to many aspects of life, it's especially evident in the proliferation of English-style pubs within the last seven years and, within the last five years, the sudden popularity of champagne bars.

These establishments go by several different names. In Spanish they're called *champanerías,* and in Catalán (especially in Barcelona where they're most popular), the name is *xampanyeries.* Since the word *champagne* technically refers to the sparkling wines of a specific region of France, the Spanish call their own version of it *cava,* and that is the product with which all kinds of Spaniards are making toasts in their newest oenophilic craze. The wines are often excellent, said by experts to be influenced by the different varieties of grapes, soil, and climate. Sometimes in professional blind tests the Spanish champagne has been pronounced better than its French counterparts.

There are more than 50 companies producing *cavas* in Spain, and each bottles up to a dozen different grades of wine. About the only way to learn about Spanish champagne, therefore, is either to visit the vineyard or to sample the products at a xampanyerie. There, between 7 p.m. and the wee hours of the following day, you can toast away with as many varieties of the sparkling wine as you want and consider yourself part of the trendy inner world of Barcelona at the same time. Most establishments offer a limited array of "house cava" by the glass, which usually costs around 375 pesetas ($2.63). You'll be offered a choice of *brut* or *brut nature* (brut is slightly sweeter). Numerous more esoteric cavas must be purchased by the bottle. The most acclaimed brands include Mont-Marçal, Gramona, Mestres, Parxet, Torello, and Recaredo. Tapas are served, usually fairly elegant morsels of everything from caviar to smoked fish or frozen chocolate truffles.

Now that you know what a xampanyerie is (ask a Catalán for the correct pronunciation), here are some addresses where you can see them for yourself:

La Xampanyeria, 236 Provença (tel. 253-74-55), is the oldest, best established, and perhaps the most frequented cava dispenser in town. Sorbets and chocolates are served with the drinks and happily consumed by the customers at the long curved bar or at marble-topped tables on one of the two levels. The inventory includes more than 50 kinds of Catalán cava, many others from throughout Spain, and a few from France.

La Cava de Olimpia, 10 Loreto (tel. 239-10-73), offers a conversation-provoking decor of vintners' memorabilia, ceramic murals of a grape harvest, and rows of champagne bottles stacked as they would be in a cellar but without the dust. You can order fresh oysters at around 1,200 pesetas ($8.40) per half dozen, as well as anchovies and an array of cheeses to go with your drinks, which can be chosen from 70 kinds of cava.

Xampú Xampany, 702 Gran Vía de les Corts Catalanes (tel. 232-07-16), one of the latest in town, has abstract paintings, touches of hi-tech, bouquets of flowers, and a color scheme of yellow and white. You'll find it at the corner of the Plaza Tetuán. There's a wide choice of hors d'oeuvres.

La Cava del Palau, 10 Verdaguer i Callis (tel. 310-09-38), in one of the old parts of town, is one of the tiniest of the champagne bars but with one of the most extensive inventories. Many customers late at night may have just come from a concert at the Palau de la Música (Palace of Music), a few steps around the corner. A salty plate of fresh anchovies, which the management claims are the best in Europe, costs around 300 pesetas ($2.10).

Xampanyeria Casablanca, 6 Bonavista (tel. 237-63-99). Someone had to fashion a champagne bar after the Bogart-Bergman film, and this is it. Potted palms, ceiling fans, and wicker chairs are what it's all about—as well as four kinds of house cava served by the glass. A plate of cured Spanish ham costs around 1,100 pesetas ($7.70). The Casablanca is close to the Passeig de Gràcia.

5. Practical Facts

For **tourism information,** go to the Oficinas de Turismo, 658 Gran Vía de les Corts Catalanes (tel. 317-22-46).

The **American Express** office in Barcelona is at 101 Passeig de Gràcia (tel. 217-17-50). Metro: Diagonal. It is open weekdays from 9:30 a.m. to 6 p.m. and on Saturday from 10 a.m. to noon.

The **Aeropuerto,** El Prat de Llobregat, is about 7½ miles from the heart of Barcelona. For information about flights, telephone 370-10-11.

The **central telephone office** is at 4 Carrer de Fontanella, right off the Plaça de Catalunya, and it's open Monday to Saturday from 9 a.m. to 1 p.m. and 5 to 9 p.m. (closed on Sunday and holidays). Be prepared to encounter one of the rudest and most uncooperative staffs in Spain!

For **medical attention,** seek out the Hospital de San Pablo, 167 Avenida San Antonia María Claret (tel. 347-31-33).

The **U.S. Consulate** is at 33 Vía Laietana (tel. 319-95-50), and it's open Monday to Friday from 9 a.m. to 1 p.m. and 2:30 to 5 p.m. It is closed weekends.

The **postal and telephone service** (24 hours) is at Plaza de Antonio López (tel. 318-38-31).

Chapter XI

BRANCHING OUT FROM BARCELONA

1. Montserrat
2. Tarragona
3. Sitges
4. Andorra
5. Lloret de Mar
6. Tossá de Mar
7. Figueras
8. Cadaqués
9. Cardona
10. Gerona (Girona)

AFTER YOU HAVE SEEN the sights and smelled the smells of Barcelona, it will be time to branch out for a series of one- and two-day excursions in all directions from this capital of Catalonia. Barcelona is like the hub of a wheel of a number of widely varied adventures. For example, about 28 miles northwest of Barcelona lies the most popular excursion from the capital, the Benedictine monastery of **Montserrat.** But there are others equally as enticing.

South of Barcelona is the too-long-neglected Roman city of **Tarragona,** of particular interest to those who appreciate history.

But lest we become too monastic or too steeped in the past, the beach resort of **Sitges,** a nugget on the "Gold Coast" south of Barcelona, returns us to today.

Other tours take us to **Andorra,** a principality in the Pyrenees that is ever growing in popularity. Andorra can be reached in a day from Barcelona, but you should definitely count on spending the night before heading back.

Finally, we'll head north along the **Costa Brava** moving toward the French frontier, taking in the "hot spots" along the coast.

1. Montserrat

The **monastery** at Montserrat, 35 miles northwest of Barcelona, is one of the most important pilgrimage spots in Spain, ranking with Zaragoza and Santiago de Compostela. Built on ground approximately 3,000 feet up, the monastery is not so spectacular, but the mountain on which it sits is—and should be of interest to Catholics and non-Catholics alike. Mother Nature must have created the mountain in a frivolous moment; it suddenly springs up from an otherwise unimpressive landscape.

The church contains a 12th-century statue of *The Black Virgin,* the patron saint of Catalonia. Thousands of the faithful touch her every year, hoping to be blessed. So many newly married couples flock here for her blessings that Montserrat has become a honeymoon center, the Niagara Falls of Spain.

The renowned boys' choir here is one of the oldest in Europe. At 1 p.m., you can usually hear choral singing in the basilica.

While at Montserrat, one of the most exciting things to do is to take the funicular to the peak, Sant Jerόni. The cost is from 425 pesetas ($2.98) round trip. The aerial ropeway goes to the summit of the mountain, at 4,119 feet, in only nine minutes. The funicular operates from 10 a.m. to 7 p.m., with departures about every 20 minutes. From there, one of the most extensive panoramic views in Spain can be seen. Passengers can see not only the whole of Catalonia, but the Pyrenees and all the way to Majorca and Ibiza.

Montserrat is easily reached from Barcelona, and the **Empresa Juliá** company, 12 Plaça Universitat (tel. 318-38-95), operates morning buses to the monastery, leaving from 5 Ronda Universitat, costing from 275 pesetas ($1.93) each way.

But the best and most exciting way to go is via the Catalán railway, Ferrocarrils de la Generalitat de Catalunya, leaving from the Plaza de España in (Plaça de España in Catalán) at 9:10 and 11:10 a.m. The central office is at 1 Plaça Catalunya (tel. 302-48-16). The train connects with an aerial cableway, which is included in the rail passage. Expect to spend around 720 pesetas ($5.04), which includes the round-trip rail passage and the aerial cable lift.

Visitors to Montserrat, even in summer, should take along warm sweaters, jackets, or coats. In winter, thermal underwear might not be a bad idea. The winds blow cold at Montserrat.

WHERE TO STAY AND EAT: Montserrat has some limited accommodations to greet the constantly arriving pilgrims. Few of us will spend the night, but most visitors will want at least one meal. If you don't care to pay a fat tab for lunch, either ask your hotel to pack your meal or do it yourself from the makings easily obtainable at one of the cafeterías in Barcelona.

You don't have to take the sacred vows to stay in the sky-top monastery. After about 800 years, the monks have gotten used to single and group pilgrimages to their retreat. As the years have passed, more comfortable quarters have been built for them, to replace the straw mats formerly handed out. The most expensive hotel is the **Abat Cisneros** (tel. 835-02-01), and the less costly is the **Residencia Monestir** (same phone). Both are at the Plaza del Montserrat.

At Abat Cisneros, the price of the excellent, attractively furnished doubles with private baths is 5,400 pesetas ($37.80), not bad for this so-called "Hilton of the monasteries." The best singles—those with private shower—cost 3,500 ($24.50). A continental breakfast is extra. The three-star hotel has an attractive lounge. Comfortable couches, simple lines, paintings, and plants—all these elements blend together to make it worthy of . . . a honeymoon at least. Meals cost from 1,500 pesetas ($10.50).

In a similar manner, the more vintage Monestir is nothing to complain to the monks about. Its pre–World War II rooms are simpler, but still modern. The prices are even more to our liking: 3,500 pesetas ($24.50) for a double room with private bath. No singles are offered. The residencia (no meals served) is open from April to October.

After leaving Montserrat and returning to Barcelona, we strike out south the next day for:

2. Tarragona

About 60 miles south of Barcelona lies the ancient Roman city of Tarragona, a Mediterranean port that is one of the grandest, but most neglected, sightseeing centers in Spain. Its Roman and medieval remains make it the principal city of historic interest on the Spanish Mediterranean coast.

Its population today is approximately 100,000 but it is believed that under the Romans the city sheltered one million persons behind its nearly 40 miles of city walls. Its architecture is fascinating, particularly the part lying inside the wall-enclosed old quarter. Many of the houses have connecting balconies.

One of the four capitals of Catalonia when it was an ancient principality, Tarragona today consists of a new town in addition to its old quarter. At some point, you want to walk along the **Rambla Nova,** a wide and fashionable boulevard, the main artery of life in modern Tarragona.

The Iberians settled in Tarragona; it was captured in 218 B.C. by the Romans, and was thus embarked on the period of its greatest glory. But wars, sieges, neglect, and plunder caused Tarragona to experience decline. Today it seems to be thriving again. The sprucing up of its historical monuments has begun. The city has a bullring, good hotels, a mild climate, and beaches, and is the center of some interesting excursions. Primarily, it is visited for the day. In a sense, it has the same kind of older sister relationship with Barcelona that Toledo has with Madrid.

You can reach Tarragona easily by either bus, train, or car.

THE SIGHTS: **The City Walls:** This is the top attraction, partially enclosing the old quarter. The base of the walls is called Cyclopean, because of the enormous size of the blocks (this part of the wall was erected by primitive people). The Romans later built on top of this earlier foundation. It's possible to take a stroll on top of the ancient walls from 9 a.m. to sunset.

The Cathedral: This 12th-century cathedral at Plaça de la Seu represents the transition from Romanesque to Gothic. It has an enormous vaulted entranceway, stained glass that sparkles like jewels, Romanesque-style cloisters, and an open choir. It is at the loftiest point in Tarragona. The main part of the cathedral may be visited free, but it costs 100 pesetas (70¢) extra to visit the museum, with its collection of Catalán art. Hours are 10 a.m. to 12:30 p.m. and 4 to 7:30 p.m.

Roman Amphitheater: On the side of a cliff, the tides of the Mediterranean washing up on it, is this gallery, the remains of an ancient amphitheater where thousands of Romans went in the 3rd century for amusement. Carved out of the side of a cliff, it lies near the grounds of Milagro Park.

Necropolis and Paleocristiano Museum: The Museu i Necròpolis Paleocristians (its Catalán name) (tel. 21-11-75), is one of the most important burial grounds in Spain, having been used by the Christians from the 3rd to the 5th centuries. It is along the Avenida de Ramón y Cajal, outside of town next to a tobacco factory. On the grounds you'll find a museum that contains a number of sarcophagi and other objects discovered in excavations. It may be visited from 10 a.m. to 1 p.m. and 4:30 to 8 p.m. in summer, from 10 a.m. to 1:30 p.m. and 4 to 7 p.m. in winter, and 10 a.m. to 4 p.m. on Sunday; closed Monday. The admission charge of 100 pesetas (70¢) also includes the Archeological Museum.

Archeological Museum (Museu Arqueologic): This museum, at the Plaça del Rei (tel. 23-62-06), houses a collection of relics from the Roman epoch in Tarragona. You'll discover such items as mosaics, ceramics, coins, silver, and countless other objects. This sculptured stone building overlooks the sea. It may be visited in summer from 10 a.m. to 1 p.m. and 4:30 to 8 p.m., in winter from 10 a.m. to 1:30 p.m. and 4 to 7 p.m., and on Sunday from 10 a.m. to 1 p.m.; closed Monday.

Finally to cap your day's sightseeing, I'd suggest a stroll around sunset along the **Balcón del Mediteranéo**—not only for its beautiful vista of turquoise-blue water but the rich vegetation in the region.

WHERE TO STAY: **Hotel Astari,** 97 Vía Augusta (tel. 23-69-11), is a resort-type establishment near the sea on the road to Barcelona. Its rather plain doubles are fresh and airy, ranging from 4,500 pesetas ($31.50) each with a private bath. Only six singles are available, each one quite good, and costing 3,000 pesetas ($21) with a private shower. A continental breakfast is extra.

The Astari rises five floors; its long balconies and terraces provide both in- and outdoor living for its guests. It also has a swimming pool, as well as a solarium and modern cafetería. The low-level dining room has wide and tall windows; the food here is praised. A complete meal—served in a friendly manner—costs 1,000 pesetas ($7). The favorite spot of most guests seems to be the outer flagstone terrace—willows, umbrella tables, orange trees, and geranium bushes. At dusk one can have drinks in the cocktail lounge, also with high windows. The hotel is open from May through October. In-the-know travelers who want to languish peacefully at a Mediterranean resort come here and let the crowds fight it out for the beachfront hotel in Sitges.

Nuria, 217 Vía Augusta (tel. 23-50-11), was built near the beach in 1967, a five-floor modern building honeycombed with balconies. It's hardly for those seeking distinguished contemporary design or super-smart furnishings. Rather, its appeal lies in its neat, pleasant rooms—each with a private bath (sometimes a shower instead of a tub) and most with balcony. A double rents for 3,500 pesetas ($24.50), singles for 2,500 pesetas ($17.50). You can dine in the sunny restaurant, where a meal featuring a plate of the day goes for 1,000 pesetas ($7). The Nuria's specialty is a romesco, a kind of zarzuela, a seafood blend.

These hotels just recommended are summer-only establishments. You might find yourself in Tarragona in the off-season. If so, the **Hotel Paris,** 4 Maragall (tel. 23-60-12), is one of your best bets. Opening onto an attractive square, it rents out 45 simply furnished but clean rooms, a double costing 4,000 pesetas ($28), a single going for 2,800 pesetas ($16.10). There is no restaurant, but you can order a continental breakfast.

Even cheaper, but not as good, is the **Hotel Urbis,** 20 bis Reding (tel. 21-61-04). Rooms are basic, but it's an acceptable choice, renting out 58 rooms, many with private bath or shower, at a cost of 3,000 pesetas ($21) in a double and 2,300 pesetas ($16.10) in a single. A continental breakfast, the only meal served, is extra.

WHERE TO EAT: **Sol-Ric,** 227 Vía Augusta (tel. 23-20-32), is the private fiefdom of the Tomas brothers, Simon and Antonio, who both prepare and serve their culinary triumphs with such panache that many guests remember the service long after the memory of the good cuisine has faded. Simon, the chef, prepares oven-baked dorado with potatoes, tournedos with Roquefort, salmon crêpes, and several kinds of somewhat exotic fish, among other specialties. A fixed-price menu is offered for 2,100 pesetas ($14.70), while an à la carte meal costs from 3,000 pesetas ($21). This pleasant place will give you food for thought as well as for your stomach, especially as you try to determine the purpose of many of the antique farm implements hanging from the rustic walls. There's also an outdoor terrace and a central fireplace, which is usually blazing in winter. The establishment, which lies about half a mile outside of town, is closed Sunday night, all day Monday, in August, and from December 15 until January 15.

Leman, 27 Rambla Nova (tel. 23-42-33). No one can ever guess in advance what chefs of this popular restaurant will serve, since so much of the cuisine tends to be based on the market availability of the ingredients. In any event, this is reputed to be one of the best restaurants in town, serving such specialties as a seafood stew, bourride of rape (a whitefish), tropical salad, and an array of well-prepared beef and fish dishes. Full meals can cost as much as 3,000 pesetas ($21), and you may wish to accompany yours by one of the house's fine wines.

Cafetería Arimany, 45 Rambla Nova (tel. 23-79-31), is an attractive, hotel-style dining room, where excellent meals are served. The shrimp in garlic oil is outstanding. Meals cost from 1,500 pesetas ($10.50).

TARRAGONA BARS: **La Zuda,** El Serrallo. One of the sights of the town is the daily routine of the local fishermen bringing part of their morning catches into this popular bar where fish and seafood provide the ingredients for most of the well-prepared tapas, costing from 125 pesetas (88¢). The atmosphere at night can be festive, and the snack food is guaranteed to make you lose your appetite for dinner.

La Cueva, Corraló de Saint Magi. When Mario Duran left off playing professional soccer with the Madrid team and married a former actress, Marisa Leza, they established this convivial pub where the food and drink attracted many people from both within and outside the world of sports and theater. La Cueva is said to have been built on top of some ancient ruins, but that doesn't prevent customers from having a good time in the here and now. Drinks cost from 150 pesetas ($1.05).

EXCURSIONS: If you have a car, you can visit two star sightseeing attractions, a 30- to 45-minute drive from Tarragona. The first stop is the **Monastery of Poblet,** 29 miles northwest of Tarragona, one of the most intriguing monasteries in Spain. A mixture of Romanesque and Gothic, it is renowned for its cloisters. Constructed in the 12th and 13th centuries, the monastery is still in use. The monks of the Cistercian order of the common observance live here and they pass their days writing, studying, farming, working with a printing press, and helping with the restoration of the building, which suffered heavy damage in the 1835 revolution. After 100 years of emptiness, a new foundation was started in 1940 by Italian monks. The most exciting feature is the oddly designed tombs of the old kings of Aragón and Catalonia. The monastery may be visited from 10 a.m. to 12:30 p.m. and 3 to 5 p.m. for an admission of 200 pesetas ($1.40).

The monks dine frugally in the stark refectory, but you can enjoy lunch at **Fonoll,** near the cloister, l'Espluga de Francoli (tel. 87-03-33), a country inn where a large, filling menu costs from 1,200 pesetas ($8.40) and up. The restaurant is closed on Thursday, however, and from December 15 to January 15. If you'd like to stay over in this enchanting part of Spain, you'll find that the innkeeper offers 17 simply furnished rooms, costing from 850 pesetas ($5.95) in a single, from 1,600 pesetas ($11.20) in a double. All the accommodations are bathless.

About three miles away is one of the most fascinating of Spanish towns, **Montblanch,** a living museum of the Middle Ages. At the entrance to this town, you'll see a map outlining the principal artistic and architectural treasures—and there are many of these. The town is unspoiled. The crumbling façade of its once-elegant baroque church fills one with awe. Taking a car along these narrow, winding streets is somewhat risky. Walking is much preferred.

3. Sitges

Lying some 25 miles south of Barcelona, Sitges is one of the most frequented resorts of southern Europe, easily reached by bus or train from Barcelona. The resort is the brightest spot on the Golden Beach, the **Costa Dorada.**

The sands of Sitges are thronged in summer by a rising, affluent crowd of young moderns from northern Europe—girls who are dead-ringers for fashion models, boys who look as if they could call Greta Garbo mom. For years the resort was patronized largely by prosperous middle-class industrialists from Barcelona and Catalán artists such as Dali, Russiñol, Casas, Nonell. But those rather staid days have gone; Sitges rocks today like its sisters down the coast (Benidorm and Torremolinos).

Reminiscent of the resorts on the Costa Brava, Sitges has whitewashed houses, horse-and-buggy streets, and flower-draped balconies. Some good and some regrettable modern envelops it. In spite of the building spree, the tides of tourists washing up on Sitges's shores have found the little resort shamefully unprepared. Its accommodations—strained in a corset squeeze in July and August—can't tuck in all the bulge. Furthermore, Sitges is caught in a spiral of rising prices that place many of its major hotels beyond the means of the average budget traveler. But I have managed to scare up a number of bargains for those willing to nail them down with reservations. By mid-October just about everything, including virtually all hotels, restaurants, and bars, is closed.

If you're planning a visit, try to schedule your arrival on a weekday. On a weekend in summer, half the population of Barcelona seemingly descends on the overcrowded place, filling up such congenial bars as the Spotted Dog, the Dubliner, the Kentucky, and the Tennessee. With names like that, you'll wonder if anyone speaks Catalán or Spanish anymore.

WHERE TO STAY: The sea and the sand are the big attractions during the day. The crescent-shaped, white sandy beach stretches along the azure bay for about 1½ miles. With that in mind, I've tried to find establishments within easy walking of the shore.

Hotel Romantic de Sitges, 33 Carrer Sant Isidre (tel. 894-06-43). Whoever composed the literature for this unusual hotel must have been a brilliant linguist or had a lot of help, because the brochures are printed in 18 Western European languages. In addition to the obvious ones, they also include Gaelic, Languedoc, Sardinian, Corsican, Bretonese, Piedmontese, Maltese, and Frisian. The multiplicity of tongues may hint at the diversity of the guests who enjoy this place.

On a quiet street in the center of town, the hotel is made up of three 19th-century villas connected together and beautifully restored. The bar and the rest of the interior are filled with artworks, although many of the guests eventually gravitate to the fountain-dotted garden where an evening meal amid the mulberry and palm trees is a treat. The hotel contains some 55 well-furnished rooms priced at 2,450 pesetas ($17.15) in a single, 4,400 pesetas ($30.80) in a double. Meals in the dining room range from 1,000 pesetas ($7). The beach is only a short walk away. The hotel is open from mid-April to mid-October.

El Galeón, 44 San Francisco (tel. 894-06-12), is a leading three-star hotel, only a short hop from the sands. It's a well-styled hostelry, blending Old Spain with modern. The public rooms, small in size, have suitable furnishings and a cozy overall feel, while the bedrooms are good-size and streamlined with wood-grain. The baths, like the public rooms, are dwarfish. Open May to October 20, the hotel charges 4,200 pesetas ($29.40) for its doubles with private bath. Singles with private bath rent for 3,000 pesetas ($21). A complete luncheon or dinner goes for 1,200 pesetas ($8.40). An attraction is the small swimming pool in the rear patio. Advance reservations are necessary.

Hotel Montserrat, 11 Espalter (tel. 894-03-00), does not put its best foot forward. Its exterior is too neutral, its position among shops and restaurants too unchic. But the Montserrat is best inside. The bedrooms, although impersonal, are spacious enough and reasonably comfortable. Many of the doubles have a private shower bath and rent for 4,500 pesetas ($31.50). The bathless singles are a bargain at 2,000 pesetas ($14) each. For 1,100 pesetas ($7.70) per person extra, you can take lunch or dinner here. In fair weather, diners enjoy the rooftop. Open April through October 5, the Montserrat is about three blocks from the beach.

Hotel Don Pancho, 2 Calle San José (tel. 894-16-62), is a modern white stucco corner hotel, with wrap-around balconies. Inside, it's been given the Scandinavian treatment—natural woods, a raised fireplace, rush-seated dining chairs. From its rather cacophonous location, Don Pancho offers fair-size and recently renovated doubles with bath for 4,500 pesetas ($31.50). Singles are 2,500 pesetas ($17.50) with private bath. A continental breakfast, not included, is the only meal served. The Don Pancho is open only from May 15 to September 30.

Hotel Florida, 16 Espalter (tel. 894-02-21), is the successful remake of an old hotel. It's centered around a large dining patio, which is surrounded by 25-foot-high walls covered with ivy and shaded by purple flowering trees—a separate little world, only a few blocks from the sea, with a swimming pool and a solarium. All of its rooms lack decorative flair, but they make up for this by their good, simple comfort. Open from June 1 to September 30, the Florida charges un-Miami prices of 6,000 pesetas ($42) for a double with private bath, 2,800 pesetas ($19.60) for a single with shower. Only breakfast is offered.

Hotel El Cid, 19 bis Calle San José (tel. 894-18-42), combines the Spain of yesteryear with that of today. Its façade suggests the 16th-century world of Segovia. Inside are beamed ceilings, a wall of natural stone, heavy wrought-iron chandeliers, and leather chairs. The same theme is carried out in the rear dining room, and even in the pleasantly furnished bedrooms. The best doubles have a private shower bath, yet rent for 3,800 pesetas ($26.60). A single with bath goes for 2,400 pesetas ($16.80). The price for a fine repast is 1,200 pesetas ($8.40) extra. Board is required in summer. El Cid lets down the drawbridge from May 1 through October 31. In summer it's a beehive of activity, attracting a handsome crowd of young Europeans with lots of Nordic joie de vivre.

Hotel Residencia Alexandra, 1 Pasaje Termes (tel. 894-15-58), is hidden on a narrow and unfashionable street, a short stroll from the beach. It's all brick-built, given added flair by its canopied balconies. The Alexandra charges 3,800 pesetas ($26.60) for a double room with private bath, 2,800 pesetas ($19.60) in a single with bath. The rooms are compact, with a complete streamlined look reflected in the wood-grained headboards and up-to-date bathrooms. A continental breakfast, costing extra, is the only meal served. Open May to September 30, Alexandra hosts an attractive "house party," with northern European sunbathing on the roof terrace, and meeting evenings in the bar.

Residencia Sitges, 5 San Gaudenci (tel. 894-00-72), is open June 1 through September 30. The bedrooms are furnished simply. Doubles run the gamut from private bath to lonely lavatory. At this little one-star residencia, a single room with wash basin rents for 1,900 pesetas ($13.30). Depending on the plumbing, a double room costs from 2,800 pesetas ($19.60) to 3,300 pesetas ($23.10) nightly. Full meals aren't served here, but Sitges maintains a snack service if you don't want to leave the premises.

One of the pleasantest bargains in town is the **Sitges Park Hotel,** 16 Jésus (tel. 894-02-50). More centrally located than most of the above, its outside is unprepossessing; but once past the desk you come into a beautiful garden with palm trees and a swimming pool. A twin with bath looking down on this peaceful scene costs 3,900 pesetas ($27.30). Singles with bath go for 2,800 pesetas ($19.60). There is a pleasant restaurant downstairs, and you can have your coffee or drinks indoors or outdoors at the hotel's café-bar. A complete lunch or dinner costs 950 pesetas ($6.65). Service is friendly and efficient. The Sitges Park is open from April through October.

Terminus Hostal, 7 Avenida de las Flores (tel. 894-02-93), in spite of its dull-sounding name, is a very pleasant place at which to stay—and it's quite reasonable: from 800 pesetas ($5.60) per person nightly in a unit with four bunk beds. A double costs 1,500 pesetas ($10.50). Most of the young people who pass through Sitges seem to stay here—if they can get in. It's that popular. It is not only clean, but friendly. The owner is Canadian and his wife Catalán. Their gracious welcome and personalities are the reasons behind the success of this place.

Hotel Platjador, 35 Passeig la Ribera (tel. 894-50-54), is one of the best economy hotels of Sitges, renting out 44 well-kept bedrooms for 2,800 pesetas ($19.60) in a single, 4,500 pesetas ($31.50) in a double. The dining room, facing the beach is known for the good cuisine, served by white-gloved waiters. Recommended are the gazpacho, paella, pescado, and, for dessert, flan. For 1,200 pesetas ($8.40), you can enjoy the set menu, including some of the specialties.

WHERE TO EAT: Sitges offers a number of commendable dining spots. Only trouble is, with all those full-board requirements at the hotels, you'll rarely get a chance to sample them. But if you do decide to sneak out, head for . . .

Fragata, 1 Passeig de la Ribera (tel. 894-10-86). Other than air conditioning, its simple interior offers little more than well-scrubbed floors, crisp napery, and some of the most delectable seafood specialties in town. Its loyal clients number in the hundreds, each appreciating the fresh ingredients that go into what a gastronomic critic might call a simple but honest cuisine. Specialties include seafood soup, roast suckling goat, crayfish cocktail with pine nuts, several preparations of squid and octopus, and flavorful meat dishes. Full meals cost from 2,200 pesetas ($15.40) and are served daily.

La Masia, 164 Paseo Vilanova (tel. 894-10-76). Its country-style decor seems a perfect foil for the Catalán specialties for which this place is well known. Despite its dedication to regional cuisine, its imaginative chefs sometimes create recipes of their own, adding zest to an otherwise traditional menu. Specialties include regional codfish, roast suckling lamb well seasoned with herbs, a wide array of fresh fish and shellfish, and the legendary local dessert, a crême catalán. Full meals cost from 1,500 pesetas ($10.50) and are served at lunch and dinner daily. If you prefer to dine outdoors, there's a pleasant garden adjacent to the main dining room.

Els 4 Gats, 13 Calle San Pablo (tel. 894-19-15), is named after a famous old Sitges café where such painters as Picasso, Nonell, Casas, and others used to congregate at the beginning of the century. This intimate, auberge-type restaurant is decorated with paintings on the walls and a paneled wood ceiling, a raised corner fireplace, and crudely styled wooden chairs. Meals range in price from 1,800 pesetas ($12.60). Specialties include sole meunière, red mullet à la Diana, veal Cordon Bleu, and shrimp cocktail. The restaurant is open from mid-April to October. It is closed on Wednesday in April, May, September, and October.

Mare Nostrum, 60 Passeig de la Ribera (tel. 894-33-93), has been around so long (nearly 40 years) that it's practically a landmark. Menu specialties include a full range of many of the seafood dishes you'll immediately think of, as well as a few you might not know about. The dining room opens onto the waterfront, offering guests a view of the sea for which the restaurant was named. In warm weather, tables are placed outside. The fish soup is particularly delectable and might make a fitting beginning for full meals usually priced at 2,200 pesetas ($15.40). The establishment is closed Wednesday and from December 15 to January 16.

4. Andorra

Once upon a time, when feudal kingdoms existed throughout Europe, Andorra was commonplace. But perhaps because of its isolation—sandwiched between France and Spain high in the eastern Pyrenees—no one got around to telling Andorra that feudal kingdoms had gone out of style. Consequently, it's a tiny but flourishing little country that is experiencing a minor tourist boom sans gambling casinos but avec duty-free goods.

The father of Andorra, according to Andorrans, is none other than Charlemagne, who gave the "country" its independence in 784. That it survived at all in the ensuing centuries is something of a miracle. With a rather amused condescension, Napoleon let Andorra keep its autonomy. Napoleon, of course, could afford to be benevolent to principalities, such as pint-size San Marino in Italy.

Andorra's a storybook country—ruled by two "co-princes," the president of France and the Spanish archbishop of Seo de Urgel—a land of cavernous valleys and snow-capped peaks, rugged countryside, pastureland, deep gorges, and breathtaking scenery. It's a highly popular summer excursion center, and recently has been gaining as a winter ski resort as well.

For centuries Andorra lay hidden from the world, one of the most insular peasant cultures in Europe. That was true even as late as 1945. But since the late '50s tourists have increased from a trickle to a flood, reaching an annual mark of 12 million. That this has created havoc with Andorra's economy is an obvious fact. What the deluge has done to Andorra is a matter of a sharp division of opinion.

There are those who have suggested that Andorra has ruined its mountain setting with urban sprawl, as taxis, crowds, and advertising have transformed the once-rustic principality into a beehive center of trading and commerce.

At first glance, the route into the country from Spain looks like a used-car lot. Virtually every Andorran at the age of 2½ gets his own automobile. When the local cars converge at the junction with the French and Spanish motorists crossing into Andorra for the day, it's bedlam. A typical sight in summer is to see, say, a Spaniard crash into a Frenchman's vehicle. While the helpless husbands stand in the background, the Latin ladies from different sides of the Pyrenees shout the blame and assess the damage. On one recent occasion a parked car filled with a French family was rammed by a bus. The French housewife, wearing only her black underwear, had been discreetly hiding behind a towel in the August heat. But the volatile woman jumped out of the car, forgetting about the protective towel, and gave the poor Catalán bus driver a taste of her pretty Gallic tongue. The spectators, meanwhile, got a taste of French striptease.

New hotels and hundreds of shops have opened in the past decade to accommodate the French and Spanish pouring across the frontiers to buy such duty-free merchandise as Japanese transistor radios, cultured pearls, suede jackets, and enough liquor to sink the *Titanic.* A magazine once called Andorra "Europe's Feudal Discount Shopping Center." In addition, because of cheap gasoline prices in Andorra, there are enough pumps to have kept all the tanks of the Allies and the Third Reich rolling in World War II.

The little principality has long been known as a smugglers' haven. But today's smugglers are the French and Spanish visitors. Once it was possible for a North American to visit Andorra, flash a passport, and be waved on. A traveler can still whiz across the border in a jiffy, but on the road to the next stopover, he or she is likely to be swooped down upon by Napoleonic policemen who check every denture for undeclared goods.

Andorra is less than 200 square miles in size. Its language is Catalán. The base for most is the small capital, **Andorra-la-Vella,** and the adjoining town, **Les Escaldes,** another prime target, with plenty of shops, bars, and hotels. Little shuttles run back and forth between the towns, but most shoppers like to walk the distance. Most of the major hotels and restaurants are either on the main street (**Avenida Meritxell**) in Andorra-la-Vella, or the main street of Les Escaldes (**Avenida Carlemany).** French francs and Spanish pesetas may be used interchangeably. Hotel, restaurant, and shop prices are quoted in both currencies. But unless you've come just to shop, you will want to leave the capital for a peek at this midget country. You might prefer to visit the nearby small villages of **La Massana** or **Ordino** by car, or take a bus leaving about every 30 minutes. That way, you'll get a better feel of the principality.

In spite of its super-abundance of hotels, shops, automobiles, and gasoline tanks, Andorra is still a bit preposterous . . . like an old Peter Sellers movie.

GETTING THERE: The ideal way to go, of course, is by car through what must surely qualify as some of the finest mountain scenery—peaks, vineyards, rushing brooks—in Europe. The tiny country may be approached from Spain, via Puigcerdá to Seo de Urgel on a passable road from Barcelona. However, allow about four hours along bad roads from Barcelona.

Another way to go is on one of the buses run by the **Alsina Graells line** in Barcelona. It's about a six-hour ride across a distance of 143 miles. The bus leaves from 4 Ronda Universidad in Barcelona (tel. 222-11-63 for time of departure). It's also possible to return to Barcelona on the same line.

There is also a mountaintop airport at Seo de Urgel, which lies seven miles across the border in Spain. It's never been popular, however, during its short existence, because of uncertain weather conditions.

If you're driving to Andorra from Barcelona, the following short detour is suggested:

On the Way—a Spanish Town in France

Llivia is a geographic freak, the Little Orphan Annie of Spanish towns. It is a man-made island, lying about four miles inside French territory and completely surrounded by France, except for a route of access that crosses French territory. If at any point you leave this road, you'll have to clear French customs.

This mongrel town has little architectural interest; in fact, it's quite poor, having experienced greater and better days (it was known to the Romans). The only reason for visiting it is because of its ironic position.

The town is approached from the Spanish border at Puigcerdá. Its curious status dates back to a long-ago border dispute between France and Spain; Llivia became a pièce de résistance to the Spanish monarchy, and France allowed Spain to retain the town, since it was grabbing up so many other Spanish villages.

A quick tour of this town will suffice, and then it's on to Andorra.

WHERE TO STAY IN LES ESCALDES: **Hotel Roc Blanc,** 5 Plaça dels Co-Princeps (tel. 21-486), was built in the early 1960s and renovated about 20 years later. You'll find many facilities here, some of them designed for the spa patients who come for thermal treatment and relaxation. On the premises are a swimming pool, a sauna, a gym, a garage, a tennis court, a collection of convention rooms, and conservative but comfortably appointed bedrooms, each of which has its own private bath and TV. The in-house restaurant, El Pi, is reviewed below. Singles rent for 4,500 pesetas ($31.50) to 5,600 pesetas ($39.20), while doubles cost 6,500 pesetas ($45.50) to 8,500 pesetas ($59.50).

Les Closes, 93 Avenida Carlemany (tel. 28-393), is a little budget find in the swing of things on the principal street in Les Escaldes. It's more like a comfortable, well-run French pension than a hotel. Open all year, it has quite adequate bedrooms, 44 in all, renting for a modest 3,500 pesetas ($24.50) in a double, 1,900 pesetas ($13.30) in a single. Only breakfast is served.

La Grandalla, 14 Avenida Carlemany (tel. 21-125), enjoys the same central location as its competitor, Les Closes, and is about the same size. Its contemporary interior lacks a lot of charm, yet nonetheless it provides a clean and safe haven. Rooms are simply furnished, costing 3,000 pesetas ($21) in a double. The hotel also operates a restaurant, and many guests stay here on full-board terms at 3,500 pesetas ($24.50) daily. The hotel is closed from January 8 to February 8.

WHERE TO DINE IN LES ESCALDES: **El Pi,** 5 Plaça dels Co-Princeps (tel. 21-486). Although this restaurant is technically a part of the Hotel Roc Blanc, it's usually thought of as an independent institution by the many visitors and locals who appreciate its cuisine. Chef Miguel García holds a diplomatic line between preparing the best recipes of France and of Spain and accompanies them with wines from both countries as well. All of these are served in a sumptuously decorated dining room one floor above street level. Your meal might consist of duckling pâté, entrecôte with Roquefort, crayfish in cream sauce, and filet of beef Stroganoff. Various signs throughout the town indicate the direction of the hotel. Many of the patrons sitting near you may be visiting the local spa facilities as part of an extended vacation. Full meals range upward from 2,800 pesetas ($19.60).

Pizza Roma, 95 Avenida Carlemany (tel. 28-538). Its French and Italian cuisine includes far more than just the pizzas its name would imply. In addition to succulent pie-shaped portions of pizza studded with anchovies, seafood, sausage, and many other ingredients, you can also order fresh pastas, an array of salads, onion tarts, grilled beef and pork, a flavorful version of osso buco, and a wide array of beer and wine. A full meal costs 1,500 pesetas ($10.50), far less if you order only pizza. You can dine within the tastefully decorated air-conditioned interior, or on the flower-dotted outdoor terrace. The establishment is open daily except Tuesday.

WHERE TO STAY AT ANDORRA LA VELLA: **Andorra Palace,** Prat de la Creu (tel. 21-072). Its balconies rise above a central location in the center of town, near many of the city's most interesting bars and restaurants. In spite of the congestion of the neighborhood, it is graced with a pleasant garden and tennis courts. Each of the 130 well-furnished accommodations has its own bath, TV, and balcony. Singles cost 5,000 pesetas ($35); doubles, 6,000 pesetas ($42). There's a gym and sauna on the premises.

Hotel Mercure Andorra, 58 Avenida Meritxell (tel. 20-773). Designed in a successful and popular chain-hotel format of balconies and streamlined furniture, this hotel rises from a noticeable position near the center of town. It contains enough facilities (outdoor pool, tennis courts, a gym, disco, sauna, and parking garage) to make it seem much more like a well-appointed resort. Each of the six dozen accommodations contains a mini-bar, private bath, and TV. Singles cost 5,500 pesetas ($38.50), doubles 6,500 pesetas ($45.50).

L'Isard, 36 Avenida Meritxell (tel. 20-092). In winter this centrally located hotel caters to the skiers who come for the Pyreneen snows. In summer the service is just as polite and efficient, although clients have the added benefit of using an outdoor pool, the garden, and the tennis courts. Each of the 55 well-furnished rooms has a private bath and a TV. Singles cost 3,800 pesetas ($26.60), while doubles rent for 4,800 pesetas ($33.60).

WHERE TO DINE IN ANDORRA LA VIEJA: Moli dels Fanals, Carrer del Doctor Vilanova (tel. 21-381). You're close enough to the French border to discover that it is indeed possible to get good French cuisine in Andorra. The establishment, directed by members of the Hetch-Fouquat family, is inside an old mill whose interior mimics the grandly bourgeois hostelries of its giant neighbor to the north. The restaurant, open daily except Monday, offers three reasonably priced meals at 1,300 pesetas ($9.10), 1,650 pesetas ($11.55), and 2,400 pesetas ($16.80). À la carte meals cost around 2,400 pesetas ($16.80) and up. The owners take their annual vacation between late June and mid-July. The outdoor terrace provides a sunny table on a pleasant day.

THE COSTA BRAVA

It is with mixed emotion that I report on the Costa Brava, that rugged stretch of coastline that begins about 43 miles north of Barcelona in Blanes, and stretches like a python toward the French frontier. The happy news is that this 95-mile stretch of shore and beach is beautiful, at least that part that has not been overly developed. The azure Mediterranean contrasts with the verdure on the hills, which often are peppered with pine and cork trees.

But now the sad part. The Costa Brava ranks next to the Costa del Sol in phenomenal growth. It is amazing how a relatively unvisited coastline, almost completely unknown to Americans, within 25 years has moved into the foreground of the most-frequented spots in Europe.

Hotels are booked from spring through fall, often months in advance. It is virtually impossible to secure an accommodation during the peak months without way-in-advance reservations. Occasionally someone secures a room, perhaps by default, in mid-August, and then reports that all those stories about overcrowding on the Costa Brava are exaggerated. Not so. The passing parade of tourists to the Spanish Riviera is in the millions. It is also a paradise for the charter-tour crowd, and that further swells the bikini-clad bodies on the overburdened sands.

Hotel construction on the Costa Brava has boomed. Little villages that hardly had a decent boarding house a decade or so ago are now resort towns. The best spot on the Costa Brava for the average North American visitor is the attractive little town of **Tossá de Mar. Lloret de Mar** enjoys immense popularity, but somehow it seems too commercial, too loaded down with hastily assembled hotels. In a poor third position is **San Feliú de Guixols,** the largest town on the coast, but old-fashioned and dated in its appeal. The most unspoiled and remote village is **Cadaqués.**

The roads between the fishing resort towns skirt dangerously close to the edge of cliffs—and great care should be taken if you're driving. Many of the smaller villages are excellent for stopovers, but not suitable as bases.

If you want to visit the Costa Brava, but simply cannot secure space in high season, you can either drive the distance or book one of the daily organized tours that leave from Barcelona. Allow plenty of time, however, for motoring. In summer the traffic tie-ups can be fierce. If you visit the coast in summer (without hotel reservation), you might—in an emergency—spend the night in inland **Gerona,** the capital of the province, where you stand a far better chance of getting a room. If you visit the Costa Brava in the early spring or late fall, your prospects improve tremendously. And if you arrive during the winter months, you can have your pick of the few hotels that remain open, hungrily awaiting the arrival of a trickle of tourists. The season here is short, in all, compared to the Costa del Sol in Andalusia, and runs from mid-June to mid-September.

5. Lloret de Mar

Lying some 62 miles from the French frontier, Lloret de Mar, like Topsy, just grew and grew. On my first visit, when Eisenhower was in office, there weren't more than a dozen hotels. But at last check it was impossible to count them at all. By the time you finish tallying them up, some orangepicker has rounded up a few army cots and opened up another less-than-scrumptious pension.

The half-moon-shaped sandy beach bordering the sea is good, as the overcrowded sands will testify. Lloret is neither chic nor sophisticated, drawing its chief clientele from low-waged Europeans—with the French, Germans, Scandinavians, and British in ascendancy. The competition for cheap rooms is fierce.

Typical of the Costa Brava towns, Lloret de Mar skips from the most impersonal of the modern box-type structures to the vintage charm of its whitewashed, flowerpot-adorned buildings on the narrow streets of the old town. Rich vegetation and a mild climate tend to give Lloret de Mar a scenic advantage, regardless of how hard Señor Hôtelier tries to blot out that asset.

From Barcelona, it's possible to take a train to the nearest railway station at Blanes (lying about five miles from Lloret by easy bus connections). Or—and this may be preferred—you can take a bus operated by **Empresa Sarfa,** leaving from the post office in Barcelona (tel. 231-79-46 for departure time). The bus goes direct to Lloret.

WHERE TO STAY: Besides the overcrowding already noted, the accommodations of Lloret present still another hurdle to the innocent pilgrim seeking a room. Many of the hotels—particularly the three-star ones—are booked almost solidly by tour groups. Those you needn't bother with, but here are some bargains if you snare a reservation:

Hotel Cluamarsol, 7 Passeig Mossèn Verdaguer (tel. 36-57-50), occupies a desirable position at the edge of a public square whose edge abuts the center of the town's seaside promenade. This is a modern, eight-story, brick-walled hotel whose ground floor contains a Victorian-style bar filled with leather-covered armchairs. There's a glass-enclosed pool on the sixth-floor rooftop, plus 87 comfortably furnished bedrooms and a big-windowed dining room overlooking the palm trees of the plaza outside. This is one of the few hotels at the resort that accepts individual bookings in high season. Open year round, accommodations contain a private bath. With half board included, the tariffs range from 5,500 pesetas ($38.50) to 6,500 pesetas ($45.50) per person, depending on the season and the view.

Hotel Excelsior, 16 Jacinto Verdaguer (tel. 36-41-37), is more or less a glorified beach clubhouse. Its six floors of 45 rooms are right on the beach esplanade, making it possible to go for an early-morning dip before facing your Spanish coffee and continental roll. The Excelsior, open from April 1 to October 30, can get you in easily off-season—although the chances are nearly nil in July and August. The hotel charges 5,800 pesetas ($40.60) for a pleasant, clean double room with a private bath, 3,500 pesetas ($24.50) in a single with bath. Although uninspired, the furnishings are modern (from the '60s anyway), and the rooms are compact and convenient. A complete luncheon or dinner is 1,200 pesetas ($8.40) extra. Board is obligatory from July to September.

Hotel Metropol, Plaza de la Torre (tel. 36-41-62). A 19th-century civic building separates the hotel's modern balconies from a view of the sea. But its guests need only to cross a plaza to reach the beach. The hotel rises eight angular stories in a concrete-walled design of green trim and iron balustrades. Open from April to October, it contains 86 simple and efficient rooms, a few of which have a private terrace. Each features built-in furniture, a bathroom, and phone. With breakfast included, singles cost 2,300 pesetas ($16.10), doubles 3,500 pesetas ($24.50). A warmly decorated contemporary bar and dining room are on the premises.

Hotel Santa Rosa, 31 Calle Senia del Barral (tel. 36-43-62). The social center of this pleasant hotel is atop the roof terrace, where a sinuously curved swimming pool is complemented with a pleasant semi-enclosed bar, disco music, potted flowers, and chaises longues. Four blocks of apartment buildings separate the hotel from the beach, whose waters are visible from some of the balconied bedrooms. Each of the 135 comfortably airy accommodations contains a private bath and phone. Most also have a balcony. Among the handful of hotels in town which accept individual (non-group) clients, this is one of the most attractive in its category. Singles cost 1,200 pesetas ($8.40) to 1,800 pesetas ($12.60), doubles 2,300 pesetas ($16.10) to 3,300 pesetas ($23.10), plus tax. The hotel is open only between March and November.

Xaine Hotel, 55 Carrer de la Vila (tel. 36-50-08), is a deceivingly large hotel (with 88 rooms) that appears small and compact. Right in the noisy center of town activity, it is only a short walk from the beach. Crisply modern, it offers above-average bedrooms, many with their own balcony and private shower bath. The most expensive doubles peak at 3,500 pesetas ($24.50) per person, dropping to 3,800 pesetas ($26.60) in a single. Full board is included in these tariffs. Xaine does business from March 1 until the end of October.

WHERE TO EAT: **Reco Catala,** 55 Carrer de la Vila (tel. 36-50-08), is at least four forks ahead of the usual hotel dining fare. From its ground-floor nest, this restaurant catches the eye with its repast, costing 950 pesetas ($6.65). It doesn't disappoint the taste buds either, offering this typical menu—cream of mushroom soup, York ham with mashed potatoes, a French omelet, and dessert (the drink's extra). The view of the passing parade is worthy of a top Nielsen rating.

El Trull, Cala Canyelles (tel. 36-49-28), is about 1½ miles outside of town, in a spot that makes the trip worthwhile. The name of the suburb is actually Urbanización Playa Canyelles. The house specialties usually include seafood in some important way. This can take the form of fish soup, a fish stew heavily laced with lobster, an omelet surprise (the waiter will give you the ingredients if you ask him), and a broad range of everything from the most common to fairly exotic fish. The decor is woodsily rustic. Full meals cost around 1,800 pesetas ($12.60). There's a swimming pool and a pleasant garden nearby.

LLORET NIGHTLIFE: Discos may or may not soon fade from the nighttime scene in Spain, but if you're an aficionado of the electronic boogie, here are some addresses. Before tripping the light (or laser) fantastic, you might want a drink at one of the city's pubs or piano bars first.

These addresses seem to be popular and safe at press time. Drinks in all of them usually average around 300 pesetas ($2.10) on a regular night, more if there's a special musical event on the night you happen to show up.

Piano Bar, 29 Paseo Marítimo, offers good drinks, tasty tapas, and relaxing piano music.

Navarro, 43 San Pedro, features what might be the most elaborate ice-cream concoctions in town, as well as a tempting array of freshly baked pastries. If eating is your pleasure, this is the place for you, and the company you meet will share your weakness. It's open daily except from the third week in November till just before Christmas.

Disco Moeff Ga-Ga, 14 Sta. Cristina (tel. 36-49-48), is the place to go after dinner. Two laser shows are presented nightly, and the music volume is toned down enough for the ears of various age groups to enjoy, while still inviting the young and the young at heart to dance. There are five panoramic bars and two open-air terraces also with musical background. Professional disc jockeys and a lighting expert make the atmosphere festive. The place is open from the first of March to the end of October.

Hollywood, Carretera Tossa-Hostalrich. Starlets of whatever gender eventually want to end in Hollywood, U.S.A., but as a way station, this trendy disco at the edge of town provides an outlet for exhibitionists and onlookers alike to be seen and to see. The place is fashionable and has an image as a hangout for the aspirants of the glamorous life. Since the street where this place is located is quite long, look for it on the corner of the Calle Gerona.

From Lloret de Mar, we head up the winding coast to:

6. Tossá de Mar

This gleaming white town, with its 12th-century walls and a labyrinthine old quarter, fishing boats, and fairly good sands, is the most attractive center for a holiday on the Costa Brava. In a setting reminiscent of the old Ava Gardner movie, *Pandora and the Flying Dutchman,* Tossá seems to have more joie de vivre than its competitors.

The little town is 56 miles north of Barcelona, 8 miles north of Lloret de Mar. It has direct bus service from Blanes (the gateway town), as well as from Lloret. In addition, it is on the main Barcelona–Palafruggel autobus run. From Barcelona, buses leave for Tossá from the Empresa Sarfa terminal, 3 Paseo de Colón. Departures are fairly frequent, and the service is good.

Tossá is one of few resorts that has withstood exploitation and retained most of its charms. No longer an outpost of British sun-seekers, Tossá enjoys a broad base of international visitors—so many, in fact, that it can no longer shelter the influx. In spring and fall finding a room may be a lark, but in summer the no-vacancy sign may make you eat crow.

WHERE TO STAY: **Mar Menuda,** Paraje Mar Menuda (tel. 34-10-00), was built in the mid-1960s with a comfortable collection of some three dozen rooms, each with private bath. The grounds around the hotel contain a pool, tennis courts, a garden, and a big parking lot. A restaurant on the premises serves competently prepared meals. Single rooms cost 2,915 pesetas ($20.41), while doubles go for 5,850 pesetas ($40.95). The hotel is open from around Easter until October.

Hotel Vora La Mar, 14 Avenida de la Palma (tel. 34-03-54). Originally built in 1957, and later enlarged in 1970, this pleasant hotel is set along a quiet street which, one block later, runs into the beach. Its severely pruned shade trees shelter clusters of outdoor café tables from the sun. There's a garden, plus a high-ceilinged dining room festooned with trailing strands of ivy. The 60 terrazzo-floored bedrooms are comfortable, and many have an angular balcony (each unit is equipped with a private bath and phone). With breakfast included, the hotel charges 2,500 pesetas ($17.50) per person, either single or double.

Hotel Avenida, 16 Avenida de la Palma (tel. 34-07-56), is a pleasant and clean four-story hotel with blue-gray trim and an angular box-like design, whose comfortable accommodations sit about a block from the beach. The lobby level contains a sunny dining room filled with ladderback chairs, a modern bar, and friendly reception. Each of the comfortable 50 bedrooms has a bath, phone, and private terrace. Open between Easter and October, the hotel charges 3,600 pesetas ($25.30) to 4,300 pesetas ($30.10) per person in high season with full board included.

Hotel Ancora, 25 Avenida de la Palma (tel. 34-02-99). Set a few yards from the sands of the beach, this hotel is composed of a pair of architecturally dissimilar buildings, the older of which was constructed in the 1930s. There's a large art deco bar set near the reception desk, and a nearby rather elegant courtyard restaurant where light and air can filter through to the crisply ironed napery via a series of lattices. Each of the 67 bedrooms contains a private bath. Many have terraces and a view either of the sea or of a narrow canal flowing beside a line of trees. With breakfast included, per person rates range from 2,100 pesetas ($14.70) to 2,500 pesetas ($17.50) in a single or double. Half board costs from 3,100 pesetas ($21.70) to 3,700 pesetas ($25.90) per person. There is an in-house garage.

Hotel Neptuno, 52 La Guardia (tel. 34-01-43). My favorite hotel in Tossá sits on a quiet residential hillside somewhat removed from the hustle of the seaside promenade. The travertine facing of its exterior is entwined with ivy. Inside, an occasional antique intermingles with modern pieces for a pleasantly personalized decor which reaches its most alluring within the beamed-ceiling dining room. There's a small but lovely swimming pool with its own terraced garden and a view of the sloping forest next door. The decor, including everything within the 50 bedrooms, is tastefully lighthearted, modern, and sunny. Open between early March and the end of October, the hotel charges 2,700 pesetas ($18.90) and 3,400 pesetas ($23.80) per person, with half board included.

Hotel Diana, 10 Plaza de España (tel. 34-03-04), is right on the waterfront, but set back from the esplanade. A former seaside villa, it was converted into a two-star hotel in 1945. All the modernized bedrooms have a private bath, and many open onto their own balcony. The 21 rooms are spacious, containing many fine furnishings. Some students of Gaudí helped with the architectural elements, and the hotel has the most elegant fireplace on the Costa Brava. Two persons pay 3,000 pesetas ($21) to 4,000 pesetas ($28) in a double with bath. Only couples or trios are accommodated. The inner patio—with its towering palms, vines and flowers, and fountains—is almost as popular with guests as the sandy "frontyard" beach. In front of the hotel is the promenade, the best place for people-watching. The Diana receives visitors from May 1 through October 31.

Hotel Cap d'Or, Paseo del Mar (tel. 34-00-81), is perched on the waterfront, at the edge of the town away from the turmoil. The 200-year-old building was originally constructed as a fish store. It nestles against the stone walls and towers of the village castle. Built of rugged stone, the Cap d'Or is like an old country inn and seaside hotel combined. It is well run and neat, and attracts a stream of visitors with its scrubbed and polished bedrooms. All of the doubles have a private bath, and only three singles are available. You can stay here in high season for about 4,200 pesetas ($29.40) per person daily, including both room and board. The food served here is good, far above the usual. The dining room—ceiling beams and ladderback chairs—is a bit old-world, and the view of the sea is pleasant. The beams came from a clipper ship that sailed to America. Outsiders are welcome to come in for a complete meal. The hotel is open April 1 to October 31.

Hotel Tonet, Plaza de la Iglesia (tel. 34-02-37), is on a plaza inside the town, only a three-minute walk from the sea, through the narrow streets. The hotel has the atmosphere of a country inn. It is built with set-back terraces on its upper floor, and as you look up, you can see potted vines and plants, and sun umbrellas where guests relax. The hotel has been classified as one-star by some bureaucrat—but what does he know? The classifier is probably a relative of one of the men who said no to Columbus. In the morning, if you have your breakfast tray brought up to the terrace, you can watch the town come alive, observing the locals entering the little church, or going out for freshly baked bread. All of the Tonet's 36 rooms have a private bath. The rooms are country simple, with natural Spanish-style wooden headboards and rush-seated chairs. The hotel is open all year. The price for a double room with bath is 2,800 pesetas ($19.60) per day, dropping to 1,900 pesetas ($13.30) in a single.

L'Hostalet, 4 Plaza de la Iglesia (tel. 34-00-88), is placed on the same plaza as the Tonet. It is a modern-looking hostelry that doesn't overlook the romantic style. The architect took full advantage of L'Hostalet's position by creating an open garden terrace on the front—simple but in good taste. This patio is shaded by lemon trees. All of the rooms are basic in their appeal, some much more inviting than others. The most expensive doubles, those with private bath, rent for 4,800 pesetas ($33.60), but doubles with a shower go for 4,200 pesetas ($29.40). Only a continental breakfast is offered, at an additional charge. Open May 1 through September 30, the hostal is sometimes known as "The House of the American Student," because of the number of Yanks who slumber here.

WHERE TO DINE: **Es Molí,** 3 Carrer Tarull (tel. 34-14-14), is the most beautiful restaurant in Tossa, set in the courtyard of a stone-walled windmill originally built in 1856. You'll be able to choose a table beneath one of three different arcades, each of which faces a three-tiered fountain whose replicas of medieval courtiers came from the balustrades that formerly adorned a nearby house. If you prefer the direct sunlight of outdoors, a cluster of iron tables, set with crisply ironed napery, sits beside the burgeoning rose bushes and trailing vines of an adjacent garden.

Alfonso Capdevila, the very competent owner, serves a platter of local grilled fish which might be the most elaborately presented in town. Other main dishes include a delightful sole amandine, fisherman's cream soup, salad Es Molí (garnished with seaweed), hazelnut cream soup, hake and shrimp in garlic sauce, crayfish flambé with Calvados, chef's style tournedos, and a long list of well-chosen wines. The impeccably dressed waiters serve tactfully and with an occasional flourish. Full meals, priced from 2,500 pesetas ($17.50), are served at lunch and dinner daily except Tuesday in April and October. Between May and September, the restaurant is open daily. It is closed between November and March.

Restaurant Bahia, Paseo del Mar (tel. 34-12-91), is a seaside restaurant whose pleasant dining room often witnesses the entrance of a talented female chef, the much-awarded Camila Cruañas, who greets her guests with a friendly smile. This place is extremely well known throughout the region, with specialties that local housewives often try to re-create at home after enjoying them here. Favorite orders include a juicy chicken marengo, an array of rice dishes containing everything from beef to salmon, seafood soup, a classic zarzuela, and frequently changing new creations. Full meals range from 2,000 pesetas ($14). The Bahia is closed on Monday from November to February.

Can Tonet, Plaza de la Iglesia (tel. 34-05-11), has one of the largest menus in town, enjoying a secluded setting on one of the most charming old squares of Tossá. Guests during the day enjoy the outside café tables, or else they can dine in the tavern-like interior with its old beams and brass chandeliers. The menu, offering meals for 1,800 pesetas ($12.60) and up, features such dishes as sopa Tonet, paella, sole Tonet, Tossá crayfish, grilled shrimp, and a zarzuela, a classic fish stew. Also at night the chef keeps the pizza oven going. The restaurant is open only from March to October.

TOSSÁ NIGHTLIFE: In the fast-changing world of coastal discos, here is an assortment of what are the most popular at press time. Drinks average around 350 pesetas ($2.45) each in all but the most glamorous.

Ely Club, Calle Pola (tel. 34-00-09). Disco lovers travel from all over the Costa Brava to dance at this favored place, where the music is said to be among the most up-to-date in the region.

Kars Bar, 17 Sant Telm, is a pub with the kind of ambience you'd be likely to find in South America. It's usually a lot of fun, a meeting place for young people, offering excellent music and cocktails. Try their special Kars cocktail or the champagne sangría. The bar is open nightly except from November to April. The establishment, formerly called Lolita, celebrates its 25th anniversary in 1987.

La Tortuga, San Raimundo de Peñafort. The live music performed here is likely to be jazz. The crowd is friendly, and people seem to want to talk. It's casual, relaxed, and international.

Casbah, Carretera Tossá-Lloret, is a popular disco about 1¼ miles from the center of town. Unlike many others, the Casbah draws crowds in winter as well as summer.

7. Figueras

A 40-minute drive from Cadaqués delivers you to Figueras, which you may want to visit for two reasons—it has one of the best places to eat in Spain as well as a museum which is one of the most visited in Spain.

First, the museum is called **Teatro Museu Dali,** Plaza Gala-Dali, and it is filled with works by the ailing surrealist artist Salvador Dali, who lives in a house nearby.

Dali, of course, hardly needs an introduction. Born in 1904 in Figueras, the Spanish painter is a leading exponent of surrealism, depicting irrational imagery of dreams and delirium in a meticulously detailed style. He's known throughout the world for his uninhibited exhibitionism. His twirling waxed mustache has perked up many a Sunday supplement.

Dali's world is often an erotic one. Chances are you'll see, say, five nude blondes swathed in polyethelene or entangled with a Bardot reptile.

At the Figueras museum you'll view much rich Daliania. Dali's oeuvre includes watercolors, gouaches, charcoals, and pastels, along with graphics and sculpture. Much is rendered with seductive and realistic imagery. He is wide ranging in subject matter, as his works are likely to depict everything from putrefaction to castration.

You enter a central domed hall, and can explore at your leisure, viewing such works as *The Happy Horse,* a grotesque and lurid purple beast, recumbent, which the artist painted during one of his long exiles at Port Lligat.

An adjoining building was purchased to permit the expansion of the museum. When a catalog was prepared, Dali said with a perfectly straight face, "It is necessary that all of the people who come out of the museum have false information."

The Dali museum is open daily from 10:30 a.m. to 1 p.m. and 3:30 to 7:30 p.m., charging 200 pesetas ($1.40) for admission. Closed Monday in winter.

For dining, my preferred choice is the **Ampurdán,** less than a mile outside of town on the old road to France (tel. 50-05-62). The daughter of the founder, Ana María, and her husband, Jaume Subirós i Jorda, welcome you to the finest meal you're likely to be served in Catalonia. Don't judge the place by its appearance, which is ordinary. The look, in fact, is institutional. But not the cuisine, as all the food-loving French who cross the border to dine here will tell you.

The family-run restaurant was founded by Josep Mercader in 1961, and he early established a reputation among U.S. servicemen in the area for his subtlety with game and fish dishes. My favorite, if the catch has been good, is called molla, which is a rare whitefish, smooth in texture. Since it needs no adornment, such as fancy sauces or whatever, it is fried in a pan—it's that good. I'd also suggest a cold bean salad, which is superb. It's called ensalada de habas frías a la menta. Meat is prepared well too, especially the solomillio de ternera a la crema sanfaina, a veal steak served with a delicately light cream sauce. Another exquisite dish is dorada al horno, a baked fish dish. For dessert, you're faced with crema catalána, a burnt-caramel custard, or a selection of sorbets.

Expect to spend from 2,300 pesetas ($16.10) to 3,500 pesetas ($24.50) for a memorable meal. The Ampurdán also rents out 42 rooms, charging 3,800 pesetas ($26.60) in a single, 5,800 pesetas ($40.60) in a double.

The other preferred place in town is **Durán,** 5 Lasauca (tel. 50-12-50). It's best to start here with the salad catalán made with radishes, boiled egg, a ham pâté, tuna fish, tomato, and fresh crisp salad greens. Other specialties include steak al Roquefort, a zarzuela (a Catalán fish stew), filetes de lenguado a la naranja (sole in orange sauce), and crépinette de sepiones a la col. Like the Ampurdán, Durán also specializes in game. Try, if featured, the grilled rabbit on a plank, served with white wine. The french fries here, unlike those served in most of Spain, are crisp and excellent, prepared just right. Finish off with a rich dessert or at least an espresso. Expect to spend from 2,000 pesetas ($14) upward for one of the top-notch meals in the provinces. You can also stay at the Durán in one of its well-furnished rooms, 67 in all. A single costs 3,000 pesetas ($21), a double renting for 5,000 pesetas ($35).

Hotel Pirineos, 1 Ronda de Barcelona (tel. 50-03-12), is a pleasant balconied hotel set beside the main artery leading into the center of town. It lies within a five-minute walk of the Dali Museum. The hotel's colorful restaurant fills most of the ground floor reception area. There's also a much-needed garage within the hotel, as well as a bar, along with 60 comfortable accommodations, each with its own phone and bath. Many also contain a balcony. Depending on the season, singles cost 2,600 pesetas ($18.20) to 3,200 pesetas ($22.40); doubles, 3,200 pesetas ($22.40) to 3,800 pesetas ($26.60).

Hostal Bon Retorn, Carretera Nacional II (tel. 50-46-23), sits near the edge of the national highway (not the autoroute), about a mile south of Figueras. To reach it from the A17 autoroute, get off at exit 4-Figueras south, then head toward town on the national highway. Owned and managed by the Gardell family, this Andalusian-style hotel contains a large and relaxing bar, a sun-flooded restaurant with an outdoor terrace, and 50 rustic Spanish-style bedrooms. Each of these has a private bath, phone, and air conditioning. Singles cost 1,800 pesetas ($12.60), doubles, 3,200 pesetas ($22.40), plus breakfast. Fixed-priced meals in the dining room go for 950 pesetas ($6.65).

8. Cadaqués

The little village of Cadaqués, despite the publicity it has received because of painter Salvador Dali, is still amazingly unspoiled and remote. There are, as yet, no high-rise apartment blocks nor garish hamburger joints, nor even shops that make "tea like your mother." The village, the last resort on the Costa Brava before reaching the French border, is reached by a small winding road, twisting over the mountains from Rosas, the nearest major center. When you get to Cadaqués, you really feel you're off the beaten path.

The village twists around a half dozen small coves, with a narrow sidewalkless street leading along the water's edge. It has no railing, so many a drunk must plummet into the water on fine summer nights.

Scenically, Cadaqués is a knockout, with its crystal-blue water, its fishermen's boats pulled up on the tiny sandy beaches, its old, whitewashed houses, its narrow, twisting streets, and its 16th-century parish up on a hill. At times the place is reminiscent of Venice, and proves equally difficult to park in when the visitor crush hits it in the summer. There is simply no place to park within the village.

The aged, ailing Dali has a home next door to Cadaqués in the tiny village of Port Lligat, opposite Port Lligat Hotel.

The only public transportation to Cadaqués is a bus that leaves twice a day from Figueras, 14 Mendez Nuñez (at 12:30 and 6:45 p.m.). It returns to Figueras at 7:30 a.m. and 5 p.m. On Sunday there's an added bus leaving from Figueras at 12:30 and 9:15 p.m. To get to Figueras, take the train.

WHERE TO STAY: **Hotel Playa Sol,** 3 Playa Pianch (tel. 25-81-00), considered the best hotel in town, sits in a relatively quiet section of the port, along the side of the bay, with arguably the best view of the thick-walled stone church at the distant edge of the harbor. The hotel is built in a 1950s balconied design of green shutters, exposed brick, and terracotta tiles. Owned and operated by the Llado family, it contains 50 bedrooms, each of which has its own bath and phone. In high season the hotel charges 4,100 pesetas ($28.70) to 4,800 pesetas ($33.60) in a single, 7,500 pesetas ($52.50) to 8,000 pesetas ($56) in a double. It is closed in January.

Hotel Port Lligat, Port Lligat (tel. 25-81-62). Many visitors find its relative isolation, at the end of a winding gravel-covered road, about a half mile outside of Cadaqués, to be its more alluring point. The terracotta tiles of its bar terrace overlook an idyllic harbor and the giant eggs and metallic profiles adorning Salvador Dali's house next door. There is a changing exhibition of surrealistic paintings in the gallery adjoining the reception lobby, plus a rectangular swimming pool ringed, hacienda style, with cabañas, a restaurant, and a snack bar. Open between April and November, the hotel contains simple, airy bedrooms with tile floors, exposed wood, and balconies. There are no singles, but doubles, with full board included, rent for 3,500 pesetas ($24.50) to 4,500 pesetas ($31.50) per person, depending on the plumbing, the exposure, and the season.

Hostal Marina, Riera San Vicente (tel. 25-81-99), is the oldest hotel in town, but many of its recent additions came in the late 1970s. It's contained within a simple white building with few pretensions, near the sea in the center of town. The Albert family's presence is very visible here. Many of their efforts go toward directing the flagstone-floored dining room, where a fixed-price meal costs 1,000 pesetas ($7). Each of the 29 no-frills bedrooms is well scrubbed, offering good value for money. Depending on the plumbing, singles cost 1,100 pesetas ($7.70) to 1,450 pesetas ($10.15); doubles, 2,100 pesetas ($14.70) to 3,100 pesetas ($21.70), plus tax.

Hostal S'Aguarda, 28 Paratge S'Aguarda (tel. 25-80-82), Carretera de Port Lligat. Its various white-walled outbuildings hug close to a curve in the road winding above Cadaqués on the way to Port Lligat. Its position enables residents to see the village's faraway medieval church and the boats bobbing at anchor in the harbor. Each of the simple, modern, airy accommodations contains French-style doors opening onto an angular terrace dotted with potted geraniums, cool tile floors, and uncomplicated furniture, along with a private bath. Depending on the season, singles cost 2,100 pesetas ($14.70) to 2,800 pesetas ($19.60), doubles 3,000 pesetas ($21) to 4,500 pesetas ($31.50).

WHERE TO DINE: **La Galiota,** 11 Calle Monturiol (tel. 25-81-87). Because of its consciously simple decor and the dozens of surrealistic paintings ringing this ultra-clean dining room, many visitors consider a meal here to be as much of an artistic experience as a gastronomic one. You'll find it behind a white façade on a steeply sloping street below the cathedral. There's a downstairs sitting room, and an upstairs dining room whose ruddy-colored stone floor is polished almost like the surface of a mirror. A menú del día costs 950 pesetas ($6.65) but most diners order à la carte, spending from 2,200 pesetas ($15.40). Specialties include paella, quiche Lorraine, baked fish, octopus, vichyssoise, beefsteak, pork cutlets, and, for dessert, soufflé Grand Marnier. Reservations are important, since the restaurant is sometimes entirely reserved for private parties. It remains open from June to October.

Don Quijote, 6 Avenida Caridad Serinana (tel. 25-81-41), on the road leading into the village, is a pleasant, intimate, bistro-type place, with a large, vine-covered garden in front. Its à la carte specialties include lamb chops, pepper steak, a zarzuela, and gazpacho. The Don Quijote cup, a mixed dessert, is the best way to end a meal. Most à la carte meals range in price from 2,000 pesetas ($14).

Sa Gambina, Riba Nemesio Llorens (tel. 25-81-27), on the waterfront, serves reasonably good food at medium prices. A Catalán salad (tomato, lettuce, peppers, butifarra, onions, and olives) is a good choice, as is the paella or the fish soup. The shrimp (gambas), for which the place was named, are always reliable. A complete meal goes for 1,500 pesetas ($10.50) up. The ambience is típico, with a cave-like back dining room.

Es Trull, Port Ditxos (tel. 25-81-96). An ancient olive press, chiseled from local granite, sits in the center of this modern cafeteria. Members of the Vehí family named their cedar-shingled restaurant after the Catalán name for this olive press, which dominates the establishment's curved inside walls. Two filling fixed-price meals are offered here, costing 825 pesetas ($5.78) and 925 pesetas ($6.48). You'll find it on a harborside street in the center of town, serving lunch and dinner daily from Easter until September.

AFTER DARK: **L'Hostal,** 8 Paseo (tel. 25-80-00), is so unusual, so consciously different from its neighbors, that its thick stucco walls have attracted some of the most glamorous names of the artistic and musical worlds. It's a Dixieland bar par excellence run by the most sophisticated entrepreneurial team in town, the German/Italian/Hungarian alliance of Veronica and Marci Pogany. Habitués still remember the time Salvador Dali escorted Mick Jagger here, much to the delight of Colombian writer García-Marquez (*One Hundred Years of Solitude*). In fact, the logo of the bar, one which appears in mosaic tiles on the doorstep and on the matchbooks which bear the beautiful Veronica's photograph, was designed by Dali himself. There's no cover charge for what is probably the best jazz music along the coast. The repertoire also includes rock and Dixieland. Some music critics have called this place the second-best jazz club in Europe. The ambience is heightened by the dripping candles, the high ceilings, and the heavy Spanish furniture. A beer costs 250 pesetas ($1.75); a Mexican sunrise, 650 pesetas ($4.55). Open all year, the establishment reverberates till 4 a.m. The best music is usually performed late.

Es Porro, 1 Portal de la Font (tel. 25-80-82), isn't overly large, but its in-house video shows and warm ambience have made it one of the most popular places in town. Drinks cost an average of 400 pesetas ($2.80).

Maritim, Centro Villa. Just by walking through the center of town you're likely to find this favored bar, with many of the local people enjoying a quick drink or two, costing from 150 pesetas ($1.05). The bar opens right onto the water, and you can drink outside under an awning or else retreat inside to a room that vaguely resembles the interior of a tugboat.

9. Cardona

On the Carretera 1410, about 50 miles to the northwest of Barcelona, the busy town of Cardona doesn't present any particular tourist interest, except for its fortified convent and castle perched high on a steep hill and dominating the town and the roads that converge there. This castle was the home of the dukes of Cardona. It has been turned into a national parador by the Spanish Ministry of Information and Tourism.

Parador Nacional Duques de Cardona (tel. 869-12-75). The castle was begun in 789 by Ludovico Pio to help secure lands conquered from the Moors. It became the property of Ramón Folch, the nephew of Charlemagne. In the Middle Ages its walls withstood many sieges. Today it's been converted into a parador of 65 rooms, all with private bath. The charge for a double is 6,000 pesetas ($42). In a single, the rate is 5,200 pesetas ($36.40). Six floors are reached by a very welcome elevator. The furnishings contain many Catalán antiques and reproductions.

Dining is in the main room of the old castle. To reach the lounge, you cross the inside courtyard where genuine wells open onto the tanks below, which were used by the dukes of Cardona when enemies were surrounding the château. A luncheon or a dinner costs 2,000 pesetas ($14). On my most recent visit I enjoyed a selection of regional hors d'oeuvres, at least a dozen, followed by spaghetti in a cheese sauce, then cod a la verde with fresh garden vegetables and a tart.

A Gothic court and chapel, part of the original structure, have been converted into a museum.

10. Gerona (Girona)

Split by the Onar River, this sleepy city with an ancient history is beginning to feel the impact of tourism, as excursion crowds from the Costa Brava dart inland for the day. One of the most besieged cities in Spanish history, Gerona has preserved parts of its old city walls, and its old quarter is from the Middle Ages.

Although Gerona is not a major tourist mecca, it can be a lifesaver for the night, particularly when hotel bookings are impossible on the Costa Brava for those who didn't make reservations. Gerona is also a good stopover station on the way to and from the principality of Andorra if you have a car; it is not recommended that you cope with the difficult bus connections to Gerona.

THE SIGHTS: The major attraction of Gerona is its magnificent **cathedral,** Plaza de la Catedral, reached by a climb up 90 steps that are centuries old and as steep as ever. The 14th-century cathedral represents many architectural styles, notably Gothic and Romanesque. The museum of the cathedral is open from 9:30 to 1:15 p.m. and 3:30 to 7 p.m. In summer, however, it remains open from 9:30 a.m. to 8 p.m. Admission is 75 pesetas (53¢).

The **Museu d'Art Palau Episcopal,** 12 Pujada de la Catedral (tel. 20-95-36), is in the former episcopal palace next to the cathedral, displaying artworks from the old Diocesan Museum and the Provincial Museum. The exhibits, which date from the 10th to the 19th centuries, are in 20 permanent rooms, with temporary displays in three other locations. The museum is open from 10 a.m. to 1 p.m. and 4:30 to 7 p.m. Admission is 100 pesetas (70¢).

While in this old quarter of the city, you might also seek out the 12th-century Arab baths, off the Pujada dei Bei Martí, open from 10 a.m. to 1 p.m. and 4 to 6 p.m. (10 a.m. to 1:30 p.m. in winter). Admission is 75 pesetas (53¢).

Two minutes' walk from the Arab baths is the **Sant Père de Galligants Archeological Museum** at Sta. Lucía in a Romanesque church and cloisters from the 11th and 12th centuries. Hours are 10 a.m. to 1 p.m. and 4:30 to 7 p.m. (10 a.m. to 1 p.m. in winter). It's closed on Monday. Admission is 100 pesetas (70¢).

WHERE TO STAY: **Novotel Gerona,** La Carretera del Aeropuerto, Riudellots de la Selva (tel. 47-71-00), lies eight miles south of Gerona. Its easy accessibility and garden-style surroundings make this efficiently modern hotel a favorite with visitors who want to explore many different areas of the surrounding resorts of the Costa Brava. Only a meadow and a well-placed copse of birches and pines separate it from the busy A17 autoroute. Yet within its verdant enclaves, you could be at a quiet country hotel. Its warmly textured public rooms include a hideaway bar ringed with exposed brick, burgeoning plants, airy lattices, and comfortable leather couches. A big-windowed dining room serves meals for 2,000 pesetas ($14), meals which many local residents make an excursion here to enjoy.

Each of the 82 efficiently designed bedrooms has its own color TV, radio, phone, built-in furniture, and private bath. Children under 16 stay free with their parents. Single rooms are priced at between 6,500 pesetas ($45.50) and 7,100 pesetas ($49.70); doubles, 7,700 pesetas ($53.90) and 8,800 pesetas ($61.60), depending on the season. There's a swimming pool on the premises, a gift shop selling well-crafted leather goods, and a spacious room with deep couches for watching wide-screen TV. The hotel lies near exit 8 (Gerona airport) on the A17.

Hotel Peninsular, 3 Nou (tel. 20-38-00), is a leading second-class hotel in Gerona, a comfortable but characterless structure near the old quarter and the river. Open all year, this good-size commercial hotel charges from 3,500 pesetas ($24.50) in a double room, from 2,300 pesetas ($16.10) in a single. Its rooms are traditionally styled and most of them contain a private bath. The Peninsular is more suited for stopovers than for longer stays. It has no restaurant, and serves only a continental breakfast, at an extra charge.

Condal, 10 Juan Maragall (tel. 20-44-62), is a bargain. It's rated third class, yet it is modern and pristine. However, its lounge is meager, the reception desk is tiny, there is no service elevator—and no meals other than breakfast are served. But these are minor concerns. The bedrooms are good and comfortable —and that's more important. Singles rent for 1,600 pesetas ($11.20), doubles for 2,800 pesetas ($19.60) with complete bath. The bedrooms are compact, some opening onto a view of a square. On the second floor is a tiny breakfast room, serving up continental fare in the morning, which is included in the tariffs quoted.

WHERE TO DINE: **Bronsoms,** 7 Avenida Sant Francesc (tel. 21-24-93), is a bustling restaurant in the heart of Gerona that was founded in 1882 by the grandfather of the present owner, English-speaking José Bronsoms. Bronsoms has a nicely integrated crowd of locals mixed with visitors, mostly European. You can get some of the best food in town here, although this is a modest restaurant. The chef knows how to make those close-to-the-hearth vegetable soups, served in good-size bowls. Another favorite choice is veal with mushrooms, a hearty dish that might fortify you for your climb up the 90 steps to Gerona cathedral. Other specialties include cannellonis, typical fish dishes, a steamed beef ragoût, and roast leg of lamb. There's also a bar if you need stronger fortification. Meals run from 1,500 pesetas ($10.50). The restaurant is closed on Saturday night, Sunday night, and from August 1 to August 15.

Chapter XII

ZARAGOZA AND PAMPLONA

1. Zaragoza
2. Pamplona

ARAGÓN AND NAVARRE, two districts of the northeast, are the wallflowers of Spain from the standpoint of the tourist. The ever-fickle sightseer, seduced by Andalusia, lured by the shapely resorts along the coastal regions, tends to neglect both these forgotten daughters. Admittedly, they don't walk off with the top prizes in the beauty contests. But those preferring the stark and rugged will pay a call on these Amazons.

Aragón, of course, was the old kingdom that united with Castile after the marriage of native son Ferdinand to Isabella. Today the term Aragón refers to the provinces of **Heusca, Teruel,** and **Zaragoza** (Saragossa in English). The pilgrimage city of Zaragoza, the largest population center in Aragón, is the major stopover in the district—for the simple reason that it lies on the most frequented route between Madrid and Barcelona.

Navarre, on the other hand, is more remote. It nestles to the east of the Basque provinces and grabs up some of the Pyreneean landscape. The province is less populated. **Pamplona** is its biggest city, and it becomes even denser with aficionados during the San Fermín fería in July, when the bulls are run through the streets. If the bulls aren't trampling you underfoot, then you may be run down by gringos—noisy, and drunk on vino. Frankly, the festival is Pamplona's big drawing card, but I like the city best at other times, when it's soft and subdued, and you can take time to appreciate the dramatic scenery surrounding it that loomed so large in the pages of *The Sun Also Rises.*

Motorists heading for Zaragoza may want to detour to the charming little town of **Medinaceli,** standing proudly above the Meseta plains. Known to the Romans, it still has a triumphal arch from that era. There are also medieval walls. If you're passing through, you can seek both food and lodging at the **Medinaceli y Restaurant Mesón del Arco Romano,** 1 Portillo (tel. 32-61-30), where seven rooms are rented to visitors, costing from 1,200 pesetas ($8.40) in a single, the price going up to 2,000 pesetas ($14) in a double. The food is good, and a complete meal begins at 1,200 pesetas ($8.40). Many regional dishes are featured. The restaurant is closed from mid-November to mid-December.

1. Zaragoza (Saragossa)

Halfway between Madrid (215 "rail" miles) and Barcelona is the big provincial capital of Zaragoza, the seat of the ancient kingdom of Aragón. This main terminus of road and rail travel has a population of more than 300,000. It's a bustling, commercial city of wide boulevards, arcades, and of the newly prosperous Aragonese, who pronounce the name of their city, Zaragoza, with each "z" sounding like a lisping "th" ("Tha-ra-go-tha").

Zaragoza has not one but two cathedrals. The city ranks with Santiago de Compostela in Galicia (the northwest) as a pilgrimage center. According to legend, the Virgin Mary appeared to St. James, the patron saint of Spain, on the banks of the Ebro, and ordered him to erect a church on that spot. The city's big festivities take place the week of October 12, with top-name bullfights, religious processions, and general merriment.

While in Zaragoza to watch the matador Antonio Ordoñez, Hemingway and A. E. Hotchner, his biographer, stayed at the Gran. But with our budget, we'd best consider overnighting in one of the following:

WHERE TO STAY: For all-around value, the champion is the **Hotel Goya,** 5 Cinco de Marzo (tel. 22-93-31), a 1965 building with excellent bedrooms that in some respects equal the much more expensive chambers at the Gran. It honors its namesake with copies of paintings placed throughout the multi-level lobby, part of which is chicly decorated with black marble and English club paneling. It is easy to find, just off the Avenida Independencia, near the Plaza de España (heartbeat of the city). The well-furnished and sufficient doubles with private bath are 6,200 pesetas ($43.40); the doubles with private shower cost 5,000 pesetas ($35). Singles with private shower rent for 4,000 pesetas ($28). A hulking giant for Zaragoza, the Goya has 150 rooms. There is a garage for your car.

Hotel Residencia Rey Alfonso I, 17 Coso (tel. 21-82-90), is clean, efficient, and a favorite with visiting business people who prefer its location in the center of the commercial heart of town. Its street corner façade has a prominent arcade, a popular countertop-service snack bar, and a crew of veteran and good-natured doormen to help visitors with their luggage. In the basement, a paneled, comfortably modern restaurant offers uniformed service, ample displays of food, and a well-prepared cuisine. Each of the 117 bedrooms contains air conditioning, musical intercom, phone, tile bath, color TV, and an efficiently serviceable decor of simple modern design. Singles cost 6,000 pesetas ($42), doubles 8,000 pesetas ($56).

Hotel Lafuente, 7 Calle Valenzuela (tel. 22-48-06). Set at the corner of a quiet and charming square, not far from an old church, this somewhat bleak-faced hotel offers dated but good budget accommodations. You'll climb a short flight of interior steps before registering in an early 20th-century lobby filled with high ceilings and accented with touches of wrought iron. There's an unusual, almost art deco bar inside, plus 65 spacious, clean, and high-ceilinged bedrooms. Depending on the plumbing, singles cost 1,600 pesetas ($11.20) to 2,500 pesetas ($17.50); doubles, 3,000 pesetas ($21), plus taxes.

Hotel Oriente, 11 Coso (tel. 22-19-60), was completely overhauled and given three stars by the government. The lobby has been modernized, and its fairly attractive and reasonably comfortable bedrooms considerably upgraded. The most expensive doubles with private bath peak at 5,800 pesetas ($40.60), and singles with bath run 3,300 pesetas ($23.10). A continental breakfast is extra. Occupying a good location, the Oriente is about a block from the Plaza de España and the Plaza de Salamero.

WHERE TO DINE: **Costa Vasca,** 13 Coronel Valenzuela (tel. 21-73-39), has for quite a while served some of the best food in the city. You enter a small bar where, if you wish, you can have a dry sherry in the Spanish tradition, then proceed to the second-floor dining room with a nautically inspired decor and uniformed waiters. The restaurant has brass studs and cedar half-paneling, and draws a dignified clientele to dine on a number of Basque specialties, with some Aragonese regional cookery as well. An elaborate set menu is offered for 2,600 pesetas ($18.20). Specialties include crêpes stuffed with mushrooms and peppers, roast lamb, Aragonese rabbit, goose liver, sole filets with smoked salmon, and turbot with anchovies and a saffron sauce. The restaurant is closed on Sunday.

Mesón del Carmen, 4 Calle de Hernán Cortés (tel. 21-11-51), is an unusually fine Aragonese restaurant, a local landmark. Most people know it only by its almost endless expanse of bar countertop, where fish-based tapas of all kinds are proudly displayed behind glass cases. After your pre-dinner snack, you might decide to walk toward the back, where a cubbyhole dining room leads into a larger chamber filled with wagon-wheel chandeliers and rustic accessories made of wood and iron. Full meals, costing from 1,800 pesetas ($12.60), include Aragonese vegetable soup, duckling with tomatoes, rabbit with garlic, jarret of veal, and codfish with garlic.

La Rinconada de Lorenzo, 3 La Salle (tel. 45-51-08), is one of the best Aragonese restaurants in town. The menu offers a blend of specialties that include such unusual dishes as fried rabbit with snails. Oven-roasted lamb or lamb hock can be ordered in advance, but lamb skewers are always available. The chef prepares several versions of a dish called migas (fried breadcrumbs), flavored with a number of different ingredients, including ham. Giant asparagus spears are often served, and if you care to go real local, try beans with pig's ear and sausage. There are several distinctly different dining rooms and a long bar. The most remote of the rooms is also the quietest. Full meals are served daily except Monday, Holy Week, in August, and on national holidays, costing around 1,800 pesetas ($12.60) to 2,400 pesetas ($16.80).

Faustino's, 3 Plaza San Francisco (tel. 35-68-68). Its starkly modern façade rises from a corner of one of the largest squares in town. To reach the establishment's heart, you'll pass between the iron tables of its sidewalk café. Stairs lead to an upstairs tea room. Perhaps you'll stop for a standup selection of tapas at the long metallic bar on the street level. After that you can descend a flight of circular steps leading into one of the most charming restaurants of Zaragoza. There, in the Bodega, you'll find a decor of mottled stone floors in shades of pink and black, an enormous copper alcohol still which nestles within the curve of the stairwell, and heavy ceiling beams fashioned from roughly textured logs. You can enjoy an array of local wines, poured from oak-sided casks placed behind the bar. Grilled specialties include veal chops, spicy sausages, entrecôte, and filet of pork. Dessert might be a temptingly caloric slice of whisky-flavored tart. Full meals cost from 1,900 pesetas ($13.30). The restaurant is open daily.

THE SIGHTS: Zaragoza has three principal sights, conveniently near each other and easy to cover in a morning.

Church of El Pilar (Basilica del Pilar)

This 17th- and 18th-century basilica, on the banks of the Ebro River at the Plaza de las Catedrales, contains the tiny statue of the *Virgin del Pilar* in the Holy Chapel. Thousands of the faithful travel hundreds of miles each year to pay homage at this important Catholic shrine. The name of the cathedral, El Pilar, comes from the pillar upon which the Virgin, according to tradition, is supposed to have stood as she made her request to Santiago (St. James). Some of the frescoes inside were painted by Francisco Goya. In the second week of October the structure serves as the backdrop for an important festival devoted to Our Lady of the Pillar, but the ceremonies merge into parades, bullfights, fireworks, flower offerings, and street dancing. The almost Oriental-looking basilica, designed by Herrera, may be visited from 8 a.m. to 2 p.m. and 4 to 7 p.m. in summer (from 9 a.m. to 2 p.m. and 4 to 6 p.m. in winter).

You can also visit the Pilar museum, which is open from 9 a.m. to 2 p.m. and from 4 to 6 p.m., charging an admission of 100 pesetas (70¢). The museum displays the jewelry collection used to adorn the Pilar statue, as well as sketches by Goya and other artists, including Bayeu. Much of the collection is quite ancient, including an ivory horn from the 8th century.

La Seo

This Gothic Mudéjar church at Plaza de la Seo, built between 1380 and 1550, is more impressive than El Pilar, but somehow seems sadly neglected. Still, in a rich baroque and plateresque setting, it manages to come off as more than a poor sister, and contains numerous artistic treasures and interesting architectural features, the most important of which is the main altar. It is a particularly fine representation of the Aragón style of Gothic architecture. In the museum is a collection of Franco and Flemish tapestries from the 15th to the 17th centuries. In the Temple of Pilar, constructed in the baroque style, the cupolas were decorated by Goya and Bayeu. Hours are 9 a.m. to 2 p.m. and 4 to 6 p.m.

Aljafería

This most unusual sight, a Moorish palace in Aragón, has been restored by the government and preserved as a National Monument. Long neglected, it is reminiscent of some of the architecture of Córdoba. The palace at Castillo was originally built in the 11th century for Moorish kings, but it has seen considerable alterations and additions since, particularly when those itinerant monarchs, Ferdinand and Isabella (who carried their kingdom with them), lived here. The palace may be visited from 11 a.m. to 1:30 p.m. and 4 to 6 p.m. weekdays; on Sunday, from 11 a.m. to 1:30 p.m. Admission is free. For information, phone 43-56-18.

AFTER DARK: Zaragoza offers at least one offbeat attraction. In the **Bar Plata,** Calle 4 de Agosto (tel. 21-11-46), opposite the Spain Square, you can see one of the last café-cantantes left in Spain. This is a good-size café, with a bar at the entrance, and an old, musty stage at the other end of the room. The café is filled with all classes of people. There's a flagstone floor, pillars covered with tiny bits of mirror, and a small balcony with more tables and chairs. Three times a day (at 2:30, 7:30, and 10:30 p.m.) there's a kind of oldtime girlie show. A wobbly three-piece orchestra whoops up the tunes, and a scantily dressed dancer comes out to warble a love song and do a couple of bumps. It's all hilariously simple and authentic. The cost is about 200 pesetas ($1.40) for a drink at a table.

Casa Luís, 8 Romea (tel. 29-11-67), is known in the town as one of the most interesting bars in the barrio of La Magdalena. You may be astonished at the array of tapas displayed out on the bar. They're reputed to be about the best in town. The fresh oysters and shrimp are among the more tempting items, or perhaps you'll settle for the razor clams "in little bundles." Tapas cost from 350 pesetas ($2.45) and are served in a modern setting of tiles and exposed oak.

Casa Amadico, 3 Jordan de Urries (tel. 29-10-41), near the Plaza del Pilar, is a popular hangout for local government workers and business people who come here after work for five or six of the tasty seafood tapas, costing from 250 pesetas ($1.75). Oysters come in three different sizes, or perhaps you'll be tempted by the smoked salmon, lobster, or Serrano ham. The place consists of a long narrow bar with a few tables in back. Women wheel baby carriages through, and men watch soccer games on TV. It's all very local. Near the cathedral, the location is on a street of bars, one of the smallest streets in the city and a bit hard to find.

Oasis, 28 Boggiero (tel. 44-10-62), would be a good choice for a place to see a spectacle, see the locals at play, and enjoy a round of drinks or even a meal. It's a former theater that was transformed into a cabaret/music hall where a changing variety of artists perform to the applause of local enthusiasts. Drinks at the bar cost around 650 pesetas ($4.55). There's a restaurant on the premises, with meals beginning at 2,200 pesetas ($15.40).

If you're motoring to Madrid after leaving Zaragoza, you'll have a rare opportunity to sample the following:

ON THE ROAD—STAYING IN A MONASTERY: Founded in 1195 at Nuevalos, the **Monasterio de Piedra** (tel. 84-90-11) is a three-star hotel open year round. It lies 136 miles from Madrid, 67 miles from Zaragoza, and was originally built as a spiritual retreat in an area known for its good climate and mineral waters. At some point, an impressive wing with comfortable rooms was added, and it is this three-story addition, with its three tiers of arches reminiscent of a Roman aqueduct, that contains the excellent bedrooms. A couple can stay here, in a room with balcony and private bath, for 5,000 pesetas ($35) nightly. Eight singles, also with private bath, are available for 4,000 pesetas ($28).

Walk through the woods and grounds to get the best of nature: a waterfall emptying into a small river, little log bridges, masses of flowering plants and trees. Dining in the great hall is a colorful, medieval event. The room has been tastefully decorated, and is a perfect background for the good Spanish meals—served for 1,300 pesetas ($9.10).

The monastery is about ten miles off the main Madrid–Zaragoza road. If you're coming from Madrid, turn east at Alhama de Aragón. From Zaragoza, turn left at Calatayud, and it'll be 14 miles from there. By train, go to Alhama de Aragón from Madrid, and from there take a taxi to the monastery.

From Aragón, we move to the province of Navarre and to:

2. Pamplona

More than half a century has passed since Ernest Hemingway wrote *The Sun Also Rises* (*Fiesta,* if you read the British edition). But the book's glamour remains undiminished for the American youths who read the novel, then rush off to Pamplona to see the running (*encierro*) of the bulls through the streets. Attempts to outlaw this world-famed ceremony have failed so far, and it remains a superstar attraction, particularly among Spanish aficionados. The festival of **San Fermín,** during which the *encierro* takes place, usually begins on July 6 and lasts through the 20th.

Nobody sleeps, which is just as well—accommodations are virtually impossible to find, unless you have a notarized letter from the Archangel Gabriel. Fireworks and Basque flute concerts are only some of the spectacles that give added color to the fiesta.

With or without Papa's book, you can bed down in sleeping bags in an emergency, or stay up carousing around the clock (by far the prevalent custom). Those who have grown weak and spoiled by capitalistic society—and who want to know they'll have a bed after watching the *encierro*—should reserve a millennium in advance at one of the city's handful of hotels or boarding houses. Or they can base in San Sebastián and visit Pamplona during the day. Pamplona has both train and bus connections to San Sebastián, 56 miles away on the Basque coast of Spain. After all, chances are that one visit to Pamplona will be enough to satisfy all but the insatiably bloodthirsty.

Hemingway, incidentally, used to give an old down-on-his-luck pal a regular yearly stipend to acquire accommodations and bullfight tickets for him. The ring at Pamplona is simply too small to accommodate the demand for tickets—so the scalpers make enough in July to get them through the winter. It helps to have a friend fending for you in Pamplona.

Actually, the bullring has recently been somewhat enlarged and tickets are now easier to obtain. Those wishing to see the running of the bulls through the streets should get downstairs by 6 a.m. Tickets for a good seat in the ring cost about 3,000 pesetas ($21), and go on sale at 8 p.m. the night before the corrida. Tickets for standing room are on sale at 4 p.m. the day of the bullfight. Seats in the *sol* (sun) are far cheaper, of course.

Pamplona, like the Roman god Janus, has two faces. One it presents only at fiesta time; the other is around for the rest of the year, when Pamplona is just a sleepy provincial capital.

Hot in summer, fiercely cold in winter, Pamplona converges at the **Plaza del Castillo,** the heartbeat of the city. Head here to check the pulse of the old kingdom of Navarre. And don't fail to spend as much time as you can exploring the nearby streets of the old town. The single most important sight is the **Cathedral of Pamplona,** Plaza de la Catedral, in the Gothic style, begun near the end of the 14th century on the site of an early Romanesque basilica that caved in. The final façade is in the neoclassical style of the 18th century and is flanked by two towers. Inside, the interior reverts to a somber Gothic style, with lots of fan vaulting. In the center of the cathedral is the tomb of Charles III (note the deftly carved figurines on his alabaster sepulchre) and his Castilian wife. From the architectural point of view, the chief interest centers on the magnificant Gothic cloisters. You can visit the Gothic Barbazan *capilla,* as well as the Diocesano Museum filled with medieval sculpture, much of which is interesting. The museum is open mid-May to mid-October from 10:30 a.m. to 1:30 p.m. and 4 to 7 p.m. Admission is 100 pesetas (70¢).

WHERE TO STAY: Residencia Eslava, 7 Plaza Virgen de la O, right off the Plaza del Cardenal Ilundain (tel. 22-22-70), is a honey. Built within the shell of an old building, it captures the spirit of old and new Spain. Its smallish living room is more like the drawing room of a distinguished Spanish family—as indeed it is. José Luis Eslava Vidaurreta, the owner, has created a congenial atmosphere at low prices. For a double with private bath, the rate is 4,500 pesetas ($31.50) nightly. Singles with shower baths are 2,500 pesetas ($17.50). The rooms, a few with balconies, are medium size, employing the same imaginative taste reflected in the public rooms. The baths are shiny clean and compact. You sip your breakfast coffee while perched on three-legged stools, and later in the day you can drink in the lounge cellar.

Hotel Orhi, 7 Leyre (tel. 24-58-00), is conveniently located in the center of town, a few steps from the bullfight ring. The 55 rooms, with private baths and a high-ceilinged design, although modernized, retain a hint of their 1930s construction. Single rooms cost 3,500 pesetas ($24.50), while doubles go for 5,500 pesetas ($38.50).

Hotel Yoldi, 11 San Ignacio (tel. 22-48-00). The 48 well-furnished bedrooms of this convenient central hotel were almost completely renovated a few years ago. Today you can be close to the bullfighting focus of Pamplona for 3,000 pesetas ($21) in a single, 4,500 pesetas ($31.50) in a double. Luckily for motorists, there's a parking garage on the premises.

Hotel Sancho Ramirez, 11 Sancho Ramirez (tel. 27-17-12), is one of the newest hotels in town, and it has quickly drawn business away from its longer established neighbors. Members of the Irigoyen family are the owners, and they do what they can to keep the 78 rooms in good order. Each of the reasonably priced units has a streamlined and contemporary decor, a private bath, a TV hookup, and a mini-bar. Singles cost from 3,800 pesetas ($26.60), doubles cost from 5,500 pesetas ($38.50). There's a garage on the premises.

Hostal Valerio, 5 Avenida de Zaragoza (tel. 24-54-66), is the leading pension of Pamplona, my economy choice. On the second floor of an old elevator building, this hostal is family run, friendly, and intimate. It is hosted by Don José Romero Aranguren, who speaks English, and who doesn't want too many changes made. He likes the hand-carved ladder-back chairs, the old pieces of furniture—everything blended to create a homey and personal atmosphere. Especially cordial to U.S. students, Don José charges 2,800 pesetas ($19.60) for singles with water basin, 3,800 pesetas ($26.60) to 6,200 pesetas ($43.40) in doubles. The functional rooms are basic, clean, and pleasant—in all, sound comfort. A continental breakfast, at an extra charge, is the only meal served. The hotel is closed in October.

Note: During the San Fermín festivities, when the town is packed, you can sometimes get rooms in private homes. Inquire at the tourist office.

WHERE TO EAT: This is quite a problem in Pamplona, where fishing for a good restaurant is easy enough, but "angling" for an inexpensive one is sometimes hard. Exceptions include the following:

Casa Marcelliano, 7-9 Calle Mercado (tel. 22-14-26). Hemingway immortalized it, and the two-centuries-old "casa" is still going strong. At the time of the festival of San Fermín it is arguably the most popular—and most crowded—place in town. Many wine-drinking visitors come just for the vino of Navarre and the tapas, but others stay to enjoy the simply prepared and low-cost meals, costing around 1,800 pesetas ($12.60). The waiters are harassed but friendly and helpful if they have the time. You are given a choice of a quartet of spacious dining areas on two floors. The menu is large, featuring many local dishes of the province. If they're in season, try pochas con chungur (ham-flavored shell beans). Or try the mussels in a garlic broth. In season braised partridge might be offered.

Las Pocholas, 6 Paseo de Sarasate (tel. 12-44-14). Its name arouses almost instant recognition, because its food is so good and because its dining salons are so elegant. Attended by a batallion of formally dressed waiters, you can enjoy such specialties as salt-cured cod with lobster chunks in a garlic sauce, sea bass baked in red wine, a champagne-laden filet of sole, seasonal game dishes, a superb roast pork, and temptingly elaborate desserts. Meals in the air-conditioned interior cost 3,000 pesetas ($21), and are served daily except Sunday night and from mid-July to mid-August.

Hartza, 19 Juan de Lebrit (tel. 22-45-68). The portions served at this popular restaurant are so generous that many first-time visitors are happily surprised. The property is the object of the hard work of the Hartza brothers, who prepare their specialties from a changing array of seasonal products which, naturally, vary throughout the year. Menu items include a steamy and well-seasoned vegetable soup, stuffed peppers, tournedos, and a selection of regional cheeses. If you're in the mood for fish, you'll find such specimens as hake and eel. The interior is air-conditioned during the hottest months of summer. Meals cost upward from 2,500 pesetas ($17.50). The restaurant is closed Monday and from July 15 to the beginning of August.

Shanti, 39 Castillo de Maya (tel. 23-10-04). Its entrance takes you through a popular tapas bar, where you might decide to linger over a drink and a predinner appetizer. Its adjacent restaurant serves a version of straightforward and honest cuisine, always very fresh, which has caused it to become one of the solidly dependable restaurants in Pamplona. Its array of traditional dishes includes grilled hake, roast loin of pork, roast lamb, and shellfish rice. Full meals, costing from 1,800 pesetas ($12.60), are served daily except Sunday night, Monday night, and in July.

PAMPLONA AFTER DARK: **Villa Concepción,** 5 Monasterio de Alberín. The name of this stylish pub has more to do with the name of the owner, Enrique Concepción, than with religion. It draws affluent guests from all over Pamplona. Expect to see a list of all the usual cocktails, wines, and beers, costing from 300 pesetas ($2.10).

Café Iruña, 44 Plaza de Castillo, dating from 1888, is a well-decorated bar and café with a popular outdoor terrace. In winter the crowd that filled the open-air tables in summer is likely to congregate around the bar, where combination plates and snacks are served in addition to the drinks, which cost from 150 pesetas ($1.05).

Es Molino, 13 Avenida Bayona. In the early afternoon, its centrally located interior serves as one of the commercial neighborhood's most popular tapas bars. Later in the evening, its ambience is more youthful, perhaps more lighthearted, and certainly more animated. It carries a full line of tapas, including fried shrimp, squid, anchovies, fish croquettes, and Russian salad. Open every day except in August.

Chapter XIII

ALONG THE ATLANTIC

1. San Sebastián
2. Guernica
3. Santander
4. Santillana del Mar and the Caves of Altamira
5. Oviedo
6. La Coruña
7. Santiago de Compostela
8. Pontevedra
9. Vigo
10. Tuy

SAN SEBASTIÁN AND SANTANDER have much in common; both are Atlantic Coast beach resorts frequented predominantly by Spaniards. San Sebastián, closer to France, of course is more international. Both are modern, with good hotels and restaurants, and both are noted for their excellent beaches. In addition, they are capitals of two of the most beautiful provinces in Spain. But San Sebastián is the queen of the Basque country, while Santander is in Old Castile, the only part of that ancient kingdom that has a coastline.

From the snow-capped **Picos de Europa** to the streets of **Laredo,** from the medieval village of **Santillana del Mar** to the nearby subterranean grottoes of **Altamira** with prehistoric paintings, the province of **Santander** offers much to see and do. Similarly attractive is Spain's smallest province, **Guipúzcoa** (capital: **San Sebastián),** which is one of the most heavily visited regions in Spain.

San Sebastián lies about 13 miles from the French border, and North Americans, among others, by the car and busload, pour over from Biarritz for a glimpse of Spain. It is safe to assume that what they see often surprises them. These Atlantic Coast provinces are not the Spain of legend, as reflected in Granada and Seville. But they form a land of fishing towns, snug harbors, inland spas, ancient ruins, towering mountains, rivers, fertile valleys, pine trees, and bays with sandy beaches.

Even farther along the coast you reach **Galicia,** which embraces the provinces of La Coruña, Pontevedra, Lugo, and Orense. It occupies northwestern Spain with **Asturias,** once the only stronghold of Christian Spain and later a principality.

A native of Galicia is known as a *gallego*. These farmers and fishermen have a reputation as a somber, hard-working people, who have had to contend with many hardships inflicted by nature. Generalísimo Franco came from El Ferrol, the most important navy base in Spain, north of La Coruña.

In the province of La Coruña, visitors can explore the *rías* country. *Rías* are what the Spanish call the lochs that cut inland from the sea, providing some of the most dramatic scenery in the country. Galicia has much to offer: stone-gray medieval villages and towns, a rugged coastline, fishing harbors, fertile valleys, mountains, a unique cuisine, sandy beaches, and some of the most colorful festivals in Spain.

The capital, **La Coruña,** is one of the legendary cities founded by Hercules. It lies some 375 miles from Madrid, and is distinguished by its *miradores,* glass-enclosed balconies on buildings facing the sea. Rows and rows of this glazed and glistening glass make for a stunning sight. The *gallegos* can sit behind them, absorb the sun, and remain sheltered from the windy Atlantic.

Interesting as La Coruña is, it must take second place to **Santiago de Compostela,** that goal of the medieval pilgrim.

Our exploration will begin, however, near the French border at:

1. San Sebastián

San Sebastián is the summer capital of Spain—hundreds of Spanish bureaucrats escape to this capital city when the Madrid sun becomes too hot. San Sebastián is a tasteful resort, and has none of the tawdry trappings associated with major beachfront cities. It is also an ideal excursion center for trips to some of Spain's most fascinating villages.

San Sebastián contains an old quarter—narrow streets, hidden-away plazas, medieval houses—but is primarily a modern city of elegant shops, wide boulevards, sidewalk cafés, and restaurants. Its most celebrated feature is its **La Concha Beach** where, it would appear, half the denizens of Spain and France spend their days under striped canopies when they're not dashing into the refreshingly cool, sky-blue waters of the bay. La Concha is half-encircled by a promenade, where the crowds parade in the evening. The adjoining beach is called **Playa de Ondarreta.**

For the best view of the city, take the funicular for 65 pesetas (46¢) to the top of **Mount Igueldo.** It operates in season from 10 a.m. to 10 p.m. It's also possible to drive up. In spring the air is scented with honeysuckle. A cliff-hanging belvedere has been built at the top, affording a fabulous view of the sheltered bay and the Cantabrian coastline.

San Sebastián, nestled ideally on a choice spot on the Bay of Biscay, is surrounded by green mountains. Its population swells enormously from June to September. It has a good, but inadequate, choice of hotels, and an excellent number of Basque restaurants that are mostly expensive. Its chief drawback—overcrowding in July, no space at all in August.

To the Spaniards, and to the civil servant in particular, San Sebastián is the most fashionable resort in Spain.

What with its bullfights, art and film festivals, sporting events, and cultural activities, San Sebastián in the peak summer months is a hub of constant activity.

San Sebastián is principally reached by rail or car, but it has both bus and airplane service. From Madrid, the TALGO departs for here from the North Station. But for approximately the same amount of pesetas it's possible to fly, and Aviaco maintains services between Madrid and San Sebastián. There's also train service from Barcelona, although it's a difficult run. In summer there is also some bus service from Madrid to San Sebastián, a distance of approximately 300 miles, but the ride is long and hard.

WHERE TO STAY: The key to hotel bargains in San Sebastián is to reserve in advance. As mentioned before, that vacancy sign in July and August is rare. But the visitor who does book space in advance will find an array of good hotel values, surprising for a resort of such international status. Assuming you do get a room at that busy time, most hoteliers will insist that you take full or at least half board (breakfast, plus one main meal).

Niza, 56 Zubieta (tel. 42-66-63), is a little 41-room hotel with character. Savored by those who like to be near the beach and esplanade, it is well appointed, combining a selection of Scandinavian modern in its bedrooms with antiques in its public lounges. The petit salon, for example, is furnished as a drawing room, with an Oriental rug, Directoire chairs, a tall grandfather clock, a rosewood breakfront. In direct contrast are the basic rooms, with wooden headboards, white walls, and usually wall-to-wall scarlet carpeting. A double room with bath costs 6,000 pesetas ($42). A single with bath is 2,900 pesetas ($20.30). In the cellar is a pizzeria.

Arana, 7 Vergara (tel. 42-69-46), attracts middle-class Spanish families who have come to stake their claim for a few feet of sand on Playa de la Concha. The Arana is on a commercial street in the shopping section, but only a block or so from the river (a five-minute walk to the beach). This year-round hotel is your best bet for an off-season visit to San Sebastián. It offers doubles with every conceivable kind of plumbing—ranging from water basin at 3,600 pesetas ($25.30), to private bath at 5,000 pesetas ($35). Singles are available with shower (no toilet) for 2,800 pesetas ($19.60). The best rooms face the street and have private "Miss Muffet" sitting rooms opening onto glassed-in bay windows. The furniture is comfortably stuffy. A continental breakfast, costing extra, is the only meal served.

Avenida, Carretera Subida a Igueldo (tel. 21-20-00), nestles on the fringe of San Sebastián on the road up to Mount Igueldo. The Avenida, graced with terraces and a swimming pool, charges 6,000 pesetas ($42) for its doubles with private bath and 4,000 pesetas ($28) in its singles, also with private bath. Accommodations are tasteful, offering a good standard of comfort. The lounge, with its French provincial pieces, has a view of the hills beyond. A guest can sit here, watching sunrises and sunsets from April through October.

Monte Igueldo, Monte Igueldo (tel. 21-02-11), is a contemporary hotel "fortress" perched like a castle on the crown of Monte Igueldo, at the edge of San Sebastián. From its windows a panoramic view of the Cantabrique Coast unfolds. Both the public rooms and the bedrooms have spacious windows to capture this view. The swimming pool terrace also juts out into space for a coastal view. This first-class "super-splurge" hotel is for festive occasions only. All of its 120 rooms contain private bath and shower, with a private balcony as well. Tariffs vary according to view, season, and room size. Doubles peak at 10,500 pesetas ($73.50), and singles at 7,900 pesetas ($55.30). All bedrooms are streamlined, with semi-modern furnishings. The atmosphere is comfortable.

The **Codina,** 21 Zumalacárregui (tel. 21-22-00), is a modern structure built in a free-form style so that nearly all of its bedrooms have a view of the bay. The compact bedrooms are comfortably furnished. From July to September, only guests taking half board are accepted. The cost for that is 4,500 pesetas ($31.50) per person. On the wide, busy boulevard is a popular café and bar. Open all year, except in February, the hotel is near an attractive residential district and close to a strip of beach.

Hotel San Sebastián, 20 Avenida Zumalacárregui (tel. 21-44-00). You'll have to travel toward the city's exit to reach this modern hotel set only a short distance from the beach. The ambience is well upholstered, with a swimming pool set into a pleasant garden. The approximately 100 rooms have private baths and rent for 6,000 pesetas ($42) in a single, 8,200 pesetas ($57.40) in a double. On the premises, you'll find an informal restaurant and a welcoming bar where the predominant color is green.

Hotel Gudamendi, Carretera de Igueldo (tel. 21-41-11), is a 1950s-era hotel with 20 rooms, some of which have panoramic views over the city. Since the hotel is surrounded by three fields used by hunters for pigeon shooting, many patrons of the hotel come here for the hunting season. Singles range from 3,000 pesetas ($21), with doubles going for 5,000 pesetas ($35) to 6,000 pesetas ($42), depending on the accommodation and the plumbing.

Hostal Bahía, 54 San Martín (tel. 46-10-83), is a top-notch little hotel just one short block from the beach and near a string of hotels. It charges 4,500 pesetas ($31.50) for the most expensive double with private bath. However, bathless doubles cost only 3,200 pesetas ($22.40). A single without bath rents for 2,250 pesetas ($15.75), rising to 2,750 pesetas ($19.25) with bath. Some of the Bahía's bedrooms are large enough to contain sofas and armchairs; others fall more into the cubicle classification. Many North Americans stay at the hostal and "commute" to Pamplona for the running of the bulls.

Residencia Parma, 11 General Jáuregui (tel. 42-88-93), has seven of its rooms with beautiful views of the ocean. It is a modern, clean hotel, featuring a snackbar downstairs. There's also a pleasant TV lobby, with armchairs and sofas. The rooms are up-to-date and cozily furnished in wood. Bathrooms are as in a luxury hotel. The best doubles with bath go for 6,000 pesetas ($42). Singles peak at 3,200 pesetas ($22.40).

At Fuenterrabia

Parador Nacional El Emperador, Plaza Armas del Castillo (tel. 64-21-40), is in a 10th-century castle. Emperor Charles V reinforced it to guard the river border with France. It is an impressive bunker, which has been restored, as have most other national paradors, with a lot of taste and imagination. Many antiques, old weapons, and standards hang from the high vault. Corridors lead to rooms of great comfort. Prices are moderate, considering the amenities. For 7,000 pesetas ($49) a single with bath is rented. Doubles, on the other hand, pay a maximum of 8,500 pesetas ($59.50). In every accommodation is a mini-bar, from which you may select your apéritif. Only breakfast is served. It's best to reserve in advance, as El Emperador has only 18 rooms.

THE BASQUE CUISINE . . . AND WHERE TO EAT IT: The Basques are considered the best cooks in Spain—and not just by fellow Basques. Both visitors and other Spaniards praise the native cuisine of these northeastern provinces. Many of the dishes, of course, would put hair on your chest—and are to be recommended only for the most adventurous stomachs. But the average diner will usually find a large and safe array of well-prepared and attractively served dishes, platters of tempting hors d'oeuvres (mainly "creatures from the sea"), and lots more. The Basques also take special care to prepare their vegetables in unusual ways. Here is a selection of the best and most inexpensive of the típico restaurants, most of them in the old quarter of San Sebastián.

Salduba, 6 Pescadería (tel. 42-56-27). Well established as one of the most solidly successful restaurants in town, this place was opened shortly after the end of World War II. It owes much of its popularity to the friendly and popular owners, who take care that the ingredients within their Basque specialties are very fresh. You can enjoy Basque-style hake, herb-laden fish soup, a confit of duckling, filet of beef, and a platter packed with the "fruits of the sea," as well as succulent beef, veal, and pork dishes. Various chocolate-laden desserts among others round off the repast, which costs from 2,500 pesetas ($17.50) and is served daily except Sunday (in winter, however, the restaurant is open daily). A cluster of dining rooms is there to choose from, and reservations are a good idea.

Casa Paco Trapos, Alvaro del Valle Lersundi (tel. 42-28-16), sits in a tiny, difficult-to-find plaza in the old section of town near an intersection of the better known Calle 31 de Agosto. Both the owner and his cuisine are proudly Basque, creating the aura of being within a comfortably appointed private house. You can enjoy dozens of varieties of Atlantic seafish here, including hake, fish soup, grilled sole, salted codfish in a green sauce, and squid in its own ink. Full meals, costing from 2,000 pesetas ($14), are served at lunch and dinner daily except Sunday and Monday at lunchtime. Annual vacation is for two weeks at Christmas and another two weeks at Easter.

Juanito Kojua, 14 Puerto (tel. 42-01-80), in the old part of town, is a little fish restaurant that has become famous throughout Spain. There is no decor to speak of, the tables are few, and there's a wait, but it's worth it. The atmosphere consists of beamed ceilings, wood-paneled walls, and stone floors. There are two dining areas on the main floor, after you pass along a narrow bar (perfect for an appetizer while you're waiting for your table), plus one downstairs—all of them air-conditioned in summer. The standard menu costs 2,000 pesetas ($14) and might include fish soup, chicken, and fruit. But you're better off ordering the à la carte specialties. Each one of the dishes is virtually a meal in itself: paella, pisto, half a besugo (sea bream), rape (a whitefish) l'americana, and lubina (sea bass). Meats are good too, but it's best to stick to the fresh fish dishes. If you order à la carte, you can escape for 2,800 pesetas ($19.60); although your tab could run much higher.

Patxiku Kintana, 22 San Jerónimo (tel. 42-63-99). The sun-flooded interior of this well-known restaurant has witnessed the passage of the most influential names of the Basque region through its portals. It's in the heart of the old city, made successful through the industry and talent of the acclaimed chef, Maritxu, and her daughter-in-law, Pepi. Many of the recipes are ancestral hand-me-downs, but despite their age, they are made only with the freshest of raw ingredients, which come out transformed into flavorful concoctions, names of which only a linguist or a Basque can accurately translate. Some of them, however, include cocido (a stew), merluza (hake) stew, squid in its own ink, and many of the veal, pork, and beef dishes that are cooked throughout much of Spain but with subtle variations. The establishment, which is closed Sunday night and Monday, charges from 2,000 pesetas ($14) for a full meal.

Gure Arkupe, Letra D. Iztingorra (tel. 21-15-09), is an intimate little restaurant where reservations are usually a good idea. The popularity of the place is certainly due in large part to the skill of the chef, whose résumé includes apprenticeships with well-known kitchens throughout Spain. Owner Manoli Iturzaeta sees to it that the cuisine offered in his place is flavorful yet unpretentious. You can feast on seafood such as shrimp with salmon and a zarzuela, as well as other fish dishes. Other specialties are homemade pâté, duckling with orange sauce, and juicy veal dishes. My preferred dessert is the thin crêpes stuffed with cream. The restaurant, closed Monday and in December, charges from 2,000 pesetas ($14).

La Oka, 43 San Martín (tel. 46-38-84). Don't come here looking for glamour, but if you're looking for a self-service cafetería with low prices, you might enjoy this place. A full, fixed-price meal costs only 650 pesetas ($4.55), and an à la carte selection goes for 1,500 pesetas ($10.50) and up. The establishment is closed Wednesday, in the evening on Monday, Tuesday, and Thursday, during the last part of May, and for a few days around Christmas. At lunchtime you can expect a cross-section of the city's office workers.

Sardines Along the Harbor

In the summer, the thing to do is to walk along the Fishermen's Harbor in San Sebastián and order a plate of charcoal-broiled sardines. At several bistros, rustic wooden tables and chairs have been placed outside rough-and-tumble restaurants that offer good food. One of the best is **Casa Panchica,** 16 Muelle, a typical dockside fish restaurant facing the harbor, where for 650 pesetas ($4.55) you can order soup, a half-dozen grilled sardines, dessert, and wine. The repast would put a twinkle in the eye of an old sea captain. One American woman reports that after having a meal of sardines here, she was stalked by two cats when she visited the old quarter.

NIGHTLIFE: **Casa Alcalde,** 19 Mayor (tel. 42-62-16). Some of the tapas on the bar have Basque names, a reminder that owner Joseba Iraizoz takes his origins seriously. The tasty canapés to go with your drinks are thinly sliced ham, cheeses, or shellfish dishes, all neatly displayed for the appraisal and selection of customers. Snacks begin at 150 pesetas ($1.05). The bar, in the center of the old town, is open daily except in October.

Kabutzia, Muelle Concha (tel. 42-57-03). Because of its location on the upper floor of the Club Náutico, the window views alone make a visit here worth the trip. There's a small dance floor with low-key music, and you can order well-prepared cocktails, costing 300 pesetas ($2.10), to help you enjoy your evening.

Maxim's, 2 Igentea (tel. 42-59-92), is owned by the Dioni brothers, who also manage the sophisticated and successful Kabutzia, visited above. Maxim's is elegant, popular, and light-hearted. Drinks begin at 300 pesetas ($2.10).

La Cepa, 9 Calle 31 de Agosto (tel. 42-63-94). If you've ever wondered whatever happened to the bullfighters of Spain when their careers in the ring are over, the answer is that many of them establish successful bars, providing relaxing rendezvous points for hundreds of guests. Many locals say that the best tapas in town are at La Cepa (the Jabugo ham is one proof of this claim). Prices begin at 150 pesetas ($1.05). The owner, known as "Barberito," is usually on the scene visiting with his many friends. The place is closed Wednesday and in November.

Negresco, 5 Zubieta (tel. 46-09-68), offers a full array of seafood tapas, costing from 150 pesetas ($1.05), the star being tartly piquant anchovies with peppers in vinaigrette sauce. There's also a wide collection of wines. The bar is closed Sunday night, Monday, in October, and in April.

Casa Valles, 10 Reyes Católicos (tel. 45-22-10). The variety of tapas, from 100 pesetas (70¢), appears almost endless here. The management doesn't exactly skimp on the wines it serves either. In any event, go for a view of the locals and an array of tidbits guaranteed to spoil your dinner. Casa Valles is closed during the latter part of both June and December.

Don Surio, 5 Manterola (tel. 46-66-65), is amid a row of bars and pubs that seem to attract many of the night owls of the city. The clientele is fairly upper crust, giving the impression that the drink price of 650 pesetas ($4.55) is not out of line.

Bataplan, Paseo de la Concha (tel. 46-04-39), offers a beachside location at La Concha, with two bars and a widely varied clientele. Drinks at this lovely place are a little less expensive than at Don Surio, which makes the place more youth oriented.

SIDE TRIPS FROM SAN SEBASTIÁN: One of the reasons for coming to San Sebastián is to use it as a base for branching out to the sight-filled environs. Readers with cars are fortunate, as buses connecting some of the more important sights are awkward or nonexistent. Our first and easiest trip is to:

Pasajes de San Juan

On the east bank of a natural harbor 6½ miles from San Sebastián is one of the most typical Basque fishing villages, Pasajes de San Juan. Visitors like to come here to dine. The village, with its codfish-packing factories, huddles close to its sheltered harbor; little fishing boats are tied up at the wharf. The architecture is appealing: five- and sometimes six-story balconied tenement-like buildings spring up from the precious land space. Many of them are in different colors, and the flamboyant laundry sailing from the porches makes Pasajes de San Juan look like the melting pot that paints the rainbow.

It is understandable why Victor Hugo lived here in the 19th century (it hasn't changed since) at building no. 59 on the narrow main street.

For a sumptuous repast, try **Txulotxo,** 82 Calle San Juan, Pasajes de San Juan (tel. 35-66-09), one of the most authentic and typical of Basque restaurants. Right on the waterside, the restaurant is in an old stone building, part of it under an arch. The kitchen is on the main street (you can peer in and inspect it). Two sides of windows encase most of the dining room, which juts out onto the harbor. A two-fork restaurant, the Txulotxo charges 1,600 pesetas ($11.20) for its menú del día. Otherwise you'll pay from 2,000 pesetas ($14) on the à la carte menu. The specialties of the casa are made from fish that is delivered at the doorstep each day fresh. On any given day you may share the restaurant with local fishermen and their families and other Basques who sometimes break into song at the finish of their meal. Closed Tuesday and in October.

Taking a car into the village in summer is not advised since parking space is at a premium. The medieval street accommodates one-way traffic only, and Pasajes de San Juan has the longest traffic signals known. All the south-moving traffic has to clear the street before north-bound motorists have the right of way.

A bus leaves every 15 minutes from Calle Aldamar in San Sebastián for **Pasajes de San Pedro,** San Juan's sister fishing village. It's possible to walk over from the neighboring village. Buses head back to San Sebastián from Pasajes de San Pedro at a quarter to the hour all day long.

After a visit to Pasajes de San Juan, you may be in the mood for a much longer pilgrimage—one to:

Loyola

This sanctuary, lying about 34 miles southwest of San Sebastián, is the most-visited attraction outside the city. Surrounded by mountain scenery, Loyola is where St. Ignatius, the founder of the Jesuits, was born. The sanctuary has an enormous regal dome, and subtle muted coloring. The **Santa Casa** (Holy House) may be visited free throughout the day.

Buses going by way of Loyola leave from 2 Plaza Guipúzcoa in San Sebastián. There are six buses a day, the first departing at 8:30 a.m. and the last at 8 p.m. The return trips run about every two hours.

Those with a car can continue northwest toward Bilbao for a visit to:

2. Guernica (Guernika)

This town that became the subject of Picasso's most famous painting, now returned to Spain, was destroyed by bombs in an air raid on April 26, 1937. Guernica is the spiritual home of the Basques and of Basque nationalism. It was the site of a revered oak tree, under whose branches Basques had elected their officials since medieval times. No one knows how many died during the 3½-hour pounding—estimates range from 200 to as many as 1,600 persons. After the bombers departed, the town had been reduced to rubble, but a mighty symbol of independence had been born.

Controversy still swirls around Guernica. The town has been attractively rebuilt, somewhat in its former style. Today it looks as if it had never seen a bomb. The quiet life goes on—old men lead heavily laden donkeys through the streets. Women gossip over the fence. The chimes of a church ring softly, and happy children play in the street. Suddenly, you'll come upon a sign: "Souvenirs . . . Remember" (in Spanish). And you will.

At the **Casa de Juntas,** the principal attraction in the town is a display of the history of Guernica. It is open from 10 a.m. to 2 p.m. and 4 to 7 p.m. in summer (closes at 6 p.m. in winter). Outside are the remains of the ancient tree, around which the Basque rulers gathered for centuries for their communal meetings. The specific symbol of Basque independence was not uprooted by the bombs.

WHERE TO EAT: **Faison de Oro,** 4 Adolfo Urioste (tel. 685-10-01). Don't be fooled by the bar area that will greet you near the front entrance of this congenial place which is directed by the Gabiola family. A sun-filled dining room occupies most of the rear section of the establishment, where the husband and wife team of Iñaki and Ana prepare a mix of international and Basque cuisine. Specialties include steamed fish, asparagus in an orange cream sauce, and French dishes such as the chef's entrecôte with béarnaise sauce. You might also order beef in a Roquefort sauce and vegetable flan. Of course, pheasant (faison) is also offered in hunting season. A full meal costs from 3,000 pesetas ($21) and can be enjoyed daily except Tuesday at supper and on Wednesday.

Restaurante Zaldua, 10 Sabino Arana (tel. 687-08-71). Specialties at this warmly decorated restaurant mainly come from the blazing grill, whose turning spits are visible to most of the dining room. Of course a wide array of seafood and fish is also available, a particular favorite being one of the denizens of the deep baked to a flaky goodness in a layer of rock salt. Full meals cost around 2,500 pesetas ($17.50). In summer the restaurant is open daily, closing Sunday night and Monday off-season. It goes on vacation from mid-December to the end of January.

On the way back to San Sebastián, try to make this stopover on the Cantabrian coast:

ONDARROA: This fishing village is considered by some to be one of the most attractive in Spain. There are, of course, many contenders for that title, but Ondarroa is certainly in the final competition. It has a snug harbor, a fishing fleet, balconied houses draped with hanging plants and vivid laundry. The people look as if they were waiting for the movie cameras to roll.

Food and Lodging

Hotel/Restaurant Vega, 8 Avenida de la Antigua (tel. 683-00-02), offers comfortable and simple rooms at bargain-basement rates of 1,000 pesetas ($7) for a single, 1,800 pesetas ($12.60) for a double. The hotel only contains some two dozen rooms, and since it's the only hostelry in town, that doesn't leave much choice for a late-night motorist in search of accommodation. Still, the setting is pleasant, and if the Restaurant Penalty (see below) happens to be closed, you can enjoy a well-prepared and honest meal here for 1,800 pesetas ($12.60). Veal, fish, fried beef, and fish soup are representative menu items. The restaurant is open daily except Thursday in winter, closing for the month of October. The hotel is open all year.

Restaurant Penalty, 32 Eribera (tel. 683-00-00), is a small, friendly restaurant at a crossroads at the edge of town. Since the number of tables is limited, it's best to reserve in advance. Meals could include a house recipe for hake that is simply heavenly, plus other specialties, nearly all of which are prepared with fish. The sopa de pescado (fish soup) will invariably be a good choice as an appetizer. Expect to pay 2,000 pesetas ($14) or more for a meal. The restaurant is a family affair, with Mrs. Francisca Osa Jayo supervising the kitchen, where her daughter, Puri Garcia-Salazar Osa, is the cook. Felipe Garcia-Salazar Osa sees to the service and well-being of customers.

After San Sebastián, we leave the Basque country and head west for Old Castile.

3. Santander

This Atlantic Coast capital is a summer festival. It is not only one of the most popular resort cities in Spain, but one of the most modern. Yet Santander is ancient. In the early '40s a fire swept over the city, destroying its old quarter and most of its colorful dwellings. The industrious people rebuilt along sane lines, and what greets the visitor is a sparkling area of wide boulevards, a promenade along the waterfront, sidewalk cafés, new buildings, shops, restaurants, and good hotels.

Santander plays host to an international *Music and Dance Festival* in August that is considered one of the most important artistic events in Spain (hotel bookings are most difficult then). At times this festival coincides with religious celebrations honoring Santiago, the patron saint of Spain.

Santander is an education center in summer, as well. Courses are presented at the once-royal palace, now the Menéndez Pelayo International University. Students and teachers from all over America, Canada, and Europe come here to study and visit.

In addition, Santander is a fit base for the sportsman. There's wild game up in the surrounding hills, and the fishing is good.

On the Cantabrian bay, this Castilian city is an important seaport, and has a prosperous commercial and industrial section.

But most visitors head for **El Sardinero,** less than 1½ miles from the city. This resort section resembles many East Coast, U.S.A., beach towns that grew up in the '20s. Besides its hotels and restaurants, Santander has three beaches, **Playa de Castañeda, Playa del Sardinero,** and **Playa de la Concha.** Under candy-striped umbrellas, you'll find the beauties and the beasts. Buses and trolleys make the short run between the heart of Santander and El Sardinero both day and night.

If these beaches get too crowded, you can take a little boat to **El Puntal** beach. The trip lasts about 15 minutes. El Puntal is a beautiful beach and is not crowded, even in August.

Those who don't like crowds *and* beaches should go up to the lighthouse, about 1¼ miles from El Sardinero beach. Views are spectacular, and there's a restaurant serving indoor and outdoor snacks. Here you can take a walk along the tops of the green cliffs, or loll in the lush grass.

WHERE TO STAY: Santander is loaded with bargains, ranging from its year-round hotels in the city itself to summer villas at El Sardinero. But the early bird who writes in advance gets the room.

In the Town

Hotel Rex, 9 Avenida de Calvo Sotelo (tel. 21-02-00), is a suitable choice if you're just passing through. This seven-story, most respectable establishment was built at the turn of the century when hotels were known for their comfort. Its large, recently modernized doubles with private bath rent for 7,200 pesetas

($50.40), but only 4,200 pesetas ($29.40) with less plumbing. Singles with bath peak at 3,800 pesetas ($26.60), and singles without bath cost only 2,200 pesetas ($15.40). The pleasant, oak-paneled lounge has comfortable groups of armchairs and couches. The Rex is open all year.

At El Sardinero

Hotel Roma, 5 Avenida de los Hoteles (tel. 27-27-00), stands in the heart of El Sardinero; it's an old mansion in the shadow of the once-grand Casino. This turn-of-the-century hotel, open from June through September, was built when life at Santander was lived on a much grander scale. Many of the classic features remain—the crystal chandeliers, the great central staircase. But when we look closely at this "birthday cake," we see that the Roma has skimped on the icing. The room furnishings, although strictly utilitarian, are clean and comfortable. The most expensive doubles—with private bath—cost from 6,100 pesetas ($42.70). Only a few singles are available, at a top price of 3,800 pesetas ($26.60). Breakfast, at an extra charge, is the only meal. Guests can play tennis and enjoy the garden.

Hotel París, 6 Avenida de los Hoteles (tel. 27-23-50), is a soul sister to the Roma. Sitting side-by-side on this hotel street, both were built at the same time and both have old-fashioned appurtenances, the Paris a bit more so than the Roma. But the summer mansion, despite its clutter, has many once-opulent bedrooms. The best have front windows overlooking the Plaza de Italia. The hotel is open from June through September. The most expensive doubles—those with private bath—rent for 4,000 pesetas ($28). Most doubles, however, contain shower (no toilet), and cost 2,500 pesetas ($17.50) a night.

Hotel María Isabel, Avenida de García Lago (tel. 27-18-50). Water lovers will appreciate the expansive vistas of the beach and the ocean available from most of the 60-some rooms of this renovated hostelry on one of the beaches of Sardinero. If you want an enclosed body of water instead of the open sea, you'll find a swimming pool on the premises. There's also a late-night disco, a parking lot, and several convention rooms, which might be in use at the time of your visit. Doubles peak at 6,000 pesetas ($42), singles at 3,800 pesetas ($26.60).

Hotel Rhin, 156 Avenida Reina Victoria (tel. 27-43-00), built in the early 1970s in a panoramic position looking out over the city's beaches, offers comfortable and clean lodgings for 4,200 pesetas ($29.40) in a single, from 7,000 pesetas ($49) in a double. The 95 rooms offer as much comfort as nearby hotels that charge more pesetas. There's a garage on the premises. The Rhin has a cafetería but no restaurant.

Hotel Sardinero, 1 Plaza de Italia (tel. 27-11-00). The façade of this centrally located hotel near the beach and the casino is worth noting for its architectural beauty. The establishment offers reasonably priced rooms for 4,500 pesetas ($16.80) in a single, 6,500 pesetas ($45.50) in a double. There's an in-house disco if you want some diversion close to home. The hotel also offers a good restaurant, Mouro, where you can order a meal for 1,400 pesetas ($9.80) up.

WHERE TO EAT: For the most part, visitors to Santander eat at their hotels or boarding houses, which—without a doubt—give better value for the money, and often more efficient service than any of the city's restaurants. However, to vary the hotel dining, a group of budget restaurants has been found, the best of which follow:

Cañadío, 15 Gómez Oreña (tel. 31-41-49). The young chef, Paco Quirós, is the owner and operator of this pleasant restaurant on the Plaza Cañadío in the center of town. Menu specialties are reputed to be among the best served in the region. Featured may be shrimp flan, hake in champagne sauce, and escalopes of ham with cheese. Meals here, where service is polite and understated, cost from 2,700 pesetas ($18.90). The Cañadío closes Monday and from early November to early December.

La Sardina, 3 Doctor Fleming (tel. 27-10-35). You'll find this restaurant in a warren of back streets in the center of the old city. Its decor is reminiscent of yachting, boating, fishing, and other pleasant sea experiences. Victor Merino prepares an inventive kind of cuisine, using wines and many other choice ingredients to concoct his delicate sauces. There are also excellent wines to accompany your meal, which might consist of such dishes as cheese mousse, beef filet with truffles and cognac, and an unusually seasoned fish salad. Service is courteous. Full meals cost from 2,300 pesetas ($16.10) up. The restaurant is closed Sunday night.

Piquío, Plaza de las Brisas (tel. 27-55-03). The view from the windows of this panoramic restaurant is only one of the many reasons to visit it. After you admire the scene of the public gardens and the beach beyond, you can enjoy the well-organized service and the menu specialties, including a full array of fish and meat dishes. Full meals average 2,200 pesetas ($15.40). Piquio is closed on Monday from October to June.

Bodega Cigaleña, 19 Daoiz y Velarde (tel. 21-30-62), is a Castilian taverna in the center of the city, dishing up the most typical of regional cuisine in a rustic backdrop—hanging hams, large wine kegs, provincial tables. What more could you ask? Popular with the young set of Santander, it serves a special menú del día for 2,200 pesetas ($15.40) from noon to 4 p.m. and 7 p.m. till midnight. The bodega changes its set menu every day so you can come often. A sample meal: sopa de pescado (fish soup), followed by shellfish paella, the fruit of the season, bread, and wine. The Cigaleña is also an ideal stopover on your bodega-hopping circuit, offering a good choice of wines from an old Castilian town near Valladolid. Ask to see its Museo de Vino.

In the evening, for a change of pace, walk or take a taxi to the fishing port, where three or four outdoor restaurants specialize in grilled sardines and other freshly caught seafood. Across the street fishermen are mending their nets. It's all part of the local color. On my last visit I had an excellent meal in **Los Peñucas,** Marqués de la Ensenada, Barrio Pesquero (tel. 22-20-91), where a set menu costs 850 pesetas ($5.95). Service is slow, but then, who's in a hurry?

SANTANDER AFTER DARK: **La Bohemia,** 25 Daoiz y Velarde (tel. 22-69-53), is one of the most popular spots for music lovers under 30 in town. Management offers musical acts in addition to the piano playing and a café/pub kind of ambience. An average drink costs 350 pesetas ($2.45).

Lisboa, Plaza de Italia, is in the city casino, drawing all kinds of people to enjoy its tap beer, from 125 pesetas (88¢), and properly mixed drinks. In summer it's especially crowded, with patrons ranging from gamblers taking a brief respite from the tables upstairs to flirtatious lovers displaying their friendship to everyone in town.

Muelle 15, 15 Paseo de Pereda (tel. 22-30-13), is a small, warm, and well-decorated bar, which is especially colorful late at night. The bartender makes good drinks, costing from 175 pesetas ($1.23). Beer and wine are popular too.

4. Santillana del Mar and the Caves of Altamira

This medieval village, considered by some to be the most perfectly preserved in Europe, lies about 18 miles southwest of Santander. Santillana is the home of one of the best known of the government-run paradors, the mansion of Gil Blas, named after the legendary rogue dear to the Spanish heart.

This sleepy little village of aristocratic mansions is a National Monument. That means that nothing can be changed, and who would want to?

If you have at least a night for Santillana, walk through its moonlit, rough, cobblestone streets, strolling back to a time when people concerned themselves with such phenomena as heretics and infidels—and Hell, Purgatory, and Paradise were more than just a poem to the villagers.

In the morning you may see men hitching up oxen to their carts or women washing their clothes in the stream, just as their ancestors did generations before them. But if you start to photograph them, you'll find that they are more sophisticated than their great-grandmothers. They'll usually stop scrubbing and start adjusting their dishevelled coiffures.

Even the most confirmed atheist can usually find a good word to say about the splendidly designed Romanesque **Collegiate Church,** with its decaying but lovely cloisters. In the center is the tomb of the patron saint of the village, Juliana. The 800-year-old cathedral holds the same rank as Westminster Abbey, and contains 1,000-year-old documents and such gems as a 17th-century Mexican silver altarpiece. The cloisters are open from 9 a.m. to 1 p.m. and 4 to 8 p.m. Admission is 100 pesetas (70¢).

The same ticket allows a visit to the rich art collection gathered in the **Convent of the Poor Clares,** now the Museo Diocesano, a restored 400-year-old-monastery. A Madrid art professor inspired some two dozen nuns to collect and restore religious paintings and statues either damaged or abandoned during the Spanish Civil War. The collection is constantly growing. It keeps the same hours as the church.

Santillana Zoo (tel. 81-81-25) is about one kilometer along the road to the Altamira Caves. So far it has limited itself solely to fauna found in Spain (wolves, foxes, reptiles, and birds). It's open from June to September. Entrance is 300 pesetas ($2.10) for adults, 150 pesetas ($1.05) for children 5 to 12 years old. Daily hours are 10 a.m. to 8 p.m.

LIVING IN A PALACE: **Parador Nacional Gil Blas,** 11 Plaza de Ramón Pelayo (tel. 81-80-00). The Middle Ages are revived in this 400-year-old palace. A heavy nail-studded doorway opens onto a front gallery lounge, elegantly informal. Guests are assigned rooms here (some with views of the garden), then they are taken up an ancient stairway to the timber-ceilinged upper hall. Large pictures of knights in armor hang in this gallery. The hand-hewn plank floor, the time-aged brass chandeliers, and the two refectory tables with bowls of fresh flowers do their part to create the mood.

Large iron keys are used to open the doors leading to the suites. Most of the 28 bedrooms are unusually large, and most have windows on two sides. Old furniture, dark with centuries of use, is combined with comfortable twin beds that have been reproduced in the old style. When the shutters are closed and the red velvet draperies are drawn, this medieval masquerade is complete. The cost? It's 10,500 pesetas ($73.50) for two persons, 8,800 pesetas ($61.60) for the most expensive single. The baths are half the size of the bedrooms, it seems, and they contain all sorts of built-in conveniences. White, freshly laundered terry-cloth dressing robes are provided. *Note:* The third floor rooms get thumbs down from readers. One wrote that they "must have been for the servants originally, as they are the smallest double rooms possible."

Four-course evening meals and luncheons are served in the great dining hall. A set meal costs 2,200 pesetas ($15.40). The palace is "fit for a king." Juan Carlos was known to stop here before he became king.

ALTERNATIVE PLACES TO STAY: **Hotel Altamira,** 1 Cantón (tel. 81-80-25), is a two-star hotel managed by David Oceja Buján near the Gil Blas, and offers another opportunity for a visitor to meet the past. This small palace, built about 400 years ago, is not as great as the government-run parador, but it holds its own, picking up the overflow. Open all year, the Altamira charges low rates for its double rooms with private bath—4,000 pesetas ($28). You can get a complete meal here for 1,200 pesetas ($8.40) even if you aren't staying over. The hotel's restaurant, seating 300 persons, is decorated in the Castilian style. The Altamira is in the center of the village. It is entered through a front garden and is enclosed behind a high stone wall, locked away in the past.

Not quite so charming as the Altamira, but more modern and comfortable, is the nearby **Los Infantes,** 1 Avenida Le Dorat (tel. 81-81-00), on the main road leading into the village. This three-star hotel, opened in 1974, features 30 rooms. The Infantes has successfully kept the old flavor of Santillana in its interior decorations. There are beamed ceilings, pretty lounges, tapestries, antiques, clocks, and paintings. The rooms are pleasant and simple, with wall-to-wall carpeting, telephones, and Muzak. Two have a small balcony. Doubles with bath cost 6,500 pesetas ($45.50); singles with bath, 5,000 pesetas ($35).

Some other bargain accommodations lie off the main road leading into the village. Most are private, two-story houses. Among them is **Hostal-Residencia Emperador,** 12 Avenida Le Dorat (tel. 81-80-54), which has only three rooms, all of them simply furnished doubles. The staff is courteous and polite, and the hospitality, for such a modest place, is gracious. The highest tariffs are charged from June 15 to September 1. At those times the double rooms rent for 4,000 pesetas ($28) per day, dropping to just 3,000 pesetas ($21) during the rest of the year.

WHERE TO EAT: Aside from eating in the parador or the Altamira Hotel, you can opt for an independent restaurant.

Santillana is tiny, yet it has long had a "whisky club," called **Los Blasones,** Plaza de la Gandara (tel. 81-80-70), a kind of bar-cum-restaurant where some of the local youths hang out. There's a dimly lit ambience in winter months. In summer the two-fork restaurant offers a set meal for 1,800 pesetas ($12.60). Barbecue specialties from the grill are also featured. Los Blasones is off the Calle del Cantón. The same establishment runs a disco, open from about 5 till 11:30 p.m. (in summer till 1 a.m.), where drinks cost 500 pesetas ($3.50).

You can get to Santillana from Santander by a direct bus that leaves the Plaza de las Estaciones in Santander. This method is faster than the train. From Santillana del Mar, consider making an important side trip to:

THE CAVES OF ALTAMIRA: About a mile and a half from Santillana del Mar are the subterranean caves of Altamira (now closed to most of the public), whose prehistoric paintings go back to the twilight when men clad in animal skins were emerging from the Ice Age. These drawings are one of Spain's greatest artistic treasures. They have been called the "Sistine Chapel" of prehistoric art.

Here on the ceiling of a cave, undetected by the world until the latter part of the 19th century, bison and horses are captured in the most vivid of reds, the darkest of blacks.

It took a long time for the world to accept the authenticity of the Altamira drawings, but once that was done, scholars, laymen, and the idly curious flocked to these grottoes, which provide a fragile link to our remote ancestors.

In fact, they flocked in such great numbers that the public caused severe damage to these long-hidden caves. Modern bacteria are the culprit. Like the celebrated Lascaux grotto in France, Altamira is still viewed by only about a dozen visitors each day, and these are by invitation only.

If you're in the area, you'll have to settle for going through a little admission-free museum at the site, which is open from 10 a.m. to 1 p.m. and 4 to 7 p.m. (on Sunday from 10 a.m. to 1 p.m.). There you can see reproductions of the artwork in the caves and buy color slides that show the subtleties in some of the caveman colors—rich vermilion, magenta, ochre. You'll also see pictures of what those bacteria did to these priceless paintings.

5. Oviedo

Oviedo is the capital of the province of Asturias on the north coast of Spain, a land with the largest coalfields in the country. Bathed by the Bay of Biscay, the old kingdom of Asturias—later a principality—is officially tabbed the province of Oviedo today. It is the Wales of Spain. Yet Oviedo, in spite of its concentrated industry and mining areas, contains some of the most unspoiled scenery in "Green Spain."

Asturias, as you may remember, was the center of Christian resistance to the Muslim invaders who took Andalusia. The Cantabrian mountains run right through Asturias, and while based at the capital of Oviedo, you can strike out for excursions in many directions, although you are likely to get rained on. Oviedo lies 16 miles from the coast, and is very pleasant in summer when much of Spain is unbearably hot.

Damaged heavily in the Civil War, Oviedo is a modern city, but it contains sections with historical and artistic monuments. Chief of these is the **cathedral,** Plaza de Alfonso II, a Gothic building begun in 1348 and completed at the end of the 15th century. Its one spire dates from 1556. Inside is an altarpiece in the florid Gothic style, as are the cloisters, which date from the 14th and 15th centuries. Hours are from 9 a.m. to 1 p.m. and 3:30 to 6 p.m.

The cathedral's **La Cámara Santa** (Holy Chamber) is famous, dating from the 12th century and much restored. Containing two chapels, the Holy Chamber possesses the celebrated cross of Don Pelayo, the cross of the victory, and that of the angels, the finest specimens of Asturian art in the world. Its hours are 10 a.m. to 1 p.m. and 4 to 6 p.m. (to 7 p.m. in summer), charging 75 pesetas (53¢) for admission.

Museo Arqueológico, San Vincente (tel. 21-54-05), occupies a former convent dating from the 15th century. Prehistoric relics discovered in Asturias are displayed, along with a numismatic exhibit. Even old musical instruments are displayed, along with some pre-Romanesque sculptures. Hours are 11:30 a.m. to 1:30 p.m. and 4 to 6 p.m.

WHERE TO STAY: Hotel La Gruta, Alto de Buenavista (tel. 23-24-50), is a family-run hotel whose owners are so determined to have a well-managed operation that they sent their nephew, Narciso Cantón, to hotel school. The public rooms are trimmed in oak, following a simple and pleasant format designed in the mid-1970s. The hotel is just outside the city limits, so that from many of the bedrooms there are views of the surrounding countryside. Each of the 55 comfortably furnished units contains a private bath and a telephone. Rates are 4,500 pesetas ($31.50) in a single, 6,500 pesetas ($45.50) in a double. There is an in-house restaurant.

Hotel Principado, 6 San Francisco (tel. 21-77-92), opposite the university in the center of town, is a well-managed hotel that was completely renovated in 1980. Many people who come here share a meal or so in the dignified dining room before retiring to bedrooms that rent for 5,000 pesetas ($35) in a single and 6,000 pesetas ($42) in a double. Each of the units contains a TV and a radio, and the hotel has access to a nearby underground parking garage, easing the problem of parking in the center of town.

WHERE TO DINE: For real Asturian cookery, I'd recommend **Casa Fermín,** 8 Calle de San Francisco (tel. 21-64-52). The chef here is the best in town. To order the most classic dish of the former principality, ask for fabada asturiana, which is a bean dish with Asturian black pudding and Áviles ham. He also prepares a tasty hake cooked in cider, the most characteristic drink of the province. In season (from October to March) venison is the specialty. Try also the traditional Cabrales cheese of the province. Expect to pay from 2,500 pesetas ($17.50) to 3,500 pesetas ($24.50) for one of the finest regional repasts in the province.

Casa Conrado, 1 Argüelles (tel. 22-39-19), is considered a city landmark almost as solidly established as the cathedral near which it stands. If you're dieting, the kitchens, directed by Pichi Niño, will prepare a low-calorie meal, although culinary self-discipline seems difficult when such an array of specialties is available. These include Asturian-style stews, seafood platters, seafood soups, several preparations of hake, escalopes of veal with champagne, and a full range of desserts. Meals cost from 2,500 pesetas ($17.50) up. The restaurant is open daily except Sunday and all of August.

ON THE ROAD: Motorists going on to La Coruña and Santiago de Compostela may want to anchor for the night in a little town, Cornellana (Salas), 24 miles from Orviedo. There the **Hostal La Fuente** (tel. 83-40-42) welcomes you to a nice little inn with more than a dozen rooms. As a thoughtful touch, the sheets and pillow cases are trimmed with embroidery. One person pays 1,400 pesetas ($9.80), a double going for 2,800 pesetas ($19.60). There's a sitting room on each floor, as well as a bath. Attached is a dining room overlooking a garden, serving a menú del día for 800 pesetas ($5.60). For that, you get three courses of attractively served good food, along with bread and wine. The place is family operated.

6. La Coruña

La Coruña, jutting out on a peninsula, is the Neptune of Spain. This capital of an Atlantic maritime province looks to the sea for much of its livelihood. Yachts, fishing boats, and transatlantic liners vie for space in the harbor. But that's not all that makes the god of the sea claim La Coruña. The government tourist pamphlet, in trying to apologize for the amount of rainfall, says that the port experiences "many days of cloudless skies." That's true, of course.

This city, with its excellent beaches, is expanding rapidly as a summer tourist resort. In July and August its population swells tremendously. **Riazor,** a good, fairly wide beach, is right in town, but the best one is called **Santa Cristina,** which is about three miles on the outskirts. There is regular bus service to and from it (the ideal way to go is on a little steamer plying across the bay).

La Coruña (known as Corunna to the English) goes back into ancient history, but, surprisingly, does not have a wealth of historical and architectural monuments, as Santiago de Compostela does. The port was known to the Celts and Phoenicians, and was conquered by the Romans.

It is, as mentioned, another of the legendary cities that points to Hercules as its founder. The city's major monument is the **Tower of Hercules** (Torre de Hércules), a lighthouse more than a mile from the center of La Coruña. It overlooks the city and the sea, and was believed to have been built by the Emperor Trajan (restored in the 1700s). But the great event in the history of La Coruña occurred in 1588 when the not-so "Invincible Armada" sailed from here to England. The following year, Sir Francis Drake and his ships attacked the port in reprisal. The admission-free tower is open from 10 a.m. to 1:30 p.m. and 4 to 7:30 p.m.

About 375 miles from Madrid, La Coruña consists of an old and new town, in addition to some fast-developing modern outskirts. The old town is ideal for walks. It has a number of historic churches and mansions. Dividing these two towns is the Plaza de María Pita. This landmark was named after the 16th-century Spanish heroine who is probably unknown to many foreigners, but to the gallegos she is Joan of Arc. María Pita is famous for her courage and bravery during Drake's reprisal attack against her city.

From Madrid, La Coruña is best reached by rail, a distance of 467 miles on the tracks (via Orense and Zamora). There is daily express service from Madrid.

If a visitor is going on to La Coruña after a stopover in Santiago de Compostela, there is a daily bus service leaving Santiago, traveling the 46-mile run.

WHERE TO STAY: You might as well stay on the beach. **Residencia Riazor,** Andén de Riazor (tel. 25-34-00), has been known to me since it first opened its doors in 1963. At that time it started a trend in hotel building of leaving the heart of town and going to the beach, making it possible for guests to arrive, check into their streamlined bedrooms, change into their swimsuits, and hit the beach —all in 20 minutes. The tall, modern establishment charges 5,200 pesetas ($36.40) in a spacious double with private bath, 3,500 pesetas ($24.50) in a single, also with private bath. A continental breakfast is extra. The residencia rises 12 stories, with an all-glass living lounge on the second floor. It perhaps takes spacious modern a bit too seriously. The lounge seems half furnished, but the existing fixtures are comfortable. The bedroom decor and equipment are a bit reminiscent of Florida early-motel design. There is a snackbar-cafetería on the premises, but no major restaurant. The friendly employees speak a lilting Spanish with a Galician accent.

Hotel Ciudad de La Coruña, Polígono de Adormideras (tel. 21-11-00). Motorists will be grateful for the easy availability of parking near this modern hotel removed from the heart of town. A view of the ocean greets many of the guests as they enter their comfortably contemporary bedrooms. These rent for 4,500 pesetas ($31.50) in a single and 5,500 pesetas ($38.50) in a double. Each unit has a private bath and a mini-bar. A garden and an outdoor pool will add to your further enjoyment. Its total of some 131 rooms makes the Hotel Ciudad de La Coruña rank with some of the biggest hotels of the town. There is a public bus stop in front.

Hotel Atlántico, Jardines de Méndez Núñez (tel. 22-65-00), is a comfortable and contemporary hotel which, with its 200 bedrooms, is the biggest one in La Coruña. It's surrounded by a large park, which draws crowds, particularly on a holiday and weekends. Parking might be a problem, but sometimes a staff member from the hotel will direct you to a vacant place after you unload your luggage at the entrance. There are a sauna, a disco, a garden, and a bar in the hotel. Each of the well-furnished rooms contains a private bath and a mini-bar. Singles cost 4,500 pesetas ($35) to 5,800 pesetas ($40.60), with doubles going for 5,500 pesetas ($38.50) to 7,000 pesetas ($49), depending on the accommodation and the season.

The establishments we have considered so far may be too expensive for your budget. If your demands are meager, there are several budget hotels which will provide you with a room for the night.

One of them is the 20-room **Almirante,** 54 Paseo de Ronda (tel. 25-96-50), which has few amenities but a pleasant reception. Good, clean rooms are rented at 3,800 pesetas ($26.60) in a double, a real bargain. There is no restaurant, but a continental breakfast will be served on order.

Mara, 49 Galera (tel. 22-18-02), is another small one-star hotel. This one rents out 19 utilitarian and clean double rooms, costing from 3,500 pesetas ($24.50) a night.

If those are full, try the first-floor **Navarra,** 23 Plaza de Lugo (tel. 22-54-00), which has 24 basic units, costing from 3,500 pesetas ($24.50) in a double and from 2,300 pesetas ($16.10) in a single. The Navarra, like the Mara, doesn't offer a continental breakfast, but there are cafés nearby where you can order one.

WHERE TO DINE: In the very heart of La Coruña, two or three blocks from the water, are several restaurants specializing in the Galician cuisine. It is customary to go window shopping for food here. The restaurants along two of the principal streets—**Calle de la Estrella** and **Calle de los Olmos**—have display counters in front of their establishments. Most of them charge comparable prices.

My favorite is **El Coral,** 15 Calle de la Estrella (tel. 22-10-82), one of the most popular restaurants at the port. Cesar Gallego Pita has been around running the place since it opened back in 1954. Galician cookery is prepared with distinction here. A two-fork restaurant, El Coral specializes in shellfish, fish, meats, and Galician wines. The chef's specialty is turbante de mariscos (shellfish). Try also the stuffed squid (calamares rellenos). A popular main course is lubina (sea bass) al horno straight from the oven. The dessert specialty is a rich and fattening "filloas." A pitcher (one liter) of Ribero wine makes for a good choice with most dishes, and you can also order Condados and Riojas wines. For a full dinner, expect to spend from 2,500 pesetas ($17.50), especially if you order the more expensive shellfish dishes. The service is polite and friendly, and the standard of cleanliness is high. The restaurant is closed on Sunday night (except in summer), and it's suggested that you reserve a table.

In the center of town, within an easy walk of the Playa del Orzan, **Naveiro,** 129 San Andrés (tel. 22-90-24), is perhaps the most typically Galician restaurant in the port. In a regional, rustic setting, this well-patronized restaurant offers inexpensive but tasty Galician specialties. It serves the classic green-and-white soup of the northwest, known as caldo gallego (potatoes and greens). But hake, that good-tasting old standby, is prepared differently in La Coruña. Here it's usually served with peppers and potatoes. Spider crabs and oysters are other popular dishes, and octopus is occasionally featured, but if that's too exotic, you can order red mullet. A small beefsteak is offered to those who've had their fill of the sea. Dinners range from 2,000 pesetas ($14). The restaurant is closed on Sunday night and in May.

7. Santiago de Compostela

All roads in Spain used to lead to this northwestern granite city that has survived intact from the Middle Ages. The tomb of the beheaded apostle, St. James, was the end of the Milky Way for the faithful medieval pilgrim—both peasant and prince—who journeyed here from all over Europe, often under the most adverse of conditions.

These wanderers risked their lives, their money, and often their virginity, to pay homage to Santiago, the patron saint of Spain. At the same time these pilgrims brought culture and learning, especially in the area of architecture, where their Romanesque influence has had a profound effect on the skylines of Spain.

Along the pilgrims' way, hospitals, hospices, and sanctuaries—many of which are still preserved—were established. Across the Pyrenees, through Navarre and León, came this never-ending stream. The pilgrimages grew so important that a guidebook, the first of the Middle Ages, was written, giving sage advice. Bits of advice: (1) The water in Solares, it seemed, was clear and sparkling—perfectly safe to drink. (2) Beware of the robbers in Asturias.

Santiago de Compostela's link with legend began in A.D. 813 when an urn was discovered mystically one starlit night. It contained what were believed to be the remains of St. James. A temple was erected over the spot, but the poor saint wasn't allowed to remain in peace. Wars, and specifically the arrival of vengeance-seeking Drake from England, necessitated removal. After a long and mysterious disappearance, the remains were later "rediscovered" and transferred back to Santiago, where whatever is resting in that silver box in the crypt of the cathedral has been "authenticated."

In addition to being the third Holy City of the Christian world, Santiago de Compostela is a university town and marketplace for gallego farmers.

It has the dubious distinction of being the rainiest city in Spain. But one can always slip under a pillared arcade—that is, unless a victim happens to be caught standing in a large plaza. The rainfalls arrive uninvited and unannounced, then take sudden leave. But they leave the ancient buildings glistening like silver. The fading sun comes out, cutting through the slight steaming mist with orange spears—and Santiago is bathed in an enchantment that must have inspired Isabella or perhaps Philip II centuries ago.

Santiago de Compostela, with its flagstone streets, churches, and shrines, is one of the most romantic and historic of Spain's great cities. The government had declared it a sacred cow architecturally, so the chances are that it will remain this way. By all means, see Santiago at dusk. The rusty-colored roofs of its moss-patched stone buildings contrast dramatically with the rich Celtic greens of the surrounding valleys and mountains. In all, the town is a Romanesque and baroque fantasy.

Santiago can be reached from Madrid by air, car, or rail. It lies about 391 miles from the Spanish capital.

Iberia has daily flights between Madrid and Santiago, as well as daily return flights from Santiago to Madrid. Santiago is easily reached from La Coruña, 39 miles away. There are daily trains from La Coruña to Santiago.

THE SIGHTS: When most visitors arrive, they head first for:

The Cathedral

This great structure on the Plaza del Obradoiro, begun in the 11th century, is considered by some to be the crowning achievement of Spanish Romanesque, the heart and soul of the Jerusalem of the West for the faithful pilgrim. Today it is still the most revered architectural site in all of northwestern Spain.

In the center of Santiago, opening onto a great plaza, the cathedral has seen a number of architects since the 11th century. Each new designer brought his own interpretation to the façades, the retables, the chapels, as well as the style of his age. Consequently, plateresque and Renaissance waltz with Gothic, Galician baroque plays leapfrog with Romanesque.

As mentioned, a silver urn in the crypt, which may be visited, contains what are believed to be the remains of the Apostle St. James. However, the glory of the cathedral does not rest on even so illustrious a tenant.

The cathedral has a number of spectacular architectural features, the most notable of which is called the Pórtico de la Gloria. Carved by Mateo in the late 12th century, this portico houses brilliantly conceived and characterized sculpture, considered the finest produced in Europe during the entire 1100s. The floor plan of the cathedral resembles a cross; it has three naves, as well as an abundance of chapels and cloisters. In the 1700s the cathedral acquired one of its most splendid façades, known as *Obradoiro.*

This Santiago landmark has the most extraordinary altar of all the major cathedrals of Spain, harmoniously blending Gothic simplicity with a baroque decor.

Don't be surprised to encounter pilgrims embracing a statue and asking for help, or inserting their fingers into openings in the "Tree of Life" for protection, or touching their heads against a stone figure three times for intelligence.

The cathedral (tel. 58-35-48) may be visited all day. However, to see the tapestries and archeological remains in the museum, a charge of 100 pesetas (70¢) is assessed; the museum is open from 10 a.m. to 1:30 p.m. and 3:30 to 7:30 p.m.

Adjoining the cathedral is the **Palacio de Gelmírez,** an archbishop's palace built in the 12th century, a most outstanding example of Romanesque. It may be visited from 10:30 a.m. to 1:30 p.m. and 4 to 7 p.m. for 75 pesetas (53¢) admission.

Hostal de Los Reyes Católicos

Founded by Ferdinand and Isabella at the dawn of the 16th century, this former hospital has been turned into one of the most spectacular hotels of Europe. Once it was a refuge for pilgrims visiting the tomb of St. James. This hotel on the Plaza de España (tel. 58-22-00) is seen at some point by most visitors to Santiago who pass through its dazzling Renaissance entranceway, seeking accommodations, meals, or drinks. Casual sightseers should announce themselves at the desk. The hotel has four huge open-air courtyards, each with its own covered walk, trees, gardens, or fountain. In addition, there are chapels, libraries, great halls, grillwork from France, and paintings (Goya, El Greco). Antiques greet the visitor at every turn. The Gothic chapel has been adapted to form the setting for weekly concerts. Imagine going in after dinner to hear the artistry of Montoya.

There is a full range of accommodations, everything from Franco's former suite to monk-like dormitories. The suites, done in original styles, often have canopied beds with ornate crests, draped in embroidered red velvet. Hand-carved chests, gilt mirrors, and oil paintings enhance the luxury. The sumptuous, palace-like double rooms with private bath cost from 8,000 pesetas ($56) to 13,000 pesetas ($91). Singles with bath go for 6,500 pesetas ($45.50). Each meal here runs to 2,800 pesetas ($19.60).

STAYING OVER: It would be ideal if one could afford the luxury of the 16th-century former hospital, but if that's not possible, Santiago has other comfortable, but less expensive establishments. In descending scale, they are:

Hotel Compostela, 1 Calvo Sotelo (tel. 58-57-00), has long been considered the grand old lady of hotels in this section. Built of native gray stone, this corner hotel has been the center for many of the elegant social events for years. It charges 6,500 pesetas ($45.50) for the best doubles with private bath. Singles with bath cost 3,800 pesetas ($26.60). The Compostela was recently enlarged, so that it now has a total of 99 rooms. Inside you'll find a carved oak staircase in the central hall, with its hand-woven carpet, as well as many salons with old-style furniture. Everywhere are huge chandeliers, oil paintings, and tapestries, and a central glass-covered patio with arches that makes it reminiscent of a monastery courtyard. Only breakfast is served.

Hotel del Peregrino, Avenida de Rosalía de Castro (tel. 59-18-50), a four-star hotel, is at the edge of town, off the main road, and although not a budget hotel, is still preferred by many readers traveling to this remote part of Spain. It has a long gallery lounge opening onto its rear garden, with centered swimming pool. Restrained furnishings and textured upholstery—everything has been tastefully selected. The modern and well-furnished double accommodations with private bath rent for 6,500 pesetas ($45.50) nightly for those who can afford to spend this much. Singles with bath cost 5,000 pesetas ($35).

Gelmírez, 92 General Franco (tel. 56-11-00), is a modern, central hotel which rents double rooms with bath for 5,000 pesetas ($35), and singles with shower for 3,500 pesetas ($24.60). No meals are served here except a continental breakfast costing extra.

Hostal La Senra, 1 General Mola (tel. 58-04-48), is a spotlessly clean, little seven-bedroom boarding house that is very comfortable. It's nicely situated, lying about a five-minute walk from the cathedral and near several main streets of sightseeing interest. The rate charged is about 2,800 pesetas ($19.60) in a double room with hot and cold running water.

Hostal Residencia Alameda, 32 San Clemente (tel. 58-81-00), is on the second floor of a building in the cathedral district. The 20 comfortable rooms are kept immaculate, and some have a bath. Doubles cost 3,200 pesetas ($22.40), dropping to 2,200 pesetas ($15.40) in a single. Only breakfast is served. The staff here is courteous and efficient. Ample parking is available adjacent to the hostal.

WHERE TO EAT: The **Restaurant Alameda,** 15 Avenida de Figueroa (tel. 58-47-96), is a second-story, two-fork restaurant, at the beginning of a tree-lined avenue. The constant stream of diners, both foreign and domestic, attest to its continued popularity. For 2,200 pesetas ($15.40) a complete meal is served, including many of the specialties for which Galicia is well known. The caldo gallego is a Galician broth that starts most meals. Americans, from the southern states in particular, may be lured by lacón con grelos, one of the most popular regional dishes of the northwest—hamhock cooked with greens. If more elegant fare is the order of the day, then the fresh fish dishes are reliable. Try the necoras (spider crabs), a real gourmet's delight. There is a cafetería-snackbar on the ground floor, handy for light meals and drinks. Guests sit at sidewalk tables.

Restaurante "El Caserío," 13 Bautizados (tel. 58-59-80), is one of the best of the seafood restaurants of Santiago. The decor is modern, and the location is near the Alameda. The main seafood specialties are usually sold by weight. Featured are spiny lobsters, spider crabs, barnacles, shrimps, prawns, and scallops. Galician soup starts most meals, followed by Galician hake, or perhaps the already mentioned lacón with grelos. Desserts include natural yogurt. If you order à la carte, your tab is likely to range from 1,200 pesetas ($8.40) to 2,500 pesetas ($17.50). Service is until midnight.

Restaurant Anexo Vilas, 21 Avenida de Villagarcia (tel. 59-83-87), stands at the edge of the city on the road leading to Pontevedra. This is a modern restaurant where head chef Juan Bello produces an unusual and savory cuisine with the freshest seafood he can find. A few of the Galician dishes are based on meat ingredients, the filet of beef with a sherry sauce being especially good. The kitchen's real creativity comes out in its fish dishes. These include all the standard kinds you can easily think of, such as fish soup, hake, and grilled shrimp, as well as many that you may not see on less elaborate restaurant menus. You'll realize that this is a family-run business, judged by the conscientious service. Open daily except Monday, the establishment charges 2,500 pesetas ($17.50) for a full meal.

La Tacita de Oro, 31 General Franco (tel. 56-20-41). The owner of this very popular restaurant arises before dawn to buy the fresh fish and produce by which this restaurant is well known. It's a favorite of lunching business people, not only because of its location in the commercial heart of town, but because of its fine cuisine. Founded in the mid-1950s, the restaurant offers such dishes as caldo gallego, fish soup, artichokes with ham, Basque-style eels, a shellfish cocktail, and a wide array of fish platters. Portions are copious, and service is attentive. Full meals cost from 1,800 pesetas ($12.60). The establishment is open daily.

8. Pontevedra

This is an old aristocratic Spanish city, on the Lérez River. The capital of a province by the same name, Pontevedra makes for an interesting stopover, as the government has installed a parador in one of the city's oldest palaces. Visitors can see the remains of the wall that once encircled the town.

Santa María Church, in plateresque, dating from the 16th century, with its avocado-green patina, is the most visited architectural sight. But try to see the beautiful Town Hall Square as well. In the old quarter of Pontevedra, you will discover many stone buildings with green trim.

This provincial Galician town is some 36 miles from Santiago de Compostela, and 521 miles from Madrid. It is often visited by the Portuguese, who cross over the nearby border for short excursions.

LIVING IN A 16TH-CENTURY PALACE: The **Parador Nacional Casa del Barón** (tel. 85-58-00), is a well-kept 16th-century palace, which the Spanish government has preserved and transformed into an excellent parador. Guests are offered an opportunity to live like landed barons, even better, as modern plumbing and central heating have been installed. The hotel contains 47 rooms which accommodate a total of 91 guests.

Off the entrance hallway is a courtyard dominated by a large old stone staircase, leading to the rooms upstairs. The inside has been maintained very much as the old *pazo* (manor house) must have looked. It includes a quaint old kitchen or *lar* (literally "heart"), which is typical of Galician country houses, furnished and decorated with characteristic items. The accommodations are large enough to have sitting arrangements; the beds are comfortable; and the furnishings attractive. Many of the rooms have views of the walled-in, formal garden. The cost is 8,000 pesetas ($56) for a double with private bath, 6,000 pesetas ($42) for single with private bath. Both luncheon and dinner are 2,200 pesetas ($15.40). Almost any dish, such as a casserole of shrimp with tomato sauce, is well prepared. The cake of the day is usually moist and delicate. The cooking is good, and the waitresses are friendly. The parador is in the old quarter of Pontevedra, ideal for exploring.

OTHER FOOD AND LODGING CHOICES: **Rías Bajas,** 7 Daniel de la Sota (tel. 85-51-00). The clientele of this hotel's 100 bedrooms tends to be the out-of-town business associates of the most conservative residents of the city. In the center of the commercial district of town, the hotel is a modern building which in some ways is a focal point of the politics in the area, since many of the city's press conferences take place in one of the convention rooms. Single rooms rent for 3,300 pesetas ($23.10) to 3,800 pesetas ($26.60), while doubles cost 4,300 pesetas ($30.10) to 5,500 pesetas ($38.50), based on the accommodation. There's plenty of parking nearby.

Hotel Virgen del Camino, 55-57 Virgen del Camino (tel. 85-59-00), is an unpretentious hotel in an unglamorous part of town, where many of the patrons have practically set up private homes. It's surrounded with all the industrial life on the edge of the city. Nonetheless, it might be suitable if nothing else is available in town, and the management is cooperative. There's an air-conditioned bar near the lobby. Single rooms cost from 4,000 pesetas ($28), and doubles go for 5,500 pesetas ($38.50), depending on the accommodation.

Urquin, 10 Alameda (tel. 84-00-10), serves its many loyal diners in several dining rooms on two stone-rimmed floors of the premises. Menu specials include a full range of fish, filet of beef with green peppers, and a chef's flan. Full meals cost 1,800 pesetas ($12.60) and up.

Casa Román, 12 Augusto García Sánchez (tel. 84-35-60), in a building development called Campolongo, is a well-decorated restaurant which serves a carefully prepared blend of seafoods that includes all the usual Spanish specialties. Full meals range from 1,900 pesetas ($13.30) and are served daily except Sunday night. It's open daily in July and August.

9. Vigo

If you continue south from Pontevedra (there are numerous buses every day), you arrive at Vigo, a distance of only 17 miles.

Vigo is a modern city, its harbor one of the most important in Spain, forming a natural amphitheater. The harbor is known for its sardine fishing fleet, and many of Vigo's inhabitants who live in white granite houses are employed in the canned-food industry.

The setting is outstandingly beautiful, the harbor surrounded by ridges, two of which are crowned by obsolete fortresses. From one of these pinnacles, the **Castillo del Castro** at 400 feet, a magnificent view of the city and the estuary unfolds before you.

The **Isles de Cies** (the ancient Insulae Siccae), a rocky archipelago at the entrance of the bay, act as a breakwater to the Atlantic, providing shelter and a handsome background for Vigo, particularly at sunset. You can take a boat tour of these islands. Sir Francis Drake did when he captured Vigo—once in 1585, again in 1589. In 1719 Vigo was once again captured by the British.

The old fishing village, the **Berbes Quarter,** bordering the bight of San Francisco, is unusual and makes for a pleasant stroll along with the milling sailors likely to be in town for the night while stationed on a Dutch, French, German, or British vessel.

The day's catch of fish is unloaded at 11 p.m., and the bustling activity is best viewed then; however, if you're an early riser, you can go there at 7 a.m. when the wholesale merchants come down to purchase the catch from the night before.

The **Samil and Canido beaches** are easily reached by bus, about a 15-minute ride from the city.

WHERE TO STAY: **Hotel Mexico,** 10 Vía del Norte (tel. 41-40-22), is a contemporary hotel in the northern part of the city, near the airport. Its more than 100 bedrooms are functional, clean, and only slightly unimaginative. Singles rent for 3,800 pesetas ($26.60), while doubles cost 6,000 pesetas ($42). The hotel has a cafetería. There's a garage for your car.

Hotel Ipanema, 31-33 Vázquez Varela (tel. 47-13-44), is one of the city's newer hotels. The in-house bar is a popular upper-crust rendezvous point in the downtown area. The more than 50 bedrooms contain pleasantly modern decor. A single will cost from 4,800 pesetas ($33.60), while doubles go for 6,200 pesetas ($43.40).

Hotel Ensenada, 35 Alfonso XIII (tel. 22-61-00), a modern hotel with some 100 rooms sits in the center of both the commercial and the historic part of the city. The in-house garage makes parking easy. If you're at the bar during one of the many civic functions that are held here, you may witness part of the inner workings of the city's social and business life. You can stay in a single room for 3,000 pesetas ($21) to 4,000 pesetas ($28), or in a double for 4,500 pesetas ($31.50) to 6,000 pesetas ($42). The hotel has a cafetería and a restaurant.

Hotel Niza, 32 Marí Berdiales (tel. 22-88-00), is a straightforward hotel with the great advantage of being almost in the exact center of town. In its comfortable interior, pleasant bedrooms are available, with singles ranging in price from 3,600 pesetas ($25.30) to 4,500 pesetas ($31.50), depending on the type of accommodation. Similarly, doubles cost from 5,500 pesetas ($38.50) to 6,500 pesetas ($45.50).

One of the most recommendable establishments in port, in terms of a bargain, is the **Estoril,** 12 Lepanto (tel. 43-61-22), which provides 45 rooms for peseta-watching visitors. It is pleasant and central, and in spite of its elegant name, relatively simple in appointments. However, it is well kept and clean, and the welcome is friendly. Expect a bill of 3,000 pesetas ($21) in a double, 2,000 pesetas ($14) in a single room with hot and cold running water.

WHERE TO DINE: **Puesto Piloto Alcabre,** 194 Avenida Atlántica (tel. 29-79-75), is one of the best-rated fish restaurants in town, but seafood is not its only achievement. The clientele returns frequently to enjoy the seafood soup, chorizos with garbanzo beans, well-seasoned rice dishes, and a wide range of regional offerings. Several continental specialties are also on the menu, which is served in an attractive room. Full meals range upward from 2,200 pesetas ($15.40). The restaurant is closed Sunday night.

El Mosquito, 4 Plaza de J. Villavicencio (tel. 22-44-41), is one of the oldest and best established landmarks in a city filled with restaurants. Chef Carmen Roel prepares a series of dishes, which, since they've been popular with the dining public for many years, no one sees any real reason to change. As you enter, you'll pass a bar area on your way to the dining room in the rear, catching as you go glimpses of huge pots steaming in the bustling kitchens. The place will probably be crowded, since it's known for serving some of the best food in town, especially its shellfish dishes, grilled sole, and roast leg of kid. Full meals cost from 2,200 pesetas ($15.40) and are served daily except Sunday, the eve of religious holidays, and from August 15 to August 31.

READER'S TOURING TIPS: "About 17 miles from Vigo lies the town of **Puenteáreas.** For the Festival of Corpus Christi, the streets of the town are carpeted with flower petals in beautiful designs. Buses from Vigo leave at 7 a.m., and the drive gives you a chance to see the beautiful landscape of Galicia, even if there's no festival going on there when you arrive.

"Along the Ría de Pontevedra there are many lovely beaches and charming villages. **Sangenjo,** which reportedly has one of the best climates in Galicia, is a pleasant town with a good beach. About a 15-minute walk over a hill (from which you have an impressive view of Sangenjo), you arrive at **Portonovo,** another colorful fishing village with an excellent beach. You can continue along the coast road enjoying the scenery, passing by the magnificent beach of **La Lanzada,** five miles in length. You'll arrive at **El Grove,** a summer resort and fishing village renowned for its fine cuisine. There is a shellfish festival held every October.

"The island of **La Toja** has now been joined to the mainland by El Grove. The island is known for its spa waters, and is covered with pine trees and surrounded by some of the finest scenery imaginable in Spain. It is a center for golf, tennis, and water sports. It also has a gambling casino" (Cecily C. Kennedy, Tuam, County Galway, Ireland).

10. Tuy

A frontier town, Tuy stands only a short distance from the historic bridge over the Minho River linking Spain with Portugal. For motorists coming from Portugal's Valença do Minho, Tuy will be their introduction to Spain.

Its age-old, winding and sloping streets lead up to the **cathedral,** a national artistic treasure dominating the *zona monumentale.* The cathedral-fortress stands like an acropolis, with its turrets and towers. It was built in 1170, although it wasn't used for religious purposes until early in the 13th century. Its principal portal, Ogival, is exceptional. If time remains, you may want to seek out the **Church of San Bartolomé,** which was built in the Romanesque style, and the **Church of Santo Domingo,** a beautiful example of the Gothic style (look for the bas-reliefs in the cloister).

Walls that were built over Roman fortifications surround Tuy. In this little provincial town, you'll find one of the finest accommodations in all of the province of Galicia.

Parador Nacional de San Telmo, Avenida de Portugal (tel. 60-03-09), appears almost like a fortress-style hacienda, jutting out on a promontory from the right bank of the Minho. The inn, with its cantilevered roof, was designed to perpetuate the architectural spirit of the province, with an emphasis on local stone and natural woods. The end result is one of elegant austerity, a building that blends perfectly with its landscape. The public rooms are enhanced by brass chandeliers, paintings by well-known gallegos, and antiques interspersed with reproductions. The main living room has a large walk-in fireplace and a tall banjo-shaped grandfather clock, along with hand-knotted rugs, 18th-century paintings, hand-hewn benches, and comfortable armchairs.

The dining room, with its high wooden ceiling, has tall windows, allowing a view of the surrounding hills. You dine in dignity on leather chairs studded with brass. Even if you don't spend the night, you can enjoy the regional cuisine here. The hors d'oeuvres alone consist of almost a dozen little dishes. The fish dishes are excellent, especially (when available) the renowned lampreys, as well as salmon, shad, trout, and succulent baby eels. Homemade cakes are offered for dessert. A complete meal costs 2,200 pesetas ($15.40).

The bedrooms, 22 in all, are sober but comfortable, overlooking hills and river and a courtyard with a colonnade. The bedrooms, furnished with Castilian-style pieces, cost 6,200 pesetas ($43.40) in a single, from 7,500 pesetas ($52.50) in a double. The baths and plumbing are modern, with a generous use of tile. Because of the limited space, reservations are essential.

Chapter XIV

THE BALEARIC ISLANDS

1. Finding a Room in Palma
2. Sampling the Cuisine in Palma
3. Majorca Attractions
4. Puerto Pollensa and Formentor
5. Ciudad de Ibiza
6. San Antonio Abad
7. Santa Eulalia del Río
8. Minorca

THE LARGEST OF the Balearic archipelago, **Majorca** (Mallorca in Spanish) is the most touristy of the Mediterranean islands, drawing millions of visitors yearly, the No. 1 tourist being Juan Carlos, the King of Spain, who comes regularly with his family to their summer residence, Marivent, in Cala Mayor. Here he, Queen Sophia, and their three children bask in the sun, relax, and enjoy life.

Majorca is boasting-proud of its 185-mile coastline. The island is most beautiful, an explorer's paradise. The northern part, with its winding precipitous roads, is mountainous, but the flatlands in the south are agriculturally fertile, devoted to raising olives and almonds. The flat landscape is occasionally broken by windmills.

With its fine beaches, little harbors, hidden mountain villages, and historical sights, the island has much to offer, both to the permanent and transient visitor. The English and Americans alike have settled in, and more are buying either homes or apartments. But the "Chopin Heights Real Estate Development" is a bit much! (Chopin and his mistress, George Sand, were the legendary vanguard of the tourists to Majorca. They spent a few months on the island in 1838.)

The natives weren't too receptive to foreigners in those days, but with the steady flow of gold into their pockets, they have become tolerant of strange new ways, such as bathing suits that don't tax the imagination.

MAJORCA

PALMA DE MAJORCA: Palma, on the southern part of the island, is the capital of Majorca, and the bustling, boom-town center of most of the hotels, restaurants, and nightlife. It has an interesting old quarter that is encircled by a flood of modern hotels. The ever-increasing new city of wide boulevards, shops, and restaurants is pushing out at its seams.

Palma's prices have been on the upsurge, but dozens of its hotels, restaurants, and boarding houses are possible on our budget. On a hot day in August, it would appear that half of the economy-minded Europeans—from Liverpool to Lübeck, from Manchester to Munich—have anchored their sun-parched bodies on the white Majorcan sands.

Swimming is possible from late April through October, when the last of the Stockholm-Hamburg-London set departs for the cold north and fast-fading tans. Don't believe the promoters selling that mild winter label in January and February. It can get downright cold, and you might catch galloping pneumonia if you plunged into the Mediterranean without a wet suit. Spring and fall can be heaven-sent, however; and in summer the coastal areas are pleasantly cooled by sea breezes.

The capital city is about 130 miles from Barcelona, and 90 miles from Valencia. The natives speak Spanish and a language of their own, a dialect of Catalán called Mallorquín that dates back to the days of the Christian king Jaime I, who drove out the Muslims in 1229. Majorca has often been the target of invasions (the Greeks and later the Romans left their calling cards in the old days). But in spite of its many conquerors, Palma has never seen anything like the present onslaught.

GETTING THERE: Most visitors head over from either Valencia or Barcelona (the preferred choice) on the mainland. The easiest, most efficient, and most expensive way to go is by airplane. A slower and cheaper method is by boat. At certain times of the year the trip by boat or plane can be pleasant. But in August the routes to Palma must surely qualify as the major bottleneck in Europe. Without advance space already booked, they're murderous, particularly the planes. Be sure you have a return plane ticket if you come in August—otherwise you may not get off the island till September.

By Boat

The **Compañía Trasmediterránea** offers regular ship services between Palma and Barcelona. The booking office in Barcelona is at the headquarters of the company's agent, Aucona Company, 2 Vía Layetana (tel. 319-81-12). In Palma the agent is at 5 Muelle Viejo (tel. 72-67-40). Schedules and times of departure must be checked in advance. What appears below is only valid at the time of research and could change dramatically before your actual visit.

The boat usually leaves Barcelona at 11:45 p.m. There are no sailings on Tuesday. It's a long run, usually arriving in Majorca at 8 a.m. They depart Palma at 12:30 p.m., landing at Barcelona at 8:30 p.m. Second-class cabin space is available for one, two, three, or four persons. The one-way cost per person from Barcelona to Palma de Majorca is 9,340 pesetas ($65.38) in a double cabin with bath and 10,730 pesetas ($75.11) for a single person in a double cabin with bath. A quad, if occupied by four persons, costs 7,800 pesetas ($54.60) per person. A triple cabin with bath occupied by three persons costs around 7,800 pesetas ($54.60) per person.

A less expensive way to go is to rent a deck seat for 4,370 pesetas ($30.59) per person, but you'll probably be awake most of the night. As mentioned above, the Barcelona-bound boat leaves Palma at 12:30 p.m. There are no departures on Wednesday.

The Compañía Trasmediterránea also has daily sailings to and from Ibiza and Mahón and frequent sailings to and from Valencia for fares differing only slightly from the cost for passage to and from Barcelona.

By Air

Both **Iberia** and **Aviaco** fly to Palma from Barcelona, Valencia, and Madrid. Daily planes are flown between Madrid and Palma, and between Valencia and Palma. But Barcelona is the major gateway to the Balearics, and it has several daily flights in summer—depending on the volume. Even so, the bookings are so tight in August that many prospective visitors to Majorca have to cool their heels at least 24 hours, sometimes more, in Barcelona, waiting for an empty seat. If you're flying—say, Iberia—on a transatlantic flight from New York to either Madrid or Barcelona, you should have Majorca written into your ticket before your departure if you plan to visit the Balearics as part of your Spanish itinerary.

Getting into Town

From the international airport, a bus, costing about 110 pesetas (77¢), will take you to the Plaza España in the center of Palma. A metered cab, on the other hand, will cost about 2,000 pesetas ($14), including tip and supplement. Naturally these fares will surely go up during the lifetime of this edition, but they provide a clue as to what you can expect to pay.

1. Finding a Room in Palma

The island of Majorca has a staggering number of hotels and boarding houses. But hold onto your reservations, for even that quantity is vastly inadequate to meet the demand in summer, particularly August.

If you stand at the hotel-booking desk at the airport, it's quite customary to see students, with knapsacks on their backs, come up to the clerk to inquire about a cheap room. In many instances the only space available would be, say, at the deluxe Son Vida. I strongly advise against going to Majorca during the peak summer visiting spree without a reservation.

Of course, Majorca in spring and fall will tempt you with many inviting rooms . . . at reduced prices. The rates quoted in this chapter are for *high season* only. Off-season, you may get substantial reductions, around 20%. But that occasionally depends on personal negotiations between you and the management.

Most of my hotel recommendations are in Palma, particularly in the **El Terreno** section, the heart of the nighttime district (don't book into one of these hotels unless you like plenty of action . . . until late at night). Those who prefer more seclusion will find that possible also at my other recommendations. Young Scandinavians, in particular, are especially fond of this section of town, and tour groups from Nordic lands often book most of the hotels en masse. However, older and more conservative readers may find it somewhat unsavory.

Palma has long ago overflowed its boundaries—and is sprawling out into the suburbs, notably **Cala Mayor,** about 2½ miles from the center. Another satellite, **San Agustín,** about three miles from the center, long ago expanded. In the **El Arenal** area, part of the Plaza de Palma, there is a huge concentration of hotels. The beaches at El Arenal are quite good, but many readers have complained of the "Coney Island atmosphere." I have a number of hotel recommendations in these suburbs for those who don't mind using public transportation. Leading off will be the pick of the hotels in Palma in descending order of preference and prices. A survey of the other moderately priced hostelries in the suburbs will follow.

HOTELS IN THE CITY: Hotel Mirador, 10 Paseo Marítimo (tel. 23-20-46), occupies a desirable position across the street from the palm-lined promenade flanking the moored boats of the marina. This attractive, relatively small hotel contains 78 comfortable bedrooms, each with a private balcony, bathroom, and phone. The spacious and conservatively modern lobby, along with its adjacent bar, has two-toned checkerboard patterns of white-and-beige marble and views of the port. Depending on the season, singles cost 2,800 pesetas ($19.60) and 3,900 pesetas ($27.30); doubles, 4,400 pesetas ($30.80) and 6,000 pesetas ($42), plus tax. The hotel remains open all year.

Hotel Saratoga, 6 Paseo Mallorca (tel. 72-72-40), with its entrance set below the modern arches of an arcade beside the medieval moat of the old city's fortifications was built in 1965. It has an airy, sun-flooded lobby, a small kidney-shaped pool on the lobby-level courtyard, a large dining room, and a seventh-floor social area. There, beside a long expanse of bar and a recirculating fountain, guests can listen to live music at twice-a-week dances from a position overlooking the city. A second swimming pool occupies the rooftop. Each of the 187 bedrooms has a private bath, phone, and in most cases a terrace or balcony. Depending on the season, singles cost 2,900 pesetas ($20.30) and 3,500 pesetas ($24.50), doubles 5,000 pesetas ($35) and 7,000 pesetas ($49), plus tax.

Hotel Bellver Sol, 11 Paseo Marítimo (tel. 23-51-42). The angles and indentations of its high rise façade were softened by rounding the corners into gentle curves, making it one of the more memorable exteriors along the harborfront. Most of the pristine but comfortable units look over the amply stocked marina, and a few even have faraway views of the island's graceful cathedral. Each room contains a private bath, softly upholstered furniture, air conditioning, and a phone. Per person rates, with a generous buffet breakfast included, are between 3,600 pesetas ($25.30) and 5,000 pesetas ($35), double occupancy, depending on the season. Occupants of singles pay a year-round supplement of 1,600 pesetas ($11.20). There's a swimming pool sunk into a concrete terrace where sun-worshippers enjoy a clear view of the sea. Several bars and a well-managed restaurant are on the premises.

Hotel-Residencia Almudaina, 9 Avenida Rey Jaime III (tel. 72-73-40). It would be hard to find a more centrally located hotel than this arcaded and balconied edifice on the main commercial street of town. The quietest rooms are in the rear, some having raised terraces with glass doors leading out. The decor of the rooms, dating from some 25 years ago, is simple. The bathrooms, although somewhat antiquated, are quite large, and the bedrooms get lots of sunlight. You'll probably be greeted in the pleasant breakfast room by a duo of cheerful Majorcan woman who seem genuinely to enjoy their jobs, as does the manager, Mateo Cabrer Parera. Single rooms, depending on the accommodation and the season, range in price from 3,000 pesetas ($21) to 3,300 pesetas ($23.10), while doubles cost 2,800 pesetas ($19.60) to 3,200 pesetas ($22.40) per person. Triples go for 2,200 pesetas ($15.40) to 2,600 pesetas ($18.20) per person. Breakfast is included in the tariffs. This is a good, medium-priced choice for a stopover in Palma.

Hotel Jaime III, Paseo Mallorca (tel. 72-59-43), is a modern hotel whose entrance lies below an angular arcade in the center of town. Formerly known as the Diplomatica, the building has a café on the ground floor, usually spilling out onto the sidewalk, a pleasantly contemporary lobby, and a restaurant/dining room. All of the double rooms have private bath, sun terrace, and up-to-date furnishings. Per-person rates in a room for two range from 2,400 pesetas ($16.80) to 3,000 pesetas ($21); occupants of single rooms pay an additional supplement of 1,000 pesetas ($7). A breakfast buffet is included in the rates. Prices vary with the season and the accommodation.

Hotel Cannes, 22 Cardenal Pou (tel. 72-69-43), is a remodeled hotel with moderately priced rooms, off an old and quiet square. Open all year, the Cannes rents doubles, all with private bath (some with shower), from 3,600 pesetas ($25.30). The most expensive singles, those with private bath, cost 2,900 pesetas ($20.30). The bedrooms have the bare essentials, and the public lounges are decorated with modern furnishings. Guests gather around the fireplace in winter, enjoy the air conditioning in summer.

Hotel Residencia Nácar, 21 Avenida Rey Jaime III (tel. 72-26-41), is small and intimate, a typically Spanish hotel of 60 well-furnished bedrooms, all with private bath and phone. Most of them contain a private terrace as well, and half a dozen also boast a sitting lounge with television. The style is modern, perhaps a little too commercial for many tastes. A twin-bedded room rents for 6,800 pesetas ($47.60), singles for 4,600 pesetas ($32.20). The hotel lies right in the center of town. The Nácar doesn't have a restaurant, but it does offer a first-class, air-conditioned cafetería. A continental breakfast is served for an extra charge. That breakfast, incidentally, is one of the best in town, featuring tasty rolls called *ensaimadas*.

Hotel Rosamar, 74 Avenida Joan Miró (tel. 23-27-23), is a Teutonic outpost in the boomtown El Terreno district. Right on the main road, within an easy walk of the Plaza Gomila, the hostelry is build around a front patio with tall palm trees. The fresh and clean bedrooms open onto balconies overlooking the patio. Most of the rooms have a private bath and rent for 3,500 pesetas ($24.50) in a double. The social life of the young and lively crowd attracted to Rosamar centers on the front terrace. The modern but slightly barren lobby contains stucco and a bar (stand-up) off to one side.

El Valle, 112 Avenida Joan Miró (tel. 23-12-43), is a modern temple for sun worshippers. Encircling balconies of bedrooms with picture windows overlook a swimming pool. You can get a double with a private bath and terrace for only 3,300 pesetas ($23.10). A single goes for 2,800 pesetas ($19.60). Lunch or dinner costs 850 pesetas ($5.95). The bedrooms are Danish style, with streamlined wooden pieces and built-in headboards. There's even central heating should you be there during those nippy winter days. In a commodious lounge, sofas and armchairs are arranged for conversation. There's also a wood-paneled drinking lounge with stools for loners, Windsor chairs for groups. Three picture windows in the dining room let in the light, revealing a display table of hors d'oeuvres, salads, and desserts. The Plaza Gomila is only a short walk away.

Borenco, 61 Avenida Joan Miró (tel. 23-23-47), is a favorite two-star hotel with Europeans who like its "touristic" location, right off the Plaza Gomila in El Terreno. From your little terrace you are likely to have a view of Bellver Castle and the Paseo Marítimo. Rooms are clean, comfortable, and modestly furnished, costing 3,300 pesetas ($23.10) in a double, 2,300 pesetas ($16.10) in a single. All units have private bath, as well as a terrace, plus phone, central heating, and music. The magnet is the rooftop pool and solarium. There's also a bar there. Spanish and international cookery is served in the air-conditioned dining room, where a meal costs 850 pesetas ($5.95).

Hotel Infanta, 10 Teniente Mulet (tel. 23-24-43), sits right in the midst of nightclub alley in El Terreno district, overlooking the Plaza Gomila. You get street noise from the adjoining video parlor. It charges reasonable prices, considering that it's a well-designed, Korean War structure. Its 51 rooms come with every sort of plumbing—water basin, shower only, shower bath, complete private bath. It charges 3,000 pesetas ($21) for a double with bath, this price dropping to 2,800 pesetas ($19.60) if bathless. Singles are rented for 2,000 pesetas ($14) without private bath. The rooms, some of which have balconies, are meagerly furnished but clean. The clientele isn't particularly chic, consisting on my last visit mainly of American sailors and scantily clad Scandinavians, but it's basically okay. The Infanta is closed in winter.

Villa Río, 115 Avenida Joan Miró (tel. 23-33-46), is a modern building in a choice position, whose rooms have balconies overlooking the bay. The location is between the heartbeat Plaza Gomila and the Club de Mar, which juts out into the water. A two-star choice, the hotel is furnished in part with reproductions of traditional Spanish pieces. The rooms, immaculately kept, are uncluttered and of suitable comfort for a long stay. Highest tariffs are in effect in July and August. The most expensive doubles with private bath cost only 2,200 pesetas ($15.40). Singles begin at 1,500 pesetas ($10.50). You can have lunch or dinner for 750 pesetas ($5.25). The hotel also has a bar, with plenty of chairs for relaxing, and a good restaurant. At midday you'll find most of the guests lounging around the swimming pool.

Hotel-Residencia Capitol, 5 Plaza Rosario (tel. 72-25-04), is one of the better two-star hotels lying within the city. It appeals especially to those who don't want to cope with public transportation. The location is just a short walk from the Mediterranean-Gothic cathedral of Majorca. Rooms are pleasantly and adequately furnished. The rate for a double room with private bath is 2,800 pesetas ($19.60), dropping to just 2,100 pesetas ($14.70) in a single with shower.

Hotel Bonanova, 5 Francisco Vidal, in El Terreno, up the hill on the road to Genova (tel. 23-59-48), is a large hotel (two stars), ideal for budgeteers. The furnishings are modern, and many rooms have a balcony with views of the ocean. There's a swimming pool, plus a bar and several pleasant lounges. Doubles with baths cost 3,000 pesetas ($21); singles with bath, 2,100 pesetas ($14.70). Breakfast is an additional charge, and other meals are 950 pesetas ($6.65) each.

Boarding Houses in Palma

Hostal Menorquina, 9 Santacilia (tel. 722-21-06). One of the most delightful hotels in its price category sits on a commemorative square in the heart of Palma near century-old rubber trees and a stone church. Its façade, like that of an identical twin across the alleyway, was designed as a private villa by a disciple of Gaudí in 1911. Its art nouveau flourishes today conceal 23 well-scrubbed, comfortable bedrooms owned and managed by the gracious Minorca-born Señora Praxedes Sintes. Each unit contains its own bath and phone. With half board included, singles cost 2,300 pesetas ($16.10); doubles, 4,400 pesetas ($30.80). The hotel's reception desk lies at the top of a short flight of stairs which begins at the back of the establishment's colorful ground floor café and art nouveau restaurant.

Hostal Borne, 3 San Jaime (tel. 72-29-42), used to be the home of Spanish nobility, but is now a large, rambling, comfortable, and homey hostal. You come in through a large, palatial entrance opening up to a pretty garden. The rooms are simple and functional. Doubles with wash basin are rented at a charge of 1,900 pesetas ($13.30) a night; with bath, doubles cost 2,300 pesetas ($16.10). The hostal's 48 rooms are available all year.

ALONG PLAYA DE PALMA: **Hotel Amazona,** 4 Calle San Bartolomé (tel. 26-36-50). So many guests run around this hotel in their bikinis, it looks like a beach club, and in a way, it is. At El Arenal, the Amazona is one of a string of beachfront hotels along this strip. Its rooms with views are often done in reproductions of traditional Spanish pieces, and each unit is complete with bath, phone, and terrace. In a double room the tariff is 3,500 pesetas ($24.50) dropping to 2,500 pesetas ($17.50) in a single. The hotel has a good-size swimming pool and is just 330 feet from the beach. A joie de vivre prevails in the bar, and the restaurant serves adequate food, a lunch or dinner costing from 1,200 pesetas ($8.40). The hotel is open all year.

Hotel Luxor, 23 Avenida Son Rigo, at Ca'n Pastilla (tel. 26-05-12), is modern with an Egyptian motif on its façade in honor of the hotel's namesake. Attracting a large number of European guests, it lies about 200 meters from the beach of Palma. In typically Spanish contemporary—no surprises—styling, it rents out 46 bedrooms, each with private bath, phone, and terrace. In a double, the full-board rate is 7,500 pesetas ($52.50) per person. Without board, singles cost 3,500 pesetas ($24.50); doubles, 6,200 pesetas ($43.40). The hotel has its own heated swimming pool, plus a garden and solarium as well. In cooler months, there is central heating. Sundowners are served in the American bar. The Luxor closes from November to mid-December.

Hotel Oasis, 25 Bartolomé Riutort, at Ca'n Pastilla (tel. 26-01-50), has been recently renovated, emerging as one of the better bets strung along the beach of Palma, about 4½ miles from the capital. The hotel is tastefully decorated, with a quiet, subdued atmosphere. Facing the sea, its 110 rooms are well maintained. Highest tariffs are charged from July 15 to September 15. At that time, a twin-bedded room with bath goes for 5,000 pesetas ($35), a single room, also with bath, for 3,200 pesetas ($22.40). A lunch or dinner, ordered separately, goes for 1,000 pesetas ($7). The Oasis is just that, surrounded by gardens and terraces, and its facilities include a bar and garage.

Neptuno, Carretera de la Playa del Arenal, Km. 11, El Arenal (tel. 26-00-00), stands right on Playa de Palma beach, its nicest feature. It might be suitable if other more attractive hotels along the strip are rented. Some rooms are pleasantly furnished, although others are quite plain and disappointing to readers. Try to get one with a private terrace overlooking the beach. The hotel's public terraces are large, and guests also enjoy the solarium. Only breakfast is served at this spacious, modern beachfront choice. A double room costs 5,200 pesetas ($36.40) a day, while singles go for 3,300 pesetas ($23.10). There is bar service both day and night, and a big private pool in the center of the complex.

Lotus Playa, 40 Maestro Ekitai Ahn, at Ca'n Pastilla (tel. 26-21-00), stands on the beach opening onto the bay of Palma, about 6½ miles to the east of the capital, next to the Marina and Yacht Club. Done in modern Spanish styling, it invites guests to enjoy its large, spacious rooms with private baths and terraces overlooking the sea. A single costs 2,800 pesetas ($19.60), the price rising to 5,000 pesetas ($35) in a twin-bedded room. Three meals a day are served in the hotel's big restaurant. The cost is 1,300 pesetas ($9.10) for either lunch or dinner. Facilities include a lounge, a bar, a solarium, a terrace restaurant, and a heated swimming pool.

STAYING AT LA BONANOVA: **Hotel Constelación,** 27 Corp Marí (tel. 40-04-61), is completely up-to-date, with an illuminated swimming pool, a flower garden, a large bar, and well-furnished rooms that open onto views of the water. There is a minibus to take clients to the beach or into town. In high season, guests are accepted who take full board at the cost of 5,400 pesetas ($37.80) per person daily, based on double occupancy. At other times of the year you can rent a room, paying only 3,000 pesetas ($21) in a single, the cost rising to 3,500 pesetas ($24.50) in a double. A continental breakfast is extra.

Hotel Majorica, 3 Calle Garita (tel. 40-02-61), at La Bonanova, is a three-star hotel with 137 bedrooms. Painted white, it is in the modern style, and from some of its rooms you'll have views of the yachts and other pleasure craft in the harbor. A family-run hotel, it has a swimming pool and a solarium. There are many facilities to entertain and amuse, including not only color TV and video films, but occasionally live acts. There is both a summer and winter restaurant as well. A minibus will take clients to the beach or into the center of Palma. Rooms are pleasantly furnished and equipped. In the summer full board is required, at a cost of 5,500 pesetas ($38.50) per person, based on double occupancy. In the off-season, the cost for a room only is 2,800 pesetas ($19.60) in a single, going up to 3,500 pesetas ($24.15) in a double.

Hotel Horizonte, 1 Vista Alegre (tel. 40-06-61), is a modern hotel just a block from the water. Large, well-furnished rooms have baths, balconies, phones, central heating, and views of the bay. Half board costs from 2,200 pesetas ($15.40) to 3,200 pesetas ($22.40) per person, depending on the season. The hotel has two pools, one for children and one full size, surrounded by a patio with a panoramic bay view, two lounges, a bar, TV, a pool table, a solarium, and a restaurant offering a selection of buffet meals. The director and desk clerk speak English.

2. Sampling the Cuisine in Palma

That any eating establishments exist at all in Palma—and haven't been nailed tight by the hoteliers—is surprising. But in spite of the octopus-grip of the full-board requirement, the restaurants are thriving—featuring old island cuisine blended with continental fare.

MODERATELY PRICED AND BUDGET RESTAURANTS: **Penélope,** 19 Plaza Progreso (tel. 23-02-69), has long been an enduring favorite. Far removed from the beach action, it sits in the commercial sector of Palma, and is well worth the trouble of finding it. The decor is in the rustic tavern fashion, with a rush-covered ceiling, immaculate napery, uniformed waiters, and a large lobster tank. Several paintings depict scenes from local seafaring life. A small bar is found at the entrance. But you don't come here for any of the above; instead diners visit to sample some of the best fish and seafood platters on the island. Specialties include lobster soup and grouper in the Majorcan style. If you want meat, the waiter might suggest a shoulder of lamb. However, it is Neptune that is the star, as reflected in the sea bass, octopus, shellfish rice, sole in champagne, baby eels (on occasion), and an old-fashioned zarzuela, a seafood stew. Meals cost from 2,500 pesetas ($17.50), money well spent.

Caballito de Mar, 5 Paseo de Sagrera (tel. 72-10-74), is often full when less successful restaurants have dozens of empty tables. There are several outdoor tables, but many guests prefer to dine inside, enjoying the lively spirit of the place and the vaguely nautical decor. Activity is sometimes frenzied around here, but that's part of its charm. Specialties include a Majorcan version of bouillabaisse, a zarzuela (a fish stew), assorted grilled fish (my favorite), oysters in season, red bream baked in salt, or sea bass with fennel. If creatures of the sea don't tempt you, try duck in orange sauce. Meals begin at 1,800 pesetas ($12.60) but could run much higher if you order the more expensive shellfish. The restaurant takes a rest on Sunday.

Fonda El Siglo, 7 Plaza Mayor (tel. 72-60-62), in the heart of old Palma, where simple sidewalk tables are set out, is a good, solid, unchic budget choice on this ancient square. Come here for hearty meals high in flavor, low on your pocketbook. Diners order for 1,200 pesetas ($8.40), a cubierto—say, macaroni and cheese, followed by pot roast, fresh fruit, and a quarter liter of wine. On the à la carte menu, specialties include chicken curry, vol-au-vent with prawns, entrecôte with mushrooms, and sole meunière. The chef is proud of his brandy soufflé, but you may be too stuffed to try it.

At the **Cellar Sa Premsa,** 35 Avenida Joan Miró (tel. 23-17-39), the typically Majorcan cuisine is served against a backdrop of wine casks, strings of garlic, log benches, beamed ceilings, tavern tables, and hanging gourds. The tavern is in the El Terreno district, right off the Plaza Gomila. The cellar is the choice of many matadors during the summer bullfight season. My most recent meal included sopa de mallorquinan, roast suckling pig (crackly crisp on the outside, moist and sweet inside), and dessert. A complete meal will cost from 1,800 pesetas ($12.60). Closed Tuesday and from mid-January to March 20.

Svarta Pannan, 5 Calle Brondo (tel. 72-10-39), in the heart of Palma, right off the Plaza Pio XII, satisfies the needs of the Swede who gets as hungry for his frikadeller (meatballs) as the Yank does for his burger. Herring with onion and potatoes is always my favorite beginning, or you might enjoy a Svarta Pannan (black pan) salad. The cook might follow with wienerschnitzel. Show up early, as the restaurant is likely to be crowded. Meals cost from 1,800 pesetas ($12.60). The restaurant stands on a narrow traffic-street in the heart of Palma.

Celler Payes, 2 Calle Felipe Bauza (tel. 72-60-36), has a set menu for 850 pesetas ($5.95) that includes soup, noodles, or gazpacho; steak or fish; plus dessert, bread, and wine. From the à la carte menu, you can select the fish of the day, which most guests prefer to have grilled. Other dishes include the classic kidneys in sherry or a simple roast chicken. Most à la carte orders will mean a tab ranging from 1,200 pesetas ($12.60) for a complete meal. The setting is cramped and intimate, with original paintings displayed on white stucco walls.

La Paloma, 16 Calle Apuntadores (tel. 72-62-59), has a set menu for 650 pesetas ($4.55), for which you get spaghetti, soup, or rice; a meat or fish dish; and dessert. Wine and bread are included. There are no frills here, but the food is good value. The restaurant is across from the most popular nightclub in the Balearic Islands, Abaco. From its simple, small dining room with oilcloth tables, it offers a typical Majorcan cuisine on the most teeming nightlife street in Palma.

La Casita, 68 Avenida Joan Miró (tel. 23-75-57), in El Terreno area, is an old standby featuring Franco-American specialties. The food is unbeatable for the price. There are ceiling fans, country-style wallpaper, and lots of exposed wood. The ambience is much improved by artworks decorating the walls of the dining room. These are the latest paintings of John Winn-Morgan, a well-known English artist. On my last visit I had roast chicken with stuffing, gravy, and potatoes, accompanied by fresh green vegetables. À la carte specialties include French onion soup, chopped chicken livers, peppered tenderloin steak, tournedos with mushroom sauce, trout with almond sauce, and homemade apple pie. Meals begin at 1,100 pesetas ($7.70), rising in cost from there, depending on what you order. It's closed Monday and Tuesday for lunch.

Gina's, 1 Plaza de la Lonja (tel. 72-64-84), off Paseo Sagrera and Paseo Marítimo, is one of the top medium-prized restaurants in Palma. There's soft lighting, tablecloths, and paintings hung on a white brick wall. The cooks take great care in the preparation of such classic Spanish dishes as paella and zarzuela, a shellfish stew. They also know how to do the Provence-inspired bouillabaisse as well. It is also a good place for such standby dishes as steak with potatoes, but the kitchen has also mastered a number of international specialties, including chicken Kiev. Another good dish to try is pescada à la sal (whitefish in salt). For dessert, try the flan with rum. If notified at the beginning of the meal, the cooks will also prepare a soufflé for two persons. Count on spending from 2,000 pesetas ($14) and up per person for a complete meal. In summer you can dine on Gina's terrace, enjoying a view of what was the 15th-century stock exchange. Gina has had a lot of practice: the owner and cooks have been at it for nearly 30 years. It is closed on Wednesday.

La Quinta, 10 Avenida Joan Miró (tel. 23-28-33), lies somewhat outside the major concentration of restaurants and bars on this popular avenue, although that may help to increase its charm. It's in a white-walled Majorcan house whose front courtyard contains plants, iron tables and chairs, and an occasional bird in an elaborate cage. If you prefer, you can dine indoors. In any event, menu items include fresh fruit and meat dishes, fondue bourguignonne, cheese fondue, crêpes gratinade with vegetable stuffing, and if you arrive in the afternoon, complete English teas. A daily menu is offered for 1,000 pesetas ($7), while à la carte meals go from 2,000 pesetas ($14). The establishment is open for lunch and dinner every day but Tuesday and on Wednesday at lunchtime.

Restaurant el Jardín, 57 Avenida Joan Miró (tel. 45-49-73). From the busy street, you'll pass under a grandly proportioned baroque stone arch massive enough to have fortified a castle. What greets you is an array of palms, an open grill surrounded by a gravel courtyard, iron tables, and scattered flowers. The bar may be the last thing you'll reach, although you can't miss it because of its Polynesian thatched roof jutting above the social life around it. All of this will be tended and managed by a team of friendly waiters dressed San Francisco style in flowered shirts and black pants, speaking a polyglot of mostly Teutonic languages. In fact the setting, with enormous candelabra dripping stalactites of wax onto the gravel pathways, might seem pure Mediterranean until you meet the Hamburg-born owners, Klau and Holger, former Lufthansa employees. Together they welcome visitors into their elaborately carved dining room in winter or into the almost tropical ambience of the garden every evening except Tuesday in summer. A strolling musician usually enhances the atmosphere for diners. The grills, as you'd expect from the stacks of olive wood waiting to be burned, are the featured dishes, and include veal, lamb chops, rumpsteak, sautéed meat Greek style, and quail in season. Liver pâté is popular, as are baked potatoes with Jardín sauce and a salad buffet. In winter, a fixed-price menu of the day is offered for 500 pesetas ($3.50), and both summer and winter, à la carte meals average around 1,200 pesetas ($8.40). The restaurant opens at 8 p.m.

Celler Montenegro, 10 Calle Montenegro (tel. 72-61-51). The street is one of the narrowest in the oldest part of town, which adds to the Mediterranean flavor of what you're about to experience. You pass behind a beaded curtain and descend a flight of stairs opening into a high-ceilinged airy room whose far wall is covered with enormous sections of wine barrels. Many of the local residents dine here, along with a colorful collection of northern Europeans and an occasional refugee from urban life in America. Daily specials are posted on a blackboard outside, none particularly sophisticated, but all making this one of the best fourth-category restaurants in town. You might enjoy pork tenderloin, roast chicken, one of the ever-present fish soups, fried fresh sardines (a specialty), and red mullet. At the far end of the dining room there's a tapas bar. The restaurant is closed Saturday night and Sunday. The rest of the week, a set menu is offered for 650 pesetas ($4.55).

One of the most popular of the chain restaurants is a collection of rooms on a side square of the main commercial street of town. Called **Click,** 8 Paseo Mallorca (tel. 72-40-26), it is in two sections. Click I specializes in hamburgers. One bearing the somewhat startling name, Hiroshima Mon Amour, is the most popular. Towering Inferno is very, very hot. Another, which I have managed so far to avoid, is El Golope, with banana and egg. Other sandwiches are available, or you can have rib steak. The place has a pub ambience. It's done in green, white, and yellow, and has sidewalk tables in front. Immediately next to Click I is Click II, which serves pizzas in a decor of marble tables, bentwood chairs, green and yellow accents, and lots of plants. Besides cheeses, there is a selection of French cheeses (La Bohème), a meal in itself, as well as all the usual pastas. Expect to pay 1,000 pesetas ($7) and up for a meal at Click.

A Horchatería

Can Joan de S'Aigo, 10 Sans (tel. 71-07-59), is the oldest horchatería on the island. It was established in 1700 and has continued to serve the refreshing mixture of crushed almonds in a frothy brew that still draws mid-afternoon customers from all over town. Other specialties are ice cream, pastries, cakes, well-brewed coffee, and several kinds of hot chocolate. Drinks cost from 150 pesetas ($1.05). It's open daily except Tuesday, from 8 a.m. to 9 p.m.

3. Majorca Attractions

Majorca is more than sun and surf. Visitors are often surprised at the wide range of activities with which they can occupy their days. Palma has a number of things to do (you can test your skill against a bull in the ring, and dance all night on a terrace overlooking the ocean), but the island itself is the big attraction, offering sights that range from caves with subterranean lakes to easily reached villages in the hills.

SIGHTSEEING IN PALMA: Most visitors don't get around to exploring the historical sights in Palma, but there are a number of places to see if you wish to break the monotony of going to the beach every day. The most important attractions are:

The Cathedral

Founded by James I (called "The Conqueror"), this Mediterranean-Gothic cathedral at Plaza Almoina took several centuries to build. Construction actually started during the reign (1276–1311) of James II, and lasted until the 17th century. Overlooking the seaside, the building stands in the old part of town. The main feature of the church is its gracefulness. Its central vault is about 160 feet, its columns rising 65 feet. The interior features a bizarre wrought-iron baldachin by Gaudí over the altar. Displayed in the Chapter House museum are panels and Gothic statues, and examples of craftsmanship in precious metals, tapestries, and liturgical ornaments. The cathedral is open from 10 a.m. to 12:30 p.m. and 4 to 6:30 p.m.; on Saturday, from 10 a.m. to 2 p.m. Admission is 100 pesetas (70¢).

Bellver Castle (Castillo de Bellver)

Erected in the 14th century, this hilltop moated castle was once the home of the kings of Majorca—during the short period when there were kings of Majorca. The castle is well preserved and has some interesting treasures. It houses the **Municipal Museum,** devoted to archeological relics and old coins. It's open from 9:30 a.m. to 1:30 p.m. to sunset. It is really the view from here that is the chief attraction.

La Lonja

This 15th-century structure at Paseo Sagrera is left over from the wealthy mercantile days of Majorca. La Lonja was, roughly, an exchange or guild, and represents an original interpretation of Gothic architecture. The Longa today is open only during exhibitions, which are announced in the local newspaper.

Baños Árabes

You can spend many hours exploring the narrow streets of the old quarter east of the cathedral. Along the way, you may want to visit the Moorish Baths at 7 Calle Serra, which are open from 10 a.m. to 1:30 p.m. and 4 to 6 p.m., to 5:30 p.m. in winter. They are closed on Sunday and holidays. These baths are the only complete remaining Moorish-constructed buildings in Palma, evoking what life was like in the heyday of the caliphate. Admission is 50 pesetas (35¢). Closed Sunday.

Palacio de la Almudaina

At the Plaza Almoina the Moors who ruled the island erected a fortress in their typical style with gardens and fountains. During the short-lived reign of the kings of Majorca, it was converted into a royal residence, evoking the Alcázar at Málaga. Now one of the most popular attractions of Palma, it is open from 10 a.m. to 1 p.m. and 3:30 to 6:30 p.m. (to 6 p.m. in winter) daily except Sunday and holidays. The price of admission is 75 pesetas (53¢). Inside is a museum displaying antiques, arts, suits of armor, and tapestries. Your attention may be torn between the beautiful flowers in the garden and the view of the harbor of Palma.

Pueblo Español

This is a collection of buildings that evoke Spain in miniature, along the lines of the already-described Pueblo Español in Barcelona. As touristy as a souvenir, it is at the Palacio de los Congresos (tel. 23-70-70), and is open from 9 a.m. to 8 p.m. Bullfights are held in its *corrida* on summer Sundays. There are mock representations of such famous structures as the Alhambra in Granada, the "Tower of Gold" in Seville, and El Greco's House in Toledo. You enter by Calle Andrea Doria. Admission is 175 pesetas ($1.23).

The Sóller Railroad

This ancient narrow-gauge railway makes the run from Palma to Sóller. The **Ferrocarril de Sóller** leaves from 7 Calle Castañer in Sóller (tel. 63-01-30) and from 1 Eusebio Estada in Plaza España in Palma (tel. 25-20-51), a one-way run costing 230 pesetas ($1.61).

Sóller is a town set in a wide basin filled with olives and citrus trees. Once you reach Sóller, it is possible to take another antique open-air tram to Puerto de Sóller, a seaside beach resort on the western coast, along with a pleasure-craft harbor and a submarine base. Like a major railway, the Sóller company offers first and second classes (only a dozen passengers can ride in the small Pullman car in first class). About two miles from Sóller, the train halts for a chance to allow its passengers to take pictures of one of the most scenic spots of the Majorcan countryside.

A School for Bullfighters

The **Cortijo Vista Verda,** at Ca'n Pastilla (tel. 26-02-12), is a farm where you can see the El Cordobés of tomorrow execute a *verónica* or a *farol.* But the surprise of the school is that it allows a neophyte matador, such as yourself, to test your skill (or lack of it), against a year-old "bull." In summer, you can visit the school on Thursday, from 4 to 6:30 p.m. The entire event costs 1,800 pesetas ($12.60). Bus transportation is available from Palma. Usually, your hotel can make all the arrangements; if not, any travel agent in Palma will book you a seat. After the bull "fight," you'll be invited into the garden to sample the regional wine and a presentation of flamenco.

Marineland

A multitude of attractions is found at Marineland Costa d'en Blanes (tel. 67-51-25), a few miles west of Palma, just off the coast road as you go toward Palma Nova. Dolphin, sea lion, and parrot shows are given daily, and you can watch Polynesian pearl divers and visit the mini-zoo. Admission is 650 pesetas ($4.55) for adults, 350 pesetas ($2.45) for children from three to 12 years old. You can go to Marineland in your own car or by bus from Palma and by taxi from Palma Nova. There's ample parking. You'll find a cafetería, picnic area, and children's playground, as well as beach facilities.

Boat Trips

In summer, boat excursions are available, some starting from the Paseo Marítimo in Palma and others at Ca'n Pastilla and in Arenal. They take you to such places as San Telmo and the island of Cabrera, even to beach parties on faraway strands. Information on such trips can be gotten from the receptionist at your hotel.

The **Flipper II,** which docks along the Paseo Marítimo, is a small boat which makes cruises from Palma to Magaluf, leaving at 10:30 a.m. and returning at 1 p.m. A trip costs 1,050 pesetas ($7.35) per person and provides good views of the Majorcan coast.

ONE-DAY EXCURSIONS: Not all the sights are confined to Palma. Majorca has several interesting caves, a legendary shrine, an artificial pearl industry—and countless other offerings. In a personal selection, I've narrowed the excursions down to the following. First, we'll head east from Palma to:

Pearl Factories and Underground Music

A good road splits the island in two in its eastward dash from Palma to the sea. A 31-mile trip will take us to the prosperous but drab little town of **Manacor,** where Majorcan pearls (artificial) are made. At cathedral square, the factory welcomes visitors, who are shown through the establishment and can actually watch the various processes necessary for the making of a pearl (if you can stand the odor). It is closed on weekends. The trade name for the world-famous pearls is **Majorica,** and visitors should be careful to avoid imitations. Across the street from the factory is a shop selling these artificial pearls in many price ranges, along with gifts and necklaces for the souvenir collector or random shopper.

From Manacor, we take the road southeast to the sea (about 7½ miles) and the beige-colored town of **Porto Cristo.** Outside this town is **Las Cuevas del Drach** (caves of the Dragon), an underground forest of stalactites and stalagmites. In this icicle-like world of many shapes, you can attribute various identities to the freakish formations: hooded monks, whatever. The most exciting aspect of the cave is its subterranean lake, where you can listen to a concert and later go boating à la Jules Verne. Beyond the steep abysses are five subterranean lakes, Martel being considered "the largest underground lake in the world." From Monday to Friday at noon, a concert (great acoustics) is given in the cave. Try to schedule your visit to coincide with a presentation of a musical performance. Price of admission: 300 pesetas ($2.10). Tours are conducted at 11 a.m., noon, and 2 and 3 p.m. Sunday to Friday from May to October. Saturday tours are at noon and 2 p.m. In the off-season tours are at noon and 2 p.m.

The least expensive way to go is to take one of the four daily buses that leave from the railroad station in Palma (inquire at the tourist bureau, Avenida Rey Jaime III for exact times of departure). The buses pass through Manacor on the way to Porto Cristo. It's also possible to book several organized excursions. Tours visit Manacor, Drach, and Hams. The **Cuevas del Ham** (Hams Caves) are about a half mile northwest of the Drach Caves and are visited from 10:30 a.m. to 1:30 p.m. and 2:30 to 5 p.m. by those wishing to see the stunning white stalactites, as exemplified by the Fishhook Chamber. These caves feature a nightclub with flamenco dancing. Admission is 275 pesetas ($1.93).

Petra

Of special interest to Americans is Petra, in the center of the island, about 35 miles east of Palma and reached by taking the C715. It was at Petra that Father Junipero Serra (1713–1784) was born. He was the Franciscan priest who founded California missions which grew into settlements and then towns and cities, among them San Diego, Monterey, and San Francisco. The **Convent of the Franciscan Fathers** can be visited. It was from the altars here that Father Serra was inspired to name the new-world missions of San Capistrano, San Fernando, and San Gabriel.

The house in which Father Serra was born was presented to the people of California as a gift from the people of Majorca, but in 1982, Spain asked that it be given back, so it is now Spanish government property. It houses the **Father Serra Missions Museum,** which can be visited free. Books about Father Junipero Serra can be found in the center of studies.

Valldemosa and Deyá

For another tour, head north to the mountains along a twisting, narrow road, for 11 miles. First stop: Valldemosa, the legendary rendezvous of Chopin and George Sand. In some ways, it hasn't changed: the olive pickers still return from the fields at sundown the way they have been doing for generations.

Valldemosa is the site of the **Royal Carthusian Monastery** (Cartúja Real Monasterio), which contains relics of what the townspeople regarded as the illicit lovebirds. It may be visited from 9:30 a.m. to 1 p.m. and 3 to 6:30 p.m. for 250 pesetas ($1.75). Off-season it shuts down an hour earlier, and is always closed on Sunday. It seems ironic that the unconventional couple the villagers could hardly tolerate more than a century ago should later be deified, in a manner of speaking. These latter-day relatives of the old contemptuous villagers know how to prosper off the romance of the Polish composer-pianist and the novelist.

It's also possible on the same ticket to visit the **Palacio de Rey Sancho,** which was constructed by one of the four kings of the island. It was also a retreat for the Moors. You're given a guided tour of the palace by a woman in Majorcan dress. If you stay for the folk dancing at 11 a.m., you'll have to pay another 100 pesetas (70¢).

From Valldemosa, we continue through the mountains for 6½ miles to Deyá.

Set against a backdrop of olive-green mountains, Deyá is peaceful and serene, with its stone houses and creeping bougainvillea. It has long had a special meaning for artists, notably Robert Graves, the English poet and novelist who used to live here, author of such historical novels as *I, Claudius,* and *Claudius the God.*

After walking through the old streets, you can stand on a rock overlooking the sea and watch a fire-red sun set over a field of silvery olive trees and orange and lemon groves. Then you'll know why painters go to Deyá and why Robert Graves once found his Shangri-La here.

To reach Deyá by public transportation, just stay on the bus that stops off in Valldemosa. Those with cars may want to consider one of the idyllic, but often expensively priced, accommodations offered in this little Majorcan village.

Food and Lodging in Deyá: Nestled between two fertile hillsides just outside the village center, **Las Residencia,** Son Moragues (tel. 63-90-11), is a super splurge hotel that seems to extract the maximum benefit from its location. It required two years for a German-born entrepreneur, Herr Axel-Ball, to bring into reality the dream which Moorish colonizers in the 10th century had struggled to produce—that of a terraced paradise rich with fruit trees and climbing vines. Sparing little expense, he combined two old farmhouses into one harmonious unit to produce one of the loveliest hotels in Spain. After parking in the roadside lot, you climb to a ringaround terrace where flowering plants vie for attention with the intricate curves of a score of free-standing wrought-iron candelabra. As you wander through the public rooms, you'll find a fascinating combination of abstract and surrealistic paintings and Spanish antiques. Each of these, as well as deep leather sofas and open hearths, is complemented by the building's thick walls, hidden courtyards, and hand-hewn beams.

There's a high-ceilinged dining room—much like something you'd find in the private home of an Iberian millionaire—called El Olivo, where nouvelle Mediterranean cuisine is brought to a fine art. The establishment contains only 33 accommodations, each different from its neighbor. Under high ceilings, above cool tile floors, huge French windows flood the collection of Spanish antiques with sunlight. Singles cost 7,000 pesetas ($49) to 10,000 pesetas ($70); doubles, 14,500 pesetas ($101.50) to 16,000 pesetas ($112), with breakfast included. Tariffs depend on the season. Fixed-price meals go for 3,800 pesetas ($26.60).

Hotel Es Molí, Carretera Valldemosa a Deyá (tel. 63-90-00), built in 1966, occupies a position above the coastal road in a stone-walled building ringed with flowers, ivy, and geraniums. Its architectural core includes the thick stone walls of a centuries-old wind-powered grist mill—hence, its name. The gardens enclose a tennis court, a large springwater-fed heated swimming pool, a terrace dotted with parasols, and a sweeping view of the nearby mountains and sea. Most of the comfortably spacious accommodations have a private terrace overlooking the panorama. Each contains air conditioning, a private bathroom, radio, and phone. The hotel's van makes four-times-a-day runs to the beach, 4½ miles away. Open between April and October, Es Molí charges 6,000 pesetas ($42) to 7,800 pesetas ($54.60) per person in a double, 7,300 pesetas ($51.10) to 9,000 pesetas ($63) in a single, with half board included. Rates depend on the season and the accommodation.

Pension Miramar, Ca'n Oliver (tel. 63-90-84), is set in an idyllic spot high above the village at the end of a winding one-lane road lined with cypresses, bougainvillea, and terraced olive groves. After crossing a small masonry bridge, you'll see a stone-walled Mediterranean villa half concealed by vines partially shading the front terrace. Antonio Masripoli maintains nine simple bedrooms inside his family house, offering it as an alluring one-star spot for budget clients. Singles cost 1,250 pesetas ($8.75), while doubles go for 1,950 pesetas ($13.65), plus breakfast. Full meals, served under the rough hewn beams of the dining room, are 850 pesetas ($5.95) each.

Mundial Ca'n Quet, Carretera Valdemossa-Sóller (tel. 63-90-10). A quick tour of the property will show why this is one of the most sought-after restaurants on the island. It's set on a series of terraces above a curve in the winding road leading out of town. The building is well scrubbed, modern, and stylish, but it has an undeniably romantic air of rustic charm and beauty. Cascades of pink geraniums ring its different terraces, and if you're lucky enough to have the time to wander over its labyrinth of sloping pathways you'll find groves of orange and lemon trees, an herb garden, barricades of roses, and a perfectly proportioned swimming pool ringed with neoclassical balustrades.

Because of its alluringly designed indoor/outdoor format, the restaurant is closed in winter (also on Monday in summer). After climbing from the roadside parking lot, you'll enter a spacious and sunny bar, and can choose between an elegant and pristine indoor dining room where a fire might be blazing in cooler weather or an upper terrace under an arbor. The owner, Francisco Arbona Puig, and his sophisticated chef, the youthful Thomas Franco, prepare full meals costing from 2,500 pesetas ($17.50). These could include a salad of marinated fish, a terrine of fresh vegetables, fish crêpes, shellfish rice, smoked salmon, duck with sherry sauce, and a changing selection of fresh fish.

Hostal Costa d'Or, Lluch Alcari (tel. 63-90-25), outside the village proper, is a former villa, situated strategically so as to have the best possible view of the vine-covered hills and the rugged coast beyond. Surrounded by private gardens filled with a swimming pool, fig trees, date palms, and orange groves, the old-fashioned estate is rather large (42 private bedrooms), and furnished with oddsy-endsy-type pieces in the rooms. But it's clean and comfortable, and the price is just fine: from 2,200 pesetas ($15.40) in a double. Bathless singles cost only 1,600 pesetas ($11.20). The bedrooms are divided between the villa and an annex, but most of the rooms have good views. From April 1 to October 31, guests can stay here, enjoying one of the good, home-cooked meals at a cost of 1,100 pesetas ($7.70).

SHOPPING: There are many beautiful and useful objects to buy in Palma, either for yourself or as gifts, ranging from handcrafts to elegant leather goods, Majorcan pearls, and fine needlework. Palma has a good-size shopping area, well supplied with bars, cafés, and restaurants where you can refresh yourself between forays into the shops.

You'll find the best shopping on the following streets: San Miguel, Calle Sindicato, Jaime II, Jaime III, Calle Plateria, Via Roma, and Paseo Borne, plus the streets radiating from the Borne all the way to Plaza Cort where the city hall stands. Some streets are for pedestrians only. Most shops close on Saturday afternoon and Sunday.

Perlas Majorica, 11 Avenida Jaime III (tel. 72-52-68), is the official agency for Majorcan pearls, of which there are many imitations with similar names such as "Mallorca" and "Majorca." This authorized agency for the authentic Majorica pearl is an elegant shop with fanciful wrought-iron and brass gates. Earlier we visited the center where these pearls are made; however, if you don't have time to go there you can browse through this shop. The pearl producers employ hundreds of artisans to turn out their stunning jewelry. The agency offers a decade-long guarantee for their product. The pearls come in surprisingly varied sizes and settings.

Casa Bonet, 3 Calle Puigdorfila (tel. 22-09-12). Elegant boudoirs throughout Europe are frequently bedecked with finely textured needlework from this famous store, whose blue-gray showroom has cove moldings embossed with bas-reliefs of cherubs engaged in the process of creating textiles from flax. Each of the sheets, tablecloths, napkins, and pillowcases is made in Majorca from the finest linen or cotton (also, for the less expensive items, from acrylic). Many are hand-embroidered, using ancient designs and floral motifs commercialized by this establishment after it was founded in 1860. A member of the staff brings out samples from the back room, unfolding them on velvet-covered tables beneath the glow of an amber-colored Majorcan chandelier.

Artesanias Pol, 43-44 Carrer Union (tel. 22-42-99), has showrooms packed with Toledo-made jewelry and Andalusian pottery, Lladró ceramics, Spanish crystal, and a host of regional pottery.

Gordiola, 2 Calle Victoria (tel. 721-15-41). This is the most amply stocked store on the island for Majorcan glassware and pottery. Dangling above the crowded showroom are so many intricate glass chandeliers and lighting fixtures that the biggest problem is in knowing which one to risk transporting home. You'll find the most unusual collection of hand-blown wine goblets in Spain, vases in one-of-a-kind spiral-shaped patterns, and some amazing centerpieces for a dining room table. The price of comparable hand-blown glassware would be much more in Venice.

Yanko, 3 Carrer Union (tel. 72-27-88). Most of its high-fashion shoes for both men and women and its leather goods are made in a modern factory in central Majorca. This address is the glossily modern showplace for the factory. Within a stylish boutique, similar to what you'd find in Madrid, is displayed a collection of not only the shoes, but also luggage and leather and suede items. Prices are more reasonable than you might expect.

La Casa del Hierro, 6 Calle Victoria (tel. 71-16-21). Many lovers of handmade artifacts consider the art of the blacksmith to be almost a forgotten part of the 19th century. This amply stocked shop, however, contains the most tempting collection of one-of-a-kind wrought-iron objects on the island. Each is fabricated within a tiny village in central Majorca by aging ironmongers who learned their techniques from long-dead teachers. You can buy door knockers or andirons shaped like a dragon's head, sets of fireplace tools, unique candelabra and wall sconces, imaginative renderings of animals in silhouette, and clusters of iron hoops for wall-mounted flowerpots.

PALMA NIGHTLIFE: Long after the sun sets over Majorca, the nightbirds of Palma start flying, after something of a late start. If visitors are just filing into their hotel dining rooms at 10:30, it's going to be after midnight before they get into the after-dark world.

The bars and bodegas are popular, but much of the more organized nightlife is likely to be expensive.

Discos and international floor shows are the biggest attractions on the nightlife circuit. For a club that's the best of its kind in Spain, we'll call on:

Tito's, 3 Plaza Gomila (tel. 23-76-42), is one of the best discos on the island. It levies a cover charge of 1,000 pesetas ($7) per person, which includes your first drink. The place opens at 9:30 p.m. for disco dancing, which continues until late at night (or early in the morning).

Broadway Night Club, 36 Avenida Joan Miró (tel. 28-52-73), offers a small and very intimate theater for the performance of sexy acts with feather-encrusted young women and an occasional sparsely dressed male. The shows grow increasingly risqué as the night advances. There's a saucy flamenco show at 11 p.m., followed by the most popular performance around midnight with a few introductory acts. A gamut of the most commonly practiced sexual expressions is likely to be presented with occasional sallies by a magician. The 2:30 a.m. show is the raunchiest and is not recommended for delicate viewers. The first drink costs 2,300 pesetas ($16.10), with second drinks going for 350 pesetas ($2.45) and 650 pesetas ($4.55), depending on what you order.

Zhivago, 34 Teniente Mulet (tel. 23-15-82), right off the Plaza Gomila in El Terreno, is one of the liveliest clubs in Majorca, packing them in at 850 pesetas ($5.95) for a drink. Frenetic dancing and live combo sounds are the rule here. On one recent inspection, a little old woman dressed in black sat on the curb nearby. As each of the scantily attired northern European young women crossed the threshold, the aging dueña crossed herself.

Abaco, 1 Calle San Juan (tel. 21-49-39), may be the most opulently decorated nightclub in all of Spain. It is in a severe stone structure in the oldest part of town, with a single enormous arch sheltering its entrance. Before the end of an evening here, the deceptively potent drinks will augment the first striking impression a visitor gets of a cross between a pasha's harem and a Russian church just before the fall of the czar. The ceiling of this early 18th-century house, which was renovated and furnished by entrepeneur Salvadore Palao after it stood empty for years, soars high above the treasure trove of 300 years of European decorative arts that simply never seem to end. The feeling I get as I wander up and down stone staircases into more rooms, each skillfully lit and jammed with art, is that I have landed in an eerily directionless party where the host has suddenly absented himself from his domicile, leaving a disconnected group of strangers amid the accumulated treasures of a lifetime.

Many motifs are represented here, but one of the strongest impressions is of some kind of religious service that might be about to begin somewhere in the dramatic interior. There are what must be millions of rose petals scattered amid all the fruits of the harvest near the entrance. These stretch up to the side of a stone construction that looks like the enormous covering for an altar. Its roof is capped with masses of exuberant gladioli, which shoot out from their vase like the flaming rays of a baroque representation of a sun disk.

There's a rectangular bar, an army of attendants serving drinks, and an enormous crowd of visitors from almost every part of Europe and America. Some of the guests seem almost in a trance—from the Mediterranean sun, the alcohol, or the overwhelming impact of so many museum pieces in a bar, or a combination of the three. Many customers eventually congregate in a stunningly beautiful courtyard with dozens of tables but one that never gives the impression of being crowded, which is unusual since at every turn there are exotic caged birds, fountains, more sculpture than the eye can absorb, extravagant bouquets, and hundreds of flickering candles. Through all this there moves a swell of vacationing art lovers who go from room to room in literal open-mouthed wonder, sometimes humming snatches of the lushly romantic music (Ravel's *Bolero*) coming from the superb sound system.

Whether you view this as a bar, a museum, or a sociological insight, be sure to go here. Special drinks range from around 1,000 pesetas ($7), including a rich, creamy, potent Irish coffee. The establishment is open from 9 p.m. to 3 a.m. every day but Sunday.

Texas Jack's, 12 Calle San Felio (tel. 72-62-87). "What do you do with a drunken sailor?" inquiries the old sea chantey. "I give 'im a kiss!" is the ingenuous response of the warm-hearted English woman who manages her beer-and-chili bar with the firmness of a captain totally in control of the ship. Eva Fox (her friends and many of the American sailors who frequent this place call her "Foxy") opens her well-disciplined club only when a ship is in port, so it's difficult to predict when it will be in business. Locals, however, claim that the stream of off-duty sailors who come to Eva's place when a ship comes into port can practically be documented by the Spanish census bureau.

Eva insists that it was her seagoing father who gave her the appreciation of a sailor's life, which enlivens this unique cross between a locker room on an all-male college campus, parole day at Huntsville State Prison, and the border patrol along the Gaza Strip. There's a pool table in an extension of the main bar, all of whose chairs have been doubly reinforced with L-shaped braces of steel so that a customer can tip back on the hind legs without peril. Tips are collected in a copper pot that clinks satisfyingly every time it collects something, at which moment one of the Majorcan waitresses enthusiastically rings a giant cowbell.

Eva's husband, Kirby (of Greenville, Georgia), makes his well-known chili, which sells for 300 pesetas ($2.10) a serving and which contains a full selection of India-grown spices hand-mixed by Eva. During her off hours Eva sells Majorcan real estate and is perhaps one of the best informed realtors on the island. The rest of the time she sells beer for 200 pesetas ($1.40) per pint.

Mam's Bar, 39 Avenida Joan Miró (tel. 28-10-40). The cramped floor space of this hole-in-the-wall bar is usually jammed with patriotic Anglo-Saxons from any one of six or seven English-speaking countries. This popular establishment, which has the honor of being the oldest American bar in town, is managed by two Englishmen, Wayne Hatley and John Lowe. They bought it when the original owner, Miriam (Mam) Steves, retired to Florida after a hard-working career of 30 years of serving drinks. Today the tiny bar is filled with posters of Marilyn Monroe and Humphrey Bogart, stand-up drinkers, and tiny tables set either claustrophobically or intimately, depending on your company, in a small courtyard on one side. There, amid plants, diners enjoy inexpensive meals, costing from 1,200 pesetas ($8.40), of chicken curry, chili con carne, spaghetti bolognese, and wine or beer. The establishment opens at noon every day except Tuesday.

Don Gomilo Pub, 7 Calle de los Consignatorios Schembri (tel. 45-45-96), is an elegant pub. This private villa's façade is semi-Victorian, with red brick, white trim, globe lanterns, and fan-shaped windows. The interior is arranged around a series of comfortable upholstered semiprivate banquettes guaranteed —with the help of potent Manhattans—to create a feeling of intimacy even with someone you happen to have just met. The pub is open daily from 7 p.m. to 4 a.m. all year. Drinks cost 450 pesetas ($3.15).

Kiss, Avenida Bartolomé Ruitort, Ca'n Pastilla (tel. 26-17-23), is noisy and crowded, and smoke will probably get in your eyes. Still, it's one of the most popular places in town for boogie hangout. Most clients are under 30, and all pay around 450 pesetas ($3.15) for a drink.

Zorbas, Avenida San Rigo, at El Arenal (tel. 26-10-71), is fun, youthful, well decorated, and often interesting. Its crowd is made up of many elements of the Majorcan night scene. Drinks cost from 500 pesetas ($3.50).

Granja Royal, 6 San Felio (tel. 71-26-58). Around 1930 there were dozens of cafeterías somewhat like this one sitting on a narrow street in the oldest part of town. What's unique about this one is how little it's actually changed since those days. Most of the customers come for the wine, the beer, the tapas, and the snacks. For 175 pesetas ($1.23), you can try one of their rich chocolate drinks served with a bowl of fluffy cream. The atmosphere is spacious, set by the high, beamed ceiling and terrazzo floors. There's a smoked-stained and "brown gravy" color scheme throughout.

The **Casino de Mallorca** (tel. 68-00-00), at the end of the Andraitx motorway (Cala Figuera turnoff), is a spot for gambling, dining, or watching a nightly international show. You can play American or French roulette, blackjack, dice, and slot machines. The casino is open from 8 p.m. to 4 a.m. Entrance is 400 pesetas ($2.80).

4. Puerto Pollensa and Formentor

Puerto Pollensa is a large resort near the far northern point of the island, nestling beside a sheltered bay whose calm waters lie between Cabo or Cape Formentor to the north and Cape del Pinar to the south. The town of Pollensa lies about 4½ miles inland from Puerto Pollensa, between two hills: Calvary to the west and the Puig to the east. From the town, the best views of the resort and the bay are from Calvary Chapel. The bay is the scene of excellent water-skiing and sailing.

Cape Formentor, "the devil's tail" and northernmost point of the island, can be reached from Puerto Pollensa via a spectacular road, twisting along to the lighthouse at the cape's end, where cliffs 650 feet high drop sharply to the sea. Part of the road is along the narrow crest of the cape. Formentor has a dramatic landscape of mountains, pine trees, rock, and sea, plus some of the best beaches of Majorca. In Cape Formentor, you'll see miradores, or lookout windows, which provide stunning views of the Majorcan fjord country, you'll snake around horseshoe turns, and you'll go through a tunnel into a region of deep valleys and high peaks.

To reach Pollensa by bus, go to the Plaza España in Palma (check for time schedules). There are four departures daily to the northern point. The buses pass through Inca (see below).

Many of the beaches along the cape are relatively isolated and can be reached by boat from Puerto Pollensa. Service is provided by **La Goviota** (tel. 53-38-14 for departures). There are five boat trips daily, costing 425 pesetas

($2.98) round trip. The last vessel sails back at 6 p.m. It's also possible to take a bus from Puerto Pollensa four times daily (no service on Sunday). The last departure from the cape back to the port resort is at 5:30 p.m. However, it's more fun to go by boat unless you're addicted to tortuous road travel.

In Puerto Pollensa, most visitors are content to stroll along the waterfront, the Passeig Saralequi. But if you want more in the way of attractions, seek out the **Anglada Camarasa Museum,** 87 Paseo Anglada Camarasa, which is open Monday, Tuesday, Thursday, and Saturday from 4 to 7 p.m., charging no admission. This celebrated Catalán painter, whom the museum honors, lived and worked here in the final years of his life.

WHERE TO STAY IN PUERTO POLLENSA: **Hotel Pollentia,** Paseo de Londres (tel. 53-12-00). Built in 1956 and enlarged in 1962, this well-managed hotel is set about half a mile from the commercial center of the resort behind a pleasant garden screen. It's my preferred hotel in town, partly because of its cool and airy spaciousness and partly because of the genial reception. The steps leading into the formally modern lobby are lined with dozens of terracotta pots overflowing with ivy and geraniums. You'll register beneath exuberant chandeliers of Majorcan glass before heading up to one of the 70 very comfortable bedrooms, each with a phone, bath, and often a private terrace. With breakfast included, singles cost 2,500 pesetas ($17.50) to 2,700 pesetas ($18.90), doubles 2,200 pesetas ($15.40) to 2,500 pesetas ($17.50) per person, depending on the accommodation. Fixed-price meals in the dining room go for 1,500 pesetas ($10.50) each. The hotel is open from early April until the end of October. It sits across the coastal road from its own bathing terrace, jutting out into the Mediterranean.

Hotel Uyal, Paseo de Londres (tel. 53-15-00), has what might be the most impressive façade in town, trimmed with Renaissance style sandstone. Inside, this former villa has been severely and blandly modernized, incorporating a jutting contemporary hotel into a more gracious older core. There is a collection of outdoor tables numerous enough for a small army, a rectangular outdoor pool, and some 100 simply furnished bedrooms, each with a private balcony and bath. Depending on the season, singles rent for 2,300 pesetas ($16.10) to 2,600 pesetas ($18.20); doubles, 4,400 pesetas ($30.80) to 4,900 pesetas ($34.30). Fixed-price meals are 1,900 pesetas ($13.30) in the dining room. The hotel sits across from its own concrete bathing terrace, fronting the coastal road, about half a mile from the center.

Hotel Miramar, 39 Passeig Anglada Camarasa (tel. 53-14-00). This centrally located hotel, one of the most grandly old-fashioned hostelries in town, occupies a desirable position across the coastal road from the beach. It has ornate frontal columns supporting a formal balustrade, as well as symmetrical groupings of jardinieres below heavily tiled eaves. Inside the lobby, you'll find clusters of antiques, a formal dining room, a beamed ceiling, and windows overlooking a pleasant seaview terrace. Each of the 69 bedrooms contains a phone and a private bath. Some of the accommodations overlooking the flowering courtyard in back have a private veranda. Depending on the season, singles cost 1,950 pesetas ($13.65) to 3,000 pesetas ($21); doubles, 2,800 pesetas ($19.60) to 4,200 pesetas ($29.40), plus breakfast. Fixed-price lunches or dinners go for 1,300 pesetas ($9.10). The hotel is open between April and October.

Hotel Sis Pins, 77 Passeig Anglada Camarasa (tel. 53-10-50), is the Catalán name for this pleasantly modern hotel that rises behind a screen of pines from a central location across from the beach. Its three balconied stories are efficiently maintained by the Bou family, who established the hotel in 1945. Behind the bougainvillea of the façade, you'll find a spacious and cool lobby containing comfortable chairs and a scattering of antiques. There are 50 tile-floored bedrooms, a few of which have a private balcony. Each comes equipped with a phone and private bath. Open from mid-March till the end of October, the hotel charges 1,550 pesetas ($10.85) and 3,100 pesetas ($21.70) in a single and 2,450 pesetas ($17.15) and 3,700 pesetas ($25.90) in a double, depending on the season and the accommodation.

WHERE TO DINE: **Restaurant Bec Fi,** 91 Avenida Anglada Camarasa (tel. 53-10-40), the best restaurant in town, offers seating between the palms of an outdoor courtyard, under a shaded arcade, or within a spacious interior covered with cool tiles. You'll find it near the center of town beside a quiet beachside square. Don't miss the opportunity to see the array of very fresh chops, meats, and fish which the establishment proudly displays in refrigerated cases. Open for lunch and dinner daily except Monday, the restaurant specializes in fish and meats grilled over a flame with a Majorcan wood known as *encina.* You can order a half dozen oysters, a grilled fish of the day, seasonal lobster (March through August only), a platter of lomo negro (baby eels), a temptingly seasoned array of brochettes, a T-bone steak, ribs of beef, and a succulent mixed grill of lamb chops, chicken, beef, pork, and kidneys. Sometimes the menu also lists rabbit. Full meals cost from 1,900 pesetas ($13.30). The restaurant is closed on Monday and from December through February.

INCA: On the road between Palma and the Pollensa-Formentor region is Inca, Majorca's market and agricultural center about 17 miles from Palma. It is the island's second largest city.

Markets are held every Thursday, with much farming equipment and livestock for sale, but tourists not interested in such merchandise will find a great variety of leather goods offered at low prices—shoes, purses, jackets, and coats.

Modernization of Inca has deprived it of its original charm, but the parish church of Santa María la Mayor and the nuns' convent of San Jerónimo are of some interest, as is the original Son Fuster inn, left over from the old village era.

Where to Dine

Cellar C'An Amer, 39 Pau (tel. 50-12-61). It was built as the subfoundation of a centrally located building in 1850. Today, its stone walls and vaulted ceiling offer the most authentic and típico cueva dining on the island. The container of local wine, which everyone here seems to drink, is tapped from one of the dozens of casks lining the walls. These, plus the wooden tables and rustic artifacts, make the handful of interconnected dining rooms memorable. The restaurant is open daily except weekends in winter. A polite staff serves Majorcan specialties in copious portions. These include *lechona frit* (a mélange of minced pork offal fried and seasoned), bread and vegetable soup, Majorcan-style codfish, seasonal thrush wrapped in cabbage leaves, roast loin of pork, and the chef's version of roast suckling pig with a bitter sauce. There is also an array of seafood and fish. Full meals cost from 1,800 pesetas ($12.60).

IBIZA

A New York art student wrote, "Even those who come to Ibiza (pronounced 'Ee-bee-tha') for the 'wrong' reason (to work!) eventually are seduced by the island's easy life. Little chores like picking up the mail from the post office stretch into day-long missions."

It is presently estimated that some 1,000 U.S. expatriates live in **Ibiza.** Some 200 of these persons introduce themselves as writers (one columnist reported that no more than "half a dozen have ever been published").

To those who may never have heard of Ibiza (if such a traveler still exists), it is the third largest of the Balearic Islands. It can be reached by both boat and air. The island is more than 225 square miles in size.

Physically, it has a jagged coastline, some fine beaches, fig and olive trees, whitewashed houses, secluded bays, cliffs, and an essentially hilly terrain. Ibiza has a warmer climate than Majorca, which makes it a better choice for a winter holiday—but it can be sweltering in July and August. Thousands upon thousands of showering tourists in summer greatly tax the island's limited water supply. But some of the pedestrians who roam the streets of **Ciudad de Ibiza** don't drain one drop from the reservoir.

Once Ibiza was virtually an unknown and relatively unvisited island, frequented only by the most esoteric of travelers. Majorca, its bigger sister, got all the business. But in the '50s, when a rising new liberated group began to chart a course through unknown waters to undiscovered lands, Ibiza was singled out. One of the more famous of these visitors was Jan Cremer, the Dutch artist who wrote the controversial bestseller (in the Netherlands), *I, Jan Cremer*. But by the time Jan-come-lately Cremer arrived, Ibiza already had the nucleus of an art colony. In fact, the artist was to have his first show here—or, to put it in his own words, "Jan Cremer came, saw and conquered."

Reputations take a long time to build . . . and to die. Many liberated travelers are still arriving, dreaming of soft drugs and hard sex. Both exist in great abundance. But there are dangers. It's common to pick up the local paper and read the list of the latest group of people deported because of *irresponsibilidad económica* (no pesetas) or *conducta antisocial*. Many young travelers, frankly, are deserting Ibiza, taking a ferry 40 minutes away to the south to the island of **Formentera** where they find less harassment (although anyone looking suspicious is likely to be checked out there, too). In Ibiza, the Guardia Civil (watch out for these guys) is known to take your passport until you can show them a one-way ticket—that is, out of the country.

Back in the '60s—the heyday of Ibiza's "in" position—one writer made the claim that "time of residence on the island is a better passport to the 'in-hip' scene than having a novel published, or a successful art show." Today, having that art show or that novel published is a better passport. Ibiza is virtually overrun by middle-class tourists from England, France, Germany, and Scandinavia. Some of the English residents have organized vigilante groups to protect their winter villas from squatters.

THE HOTEL OUTLOOK: The chances of finding space in peak summer months are dismal, the worst of any Mediterranean resort in Spain. At other overcrowded resorts, such as those on the Costa Brava and the Costa del Sol, a visitor—faced with the no-vacancy sign—can always press on, even go inland to find a room for the night. But in Ibiza, because of infrequent transportation, a visitor without a reservation in July and August can land in a trap. Cremer relates that he slept in caves when he first visited the island. But that was for financial reasons. You may end up sleeping on the beach on an air mattress (if the police let you; there are camping areas), even though your pockets are bulging with pesetas.

The island of Ibiza is not always prepared for its hordes of international tourists. The hotels can't be built fast enough. Many of the hastily erected ones sprouting up in San Antonio Abad, Santa Eulalia del Río—even on the outskirts of Ciudad de Ibiza—are more frame than picture.

At most resorts you can write ahead to make a reservation. But at hotel after hotel on the island of Ibiza, you can't do this. Individual bookings in most establishments range from horrifically difficult to impossible. In many cases hoteliers don't bother to answer requests for space in summer. Armed with a nice fat contract from a Midlands tour group, they're not interested in the plight of the stranded pilgrim.

Don't—repeat don't—go to Ibiza in summer without an iron-clad reservation, unless you're reasonably attractive, at least a good enough looker to assure yourself that you'll get an invitation to share someone's place in the old town.

GETTING THERE: The easiest way to reach Ibiza is by an **Iberia** or **Aviaco** flight from Palma, Barcelona, or Valencia. At the airport in Ibiza, taxis transfer four people at one time to one of the resorts. From the airport into town costs $8 (U.S.) in a taxi, but only 150 pesetas ($1.05) on a bus to the terminal.

The shipping line **Compañía Trasmediterránea** maintains services between Ibiza and Barcelona, Palma de Majorca, Valencia, Alicante, and Mahón. There are local booking offices in Ibiza (Avenida Bartolomé Vicente Ramón; tel. 30-16-50), Barcelona (2 Vía Layetana; tel. 319-81-12); Palma de Majorca (5 Muelle Viejo; tel. 22-67-40); Valencia (15 Avenida Manuel de Soto; tel. 367-65-12); Alicante (2 Explanada España; tel. 20-61-09); and Mahón (Nuevo Muelle Comercial; tel. 36-29-50).

In winter, runs between the various ports are limited, although they increase in number to meet the capacity. To get to Ibiza from Barcelona, you can catch a ferry in summer at 10 p.m. daily except Sunday, which makes a stop at Palma and gets into Ibiza the next day. As of this writing, but subject to change, passage from Barcelona to Ibiza costs 6,900 pesetas ($48.30) per person in a (tiny) double cabin with bath and 5,990 pesetas ($41.93) per person in a triple with bath. Prices are even lower for passage in a quad, where each person pays 5,740 pesetas ($40.18). The cheapest passage of all is in a deck chair for 3,120 pesetas ($21.84), but after a long night awake, it's doubtful that you'll find anything romantic about a morning sunrise over an early-morning Mediterranean. Prices from Valencia to Ibiza are roughly the same as prices from Barcelona to Ibiza.

Again, as with Palma, if you come in August, be sure you have a return ticket (although boats are easier than airplanes in this regard) and a reservation. Stories abound of passengers who were stranded for days in Ibiza in midsummer until a seat miraculously opened up or until they purchased someone else's boarding pass for many times the original amount.

5. Ciudad de Ibiza

Ibiza is the capital of the island. Founded by the Carthaginians 2,500 years ago, it is graced with a harbor filled with boats and yachts. The town is not a resort, consisting of a lively **Marina** district around the harbor and an old town **(Vila)** with narrow, cobblestone streets, and flat-roofed, whitewashed houses that climb a steep hill.

The Marina quarter is usually yacht clogged, and its mainstreet paseo, **Vara del Rey,** has a distinctive personality of long ago, but it is the people—the skeptical natives and the expatriates—who provide the ever-continuing spectacle. It is a study in contrast. The old fishermen, long accustomed to Ibizan women swathed in black, are treated to sights that pop their eyes, as the fair-skinned American and northern European Mary Janes parade around in bikinis and halter tops. In addition to its people, the Marina quarter is intriguing for a stroll because of its art galleries, discos, boutiques, and foreign-operated bars and restaurants—an amazing conglomeration best viewed at night.

WHERE TO STAY: The hostelries in the town are limited and often lack style and amenities. An exception follows.

El Corsario, 5 Calle Poniente (tel. 30-12-48). It's rumored that a 16th-century pirate built this villa's terraces with his ill-gotten gains. It sits beside a steeply sloping alleyway just below the foundations of the fortress crowning the highest point in the old city. The location is within a labyrinth of pedestrian walkways with slippery cobblestones. You'll have to walk the last 500 feet to reach the place, after your taxi deposits you near a church some distance down the hill.

The owner of the house, which was built in 1570, is the German-born Anna von Osterburg, who returned to Ibiza after several years in El Salvador. She rents 14 simple but pleasant bedrooms, all but two of which contain a private bath. Some overlook an enclosed garden ripe with trailing bougainvillea and carefully cultivated flowers. The tactful manager, Jaime Alcázar, quotes singles at 3,400 pesetas ($23.80), doubles at 5,600 pesetas ($39.20), plus breakfast. The in-house restaurant is one of the most romantic places to dine in town (see the restaurant recommendations following).

Playa de Figueretes

On the edge of town, around some fair sands, a number of modern beach hotels have sprouted up, far superior to the ones in the city. With few exceptions, most of these are booked solidly in summer by tour groups.

Hotel Cénit, Archiduque Luís Salvador (tel. 30-14-04), is your best choice along this playa. Circular shaped, it looks like a quartered wedding cake. In the pueblo fashion, each floor has been staggered so as to provide a terrace for the rooms above. In high season, a person can stay here in a double with bath for 4,200 pesetas ($29.40), 3,000 pesetas ($21) in a comparable single. The rooms are routine, but not so bare-boned that they lack comfort. All the 62 accommodations contain a private bath (some with a shower, but no toilet). The curved dining room, with its picture windows, is a pleasant place to enjoy a continental breakfast, not included in the room rates. The Cénit, which has a pool, is perched on a hillside, a short walk down the beach. It's open from April to October.

Hotel Palaú, 12 Galicia (tel. 30-23-50), is one of the more laudable contenders near the beach, having been built in 1965 to house the northern invaders. You can book a fairly pleasant but spartan double room (all with private bath) for 4,500 pesetas ($31.50), 3,300 pesetas ($23.10) single. A continental breakfast, costing extra, is the only meal served. In sum, it's an agreeable spot to stop, only a short block from the beach. The hotel is open from April 1 until the end of October.

Hotel Marigna, 18 Al Sabini (tel. 30-49-12), is an inexpensive one-star hotel built on a hill, encompassing views of the city and water. Like nearly every other hotel around here, it's hooked up to the umbilical group cord—notably English and German—but it will accept those who write in advance. Its bedrooms are efficient, good size; nearly all of them have a compactly modern bath and a balcony. As for the decor, someone tried, making for a welcome relief from the utter vacuousness of many of its competitors. Doubles with bath cost 3,500 pesetas ($24.60) to 4,000 pesetas ($28). Singles, depending on the plumbing, range in price from 2,200 pesetas ($15.40) to 2,800 pesetas ($19.60). A continental breakfast, costing extra is the only meal served. The hotel is open from May to October. Guests can use the pool of the nearby Cénit.

WHERE TO EAT: In recent decades Ibiza has become the dining room of the world, with a wide international cuisine, hoping to appeal to most tastes. Some of the dishes lose a lot in translation to the Balearics, however, and that is why the wise diner will stick to the fresh fish on which the islanders have lived for years.

Restaurant Sa Oficina, 6 Avenida de España (tel. 30-00-16), is one of the better restaurants of the city. It specializes in Basque cuisine from a position in the center of town. You might be surprised by the large portions served when you dine in the pleasantly decorated place, but judging by the increase in business since the restaurant opened in 1982, the owners are doing things right. Specialties include a combination shellfish and shrimp platter, hake with shellfish sauce, veal dishes, and a seafish soup with large chunks of crustaceans. Full meals, served at lunch and dinner daily, average 2,200 pesetas ($15.40). Closed Sunday.

Mamma Mia, 10 Garijo (tel. 30-26-73). Owner Claudio Testa gives his diners the chance to switch from the Ibizan culture outside his restaurant to a little corner of Italy within. Specialties, as you may have suspected, are pizza, spaghetti with garlic, and veal scaloppine pizzaiola. Full meals, served daily from mid-October to mid-May, average around 1,800 pesetas ($12.60). The pizzeria opens onto the waterfront, with views of the ships in the harbor. You can select a table outside among the milling throng or else retreat inside if the weather is nippy. The place is gaily decorated with red-and-white-checked tablecloths.

El Brasero, 4 Barcelona (tel. 30-71-68). There's a sidewalk café section where the view of your fellow diners might be (because of the better light) even more revealing than the view inside. Indoors or out, however, this is one of the best known, best established, and most popular places on the island, catering to a covey of nationalities with aplomb and grace. Menu choices represent international specialties. These include chicken salad, grilled meats, asparagus gratinade, duckling with honey, beef filet in hot sauce, and a steamy fish stew. The restaurant is closed in January and February and on Monday in winter. Full meals will cost 2,200 pesetas ($15.40) and up.

Restaurant Formentera, 4 Eugenio Molina (tel. 30-00-54), was established as a center for the preparation and service of recipes which originated in Ibiza. Today it's one of the few restaurants on the island which maintain these traditions strictly. The owner, Juan Tur Ramis, offers a complete wine list, good service, and a daily fixed-price menu for 1,200 pesetas ($8.40). Your meal might consist of well-spiced seafood dishes and such other specialties as spinach Ibizan style and an array of rice dishes, some with fish. Full meals cost from 2,000 pesetas ($14) à la carte, and are served every day except in November. You'll find the restaurant in the center of the city's seaside promenade. However, a rear entrance opens onto a pedestrian alleyway, and in fair weather the tables placed outside are more sought after than those in the interior. You dine in green painted chairs on green checked tablecloths. Inside you'll also find a prominent bar.

El Corsario, 5 Calle Poniente (tel. 30-12-48). Its accommodations are reviewed separately, but its dining room with its panoramic view is so romantic that it deserves special mention. This 400-year-old flower-draped villa sits near the top of the hill whose fortress dominates the skyline. Your taxi will deposit you about 500 feet down the hill in a plaza fronting an old church, and you must climb the slippery cobblestones to reach it. For dining, you enter a pleasant pair of rooms filled with a standup bar, a handful of neat tables, and a view of the harbor. Manager Jaime Alcázar will offer you such menu specialties as six kinds of spaghetti, four kinds of pasta, and two different preparations of lamb. Full meals, served daily between May and October, cost 2,500 pesetas ($17.50).

La Solera, 8 Plaça Sa Tertulía (tel. 31-11-71), an enterprise of the Sánchez family for a number of years, is quiet and intimate, a reliable place to sample some of the best mainland-style tapas on Ibiza. A few of those displayed at the bar are served in bigger portions at tables in the two dining rooms, where full and well-prepared meals of typically Spanish dishes average around 1,600 pesetas ($11.20). The establishment is open daily except from mid-October to mid-March.

Alfredo, 16 Paseo Vara del Rey (tel. 30-10-00), is where you can order a belt-loosening meal for 1,000 pesetas ($7). The first course might begin with a homemade fish soup, then follow with a plate of freshly caught fish, plus a good steak with fried potatoes, finishing off with fruit or caramel custard, not to mention freshly baked bread and a regional wine. The waiters in their tidy white jackets are attentive. After the dessert, you can have your coffee on the terrace. Don't be put off by the rather junky looking façade. The interior is spacious and clean, with white napery and cool tile floors. Mirrors and bentwood chairs add to the harmony. It is closed on Saturday.

Restaurant Victoria, 1 Calle Riambau (tel. 31-06-22), is a pleasant little bistro with a limited but most economical menu. The crowd usually consists of budget-conscious visitors drawn here by the fresh fish dishes, including grilled hake, octopus in sauce, clams, sole, fresh sardines, and shrimp. You might begin with one of the freshly made soups or the salad of the house, perhaps an omelet made with ham or cheese. Meat dishes are standard and very limited. A meal costs from 1,200 pesetas ($8.40). It has a conservative decor of simple walls, checked tablecloths, graceful wooden chairs, and a handful of original paintings. Now run by Mrs. Josefa Costa, it was established some 46 years ago by her family. She's seen life in Ibiza go through many changes, but continues over the years serving the same wholesome meals. Her place is closed in November, reopening in April.

THE CHIEF SIGHTS: Ibiza is an island to strike out for if you're seeking sun and fun. But there are two sightseeing attractions worth a special visit.

The archeological museum, **Museo Arqueológico de Dalt Vila,** 3 Plaza de la Catedral (tel. 30-12-31), contains all archeological finds from the islands of Ibiza and Formentera except those from the necropolis of the Puig des Molins (see below). Prehistoric artifacts and a fine collection of Punic (Phoenician) relics may be seen here, including a collection of Carthaginian amulets and rose-painted Punic vases. Another display consists of a group of intriguing terracotta figurines as well as Hellenistic busts from the 2nd century B.C. Still another section of the museum is devoted to a collection of vases and urns, some dating from the 6th or 7th century B.C., along with many fragments of ceramics, glassware, and artifacts from the imperial Roman period. A numismatic exhibit contains only coins found on the island and dated between the 4th century B.C. and the end of the Roman empire. This museum is open from 10 a.m. to 1 p.m. except Sunday and holidays.

A ticket costing 100 pesetas (70¢) will admit you to the Dalt Vila museum and also to—

Museo Monográfico del Puig des Molins, 31 Via Romana (tel. 30-17-71), at the foot of the necropolis. This museum houses only objects found in the area which served as a cemetery for the city's inhabitants from 654 B.C., the accepted date for the founding of Ibiza, to the 1st century A.D. This is the site where Carthaginian and Roman funerary remains were excavated. The necropolis is 550 yards from the center of the city. This museum is open from 4 to 7 p.m. daily except Sunday and holidays.

AFTER DARK: **Montesol,** 2 Vara del Rey. In the evening the menagerie at this hotel bar is likely to include both the well-established foreign community, the newly arrived hopefuls looking for a "hook" into Ibiza's inner circles, and a covey of Spaniards coming along for the view. In many ways this is the greatest multi-ring circus in town, made more pleasant by the well-prepared tapas and the generous drinks, costing from 125 pesetas (88¢). To see more action, sit at one of the sidewalk tables. However, in cooler weather you can retreat inside to an interior of white tiles, mirrors, and solid modern tables and stools with tones of brown and pink. The location is in what used to be the oldest hotel in town, a neoclassic building with Ionic inset on the main street, a short walk from the harbor.

La Tierra, Callejón Trinidad, is another of the city's watering holes where every fashionably trendy starlet of major and minor theater will eventually appear for a tapa and a drink, from 125 pesetas (88¢). The crowd contains cross-sections of urban life of most of northern Europe, so be prepared for what you get.

Tango, 4 Pou. The special cocktails of this place, costing from 550 pesetas ($3.85), are guaranteed to make you even more appreciative of the expensive terrace and the varied crowd. Ask for the special Tango cocktail. It's closed from October until Easter.

Zoo, Puerto. This is not a place for intimate conversation (with a name like Zoo, what would you expect?), but still you're likely to get a view of many of the passers-through of the island. The bar, one of the most popular in the old city, stands right on the waterfront, with deep-red high tables and rush-bottomed stools. You can sit on candy-striped banquettes any time from 7 p.m. to 2 a.m., and if you have a very, very revealing snapshot of yourself in a bikini, management might post it on the bulletin board. Beer begins at 300 pesetas ($2.10).

Amnesia Nightclub, San Rafael (tel. 31-41-36), is a disco hangout for the trend-conscious youth of the island, who observe and meet their peers from other parts of the island here. The Amnesia is about 3¾ miles from the center of town, in an area called San Rafael. This disco operates between June and September. World-renowned celebrities, including movie stars, artists, and singers, spend their holidays on Ibiza and make a point of visiting Amnesia. People dance all night, often until they can watch the sun rise. Drinks aren't cheap, averaging around 1,200 pesetas ($8.40).

Pacha, Paseo Marítimo (tel. 30-38-76), offers the most consciously elaborate display on the island. It includes special lighting effects, well-amplified music, a restaurant, a dance floor, and a swimming pool. This place is popular in summer, when it's open daily. In winter it opens only on weekends. Throughout the year drinks cost around 1,500 pesetas ($10.50).

6. San Antonio Abad

Known as Portus Magnus to the Romans, this thriving town is the chief resort of Ibiza. Lying ten miles west of Ciudad de Ibiza, San Antonio Abad as a resort was discovered largely in the '50s.

In summer you have as much chance of finding a room here as you would of booking a reservation on the last flight to the moon if the earth were on fire. Virtually all the hotels have a direct pipeline to tour-group agencies in northern Europe, which feed constant plasma directly into the bloodstream of San Antonio. The individual probably won't get the time of day. The hotel clerk will be too busy rerouting army cots, as he's already overcrowded on his tour clientele.

The resort is built on an attractive bay. A four-minute ferry ride takes you across the bay to the popular beaches. With all its influx, San Antonio does have a joie de vivre, plus lots of mildly entertaining nightlife. Even if you're staying in Ibiza or Santa Eulalia, you may want to hop over for the day or evening. A bus leaves every half hour from Ciudad de Ibiza to San Antonio and vice versa.

San Antonio is not for the conservative visitor. It's not unusual to see topless women not only on the beach but at the discos as well. Many attractive young women are openly "pawed" on the narrow streets of town, and of course the smell of marijuana is commonplace by now. Remember, however, that buying and selling marijuana is strictly against the law.

When the revelers have had too much cheap booze and vino, San Antonio can get dangerous, particularly if you're caught in the middle of a fight. Some tour-group Britons openly admit that their only reason for going to San Antonio is "to get drunk."

First, I'll survey a handful of the budget hotels for the off-season visitor. Some might possibly grant you a reservation in summer if you give them plenty of notice.

WHERE TO STAY: **Arenal Hotel,** Avenida Doctor Fleming (tel. 34-01-12), built in 1966, ranks among the top hotels in San Antonio Abad, offering value comparable to that of its more expensive neighbor, the Hotel Palmyra. During high season the groups take over, but in October and from April to mid-May you can generally get a reservation if you write two weeks in advance. Off-season, all you need do is arrive. At the edge of town, on its own beach, the Arenal is a long, four-floor balconied establishment with a swimming pool. Contemporary architecture and furnishings are used throughout. Simple and attractive, the rooms offer comfortable beds. All units contain a private bath and a balcony opening either onto the sea or the little front garden lawn with palm trees. A double costs 5,000 pesetas ($35); a single, 3,000 pesetas ($21). Lunch or dinner is another 1,400 pesetas ($9.80). Off-season note: One living room has a circular raised fireplace with surrounding banquettes.

Hotel Palmyra, Avenida Doctor Fleming (tel. 34-03-54), is a five-story modern hotel with deeply recessed balconies set just outside the commercial center of town. Its attractive decor is enhanced by the hotel's policy of reserving half of its 160 spacious bedrooms for individual clients, making this one of the best bets in town for travelers who are not members of organized tours. There's a small but verdant garden in front near a large swimming pool ringed with plants and reclining chairs. A marble-sheathed lobby opens directly onto the sands of a private beach. Bedrooms contain private baths, phones, summer furniture, cool tile flooring, and balconies. Depending on the season and the view, singles cost 5,500 pesetas ($38.50) to 6,000 pesetas ($42); doubles, 5,000 pesetas ($35) to 5,500 pesetas ($38.50) per person, plus breakfast. Fixed-price meals go for 2,300 pesetas ($16.10).

Hotel Tropical, Cervantes (tel. 34-00-50). Its garden and swimming pool sit across a quiet street from its blue-and-white balconied façade. Their separation seems to create almost a public park around the water, ringed with hundreds of reclining chairs and a handful of billiard tables. The hotel is set away from the port in a commercial center of town. It was built in the early 1960s with a russet and white-marbled lobby filled with armchairs. Each of the 142 modern bedrooms has a private bath and phone. Depending on the season and the accommodation, singles cost 1,650 pesetas ($11.55) to 2,200 pesetas ($15.40); doubles, 3,000 pesetas ($21) to 3,700 pesetas ($25.90), plus breakfast.

Hotel Tanit, 7 Mateo Obrador (tel. 45-13-73), at Cala Gració. Because it's set in an isolated position outside the center of the resort, its architects tried to make it as self-contained as possible. Its angled balconies jut off from the sand-colored façade. Once you pass through the airy lobby, you'll be amid a dense crowd of vacationing Europeans, who cluster by the dozens around the perimeter of the large swimming pool. A series of steps leads through a grove of pines down to the beach, but the true heart and soul of the place lies near the terraced snack bars and outdoor tables between banks of geraniums and fragrant oleander. This large property offers more than 700 beds in rooms, which each contain a private bath, phone, and private terrace. Depending on the season and the accommodation, with half board included, singles cost 3,400 pesetas ($23.80) and 6,700 pesetas ($46.90); doubles, 2,600 pesetas ($18.20) to 5,200 pesetas ($36.40) per person. The hotel is closed between November and March.

Residencia Mitjorn, 10 Calle del Faro (tel. 34-09-00). This well-scrubbed, pleasantly friendly hotel contains 18 modern rooms, each of which has a private bath. Señora Maria Prats, the genial owner, is likely to be serving drinks in the lobby-level bar when you enter to register. The simple but comfortably airy bedrooms rent for 1,500 pesetas ($10.50) and 1,600 pesetas ($11.20) in a single, 2,400 pesetas ($16.80) and 2,600 pesetas ($18.20) in a double. You'll find the entrance to this hotel's secluded front courtyard on a quiet street that parallels the harbor, one terraced block uphill from the waterfront road. The hotel closes in winter.

Hotel Coves Blanques, Playa de Coves Blanques (tel. 34-11-12), is a small hotel (26 doubles) built at the water's edge in 1965. Well styled, its lounges are restful and pleasant, using simple leather and natural wood furniture. The rooms open onto a terrace facing the sea. Every bedroom has a private bath, is good-sized, and contains up-to-date, comfortable furnishings. An added bonus is the private sun balconies. The cost of a double room is 3,200 pesetas ($22.40). The hotel is open daily from April 1 to October 31.

WHERE TO DINE: **Restaurant/Bar Rias Baixas,** 4 Calle Ignacio Riguer (tel. 34-04-80), lies behind wrought-iron window bars on a quiet sloping street in the commercial heart of town. It's named after the low Galician tides in the north of Spain that uncover rich beds of oysters, scallops, and clams. In fact, Galician seafood, flown in fresh every day from the north of Spain, is the restaurant's specialty. You'll dine in a rustic Iberian dining room filled with thick stucco arches, ceiling beams, and an open fireplace. Full meals cost from 2,500 pesetas ($17.50) and include trout zingara, veal, pork, and beef dishes. But the specialties are the chef's style mussels, Galician clams, crabmeat soup, caldo gallego, trout meunière, and Bilbao-style eels, each dish accompanied by a selection of Galician wine. The restaurant serves lunch and dinner daily except between December 15 and February 1.

Sa Capella, Carretera de Santa Inés (tel. 34-00-57), as its name implies, is housed within a deconsecrated 600-year-old chapel whose stone vaulting soars dramatically over its clusters of wooden tables. As you dine, you'll notice ecclesiastical hints of an earlier function of this building, including a primitive rose window, radiating alcoves, balconies, and brass or wrought-iron chandeliers that can be lowered on pulleys from the overhead masonry. You'll pass beneath an arbor of magenta-colored bougainvillea before being ushered to your table by a waiter dressed in a red-and-white traditional Ibizan costume. Full meals cost from 2,500 pesetas ($17.50) and include fisherman's soup, seafood cocktail, sole meunière, eels Bilbao style, Basque-style rape (a whitefish), marinated mussels, rabbit, and pepper steak.

NIGHTLIFE: **Summum Disco,** Carretera Port des Torrent, Bahía San Antonio (tel. 34-20-10). This is considered the most unusual and interesting disco in town. Designed by an architectural team from the Costa Brava, it has plaster replicas of flying angels suspended beneath the ceiling and simulated clouds moving above a popular dance floor ringed with delta-shaped marble chairs. The music is danceable and recent. There's a 600-peseta ($4.20) entrance fee, after which beer costs 150 pesetas ($1.05). Go late for the most varied crowds.

Es Paradis, Pasaje de Can Mañá (tel. 34-28-93), is scattered over a wide floor area that includes seven different bars and more than one dance floor, with boundaries usually accented with copies of Greco-Roman columns. The largest and most central of the dance floors has a fountain in the middle. A full range of mixed drinks is available. It charges a cover of 1,800 pesetas ($12.60) which includes the first drink. If you're hungry, you can order hamburgers, salads, and snacks.

7. Santa Eulalia del Río

Five miles north of the Ciudad de Ibiza, on the estuary of the only river in the Balearic Islands, is Santa Eulalia. Formerly patronized by expatriate artists from the capital, it presently draws a broader base of tourism—largely middle-class northern Europeans.

Santa Eulalia nestles at the foot of the Pui de Missa, crowned by an ecclesiastical compound gleaming white in the Ibizan sun. The church dates from the 16th century. The hill lies between the river and the resort. The best beach is El Caná, cosmopolitan in character.

Santa Eulalia is relatively free of some of the plastic quality of San Antonio Abad. Sometimes a visitor has a better chance of finding an accommodation here, despite its location and limited choice of lodgings, than in the other two major towns.

WHERE TO STAY: Hotel Ses Estaques, Ses Estaques (tel. 33-02-00), is my favorite hotel in the resort. It occupies a desirable position close to the crashing waves of a peninsula at the edge of town. A beautiful garden of roses, well-ordered palms, and cascades of ivy ring it, coming right to the edge of a pine-sheltered swimming pool. It's filled with thoughtful extra touches and hideaway corners of charm. There's an aquarium in the spacious lobby, plus a pleasant tropical-style restaurant in an outbuilding on the beach a short walk away, a tennis court, and a comfortable collection of stay-a-while chairs beside the pool-side snack bar. Each of the 165 terrazzo-floored bedrooms has a balcony illuminated by a wall sconce shaped like a trout, dangling a light as it would a fly from its mouth. There's a phone and a private bath in each room as well, along with a view of either the garden or the sea, depending on your preference. With half board included, doubles cost 2,600 pesetas ($18.20) to 3,600 pesetas ($25.30) per person daily; singles 2,900 pesetas ($20.30) to 3,900 pesetas ($27.30), plus tax. The hotel is closed between late October and early May.

Hotel Tres Torres, Ses Estaques (tel. 33-03-26). It's modern and stylish, designed in a harborview style of boxy angles and prominent balconies. Many of the angled windows overlook a pair of swimming pools ringed with reclining chairs. There's a disco on the premises, plus a comfortable lobby filled with neo-Victorian wicker chairs. An airy and sun-flooded dining room has a view of the water. There is also a handful of places to enjoy refreshing drinks. Each of the comfortably furnished bedrooms has its own balcony. With half board included, singles cost 4,800 pesetas ($33.60); doubles, 4,300 pesetas ($30.10) per person. The hotel closes in winter.

Hotel Riomar, Playa Dels Pins (tel. 33-03-27), brings a host of modern comforts to service the needs and whims of the guests it welcomes from April through October. Built smack on the beach, it is graced with six floors of good-size, nicely furnished bedrooms (120 in all), each with a wall of glass opening onto a pigmy balcony. But try to garner one of the sea-view rooms. The 4,000 double rooms have either private tub or shower bath. The cost for a double is 4,000 pesetas ($28), 3,000 pesetas ($21) in a single. For lunch or dinner you pay 1,500 pesetas ($10.50) per person extra. From the living room lounge, you can make a quick dash for a plunge into the waters of the Mediterranean.

Hotel Ses Roques, Calle del Mar (tel. 33-01-00), is modern but basic. It provides May to October accommodations right beside the sea, three floors of 34 rooms—all with private bath (either shower or tub), plus a private balcony. The furnishings are contemporary, and everything's scrubbed and polished daily. The meals are served near the water. Doubles cost 3,600 pesetas ($25.30); singles, 2,000 pesetas ($14).

WHERE TO DINE: **Doña Margarita,** Paseo Marítimo (tel. 33-06-55). Margarita Ribas Prats is the guiding energy behind this large, simple, yet surprisingly elegant restaurant on the Paseo Marítimo. She is almost always on hand to direct the service and supervise the preparation of the solidly traditional menu items that seem to please so many of her local customers. The dishes include mussels marinara, paella, filet of beef with peppers and gratinade of asparagus, salmon with green peppercorns, calves' kidneys with fried onions, and beef stew. Full meals in the air-conditioned interior or on the panoramic sea-view terrace cost around 2,500 pesetas ($17.50) and up. In summer the restaurant closes on Monday at lunchtime, and in winter on Sunday night.

Sa Punta, Isidoro Macabitch (tel. 33-00-33), which seems dedicated to producing a constant supply of fine food, has a dramatically opulent decor. In warm weather many patrons prefer to dine on the flowered outdoor terrace where the view encompasses the sea. Some of the dishes reflect nouvelle cuisine touches, as exemplified by the lobster and kiwi salad. Other selections include hake with a leek sauce, seafood crêpe, fresh grilled salmon, a zarzuela (shellfish stew) Sa Punta, and hot mussels Belgian style. Full meals cost upward from 2,700 pesetas ($18.90). The establishment is closed Sunday night and Monday at lunchtime, as well as from mid-January to mid-February.

El Naranjo, 31 San José (tel. 33-03-24). Naranjo means orange in Spanish, and many foreign visitors refer to this place by its English name, calling it simply "The Orange Tree." A chic rendezvous at night, it carries out the theme with its orange tree patio, the verdant setting enhanced by flowering bougainvillea vines —altogether the most beautiful courtyard restaurant at the resort. The location is up in the town, several blocks from the water, but that doesn't prevent a steady stream of diners seeking it out in the evening. In fact, reservations are needed. If your table isn't ready when you arrive, you can enjoy an apéritif in the cozy bar. The menu is beautifully prepared and served. One newspaper called the chef "an artist," and unlike many people, he is said to "love his job." The menu is international, including fresh fish and such standard dishes as duckling in an orange sauce. As a concession to visiting British guests, the Sunday menu features roast beef with Yorkshire pudding. The Orange Tree doesn't bloom on Monday.

Pizzería Pinocho, 49 Calle San Vicente (tel. 33-14-20), is a simple Italian restaurant that offers one of the best bargain dining values in Santa Eulalia. Here you get not only pizzas, but good meat courses and freshly made pasta dishes along with good regional wine and a range of desserts. It draws an international crowd anytime between noon and 1 a.m. from March to October. Count on spending from 1,200 pesetas ($8.40) and up for a meal here.

Dining at Santa Gertrudis

Restaurant Ca'n Pau, Carretera de Ibiza (no phone). Despite the fact that the cooking here is solidly traditional, without any particular elaborations or innovations, this is still one of the most sought-out spots on the island. It's run by members of the extensive Pau family, who oversee the efficient and friendly service. They serve such specialties as cannelloni, grilled meats and fish, fish or meat stew, cocidos, and a rich version of dessert flan called crema catalana. Meals cost from 2,200 pesetas ($15.40). A garden surrounds the restaurant, which is open only for dinner from June to September. The restaurant is 1¼ miles from the center of town.

AFTER DARK: **Mozart,** 33 San José. In summer this place is noisy and convivial. In winter it's more appropriately called a pub, with quiet conversations over well-made drinks, beginning at 250 pesetas ($1.75). On one of the back streets of town, it has a canopied entrance.

Top Hat, 34 Isidoro Macabitch, is one of the town's best established pubs, filled with people who know one another but don't seem averse to greeting a newcomer. Beer costs from 150 pesetas ($1.05). However, the bartender specializes in fruit drinks with a tropical flavor, which he serves from 9 p.m. to 3 a.m. Slick, glossy black accents and comfortable banquettes add an elegant note. After all, its name is Top Hat, à la Astaire and Rogers.

Anita, San Carlos, north of Santa Eulalia. If you haven't seen *The Big Chill* and wonder whatever happened to the flower children of 1965, you might meet a few more or less well-preserved examples at Anita's. A fixed-price meal is offered for 650 pesetas ($4.55), along with a selection of liqueurs and wines.

8. Minorca

Minorca, still unspoiled after 7,000 years of visitors, is one of the most beautiful islands in the Mediterranean, with miles of sunswept beaches. It is relatively unknown to Americans, but has long been a favorite vacation spot for the English, Germans, French, and Scandinavians.

After Majorca, it is the second largest of the Spanish Balearic islands, but it has more beaches than Majorca, Ibiza, and Formentera combined. These beaches range from miles-long silver or golden crescents of sand to tiny beaches inside great rocky coves, or *calas* as they are called here. These calas are reminiscent of the fjords of Norway.

Minorca, barely 9 miles wide and less than 32 miles long, lies 130 miles off the coast of Spain and 27 miles northeast of Majorca. Its principal city is Mahón, a city of 25,000 people on a rocky bluff overlooking the great port which was fought over for centuries by the British, French, and Spanish.

Minorcans are friendly and prosperous—unemployment is virtually unknown here—and it has not had to depend on tourism, a fact that has kept it so unspoiled. The Minorcans have yet to discover tourist traps and double pricing.

The beaches are the island's greatest attraction, and there is nude bathing at many, although the practice is frowned upon by Spanish law. There are many items of interest for those interested in history, archeology, music, and art. Everywhere you look there is also a restaurant or disco.

A BIT OF HISTORY: The island has been occupied over the centuries by the Phoenicians, Greeks, Romans, Vandals, Byzantines, Moors, Normans, and finally the Spanish. It was occupied for almost all of the 18th century by the British, with one interruption by the French who used the occasion to discover *salsa Mahonesa,* mayonnaise. The island is as famous for its gins as for its *Mahónaise.* At least two distilleries are open to the public for free tasting and sales. Inquire at the tourist office, 13 Plaza de la Constitución (tel. 36-37-90), in Mahón for details.

The first American midshipmen were trained in the port of Mahón by Admiral James G. Farragut until the U.S. Naval Academy opened at Annapolis in 1845. There is a small American cemetery in the harbor, with graves of young men who died in the service of their country more than a century ago.

Archeologists say Minorca was first occupied as much as 7,000 years ago by a strong, athletic race of tribesmen who emerged from their caves to build underground villages, the oldest housing in Europe. The island is dotted with prehistoric monuments still a mystery to scientists. The most spectacular are the *taulas,* Stonehenge-type structures made of a great slab of rock lying atop a vertical slab to form the letter "T." There are also *talayots,* huge circular stone towers. Their purpose is also a mystery.

A PREVIEW OF THE ISLAND: **Mahón** and neighboring **Villacarlos** still show traces of the long British occupation—casement windows that slide up and down, the only place in Spain where they don't swing out; beautiful Georgian architecture including Golden Farm, the magnificent Georgian mansion overlooking Mahón harbor and where (according to local legend) Admiral Lord Nelson and Lady Hamilton lived in sin.

Cludadela, on the opposite end of the island, is pure Spanish with its heavy Moorish accents. It is the ecclesiastical capital of Minorca and contains many beautiful palaces and churches. The streets are narrow, flanked by vaulted passages and Arabian-style arches whitewashed and gleaming in the sun. It is noted for its manufacture of women's fine-quality shoes, one of the great bargains of the island. Bargains in men's shoes can be found in Alayor, farther east.

Many artists live in Minorca, and there are frequent exhibitions, listed in the local paper. The **Cathedral of Santa María** in Mahón has one of the great pipe organs of Europe, and world-famous organists give frequent free concerts.

Golf, tennis, and sailing are available at comparatively small fees, and details on these can be obtained from your hotel or the Oficina de Turismo in Mahón or Ciudadela—there are signs all over both towns pointing to these offices. Windsurfing is available at every major beach.

GETTING THERE: The high season is, of course, the most delightful time to visit Minorca, but one can swim as early as May (cool evenings) and as late as October (cool evenings and occasional rain).

There are air connections from both Madrid and Barcelona. It's also possible to fly over from Palma if you are already in Majorca and wish to extend your vacation in the Balearics.

If you want to travel by ship, there is regular service (which increases in summer) between Minorca and Barcelona, Palma de Majorca, and Ibiza. Service from Barcelona is aboard a moderately luxurious liner, requiring a passage of about nine hours. The lowest fare is around 4,080 pesetas ($28.56) for a deck seat, while the most expensive would be for a single person occupying a double cabin for 10,030 pesetas ($70.21). Two persons in a double cabin with a tiny bath pay 8,730 pesetas ($61.11) per person. If you're on a rock-bottom budget but still want some semblance of a night's sleep, you can always stay as one member of a quad for 6,430 pesetas ($45.01) for passage plus bed. Incidentally, a bunk in a four-person cabin is about the same price as a chair in the lounge. Meals can be purchased in a self-service restaurant on board or else brought along if you're doing some serious economizing.

If you're already in Palma and want to come to Mahón for a few days, a double room, double occupancy, costs 6,900 pesetas ($48.30) per person with bath. On that routing, the cheapest passage is a deck chair for 3,120 pesetas ($21.84) per person.

All prices listed here are those available at press time and could (and frequently do) change without warning from one season to another.

In Mahón, for ticket information and departure times, check at the offices of the **Compañía Trasmediterránea,** Nuevo Muelle Comercial (tel. 36-29-50). For addresses of the ship company's offices throughout the Balearics, see the "Getting There" section for Ibiza.

TRANSPORT ON THE ISLAND: The best way to travel around Minorca is by car. Rentals run from about $125 (U.S.) and up a week for a small Seat (Spanish-made Fiat) to nearly $250 for a large French Renault 12. Vespas rent for 1,000 pesetas ($7) and up per day. Taxis are fairly expensive—about 750 pesetas ($5.25) from the airport to Mahón. Bus service is excellent and cheap, and the fare from Mahón to the airport is 60 pesetas (42¢). Bicycles are comparatively cheap but impractical because of the distance to the beaches and the hills en route.

ACCOMMODATIONS: Hotels are generally booked solid through the favorite vacation months of July and August, and it is well to make reservations far in advance.

In hotels, facilities range from the luxurious and expensive four-star Hotel Port Mahón overlooking the beautiful harbor, to small residencias with communal showers. Some of these small residencias have double rooms for as little as 1,800 pesetas ($12.60) a day.

In Mahón

Hotel Port Mahón, Avenida Fort de l'Eau (tel. 36-26-00), is a four-star hotel of substance and comfort, considered the best on the island. Those who want to splurge can obtain bookings at this charming, up-to-date hotel with its many traditional features, such as its fine furnishings. The location on the cliffs opens onto what many visitors have considered one of the best views in the Mediterranean. Rooms are handsomely equipped, containing private plumbing. A double room with bath and balcony overlooking the harbor is 8,000 pesetas ($56). Even cheaper doubles are rented for 6,500 pesetas ($45.50). Singles range in price from 5,500 pesetas ($38.50) to 6,000 pesetas ($42).

The hotel has a fine restaurant at which you can dine even if you aren't a guest of the hotel. Meals cost from 2,000 pesetas ($14). Guests walk through the gardens by day, enjoying the sunny terraces and the private swimming pool, then retreat to the hotel's nightclub after dinner.

Hotel Capri, 8 San Estebán (tel. 36-14-00), is a comfortable modern hotel with 75 rooms, conveniently situated in the center of town. Motorists will appreciate the in-house garage. Each well-furnished room contains a TV. Singles rent for 2,800 pesetas ($19.60), while doubles cost 4,500 pesetas ($31.50).

If the luxury retreats recommended so far are too much for your budget, you can descend to **San Roqueta,** 122 Virgen del Carmen (tel. 36-43-35), a one-star hostal-residencia. At this simple place, a double room with private bath rents for 1,900 pesetas ($13.30); a single, also with bath, goes for 1,500 pesetas ($10.50).

The one-star **Reynés,** 26 Comercio (tel. 36-49-59), has uncluttered, well-maintained, basic rooms. This hotel is quiet and friendly, with rooms costing 1,900 pesetas ($13.30) in a double with a bath down the hall. The food is acceptable, a lunch or dinner costing from 1,000 pesetas ($7).

A typical two-star hostal in Mahón is **El Paso,** 157 Cos de Gracia (tel. 36-12-00). The entrance is somewhat depressing, but the big rooms inside have a fine view of the city. A double with bath costs two persons 2,200 pesetas ($15.40) per day. A bathless double rents for 1,800 pesetas ($12.60). This hotel might be considered only as an emergency stopover, as the noise from traffic and the downstairs bar (open until 3 a.m.) might keep you awake. A little more elbow grease in some of the rooms would help, too. An inexpensive bar/restaurant is in the same building.

At Villacarlos

The leading hotel in Villacarlos is the **Hotel Agamenón,** 18 Paraje Fontanillas (tel. 36-21-50), a gleaming white, six-story hotel overlooking the harbor at a point which, according to local legend, receives the first morning sun in Spain. It has everything from a swimming pool to its own disco. There are plenty of terraces for soaking up the sun. Rooms are attractively, but simply, furnished, and guests can book in here anytime between April and October. Rates run 6,000 pesetas ($42) in a double room, 4,000 pesetas ($28) in a single. Either lunch or dinner runs the bill up an extra 1,500 pesetas ($10.50).

Hotel Rey Carlos III, Miranda de Cala Corp. (tel. 36-31-00), is a functional and comfortable hotel containing 87 rooms, set at the edge of the sea. It's open only from April till October, during which time the management has some of the public rooms, including the dining rooms, air-conditioned. Single bedrooms rent for 4,800 pesetas ($33.60), and doubles go for 6,300 pesetas ($44.10).

There are some real bargains in Villacarlos. In Horizonte (Horizons), a housing development on the edge of the city, there is the one-star hostal, **Horizonte** (tel. 36-29-22), a small and immaculate hotel where double rooms with bath are 3,600 pesetas ($25.30) per day. Lunch or dinner is another 1,200 pesetas ($8.40). Nice and clean Horizonte may be, but take note: it is utterly devoid of charm.

On the Outskirts

Hotel del Almirante, Carretera Villacarlos, Puerto de Mahón (tel. 36-27-00). At the end of the 18th century British Admiral Collingwood built this beautifully detailed house which today has been transformed into a hotel containing some 40 rooms. Of course they have been renovated several times since the British controlled the island, yet they are nonetheless clean, comfortable, and well managed by Francisco Pons Montanari. Singles cost 2,400 pesetas ($16.80) to 3,400 pesetas ($23.80), while doubles go for 3,300 pesetas ($23.10) to 5,000 pesetas ($35). All rooms have a bath. The hotel has a swimming pool, a tennis court, and large gardens. It's open from April to October.

Hotel Rocamar, 32 Fonduco, Puerto de Mahón (tel. 36-56-01), is an agreeable hotel directly on the port, in the same building as a restaurant under the same direction. The three dozen rooms rent for 1,200 pesetas ($8.40) for a single, from 1,800 pesetas ($12.60) in a double. Parking facilities are nearby. Open May to September.

Cala Galdana Beach (Ferrerias)

Every major beach in Minorca has a large resort hotel, as fully equipped as a cruise ship, with swimming pools, discos, restaurants, and bars. A typical one is **Hotel Los Gavilanes** (tel. 37-31-75), one of the more beautiful on the island. The big (357 rooms) hotel with a magnificent view of the Mediterranean charges 8,200 pesetas ($57.40) for two persons in a room with bath. Singles cost 6,300 pesetas ($44.10). Meals cost from 2,000 pesetas ($14). Open May to October.

Ciudadela

Hotel Esmeralda (tel. 38-02-50). If you want a hotel beside the sea in the center of town, with a modern format dating from the early 1960s, this may be the place for you. Its 135 nicely furnished rooms rent for 4,800 pesetas ($33.60) to 7,100 pesetas ($49.70) in a double, 4,800 pesetas ($33.60) in singles also. Guests have free use of the swimming pool, the garden, and the tennis courts.

Hotel Almirante Farragut, Avenida de los Delfines (tel. 38-28-00), is an immense hostelry (almost 500 rooms), but it's fairly luxurious and comfortable nonetheless. On the premises is just about everything a vacationer would want, including a collection of boutiques, a swimming pool, a view over the sea, a mini-golf course, a disco, and an extensive garden. Comfortably appointed single bedrooms rent for 3,500 pesetas ($24.50) and up. For doubles, you pay 4,000 pesetas ($28) to 7,500 pesetas ($52.50). The wide variation in prices is the seasonal swing. The hotel is open May through October.

Cala Blanca, Urbanización Cala Blanca (tel. 38-04-50), is a pleasant hotel set amid a collection of recently built chalets in a housing development just outside of town. The 147 suitably furnished rooms rent for 3,300 pesetas ($23.10) to 5,600 pesetas ($39.20) in a single, 4,000 pesetas ($28) to 6,000 pesetas ($42) for a double. On the premises are a garden, a swimming pool, a parking garage, and a restaurant. In many ways this is one of the best hotels in Minorca.

A typical fonda is the **España,** 13 Calvo Sotelo (tel. 38-02-88), where a double room rents for only 2,600 pesetas ($18.20), a single going for 1,500 pesetas ($10.50). The shower is down the hall.

There are also dozens of *casa de huespedes,* usually private homes that take in roomers. A typical one is **Valldemosa,** 84 República Argentina (tel. 38-15-36), where a double room—simple, basic, uncluttered—rents for only 1,200 pesetas ($8.40) a day, a single costing 750 pesetas ($5.25). There is a communal shower. This is one of the best bargains on the island.

At San Cristóbal

Hotel Los Condores, Playa de Santo Tomás (tel. 37-00-50), offers fairly spacious bedrooms in an air-conditioned building constructed in the early 1970s. It sits in a park at the edge of the sea, about 13 miles from Mahón. Most guests prefer to bathe in the swimming pool set into the garden, although the hotel has access to a stretch of beach. There's a mini-golf course on the grounds for added diversion. Depending on the room and the season, the 188 units rent as follows: 6,300 pesetas ($44.10) for a single, 8,200 pesetas ($57.40) in a double.

WHERE TO DINE: As some wit said, the British landed in 1709, and Minorca is still studded with fish-and-chips places. There are also pizza parlors and a few hamburger joints. Restaurants come and go on Minorca almost as often as the tourists, but a few landmarks remain.

Food is more expensive on Minorca than on the mainland, because of the extra cost of shipping. Even in simple restaurants, a menú del día is likely to cost from 750 pesetas ($5.25). The meals, however, are likely to be rather substantial.

The best buys for lunch are the innumerable beach restaurants, where you traipse in barefoot in your swimming togs. Most specialize in freshly caught seafood. The menus are in Spanish, English, French, and German, and the prices are low.

You can eat for very little at some of the fast-food restaurants now found throughout much of Minorca. There are literally hundreds of restaurants in Minorca, and it is better to avoid the complete "pension" at your hotel so you can sample them.

At Mahón

One of those landmarks referred to is **Rocamar,** 32 Fonduco, on the Mahón harbor (tel. 36-56-01). Here a dinner for one with wine will run about 2,200 pesetas ($15.40). Some prize varieties of fish can be expensive, but not the small rougets or red mullet which are not only moderately priced, but delicate in flavor. Often the fish of the day is prepared with wild fennel which is then flamed under the catch. Try also the shellfish crêpes. Closed in November and on Monday in winter.

Restaurante Pilar, 61 Cardona y Orfila (tel. 36-68-17), is an extremely good island restaurant where the specialties are almost always based on authentic Minorcan recipes. Pilar Pons, the owner and chef, labors over her shopping (she uses only the freshest ingredients and bases her cuisine on what's available that day in the market). Her cooking and service receive the same personal attention. The four best tables in the place are on the patio at the rear of the restaurant, and must be reserved in advance. If you simply show up, however, you will probably be seated in the pleasant dining room amid a crowd of local residents who know and appreciate Pilar and her excellent cuisine. Featured dishes include chicken with shrimp, a wide array of shellfish prepared in stews, soups, and casseroles, and deftly prepared meats. Desserts are chosen from a buffet. Full meals cost from 2,400 pesetas ($16.80), but could go higher. The establishment is closed Monday and in November.

Restaurante Es Moli de Foc, 65 San Lorenzo, San Clemente (tel. 36-41-37), is three miles from Mahón. Although the decor is traditional to the island, the cuisine here is unabashedly French. It's prepared by Yvette Bouvière, the owner, who has a frequently changing list of specialties which vary with the availability of their ingredients in the marketplace. The restaurant expands in summer onto a flowered terrace, where the aromas of the kitchen give promise of the excellent dishes. These could include several forms of house pâté, quiche Lorraine, beef bourguignon, and chocolate profiteroles. Full meals cost from 2,000 pesetas ($14), and are served daily except Monday and in March. Only supper is offered from June to October 15.

Chez Gaston, 13 Conde de Cifuentes (tel. 36-00-44), is a small restaurant with a French name and Spanish decor, owned by a British woman named Lis and her husband, Hans, the chef. It's a block from Plaza Esplanade. The menú del día is 750 pesetas ($5.25). However, you do better choosing such à la carte dishes as entrecôte, escalope milanese, cannelloni, squid in garlic, and a luscious dessert called meringue Waldorf. A three-course à la carte meal will cost from 15,000 pesetas ($10.50). The restaurant is closed Sunday and from December 10 to January 15.

At Fornells

This north coast fishing village, overlooking a yacht harbor, lies about 18½ miles from Mahón. If you have a car, you might want to drive there to sample the food at the following well-recommended place:

Es Plá, Passaje d'Es Plá (tel. 37-51-55), is another classic Minorcan restaurant, a favorite of King Juan Carlos. It does a number of fish dishes. Try, if featured on the menu, such specialties as mero (brill) which is grilled and served with a mayonnaise sauce, and calamares (squid) which is also grilled. With wine, salad, and dessert, your dinner should run as low as 1,800 pesetas ($12.60) per person. However, Es Plá is known for its local specialty, caldereta de langosta, a peppery soup that contains chunks of spiny lobster. But lobster is very expensive, the cost varying from week to week. Es Plá is closed in November.

At Ciudadela

Like Rocamar at Mahón and Es Plá at Fornells, the third "classic" restaurant is **Casa Manolo,** 117 Marina (tel. 38-00-03), in the yacht basin at Ciudadela.

It is also a favorite with the king of Spain. The specialty, as in most Minorcan restaurants, is seafood. Dinners run around 2,500 pesetas ($17.50) per person, and reservations are necessary.

On the Outskirts

A typical British restaurant is **El Picadero** (tel. 36-32-68), on the road between Mahón and San Luís. Prime steaks will run around 1,600 pesetas ($11.20) per person, and owner Terence Hazzard will let you mix your own dry martini at the bar. He also offers a Sunday luncheon buffet—as much as you'd like to eat and drink—costing only 2,200 pesetas ($15.40), which is one of the bargains of the island.

A brilliant country restaurant is **Biniali,** 50 Suestra (tel. 36-17-24), just outside San Luís on the road to Binibeca. Biniali is an exquisite nine-room hotel furnished with Spanish antiques. Incidentally, it rents a double room with bath for 7,200 pesetas ($50.40) in case you'd like to stay here. Again, the specialty is seafood, served by waitresses wearing such modern fashions as Nancy Reagan–type bloomers. Dinner with wine will run around 2,500 pesetas ($17.50).

AFTER DARK: At night vacationers seeking amusement often resort-hop, sampling the excitement (or lack of it), then moving on to another late-night spot.

Cala en Porter

Cala en Porter has the most spectacular disco, **Sa Cueva d'en Xoroi,** a vast cave overlooking the sea 100 feet below. Dancing is usually to recorded music, often American, in the daytime, a lively disc jockey and a nightclub atmosphere prevailing at night. The first drink costs 250 pesetas ($1.75) during the day, 500 pesetas ($3.50) at night. It takes a vacation from November to May.

Ciudadela

Es Moli, Plaza Alfonso III, is one of my favorite bars in town. It was constructed inside an old mill whose thick beams and rough walls contribute to the country-style and very tasteful decor. This is a bar above all else, which gets more and more popular as the night rolls on. Beers cost from 150 pesetas ($1.05).

Ca's Quintu, 4 Plaza Alfonso III, contains all the trappings of a small-town café in Spain. Someone will be sipping wine regardless of the time of day, so if you're a drinker, you won't be alone. There's a simple dining room in the back where you can get a meal for 1,500 pesetas ($10.50).

Adagio's, Son Oleo. If you stay here long enough, the music will change styles so you're bound to hear something you like eventually. The place is spacious and illuminated with an array of colored lights which at times may be almost too bright. There's lots of room to move around in if your private party (of one, two, or more) gets too claustrophobic. Drinks cost from 350 pesetas ($2.45).

Mahón

Menta, 36 Costa d'en Ga. Many guests never leave the confines of the popular bar area near the entrance, although if they eventually grativate toward the well-appointed, table-filled area in back, they're usually grateful for a seat. This is a combination disco and bar, which seems to be the right place for either thinking alone or talking to people. Drinks cost from 400 pesetas ($2.80).

Tonic, Afueras Villa, is a disco set into the confines of a natural cave. Here the music is danceably loud and rhythmic, attracting many of the younger members of the city's night scene. Drinks average 500 pesetas ($3.50).

Villacarlos

Bananas, Fort de l'Eau, is decorated jungle style with lots of plants and bamboo. In warm weather clients enjoy the outdoor terrace, sipping on drinks, many of which are made with a base of tropical fruit juices. These can come with or without a heady dose of alcohol. At night the ambience can get lighthearted and fun.

Chapter XV

GIBRALTAR

1. Where to Stay
2. Where to Eat
3. What to See and Do
4. The Rock After Dark

WHERE ELSE WOULD you find a town that is also a country? Gibraltar is only 2¼ square miles in size, with a population of 30,000, but it has its own airport, currency, postage stamps, naval and military garrisons, two cathedrals, its own newspapers, radio, and TV—and a casino. "The Rock" enjoys a healthy climate and has a recorded history dating from A.D. 711 and traces of cave occupation 40,000 years ago.

The Rock of Gibraltar is a massive limestone rock rising out of the sea to a height of 1,396 feet, often referred to as the Gateway to the Mediterranean. It was originally a Phoenician trading post called Calpe. In Greek mythology it was the northern bastion of the Pillars of Hercules. Abyla (now Jebel Musa at Ceuta) was the southern bastion. Hercules is said to have stood with a foot on each "pillar," pushed them apart, and formed a bridge across the straits. During Phoenician domination of the Mediterranean, it was also recorded that Calpe was the end of the world, the point beyond which no trader should venture.

In 711, a Berber called Tarik Ibn Zeyad landed and named the rock Gibel Tarik (mountain of Tarik), from which the name of Gibraltar is derived. The rock was captured from the Moors in 1309 by the marauding Guzman El Bueno, then recaptured by the Moors in 1333. In 1462 Spain seized and fortified the prestigious rock against further attack but, in 1704, during the Spanish War of Succession, a joint Anglo-Dutch fleet, under the command of Prince George of Hesse-Darmstadt, made a surprise attack, capturing the fortress with little opposition.

The Spanish and the French have since made attempts to conquer the Rock by siege, bombardment, tunneling, and, finally, with specially reinforced ships, upon which the British rained red-hot cannon balls that set the ships afire.

There have been three treaties confirming Gibraltar as a British possession —Utrecht, 1713; Seville, 1727; and Versailles, 1783. In two world wars, the Rock was invaluable in keeping the Mediterranean open in spite of aerial bombardment. Its only land frontier—referred to by many Gibraltarians as the Garlic Wall—was closed by the Spaniards in 1966, in an attempt to enforce Spanish sovereignty on the people. The Spanish finally banned all trade to Gibraltar in 1969 in an attempt to bring further pressure to bear. But the Gibraltarians, in a free vote, decided by 12,138 to 44 to remain under British rule.

The Franco government closed the gate to Gibraltar, creating a blockade and causing much hardship for people on both sides of the frontier. Under King Juan Carlos, the frontier has been reopened to tourists.

Two languages are spoken, English and Spanish. The community is made up of Gibraltarians, Britons, Spaniards, some Moroccans, and a few Italians and Indians. The Spaniards who could not work on the Rock during the years the frontier was closed are back in force, and Spanish is heard constantly on the streets. With this and the departure of most of the British military, Gibraltar has ceased to be the proud little enclave it once was and is much more part of the mainland.

The town of Gibraltar lies on the west side of the rock around the harbors.

GETTING THERE: Gibraltar, for the foreign tourist, can be reached by land, air, or sea.

Now that the frontier is fully open, Gibraltar is linked by road to Spain once again. Provided your passport is in order, you can easily and quickly cross the frontier **on foot** in either direction. There is sometimes a delay if you wish to cross by **car,** as there is a stream of vehicles in both directions at times.

Because it is under the British Crown, Gibraltar benefits from advantageous airfares from Gatwick Airport in London, and you may find this an ideal gateway for your subsequent tour of southern Spain or northern Africa.

Scheduled flights are operated out of London by **British Airways, Air Europe,** and **Gibraltar Airways** (Gibair), which also provides service to Tangier. Don't be surprised if you hear the plane making that trip referred to as "Yogi Bear," as this is the affectionate name Gibraltarians have for their air link with Morocco. The Gibraltar–Tangier flight costs £29 ($43.50) each way.

The old ferryboat which provided straits crossings for many years has been replaced by a catamaran operated daily except Monday, taking people to and from Tangier at £12 ($18) one way for the 1½-hour voyage. A round-trip ticket is £20 ($30), but if you make the trip within the same day, the price is only £18 ($27) for the round trip. Children under 12 travel for half fare. The general sales agent is **Seagle Travel Ltd.,** 9B George's Lane, Gibraltar (tel. 71415). The hydrofoil that has operated between Gibraltar and Tangier for some years still exists, but the service is very erratic because of weather conditions and mechanical problems. For information, contact **Batmar Ltd.,** The Arcade, 30 Main St. (tel. 77666).

Once across the border at La Linea, Spain, you will find a lot of taxis and a board attached to the fence giving the cab fares to various places; to Málaga Airport, 9,000 pesetas ($63); Torremolinos, 8,600 pesetas ($60.20); Sotogrande, 1,600 pesetas ($11.20); Granada or Seville, 1,800 pesetas ($12.60); and Jerez de la Frontera, 11,500 pesetas ($80.50). It costs 1,500 pesetas ($10.50) to go to Algeciras, and you can take ferries from there to Morocco or Ceuta. If you plan to use a taxi for a sightseeing trip, figure on paying 900 pesetas ($6.30) per hour waiting time. A tour of La Linea (where there's not much to see) is 1,000 pesetas ($7).

1. Where to Stay

Accommodations in Gibraltar are limited, and tend to be more expensive in general than those in Morocco or along the Costa del Sol in Spain. During the summer, the British book most of the rooms, so reservations are strongly recommended. I've included the following listing of hotels, many of which are, frankly, over our budget, but could be handy to know about if you find yourself staying over in Gibraltar.

Montarik Hotel, Main Street (tel. 77065), is a charming collection of awnings and balconies above the shops of this major artery. The entrance is down

Bedlam Court, opening into a bare lobby with an Elizabethan Room for candle-lit dinners or substantial lunches. A cheerful, friendly bar makes up the ground floor. Rooms are neat with good beds, and all have a bathroom or shower as well as a phone. On the roof the sun terrace offers a certain amount of privacy among the rooftops of the town. It is open only in July, August, and September.

A single room with shower or bath goes from £16 ($24) to £17 ($25.50) and a double with shower for £22 ($33), increasing to £23 ($34.50) with private bath. There are some three-bedded rooms at £27 ($40.50). Tariffs include a continental breakfast. Tea, coffee, and basic supplies can be made ready for your arrival, and the shops of Main Street and the market are just outside. Stanley Norton rules the hotel with a steady hand, seeing that the place is kept spotless. A three-course table d'hôte lunch costs £6 ($9).

Bristol Hotel, Cathedral Square (tel. 76800), is a bright white building on a square opposite the Anglican cathedral and across from the Tourist Board. The restaurant is reached by a covered bridge across a narrow side street and down into the hotel's garden. As all catering is done on this side, room service can only be provided when you are ill or otherwise confined to your room. There is a leafy garden surrounding a small swimming pool. Rooms have been recently refurnished. Rooms with complete bath rent for £22.14 ($33.21) in a single, £34.40 ($51.60) in a double, and £40.81 ($61.22) in a triple. With private shower, the charges are £20.90 ($31.35) single, £30.35 ($45.53) double, and £35.75 ($53.63) triple. A 12½% service charge is added to all bills. A table d'hôte lunch costs around £5.50 ($8.25).

Mr. Olivero, the manager, is very eager to update and improve the service offered to all guests. All units have radio and color TV. An English-language program is broadcast nightly from 7 to midnight. Lunches in the Garden Club are simple but tasty, and if you don't want the set menu, there's a reasonable à la carte choice. Picnic lunches are available if you give the staff time enough to prepare. Only bar snacks are served in the evening.

Queens Hotel, Boyd Street (tel. 74000), lies close to the bottom station of the cable car that travels to the top of the rock. It's a rather plain, tall building surrounded by busy streets. The furnishings are very Spanish, with roughcast walls and dark wood beams in the bar and lounge. There is an elegant dining room with a front terrace for coffee and drinks. Bedrooms are large, and many have communicating rooms for family occupancy. Most have a balcony and private bath or shower. A bathless single rents for £14 ($21), going up to £18 ($27) with private shower or bath. Without bath, a double or twin ranges from £18 ($27), going up to £35 ($52.50) in a twin with bath and sea view, plus 12½% added for service. There is a friendly atmosphere.

Continental Hotel, Engineer's Lane, off Main Street (tel. 76900), is entered by going through the Continental Fast Food Restaurant on Main Street to reach the hotel's elevator. Above the street, there is an elegant paneled lobby leading to neat, well-furnished bedrooms, all with comfortable beds with duvets, complete bath, and color TV tuned to Gibraltar, Spain, and Morocco. Colors are muted, with browns predominating. Rooms rent for £28 ($42) in a single and £38 ($57) in a double. If you wish, you can have breakfast downstairs in the spotless, marble-floored restaurant that's quiet and pleasant in the morning, although it gets somewhat raucous later in the day. The hotel is in the heart of town, but the double-glazing of the windows makes it quiet and peaceful.

The two splurge hotels in the town are as follows:

Holiday Inn, Governor's Parade (tel. 70500), stands on a tree-lined square in the old and interesting part of town, within steps of Main Street. A friendly, pleasant place, it has a large bar, lively with talk and chatter, furnished with deep leather chairs. In the basement, the coffeeshop serves hamburgers, fried fish, calamares, omelets, salads, and other light meals. Breakfast is a help-yourself affair costing £5 ($7.50) for a selection of fruits, yogurts, bacon, and eggs. A set lunch or dinner costs around £10 ($15). On the roof, the eighth floor, is a glass-walled terrace and swimming pool. Singles are £45 ($67.50); doubles and twins, £52 ($78). All units have a bathroom, television set, telephone, radio, and air conditioning.

Rock Hotel, Europa Road (tel. 73000), is set in beautiful nine-acre grounds on the Rock's sunny western side with magnificent views of Spain and North Africa. This is *the* place for the traditionalist. There are gentle walks through the geranium-bright gardens, as well as a wisteria-covered terrace for a sundowner. The bar is sober with leather armchairs and naval battle scenes on the walls. The large, air-conditioned dining room has a dance floor with dancing to live groups on occasion. A single facing the Rock costs £35 ($52.50), a sea-facing single with bathroom and balcony going for £44 ($66). Doubles, all with private bath, go from £40 ($60) to £49 ($73.50). The swimming pool across the road from the hotel is available in season in the garden with a restaurant and bar service.

Caleta Palace Hotel, Catalán Bay (tel. 76501), lies at the end of the bay, on the east side of the Rock. A holiday hotel, it was built out on rocks over the sea with sun terraces and a swimming pool, with steps down to the water. In all, it's an easy place to stay and relax in. Most rooms have a balcony and overlook the sea. There are several bars, and guests dance in the Reflexions Disco. The Arcadia Coffee Shop offers al fresco dining. You can enjoy the quiet lounges or the more boisterous games room. The hotel has a hairdressing salon and a boutique, which stocks a wide selection of useful souvenirs and beach clothes. A single with a bath and a view of the Rock rents for £23 ($34.50), the tab rising to £31 ($46.50) with a sea view. A Rock-view twin with bath costs £41 ($61.50), the price jumping to £46 ($69) with a view of the sea. All units have a private bathroom, and a continental breakfast is included in the rates. A meal in the grill room will average about £12 ($18) per head.

YOUR OWN APARTMENT: Gibraltar Beach Hotel and Apartments, Sandy Bay (tel. 76191), is a long, low, four-storied apartment complex stretching along the length of Sandy Bay. The units have direct access to the sands and the crystal-clear Mediterranean; they offer one or two twin-bedded bedrooms, baths with shower, and well-equipped kitchens, plus patio-balconies overlooking the bay. There is twice-weekly maid service, and, if you decide not to cook dinner, the hotel's restaurant will serve an al fresco meal or else one in the dining room. In the complex are bars and a supermarket, and, in summer, a beach grill and barbecue. There's also TV, table tennis and bars. In addition to the sea, there is a swimming pool. In summer an excellent babysitting service is provided as well as a supervised playroom for children. A two-bedded unit rents for £20 ($30) per person per day; a four-bedded apartment, £18 ($27) per person. Sole occupancy of an apartment costs 50% on top of the room rate.

The complex also has the Battle of Trafalgar Restaurant and Grill and Upper Deck Bar. On Sunday they serve a traditional three-course lunch. The average meal costs from £6 ($9). They also do a "take-away" service in case you want to bring food back to eat in your apartment.

Ocean Heights, Montagu Place (tel. 75548), is back in town, two minutes from Main Street and close to the harbor, within easy reach of the fish and general markets for those who really want to integrate and shop alongside the Gibraltarian housewives, where the produce is fresher. In fact, it's only about a two-minute walk from the center of Gibraltar life—stores, shops, banks, restaurants, and bars. The upper floors have good views over the harbor. Apartments consist of studios, or one-, two-, or three-bedroom units, simply but well furnished with bathroom or shower room, kitchen with stove, refrigerator, and waste disposal. There is a cleaning service and also a launderette with ironing facilities. Apartments sleep two to six persons and range from £16 ($24) to £28 ($42) per person per night. Beside the restaurant is a swimming pool plus an open sun terrace. Below the block is Romano's restaurant and bar, offering grills and more complicated dishes, flambé grills, and crêpes, plus a wide choice of à la carte and table d'hôte meals. In summer, light lunches are served daily on the terrace, and on Friday and Saturday nights a dinner dance is held. The complex contains two elevators. The Ocean Heights Health Club features a range of fully equipped facilities, including saunas.

2. Where to Eat

In town, Main Street and Irish Town, which run parallel from Close to Casemates Gate, contain many of the most popular restaurants. This is where you'll find a multitude of English-sounding pubs, such as the Bull and Bush, the Captain's Cabin, the Royal Oak, or the Mason's Arms.

The Free Press, 79 Irish Town (tel. 75566), is a large room reached through a bright, smart bar with more atmosphere and polish than many in Irish Town. There's less emphasis on bar snacks and more on the ambience. In the restaurant, Henry Xiberras, the owner, has expanded his menu to suit the demands of the influx of international tourists. The day's fresh-fish prices are posted on a blackboard, and you can order your selection grilled, fried, or in one of the specialty dishes such as bouillabaisse. There is also a wide variety of meat dishes, pasta, poultry, curries, and vegetarian dishes. A meal will cost about £10 ($15).

The restaurant is open daily from noon to 3 p.m. and from 7 p.m. to midnight.

Irish Town Fisheries, 39-41 Irish Town (tel. 74970). You can eat in style here in the York Room Restaurant, where the fish overhangs the edge of the plate. But for many, the delight of this fish-and-chips shop is that the owners still wrap the fish and chips in newspaper after smothering them in vinegar and salt (you can have it au naturel if you wish). Or you can have a large portion of cod or haddock cooked in their "secret recipe" batter. The price of a meal of plaice and chips, with a glass of wine and ice cream, is £5 ($7.50).

La Mancha, 6 Lynch's Lane, off Main Street (tel. 75300), is a simple room with a high arched roof and Quixotic memorabilia decorating the walls. A bar at the entrance is home base for Alan and Susie Dowley, who serve drinks, take orders, set tables, and generally cajole the chef, placate the waitresses, and greet customers. Drinks are typically European. Fish such as sole and swordfish are only included on the menu when they are absolutely fresh. You might settle happily for a tournedos steak, including vegetables and potatoes, or else a poached lemon poisson, which is the specialty of the house. Desserts include the ever-popular "boozy pud." Meals begin at £10 ($15), ranging upward. Susie manages to operate very efficiently in her tiny kitchen at the end of the room and periodically comes out for air to look around the red-checked tables to see if her efforts are being appreciated. The restaurant is open daily except Tuesday from noon to 3 p.m. and 6 p.m. to 1 a.m. (last orders at 11:30 p.m.).

The Spinning Wheel, 9 Horse Barrack Lane, off Main Street (tel. 76091), is owned by Norman Birch, an ex-Flying Squad policeman from London and his wife, Raqui. He claims to be general factotum in his restaurant, cleaner, potman, and washer-up. The food has an international flavor, which is coupled with comfortable, continental-style surroundings. Lobster is cooked in a variety of ways, and poached salmon is among the specialties. The accent is on a variety of prawn and scampi dishes, and you can also order swordfish steak. Chicken, lamb, veal, and a variety of steaks, including a Chateaubriand, are also featured, and vegetarian dishes are prepared as well. Count on spending from £13 ($19.50) up for a meal here. Of course, the experienced chefs will, given time, prepare whatever suits you, as all food is cooked to order. An adjoining lounge will allow you to relax over coffee and liqueurs, in air-conditioned comfort. In the same courtyard, a grill bar is open all day, providing hot and cold snacks.

Jim's Den, 25 Prince Edward's Rd. (tel. 71289). Up the hill from the Holiday Inn, you come to the black doors and large window of an old warehouse. It's the lair of Jim Wright and his wife Denny, who have created a pleasant, relaxed restaurant. A long bar is presided over by the tall, good-looking Mohamed. Singles are asked to eat at the stools there when the tables are filled. The wooden tables are always scrubbed clean, and rugs add color to the stone floor.

Anchors and a ship's bell provide the decor, and you can turn your entire concentration on the menu and the succulent steaks cooked at the open barbecue by Jim. Portions are huge. A T-bone, more than 16 ounces in weight, is a favorite dish, as are the rump steak and the filet. As a side order, try a fresh salad, french fries or new potatoes, or Jim's special fried onions. Desserts include a variety of crêpes. Jim claims to have been the first restaurant in Gibraltar to put them on the menu. Fillings range from simple—lemon and sugar—to spectacular—an alcoholic one flambéed in Grand Marnier. Jim also serves more than a dozen special coffees—Gaelic, Highland, Jamaican, Calypso. Of course, you can also end your meal with straight coffee. A royal feast of prawn cocktail, a "small" (really three chunky pieces) filet with onions and french fries, then a crêpe will cost around around £12 ($18) per person. Open 7:30 to 10:45 p.m. Closed Sunday.

Strings, 44 Cornwall's Lane (tel. 78800), is owned and run by Peter Wheatley, who claims to be found nightly in one of two places—behind the bar with a drink in his hand, or else under the table by the door (letting his friends do his work for him). Actually, I've only seen him perfectly "sober" and behind the bar hard at work. Strings is a converted warehouse with a wooden ceiling and a carpet-covered stone floor. Tables are in booths with high-backed bench seats and old pictures on the walls. Lighting is by candles stuck in wax-covered bottles. At a small bar built from barrels you can meet the aforementioned Peter and contemplate the blackboard with the day's specials. I always select either the day's fish catch, or fresh game when it's featured. You'll have to wait for your meal once you've ordered, as everything is prepared to order.

Appetizers include a large prawn cocktail (more prawns than greenery), a Mediterranean seafood soup with brandy, Peter's chicken liver pâté served with red currant jelly and toast. Main courses include a ten-ounce filet steak, chicken crêpes with white wine sauce, and a vegetarian platter served with jacket potatoes, "chips," and various vegetables and a salad. All desserts are homemade and succulent, enticing if you still have room. A meal will cost around £10 ($15) if you last through three courses. A 10% service charge is added to your bill. The establishment is open daily from 8 p.m. to midnight except Sunday at lunchtime and Monday.

Woods, Marina Bay (tel. 79241), is a pleasant place run by William White, who owns the Holiday Inn. The place is cool and elegant, with pink tablecloths, wooden tables and chairs, and lots of ferns and hanging plants. Guests can enjoy drinks in the bar, seated in wicker chairs. Set lunches are served, with two courses costing £7.50 ($11.25) and three courses going for £10 ($15). You might choose a soup, to be followed by pâté, steak-and-kidney pie, roast pork, or scallops, plus a selection of desserts made on the premises. At dinner, the menu offers such appetizers as a feuilleté of chicken livers and smoked salmon with asparagus and toast. For a main dish, choices may include grilled fresh hake with asparagus, chicken cooked in cider with ham and cheese, chicken in peanut sauce, and pork dijonnais with mushrooms and mustard sauce. For dessert, I recommend the whisky sabayon with walnut ice cream. Dinners begin at £12 ($18). The restaurant is open for lunch from 12:30 to 3 p.m. and for dinner from 7 to 11 p.m. Closed Saturday and Sunday at lunchtime.

Among the budget places in town, the **Capri Restaurant,** 45 Main St., must be one of the best. The place hums with lively banter and laughter. The butt of much of the humor is the owner, Joe Hill, who normally is behind the bar except when he is away with the hockey team. Your selection is likely to include curry and rice, fish and chips, calamares (squid), meatballs and potatoes, or if you want lighter fare, hamburgers and salads. Sandwiches and omelets are prepared, as is a jacket potato with cream or butter. Meals cost from £5 ($7.50) to £6.50 ($9.75), and hours are Monday to Saturday from 9 a.m. to 10 p.m.

The **Oliver Twist Bar,** 78b Irish Town (tel. 76097), serves steak pie and chips and scampi and chips, with light meals costing about £4 ($6) and up. There is a separate room with two pool tables, plus video and other gaming machines.

Paddington's, The Arcade, off Main Street (tel. 75387), is the domain of Brian Strange. Snacks and tapas are available at the bar during lunchtime, and in the evening tables are set out in the narrow alleyway between balconied houses to augment those inside the restaurant. Appetizers include fresh melon with port, harida (a rich Moroccan soup), and sweet corn. Main dishes feature Chateaubriand with brandy sauce for two, steak au poivre, and fresh swordfish au gratin. Meals cost from £12 ($18). Open seven days a week.

Casa Antonio, Waterport (tel. 77069), is upstairs above what appears to be a real harbor bar. It is a large, airy room with windows the length of the place, overlooking the boats and harbor life. William Hernandez specializes in fish, and his menu has a distinctly Spanish flavor. Soups include gazpacho, shellfish, and garlic with egg. The season's salad is always offered. Paella for two is also available, and fresh grilled or fried hake, bream, or swordfish form the usual catch of the day. Steaks and chops are also offered. Count on spending from £10 ($15) up for dinner. A set luncheon is featured for £5 ($7.50). Very popular with locals, the restaurant is open daily except Sunday, from 12 noon to 3 p.m. and 8 p.m. to midnight. A lower cafeteria serves tapas, ranging from calamares to *pulpo* (octopus), as well as crab and hake. The cafeteria serves from 7 a.m. to 1 a.m.

Wesley House Restaurant, Main Street (tel. 78493), is run by the Methodist church. This must surely be the most economical place on the Rock for a square meal, costing around £4.50 ($6.75). From the serving counter, the meal of the day is likely to begin with a soup, then include a meat dish, such as braised steak, potatoes, and vegetable, and follow with a dessert. The place is open Monday to Friday from 9 a.m. to 8 p.m., on Saturday from 9 a.m. to 3 p.m.

Pat's Pantry and Bistro, 9-13 Governors Parade (tel. 74124), is one of the few places where you can sit outside in the pleasant square, opposite the Holiday Inn, savoring the sunshine and sampling the fare offered by Mr. and Mrs. Barnard. You can have just a coffee, a hamburger, or else a big meal from the menu which offers fresh salads, a T-bone steak, grills, coq au vin, and chicken suprême. I recently ordered a juicy melon followed by homemade vegetable soup, mixed grill, and apple pie and cream, all for £8.40 ($12.75). The place is open from 9 a.m. to 10 p.m. seven days a week.

Chaplin's Bistro, 150 Main St. (tel. 72832), managed by Steve Shaw, is open most days for lunch and dinner. It's a bright, cheerful place with a red-checked carpet, pictures of Charlie Chaplin on the walls, marble-top tables, and cane chairs. The blackboard shows specials, or there is a menu offering such dishes as swordfish and chips, veal à la crème, and filet steak. A meal costs about £7 ($10.50). In the evening, piano music is played in the bar.

A leading splurge restaurant is **Country Cottage,** 13-15 Giro's Passage, off Main Street across from the Roman Catholic cathedral (tel. 70084). There is a tiny bar where you pick your menu before taking one of the polished tables with flickering candles and high-backed settles. The à la carte menu includes house specials such as prawn cocktail with mushrooms and pineapple. Other dishes include seafood crêpe with cheese sauce and butter-roasted spring chicken, each main course served with fresh vegetables, potatoes, and hot garlic bread. A blackboard menu displays specials such as fresh salmon and other seasonal dishes, including lobster and duck. Desserts from the trolley are wheeled out, and unlimited coffee is served with chocolate mints. Meals cost from £10 ($15) up. The Cottage is open daily, except Monday, for dinner only from 7:30 to 11 p.m. Reservations are recommended.

English Tearooms, 9 Market Lane, is an attractive tea room with white tables set close together. The staff is friendly, and service is from 9 a.m. to 6 p.m. Monday to Friday (from 9 a.m. to noon on Saturday). Meals start with an English breakfast at £2.50 ($3.75), consisting of juice or cereal, bacon, egg and sausage, toast and marmalade, coffee or tea. Lunch will find you ordering farmhouse soup, eggs and bacon, omelets, or a ploughman's lunch. The set lunch at £3 ($4.50) is likely to feature soup or juice, a salad with ham or cheese, an omelet or spaghetti, ending with dessert, and tea or coffee. You can also drop in after sightseeing for an afternoon tea, British style, with sandwiches, costing around 50p (75¢).

Over in Catalán Bay, the **Village Inn** has an excellent seafood menu of snacks and tapas, priced from £1.80 ($2.70), to be eaten on the patio not 30 paces from the beach. They specialize in light meals—for example, swordfish, salad, and chips for £3.50 ($5.25).

Next door, **Seawave** also has salads and seafood snacks beginning at £1.50 ($2.25). Both are open most of the day and until midnight.

Also at Catalán Bay is the **Piccolo Bistro,** run by an English family—Sam, Edith, and daughters Karen and Paula—at 15 Sir Herbert Miles Rd. (tel. 72373), a bistro with sun-drenched terraces front and rear. The menu is traditional English, varied and at low prices. You can have pub-grub snacks or select from a full à la carte offering, including pizza, roast beef, steak-and-kidney pie, seafood, salad, and grills. Two local favorites are roast beef and Yorkshire pudding on Sunday and fish and chips daily. The bistro is open from noon to midnight seven days a week year round. A full dinner will cost around £10 ($15), including wine.

3. What to See and Do

Your starting point is the frontier at **La Línea,** Spain, just beyond the airport, called by the Gibraltarians the Garlic Wall. There is little to see other than two sets of gates, a rather bored Guardia Civil in the distance, and the odd dog who knows no frontiers. Cross the airport runway with the sea on either end. On your right you see the Victoria Stadium and Sports Center.

At Sun Dial, turn left (east) and you drive straight to **Eastern Beach,** then on to **Catalán Bay** and **Sandy Bay.** Between these two bays, the major Water Catchment Area rises to your right; an enormous area of mountainside, 34 acres of specially treated corrugated iron sheets. Thousands of tons of water are stored in reservoirs inside the Rock, where it is purified and pumped to the town and the docks for use by naval and other vessels in the harbor. Shortly after leaving Sandy Bay, you enter one of Gib's famous tunnels, the **Dudley Ward,** some 800 meters in length. It emerges above Boathouse Cove and the Gibraltar clay-pigeon shooting club on Europa Advance Road. The shooting club is on the left, and visitors are welcomed.

Continue on south to **Europa Point,** called by many the end of Europe. The most southerly point in Europe is actually Tarifa, Spain, which can be seen in the distance from the boat crossing to Tangier. At Europa Point is the lighthouse built in 1841 by Trinity House, the general lighthouse and pilotage authority for Great Britain, incorporated in 1514 by Henry VIII.

Standing by the light, you can see across the straits to the west of Ceuta to Jebel Musa (formerly Mount Abyla), the other Pillar of Hercules. Here also is Lloyd's of London's only foreign spotting station, recording every merchant ship to enter or leave the Mediterranean. Some 80 to 100 ships pass by during a 24-hour period, and also many yachtsmen voluntarily report their presence and intentions. Lloyd's will, on request, without charge, notify a friend or relative through their local yacht club.

On the Europa Road, back toward the town on the east of the Rock, is the **Chapel of Our Lady of Europa.** The chapel is much venerated and often saluted by passing vessels. Before the lighthouse was built, the small chapel kept a light burning day and night to warn passersby of the treacherous rocks and the narrowness of the passage.

From here you can travel through Keightley Way Tunnel to reach the 100-ton gun. It is said that the first time the British attempted to fire it, the shot remained in the cannon barrel. A volunteer was called for to crawl down the barrel, and the only one to step forward was the drummer boy. Probably with a hard push from behind, he climbed down the muzzle head-first and freed the cannon ball. For his bravery, he was promoted on the spot to sergeant, and was for years the youngest to hold this rank in the British army.

You now rejoin Europa Road by way of South Pavilion Road, then take a sharp right beyond the filling station to Witham's Road. At South Barracks Parade, keep right past the hospital to the casino on Europa Road. Turn right and take Engineer Road climbing toward the top of the Rock. As you climb, notice the large iron rings set in the rock walls, which were designed to haul the old naval cannons to the top. The cannons were hauled up and placed in such strategic positions as O'Hara's Battery just below the summit. After Engineer Road, turn left on to Queens Road until a sharp right-hand turn takes you to—

St. Michael's Cave (tel. 73130), which is open from 9:30 a.m. to 7 p.m. in summer (to 5:30 p.m. in winter). The Lower Cave and lake, open to the public under special permission, are connected to the Upper Cave (which is open to the public) by a passage spanning the 50- to 150-foot difference in depth. The endless stories of adventures in the labyrinth of passages that have formed naturally in the porous rock are an attraction to speleologists, and it is possible for even an amateur to travel miles underground. For further details, get in touch with the Speleological Section of the Gibraltar Society, known as the Gibraltar Caving Society, c/o the Tourist Office, Cathedral Square, Gibraltar. If you are fortunate enough to be in Gibraltar when the **son et lumière** program is on, I can recommend it as the evening entertainment. Otherwise, just enter the caves and listen to the carefully chosen music. Admission is £1 ($1.50) for adults, 60p (90¢) for children.

On leaving the caves, rejoin Queen's Road, then take the left fork on to Old Queen's Road to visit the **Rock Apes.** Although almost universally known as Barbary Apes, they are actually tailless monkeys (macaques). Legend has it that the first apes were either brought in by the Moors or that they found their way through a tunnel that linked St. Michael's Cave with Africa and that, when Africa and Europe were joined together, there were many more monkey packs. Today there are only two packs, some 40 apes in each. Each pack has its leader and its own den halfway up the Rock. Regular mealtimes—the apes are fed daily at 8 a.m. and 4 p.m. by a member of the Gibraltar Regiment—have helped to stop their descending to the town. It was not funny to find one of these still-wild creatures in your kitchen. The apes are carefully tended and protected by the British, since they have a saying that "when the apes leave the Rock, so will the British."

On along Old Queen's Road toward the mainland you pass beneath the cable car and then through a gap in the ruined Moorish Wall, the Wall of the Arabs. Little remains of this early fortification which ran from the sea to the summit, but you can still see its upper stages zigzagging toward the peak.

There are fine observation points along the road with views over the harbor and then toward Spain. At the end of the road you reach the **Upper Galleries,** which are open from 9:30 a.m. to 7 p.m. (earlier in winter). Admission is 80p ($1.20) for adults, 50p (75¢) for children (tel. 78007). These are not picture galleries, but large tunnels hewn in solid rock which are used mostly as vantage points for guns hauled up the Rock to protect it from the mainland.

St. George's Hall, the largest and best known of the galleries, was the site of a magnificent banquet given by Lord Napier in honor of U.S. Gen. Ulysses S. Grant.

The road winds back, past the waterworks, and Willis's Road takes you down to the **Tower of Homage** (tel. 71566) of the old **Moorish Castle,** which is open from 9:30 a.m. to 7 p.m. (closes earlier in winter). Admission is 30p (45¢) for adults, 20p (30¢) for children.

The tower and adjoining walls are floodlit, a magnet to the eyes of visitors and ships' passengers passing through the straits. Little remains of the original castle, 12 centuries old, other than parts of the outer walls running between the castle, the harbor, and the Moorish Pier, marking the considerable area of the castle and its defenses. The rest of the sights are best seen on foot, as parking is not easy in the town.

The **Gibraltar Museum,** Bomb House Lane (tel. 74289), is open Monday to Friday from 10 a.m. to 6 p.m., Saturday 10 a.m. to 1 p.m. Admission is 50p (75¢) for adults, 10p (15¢) for children. The museum is built over a Moorish bath in the town center, close to the Roman Catholic cathedral, just off Main Street. To anyone who has become intrigued with the history of Gibraltar, the exhibits are fascinating. There is a large scale model of the Rock, showing every dwelling existing in 1865. Other exhibits depict the history, from prehistoric cave-dwelling days to the present. There is a mass of artifacts, cannon balls, weapons, and military uniforms, plus a modern display on natural history.

The Convent and King's Chapel, Main Street, is the official residence of the governor, the Queen's representative. The Changing of the Guard takes place every Tuesday at 10:30 a.m.—a ceremonial occasion with full band and the governor and his family on the balcony to take the salute. The convent was so named in 1531 when a wealthy Spaniard gave the Franciscan friars land, materials, and money to build a convent and a chapel for the burial of himself and his family. There is no sign today of their graves. King's Chapel is open to view, but the convent, a private home, is not. There is a 1,000-year-old Dragon Tree in the grounds which you can see if you look down from the hill behind the Roman Catholic cathedral.

Main Street runs from Casemates Square and proceeds between old buildings and modern stores past the Main Post Office and on to the Piazza, a colonnaded entrance to a paved square where people drink, children play, and desultory business is conducted. There is a flower-seller as well as a newspaper kiosk, ice-cream vendor, a cafeteria, an information office, a taxi rank, and, very important, public toilets.

Narrow lanes and streets lead into Main Street. Do wander along them, as there is so much of the past history of the Rock to see between the high walls.

You come next to the square facing the Roman Catholic cathedral, which is a converted mosque, an impressive structure, and one of the first buildings on the Rock. Then it's on to the Cathedral Square with the Anglican cathedral facing a green garden and the harbor. Also in this square is the **Tourist Office** (tel. 76400), where an enthusiastic staff has a vast selection of brochures on the various attractions of the Rock. They will produce information on almost any question you can think to ask.

Note: The main Information Centre of the Tourist Board is at the Piazza on Main Street (tel. 75555). Hours are 9:30 a.m. to 6 p.m. Monday to Friday, and 10 a.m. to 2 p.m. on Saturday. A team of charming and helpful young women will dispense information, maps, and other free publications.

Farther on you come to King's Chapel and then the convent, and the street ends at the other end of town at Southport Gates, built into the defense wall of Charles V of Spain.

Just outside the town gate, where there was once a drawbridge and a moat, is the **Trafalgar Cemetery,** a charming garden blazing with geraniums. Tombstones commemorate many who fell at the Battles of Algeciras, Trafalgar, Cádiz, and Málaga in the early years of the 19th century.

Farther on up Europa Road, the **Alameda Gardens,** now covered with subtropical trees and flowers, were once the site from which the Arabs drew water and piped it through the town to Waterport to supply their ships. The Spanish also drew water there. Nowadays there are monuments to the Duke of Wellington and to General Eliott, an open-air theater, tennis courts, and crazy golf.

On Red Sands Road just below the gardens is the Lower Station of the **cable car** which rises to the top of the Rock. The cost is £2.50 ($3.75) to the top, a round-trip charge. You may prefer to walk along the path to the highest point, 1,398, and then down to St. Michael's Cave or along the ridge to Poca Roca Cave and down to the road near the Upper Galleries. The cable car also stops at the Apes Den halfway up the cliff. At the top is a refreshment place.

GETTING AROUND: There are four basic ways of getting around the places of interest on the Upper Rock—self-drive car, taxi, tour bus, or a combination of cable car, public bus, and on foot. The last, however, involves much uphill walking and is only recommended for the young and strong of heart who also have the time.

If you want a self-drive car, **Budget Rent-A-Car,** Peninsular Ltd., P.O. Box 327, Gibraltar (tel. 79666), will rent you a small Vauxhall documented for Spain as well as the Rock for £109 ($163.50) per week, including Green Card insurance, bail bond, and collision damage waiver, all necessary for Spain. **Pegasus RentaCar,** 238 Main St. (tel. 70392) has a special weekend rate of £40 ($60) for a Fiat Uno or Opel Corsa, fully documented for a quick trip into Spain. All rates include unlimited mileage. At La Línea, just steps from the frontier gate, **Gibralturis,** Acera Parque Princesa Sofia (tel. 76-11-93), offers a Panda Sprint on an unlimited mileage basis for the weekend at 6,600 pesetas ($46.20), 2,150 pesetas ($15.05) per day for three days or more. Again insurance is included. Renting here avoids a possibly tedious wait to drive across the frontier.

A complete **taxi tour,** which takes about three hours and includes Europa Point, the east coast area, St. Michael's Cave, the Apes, Upper Galleries, the Moorish castle, and the Spanish frontier costs £14 ($21) for up to four persons. Rental charges are also available for longer periods. All taxi drivers are required to carry and display a tariff card. Tariffs are set by the government. Calls for a taxi should be made to the Gibraltar Taxi Association, 12 Cannon Lane (tel. 70027).

Gibraltar Motorways, 75 Irish Town (tel. 77228), offers a Rock Tour daily at 11 a.m., costing £5 ($7.50). The three or four bus companies running regular services from the city around the Rock and between other points on the peninsula charge 20p (30¢) for adults to go anywhere on Gibraltar, 10p (15¢) for children under 12.

DOLPHINS AND 'ROUND THE ROCK: In Sheppard's Marina at the bottom of Glacis Road lies a fleet of yachts and cruisers of all shapes and sizes. Mary and Mike Lawrence live on **Cosmic Star,** an ocean-going sailer in which they planned to travel around the world. They got as far as Gibraltar and stayed. Mike now owns a deep-sea fishing boat with which he operates 2½- to 3-hour cruises out into the Bay of Algeciras to see the dolphins. Over the past 15 years Mike has become their friend and, on good days, great schools of more than 400 arrive to leap around the boat. Some are so friendly you can stroke their backs.

It is a photographer's paradise, and a free drink is offered to the first passenger to spot a dolphin. Afterward you cruise around Europa Point under the lighthouse and along the east coast of the Rock, past romantic cave entrances, to Sandy Bay and Catalán Bay before returning to harbor. Mike, ex-Royal Air Force, gives an amusing and factual commentary. He takes various friends and relatives as crew. Beer and Cokes are carried on board for sale at nominal prices. The trip costs £10 ($15) per person. Telephone 71914 for departure times and other information.

WRECK AND REEF DIVES: **Gibaqua Ltd.,** 6 Rosebay Court, Naval Hospital Road (tel. 79763), offers wreck and reef dives to qualified divers. Among the sights are SS *Excellent,* sunk in 1888 and lying upside down, affording a good swim through from amidships to bow, and a Bristol Bombay aircraft wrecked in 1939 and lying in 115 to 140 feet of water. Reefs include the Seven Sisters with excellent marine life, Los Pecos, and Europa Reef. The cost per dive is £10 ($15), or six dives for £55 ($82.50). There is an introductory Resort Course for the non-diver at £32 ($48). Equipment can be rented, costing from £1.70 ($2.55) a dive for a full wet suit, 60p (90¢) for mask, snorkel, and fins. All rates include air, cylinder, and weights.

BIRDWATCHING: With the cliffs of the Bosporus, Gibraltar is one of the major staging points in Europe for migrating birds. The craggy cliffs are the breeding grounds of kestrels and alpine swifts, peregrines, and the more exotic Sardinian warblers, blue rock thrush, and Barbary partridge. Honey buzzards, booted and short-toed eagles, Egyptian vultures, and white storks, plus a multitude of seabirds, pass through each year. Warblers, chiffchaffs, redstarts, robins, and nightingales "fall" here in spring and autumn. More than 200 species have been recorded on the Rock. Take the cable car to the top and walk in the less populated areas.

There are also more than 800 species of wildflowers, some quite exotic.

PHILATELY: There is a current set of stamps as well as five commemorative issues each year. A special sales counter at the General Post Office on Main Street is open from 9 a.m. to 1:15 p.m. and 2:15 to 4:30 p.m. Monday to Thursday, closing at 4 p.m. on Friday. Hours may differ slightly in summer. The Post Office also operates a mail order service. Those interested should write to the Gibraltar Philatelic Bureau, P.O. Box 5662, Gibraltar.

SWIMMING: Outside the Police Station in Irish Town, a notice states which beaches are safe to swim at that day. Most beaches have changing rooms and, for a small cost, showers and tents can be had.

4. The Rock After Dark

There are four cinemas with two programs nightly and matinees on weekends. The program is changed twice weekly, so if it rains you have a selection of films to see.

DISCOS: Penelope's, 8 Corral Rd. (tel. 70462), is built in one of the old defense walls, a cavern with a long friendly bar for drinks and good snacks and plenty of room just to sit and hear the music. When you enter, expect to be greeted in a warm and friendly manner by one of the dynamic trio running the club, Charlie, Elio, or Joe. There are several caves with low lights, low stools, and tables for intimate conversation, and another cave, brilliant with lights and vibrating with noise for freaking out.

Admission is free for couples, whereas stags pay from £2 ($3). You'll be refused entry if you're wearing jeans, or are untidy and/or noisy. During the summer months the terrace restaurant is open, and you can enjoy live entertainment. Snacks might include the ever-popular pinchitos (Moroccan kebabs). A normal drink, such as a Scotch and soda, will cost from £1 ($1.50).

Cornwall's, Cornwall's Lane (tel. 72011), is probably the only place on the Rock where you disco-dance and eat after midnight. Bob Massey, the owner, found this Moorish building and converted it perfectly, preserving the arched vaults in the disco and an original plaque dating from 1789 in the bar. Upstairs is the Bistro where visitors are admitted free if there's room. It serves soups, tapas, stews, pâtés, chili, and grilled steaks. Downstairs in the old cellars is a membership-only disco, a very attractive bar with brass footrail and copper-covered tables in the split-level seating area. The bar is beneath the arches and the old beams of this building. You go through the bar to a mirrored dance floor with its constant pulsing beat. Basket meals, such as chicken and scampi, are available throughout the evening downstairs. They have a 22-hour license, and, in summer, will stay open longer than ever. Membership is reasonable: £1 ($1.50) per person nightly. Drinks cost from £1.25 ($1.88).

GAMBLING: The Casino and Royale Restaurant, 7 Europa Road (tel. 76666), is entered from the street, through a cave bar with trickling streams and rock pools. Guests head upstairs to the large room where slot machines clang and rattle from 10 a.m. There is a wide terrace overlooking the lights of the harbor where dinner is served by candlelight, and bars are open all day. The Pigalle Night Club provides Bingo seven nights a week. The gaming room provides games such as roulette, baccarat, craps, black jack, boule, and chemin de fer. It is open daily from 8 p.m. and there is no limit on the stakes. Entry fee is £1 ($1.50). On Saturday the management holds barbecue dinner dances under the stars in the Japanese Gardens, surrounded by tropical flowers and waterfalls. The cost is from £10 ($15).

The casino disco operates every Friday and Saturday from 10 p.m. to 2 a.m., charging £2 ($3) for entrance.

Chapter XVI

THE CANARY ISLANDS

1. Gran Canaria (Las Palmas)
2. Tenerife
3. La Palma
4. Lanzarote
5. Fuerteventura

OFF THE COAST of West Africa lies the spring-year-round cluster of islands and islets known as the Canaries. According to ancient myth these Spanish-ruled islands may well be the peaks of the lost continent of Atlantis (a position also claimed by the Portuguese-controlled Azores). Legends have also referred to the islands as the Elysian Fields and the Garden of Hesperides.

This outpost of Spanish civilization in the Atlantic is dubbed the "Islas Afortunadas," or the fortunate islands. The archipelago, 70 miles from Africa, consists of seven principal islands, the largest being Tenerife. Others include Gran Canaria, Lanzarote, Fuerteventura, La Palma, Gomera, and Hierro.

Geographically part of Africa, since 1927 the Canaries have been two provinces of Spain, Las Palmas and Santa Cruz de Tenerife. The islands are volcanic, and eruptions were frequent as late as the 19th century. At one time the archipelago was believed to have been a single land mass.

HISTORY: The first Canarians were the tall, fair-haired Guanches, who were cave-dwellers. Their origins remain an enigma, although some people believe they migrated from the southwest of France around 2000 B.C. After colonizing the islands, the Guanches appear to have lost their art of navigation and did not even travel among the islands. This accounts perhaps for the different characteristics of the denizens of each islet.

The Guanches worshipped the summits of the mountains, which were considered the homes of their deities—Teide on Tenerife, Bentaiga on Gran Canaria. Their kings and nobles were embalmed, and many interesting relics remain from those days to be examined in the museums on the islands.

Colonizing Romans discovered and explored the islands in 30 B.C. The Romans charted the flora and fauna and took back with them two Canary dogs. In 1016 the Arabs came looking for slaves, particularly on Lanzarote, the island nearest to Africa.

Then in 1402, Jean de Bethencourt, a Norman, led his first expedition to the islands. After conquering Lanzarote and building a fortress at Fuerteventura, he returned to Spain. Henry III of Castile financed his next expedition. By 1483, after a five-year struggle, Gran Canaria fell to the Spaniards. Tenerife and La Palma succumbed by 1496 to attacks ordered by the Catholic monarchs, Isabella and Ferdinand. The islands were, at last, Spanish.

Dutch and English sorties in the 16th and 17th centuries rocked the islands. In 1797 Lord Nelson lost an arm shot off by a cannonball during an attack on Santa Cruz de Tenerife. That cannon is still shown in the town today.

GENERAL TIPS: Food prices tend to be higher on imported goods from Spain. Liquor is duty free and therefore cheap, with the exception of whisky. The local drink is rum, distilled throughout the islands. Wines are generally imported from the mainland, but there are some interesting local vintages as well. Ask for the Malvasia of Lanzarote and the mellow reds from Monte in Gran Canaria.

In shopping, it's best to purchase luxury goods in the free port of Las Palmas. Store hours are from 9 a.m. to 1 p.m. and 4 to 7 p.m. Closings are usually on Saturday afternoon, all day on Sunday, and on feast days. Bazaars on the islands remain open as long as there is someone around to buy.

Outside the main towns, the local shops and bars are often unobtrusive in the extreme. Look for a half-open, green-painted door with a faded Coca-Cola sign. It may take some nerve to walk into the dark interiors of these bars, as strangers stick mainly to the well-trodden tourist paths. Once in, however, you'll be treated courteously; your drink will be enormous, and everyone will try to tell you where to go and what to see.

Water is plentiful in both Las Palmas and Tenerife. Outside big towns, reliance on rainwater is heavy. However, you'd better not drink it, unless you have a cast-iron stomach. Bottled water with or without gas can be purchased everywhere at a small cost. In Lanzarote there is a shortage of water, and most of it is supplied to outlying areas from the *potabilizadoras* which distill sea water. Unless you know the source of your water, it's best to avoid getting sick by sticking to the bottled variety.

As for food, the large hotels and tourist restaurants offer dishes tempered to the international palate. If you wish to sample the local delicacies, you must seek out the places where the Spaniards eat and join them. Fresh fish is the most recommended bill of fare. *Sama, vieja,* and *burro* are native to the area. Fish is usually grilled or broiled and served with *mojo picón,* a sauce made with olive oil, vinegar, salt, hot peppers, and such spices as coriander and cumin.

Puchero is the main meat dish, a stew of any and every vegetable with meat. Many thick soups are recommended. Sometimes these soups are difficult to tell from the main dish because of their virility and substance. The best known one is *potaje de berros y jaramagos* (made of watercress and herbs). Spanish omelets or tortillas are common. The celebrated wrinkled potatoes are *papas arrugadas,* potatoes boiled in their skins and served with a hot sauce. Something to try as well is *gofio.* It's a loaf made from ground toasted corn or wheat and used to sop up a gravy or sauce. It would make a health-food addict jump for joy, and is not unlike the couscous of North Africa. A favorite local dish is *sancocho,* a stew of salted fish with potatoes. *Churros,* a sort of doughnut, very crisp and deep-fried, is served hot with your morning coffee. Some good local cheeses are *guia* in the Gran Canaria and a bland white goat's cheese, *queso blanco,* served with wine, usually as a pre-dinner bar snack on Lanzarote.

Of course, the main reason to go to the Canaries is sunshine. There is a saying in Las Palmas that there is sunshine somewhere on the island every day. For that reason in both Gran Canaria and Tenerife, hotel complexes stand on the southern sandy dunes and beaches.

The average temperatures range from 64° Fahrenheit in January to 76°

Fahrenheit in August. The islands are subjected to southwesterly winds across the Atlantic which account for the muggy atmosphere in the north of the islands where the wind has to cross the mountains. Lanzarote and Fuerteventura are not affected—they have no central mountains and are exposed to the warm dry winds from Africa.

Each of the four major tourist islands now has a **Tourist Information Hotline to the Sun** on which you will be given up-to-date tourist information. Don't expect things to be explained in clear English, but you will probably be able to pick up the essentials of the events. The numbers are: Gran Canaria, 26-46-23; Tenerife, 38-60-00; Lanzarote, 81-18-60; and Fuerteventura, 85-12-62.

Throughout the islands there are manned telephone booths where you can call all over the world and pay for the call at the end of the conversation. However, you must pay a deposit before the call to cover possible costs in case you thought about running away without paying—or just forgot. Don't be offended when you're asked to pay in advance.

Regarding water sports and waterborne activities, many of the businesses or groups involved do not have addresses or phone numbers. People are expected to go to the place mentioned, and they will find all is in operation.

GETTING THERE: **Iberia,** the national airline, has flights from many European cities and connections via Madrid to North America. These flights can often be incorporated as a stopover into ongoing air tickets for very little extra cost. Consult a travel agent for the best bargain.

Iberia also operates a "mini tariff" on its domestic routes, including the Canary Islands, at a discount of 40% of the normal charge. Tickets must be purchased and paid for before the trip begins. They are valid for three months, and your schedule must allow for a Saturday night between the beginning and end of the journey. You may also face cancellation charges and amendment fees. Seats are sold at the reduced fares subject to availability.

In addition, steamship services from Spain and other ports run to the Canaries. Ferryboats from the mainland of Spain are all operated by the **Compañía Trasmediterránea,** which has put its two most modern vessels on the Canaries run. The *J.J. Sister* and the *Manuel Soto* leave Cádiz every Friday at 9 p.m., arriving at Las Palmas on Sunday morning and at Santa Cruz de Tenerife Sunday evening. The vessels then return to Las Palmas Sunday night and sail overnight from there to Lanzarote. The return voyage leaves Lanzarote on Monday night and calls at Las Palmas and Tenerife on the way back to Cádiz and the Mediterranean ports of Málaga, Almería, Palma de Majorca, and Genoa in Italy. A trip from Cádiz to Las Palmas, Tenerife, or Lanzarote ranges in price from 31,890 pesetas ($223.23) for a single cabin with shower and toilet to 11,960 pesetas ($83.72) for a berth in a showerless, four-berth cabin. A berth in a two-person cabin with shower is from 26,470 ($185.29) to 28,700 pesetas ($200.90) per person, 26,470 pesetas ($185.29) per person in a three-berth accommodation with shower, and 22,000 pesetas ($154) per person in a four-berth cabin with shower. Return fares are the same amounts as one way. The one-way charge for a small car is 10,700 pesetas ($74.90).

1. Gran Canaria (Las Palmas)

Almost circular in shape, Gran Canaria is often described as a continent in miniature, because such a wide variety of scenery is packed into so small a place. The topography is dominated by deep ravines, running from the rugged heights of the central massif down to the edge of the sea.

The dachshund-shaped provincial capital is **Las Palmas,** the major metropolis on Gran Canaria. It's also the largest port in Spain. The town is roughly

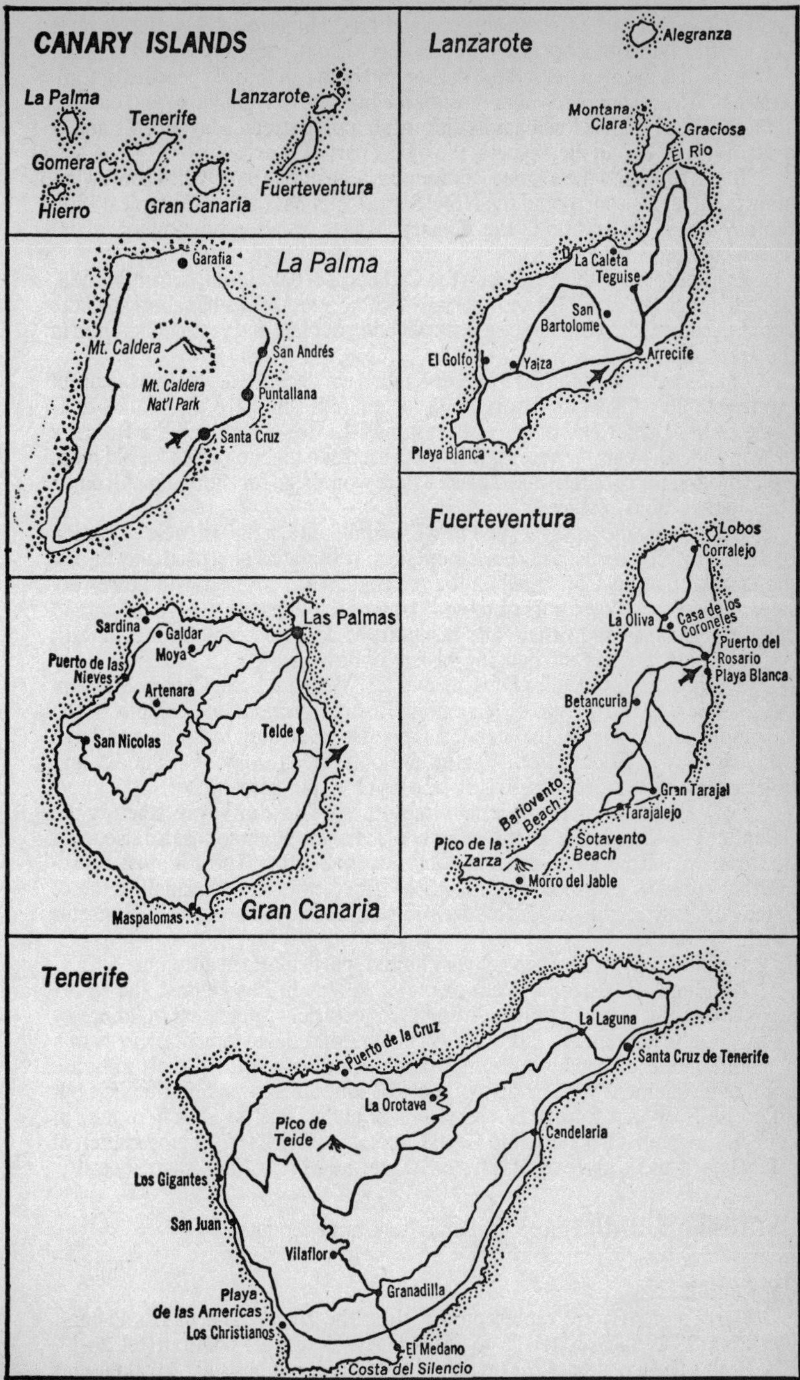
CANARY ISLANDS
La Palma
Tenerife
Lanzarote
Gomera
Hierro
Gran Canaria
Fuerteventura
Lanzarote
Alegranza
Montana Clara
Graciosa
El Rio
La Caleta
Teguise
San Bartolome
El Golfo
Yaiza
Arrecife
Playa Blanca
La Palma
Garafia
Mt. Caldera
Mt. Caldera Nat'l Park
San Andrés
Puntallana
Santa Cruz
Fuerteventura
Lobos
Corralejo
La Oliva
Casa de los Coroneles
Puerto del Rosario
Playa Blanca
Betancuria
Barlovento Beach
Gran Tarajal
Tarajalejo
Pico de la Zarza
Sotavento Beach
Morro del Jable
Las Palmas
Sardina
Galdar
Moya
Puerto de las Nieves
Artenara
San Nicolas
Telde
Maspalomas
Gran Canaria
Tenerife
La Laguna
Puerto de la Cruz
Santa Cruz de Tenerife
La Orotava
Pico de Teide
Candelaria
Los Gigantes
San Juan
Vilaflor
Granadilla
Playa de las Americas
Los Christianos
El Medano
Costa del Silencio

divided into two parts: the harbor area and Las Palmas town. The **Puerto de la Luz** is a free bunkering port used by passenger liners, cargo boats, and tankers. Adjoining it is the area behind the harbor and between the two beaches of **Canteras** and **Alcaravaneras,** where most of the big hotels, nightclubs, and bazaars are found. Las Palmas town has its elegant shopping street, **Mayor de Triana,** a residential areas, and the **Vegueta,** the oldest part of the city.

To the south lies the **Parque Doramus,** a large public park with a zoo, swimming pool, tennis courts, and the Hotel Santa Catalina, built in the typical 18th-century style. In addition, the **Canary Village** is an exhibition of island architecture and folklore.

Farther south in the Vegueta is the **Cathedral of Santa Ana,** still unfinished. Its style ranges from a lofty and spacious Gothic interior to a neoclassic façade. For 25 pesetas (18¢) you can see a fine collection of plate and vestments stored in the Treasury.

Opposite the cathedral is **Plaza de Santa Ana,** decorated with two beautiful bronze statues of Canary dogs, the fierce animals that gave the islands their name. At the other end of the square stands the Town Hall and the Bishop's palace. Like all Spanish squares, this one is used as a meeting place for old men, a playground for children, and a place where women go for shopping. All day it rings to the sound of voices.

A short distance away is the **Plaza Espiritú Santo,** a tiny triangle of garden bordered by busy roads. There is a fountain and a small chapel used only during the feast of Corpus Christi, when the pavements are covered with flower designs. This is the oldest part of town. Many of the houses have typical carved wooden balconies and ornate and heavy front doors opening onto cool dark courtyards with palms and hanging baskets of flowers.

On the corner of Calles Dr. Chil and Dr. Verneau is the **Canary Museum** (tel. 31-56-00), with a large collection of Guanche remains and exhibits of the geography and biology of the island. It is open from 10 a.m. to 1 p.m. and 3 to 6 p.m. Monday to Friday (from 10 a.m. to noon on Saturday). On Sunday and holidays it is closed. Admission is 50 pesetas (35¢) per person.

Columbus lived here while he fitted out his ships for voyages across the Atlantic. The **Casa de Colón,** the former palace of the governors, is a museum of fine arts, open from 9 a.m. to 1 p.m. daily except Sunday. There is also a museum that contains maps and documents of his voyages and the small statue of Santa Ana to which he prayed for success in his journey. Admission is 25 pesetas (18¢).

Warning: Las Palmas can get very humid, particularly in autumn.

Although most people seem to prefer to stay in Las Palmas, the resort areas are in the south. You won't find architecturally interesting buildings or many good restaurants in this area. As in Tenerife, development consists of a conglomeration of concrete "boxes" constructed as hotels. There's in-house hotel entertainment such as discos, movies, folklore shows, and the like, but little else is offered to interest the visitor at night. The beaches here are, of course, the main attraction, and Gran Canaria's south has a lengthy stretch of sandy beach and is more southerly, and therefore a bit warmer, than Tenerife.

GETTING AROUND: Transportation is basic but adequate.

Car Rentals

Hertz and **Avis** are represented both at the airport and in Las Palmas. Hertz is at 27-29 Sagasta (tel. 26-45-76), and Avis is at José M. Duran (tel. 26-13-62). Both offer a compact car on an unlimited-mileage basis for 3,050 pesetas

($21.35) to 3,350 pesetas ($23.45) a day. **Carop** operates through Autos Maroso, 22 Venegas, Las Palmas (tel. 36-30-22), at 2,350 pesetas ($16.50) a day. Tax and insurance are extra. The availability of small cars is very limited, so it's wise to reserve one well in advance. Otherwise, you may be forced to pay for a more expensive car.

Motorcycles

This is a popular means of touring the island, especially for young people. Motorcycles are rented from **Puíg,** 4 Montevideo (tel. 27-49-01). A Vespa scooter costs 1,500 pesetas ($10.50) per day or 9,000 pesetas ($63) per week. A minimum deposit of 4,000 pesetas ($28) is required. Many of the hotels on the southern part of the land also have bicycles and tandems for rent.

Taxis

There are ranks throughout Las Palmas and the airport. Rates are inexpensive and taxis are metered. Drivers are allowed to charge extra for luggage. If you arrive by boat, it's best to ask for the price of a particular trip, as drivers are entitled to collect various surcharges for the transporting of bags and extra passengers. A charge ranging from 20 pesetas (14¢) to 50 pesetas (35¢) is levied, depending on the size of the baggage.

From the airport to Las Palmas, a taxi ride costs 1,800 pesetas ($12.60); from the airport to Maspalomas, 2,000 pesetas ($14); and from the air terminal to the center of the city, 250 pesetas ($1.75). From the harbor to the city center depends on which jetty you take, as the rates range from 380 pesetas ($2.66) to 750 pesetas ($5.25).

Tariffs increase after dark. Always ask how much the fare is before you get in. Prices are posted at the airport, showing rates to various parts of the island. Taxi drivers also have a price list for out-of-town meter areas, and all tariffs are strictly controlled by the government. If you get cheated, it's your own fault.

For radio taxis, call 25-07-77 or 20-21-00.

Buses

There is a very efficient and frequent bus service throughout the island. The main bus station is on Calle Raphael Cabrera opposite the **Parque San Telmo.** Information on times and prices can be obtained by telephoning 36-86-31 for service to the south, and 36-01-79 for central and northern information, but you'd better speak Spanish. Timetables and prices are also available at the tourist office, Parque Santa Catalina, Las Palmas.

The cost of a journey from the airport to the air terminal in Las Palmas is 125 pesetas (88¢). You can buy vouchers for use on the buses from various points in Las Palmas.

Besides regular bus service, a microbus system is operated by a cooperative on the island. These microbuses are known to everybody as *gua-guas* (pronounced "waa-waas"). Don't ask for a microbus, as no one will know what you're talking about. These small buses depart from various points in Las Palmas. Expect to pay about two-thirds of the big bus fare. But be warned, gua-guas stop at almost every street corner and are a strictly local service. The minimum charge is 35 pesetas (25¢), rising according to the distance you travel. The best way to learn more about this economical service is to use the general information leaflet available at the tourist office.

Tartanas

These are horse-drawn carriages available sometimes on the Calle Simón Bolívar, opposite the Plaza Santa Catalina. Most routes are slow and gentle, following the Generalísimo Franco. Negotiate the price before you embark—around 400 pesetas ($2.80) per person for one hour or 1,000 pesetas ($7) for four persons. The one-hour drive includes the docks, market area, and seafront.

Excursions

Cyrasa, Intersol, and other companies operate excursions by coach with a guide to Bandama (half day), Tejeda (full day), and within the city itself. The trip to Tejeda, without lunch, is 1,350 pesetas ($9.45). A full-day trip to Maspalomas goes for 2,000 pesetas ($14), excluding lunch, and a full day's jaunt to Puerto Rico and Sioux City, without lunch, comes to 2,300 pesetas ($16.10). A day trip by air to Lanzarote, including a tour of the island and lunch, costs 15,000 pesetas ($105); and to Tenerife by jetfoil, including a coach drive through the mountains and villages, is 7,500 pesetas ($52.50).

WHERE TO STAY: The **tourist office,** at the Parque Santa Catalina (tel. 26-46-23), has a list of accommodations in all price ranges. Hours are from 9 a.m. to 2 p.m. and 5 to 7 p.m. (on Saturday from 9 a.m. to 2 p.m.; closed Sunday and holidays).

Paradors, previously mentioned in the section on mainland Spain, are the most popular form of hotels in the Canaries. For those who wish to reserve in advance, just one letter or telephone call to Madrid will solve the problem. Address your request to **Paradors in Spain,** 18 Veláquez, Madrid 1 (tel. 435-97-00). The office is open Monday to Friday from 9 a.m. to 1:30 p.m. and 4:30 to 7:30 p.m.

Hotel Cristina, 6 Gomera, Playa de las Canteras (tel. 82-75-00), is a big, modern hotel just a road back from the Canteras promenade. A single or double rents for 12,000 pesetas ($84). You can dine here for 3,500 pesetas ($24.50) in the hotel's restaurant, or you might prefer to take your meals at the snackbar, Trident's. There's also a bar. The hotel's swimming pool overlooks the beach, and for evening entertainment, you can try the disco, El Coto.

Hotel Faycan, 61 Nicolas Estevanez (tel. 27-06-50), stands just half a block from Canteras beach. If you look sideways, you can see the sea from many of the rooms. You enter a typical dark, cool lobby, with a convenient bar patronized by locals and residents alike. The clean, simple rooms are equipped with private baths and toilets, renting for 2,800 pesetas ($19.60) in a single, from 3,500 pesetas ($24.50) in a double. If you're traveling with a child, ask about a three-bedded room, going for 3,000 pesetas ($21). Tariffs include a serve-yourself breakfast.

Residencia Verol, 25 Sagasta (tel. 26-21-04), is one block from Canteras beach. The place at first looks like a bar, as the entrance is right on the corner. You climb steps to a bustling coffeeshop with an ever-flickering TV. Sandwiches and hamburgers are sold here, along with coffee and beer. The tiny reception to Verol is behind the bar, although it has a small entrance from the street on its own. Safe-deposit boxes are provided for residents—not so much as an indication of danger, but as a precaution against petty theft. Rooms are basic, but adequate nevertheless. Most units contain private bath or shower, and the prices are very reasonable: 3,000 pesetas ($21) in a single or double. An elevator leads to the upper floors.

Hotel Gran Canaria, 38 Paseo Canteras (tel. 27-50-78), is grander than many of my choices. It's right in the center of life, overlooking the beach, although many of its rooms don't have a sea view. It has plenty of lounges and a restaurant serving international dishes. Singles with shower rent for 4,200 pesetas ($29.40) in high season, and doubles with bath go for 5,800 pesetas ($40.60).

A main meal such as lunch or dinner costs 1,600 pesetas ($11.20). Gran Canaria is well situated and comfortable.

The **Reina Isabel,** 40 Alfredo L. Jones (tel. 26-01-00), right on Canteras beach, is the splurge place to stay in Las Palmas, the only hotel actually on the water. You can have a room with a city view or with a sea view over the Paseo Marítima, with occasional glimpses of Mount Teide on Tenerife. Singles range from 7,000 pesetas ($49). Doubles rent for 10,500 pesetas ($73.50). Sea-view rooms carry a 400-peseta ($2.80) supplement. A four-course meal in the Reina Garden restaurant costs 2,800 pesetas ($19.60), or you can order a sandwich of cheese, roast beef, chicken, or veal Pepito (a sort of minute steak).

The ground-floor lounge, just off the hotel lobby, is elegant, with large, comfortable armchairs. The covered open terrace, the Reina Bar, is open from 10:30 a.m. to midnight. The terrace is filled with potted plants and bamboo furniture, a fountain splashes, and cool breezes come in from the sea across the sandy Canteras beach. Opening onto the promenade is the Captain's Cabin, a replica of an English timbered pub. It's open from 8 a.m. to midnight. Irish coffee goes for 250 pesetas ($1.75) and half a pint of draft beer is 125 pesetas (88¢). They also have toasted sandwiches. Reina Isabel has become the best five-star hotel in Las Palmas.

Hotel Los Frailes, Tafira (tel. 35-12-06). Some 21 years ago Thomas Hutley, who had owned a pub near Henley, England, visited Las Palmas, liked what he saw, and bought Los Frailes. He has been there ever since. The hotel is reached along a tree-lined avenue. A monastery since before the Spaniards arrived on the island, the building still retains the cloisters. The dining room was the old chapel. Set in extensive gardens, the converted hotel surrounds a patio where you can sit and admire the view in peace, yet you are only 20 minutes from the center of Las Palmas. In the evening you can hear crickets chirping in the bushes. There is a large lounge with comfortable chairs and television (in Spanish), and the bar has been added to the old building with Canary-style furnishings. Rooms are comfortable; some have a private bath, and rent for 1,000 pesetas ($7) in a single, 1,500 pesetas ($10.50) in a double. A lunch or dinner costs 1,000 pesetas ($7). A bell rings to summon you to meals. This is a delightful retreat away from the bustle of the harbor area, and it's an ideal spot from which to tour the interior of the island.

Hotel Don Gregory, 11 Las Dalias (tel. 76-26-62), is my super-splurge hotel for the south of the Gran Canaria. It's a beachside hotel that offers many free facilities in sunny San Agustín, a fast developing area. The Don Gregory manages to provide an oasis in the jungle of high-rise hotels and apartment blocks. A double goes for 6,500 pesetas ($45.50) per person in low season, 12,000 pesetas ($84) per person in high season. Singles range from 8,000 pesetas ($56) to 15,000 pesetas ($105). You can enjoy breakfast on a covered patio by the pool. Lunch, also buffet, costs 3,000 pesetas ($21), and for that same price you can have a more formal, four-course dinner in the evening. For full board, add 2,500 pesetas ($17.50) per person to the room rate.

Bedrooms all have balconies overlooking the sea, and are decorated in British nautical style, with much use of wood, brass, and tartan furnishings. Well-equipped bathrooms provide plenty of space for your bits and pieces. The built-in radios work, and there is a good telephone service for quick room service. Included in your room rate are a wind-sheltered, heated swimming pool, a tennis court, pedalos, catamaran sailing boats, and scuba-diving in the swimming pool. You can also borrow fishing rods if you wish to join the Spaniards fishing off the sandy beach. Golf is available free at Maspalomas, but you must get there yourself—it's not far. Moored out in the deeper water of the bay is a diving raft.

Your evening is occupied with cocktails, a well-cooked dinner, and then films in the lounge, or perhaps live band disco-dancing in the bar overlooking the pool, a fashion show, or other entertainment. The staff is friendly and efficient.

Hotel Residencia Olympia, 1 Dr. Grau Bassas (tel. 26-17-20), is a clean establishment in a street that runs to the Canteras beach. The hosts may not speak much English, but their welcome is warm. All rooms have a bath, shower, toilet, phone, and cable music. Singles cost 2,500 pesetas ($17.50) to 2,900 pesetas ($20.30); doubles, 3,000 pesetas ($21) to 3,400 pesetas ($23.80). There's a bright snackbar where breakfast and light meals are served.

Apartamentos Aguas Verdes, 47 Playa de las Canteras (tel. 26-84-50), is a rarity in the islands, an apartment block where accommodations are not committed year round to tour operators from Europe. All apartments have a balcony, some overlooking the beach and the sea, as well as a bath, kitchen with hot and cold running water, phone, and piped-in music. A swimming pool and solarium are on the roof, and the place is near food and provision stores if you go in for self-catering. A double with sea view goes for 4,000 pesetas ($28) per day, with accommodations at the back costing 3,000 pesetas ($21) for a double.

WHERE TO EAT: Las Palmas is divided into two main sections: the southern industrial, mercantile part, containing the cathedral and the oldest part of town; the northern, resort area with the Puerto de la Luz, the bazaars, the Canteras and Alcaravaneras beaches, plus the main hotels and restaurants. There are many places to eat, providing food from all countries at prices ranging from "give-away" to extravagant. My choices follow.

Kim's Steak House, 19 Alfredo L. Jones, Puerto de la Luz. You're assured of a welcome from Joan and Gordon Gray, as well as good food. Even the locals eat here, as the steakhouse has been established for many years now. The menu of the day, which changes daily, goes for 750 pesetas ($5.25). If you want to order à la carte, I'd recommend a New York-cut steak, tournedos Rossini, or filet béarnaise. The Grays specialize in coffees—Irish, Jamaican, Mexican, Spanish, or American. The house wine is Siglo. Expect to pay about 1,500 pesetas ($10.50) for a meal, not including the cost of your wine. Mr. Gray was a film editor in England, and later he helped start independent television there. He has many interesting tales to relate about the beginnings of commercial television in England.

El Cortijo, 3 Diderot (tel. 27-59-55), is a small place in a street away from the main promenades of the Puerto de la Luz, within walking distance. *El jefe,* a *maestro asador,* brought many recipes with him when he came from northern Spain. He is a big man who obviously enjoys his own cooking and throws himself wholeheartedly into the running of his restaurant. Try his homemade sausages along with a drink while you scan the menu. You might choose one of the house specialties, such as roast leg or rib of lamb served in thick chunks in a special sauce or a northern Spanish stew of meaty knucklebones served with vegetables. Veal steaks, juicy pink lamb chops, and fresh fish are also featured. A meal, including a half liter of wine, costs around 1,500 pesetas ($11.90). This seems to be the place where other restaurateurs eat on the days their own places are closed.

Bar La Strada, 58 Tomás Miller (tel. 27-33-51), in Las Palmas, is on the ground floor. At the bar there is the best selection of tapas (hors d'oeuvres) in town, a tempting array including fish, meat, and vegetables dishes. Some 50 different dishes are offered, including a plate of Serrano ham, and priced according to your choice and whether you request a half or full portion. Everything is on display, so selecting is easy—you simply point. The bar is traditional, with smoked hams hanging from the ceiling and a long wooden counter with high stools. It's open from 8 a.m. until late at night. Upstairs is a self-service smörgåsbord where a meal costs 700 pesetas ($4.90). As you leave, the staff will present you with a card granting 25 pesetas (18¢) off your next meal.

El Cerdo que Rie (The Laughing Pig), 31 Paseo de Las Canteras, is open in the evening only. The menu of the day at 550 pesetas ($3.85) is served from 5 to 7 p.m. Otherwise you make selections à la carte. These might include the soup of the day, goulash, or hot pepper soup, salad, avocado or asparagus vinaigrette, shrimp cocktail, escargots, a fish or meat of the day, or flambé specialties. Your meal will cost 1,050 pesetas ($7.35) to 1,400 pesetas ($9.80). To accompany it, you might enjoy a glass of wine or local beer.

Restaurant Skandinavia, 26 Alfredo L. Jones (tel. 27-62-01), is a popular eating place for many American tourists who recognize good value, good food, and cleanliness, all offered in this typical Scandinavian eatery. Spotless white napery and comfortable chairs help you accept the somewhat slow but cheerful service from noon to 11 p.m. Appetizers include soups, omelets, and a plate of herring and prawn cocktail. For a main dish, you might choose sole à la maison with vegetables, wienerschnitzel and french fries, a pork chop with cabbage and potatoes, or a Chateaubriand for two with potatoes and salad. Perhaps you'd like one of the less expensive courses, such as fried liver and bacon, hamburger and french fries, or hot dogs with mashed potatoes. Salads are served with all dishes. If you choose the menu of the day, you'll be served a herring plate and then select from six different main dishes, with coffee for your beverage. Expect to pay 1,150 pesetas ($8.05) for a complete à la carte meal.

La Cafetera, Calle Alfredo L. Jones, at the corner of Dr. Miguel Rosa (tel. 26-05-72), has as its main clientele young, urbane Spaniards who gather for afternoon tea and coffee around the marble-topped tables of the bistro-style café. From 4 to 11 p.m. the café is transformed into a crêperie, offering some 12 savory pancakes, made with ingredients ranging from spinach to eggs, cheese, and ham. They are large and filling, but if you have room, you might enjoy a banana crêpe, one made with strawberries and cream, or the chocolate and vanilla cream crêpe. One of the tasty delicacies will cost 220 pesetas ($1.54) to 475 pesetas ($3.33). Annemarie Schaefer and Christine Hansen also offer cheesecake and Black Forest tarts made from old German recipes.

Restaurant Buffet International, 67 Tomás Miller, Puerto de la Luz, offers as much as you can eat, costing from 750 pesetas ($5.25). Service is from noon to 11 p.m. The tables are set for six or eight diners, so there is every chance that you'll share it with international company. Help yourself from the circular buffet to a variety of cold dishes, and you'll also find several hot selections, such as sardines or chicken with vegetables. The bright and rather commercial atmosphere is broken by potted plants. As you leave, you'll be given a card entitling you to 25 pesetas (18¢) off the price of your next meal.

Cafetería Piccadilly, 33 Alfredo L. Jones (tel. 27-95-35), is a clean bar, stretching back off the pavement into a dark interior. Here you can get a multitude of dishes from 11:30 a.m. to 11:30 p.m. Specialties include solomillo, potatoes, and salad; pescado (fish) a la plancha with fried potatoes and greens; and mixed cold meats, cheese, olives, and potato salad. Ham sandwiches are available, as is a hamburger. Earlier in the day the cafetería serves a breakfast of bacon, fried egg, toast, marmalade, fruit, and coffee. A meal will cost 500 pesetas ($3.50) to 900 pesetas ($6.30). You can enjoy good tapas, including paella, at the bar.

Part of the **Concorde Hotel,** 85 Tomás Miller (tel. 26-27-50), is the plate-glass-fronted Snack Bar with waitress service. Fresh flowers adorn the spotless tables, and it's open from 8 a.m. to 1 a.m., serving breakfast and fresh fish and meat. Marinated herring with vegetable salad and wienerschnitzel with french fries and salad are featured. A three-course meal costs around 1,200 pesetas ($8.40).

Mesón Vasco Kai-Alde, 35 Dr. Grau Bassas, is a typically Spanish restaurant with stone walls and metal-grilled windows. Its nice, cool, dark interior offers a haven from the heat and humidity of summertime Las Palmas. At a small bar in one corner you can order a drink before adjourning to one of the tables covered with blue-checked cloths. The menu offers a tomato and green salad, melon and ham, homemade soups such as fish soup, fish dishes from blackfish Romana to eel Aguinaga. Meat dishes include chicken stew, kidney in sherry sauce, lamb cutlets, and filet steak. Complete meals begin at 1,000 pesetas ($7), excluding wine. The tall, elegant Spaniard who serves behind the bar is the owner, and he keeps an eye on the service.

El Rayo, 3 Ripoche, Puerto de la Luz, stands behind the Bar Central on the Parque Santa Catalina, a spotless little restaurant a few steps down from street level. It offers food very like home-cooking, Spanish-style. The menu of the day goes for 500 pesetas ($3.50), with a choice of fish soup, noodle soup, or Russian salad, then a selection of veal or fish, followed by fresh fruit and ice cream. Bread and a half liter of wine or water (bottled) are included. For those who want a slightly wider choice, there is an à la carte menu from which you can select a three-course meal for around 1,200 pesetas ($8.40).

Restaurant Don Quijote, 74 Secretario Artiles (tel. 27-83-17), is a white arched place with typically Spanish upright, high-backed chairs set around wooden tables on a polished red-tile floor. Service is from 1 p.m. to midnight except Monday. Background music is played during the day, and in the evening a live guitar player entertains. Terracotta-covered lights hang above the tables, giving a warm and friendly glow to the bare white walls. Specialties include gazpacho Andaluz, seafood cocktail Don Quijote, sole au champagne, fondue bourguignonne, steak tartare, and fried Camembert. Dining à la carte can cost more than 1,800 pesetas ($12.60) per person, and a set menu is presented for 1,200 pesetas ($8.40).

El Gallo Feliz, 35 Las Canteras, is in an old stone building with high shuttered windows which are opened in the evening so that diners can view the promenade and sea. Candles on the dark wooden tables flicker on the wooded arched ceiling, and settles divide the dining area into more intimate alcoves. House specials are swordfish steak Mexican style and elephant ears steak. The cheapest way to dine here is to order the menu of the day at 1,000 pesetas ($7), a good meal—bread and consommé, chicken in wine, ice cream, and half a bottle of the house wine. An à la carte meal can cost 2,000 pesetas ($14). The standard of cooking and the service is high. It is open from 6 to 11:30 p.m. daily.

In the **Lord Nelson,** 8 Las Canteras and 43 Sagasta, Puerta de la Luz, you'll encounter a nautical decor and cannons. The German-owned pub offers bar snacks, as well as complete meals, and allows you to sit and watch the world go by. A good medium-priced meal for two persons will cost around 2,000 pesetas ($14), and you can order between 1 and 11 p.m. Spaghetti and pasta dishes are featured, along with the invariable seafood cocktail. Roast duck or chicken is alluring, as are the more expensively priced steaks. The dessert specialty—served only for two guests—is bananas flambé. You can eat inside or at tables on the promenade, right beside the beach.

Undoubtedly, the splurge meal in Las Palmas is to be had in the **Grill Room** of the Reina Isabel Hotel, Playa de las Canteras. Take the elevator from the lobby to the top floor (tel. 26-01-00 for reservations). There is a club-style lobby with chintz armchairs for your pre-dinner drink. Then you go into an elegant dining room. Try to get a table by the window—high over the Canteras beach and the city. Appetizers include seafood cocktail, Cantabrican oysters in season, young eels on toast au gratin, and smoked salmon. Soups range from Malagueño garlic to a cold crab bisque with champagne. There is always fresh fish, served with well-blended sauces, and such main dishes as pheasant cooked with whisky, partridge in rum, filet of pork with whisky, and filet steak à la Mexicana. Fresh lemon, papaya, or avocado sorbet will clear your palate before you try a dessert such as a soufflé or stuffed crêpes. A meal will cost from 3,000 pesetas ($21), tax and service included. Imported wines are served here. The atmosphere is sophisticated and relaxed, and the service is good. Afterward you can join the disco dancing in the Fiesta Bar.

On the Parque Santa Catalina, the **Bar La Peña** does a very good menu of the day for 525 pesetas ($3.68), including an appetizer of soup or salad, then spaghetti bolognese or fried fish accompanied by bread and a glass of wine. You might, however, prefer the red mullet. An à la carte meal costs from 750 pesetas ($5.25).

Next door is the **Bar Marisquería el Guanche** (tel. 27-92-76). The bar and restaurant spreads from its place along the side of the square into a roofed area of the parque. The entrance is decorated with a display of the day's fish, shellfish, and meat. Temptations include langostinos (crayfish), octopus Galicia, and squid à la romana for appetizers. Main dishes offered are such regulars in the Spanish repertoire as hake cooked Basque style. They also do flambé dishes and international specialties. A complete meal will cost around 1,600 pesetas ($11.20) from the à la carte menu, or you can order a set meal for 775 pesetas ($5.43).

Both of these establishments open right onto the Plaza Santa Catalina, and tables are set out onto the square. You need not come here to eat; you may prefer only a drink and various tapas, as it's the sort of place where everyone rests after sightseeing or shopping.

In the old part of town, the best place for tapas and Canary Island specialties is **Bar Herreno,** 23 General Mola. It's behind the market, close to the cathedral. English is spoken, and it's well worth investigating.

Down in the south where San Agustín turns into Playa del Inglés, and then into Maspalomas, stands **Loopy's Tavern,** 31 Las Retamas, San Agustín (tel. 76-28-92). It looks thrown together, a complex of huts and shanties, decorated with wagon wheels, postcards, and Victoriana. Basically, it's a ranch-style building, with lots of wood and nails, plus an outside barbecue grill for charcoal steaks, which, including T-bones, are the specialty of the house. In a cozy, intimate atmosphere, a special feature is the king-size hamburger, or you might prefer chicken in the basket. A favorite beverage here is the authentic Irish coffee. A meal in the tavern costs from 650 pesetas ($4.55), much more if you order steak. The owner has a pizzeria operation below the tavern. Here you can select from 17 different kinds of pizza ranging in price from 500 pesetas ($3.50) to 750 pesetas ($5.25). The tavern is open from early in the day to 2 a.m.

The island's parador is the **Parador Nacional de Turismo,** Cruz de Tejeda (tel. 65-80-50), some 22 miles from Las Palmas, and it is suitable for dining but at the moment doesn't rent rooms. Right in the center of the island, it nestles against a hillside of pine and jagged rocks, in a col between the north and south of the island. A good road leads all the way from Las Palmas. But, on the other side, the roads to Maspalomas and Mogan pass the Roque Nublio and are steep —often little more than dirt tracks. It's a fascinating drive, but not a fast one. The parador is an attractive building in the Spanish style, with a courtyard, designed by Nestor de la Torre. The lobby is cool with a polished floor, and from the lounge magnificent views open over the forest and the valleys of the south. You can drive out for lunch or dinner at a cost of 1,800 pesetas ($12.60). The typical Spanish menu makes few concessions to foreigners, other than printing the menu in English.

NIGHTLIFE: Cards advertising strip clubs, nightclubs, and discos are given out on the streets. It's wise to be cautious, although most places in Las Palmas are comparatively harmless for the person who's sensible. The police keep a pretty stern eye on most operations.

Nightclubs come and go in Las Palmas. Most are expensive and not of a very high standard, as is usual in a busy international port. Visitors seeking nighttime entertainment should inquire when they arrive on the island as to what is currently the rage.

The **Fiesta Bar** on the roof of the Reina Isabel Hotel, by the swimming pool and outside the Grill Room, offers disco dancing from 10 p.m. to 2 a.m. nightly. Admission is free to "respectably dressed" residents and nonresidents, but the management reserves the right to charge admission to those wearing jeans, Hawaiian shirts, and other super-casual clothes. Ties are not obligatory but are preferred. Decor is blue and gold with bamboo tables and chairs, and potted plants give a touch of green to what is one of the city's most popular discos.

Lord Nelson, 8 Las Canteras, in Las Palmas, has a smashing disco in the cellars from 10 p.m. to 3 a.m. each night. Regular admission is 400 pesetas ($2.80), rising to 700 pesetas ($4.90) on weekends and holidays. You enter the disco past portholes behind which fish swim. Many guests like to take a meal here, ordering one of 13 platos combinados (meat and vegetable plates with salad garnish), ranging in price from 450 pesetas ($3.15) to 750 pesetas ($5.25), the latter the cost of a plate of grilled sole with two vegetables.

El Bombin Discoteca, 39 Dr. Grau Bassas. The "Bowler Hat" disco is a cheerful, friendly place behind the Hotel Gran Canaria, just off the Canteras promenade. Drinks cost around 350 pesetas ($2.45), although whisky, always expensive in the islands, goes for around 450 pesetas ($3.15) a drink. However, if you arrive before midnight, the prices are lower. Bill, a friendly Englishman, and his Swedish wife, Monica, keep the crowd happy with good, noisy music.

Wilson Discoteca, 20 Calle Franch y Roca, is one of a chain of well-run, orderly discos with flashing mirrors and lights, plus deafening sound. Admission charges vary with the day and the hour. Drinks are 500 pesetas ($3.50).

Armstrong Dancing, 23 Alfredo L. Jones, is a well-run place with live music every night. Two orchestras and disco music invite you to go dancing far into the night.

You can try your luck at gambling at the **Casino Gran Canaria,** in the Hotel Tamarindos with its own entrance from the road at Playa San Agustín (tel. 76-27-24). It is open from 9 p.m. to 4 a.m., except Saturday and holidays when its hours are from 9 p.m. to 5 a.m. An admission card is obtainable by presenting your passport or identity document and the payment of the appropriate fee. A one-day card is 500 pesetas ($3.50), a week's card, 2,500 pesetas ($17.50). Games include French and American roulette (one zero), blackjack, chemin de fer, and punto y banco. Decor in the large gambling room is the usual dark wood and warm furnishings. The bar operates throughout the open hours, and the gambling is strictly controlled by a government representative on duty throughout the evening. The operators are not allowed to close down a table without his permission. At present the Casino does not have its own restaurant and uses the facilities of the Tamarindos Hotel, which offers a high standard of service and cuisine.

EXPLORING THE ISLAND: The north of the island is lush. Here are banana plantations and small fishing villages clustered around small rocky bays, with waves constantly breaking against the rugged shore. At **Galdar** and **Cenobio de Valerón** there is much evidence of the Guanches. The cliffs are honeycombed with caves, and at Galdar is a grave enclosure that may have been the burial place of the local Guanarteme (king) and his family. At **Arucas** a Gothic church rises out of banana trees and orchards. At **Agaete** are sugarcanes and the island's first sugar refinery. This part of the island is not often visited by tourists, and, perhaps because of that, it retains much of its pristine character. It's well worth a day or two of exploration.

South of Las Palmas, a motorway runs to the airport of Gando. This is a more barren part of the island, with a wide coastal plain, sloping to small sandy beaches separated by rocky headlands. At **Cuatro Puertos,** a sacred cave was dug into the hillside. Its use by the Guanches is uncertain, but it may have been an embalming place or a sanctuary.

Running from Telde inland to Santa Brigida, the **Atalaya Valley** is a steep and narrow enclave where people still live in caves in the rocky hillsides. The silence is broken only by the tinkle of a goat's bell or the bark of a dog.

Past the airport, the road continues south to **San Agustín, Playa del Inglés,** and **Maspalomas.** Once a quiet and deserted area of sand dunes and palm trees, this is the area of the big hotels, discos, and tourists. It's a paradise of sun and sea, yet an entirely commercial area.

Beyond the lighthouse on the southern tip of the island the road continues to **Puerto Rico,** an artificial harbor and development of apartments and villas. Here it's possible to go deep-sea fishing or out on yachting trips.

Right in the center of the island is the **Cumbre,** the mountain. Its northern face is covered with thick pine forests. Its eastern side, with steep valleys, is dotted with tiny rough houses. However, to the south and west it is almost barren. The road from Las Palmas climbs up through rich agricultural land and villages of large houses and estates to **Cruz de Tejeda** where there is a parador. When the sky is clear, the views of the island are remarkable.

From here, you can see the jagged peak of the **Roque Nublio** and the other sacred mountain of the Guanches, **Bentaiga.** On a clear day, it's possible to view all the way to Teide on Tenerife, some 60 miles away. The descent from Tejeda to Maspalomas is unforgettable, a twisting track between peaks and valleys to **San Bartolomé,** a sudden oasis of a village with flowers and pleasant gardens.

Even if the weather is overcast in Las Palmas, you can nearly always be sure of sunshine in the south of the island.

About eight miles from the center of Las Palmas, the **Bandama Crater** is just over a half mile across and about 600 feet deep. Its claim to fame: it is the only crater in the world where a small settlement of people lives all year. It also qualifies as having one of the world's most bizarre golf courses, an 18-holer laid out on the outer and lower slopes. See "Outdoor Activities" for greens fees.

MISCELLANY: The **Pueblo Canario** (tel. 24-35-93) is the Canary Islands village in the Parque Doramas, which also contains the old Spanish-style Hotel Santa Catalina. This was created by Nestor, who did much in the Gran Canaria to promote concern for traditional island architecture and customs.

The village includes a chapel, an inn, and other period buildings grouped around a central courtyard, on which folk dancing takes place on Thursday between 5:30 and 7 p.m., and on Sunday at 11:30 a.m. This is an attractive spectacle performed in the traditional style by local dancers. There is no charge, but if you sit at the bar, a varying amount will be added to the cost of your drinks.

El Mercado Municipal is nicknamed "The Market of the Forty Thieves," because there are that number of stalls. Off León y Castillo, toward the harbor, most of these stalls sell leather goods and souvenirs. But you can also buy meat, vegetables, and other household goods—you name it, it's there. Bargain as you will or just walk around watching the people and the deals they conclude.

The **Nestor Museum** contains a collection of his works, and is open from 10 a.m. to noon and 4 to 7 p.m., Monday, Tuesday, Thursday, and Friday. On Saturday, hours are from 10 a.m. to noon only, and on Sunday and holidays, 10:30 a.m. to 1:30 p.m. Admission is 25 pesetas (18¢).

In winter, the **Teatro Perez Galdos,** on Lentini (tel. 21-54-69), just before you get to the Barranco, gives performances of plays, ballets, and concerts. It also benefits from visits by some of the best-known orchestras in Europe. Information on performances is available from the tourist office or from one of the daily newspapers. The fine building in which it's housed is another example of the work of Nestor. It was opened in 1927. The huge foyer is decorated with paintings of Canary fruits, the theme of the magnificent carved balustrade. Buses pass the theater, so it's quite easy to get back to the Puerto de la Luz end of town.

The **Parque Santa Catalina** is the hub of national and international life, in the Puerto de la Luz part of Las Palmas. It's a large tree-shaded patio bordered on three sides by streets and on the fourth by cafés and shops. The cafés spill onto the paved square (see "Where to Eat"), and you can while away many hours with a coffee or a beer. Here a bootblack, there a letter writer or reader of newspapers. Photographers, lottery-ticket sellers, and many others may seek you out. Moorish Africans have their stalls here, selling leather goods, kaftans, and sandals. Characters abound.

Chess and domino games are played here. You can obtain a ticket from the photographer who stands close by, and then you wait your turn to challenge the resident player. Local women walk between the people, selling lacework. Expect to pay a half to a third of the asking price.

If you're offered gold or other jewelry, beware, for chances are it won't be entirely what it's claimed to be. For those who need them, there are clean toilets with an attendant at the old city end of the Parque. The attendant deserves the customary tip of 25 pesetas (18¢).

Across the street, from which the Tartanas depart, lies the tourist office in another one of Nestor's buildings. Duty-free shops line the square and nearby streets. There is little, however, that is now a bargain for North Americans.

The **British-American Clinic,** 5 Sagasta, Puerto de la Luz (tel. 26-45-38), is operated by the dapper Dr. Stanley S. Pavillard, who always sports a carnation in his buttonhole. The clinic offers 24-hour emergency service with two ambulances. It does not, however, have beds, although the staff will make all the necessary arrangements if you're really ill. It does offer an X-ray department and ECG. Subsidiary clinics are at the Playa del Inglés (Hotel Buenos Aires), 1 Avenida España (tel. 76-27-42); at Puerto Rico, Center Cívico Commercial (tel. 74-57-41); and at Puerto de Mogan, Urbanización Turistica Puertó de Mogan (Local X-105). These clinics are at the biggest tourist centers on this island, and may be of great help to readers who might need their services.

Holy Trinity Church, 11 Calle Rafael Ramirez, Garden City, is basically Church of England, but it offers a haven and a sincere welcome to all denominations. To get in touch with the resident chaplain, call 26-72-02. The church is near the municipal offices overlooking the port.

Canary Tourist Radio, 1275 kHz, broadcasts at 9 a.m. daily except Sunday. You'll hear world news and tourist tips in several languages. Established in 1963, it is produced by Xavier Ingemar Palin.

On the beaches of **Las Cantera** and **Alcaravaneras** chairs cost 150 pesetas

($1.05) daily; umbrellas, the same. Use of the changing rooms on Canteras beach is 50 pesetas (35¢). However, in the southern resorts expect to pay 20% more than in the north. On Las Canteras beach, a first-aid station is available.

On the main road to the south, just before San Agustín, on the right is **Cañón del Aguila,** the home of the Sioux City (tel. 76-25-73). Suddenly, you're transported to the Old West. Admission is 1,000 pesetas ($7); children, 775 pesetas ($5.43). Hours are 9 a.m. to 8 p.m. daily except Sunday. A minibus takes you up to the "Canyon City." Built originally as a film set, everything was imported from the U.S., including the cattle in the corral. There is a bus from Playa del Inglés to the cañón. Shows lasting 1½ hours take place at noon and at 2:30 and 6 p.m.

At the **Western Inn Bar,** in Cañón del Aguila, a beer is 150 pesetas ($1.05). You can also buy a gunbelt or a cowboy hat from the Wells Fargo Company or the Miners' Union Shop. At the three-star saloon with its long bar, light meals cost from 1,000 pesetas ($7). A ride on a well-trained horse is 700 pesetas ($4.90) for 30 minutes. The saddles are, of course, western.

At set intervals an announcer lets you know the attractions, including a cattle drive and an Indian trick-rider. Naturally you can expect a bank robbery, with bloody killings and a fight, not to mention a jailbreak. Handcuffs, "Wanted" notices, axeheads, and arrows are sold. At the inn, oldtime wrestling shows are staged. Madame Rosa runs a Turkish bath for men.

OUTDOOR ACTIVITIES: In a setting of sun and sea, the sporting life is practiced with much enthusiasm.

Puerto Rico is the center for nautical activities in the south of the island. Several man-made harbors combine around a complex of holiday apartments, in an area that was once barren. The facilities have attracted a number of sailors as well as private yachtspeople.

Nudist Beaches

There are now two nudist beaches, apparently accepted by the Catholic church in recognition of the tourists' dollars. One is at **La Cañada de la Pensa;** the other **Playa del Inglés.** There is also a naturist zone at **Playa de Maspalomas,** popular with the gay crowd, where you can manage to lose yourself in the sand dunes.

Sailing

For the romantic, there are two sailing ships, the windjammer **San Miguel,** Spanish owned and run, and the topsail schooner **Gefion,** owned by a Dutchman and sailed under a Spanish flag.

The *San Miguel* sails daily, except Monday, from the Pasíto Blanceo, Puerto Rico, at 10 a.m. For advance reservations, call 76-00-76. A day's cruise, including lunch and wine, is 2,500 pesetas ($17.50). At the bar drinks are extra but sold at normal prices.

The *Gefion* is claimed to be the oldest topsail schooner still in action, built in 1894 in Sweden and used transatlantic to Newfoundland. In 1940 she was engined for the first time. After some years of neglect, she was restored in 1970 by her owner to her present glory—the only change from her original shape being the conversion of the hold into a comfortable salon. She's not fast but she's strong and powerful, and you can spend the day helping to sail her, sunbathing, or scuba-diving. You can also fish or just chat below decks to the background of romantic music. Lunch is included in the day's price of 2,750 pesetas ($19.25), a cocktail followed by a cold buffet, wine, coffee, and brandy. The day starts from

Puerto Rico at 10 a.m., returning at 4:30 p.m. Reservations can be made by calling 76-18-97 from 5 to 7 p.m.

If you don't want a full day at sea, take a trip in M/Y **Salmon** from the jetty by the beach at Puerto Rico. She sails at 1 and 3 p.m. daily except Sunday for a 1½-hour cruise along the coast toward Mogan. A bar is on board, and there will be time for a swim in the crystal-clear waters of the Atlantic. A trip costs 1,000 pesetas ($7) per person.

Diving

This is one of the activities offered at the **Sporting Center** of the Hotel Don Gregory, San Agustín (tel. 76-26-62), to the south of the Gran Canaria. A six-day diving course costs 18,000 pesetas ($126), including equipment and transportation, plus instruction in English as well as Spanish. If you are already proficient, a day's excursion to one of the best diving areas on the island is offered for 3,500 pesetas ($24.50) per day or 15,000 pesetas ($105) for six days, equipment and transportation included.

Windsurfing and Sailboat Operation

The **Sporting Center** of the Hotel Don Gregory (see above under "Diving") offers instruction in sailing or windsurfing, a five-day course costing 7,000 pesetas ($49), but only 6,000 pesetas ($42) if you bring your own equipment. All instruction and gear used by the center for these two sports, as well as for diving, is approved by the Spanish navy, and standards are high.

Bullfights

From November to April, bullfights occasionally take place on Sunday at the Plaza de Toros, Playa del Ingles. If a fight is planned, you'll see all sorts of advertisements about it. There is usually a bullfighter and one assistant, with four bulls to be fought seriously, plus light relief in the form of comic "toreadors," as well as participation in a mock fight by the spectators. The price of admission varies with the skill of the matador.

Donkey Safaris

These operate daily from **Viajes Canyrama,** 49 Nicolas Estevañez in Las Palmas (tel. 27-65-53). Participants are taken by bus to Barranco de Guaya de Que to ride the donkeys to a Canary village for a lunch of paella and wine before returning to Las Palmas. The cost is 2,500 pesetas ($17.50), including lunch.

Golf

The excellent course at Bandama, **Club de Golf de Bandama,** Las Palmas (tel. 35-10-50), charges 3,000 pesetas ($21) for greens fees. Caddies cost 500 pesetas ($3.50) to 750 pesetas ($5.25), or you can rent a club cart for 125 pesetas (88¢).

Cock-Fighting

For those who have the stomach for it, or who are compulsive gamblers, cock-fighting takes place from February to May on Sunday at 11 a.m. in the **Polideportivo López Socas,** Escaleritas, Las Palmas. Admission is free and the meetings last about two hours. The Tourist Board has further information on this and on fights elsewhere in the island.

2. Tenerife

The largest of the Canary Islands, Tenerife is the capital island of the province that bears its name. The province consists of not only Tenerife itself, but La Gomera, La Palma, and Hierro. The last two islands are comparatively small and isolated. La Gomera is reached from Los Cristianos in the south of Tenerife and is worth at least a day's visit. La Palma is covered separately in part 3 of this chapter.

Tenerife's capital is **Santa Cruz de Tenerife,** which, with 150,000 inhabitants, is the second-largest port in the Canaries. Right in the center of the seafront lies the **Plaza de España,** with its memorial to the fallen in the Civil War. This square has a complicated traffic pattern, with many whistling policemen, shouted insults, streetside cafés, the tourist office, and a perpetual smell of oil and diesel. If you arrive by boat, this is your first view of the island. It's best to stop for a coffee to collect yourself before embarking upon further exploration.

Streets of shops extend up from the front. To the west of the plaza lies the **Plaza de la Candelaría,** with a statue of the Virgin of Candelaría atop an obelisk, and beneath three Guanche kings who were converted to Christianity. Here, too, is the **Church of the Conception,** with a tall, lantern-shaped tower once used by sailors as a landmark. Visit, too, the **Church of San Francisco,** a fine example of colonial architecture but with an elaborate interior and altars of gilded wood.

Up the hill from the port is the **Parque Municipal,** filled with subtropical plants, and at its entrance, a floral clock. There's also a small zoo here.

The **Municipal Museum,** on José Murphy, up from the port and opposite a tiny dusty square in the center of town, houses a fine collection of pictures by Spanish artists.

The nearest bathing beach is the man-made one at **Las Teresitas,** a few minutes outside town to the north and beyond the Nautical Club and the main harbor installations. It was built behind a breakwater, with a wide stretch of white sand. The water is clean, the bathing safe.

Although the seaport and provincial capital, Santa Cruz de Tenerife, is the choice of some short-stay visitors, the island's best and most established resort area is **Puerto de la Cruz,** known locally as just Puerto. Areas such as Los Cristianos and Playa de las Americas are still developing and not really very enjoyable places in which to stay unless you wish to center your visit solely on your hotel and enjoy the arguably better climate of the south.

Los Gigantes, so named for the imposing sea cliffs, has a certain elegance and some activity around its harbor. It does not have the preponderance of 25-story, up-ended concrete matchbox hotels of the other southern resorts. There is no good beach in Tenerife, with the possible exception of El Medano.

It is almost impossible to rent apartments or villas unless you go to the island and make inquiries in person, as there is a dearth of agents handling rentals.

JET FOIL: **Trasmediterránea** now operates a jet foil between Las Palmas and Santa Cruz on Tenerife. The 1¾-hour journey is very popular with business people who can get between the islands with time for a full day's work in between. For the visitor, the service takes a lot of pain out of the ferry crossing, which can sometimes be quite rough. There's a maximum baggage allowance of 14 kilograms per person, and you'll have to negotiate to take much more with you. Heavy or bulky pieces are handed to the baggagemen at the gangway in exchange for a tag. Coffee and crackers are served free during the crossing, which costs 4,040 pesetas ($28.28) for a one-way ticket. There are reductions for round trips and excursions. The best seats are at the front downstairs.

ABOUT YOUR ARRIVAL: There are two separate airports serving the island. The old one in the north of the island is **Los Rodeos;** the newer and more sophisticated one in the south is **Reina Sofia.** There is very little consistency over which airport planes will arrive at or depart from. You could, in fact, arrive at one airport, only to find that your inter-island flight was leaving from the other. So be sure to reconfirm your onward flight and double-check the departure airport.

If you happen to be staying in Puerto de la Cruz, you can take a taxi, which will cost about 6,000 pesetas ($42) or use the cheaper method of a self-drive car, which even for one person goes for about 3,500 pesetas ($24.50). There are no drop-off charges if you use Hertz or Avis, and you have the vehicle for 24 hours. This is not practical if you are leaving or arriving at Los Rodeos in the north. Otherwise, a bus from Reina Sofia to Santa Cruz costs 400 pesetas ($2.80) for the one-hour journey. A bus from Santa Cruz to Puerto, a 50-minute journey, via La Laguna and the Rodeos airport, goes for 290 pesetas ($2.03). If you're planning to use the bus between the two airports, be sure to allow plenty of time. One leaves roughly every half hour in both directions. The bus station in Santa Cruz is just outside the town close to the freeway. To reach the center of the city, take the local bus 19 to the Plaza de España for 20 pesetas (14¢).

GETTING AROUND: By car or coach, ferry or bus, the island enjoys a respectable system of transport.

Car Rentals

Hertz and **Avis** are represented at the airport and in Puerto de la Cruz. Hertz in Puerto is at Plaza de Agustín de Betancourt (tel. 38-45-60). In addition, it has another office at Playa de Las Américas, Grupo Urbania (tel. 79-08-61). Avis is on Avenida de Venezuela, Puerto de la Cruz (tel. 38-45-52), at the airport (tel. 77-06-56), and at Playa de las Américas. The Avis address at Playa de las Américas is Urbanisación Paraíso del Sol (tel. 79-13-02). Both companies charge about 2,850 pesetas ($19.95) to 3,300 pesetas ($23.10) a day for a Seat Fura, 3,500 pesetas ($24.50) a day for a Panda with unlimited mileage, although tax and insurance are extra. There are several smaller local car-rental companies which offer good service.

Care should always be taken in reading the insurance clauses.

Motorcycles

Very few scooters are now available on the island, but many of the smaller car-hire companies also rent out Suzuki motorbikes (125-cc, 185-cc, and 250-cc). If you're interested in such a rental, you might try **Motos Rueda,** 26 Calle la Verdad, Puerto de la Cruz (tel. 38-29-02), or **Rent-a-Bike,** 59 Calle La Hoya, Puerto de la Cruz (tel. 38-33-70). Charges range from around 1,300 pesetas ($9.10) to 1,900 pesetas ($13.30), plus insurance and taxes. Helmets are rented for 150 pesetas ($1.05), and a deposit of 6,000 pesetas ($42) is required.

Taxis

These are quite inexpensive and available from ranks at the airport and in Santa Cruz and at Puerto de la Cruz. Make sure they work on the meter. They're entitled to charge you for each case or bundle. If you want to rent one for the day, agree on the price first, of course. If you go to a remote part of the island, ask the driver to wait while you sightsee. Typical fares are as follows: from Puerto to Los Rodeos Airport, 1,700 pesetas ($11.90); to Reina Sofia Airport, 6,000 pesetas ($42); to La Laguna, 2,000 pesetas ($14); to Santa Cruz de Tenerife, 2,400 pesetas ($16.80); and to El Medano, 6,000 pesetas ($42). In the city area, the price is 45 pesetas (32¢) to get into the taxi and 40 pesetas (38¢) per kilometer (.62 miles).

Buses

There is a good network of bus routes, with a modern **terminal** being situated on Avenida Tres de Mayo (tel. 24-30-23). Buses run to all parts of the island, every half hour to Puerto de la Cruz and every hour to Las Américas and Los Cristianos. One bus goes to Las Cañadas del Teide daily at 8:30 a.m., returning in the afternoon. A one-way ride costs 375 pesetas ($2.63). Other journey costs: Santa Cruz to Puerto de la Cruz, 300 pesetas ($2.10) one way; Santa Cruz to Las Américas, 495 pesetas ($3.47); Reina Sofia Airport to Santa Cruz, 400 pesetas ($2.80); and Los Rodeos Airport to Santa Cruz, 150 pesetas ($1.05). The buses from the airports run according to the flight timetables.

In addition to the regular buses, there's a microbus service on many routes. It's quite possible, given time, to tour the whole island this way, stopping at villages you didn't know existed. The tourist office will provide information on the various departure points and fares.

The cable cars to the peak of the Teide run from 10 a.m. to 4 p.m., and the round-trip fare is 475 pesetas ($3.33) for adults, 275 pesetas ($1.93) for children.

WHERE TO STAY: In the tourist office at Santa Cruz, on Calle Marina, and at Puerto de la Cruz, Plaza de la Iglesia, you can obtain lists of accommodations of all types and prices. Also at Santa Cruz, on José Antonio Primo de Riveira, the **Patronato de Turismo de Tenerife,** can provide advice on hotels and restaurants throughout the island.

Santa Cruz

Hotel Residencia Pelinor, 8 Bethencourt Alfonso (tel. 24-68-75), is easily found just off the Plaza de España. In a modern block, it is surrounded by shops of all sorts as well as snackbars, making it ideal for business or pleasure. Run by Don Laureano Cruz, the hotel-residencia offers eight floors of small and simple rooms, all with bath. Accommodations are fresh smelling and well cleaned. Singles rent for 2,000 pesetas ($14); doubles with bath, 3,800 pesetas ($26.60). No meals are served, but there are plenty of opportunities for dining nearby. English is spoken at the hotel. There's a friendly, cheerful atmosphere, plus a rooftop solarium.

Hotel Anaga, 17 Imelda Seris (tel. 24-50-90), is also just off the Plaza de España. A typical commercial overnight stop, it is unremarkable but clean and convenient. The rooms are plainly furnished with telephones—but no radios or anything. The closet space is good, and shiny linoleum covers the floors. Many of the accommodations contain a private bath, and there are adequate public facilities as well. Singles with bath range from 2,400 pesetas ($16.80). Doubles with bath start at 3,000 pesetas ($21). The restaurant on the first floor is light and clean, serving a set dinner for 950 pesetas ($6.65), and there is a terrace on the roof for sunbathing.

Hotel Diplomatico, 6 Antonio Nebrija (tel. 22-39-41), stands up the hill from the bustle of the port, on a quiet street behind the market. All rooms contain private bath and a tiny balcony overlooking the town to the sea. Spotlessly clean and comfortable, the accommodations rent as follows: 2,400 pesetas ($16.80) in a single with bath, 4,000 pesetas ($28) in a double with bath. There is a swimming pool and rooftop terrace, plus a bar.

Residencia Tamaide, 118 Rambla General Franco (tel. 27-71-00), is a suitable choice. The "rambla" is a wide, two-way road running across the top of the town. The Tamaide is in the residential part of town—more elegant, where the air is fresher, yet it's within walking distance of the port and commercial sector. All rooms have a balcony and bath or shower, and are neatly and simply furnished. Only doubles are rented, costing 3,800 pesetas ($26.60). There is no restaurant, but they abound in the neighborhood, including a Chinese one. A swimming pool and sun terrace make the atmosphere even more pleasant.

Puerto de la Cruz

Hotel San Borondon, 4 Calle Puerto Viejo (tel. 38-35-40), is, as its address suggests, behind the old port, although still within easy reach of the tourist attractions. It's entered through a pretty flower-covered arch. The rooms are grouped around a grassy sunken garden and seawater swimming pool—a sun trap between high hedges. The accommodations are reached along covered walkways. All have private bath or shower. Well furnished and comfortable, the doubles cost 3,500 pesetas ($24.50) to 4,000 pesetas ($28); singles, 3,300 pesetas ($23.10) to 3,800 pesetas ($26.60). Lunch or dinner goes for 1,000 pesetas ($7) to 1,500 pesetas ($10.50). It's a quiet and peaceful oasis, and English is spoken.

Residencia Bambi, El Lomito (tel. 38-45-51), stands on a small street one block up from the Promenade. All rooms have a tiny kitchenette with freezer/refrigerator, crockery, cutlery, but no cooker. All the accommodations have private bath. Doubles with bath cost 2,800 pesetas ($19.60) to 3,400 pesetas ($23.80); singles, 2,500 pesetas ($17.50) to 2,800 pesetas ($19.60). An elevator services all floors. The bar is pleasant, with wood beams. The Bambi is unremarkable, but the value is good. The hotel is used extensively by a tour group, and reservations are entirely on a person-by-person daily basis. No advance bookings are accepted.

Hotel Marquesa, 11 Quintana (tel. 38-31-51), overlooks the gardens in front of the parish church. The oldest hotel in Puerto, it boasts more than 100 years of service. When you look at the attractive building, with its typical Spanish balconies and shuttered windows, you will know this is so. Family owned and run, the old building has been adapted to modern standards with the addition of a new wing at the back. The central courtyard has been roofed in and made into a large and cheerful lounge, off of which run the bar and dining room. The hotel has been entirely redecorated, and the bedrooms are simply but adequately furnished. In the new part the accommodations contain modern baths. In the old part, reached off the gallery around the courtyard, the ceilings are high (some of the doorways are eight feet high). Bathrooms have been built into these lofty chambers. Some of these rooms have balconies overlooking the square. The antique part is even furnished with heavy old Spanish pieces, including interesting pictures on the stairway and a beautiful old balustrade which must have felt a million hands.

Rates are reasonable: 3,300 pesetas ($23.10) in a single, from 5,000 pesetas ($35) in a double. The half-board rate is 1,500 pesetas ($10.50) to 2,200 pesetas ($15.40) per person in addition to the room tariff. The cool, paneled dining room offers a table d'hôte menu for 2,000 pesetas ($14). The cooking here is authentically Spanish, although some concession is made to the international palate. There is a roof solarium at the Marquesa that gives access to the small pool of the Residencia Condesa, which is under the same ownership.

Hotel Marquesol, 3 Calle Esquivel (tel. 38-37-53), offers 23 rooms serviced by an elevator. The units each contain a private bath and radio, and 18 have a balcony. Many of the accommodations are large, overlooking the beautiful tile roofs of the old houses and the sea. On the roof facing the water is a solarium, and in the basement is a well-stocked bar complete with tapas. A single costs 2,500 pesetas ($17.50), a double going for 3,400 pesetas ($23.80).

Hotel Monopol, 15 Quintana (tel. 38-46-11), is another Spanish-type building which has been added to. The enclosed courtyard has been filled with green plants and white seats, making it a peaceful resting place to escape the heat of the day. The newer part is reached through the courtyard toward the sea. A bar overlooks a small swimming pool and terrace and, in the distance, the Atlantic rollers. Bedrooms are neat and functional, some with a flower-bedecked balcony overlooking the square, others in the modern part fronting the sea. All have a private bath. Singles cost from 2,200 pesetas ($15.40) to 3,000 pesetas ($21), while doubles go for 3,800 pesetas ($26.60) to 5,800 pesetas ($40.60), breakfast included. The menu of the day is priced at 1,000 pesetas ($7). Picnic lunches are also provided, if desired. The hotel has undergone a careful restoration and is in good condition.

Hotel Los Príncipes, Calle Dr. Victor Perez (tel. 38-33-53), is a modern building, facing a charming plaza with flowers and palm trees. It's in the old part of town, near the fishing harbor and market, standing on the same street as the previously recommended Marquesa. At the hotel's coffeeshop, facing the square, you can order drinks, sandwiches, tapas, and light meals. There is also a restaurant. After passing through the cool, spacious lobby, you are shown to neatly furnished bedrooms, all of which have a private bath and phone (some have a balcony). Singles cost 2,400 pesetas ($16.80) to 3,000 pesetas ($21); doubles, from 4,000 pesetas ($28) to 5,000 pesetas ($35). These tariffs include a continental breakfast. On the roof is a heated swimming pool with wide sun terraces, and the beaches and public pools are only minutes away. The hotel is nice, with a quiet situation and a cheerful atmosphere.

Hotel Martianez, 19 Avenida del Generalísimo (tel. 38-06-00), is a modern high-rise block just up from the beaches. It is best known for the flamenco show it offers. The lobby is pleasant, as are the lounges and bar. The bedrooms are decorated in a typical Spanish style, with good beds and flowery balconies. All contain a private bath. A single goes for 4,000 pesetas ($28), a double for 8,000 pesetas ($56) to 9,600 pesetas ($67.20)—good value for those wanting a bit of luxury. Meals run around 1,150 pesetas ($8.05).

Hotel Residencia Puerto Azul, 28 Calle de Lomo (tel. 38-32-99), in the old part of town where restaurants and bars abound, is a clean little place on Lomo, which is closed to traffic at that point. Simply furnished rooms cost 2,300 pesetas ($16.10) to 2,800 pesetas ($19.60).

A splurge hotel of the island is the **Hotel San Felipe Sol,** 13 Avenida de Colón (tel. 38-33-11), lying along the waterfront, a bit away from the Manrique complex but within easy walking distance of the shops and promenades of the resort. The hotel has been completely revamped and is a comfortable luxury establishment where the friendliness and helpfulness of the staff is one of the first things you notice. A high-rise building, it has bedrooms facing either the sea or Mount Teide and the tropical garden. Rooms are well furnished with good storage space, balconies, and private baths. Singles rent for 9,000 pesetas ($63), doubles for 12,000 pesetas ($84) to 15,000 pesetas ($105).

Lunch is an informal warm and cold buffet in the swimming-pool bar or a more formal meal in the bright, light dining room. In the gardens is an Olympic-size swimming pool with excellent diving boards, as well as tennis courts floodlit in the evening. All sorts of other services are offered—use of a TV room, bridge, a library, hair-dressing, massage, sauna, table tennis, and a pool and playground for children. The hotel has a boutique, dances every night, and professional shows.

El Medano

El Medano is at the southern tip of the island where complexes of hotels have been built. It's reached by a metalled road. The modern airport, some three to four miles from the heart of town, has made this part of the island more accessible to visitors. However, it has not increased the noise at El Medano, because flight paths do not cross it. The taxi ride from Reina Sofia is only about 12 minutes. El Medano still has some of its vintage Spanish character. It cannot accommodate unlimited tourists, which makes it a place where you can get acquainted with the locals if you're lucky enough to be able to get a room here.

Hotel El Medano, Playa de El Medano, Granadilla de Abona (tel. 70-40-00), lies at one side of a sand bar, built on a pier so that it's possible at high tide to dive from the sun terrace straight into the sea. But don't try this stunt at low tide, as there's nothing but sand beneath. The lobby leads to a pleasant dining room, lounge, and bar. Beyond is a sun terrace, with loungers and chairs. The public rooms are furnished with comfortable chairs in light colors. The rooms all look onto the sea, and most of them have a private balcony. Some are very large, and all have a fully equipped bathroom. The furnishings are basic, as in the typical seaside hotel where little time is spent in your room. The floors are of stone. Beds are comfortable, and extra pillows and blankets are supplied willingly. Singles cost 3,500 pesetas ($24.50); doubles, 5,200 pesetas ($36.40). Lunch or dinner goes for 1,500 pesetas ($10.50). The hotel is within easy reach of Santa Cruz, the Playa de las Américas, and Los Cristianos complexes. However, Teo López, who runs the hotel, gives film shows and other diversions in the evening for those who don't wish to join the locals in one of the many, many bars in the small town. Mrs. López, who is English, looks after the housekeeping.

Hostal Residencia Carel, Avenida de los Principes (tel. 70-42-50), is run by Don Manuel Ramos and his family. About 300 yards from the sea, their hotel lies a little above the beach right in the middle of this small town. A relatively new building, it has a nice restaurant as one of its main features. Mrs. Ramos speaks English. The menu of the day goes for 550 pesetas ($3.85). A complete à la carte meal will cost about 900 pesetas ($6.30). Rooms, 24 in all, are pleasantly furnished and comfortable, renting for 2,600 pesetas ($18.20) in a double, 1,800 pesetas ($12.60) in a single. The management has installed a small disco with free admission and drinks at average hotel prices. However, the management reserves the right to require its guests to be tidily dressed and sober.

Hotel Playa Sur Tenerife, Playa de El Medano (tel. 70-41-50). At the far end of the sandy bay, this building, which has been a hotel for many years, has been refurbished and freshly decorated. German owned but with a Spanish manager, it caters very much to a windsurfing fraternity. There's a pleasant lounge and dining room with a wooden ceiling, along with ample tables and comfortable chairs. They boast an international cuisine with Spanish specialties, and vegetarians and other dieters will find special menus. By the sheltered swimming pool is a pleasant bar, and there's also a sauna and massage parlor in which you can relax after windsurfing or whatever. Bedrooms are prettily furnished, and each has a balcony and a sea view. A double with shower, toilet, and phone costs from 8,000 pesetas ($56) daily, including a buffet breakfast. A single goes for 5,500 pesetas ($38.50), so it's not cheap, but there are reductions for stays of one week or more. Dinner costs 1,500 pesetas ($10.50). They have a minibus for transfers to the nearby Reina Sofia airport, a ten-minute journey.

Puerto de Santiago

Hotel Los Gigantes Sol, Urbanización Los Gigantes (tel. 86-71-25), may seem isolated, but even a short stay will convince you of the advantages of staying near a small Spanish town in an area of magnificent scenery away from the concrete jungles of Las Américas. The hotel is built right on the edge of the sea, with swimming pools set in the rocks and steps down to the beach below. The hotel has simple rooms. Depending on the season, half-board accommodation costs 2,600 pesetas ($18.20) to 4,800 pesetas ($33.60) per person daily. Among the activities available are tennis, squash, miniature golf, and indoor games, and the hotel has a library. Regular bridge tournaments are an added attraction. The yacht marina beneath the hotel offers waterskiing and sailing. And just in case, a medical emergency room is connected with the hotel. From here you can take excursions to Puerto de la Cruz, Teide, the villages of the north coast, and Santa Cruz.

A Parador in a Crater

Parador Nacional Canadas del Teide, Apartado 15 de la Orotava (tel. 33-23-04), lies in the crater of the ancient volcano, which now forms a plateau at the highest part of the island from which the peak of Teide rises, 3,700 yards from the sea. The parador was built to withstand differences in temperature, as it can be cold at night, and there is often snow on the peak. The building is like a chalet, with balconies and shutters. In the dark wooden interior, huge log fires burn in the lounge and bar. The food in the dining room is uncompromisingly Spanish. A lunch or dinner at 2,000 pesetas ($14) will fill the best trencherman. Local wine is served unless you ask for a bottle from the mainland. The bar also serves snacks. A double room costs from 5,500 pesetas ($38.50). A single goes for 4,500 pesetas ($31.50) with a terrace. There's a swimming pool for the many days when the temperature is in the 90s.

WHERE TO DINE: My survey of places to eat, snack, or drink will range around the island, beginning first in the capital of:

Santa Cruz

La Riviera, Avenida General Franco (tel. 27-58-12). Judging by its clientele, this restaurant is used regularly by discerning Spaniards for the excellence of its menu, the pleasant surroundings, and superb service. A small terrace bristling with potted trees leads to the bar, where you can relax in one of the soft chairs to one side or sit at the bar on the other, enjoying a drink while the dining room prepares for your arrival. Upstairs, you dine amid green baize walls and floor, green table linen, sparkling silver-edged dishes, good crystal and silver, and attentive service. Santiago, the owner and maître d'hôtel, a gentle giant with a delightful smile, rules benevolently over a crew that includes several charming and well-trained young women. Among the appetizers are avocado Dacil (a warm avocado dish) and vichyssoise. Main dishes include filet Cordon Bleu, entrecôte minute, charcoal-grilled lamb chops, and Chateaubriand for two. For dessert, you can choose from the ices and flan, or try the Riviera banana flambé or crêpes Suzettes. Meals cost around 2,500 pesetas ($17.50).

Restaurante-Cafetería Olympio, Plaza de la Candelaría (tel. 24-17-38), is a modern complex right on the corner of the square, overlooking a war memorial and, beyond, the harbor and its ships. The first floor has a balcony of tables for those who wish to eat outside. Inside is a large dining room, ideal for a quick meal. Prices depend on where you sit, the bar being cheaper. Soups range from consommé to shellfish, and the salads are also tempting. A minute or ham steak is also offered, served with tomatoes, salad, and french fries. Desserts are standard. A combined dish of meat, fried potatoes, egg, tomatoes, and sausage costs 650 pesetas ($4.55) at a table, less at the bar. A good breakfast costs 550 pesetas ($3.85).

La Masia, Mendez Núñez y San Fernando, is an expensive and luxurious retreat for a quiet, elegant meal. It is very much patronized by local people, so go early if you want a table. Grilled wooden portals lead to a dark dining room with wooden panels. You might begin with mushrooms with garlic, or perhaps Costa Brava anchovies. The fish dishes, of course, may vary depending on the catch of the day. You can also enjoy fully garnished steaks, chops, and escalopes. Expect to pay around 2,000 pesetas ($14) for a complete meal.

Fontana del Oro, 127 Avenida General Franco, is one of the most popular places in town for quick, appetizing food. Beneath the Edificio Strelitzia, a long, shallow basement room going back to the gardens has a long counter from which you choose your meal. Just point to the foods you want and your plate will be served: a selection of salad, Russian eggs, prawns with vinaigrette, squid romana, hamburger, spaghetti, and/or meat stews. You'll be charged about 660 pesetas ($4.62) for a good cheap meal.

Pizzaría, 129-131 Avenida General Franco, is a pizza- and pasta-lovers' paradise. It boasts 18 different varieties of pizza, spaghetti with seven sauce selections, four choices of ravioli fillings, two cannelloni, and two lasagnes. Various egg and combination dishes are also on the menu. If the pasta is more than you can handle, you might prefer the tapas, which include prawns, ham, and vegetable salads, or one of the sandwiches offered. You can feast on pasta or pizza, accompanied by a German lager, for around 650 pesetas ($4.55). This place is popular with the locals, who like to eat at its clean tables with the smart checkered cloths.

Cafetería Restaurante El Aguila is to be found at the top end of the Calle de Bethencourt Alfonso, up from the harbor on a small triangular square with palm trees providing an oasis in the busy town. Tables are on the pavement and in the air-conditioned interior. Freshly squeezed orange juice, good tapas, sandwiches, shrimp in the basket, chicken in the basket (spit-cooked before your eyes) are served. Specials include chili con carne, chicken curry, escalope of veal, and spaghetti bolognese. Meals cost from 1,200 pesetas ($8.40). English is spoken here, and the toilets are clean. Women selling tablecloths go among the customers at the tables.

Puerto de la Cruz

This town, contrived entirely for tourists, boasts many bar/cafés that sell *perros calientes,* hamburgers, french fries, soft drinks, wine (generally not local), and coffee.

The **Cafetería Oasis,** 11 Avenida de Colón (tel. 38-16-07), is owned by Anna Welsch. She, along with the piano and organ music, is as popular as ever. You may be content with something light, such as soup, salad, and perhaps a dessert, but there are such tempting offerings as prawns in garlic butter, steak baked in pastry, and avocado with prawns. A complete meal will cost from 1,500 pesetas ($10.50) à la carte or 550 pesetas ($3.85) for the menú del día.

Café de Paris, Avenida de Colón, is a coffeeshop next door to the Hotel Valle Mar. It's an attractive pavement place. Large and busy from morning till night, it's an ideal place to rest from sightseeing, as it is right on the main street.

A coffee or drink can be spun out for as long as you like. It has a bakery, a croissant bar, a sweet shop, and a cake shop in the side street. The lovely, open continental café serves breakfast, coffee, drinks, lunch, and afternoon and evening meals. Along with the cakes, there are ice cream concoctions decorated with fruits and favors, a menu of fish dishes, several Italian pasta dishes, grills, and fried dishes. The menu of the day costs 950 pesetas ($6.65), but you're more likely to spend 1,200 pesetas ($8.40). Beside the garden café is a nightclub decorated with dark wood and red plush. It has a small dance floor and live music from 9 p.m.

Restaurant Viking, Avenida General Franco (tel. 38-29-57), is on one of the main streets of Puerto, beneath the Hotel Martina. Patrons find it a cool spot for just a drink or a coffee, but they can stay to order a set meal for 550 pesetas ($3.85). A meal on the à la carte menu is likely to run around 1,000 pesetas ($7) or less. For that, your choices are likely to include matjes herring served with "long" potatoes, a salad with tomato, onion, cucumber, and lettuce, filet mignon Viking, and dessert. Portions are large. The owner is Scandinavian, so you are going to get reasonably authentic dishes. The place is open daily except Monday from 11 a.m. to 11 p.m.

Restaurante El Pescado, 3B Avenida Venezuela (tel. 38-28-06). If you turn left up from the sea by the Café de Paris, you come to the cul-de-sac Venezuela. At El Pescado there are two small dining rooms separated by a central kitchen and decorated with dark wood paneling and tables with upholstered bench seats. Hours are from 12:30 to 2:45 p.m. and 6:30 to 10:45 p.m. Live guitar music is presented in the evening. Fishermen's soup with Pernod or garlic soup Catalán style await your selection. The chef obviously specializes in fresh fish, and the menu depends quite a lot on what fish is caught. When I was last there squid, clams, halibut, cigalas, lobster, and langostinos were available. A paella valenciana for two overflows with shellfish and chicken. A Canarian puchero, a meat stew (the first time I have found it in a Puerto restaurant), can only be ordered for four people or more. You must, however, wait some 45 minutes for paella or puchero to be prepared. The day's catch of fish is marked on a blackboard outside the restaurant in traditional style with weights and prices. The cost of a complete meal can vary widely—from 1,500 pesetas ($10.50) to 2,600 pesetas ($18.20)—depending on what you select for your main dish. Make sure you enter through the proper door, or you'll find yourself in the backyard in the midst of the trash cans.

For the best selection of budget restaurants, head for the **Calle de San Felipe,** a street for good, inexpensive, international food establishments. At last count, there were nearly a dozen such restaurants. In a five-minute walk, you can have a selection of Spanish, French, German, Peruvian, or Italian dining spots. It's possible to eat a three-course meal at lunch, with bread and a quarter of a liter of wine, for 500 pesetas ($3.50) all day and late at night.

Restaurant El Inca, Calle de San Felipe, is in the old part of town, on a small street running off the Plaza General Franco. It is attractive, with iron grills and clean tables. The chef specializes in Peruvian dishes and fresh local foods. The menu includes such selections as melon with ham, cebiche mixto (marinated fish), and garlic soup Peruvian style. Main-course specialties include sole a la Inca, ox heart en brochette, duck with rice, and chicken with a special sauce. Desserts include the usual offerings, but also banana flambé. Complete à la carte meals begin at 1,200 pesetas ($8.40). The least expensive way to dine here is to order the menu of the house for 650 pesetas ($4.55), including, say, garlic soup, a Peruvian-style grilled halibut in a special sauce, plus wine, bread, and ice cream. The restaurant is closed Wednesday.

Rancho Grande, Calle San Telmo, is built in the typical Spanish style, with a wooden balcony overhanging the walkway and the sea in the old part of town. Try for a seat on the balcony where you can watch the world go by and see the water breaking on the rocks below. They serve food throughout the day starting with breakfast. Lunch can include an avocado pear or melon and ham. Main courses include lamb chops, spareribs, skewered meat, and pepper steak. T-bone steaks are well prepared, and diners usually order salad to go with them. Afterward there's a large selection of mouthwatering cakes and pastries from which to select your dessert. These include apple pie and sponge cake with real strawberries topped with mounds of whipped cream. Make your selection at the buffet and wait for the waiter to bring it to your table. The menu of the day, changing daily, costs 1,050 pesetas ($7.35) and may include beef soup, rump steak, french fries, salad, and a pastry. If you prefer to order à la carte, expect to spend 1,500 pesetas ($10.50) and up.

La Papaya, 14 Calle del Lomo (tel. 38-28-11), occupies the converted ground floor of an old Canary house in the old town near San Felipe, the street of restaurants. Luís Gimenez, the owner, greets everyone with a glass of sherry, while diners make their selections from his typical Spanish menu. The simple house has windows opening right onto the street. There are several rooms with small tables everywhere. Humming with life, it's very popular with local business people. The menu changes often but always includes fresh fish, sama with Canary potatoes and mojo, a zarzuela (mixed fish and shellfish stew), and paella. Rabbit, roast beef, pepper steak, and pork chops are always available. Most of the fresh vegetables and salad greens come from Luís's own garden. The average cost for a meal that's almost more than you can eat ranges from 1,300 pesetas ($9.10) to 1,800 pesetas ($12.60). You can sit out behind the house, enjoying an apéritif before you're called in to dinner.

Capitán Metro Steak House, 6 Calle Cologan (tel. 38-04-44). A cheerful nautical air permeates this spotless place, with its bright tables decorated with fresh flowers. The menu is whimsical and very good. You may want to start off with one of the tasty soups or a salad, and follow with one of the well-prepared fish dishes. As the name implies, steaks are the specialty, from pepper steak through filets, ranch house, and T-bones, cooked to your taste. You can dine well here for 1,800 pesetas ($12.60) and up. The service is quick and efficient.

At Icod de los Vinos

Agustín y Rosa, 15 San Sebastián (tel. 81-07-92), is on the north coast of the island, to the west of Puerto de la Cruz. The town of Icod is famous for its dragon tree, the oldest on the island. Visitors may like to slake their thirst and break their fast at this friendly place, run by Agustín and his wife, Rosa, with a little help from their friends. In the middle of town, a short walk from the dragon tree, you enter through the bar to a large, well-lit dining room overlooking Icod to the sea. Simple white cloths are placed on wooden tables, with a wide menu of Spanish food served to the accompaniment of much chatter and laughter. If you don't understand anything, you get a passable explanation in Spanish. Here you can sample the Canary Island dessert of "Bien-me-Sabe," a meringue with almonds and honey. Also I recommend trying the local Icod wine, which has a distinctive bouquet. A bottle costs about 350 pesetas ($2.45). A set meal goes for 550 pesetas ($3.85). If you'd like to spend the night, you'll find double rooms renting for 1,900 pesetas ($13.30).

Hostal del Drago is an old Spanish building on one corner of the Square where the dragon tree stands. Although called a hostal, it does not have any accommodations, but you can get tapas in the bar, where they have a large selection. In the restaurant or at one of the tables in the garden, you can have a meal from an extensive menu ranging from soups and asparagus to grilled fish, steaks, and chicken to the ever-popular flan for dessert. A three-course meal will set you back 1,000 pesetas ($7) or more, according to your choice. There is also a large souvenir and postcard shop. If you go in at lunchtime, don't be surprised to find the family dining at their own table in a line watching color television. All is very Spanish, but there is an English menu which the waiter will understand only if you point to what you want.

Garachico

On the north side of the island, a few miles from Icod, this small town was completely engulfed in lava when Teide erupted in 1706. Surrounded by vineyards and banana plantations, it is now a busy little town with a pleasant square dominated by the Church of Santa Ana.

As you drive into the town, the **Castle of San Miguel** stands beside the sea. Built in 1575 to protect the city from pirate attack, the fortress managed to escape the lava. Today it is lovingly cared for by students from the local college who sell pictures and books on the history of Garachico and the island. There is no admission charge, but you are expected to make a contribution toward the castle's upkeep. From the large, cool hall, take the stairs to the roof for a panoramic view of the town and the sea.

The **Church of Santa Ana** is also worth a visit. Not much remains of the 16th-century structure, which was engulfed by lava in the volcanic disaster of 1706. The present church has grown through the 18th and 19th centuries to become a magnificent parish church of Canarian architecture with priceless treasures and statues.

Restaurante Isla Paja and **La Tasta Snack Bar,** Mercadilla Restaurante (tel. 83-00-08), are in a traditional Spanish house with great, 15-foot double doors leading into a cool courtyard surrounded by lofty cool rooms that house an exhibition of ancient Garachican relics. Here you'll see a wooden dugout boat that survived the lava, a traditional water purifier, and a fascinating model of the area and the town showing, with light effects, how the volcanic flow engulfed the town.

Beside the entrance is La Tasta Snack Bar, a narrow room where you can select cold meat, bacon, french fries, and salad, an octopus salad, or sausages and french fries, as well as coffee or soft drinks. There are tables outside where you can sit and gaze out over the turquoise sea with the castle in the foreground. A light meal from the snackbar will cost about 400 pesetas ($2.80). The restaurant is upstairs in a cool, wooden room where more substantial meals include fresh fish and vegetable soups, avocado and shrimp salads, fresh-caught fish grilled with mojo, fresh sardines or bocorones, local dishes such as pickled rabbit with salmorejo sauce, and paella. The menu of the day, costing 800 pesetas ($5.60), will allow you to enjoy soup, veal escalope milanese or fresh grilled fish, salad, potatoes, and ice cream, as well as bread and wine. If you prefer to order à la carte, expect to pay 1,000 pesetas ($7) or more for a complete meal.

Remember that Spanish lunch does not start until around 2 p.m. The fish must be caught and prepared first, so don't go early.

La Perla de Garachico, Calle de 18 de Julio (tel. 83-02-86). There is the usual plain, clean room with a bar offering drinks, coffee, and tapas. From the dining room, a spotless kitchen is visible. Señor Alfredo Rodriguez, who owns and operates La Perla, will show you the fish you are going to eat before it's prepared, or you can choose the steak you prefer. A three-course meal costs 650 pesetas ($4.55), a four-course repast goes for 750 pesetas ($5.25).

On the Calle Esteban de Ponte, behind the church, is a tiny house, the **Casa Ramón** (tel. 83-00-77). The front room gleams with polished wood and bright red-and-white-checked tablecloths. While Ramón is out fishing, his smiling wife cleans and prepares the food. Then at 2 p.m. they serve a set meal of soup or salad or beans followed by the fish you have just watched Ramón cook, either grilled or boiled in fresh water, salad, and potatoes. Served separately if you prefer is a spicy sauce, mojo. Dessert is flan or ice cream, and the whole repast costs 900 pesetas ($6.30). You can enjoy the local wine at 450 pesetas ($3.15) for a large flagon. In keeping with the local custom, there is a washbasin in the restaurant in which you can wash your hands if you decide to eat with your fingers. This totally unsophisticated and charming little place is popular, and you may have to go to a nearby bar while waiting for a seat.

If you're driving from Icod to Garachico to visit the crater of Teide, or the beaches of the south, you can climb up the mountain through banana trees to the **Mirador de Garachico,** which has fine photographic views. There you can sit with the lava behind you, the sea beneath you, and eat sandwiches and smoked meats, buy provisions for a picnic, or else browse in the Bazar Típico which is full of unusual souvenirs of the island. For a snack, try orejas de elefante (elephant's ears), sweet, crisp fritters with an apple center, at 60 pesetas (42¢) each.

From Garachico west along the coast to Buena Vista, then El Palmar and Masca to Santiago del Teide, is a dramatic mountain drive, one of the finest I know of in Europe covering so short a distance. After Buena Vista, the road climbs and twists upward some 5,000 feet through valleys, peaks, and sheer rock faces. Around every bend a village clings spider-like to the rocks, and you see restaurants dotted out on cliff piers. Masca is a lovely old village, an ideal place to have a quiet drink in the main square before continuing to Santiago down on the main route. The road is good and drivable except for someone who suffers from vertigo.

El Medano

Fishing boats are drawn up on the beach and on the wide promenade where at festivals there is dancing, but on any day the old men sit and smoke.

At **Casa Mario,** Calle Marcial, Mario and his two brothers run the bar, and the women of the family do the cooking. It is a small spotless room opening onto the promenade, with three or four tables, plus the bar. A few tables are placed outside on the pavement. On Wednesday at lunchtime they do a special Canary meal, making so much food there is plenty left over for the evening as well. In huge pots in the spotless kitchen simmers a fish stew to be eaten with a sauce made of garlic, lemon, oil, and coriander, or else a *punchero,* a typical stew of meat with a vast array of vegetables in a luscious herb-flavored juice. A Canary soup with chick peas or a fish soup jostles for position on the stove. You're invited to inspect the pots and choose what you'll have as your meal. When you've finished one helping, you can go back for more. A glass of wine completes the meal, and you'll rise replete for the small cost of about 550 pesetas ($3.85) per person. The bar is the meeting place for the locals, who congregate to listen to *fútbol* on the radio—played loud—or else to argue violently in Spanish. The bar is popular in the evening when tables are set out on the tile patio for drinking. Closed Tuesday.

Bar Familiar has a large bar downstairs where tapas are sold. Selections include prawns, potato salad, octopus in mojo. Upstairs is a restaurant where the menu of the day goes for 540 pesetas ($3.78), including three courses with wine. Otherwise, on the à la carte menu, the fish soup is preferred as an appetizer. Fish is sold by weight, and you can make your selection before it is cooked. Sole and langostinos are the usual orders, although many guests prefer the squid. A Chateaubriand for two is offered. Complete à la carte meals average 1,000 pesetas ($7), but may rise to 1,800 pesetas ($12.60).

Bar Restaurant Angelo's Way, 3 Avenida Amalia (tel. 70-43-75), has lots of tables outside on the patio just up from the Hotel Medano and across the promenade from the beach. Downstairs, the wide doors of the bar open right onto the patio. During the day, bar meals include sweet peppers with french fries and mushrooms; corned beef with a fried egg, asparagus, french fries, and a salad; and hamburger with french fries and salad. There are also sandwiches and filled rolls containing Serrano ham or chicken and cheese. Upstairs, there is a more formal restaurant, with neat tables and high-backed chairs, candles, green tablecloths, and a view of the open-plan kitchen. For an appetizer, you can select fish soup, asparagus with mayonnaise, or a salad, either mixed or Angelo's Way. If you don't want fish for your main dish, you can have grilled giant prawns, filet steak, pepper steak, or rabbit Canary style. A banana split, butterscotch cream, or strawberries and cream are among the desserts offered. In the bar downstairs you can order a set lunch for 500 pesetas ($3.50) or make an à la carte selection for less than 600 pesetas ($4.20). In the upstairs restaurant a complete meal will cost around 1,400 pesetas ($9.80) if you're that hungry.

The **Bar Avencio** (tel. 70-40-97) is narrow and dark, the entrance almost covered by bushes. It's well recommended for its prawns fried in garlic butter. The onion soup is very substantial, and the house wine can be recommended. Clams or oysters in season are a feature, and lobster and mussels are the house specialties. The menu of the day costs 550 pesetas ($3.85). The place has a friendly atmosphere, and Canary artifacts and fishing gear hang from the walls. This is a magnificent repast for the aficionado. Closed Monday.

Juani's Disco Pub, 10 Esplanada, is right down by the edge of the beach, its wide windows opening the bar out to the pavement with its colorful tables and umbrellas. Inside, the proprietor and his family dispense the usual drinks from a long curved bar. For lunch they serve large portions of fresh fish from the day's catch, along with a salad and potatoes. If they've got them, do order the fresh grilled sardines. Calamares are also popular. Pork chops and a meat stew are featured also. You can eat well for around 650 pesetas ($4.55).

Los Cristianos

Restaurante Casa del Mar, Esplanade Muelle de los Cristianos (tel. 79-11-23), stands down by the harbor. This restaurant is on the third floor of the Instituto Social de la Marina, a modern building on the quayside by the car park. It has a fine view over the harbor and out to sea, and is open daily for lunch and dinner. It has an English menu, but only Spanish is spoken. In fine weather you can eat on the balcony. You can order paella for two including salad and french fries. Other fish dishes are available, as are chicken and other meats. Expect to pay from 1,200 pesetas ($8.40) and up for a complete meal.

San Juan

This small fishing village lies on the west coast of the island, beyond the modern complexes of the south. It is between the banana plantations and the sea on the old coast road. It is minus the sophistication of Los Cristianos, and that forms part of its charm.

The restaurant, **Brisas del Mar,** Playa San Juan (tel. 86-79-54), overlooks the sea and fishing boats that bring in the catch. It's so popular with the locals that it's often difficult, especially on weekends, to find a table. But it's well worth trying if you're in the area. (Tourists, however, mainly eat in the more expensive place across the road.) The available fish dishes are written on a blackboard, and you'll be invited to go in the kitchen to select the catch you want prepared for you. A salad comes with the fish plate. A meal costs 650 pesetas ($4.55), not including wine. At a wash basin, you can clean up after you've eaten your prawns with your fingers, as the locals do. Eating begins at noon, finishing at 10 p.m.

Puerto de Santiago

Bar-Restaurante El Ancia, Poblado Marinero, Acantilado Los Gigantes. Right down by the harbor in Santiago de Teide, once voted the cleanest and smartest village in Tenerife, is this spotless little restaurant with tables on the quayside and the great cliffs towering behind. The menu for lunch, served until 4 p.m., and for dinner starting at 6 p.m., offers fish or onion soup, melon and ham, prawn cocktail, and avocado with prawns for appetizers. Main dishes may be grilled hake, cherne with parsley sauce, sole, prawns, a plate of mixed grilled fish for two, paella for two, and fish stew. A good à la carte selection can cost 1,400 pesetas ($9.80) for a complete meal.

Bamboo Restaurant and Pâtisserie is a modern building decorated in Spanish style, with lots of wood. A large, bright patio leads to openwork bamboo screens, high-backed chairs, and round wooden tables with rush mats. Lights are subdued by rush lampshades. Fish dishes include half a lobster Buena Vista, king prawns with two sauces, and grilled sole. If you're in the mood for meat, try the entrecôte bordelaise, the steak au poivre, or wienerschnitzel. Specialties to be ordered in advance are duck with orange, Spanish-style lamb, leg of lamb for two, and Chateaubriand for two. There is a wide selection of desserts from the trolley, or you can have crêpes Suzette for two. Unusual in the islands is a cheese board. A complete meal will come to 1,500 pesetas ($10.50) or more. Next door is the pâtisserie, where you can buy cakes and pastries to eat there or take away.

NIGHTLIFE: It's spread out among the various resorts. My favorite spots follow.

Puerto de la Cruz

Nightclub Plaza de Toros La Rueda, Las Cabezas (tel. 38-29-60), is open every night for an hour's dancing at 9 before the show begins at 10. Acts include a good comedian, flamenco dancing, and a mini-bullfight where you can join in if you wish. The entrance is 1,500 pesetas ($10.50). For that, you can drink all you want until 1 a.m., from a range of beers, sangría, wines, and Spanish champagne. In all, it offers good clean entertainment and puts on quite a show.

The best place for flamenco is probably the **Hotel Martianez** (tel. 38-06-00 for reservations). You enter the nightclub from the Calle Valois entrance into a spacious typical Andalusian room, with grills, plants, wooden tables, and rush chairs. It is air-conditioned. A big band plays for dancing, and a superb flamenco troupe performs at 10:30 and again at 11:45 p.m. Entrance and the first drink cost 1,500 pesetas ($10.50).

Between the Avenida de Colón in Puerto de la Cruz and the sea, Cesar Manrique has devised a fabulous complex, Costa Martianez. There are several swimming pools here bordered by sun terraces. Those who do not want to risk the black sand and dangerous undertow of Martianez Beach can swim and sun among the palms. Loungers are available. Admission to the pools is 200 pesetas ($1.40), 100 pesetas (70¢) for children. Beyond the pools is a "Willow Pattern" bridge leading to the **Isla del Lago** (island in the lake), a unique architectural and landscaping masterpiece. By day it's an upstairs terrace, cafetería, and restaurant. But at night the whole place is transformed, with lights dancing on the water. An incredible nightclub is built inside the island below sea level, and it offers disco dancing and a spectacular floor show. The dance floor is open to the sky, and it's like being in a cave. Entertainment is offered nightly, costing 2,000 pesetas ($14) for the dancing and show, with unlimited wine included. Those who don't feel like going in can stay above ground in the bar and listen to the music under the night sky. For reservations, phone 38-38-52.

La Cueva, La Longuera, Los Realejos (tel. 34-08-05), stands high on a cliff above Realejos, with views over the ocean. The nightclub is in a Guanche cave, containing a restaurant and stage for the twice-nightly floor shows which take place there. It's mostly patronized by people who come on the set excursion, which includes transportation from Puerto, dinner, wine, and dancing to the live band in between shows. The trip costs 2,500 pesetas ($17.50) per person. Without a meal, the bill is 1,500 pesetas ($10.50). Evenings are lively. The entertainment might be South American, African, whatever.

For the same price, there is a nightly Hawaiian show at the **Hotel Parque San Antonio** (tel. 38-29-60), from 8:30 p.m., including dinner and dancing, followed by a spectacular show at 10:30 p.m.

If you're interested in gambling, the majestic old Taoro Hotel has been revamped in part to contain the **Casino Taoro,** Parque Taoro (tel. 38-05-50). There is a splendid restaurant where a good three-course meal costs 1,800 pesetas ($12.60) per person, a bar with muted lights and trailing ferns and, of course, the gaming room, a sunken area beneath the bar and restaurant where blackjack, roulette, baccarat, and slot machines are played. Admission for one day is 500 pesetas ($3.50), and other charges and conditions are the same as those for the Casino in Gran Canaria. The management reserves the right to refuse entry to minors under 18 years old and prefers male guests not to wear jeans.

EXPLORING THE ISLAND: To the northeast of Santa Cruz lies a rugged pine-covered area, the **Montanas de Anaga** and the **Forest of Las Mercedes.** It's well worth a visit, as it's an area of great beauty and contrasting scenery.

To the south and north of Santa Cruz, *autopistas* (motorways) run to the beaches of Los Cristianos and Las Américas and to the airport and Puerto de la Cruz.

The northern motorway also brings you to **La Laguna,** the first capital of Tenerife and the seat of the only university on the island. This is a lovely old town in which to walk, visiting the **Nava Palace** owned by the father of the man who later founded the Botanical Gardens, the **Convent of Santa Catalina,** and the **Church and Monastery of Santo Domingo.** Also to be seen are many old seigneurial houses, with their coats-of-arms and sculptured lava façades; the **cathedral,** a modern building dating from 1913; and the **bishop's palace,** plus a mass of other beautiful churches and buildings in the traditional style.

After La Laguna, the motorway bears west and descends to **Puerto de la Cruz.** Once only a tiny fishing port, it was taken over first by the wintering wealthy, then developed as a broader-based all-year-round holiday resort. There is a wide promenade, with swimming pools, amusement parks, and gardens, as the beaches are rocky or made of black pebbly sand. Hotels tower in all directions, and it is only by searching that you find any traces of the old town. The **Church of Nuestra Señora de la Peña,** on the Plaza de la Iglesia, is early 17th century, and has a particularly fine baroque altarpiece in the usual gilded wood.

A market near the fishing port is open from 9 a.m. to 1 p.m. and 4 to 7 p.m. daily except Sunday.

Also right on the seafront is the tiny **Chapel of San Telmo,** built in 1626 by local fishermen and dedicated to their patron saint. It is now used by Catholic visitors, and masses are said in many European languages each Sunday.

The former **Royal Customs House,** 1 Calle Las Lonjas (tel. 38-30-61), in Puerto de la Cruz, lies between the Town Hall and the fishing harbor. Built in 1620 as a private residence, it is the oldest house in Puerto. It offers a 22-minute audio-visual presentation of the history of the island—from the Spanish conquest in 1496 up to the present day. Shows are given every half hour from 10 a.m. Admission is 100 pesetas ($70¢). The English owners are glad to answer questions. A shop selling real Canary crafts, South American artisan work, and Spanish Toledo work is to be found in this house and also at **Casa de Miranda,** at the end of the same street. This is also a historic structure built in 1730 and belonging to the Canary Island parents of Francisco de Miranda (1750–1812), the precursor of Latin American independence.

On the road down from the motorway to Puerto, on the right, lie the **Botanical Gardens.** These merit exploration even if you're not interested in gardening, as some of the trees and flowers are exotic and fantastic. A guide is available at the gate to identify the more extraordinary ones. The gardens are open all day from 9 a.m. to 7 p.m. in summer, to 6 p.m. off-season, charging an admission of 100 pesetas (70¢) per person. They were founded in 1788 for the purpose of acclimatizing exotic plants brought back by the Spanish Conquistadores. Bromeliads and aroids can be seen on the trunks and branches of trees, and morning glory covers the stone walls. There are palm trees and giant rubber-tree plants from South America, as well as the delicate strelitzia, which is now entirely adapted to the islands.

Behind Puerto, in a deep valley leading upward to the slopes of Teide, lies the town of **La Orotava.** One of the earliest to be established on the island by the Spanish, it was built on the site of the old Guanche kingdom of Bencomo and still retains much of its original splendor. Even today, it is the home of noble and well-to-do families, with lovely old houses and interior staircases and balconies of carved wood. Many flowers decorate the streets. The **Casa de los Balcones** now displays a collection of local arts and crafts which are for sale.

Along the north coast of the island, to the west of Puerto, lie many small villages, nestled between the foothills of Teide and the sea. Among these, **Icod de los Vinos** is probably the best known because of its dragon tree, reputed to be 3,000 years old. The town lies in a fertile wine-growing area, and its local wines are rather special. Above the dragon tree lies a small tree-shaded square surrounded by pretty Spanish houses. It's the most charming place in town, with views out over the sea and the countryside.

On the west side of the island are the massive cliffs of Los Gigantes, then a series of attractive little fishing ports lying between the sea and the banana plantations. These are passed before you arrive at the southern tip of the island and the urbanizations of **Las Américas, Los Cristianos,** and **Ten Bel.**

From here, the Autopista del Sur leads all the way to Santa Cruz, a journey of some 50 minutes. You'll pass **El Medano** which still seems to remain unchanged despite the proximity of the big hotels and the new airport inland.

In the center of the island, the peak of **Teide** is the focal point. It is set in a wide crater of barren rocks, **Las Cañadas,** and rises far above the pine-covered slopes which descend to the coastal plain, wide in the south, narrow in the north.

As you climb up and enter the Cañadas, you'll be amazed at the wide, barren crater stretching in all directions. The rocks are of fantastic colors, and there is a great silence. Beneath the peak is a parador, and on the side of the peak, within walking distance of the summit, a refuge.

For the lazy, a cable car runs to the upper station. From there, it's just a short walk to the edge of the cone. The altitude is high, however, and many visitors experience difficulty breathing. The cable cars run from 10 a.m. to 4 p.m., and the last one leaves the upper station at 5 p.m. A round trip costs 475 pesetas ($3.33).

From the Cañadas there is an excellent road running along the spine of the island to the airport at Los Rodeos. Beautiful views unfold on both sides. At some points you can see the sea on both sides of the island at once. It's lovely if the weather is good, rather mysterious if the clouds descend and isolate you.

Excursions by Coach

Viajes Marsans, 1 San José (tel. 24-26-18), Santa Cruz; **Meliá,** 9 Pilar (tel. 24-41-50), Santa Cruz; and **Wagons-Lits/Cook,** 9 Pilar (tel. 24-67-36), operate coach tours from Santa Cruz.

A day's drive up the spine of the island through the Cañadas to Teide, returning via La Orotava and Puerto de la Cruz, costs 1,600 pesetas ($11.20), excluding lunch. A trip to the Mercedes pine forests of the north on a Saturday afternoon goes for 1,500 pesetas ($10.50) and a day's tour of La Orotava, Icod, Los Gigantes, and Los Cristianos and their beaches, including lunch, is 3,000 pesetas ($21).

From Puerto de la Cruz, **Cyrasa,** Avenida Cristóbal Colón (tel. 38-05-66), operates a half-day jaunt that takes in the northwest coast. That tour goes to Icod to see the dragon tree, then to Garachico, a small fishing village that was almost entirely engulfed by a volcano. This costs 1,250 pesetas ($8.75). Cyrasa also offers a full-day tour of the island, which includes a visit to La Laguna, going for 2,300 pesetas ($16.10), including lunch.

ODDS AND ENDS: In Puerto de la Cruz, close to the tiny fishing harbor where you wonder how they get their boats in and out, is **La Fregata,** Edificio Bahía (tel. 38-34-33), the frigate pub. It's surrounded by fishermen mending their nets, selling fish, and talking. For several years it's been run by Tony Pestaille, and it's entirely like an English pub with a long bar, polished tables, and beer mats. A half pint of real English beer costs 150 pesetas ($1.05). Tony knows the island and is willing to help tourists with local information. The atmosphere and the talk are so cosmopolitan that it's almost a shock to walk out and be back in Spain again.

Another English pub, the oldest one at Puerto de la Cruz, is **Dick Turpin Tavern,** 24 Calle La Hoya. This one has live music and up-to-date music by cassette straight from Britain. You can relax in the cozy atmosphere of the pub from 11 a.m. to 1 a.m. drinking local beer at 150 pesetas ($1.05) a pint.

Casa Iriarte, 21 Calle San Juan (tel. 37-15-93), in Puerto de la Cruz, is a 300-year-old house with galleries surrounding a patio now devoted entirely to craftspeople from the islands. You can watch them embroidering, fashioning filigree silver and gold, hand-tooling leather, carving wood and ivory. The artisans sell their produce, and prices are lower than in the stores. Casa Iriarte is considered a National Historic Monument and is the only old Canary mansion left that is open entirely free to the public. Built before 1790, it is one of the few real Spanish houses containing a courtyard left in Puerto that you can enter.

A part of Casa Iriarte houses the only Nautical Museum in the Canary Islands, with a huge exhibition of maps and perfect-scale model boats, including all the Tall Ships that participated in the American Bicentennial Atlantic crossing. This museum is unique in that it shows the history of Tenerife as it relates to the sea, from its ancient discovery, as a stepping stone to the New World, and throughout history to the present. The entrance charge is 200 pesetas ($1.40).

Loro Parque, Punta Brava (tel. 38-30-12), just outside Puerto de la Cruz, attracts the family trade. Reached by free bus service from the Café Columbus on the Martianez Beach every 20 minutes, it is a tropical garden where exotic birds and animals fly or play free among the branches. The huge garden contains more than 500 palm trees and many blossoming hibiscus plants, sheltering what is one of the world's most important parrot collections. For the price of your coffee and cakes, whisky or Coca-Cola, you can watch parrots play ball, ride bicycles, roller-skate, count, add, and raise flags. The Black Continent contains specimens of all the parrots of Africa as well as chimpanzees, plus Lorovision, an impact film that is one of the latest novelties in the world of cinema. It allows you to see man's crazy world through the eyes of a parrot.

If you don't want to watch one of the exhibitions, you can just walk through the gardens past flocks of flamingos, to the colibrí free-flying hall, and then among the chimpanzees, also seeing the Galapagos turtle. The park is open daily from 8:30 a.m. to 6 p.m. Parrot shows are given at 9:30, 10:30, and 11:30 a.m. and 12:30, 2, 3, 4, 5, and 6:05 p.m. Lorovision is shown all day at ten minutes after the hour. The entrance fee is 600 pesetas ($4.20). There is a grill restaurant at the park with reasonable prices. Your entrance fee covers bus transportation from and back to Puerto.

Above Puerto at Las Arenas, the pottery shop, **La Calera** (tel. 37-02-26), sells all sorts of local products made on the premises. They range from ashtrays to gigantic Ali Baba vases.

Back in Santa Cruz, **Artespaña** is a big chain of stores created by the government to offer and sell representative Spanish handcrafts. Artespaña has two of these shops in Tenerife, one downtown in Santa Cruz at 8 Plaza de la Candelaría, just off the Plaza de España (tel. 24-62-75), and the other one in a 17th-century balcony house in La Orotava, 5 Calle de San Francisco (tel. 33-03-42). These shops give you the opportunity to acquire the most interesting examples of the country's popular arts, such as ceramics, Canary Islands embroideries and lace, Toledo swords, shields, and jewelry.

A five-minute walk from the Plaza de España, at the end of Puente Serrador, takes you to the **Market.** On the Calle José Manuel Guimera and Hernández Alfonso, fruit, vegetables, clothes and shoes, flowers, pottery, earthenware—everything—is for sale. It's the Petticoat Lane or flea market of Santa Cruz. The street is wide, tree-lined, and cool on a hot day. On Sunday the market is devoted to stamps and stamp-collecting, a popular Spanish hobby.

Next door is the **Mercado de Nuestra Señora de Africa,** a two-story building housing many open-sided shops in cloisters around a central courtyard with a fountain. Flower sellers in big straw hats are grouped around. Outside the market, record sellers play their wares, seemingly oblivious of each other, making a cacophony worth experiencing.

El Barco, Tenerife Pottery, 87 Las Arenas (tel. 37-16-23), in Puerto de la Cruz. Everything here is made in the pottery from Mount Teide clay and painted by hand. You can watch the craftsmen at work and order tiles to take home as a souvenir. Also made in the pottery and for sale there is ceramic jewelry. The Canary Craft Corner has a wide selection of local handiwork, lace and embroidery, along with hand-tooled tin and leatherwork. Refreshments are available on the terrace, and a free bus leaves from the Café Columbus in Puerto de la Cruz several times a day. The pottery lies high above the town. It's open daily except Sunday and holidays.

Safari Shangri-La, Finca el Patio, Santiago del Teide (tel. 86-31-72), is a donkey trek into the heart of the Tinerfeño countryside. At 2,000 feet below rugged cliffs lies the village of Masca. Until recently, this village could only be approached by mule-train. Now there is a road, but the Safari follows the old tracks past native houses where it seems time has stood still. You will pass 400-year-old *fincas* (farmhouses) using the traditional methods of cultivation and see the inhabitants wearing, as everyday clothing, the costume now usually only associated with the folklore of the country.

The owners and breeders of the donkeys provide their own interesting story. Hank and Diane Young visited Tenerife during a world cruise in their own yacht, after having sold out in their home state of California. They fell in love with the island, particularly the area around Santiago del Teide, and sold their boat and bought a dilapidated finca. They set about restoring the house and revitalizing the farm, building stables and a large paved corral. The finca has now been declared a National Monument, and the Youngs have to get permission before they can even put a coat of paint on the old buildings. They and their two Siamese cats are making a local name for themselves, not only for the safaris but for the prowess of their male donkey, who has sired more than 70 foals and stands at stud to the local farm mares. The herd is now 49 in number, including a set of twins, the only known pair alive in the world as of this writing. The donkeys, fit, well fed, and rested, make little of the breathtaking journey up to Masca, a lovely old village high in the mountains. During your trip, you break for lunch, which is accompanied by guitar music. The cost of the day, including transportation, lunch, wine, and the donkey, is 3,200 pesetas ($22.40) per person.

Bananěra el Guanche, La Orotava (tel. 33-18-53), is a banana plantation, open daily from 8 a.m. to 7 p.m. Every 15 minutes the bus leaves from the Café Columbus on the promenade in Puerto, so the plantation is within easy reach. The whole process of banana growing is explained in a simple fashion, and you are given a drink of banana liqueur and a Canary banana. In the shop all sorts of souvenirs are available, and you can buy seeds, rum, rum honey, flowers, and avocados. The entrance fee is 350 pesetas ($2.45).

On its journey back to Puerto the bus stops at **La Calera,** a fascinating pottery on Las Arenas, Puerto de la Cruz (tel. 37-02-26). It's well worth a visit to see the pots being thrown, baked, and painted. They are very beautiful and a charming souvenir of the island. In addition to the free bus ride, you get a free banana and a shot of banana liqueur served to you by young women dressed in national costumes.

El Castillo, at Los Realejos in the Orotava Valley, ten minutes from Puerto de la Cruz, is a fascinating place with a museum displaying graphic and factual representations of the story of the Canary Islands from the early times of the Guanches to the 19th century, including Nelson's attack on Tenerife. The gardens contain orchards of avocado pear trees, papayas, mangoes, and bananas, and there is a cactus garden. You can play *petanca,* a Mediterranean game of bowls, or relax in the solarium. Souvenirs of the islands are available in the gift shop, or you can have a drink at the patio bar. Open daily from 9 a.m. to 7 p.m., to 6 p.m. in winter. There is a free bus transfer from the Café Columbus in town.

OUTDOOR FUN: This is a marvelous island for walking, as one is rewarded with such beautiful views. It's possible from the top of Teide at dawn to see every island in the archipelago.

Walking and Climbing

The tourist office in Santa Cruz can supply a series of ten excellent maps of the **Senderos Turisticos** (tourist pathways). Available in English, they give routes and useful information as to refuges, camping sites, and picnic places. Bus stops and telephone locations are shown, together with the phone numbers of various taxi stands, the police, and the forestry bureau. As they also show main roads, these maps are excellent for the motorist.

Golf

At El Penon, Tacoronte, 8½ miles from Santa Cruz, 13½ miles from Puerto de la Cruz, is an 18-hole course. Greens fees are about 900 pesetas ($6.30) Monday to Friday, rising to 1,100 pesetas ($7.70) on weekends and holidays. Rental of clubs is 250 pesetas ($1.75), and caddies are available at a cost of 500 pesetas ($3.50) per hour. There is also a snackbar and restaurant on the grounds. For more information, telephone 25-02-40.

Fishing

To practice surf casting, you can get in touch with **Club de Pesca Neptuno,** 21 Calle Pérez Galdos (tel. 28-13-21), where you will get information as to the best places for this sport.

Bullfights

This takes place in the bullrings on the Rambla de General Franco in Santa Cruz. It's not a regular event, although times of bullfights are posted throughout this island.

Boating

You might enjoy a day aboard the *Marino Riquer,* a sailing ship more than 100 years old. During the day's coastal voyage you can bathe or fish or just lie on deck, watching the other passengers hard at work. Departure by coach is from Café Columbus in Puerto de la Cruz at 9 a.m., the return at 5:30 p.m. The cost, including transport and food, is 3,000 pesetas ($21) per person.

FERRY TO GOMERA: This is a motorway over the sea. In the south of Tenerife, almost hidden among the high-rise hotels, the car-ferry, *Benchijigua,* runs a trip from the old port of Los Cristianos to the port of San Sebastián on the island of Gomera. The cost of a round trip is 2,480 pesetas ($17.36) for adults, 1,340 pesetas ($9.38) for children. The cost of taking a small car over and back is 4,400 pesetas ($30.80). There is bus service from Santa Cruz to Los Cristianos 1¾ hours before the boat sails at 10 a.m. The bus round trip costs 750 pesetas ($5.25).

The Parador Nacional (tel. 87-11-00) is really the only place to eat at Gomera. A taxi from the harbor costs 275 pesetas ($1.93). It is a beautiful low building erected around a shady courtyard with much antique furniture. There is a delightful formal drawing room and a cool dining room with a polished floor and sparkling tables. The menu of the day costs 2,000 pesetas ($14), consisting of a lunch of three substantial courses. A bottle of Gomera wine (mostly white) is an additional 250 pesetas ($1.75). If you wish to spend the night, a double with bath will cost 8,000 pesetas ($56); a single, 5,500 pesetas ($38.50). However, just for lunch the parador is good value. It also has a swimming pool set in gardens high above the sea.

For a low-cost overnight stay, try **Hotel Garajonay,** 17 Ruíz de Padron, San Sebastián de la Gomera (tel. 87-05-50), which lies in the small harbor town. At this simple place only doubles are rented, costing from 2,000 pesetas ($14).

A taxi ride of about 3½ hours to Vallehermoso and back to the parador costs about 6,000 pesetas ($42), or a drive around to Vallehermoso and on to Valle Gran Rey and Playa Santiago costs about 8,500 pesetas ($59.50) by taxi. Although these rates are high, the cost can be divided among four passengers. The roads are tortuous, the progress slow.

At Hermigua, a typical house, **Los Telares,** has been restored and is worth a visit to see how workers wove cloth and ground corn. Souvenirs are available.

Around Agulo in the north is a rich region of vines and fruit trees. High above the town is the **Restaurant Las Rosas,** with a daily menu offered at lunch for 700 pesetas ($4.90). From here, you can look across at neighboring Tenerife with magnificent views of Teide.

Self-drive cars are available from the harbor, but it is well to book in advance if you want to be sure of a car.

Excursions to Gomera are available from Puerto de la Cruz and Santa Cruz, covering the drive to Los Cristianos, a ferry, and a coach drive around the island, including lunch. The cost is from 7,000 pesetas ($49), and you must start out at 6:15 a.m. You won't be home until around 9 p.m., making it a long, tiring day.

The *Benchijugua* has two large lounges with a bar and snacks as well, plus a restaurant, to while away the 1½-hour journey.

3. La Palma

La Palma, the most northwesterly island in the Canary archipelago, is a fast-rising tourist area like Fuerteventura, its distant cousin in the east. In relation to its size of 290 square miles, it is the world's highest island. Its name, La Palma, is not to be confused with Las Palmas on Gran Canaria, and its major town, Santa Cruz de la Palma, is not to be confused with other Canarian Santa Cruzes.

There are a few beaches of poor dark sand and rocks, yet it is eagerly sought out by some tourists as a remote hideaway. For most of its modern history, the island has been left undisturbed. The majority of its friendly people have engaged in agriculture, growing bananas in the south, tobacco and cereals in the central area. Throughout the island are found almond and fruit trees, as well as potatoes and other vegetables. A good water supply from rain and underground sources makes the island lush. Large beech and pine forests abound on the island, but little flora. As for fauna, kestrels, pigeons, and rabbits are plentiful. Farm animals are purely for local domestic use.

There is an average temperature of 68° Fahrenheit, with a winter minimum of around 59° and a summer peak of 85°.

GETTING THERE: **Iberia,** the national airline, has daily flights to La Palma from Tenerife and Gran Canaria, and **Compania Transmediterránea** operates a regular boat service from Santa Cruz de Tenerife three times a week in each direction. There is also a boat once a week from El Hierro, the island on the horizon to the south. The boat fare from Tenerife to La Palma is 3,380 pesetas ($23.66) for a seat in the large and comfortable lounge, going up to 9,000 pesetas ($63) for a berth in a two-berth cabin with shower and toilet. The ships are large and stable, and there is usually a buffet bar. Once at La Palma, a taxi from the airport to the city center is 650 pesetas ($4.55) plus tip, for up to four passengers and their baggage. From the docks to the city center is about 200 pesetas ($1.40).

WHERE TO STAY: Accommodations are limited, so always arrive with a reservation.

Parador Nacional de Santa Cruz, 34 Avenida Marítima, Santa Cruz de la Palma (tel. 41-23-40), is a typical Spanish building with balconies on the upper floors, a stone-floored lobby, and an elegant staircase leading to a wide lounge with comfortable chairs grouped around the inevitable TV. Bedrooms, all with bath, vary in size from small to spacious, and you may be lucky and get the first-floor corner room which was occupied by King Juan Carlos on his visit to the Observatory at the top of the island. The beds are comfortable with spotless linen, and many have marvelous views out to the sea across the promenade. Doubles go for 5,500 pesetas ($38.50) a night. There are only two singles, so you may find yourself paying for a double even if you're alone. Breakfast is a casual help-yourself affair. Dinner at 1,900 pesetas ($13.30) includes homemade soups and a choice of appetizers such as prawns with avocado, followed by a good fresh fish dish or perhaps a grilled steak or pork chops.

Hotel Mayantigo, 68 Alvarez de Abreu, Santa Cruz de la Palma (tel. 41-17-40), is a very simple place one floor up in a building lying one block from the seafront in the central part of town. Clean, basic rooms with private bath rent for 2,200 pesetas ($15.40) in a single, 3,400 pesetas ($23.80) in a double. Breakfast is the only meal served. A friendly staff goes a long way toward creating a homey atmosphere, but no one speaks anything other than Canarian Spanish.

Hotel San Miguel, 31 Avenida de José Antonio, Santa Cruz de la Palma (tel. 41-12-43), is quite a large place, lying up a broad avenida from the sea. The street level is taken up with a bar and a snackbar where you can order light meals or breakfast. The clean but simple accommodations rise some ten floors above, with singles renting for 2,500 pesetas ($17.50), doubles for 3,600 pesetas ($25.30), each with private bath. An apartment for two with a sitting room costs 4,000 pesetas ($28).

WHERE TO EAT: **Restaurante Canarias,** Avenida Marítima, Santa Cruz de la Palma (tel. 41-31-82), is a busy and bustling place, spotlessly clean, standing on the main promenade of town with a small balcony. Don Amadeo dispenses food and drink almost every day of the week from early morning until late at night. Portions are generous, and the paella for two is large enough for four. A good mixed salad is a meal in itself or you can enjoy the more luxurious shrimp with garlic. Poultry and meat dishes are fresh. For the less ambitious a menu of the day begins at 750 pesetas ($5.25). I tend to favor places where Spaniards eat, and this restaurant is popular with young Palmerans.

Bodegón Tamanca, San Nicolás, Las Manchas (tel. 46-21-55). As you drive through the south of the island, ignore the more obvious bodegón that you pass after Fuencaliente and drive on to Las Manchas and this delightful bodegon built into the side of the cliff, a warren of dimly lit cavernous rooms. The bar is dominated by barrels of beer and wine from which you drink by the small glass or the jug. Hanging among the barrels are hams and dried carcasses, fish and animal. There is no menu. Just ask for such dishes as jamón (ham) serrano, salads, or papas arrugadas. If you feel adventurous, try the plate of local delicacies, all sorts of sausages of the island, including morcilla dulce made from hazelnuts, blood, and onions. You can also order a small pork filet and a tiny beefsteak. A meal is likely to cost from 750 pesetas ($5.25). Mojo sauce accompanies almost every dish. Clients are usually islanders out for a jaunt, and the bar is often full of happy talk and banter.

EXPLORING THE ISLAND: As there is no regular coach tour around the island, a self-drive car is usually the way to tour. Car-rental companies tend to be helpful with advice and maps as to what to see, where to eat, and which roads are really only suitable for locals who know them well.

It's best to divide the island into two or three parts. The north; the center including the capital, the Observatory, and the Caldera de Taburiente National Park; and the southern part of the island.

A drive to the north will take you through Puntallana, a town of about 1,500 inhabitants in an area of natural and luxuriant vegetation, to Punta Salinas where you can watch underwater scuba and surface fishing. Then it's on to **San Andrés** for a swim in the Charco Azul, a natural sea swimming pool. San Andrés lies 17 miles from Santa Cruz in one of the most fertile areas of the island. The town is one of the most beautiful, with lovely old buildings and flowers on every corner and balcony. Later you can drive to **Puerto Espíndola,** a fishing port where you can enjoy fish straight from the boats in one of the small local bars and watch the fishermen at work on their nets.

From here the road deteriorates and begins to twist and wind up the mountain slopes so it is only the adventurous who should continue on the dirt road north to Barlovento through rich banana plantations. Here is where you can purchase a straw hat or basket and some of the typical hand embroidery of the region. Very winding roads lead to Garafia. It's only about 22 miles, but even the bends have bends so you can't get up any speed. There are several legendary dragon trees in the area and at Fuente de la Zarza a "guanche" cave.

A drive south from Garafia to Puntagorda and Tijarafe takes you to **Cueva Bonita,** the "pretty cave" where seawater flows into a large cavern and gives a bluish light, filling the entrance and then breaking into glittering particles which give off all the colors of the spectrum. This is a spectacular display which seems to be more artificial than natural, but it is entirely natural. The road continues through El Time, Los Llanos de Aridane, and El Paso. There you will see the road to the left to La Cumbrecita, a viewing point over the **Caldera de Taburiente,** the majestic crater in the center of the island. A 9½-mile drive will take you back to the capital.

A drive to the south is a more leisurely affair along the coast. It's less attractive but the road is good almost all the way. Some eight miles from Santa Cruz takes you to Mazo where the old and new meet for the island airport's impressive runway. Down by the water is the **Belmaco Cave** decorated with ancient paintings of great archeological importance and rock engravings relating to the Megalithic period of the Atlantic coasts of Europe.

As you drive on south you will see the island of El Hierro on the horizon. At Fuencaliente you will come to an area of the most recent volcanic activity. In 1971 **Teneguía** erupted. There is a road to the volcano, and you can also walk to the older volcano of San Antonio. The road now turns north to Los Llanos de Aridane where you can head east across the island to drive back to Santa Cruz through El Paso.

A visit to the new **Observatory** at Las Muchachos is worth while, but it involves a lot of problems. The actual buildings are open to the public only on the 15th day of each month. The buildings house the giant Isaac Newton landscape telescope with computers and electronic devices, joined by the William Herschel reflector, the third-largest telescope in the world.

However, even if it isn't possible to visit the buildings, you can drive through the National Park, going first through thick forests of pine and chestnut. The forests give way to enormous craggy craters and sheer rock faces. Be warned: the road is good but rocks occasionally fall and the barriers are inadequate. The faint-hearted are advised to think twice before embarking on the drive of about 1½ hours up, then back along the same route.

Those who make the trip will be rewarded with magnificent views and, at the top, be able to stand on two rocks called Los Muchachos (two boys), which is now a viewing area created at the same time as the observatory. The road is wide enough for passing traffic as it was built to enable construction of the observatory.

WHAT TO SEE IN SANTA CRUZ DE LA PALMA: The area just back from the sea around the **Church of El Salvador** is the oldest part of town. The church was started in 1503 and is worth a visit to see its beautiful Moorish type roof-work and the baptismal font carved in the Renaissance style from Carrara marble. The painting of the *Transfiguration* on the high altar is by Esquivel, the romantic painter of the Seville school.

The **city hall** dates from the mid-16th century, and there are several ancestral homes along the Calle Real which once belonged to the various aristocratic families of the island. The oldest and most attractive are on the Avenida Marítima where their ancient wooden balconies jut out over the pavement.

The well-equipped **National History Museum,** La Cosmologica, on Pedro Poggio dates from 1881. The **Castle of Santa Catalina,** also known as the Royal Castle, formed part of the defenses of the island from the 16th to the 18th centuries against attacks from pirates. The most infamous was Peg-Leg, the French corsair who ransacked and burned the city in 1553. In 1585, Sir Francis Drake had his flagship sunk beneath him when it was hit by a cannon ball from the castle.

On the edge of the capital is the **Sanctuary of Nuestra Señora la Virgen de las Nieves.** The building dates from the 16th century with 17th and 18th century additions. Its most precious possession is, without doubt, the small Gothic sculpture in glazed and painted terracotta, depicting the 14th century Señora de las Nieves, patroness of La Palma. Her feast day on August 5 is a joyous day throughout the island. Other annual festivals include the Dance of the Dwarfs and the Dialogue between the Castle of Santa Catalina and the Ship, a replica of Columbus's caravel, the *Santa Maria,* which lies alongside the Avenida de las Nieves and contains a Naval Museum.

4. Lanzarote

Lanzarote is the most easterly of the Canary Islands and the closest to Africa. Like the other islands in the archipelago, the south is bare, dry, and sandy, the north lusher and more cultivated. But on Lanzarote you don't have the marked difference in temperature and climate found on the sister islands. No central mountain creates rainfall in the north, leaving Lanzarote exposed to the hot breezes from Africa.

The island is still unspoiled by tourism, although roads have been paved leading in from the airport, so visitors no longer disappear in a cloud of dust. However, the two main resort areas of Puerto del Carmen and Playa Blanca are developing rapidly. The style of new development is pleasant and inoffensive—no high-rise buildings have been allowed since the 1970s. There are many reasonable restaurants, some good sea-village fish places, bars, discos, and supermarkets, a number of which seem to be open at all hours.

With such rapid development, businesses in existence one day may disappear within the next month or so. Therefore, I have kept to the tried and established places, usually owner-run. I know you'll find many more good places to stay, to eat, and to enjoy yourself, such as the new Cave Concert Hall next to the grotto of Jameos del Agua where prestigious entertainment is presented.

The island is booming, and prices are rising. There is a general drug problem throughout Spain since relaxation of the laws. This has led to increased crime and necessitates an extended baggage inspection at airports. Because of this, the rather slow Lanzarote Airport Customs check can be even slower, and you may have to wait up to two hours after landing before you can clear the baggage hall. Preference is given to Spanish flights, which can add to the delay.

Still, Lanzarote has a magnetic power which draws people back year after year. You may choose to stay in an apartment or villa, but if so, you will find that basically, as with the other islands, you'll find out about these mainly by personal contact after your arrival.

The capital is **Arrecife,** a busy town with a fish-canning factory, salt pans, and a thriving harbor where the large fleet of fishing boats unload their catches and where ocean-going vessels call. On the main street, León y Castillo, very few people speak English. But don't let that put you off, as the island people are generally very kind, from the policeman to the attendant in the chemist shop.

On the reef from which the town takes its name is the **Castillo de San Gabriel,** a squat fortress housing a museum of archeology and anthropology. It's usually open from 9 a.m. to 1 p.m. and 3 to 7 p.m. The custodian has studied his subject with care and will willingly tell you—in Spanish—about the collection of relics from the island's past.

In the big-ship harbor is the **Castillo de San José,** another fortress skillfully adapted by Cesar Manrique, the island's favorite son. It contains a good exhibition of modern painting and sculpture. At its restaurant, you can dine well for 1,500 pesetas ($10.50) to 2,800 pesetas ($19.60), choosing from such dishes as melon and Serrano ham, asparagus with mayonnaise, squid, pepper steak, and fondue bourguignonne. It's pleasant to have a drink at the black leather bar. The tiny, rocky garden jutting right over the harbor is tranquil, too. At night the harbor is floodlit.

In town stands the **Church of San Gines,** named after the patron saint of the island, whose festival on August 24 and 29 is an occasion for frantic celebrations and processions.

GETTING AROUND: You'll find the usual methods, as outlined below.

Car Rentals

Hertz and **Avis** deliver to the airport. Avis has an office at Puerto del Carmen by the Fariones (tel. 82-52-54). Either charges 3,600 pesetas ($25.30) per day for a Seat Fura, 3,870 pesetas ($27.09) per day for a Panda with a sun roof, plus tax and insurance. All rentals are based on unlimited mileage. If you rent a car for a week, they give you the car free one day in every season.

Taxis

There are ranks at all major hotels and at the airport. Usually it's better to ask your driver to wait at an agreed price if you use a taxi for a whole day's exploring. Prices are reasonable, but always agree in advance, of course. From the airport to Puerto del Carmen costs 800 pesetas ($5.60); from the airport to Arrecife, 425 pesetas ($2.98).

Many of the taxi drivers now speak a little bit of English. Most certainly they are knowledgeable about the island. A tour of the north of the island should cost about 5,470 pesetas ($38.29); to the south, 4,590 pesetas ($32.13); or an evening visit to Jameos del Agua, (see below, "Exploring the Island") will run about 2,790 pesetas ($19.53). Waiting time, at 900 pesetas ($6.30) an hour, is extra. These prices quoted are valid from Puerto del Carmen or from any of the urban developments and hotels on the southeast coast.

Buses

There are three bus routes—north, central, and south. On the whole they cater to working people who come into Arrecife in the morning and return to their villages at night. From Playa Blanca (Yaiza) to Arrecife costs 180 pesetas ($1.26); from Puerto del Carmen to Arrecife, 90 pesetas (63¢).

Information on both buses and taxis (which are all state controlled) can be obtained by calling 81-15-46. It's not difficult to use the system. No one will speak English, but everyone will try to help see that you're going in the right direction.

WHERE TO STAY: I'll begin my hotel recommendations on Lanzarote at:

Arrecife

Hotel Residencia Miramar, 2 Calle Coll (tel. 81-04-38), overlooks the Puento de las Bolas and the Castillo de San Gabriel on the Arrecife seafront. An unobtrusive façade leads to a small lobby with a tiny lounge overlooking the castle. Rooms are simple but clean, renting for 2,800 pesetas ($19.60) in a single with bath, 4,000 pesetas ($28) in a double with bath. The Miramar is good to know about, as pleasant, modest accommodations are scarce in Arrecife. The hotel doesn't have a restaurant, but you can order a continental breakfast, and you are only five minutes from the center of town and the Arrecife Gran, where there are many restaurants. The establishment is also handy if you arrive by ship, as it lies on the dock side of town.

Apartamentos Arrecife-Playa, 40 Avenida de la Mancomunidad (tel. 81-03-00), is one of the places where you can be pretty sure of finding an apartment for one night, two weeks, or three months, for this establishment is not tied to any tour operators. It is a large building opposite the Arrecife Grand Hotel, with a lobby decorated with seashore pebbles, an erratic elevator, and roomy apartments, all of which have a wide terrace with views over the sea. Furnishings are simple, but the accommodations have all the necessary equipment for a comfortable life. All you need to add is food and drink. Downstairs are many restaurants and bars, so you don't have to go hungry if you don't stock your larder. Apartments go from 4,800 pesetas ($33.60) to 5,400 pesetas ($37.80) with less attractive views, 6,000 pesetas ($42) to 6,500 pesetas ($45.50) for those with larger living rooms and better outlooks. All, however, have a kitchen and bath.

Puerto del Carmen

Hotel los Fariones, at Puerto del Carmen (tel. 82-51-75), is a long-established hotel with a long palm-lined terrace leading to tropical gardens where exotic birds sing and down to a sandy cove, also palm lined, where the sea laps gently against the protecting rocks. There are two swimming pools, mini-golf, tennis, and indoor games for the energetic. For the less active, a large lounge and busy bar open onto the terrace. At night the boîte, La Cueva, hums with life—at a peaceful distance from the hotel. Rooms are well furnished, having sea views and balconies. Singles, including a continental breakfast, rent for 6,000 pesetas ($42); doubles, 8,200 pesetas ($57.40). For half board, add an additional 3,200 pesetas ($22.40) per person daily.

Hostal Residencia Magec, 8 Calle Hierro (tel. 82-58-74), is on a quiet road off the main street of the old fishing village. Some rooms look out over the sea along the street, while others have no view except neighboring buildings. All are simply furnished, with basic fixtures. Singles with wash basin rent for 1,400 pesetas ($9.80). Bathless doubles cost 2,200 pesetas ($15.40), and doubles with bath or shower go for 2,600 pesetas ($18.20). Half board is available for 1,400 pesetas ($9.80) per person. The downstairs café is open daily.

Playa Blanca

Salvador, who runs a restaurant, Casa Salvador, nearby (see "Where to Eat"), and his family also own and operate the **Hostal Playa Blanca** (tel. 83-00-46), built on rocks overlooking the bay. Only ten rooms are available, and they are well kept and simply furnished. The cost of a double room is 1,600 pesetas ($11.20) to 1,800 pesetas ($12.60) per day. Write for an accommodation, or else ask at the bar when you arrive. A continental breakfast is served down in the bar.

Playa de los Pocillos

For those who can afford it, **Hotel San Antonio,** Playa de los Pocillos (tel. 82-50-50), is right on the sea between long sandy beaches south of the airport. All rooms overlook the water and subtropical gardens full of lush vegetation planted in volcanic ash. The hotel has its own desalinization plant so the water is safe to drink. There is an excellent quick laundry and dry-cleaning service as well. You can sink into one of the soft chairs in the lounges and bar with your favorite cocktail. There is live music for dancing every night, as well as a popular disco. Other facilities include a super swimming pool, tennis courts, and game rooms. In the dining room, the chef offers a wide range of international dishes. There is a cold buffet by the pool every day for lunch and a barbecue every Sunday. In this island where water and amenities are scarce, the San Antonio is a haven at a cost of 4,800 pesetas ($33.60) per person, based on double occupancy. A single rents for 5,800 pesetas ($40.60). For full board, add another 5,200 pesetas ($36.40) per person daily. Pedro Cabrera is the manager.

Your Own Villa

There are many privately owned villas and apartments on the island—mainly in the complexes around the Fariones hotel. Many are rented out for short or long periods when not required by their owners. Although they vary in size, some accommodating up to ten persons, most of them shelter four adults with room for cots for small children. These villas or apartments are fully furnished, and a maid comes in daily except Sunday. Pre-arrival groceries can be provided upon request.

For further information, get in touch with **Lanzacasas S.L.**, Plaza San Antonio, Playa de los Pocillos, Lanzarote (tel. 82-60-20). A one-bedroom apartment for two persons will cost from 31,750 pesetas ($222.25) per week, from 48,000 pesetas ($336) per week for a two-bedroom apartment for four persons.

The Super-Splurge

Hotel Las Salinas-Sheraton, Costa Teguise (tel. 81-30-40), lies about eight miles to the north of Arrecife, toward Arieta and Jameos del Agua. The hotel stands like an oasis among lava fields, right on the coast. Las Salinas is set in gardens, contrasting with the black of the lava. It is a white cantilevered building, surrounded by palms, grass, and a mass of bougainvillea on every balcony. The cool, marble-floored lobby leads to a large water garden, open to the sky. Around this garden, rooms are grouped on three floors. There are interesting nooks full of comfortable armchairs, as well as a large lounge. The dining room is large and airy, overlooking the swimming pool and bay. There are three bars, in addition to the one at the pool. The swimming pool is an architectural masterpiece, reflecting, as does the whole hotel, the hand of Cesar Manrique, who designed it. You can swim around islands, under bridges, in deep or shallow water.

The bedrooms have large beds, baths, and separate toilets, color TV, video movies, radios, and direct-dial phones, plus mini-bars. Each has a terrace surrounded with flowers and ferns that is totally invisible from all other rooms, so you can let yourself go if you want to. The charge is 18,000 pesetas ($126) in a single, 23,000 pesetas ($161) in a twin-bedded unit. If you take full board, expect to pay 7,500 pesetas ($52.50) per person additional. Lunch or dinner costs 3,500 pesetas ($24.50).

Breakfast is served in your room or at the buffet beside the pool. You can eat as much as you like. Lunch is either table d'hôte in the dining room, or, again, you can eat from a poolside buffet with a choice of some 38 cold main dishes, two hot dishes, including a mix-your-own sauce for pasta to be made up from 20 different spices and relishes. Follow that with a choice from some 16 desserts. Dinner is a four-course delight—even the table d'hôte offers three or four choices with each course. There is also an à la carte menu. The cuisine is of a high standard. Activities included in the room tariffs are tennis and windsurfing. There is also a nine-hole golf course. You can make use of the complete body-building center with a monitor.

WHERE TO EAT: My recommendations range throughout the island, beginning in:

Arrecife

Cafetería Avenida, Avenida de la Mancomunidad, is one of a row of cafés on the main promenade of town. Under a large awning, you can sit on the terrace and watch the world go by for the price of a sangría or beer at 150 pesetas ($1.05). Tapas (bar snacks) are good at a cost of 150 pesetas ($1.05) to 250 pesetas ($1.79) a portion. It caters more to those seeking snacks and sandwiches. However, the cook will prepare pork chops and french fries, or steak with fries. You can fill up for around 750 pesetas ($5.25). This place is used a lot by the locals, which indicates that it's reliable. It's certainly a very pleasant place at which to write your postcards.

La Marísquería del Molino, Muelle Pescador, Puerto de Naos, is presided over by Don Jacinto Duque Carabello. In the scruffy part of town, it's right on the fishing quay. Smart expensive cars are usually parked outside, as the restaurant attracts local business people drawn to its good food. You eat either in the small bar downstairs, jostled by waiters and hurried drinkers, or upstairs in the smartly decorated restaurant. The fish—squid, mero, langostinos, cigales, viejas, or percebes—is delivered daily from the boats across the road. The price varies a little according to the catch of the day. For 1,500 pesetas ($10.50) and up you can have a satisfying fish dinner, including potatoes and a salad. Half portions of fresh fish go for half price. Local wine is served. In the downstairs bar, tapas of octopus, rabbit (a local specialty), vegetables, and fish salads are excellent.

Restaurant Martín, 11 Plaza Calvo Sotelo, is run by Señor Martín, who caters to local shopowners and dignitaries. The restaurant is a simple room, packed with tables. At the back is a bar where you can order half portions of many of the regular dishes at less than half price. The menu of the day costs 675 pesetas ($4.73) for two dishes, soup or salad, then meat or fish with vegetables, bread, a dessert, and a quarter liter of wine. On the à la carte menu your tab can easily climb to 1,200 pesetas ($8.40). Typical selections are prawns in garlic, squid, tongue, ham with peas, and meatballs, followed by pineapple with kirsch. The restaurant offers excellent value, as well as fascinating local color, but it's best to arrive early as it is very busy around 2 p.m. and you'll most likely have to wait for a table.

Marísquería Abdon, 54 Calle Canalejas, lies on a back street behind the Café Avenida. At this restaurant you can select your own fish swimming in a tank. It's another owner-run place, where Señor Abdon Betencort presides behind the bar and cooks your meal as it's ordered. A substantial menu of the day costs 900 pesetas ($6.30). You can also order à la carte—selecting such dishes as seafood soup, asparagus in three sauces, paella with seafood, large boiled crawfish, squid (fried or grilled), and mussels marinara. Complete meals ordered this way begin at 1,400 pesetas ($9.80). Have the local wine by the carafe. The place is very popular with tourists and locals alike, and its atmosphere is so nice and friendly it's like being part of a family.

Or if you're not in the mood for fish, try the **Restaurant Chino Taiwan,** next door. Local workers often gather here to try the usual Chinese dishes: prawn crackers, chop suey, the special of the house, and other Oriental cuisine. A three-course meal will cost from 950 pesetas ($6.65) to 1,400 pesetas ($9.80).

They also do take-away meals, and are open from 11:30 a.m. to 11:30 p.m. seven days a week.

Bar Brasilia, 5 León y Castillo. When you go into town—to the bank or the pharmacy, for example—stop at the Brasilia for coffee and churros, those doughnut-like sticks, deep-fried and sweet, served in a pile wrapped in a napkin. Order one portion for two people, unless you're a good trencherman (or woman). This is the traditional morning snack of the local shopkeeper, banker, or passerby. The bar stretches far back from the street, a noisy passageway of tables flanking the long bar. A dull roar of chatter bounces off large black-and-white photos of old Lanzarote. There are clean, functional toilets, and in the Brasilia itself, hurried, anonymous service. They also do such tapas as Russian salad, fish-and-potato pie, sandwiches, and stuffed rolls, at a cost ranging from 85 pesetas (60¢) to 175 pesetas ($1.23). Coffee is 65 pesetas (46¢). But it is for the churros that I recommend this place. Have a look at the churros-making machine.

Arrieta

Bar Miguel lies on the edge of the sea, with tables on the terrace. The fish has only a few yards to travel from sea to pan. As with so many of the really good fish restaurants, Miguel's is a very simple place. It's really just some long lines of oilcloth-covered tables, plus a bar. At first glance it might look uninviting, but it's clean and the cookery is very good. The menu includes such delicacies as sancocho Canario, caldo de pescado, and escoldones de gofio, along with calamares a la romana, plus pulpos en aceite y vinagre. There is always a mixed salad along with papas arrugadas or french fries served with the fish. Local cheese and ice cream make up the selection to end your meal. The fresh fish of the day is served fried or grilled. Expect to pay around 1,000 pesetas ($7) per person for a meal, including some local wine. Closed Monday.

Teguise

The **Bar-Restaurant Acatife** is on the main square opposite the church and the Palace of Spinola, with the inevitable half-open green-painted door. It opens onto a large bar and then a restaurant in which you can order soup, rabbit, paella, and desserts, a meal costing from 550 pesetas ($3.85). White wine is available.

Caleta de Famara

The village lies on the north coast of the island at the end of a long beach dominated by the cliffs on which perches the Mirador del Río. Across the water you can see Graciosa. To get there, drive past the Monumento toward Teguise, then turn off through the fields to Caleta de Famara.

Bar Restaurante Bajamar, Casa Garcia, is two lofty, airy dining rooms joined and divided by window boxes, tables decked in clear blues and greens, and a spanking white bar on one side. I always ask for the fish of the day, which the cook prepares as you like it—grilled, fried, breaded, or in batter. You'll also receive a large dish of beautifully cooked mussels to be eaten with salad and potatoes. Look out for the homemade mojo verde, surely the strongest on the island. A complete meal, not including wine, will cost from 1,800 pesetas ($12.60) to 2,000 pesetas ($14), depending on the kind of fish you have. You can drink local or imported wine or else local beer.

Puerto del Carmen

The **Victoria Inn,** Puerto del Carmen, is run by Ted Martin, who is English. He is found behind the bar from 6 p.m. till midnight except Thursday, when it's shut all day. The kitchen keeps the same hours. Drinks are good measures at reasonable prices, with bottled English beer going for 110 pesetas (77¢). Juan helps with the waiting and serving, and Honorio reigns in the kitchen, turning out a good pepper steak. Only ask for *muy fuerte* (very hot) if you mean it. There is no daily specialty, except on Sunday when it's likely to be roast pork with all the trimmings. Otherwise, the menu carries such items as soup, shrimp cocktail, scampi provençale, pork filet with cheese sauce, or grilled sole. Expect to pay 1,800 pesetas ($12.60) for a three-course meal. All dishes are served with potatoes and a vegetable or salad, and the portions are ample. Apple pie with ice cream is good and popular, as are the strawberry crêpes. Wines are a fine value. The atmosphere is very cosmopolitan, with mainly English-speaking tourists, and the food really good.

Las Vistas Terraza Bar, 20 Calle Guardilama (tel. 82-50-10), is up the hill from the sea, among apartments. A cheerful lighted doorway leads into a courtyard where you can eat lunch or take your coffee and drink. You wait for your table in a small bar and lounge. Then you're shown into a bright, busy restaurant of bench seats, red-and-white tablecloths, and candles under an arched roof. You dine to music from strolling guitar players. The menu is international, but always there is fresh fish. The fish is cooked to your specifications. Several soups are featured, the favorite being seafood. Other openers might include melon and ham or shrimp with garlic. Main-dish selections include pork chops, spaghetti bolognese, grilled sole, and pepper steak. The chef also does an excellent kebab—pinchitos—with various meats. A plateful of giant prawns with sauce is almost too large. The least expensive way to dine here is to order the menu of the day at 850 pesetas ($5.95), including two dishes, bread, and one-quarter of a liter of wine. Otherwise, if you order à la carte, expect a final tab of 1,800 pesetas ($12.60). The restaurant is popular with tourists, as it offers good value and more comfort and elegance than many of the local restaurants. It is also air-conditioned. Closed Monday.

Bar Playa, Puerto del Carmen, is a good choice for a sunny lunch. Right on the old fishing quay, it's a place where everybody rushes outside, joining a cosmopolitan crowd. You can sip a beer, a Cuba libre, sangría, or wine while you relax. Tapas of octopus with mojo verde, sardines, and salad of egg, bean, tuna, and onions are served. Other food includes all the standard fish dishes, pork chops, squid, and salad, as well as paella, which must be ordered for two. A meal will cost from 1,200 pesetas ($8.40) up. The place is noisy and cheerful. You can visit in your swimming trunks or bikini—no one minds.

Restaurante Romantica I, Centro Olivin, is tucked away up a small alley beside the excellent fish and meat shops on the road leading down from the Fariones to the old town. This small grill and restaurant serves the best steaks on the island—by my tastes and those of many others. It is small, with only five tables, each seating six people, and a tile floor and white walls. Service is good, and the menu is simple. Everything is cooked on a charcoal grill, served on a wooden platter, and dishes are accompanied by a baked potato and salad. A highly satisfactory meal I have enjoyed is filet mignon, garlic bread, and, as mentioned, the potato and salad. If you don't want a steak, I can recommend the plaice or one of the other fish dishes. Expect to spend around 1,400 pesetas ($9.80) for a complete meal.

El Tomate is on the little road to the right as you go down into the village by the water catchment. It's a tiny place with chairs and tables higgledy-piggledy just inside the door and upstairs. The service seems slow, but you must remember that everything is cooked or assembled to order, and portions in this Teutonic eatery are ample, even sometimes huge. French onion soup with baked cheese, tomato soup with green peppers and gin, avocado and shrimp, stuffed tomatoes with basil, and baked Camembert with wild red currants are among the appetizers. For a main dish, you might have pork filet either with tarragon or Hawaiian style with fruit, filet of sole with shrimp and cream sauce served with saffron rice, a Stuttgarter filet "pot" stuffed with meat and vegetables, fishpot Olivin, or filet Stroganoff. Meals cost from 2,500 pesetas ($17.50).

La Finca, 134 Carretera a Macher, looks just like a café, with a pottery and souvenir shop alongside, at the edge of the main road going south from the village. You'll find plenty of parking space and a small, cluttered bar/restaurant which dispenses mainly drinks and snacks during the day. It comes into its own in the evening, however, when it is usually necessary to reserve a table. Owned by Petra Beyerle, the place has nine tables for four grouped around the bar and in the sun lounge. Appetizers include such soups as gazpacho and shrimp with garlic. Main courses are often cooked and served from the grill barbecue, on an adapted camel saddle beside the bar. They include pork filet, pinchitos, rabbit, sole, and squid a la romana from the freezer. For dessert, you might have fresh fruit with ice cream or hot apple tart with cream. Meals cost from 2,500 pesetas ($17.50).

El Varadero, in Puerto del Carmen, is one set of "Green Doors" you'll want to venture behind. Revamped and altered, it is now a gourmet restaurant, owned and run by Caspar von Tangen-Jordan, a Norwegian who trained in the Swiss hotel school and has diplomas on the walls on view for all to see. He is so well known that his place is often called simply Caspar's. Down below the Victoria pub by the boat slipway, the old fish warehouse has been attractively converted into a very pleasant restaurant, with high ceilings (much use of white and green paint), hanging plants, and fishing gear. Some tables are downstairs; others are up among the rafters at the rear of the place. The limited menu offers a choice of international dishes, including sole Walewska, pork with rice and pineapple, beef Stroganoff, all served with superb sauces. Prices are on the high side, a three-course meal costing from 2,800 pesetas ($19.60). Closed Tuesday.

Restaurant Romantica II, Centro Atlántico, on the Avenida de las Playas, stands between the Fariones and the San Antonio Hotels. It's a first-floor restaurant, decorated in the Spanish style, with large or small tables. There's a bar where you can wait for your table or your friends. A pianist plays throughout the evening. All steaks are cooked on the charcoal grill in full view of the diners. They come skewered on an alarming variety of swords, daggers, and spears, and are eaten with a salad and jacket potatoes. There is also a special Canary dish, a whole fish cooked in the oven, baked in a thick jacket of salt which has to be broken away by force, leaving the delicate fish ready to eat. Appetizers include garlic bread with tomatoes or ham, soups, and salads. A meal will cost around 1,800 pesetas ($12.60) or more per person.

Yaiza

In Yaiza, but unknown to coach trippers and hardly ever found by other tourists, is the **Restaurant El Volcan,** next door to one of the souvenir shops. Go here for Sunday lunch—at around 2 p.m. That's when the locals come in from the fields (yes, on Sunday they look after the family plot). They order *puchero,* the stew made from braised meat and vegetables, served only on Sunday, and accompany it with local wine from the barrel. The menu of the day costs 900 pesetas ($6.30) and is quite filling. A bottle of the local wine goes for 450 pesetas ($3.15). The restaurant is open for lunch only. El Volcan lies just near the road up to the Fire Mountains and makes a good stopping place after a visit there.

La Era is one of the longest established restaurants on the island. It is recommendable for its situation alone, but the food is good, too. The house is 200 years old, a farmhouse built around a courtyard with the grain stores and stables now serving as small dining rooms. Each is carefully decorated to enhance its allure, with ferns and ceramic pieces. You dine by candlelight. There is a standard set menu for 1,050 pesetas ($7.35). From the à la carte menu, you can order soup, melon, rabbit, pincho, a pork chop, mixed grill, and squid, a dinner averaging around 1,800 pesetas ($12.60). You drink your coffee sitting in the courtyard, or else you can wander into the garden, filled with palms and local plants along with bougainvillea and mimosa. For entertainment nightly, there is a small disco with a view of an enclosed greenhouse containing numerous exotic flowers and plants, including white orchids.

Playa Blanca

Restaurant Playa Blanca is a cool white structure with windows the whole length of the building, open and overlooking the shimmering sea and the waves lapping the sandy shore of the bay below. This must be one of the best located places on the island, about 100 feet back from the sea and protected from prevailing winds. You have a choice of a table outside and the free use of a lounger or a table inside surrounded by plants, with gentle background music. The standard of cookery is high, with much use of the fresh fish landed just along the bay. Meals are served throughout the day. Specialties include a mixed fish grill, a zarzuela, paella with shellfish, prawns in garlic, and chicken a la Cazadora. They do enormous steaks served with salad and potatoes, pork chops, beef burgers, and spaghetti. A meal will cost around 1,400 pesetas ($9.80), and a bottle of Vina Sol or Sangre de Toro goes for an extra 750 pesetas ($5.25).

Restaurante Playa del Sol is a crowded, hot little eating place in the Hostal Playa del Sol, with nothing but the hotel terrace between it and the golden sand of the tiny bay. The restaurant service is slow but cheerful. Besides the customary appetizers, you can choose from among excellent fish dishes, including grilled sole, or you may prefer steaks or veal escalope. A meal will cost about 1,400 pesetas ($9.80) per person, including wine. The atmosphere is good but noisy. The hostal would be a good place to stay except that it's closely linked with a German tour operation so that it's difficult to get a room if you're an outsider.

Restaurant Casa Salvador, on the bay, is where everyone goes to drink in the evening. The tiny bar is full of tourists and locals alike, and conversation jumps from topic to topic and language to language. The large restaurant looks out over the sea. The menu of the day, at 800 pesetas ($5.60), includes half a liter of wine. On the à la carte menu, you'll find soups, omelets, paella, half a roast chicken, and those tasty langostinos (crayfish), which are priced according to their availability. A complete meal of your personal selections will cost around 1,400 pesetas ($9.80).

Playa de los Pocillos

La Gaviota, Marina Bay (tel. 82-50-50), close to the San Antonio Hotel, is where you might see King Hussein of Jordan dining during one of his visits to his villa on the Costa Teguise. You can dine between 7 p.m. and midnight daily in the elegant room with cool, blue decor and striking views over the bay and the sea. There are also tables outside, if you prefer to eat al fresco. Menus include gazpacho, lobster bisque, seafood soup, couscous, and asparagus with whipped butter among the appetizers. Main dishes are local Canarian fish, lobster and chicken flambé, escalope of veal, tournedos, leg of lamb a la Castille anguillas, and filet of sole in champagne sauce. Meals begin at 2,800 pesetas ($19.60), going up. Beside the restaurant is the cocktail bar, La Barca, an elegant and extensive collection of small rooms and crannies where you can enjoy before-dinner drinks.

Haria

Los Helechos, above Haria in the north of the island, is perched on the edge of the Famara cliffs, offering fantastic views down to the sea at Arrieta and to Haria. The latter is an almost biblical-looking town of white houses and hundreds of lofty date palms. The restaurant takes its name from the delicate ferns which hang in baskets throughout the dining room. Try to get a table by the window. As soon as you arrive, order paella—it's the best on the island, prepared specially for you so you'll have to wait, browsing in the souvenir shop or nibbling cold meats with your drink. For that nibble, I always prefer the Lanzarote goat cheese or else the fresh cooked ham or pork from the bone. The paella then arrives, and it's beautifully decorated, bursting with shellfish and meats to be accompanied by cold local white wine. The paella for two people is an ample dish. A menu of the day goes for 650 pesetas ($4.55), and local wine is sold at 400 pesetas ($2.80) a bottle. This is a notable stopover on your way up to the Mirador del Río.

At Mirador del Río

Right in the north of the island, at the **Mirador del Río,** only tapas at the bar are served. But these are sometimes fresh fish and vegetable salads as well as succulent sponge cakes decorated with chocolate or fruits. Try queso blanco, a white goat cheese, with a glass of either cold white or the red local wine.

Bar Restaurante Los Roques, Orzola, is the official name of Rafael's restaurant in the north of the island in the village from which the boats go over to Graciosa. Rafael will usher you into the long, narrow restaurant and seat you, talking all the time—offering drinks, organizing the kitchen, and shouting to his assistant, a small boy of about 10 or so.

If the weather is good, you should insist on sitting outside, where massive wooden wheels are used as tables, and starfish and sea urchins are laid out to dry in the sun. There is a massive barbecue piled with fuel and lit with great panache by another member of the family. There is no menu. You are brought plates of olives, white goat cheese, figs, and jugs of Lanzarote wine. This is followed by papas arrugadas and heaped plates of salad, after which comes the fish fresh from the sea, grilled in the kitchen or marinated in mojo and tossed on the red-hot barbecue grill. The meal continues with bottles of brandy and banana liqueur placed on your table for unlimited consumption. There are flans and ice creams if you want them, plus coffee.

The meal will cost 1,800 pesetas ($12.60) per person, unless you're fortunate enough to arrive when lobster has been caught, when you can have a whole boiled one for about 3,500 pesetas ($24.50). Don't go to Los Roques unless you're ready to eat fish. You'll incur Rafael's wrath if you try to order something simple, such as a delicate French omelet. I learned the hard way.

NIGHTLIFE: My recommendations begin first in the town of Arrecife, then branch out to the beach resorts.

Arrecife

The red-light district is on the main Arrecife–Tahice road. You can't miss it, if that's what you're looking for.

Otherwise, the best nightclub is **Snipe Disco,** behind the Café de París on the Avenida Mancomunidad, next to the Café Avenida, almost opposite the Arrecife Grand Hotel. The club is open daily from 8 p.m. until around 3 a.m. In this hot, dark atmosphere, mainly disco music is played, but occasional groups are featured. Admission is 500 pesetas ($3.50), which includes the price of your first drink, but tourists showing their passports get in free.

At the **Bar Mexicana,** on the Avenida Mancomunidad between the Lancelot Playa and the Cafés Avenida and de París, the atmosphere becomes noisier and more informal as the evening progresses. The guitarist encourages people to sing with him. Before you know it, you're involved in a full-scale sing-along. Don't worry if you don't know the words. Drinks are at normal prices, and there is no admission charge, as this is a bar, not a club. You can also order fish, prepared Mexican style, at 800 pesetas ($5.60), or a steak at 950 pesetas ($6.65).

Playa de los Pocillos

The Hotel San Antonio has a good disco nightclub, the **Beach Club,** on the edge of the beach, with good parking above. The entrance fee of 600 pesetas ($4.20), which includes your first drink, is not charged for residents of the hotel. If you're tidily dressed and it's early in the evening, you'll probably get in free. The decor is plushy red, with deep settees and flashing lights, a throbbing beat pounding ceaselessly. The place is very lively and popular with young people. Go after 9:30 p.m. and drink sangría by the jug for 650 pesetas ($4.55). Other drinks cost from 400 pesetas ($2.80).

Puerto del Carmen

Let's face it, most of the tourists are here.

In the Fariones complex is the **Bierkeller,** run by Peter. It's what you'd expect: a stone floor, scrubbed wooden tables, and stools. German beer is 150 pesetas ($1.05) for a small stein, and lively songs are sung to the accordion and guitar.

Wilson Disco on the Calle Reina Sofía is a lively and popular place for holiday-making young people, and also used by a surprising number of middle-aged vacationers who happily rub shoulders with those of more tender years. The place is large and glittering with electronic lights and pulsating beat. Entry is free until midnight, but you pay high prices for drinks.

Bourbon Street Jazz Club, Roque Nublo (tel. 82-52-08), is a plush place with overstuffed chairs around small tables, a long bar, and live jazz nightly. The music is somewhat dictated by the patrons, for while many would love to concentrate on the real thing, the program has to include more popular choices for the uninitiated. Entrance is free. You can get pita bread with lamb and salad for 550 pesetas ($3.85). The club is open from 9 p.m. until the wee hours.

EXPLORING THE ISLAND: From Arrecife, the road to the north leads to **Teguise,** the ancient capital of the island, with a peaceful square bordered on one side by the 18th-century **Palace of Spinola,** a beautiful old house restored to its former glory. The palace is well worth a visit to see its elegant salons with old paintings and a lovely collection of polished seashells. The antique kitchen has been restored to show the old water purifiers. The water drips from one stone bowl in which lichens grow, into another and then through the stone into your cup. From the small walled garden there are steps to the roof for a very photogenic view of the steeple of San Miguel. The palace is open from 10 a.m. to 1 p.m. and 3 to 6 p.m. It is closed all day on Sunday and on Saturday afternoon. Admission is free, but it's nice to tip the custodian.

The palace is owned by Union Explosives Rio Tinto Mining Company of Spain, which promotes a vast tourist complex, Costa Teguise, where there is a nine-hole golf course (see "Outdoor Activities").

Across the square is the **Church of San Miguel,** hiding beneath its simple exterior a spotless colorful interior with beautiful statues. The Virgin on the high altar is from the 16th century. The **Convents of Santo Domingo** and **San Francisco** are in the process of being restored, with carefully chosen materials, to their

original states. The convents are not generally open to view, unless you can persuade someone to let you see inside. In the town there remains the local craft which has survived centuries—that is, the making of timples, the small guitar-like instrument played throughout the islands.

Near Teguise on the road north is the **Castle of Guanapay,** placed most strategically on a hill as a defense against the Moors. Perched on the edge of a volcanic crater and entered across a drawbridge, it must have been almost unassailable. There are magnificent views across the island, and the silence is almost deafening.

The road to the north passes through **Los Valles,** a beautifully kept area of cultivation, before coming out above the Arabic-looking village of **Haria.** It nestles among tall waving palm trees at the bottom of the valley. The white houses are covered with bougainvillea and geraniums. The village square is tree lined and paved with tiles, produced locally.

The road continues through increasingly barren land to the **Mirador del Río,** a lookout blasted into the rock of the cliff overlooking the island of **La Graciosa.** This is another creation of favorite son Manrique. Admission is 125 pesetas (88¢), and it's open from 11 a.m. to 7 p.m. (closes earlier in winter). At the previously recommended bar, the view is not only over Graciosa but of the Montana Clara and Allegranza. Far below, at the bottom of cliffs, are salt pans, glowing red at the edge of the Río, the stretch of water separating the island from Lanzarote.

To get there, you must take a boat from the tiny little port of Orzola. Once on the island, you'll find a lovely bathing beach, although the accommodation is rawboned.

In the area of ancient volcanic activity in the north lie the **Cuevas de los Verdes,** an underground gallery running for nearly four miles, from the volcano that created it to the sea. A 50-minute guided tour of the multicolored lava costs 300 pesetas ($2.10). Hours are 11 a.m. to 6 p.m.

Created by the same eruption, the **Grotto Jameos del Agua** has been transformed into a restaurant and nightclub. It's open during the day and on Tuesday, Thursday, and Saturday from 10:30 p.m. till 3 a.m. when men are required to wear a jacket and tie. During the day music is piped through the cavern. Even chattering tourists can't completely spoil the mysterious appearance of the cave, with its subterranean lake inhabited by thousands of tiny blind white crabs. Birds fly through from the restaurant to the gardens at the other end of the cavern, and turtles swim in the pool in the pretty garden—you can join them if you wish. Menuhin played in the cave, finding it acoustically superb. The entrance fee is 300 pesetas ($2.10) during the day, 600 pesetas ($4.20) on the nights when there is a cabaret with dancing.

The Gent's, to misquote Noel Coward, is very definitely a loo with a view, a must for anyone who can visit it. It overlooks a subterranean grotto and is tastefully lit to show up the lava and rocks.

A road runs straight across the island from Arrecife. At the crossroads, right in the middle, is favorite son Manrique's **Monument to Lanzarote Man** or, some people say, fertility. Others claim it represents a man and his camel. At any rate, it's an incredible modern construction of metal towering above the fields and contrasting sharply with the life that goes on around it. Women stil ride donkeys past it and till the fields with camel and wooden plowshares.

What used to be a humble farmer's cottage beneath the monument ha been transformed into a restaurant and museum of island crafts. It's known a Manrique's **El Monumento.** An attractive courtyard contains yokes and farmi implements, an old camel plow, and donkey and camel saddles. There is als small bodega where you can taste the local wines—they vary a lot from village

village. The restaurant serves a fascinating variety of local foods—tortillas de carnival to be eaten in the fingers, juicy with honey and spices, sweet potatoes, papas arrugadas, dried fish, rabbit stew, and, if you have puchero, the staff will make specially for you gofio balls, which are rolled in a piece of goatskin for shape before being fried and dunked into the soup. The entrance to the cottage is free. The monument is open from 10 a.m. to 5 p.m. weekdays, from 10 a.m. to 7 p.m. on Saturday and Sunday.

To the south of Arrecife the road passes the airport and the wide beaches of the southeast coast before coming to an area known as **La Geria.** When the volcano erupted in 1730, this area was devastated. Casting about for a way to make a living, the local people realized that the lava pebbles retained moisture from the heavy night dew. They devised an incredible way of cultivating their vines. The result was to produce the famous Malvasia wines. The growers dig craters 10 to 20 feet wide down into the earth. These are then surrounded by loose stone walls. The vine is planted, and the whole pit covered with a layer of picon (lava granules). The vine flourishes in this soil, watered by the moisture in the picon in this otherwise arid land. Coming suddenly upon this region, you might think you've landed on the moon, as acre upon acre of walled-in pits look like the holes in cheese.

This part of the island is mostly lava, and it's possible to see the paths it took when the mountain erupted in 1730. Palm trees, standing tall against the sky, and the low whitewashed houses give the area an African look. **Yaiza,** the capital of the south, lies on the very edge of the lava flow. Beyond, the road forks, one direction leading to **Playa Blanca** in the south. The other heads to **El Golfo,** a crater right on the edge of the sea. On the sea side the wall has fallen away, leaving a semicircular lagoon of brilliant green water. No one knows how deep it is, or why it's green, perhaps because of a strange fungus growing there. It's a good picnic spot, and excellent bathing is possible in the salty water of the lake. Also on this road, at **Janubio,** are the largest salt pans on the island. There's a road down to the entrance, where you can see the various processes of extracting salt from seawater.

The **Montanas del Fuego** (Fire Mountains) are the most spectacular feature of the island. This is the region of the eruptions of 1730–1736, protected now as a tourist attraction. The entrance to the area costs 450 pesetas ($3.15) per car, and visiting hours are 9 a.m. to 5 p.m. You drive your own car through in a convoy with a leader and an escort but no commentary. The road leads through the jagged lava fields past sinister craters to the **Islote del Hilario,** a circular restaurant and bar built on the site of the old hermit Hilario's hut to which he returned with his donkey after the devastation. He planted a fig tree, the only vegetation in the area, an ancestor perhaps of the one that now grows through the middle of the restaurant. In all directions the view is of lava and craters. The ground is so hot you can fry an egg on the natural barbecue, set fire to brushwood, and cause geysers by pouring water into ready-made gushers.

Timanfaya is the biggest mountain. For the ardent explorer, it's possible to take a camel ride up Timanfaya from the station just before you enter the park. The cost is 500 pesetas ($3.50) per person. It's an eerie sight to see the camels wind their way up the side of the mountain to the crater. The camels go home at lunchtime, as they have to work in the fields in the afternoon.

North of Fire Mountains, the lava stops suddenly just short of the tiny village of **Mancha Blanca.** There's a legend that Our Lady of the Sorrows appeared and commanded the lava to stop, thus saving the village from engulfment. A church was built in the village, and each year there's a festival in her honor.

The best bathing beaches in the island are those on the southeast coast and

right in the south at **Punta Papagayo.** Here the sand is golden, the sea crystal clear, and the beaches almost deserted except on weekends.

On the road from Arrecife to Yaiza along the coast at Uga is the **Ahumadería** where Wolfgang and Erika Lündstedt run a thriving cottage industry, smoking imported salmon and local eels. Wolfgang, an electronics engineer, came to the island some time ago, liked it, and set about finding a way to stay. His fish is not cheap, but it's smoked to a secret recipe of special woods, some of it imported, and the taste is superb. His produce travels well and keeps for ages if chilled or frozen.

Excursions

These are available from **Viajes Cyrasa** at Puerto del Carmen, Avenida de las Playas, local 60 A (tel. 82-58-51), from 9 a.m. to 1 p.m. and 4 to 7 p.m. daily (from 9 a.m. to 1 p.m. Saturday). A full day's jaunt to Fire Mountains, El Golfo, and the south, including lunch at Yaiza, costs 3,000 pesetas ($21). A half-day to the north and the Mirador del Río, Cueva de los Verdes, and Jameos del Agua goes for 1,975 pesetas ($13.83). On Tuesday and Saturday, there are evening excursions to the nightclub, Jameos del Agua, costing 2,000 pesetas ($14). At Uga, an attractive Fiesta Canaria with folklorica and a typical dinner with unlimited wine costs 2,900 pesetas ($20.30).

OUTDOOR ACTIVITIES: From deep-sea fishing to windsurfing, there's plenty to do.

Undersea Diving

Beyond the Victoria Inn in Puerto del Carmen, Bob Wright, an Englishman who with his partner Dennis Wright also runs a school in Poole, Dorset, England, has started a highly professional and successful diving school, **Clubulanza,** in Puerto del Carmen (tel. 82-60-61). They have compressed-air facilities. If you are already proficient, each dive costs about 2,750 pesetas ($19.25), including full use of all equipment. There is a terrace for relaxing on and a bar. A delightful, informal atmosphere prevails, yet a wonderful businesslike approach to a sport that can be dangerous if not approached sensibly is evident. Bob is ex-Royal Navy, quiet and friendly, as well as passionately interested in diving.

Golf

The golf course at **Costa Teguise** lies at the foot of a volcano, a unique links of Bermuda grass and black sandy bunkers. Only nine holes are in operation at present, but they offer an interesting challenge to the sportsperson on a holiday. Designed by an Englishman, John Harris, the course winds and twists through lava fields, past lush watered flowering bushes and stark palm trees. There's a pleasant clubhouse for a relaxing drink after your round. Greens fees, unless you're staying at the Salinas-Sheraton, are 1,700 pesetas ($11.90) for nine holes. There is a pro available as well as a practice ground for beginners.

Sports Center

Club Viajes Insular, Urbanización Playa Blanca, junto Hotel los Fariones, Puerto del Carmen. A large area in the middle of the village has been leveled, tiled, and planted to make a sports area, with a swimming pool, sun terrace with sunbeds, tennis courts, table tennis, and projected squash courts. Tennis courts are 400 pesetas ($2.80) an hour in daytime, 600 pesetas ($4.20) at night when lights are needed. There is a tennis teacher with whom you can negotiate for instruction. Use of the pool is 200 pesetas ($1.40). There are changing rooms and showers. At the poolside café you can purchase beer, soft drinks, coffee, and whisky. You can also have a good lunch. This is an ideal spot to spend the day if you're tired of sea bathing.

5. Fuerteventura

Separated from Lanzarote by a narrow channel, the island's capital, **Puerto del Rosario,** is a good base for excursions into the interior. Many unspoiled beaches dot the coastline. Fuerteventura is rated among the world's Top Five as a windsurfing paradise.

GETTING THERE: From the harbor at Playa Blanca there is now a car-ferry service to Corralejo in the north of Fuerteventura. The service is on the *Alisur.* This is very much a local service, carrying produce trucks, tanned surfers complete with boards, family parties including granny and the baby, and tourists with peeling noses.

The *Alisur* makes three round trips daily. Times of sailing are well advertised, and tickets are on sale at the harbor as well as in Arrecife and Puerto del Carmen. The cost is 1,500 pesetas ($10.50) each way. Children go for half price. Cars cost from 2,500 pesetas ($17.50) to 3,500 pesetas ($24.50) one way, the charge depending on the length of the car. The round-trip price for a car is from 3,500 pesetas ($24.50) to 4,500 pesetas ($31.50). For information, get in touch with *Alisur,* 16 León y Castillo, Arrecife (tel. 81-42-72).

There is a hydrofoil service "for passengers only" on Wednesday, Thursday, and Friday from Corralejo at 9:20 a.m., returning from Playa Blanca, Lanzarote, at 5:40 p.m. for the 15-minute journey. The fare is 1,900 pesetas ($13.30) one way, 3,800 pesetas ($26.60) round trip; half price for children.

Excursions are also run from Lanzarote, costing about 7,000 pesetas ($49) per person, including the pickup at your hotel, the coach drive to Playa Blanca, the ferry trip, and a bus ride around Fuerteventura. After visiting Betancuria, the old capital of the island, as well as Lajares and La Oliva, a stop is made for lunch; then the bus returns to the ferry and Lanzarote by way of the beautiful beaches of Corralejo. The ferry has a bar and a snackbar, serving hot and cold drinks, along with sandwiches and rolls.

LODGINGS: There is an attractive Moorish-style parador near the airport.

The **Parador Nacional de Fuerteventura,** Playa Blanca, Puerto del Rosario (tel. 85-11-50), is entered through a high arch in the wall leading to a courtyard and then to a pleasant wooden-floored lobby. Wooden staircases and passages continue on to the rooms. There are simply furnished but comfortable, some with a private terrace leading out into the garden. In the garden, right on the edge of the sea, is a swimming pool. Stretching away beside the hotel is a wide sandy beach, but currents make bathing dangerous. Singles cost from 5,000 pesetas ($35) to 5,500 pesetas ($38.50), depending on the season. Doubles go for 5,500 pesetas ($38.50) to 6,500 pesetas ($45.50). A lunch or dinner is offered for 1,900 pesetas ($13.30).

You can also try the **Hotel Valeron,** Candelaría del Castillo, Puerto del Rosario (tel. 85-06-18), which has rooms available for one or two persons at 2,500 pesetas ($17.50) per night. Dinner here costs 1,000 pesetas ($7). This is a very Spanish place and a good alternative to the parador. It's also cheaper.

Hotel Corralejo, Playa Corralejo (tel. 86-60-67), lies right beside the sea with views out over the harbor to Lobos. Simple rooms with bath or shower go for 4,000 pesetas ($28) for two. A set dinner is offered for 800 pesetas ($5.60). The menu features local cheese, fresh fish, poultry, and meat dishes. À la carte meals cost around 1,500 pesetas ($10.50), including a half liter of Canary wine.

Hotel Oliva Beach, Playa de Corralejo (tel. 86-61-00), is a long-established hotel among the dunes by the sea. There are large lounges and bars, if you tire of the open air. If you don't, the hotel has a swimming pool, a solarium, and games such as volleyball, *petanca,* and table tennis. Evening entertainment comes in the form of a disco, and there are often evening shows. You have your own table in the self-service dining room all during your stay, and you can occupy it all evening if you wish. Enormous buffets are laden with hot and cold dishes, and you can eat as much as you want. Single rooms rent for 4,500 pesetas ($31.50) and doubles for 7,800 pesetas ($54.60), with reductions for children.

Right in the north of the island, overlooking the island of Lobos and across to Lanzarote, is the splurge:

Hotel Tres Islas, Playa de Corralejo, La Oliva (tel. 86-60-00), is set in splendid isolation on a marvelous stretch of golden beach, where barbecues are held. It is self-supporting in the way of entertainment, as there is nothing for miles around. Facilities include a large swimming pool, tennis courts, and a bowling alley, plus a hairdressing salon, shops, and a chemist. In addition to a restaurant and grill room, a snackbar serves hamburgers, sausages, and other light meals. There are film shows, a pool bar, a beach bar, a disco, sailing and windsurfing nearby—you name it. Skin-diving and beach games occupy many a day. All in all, it's one of the most beautiful spots in the Canary Islands. But this retreat has a price tag. Singles cost from 9,000 pesetas ($63) to 10,500 pesetas ($73.50). The charges in a double are 8,500 pesetas ($59.50) to 9,500 pesetas ($66.50) per person, all tariffs being for full board. A set dinner goes for 2,500 pesetas ($17.50).

WHERE TO EAT: **Bar Restaurante Marquesina,** on the corner of the Calle la Iglesia in Corralejo, has a menu of the day for 550 pesetas ($3.81), but this bright and cheerful place is so reasonable that you will probably prefer to choose from the à la carte dishes. Offered are several soups, mixed salad, shrimp in garlic, omelets, fresh seafood, meat, and steaks. Paella for two is the specialty.

Restaurante Bar Oscar, off the old square in Corralejo, is owned by one of the four top families of Fuerteventura. It has a tile floor, great wooden pillars supporting the roof, and red-checked tablecloths. The menu is typical of the islands, with a large chef's salad, goat cheese, soups, several fresh fish dishes, shrimp in garlic, paella, a mixed grill Oscar, and a T-bone steak served on a big wooden platter. Flamed meat dishes are a feature. Bananas flambé and crêpes are special desserts. Meals cost from 2,000 pesetas ($14).

Restaurante El Pàjaro Chino is reputed to be the best Chinese restaurant in the islands. The chef is from Taiwan, and you can watch him at work in the kitchen among the woks and kettles. The dining room has an elegant tile floor and pink-and-white tables with bamboo chairs and plenty of fresh flowers. A large and satisfying meal costs from 1,500 pesetas ($10.50), with beer or wine. You'll be offered a free liqueur, plus a bonbon as you leave.

NIGHTLIFE: There's not much besides the bars and cafés of the town. However, one establishment, **Freddy's Discoteca,** 29 Calle la Iglesia, Corralejo (tel. 86-61-78), is a bright and friendly spot for energetic persons. It's popular with the windsurfing crowd. Men are charged 400 pesetas ($2.80) to enter, which includes a free drink. Women pay nothing, but they don't get a free libation.

WATER SPORTS: The island is known worldwide for the excellent conditions for windsurfing, and in the south is the place for speed surfing, where world records have been set and broken in the perfect conditions. The beaches of the north are crowded with wave surfers. Boards can be rented for 800 pesetas ($5.60) to 1,000 pesetas ($7) per hour, 2,500 pesetas ($17.50) to 3,000 pesetas

($21) per day, depending on the type of board you rent. This island is for the experienced windsurfer, and little instruction is available. Experienced surfers can get advice and equipment from Rick Crampton, a young Englishman who, with his wife, Elaine, operates a workshop to repair and replace surfboards after accidents. Rick and Elaine live at **Villa Sol y Mar** (tel. 86-60-23), and they also offer accommodations in their home in two-, three-, and four-bedded rooms.

Underwater enthusiasts can go to Miguel Abella's **Barakuda Club Corralejo,** 20 Calle José Segura Torres, Corralejo (tel. 88-62-43), where a beginner's diving course costs around 16,000 pesetas ($112). Certified divers can take plunges from the club's boat for 1,800 pesetas ($12.60) per dive.

Part Two

MOROCCO

Chapter XVII

MOROCCO ON $40 A DAY

THE KINGDOM OF MOROCCO, the westernmost point of North Africa, has, since the dawn of travel, evoked an image of romance. Long before the present massive invasion, Morocco was known to film-goers—whether they went there with Marlene Dietrich in *Morocco,* Gary Cooper in *Beau Geste,* Humphrey Bogart and Ingrid Bergman in *Casablanca,* or Hope, Crosby, and Lamour in *Road to Morocco*.

Morocco is the most accessible of the far-off lands for those who live in Western Europe or the eastern U.S.

Geographically, Morocco is bounded on the east by not altogether friendly Algeria, on the west by the Atlantic, with its stretches of fine sands and pine forest, on the north by the Mediterranean, with its rugged coastline, and on the south by the forbidding Sahara. Because of its location in the temperate zone of the northwest corner of Africa, it boasts 300 days of guaranteed sunshine per year. In winter this comes as a welcome relief; in summer inland cities in particular can be stifling. However, Morocco's 1,000 miles of beach keep the summer visitors pouring in.

1. Flying to Morocco

Established in 1946 as the official airline of the Kingdom of Morocco, **Royal Air Maroc** offers safe, well-monitored transatlantic flights on twice-weekly departures from New York's JFK airport. With its fleet of well-upholstered 747s, it is the only airline to fly nonstop between North America and Morocco, and the only one to connect the many cities of the country's far-flung territories. Flights depart every Tuesday and Saturday in both directions from New York and Casablanca.

The airline's bargain fare is the midweek Super APEX ticket, which requires Tuesday travel in both directions, a delay of between 7 and 30 days before using the return half of your ticket, and a 7-day advance purchase. Round-trip low-season fares at present are $499, while high-season round-trip fares go up to $570. A slightly more expensive, and more popular, fare is the "Magical Kingdom Fare," requiring a 7-day advance purchase, a minimum sojourn of 7 days, and a maximum stay of 60 days (twice as long as its less expensive sister). Some travelers consider that its flexibility about departures and returns (you can fly on a Saturday in either direction if you wish) adds to the ticket's allure. Subject to change, low-season fares are $545, going up to $599 in high season.

If you want to revel in Morocco's pleasures for a full season, a recently inaugurated three-month APEX ticket allows up to 90 days delay before returning home, encouraging many budget-conscious travelers to begin and end their tours of Europe from a base in Morocco. This strategy requires a bit of comparison shopping and a clear idea of which European countries are important to your vacation goals. But because Royal Air Maroc's hub of Casablanca is so close to Europe, and because it offers such low-priced fares to the continent when passage is booked before your departure, many travelers consider this as a serious alternative.

At present, a three-month APEX ticket costs $620 round trip in low season, $722 in high season. If you're interested in this type of ticket, don't forget to ask a reservations clerk about flying into Casablanca from New York on Royal Air Maroc and flying back to New York from Madrid on Iberia Airlines for the same cost as a round-trip passage to either city from New York. (The passage between Casablanca and Madrid, of course, is extra.)

In addition to attractively priced fares from either Europe or North America to Morocco, Royal Air Maroc offers an inexpensive alternative to traveling within Morocco by car. A one-way passage from Casablanca to either Marrakesh or Tangier costs about $17 or $25 respectively—one of the true air-travel bargains, considering the distance, the time, and the high price of gasoline and car rental. A one-way passage from Marrakesh to Tangier is $41, an option for visitors wanting to catch the ferry boat or hydrofoil to southern Spain.

Information and up-to-date fares (the ones I've cited are only to be used as a general guideline) may be obtained from one of Royal Air Maroc's helpful reservations clerks. For more information, call 212/974-1077 in New York City toll free 800/345-3556 in New York State, and 800/223-5858 from the rest of the United States.

AIRLINES/AIRPORTS: If you're in Europe, Paris is a good transfer point to Morocco, as both Royal Air Maroc and Air France fly from there to Tangier and Casablanca. Of course, you can also fly directly from New York to Morocco using a method of transport I have just described.

Once in Morocco, you can travel to major destinations by plane, availing yourself of Royal Air Inter's domestic routes. Fez, Meknes, Tetuan, Oujda, Quarzazate, Agadir, Marrakesh, and Rabat are just some of the cities connected by this airline.

Most international flights come into Casablanca (rather, the airport at Nouasseur). Royal Air Maroc has connecting flights to Rabat (Salé). Another popular routing is to take a Royal Air Inter flight to Tangier, from which you can either fly to the already previewed sections of Gibraltar or else Málaga on Spain's Costa del Sol.

Mohammed V International Airport at Casablanca is about 12 miles south of the city. A C.T.M. bus will take you into the city terminal for a fare of 20 DH ($2.20). If you go by taxi, the legal rate is about 100 DH ($11), although many drivers will try to charge you far more.

For airport information, telephone 33-91-00.

If you're booked on a domestic flight from Casablanca, you have to leave from a different airport, **Casa-Anfa,** some three miles out of town if I clocked the mileage accurately. Regrettably, there is no bus service from this airport, and you must throw yourself on the mercy of a Casablanca taxi driver.

2. Traveling Within Morocco

It's easier to travel through Morocco than you might imagine. Train connections, for example, between the major cities are good, and **Royal Air Inter** has domestic flights to most of the principal tourist zones. The best way to capture the magic of Morocco is to travel by road. For the most part, roads connecting the major cities and coastal towns are good, less so if you go to remote inland points. Except for the approaches to Casablanca, there is little bumper-to-bumper driving (in many places you won't see a car or truck for miles, although you'll have people, donkeys, and sheep herds to cope with). You can reach the sights recommended in this book by rented car or bus, not always by train or air. Generally, your point of entry into Morocco will be either Tangier or Casablanca. At either of these cities, you can rent cars, as well as make bus and train connections.

TRAVEL AGENTS: Each city or town has many travel agents where you can pick up information and purchase tickets on buses, trains, and planes.

In Casablanca, I have always found the Anglo-Moroccan-owned **Olive Branch Tours,** 76 rue de Foucauld (tel. 22-35-64), especially helpful. They can also assist you with sightseeing tours and often cash traveler's checks as well.

There's also a branch of Olive in Marrakesh at Palais El Badia (tel. 303-81); in Tangier at 11 rue Omar Ibnou El Aass (tel. 380-83).

Travelers to Tangier might also patronize **Wagon Lits/Cook,** 86 rue de la Liberté (tel. 316-40). In Fez, Wagons Lits/Cook has a small office in the Grand Hotel building; and in Meknes, at the rue du Ghana.

TRAINS: Fares are moderate to low. Children 4 to 10 travel for half fare. The major cities—Tangier, Fez, Rabat, Meknes, Casablanca, and Marrakesh—are serviced by trains. Note that there are supplements for air conditioning and express trains.

In Casablanca, the offices for the Moroccan Railways, called **Chemins de Fer du Maroc** are at Casablanca Voyageurs station, Boulevard Ba-Hammad (tel. 24-58-01); and at Casablanca-Port station, Boulevard Al Hansali (tel. 22-30-11).

BUSES: **C.T.M.** and **SATAS** are the major bus companies, both employing an older Greyhound-type bus that is moderately comfortable but not always spotless. C.T.M. operates all over Morocco, and SATAS operates between Casablanca, Agadir, and the section south of Agadir. It does get crowded at times, and occasionally somebody gets on with a chicken or two. Be warned that you'll have meager toilet facilities in some of the smaller villages—a squat toilet only, if that. Bus fares are low: about 15 DH ($1.65) in a deluxe seat and 12 DH ($1.32) in a first-class seat per 100 kilometers. Always pay a little bit extra for a reserved seat.

Try to book long journeys in advance. The first-class buses are, on the whole, more reliable than the deluxe vehicles which tend to break down, stranding you in some outlying village until the next one comes along next day. Prices are: Tangier–Rabat, 48.70 DH ($5.36); Tangier–Casablanca, 64.75 DH ($7.12); Tangier–Fez (a 5½-hour journey), 45.05 DH ($4.96); and Tangier–Tetouan, 7 DH (77¢).

In Rabat, the C.T.M. office is on Avenue Hassan II; in Casablanca, at 23 rue Léon d'Africain; and in Marrakesh at Djemaa el-Fna square.

TAXIS: They come in two sizes. The cheaper vehicles, called **petit taxis,** seat three passengers and are used in the bigger cities or towns. These taxis charge about half the price of the larger cabs which travel out-of-town. Most of the taxis in Moroccan cities (with the exception of Marrakesh) are metered. If a taxi isn't metered, agree on the price to be charged to avoid a scene later. Fares vary from city to city, but tend to be low. For example, in Tangier it costs about 8 DH (88¢) to take a petit taxi, rising to 10 DH ($1.10) if you go from one side of town to the other. Expect to pay 25% more at night.

To dial a taxi in Rabat, call 205-18; in Casablanca, 203-93; in Tangier, 355-17; in Fez, 41 or 195; in Meknes, 161; and at Oujda, 21-21.

HITCHHIKING: Ever since I learned about two American girls who hitched a ride outside Marrakesh in the late 1960s, and were never heard from again, I have never recommended hitchhiking in Morocco. Hitchhiking, of course, can be extremely hazardous anywhere in the world, including America (remember Truman Capote's *In Cold Blood?).* You have to be adventurous indeed to set out with all your traveling possessions and an outstretched thumb into the far reaches of Morocco. If you must hitch a ride—and then the reason should be strictly financial necessity—fellow tourists are your best bet. And even then, I'd suggest great caution.

CAR RENTALS: Because of the irregularity of bus schedules, the relative lack of trains, and the far-flung nature of the country, you'll probably get the most out of Morocco if you visit it by car. When two or more persons travel together, renting a car often becomes the most efficient way of seeing the geographically diverse areas of the country, especially if expenses are shared.

Drivers, however, need to exercise cautionary techniques. Even the secondary roads are almost always tarred and often well maintained in all but the most remote areas. In unpopulated areas, however, they tend to be narrower than their urban counterparts, with soft shoulders and sometimes open ditches on either side. This encourages driving toward the center of the road for trucks and cars alike.

Don't be afraid to blast your horn while negotiating narrow mountain curves, because disconcertingly often a car will be just on the other side of your blind corner. Night driving can be hazardous as well, because it's sometimes difficult to see dark-robed Moroccans walking, sometimes with sheep or goats, beside the road. On the other hand, in crowded cities, streams of pedestrians and animals on the streets sometimes present unnerving obstacles.

Other drivers, however, tend to be more considerate, often giving wide berths when passing or being passed on narrow desert highways.

A final word of caution: Experienced drivers in unpopulated regions, never, repeat never, allow their gas gauges to drop below the halfway mark if they can help it. You never know when the only gas station within 75 miles will be closed and locked (or, more disconcertingly, open but out of gasoline).

Still, the Moroccan countryside is often almost incredibly beautiful, filled with a visual splendor, and is well worth the trouble of motoring through it.

Several North American car-rental companies are represented in Morocco, plus a host of regional rental companies. All of them seem to compete for the attention of newly arrived visitors as they enter the arrivals hall of the Casablanca airport. Although at first glance, the rates of the regional companies might appear less expensive than those offered by their U.S.-based counterparts, potential renters should exercise caution. On a recent research trip, the local company whose kiosk I approached charged me $120 for what I considered a badly maintained car for a four-hour drive between Casablanca and Marrakesh. The car broke down *only* once. Unless you intend to do practically no driving, you'll probably be better off renting a car on an unlimited mileage basis, reserving it at a favorable rate with one of America's big three rental companies before leaving home.

For the second part of my most recent research trip on this guide, I rented a car from **Budget Rent-A-Car.** I drove it hard for hundreds of miles, and was pleased with the car's level of maintenance, service, and price.

Budget maintains offices in Casablanca, Marrakesh, Agadir, and Tangier. If it's reserved two business days in advance, a car can be waiting for you at an airport or delivered directly to your hotel. Budget charges 1,680 DH ($184.80) weekly for its least expensive car, a Renault 4, which has a theoretical seating capacity for four persons, plus their luggage, and manual transmission. A more luxurious car, a Talbot Horizon, also with manual transmission, has a seating capacity for five persons, costing 3,500 DH ($385) per week, with unlimited mileage, plus 19% tax. A collision damage waiver at $2.75 per day is an attractive option if you're unwilling to pay the first $177 of any potential damage to your car. I always take the extra coverage. All cars are equipped with safety belts (or should be), and luggage racks are available upon request (however, if you use one, you can't leave your car unguarded at any time).

It's important to note that an automatic transmission is considered an unnecessary and extremely difficult-to-repair luxury in Morocco. Neither Budget, Avis, nor Hertz offer automatic transmissions in any of their Morocco-based cars as of this writing. Avis and Hertz both offer the almost identical array of well-maintained cars as Budget, but at higher prices and on less convenient terms than those offered by Budget.

For more information, and to comparison shop, call **Budget's** toll-free reservations system at 800/527-0700, **Hertz's** at 800/654-3001, and **Avis's** at 800/331-2112.

Driving Requirements

Vehicles, including motorcycles, can remain in Morocco for six months free of duty; after that, they are subject to the usual import restrictions. In general, your valid hometown driver's license should be sufficient, particularly if you're dealing with the big companies such as Budget, Hertz, and Avis. However, I have found that some of the smaller car-rental agencies insist on an international driving permit.

You must have adequate insurance to drive in Morocco. The **Carte Verte** (green card), the international insurance certificate, is now recognized and valid in Morocco. Your car-rental agency will arrange insurance for you as part of the rental agreement. Otherwise, if you're bringing in that new car you just purchased in Europe, you can get local insurance at all ports of entry, such as Casablanca and Tangier. The cost is about 70 DH ($7.70) for ten days, 185 DH ($20.35) for one month.

Third-party insurance is compulsory in case a driver doesn't possess a green card. This third-party insurance may be obtained at Customs upon arrival in Morocco.

Traffic drives on the right, and the French highway code is used. Inside Moroccan cities and towns and on its national highways, signposts conform to international codes and standards.

In Morocco, chances are you'll encounter very little vehicular traffic on the main roads between the imperial cities. However, the ever-flowing stream of people and animals such as donkeys means that you have to drive with extreme caution. Whenever possible, it is not recommended that you drive at night, unless it is some sort of emergency. Dark-robed Moroccans, as mentioned, are hard to see at night along unlit roads.

In most towns, you will find official parking men who display badges and will look after your car for you. Tip 2 DH (22¢) for the service.

Gasoline

Morocco is not one of the rich Arab oil countries, but gas or "petrol" is available here. You'll spot such familiar signs as Mobil, at least in the main cities and towns. I've discovered that prices vary from day to day. The farther south you go, the steeper the gasoline prices. Obviously, if you're planning a long stretch of travel into the remote countryside, make sure you have a full tank and know how far down the road the next filling station is.

Before you set out on the open road, be sure you know which type of gas your rented car needs. Only the cheapest, most primitive engines (often those in heavily polluting trucks or farming equipment) use the relatively inexpensive "pétrol mélangé." This means a mixture of gasoline and oil which is suitable only for certain low-performance engines. If you're in doubt, ask for "super" or "pétrol super." This contains a lesser octane rating than its counterpart in North America, but it is suitable for most up-to-date rental cars in Morocco. Service station attendants are usually friendly and helpful.

ITINERARIES: If you have a car, I'd suggest the following two-week excursion through Morocco. It's only a preview of the highlights, but you can save the rest for another trip. Most visitors will arrive at the gateway to Morocco, Casablanca, perhaps in time to recover from jet fatigue from their transatlantic flight. Fully recovered the next day, you will then be prepared to embark on your goal of discovery, beginning with—

Day 1: Drive north to **Rabat** (for distances between cities, refer to our mileage chart). Take in the attractions there and spend the night.

Day 2: Continue driving along the coast, bypassing Ksar-El-Kebir with a luncheon stopover at the small Hotel Riad in Larache (part of the Diafa chain), which offers reliable food. Overnight in **Tangier.**

Day 3: Continue your stay in **Tangier,** as it's one of the most interesting cities in North Africa, and you will have spent a good part of Day 2 just getting there from Rabat.

Day 4: Drive south to **Meknes,** stopping to inspect Chechaouèn. This drive and stopover will take up most of your day.

Day 5: From Meknes, visit Volubilis and Moulay Idriss before making the relatively short journey east to **Fez,** where you can spend two nights.

Day 6: Explore **Fez** and its environs.

Day 7: Drive south through the Middle Atlas, with **Erfoud** as your eventual destination for the night. Have lunch in Er Rachidia providing you got an early start from Fez. Continue south to the desert oasis of Erfoud which will put you at the gateway to the Sahara. Overnight in Erfoud, perhaps in a palm grove.

Day 8: From Erfoud (and to avoid returning on the same road to Er Rachidia), a decent road cuts northwest across a bleak countryside to Goulmima. Take it. However, once at Goulmima, head west for an overnight stopover in **Tinehir.** There should still be enough daylight for you to drive the short distance through a lovely valley to the Gorges of Todra.

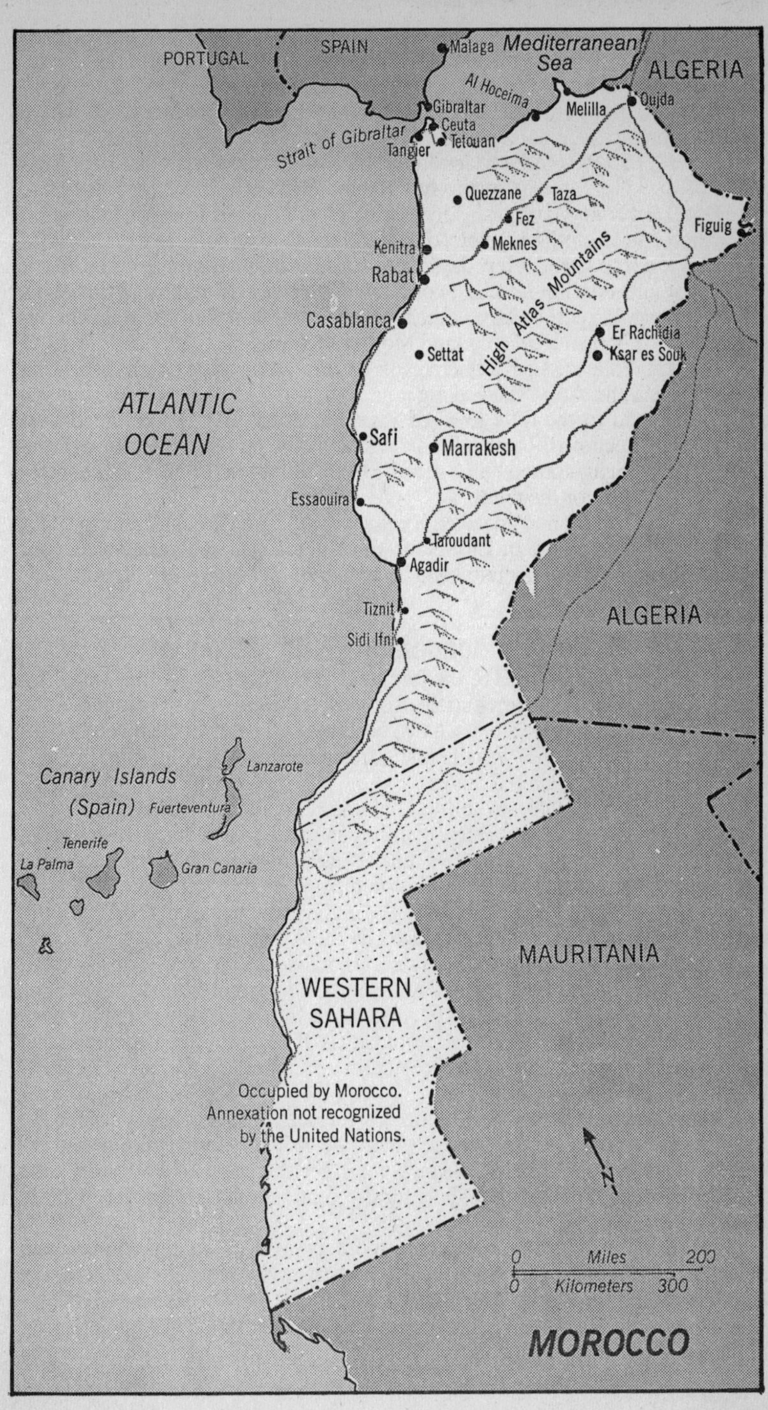
PORTUGAL
SPAIN
Malaga
Mediterranean Sea
ALGERIA
Al Hoceima
Gibraltar
Ceuta
Melilla
Oujda
Strait of Gibraltar
Tangier
Tetouan
Quezzane
Taza
Fez
Figuig
Kenitra
Meknes
Rabat
High Atlas Mountains
Casablanca
Er Rachidia
Ksar es Souk
Settat
ATLANTIC OCEAN
Safi
Marrakesh
Essaouira
Taroudant
Agadir
Tiznit
ALGERIA
Sidi Ifni
Canary Islands (Spain)
Lanzarote
Fuerteventura
Tenerife
La Palma
Gran Canaria
MAURITANIA
WESTERN SAHARA
Occupied by Morocco. Annexation not recognized by the United Nations.
N
0 Miles 200
0 Kilometers 300
MOROCCO

Day 9: From Tinehir, continue west toward **Ouarzazate** "at the crossroads to everywhere," detouring, however, for a preview of the Gorges of the Dadès. Overnight in Ouarzazate, which has several good, moderately priced hotels.

Day 10: Drive across the mountains to the fabled city of **Marrakesh,** where you can spend two nights.

Day 11: Many consider **Marrakesh** one of the world's most fascinating cities, and you will want to allow this full day and night to take in its attractions.

Day 12: From Marrakesh, drive west to the coastal town of Essaouira. Once there, head south to **Agadir,** one of the beach resort bargains of the world (you may want to spend a few days there relaxing if you have the time). Or, if you're not interested in beaches, continue that same day on a road through a fertile valley going east to **Taroudannt,** which is much smaller, far more charming, and full of lots of local color and Moroccan flavor.

Day 13: While based in either **Agadir** or **Taroudannt,** you can make a swing south through the Anti-Atlas, along a narrow, sometimes dangerous, but still fascinating road to the little town of Tafraout. After lunch there, head west again in the direction of Tiznit. (Frankly, I'd skip the far southern town of Goulimine and its highly touted "blue men.") Head north, returning to either Agadir or Taroudannt for the night.

Day 14: The next and final day, continue north along the coast, stopping for lunch either at Essaouira or El Jadida. You will reach **Casablanca** before dark where you can check into a hotel and be prepared for your return flight.

3. Getting Acquainted With Morocco

Morocco is accustomed to the foreigner. The Phoenicians once came this way, as did the Carthaginians and the Romans, followed by the Portuguese, the French, the Spanish (who still have two enclaves in the north, Ceuta and Melilla). Historically, Morocco was the first African nation to sign a treaty (in 1787) of friendship with the United States.

If you speak French, even the la-plume-de-ma-tante variety, you'll fare better in Morocco than with English, although in the past years English has become more common. But it is the French presence—a holdover from colonial days—that lingers. Recently, King Hassan II has been trying to get rid of French influences, a policy reflected, for example, in the street names of the capital city of Rabat. The word *rue* is being replaced by the Arabic *zankat.*

The nation is Muslim, but it tolerates religious freedom. For example, many Jews in the imperial city of Meknes fled to Israel after Morocco was granted independence in 1956; others stayed to live peacefully in the medina. The king ordered new housing on the outskirts of Casablanca and decreed that Jews and Arabs would live in the project on a communal basis, an experiment that so far has worked.

Note: A word of warning to serious sightseers. The greatest specimens of Moorish architecture, the mosques, cannot be visited by non-Muslims (an exception is the one in Meknes). If you want to see the inside of a mosque, head back to Córdoba, Spain (although, naturally, a cathedral has been placed inside the mosque).

All in all, whether you're planning a desert safari or want to go mountain skiing, you'll find a wide range of activities in Morocco. The late Truman Capote once summed up Morocco's peculiar charm when he advised prospective visitors "to have yourself vaccinated against typhoid, liquidate your bank account, and say goodbye to your friends. Who knows when you

MILEAGE BETWEEN MAJOR CITIES (MOROCCO)

Distance in Miles

	Agadir	Casablanca	Ceuta	El Jadida	Erfoud	Er Rachidia	Essaouira	Fez	Marrakesh	Meknes	Melilla	Ouarzazate	RABAT	Tangier	Taroudannt	Tetuan	Tiznit
Agadir		323	590	263	474	423	108	490	190	470	691	234	381	552	50	562	56
Casablanca	323		349	60	370	308	218	182	147	138	393	274	58	229	373	239	379
Ceuta	590	349		355	466	397	484	205	414	187	295	534	209	63	639	26	646
El Jadida	263	60	355		412	432	158	242	122	205	455	243	118	289	313	299	332
Erfoud	474	370	466	412		63	461	261	355	273	355	234	334	422	418	386	516
Er Rachidia	423	308	397	432	63		416	198	310	210	292	189	272	559	373	317	477
Essaouira	108	218	484	158	461	416		399	106	362	611	227	275	446	158	456	164
Fez	490	182	205	242	261	198	399		301	37	201	422	124	203	441	172	547
Marrakesh	190	147	414	122	355	310	106	301		280	502	121	200	371	140	522	238
Meknes	470	138	187	205	273	210	362	37	280		238	401	87	174	420	180	518
Melilla	691	393	295	455	355	292	611	201	502	238		623	335	306	642	270	740
Ouarzazate	234	274	534	243	234	189	227	422	121	401	623		321	492	184	497	288
RABAT	381	58	209	118	334	272	275	124	200	87	335	321		171	430	182	437
Tangier	552	229	63	289	422	559	446	203	371	174	306	492	171		601	35	608
Taroudannt	50	373	639	313	418	373	158	441	140	420	642	184	430	601		600	98
Tetuan	562	239	26	299	386	317	456	172	522	180	270	497	182	35	600		618
Tiznit	56	379	646	332	516	477	164	547	238	518	740	288	437	608	98	618	
Zagora	338	377	645	347	158	220	331	526	225	505	526	104	425	596	288	603	386

will see them again?" (Capote meant you'll be taken in by the charm, not the natives.)

HISTORY: Stretching along the Mediterranean, around the tip of Africa where Tangier stands, and down the Atlantic coast, Morocco is a country whose history has been molded by its geography. The earliest known inhabitants of this land were nomads, called Libyans by the Greeks and Numidians and Mauri (thence Moors) by the Romans. These Berber-speaking people were here at least 2,000 years before the birth of Christ. During the 12th century B.C., Phoenicians set up trading posts along the south shore of the Mediterranean, and their descendants, the Carthaginians, had settled on the shores of the Atlantic by the 5th century before Christ.

There seems to have been a kingdom of Mauritania in this area from about the 4th century B.C., but no records remain, although the Carthaginians' Punic language was spoken in coastal sections. A Berber kingdom, ruling about half of today's Morocco, was established after the fall of Carthage about a century and a half before the Christian era. The Romans gained brief power over the land but withdrew from much of the territory in about A.D. 253, after which Christian and Jewish refugees from Rome moved in. Rome clung to a coastal frontier to protect its claims on Tangier and the Straits of Gibraltar.

The Vandals came over from Spain, but they made little change in the Berber tribal claims other than seizing Ceuta. It was soon after the brief Vandal visit that invaders came from the east, changing forever the history of Morocco. These were warlike Arabs, newly converted from paganism to the Islamic faith inaugurated by the Prophet Mohammed in 622. They swept across North Africa, and by 683 were claiming the land and many converts among the Berbers. These Arabs were fair to the people living in the conquered lands, accepting Christian and Jews but striving most to convert the pagan Berbers. Having established control over the northern plains of Morocco, the followers of Mohammed used Tangier as the jumping-off place for conquest of Spain in A.D. 711 (see The Spanish, Chapter II).

Berber Muslims never quite saw eye to eye with the Arabs except in matters of religion, and there was a long, long period now of unity, now of conflict, between the two Islamic peoples.

After the expulsion of the last Moroccan caliph from Spain (1492), things were lively along the Mediterranean's southwestern coast. By the 19th century, with the Alaouite dynasty ruling by virtue of descent from the Prophet, part of the country came under Spanish rule and the rest became a French possession by the early 20th century. Spanish and French protectorates, they were called. Britain hung onto Gibraltar but otherwise bowed out of Moroccan affairs, since it had Egypt to see to.

The Moroccans were not happy under the European mandates. Sultans, sherifs, and tribal leaders kept up a series of strikes against the Europeans from about 1911, and after World War II the French and Moroccans were locked in conflicting ideologies. France lost. A rebellion against French control ended in independence for Morocco in 1956. The heir to the throne of the Alaouite dynasty, who had been exiled by the French, came back, and his son, Hassan II, is King of Morocco today.

Spain recognized the independent nation, ceding all of Spanish Morocco to the nation but retaining Ceuta and Melilla as Spanish enclaves. The Spanish Sahara, still a trouble spot to Morocco, was divided in 1976 between that country and Mauritania. Guerrillas are battling for independence of the area—far, far from the parts of Morocco visited by tourists.

GOVERNMENT: The present monarch is King Hassan II, who is both head of the civil state and leader of the Muslim religion in his country. Morocco is a hereditary constitutional monarchy, and the sovereign has wide powers. For example, he must approve all legislation, and he may dissolve the House of Representatives. He can also declare a state of emergency and suspend parliamentary government, as has been done.

Otherwise, the parliament of Morocco is bicameral. The major legislative body is the House of Representatives, and there is also the House of Councillors. The king heads the Supreme Council of Justice, which is independent of the executive and legislative branches.

A word of advice: It is extremely unwise to criticize the king while you are a guest in his country. If you object to the manner in which the country is run, save your barbs until you're back in Europe or North America.

LANGUAGE: Arabic, of course, is the national language, but French and Spanish are widely used. Since the 1960s English has made great inroads, especially in hotels, restaurants, and nightclubs in the major cities, where you can almost count on its being spoken. And if you've got some dirhams in your purse, shopkeepers will speak any language you want them to.

CULTURE: Moroccan literature, art, drama, and music partake of both Western and Middle Eastern influences.

Literature

Early Arabic literature had as its forms poetry, essays, and history, with modern additions being novels, short stories, and drama. Because of the difficulty of using either classical or dialectic Arabic in the newer genres, writing, even of the protest literature of the early 20th century, was mostly in French. Oral literature is more prevalent than written, professional storytellers still being found in the marketplaces of some towns and villages.

Art and Architecture

Paintings on cave and rock shelter walls in Morocco date from Neolithic times, with the next art of any note found in North Africa being from Roman times—statues, portraits in bronze, weapons, and the like. In the field of architecture, few if any relics of pre-Roman builders' art exist. As in other countries once under Roman domination, however, excavations in Morocco, especially in Volubilis, reveal arches, forums, villas, and baths.

The 7th-century Arab invaders brought to Morocco's cities not only the Islamic religion but also architectural forms and decorative embellishments. The style of architecture known as Hispano-Moorish has its roots in 8th-century Spain but came to full flower from the 12th to the 14th centuries in Morocco. This is the style used in mosques and Islamic schools and to some extent in gates, city walls, and palaces. Gateway arches, colonnades, courtyards, use of mosaic tiles, stone filigree, and other decorative effects are seen.

Artisans of Morocco still carve plaster panels and wood stalactites, as well as producing delicate wall decorations in glazed clay. In outlying villages, traditional patterns are used to produce jewelry and weapons.

Painting pictures other than as decoration for buildings inside and out is fairly new in Morocco, having been discouraged by the Islamic prohibition of representative art. Today, however, a school of young painters has developed, with their subjects including street scenes with human figures as well as Western-style abstract paintings. Brilliant colors are used.

Household articles are usually decorated in some way, whether they're made by family members or by skilled craftspeople. Leather, pottery, rugs, textiles, and items of wood, brass, iron, and copper are appreciated for their beauty as well as for their usefulness.

Music and Dance

In Morocco, you can hear Arab, Berber, popular, and classical music, the last named being of 10th- to 15th-century Andalusian derivation, with lyrics done in classical Arabic or in the dialect of Andalusia. The orchestras which produce this complicated form are made up of the *tar* (a type of tambourine) and three stringed instruments—the *rebab* (the rebec in Europe), the lute, and usually a European violin which has widely replaced the *kemanjah* once common. Sometimes the *darbuqa*, a funnel-shaped drum, is used.

Popular Arab music is not as complicated of structure as the classical, and it uses the common language. Called *griha,* its lyrics may be about war, love, sorrow, or adventure. Berber regional life is varied and so is the music, but it's all mainly connected to dancing. Drums and tambourines provide the rhythms, the melody being produced by a flute or one-string rebab. Berber country dances celebrate the harvest, marriage, and religious occasions.

In Morocco, music is very much a part of such events as funerals, circumcision rites, weddings, and religious holidays, and you'll hear it in homes, at cafés, and at concerts.

FOOD AND DRINK: If you think the Spanish are proud, wait till you get to Morocco. They're fierce. Some Moroccans claim their cuisine is the finest in the world. Others less chauvinistic rank it after France and China. What you'll usually find in the first-class and deluxe hotels is a cuisine that is mainly French and continental, although each establishment is likely to have a Moroccan room serving local specialties. To go truly native, you'll have to sit with robed Berbers and chew on fried locusts, as you watch the deadly, but defanged, cobra coil slowly upward from his basket to the music of a snake charmer.

The national soup is called **harrira** and is prepared in many different ways. It usually contains diced mutton and such spices as saffron and coriander. It's served piping hot, usually accompanied by dried dates as well as lemon slices and cinnamon sprinkled on top.

Couscous is the national dish. It is made with a base of steamed semolina, and its ingredients vary widely, depending on the chef or what was available at the market. Usually, mutton with vegetables is the order of the day. Couscous is most often served in a ceramic circular bowl, with a matching cover.

What North Americans refer to as shish-kebab in Morocco is called **brochette,** as in French. Brochettes are made with a number of meats, such as veal, beef, and lamb. A simple **kefta** is ground beef or lamb seasoned with herbs and skewered over a charcoal fire. **Tajine** (or tagine) is another common dish. It is a

Moroccan stew made with almost anything, perhaps camel meat. A favorite version of this dish is with lamb and prunes.

While in Morocco, you'll want to try the classic **lemon chicken.** In fact, if you find yourself in a typical Moroccan restaurant and think you're going to lose your appetite, this is your safest bet, because it contains ingredients you can readily identify. It is also superb in flavor. Other dishes include **pastilla,** a thin pastry filled with chicken or pigeon meat and flavored with ground almonds; **spices and sugar** served as an hors d'oeuvre; and **cornes de gazelle** (kaab el ghzal), horn-shaped pastries filled with almond paste (these are served with tea). **Mechoui** is a dish for festivals, when a lamb is cooked in a tight-fitting pot with raisins and almonds.

Most visitors to Morocco worry about their health. A stroll through the markets, where meat hangs out in the open, often fly-covered in hot months, only forces concern. However, most Moroccan dishes are simmered for long periods of time in tight dishes or cauterized over a hot flame on an open-air brazier (only the toughest of microbes hold up under these inferno baptisms), so you can relax somewhat.

The Moroccans eat with the fingers of their right hand. However, spoons and forks will be provided. Don't worry about messy fingers. Warm water placed beside a basin is presented to each guest before and after the meal. The water is then poured over the hands, which are held over the basin.

If you're being really native (or if you don't care for it) you won't drink wine—or anything—with your meal. However, you can get a glass of something when you feel like it. Moroccan wines are good and inexpensive, and should be better known. The wine-growing regions south of Meknes and Fez produce some excellent wines, including an interesting *gris* which is lighter than a rosé but not clear enough to be white wine. The names to look for are Ksar and Château Toulal (the most popular reds), Guerrouane and Boulaouane. The few restaurants and hotels that offer imported French wines charge prices that are very high. A good accompaniment to many a meal is mineral water from Sidi Harazem (said to cure kidney disorders, it also tastes good). In addition to the still water from Sidi Harazem, try the still mineral water from Sidi Ala. For sparkling water, the spring is at Oulmes. Coffee in Morocco is usually strong and black. If you want yours decaffeinated, better take it with you on your trip, as it is only available in the most expensive hotels. A meal usually concludes with mint tea, ideally made with fresh young mint. This is a refreshing drink if it's made properly.

Drinking Water

It is generally safe, at least in the big cities and towns. I'd avoid it in some of the remoter places, and drink mineral water instead. As a matter of personal taste, I find the water of the south, although safe, much too salty. Perhaps you will too. If so, stick to mineral water. See above.

Alcoholic Beverages

Muslims view the consumption of liquor quite differently from North Americans and Europeans. Many Moroccans prefer to get high on hash instead. In fact, it is illegal—at least in theory—to sell liquor to Muslims. Therefore, you should exercise caution in inviting someone for a drink.

Instead of traveling around with a bottle, it's best to confine your consumption of liquor to that regularly sold in bars, restaurants, nightclubs, and such.

There you'll be on safer ground. Don't expect to be served alcoholic beverages in certain local restaurants in the "medinas" of various towns and cities.

4. The ABCs of Morocco

Regardless of where you've traveled in Europe, Morocco is an entirely different trip. Don't be deceived by the short boat trip from Algeciras, Spain. You've entered an entirely different world when you step on the shores of Africa, and because of that, these "facts of life" may assume even greater importance. Knowing how to cope in your "gateway" to Africa can help ease your adjustment into this always-fascinating, often-perplexing land.

BANKS: In general, banks are open at 8:30 a.m., conducting business until 11:30 a.m. when they close for lunch. They're open again at 2:30 p.m., staying so until 4:30. Business days are Monday to Friday, as in most American cities.

If you arrive by plane in Casablanca, you'll find the **Banque Marocaine du Commerce Extérieur** open to exchange foreign currencies into dirhams. It's important to keep a record of all your transactions with banks in case you encounter any difficulty in leaving the country.

Likewise, such exchange facilities are available to those passengers arriving by either boat or plane in Tangier. Sometimes exchange bureaus operate on boats leaving from Algeciras, heading for Morocco.

Since there is no local American Express office to exchange money, it's important to have a reliable bank. I patronize the Banque Marocaine du Commerce Extérieur, whose head office is at 241 Boulevard Mohammed V in Casablanca (tel. 30-61-80); on Avenue du General Kettani in Agadir (tel. 219-93); at 4 rue Richard d'Ivrey in Rabat (tel. 230-65); and on Boulevard Pasteur in Tangier (tel. 310-44).

BICYCLE RENTALS: In Tangier, it is possible to rent bicycles and motor bikes from **Meshbahi et Cie.,** 7 rue Ibn Tachfine (tel. 409-74). This is a small office in a street leading up from the Avenue des F.A.R. where Abdullah Scullion, a quiet American from Ohio, rents pedal bikes at 60 DH ($6.60) per day and 50cc motorbikes at 165 DH ($18.15) per day, 350 DH ($38.50) for three days, and 600 DH ($66) per week. Insurance is included. You must pay a refundable deposit of 1,000 DH ($110). Helmets are not compulsory, and it is unlikely that you will be able to rent one.

BOOKSTORES: For English-language books, magazines, guides, and maps, go to the **Librairie des Colonnes** at 54 Boulevard Pasteur (tel. 369-55) in Tangier. The English-speaking staff also sells etchings and art reproductions.

In Rabat, the **Librairie-Tabacs-Journaux** of the Rabat Hilton (tel. 721-51), carries a line of English-language books, along with newspapers, journals, and magazines, and also sells guides, maps, and postcards. It's open from 8 a.m. to 8 p.m.

CAMPING: There are at least 30 camping sites throughout Morocco, including grounds outside the major cities, where you'll find adequate shower and toilet facilities. The Moroccan tourist office will provide more information and details. Camping along the southern border of Morocco is to be avoided because of potential danger. The cost is 2 DH (22¢) per person, plus another 2 DH (22¢) for the site.

CLIMATE AND CLOTHING: Morocco experiences weather extremes, and what you wear will depend on the time of the year, where you go, etc. Remember that you can freeze to death in the sky-high Atlas and burn to a crisp in the Sahara. The mountain resorts around Marrakesh can require much protective wool, even light woolen attire at certain times in the summer.

In winter, when many North Americans favor Morocco (these are the so-called rainy months), cities such as Tangier, Casablanca, Fez, Rabat, and Meknes have a climate like Southern California. When the sun goes down, you'll need light coats or jackets; but during the sunny hours you can sunbathe with comfort in wind-protected areas. Swimming in heated pools is popular in winter, although ocean bathing is not, unless you're a Finn. Cold Atlantic winds can sweep through Tangier and Casablanca, yet light woolen clothing is generally adequate.

In summer, the entire picture changes. Light summer apparel is suitable in Casablanca and Tangier, but it gets unbearably hot the farther south you go, especially in Marrakesh and the Sahara. Moroccan residents learn to protect themselves from the stifling heat. Those who can afford to do so retreat to the mountains.

Records show that Marrakesh has the highest percentage of sunny days in Morocco, Casablanca the lowest, with Tangier and Agadir somewhere in between.

For more specific information, refer to "Temperatures," in this section.

CONSULATES AND EMBASSIES: In general it's best not to telephone. If you've got business to transact, go there in person during regular office hours Monday to Friday.

In **Rabat,** the U.S. Embassy is at 2 Avenue de Marrakesh (tel. 622-65).

In **Casablanca,** the U.S. Consulate is at 8 Boulevard Moulay Youssef (tel. 22-42-84).

In **Tangier,** the U.S. Consulate is at rue El Acouak (tel. 359-04), the British at 52 rue d'Angleterre (tel. 358-95).

CRIME: In all the major cities, you will be pestered by characters wanting to guide you, and you only have to ask the way to someplace to acquire at least one companion for the trip—and he will expect recompense for his pains. On the whole, a very firm "no" and complete uninterest will discourage the would-be "guides" and the "students of language." It is not wise to distribute money in the streets, except perhaps for a photograph, unless you want to be mobbed. There are clip joints and nightclubs where you will be shamelessly ripped off, but then you have to learn to spot those a mile off.

It is not advisable to leave luggage in your car, even when it is locked, and don't examine the contents of your wallet in the street. This is just asking to have it lifted.

Official guides, who display badges, can usually be relied on to protect your interests and recommend places to go where you will not be threatened or ripped off. See "Guides" below.

In particular, go to Tangier at your own risk! My own personal experience and mounting outcries from readers lead to the conclusion that Tangier is a very dangerous city, and you should exercise extreme caution. Unless you're looking for trouble, don't go wandering around at night, particularly through the narrow streets of the Medina and the Casbah. You especially flirt with danger should you go into any dive accompanied by a man who accosts you on the street with a tempting tale of a "little hot spot." One man from Howard Beach, New York, writes: "After supper, I took a walk. A character accosted me, knew of a nice native club, pretty girls, drinks for nothing, wine only two dollars a bottle. So, I went. To be brief, after two bottles of 'champagne,' which he first said was wine, but still was only two dollars a bottle, and after I had given him a few dollars for his 'trouble,' plus drinks for him and a 'B' girl, I said to myself it was time to go, and asked for the check. I was there 20 minutes. So I got the bill for $85. When I protested violently, I was surrounded by half a dozen cutthroats. I had to empty my wallet of $50 in Spanish, American, and Moroccan money, and then sign over two $20 travelers checks. I didn't think these guys would hesitate to dump me in the ocean with a knife in my back."

Tangier may be one of the most dangerous cities of Morocco, but the warning sounded there is still valid wherever you travel in the country.

About Hashish

A band of young Americans and Canadians have "gone Moroccan" in Marrakesh—that is, they've bought djellabas and put a pair of babouches on their feet. You'll see them sitting around Djemaa el-Fna square at night, eating a typical Moroccan meal and smoking kif.

For many of these expatriates, the monetary title of this book represents a far more luxurious standard of living than they would want to indulge in. Many know how to live—or at least survive—in the Medina for a dollar or two a day. However, many of these unwanted visitors have largely disappeared from the scene following a crackdown by the police who weren't too happy about their hash-smoking ways.

Kif, a raw-leaf marijuana, is still sold openly. It is commonly smoked in public in a clay pipe. Despite this rather blatant display, note that the sale of kif, as mentioned, is *illegal* in Morocco. In one year alone, some 100 foreigners were arrested on drug counts.

Moroccan laws make the buying, selling, and exporting of pot or hash a very risky business. The maximum penalty has been raised from five to ten years in jail, and the minimum from three months to five years for most types of offenses. Fines have been increased considerably, up to 500,000 dirhams ($55,000).

Moroccan authorities consider many foreigners an "evil influence" on local youth, and the national law makes it a "major crime" to corrupt minors by inciting them to take drugs.

CURRENCY: Here's how the U.S. dollar translates into Moroccan currency. The basic unit of Moroccan currency is the **dirham** (abbreviated DH). This chart is based on the exchange rate of 9 dirhams to $1 U.S. One dirham is worth about 11¢ U.S. As we go to press, this rate appears fairly stable, but, with world economic conditions being what they are, it's always best to confirm the up-to-date official rate of exchange before you go to Morocco by checking with your bank at home.

The Moroccan dirham is divided into 100 centimes. Dirhams come in coins of 1 and 5; centimes in 5, 10, 20, and 50. In bills, you are issued denominations of 5, 10, 50 and 100 dirhams.

Dirhams	U.S.$	Dirhams	U.S.$
1	$ .11	30	$ 3.30
2	.22	35	3.85
3	.33	40	4.40
4	.44	45	4.95
5	.55	50	5.50
6	.66	60	6.60
7	.77	70	7.70
8	.88	80	8.80
9	.99	90	9.90
10	1.10	100	11.00
15	1.65	125	13.75
20	2.20	150	16.50
25	2.75	200	22.00

CUSTOMS: The following items may be temporarily imported to Morocco duty free: still and movie cameras with two rolls of film for each; personal clothing and jewelry; binoculars; portable typewriters; camping material; and sports gear. Most foodstuff is allowed, but in "reasonable quantities." The visitor is allowed to bring in 400 grams of tobacco, or 200 cigarettes or 50 cigars, and one bottle of wine or spirits. Firearms and cartridges may be imported subject to a license issued by the police department in Rabat (Direction de la Sureté Nationale).

Citizens of the United States who have been outside the country for 48 hours or more are allowed to bring back to their home country $400 worth of merchandise duty free—that is, if they have claimed no similar exemption within the past 30 days. If you make purchases in Morocco, it is important to keep your records.

Warning: After a tour of Morocco, if you are returning to Spain by car, know that your vehicle will probably be searched thoroughly, as Spanish Customs look for hashish (kif). Sometimes it takes hours to gain clearance. And from what I hear, Spanish jails aren't the Hilton.

DOCUMENTS FOR ENTRY: Very liberal visitor regulations make it easy to enter Morocco. A valid individual or joint passport is necessary. For U.S., Canadian, and United Kingdom visitors, no visa is required, and tourists may stay in Morocco for three months. Those wishing to stay longer must apply to the local police department for an extension. No vaccination certificate is required to enter Morocco.

DRUGS: My advice is to take whatever medication or drugs you'll need with you. I've experienced great difficulty in getting a prescription filled in certain parts of Morocco. American brands do not exist in certain places (the French seem to have cornered the market here).

If you're in a dire emergency, ask the concierge at your hotel to direct you to the nearest pharmacy. Perhaps it would be wise to have him or her call ahead and explain your needs to the druggist there in case there's a language problem.

Moroccan pharmacies operate in accordance with the French *Codex*.

For an all-night pharmacy in Casablanca, telephone 743-13. In Rabat, call 261-50; in Fez, 220-62; and in Marrakesh, 304-15.

ELECTRIC CURRENT: Nowadays, it is generally 220 volts, but you'll occasionally come across 110 volts.

EMERGENCY: In **Tangier,** to telephone the police, call 19, and don't be surprised if they're indifferent, especially about thefts. The emergency hospital number (the Hospital Al Kortobi) is 342-42.

In **Rabat,** phone the police at 19, an ambulance at 228-78, and report a fire by calling 15.

In **Casablanca,** some good numbers to know are as follows: police, 19; ambulance or fire, 15.

In **Fez,** reach the police at 19, an ambulance at 227-76.

In **Meknes,** call the police at 19, an ambulance at 228-05.

In and around **Agadir,** dialing 19 gets you the police, 224-77 an ambulance.

In **Marrakesh,** the emergency numbers are as follows: 19 for the police, 15 to report a fire, and 16 to call an ambulance.

EXCHANGING MONEY: At the border, foreign visitors are obligated to declare to Customs the amount of foreign currencies and Moroccan money (dirhams) in their possession. The carrying of Moroccan banknotes into the country is officially forbidden. Those bringing in Moroccan dirhams risk having them confiscated upon entry.

You may convert foreign currencies or traveler's checks at any exchange office throughout Morocco. Many exchange counters are in hotels, and at all ports of entry. To change foreign currencies outside official exchange offices is a considerably risky practice. Further, it is strictly prohibited to give foreign currency to a resident of Morocco in exchange for goods or services. Payment must be in dirhams only.

Foreign nonresidents upon leaving Morocco can reconvert dirhams up to 50% of the amount mentioned on their exchange statements if their stay exceeds 48 hours—and up to 100% if their stay does not exceed 48 hours. It is officially forbidden to export Moroccan banknotes.

GUIDES: The sights in the medinas of Morocco are usually covered by foot. This is unquestionably preferable, allowing you to savor everything at your own speed. If you do want some help rather than an organized tour, I recommend engaging an English-speaking guide for a half day of general orientation. Maps are usually inadequate, and many of the sights described simply can't be found on your own, unless you have unlimited time to do so.

City-licensed guides are available either through your hotel or by going to the **Syndicat d'Initiative,** which is the tourist office. You'll find one in every major city. Hiring an official guide is less expensive than you think. Prices are regulated; but it's important to have a clear understanding of the rate and the hours he or she is to work. The cost is the same from city to city. For a half day it is 30 DH ($3.30), and for a full day 50 DH ($5.50).

For a warning on unscrupulous "guides," see "Crime" above.

HAIRDRESSERS: Of widely varying quality, these salons are found in all the major cities and towns (ask at your hotel for the most recommendable one nearest you). For a shampoo and set, women pay from 30 DH ($3.30) to no more than 75 DH ($8.25) in the most deluxe establishments; and for a haircut (not styling), men are charged from 20 DH ($2.20) in a simple barbershop to around 45 DH ($4.95) for a more first-class job.

HOLIDAYS: Official holidays include March 3, the Fête de Trône, which is Moroccan independence day, marking the accession of King Hassan II; May 1, Workers' Holiday; May 23, National Holiday; July 9, the king's birthday; August 14, celebration of reclamation of land from the desert; and November 6, date of the Green March, the peace march to claim the Sahara from Spain. November 18, another holiday, commemorates the accession of King Mohammed V. Religious holidays vary according to the Muslim calendar. Aid-es-Seghir is celebrated as ending the fast of Ramadan; Aid el-Kebir commemorates Abraham's sacrifice; Mouloud honors the Prophet's birth; and Achoura, the tenth day of the Muslim year, celebrates the beginning of the Hegiran year.

All banks and shops are closed on these religious holidays. Check with the tourist office for actual dates in the year you plan to travel.

LAUNDRY: Take along some drip-dry clothing, as laundry and dry-cleaning can be highly erratic in Morocco. It's best to stick to the services of your hotel. In an emergency I often tip the maid to launder and press a shirt. For the regular hotel laundry, expect to pay about 16 DH ($1.76) per shirt. To have a woman's dress dry-cleaned in Morocco costs about 25 DH ($2.75), and a man's two-piece suit can be cleaned for about 45 DH ($4.95).

METRIC MEASURES: Morocco uses the metric system of weights and measures (refer to the ABC section on Spain).

MOSQUES: Many North Americans and Europeans visit Morocco with the mistaken notion that they will get to go inside mosques or religious shrines, as part of that country's sightseeing attractions. It simply isn't possible, as frustrating as that revelation may be.

If you're not a Muslim, you'll be committing a grave offense in entering a mosque, and may get yourself in a lot of trouble. To enter certain holy shrines in the countryside is to court suicide. Remember, in this land, you're the "infidel."

Occasionally you'll come across some old *medrassa* that are no longer in use as places of worship, and there you'll get a tantalizing preview of what a mosque looks like inside. When a functioning mosque is open, and Moroccans are at prayer inside, do not linger outside on the threshold peering in. It's considered very bad form, as few Muslims want infidels to view them at these personal, private moments.

NEWSPAPERS: From Paris, The *International Herald Tribune* is flown to Casablanca and Rabat. Chances are, you can enjoy it in the late afternoon. It's likely to arrive later in other cities in Morocco. Some English newspapers filter in through Gibraltar.

PETS: An international health and inoculation certificate is necessary for pets to be taken into Morocco.

PHOTOGRAPHY: Provincial Moroccans do not like to be photographed. It is considered very bad manners. Under no circumstance should you ever try to take a picture of a woman. Such cities as Marrakesh and Tangier are so used to tourists at this point that it often rarely matters, but exercise caution, nevertheless.

Most film sold in France is available in Morocco as well. Color slides and photographs can be developed here, but I've found the services unreliable and time-consuming; therefore, I'd suggest that you wait until you return home.

Because light in Morocco is often filtered through a veil of dust (or mist), a photoelectric exposure meter should be carried along if you plan to do much photography.

POST OFFICES: In the large cities of Morocco, including Casablanca, Rabat, and Tangier, post offices are open from 8:30 a.m. to 6:30 p.m. In smaller places, they are likely to shut down between noon and 3 p.m. The clerk at your hotel will direct you to the post office branch nearest you.

It costs 3 DH (33¢) to send an airmail postcard to Canada or the United States, 3.50 DH (39¢) to send a letter (up to 20 grams). These tariffs are subject to change, so check at the local post office before you mail.

Stamps can also be purchased at tobacconists, as in France.

RELIGIOUS SERVICES: In all towns with a European population you'll find Catholic churches (not always Protestant). In the cities, however, there exist not only Catholic, but Protestant and Orthodox as well.

Jewish worshippers in Casablanca can attend the synagogue, **Ein Habanim,** 14 rue Lusitania (tel. 26-69); in Fez, the **Ruben Sadoun** synagogue on rue Fréjus; in Marrakesh, the **Attias** synagogue at 3 rue Ibn Tourmert; and in Tangier, the **Temple Nahon,** rue des Synagogues (tel. 396-36).

In Tangier services are held at the **American Church,** 34 rue Hassan Ibn Quezzane, sometimes still known as rue Léon l' Africain (tel. 327-55), at 11:30 a.m. Sunday. **St. Andrew's Episcopal Church,** 50 rue d'Angleterre, also has services each Sunday, at 11 a.m. This church is an interesting mix of European and Arabic architecture. There's also a pleasant churchyard, where you can sit in peace away from the noise of the city.

In **Meknes** Catholic services are conducted at the **Church of Notre-Dame,** Avenue Mohammed V.

In **Casablanca,** there's a Roman Catholic Church, the **Cathedral of Sacré-Coeur,** on Boulevard Rachidi, and an Anglican church on rue Guedj. In addition, there's also a Protestant church at 33 rue Azilal.

REST ROOMS: All modern airports and rail and bus terminals have toilets, maintained more or less well. Public toilets in the major cities and towns are often cesspools, and I'd recommend that you avoid them unless it's a case of dire emergency. It's best to patronize the rest rooms of major hotels and restaurants. The squat toilet is still very much in evidence in Morocco. (See "Toiletries" for a further tip.)

SHOPPING: Shopping is another strong reason visitors go to Morocco, although they must learn to haggle for bargains in the *souks* of Meknes, Fez, and Marrakesh. Advised one Moroccan: "Never pay the third price asked." I've always been able to cut prices quoted by at least half and often two-thirds. Even then, I'm sure the shopkeeper has made a generous profit.

Moroccan handcrafts enjoy world renown. Even if you're not in the market for anything, sellers will seek you out. Everybody from the smallest child in the street to the clerks at the more modern stores will try to sell you something . . . anything! Brightly colored Rabat carpets, embroidered tablecloths and matching napkins (always too small), silver boxes, gem-studded slave bracelets, engraved daggers, silk brocade caftans (a graceful T-shaped garment sold in every known color, with every conceivable type of adornment), even antique rifles—the merchandise is here. Brassware is good value if you pick the weighty pieces, as the thin and tinny pieces will tarnish and turn black when you get them home. Moroccan leather goods are world famous—jackets, skirts, shoes, and handbags. Wallets make good souvenirs as well as being practical and available at reasonable prices. Spices are good bargains in local markets, and if you need good luck, tradition has it that you must buy a Fatima's hand, with its stylized three fingers and two thumbs.

If you detest haggling, you should be able to go to certain outlets in every major city which feature fixed prices. You'll end up paying more, of course; but then you don't have to embarrass yourself.

STORE HOURS: Most shops and stores are open from 8:30 a.m. to noon, reopening at 2:30 p.m. and conducting business until around 7 p.m. (some stay open even later). Many shops are closed on Sunday, and, because of the special way the Muslim week works, can also be shut down on Friday.

TELEGRAMS: As in many European countries, telegrams are sent from the post office.

TELEPHONE: In Morocco the telephone services operate through the post office. Calls within cities such as Tangier and Casablanca can be made at public phone booths. As of this writing, international phone calls are routed through the capital city of Rabat. Therefore, expect delays of 2½ to 3 hours (my latest call from Fez to New York took four hours).

The large cities are linked by automatic telephone. In these cases, all you have to do is simply dial the number after you've learned the area code. Consult the phone directories of the *Postes Chérifiennes.*

TELEX: Chances are your hotel will send one for you. However, smaller inns and hotels, most likely, won't be equipped to send a Telex.

TEMPERATURES: The chart below lists average temperatures in Fahrenheit.

	Jan.	Feb.	Mar.	Apr.	May.	Jun.	Jul.	Aug.	Sep.	Oct.	Nov.	Dec
Agadir	69	70	72	74	76	77	80	80	79	78	76	69
Casablanca	63	63	66	68	72	75	81	81	82	77	68	64
Essaouira	64	64	64	66	68	68	72	70	70	70	68	66
Fez	61	63	66	72	79	88	97	97	90	81	66	61
Marrakesh	66	66	73	79	84	91	102	101	91	82	70	66
Meknes	59	61	64	70	77	84	93	93	86	79	66	61
Ouarzazate	63	67	73	80	86	96	102	100	91	80	70	62
Rabat	63	64	66	70	73	77	82	82	81	77	68	64
Tangier	59	61	62	66	72	77	80	82	79	73	64	61
Taroudannt	72	73	79	81	86	90	99	100	95	90	77	72

TIME: Greenwich Mean Time (GMT) is in force all year in Morocco. The country is five hours ahead of Eastern Standard Time (six hours in summer).

TIPPING: A nightmare! Everyone seems to have a hand out; and one is tempted to draw a Moroccan veil and face away without parting with a dirham. Nevertheless, certain tips are expected—and rightly so. Here are the guidelines. Take every opportunity to fill your pockets with 1-dirham and .50-dirham pieces. They'll go quickly enough. Most restaurants and hotels include a service charge, usually 15%—but don't take that too seriously. The waiter expects something extra. Give 3 DH (33¢) per bag to the porter for taking your luggage to your room, 3 DH to the taxi driver unless the ride has been unusually long. Attendants who watch cars at the entrance to restaurants or sights expect at least 2 DH (22¢). Guides who show you through museums expect at least 3 DH (33¢). Train and boat porters also expect 3 DH (f they don't get it, they are likely to chase after you). If you've required the assistance of a hotel concierge for a stay of at least three days, then about 25 DH ($2.75) is adequate.

TOBACCO: American and British cigarettes are sold in the big cities. You can also purchase Moroccan brands. I find the Moroccan Gauloises cheap but atrocious. You can purchase tobacco not only in tobacco shops but in most food markets and cafés. A popular Moroccan brand of cigarettes is called "Casa Sports," made with black tobacco, costing from 2.60 DH (29¢) per package. A package of American cigarettes sells for around 12 DH ($1.32).

TOILETRIES: Take what you'll need, as you may not find your local product in Morocco. It is wise to travel with insect repellent if you're going to tour. Certainly if you're visiting some spots in the Sahara in the summer, it's also discreet to carry along a supply of salt tablets. Naturally, suntan lotion is essential. To be on the safe side, I'd also recommend to the smart traveler that he or she take along a "stash" of toilet paper. When you've visited certain Moroccan toilets, you'll understand why!

TOURIST INFORMATION: Before you go, you can obtain information and have many of your questions answered by writing or calling the **Moroccan Tourist Office,** 20 East 46th St., New York, NY 10017 (tel. 212/557-2520).

In Morocco, there are many national and city tourist offices dispensing information to the traveler. English is spoken in all these offices.

In **Rabat,** tourist information is given out at the **ONMT** (the Office National Marocain du Tourisme), at 22 Charia Al-Jazair (tel. 212-52), and there's also a Syndicat d'Initiative on the corner of rue Patrice Lumumba and rue Van Vollenhoven (tel. 232-72), which is run by the city.

In **Casablanca,** the national tourist office is at the ONMT office, 55 rue Omar Slaoui (tel. 27-11-77), and the city information office is at 98 Boulevard Mohammed V (tel. 22-15-24).

In **Tangier,** the ONMT office is at 29 Boulevard Pasteur (tel. 382-39), and the Syndicat d'Initiative is at 11 rue Velásquez (tel. 354-86).

In **Fez,** national tourist information is presented at the ONMT office, Immeuble Bennani, Place de la Résistance (tel. 234-60), and city information at the bureau of the Syndicat d'Initiative on Place Mohammed V (tel. 247-69).

In **Meknes,** the national tourist office is at Place Administrative (tel. 212-86), and city information is given out on the Esplanade de la Foire (tel. 201-91).

In **Tetuan,** you can seek information at the ONMT office on 30 Avenue Mohammed V (tel. 44-07).

In **Agadir,** the national tourist office is on the Avenue du Prince Héritier (Sidi Mohamed) (tel. 28-94), and the Syndicat d'Initiative is on Avenue Mohammed V (tel. 226-95). Don't expect any great help at either one of them, however.

Finally, in **Marrakesh** go to the ONMT office at Place Abdelmoumen Ben Ali (tel. 302-58), or the Syndicat d'Initiative at 170 Avenue Mohammed V (tel. 32-97).

Chapter XVIII

TANGIER AND THE NORTH

1. Tangier
2. Ceuta
3. Tetuan
4. Chaouen (Chechaouèn)

BEACHES AND VACATION VILLAGES attract thousands of tourists each summer to the Mediterranean coast of Morocco. The major destination in the north, **Tangier,** has long been a city associated with glamour and intrigue. Legend claims it was founded by the mythological Greek figure Antea.

The coastline for the most part is relatively calm, and nearly all the beaches are uncrowded. Outside of Tangier, if you're touring in the area, one of the most popular destinations is **Tetuan,** founded in 1307 by the Merinid ruler, Sultan About Thabit. During Spain's Inquisition, thousands of Jews and Muslims took refuge here to avoid persecution or perhaps death. Tetuan, even today, still shows traces of its Andalusian culture. Tetuan is the main town in the Rif area, and you can see many peasant women wearing their traditional red, white, and blue striped skirts.

Chaouen, on the other hand, was founded in 1471 and is nestled in a fold of the Rif mountains. Its name in Berber means "The Horns." Many of its buildings resemble those found in southern Spain.

Should you wish to sample a more undiluted version of Spain on the North African coast, you can drive east from Tangier to a military enclave of Spain, **Ceuta,** a real Andalusian town. Spain refused to surrender this enclave when Morocco was granted independence in 1956, and it also still clings to the outpost of Melilla, farther east on the route to Algeria.

Whether you're coming from Algeciras or Gibraltar on the Spanish mainland, or perhaps winging in, the first destination of most travelers is—

1. Tangier

By ferryboat from Algeciras you can be in Tangier in 2½ hours. A hydrofoil takes only an hour. The ride from Spain is so short that it's hard to imagine you have entered a whole other way of life. The world is now Islam, and you can hear the special sounds that call the faithful to prayer. Catholic Spain is far, far away—even though you can look out across the strait and see it.

A white sandy beach—about 2½ miles long—stretches in front of Tangier, a potent attraction in summer to Americans and Europeans. Because of its hard-hit economy following the collapse of Tangier's status as an international city in 1956, the government is making a strong bid for tourism. It casts a lean and hungry eye on the hordes of people who descend on the less desirable beaches of the Costa del Sol, and wonders why the crowds don't get the message and come on over. The so-called Moroccan Riviera with its beautiful beaches is so uncrowded in summer that tourists can swim nude near one of the Caves of Hercules.

By all means, spend the night in Tangier, although it is important not to let your guard down here (see "Crime," Chapter XVII). Too many visitors arrive on one of those one-day excursions, then rush through the city—and everything becomes a blur. There's enough to see and do to jam-pack many days. Now let's zero in and find out what it's like.

The dazzling white city of Tangier is fickle: it winks at the Mediterranean with one eye, while casting a flirtatious glance at the Atlantic with the other. Tangier does not look dark and mysterious, but bright and airy, with palm-lined boulevards, comfortable, white-painted hotels. However, once you've docked, once you've penetrated deep into the city (the Medina and the Casbah), you'll surely change your mind.

Tangier is a city of contrasts. Women in white haiks who look like mummies walk down the old streets, the way their grandmothers did before them, and their grandmothers' grandmothers before them. The modern Moroccan woman, on the other hand, may wear a dark djellaba. Once virtually every Moroccan woman peered over a veil at her liberated European counterpart. Today increasing numbers are veil-less, and their new-found freedom is also reflected in high-heel shoes and nail polish. At night, too, in the cabarets, you'll find that modesty is not mandatory for Moroccan women. The belly dancers don't even wear diamonds in their navels.

The contrast is seen in the men, as well. Old bearded relics of another day hobble down the alley-like streets with their weary donkeys; they look as if they had stepped fresh out of Jerusalem before the birth of Christ. More modern men pay homage to their Muslim traditions by wearing camel-hair robes. In total disregard of their origins, some of the young men wear blue jeans and leather jackets (in the cooler months), and would fit in the Bronx.

Tangier is a city whose origins dip deep into antiquity; many conquerors have presided over the Casbah. From around the time of World War I until '56, Tangier was an international city. It had acquired associations then, particularly during World War II, which it has not lived down today. It is often considered a wicked city, a hot-bed of intrigue, prostitution, money changers, and narcotics. The government, in an attempt to remove some of the stigma of this reputation, has cracked down on houses of prostitution, forcing the women to take to the streets. The situation has been made tough for the money changers, but they blithely go on their way, offering you extra dirham if you'll convert your pesetas or dollars. The drug trade flourishes in Tangier; the odor of kif (a kind of marijuana) permeates the air in some parts. However, foreigners caught with drugs, particularly if they're on the dealing end, are not dealt with lightly in Morocco, as is attested to by the presence in Moroccan jails of several Americans. So take care!

Moroccans are quick to point out that Tangier is the most religious city around, since its three different sects—Jews, Christians, Muslims—celebrate their holy day on a different day of the week. In a sense, the city has three sabbaths.

How to describe it? Tangier is a city of mosques, modern hotels, white- and purple-washed houses, exotic markets, foreign and Moroccan restaurants—and there's even a place where you can ask a Yank to serve you a hamburger, light on the onions if you wish.

A warning: One thing that is very confusing in Tangier is that all roads have two names, one European, such as rue des Vignes, and one Moroccan, as rue Prince Héritier. You can never be sure which one you'll get when you ask for directions. Most of the road signs are obliterated anyway so it's often a hit-or-miss affair. However, with concentration and patience, you will soon find your way around.

GETTING THERE: A gateway to the Mediterranean, Tangier is naturally most often reached by sea or air. The most popular method is to take a ferry from Algeciras in Spain. Tickets in Algeciras can be purchased at Estacíon Marítima (tel. 65-03-55). In summer, ferries run about four times daily, the trip taking 2½ hours and costing about 2,200 pesetas ($15.40) per person. For about the same price, you can take a hydrofoil from Tarifa to Tangier; the travel time here is only an hour. Depending on the weather, vessels leave twice a day except on Sunday.

If you're flying, you can take either an **Iberia** or a **Royal Air Maroc** flight between Madrid and Tangier. Iberia also maintains connections between Tangier and Málaga. **Air France** hooks Tangier up with Paris, and **British Airways** maintains a London–Tangier run. For connections from Gibraltar, refer to Chapter XV.

WHERE TO STAY: Tangier offers a number of hotels within our price range. Most of them lie somewhere between the **Boulevard Pasteur** (main shopping and business street of the international section) and the beach, and many are within easy walking distance of either area. Some are built on sloping streets, affording views of the bay.

Rif Hotel, Avenue d'Espagne (tel. 359-10), is the place for the visitor who requires comfort and elegance with total Moroccan style. A six-story building, it faces the beach and the broad waters of Tangier Bay, with a welcoming, cool marbled lobby with deep, comfortable leather armchairs. The lounges and public rooms mainly overlook the sea and are decorated in extravagant Moorish style. The mosaics on the walls are handmade, and the carved wooden ceilings are carefully fashioned. Modern furnishings blend well with the traditional, and the fresh cool dining room and the leather-covered bar look out on to the sheltered patio and pool area. Cool green trees and shrubs climb behind and overhang the pool and grotto; loungers and chairs are dotted among the palms and creepers.

All rooms overlooking the bay are in the traditional style with Moorish filigree woodwork on the cupboards and friezes. Good beds and balconies are another plus, and bathrooms are efficient. At the back, overlooking the garden, the rooms are furnished in a contemporary style, and there are several duplex apartments designed and decorated by Patrick Frank, a French antiquarian who, like so many, has settled in Morocco. Again there is much adaption of the ancient styles with Moorish lanterns providing a soft light, lush carpets, and carved woodwork reflecting the glow. Lunchtime salads and sandwiches are available around the pool if you do not wish a set meal in the dining room, costing 100 DH ($11). Rooms are 265 DH ($29.15) for two persons, 190 DH ($20.90) for singles. Duplexes are more expensive. Half board is obligatory from April to October, costing from 290 DH ($31.90) per person.

The Rif maintains, as always, its position as the doyen of Tangier hotels. Its special feature is the excellence of the staff, who, without exception, are friendly and well trained. The barman remembers your usual order and has your drink lined up before you've asked for it. The headwaiters and the section leaders are eager to find out what fish arrived today, to squeeze fresh oranges for your breakfast juice, and to cater to your special requests. Mr. Serfati is very ably assisted and supported by Simon Cohen. Tennis with a pro is available, and there is a sauna.

Rembrandt Hotel, Boulevard Mohammed V (tel. 378-70), is built on a hillside right on the main boulevard, as it climbs toward the Place de France. A cool lobby leads to a smart bar and neat dining room, and there are lounges with TV and air conditioning. You can take the stairs or else a somewhat erratic (but safe) elevator to the upper floors where many of the rooms look over the bay and harbor. Some units are simple, and others contain a tiny balcony, plus a sitting room with TV. All have a private bath and toilet. A single with bath and toilet rents for 185 DH ($20.35), a double with the same plumbing costing 235 DH ($25.85). A lunch or dinner goes for 85 DH ($9.35). For that, you are likely to get a meal beginning with soup, salad, or juice, following with a meat and vegetable dish (or else a Moroccan specialty), plus dessert. A small à la carte menu offers grills, fresh fish (when available), and both international and Moroccan dishes.

Outside is a pleasant, private garden, with a small, clean swimming pool. You are five minutes from the harbor and within easy walking distance of the main restaurants and shops. You'll probably still want to take a taxi to the Casbah, but the markets are not too far away.

Tarik Hotel, Route de Malabata (tel. 409-44), is the place for those who don't want to be right in the city and prefer to be able to walk out onto the sandy beach from their hotel. At the other end of the bay near the five-star Malabata Hotel, the Tarik is essentially a summer place with a bar and restaurant opening onto a terrace with a swimming pool and lounges for sunbathing. The beach stretches for miles around the bay and back into the town. The hotel has 154 bedrooms, plain and comfortable, with extra beds if necessary, balconies, hot showers, and toilets. Singles rent for 120 DH ($13.20) and doubles for 150 DH ($16.50). For 55 DH ($6.05), you can dine on the tourist menu which includes such dishes as couscous with vegetables, roast chicken, or grilled fish. You may choose for dessert orange salad with cinnamon, fresh-baked pastries, or ice cream. The enthusiastic manager, Pepe Mermolejo, arranges evening entertainment at the hotel, so don't be surprised to be roped in for the knobby-knees competition. The bus into town costs 1.20 DH (13¢), or you can walk up to the Hotel Malabata and take a taxi from the rank for 10 DH ($1.10), sharing with others if necessary.

Grand Hotel Villa de France, 143 rue Hollande (tel. 314-75), has lost some of its chic and is a little dilapidated in some parts today, but it's still a nice old place with a tile courtyard leading to the bright, noisy bar beside the swimming pool in sheltered gardens and to the main hotel with its TV lounge, bar, and lofty restaurant. Bedrooms are basic, and the bathroom plumbing is antiquated, but most units have nice views over the terraces to the town and the sea. Rooms go for 230 DH ($25.30) for two, including a continental breakfast served in the majestic dining room. There is some reduction for a single occupant, depending on the room. For full board, the charge is 95 DH ($10.45) additional per person. Dinner costs from 80 DH ($8.80) to 105 DH ($11.55), the latter price for the gourmet menu. There is parking for cars, and the large gardens are pleasant. You can walk across to the nearby Hotel El Minzah, arguably the best in town, for a drink or dinner or just to see the lovely old building, formerly a private house built in Spanish style with courtyards and peaceful gardens.

Hotel Miramar, Avenue des F.A.R. (tel. 389-07), is as close as you can get to the wide and long beach. The Miramar is modern, and has much to offer. All of its quite good rooms, kissed by sea breezes, have private bath or shower. A single with bath costs 75 DH ($8.25), a single with shower going for 60 DH ($6.60). Doubles cost 95 DH ($10.45) with bath, dropping to 75 DH ($8.25) with shower. Tariffs include service and tax. A tourist menu costs 35 DH ($3.85). A typical dinner might start with a fresh melon, followed by filet of swordfish, then a grilled entrecôte or roast chicken, topped by a fresh fruit salad. From most of the rooms, you can see high-rising Gibraltar and the southern tip of Spain.

Hotel Panoramic Massilia, 3 rue Marco Polo (tel. 350-15), midway between the beach and the Boulevard Pasteur, is built on a hillside, giving many of the bedrooms a view of the sea. The furnishings are relatively modern, and the beds quite comfortable. A single with shower and with or without toilet costs 75 DH ($8.25). Doubles with shower and toilet cost 120 DH ($13.20). All rates include a continental breakfast, taxes, and service. In all, the Massilia offers modest amenities, good service, and one of the best and most scenic positions of the low-cost hotels in Tangier.

Hotel d'Anjou, 3 rue Ibn Al Bana (tel. 342-44). The owner is a considerate host who welcomes you to his little hotel. A single with bath (no toilet) rents for 75 DH ($8.25), going up to 95 DH ($13.20) with toilet. Doubles with bath and private toilet cost 120 DH ($13.20). The hotel has hot water, and, in the cooler months, central heating. A continental breakfast, French style, is the only meal served, but the hotel is most central, well furnished, and quiet. It stands down a steep road beside the Rembrandt Hotel (previewed above), with marvelous views of the harbor and the straits. I consider the d'Anjou one of the best bargains in Tangier.

El Djenina Hotel, 8 rue El Antaki (tel. 360-75), may be too somnolent for some, but I think its bright, polished air, clean smell, and abundant hot water go a long way to make it recommendable as a place to relax and recharge your batteries. Back a little way from the seafront and up the steep hill, it has a pretty little garden with chairs and tables, all shaded by vines and flowers, and inside is a small bar and restaurant. The rooms, all with bath, rent for 95 DH ($10.45) in a single and for 112 DH ($12.32) in a double. Set meals cost 45 DH ($4.95). El Djenina is down from the Bristol and in my opinion offers better value.

Hotel Marco Polo, Avenue d'Espagne (tel. 382-13), is right on the seafront, with an entrance from the Avenue d'Espagne up steep steps to the delightful patio entirely covered by a rampant vine. The hotel's bar has wide windows and doors opening to include the patio. The German-run establishment has nine rooms, all with bath or shower, which cost 95 DH ($10.45) in a single, 100 DH ($11) in a double, with a continental breakfast included. There is an excellent restaurant with a long menu. You can order goulash or fish soup, salade niçoise, eggs mayonnaise, shrimp pil-pil, half a roast chicken with vegetables, or a filet steak Marco Polo. At night the bar is busy with expatriates and tourists.

Hotel Madrid, 140 rue de la Plage (tel. 316-93), is a hard place to beat for a really good bargain. Right across from the harbor entrance, the railway station, and the buses, halfway up the rue de la Plage, it's clean and simple. Rooms have running water, and some have a shower. A single goes for 40 DH ($4.40), a double for 55 DH ($6.05). No meals are served.

Hotel Valencia, 72 Avenue d'Espagne (tel. 317-14), is as convenient to boats, trains, and buses as the Madrid. The managers are helpful and friendly. Singles with showers cost 85 DH ($9.35); doubles, also with showers, rent for 115 DH ($12.65). It's easy to get to the market area from this hotel.

Hotel Bristol, 14 rue El Antaki (tel. 310-70), stands on a street that climbs away from the sea. It has an elevator, central heating, and cool breezes, since it stands about 100 yards from the beach. For a single with shower, the charge is 75

DH ($8.25), rising to 95 DH ($10.45) for a single with bath. Doubles cost 90 DH ($9.90) with shower, 112 DH ($12.32) with bath. No meals are served, not even breakfast, but you can enjoy coffee and croissants at one of the nearby cafés in front.

For a true bargain in a pleasant establishment, try the **Hotel Continental,** 36 Dar Baroud (tel. 310-24), on a hill adjacent to and just inside the old city, a five-minute walk from the port it overlooks. The new owner has totally renovated the premises, and fortunately the manager of some 30 years' duration, the friendly Abslom, who speaks perfect English, is still here. The hotel is a magnificent large building, and by the time you visit, the plans to build a restaurant and bar on the roof may have been realized. The rates for pleasant bathless rooms are 20 DH ($2.20) in a single, 30 DH ($3.30) in a double, and 40 DH ($4.40) in a triple. With private baths, the prices go all the way up to 28 DH ($3.08) in a single, 38 DH ($4.18) in a double, and 42 DH ($4.62) in a triple. There is a large patio looking out over the bay and the beaches.

Staying in the Medina

Hotel Mamora, 19 rue des Postes (tel. 341-05), near the "Socco Chico," is for those who want the experience of living in the Medina. Comfortably furnished doubles with shower (no toilet) are 85 DH ($9.35). The best doubles, with private bath, rent for 95 DH ($10.45), and a single with shower costs 75 DH ($8.25). And if you wish, you can join the sunbathers on the roof terrace, with its excellent views of the Medina and the Casbah.

WHERE TO EAT: Food in Tangier tends to be expensive, but moderately priced meals are available. The international cuisine generally represents French, Moroccan, and English cooking. Some of the more elaborate Moroccan restaurants charge high prices, but they provide entertainment and a sultan-posh decor, in addition to specially prepared meals. Here are the restaurant selections:

French

La Grenouille, 3 rue El Jabha El Quatania (tel. 362-42), is run by two brothers, Ahmed and Hamid. On a small side street off the Boulevard Pasteur, it is one of the best gastronomic bargains in all of Morocco. The restaurant is on two levels, and decor includes soft lighting, rattan chairs, red upholstered divans along the walls, plus a cozy bar at one end. Courteous, efficient waiters will place bamboo placemats before you. On the walls are Moroccan metal plates. For 50 DH ($5.50), plus 15% tax, you have a wide choice of dishes. Begin with a salade niçoise or soup or raie au beurre noir, or baked macaroni and cheese, even snails or sardines. The second course might be a filet mignon or roast chicken or veal liver or wienerschnitzel, accompanied by potatoes, a salad, and vegetable; then a dessert of peach Melba, a special cake, or cheese. It all makes a memorable dining experience. The clientele is discriminating, mostly English and French residents.

La Dolce Vita, 18 rue Samuel Pepys, near the Fez market (tel. 396-78), serves tasty French and English dishes. The cost of three full courses is 35 DH ($3.85), plus whatever wine you order. You can ask for wine by the bottle or glass. There is a wide selection for each course offered. The proprietor, Larbi, supervises and is very courteous, speaking good English. He can also offer various suggestions about Tangier's attractions.

Restaurant Number One, 1 Boulevard Mohammed V (tel. 318-47), is across a small side street from the Rembrandt Hotel, right in the city center. On a set menu, costing 50 DH ($5.50), they serve salad, fish soup, fruit juices, grilled chicken or veal kidneys, and flan to finish. If you prefer to order à la carte, expect to spend from 90 DH ($9.90) for a meal, which might consist of grilled squid, skate with black butter, escalope of veal, rabbit chasseur, or calves' brains grenobloise.

Spanish

Restaurant Romero, 12 Avenida Moulay Abdellah (tel. 322-77), is for those with nostalgia for a Spanish budget restaurant. It's crowded with small tables with fresh paper cloths for each party. A cold chest displays the day's catch from the sea, and during your meal, a couple of successful fishermen may arrive with some very fierce, very fresh lobsters to be added to the selection. You choose from the à la carte menu at both the busy lunch and dinner hours. Among the appetizers are chanquettes (a small sort of whitebait), squid, shrimp mayonnaise, monkfish a la Romano, salade niçoise, and asparagus or artichokes mayonnaise. Many low-priced omelets are offered, and meat dishes include pork chops, grilled kidneys, and tajine marocaine. If you insist on eating Moroccan, a bowl of couscous will be served along with brochettes of meat, liver, kefta, and fish. A large and satisfying meal will cost around 80 DH ($8.80). Try a bottle of Toulal red wine or a half bottle of Valpierre. Mohammed, the owner, controls the place from his tiny office between the kitchen and the restaurant.

Moroccan

Le Detroit, Riad Sultan (tel. 380-80), at the old gate to the Casbah on the top of the hill, is a former palace that has been transformed into the most exciting restaurant in Tangier. The view is spectacular: the southern coast of Spain lies before you (on a clear day you can see Gibraltar). With taste, the best of traditional Moroccan architecture has been re-created. Native music is played, and belly dancing is featured. You can sit, sultan fashion, on low, cushioned seats, as the most typical Moroccan dishes are brought to your table. The couscous with seven vegetables is everybody's favorite, and if you're really a big spender, you can try a gourmet dish of Morocco, pastilla. (If you thought old King Cole had it good, wait till you try this cinnamon and sugar-coated pigeon pie.) For an à la carte dinner, expect to spend from 90 DH ($9.90).

Marhaba Palace, nearby, on the rue de la Kasbah, is just outside the entrance to the Casbah. It is a real, old Moroccan residence, with arches and tiling. In the afternoon, it's the best place to go for mint tea. The palace features an orchestra seated on a rostrum, plus at least one dancing boy who does the Rif tray dance. Moroccan dinners cost from 90 DH ($9.90).

Damascus, 2 bis rue Moulay Abdellah (tel. 347-30), is in the typical Moroccan style, offering specialties that represent some of the best of both the French and Moroccan kitchens. It is, in addition, a bar as well as a salon de thé (tea room). Unlike some of the country's so-called Moroccan restaurants, this serves a fine version of *la haute cuisine marocaine,* including pigeon pies, tajines, and kebabs, along with more familiar French dishes. Meals begin at 85 DH ($9.35).

Restaurant Hamadi, 2 rue de la Kasbah (tel. 345-14), is a good place for a traditional Moroccan evening, with harira soup, lamb couscous, lemon chicken with olives, fresh fruit, and wine served by the glass or bottle. It all costs around 105 DH ($11.55) per person. This establishment, serving some of the best Moroccan food in the city, is popular with tourists.

International

On the beach opposite the Hotel Solazur is the **Windmill,** Avenue des F.A.R. (tel. 409-07). This terrace restaurant and bar offers a wide variety of snacks, fresh fish and seafood, and sometimes couscous. This is the best place for bacon, eggs, and tomatoes, served with bread and a pot of tea—if you're yearning for English-type food. It's one of the few places in the city bacon can be found. Full meals cost from 90 DH ($9.90).

A Street of Budget Restaurants

If you can't afford to sample the Moroccan specialties at some of the places already considered, and must keep costs bone-trimmed, climb the steep and narrow **rue Salahe Dine Ayoubi** (formerly called the rue Plage). Here you'll find several restaurants serving full, low-cost meals. My favorite of these is the **Restaurant Africa,** 83 rue Salahe Dine Ayoubi. Couscous is made here with either chicken or lamb, and the portions are generous and filling. Occasionally they'll also offer fresh fish. Meals cost from 30 DH ($3.30).

The Most Popular Bars

The **Café de Paris,** 1 Place de France (tel. 384-44), is a kind of social center of the town, where all rumors are spread. Few visitors are in Tangier for more than 24 hours without paying at least one call on this centrally located café. It's a natural meeting ground for both Europeans and Arabs. Real-estate transactions take place here, as well as assignations of every conceivable type—and you can also have a cup of coffee or chilled drink. No one insists that you vacate your table. For around 4 DH (44¢) for sipping rights, you can sit and watch the passing Parade. Five of the principal streets of Tangier rendezvous on the Place de France, as do all of the principal players.

The **Tangerinn,** beneath the Hotel El Muniria in rue Magellan, is open from 9 p.m. to 1 a.m. The small corner bar is generally crowded with British and U.S. expatriates, so you may have to sit in one of the two rather bare rooms, one with a grand piano for anyone who wants to play it. The roof is tented to soften the starkness of the place. Run by John Sutcliffe and Peter Tuckwell for more than 20 years, there is no better place for tourists in need of information on the country or the city. Here, you're sure to find someone who knows exactly where to find what you seek. This interesting and cosmopolitan place has to be the successor to Lily's famous Parade Bar, now defunct. No food is served here.

Tea for Two

Madame Porte, corner of Avenue du Prince Moulay Abdellah and rue El Mouttanabi, is an institution, attracting those who wouldn't be caught sipping mint tea in the Medina. The tea at 8 DH (88¢) and the French pastries are good and proper. The British writer Alec Waugh reports that Porte serves "the best dry martinis I have ever tasted. They are lagoon-size, ice cold, served in a German-type wine glass with a long, thin sliver of lemon peel curving around the rim, and cost 25 DH ($2.75). One of them is as much as I can manage." Madame stays open till 9:30 p.m.

WHAT TO SEE AND DO: Here follows a potpourri of things to do and see in Tangier, including such adventures as a visit to the Casbah and excursions to the Caves of Hercules.

The Casbah

One of the most famous lines from the movies actually was never spoken. It was the invitation reputedly extended by Charles Boyer to Hedy Lamarr in *Algiers:* "Come with me to the Casbah." Even though the invitation was never extended in actuality, popular legend has it so. The mythical line sparked a whole new meaning for romance, glamour, and intrigue. Even if Mr. Boyer actually didn't extend the invitation, surely he meant to, and for that reason, few foreigners who visit this part of the world can resist exploring the Casbah of Tangier, which has many similarities to the Casbah of Algiers, and in fact to all the Casbahs of North Africa. Although a number of expatriates have moved in, the Casbah still is the old Arab residential quarter of the city. It sits proudly on a hill, looking down at the bay and the streets of the Medina, another residential and also commercial district. The best way to reach it is to continue north from the Grand Socco on the rue d'Italie, then turn right and pass through the old gate. It's quite a climb, so wear your walking shoes.

The major sight to be visited here is the former **Palace of the Sultans,** now a museum (free). Run by the government, this old palace shows the Moorish architecture, and contains a handsome display of Moroccan handcrafts. Its patio was once accustomed to the bare feet of dancing girls; its great treasure boxes, now empty, once held gold and jewels. The museum also shows archeological finds from the surrounding district.

After your visit here, you can begin your exploration of the narrow, winding streets. Don't be surprised if you run into a snake charmer; give him 2 DH (22¢) if you'd like to see him make the snake rise.

The Soccos of the Medina

Both the **Big Socco** and the **Little Socco** (sometimes called *Petit* or *Chico*) make up the teeming life of old Tangier. A trip through the markets can be fascinating. Smell the exotic spices; drink the mint tea. Surely Tangier has the world's largest oranges. In and around the Soccos you'll find the shops, the bazaars, and the vegetable markets for which the city is so well known.

The Big Market has been cleaned up considerably and "beautified," but not all the colorful Arab life has been chased away. Next to the Big Socco is the **Mendoubia,** a garden with an 800-year-old dragon tree (that's what the tourist people claim) and about three dozen cannons used during one of the sieges of Tangier.

The Little Socco is not a market, but a small plaza almost completely surrounded by cafés. It's the meeting place for foreigners and visitors—plus what one resident termed as "some rather doubtful locals."

The Dar el Makhzen

When this edifice was constructed in the late 17th century, the English had just evacuated Tangier. To celebrate his reconquest of the city, Sultan Moulay Ismail erected this palace, which was enlarged and embellished around 1750. Later it became the residence of the pashas of the city before it became a museum.

The sections of the museum include **Le Musée des Arts marocains** and **Le Musée des Antiquités.** The former, centered around a tile patio, contains six rooms filled with Moroccan antique carpets, jewels, Hispano-Moorish artifacts, Bedouin craftsmanship, wrought iron, antique furniture, and silk embroideries. The museum of antiquities has a courtyard graced with a Roman mosaic depicting the navigation of Venus, accompanied by a host of attendant cherubs and deities, in a barque rowed by the Three Graces. In the rooms, you'll see prehistoric carvings found throughout the countryside around Tangier, including sarcophagi and Roman relics, plus artifacts from the Portuguese and English occupations. An annex of the museum contains the Bit et Mâl, a noteworthy piece of Moorish architecture whose coffers once contained the sultan's treasures.

Guided tours are available from 9 a.m. to noon and 3 to 7 p.m. On Friday, morning hours end at 11:30 a.m. Everything is closed Tuesday. You'll be expected to tip your guide.

The New Mosque

This structure, on Place de Kowelt, a few blocks up from the Art Center, is one of the largest mosques in North Africa. Non-Muslims are allowed into the courtyard, but men must not wear shorts, and women must wear dresses and have their shoulders covered (no pants suits or jeans).

The Old United States Legation

The Tangier Legation building, now a museum and study center, 8 Zankat/rue d'Amérique, is the oldest diplomatic property of the United States to be continuously owned. In the Medina of Tangier, it is the first real estate the U.S. government (it is believed) ever acquired abroad. In 1821 Sultan Sidi Moulay Suliman gave it to the American people. The legation is maintained by the staff of the American consul-general through their voluntary efforts and through contributions. It offers one of the finest lithographic collections I've seen.

Long a seat of U.S. diplomatic representation to the sultans of Morocco, the building ended that role in 1961 with the construction of the new U.S. consulate building. In later years, as it gradually fell into disrepair, it was used as an Arabic-language school for American diplomats and later as a Peace Corps training center. As a special Bicentennial project, it was restored to some of its former glory. The jewel of the additions is a Moorish pavilion overlooking a courtyard.

Note in particular the carved doors leading from the terrace into the pavilion; they are more than 400 years old. The antique doors, shutters, ceilings, and tiles within the pavilion were found in Fez and other parts of Morocco.

Sports

Tennis: Courts are available at Ensallah Gardens, near the Craft Center in town. You can rent rackets. Open from 7 a.m. to 6 p.m.; later hours in summer.

Horseback riding: Club de l'Etrier, Boubana (tel. 389-84), in the Ahlen Valley on the way to the airport, offers riding at a cost of 50 DH ($5.50) per hour, with or without instruction.

Golf: At the Royal Country Club, Boubana (tel. 389-25), the greens fees are 25 DH ($2.75), and a caddy costs 12 DH ($1.32) for nine holes, 18 DH ($1.98) for an 18-hole round. Clubs can be rented.

Water sports: A temporary membership at the Yacht Club (tel. 385-75) will enable you to enjoy the private beach for sunbathing, windsurfing, and pedaloing.

In the Environs

The environs of Tangier have some interesting Roman and Phoenician ruins, but the best two excursions from the city are to **Cape Spartel,** the most northwestern tip of Africa, and to the **Caves of Hercules.** A bus tour from Tangier costs 55 DH ($6.05).

On Cape Spartel is a lighthouse, built by an engineer about a century ago on the spot where the Mediterranean meets the Atlantic. It's some five miles from Tangier to the cape. The view from here is magnificent.

From Spartel, it's about a mile to the Caves of Hercules, where many prehistoric remains have been found. The caves have been greatly enlarged by workers carving out millstones.

The miles and miles of beach viewed from here point up an enormous potential tourist development for Morocco.

TANGIER NIGHTLIFE: From belly dancers to discos, Tangier tries to please all tastes. Forget all those '40s movies about espionage or whatever. Bogart is long dead, and Hedy Lamarr is in retirement. The nightlife of Tangier has long surpassed its heyday in the '50s. Its bars and nightclubs today often attract very unsavory characters, such as pimps and thieves. You can risk your life going into the wrong places. At best, you risk your wallet. You'll be taken for whatever they think they can get from you in some places. It's not a pretty picture unless you pick and choose carefully among the offerings.

Belly Dancing

Morocco Palace, 11 Avenue Prince Moulay Abdallah (tel. 39-81-14), is about the best place to see belly dancing in Tangier. Count on spending around 65 DH ($7.15) for a drink and the show. The decor includes Moroccan inlaid tiles on walls and pillars, with small tables and settees. An orchestra usually plays at night, and one of the numbers consists of a girl dancing with a tray of drinks and lit candles balanced on her head.

Discos

There are some excellent discos in the big hotels, safer than some of the joints in town, although you may feel isolated and insulated from the country and the locals. The Solazur and the Rif Hotels, both on the Avenue des F.A.R., have good facilities, and it's hard to beat **Up 2000,** the flying saucer–shape disco on the top of the Hotel Almohades, also on the Avenue des F.A.R. In town, **Regine Disco** on rue el Mansour Dahbi is popular. Admission is free. In the smaller places, you should check on the price of drinks before ordering the more exotic concoctions offered.

The Ranch Discothèque, 17 rue Omar Ibn Al Hass (tel. 382-66), is considered one of the best discos of Africa. It's done up like an Old West saloon. Sometimes there are spontaneous jam sessions with visiting musicians, and guests can always count on a reliable piano player. It's a place at which you not only can enjoy yourself, but meet friends from all over the world, as you listen to records from Gordon Lightfoot among others. For 12 DH ($1.32), you're not only admitted but given a drink.

READER'S TOURING SUGGESTION: "My brother and I 'stumbled' upon a small city, **Asilah,** that's absolutely perfect to see. It's some 30 to 40 kilometers outside Tangier, lying right on a beach. It's a small place, complete with a market (the usual bargaining) and camels. There are several hotels and campsites there, and it seems to attract many German and French visitors. This is an ideal place to visit if you want a taste of Morocco, but don't want to travel far into the country and don't want to deal with the hassles of Tangier" (Howard S. Smith, Kingston, N.Y.). [*Author's Note:* A coach tour goes there on a four-hour roundtrip for 80 DH ($8.80) per person.]

2. Ceuta

Ceuta is a Spanish enclave on the North African coast. When Morocco was given its independence in 1956, Spain held onto two military enclaves, Ceuta and Melilla. Ceuta is really an Andalusian-style town, characterized by gleaming white buildings and wrought-iron balconies filled with flowers.

The town sits on the promontory of Monte Acho, which is the southern tip of one of the two so-called Pillars of Hercules. The other one is Gibraltar. These two pillars formed the gateway to the ancient world. You can climb Monte Acho for a panoramic view of the Mediterranean that includes Gibraltar on a clear day. There's a military outpost, Fort Acho, which was a penal colony. You can only look at it from the outside.

HOW TO GET THERE: Car ferries run from Algeciras to Ceuta daily. The trip takes between 1 and 1½ hours, and departures from Algeciras are from 8 a.m. until 8:30 p.m. (about 12 sailings a day). In summer some extra ships are put on. There are two ship lines serving the route—Compañía Trasmediterránea and ISNASA. The cost of a ticket is the same for both lines: around 1,200 pesetas ($8.40) for adults, half fare for children from 2 to 7 on Trasmediterránea from 3 to 9 on ISNASA. Tickets may be purchased in Madrid from the Compañía Trasmediterránea at 63 Alcalá (tel. 225-21-10 or 225-51-10), or from authorized travel agencies. In Algeciras tickets are available at the Maritime Station or travel agencies for both companies.

WHAT TO SEE: The sights of Ceuta (Sebta in Arabic) are limited, but they include: the **Church of Our Lady in Africa** from the 18th century; the **San Felipe moat** from the days of the Portuguese occupation, plus a tiny **Archeological Museum,** a few pretty squares, and a main shopping street. Chances are you'll be moving on after a half day to Morocco proper.

WHERE TO STAY: Biggest and best in Ceuta is **Gran Hotel La Muralla,** 15 Plaza Virgen de Africa (tel. 51-49-40), right in the heart of town on a pretty, palm-lined square, with the Church of Nuestra Señora de Africa across the street. You can get a double room with bath for 7,500 pesetas ($52.50), a single with bath for 5,900 pesetas ($41.30). A continental breakfast is an additional charge. This four-star hotel has many amenities, including a swimming pool, bar, air conditioning, even a nightclub. The hotel has a somewhat secure parking lot between the hotel and army post. At the other hotels in town, you leave your vehicle on the street, an unwise situation.

Cheaper is the three-star **Africa,** 9 Muelle Cañonero Dato (tel. 51-41-40), overlooking the ocean, a little bit out of town. Its doubles with bath rent for 4,800 pesetas ($33.60); its singles with showers cost 2,500 pesetas ($17.50). A continental breakfast is the only meal served, costing extra.

WHERE TO EAT: **El Mesón de Serafín** (tel. 51-40-03), is spectacularly situated on top of Monte Acho, providing sweeping views of the Mediterranean. In true mesón style, it has a rustic decor created by hanging hams and the like. Spanish regional dishes are featured. Figure on spending about 2,000 pesetas ($14) for the daily menu.

Restaurant La Torre, Plaza de Virgen de Africa (tel. 51-49-40), is a well-rated restaurant contained within the Hotel La Muralla. Before eating, you may want to walk out to the pool set in the garden. Menu items include all the specialties of Andalusia, such as fish dishes, stews, soups, and grilled meats. A fixed-price menu is offered for 2,600 pesetas ($18.50).

Sombrero de Copa, 4 Padilla (tel. 51-82-84), would be a good choice for budgeteers looking for an honest meal at bargain rates. The unpretentious cooking includes a fish-based fixed-price meal for around 1,500 pesetas ($10.50). The establishment is closed Sunday evening and all day Monday.

Those on a shoestring should head to **Las Fuentecitas, Mercado,** inside the Ceuta market. There are no frills in the *económico,* just a half dozen tables, rotating fans in summer, and simple home-cooking. The tab for a four-course meal comes to 800 pesetas ($5.60).

Once you've seen the little there is to see in Ceuta, you can take the bus to Tetuan. Buses leave every hour from the Paseo de Colón, starting at 6 a.m. and running till 10 p.m.

3. Tetuan

Until April of 1956 Tetuan was part of the Spanish Protectorate in North Africa and was, in fact, the capital of Spanish Morocco. Thus the Spanish influence, even today, is still stronger than the French. This is true not only as regards the language spoken, but also in respect to a more integrated city. For example, residents fairly well shun the "native" and "European" quarter concepts. Although there is a small medina, the two cultures blend easily in what might, in many respects, be called a Spanish city, characterized by fountains and balconied houses in the Andalusian style.

A Traveler's Advisory: Go to Tetuan at your own risk. The place is crawling with unsavory characters who will pick your pockets or worse. The medina is notoriously dangerous at any hour of the day or night. The police seem to turn a deaf ear to complaints from foreigners.

GETTING THERE: Tetuan lies 24 miles south of the Spanish enclave of Ceuta, a short drive by car or bus. Coming from Ceuta, the road to Tetuan skirts what has been called the Moroccan Costa del Sol, a long stretch of Mediterranean beach. In the background you can see the Rif mountains.

The Moroccan buses leaving the Bab Sebta, the border station between Ceuta and Morocco, cost 8 DH (88¢) per person. The C.T.M. first-class buses leave Ceuta at 9:30 p.m. and get into Tetuan at 10:30 p.m. From Tetuan to Ceuta, they leave at 4:15 p.m. There are also numerous second-class buses.

The formalities at the border between Spanish Morocco and Morocco proper are tedious, often taking an hour or more.

THE SIGHTS: Tetuan is still a walled city for most of its perimeter, and numerous turrets and crenellated ramparts can be seen from its former fortifications as well as seven large gates.

The **Medina,** if you dare, is entered through the city gates and filled with 17 white mosques (entrance forbidden to foreigners). It's characterized by its *souks,* narrow, arched passage ways, and little shops. Tinsmiths, silk merchants, tanners, hustlers, drug dealers, and others ply their age-old trades. On market days, the Medina teems with the people from the Rif mountains, who wear red-striped *foutahs* and *esparto* hats with blue tassels.

Other main sights include the **Royal Palace** (Palais Royal). On the Place Hassan II, it dates from the 17th century, but was completely restored in 1948. It's an example of the Hispano-Moorish style of architecture, and its old walls witnessed the nightly rituals of the caliphs.

The **Archeological Museum** is also interesting. It's open daily, except Tuesday, from 9 a.m. to noon and 2:30 to 6 p.m., charging 5 DH (55¢) for admission. It contains exhibits found at two ancient Roman cities of North Africa, Lixus and Tamuda. Bronzes, pottery, and mosaics make for good viewing. Of the mosaics, the most outstanding is the *Three Graces of Lixus.*

BEACHES: The closest beach to Tetuan is the one at **Martil** (formerly known as Rio Martin), eight miles away. By car, you can take the road toward Ceuta for less than a mile, then turn right to Martil, which is Tetuan's port. The beach is about 6½ miles long and has restaurants and cafés (the latter don't serve alcoholic beverages, however). There are also bus services. Check at your hotel or at the tourist office in Tetuan at 30 Calle Mohammed V (tel. 70-09).

WHERE TO STAY: About the best all-around economy hotel is the **National,** 8 Boulevard Mohammed Torrés (tel. 32-90). It has a restaurant and a bar, and is well kept. Most of its rooms contain a private bath. Double accommodations cost 75 DH ($8.25); singles, 62 DH ($6.82).

Those on a tighter budget might try the **Régina,** 8 rue Sidi El Mandri (tel. 21-13). It has 86 rooms, only three of which contain a complete private bath, but 17 of them offer a shower. It provides only minimum comfort, and it charges 65 DH ($7.15) in a double.

For those wanting to overnight in more style, I'd suggest the **Dersa,** 8 rue Général Franco (tel. 67-29), which has 75 rooms, 50 of them with bath. All have a phone, incidentally. Even though this is one of the best hotels in town, it is still modest. However, it has more facilities than the above mentioned choices, including a restaurant, bar, and nightclub. Doubles peak at 100 DH ($11), singles at 82 DH ($9.02). A tourist menu goes for 50 DH ($5.50).

BUDGET DINING: **Zarhoun,** 7 Avenue Mohammed Torrés (tel. 66-61), is about your best bet if you want a typically Moroccan meal. Near the bus station, it is decorated in the traditional Moorish style, and offers a complete tourist meal for 55 DH ($6.05). You dine in a Moroccan salon, on low-slung sofas, around a brass table from Fez.

The **Restaurant Nacional,** 8 Boulevard Mohammed Torrés (tel. 32-90), in the previously recommended Hotel National, serves some of the best and most economical dishes in town. There is a surprising international menu of grills and fish dishes mixed with couscous and the local brochettes. A tourist menu costs only 45 DH ($4.95).

4. Chaouen (Chechaouèn)

The town of Chaouen, nestled among the Rif mountains, is a beautiful white town tucked right at the base of three magnificent mountain peaks. There is a weekly open market, and pretty blue-and-white houses cling to the steep slopes on which the town is set. There is also a workshop where you can watch local craftspeople at work on woolen and woven goods. The air is clean and crystal-clear, and the panoramas are spectacular. Lying about 100 miles from Tangier and just over 50 miles from Tetuan, Chaouen is reached by a good highway.

The ancient town fortress has been converted into a lovely **Jardin Municipal** (city garden), with the Rif mountains as a striking backdrop to palm trees and brilliant tropical flowers. You can stroll through the garden in the casbah, entered via Place Uta el Hammam.

Reader Charles E. Colson, Oak Brook, Illinois, says of his visit to Chaouen: "It was a joy to get up in the morning, stroll through the streets as the town gradually came to life, and then purchase the day's supply of fruits and Sidi Harazem for our journey. The finest moments, however, are in the evening after dinner, when you listen to the muezzin finish his call for evening prayer. Then, as the final tones of his voice are fading, a lone flute begins a serene melody. A second flute and then a third also begin, playing together or in counterpoint to each other. And as you walk through the streets, the shops now closing and the people going to prayer and then home to eat, and listen to the mournful sounds of the flutes before they drift off into the surrounding mountains, it is possible to feel closer to Morocco than during any other part of your trip."

WHERE TO STAY AND EAT: You can find food and lodging at the **Hotel de Chaouen** (tel. 63-24), which was once part of a government parador but is now run as a link in the Maroc-Tourist chain. Rooms, 37 in all, are pleasantly and attractively furnished and well kept. The best double with private bath costs only 150 DH ($16.50) nightly, a single costing 115 DH ($12.65). A continental breakfast with croissants fresh from the town's baker is served. As a welcome relief, the hotel also has a swimming pool. It's not the best hotel in town (the Hotel Asma, granted four stars, has that honor), but it's the best we can do on our budget. You can enjoy a Moroccan dinner in the evening for 60 DH ($6.60).

Chapter XIX

MEKNES, FEZ, AND THE MIDDLE ATLAS

1. Meknes
2. Volubilis and Moulay-Idriss
3. Fez
4. Sidi Harazem
5. Immouzer du-Khandar
6. Azrou

TWO OF THE MOST popular tourist destinations in Morocco are the old imperial cities of **Meknes** and **Fez.** These historic towns lie less than 37 miles apart. Meknes stands on the national highway linking the capital at Rabat with the eastern part of Morocco which borders Algeria. Meknes, founded in the 10th century, grew up at a location south of the Rif mountains. A visit to Meknes is traditionally tied in with excursions to **Moulay-Idriss** and **Volubilis,** which are described below.

Fez, to the east, is the most exciting tourist city in all of Morocco, in the opinion of many. It is actually composed of three cities which we'll visit later. Fez grew rich from the Mohammedans driven out of Córdoba and, in time, it became the religious center of Morocco. It is often used as a base for exploring the Middle Atlas, a land rich in folklore and tradition which is inhabited by sedentary Berbers and traversed by nomads whose tents dot the pastures. Following a visit to Fez, we will take some of the most interesting excursions to the south, penetrating deep into the Middle Atlas.

1. Meknes

One of the four Imperial Cities of Morocco, Meknes is encircled by a triple enclosure of 28 miles of ramparts and bastions. Nine gates with their four-cornered towers pierce these ramparts; minarets stud the cityscape. In spite of its massive, sober look, Meknes is also a city of gardens.

The commercial life, including the hotels and restaurants, is found in the "Ville Nouvelle," but the sights are in the Medina and the "Ville Imperiale."

It was the Alaouite sultan, Moulay Ismail, who made Meknes "imperial." During his long 55-year reign, which began in 1672, his extensive building program, often carried out by slaves, earned for Meknes the title of the "Moroccan Versailles." Traditionally, Meknes has been a bitter rival of Fez.

Meknes is serviced by the same train and bus connections from Rabat, some 70 miles west on the coast.

THE SIGHTS: Most tours start at **Bab Mansour,** the city's most interesting gate, begun during the reign of Moulay Ismail and completed by his son and successor, Moulay Abdullah, in 1752. The decorative gate is characterized by an ogival horseshoe-shaped archway. Opposite the gate sprawls the vast rectangular square (about 650 feet in length, 330 feet in width), the **Place El-Hedim,** It is bordered by the Bab Mansour gateway and one called **Bab Djama En-Nouar,** smaller and dating from the 18th century. If you're driving, incidentally, you can leave your car here (tip the attendant).

At the far end of the square stands **Dar Jamal,** a palace constructed by the vizier Djamai during the reign of Moulay Hassan (1873–1894). It has been turned into a museum of Moroccan handcrafts, although it has served many functions in its day—once a military hospital, also a harem. Passing through the handsome courtyard, you proceed through one ornamental salon after another, observing the handcrafts, including such items as antique Meknes embroidery and old Berber silver jewelry. The reception room is furnished in the classic Moroccan style. Copies of the Koran on display date from the 17th century. The admission is free, but you're expected to tip the guide, as always. Closed Tuesday.

From the Dar Jamal, walk down the rue Sekkakine, with its mélange of jewelry shops and hardware merchants, to the gateway of **Bab Berrima.** This leads to the **Mosque of Bab Berrima,** built during the reign of Sidi Mohammed Ben Abdullah (1757–1790). The mosque forms a corner of the Berrima quarter, which used to be the Casbah. The quarter is surrounded by a high four-cornered wall, and is separated from the **Mellah,** the former Jewish quarter, by another wall. The Mellah is inhabited mainly by Muslims today, following a mass exodus to Israel of most of its Jewish inhabitants after Morocco was granted independence in 1956.

The **Medina of Meknes** is not special, nothing like the one at Fez. But it is, nevertheless, a bustling center of activity—especially in the Berbers' rug-making section. While in the Medina you may want to visit the **Medersa Bou Inania,** a college whose construction was launched during the reign of the Merinide sultan, Abou El-Hassan (1331–1350). Note especially the bronze door and intricate carving. If you stand in the courtyard, with its large ablution basin, and look up, you'll see where the students were lodged. Another medersa worth seeing is the **Filala,** which was built during the reign of Moulay Ismail near the Great Mosque.

The Imperial City

This quarter, entered through the Bab Mansour, was almost completely the work of Moulay Ismail. Much of what remains of the Ville Imperiale is in ruins, including the palace of the former sultan, **Dar Kebira.** Now hardly more than a shell, the palace, dating from 1697, at one time comprised nearly two dozen buildings. By passing through the Bab Filala, you reach the **Koubbet El-Khiyatine,** a pavilion where Moulay Ismail used to receive foreign ambassadors.

At the opposite side of the Place Lalla Aouda stands the **Mausoleum of Moulay Ismail.** This is the only mosque in Morocco that a non-Muslim can visit, and even then you can't go in to see the actual tomb. However, you enter a main courtyard and that in turn is followed by yet another smaller courtyard (it's imperative to remove your shoes in this one).

From the mausoleum, you can walk across the grounds to a music school. There a guide will take you down some steep steps nearby to an old **Christian prison**—severe, damp, spooky. Perhaps you won't get lost in these catacombs and will emerge before the thick door at the top of the steps is locked.

Passing on through the **Bab Er-Rih** (Gateway of the Wind), you reach the

Dar el Makhzen, the imperial palace where King Hassan II stays whenever he is in town. Nearby are the **Gardens of the Sultanas,** with ornamental ponds and fountains as well as an arboretum.

Other sights of the Imperial City include the **Borj El-Ma** (Bastion of Water), the **Casbah of Hedrache** (formerly a barracks), and the **Heri** (storehouse). The latter monument was really a granary, with large vaulted underground silos (the storerooms were above). From the Heri, a lane leads to the **Dar el Beida,** an 18th-century fortress, now a military academy. Nearby is an **Ostrich Farm,** also dating from the 18th century.

Beyond, you arrive in the **Jbabra section** to visit the **Roua,** the great stables of Moulay Ismail, said to have sheltered 12,000 horses and mules at one time. In ruins and exposed to the sky, these vast chambers are foreboding in their immensity. The former stables are enclosed by walls and divided by arches. A palace, now gone, had been built over the stables, and contained nearly two dozen pavilions. The barracks of the king's Black Guard were here as well. The descendants of these former slaves are reputed to form King Hassan II's bodyguard today. Nearby, some 50,000 slaves once dug out a pleasure lake which serves as a reservoir and comprises nearly ten acres.

READER'S SIGHTSEEING TIP: "The high point of our trip was the **fête for Mouloud.** We did not stay too long because the crowds were getting large. Our guide said that the city has a 450,000 population and receives 2,000,000 visitors for this week-long festival. As we left, we passed people coming in trucks, packing buses, and walking in groups to the city. If someone plans to be in town for such a festive occasion, I suggest they pick the first day, because I am sure the crowds would lessen the enjoyment of the sights by the end of the week. The horsemen with gorgeous Arabian steeds, highly decorated saddles, and long guns looked straight out of *Lawrence of Arabia.* The Berber women with gilded scarves were also striking. The riding areas were surrounded by nomad tents of many different groups. It was exciting, but our guide seemed nervous as we walked around the fairgrounds. Not to be missed—but watch your pockets" (Linda Heutwick).

WHERE TO STAY: The splurge hotel in Meknes is **Hotel Transatlantique,** rue El Meriniyine (tel. 200-02). It boasts five stars which gives promise of guests being able to get a lot of personal attention, such as getting washing and drycleaning done, as well as relaxing in comfort. It is an elegant building, long and low, with views over the Medina and within earshot of the muezzin when he calls the faithful to prayer (this may seem less than a joy at daybreak, around 3:30 a.m. in summer). Bedrooms have well-equipped bathrooms, TV, and phones, as well as mini-bars which are stocked to order. Singles rent for 375 DH ($41.25), doubles for 500 DH ($55), and triples for 600 DH ($66). The hotel has a good bar with comfortable chairs and tasty things to nibble on, plus a fine restaurant with international cuisine and a Moroccan restaurant somewhat reminiscent of a clinic. There's a snackbar between the two swimming pools, where filling sandwiches and salads are served.

There is ample parking, and you can take a taxi to the center of town for about 10 DH ($1.10), or you may prefer to walk through the pleasant suburban streets. The Transatlantique is the only hotel in town which can suitably accommodate tour groups, so don't be surprised to find yourself surrounded by other visitors to the country, en masse.

Hotel Rif, 10 Zankat Accra (tel. 225-91). The accommodations are adequate, with most units opening onto the inner courtyard with its swimming pool. The bedrooms have many built-ins. Singles go for 260 DH ($28.60); doubles, 265 DH ($29.15). The entire hotel has a pleasing decor, the use of chalk white effectively offset by bold colors. There's one color to a floor. The dining room overlooks the courtyard. An afternoon sit-down mint tea is recommended in the Moroccan-style salon. In the evening there's belly dancing and dancing to records in the lower-level nightclub, where drinks go for 40 DH ($4.40) and up. There is also a rooftop sunbathing terrace with a bar.

Hotel de Nice, 10 Zankat Accra (tel. 203-18), is a small, semi-modern hotel, which was refurbished in 1974 and features a restaurant and a "New York" bar. It offers well-maintained and fairly comfortable bedrooms, 33 in all, 30 of which contain a bath. Doubles with full bath cost 150 DH ($16.50) for two, 115 DH ($12.65) for one. Service and taxes are included. This hotel is excellent value. Its restaurant, Valpierre, is considered one of the best in Meknes. A tourist menu, costing 50 DH ($5.50), includes main dishes such as veal, steak, or chicken with couscous or rice and vegetables.

Palace, rue du Ghana (tel. 204-45), is a fairly modern, three-floor (no elevator) hotel in "downtown" Meknes. You'll find neon lighting and plastic furnishings; however, the bedrooms are compact and scoured daily—and the rates are not bad. A single with shower costs 85 DH ($9.35), rising to 105 DH ($11.55) with bath. Doubles with shower cost 112 DH ($12.32), going up to 135 DH ($14.85) with bath, all tariffs including a continental breakfast, service, and taxes.

Majestic, 19 Avenue Mohammed V (tel. 220-35), is owned and managed by a zealous collector of memorabilia and handcrafts from all parts of Morocco. His hobby is displayed on the walls and ceilings of the reception lounge and in the corridors. A traditional Moroccan-style tea salon was installed, but the general decor suggests a dark barn of a place. Some of the bathrooms are utterly simple, the showers merely showerheads and the drain in the corner of the bathroom. Singles rent for 75 DH ($8.25), doubles for 90 DH ($9.90), all with shower. A continental breakfast, costing extra, is the only meal served. The manager suggests that you eat "around the corner" in a cheerful little place with a tourist menu costing 50 DH ($5.50).

Grand Hotel Volubilis, 45 Avenue des F.A.R. (tel. 201-02), close to the C.T.M. bus station, is another simple but clean and pleasant place with good-size bedrooms mostly with shower and toilet, phone, and central heating. A single costs 115 DH ($12.65), a double or twin 145 DH ($15.95), and a three-bedded room 190 DH ($20.90). There is no restaurant.

WHERE TO EAT: **La Hacienda,** Route des Fez-Meknes (tel. 210-92), is a country-style inn about two miles outside of Meknes on the road to Fez (signs point the way through a woodland). It's ideal for long, leisurely luncheons or dinners in a holiday atmosphere. A large rustic dining room and buildings are built hacienda-style around a swimming pool. Inside it's more rustic—rough plaster walls, a beamed ceiling, straw lanterns, brass sheep horns, and farm tools. The menu offers many French dishes, such as a dozen escargots or the potage du jour. Main dishes include entrecôte with anchovies and hamburger, the latter a fine luncheon choice on a hot day. Finish with a basket of fruit. Expect to spend from 90 DH ($9.90) for a complete meal, unless you order the house specialty. If you do, a small charcoal stove is placed on your table so that you can cook the meats to your satisfaction. You are given a kebab or two, sausages, a lamb chop, and a small beef steak. In the evening there is entertainment in the basement night club. Often you get to see folk dancing from the Middle Atlas. Admission is 20 DH ($2.20), including one drink. The club section is open from 10 p.m. to 1 a.m. If you take a taxi there, the cost is about 20 DH ($2.20), and the staff will call another cab for you when you're ready to return to your hotel.

Bar Restaurant La Coupole, Avenue Hassan II (tel. 224-83), close to the Rif Hotel, is a large, clean room filled with tables covered by bright orange cloths. It's not particularly chic, but it serves good food in a pleasant atmosphere. The tourist menu, costing 50 DH ($5.50), includes hors d'oeuvres, salad niçoise or tomato, then entrecôte with vegetables. The à la carte selection is made up of many appetizers (salads, fish, and vegetables), tajine of lamb with prunes or lemon and olives, kebab El Maghour, Chateaubriand, and rabbit with mushrooms. Pastilla and mechoui are available on request.

Rôtisserie Karam, 2 Avenue Ghannah (tel. 224-75), is a place for a good and low-cost dinner, lying in the Ville Nouvelle one block from the Palace Hotel. The dining rooms is clean, and the service is courteous and speedy. You can order a salad, followed by a meat or chicken dish, along with french fries, bread, dessert, and a beverage for 45 DH ($4.95), quite a bargain. You can't do much better than this if you want good food at such an inexpensive cost in the new town.

A reasonably priced dining choice is the **Novelty,** 12 rue de Paris (tel. 221-56), close to the Rif Hotel. It offers a meal for 38 DH ($4.18), with an alternative menu going for 32 DH ($3.52). Both include a choice of soup or salad, hors d'oeuvres, a main course, and dessert. The chef's specialty is lamb couscous. The daily special could be steak with french fries or couscous. The Novelty has a typical French family-restaurant atmosphere and is close to the major shops. Wine, beer, and common mixed drinks are available. Many French and some Americans eat here regularly, as well as Moroccans. It isn't fancy, but the food is good.

2. Volubilis and Moulay-Idriss

Nineteen miles north of Meknes lie the finest Roman ruins in Morocco, **Volubilis,** one of the country's most ancient cities. It's on a windswept plain, reached after passing through some dramatic scenery. During the reign of Juba II (25 B.C.–A.D. 23) it became a royal residence and the capital of Mauretania Tingitana. Eventually it was annexed to the Roman Empire. Rome abandoned the colony in 285, and the city drifted along until the appearance of Islam in 684. Again, in the course of time, Volubilis fell into decay. Serious excavations were begun in 1915.

Chances are you may have seen more dramatic ruins than these; but their scope is impressive, nevertheless. Volubilis sprawls over 100 acres encircled by a 2nd-century rampart approximately 1½ miles long.

Guides at the entrance will offer to direct you through the ruins for a fee. You must buy an admission ticket costing 6 DH (66¢). Hours are from 8 a.m. to 6:30 p.m. (closes at 5:30 p.m. in winter).

The most notable buildings include the House of Orpheus (named for a large mosaic in the reception room depicting Orpheus at play with a group of animals); the Baths of Galius (the most important ones found in Morocco, although badly decayed); an Arch of Triumph ordered constructed by Silvius Aurelius Sebastianus; the Basilica with two good-size apses; the Forum, from the 3rd century; the House of the Youth, typical of the private villas of that time in that it was built around a patio; the mosaics of the House of the Labors of Hercules; the House of the Beasts, noted for its mosaics of wild animals; and the colonnade of the Palace of Gordius, ranging upward to the Tangier Gate, from which there is a superb panorama of the archeological garden.

Lying only a short ride from Volubilis is **Moulay-Idriss,** 21 miles from Meknes. It is one of the most venerated sites in Morocco. On two rocky spurs split by a deep gorge is this ancient city, considered sacred because it contains the *zawiya* of Moulay-Idriss, the founder of the Idrisside dynasty, the first Arab dynasty to rule over Morocco. His mausoleum, whose green-tile roof dominates the city, is the site of a colorful yearly pilgrimage—called a *mousem*—in August and

September. If you are not of the Islamic world, then the entrance to the mosque is, of course, forbidden. In fact, foreigners at one time were not welcomed in Moulay-Idriss, but happily that state has changed.

Even if Moulay-Idriss were not a holy city, you might still want to visit it just for its dramatic scenery. You pull your car into the market square, where it's easy to secure the services of a guide. He will rarely speak English (except for a few words), but you should consider his services nevertheless. The reason is that although a walk through the town is of interest, the most moving sights are in the surrounding hills. You'll need help to get you up and down the narrow streets and over the encircling roads (many of which lead to blind alleys). Outside the town, incidentally, are hot springs once used by the Romans.

You may want to conclude your tour by walking through the teeming *souks* of the Medina. The town hasn't quite arrived in the 20th-century, but electricity has been installed in some places. As of yet, there is no recommendable hotel or restaurant. If you're hungry, and not fastidious, you can get lamb kebabs grilled over an open charcoal brazier in the marketplace.

There is no set tour offered from Meknes, so that means most visitors have to rent a taxi for the day's drive out. Bargain over the price, but it should run around 300 DH ($33) per day.

3. Fez

Fez has been called "the most complete example of Oriental civilization." It is three cities in one: the pearl-gray rampart-enclosed ancient town, **Fes El Bali,** is on the right bank; the "New Fez," **Fes El Jedid,** is on the left. Then there is an even newer town, the European quarter founded in 1916 three miles west of the Medina. It is called **Fez Debibagh,** named after a mosque found there.

Fez is on the north-south caravan route between the Sahara and Tangier, 100 miles inland from the Atlantic. It stretches out between low hills, and is crowned by ruins of old fortresses. The most ancient of the Imperial Cities of Morocco, Fez was founded in 808 by Idriss II. It reached the apex of its fame and influence under the Merinides in the 14th century, and its reputation as a seat of learning was renowned throughout Europe.

After Granada fell to Isabella and Ferdinand, Fez became a center for refugees, who brought with them a spectacular knowledge of arts, science, and crafts. Those crafts are still practiced today. In fact, a walk through the Medina of Fes El Bali is like plunging back to the Middle Ages. Fez became known as a "city of mosques" (there are more than 300, including the world-famed Karaouyine, the largest in Africa).

On the banks of the Fez River, an effluent of the Sebou, Fez is best approached by a high road on a hilltop crowned by the Merinid tombs. From the vantage point, the minaret-studded city—best viewed at sunset—spreads before you.

WHERE TO STAY: Hotels tend to be heavily booked at peak tourist months, so reserve.

Hotel Palais Jamai, Bab el Ghuissa (tel. 343-31), is right on the edge of the Medina of Fes El Bali, and part of the hotel is the beautiful 19th-century palace of the Grand Vizier Jamai for "rest and evasion, the pleasure of the eyes and the peace of the soul." Many of the bedrooms are in the old palace, although those in the new wing have better views over the roofs of the Medina. Doubles cost from $70 (U.S.). The entire hotel is surrounded by sculpted gardens inhabited by a raucous peacock. There is a swimming pool with a good poolside bar where snacks are available. If you spend a night here, you can breakfast on the balcony overlooking the gardens and across the Medina roofs to the hills beyond. Even if you don't stay here, this is a perfect place for a leisurely drink and a rest after a hot, busy day of sightseeing before returning to your hotel in the new town.

Hotel Zalagh, 6 rue Mohammed Diouri (tel. 255-02), is listed as first class by the government and is one of the members of the Salam chain. You pay 220 DH ($24.20) for a double room with complete bath, 175 DH ($19.25) in a single with bath. French windows open onto your own balcony, where you can enjoy the view and have a breakfast of coffee and croissants for an extra charge. All of the bedrooms contain a private bath, but only the public rooms are air-conditioned. There is, however, a swimming pool surrounded by a flagstone terrace. Meals, costing from 85 DH ($9.35), are a Moroccan event here, and the dining room decor is sumptuous.

Hotel de Fes, Avenue des F.A.R. (tel. 250-02), is a modern hotel in the Ville Nouvelle with a beautiful large lobby furnished with armchairs and valuable rugs. Off the lobby are a coffeeshop and a shopping arcade leading to the gardens and pool. El Minzeh Restaurant has a long menu of Moroccan and European dishes, including cassolette d'escargots, filet au poivre or with mushrooms, suprême of turbot, and sole meunière. A meal of an appetizer and a main course will cost from 140 DH ($15.40). A light meal in the coffeeshop is available for 45 DH ($4.95) and up. Bedrooms, well-furnished and comfortable, cost from 380 DH ($41.80) for one person, from 455 DH ($50.05) for two.

Splendid, 9 rue Abdelkrim El Khattabi (tel. 221-48), is a 76-bedroom hotel which has an intimate Scandinavian lounge with original artwork. White is used throughout the accommodations, relieved by vibrant colors. Some of the units are new, with modern decor, and all have a toilet and bath or shower, plus central heating. Singles rent for 130 DH ($14.30) and doubles for 160 DH ($17.60). Many of the bedrooms open onto a courtyard garden where you can order drinks at one of the patio tables, and the hotel has a cocktail bar and a TV lounge on the first floor. The Splendid is in the center of the Ville Nouvelle, overlooking a square. A French and Moroccan restaurant, L'Adour (see below) is on the premises.

Le Grand, Boulevard Chefchaouini (tel. 255-11), is contemporary and traditionally Moroccan at the same time. It offers 98 rooms with a wide range of plumbing. Doubles with complete bath, either tub, or shower, are 165 DH ($18.15). The more expensive singles, with complete bath, cost 135 DH ($14.85). The furnishings are comfortable, if not always new, and most of the rooms are spacious. All of the public rooms are air-conditioned, as are some of the bedrooms. A continental breakfast or an English one—ham and eggs—is extra. A tourist menu of three courses at 70 DH ($7.70) or a gastronomic menu at 85 DH ($9.35) are both served in the hotel's La Normandie Restaurant.

Hotel Volubillis, Avenue Allal Ben Abdellah (tel. 230-97), is a bit like a resort. Two floors of air-conditioned private units and public rooms open onto a large garden with swimming pool, palms, and flowering bushes. It's informal living, with emphasis on the relaxed life. The room decor is severe yet attractive, with warm wall colors and good modern furniture as well as picture-window doors leading out onto private terraces. All rooms have a complete private bath. The rate is 270 DH ($29.70) in a double, 205 DH ($22.55) in a single. Most dining room tables have a view of the garden, and you can order a complete luncheon or dinner here for 85 DH ($9.35). The hotel also has a bar and snackbar. At night a disco opens and plays the latest international records. There's no cover charge, just the price of your drinks.

WHERE TO EAT: Most visitors dine in their hotels, taking the half-board plan (a room with breakfast and one main meal, usually dinner). However, there are several independent restaurants.

Palais des Mérinides, 99 Zkak et Rouah (tel. 340-28). Don't try to find this place without a guide—you'll surely get lost. You'll follow a trail through narrow streets to what from the outside doesn't even look like a restaurant. You enter a magnificent palace where the ground floor is an Ali Baba's cave of priceless carpets—old, modern, brightly colored, patterned, or plain in desert colors of the Berbers. Upstairs, in cool rooms off the balcony, low chairs and sofas surround small tables beneath tented ceilings in what is one of the finest restaurants in Fez, although it charges moderate tariffs. Each of the rooms has a different decor. You can be served a Moroccan feast, perhaps including one of the finest bastillas in Morocco. As mentioned, bastilla is pigeon pie, which Moroccans eat with their fingers. It is covered with cinnamon and powdered sugar and is given added flavor through use of sugared almonds. You can dine here for a total cost of 60 DH ($6.60) to 90 DH ($9.90) per person.

Haj Mohamed Lahlou, the gentle owner of the place, will assist you if you're interested in purchasing one (or more) of the carpets downstairs. He speaks little English, but you can get by with basic French, and besides, when it comes to buying the carpets, figures seem to be universally understood. M. Lahlou will arrange packing and shipment to your home, "charges forward," and he accepts major credit cards. The carpets range from 300 DH ($33) to 1,250 DH ($137.50) per square meter.

Pavillon L'Anmbra, Laraichi, 47 bis Route d'Immouzer (tel. 416-87), is a totally Moroccan experience that's worth the price. It draws upon the styles of the 14th century and is richly decorated with many antiques and handcrafts. In spacious surroundings, you dine on low sofas, with all the Aladdin's-lamp trappings. For a complete meal, including two Moroccan specialties, such as pigeon pie, figure on spending 120 DH ($13.20). Called bsteelah (bastilla), the pie is the supreme glory of Moroccan cuisine. I'm also fond of the chicken with olives, lemons, and almonds. This price includes mineral water, fresh fruit, ice cream and mint tea, as well as service. All dishes are à la carte. The ovenbaked lamb, the keftas (skewered meat), and tajine (meat and vegetables simmered in earthenware dishes) are recommended. The restaurant has a patio overlooking the garden where guests can order soft drinks, ice cream, tea, and coffee from 9 a.m. to 10 p.m. Lunch is served daily from noon to 3 p.m., dinner from 7 to 11 p.m. The location is out toward the airport, about 3 miles from the center.

L'Adour Restaurant, 9 rue Abdelkrim El Khattabi (tel. 221-48), part of the Splendid Hotel, is your best bet for French cooking in the Ville Nouvelle. A tourist menu is offered for around 65 DH ($7.15), and snacks are available, such as sandwiches and salads, for from 30 DH ($3.30). There are also à la carte selections. You pay 80 DH ($8.80) for a complete meal, including tax and service. I recently enjoyed some tempting hors d'oeuvres, followed by a Moroccan tajine and a selection of fruit for that price. At lunch, try the spaghetti bolognese or an omelet. The sole meunière is also fine. Many Moroccan dishes, such as couscous, are also served. L'Adour is a good, safe bet for those who've had too much local color.

Dar Tajine, 15 Ross Rhi (tel. 341-67), is a delightful place only three short, narrow streets into the Medina, but you will probably be wise to have a guide when you make your first visit. While it is quite safe to walk there unaccompanied, there is still the chance of getting lost in the maze of alleys. The unobtrusive doorway marked only with a small sign leads into what one reader described as a pasha's palace, 130 years old and the home of the Lebbar family for most of that time. The dining room is a beautiful, quiet, lofty place with tall decorative columns and a tile floor with a small fountain playing languidly. Far above, birds flit between the rafters of the transparent roof. In the Moroccan tradition, there are no windows, for it is not considered polite to demonstrate one's wealth to a neighbor who might not be so fortunate. Around the walls are small chambers with low sofas and tables, some downstairs and some high on the gallery above. Boys in scarlet breeches and tarboushes wait attentively on the tables.

Lunch at 125 DH ($13.75) is a choice of several salads which fill the table: tomato and onion, spinach with sauce, potatoes in mild tomato, beetroot, and a fiery tomato one. Among main dishes, you might have brochettes of kefta or meat, tajine, or couscous, rounded off with fresh fruit presented in a large bowl. In the evening, the meal is more elaborate at 150 DH ($16.50) for soup, kefta or brochette, salads, lemon chicken, pastilla (for which a supplement is charged), or mrouzia, a dish not often seen for it is usually only prepared when a lamb is slaughtered. Lebbar Omar, the owner, is proud that it appears often on his menu. It's a joint of lamb simmered with dry raisins to make what the French call a *confit.*

Lebbar Omar trained in England, returning to Fez with the desire to convert his home into a restaurant where he could offer the best in Moroccan hospitality. If you go for lunch, served from noon to 3 p.m., it's best to be early or late to avoid the groups which fill the courtyard, chattering like the sparrows in the roof above. Despite the crowd, the owner manages to greet everyone and welcome them to his home. It's a good idea to go at lunchtime and arrange your menu for the evening meal, served from 7 to 10:30 p.m.

24/24, Abdullah Ben Chekrun, Boulevard Mohammed V (tel. 236-97), is the closest thing to a fast food place you'll find in Morocco. The simple restaurant with metal tables and hard chairs is run by Abdelali Bennani from his position behind the high counter over which sandwiches, hamburgers, and omelets are dispensed. A veal brochette here is excellent. Meals cost from 50 DH ($5.50). The place is clean and bright, the service cheerful, and the atmosphere pleasant. It's open 24 hours a day, hence the name.

Restaurant Le Coq D'Or, Boulevard Mohammed V, does not have a telephone, so you must take a chance on getting a table for dinner. Inside, the atmosphere is one of elegance and gentility, with high-back tapestry-covered chairs around tables with white napery and gleaming silver. The menu includes Moroccan dishes as well as such European courses as wienerschnitzel, entrecôte bordelaise, and spaghetti bolognese. A meal of two courses will cost 55 DH ($6.05) to 85 DH ($9.35). Wine of the country is served.

Dar Firdaous, 10 rue Jenjfour, Bab el Guissa (tel. 343-43), is just outside the courtyard of the Hotel Jamai. Here, the courtyard of an old Medina house is covered with a drapery like a tent, and tables are grouped in the court and in the small rooms around the walls. Dinner, chosen from the menu of Moroccan foods such as harira soup, tajine, couscous, and mechoui, will cost 120 DH ($13.20). At 9 p.m., a spectacular show with dancers and entertainers is presented, costing 20 DH ($2.20) per person extra.

FEZ NIGHTLIFE: Not much. Your best bet is **Night Club Oriental,** Le Grand Hotel, Boulevard Chefchaouni (tel. 255-11), which features a nightly cabaret—complete with Moroccan folkloric presentations and disco dancing—for 50 DH ($5.50), including your first drink. The show starts at 10:30 p.m.

EXPLORING FES EL BALI: In the ancient city, or Medina, you'll find the greatest collection of palaces, mosques, *souks,* national monuments, and *medrassa* (former schools or colleges, now relatively abandoned). If you venture deep into the Medina, you may never return. Not that you'll be so enraptured by it, although that's a likely possibility. Rather, you may never find your way out. A guide is absolutely essential, even for those who pride themselves on getting around Moroccan cities without hired help.

The streets, a labyrinthine maze of alleyways, are extremely narrow. The houses rise high, blocking sight of the sun. Inside, the buildings are often dark, musty, even gloomy, especially so in winter. Yet many of the buildings, in spite of their unprepossessing façades, conceal private courtyards and sumptuously decorated salons.

Aside from the historical monuments outlined below, take time to observe the everyday life—by far the most enduring attraction of the Medina. For example, women make the dough for their bread at home, then take it to the baker who pops it in his ancient oven. Except for the mosques and private homes, you can wander past almost any door and watch the craftspeople practice their age-old secrets.

Throughout the Medina is a maze-like serpentine collection of *souks,* with hustlers trying to lure you inside. The teeming crowds rub shoulders as they make their way through, giving way only to the heavily laden donkeys, the "taxis" of Fez, which stubbornly knock you down with the load jutting out from their backs if you don't get out of the way. Each craft has its section. Thus you'll find the weavers, the goldsmiths, the spice merchants, the dyers, the bookbinders, the coppersmiths, even the barbers, huddled near each other and, needless to say, madly competitive.

You won't need a guide to take you to the **Tanners' Quarter.** Just follow your nose. In one of the most serious recommendations in this guide, I suggest you buy a sprig of mint from one of the many vendors in the alleyways before venturing into this grotesquerie of medieval horror. You're taken first through the section of vats where the animal hides are treated by scantily clothed men, the stench from the slain beasts rising to greet you. You proceed to a terrace where you can look down at the many-hued dyes resting in vats in which the treated hides are submerged. Thrilling, most certainly. But you won't want to linger.

In the Andalusian Quarter, you'll find the **Quartier des Potiers** (potters). As you approach the sector, and if you don't already have a hired guide, you'll receive countless offers from young boys to show you through for a fee. The potters practice their craft with consummate skill, most of the workers trained by their fathers who in turn were trained by their fathers, ad infinitum.

The quarter takes its name from the **Mosque of the Andalusians** (no admission to non-Muslims) built for the refugees from Córdoba and dating from the 9th century. The present structure, however, is mainly from the 13th century. You can't go inside, but can admire the restored porch roof over the north doorway.

The Medina is traditionally entered through the **Bab Boujeloud,** actually two gates, the newer one built in 1913. You come first to the **Dar Batha,** a 19th-century palace turned into the **Museum of Moroccan Art and Handcrafts.** It is in the Hispano-Moorish style of architecture, and can be visited daily except Tuesday, from 9 a.m. till sunset. There is no admission, but tip the guide.

Inside are collections of embroidery, tapestries, pottery, ceramics, manuscripts, wool carpets, funereal art, jewelry, leatherwork. The Moorish garden is especially attractive.

From the palace, you can make your way to the **Bou Inania Medersa,** a former college complex dating from the 14th century and a fine example of Merinid architecture. Note the mosaic-covered walls, the carved plaster, and the elaborate cedarwood friezes. Its pentroof is superbly decorated as well; and its courtyard is paved with onyx and pink-and-white marble. Upstairs are the rooms that housed the former students. The so-called clock, perhaps a former carillon, is a curiosity. Men only are admitted to the Hall of Ablutions. Finally, staircases lead to the Mosque of the Dead. It is open daily except Friday morning.

Another college to be visited is the **Attarine Medersa,** on the rue de Souq el-Attarine, which is even older than the Bou Inania. It is also a smaller complex, and in some ways more graceful. It, too, dates from the 14th century, 1325 to be exact. If you climb to the terrace, you'll enjoy a view of the monumental **Karaouyine Mosque,** founded in the 9th century and still the largest in North Africa, with its 270 columns and 16 naves. It literally dominates the Medina. Of course, non-Muslims are forbidden to enter; but nobody stops you if you walk around, glancing into the many doorways.

A short walk from the Karaouyine Mosque and you're at **Nejjarine Square,** one of the most delightful spots in the city. The plaza is known for its mosaic fountain. The much-photographed **Nejjarine Fondouk** has an entrance surmounted by a handsome pentroof. A *fondouk* was a caravansary or stable that also offered lodgings to men in its upstairs rooms. This one dates from the 18th century. From this point, you can venture into the Nejjarine *souk,* with its compelling odors of thuya and cedarwood worked by cabinetmakers. Continuing on, the ancient **Kissaria** just isn't what it used to be, as the fabric market was destroyed by fire. But the animation and the flamboyantly colored fabrics—many with gold embroidery—are still there. Perhaps you'll get to see an auction.

Near the Nejjarine Fondouk is the **Zawiya of Moulay Idriss,** a sanctuary dedicated to the founder of Fez. It is a much revered sight, sacred to Moroccans, and visitors are asked to respect that. Wooden beams bar the streets leading to it, marking the limit of the so-called *horm* or holy asylum. You definitely cannot go inside the sanctuary. In fact, you're advised not to get too close to the *horm* limit.

In our final round-up of the sights of Fes el Bali, make sure your guide has taken you to the **Seffarin Medersa,** the oldest in Fez, dating from 1255. It is near the sector where the coppersmiths ply their trade, on the Place Seffarine.

The **Cherratine Medersa,** from 1670, is the largest in Fez. It does not have the interest that the Merinid medrassa possess; note the bronze-faced doors, however, on the rue Cherratine.

Incidentally, all of the medrassa, unless they are being restored, are open daily except Friday morning. Always tip the guide in charge.

Finally, the **Tetuani Fondouk** was named to commemorate its past function—a way station to serve the merchants and their camels who came down from Tetuan. See especially its delicately carved wood ceiling from the 14th century. The goods and camels were kept downstairs, the beds placed in cramped quarters above.

Crossing through the **Bou-Jeloud Gardens,** you leave Fes al Bali, and enter—

FES EL JEDID: Less colorful, but interesting nevertheless, the so-called New Town contains the **Dar el Makhzen,** the imperial palace complex where King Hassan II stays when he is in town. The palace, its grounds, and adjoining buildings occupy nearly 200 acres.

The **Mellah,** the old Jewish quarter, lies in this sector, enclosed behind its own walls. It dates from the early 14th century, and today this former ghetto has far fewer Jews than Muslims; however, some of the most fascinating shops are run by Jewish goldsmiths. In addition to a Jewish cemetery, there are a few synagogues in the Mellah as well. Unlike the mosques, the synagogues can be visited (see especially the Serfati and the Fassiin or Fasyne or Fasiyin—take your own choice of spelling).

Perhaps what will interest you most about Fes el Jedid is the **Old Mechaouar** courtyard, which is surrounded by high walls. On an afternoon, jugglers, fortune tellers, soothsayers, acrobats, and dancers entertain. However, this spectacle has lost many adherents over the years.

Also in this district is the Great Mosque, founded in 1276, and the **Mosque of Moulay Abdellah,** surrounded by an interesting quarter of the same name.

THE CORNICHE ROUTE: Before the sun sets, strike out by car for the **Route du Tour des Fes,** a corniche highway above the town which encircles Fez for about ten miles. If you stop for drinks on the terrace of Des Mérinides Hotel, you can enjoy a view not only of the Old Town but the Sebou River, Mount Senhadia, and east to the Atlas range as well.

You might also want to stop over at the badly deteriorated **Merinid necropolis,** on El Kolla hill. Most of the tombs of the sultans date from the 14th century.

Housed in a small fort nearby is an **Armory Museum** containing a collection of weapons from around the world, including Spain, Iran, Tunisia, Japan, France, Turkey, and Senegal. Even prehistoric weapons and American-made Colts and automatic pistols are displayed. Note especially the 16th-century Milanese armor and the 15th-century Moroccan cannons. Admission is 3 DH (33¢), and tip the guide. It is open daily except Tuesday, from 8 a.m. to noon and 3:30 to 7:30 p.m.

EXCURSIONS FROM FEZ: Fez is the hub of an excursion wheel, its spokes branching out in all directions. The most popular day's jaunt—to the Roman ruins of Volubilis and the Sanctuary of Moulay-Idriss—is described earlier in this chapter. But there are many other sights.

4. Sidi Harazem

Heading east from Fez, on the road to Taza that ultimately leads to Algeria, after 11 miles you come to a turnoff on the right marked Sidi Harazem. Although it was known to the Romans, this resort oasis has only recently been developed, and is one of the leading spa centers of Morocco.

Once the storks perched on top of the mud houses and the Berbers had Sidi Harazem pretty much to themselves. Nowadays an influx of spa-loving Germans and off-the-record Algerians is pouring in. Can other Europeans, and eventually Americans, be far behind?

The hot (93 degrees) artesian springs at the spa are said to cure everything from kidney stones to gout. The bottled Sidi Harazem natural mineral water remains the most popular drink with meals in Morocco. Incidentally, near the springs is a prehistoric stone circle of 26 monoliths, the Stonehenge of Morocco.

Those wanting to escape the stiffling heat of Fez in summer often book a room here at the following:

The **Hotel Sidi-Harazem** (tel. 455-22), is an ingeniously conceived resort hotel—part of the spa complex and centering on an array of mineral water swimming pools and baths, as well as spacious gardens. It's a combination of a modern hotel and a first-rate spa facility. Yet the price is quite reasonable: 175 DH ($19.25) for a single, 215 DH ($23.65) for a double, both with private bath. You pay another 85 DH ($9.35) for a complete, many-course luncheon or dinner.

5. Immouzer du-Khandar

Our final excursion from Fez is to Azrou, south of the city on the road to Marrakesh. Passing through interesting countryside, you arrive first at the Berber village of **Immouzer du-Khandar** (alt. 4,400 feet; 21 miles from Fez). It sits on a rocky plateau overlooking the Sebou plain in a setting of mountains, pine forests, and several fine fishing lakes. It appears that sleepy Immouzer du-Khandar will one day become an important mountain resort.

Adjoining the hillside marketplace is a series of caves inhabited by Berbers. For a few dirhams the dwellers will show you the inside of their primitive homes.

Hotel Royal, Avenue Mohammed V (tel. 630-80), is a village inn, right in the town center. It's a third-class hotel, modest in scope, with a dining room opening onto a pond and garden. There is no lounge to speak of—only a large bar and a dining room. Most visitors stop by for a meal of gargantuan portions. If you just "leave it to the chef," chances are you'll have everything from hors d'oeuvres to freshly caught fish fried in butter, followed by a meat course, cheese, dessert, and coffee, all for 65 DH ($7.15). You can dine for less, of course. The upstairs bedrooms are immaculate. One person pays 115 DH ($12.65) for a room; two, 140 DH ($15.40). Rooms contain a shower or bath.

The king maintains a handsome and stately chalet here, by the way (you can't miss seeing it, as well as the villa across the way where he houses overflow guests).

6. Azrou

You next arrive at the fashionable little summer resort and winter sports center of **Ifrane,** 37 miles from Fez. At an altitude of 5,250 feet, its setting is idyllic, in the center of a wooded plateau of oak and cedar. The climate, especially the air, is invigorating. Seven miles from Ifrane is the **Tizi-n-Tretten** pass, which is snowcovered for most of the year. Skiers are attracted to its slopes, especially to the sports resort of **Mischliffen,** with its ski lifts and marked courses.

But back to the main road. From Ifrane, the highway cuts across the cedar forest to our final destination, **Azrou** "The Rock." (Bus connections are possible from Fez.) Azrou lies 11 miles from Ifrane. The town is at an altitude of some 4,000 feet, and is noted for its handcrafts, especially its cedarwood carvings and Beni M'Guild carpets. In the center of Azrou is a handcrafts cooperative where on any day of the week, except Friday, you can see women at the looms making the carpets, as well as purchase a selection of the cedarwood carvings in an adjoining aisle. The 17th-century Casbah here, built by Moulay Ismael, is also interesting but run-down.

Azrou is a pleasant place lying at the foot of pine-covered mountains with fresh clear air and an air of prosperity. Apart from the handcrafts co-operative, there are attractive little green-tile market stalls lining the steep streets, and on Tuesday the large market place is full of people from the surrounding countryside buying, selling, and exchanging wares.

For food and/or lodgings, try the **Hotel du Panorama,** outside the center (tel. 20-10), an all-purpose mountain lodge, open all year to attract travelers who either want to escape the summer heat or ski in winter. In spring or fall, fishermen show up. It's outside town, set on the rise of a hill. The owner, a French woman named Madame Duffal, runs everything well, seeing to it that the large tavern bar, the dining room, and the bedrooms are well kept. Most of the accommodations contain a private balcony opening onto the panoramic views—hence, the name of the hotel. The price of rooms for two with hot and cold running water is 62 DH ($6.82), 78 DH ($8.58) with a shower. An average meal, including service charge, costs 60 DH ($6.60). Board is required on national holidays.

You can also visit Azrou from Meknes, a route to that delightful little town in the Moyen Atlas that's far more attractive than the road from Fez. You pass through some 15½ miles of rolling farmland made up of huge acreage of big farmers, perhaps being harvested by big combines (harvesters) as you pass by, interspersed by equally fertile, postage-stamp size plots of local owners, who cultivate it by donkey-drawn plow after the family has sowed the grain by hand and is waiting to harvest it by hand.

Along this road, you come to **El-Hajeb,** perhaps the cleanest village you'll see in Morocco. An old fort and lovely old steps carved into the hillside are seen, as well as bright, primitive pictures carefully painted on the walls of the buildings you see as you drive through. This is the wine-growing region, and you soon see the fields spiky with vines. The road starts to climb, and the scenery becomes more rounded, with fir trees clothing the slopes and heavy cows grazing in lush green fields. Houses are built to withstand low winter temperatures, when heavy snow must be kept, when possible, from windows and doors.

You'll see a sign on the right, **Auberge Amros,** just 3 miles before you reach Azrou and 38½ miles from Meknes. Turn into the yard and wander into the tiny, dark, highly polished bar where more than six people make a crowd. The spotless dining room, with its red-checked tablecloths, is not always open at lunchtime, but you may decide to return here for the night, in order to spend it in the silence of the countryside, broken only by the creaking of storks nesting on the roof and in every available fir tree around. Bedrooms in the garden are simple, as is the plumbing, with rent being 30 DH ($3.30) for a double. Dinner will consist of whatever is available, the charge being based on what and how much you eat. Even this paradise of quiet can become busy when locals drive out to eat in the garden around the swimming pool. Hamid Tarsi is the owner of the auberge. The telephone number is 5 "par la poste," which means you must ask for the post office at Azrou and ask to be connected with the establishment.

Drive on into the ugly, modern commercial part of Azrou, where gasoline is refined, passing on into the old town. After lunch at the Hotel du Panorama, you'll have time to drive down to Fez and back to Meknes. If you have the time to spare, turn off the Fez road before Immouzer for the **Tour Touristique des Lacs,** a drive around five tranquil lakes of about 34 miles through beautiful country.

At the entrance to the lakes is the **Chalet du Lac,** Dayet-Aoua, south of Immouzer du-Khandar (tel. 0 "par Ifrane"). The place has a marvelous position at the top of the first lake, with a restaurant looking straight down the lake to the mountains. Most of the bedrooms have the same view. A single rents for 55 DH ($6.05) and doubles for 70 DH ($7.70). Dinner is 100 DH ($11). The chalet is open throughout the year except during the month of Ramadan.

Chapter XX

RABAT, CASABLANCA, AND THE ATLANTIC COAST

1. Rabat
2. Casablanca
3. El Jadida
4. Essaouira
5. Agadir
6. Taroudannt
7. Tafraout
8. Tiznit
9. Goulimine

THREE OF THE MOST famous destinations in Morocco—Casablanca, Rabat (the capital), and the beach resort of Agadir—are covered in this chapter. Not only that, but we'll visit several more esoteric beach destinations along the Atlantic coast before we dip inland into the deep southwestern part of Morocco to visit the most rewarding targets in a mountain range known as the "Anti-Atlas."

Rabat, our first destination, dates from the time of Ptolemy or even before. In the 11th century it was the stronghold of Almohad, and once it was a hideout for the corsairs who enjoyed their women and their loot before venturing out once again to menace shipping in the Atlantic. In time, the French would make Rabat the capital of the protectorate. Many readers have questioned the charm of Rabat, although frankly I like it. Certainly, however, it doesn't have the allure of such cities as Fez or Marrakesh. But if you have at least a day, it can be a rewarding target, especially if you take a visit to the nearby whitewashed town of Salé, which has far more local color.

Casablanca, the biggest city in Morocco, is often your gateway to Africa, particularly if you're flying from North America. Lying 63 miles south of Rabat, it has grown by leaps and bounds, often unattractively so. In Arabic, it's called

Dar al'Beida or "the white house," from which comes the Westernized name of Casablanca. This city is hardly one of the great attractions of Morocco, and many visitors say that the best thing about it is in leaving it. But since it's one of the biggest ports in Africa, you'll probably find yourself there. If so, you'll discover some surprisingly good hotels charging moderate prices and many restaurants featuring a good cuisine. Those who are apologetic about its lack of sightseeing targets speak of "the vitality" of its people.

If you want to escape the crowds, and are seeking an African Atlantic coast beach resort, then try either **El Jadida** or **Essaouira,** coming up. However, those wanting to be smack in the center of the beach action should continue south to **Agadir,** which is crowned by a kasbah fortress built in the 16th century. This is where the Souss Valley, the Atlantic, and the Anti-Atlas mountains come together. Agadir offers thousands of beds in all price ranges.

When you tire of the beach, you can heed the call of the Deep South, plunging into that mountainous barrier, the Anti-Atlas, which shields the Souss from the drying winds of the Sahara. In the concluding sections of this chapter, we'll visit the most rewarding targets in the Anti-Atlas: **Taroudannt, Tafraoute,** and **Tiznit.**

1. Rabat

As the capital of Morocco, Rabat is the primary home of King Hassan II, who maintains elaborate palaces in the other Imperial Cities as well. Founded in the 12th century, and once known as the Camp of Victory, Rabat today is essentially a modern city of gardens and monumental gateways. The third-largest city in Morocco, it lies on the Atlantic coast, 57 miles northeast of Casablanca. It is separated by the Bou Regreg from its sister city, **Salé,** on the opposite bank.

THE SIGHTS: Most visits begin at the **Quadias Casbah.** The Casbah, surrounded by a wall with bastions, is reached by a splendid gateway (*bab*) constructed in the reign of Yacoub El Mansour (1185–1199). The gate leads to the inner garden, designed in 1915 and richly planted with orange trees. Bougainvillea drape the walls, and storks find places for their nests on the battlements. After a stroll through the gardens, the visitor can stop off at the **Moorish Café,** with its belvedere overlooking the city of Salé on the opposite side of the river. Coffee or the traditional mint tea are available, but you may find the pastries too sweet.

Installed in the gardens is the **Museum of Oudaïa** (tel. 315-37), housed in a small palace built in the 17th century during the reign of Moulay Ismail. Various Rabat carpets are exhibited in the old oratory chamber. After seeing them, you pass into a patio with a pond. Moroccan ceramics are displayed in the loggia. One salon is devoted to jewelry, including gold pieces and silver filigree. Decorated in the traditional Moroccan style, another salon is complete with brocaded divans, antique Rabat carpets on the floor, a finely chiseled copper incense burner, as well as sculptured cedar chests and embroidered cushions. Perhaps the section devoted to costumes, such as Rif dress, is the most interesting. One tableau depicts a Berber wedding ceremony; others show the dress of the natives who live in the High Atlas. Hours are daily except Tuesday, from 9 to 11:30 a.m. and 3 to 6 p.m.

The **Tower of Hassan** rises over the ruins of a large mosque; the 144-foot tower was originally its minaret. The minaret, incidentally, was built to rival the Giralda in Seville. Construction started in 1184 on orders from Yacoub El Mansour, who wanted a mosque big enough to shelter his entire army. Work stopped upon the death of the sultan. At many points in its sad decline, the mosque was used as a quarry for building materials. Finally, the 1755 earthquake that struck Lisbon did further damage. A ramp climbs to the pinnacle, from which you can look out over the rooftops of Salé. At the eastern end of the grounds is the constantly guarded memorial and **mausoleum of Mohammed V,** who died in 1961. He was the father of the present king, Hassan II, and was instrumental in liberating Morocco from Spanish and French rule.

The **Medina** has been likened to that of an Andalusian town. In fact, many Muslims driven from Spain did settle in the Medina, erecting the Andalusian wall in the 17th century. The Old Town was built between this wall and the Almohad walls from the 12th century. Here life holds forth in *souk* after *souk*. You may want to purchase a Rabat carpet, the craftsmanship enjoying world fame. The Medina is mainly for strolling and shopping, as it holds few monuments of interest. At the old wool market, the Place Souq el Ghezel, you could, in the 16th century, purchase a Christian slave—real cheap! At one time foreign emissaries were obliged to live on the rue des Consuls, but that requirement has long ago been dispensed with. This street leads to the Place du Mellah. Branching off from here are the houses and shops of the **Mellah,** or Jewish quarter.

The **Mechouar** is the enclosure that contains the royal palace where King Hassan II and his family live. Nearby are the barracks of the "Black Guard," descendants of West African slaves.

The **Museum of Antiquities** (Musée Archéologique), on Zankat al Brihi, contains a reproduction of a geometrical mosaic floor from Volubilis and the statue of Ptolemy, son of Juba II and Cleopatra Selenea. The main entrance and first floor contain many displays of Roman life and crafts of ancient Morocco, as well as artifacts from prehistoric periods. Hours are 9 a.m. to 6 p.m. Admission is 3 DH (33¢). Closed Tuesday.

Outside the city walls, **Chellah** was the last Roman city (Sala Colonia) to go up on the Atlantic coast. Next to Rabat on the Bou Regreg estuary, it lies in ruins today. Once non-Muslims weren't allowed through the gateway, but in this more democratic day they can pass. The gateway, richly decorated, was begun by Abou Said (1310–1331) and completed by his son, Abou El Hassan, in 1339. Inside the walls you can see the marble tombs of the former sultans and an inner courtyard of a sanctuary, as well as a mosiac-decorated minaret crowned by a stork's nest. The remains of a Roman bath and two ancient villas were discovered. The rest of the former necropolis is planted with gardens; and a path leads down to a spring. It's a serene oasis on a hot afternoon.

WHERE TO STAY: **Rabat Chellah Hotel,** 2 rue d'Ifni (tel. 640-52). Because this hotel's entrance lies kitty-corner from the Royal Palace, you'll be able to gaze upon the green-tiled roofs of the king's residence. It opened in 1972, but its copper-trimmed façade still looks fairly new. You register in a brick-floored lobby sheathed in elegantly crafted tilework. This is a well-run, very clean hotel with style and a good design. On the ground floor is an alluring bar, plus one of my favorite restaurants in town, the Kanoun Grill (see the dining section for Rabat). Each of the comfortable bedrooms has a private bath, air conditioning, and a phone. Singles cost 215 DH ($23.65), doubles, 270 DH ($29.70). Half board is offered for a supplement of 160 DH ($17.60) per person.

Hotel Belere, 33 Avenue Moulay Youssef (tel. 699-01). Its entrance is set beneath a modern stone-slabbed arcade in a central part of the city. Built in 1976, it has a marble-floored lobby with a scattering of Oriental rugs, unusual bas-reliefs hammered from copper, and a pleasant restaurant. It's about a minute's walk from the train station of "Rabat-Ville." The hotel contains 90 attractive but sparsely decorated bedrooms, each with its own bath and phone. Ask for a fifth-floor accommodation because, although the cost is the same, you'll get a sunny balcony and a view of the skyline of modern Rabat. Singles rent for 210

DH ($23.10), doubles for 275 DH ($30.25). Full meals in the air-conditioned dining room go for 85 DH ($9.35).

Hotel Oudayas, 4 rue de Tobrouk (tel. 678-20). Named after the elegant district of the city in which it sits, this modern hotel is one of the most dramatic hostelries in the neighborhood. Its lobby, sheathed in a combination of black marble and beige stone, has a restrained French theme. Each of the comfortable 37 bedrooms has a private bath and a tasteful but somewhat spartan decor. Singles rent for 180 DH ($19.80), doubles for 225 DH ($24.75), with fixed-priced meals costing 70 DH ($7.70) each.

Hotel Balima, 173 Avenue Mohammed V (tel. 677-55). Built in 1932, this pleasant hotel has an inviting tree-shaded courtyard filled with café and restaurant tables on its quieter side. Its official entrance lies in a bull's-eye position along Rabat's major avenue in the commercial heart of the city. You'll register in a marble-sheathed high-ceilinged lobby filled with lattices and art deco touches. The 71 high-ceilinged bedrooms are very clean and sunny, with slightly dated bathrooms, a decor a bit like you might have found in colonial Cairo. Singles cost 120 DH ($13.20); doubles, 150 DH ($16.50), plus breakfast. A fixed-price meal in the restaurant (see the dining section for Rabat) costs 65 DH ($7.15).

Hotel Shéhèrazade, 21 rue de Tunis (tel. 222-26), was built in 1972 in a modern architectural design, with vertical zigzag bay windows on the front, allowing extra bedroom space and views up and down the avenue. For such a superior hotel, the prices are moderate: 150 DH ($16.50) in a single with bath, 205 DH ($22.55) in a double with bath. A person can take lunch or dinner for an extra 65 DH ($7.15). The entire hotel is tastefully conceived and furnished; the lounge, bar, and dining room have a subtle Moroccan theme, and there is an attractive rear courtyard.

Hotel Dahir, 429 Avenue Hassan II (tel. 330-25), is a modern hotel built in 1980 whose façade is a geometric pattern of distressed concrete. Popular with both tourists and commercial travelers, it contains 126 bedrooms, in such colors as green, turquoise, and saffron. Each of the accommodations contains a tile bath, and each has a tiny geometrically shaped balcony, opening onto a commercial neighborhood. Singles rent for 95 DH ($10.45), doubles for 110 DH ($12.10). There is a restaurant on the premises.

Grand Hotel, 19 rue Patrice Lumumba (tel. 272-85), is a well-located little hotel that dates from the early 1930s. It's a simplified version of a small hotel where Bogie (or Rick in *Casablanca*) might have stayed. It has quite a bit of character, with art deco armchairs, large tile baths, and an occasional antique wall phone. An elevator leads to 52 comfortable bedrooms, renting for 60 DH ($6.60) to 95 DH ($10.45) in a single, 75 DH ($8.25) to 110 DH ($12.10) in a double, plus breakfast. The hotel has central heating and a good restaurant and bar.

Hotel d'Orsay, 1 Avenue Moulay Youssef (tel. 613-19), is a modern white-walled establishment, close to the rail station of "Rabat Ville." The stairs leading up to the second-floor reception lobby are separated from the sidewalk outside by a wrought-iron gate crafted into art nouveau patterns. The hotel contains a sunny TV lounge and a handful of uncomplicated bedrooms, costing from 120 DH ($13.20) in a single to 150 DH ($16.50) in a double, plus breakfast. Each accommodation is clean, with a shower set into the corner.

Hotel Splendid, 2 rue du 18 Juin (tel. 232-83), lies two blocks east of the intersection of Avenue Hassan II and Boulevard Mohammed V, within walking distance of the Medina. Understanding of the 20th-century tourist's needs, the staff of the hotel offers safe luggage storage, spacious and clean rooms, plus friendly, understanding service. The hotel is often patronized by American

Peace Corps volunteers, and the staff is able to speak several languages, including English. Rooms with a shower rent for 61 DH ($6.71) in a single and 75 DH ($8.25) in a double. Without a shower, the rates are 51 DH ($5.61) single, 63 DH ($6.93) double. There's a lovely garden where the guests gather.

Hotel Central, 2 rue Al Basra (tel. 673-56), provides basic accommodations in an excellent section. The reception area is nil; but the rooms are fairly clean and comfortable, a good buy if you're really watching those dirhams. The price for two persons in a twin-bedded room with bath is only 75 DH ($8.25), 48 DH ($5.28) in a room with hot and cold running water only. You'll be charged 38 DH ($4.18) to 55 DH ($6.05) in a single, depending on the plumbing.

WHERE TO DINE: **Koutoubia,** 10 Zankat Pierre Parent (tel. 601-25), is for Moroccan specialties. It's in the traditional style, with colored glass and booths. The restaurant features such dishes as three types of couscous and seven tajines. A good opening is the Moroccan soup. Specialties include chiche kabbat in the Tunisian style and a brochette of lamb. The Koutoubia is among the finest in its field, yet reasonably priced. Expect to spend from 100 DH ($11) for a complete meal. Your host, Bennani-Ahmed, speaks English and is most gracious and considerate. The King of Morocco occasionally dines here.

Kanoun Grill, Rabat Chellah Hotel, 2 rue d'Ifni (tel. 640-52), is the better of the two restaurants contained within this already recommended hotel. Its decor is so rustically alluring and its grilled food so flavorful that many of its clients, often employees of nearby foreign embassies, swear by it. The restaurant's low-hanging ceiling is interspersed with massive hand-hewn beams, some of which jut down between the limited number of tables. The focus of attention centers around the activity near the large grill, which is concealed in a sort of caged-in cubbyhole much like something in a casbah.

The restaurant is named after a terracotta brazier used by the Bedouins to cook food. The ample menu includes many of Morocco's most famous dishes, including harira, the soup consumed at Ramadan, along with filet of loup or sea bass flambé, grilled or poached turbot, an array of juicy tajines, roast lamb, kebabs, and a goodly selection of Moroccan wines. Full meals cost from 120 DH ($13.20) and are served at lunch and dinner daily except Sunday.

Restaurant Casabella (Chez Marcel), Zankat Moulay Abd Al Aziz, sits in a well-heeled neighborhood a few steps from the entrance to King Hassan's Royal Palace on the street level of an art deco apartment house. Its allure and cuisine is French, but from the exterior it looks a bit like a tongue-in-cheek version of a fortified casbah. During Ramadan it's open only in the evening after 8, but for the rest of the year it serves lunch and dinner daily for 110 DH ($12.10). Specialties include crayfish pil-pil, stuffed mussels, Burgundy-style snails, sole amandine, rabbit with mustard sauce, brains in black-butter sauce, and coq au vin.

Restaurant Balima, Hotel Balima, Avenue Mohammed V (also 137 rue Jakarta). Its address is officially on the major artery of town, but you'll find its most pleasant entrance along a parallel street in back. It's owned by the already recommended Hotel Balima. Its spacious outdoor terrace is almost completely covered with a screen of well-trimmed trees, creating an oasis of calm and quiet in the middle of a busy neighborhood near the Moroccan Parliament. You can dine on the terrace or inside a semi-modern room. Two fixed-price meals go for 50 DH ($5.50) and 70 DH ($7.70), including such specialties as house-style ravioli, seasonal lobster, grilled sea bass with a béarnaise sauce, pepper steak, veal kidneys with madeira, and an array of tajines and kebabs.

Those with a yen for Chinese cookery can try the **Hong Kong,** 361 Boulevard Mohammed V (tel. 235-94), where a sharkfin soup might get you going, followed by a selection of Vietnamese specialties, which are hot and spicy.

Count on spending around 65 DH ($7.15) and up for a meal here. After ascending a steep flight of stairs, you will be greeted by a simple Chinese decor. Some tables have a view of the street.

Café et Restaurant Saadi, 81 bis Avenue Allal Ben Abdellah (tel. 699-03). English-speaking Lahcen Anjar is a gracious host, welcoming visitors to his tiny restaurant near the Place Mohammed V. The restaurant stands in an arcade. Among other offerings are two different versions of a menu touristique, costing 55 DH ($6.05), a remarkable bargain considering the quality of the food. The cook specializes in tajines (my favorite is the chicken with citrus). You might begin with a Moroccan salad, following with couscous. You're presented with a selection of local pastries or the fruits of the season. Naturally, every diner finishes off the dinner with a mint tea.

El Bahia, Avenue Hassan II (tel. 345-04), has a dozen gaily decorated tables in the courtyard, up against the old walls of the Medina. A plate of the day is reliable, and Moroccan specialties are featured, including couscous, but also three kinds of tajines and four different brochettes. You can also order fresh fish, perhaps squid in sauce. Everything tastes better if accompanied by a Moroccan salad. There is a pleasant patio with more tables and sunshades; a fountain in the center with goldfish; ivy-covered walls; plus more tables inside the buildings as well as upstairs. You enter the patio through two huge doors with great nails and a heavy knocker. You'll spend from 75 DH ($8.25) for a meal.

Jour et Nuit, 4 Place Ali Janah (tel. 203-34), is open day and night, as its name suggests. Three dining rooms provide both table and counter service. Yet many visitors prefer a table in the courtyard, opposite the Jardins Triangle de Vue. If you're visiting for lunch, you may enjoy the ham omelet, preceded by a bowl of vegetable soup. For dessert, dare you try a Moroccan banana split? Featured throughout the day are such reliables as hamburgers, steak sandwiches, and spaghetti bolognese. If you want to order a complete meal, expect to pay from 75 DH ($8.25). The place attracts a clientele of well-heeled Europeanized Moroccans.

AN EXCURSION TO SALÉ: Salé is the sister city of Rabat, lying on the opposite side of the Bou Regreg river. Once famed as a pirates' nest, in the 17th century it flourished as a center of the corsairs, much to the horror of the French and English fleets. Robinson Crusoe, you may recall, was captured by the "Salee rovers."

In the Middle Ages it became known as a merchant port and entrepôt of the west coast of Africa. The town is believed to date from the 11th century, although the Merinides built the encircling ramparts in the centuries to follow. The Merinides were also responsible for the **Bab Mrisa,** the former entrance to the harbor. The 13th-century gateway leads to the **Mellah** or Jewish quarter. The Merinides are further credited with the **Medersa of Abou Al Hassan,** a college built in 1341 by the "Black Sultan." It is across from the **Great Mosque,** which dates from the 12th century (you can observe it only from the outside). If you're traveling with a guide (highly recommended), ask him to point out the **Fondouk Askour,** 14th-century hospice noted for its gateway, and the most prized monument of Salé, the **Tomb of Sidi Abdallah ben Hassoun,** the city's patron saint. It is characterized by its curious dome and its galleries in many colors. These are but some of the monuments that have earned Salé the reputation as a "city of sanctuaries."

Of course, most of your time will be spent walking through the narrow streets and looking at the shops. Salé is known for its matting work, a specialty of the local craftspeople. On the rue Kechachine, you'll find carpenters and stone carvers, and on the rue Haddadine, blacksmiths and brass workers. Many Andalusian Moors, fleeing Spain after the reconquest, settled in Salé, and perhaps for that reason the appearance of the town is often compared to that of a Muslim town in Andalusia before the fall of Granada.

Allow at least half a day for exploring Salé. You'll need that or more. (The best way of reaching Salé is to take a ferry near the Casbah des Oudaïs.)

RABAT AFTER DARK: **The Rainbow Club,** Hotel Balima, Avenue Mohammed V (173 rue Jakarta) (tel. 686-25). Its entrance is set within the courtyard of the already recommended hotel in the center of the city. It offers an all-encompassing array of disco music and folkloric programs of Moroccan music as a sort of showcase for musical artists. Call for a reservation if you want to see the show, which begins after 10 p.m. Entrance costs 38 DH ($3.85).

2. Casablanca

Casablanca is the gateway to North Africa. Morocco's commercial and industrial capital is essentially a modern city, and that means you won't be spending much time viewing historical monuments as you would in Fez and Marrakesh.

Big and bustling "Casa," as it is affectionately known, charms many, but strikes others as cold and impersonal. Most travelers to Morocco eventually pass through the city, often staying over one or two nights to catch boats or make plane connections. That time can be well spent.

Casablanca, "white house" in Spanish, lies south of Rabat on the Atlantic coast. It grew haphazardly and dramatically in the 20th century. Its history before that has been confused; only in modern times has it begun to shake off its varied colonial overtones and emerge as a truly Moroccan city.

In the 18th century Sultan Sidi Mohammed ben Abdallah rebuilt Casablanca. It had first been destroyed by the Portuguese in 1468 because it sheltered a den of pirates menacing Christian shipping on the Atlantic. The Portuguese occupied the city in 1575, staying there until 1755 when the earthquake struck Lisbon. The French occupied Casablanca in 1907.

Once all life in Casablanca was concentrated in the **Old Medina,** the original Arab settlement. Parts of it still lie behind ramparts. Like most such quarters in Morocco, the Medina is a maze of narrow streets and whitewashed buildings. It has a teeming center, and it's interesting to watch many craftspeople at work, and to visit the *souks,* but I find the Medina here far less appealing than those in most other Moroccan cities, including Tangier. Lying northwest of the heartbeat Place Mohammed V, the Old Medina contains a Great Mosque erected under the rule of Sidi Mohammed ben Abdallah (1757–1790), but you have to appreciate it from the outside unless you're a Muslim. Three gateways—Bab Kedim, Bab El-Assa, and Bab El-Marsa—connect the Old Medina with the port.

THE SIGHTS: The **Harbor,** one of the largest in Africa, is an audacious engineering achievement. It paved the way for Casablanca's expansion and development. It is reached from the Place Mohammed V by going along the Boulevard El Hansali.

Many visitors find the **New Medina,** built by the French beginning in 1921, more intriguing than the old. It looks like a filmmaker's conception of what a medina should look like. It grew up around a palace built by a sultan after World War I and set in a high walled garden. Its chief architectural monument today is still this Royal Palace, where King Hassan II stays whenever he is in Casablanca.

You can sit on the Mahkama (court of justice), built in 1941. More enticing is the *joutiya,* or handcrafts market, where you can bargain for copperware and Mediouna carpets.

The **United Nations Square** (Place des Nations Unies) is the most monumental square of Casablanca. Here you'll find the central Post Office, the Municipal Theater, and the Prefecture (City Hall).

Nearby is the magnificent rectangular park, **Arab League,** with its promenades and ornamental lakes.

Although you can't visit any mosques, there are two places of worship, both Catholic, worthy of being listed as sightseeing attractions. On the Boulevard Rachidi stands the gleaming white **Cathedral of Sacré-Coeur,** built in 1930 and named after the Sacred Heart church in Paris. Another European church, **Notre-Dame de Lourdes,** on the Boulevard Mohammed Zerktouni, is noted for its remarkable stained glass.

WHERE TO STAY: With very few exceptions, the third-class hotels of Casablanca are definitely third rate, and some of the best bargains don't appear to be a safe haven for the average visitor. Therefore, in a most serious recommendation, I suggest that if you're going to be staying in Casablanca, either for a short or longer time, you spend more than our usual budget allows if you want clean, respectable, and more secure accommodations. With that thought in mind, I'll lead off with some . . .

Super Splurge Choices

Casablanca Hyatt Regency, Place Mohammed V (tel. 22-41-67), since it was built in the early 1980s, has become a synonym throughout Europe and the Arab world as the most stylish and innovative hotel in North Africa. Before he received its commission, the hotel's interior designer was known as the favorite decorator of King Hassan II because of the refreshingly tasteful avant-garde esthetic he repeatedly brought into the Moroccan capital.

The super-splurge hotel rises in a well-proportioned cube of rose-colored glass, slate-colored masonry, and hot-pink vertical trim, above the best known square in Casablanca. A team of well-trained doormen will carry your luggage from the entrance portico into the glistening marble lobby, whose deep black surfaces are highlighted with ruby-colored Rabat carpets and swathes of intricate tilework. Throughout the public room, the dozens of high-tech touches are softened with such hints of Moroccan traditionalism as splashing fountains, deeply comfortable seating niches, and a sandstone replica of an intricately chiseled dome-covered courtyard. Everywhere, Regency-style armchairs mingle with carved masks from Central Africa, a life-sized menagerie of carved horses and camels from 19th-century Venice, and one of the best staffs in Morocco.

On the premises is a collection of interesting restaurants, a few of which are reviewed separately in the "Where to Dine" section. There's a replica of Humphrey Bogart's "Rick's Bar," a resort-style outdoor swimming pool with ringaround landscaping of bamboo, palms, and potted flowers, and the most modern weight and health club in Casablanca.

Perhaps most important, the Hyatt's plushly upholstered bedrooms are skillfully arranged into the most sophisticated division of spatial areas I've ever seen. Their aura is like something an ultra-sophisticated decorator might create within an elegant private apartment in Rome, Paris, or New York. Each has mirrored surfaces, a walkaround bar, luxurious carpeting, curtains, upholstery in shades of blue-gray or persimmon, air conditioning, one of the most stylish bathrooms in Morocco, U.S.-based news broadcasts, and the kind of video movies you wanted to see back home but never did. Single rooms cost between

750 DH ($82.50) and 850 DH ($93.50); doubles, 850 DH ($93.50) and 1,000 DH ($110), with service and taxes included. For reservations and information within the U.S. call Hyatt's toll-free reservations number, 800/228-9000.

Hotel El Mansour, 27 Avenue de l'Armée Royale (tel. 31-21-12). Before the Casablanca Hyatt was built to usurp its position, this 1950s era hotel was regarded as the most desirable address in the city. Set near the heartbeat Place Mohammed V, it greets visitors with a high-ceilinged, lattice-accented lobby sheathed with stone and marble, a pair of octagonal reflecting pools within a glass-sided courtyard, and a plush covering of thick carpets and velvet-covered armchairs. Each of the 250 bedrooms has its own bath, air conditioning, radio, and TV. Singles cost 380 DH ($41.80); doubles, 450 DH ($49.50), plus breakfast. A fixed-price dinner in the main dining room is 110 DH ($12.10). A bar, a Moroccan specialty restaurant, a coffeeshop, a parking garage, and a sauna add additional diversions and attractions.

Less Expensive Choices

Hotel Riad Salam, Boulevard de la Corniche, at Aïn Diab (tel. 36-35-35). Set on the glamorous sea-fronting road of this prosperous suburb, this lovely hotel sits behind a mock fortified façade of white stucco and flowing water, before entering an extravaganza of Moorish carved filigree. You'll descend a teakwood staircase, past cascades of arabesques and tile work. The accommodations encircle a series of simulated lagoons, crossed with footbridges, and a huge circular fountain whose waters drip into an elliptical swimming pool. Each of the units has its own terrace or balcony, TV, mini-bar, radio, and private bathroom, and is furnished in the "casbah-boudoir" style. Singles cost 450 DH ($49.50), doubles 550 DH ($60.50). Fixed-price meals in the main dining room go for 165 DH ($18.15). The establishment has three other specialty restaurants for musical evenings of Moroccan song and dance.

Hotel Safir, 160 Avenue des F.A.R. (tel. 31-12-12), was designed as one of the most prominent skyscrapers in the city. Built in 1983, it has 16 floors of clean and attractive bedrooms, each of which offers a private bathroom, radio, alarm clock, color TV, soundproofing, and phone. Singles cost 430 DH ($47.30); doubles, 480 DH ($52.80). Inside you'll find a cool stone-trimmed lobby with a trio of tile Moroccan arches, in back of which pours a sheet of dripping water. There's a swimming pool on the third floor, massage facilities, a trio of restaurants, and two bars.

Hotel Les Almohades, Avenue Moulay Hassan ler (tel. 22-05-05), sits on one of the busiest streets of town, but its stippled façade is softened with a small cascade of water and a screen of banana and papyrus plants. A slickly modern entrance leads into the lobby, where a circle of low couches frames a view of a tile courtyard and a green-and-white reflecting pool. This very attractive hotel has 138 well-furnished bedrooms, each of which has its own mini-bar, TV, phone, and private bath. With breakfast included, singles cost 240 DH ($26.40), doubles 310 DH ($34.10). A pair of restaurants, one international, one very elegant Moroccan, offer dining options.

Hotel Toubkal, 9 rue Sidi Belyout (tel. 31-04-50). Its position near Place Mohammed V makes it a convenient choice, and its "Moroccanized" art deco style makes it almost irresistible. Behind a glamorous façade of black marble, Muslim-style slats and lattices, river-smoothed rocks, and lush planting, you'll find a lobby accented with ziggurat-shaped arches and double-reflecting mirrors. This hotel was built in 1971, and a renovation in the early 1980s transformed its public areas into something approaching high style. Each of the 66 sunny bedrooms has comfortable furniture, a private bath, TV, phone, and mini-bar. The quietest rooms overlook a rear garden filled with palms. With breakfast included, singles cost 230 DH ($25.30), doubles 310 DH ($34.10). There's a disco on the premises.

Transatlantique, 79 rue Colbert (tel. 61-62-63), is a substantial, rather old-fashioned, 57-room hotel, offering abundant facilities and conveniences. On a quiet and narrow street in the heart of the city, it lies about three blocks from the Medina and is near many airline agencies, as well as the bus terminal. The salon is very Moorish; and in summer a small garden is put to use. You can get a double room for 220 DH ($24.20), a single for 175 DH ($19.25).

Hotel Georges V, 1 rue Sidi Belyout (tel. 31-24-48), sits impudently across from one of the most glamorous hotels in Casablanca, the deluxe El Mansour. Yet the Georges V, built in the 1930s, maintains moderate prices. The small 35-room hotel is quite plain inside, with a "leather chair lobby," a two-passenger elevator, and painted furniture in the bedrooms. The most expensive rooms are the twins with bath, at 110 DH ($12.10). Singles with bath go for 95 DH ($10.45). Bathless doubles—hot and cold running water only—are 75 DH ($8.25).

Excelsior, 2 rue Nolly (tel. 26-22-81), has a "core of the apple" position, just off the Old Medina—right between the life there and the promenade on Casablanca's major boulevard. It was the first "grand hotel" in Casablanca, built in 1918. It is old-fashioned, with high ceilings and an art deco lobby, but it serves well. Depending on the plumbing, singles range in price from 55 DH ($6.05) to 95 DH ($10.45); doubles, from 75 DH ($8.25) to 110 DH ($12.10).

WHERE TO DINE: **Restaurant Valentino,** Casablanca Hyatt Regency Hotel, Place Mohammed V (tel. 22-41-67). This winning combination of high-tech architecture and flavorful Italian food draws an animated crowd from throughout Casablanca, many of whom consider an evening amid the dramatic architecture of the Hyatt Hotel to be entertainment of its own. You'll have to traverse the hotel's shopping arcade and climb a flight of stairs before a uniformed maître d' will seat you. Regardless of which table you select, you'll have the best view in town of the other diners because of the restaurant's placement in a series of balconies ringing a skylit atrium.

In many ways, it evokes the see-and-be-seen ambience of a 1930s nightclub, complete with palms and the kind of "Desert Sheik" decor which Valentino himself might have enjoyed. Banquettes are of white Naugahyde, the curved pastel-colored balustrades give a hint of art deco, and the tuxedo-clad waiters offer monochromatic touches of class. A theatrically arranged buffet of lavishly decorated desserts and another of colorful antipasti offer visual temptations as soon as you enter. You can order such specialties as tomato and mozzarella salad, eggplant parmigiana, good pasta including tagliatelle, spaghetti, and fettuccine prepared according to your taste, saffron-flavored risotto, sea bass with fennel, saltimbocca, and T-bone steaks. Full meals cost from 110 DH ($12.10) and are served every day at lunch and dinner. Full breakfasts with cappuccino are served every morning from 6 a.m. till 1 p.m., costing 50 DH ($5.50) to 70 DH ($7.70), depending on what you order.

Restaurant Wong Kung, Casablanca Hyatt Regency, Place Mohammed V (tel. 22-41-67). Other than an initial murmur of cross-cultural confusion, you'll quickly settle into the relaxed ambience of one of the most elegant Chinese restaurants in town. It's set behind pagoda-style columns near the Moorish dome in the lobby of the Hyatt Regency Hotel (see "Where to Stay"). You'll sit at lacquered tables in a quadrangle of four huge enamelled vases on teakwood pedestals. The sophisticated veteran of restaurants throughout Europe, maître d'hôtel Abdel Daif, will seat you near a lacquered screen, then take your order for such well-prepared specialties as won ton soup, corn-and-crabmeat chowder, Hunan-style beef, sweet-and-sour veal, cold soya-stuffed duckling, fried Cantonese ravioli, and many excellent seafood dishes. These include Szechuan shrimp, fresh lobster sautéed with black beans and chili, and fresh fish platters with Chinese vegetables. Fixed-price meals cost 160 DH ($17.60) to 200 DH ($22) and are served only at dinnertime, every day except Sunday. Because of this establishment's popularity with nonresidents of the hotel, reservations are suggested.

Restaurant La Cambuse, Boulevard de la Corniche (tel. 36-15-56) is considered one of the very best seafood restaurants along the coast. Its most popular, and perhaps its most animated, dining spot is within the ground-floor brasserie, where big windows illuminate the knotty paneling and crisply ironed napery. There's a more sedate upstairs dining room, with fewer tables, marine-inspired frescoes, and panoramic windows. For the greatest possible exposure to the elements, you can choose the rooftop terrace where a parasol might be your only protection from the glittering sea and the sparkling air.

Owner Achak Kacem makes himself personally responsible for the day's shopping, looking throughout the city's markets for the freshest fish. A particularly delicious house specialty is an original version of filet of John Dory au gratin, studded with shrimp and fresh mussels. Other dishes include veal kidneys with madeira, Norman-style sweetbreads, fondue bourguignonne, couscous royale, house-style stuffed mussels, scallops provençale, lobster thermidor, and, for dessert, bananas flambé. Full meals cost from 135 DH ($14.85), and are served every day at lunch and dinner.

Restaurant La Mer, Boulevard de la Corniche, Phare d'el Hank (tel. 36-33-15), is a chic, French-style seafood restaurant where you're likely to rub elbows with some of the most discerning diners in town. It's on a sunwashed seaside road, several miles from the most congested part of the city, within view of the tidal flats where neighborhood children sometimes search for shellfish. You'll pass through a lovely rock garden, whose incline gives you the impression of entering a grotto. Once inside, you'll be seated in one of a pair of lattice-decorated dining rooms filled with crisply ironed napery, exposed cedar, and huge windows overlooking the coastline. The nearby lighthouse of El Hank thrusts an illuminated version of a seaside minaret into the air. Menu specialties focus on fresh fish and shellfish, such as oysters marinara, grilled filet of sole, red mullet en papillote, John Dory au gratin, grilled seabass flambéed with fennel, a classic fish soup, and a changing array of daily specials. A limited number of meat dishes includes filet mignon with shallots, succulent lamb chops, and veal. Full meals cost from 200 DH ($22) and are served every day at lunch and dinner. Reservations are suggested.

Al Mounia, 95 rue du Prince Moulay Abdallah (tel. 22-26-69), is one of the finest Moroccan restaurants in Casablanca, yet it is reasonably priced. The air-conditioned setting is palace-like; outdoor tables are placed in the front garden in summer. Two sisters, Madame Berrada and Madame Laïdï, operate the restaurant in this century-old villa, which is entered through a filigree stone gate opening onto a courtyard. A pair of intensely ornate rooms open off the central corridor, with a painted ceiling and filigree work. The traditional opener to any Moroccan meal is the local soup harrira. Main-dish specialties include tajine with almonds, couscous, and pastilla. Moroccan pastries and mint tea round out your dining adventure, which will cost from 130 DH ($14.30).

If you're in the mood for Spanish food, then seek out **La Corrida,** 59 rue Gay-Lussac (tel. 27-81-55). The restaurant, set in a Spanish garden, is in the center of town. Go here in the evening when you dine under palm trees by candlelight in summer. House specialties include the paella and zarzuela de pescados, a savory fish stew. You can order a set dinner for about 120 DH ($13.20), including wine. The restaurant, owned by Solange Marmaneu, is open from 11 a.m. to 2 p.m. and 7 to 11 p.m.

Restaurant des Fleurs, 42 Avenue des F.A.R. (tel. 31-27-51). From its unpromising outside, it looks like a 1950s commercial building, but inside, it opens into an elegantly decorated multilevel dining emporium. You'll find it at the congested angle of two major avenues, near the El Mansour Hotel. There's a ground-floor restaurant with a menu and a decor which is a bit like a brasserie on the Grands Boulevards of Paris. This section remains open 24 hours a day for drinks and snacks, which include salads, plats du jour, and other pick-me-ups.

The allure of the place, however, isn't visible until you reach the second floor. There, you'll find two radically different, very elegant dining rooms. You can dine on low banquettes in one of the most elaborately tiled Moroccan settings in town. If you prefer a European ambience, there's a darkly paneled, spacious, French-style dining room with crisp napery and all the accoutrements of a restaurant in Paris. The waiters are flexible about offering the Moroccan menu in the European dining room and vice versa. In either section, you can enjoy sole with almonds, swordfish in a white wine sauce, red mullet en papillote, and an array of shellfish (including lobster) priced by the gram. The list of classic Moroccan dishes includes a pastilla of pigeon, couscous, chicken with almonds, and kebabs. A set meal costs 90 DH ($9.90), while à la carte goes for around 110 DH ($12.10).

CASABLANCA AFTER DARK: **Casablanca Bar,** Casablanca Hyatt Regency Hotel, Place Mohammed V (tel. 22-41-67). Its 1930s-style ceiling fans and Foreign Legion decor re-create the kind of setting where Humphrey Bogart might once again captivate Ingrid Bergman's heart. Its speakeasy-style entrance is near the reception desk of one of the most dramatic hotels in town (see "Where to Stay"), but much of its business seems to come from affluent residents of the city. It's a bit like an elegant version of a French-Moroccan desert outpost, with lots of exposed hardwood, a dark oak floor on which you can almost smell the imaginary sawdust, movie posters of Hollywood's romantic couple, and a beat-up piano waiting for Sam to play it again. A scotch and soda costs between 40 DH ($4.40) and 60 DH ($6.60), depending on which brand you order. Here's looking at you, kid.

ANFA AND AÎN DIAB: The most beautiful residences, heavily Europeanized, lie in the suburb of **Anfa.** This quarter, reached from the Place Mohammed V, along Hassan I Boulevard, was the site of the world-famous Anfa Hotel (torn down in 1973), the meeting place of Churchill, Roosevelt, and De Gaulle for the Casablanca Conference of World War II. The conference, in January of 1943, planned the invasion of Sicily, and here Roosevelt announced that "unconditional surrender" was demanded of the Axis powers.

The coast road to **Aîn Diab** passes the **Casablanca Aquarium,** Sidi Mohammed Ben Abdallah (tel. 27-60-88). Facing the sea, the aquarium shelters much evidence of Moroccan underwater life, both freshwater and saltwater species. Land and sea reptiles are exhibited here, as well as sea turtles and crocodiles. Admission is only 3 DH (33¢), money well spent. After a stopover here, you can head on out along the Corniche for a day at the beach.

Food and Lodging

Should you like to overnight or dine in this sector, I recommend the **Hotel Bellerive,** Boulevard la Corniche, Aîn Diab (tel. 36-71-92), fine during hot weather as it faces the ocean. It's on the outskirts of Casablanca, about a ten-minute drive from the heart of the city. Most bedrooms face the ocean and have

pal building than a hotel. One of its outlying poolside buildings housed soldiers during the French occupation of Morocco, but after their departure in 1956 the barracks were transformed into some of the most alluring accommodations in the hotel. Other units, each fronted with vines and flowers, ring a large courtyard, and in the center is a swimming pool and a modernized version of a Bedouin's tent. There's a cedar-paneled bar with large windows overlooking the bathers, and traditional, rather formal bedrooms in the main building. Each of these accommodations has dark paneling, big windows, and a renovated bathroom. Singles cost 200 DH ($22), doubles 260 DH ($28.60). Fixed-priced meals in the dining room go for 100 DH ($11).

Hotel Tafoukt, 58 Boulevard Mohammed V (tel. 2416). Translated from a Berber dialect, the name of this pleasant and friendly little hotel means "sun." In many ways, its 40 very clean bedrooms offer the best value in town, particularly since the management genuinely seems to welcome foreign visitors. Built in 1977, the hotel sits across the street from a promenade flanking the beach in a flower-dotted residential section of town. Its three-story green-and-white façade has concrete flowerboxes, wooden balustrades, and a sprinkling of private balconies. Each of the sun-flooded bedrooms has a private bath, phone, and simple modern furnishings. Singles cost 140 DH ($15.40); doubles, 175 DH ($19.25); and triples, 230 DH ($25.30), plus breakfast. Fixed-price meals in the inviting dining room go for 65 DH ($7.15). Don't overlook the ground-floor pair of Moroccan tea rooms, where elaborate geometric tilework contrasts attractively with the glossy tuya and lemonwood paneling of the other public rooms. The hotel is an excellent choice for the budgeteer.

WHERE TO EAT: For dining, everybody seems to head for **Chalet de la Plage,** Boulevard Mohammed V (tel. 21-58), a club-bistro across from the beach, which has good specialties—none finer than its shellfish and well-seasoned whitefish dishes that are the pride of the chef. Both the service and the food are excellent, a meal costing around 55 DH ($6.05).

However, the most adventurous readers will stroll along the quayside of the port, having a lunch of freshly grilled sardines straight from the sea. Many vendors there will be happy to oblige. Just follow your nose along this scent trail.

5. Agadir

The center of southern Morocco's resort area, Agadir overlooks five miles of white sands and sea where the climate permits swimming all year long. Along the Atlantic seaboard, the beach is said to offer the safest bathing on the coast. In winter and early spring, expect daytime temperatures in the mid-70s. Summer temperatures climb to around 85; however, that is mild compared to the caldron, Marrakesh. Agadir is protected by the rugged High Atlas mountain range to the north and the Anti-Atlas range to the south. Promoters of the resort claim that it has the most days of sunshine on an annual basis of any resort lying within a 3- to 3½-hour flight of the big cities of Europe. It is estimated that at least 350 days of the year are "suitable beach weather." Blatantly commercial, it is the Moroccan Miami Beach.

It has rapidly bounced back from the disastrous earthquake of February 1960, whose violence almost completely destroyed Agadir. The old districts were demolished by the sudden devastation, a tale vividly recounted by Robin Maugham, nephew of W. Somerset Maugham. Some 15,000 casualties were reported, and on the periphery of Agadir entire villages were wiped out.

But over the past 25 years the recovery has been so rapid that Agadir has quickly regained its position as the chief tourist center of south Morocco—not that it has much competition for that title. Windsurfing, sailing, and waterskiing are available. You'll also find such distractions as riding a camel through the rippling surf or skipping along the white sands at 50 miles per hour on the back of a speed sail.

Seismologists predict that the chances of another such earthquake occurring are slim indeed. New buildings incorporate antiseismic features. The earthquake did not entirely destroy the fishing port, which has been enlarged.

Some readers have found prices in the shops of Agadir higher than those charged at Marrakesh. Granted, the merchandise is often exquisite and much of it is geared to European and North American tastes. If you're planning day trips, hold off on serious purchases until you visit the *souks* of such places as Taroudannt, where items are much more reasonably priced. In Agadir you might want to visit the municipal market on Avenue Hassan II, a two-story mall filled with shops selling every item from kaftans to silver jewelry. The air is scented with such spices as cumin and coriander.

Because Agadir is so modern in appearance, one tends to forget that it has had a long and colorful history. That is, of course, because of its strategic location, at the crossroads between the Atlantic coast and the Atlas mountains, lying as it does at the mouth of the fertile Souss Valley. Until destroyed by that already mentioned earthquake, a large Casbah had crowned the highest point in Agadir since the 16th century. For centuries, this fortress protected Agadir from pirates and other invaders. Today you can visit the ramparts of the Casbah, which survived the earthquake, for a spectacular view of the coastline. However, as you view it, you are likely to be hassled by all sorts of peddlars and hustlers.

WHERE TO STAY: Agadir has one of the wealthiest concentrations of hotels in all price ranges of any place in North Africa. It is also very reasonable in price, and, when visiting the resort, the budget traveler may want to indulge in a bit of luxury and stay at more highly rated and starred hotels than would be possible in one of the famous beach resorts of America or Europe.

Club Agador-Tamlier, Secteur Balnéaire (tel. 20078). Its sprawling array of facilities makes this one of the most complex and all-encompassing resort facilities at Agadir. It originated in the early 1980s when the Residence Tamlier was built as a casbah-style collection of studio apartments with kitchenettes. Since 1986, when the adjacent construction of the modern Club Agador more than tripled the size of the original hotel, the accommodations within the older section became the least expensive within the complex. In many ways, however, I prefer them to their younger sisters.

The older complex is designed like an updated and glamorized version of a Moroccan ghetto, within a labyrinth of stairwells, plant-lined walkways, and courtyards. Each accommodation has its own hidden terrace, thick walls, rustic furniture, and a small kitchenette. With breakfast included, these units cost 220 DH ($24.20) for a one-bedroom apartment, 275 DH ($30.25) for a two-bedroom apartment. Clients in this original section have full access to the resort's newer facilities. These include a cluster of swimming pools landscaped between rolling hillocks, scattered bars with palm-frond roofs, a handful of unusual restaurants, and a burgeoning nightlife. From an island in the center of the biggest pool, palms and vines create a feeling of a tropical lagoon.

Accommodations in the newer section are arranged around a series of courtyards, each of which has such traditional Moroccan touches as splashing fountains, high arcades, and banks of flowers. Concealed behind cedar doors, each room has stylish renditions of Moroccan furniture, slick tiles, and glossy accessories. None of the newer units has a kitchenette, however. With half board included, singles cost 350 DH ($38.50), doubles, 550 DH ($60.50).

Residents have a wide choice of dining options, including an à la carte restaurant raised on wooden stilts somewhat like a Moorish adaptation of a Japanese tea house. Added together, there are more than 500 accommodations in the two sections of this place, plus a huge array of planned activities.

Hotel Europa Maroc, Boulevard du 20 Août (tel. 21212). The architect of this coolly tiled hotel designed its pool, its courtyards, its lobby, and many of its public rooms in a series of hexagons. Behind its stylishly streamlined façade lies a dark blue lobby, a rock garden with vines, a dining room with folkloric entertainment (such as snake charmers and native dancers), and 240 well-furnished and comfortable bedrooms, each with air conditioning. Each of the units also has a balcony, usually with a view of the pool and the surrounding lawns, as well as a private bath. With breakfast included, singles cost 340 DH ($37.40); doubles, 420 DH ($46.20). Fixed-price meals in the dining room go for 90 DH ($9.90).

Hotel Argana, Boîte Postale 93 (tel. 22070). Set on the stylish Boulevard Mohammed V, this pleasant hotel has a façade strongly marked by deeply recessed white balconies. Some of its 174 bedrooms are arranged around a sun-flooded atrium filled with planting. Others overlook either the sea or the hotel's circular swimming pool. Each accommodation contains its own bathroom, plant-lined balcony, built-in furniture, and Moroccan carpet. Constructed in the mid-1970s, the hotel charges 220 DH ($24.20) in a single, 275 DH ($30.25) in a double. On the premises is a darkly Oriental plush bar, a restaurant, and an English-speaking staff.

Club Hotel Tagadirt, Boulevard du 20 Août (tel. 23355). Blue-and-white lattices, climbing roses, and trees cover parts of the many buildings that compose what looks like a well-maintained Moroccan village. It was built along a steep hillside in a central part of town. Contained within these scattered and verdant outbuildings, the comfortably airy accommodations cost 240 DH ($26.40) in a single, 370 DH ($40.70) in a double, with half board included. The clubhouse of this establishment is appealing, dotted with lattices, chastened brasswork, plants, comfortable sofas, and brass chandeliers. The semi-concealed swimming pool is ringed with plants, flowers, and dazzling sunshine. Fixed-price meals in the dining room go for 70 DH ($7.70) each.

Hotel Marhaba, Avenue Hassan II (tel. 2670). Built in 1968, this was one of the first hotels reconstructed after Agadir's devastating earthquake. In many ways, it was able to grab one of the resort's choicest locations, only a short walk down a flower-dotted hillside to one of the best beaches in town. It has lovely gardens, filled with mature palms and cactus, whose spiney branches are reflected in the sapphire waters of a 12-sided swimming pool. Each of the 75 clean and airy bedrooms has a private bath, phone, and radio, and all but a few contain a private balcony overlooking the pool or sea. Singles cost 215 DH ($23.65); doubles, 275 DH ($30.25). Fixed-price meals in the dining room are 85 DH ($9.35).

Hotel Mabrouk, Avenue du 20 Août (tel. 22606), stands on one of the city's most prestigious avenues near much more expensive hotels. Its prices are as low as something you might find in an unpretentious corner of the Casbah, however. It sits behind a brick-and-iron fence and a stretch of lawn. A cluster of rubber trees softens the boxy angles of its balconied façade. Each of the 41 bedrooms contains a private bath and a phone. The hotel was built in 1966, and many pieces of its original furniture still remain. Singles cost 145 DH ($15.95); doubles, 170 DH ($18.70). There's a pool on the premises.

Hotel Royal, Boulevard Mohammed V (tel. 22475), was built in 1970 and tastefully renovated in 1982. My favorite accommodations are the roughly textured bungalows with vine-covered entrances amid the verdant labyrinth of the gardens. Four gardeners keep the grounds immaculate. Many other visitors prefer the airily modern decor of the accommodations in the main building. A swimming pool sits near emerald lawns where clusters of rocks appear at scattered intervals near banks of bougainvillea. One of the hotel's most romantic hideaways is the intimate bar where a Moorish fountain drips water into a marble basin. There's a rooftop terrace with a panoramic view of Agadir and a sun-flooded restaurant with big windows and a high ceiling. The 73 comfortable accommodations each contain a private bath, plus a balcony or terrace. Bungalows and rooms cost 140 DH ($15.40) in a single, 170 DH ($18.70) in a double. Fixed-price meals go for 70 DH ($7.70) each.

Hotel Atlas, Boulevard Mohammed V (tel. 23232). Among the dozens of hotels in Agadir, this pleasant establishment is perhaps a bit better managed and more imaginatively furnished than many of its competitors. Its modernized Moroccan decor was installed when the hotel was built in 1970. It sits at the edge of town, rising high above the wide boulevard flanking it. The hotel contains 156 bedrooms with private bath, a stylishly contemporary earth-tone decor, and a balcony. Singles cost 240 DH ($26.40), doubles 340 DH ($37.40). Many residents prefer one of the 40 bungalows sitting on terraced gardens along the hillside below. There's a swimming pool surrounded by a lawn and festoons of flowering vines strung out on arbors above the entrance to the bungalows. Fixed-price meals in one of the hotel's two restaurants are 90 DH ($9.90) each.

WHERE TO EAT: **Le Doyen,** Boulevard Mohammed V (tel. 22153), is considered one of the best restaurants in town, with a chic decor of pink velour, gilded brass, and art deco accessories. A sweeping wall of glass overlooks the faraway water. The elaborate table settings are arranged so that most seats have a view of the live bands who play from 7 to midnight every night of the week except Sunday. A small dance floor, raised on a dais, attracts anyone who's interested, and a secluded outdoor terrace offers extra seating. A charming and well-trained staff serves meals costing from 100 DH ($11). Dishes include both fish and meat, including pepper steak, Valencian paella, a tajine du jour, grilled sole, fried squid, grilled sea bass with fennel, lamb flavored with thyme, and a dessert soufflé flavored with Grand Marnier. The restaurant is open from 10 a.m. to midnight daily.

Jazz Restaurant, Boulevard du 20 Août (tel. 20208), is one of the best restaurants that stretch along this tourist-oriented boulevard. In the Complexe Igoudar, it has a nautical decor and imaginatively arranged pink napery. Guests can dine inside or else out on a big outdoor terrace. The uniformed staff is charming and polite and will guide you through a menu likely to include Jazz tenderloin steak, various brochettes, and fresh fish dishes. You might begin with a fish or shellfish soup, finishing your meal, costing from 100 DH ($11), with a soufflé Grand Marnier.

Restaurant Chateaubriand, 12 Complexe Tamlait (tel. 21673), is set within a well-designed mini-village of restaurants, boutiques, and bars. This is considered one of the best dining spots in town, offering an elaborate, high-ceilinged pair of dining rooms, each richly paneled with two varieties of hardwoods. Its ambience is one of the most intimate in Agadir, particularly when the candlelit tables in the tree-dotted square outside cast a romantic glow through the picture windows. A handful of tables sit under a bamboo-roofed arcade outside. A friendly staff serves meals costing 100 DH ($11). Dishes include fish soup, shrimp au gratin, ravioli, house-style Chateaubriand, pepper steak, grilled filet of sole, and lasagne. The Moroccan specialties include four kinds of tajine, couscous, and an array of well-seasoned grills. Regardless of the cuisine you order, you can top it off with bananas flambé.

Le Grill du Soleil, Résidence Club la Kasbah, Boulevard Mohammed V (tel. 23636). Technically, it's connected to one of the city's resort hotels, but since it sits directly on a busy boulevard its warmly rustic decor attracts dozens of independent diners. You can eat on the front terrace under a parasol or in the earth-toned interior. The walls are accented with bas-relief sculpture in terracotta of desert animals. Full meals cost from 100 DH ($11) à la carte or 80 DH ($8.80) on the daily fixed-price menu. You can enjoy filet mignon of pork with an essence of thyme, fish soup, three kinds of salads, a brochette of monkfish, several different pizzas, squid, and seven different preparations of beef. The pork, the vegetables, the rabbits, ducks, and geese served here are strictly fresh, coming from a farm a few miles outside of town. The restaurant is open daily except Tuesday.

On Agadir Beach, **Jour et Nuit** (tel. 224-48) lives up to the promise of its name. It's a grill room and snackbar open all day and night, attracting a lively crowd that seems to grow more exotic the later the hour. Snacks are from 22 DH ($2.42).

THE ANTI-ATLAS

If you have a taste for the exotic, often eerie landscape, then a trek through the Anti-Atlas Mountains to the southwest of Agadir will prove a rewarding excursion. New and improved hotels, attracting an international clientele, have eased some of the burdens travelers of yore reported. The Anti-Atlas lie on the doorway of the vast Sahara, from which the famous "Blue Men" emerge to trade in such villages as Tiznit and Goulimine.

Roads have been upgraded by the Moroccan government. Several travel agencies in Agadir run excursions in air-conditioned motorcoaches to these points. More adventurous readers can strike out in a Landrover with a Berber tent.

The Anti-Atlas are a mountainous barrier that shields the Souss from the dry winds of the blistering Sahara. The Souss form a near rectangle. Agadir, Taroudannt, Tafraoute, and Tiznit are the four points, and for others the desert outpost of Goulimine is also a lure.

However, a severe warning must be issued. If you venture into the Anti-Atlas in summer, especially July, you'd better be able to take the heat.

6. Taroudannt

This very old place is a town of stone carvers, and it's encircled by tawny, well-preserved, thick battlements and bastions. In 1520 it was the capital of the Saadian dynasty. Outside the crenellated walls are beautiful gardens and olive groves in a sun-bathed landscape. You can reach Taroudannt by daily bus service from Agadir, 50 miles away. The trip goes through the fertile Souss Valley.

A tour of the walls is most popular. Frankly, I prefer it under moonlight, although others like to get up at sunrise for a trek. The journey is a distance of three miles. Later, you can visit the souks, as Taroudannt is famous for its craftspeople. Daggers, richly ornamented rifles, Berber jewelry, carpets, and hundreds of trinkets are for sale. The souks of local handcrafts are in the center of town.

FOOD AND LODGING: **La Gazelle d'Or** (tel. 2039). Acceptable by European standards but stratospheric by Moroccan prices, the tariffs charged by this world-famous hotel place it into the super-splurge category. Still, because of its beauty, some readers will consider it well worth the price of 925 DH ($101.75) in a single and 1,350 DH ($148.50) in a double, with half board included.

The fertile land it sits on was bought in 1938 by the French-born Baron von

Pellenc, who dreamed of building a vacation paradise for himself and a handful of occasional visitors. His marriage a few years later to an American millionairess and artist enabled him to establish huge tracts of orange groves, set up the most beautiful gardens in the region, and to build the stone-walled structures you'll see today. Most of these date from the 1950s and are filled with the kinds of exotic artifacts and paintings that at the time created a legend in the glamorous salons of Europe and America. David Rockefeller referred to it as "one of the loveliest inns we know anywhere." Ronald Reagan visited when he was governor of California, and Prince Bernhard and Queen Juliana of the Netherlands came once to visit, as did Barbara Hutton (who stayed for weeks). Even the Queen of England has "dropped in."

The accommodations are contained within 30 one-story bungalows with walls and terraces entwined with lavish vines and flowers. Each contains a stylishly Moroccan decor, full bathroom, mini-bar, and a fireplace. There are two tennis courts, spring-fed cascades of water rambling beside exotic European and African trees, a sapphire-colored swimming pool with lunchtime buffets, and dozens of meandering pathways flanked with roses. The main clubhouse has an elegantly exotic dining room, the kind of bar where guests enjoy seeing and being seen, and a Moroccan-inspired zodiacal chart set in mosaics into the floor of one of the salons. Since 1981, a group of Moroccan investors has poured more than $2 million into its decor and gardens. The hotel is closed between July 20 and September 1, the hottest part of the summer.

Hotel Palais Salam (tel. 2501). The core of this exotic hotel sits within the 18th-century walls of a Moorish palace, the foundation of which skirts the inner walls of the town's medieval fortifications. It became a hotel in the 1940s and ever since has offered hints of pasha-style grandeur to residents of its 97 rooms. You register in a lavishly tiled reception area where a wall fountain splashes into a marble basin. The newer accommodations are scattered in bungalows along pathways draped with vines, flowers, and trees. The older accommodations, those which originally formed part of the palace, ring themselves around a handful of very old courtyards where symmetrical pathways converge at Moorish fountains amid a small grove of banana trees. All but the oldest rooms contain air conditioning; however, their high ceilings compensate a bit for the sometimes oppressive heat. Each accommodation has a private bath, phone, and radio. With half board included, singles cost 340 DH ($37.40) and doubles are priced at 525 DH ($57.75).

On the premises are two lavishly decorated Moroccan restaurants, a less dramatic restaurant serving international food, a bar/salon covered with some of the most elaborate tilework in town, and a friendly and cooperative staff which includes ten gardeners. Within the shadow of the crenellated defenses which flank part of the gardens, a colony of arrogant peacocks shrieks and squawks near the arabesque curves of the swimming pool.

Hotel Saadien (tel. 2589). This attractive hotel is inside the Medina, standing to the side of a dusty street barely wide enough for two cars. Built in 1980, it contains 56 pleasantly simple rooms filled with Bedouin-inspired furniture and at least one Moroccan carpet. Throughout, the hotel is clean, serviceable, and attractive. The otherwise modern reception lobby is capped with an intricate filigree ceiling and sheathed in cedar. No alcohol is ever served in the Moroccan tea room upstairs. Berber artifacts and chastened brasswork are clustered throughout many of the public rooms. There's a panoramic lounge for breakfast on the rooftop, with plants, big windows, and a terrace open to the brilliant sky and a view of the rooftops of the Medina. Open all year, the hotel charges 50 DH ($5.50) to 100 DH ($11) in a single, 60 DH ($6.60) to 120 DH ($13.20) in a double, depending on the plumbing. The more expensive rooms contain a clean tile bathroom.

Hotel Taroudannt, Place Assarag (tel. 2416), is lusher, more verdant, and more exotic than you might have imagined from seeing only its unpretentious exterior. It's also the bargain of town, sitting at the side of the main square just at the edge of the labyrinth of streets intersecting the Medina. You'll register at a bar whose 1930s Foreign Legion decor sits closest to the entrance. An employee will usher you through a pleasant restaurant lined with dozens of oil paintings, through a Moroccan sitting room with tile walls, and into a beautiful courtyard. The entrances to the 20 very simple and most basic accommodations are set beneath arcades flanking the edges of the garden. Plumbing varies widely, but is very complete in the more expensive accommodations. Each room is decorated in a pleasantly exotic combination of Bedouin artifacts and textiles. None has air conditioning. Singles or doubles begin at 45 DH ($4.95), rising to 85 DH ($9.35) for the more expensive units. Fixed-price meals cost from 52 DH ($5.72) in the dining room.

SHOPPING IN THE MEDINA: Magazin Lichir, 36 Souk Smata (tel. 2145). There are dozens of shops throughout the Medinas of most Moroccan cities, but this one is so unusual that it deserves special mention. It's set within the labyrinth of the most exotic part of the souk, surrounded by spice vendors and coffee merchants. Its two floors of merchandise contain genuinely antique jewelry, intricately woven carpets, and furniture in a profusion rarely matched by other dealers. There's also a valuable collection of 18th- and 19th-century Moroccan arms and pistols which any collector would be proud to display. It's perhaps the establishment's Bedouin carpets that attract the most attention. The owner is a polite Moroccan man who traverses the desert on seasonal buying trips, obtaining brilliantly colored primitive carpets which often look stunning in Western homes. Lahoucine Lichir will, without undue pressure, unfold dozens of carpets until you see something that strikes your fancy. Good natured negotiations are welcomed.

7. Tafraout

From Tiznit to Tafrout, a fair road cuts through 69 miles of striking countryside of mammoth boulders and Anti-Atlas valleys to reach this town of jumbled rocks, lying under a ring of red boulders and granite cliffs. The highest point along the road is the Kerdous Pass at 3,600 feet. At Tafraout, the houses almost seem to huddle among the rocks, as they look out toward the Valley of the Cyclops. If you came here seeking an exotic landscape, you will surely have found it. Palms and gardens soften the austerity, and at almond-blossom time in mid-February, the countryside is as stunning as Portugal's Algarve Coast. From Agadir an alternate way to reach Tafraout is not via Tiznit, but along the S509 by way of Blougra and Ait-Baha. Here you'll cut through some of the most beautiful valleys of the Anti-Atlas along a highway that is treacherous in points and therefore recommended only to skilled drivers. The best time to visit is on Wednesday, the market day.

Some of the pink casbahs of Tafraout perch on spurs of rock or cling tenaciously to the walls of the cliff. Their façades are often painted with unusual designs in ochre or white.

For a stopover or a meal, there's the **Hotel Les Amandiers** (tel. 8). Its position atop a hill, and its fortified design of pink crenellations and very thick walls, make it the most prominent building in town. It was constructed in 1920 outside the commercial center and later enlarged in 1960. There's a swimming pool but it may not necessarily be filled unless you arrive in the peak of midsummer. Some of the older rooms, the ones with the highest ceilings, are arranged around an interior courtyard with an octagonal fountain. The public salons contain dozens of deep armchairs, filigree ceilings, and lots of unused space. The hotel's electricity is generated on the premises, so the electricity is sometimes deliberately shut off during certain hours of the day. The plumbing varies from room to room. Singles cost 100 DH ($11) to 155 DH ($17.05); doubles, 125 DH ($13.75) to 200 DH ($22), plus breakfast. Fixed-price meals in the slightly faded dining room go for 70 DH ($7.70).

8. Tiznit

Enclosed by towered walls, Tiznit is a charming sight. Its walls, four miles long, are red-washed, and machicolated gates lead to squares. Palm trees pierce the sky, and its garden oases sometimes attract the nomadic "Blue People" of the desert. In other words, Tiznit is something of a stage setting, except it is for real. Tiznit seems like a bit of greenery, surrounded by a vast expanse of sand.

On the road directly south from Agadir, Tiznit used to be a stopover point for excursionists heading for Goulimine. That desert outpost now has suitable accommodations itself (see below).

Founded in 1882, Tiznit lies some ten miles from the coast. Copper and silver-chased daggers are made and sold here. In addition, much interesting Berber jewelry of engraved silver is made here by craftspeople. A guide will be only too happy to show you through the souk of jewelers.

The town's accommodations range from fair to poor.

The best in town, **Hotel Tiznit** (tel. 2411), a three-star hotel, is set at the edge of the city near a commercial crossroads within sight of the old fortified city. It contains 40 comfortable bedrooms, each with big windows and its own bath and phone. Singles rent for 145 DH ($15.95), doubles for 175 DH ($19.25). You pass beneath the Moorish arch of the hotel's entrance before registering within sight of a pleasant courtyard. There's a swimming pool on the premises, banks of oleander, and a large and sunny restaurant one floor above ground level, serving meals for 70 DH ($7.70). The staff tends to be friendly, working hard to make visitors comfortable.

9. Goulimine

This westerly oasis could be a backdrop for *Lawrence of Arabia.* It's possible to reach it by a decent highway south from Agadir, but the run is 125 miles. It is known as a port, but only for camels, as it's surrounded by a sea of sand.

Goulimine today is a dull, desert outpost. Its once-famous camel market is, as of this writing, mainly abandoned because of the war between Morocco and the Polisario guerrillas. However, the town is still famous for its so-called Blue People, who are actually nomads who wander the desert in their indigo cloaks. They emerge from the vast desert to enjoy a rest stop at Goulimine, then seem to disappear again into the vastness of the sandy sea. Many know the route all the way to Timbuctu.

You can see the Blue People in the evening at one of their camps, eating black date bread. Sometimes, usually Saturday or Sunday, you can watch the Guedra ritual, a provocative dance, almost erotic, by the campfire. The female dancer performs on her knees, and is almost entirely concealed by a midnight-blue robe. To guttural chants that sound like a heartbeat, she dances a spellbinding rhythm. The dancer's hands are most expressive, filled with gestures created and passed down by dancers through centuries. The intensity of the earthenware drums echoes through the camp. However, this dance seems to be staged mainly for tourists.

The place can be a caldron in summer, with temperatures climbing up to 120° Fahrenheit. Water can get very scarce here.

The market begins at dawn on Saturday morning, as djellaba-clad Chleuh Berbers mix with nomadic camel drivers, each trying to work the best deal.

The best hotel in this desert outpost is **Hotel Salam,** Avenue Youssef Techfne (tel. 2057), built in 1968. The tiles of its blue-and-yellow façade are set on a dusty and crowded commercial street in the center of town. Its 20 rooms are arranged around a central enclosed courtyard one floor above the reception area. The walls of the stairways are covered with hand-painted frescoes of desert warriors and with lush vines and leaves, adding touches of interest to the thick concrete construction. Each room has a bath, phone, and simple furniture. Singles cost 145 DH ($15.95); doubles, 175 DH ($19.25). Fixed-price meals in the Moroccan restaurant go for 65 DH ($7.15) each. There's a sun-flooded terrace on the top floor with a view of the city.

Chapter XXI

MARRAKESH AND THE DEEP SOUTH

1. Marrakesh
2. One-Day Excursions from Marrakesh
3. Ouarzazate
4. Zagora
5. El Kelaa des M'Gouna
6. Boumalne-Dades
7. Tinerhir
8. Er Rachidia
9. Erfoud

MARRAKESH IS DEFINITELY the star of this chapter, but this ancient caravan city, a fabulous place of gardens and palaces, in a larger sense belongs to the Sahara. It sits poised on the gateway of an adventure rarely enjoyed by the average North American visitor. So, if you can afford the time, it would be good to see not only **Marrakesh** itself, but to go exploring in the High Atlas and take the "route of the casbahs" across the wilderness, finding oases as you go along the trail.

After one-day trips to some exciting targets on the doorstep of Marrakesh, you can take a five-hour drive over the High Atlas to **Ouarzazate.** This old town lies at the crossroads of four major traffic patterns: the desert road to Agadir, the Tizi-n'Tichka Pass, the Draa Valley, and the Dades Valley.

After exploring Ouarzazate, you can head east to a land rich in folklore and scenery and filled with villages that offer examples of Saharan-style architecture. These mud-red houses look even redder under clear skies of piercing blue.

Ouarzazate stands on the threshold of the Sahara. In your journey through the Deep South of Morocco, with the desert outpost of **Erfoud** as your final destination, you'll go along a vast desert plateau which is then relieved by casbahs and oases with welcoming palm groves. As you make your way along the valley of the casbahs, you'll be taking the same route that the ancients did in their caravans from black Africa. They brought gold, slaves, and exotic spices—that is, if they didn't lose them to the raiders of the desert.

Of course, once they reached the safety of the casbahs, these traders were offered lavish food and sensuous dances by the light of great open fires. The hammering of bendir drums cut through the night.

As you explore this most fascinating of regions, you'll hear that each new day is a gift from Allah.

1. Marrakesh

The red city of Marrakesh is a palm-treed oasis at the threshold of the Sahara. Second oldest of the imperial cities, Marrakesh (famed for its red ochre color) was founded by the Almoravids in the 11th century. Legend has it that Marrakesh grew from a crossroads on caravan trails, a site besieged by a tribe from beyond the Atlas Mountains whose food supplies contained many dates. During the siege, so many years passed and so many date pits were trodden into the sand that a palm grove sprang up in time to make the place an attractive spot in which the Saharan nomad Almoravids could settle down. During its rich history, this city has seen dynasties and fortunes come and go. It was already a handsome city when its great sultan, Yacoub El Mansour, made a military expedition to Muslim Spain to shore up the Arab rule there, with the result that many intellectuals from Andalusia came to the Marrakesh court, including philosophers and writers, as exemplified by the famous Andalusian thinker, Doctor Averroes.

After a few centuries of decline following this greatness, the city again came into the spotlight when the Saadians arrived from Arabia, amassing great wealth and defeating efforts of the Portuguese to annex parts of Morocco. By the late 19th century, the whole country now known as the Kingdom of Morocco was called the Kingdom of Marrakesh by Europeans. The name Morocco was derived from the city's name. Today it is the capital of southern Morocco, and as such is a jewel of the Islamic world. Its chief monument is its Koutoubia Mosque, built by the Almohads with a characteristic minaret that dominates the cityscape.

Some have called Marrakesh the most mysterious town in all of Africa. Here you'll be far removed from the Mediterranean—Tangier and Casablanca may look toward Europe, but Marrakesh is deeply rooted in Africa.

It is at its best in winter, when snow covers the peaks of the Atlas Mountains in the background. For years it was known as a winter playground of the rich (Winston Churchill used to be a frequent visitor, spending many hours painting the date palms and mountains). In winter the temperature averages around 68° Fahrenheit, but in July and August, midday temperatures of 110° are frequent. Of course, the heat is dry, and the high temperatures seemingly don't deter the huge influx of visitors during the summer. Winter remains the best time to visit.

GETTING THERE: Royal Air Maroc and British Airways fly from London, and both Royal Air Maroc and Air France leave from Paris several times weekly. If you're visiting Gibraltar, you can fly BA to Marrakesh. Royal Air Inter Lines connects Marrakesh to most major Moroccan towns; and the air-conditioned Moroccan railways maintain daily service from Casablanca, 150 miles away. The least expensive but most uncomfortable way is to go by bus, which connects Marrakesh with Tangier, Fez, Rabat, and Casablanca.

WHERE TO STAY: Marrakesh offers some of the best hotel bargains in North Africa. Many of the hotels are new, complete with air conditioning and swimming pools. If you're willing to settle for fewer extras, you can live quite reasonably at a good standard in Marrakesh.

Some Upper-Bracket Choices

Hotel Es Saadi, Avenue Quadissia (tel. 488-11), built in 1966, is a high-rise, action-oriented hotel with a glittering theme somewhat like what you'd find in Las Vegas. It contains one of Morocco's two casinos, a vibrantly active poolside patio, a high-ceilinged sun-flooded lobby where masses of people always seem to be checking in or out, and 150 comfortably modern bedrooms. Each of these accommodations has TV, a refrigerated bar, radio, balcony, private bathroom, and air conditioning. Singles cost 340 DH ($37.40), doubles, 410 DH ($45.10). Fixed-price meals go for 160 DH ($17.60). The hotel sits in a Europeanized neighborhood of Marrakesh amid a flowering garden, the focal point of which is the ever-popular pool (its central island boasts a palm). A sauna, an exercise room, massage facilities, a hair dressing salon, an outdoor snack bar for poolside lunches, and tennis courts complete the facilities.

Hotel Palais El Badia, Avenue de la Ménara (tel. 330-77). Originally built as a Holiday Inn, and later purchased by a Moroccan hotel group, this modern facility was designed around a chain-hotel formula but softened with regional accessories. It's set in what used to be an open field at the edge of town in a neighborhood where clusters of other vacation-oriented hotels have sprung up to profit from the desert sunshine. You'll enter a lobby filled with an elaborately carved wooden ceiling and dozens of red wool carpets. Rooms sprawl around a U-shape courtyard in the center of which a tree-dotted lawn encompasses a hexagonal swimming pool. Each of the 300 comfortably international bedrooms contains air conditioning, phone, and radio. Singles cost 280 DH ($30.80); doubles, 340 DH ($37.40). Fixed-price meals go for 100 DH ($11). On the premises are two Moroccan restaurants, an international dining room, a bar with folkloric singing and dancing, tennis courts, and access to golf and horseback riding facilities.

Moderately Priced Hotels

Hotel Les Almoravides, Arset Djenan Lakhdar (tel. 251-42), gets a four-star A rating from the government. It was built in 1972. It has its own garden and swimming pool, with pert umbrella tables where you can order poolside refreshments. More than half of the 100 modern, streamlined bedrooms overlook this garden, and also have a view of the minarets (you'll hear the wailing prayers five times a day). All of the units are air-conditioned, and have a dressing room and full bath. Sliding glass doors open onto private balconies. Single travelers pay 220 DH ($24.20); couples, 265 DH ($29.15). The general atmosphere is plush, and you'll find an American bar which emphasizes comfort and style.

PLM N'Fis Hotel, Avenue de France (tel. 487-72). Designed like something you might find in a Spanish-speaking island in the Caribbean, the desert-colored stucco façade of this establishment towers above virtually every other hotel nearby. It's in a residential suburb, amid a handful of other resort-style hotels. The visual focus of the glamorous lobby is a huge star-shaped fountain sheathed in emerald-green tiles. A harem-style skylight illuminates the Moroccan carpets, brass tables, and the otherwise modern design. In back, you'll find a brilliantly landscaped pool area ringed with multi-level terraces, bars, intricate tilework, and scantily dressed Europeans. This is a hotel where there are many planned activities. The Dahlia nightclub has ringaround leather-covered banquettes. Its very French clientele appreciates the pair of restaurants, the bar, and the 284 bedrooms contained within a trio of outlying buildings. Each of these has its own phone and private balcony. Singles cost 270 DH ($29.70); doubles, 370 DH ($40.70). Fixed-price meals go for 95 DH ($10.45). The hotel's confusing and hard-to-pronounce name is derived from a Moroccan river.

Chems, Avenue Homane el Fetouaki (tel. 348-13), is in a newer section of town, yet within an easy walk of the Medina and Djemaa El Fna. When you swim in the magnificent pool of the hotel garden, you can see the towers of the Koutoubia. This 140-room hotel with eight bungalows was built in 1972 amid a grove of orange trees. For such good accommodations, the rates are low: 220 DH ($24.20) in a double with either private bath or shower, 185 DH ($20.35) in a single. Rates include taxes and service. Popular and enjoyable are the cocktail lounge, the garden, the solarium, and a disco.

Hotel Le Marrakesh, Place de la Liberté (tel. 343-51). The design of this modern hotel was heavily influenced by traditional Moroccan themes. Its busy interior contains a pair of covered oval atriums, lots of exposed paneling, and dozens of carpets. It welcomes many members of French and German tour groups who transform the terrace ringing the outdoor pool into one of the busiest social centers in town. The hotel boasts a lush collection of paintings, dozens of organized activities, and some 350 pleasant bedrooms, each containing air conditioning, a private bathroom, and a phone. With half board included, singles cost 325 DH ($35.75) and doubles cost 500 DH ($55) per day.

Hotel Toubkal, rue Haroun Er Rachid (tel. 329-72). Partly because of the roses which surround it, this is one of my favorite hotels in Marrakesh. It's set in a quietly isolated position in a residential neighborhood filled with manicured gardens and flower-dotted lawns. The hotel's salmon-colored stucco exterior has evergreens and lush rubber trees which almost conceal it from view. Inside, low-slung couches provide comfortable seats in a high-ceilinged, warmly masculine bar with big windows overlooking the gardens, the pool, the lawns, and the dozens of scantily clad sunbathers. The hotel has a disco on the premises with live music and a circular dance floor, a second-floor restaurant (El Minzah, reviewed separately), tennis courts, and an impeccably uniformed staff.

The 120 breezy and comfortable accommodations are in five-story wings flanking two edges of the garden. Each has air conditioning and a private bathroom. Singles cost 220 DH ($24.20); doubles, 275 DH ($30.25); and triples, 340 DH ($37.40). Fixed-price meals cost from 85 DH ($9.35) each.

Hotel Safir Siaha, Avenue du Président Kennedy (tel. 342-52). Its salmon-colored façade sits within nine acres of manicured gardens with pines and tile-covered pathways that give the grounds an almost Biblical aura. Its sprawling interior lobby has modernized Moroccan designs set into the elaborate tilework, walls of glass, and access to a landscaped swimming pool ringed with tables, bougainvillea blossoms, drinking facilities, and bikini-clad bathers. The almost 200 bedrooms line upstairs hallways filled with Moroccan carved trunks and Bedouin artifacts. Rooms contain updated versions of desert-style frescoes, plush upholstery, a full bathroom, a balcony, a cozy corner salon, radio, and TV. Suites have provocatively positioned windows that allow views from the bedroom into the bath area for anyone who's interested in the theatrical value of an occupied bathtub. Singles cost 220 DH ($24.20), doubles are priced at 275 DH ($30.25).

Hotel Tafilalet, Avenue de Casablanca (tel. 345-18), considered one of the best small hotels in town, sits behind a barricade of semi-tropical plants along an outlying road filled with bigger, and sometimes less desirable, hotels. It has a low-slung façade covered with vines, a spacious lobby sheathed with honey-colored slabs of marble, and airy comfort enhanced by the courtyards. The gardens surrounding the swimming pool are among the best maintained in town. They're laid out in brilliant banks of roses, pansies, petunias, geraniums, and phlox, each segregated by color, each lining the edges of palm-fringed walkways.

The 84 accommodations are clustered into a handful of Navaho-style buildings with log detailing and thick walls—a study in artful rusticity. Each room has its own spacious tile bathroom, a balcony or terrace, air conditioning, radio, and phone. Singles cost 215 DH ($23.65), doubles go for 275 DH ($30.25). A third person sharing a double pays a supplement of 65 DH ($7.15). Fixed-price meals cost 100 DH ($11). The Le Rissania Restaurant offers flavorful meals, accompanied in the evening by folkloric song and dance. The hotel is named after the region of Morocco where King Hassan II was born.

El Andalous, Avenue du Président Kennedy (tel. 48-226). The decor of this pleasant establishment celebrates the era when all of southern Spain was a Moorish dominion. It's set at the edge of a wide boulevard within walking distance of the medieval ramparts. Its buff-colored façade could easily have been designed by a Spaniard because of its neo-Romanesque trios of arches and its Andalusian-style wooden balconies. You'll register beneath a lobby ceiling intricately covered with filigree plasterwork. Acres of gleaming white marble accentuate the leather upholstery and emerald tiles. A swimming pool in back is partially ringed with green lattices and green-and-white herringbone tiles. Each of the 195 comfortable bedrooms contains its own loggia, bathroom, phone, air conditioning, and radio. Singles cost 215 DH ($23.65), with doubles going for 270 DH ($29.70). A third person sharing a double room pays another 60 DH ($6.60). Fixed-price meals in one of the three restaurants cost between 85 DH ($9.35) and 110 DH ($12.10).

Hotel de la Menara, Avenue des Remparts (tel. 473-54), is a modern hotel offering a surprising amount of style and comfort for your dirhams. It's quite beautiful in parts, as exemplified by the sunken lounge with one of the most ornate filigree ceilings in town. There's lavish use of painted ceilings, tiles, Oriental carpets, and mosaics. Its bedrooms have good-size balconies overlooking a palm-studded garden and courtyard. Vines climb the balconies, water bubbles up in the sunken fountain, and guests splash in the swimming pool. Rooms are spacious, and all have a bath. A double or twin-bedded room is 220 DH ($24.20), including a continental breakfast, service, and taxes. A set lunch or dinner costs 90 DH ($9.90). The hotel is a ten-minute stroll from the Old Town.

The Best Bargains

Hotel Koutoubia, 51 Boulevard El Mansour Eddahbi (tel. 309-21). Its ornate iron railings and elaborate mosaics make its façade look a bit like that of a mosque. Inside, you register beneath an elaborately inlaid ceiling before being ushered to your clean and comfortable bedroom, where simple paneling accents the traditional woven fabrics which serve as bedspreads. Depending on the plumbing, the 60 bedrooms cost between 75 DH ($8.25) and 115 DH ($12.65) for a single, between 105 DH ($11.55) and 145 DH ($15.95) in a double. A swimming pool in the rear garden is ringed with palms and rubber trees. The high-ceilinged dining room offers a pleasant mixture of Moorish accessories and cooperative service. A TV room whose entrance opens onto the sun-flooded courtyard is in the typical Moroccan style, with geometric paneling and filigree ceilings. The hotel is a good choice for pleasant and comfortably exotic accommodations near the center of town.

Hotel Grand Imilchil, Avenue Echouhada (tel. 314-53), with a modern salmon-colored façade, is in Hivernage, a district midway between the European community of Guéliz and the Medina. Near its entrance, an elaborate four-tier fountain splashes water into a plant-ringed reflecting pool. The charming restaurant on the premises serves fixed-price meals for 80 DH ($8.80). A small swimming pool in the rear garden welcomes sun-worshippers to its ringaround terrace. The 97 comfortable, modern bedrooms rent for 140 DH ($15.40) in a single, 170 DH ($18.70) in a double. A third person in a double room pays a supplement of 55 DH ($6.05). Each unit has a balcony, bathroom, phone, and air conditioning.

Hotel La Renaissance, 89 Avenue Mohammed V, in Guéliz (tel. 312-33), is known for its sixth-floor "La Mirador," a panoramic terrace that takes in an overall view of Marrakesh and, on a clear day, the foothills of the Atlas Mountains in the south. The hotel has no seductive garden or a swimming pool, but it is a reasonable choice nevertheless. Each of its simply furnished units, 45 in all, contains either a private bath or shower. The most expensive singles cost 155 DH ($17.05), a double going for 190 DH ($20.90). The centrally heated hotel also has two restaurants: the first is on the ground floor, with a big terrace and a tea room attached, and the other is one floor above, containing a bar.

WHERE TO EAT: After dark, the most adventurous of readers will head for the **Djemaa El Fna** for dinner. If you're interested in native food, you'll find it here. . . and how! You won't come across restaurants, but instead you'll find open-air stands where each chef is noted for a different specialty. At one, tiny fish will be deep-frying; at another a young boy will be cooking chunks of lamb on a charcoal brazier; then there are the large bowls of food, both salads and spicy dishes. You sit at benches and place your order with the main cook. Everything is accompanied by the round loaves of barley bread. Frankly, many people are horrified at the sanitation conditions here; I think you will be, too, unless you had Ma Kettle for your mom. Nevertheless, Djemaa El Fna for many travelers remains a long-standing dining tradition. I suggest you skip it and sample the fare at one of the establishments recommended below.

La Trattoria de Gian Carlo, 179 rue Mohamed El Begal, Guéliz (tel. 326-41), was established by a likable and enterprising Italian, a former resident of Rome, whom everyone in Marrakesh calls simply "Gian Carlo." The restaurant is contained within an art deco villa which, after its construction in 1927, served first as the residence of a Russian prince and later as the headquarters for a French-language radio station. Today its plushly Oriental decor includes elaborate plaster ceilings, ornamental brasswork, pasha-style upholstery, working fireplaces fashioned from a Berber technique of polished lime called tadlak, and art deco chandeliers.

The restaurant stands behind a lovely courtyard filled with palms and flowers. Full meals cost from 150 DH ($16.50) and include a large selection of such pastas as spaghetti with clams and tagliatelle with salmon. The many veal and fish dishes include saltimbocca, osso buco, veal marsala, and several dishes named after local celebrities. The dessert extravaganza is a temptingly caloric zabaglione. An array of wines can accompany any dinner, and service is impeccable. Full meals are served daily except Monday.

For a meal in the Medina, head for **Gharnata,** 5 Riad Zitoun Jdid El Arsa (tel. 452-16). In a palatial setting, seated on low sofas, you are entertained by folkloric groups while you dine on authentic Moroccan dishes. Have your hotel call to make sure you tie in your visit with one of the presentations. A local soup makes an excellent beginning, followed by one of the typical dishes, such as chicken with lemon, pigeon pie, and pigeon filled with almonds. Order milk of almonds, a nectar worthy of the gods. Moroccan pastries and a mint tea round out your repast, which will cost around 100 DH ($12.10). Service and tax are extra. A guide hired by the restaurant usually waits for visitors in a nearby square, and he'll direct you to the right restaurant. Otherwise, you'll never find it.

Le Riad, Rue Arset El Maâcch Marrakech, Medina (tel. 454-30). This famous restaurant was built around the core of a 150-year-old villa, but the lush and elaborate Moroccan decor you see today was installed in 1971. It's considered one of the best independent restaurants in Marrakesh, often attracting a glamorous clientele of European residents. It stands on a quiet street of the Medina, away from the clusters of shops and souks. You climb a stately flight of tile-covered stairs to reach the huge second-floor dining room. There, low-slung brass tables require seating on plushly upholstered banquettes.

A polite and charming staff of uniformed waiters serves such Moroccan specialties as pigeon tart, pigeon with almonds, couscous, chicken with lemon, and a delectable version of lamb with prunes and almonds, followed by a temptingly sweet collection of dessert pastries. Clusters of roses are placed on every table, and there is plenty of visual distraction provided by the folkloric dancers who present a show every evening. Full à la carte meals cost from 190 DH ($20.90), including the show. Most visitors, however, order one of the five-course fixed-price dinners which offer a sampling of many of the culinary specialties of Morocco at a cost of 135 DH ($14.85). Reservations are needed, and lunch and dinner are served every day of the week.

Villa Rosa, 64 Avenue Hassan II (tel. 308-32), is an intimate Italian restaurant behind a high wall beside a busy boulevard in the European section of Guéliz. You can dine on a sheltered outdoor terrace beneath orange trees near clusters of flowers or within a pair of candlelit dining rooms. Pink napery and a tiny apéritif bar in one corner add to the allure. Reservations are important, and only dinner is served. Fish and different versions of spaghetti are the house specialties. You can order ten kinds of pasta, including carbonara, matriciano, a double-cream tagliatelle, tagliatelle with mushrooms, three kinds of soup, spicy shrimp served pili-pili style, four kinds of veal, seasonal asparagus, filet Stroganoff, three kinds of sole, monkfish with pink peppercorns, and poached filet of John Dory. Madame Clélia Vasary is the Italian-born owner, serving meals costing from 135 DH ($14.85) every evening.

El Minzeh Restaurant, Hotel Toubkal, rue Haroun Er Rachid (tel. 329-72), is one of the dozens of specialty restaurants contained within the hotels of Marrakesh, but because of its garden setting, amid a riot of flowering plants, its well-prepared food, and its polite service, it deserves a special mention. It's on the second floor of the well-recommended Hotel Toubkal (see the accommodation recommendations). You can dine in a pleasantly sunny and airy room amid immaculate napery, within sight of an open grill, or on the terrace under parasols above the lush gardens of the swimming pool. Full meals cost from 95 DH ($10.45) per person and might include medallions of veal in a cream sauce, steak au poivre, an emincée of beef Stroganoff, several different kinds of grilled meats, the grilled fish of the day, veal kidneys, and an array of omelets. Several Moroccan specialties include tajines and brochettes and a goodly selection of Moroccan wines. The restaurant is open daily for both lunch and dinner.

Restaurant Chaouia, Route de Guémassa (tel. 229-15), caters to groups who usually arrive en masse by motorcoach in time for the elaborate displays of horsemanship, dancing, and music. Some visitors have said that the well-choreographed races, swordplay, and exhibition combat presented here were some of the high points of their trip. The art is to phone ahead and learn when a show will be performed, then reserve a private table for yourself and your party. Dining is within about a dozen Bedouin-style tents flanking the edges of a grass-covered playing field. The restaurant lies in Ménara, close to the airport, 1½ miles outside of town. Fixed-price meals cost from 120 DH ($13.20), including typically Moroccan tajines, brochettes, and grills. À la carte meals cost 160 DH ($17.60). In theory, this loosely organized establishment is open 24 hours a day, seven days a week (you can always drop in for tea). But you should never go out there without calling first and finding out about the evening program.

A good place to sample Moroccan specialties is at the **Restaurant de Foucauld,** next to a hotel of the same name on Avenue El Mouahidine, near the Koutoubia and Djemaa El Fna (tel. 454-99). Each day at either lunch or dinner you're given a range of at least 14 typically Moroccan dishes, including pigeons stuffed with almonds or poulet with prunes. Naturally, you get couscous prepared either with mutton or chicken. Tajine comes in a number of ways (one method is with fish). For those with American or European tastes, the chef will also prepare you an entrecôte or steak, perhaps a tournedos, even some spaghetti and an American hamburger. Should you prefer the set meal to the à la carte offerings, you'll be presented with a three-course dinner for 55 DH ($6.05). A good French dish in season is the roast rabbit (lapin) with mustard sauce. For an à la carte repast, expect to spend from 100 DH ($11). The restaurant, naturally, is Moroccan-style, a quiet and shady spot on a hot summer day.

If economy is a major factor in your dining, then try the curiously named **Iceberg,** Avenue El Mouahidine, near the Koutoubia (tel. 429-51), a café-restaurant proud of its *salle climatisée.* Upstairs, the Iceberg is a small café with a few sidewalk tables; downstairs is the large basement restaurant. It specializes in Moroccan dishes and features mint tea with sweet pastries. Best bet is the five-course meal for 40 DH ($4.40). Considering its quality and scope, I consider this the best value in Marrakesh. For example, I recently enjoyed a selection of hors d'oeuvres, followed by an omelet, then leg of lamb, potatoes, and dessert (cheese, flan, or strawberries in season). Lemon chicken is a specialty. English is spoken by the affable, engaging owner, Moulay Driss Alaoui. If you're planning to return to his restaurant, he'll often suggest a special dinner for you, which he insists you eat Moroccan style—that is, with your fingers. Perhaps it'll be his large and tasty tajine, a dish made with lamb and cooked with olives and fresh hearts of artichoke in a savory sauce.

Sidewalk Cafés

One of the most popular pastimes in Marrakesh is sitting and sipping at a sidewalk café. The most interesting panorama unfolds at the pretentiously named **Café de France** (tel. 223-19), right on the heartbeat Djemaa El Fna. The café is utterly simple, but not the action taking place in front of it. An inside staircase leads up to an unobstructed view of the marketplace from a terrace, affording a panoramic vista. A coffee in the café costs only 2.50 DH (28¢), probably the cheapest entertainment in the city.

In Guéliz, seek out the **Brasserie des Négociants,** 11 Avenue Mohammed V (tel. 310-94), which is right in the hub and rather attractive, decorated in a tropical motif. Should you wish to spread a rumor around Marrakesh quickly, launch it here. As you sit sipping a coffee at 2.50 DH (28¢), at least ten boys will offer to shine your shoes. Often the same ones will approach you two or three times, just in case you should change your mind.

THE SIGHTS: The peculiar charm of Marrakesh certainly isn't reflected in the New Town, **Guéliz,** which was founded in 1913 about 1½ miles west of the Medina. Unlike the old town, Guéliz is characterized by wide boulevards, palaces, gardens, and many modern structures. You'll spend much time in this quarter, as the majority of the hotels and restaurants are here. However, life in Marrakesh really centers on . . .

Djemaa El Fna

The largest souk in Morocco is a world unto itself. Camera-carrying tourists from the Mamounia Hotel and kif-smoking young people rub shoulders with Berber men in town from the Atlas Mountains or wandering tribesmen from the Sahara in their indigo-blue robes. If you go at 2 o'clock on a winter afternoon (4 or 5 o'clock in summer), you'll meet the cast of characters ranging from occasional acrobats of Amizmiz, monkey trainers, soothsayers, palm readers, trick cyclists, pate-polishing barbers, magicians, jugglers, fellahs (small farmers), flame eaters, lottery sellers, acupuncturists, scribes. To be frank, this square isn't the three-star attraction it used to be. One Moroccan explained it this way: "Many of us have TV now. We stay home and watch a show in our living room and don't have to go to the square to see one."

The most characteristic star in this drama is the red-clad water seller, a goatskin sack draped across his back, a necklace of brass cups dangling from his throat. Tinkling his bell in your ear, he makes his way through this mass of humanity. Today he earns more money posing for tourists (give him at least 2 DH, or 22¢) than he does selling water from the gold faucet of his goatskin sack.

Everybody in Djemaa El Fna has something to sell, and you are the prime target. The merchandise is varied, ranging from a gigantic brass ant to a live chicken (what the mountain man thinks you're going to do with a live chicken I don't know, unless he suspects Westerners of voodoo).

Snake charmers are here too. With one eye on a defanged black cobra, another on you, the snake charmer will take the snake from its rush basket, his tongue darting out in rhythm with the snake's. Then he'll put the snake away and rush over to collect a dirham from you as entertainment tax. Only the most mercenary visitor walks away without paying his price. After all, the charmer earns his living from this exhibition—not to mention the money for snake food.

Don't think this square was conceived as a tourist attraction. Its origins lie deep in the traditions of Marrakesh, and if you look hard enough you'll find a circle of Arabs around an ancient man who spins tales straight from a *Thousand and One Nights.*

If Allah is smiling on you during your visit you'll get to see a performance by the black Muslims of Mauritania, who are known for their acrobatic feats and barefoot dancing. Scarlet-colored sashes are slung around their ivory-toned garb, a dramatic sight in movement to the tam-tam.

Although the drama peaks in the afternoon, the square is an experience at any time of the day or night. Many get up at sunrise to see it come alive, listening to the solitary sound of the fluteplayer.

Incidentally, the name of this square is translated roughly as "Rendezvous of the Dead." It must be the worst-named square in Morocco.

Djemaa El Fna lies in the shadow of . . .

The Koutoubia

Dominating the city, this mosque is graced with a minaret 222 feet high. It was built in the 12th century from pink sandstone from the former quarries at Guéliz. Abd El Moumen started the mosque, and it is said to have been completed by Abdoul Yussef, the second ruler of the Almohad dynasty, who reigned until 1184. The tower is crowned by three decorative gilt balls which, according to legend, were presented by the wife of the sultan Yakout El Mansour, "The Victorious One." The Koutoubia, the "Mosque of the Scribes," is the sister of the Giralda Tower at Seville and the Tower of Hassan at Rabat—both frank imitations. The sides, each one different, are covered with beautiful decorative facing. The Koutoubia was erected on the site of the "Palace of Stone," in which the Almohads lived. All in all, this mosque makes Marrakesh one of the great cities of the Islamic world, and represents a triumph of Moorish architecture. Regrettably for sightseers, non-Muslims are forbidden to enter this most enduring and characteristic monument of Marrakesh.

The Djemaa El Fna provides an excellent gateway to the labyrinthine alleyways of . . .

The Souks of the Medina

After you've learned the ground rules of the market square, you'll be ready to venture into the nearby maze of souks, beginning at the northern edge at either the Bab er Robb or Bab Agnaou gateways. Some of the finest craftspeople in Morocco are found on these narrow streets.

Everybody heads for the dyers' souk, as it is, naturally, the most colorful (but not on Friday). Hanging on lines strung across the streets are silk and woolen skeins in every hue of the rainbow. Leather workers, bookbinders, shoemakers, brass and copper artisans ply their age-old crafts, the rules changing little from generation to generation. The aromas alone will lure you to the exotic spice section. Fabric is sold in the *Kissarias,* and the bright sunlight only enhances the brilliance of the gold embroidery.

Some of the alleyways are covered with latticework, casting slanting shadows on the ground and making everybody and everything zebra-striped. Lop-eared donkeys, heavily laden with goods, ply their way through the crowds of locals and foreigners. Merchants try to lure you into their souks, tempting you with all sorts of kettles and braziers, wrought-iron lanterns, daggers in silver, camel-hair blankets. Perhaps the rugs will catch your eye—especially those from Chichaoua, with their red backgrounds and geometric designs. Or those from Glaoua with black stripes splashed with color.

During your tour of the Medina, you can visit . . .

Medersa Ibn Yussef

This monument was built in the reign of Aboul Hassan, a 14th-century Merinid sultan. The Saadian monarch, Moulay Abou Abdallah, rebuilt it in 1565. The style is traditional, with a quartet of ornately decorative inner façades surrounding a central courtyard. Look for the 11th-century marble basin with its heraldic birds. Until 1956 the medersa was used as a university, filled with medical students who lived in the cell-like rooms upstairs. The monument is open daily, except Friday morning. (Tip the guide.)

The Saadian Tombs

These tombs, built during the reign of the Saadian monarch Ahmed El Dehbi in the 16th century, are elaborately decorated. They contain the remains of all but five of the Saadian rulers. The royal burial ground, in back of the Casbah Mosque, wasn't discovered until 1917. All in all, the necropolis forms the most dramatic architecture in the city, and of the three halls, the most elegant is the Chamber of the 12 Columns. Many of the tombs contain the remains of children. The mausoleum may be visited daily, from 8:30 a.m. to noon and 2:30 to 6 p.m. (free, but tip the guide).

After visiting the tombs, ask your guide to show you the nearby **Mellah,** the old Jewish ghetto of Marrakesh. Jews were housed here ever since the 16th-century orders from the Saadian monarch Moulay Abdallah. Many jewelry shops are found here.

North of the old Mellah lies the . . .

Bahia Palace and Gardens

If King Hassan II isn't putting up a special VIP guest or one of his relatives isn't in town, you can visit this splendidly decorated palace, built between 1894 and 1900. Called the "Brilliant Palace," Bahia is noted for its decoration and its Moorish gardens. Incidentally, these gardens—imbued with the smell of sweet jasmine—are irrigated by water from an artificial lake. In the palace you proceed haphazardly through tiny courtyards and sumptuously decorated salons (the former harem has now given way to a reception room). The hours vary but in summer are from 8:30 a.m. to noon and 2:30 to 6 p.m. (but don't count on that).

Dar Si Said

Now an arts museum (tel. 224-64), this second palace was erected at the end of the 19th century by the brother of Ba Ahmed, grand vizier of King Moulay Hassan. You enter via a sweet-smelling patio garden, graced with the sound of chirping birds. The collection is interesting, especially the handcrafts from the High Atlas Mountains. The rugs and capes are exceptional, as is the jewelry. The room of engraved daggers, muskets, and powderhorns evokes old Buster Crabbe movies about the French Foreign Legion. Note also the waterbags of camel skin, the copper and brass work, the Safi and Zagora pottery, even the decorated doors to Berber houses. The admission-free museum (tip the guide) is open daily except Tuesday, from 9 a.m. to noon and 4 to 7 p.m.

The **Royal Palace,** where King Hassan II lives when he is in Marrakesh, cannot be visited, but visitors are fond of riding around it in a horse-drawn carriage. It's a huge place, the trip around its high walls about two miles. The palace is known as Dar el-Makhzen.

A Garland of Gardens

Marrakesh is famous for its gardens. The best known is the two-mile-long **Aguedal,** a splendid imperial garden laid out by the Almohads in the 12th century. The garden, studded with olive trees, is irrigated by pools. At certain times of the year this oasis has an especially sweet scent. The sultan Moulay Abd Er Rahman is credited with giving Aguedal its present form in the 19th century.

Surrounded by an adobe enclosure, the **Menara Gardens** are about 1,200 yards long and 800 yards wide. These gardens of olive trees were originally laid out by the Almohads. In the 19th century, Sultan Abd Er Rahman erected a pavilion surrounded by a 12-foot-wide parapet. Apparently, the sultan met his "favorites" here in this tranquil setting.

Yet a third garden is the **Mamounia,** the same garden in which the deluxe hotel of the same name stands. It is cool and tranquil, dates from the Saadian era, and offers many a shady walk through its orange and olive trees.

Finally, no trip to Marrakesh is complete without a tour of the celebrated **Palm Grove** and a horse-drawn carriage ride around the **ramparts.** Frankly, the cost depends on your negotiations with the driver. But expect to pay from 80 DH ($8.80). Stretching on for nearly 12 miles, the palm oasis embraces an area of about 30,000 acres; the number of trees is usually reported at 150,000. At some point, you may want to stop off and mount a camel. Before your visit to the Grove, you can circle the ramparts. Trips usually begin at the **Place de la Liberté,** and last for nearly five miles. This way you'll get to see the interesting gates of Marrakesh. The word for gateway is "Bab," and you'll pass by **Bab Doukkala,** of Almoravid origin, and the especially delightful **Bab Agnaou,** from the 12th century.

A TOUR OF THE TOWN: The heartbeat of Marrakesh is in the Djemaa El Fna, the open marketplace overshadowed by the minaret of the Koutoubia. For a walk through the town, for which I advise you to secure the services of a guide although you can do it on your own if you choose, you turn right with your back to the old city, into the Avenue Mohammed V as far as a crossroads with a fountain in the middle. To the left is the Avenue El Yarmouk which runs along the side of the ramparts. When the fortifications turn from the avenue at right angles, enter the Medina, choosing one of two gateways, Bab er Robb or Bab Agnaou.

Inside is the casbah and the Grand Mosque, with the Saadian Tombs in a walled garden nearby. After seeing the tombs, turn right into the rue Kasbah and take the second street on the left to go to Bab Berrima and El Badi Palace, now in ruins but used as a setting for the annual folklore festival. Farther along to the right, you go around the Dar El Maghzen, a royal residence, to the external and internal *mechouars* which are separated by a wall from the Agdal gardens, which were laid out in the 13th century and are planted with ancient olive trees.

Back at the Koutoubia, go through the quarters on the right, known as Riad Zitoun Kebir and Riad Zitoun Jedid, coming to the Bahia Palace and its lovely gardens and the Dar Si Said Palace, with its art museum. Take the street on the left on the far side of the Djemaa El Fna, and enter the covered alleyways lined with shops selling rugs. After this parade of handcraft from Chichaoua, Ouarzazate, and the Great Atlas, you come to a maze of small streets redolent of cedar, sandal, and thuya wood being used by cabinetmakers. Visit a little square with a country air, and go under a "bridge" of skeins of wool of all colors strung across the way in the dyers' souk.

Farther on is the Moulay Youssef mosque near which, on lower ground, is a very old koubba shrine dating back to the 11th century. Near the Ben Youssef mosque, you can visit the medrarsa (college) of the same name, used by students since 1565. Here you see a fine fountain decorated with stalactites and woodcarvings inscribed with kufic and cursive Arabic script. This is the Chrob ou Couf fountain (drink and admire). Farther on are the zaouias of Sidi Ben Abbes es Sebti, Sidi Ben Slimane and Jazouli, Sidi Abdelaziz, Kaid Ayad, Sidi El Ghezouani, and Sidi Es Soyhli. On the way are the Grand Mosque and several fine fountains. After this, you can retrace your steps, returning to the Djemaa El Fna.

MARRAKESH NIGHTLIFE: For a big night on the town, head for the **Casino de Marrakech** (tel. 320-11), the chicest one in North Africa, set in gardens by the Es Saadi Hotel. You need both 5 DH (55¢) and your passport before you enter the gaming rooms. Baccarat, blackjack, roulette, and craps get going at 9 every night of the week. Far more interesting—to me at least—is the show downstairs. The budget-bursting dinner spectacle costs 160 DH ($17.60). For that price, you'll be entertained by the usual array of snake charmers, acrobats, belly dancers, and folk dancers from the Rif.

2. One-Day Excursions from Marrakesh

Separating Marrakesh from the Sahara Desert is the Great Atlas Mountain range. You can spend more than a week making excursions from Marrakesh into the Atlas, but few are blessed with such time or money. Unless you have your own car, tours to the Atlas tend to be super-expensive.

The jaunt to the **Ourika Valley** is one of the most popular excursions. After leaving Marrakesh, the road is dull, but suddenly you're in the foothills of the Atlas—and the scenery improves.

One of the first Berber villages you come to is called **Dar Caid Ouriki,** noted for its painted minaret. Your final destination for the day is usually the village of **Setti Fatma,** at the end of the valley, a distance of 42 miles from Marrakesh. It is charming in a primitive way, with a nicely decorated earthen *zawiya.*

THE OURIKA VALLEY: Of course, many will want to stop over at one of the inns or hotels in the valley for lunch. The first hotel you'll come to is the **Ourika,** Vallée de L'Ourika, Route S513, Arbalou (tel. 04), an unexpected island of sophistication in the foothills of the Atlas, 28 miles southeast of Marrakesh. It's lodged on a ledge above the road that splits the Ourika Valley, and from nearly every bedroom there's a view of the mountain range. A winding driveway leads past trees and banks of roses to the balconied gray and brown façade which rises on stilts above the sloping hillside. There's a view of a mudwalled village in the distance, the sound of a rushing stream, and an ambience a bit like a Moroccan version of an alpine hotel. There's even a fireplace in one of the sun-flooded public rooms, to take off the midsummer chill of a high-altitude climate which is considerably colder than that of nearby Marrakesh. Each of the 22 pine-trimmed rooms contains a private bath. Most have a terrace. Singles cost 185 DH ($20.35); doubles, 230 DH ($25.30). Fixed-price meals in the pleasant dining room go for 55 DH ($6.05) and 90 DH ($9.90). Even if you can't stay overnight, I recommend a stop for lunch.

An alternative choice farther up the road is **Hotel Ramuntcho,** Vallée de L'Ourika, Route S513, Arbalou Par Marrakech (tel. 118 Arbalou), a roadside inn on the lower portion of the winding road cutting through the Ourika Valley. The inn, owned by René Dufour, has for decades been known for its hearty food and pleasant rooms; its cluttered atmosphere has a peculiar fascination. Overlooking the river is the terrace dining room, partially shaded by orange trees; inside, the atmosphere is that of a country tavern, with rugged stone walls, a raised hearth, and large windows. In spite of his many years in Morocco, Monsieur Dufour is as French as a Parisian bistro. He offers a six-course meal for 80 DH ($8.80), including a wide choice of hors d'oeuvres, a fish or egg dish, followed by eight main choices, such as pastilla (pigeon pie) or tajine (lamb, veal, or chicken cooked with prunes or onions), then a salad course, followed by a selection from the cheese board, and finally, dessert. Half-board rates are 200 DH ($22) per person.

OUKAIMEDEN: You can branch off the Ourika Valley road to the winter resort of the Atlas, **Oukaimeden,** about 50 miles from Marrakesh. The road to it is paved, but likely to be dangerous for inexperienced drivers. The resort is perched high up at 7,742 feet and boasts one of the highest ski lifts in the world (10,498 feet).

A good hotel has been built, the **Imlil** (tel. 591-32), offering 34 rooms with a toilet and bidet, another ten with a complete bath, and even more facilities often rented to large families or groups. Only full-board guests are accepted at rates ranging from 175 DH ($19.25) to 225 DH ($24.75) per person daily. The hotel's chef serves a good, well-prepared cuisine with meals costing from 85 DH ($9.35), and in the bar guests enjoy a musical ambience. The resort also has a nightclub, Zin Zin, with its salle de cinéma. Ski instruction is available, and all equipment can be rented on the premises. It is open only from December to April.

ASNI: Another excursion south of Marrakesh is to this Berber village, noted for its Casbah. Many of the city people go there to escape the heat of summer as the town is at an altitude of 4,000 feet, surrounded by the highest peaks of the Great Atlas (Mount Toubkal, 13,664 feet, looms behind the village). The view is impressive. Since Asni is 32 miles from Marrakesh, it is easily reached on a morning's excursion. If you're stopping over—either for a meal or overnight—then try:

Grand Hotel du Toubkal, Km. 45, Route Taroudannt (tel. 3 Asni). You drive for miles through vivid and sparsely populated scenery before reaching the sienna-color façade of this casbah-style hotel. It was built in 1945 and heavily restored in 1970. The architects did everything they could to retain the filigree stone ceilings, the exposed wood, and the intricately patterned mosaics. The establishment's reception desk fills an unlikely corner of the high-ceilinged dining room whose big windows encompass the snow-covered peaks of the Atlas Mountains. Clusters of iron tables provide seating beside a rose garden and a grove of apple, pear, and cherry trees. Each of the 31 bedrooms is clean and sunny, with handwoven bedspreads and tile floors, and a few have a balcony and a spacious tile bath. With half board included, single rooms with bath cost 230 DH ($25.30), doubles with bath 345 DH ($37.95). Even if you don't stay overnight, the courteous staff will welcome you if you stop for lunch. Fixed-price meals cost 70 DH ($7.70) and feature Berber specialties.

OUIRGANE: To discover one of the loveliest and most tranquil retreats in the environs of Marrakesh, you can continue another eight miles from Asni to Val d'Ouirgane and the following oasis.

La Roseraie, Val d'Ourigane, Km. 60, Route de Marrakech–Taroudannt (tel. 4 Ourigane), was established shortly after the end of World War II by the German-born Count Meckenheim, who lavished time and money on the 54 acres which still surround it. His ambition was to develop a self-supporting fruit plantation, but the lovely gardens and stone-walled buildings that served as his home and headquarters are perhaps his most lasting legacy. In the 1970s, the property was bought by Moroccan entrepreneur Fenjiro Abdelkader, who built a cluster of well-furnished bungalows, added a rectangular swimming pool, and transformed it into one of the most charming hotels in all of Morocco. A dozen gardeners maintain the thousands of burgeoning roses in showcase condition. The hotel has a water cascade flanked with lilies, a labyrinth of brick sidewalks which connect the many outbuildings, a sauna, earth-bottom tennis courts, and a stable of rentable horses. The verdancy of the property is the most unusual thing about it, especially when visitors remember the dusty countryside through which they drove to reach it.

The European restaurant has a roughly textured fireplace assembled from smooth river rocks. There's also a Moroccan specialty restaurant. The honey served at morning breakfast comes from bees which are bred on the property, where many of the teas, tisanes, and herbs which are served are also cultivated and collected.

There are 30 accommodations, scattered among outlying bungalows. Some contain a kitchen, others are considered suites, and a few have an open fireplace to ward off the high-altitude chill. Each contains a private bathroom, exposed stone walls, and a simple decor of artfully primitive Bedouin-inspired furniture. With half board included, singles cost 330 DH ($36.30) to 500 DH ($55), doubles 500 DH ($55) and 680 DH ($74.80) per day, depending on the accommodation. The hotel is open all year long.

From Asni you can continue southwest on the Taroudannt road to **Tizi n'Test,** at 6,890 feet, one of the most magnificent mountain panoramas in the Atlas, with the Valley of the Souss spread before your feet.

THE EDGE OF THE SAHARA

If you'd like to go on the trail that Marlene Dietrich took when she followed Gary Cooper into the desert in the 1930 version of *Morocco,* then the Deep South—south of the Atlas Mountains—is just the place to experience that Foreign Legion–type exotica. Rich in folklore and scenery, this is a land of sand and more sand, with an occasional quiet village surrounded oasis-like with olive groves and orchards. The sky is an incredible intense blue, lighting the red Saharan houses that stand baking in the sun.

A few comfortable government-built hotels that represent Saharan-style architecture are found along this trail, but you must always call ahead for a reservation, since many places are completely booked by French-speaking tour groups. Names here evoke an *Arabian Nights* fantasy. The heat is dry, although in summer the mercury is likely to hit 107° Fahrenheit.

Marrakesh is the major starting point for people who want to experience this mysterious land, much of which looks unchanged since biblical times (definitely Old Testament). From Marrakesh, you can take a southern route, going first to Ouarzazate and on to Zagora, then heading east to Tinerhir, Er Rachidia (with a detour to Erfoud), before turning north via Midelt and Azrou to Meknes. It's possible to travel by bus along this route.

After leaving Marrakesh, you come to the—

TIZI N'TICHKA PASS: It can be visited on a day trip from Marrakesh. At a peak of 7,415 feet, it offers a vast panoramic view of the Atlas. From December to April, the pass can be closed temporarily until snowplows clear it. The road was constructed before World War II. Before that, it took almost two weeks to cross the pass, and travelers were victimized by mountain bandits. From the pass, you can travel to—

TELOUET: This round-trip journey from Tizi n'Tichka is less than 35 miles. The road rises to 5,900 feet. Once at Telouet, you'll find one of the most fascinating casbahs in Berber country. At the end of the road stands Dar Glaoui, the former residence of the caid. It lies on a hill looking down over the valley. After having a simple lunch in this large village on the south slope of the Atlas range, you can journey back to the pass and return to Marrakesh, having traveled a distance of about 180 miles. Or you can continue south to—

3. Ouarzazate

This is a *Beau Geste*–looking town, reached in half a day's journey from Marrakesh. A distance of some 127 miles from "the red city," Ouarzazate is like an oasis of palm trees, appearing after the wasteland of the desert. At the head of two valleys, it lies on a river from which it takes its name. Ouzguita tribesmen can be seen on its hot streets, selling their carpets.

Established in 1928 as a military outpost, earthy-pink Ouarzazate has only a small population and is dominated by a fortress sheltering the royal army. About two buses leave every day, one heading north to Marrakesh, another east to Er Rachidia (formerly known as Ksar-es-Souk).

Guides who will immediately attach themselves to you will show you the few sights. One is a small museum of arts and crafts in regional government offices (on the right of the road to Taourirt). You will also be directed to a carpet weavers' cooperative shop where Berber jewelry and stone articles are for sale.

About a mile east on the Boumalne road stands the **Kasbah of Taourirt,** a fortress that is a typical example of the Saharan casbah style. This is one of the most beautiful casbahs in Morocco, the work of much restoration. A true fortified city, it was a residence of the Glaoui, the Lords of the Atlas. It is characterized by angled walls and square-based towers, each pierced with openings and crenellated tops. Private houses are built around the base of it, almost one on top of the other, rising up the slope. You are shown through rooms used by the Glaoui, including a chamber reserved for "the favorite." Admission is 3 DH (33¢), and hours are from 8 a.m. to 6 p.m.

Eight miles west on the route to Zagora, stands the **Kasbah of Tiffoultoute** (take the turn-off onto Route P31, the Marrakesh road, for a distance of two miles). This casbah dominates the palmy valley of Ouarzazate. Houses in earth tones climb up to the base of the fortress, which was another residence of the powerful Glaoui. From here you'll have a beautiful view of the High Atlas. Visits are possible from 8 a.m. to noon and from 3 to 7 p.m.

FOOD AND LODGING: **Hotel Karam Palace** (tel. 2225) was designed to look as much like a modernized version of a casbah as possible, ringed with crenellated walls of the same color as the desert around it. Surprisingly, it opens into one of the most luxurious modern interiors in south Morocco. This is one of the newest hotels of the PLM chain and considered something of a showcase. A rectangular swimming pool is set near the terrace where the enclosing wall looks out over an arid valley and part of a mud-walled city beyond.

There's a pleasant lattice-ringed outdoor café-bar, along with well-ordered plantings, arbor-covered walkways, and 150 accommodations. These are scattered in an artfully unsymmetrical cluster of two-story bungalows, interconnected with above-ground indoor/outdoor passageways interspersed with contemporary interpretations of Moorish courtyards. Each of the cozy modern rooms has a radio, a private bath with its own harem-style dome, and a phone. Single rooms cost 280 DH ($30.80), doubles going for 365 DH ($40.15), plus breakfast. Fixed-price lunches or dinners are 90 DH ($9.90). You'll find this hotel in an isolated position on a plateau above the oldest part of the city.

Hotel Azghor (tel. 2612) sits in a Europeanized suburb on a hillside away from the oldest part of the Medina. Its earth-color tower is part of an older mud-brick hotel built in 1953. The better-maintained newer sections were constructed about ten years later. Its social center is a rectangular swimming pool with a breathtaking view over the valley and the arid mountains nearby. The 150 accommodations sit behind cedar doors along the upstairs hallways. Units have a private bath, a simple and functionally modern decor, and lots of wooden trim. Singles rent for 215 DH ($23.65), doubles for 275 DH ($30.25), and triples for 340 DH ($37.40). Fixed-price meals cost 90 DH ($9.90) each. There's a pleasant bar on the ground floor filled with modern furniture and Moroccan-made brass chandeliers. The hotel's name translates from the Berber dialect as "big tree," for the noble tree that stood here before the hotel was built.

PLM Hotel Zat (tel. 2521) is modern (1973), pleasant, clean, and serves the best food in town. Named after the river which flows near the town, it contains 60 comfortable air-conditioned bedrooms, each of which has a phone and private bath. Rates are 215 DH ($23.65) in a single, 275 DH ($30.25) in a double. Fixed-price meals cost from 85 DH ($8.35) each. The hotel has a rectangular swimming pool on a flower-dotted terrace, a gracious and high-ceilinged restaurant with a particularly charming staff, a disco, and a well-stocked lobby-level gift shop.

Hotel Gazelle, Avenue Mohammed V (tel. 2151). Built in the mid-1970s, some of its high-ceilinged bedrooms carry just the slightest hint of what the French colonials left. Suitable for serious economizers, it offers 30 simple, basic rooms, each of which has its own shower and toilet. Singles are a bargain at 75 DH ($8.25), doubles at 100 DH ($11). Don't expect the Ritz, because this isn't it, and you might get just a whiff of something a bit musty. Still, the staff is friendly and cooperative, and the plain dining room serves well-prepared dinners either inside, under plaster filigree friezes, or outside on the pleasant terrace. Fixed-price meals begin at 45 DH ($4.95).

4. Zagora

This is the last stop before the gazelle country and the desert. Zagora is a thriving village in the Draa Valley, lying 107 miles south of our last stopover at Ouarzazate. From the top of Djebel Zagora, you can look out onto a panoramic view of the desert and valley. The town, whose main boulevard is the Avenue Mohammed V, contains the remains of a fortress built in the 11th century by the Almoravides.

The most interesting excursion from Zagora is to **Tamegroute,** 14 miles to the south, where there is an ancient library with illustrated Korans written on gazelle skin. The oldest of these date from the 13th century. The antique Korans are displayed at the Zaouia Nasseria. In the village are several potteries.

The highway doesn't actually end in Zagora or even in Tamegroute but continues to M'Hamid, which is the final outpost before the desert. If you're traveling south from Zagora, you must apply for special permission at the offices found at Cercle de Zagora.

The journey to **M'hamid** is a distance of 56 miles over rough roads (you are likely to be stopped by the police several times on the way there). It is at M'Hamid that the water of the Draa Valley comes to an end. After M'Hamid the vast wasteland of the Sahara opens up. Frankly, I'd skip this latter excursion because of its discomfort and uncertain conditions. However, the most intrepid do press on, and, if so, they should time their visit for a Monday when the "Blue Men" of the desert can be seen at the souk.

Back in Zagora, weary travelers take delight as they approach **Hotel Tinsouline** (tel. 22), the southernmost I recommend in Morocco. It offers 90 pleasantly furnished rooms decorated in a stylized fashion, all with private bath or shower and air conditioning. A single costs 120 DH ($13.20); a double, 150 DH ($16.50). The swimming pool is a welcome sight after a trek through the desert. The overall setting of this clay-built structure is one of peace and serenity. The bar, decorated in the local style, the restful lounges, and the restaurant are appealing. The restaurant offers a tourist dinner for 75 DH ($8.25).

5. El Kelaa des M'gouna

This oasis, with its huge collection of strung-out *ksour,* makes a stopover between Ouarzazate and Tinerhir. The hamlet sits on a Saharan plateau. Kelaa is a village of roses, and there is a festival every spring. Instead of the usual date palms, you'll see fruit and nut trees as well.

Hotel des Roses du Dades (tel. 18) is so isolated, and the town around it is so dusty, that you'll be surprised that this hotel is as elegantly modern as it is. It's contained within a pair of sienna-color casbah-style buildings to which dozens of modern touches have been added. The main building contains a pair of inviting courtyards and a coolly echoing decor of tile, wood, and marble. A spacious and modern dining room offers views of the desert. Upstairs, on a raised terrace, a lovely pool offers an oasis from the scorching sun. There's an unusual bar with lots of exposed wood and a nighttime ambience a bit like a disco, especially when two or more tour buses have deposited their passengers en masse. The 102 accommodations are artfully spartan, usually with a raised platform, tile surfaces, and consciously simple furniture. Single rooms cost 175 DH ($19.25), doubles 230 DH ($25.30), and triples 280 DH ($30.80). Fixed-price meals begin at 90 DH ($9.90) each. The well-stocked gift shop in an alcove of the lobby offers some of the best values in the region on hand-woven Bedouin carpets, although you'll have to negotiate hard to get a really good price.

6. Boumalne-Dades

Moving ever eastward from Ouarzazate, you'll be passing through the famed route of the casbahs. The number of them is staggering; one estimate was 1,000 casbahs. One stopover along the way is at Boulmane-Dades where the Glaoui, or lords of the Atlas, put a large ksar above the entrance to the **Gorges du Dades,** one of the most stunning natural attractions in Morocco, directly north of this town.

As you go along the Dades Valley, heading for M'Semrir, the road will pass several imposing *ksour,* ranging from palatial palaces to medieval fortresses which seem to emerge from palm groves and tamarisks. At a distance of some 14 miles you may want to turn back. The terrain the rest of the way is strictly for the most adventurous of explorers. The road is narrow, and the bends are hairpins. However, the mountain scenery is of exceptional beauty, and the gorges are full of greenery. The rocks are red or mauve in color, depending on the light and the time of day. You'll travel through the hamlet of Tinjdad where a pastoral people make little bonnets and weave wool for djellabas. From Aremba Cliff, there is a panoramic view.

Back in the town of Boumalne-Dades, you'll find little of interest. But you may appreciate the following stopover.

PLM Hotel Madayeq (tel. 31), from the outside, looks a lot like a heavily fortified mud-walled casbah, but inside, you'll find a handful of courtyards filled with plants, a spacious café decorated with geometric Moroccan-inspired designs, and an imaginatively decorated collection of comfortable public rooms. Built in 1974, the hotel contains 100 comfortable bedrooms, with roughly textured stucco walls in shades of green or yellow, terrazzo floors, tile baths, small terraces, and phones. Single rooms cost 175 DH ($19.25), doubles going for 230 DH ($25.30). There's a particularly pleasant restaurant well worth a luncheon stopover, with a view over the nearby desert, where fixed-price meals cost from 75 DH ($8.25). Residents appreciate the ten-sided swimming pool whose blue tiles are sunk into the rooftop terrace.

7. Tinerhir

This town—standing on a hill dominating an oasis—was once a garrison of the French Foreign Legion. The ksar of Tinerhir, a palace, can be visited; and numerous casbahs, also worth a visit, rise like tall silhouettes, looking out upon palm groves, an oasis of olive trees, and walnut trees. The flowers from the walnut trees are processed to extract the oil.

From Tinerhir you can take excursions to the **Todra Gorge.** The red ochre flanks of the mountains hem in the Todra Valley and its palm groves. The narrow Todra Gorge—some nine miles north from Tinerhir—lies between steep rocky walls. The trail takes you to the top of some naked summits. From there, other trails branch off, going either to the Plateau of the Lakes (via the Tizi Tirhourghezine Pass) or over to the Upper Dades Valley, a rough journey in any direction.

At Tinerhir, the **Hotel Sargho** (tel. 01) is a casbah-style hotel that appears so stern and imposing you'll think at first you've arrived at a red ochre fortress. Behind its thick walls, you'll enjoy comparative luxury, delighting in the coolness of some 60 comfortably furnished bedrooms, each of which has air conditioning, and contains either a private bath or shower. Rates are 200 DH ($22) in a double, dropping to 180 DH ($19.80) in a single. A continental breakfast costs extra. In the middle of the patio is an inviting swimming pool. The hotel also has a bar and restaurant, serving a tourist menu for 85 DH ($9.35) and up. From its terraces there is a panoramic view.

8. Er Rachidia

Once known as Ksar-es-Souk, this is a large palm grove, with a bustling market on the main square. If you're coming from Erfoud, you can visit the **Blue Springs**—noted for their limpid water—at Meski, which is 11 miles north of Er Rachidia. Another excursion is to the **Cirque de Jaffar,** a natural amphitheater near Midelt, which is 75 miles from Er Rachidia.

Er Rachidia lies in the valley of the Ziz, at the crossing of two age-old routes, the road from Meknes to the oasis of Tafilalet and the Deep South Atlas highway to southern Algeria. From both Meknes and Erfoud, there is bus service to Er Rachidia.

FOOD AND LODGING: Hotel Rissani (tel. 2584). Lovely gardens surround this modernized, very Moroccan hotel that first opened for business in 1972. It offers a green-and-white dining room filled with plants, a rectangular swimming pool, and an outdoor terrace with a view of the nearby village. Each of the 60 bedrooms has a private bath, a phone, terrazzo floors, big windows, and a color scheme of ruddy and sandy earth tones. Singles cost 175 DH ($19.25), doubles are 230 DH ($25.30), and triples come to 275 DH ($30.25). Fixed-price meals go for 90 DH ($9.90) each.

Hotel Meski (tel. 20-65), with a salmon-color, heavily crenellated façade, sits beside the dusty main road leading into town. Although it was built in 1974, the designers took great pains to add intricately carved expanses of plaster filigree to the ceiling of the ground-floor café. There are a second-floor guest lounge with a sun-flooded terrace, a small oval swimming pool with an intermittent supply of water, and high-ceilinged upstairs hallways leading to 25 simple but comfortable bedrooms. A true no-frills bargain, the hotel charges 50 DH ($5.50) to 75 DH ($8.25) for a single, 60 DH ($6.60) to 95 DH ($10.45) for a double, depending on the plumbing and the accommodation. The hotel's name is derived from a nearby water source.

9. Erfoud

This town of ox-blood red buildings—shaded by pepper trees and eucalyptus—is a gateway to the Sahara. At an altitude of 3,051 feet, Erfoud stands near the Ziz River, at the foot of the Djebel. You can explore its *souks,* usually crowded with men in huge white turbans and veiled women. The local Jewish women are seen in their distinctive headdresses and vermilion skirts. At Erfoud you can enjoy beautiful desert sunsets over the palm groves. The best vantage point for seeing this is to take the steep trail up to the small **Bordj Est',** an old fortress.

South of Erfoud takes you to the charming oasis known as **Tafilalet,** which is kept green by the underground waters of the Ziz and Rheris. Here vegetation seems to come to an end, but, before doing so, the effect of vegetation is glorious, with fruit trees, tamarisks, and date palms. The oasis, which is about 12 miles long, is noted for its dates.

You can drive south for 14 miles to **Rissani,** with its casbahs and barracks. While here, you can visit a fascinating souk on Tuesday or Thursday morning around 10 o'clock. If you go on Sunday, you'll get to see an authentic Saharan camel market. In the hamlet is a colorful mosque with a graceful minaret.

From Rissani, it is 1½ miles to the venerated and much restored **Mausole-**

um of Moulay Ali Cherif, the ancient ancestor of the Alaouite dynasty. This bearded man was most pious, devoting (according to legend) one year to study, followed by an entire year of prayer.

To the west of Rissani lie the ruins of **Sijilmassa,** the famous "red town." Trans-desert caravans of long ago used to arrive here, bringing gold from the Sudan. Sijilmassa was the most westerly terminus across the Sahara. Its counterpart was Timbuctu in the South.

One of the most dramatic and difficult excursions from Erfoud is to **Merzouga,** where civilization ends and the vast wilderness of the Sahara begins. The location is 31 miles south of Erfoud. You may already be familiar with the scenery, as it was used in such films as *The Little Prince* and *Marco Polo*. It's customary to go to Merzouga with a guide in the early, early hours of the morning. That way, you can watch the sun come up over the Sahara. Some have found this sunrise a mystical experience.

You'll need a guide, as mentioned, if you plan to witness this visual panorama, as the road is not clearly marked. It's possible to drive to Merzouga in a regular vehicle, but because of poor road conditions, even that can be a bit risky. For example, you might find your tires sinking into the sands.

Thousands of tourists every year pay a visit to Merzouga, as it offers a genuine Saharan landscape and the feeling that one is gazing out upon a vast ocean of sand.

FOOD AND LODGING: The leading hotel of town, the **Sijilmassa** (tel. 80), rises imposingly in pink-sided splendor above a lush oasis with waving palms that evoke Biblical images. Casbah-style, the entrance is reached via a set of steps which direct visitors under a set of early 1960s-style chandeliers. There's a swimming pool, a comfortable bar, a very large dining room with enormous greenhouse-type windows, and 75 comfortable, renovated bedrooms. Each has a modern bath, air conditioning, a phone, and a terrace. Do your best to rent a room with a view of the oasis, because its unspoiled verdancy might be one of the longest-lasting visual memories of your trip. Singles rent for 180 DH ($19.80), doubles for 230 DH ($25.30). Fixed-price meals cost from around 70 DH ($7.70) each. This hotel has an engaging staff, courtliness, and a great deal of frontier-style charm.

Hotel Salam (tel. 264). Conceived in a casbah-inspired design of flair and drama, this 98-room hotel opened in 1986. Its engineers chose traditional Berber construction techniques for its two-story design, combining a cement core with an exterior covering of dried mud and chopped straw for a look much like that of the oldest fortified towns in Morocco. The bone-dry desert approaches the very foundations of this unusual hotel, but inside the double courtyards, a sapphire-color swimming pool and newly planted gardens bring the feeling of an oasis. Each of the small but cozy bedrooms has a beamed and plank-covered ceiling, tile-covered floors, and a Bedouin-inspired decor of consciously primitive furniture. Each contains a private tile bath, a phone, and air conditioning. Single rooms rent for 220 DH ($24.20), doubles for 275 DH ($30.25). Fixed-price meals cost 90 DH ($9.90). You'll find this hotel outside Erfoud, beside a road leading off into the desert toward Rissani.

Appendix

SPANISH FOOD AND LANGUAGE

1. Menu Translations
2. Capsule Vocabulary

IF YOU FIND yourself gaping at a menu all in Spanish or at a loss for words—that's where this Appendix comes in.

1. Menu Translations

Spanish menus are a bit bewildering in that regional specialties, from Andalusia to Galicia, crop up regularly to confound the foreign visitor who has successfully learned that a *tortilla* is an omelet. If it's any comfort, vacationing Spaniards are often confused in their own country, particularly after each chef has asserted his individuality by tacking a flowery phrase on the end of such common fare as beans. Nevertheless, a basic knowledge of the essentials of the Spanish diet, from soup to specialties, from salads to salt, can save the foreign diner from the clutches of an octopus and unite him or her happily in the embrace of a lobster.

SOUPS (SOPAS)

sopa de ajo	garlic soup	**sopa de guisantes**	pea soup
sopa de cebolla	onion soup	**sopa de verduras**	vegetable soup
sopa clara	consommé		
sopa espesa	thick soup	**sopa de lentejas**	lentil soup
sopa de fideos	noodle soup	**sopa de pescado**	fish soup
caldo gallego	Galician broth	**sopa de tomate**	tomato soup
caldo de gallina	chicken soup		

EGGS (HUEVOS)

huevos escalfados	poached eggs	**huevos pasados por agua**	soft-boiled eggs
huevos fritos	fried eggs	**huevos revueltos**	scrambled eggs
huevos duros	hard-boiled eggs		
huevos y "bacon"	eggs and bacon	**tortilla**	omelet

FISH (PESCADO)

almejas	clams	**langostinos**	prawns
anchoas	anchovies	**lenguado**	sole
anguilas	eels	**mejillones**	mussels
arenque	herring	**merluza**	hake
atún	tuna	**necoras**	spider crabs
bacalao	cod	**ostras**	oysters
calamares	squid	**pescadilla**	whiting
cangrejo	crab	**pijotas**	small whiting
caracoles	snails	**pulpo**	octopus
centollo	sea urchin	**rodaballo**	turbot
chocos	large squid	**salmonete**	mullet
cigalas	small lobsters	**sardinas**	sardines
gambas	shrimp	**trucha**	trout
langosta	lobster	**vieiras**	scallops

SPECIALTIES

cochinillo asado	roast suckling pig	**gazpacho**	a cold soup: raw tomatoes, cucumbers, peppers, olive oil, vinegar, garlic
cordero lechal asado	roast lamb	**jamón serrano**	cured ham
entremeses	hors d'oeuvres	**paella**	saffron rice with chicken, seafood

MEAT (CARNE)

albondigas	meatballs	**higado**	liver
bistec	beefsteak	**jamón**	ham
callos	tripe	**lengua**	tongue
cerdo	pork	**riñón**	kidney
chuleta	cutlet	**rosbif**	roast beef
cocido	stew	**solomillo**	loin
conejo	rabbit	**ternera**	veal
cordero	lamb	**tocino**	bacon
costillas	chops	**vaca**	beef

POULTRY (AVES)

gallina	fowl	**pavo**	turkey
ganso	goose	**perdiz**	partridge
paloma	pigeon	**pollo**	chicken
pato	duck		

VEGETABLES (VERDURAS)

aceitunas	olives	**guisantes**	peas
alcachofa	artichoke	**judías verdes**	string beans
arroz	rice	**nabo**	turnip
berenjena	eggplant	**patata**	potato
cebolla	onion	**pepino**	cucumber
col	cabbage	**remolachas**	beets
coliflor	cauliflower	**setas**	mushrooms
esparragos	asparagus	**tomate**	tomato
espinacas	spinach	**zanahorias**	carrots

SALAD (ENSALADA)

ensalada verde	green salad	**ensalada de pepinos**	cucumber salad
lechuga	lettuce		
ensalada mixta	mixed salad		

DESSERTS (POSTRES)

buñuelos	fritters	**helado**	ice cream
compota	stewed fruit	**pasteles**	pastries
flan	caramel custard	**queso**	cheese
fruta	fruit	**torta**	cake
galletas	tea cakes		

FRUIT (FRUTAS)

albaricoque	apricot	**limón**	lemon
aquacate	avocado	**manzana**	apple
cerezas	cherries	**melocoton**	peach
ciruela	plum	**naranja**	orange
datil	date	**pera**	pear
frambuesa	raspberry	**piña**	pineapple
fresa	strawberry	**plátano**	banana
granada	pomegranate	**toronja**	grapefruit
higo	fig	**uvas**	grapes

BEVERAGES (BEBIDAS)

agua	water	**cerveza**	beer
agua mineral	mineral water	**ginebra**	gin
café	coffee	**jerez**	sherry

jugo de naranjas	orange juice	**sifon**	soda
jugo de tomate	tomato juice	**té**	tea
leche	milk	**vino blancho**	white wine
sangría	red wine, fruit juice, and soda	**vino tinto**	red wine
sidra	cider		

CONDIMENTS (CONDIMENTOS)

aceite	oil	**pimienta**	pepper
ajo	garlic	**sal**	salt
azucar	sugar	**vinagre**	vinegar
mostaza	mustard		

MISCELLANEOUS (MISCELÁNEO)

hielo	ice	**cocido**	broiled
mantequilla	butter	**frito**	fried
pan	bread	**poco hecho**	rare
panecillo	roll	**asado**	roast
tostado	toast	**muy hecho**	well done
empanado	breaded		

2. Capsule Vocabulary

		Pronounced
Hello	**Buenos días**	bway-noss dee-ahss
How are you?	**Como está usted?**	koh-moh ess-tah oo-steth
Very well	**Muy bien**	mwee byen
Thank you	**Gracias**	gra-theeahss
Good-bye	**Adiós**	ad-dyohss
Please	**Por favór**	pohr fah-bohr
Yes	**Sí**	see
No	**No**	noh
Excuse me	**Perdóneme**	pehrdoh-neh-may
Give me	**Deme**	day-may
Where is?	**Donde está?**	dohn-day ess-tah
the station	**la estación**	la ess-tah-thyohn
a hotel	**un hotel**	oon-oh-tel
a restaurant	**un restaurante**	oon res-tow-rahn-tay
the toilet	**el servicio**	el ser-vee-the-o
To the right	**A la derecha**	ah lah day-ray-chuh
To the left	**A la izquierda**	ah lah eeth-kyayr-duh
Straight ahead	**Adelante**	ah-day-lahn-tay

I would like	**Quiero**	kyehr-oh
to eat	**comer**	ko-mayr
a room	**una habitación**	oo-nah ah-bee-tah-thyo-n
How much is it?	**Cuánto?**	kwahn-toh
The check	**La cuenta**	lah kwen-tah
When	**Cuándo?**	kwan-doh
Yesterday	**Ayer**	ah-yayr
Today	**Hoy**	oy
Tomorrow	**Mañana**	mahn-yah-nah
Breakfast	**Desayuno**	deh-sai-yoo-noh
Lunch	**Comida**	co-mee-dah
Dinner	**Cena**	thay-nah

1 **uno** (oo-noh)
2 **dos** (dose)
3 **tres** (trayss)
4 **cuatro** (kwah-troh)
5 **cinco** (theen-koh)
6 **seis** (sayss)
7 **siete** (syeh-tay)
8 **ocho** (oh-choh)
9 **nueve** (nway-bay)
10 **diez** (dyeth)
11 **once** (ohn-thay)
12 **doce** (doh-thay)
13 **trece** (tray-thay)
14 **catorce** (kah-tor-thay)
15 **quince** (keen-thay)
16 **dieciseis** (dyeth-ee-(sayss)
17 **diecisiete** (dyeth-ee-sye-tay)
18 **dieciocho** (dyeth-ee-oh-choh)
19 **diecinueve** (dyeth-ee-nywaybay)
20 **veinte** (bayn-tay)
30 **trienta** (trayn-tah)
40 **cuarenta** (kwah-ren-tah)
50 **cincuenta** (theen-kween-tah)
60 **sesenta** (say-sen-tah)
70 **setenta** (say-ten-tah)
80 **ochenta** (oh-chen-tah)
90 **noventa** (noh-ben-tah)
100 **cien** (thyen)

NOW, SAVE MONEY ON ALL YOUR TRAVELS!

Join Arthur Frommer's $25-A-Day Travel Club™

Saving money while traveling is never a simple matter, which is why, over 24 years ago, the **$25-A-Day Travel Club** was formed. Actually, the idea came from readers of the Arthur Frommer Publications who felt that such an organization could bring financial benefits, continuing travel information, and a sense of community to economy-minded travelers all over the world.

In keeping with the money-saving concept, the annual membership fee is low—$18 (U.S. residents) or $20 (Canadian, Mexican, and foreign residents)—and is immediately exceeded by the value of your benefits which include:

(1) The latest edition of any TWO of the books listed on the following page.

(2) An annual subscription to an 8-page quarterly newspaper *The Wonderful World of Budget Travel* which keeps you up-to-date on fastbreaking developments in low-cost travel in all parts of the world—bringing you the kind of information you'd have to pay over $25 a year to obtain elsewhere. This consumer-conscious publication also includes the following columns:

> **Hospitality Exchange**—members all over the world who are willing to provide hospitality to other members as they pass through their home cities.
>
> **Share-a-Trip**—requests from members for travel companions who can share costs and help avoid the burdensome single supplement.
>
> **Readers Ask . . . Readers Reply**—travel questions from members to which other members reply with authentic firsthand information.

(3) A copy of *Arthur Frommer's Guide to New York.*

(4) Your personal membership card which entitles you to purchase through the Club all Arthur Frommer Publications for a third to a half off their regular retail prices during the term of your membership.

So why not join this hardy band of international budgeteers NOW and participate in its exchange of information and hospitality? Simply send $18 (U.S. residents) or $20 U.S. (Canadian, Mexican, and other foreign residents) along with your name and address to: $25-A-Day Travel Club, Inc., Gulf + Western Building, One Gulf + Western Plaza, New York, NY 10023. Remember to specify which *two* of the books in section (1) above you wish to receive in your initial package of members' benefits. Or tear out this page, check off any two books on the opposite side and send it to us with your membership fee.